THE OXFORD HANDBOOK OF

LAND ECONOMICS

THE OXFORD HANDBOOK OF

LAND ECONOMICS

Edited By
JOSHUA M. DUKE
and
JUNJIE WU

OXFORD
UNIVERSITY PRESS

OXFORD
UNIVERSITY PRESS

Oxford University Press is a department of the University of Oxford. It furthers the University's objective of excellence in research, scholarship, and education by publishing worldwide.

Oxford New York
Auckland Cape Town Dar es Salaam Hong Kong Karachi
Kuala Lumpur Madrid Melbourne Mexico City Nairobi
New Delhi Shanghai Taipei Toronto

With offices in
Argentina Austria Brazil Chile Czech Republic France Greece
Guatemala Hungary Italy Japan Poland Portugal Singapore
South Korea Switzerland Thailand Turkey Ukraine Vietnam

Oxford is a registered trademark of Oxford University Press in the UK and certain other countries.

Published in the United States of America by
Oxford University Press
198 Madison Avenue, New York, NY 10016

Library of Congress Cataloging-in-Publication Data
The Oxford handbook of land economics / edited by Joshua M. Duke and Junjie Wu.
pages cm
Includes bibliographical references and index.
ISBN 978-0-19-976374-0 (alk. paper)
1. Land use. 2. Economic development. I. Duke, Joshua M. II. Wu, JunJie.
HD111.O94 2013
333.73—dc23
2013024328

1 3 5 7 9 8 6 4 2
Printed in the United States of America
on acid-free paper

Contents

PART II ENVIRONMENTAL AND SOCIOECONOMIC CONSEQUENCES OF LAND USE AND LAND USE CHANGE

PART III METHODOLOGICAL DEVELOPMENTS

Foreword

Few human sentiments are more urgent than place—the place we are born, the place we become sentient, the place we engage others in a variety of pursuits, and finally the place we will become dust. Some creatures *have* their territory. Humans are creatures *of* their territory.

It cannot therefore be a surprise that place becomes conflated with land, and vice versa. The primacy of land can be seen in a number of ways. In some societies, "property rights"—shorthand for some presumptive imaginings about individual control over land—often seem more important than "human rights" (whatever they might be). History reveals the military and political importance of land. In agrarian societies the connection between land and economic well-being is obvious. In that regard, it has been claimed that economic development and attendant urbanization will diminish the economic importance of land. This now seems improbable. Indeed, one could make a plausible argument that land will become of increased importance in the future. The contents of this marvelous volume would certainly support that hypothesis.

Those of us who are modern know well the Lockean Creation Myth—God gave land to all in common and then admonished us to take control of it and make it flourish. From this mischief all manner of tragedy has followed, whether we have in mind the near-complete annihilation of indigenous peoples the world over, or the near-misses of European wars of mutually assured destruction throughout recorded history. Land is always worth a good (or bad) fight.

Happily for those of us who are economists, land is also—and always will be—worth a good debate. And good debates lead to good science.

The chapters included here offer profound insights into many of those debates. Josh Duke and JunJie Wu have arranged for an impressive lineup of experts to address, with clarity and rigor, the important issues requiring good analysis and coherent solutions.

An important undercurrent here, and one that explains many of the difficulties in crafting workable public policy to address problems in land use and land use change, is the conceptual inconvenience that land is a *fictitious commodity* [Polanyi, 2001].[1]

> ... labor, land, and money are essential elements of industry; they also must be organized in markets; in fact, these markets form an absolutely vital part of the economic system. But labor, land, and money are obviously not commodities; the postulate that

[1] Karl Polanyi, *The Great Transformation*, Boston: Beacon Press, 2001.

> anything that is bought and sold must have been produced for sale is emphatically untrue in regard to them.... Labor is only another name for a human activity which goes with life itself....; land is only another name for nature, which is not produced by man; actual money... is merely a token of purchasing power... which comes into being through the mechanism of banking or state finance. None of them is produced for sale. The commodity description of labor, land, and money is entirely fictitious [Polanyi, 2001, pp. 75–6].

The inconvenience of land as a fictitious commodity arises because economic models can only do the necessary work when they are deployed in the service of answers to questions that motivated their creation in the first place. All models are context specific, and they are only useful if their deployment in new settings is consistent with the assumptions underlying their essential structure. The test of all models is whether or not they are good to think with.

For most economic models, various quantities of a particular commodity can be arrayed along one axis, and the various prices of that commodity can be arrayed along another axis. Unfortunately for land and land use changes, the commodity fiction renders this problematic. It is, of course possible to plot acres/hectares of land along one axis, and it is possible to refine that depiction by incorporating some index of "quality." But that may not satisfy some who refuse to see land in that light. Equally problematic, the *other* axis in our models reflects yet another fictitious commodity—money.

Suddenly we see why there are so many profound debates about land. The very concepts and models that allow us to analyze markets for "real" commodities—toothpaste, bread, houses, cameras—offer up seriously contested concepts when we must deal with land (nature). Two obvious problems arise. First, many people refuse to accept money as a plausible measure of the value of land—the one fictitious commodity cannot be mapped into the other fictitious commodity. Second, many people refuse to accept the idea that land (nature) is a commodity. Note that for the concept of a commodity to have any meaning in economics it must be capable of assignment (ownership). This introduces the concept of "belonging to." Native people say that land does not belong to them—they belong to the land. The implication of this notion may warrant a brief elaboration. Recall that the essence of a normal commodity is that when it moves through markets the only thing that really matters is that there is a change in its ownership. That is what markets do—they mediate *changes in ownership* of those commodities that "pass through" markets. And since ownership is itself yet another social construct, we see the layering of contestation that will always attend economic analysis of land, land use, and land use change.

We disregard these concerns at our peril. If we hope to produce policy relevant insights concerning the contested realms of land, we must speak to a large audience of sapient adults who refuse to accept quite fundamental presumptions in our models. Science practiced in disregard for shared human meanings is impertinent.

The various chapters here admirably spell out the contested nature of figuring out how to think about what is better to do with respect to land. I like to say that there is no such thing as land, there is only land tenure—social rules that bestow on certain individuals a circumscribed suite of capacities concerning what can and cannot be done with that thing we call land. And this reminds us that when we study land we are really poking around at the outer limits of presumptions concerning who gets to define the rules by which land use—and land use change—shall be determined. It seems we are back to the matter of presumptive "rights" over land. And as we know, rights are not inherent but *worked out*:

> Only those economic advantages are rights which have the law back of them... whether it is a property right is really the question to be answered [Justice R. Jackson, Willow River Power Co. 324 US 499, 502 (1945)].

In other words, economic advantages are not protected because they are rights. Rather, those settings and circumstances that a society chooses to consider valuable are given protection under the cover of "rights." We see that economic advantages are bestowed by the political class. Suddenly we grasp the fount of contestation over the manifold advantages of owning this thing called land.

Daniel W. Bromley
Madison
October, 2011

Preface

Land use change is arguably one of the most pervasive socioeconomic forces affecting ecological systems, economic systems, and human wellbeing. Almost all major environmental problems, including climate change, water pollution, and habitat destruction, are rooted in land use change. Many socioeconomic phenomena, such as urban sprawl, suburbanization, urban redevelopment, and economic segregation, are also deeply ingrained in land use change. In response to the great need to study these environmental and socioeconomic phenomena, many new developments have taken place in the field of land economics during the past decade, justifying a new handbook in the field.

This volume draws on recent advances in several literatures that investigate land use behavior and policy, including natural resource economics, environmental economics, regional science, and urban economics. The contributors of this volume are the eminent scholars in the field and the newer experts, who work at the frontier of the field. Starting from inherited theories and analyses, this forward-looking handbook seeks to become a "must" reading, not only for those who are new to the field, but also for those who want to extend their knowledge to the frontier of land economics.

There are various ways to use this handbook. This comprehensive treatment of land economics provides an excellent source of readings for a graduate course in land or resource economics. Although the length and diversity of methods may make it difficult to cover in a single semester course, instructors may seek to focus on a subset of chapters. For instance, a course might be structured around the chapters on the ecosystem services of land and a few related methods chapters. Or, the focus might be on cutting edge methods in land economics, supplementing the methods chapters with seminal articles in general economics on equilibrium modeling, auction theory, and specific econometric techniques. Researchers and policy analysts will find that the book offers the state-of-the-art in land economics research. The depth of coverage on the methods chapters offers researchers a structure for setting up their own analyses. The applied chapters can serve either as a starting point for learning about markets and incentive problems associated with land topics, or as a source of citable research results and synthetic conclusions from experts in the area. Those with less familiarity with economics can also use this handbook to understand what is known and unknown on a given topic area. This will help noneconomists, policy makers, and grant funders to articulate better hypotheses, policy goals, and funding opportunities.

We are profoundly grateful to our chapter authors for their outstanding contributions to this handbook. We also acknowledge the insights of our colleagues around the world, who inspire us with their research and collegiality. Among a very long list, we would like to single out Daniel Bromley and Kathy Segerson as our mentors, who shaped our lives—research and otherwise—at a deep level and to whom we owe a great debt. We would also like to recognize the other leading lights in our professional lives, including Emery N. Castle, Richard M. Adams, Bill Boggess, and David Zilberman. Finally, we thank our friends and colleagues for their advice and encouragement during the long process, especially Titus Awokuse, Kathleen Bell, Rob Johnston, Lori Lynch, Kent Messer, and George Parsons. Finally, we are grateful for the support of our Universities, whose combined land grant missions have promoted the advancement of integrated land economics research.

Joshua M. Duke, *Newark, Delaware*
JunJie Wu, *Corvallis, Oregon*

List of Contributors

Richard M. Adams is Professor Emeritus in the Department of Applied Economics at Oregon State University.

Ruth Aisabokhae is Economist, DuPont Pioneer, Lagos, Nigeria.

Christopher M. Anderson is Associate Professor in the School of Aquatic and Fishery Sciences at University of Washington.

Witsanu Attavanich is Lecturer in the Department of Economics at Kasetsart University in Thailand.

Edward B. Barbier is the John S. Bugas Professor of Economics in the Department of Economics and Finance at University of Wyoming.

Dana Marie Bauer is Assistant Professor in the Department of Geography and Environment at Boston University.

Daniel W. Bromley is Professor Emeritus in the Department of Agricultural and Applied Economics at the University of Wisconsin-Madison.

Seong-Hoon Cho is Associate Professor in the Department of Agricultural and Resource Economics at University of Tennessee.

Roger Claassen is a senior agricultural economist in the Resource, Environmental, and Science Policy Branch of the US Department of Agriculture Economic Research Service.

Joseph Cooper is Chief of the Agricultural Policy and Models Branch in the Market and Trade Economics Division of the US Department of Agriculture Economic Research Service.

Christine L. Crago is Assistant Professor in the Department of Resource Economics and Commonwealth Honors College at University of Massachusetts Amherst.

Joshua M. Duke is Professor in the Department of Applied Economics and Statistics at University of Delaware.

Joel B. Eisen is Professor of Law at the University of Richmond School of Law.

Jeffrey Ferris is a Graduate Student in the Department of Agricultural and Resource Economics at University of Maryland.

Ekaterina Gnedenko is Lecturer in the Department of Economics at Tufts University.

Dennis Heffley is Professor in the Department of Economics at University of Connecticut.

Ian Hodge is Professor in the Department of Land Economy at University of Cambridge.

Elena G. Irwin is Professor in the Department of Agricultural, Environmental, and Development Economics at the Ohio State University.

Robert J. Johnston is Director of the George Perkins Marsh Institute and Professor in the Department of Economics at Clark University.

Scott Kaplan is an undergraduate student at the University of California, Berkeley.

Madhu Khanna is Professor in the Department of Agricultural and Consumer Economics at University of Illinois.

Eunice Kim is Program Administrator in the Department of Agricultural and Resource Economics at University of California, Berkeley.

Seung Gyu Kim in Assistant Professor of Agricultural Economics at Kyungpook National University in South Korea.

H. Allen Klaiber is Assistant Professor in the Department of Agricultural, Environmental, and Development Economics at the Ohio State University.

Nicolai V. Kuminoff is Assistant Professor in the Department of Economics at Arizona State University.

David J. Lewis is Associate Professor of Applied Economics at Oregon State University.

Rebecca Lewis is Assistant Professor of Planning, Public Policy and Management at University of Oregon.

Lori Lynch is Professor in the Department of Agricultural and Resource Economics at University of Maryland.

Bruce A. McCarl is Regents and Distinguished Professor in the Department of Agricultural Economics at Texas A&M University.

Kent D. Messer is Associate Professor and Unidel Howard Cosgrove Chair for the Environment in the Department of Applied Economics and Statistics at University of Delaware.

Thomas J. Miceli is Professor in the Department of Economics at University of Connecticut.

Edwin S. Mills is Emeritus Professor of Real Estate and Finance in the Kellogg School of Management at Northwestern University.

Claire A. Montgomery is Professor in the Department of Forest Engineering, Resources and Management at Oregon State University.

Jianhong E. Mu is Postdoc Scholar in the Department of Applied Economics at Oregon State University.

Mark Musumba is Postdoctoral Research Fellow at The Earth Institute of Columbia University.

Erik Nelson is Assistant Professor of Economics at Bowdoin College.

Cynthia J. Nickerson is an agricultural economist in the Resource and Rural Economics Divison of the US Department of Agriculture Economic Research Service.

Dawn Cassandra Parker is Associate Professor in the School of Planning at University of Waterloo.

Mark D. Partridge is the C. William Swank Chair of Rural-Urban Policy at The Ohio State University and a Professor in the Agricultural, Environment, and Development Economics Department.

Andrew J. Plantinga is Professor of Natural Resource Economics and Policy in the Bren School of Environmental Science and Management at University of California, Santa Barbara.

Benjamin S. Rashford is Associate Professor in the Department of Agricultural and Applied Economics at University of Wyoming.

Dan S. Rickman is Regents Professor of Economics and Oklahoma Gas and Electric Services Chair in Regional Economic Analysis in the Department of Economics and Legal Studies in Business at Oklahoma State University.

Roland K. Roberts is Professor and Director of Graduate Studies in the Department of Agricultural and Resource Economics at University of Tennessee.

Cristina Salvioni is Associate Professor of Agricultural Economics in the Department of Economics at University of Chieti-Pescara, Italy.

Kathleen Segerson is Philip E. Austin Professor in the Department of Economics at University of Connecticut.

Edward Stone is a graduate research assistant in the Department of Applied Economics at Oregon State University.

Stephen K. Swallow is Professor and DelFavero Faculty Fellow in the Department of Agricultural and Resource Economics and the Center for Environmental Sciences and Engineering at University of Connecticut.

Charles Towe is Assistant Professor in the Department of Agricultural and Resource Economics at the University of Maryland.

Emi Uchida is Assistant Professor in the Department of Environmental and Natural Resource Economics at University of Rhode Island.

Marcella Veronesi is Assistant Professor in the Department of Economics at the University of Verona, Italy and the Institute for Environmental Decisions at ETH Zurich, Switzerland.

Douglas H. Wrenn is Assistant Professor in the Department of Agricultural Economics, Sociology, and Education at the Pennsylvania State University.

JunJie Wu is Emery N. Castle Chair in the Department of Applied Economics at Oregon State University.

Wendong Zhang is a doctoral student in the Department of Agricultural, Environmental, and Developmental Economics at the Ohio State University.

David Zilberman is Robinson Chair in the Department of Agricultural and Resource Economics at University of California, Berkeley.

INTRODUCTION

Land as an Integrating Theme in Economics

JOSHUA M. DUKE AND JUNJIE WU

1. Land Markets and Welfare

This handbook explains what economists know about land—and how they know. The innumerable decisions about how to use land and how to change land uses over time pervade society, affecting human well-being both directly and indirectly through changes in the performance of economic and ecological systems. Large shares of major environmental problems (air pollution, water pollution, climate, habitat destruction, to name a few) are rooted in land use change. Socioeconomic phenomena such as urban sprawl, suburbanization, urban redevelopment, and jurisdictional fragmentation are essentially land use changes by another name—and they affect opportunities for further land use change. Fomenting all these forces are the inescapable land policies, which sanctify winners, disappoint losers, and provide a setting for the baser forms of modern civil disputes. The special status of land in history and culture serves to intensify these disputes.

With so much at stake and so many pressing environmental and socioeconomic challenges inextricably linked to land and land use change, future progress requires clear economic insight about the functioning of land markets and the drivers of land use behavior. Economists have long offered explanations about why land decision makers behave suboptimally and how policy might redirect these decisions to enhance social welfare. These insights often involve measuring utility impacts outside of markets, altering incentives with policy change, and creating markets to improve the allocation of society's resources. Economists seek to understand how land markets adjust in the face of policy changes and changes in relative scarcity of resources, anticipating opportunities to enhance the effectiveness of policy. As research over the past few decades has shown, explaining the processes of land use change poses great challenges because of the simultaneous cause and effect of price changes in land markets and the oft-times confounding role of local policies. Land economics covers more than explanation.

Economists use recent advances in theory and methods to predict the likely impacts of novel and unimplemented policies. The large set of recent developments in land economics warrant a new handbook for the field.

This handbook draws broadly from advances that investigate land use behavior, markets, and policy, showing that land is a theme that integrates several fields of economics. These fields include natural resource economics, environmental economics, regional science, and urban economics. The emergence of the new economic geography and the increasing recognition of the role of natural endowments and amenities in determining urban development patterns and the spatial distribution of economic activities has led to a blurring of the lines among the traditional fields, with land use and land use patterns as an integrating theme. The alignment of interest and the development of spatial modeling approaches have made the potential gains from collaboration and cross-fertilization across fields much greater. One goal of this handbook is to stimulate further collaboration and cross-fertilization among the economics fields related to land use markets, behavior, patterns, and policy.

This handbook presents studies of land use and land use changes from various economic perspectives. Several other disciplines also take land use as their subject matter of study, including geography, anthropology, and sociology. What distinguishes economics from those disciplines is that land economists largely focus on explaining the economic incentives or institutions that drive land use behavior and policy. Land economics investigates the benefits and costs of land use decisions and change. These benefits and costs are broadly defined to include those associated with both economic and ecological impacts, as well as the feedback effects from those systems.

Land economics emphasizes economic efficiency in land allocation. As the reader will discover, many chapters in this handbook will be distinguished by whether the authors assess efficiency in partial and general equilibrium settings. These approaches involve tradeoffs in explaining the substantive and complex problems associated with land. When benefits are difficult to measure, land economists often turn to cost effectiveness in achieving a goal when evaluating a policy.

This handbook is organized into four sections. The first section investigates the major drivers of land use behavior and land use change. The second section evaluates the environmental and socioeconomic implications of these forces, including chapters focusing on the impact of land use change on water, habitat, climate, and other ecosystem services. The third section presents recent methodological advances in land market modeling, involving spatial modeling techniques, agent-based approaches, econometric methods, quasi-experiments, and experiments. The fourth section focuses on the pervasive set of institutions from law and policy that direct land use behavior and change. The handbook concludes with a discussion of future research directions in land economics. The remaining parts of this introduction establish a setting and offer a brief overview of each section, in turn.

2. Determinants and Drivers of Land Use and Land Use Change

Numerous societal changes, including economic development, technological progress, and urbanization, drive land use change. Land use change in turn influences societal changes. The complexity of the relationships among land use, societal change, and the spatial distribution of economic activity have been increasingly recognized with the emergence of the new economic geography and new growth theory. Consequently, much effort has been devoted to the development of spatially explicit models that identify the nature of forces that shape the spatial distribution of economic activities and land use patterns.

The first section of this handbook reviews the economic literature for recent advances in the analysis of the major drivers of land use change. It starts with Chapter 1 by Partridge and Rickman, which examines the relationship between economic development and land use change. The chapter contends that two largely distinct literatures have emerged in regional economic development and land use economics, despite their fundamental interrelationship. Partridge and Rickman argue that a lack of integration is a shortcoming in both approaches and that a spatial equilibrium framework is especially suited for a systematic understanding of the various feedback mechanisms that affect development and land use.

Technological progress is another major force driving land use change. The astonishing increase in agricultural productivity enables the consistently decreasing number of farmers to feed the consistently increasing number of people in the world. Technological advances in seed varieties, irrigation, and fertilizers, among many others, led to these productivity gains. Although the negative impacts of intensive agriculture may garner disproportionate attention in the developed world's popular press, it is difficult to overstate the importance of technology in land use—especially when one recognizes that a more technologically efficient, intensive use of farmland directly impacts outcomes in urban land markets (which will be encouraged to grow up, not out) and forests (which will be less likely to be converted to agriculture). In Chapter 2, Zilberman, Khanna, Kaplan, and Kim offer a comprehensive assessment of technology and land use. They focus on adoption as an investment, and present results associated with the threshold model, input use efficiency, diffusion, credit, learning, and risk.

Land use change is ultimately determined by the relative value derived from the alternative uses. Since Ricardo and von Thunen, economists have sought to understand the determinants of land values and land use patterns. Modern manifestations of this work include explaining urbanization and suburbanization processes and the external costs from development at the fringe, which is the economic approximation of the widespread notion of "sprawl." In Chapter 3, Mills discusses the role of the metropolitan area in explaining urbanization and suburbanization and assesses the impacts of proximity and density on the costs of various land uses. Mills's discussion of economies of scale and scope and of congestion and pollution helps build a theory on the size and growth of metropolitan areas, predicting that suburbs will continue to grow rapidly, at least in the United States.

The relative value derived from alternative land uses is ultimately affected by the relative value of services or outputs from the land uses. Land can be used to produce bioenergy crops. As returns to energy production increase either due to market forces or policy changes, more land will be allocated to energy production. In Chapter 4, Khanna, Zilberman, and Crago evaluate the phenomenon of biofuels—an emerging issue that has propelled land allocation into public debates about "food or fuel." The models reviewed directly link land markets with energy markets; interestingly, these models show that government policies other than zoning can trigger substantive land use changes. Although the reviewed models lack agreement about the extent of land use change needed to meet governmental biofuel targets, Khanna, Zilberman, and Crago anticipate a moderate increase in crop prices. Technology will mitigate some of the anticipated adverse impacts from large-scale biofuel production.

In Chapter 5, Nickerson and Zhang tackle perhaps the longest standing challenge in land economics: explaining farmland value. They focus on hedonic estimations of models in which land rents are capitalized, considering both cross-sectional and dynamic analyses. Nickerson and Zhang review the tools for addressing spatial dependence, spatial heterogeneity, and sample selection bias, and then discuss recent innovations in nonparametrics, quasi-experimental design, panel data, and structural econometric models.

In the developing world, agriculture comprises a comparatively large part of the economy and remains labor-intensive. The expansion of cultivation in the developing world continues to decrease forests and other natural land uses. In the final chapter of this section (Chapter 6), Barbier considers whether this farmland expansion will lead to the same level of economic development experienced from similar patterns in the past. Barbier models the processes of this "frontier economy," in which a traditional sector converts available land to produce a nontraded agricultural output, and a fully developed, commercially oriented sector exploits available land and natural resources for a variety of traded outputs. The model accounts for population increases, migration, and unskilled labor. The results suggest that although the frontier can help mitigate the adjustments of economic growth, it also induces considerable costs, such as those associated with boom-and-bust cycles. The results provide a plausible explanation for why land use expansion in developing economies may not be generating greater economy-wide benefits.

Together, the chapters included in this section provide a critical assessment of the recent analyses of the major drivers of land use change. They also lay a foundation for understanding the environmental and socioeconomic impacts of land use change, which are explored in the next part of this handbook.

3. Environmental and Socioeconomic Consequences of Land Use and Land Use Change

Land use changes, such as deforestation, urbanization, intensification of agriculture, and innumerable other human activities have substantially altered the Earth's landscape. Such disturbances affect important ecological processes and the provision of ecosystem services, causing wide-ranging and long-term environmental and socioeconomic consequences. The second section of this handbook presents economic research efforts that examine the environmental and socioeconomic impacts of land use and land use change. It shows the breadth of research in this area, and highlights the need for more economic research that focuses on the socioeconomic impacts of land use and land use change.

3.1 The Land Use and Environment Nexus

Land use is arguably the most pervasive socioeconomic force affecting the processes and functions of ecosystems. Forests provide a clear example of the relationship between land use and ecosystem services. Forests support biodiversity, provide critical habitat for wildlife, hold carbon dioxide out of the atmosphere, intercept precipitation, slow surface runoff, reduce soil erosion, and mitigate flooding. These ecosystem services significantly affect human well-being, although they are rarely priced by markets. Substantive welfare losses may result when the ecosystem services of forests are ignored in decisions to convert forest to agriculture or urban development. In one current and leading example of these phenomena, deforestation substantially alters and fragments the Earth's vegetative cover. Such disturbance can change the global atmospheric concentration of carbon dioxide, the principal heat-trapping gas, and is suspected to affect local, regional, and global climate by changing the energy balance on the Earth's surface (Marland et al. 2003).

Agriculture is a dominant form of land use, with 38% of land in agricultural uses globally (Food and Agricultural Organization [FAO] 2004). Agro-ecosystems generate beneficial ecosystem services, including food and materials for human consumption, but intensive agriculture can have a wide range of negative ecological impacts. For example, it has long been recognized that agricultural land use and practices can affect water quality and quantity, and the effect is influenced by government policies. Soil erosion and nutrient runoff from agricultural lands are a leading source of water pollution both in inland and coastal waters.

Urban development has also been linked to many environmental problems, including air pollution, water pollution, and loss of wildlife habitat. Urban runoff often contains nutrients, sediment, and toxic contaminants, and it can cause large variations in stream flow and temperatures. Habitat destruction, fragmentation, and alteration associated with urban development have been identified as the leading causes of biodiversity decline and species extinctions (Czech et al. 2000; Soulé 1991). Urban development and intensive agriculture in inland and coastal areas damage the health, productivity, and biodiversity of the marine environment throughout the world.

The first five chapters of the second section present economic research efforts to understand the linkages between land use decisions and environmental outcomes. Chapters 7, 8, and 10 all address habitat conservation, but with three different foci. In Chapter 7, Lewis and Nelson evaluate the effectiveness of three leading approaches to securing the public goods associated with wildlife conservation: regulation, direct purchase, and incentive-based policy. They evaluate the challenges to these policies, including the perverse result of preemptive habitat destruction, or "shoot, shovel, and shut up," and issues arising from spatially dependent benefits.

In Chapter 8, Johnston et al. offer a review of the most current methods for determining the nonmarket values of ecosystem services. The authors show that economists' focus on valuation methods—that is, how ecosystem services are evaluated—is only one part of a very complex process. Researchers must also determine what ecosystem services are to be evaluated and at what scope and scale. These latter two challenges involved many uncertainties, including unknown scientific information on the processes and the linkages among various services.

In Chapter 10, Attavanich et al. develop an integrated model to predict the joint effect of climate change and resulting land use responses on a specific ecosystem service (waterfowl productivity). Land use change in a specific location (the Prairie Pothole Region of North America) is explicitly modeled as a function of climate change. One important finding from this analysis is that land use response to climate change exacerbates the direct negative effects of climate change on waterfowl populations.

In Chapter 9, McCarl et al. present a thorough assessment of what is known about land use and climate change. Although climate change is an area with massive uncertainties, economists offer a great deal of recent research on how climate change and land use interact; for instance, this research predicts how agricultural growing regions will alter with a warming planet. McCarl et al. divide the research results into three types of studies: vulnerability, adaptation, and mitigation research.

In Chapter 11, Montgomery provides a comprehensive treatment of the topic of fire as an agent and a consequence of land use change. The chapter presents the literature on the economics of fire management, institutions, and policy and examines emerging challenges for fire policy. Montgomery also discusses the three core themes in the economics of wildfire: spatial externalities, incentives, and risk-based decision analysis.

These chapters highlight two challenges for the evaluation of environmental impacts. The first is related to the challenges of linking specific ecosystem functions to land use decisions. Two of the chapters offer examples of how economists are beginning to overcome this challenge. Johnston et al. offer a bioeconomics model linking specific land management decisions with bird habitat outcomes for a specific species (bobolink) in a specific location. Similarly, Attavanich et al. develop an integrated model to predict how a specific ecosystem service (waterfowl productivity) will change as a result of land use changes.

The second challenge is related to the problem of asymmetric information, a theme arising throughout the handbook. Chapter 7 addresses this challenge in the context of the design of incentive-based policies for habitat conservation. Several other chapters study various manifestations of this problem (see for instance Chapter 15 on empirically modeling landowner returns, Chapter 19 on private information in conservation auctions, and Chapter 26 on landowner information on reservation value and land assembly).

This information asymmetry problem refers to the policy maker's inability to design first-best or cost-effective mechanisms when landowners have private information about their willingness to accept compensation to provide ecosystem services. With constrained budgets, policy makers would prefer to secure the greatest ecosystem services supply possible, which in theory means paying each landowner their minimum willingness to accept compensation. However, information asymmetry prevents policy makers from targeting the least-cost suppliers, manifesting as at least three overlapping problems examined in recent literature. First, fiscal inefficiency occurs when a landowner is paid more than his or her minimum willingness to accept because the policy maker cannot sort by types. For instance, Kirwan et al. (2005) find evidence that 10–40% of the US Conservation Reserve Program expenditures were rent premiums. Second, adverse selection occurs when a landowner is paid for supplying an ecosystem service even though he or she would supply that service in the absence of the policy. Third, additionality is not achieved when a current supplier of ecosystem services is credited for future supply, even though that supply currently exists and would likely continue had no policy been implemented. Much research has explored solutions to these problems for the design of conservation and environmental policies. For example, economists have developed contracts to achieve second-best outcomes in the face of these information problems when targeting land for conservation (Smith 1995; Wu and Babcock 1996). Several methodological chapters in this handbook address economic techniques to predict and/or sort by types, given the underlying censoring from this information asymmetry.

3.2 Socioeconomic Impacts of Land Use Change

Perhaps the most visible social impacts of land use change are those associated with urbanization and suburbanization, which affects both urban and rural communities. As more people leave rural areas to live in cities, demand for housing increases, congestion intensifies, and urban air quality declines. All these changes will drive up housing prices in desirable locations, which some see pushing "the new labouring poor into great morasses of misery outside the centres of government and business and the newly specialised residential areas of the bourgeoisie" (Hobsbawm 1962, Chapter 11).

The locational pattern of different income groups and community characteristics, such as economic segregation and jurisdictional fragmentation, are strongly influenced by the spatial distribution of environmental amenities (Wu 2006). For example, it has been suggested that "the almost universal European division into a 'good' west end and a 'poor' east end of large cities" documented by Hobsbawm (1962, chapter 11) is "likely due to the prevailing south-west wind which carries coal smoke and other airborne pollutants downwind, making the western edges of towns preferable to the eastern ones."

As congestion associated with urbanization surpasses an acceptable cost level, a reverse pattern of migration, known as suburbanization, may occur. In fact, during the past 50 years, the proportion of the US population living in suburban areas increased from about one-third in 1960 to 63% in 1998 (US Department of Housing and Urban Development [USDHUD], 2000). With suburbanization, cities tend to gain lower income residents and lose upper income population, causing income segregation and economic disparities between urban and suburban communities to manifest and intensify. From 1969 to 1998, the share of low-income families in central cities grew from 21.9% to 25.5% compared with a decline from 18.3% to 16.6% for high-income households (USDHUD, 2000). The change in income mix led to a smaller tax base and more need to finance social services in urban communities. Wu (2010) developed a spatially explicit model to investigate how urban and suburban communities evolve differently with changes in local economic fundamentals such as rising income or falling commuting costs. The model highlights the importance of environmental amenities and the economy of scale in the provision of public services as determinants of urban spatial structure.

Urbanization has also changed rural communities. In some areas, migration to cities has turned once-viable rural communities into ghost towns. In other rural areas, urban sprawl has encroached to such an extent that the community itself has been lost (Wu et al. 2008, vii). Urbanization also presents challenges for farmers on the urban fringe, especially those who lease and therefore do not benefit from land appreciation. As neighboring farms are converted to development, farmers will no longer be able to take advantage of economies of scale from information sharing and business relationships with neighboring farmers. Urbanization may also cause the "impermanence syndrome," leading to a reduction in investment in new technology or machinery or idling of farmland (Lopez et al. 1988).

As urbanization intensifies, agricultural and nonagricultural land use conflicts become more severe (Lisansky 1986). This may lead to an increase in local ordinances designed to force farmers to internalize some of the negative externalities normally generated by agriculture. As the nearest input suppliers close because of insufficient demand for farm inputs, a farmer may have to pay more for inputs or spend more time to obtain equipment repairs (Lynch and Carpenter 2003; Wu et al. 2011). Competition for labor from nonagricultural sectors may raise farmers' labor costs. When the total amount of farmland falls below a critical mass, the local agricultural economy may collapse (Wu et al. 2011).

Urbanization also presents opportunities to farmers. The emergence of a new customer base provides farmers with new opportunities for higher value crops. For example, vegetable producers receive higher prices in urbanized areas (Lopez et al. 1988). Many farmers have shown remarkable adaptability in adjusting their enterprises to take advantage of new economic opportunities at the urban fringe. They farm more intensively in areas with high population density (Lockeretz 1988). More than half the value of total US farm production is derived from counties facing urbanization pressure (Larson et al. 2001).

Although there is strong evidence that land use change affects social structures in both rural and urban communities, relatively few studies have focused on the socioeconomic impacts of land use change. Nechyba and Walsh (2004) recognized this gap. After an extensive review of the literature, Nechyba and Walsh point out that, although many previous studies have investigated the drivers of urban development, relatively few have examined how city landscapes evolve within expanding boundaries. Chapter 12 by Stone and Wu, focuses on a fundamental problem in analyzing the socioeconomic impacts of urbanizing land use: household location choice. Stone and Wu first survey the most significant developments in theory and analyses that examine the interactions among household location decisions, land use patterns, and municipal profiles and then explore strategies to model these interactions using a case study from Portland, Oregon. We hope this chapter will help stimulate more research on the socioeconomic impacts of land use change.

4. Methodological Developments

The increasing importance of the environmental and socioeconomic issues associated with land use and the increasing complexity of land policy has led researchers to develop ever more sophisticated methods. Section III of this handbook addresses six cutting-edge approaches in three general categories. The section also includes a synthetic chapter critically reviewing methodological advances.

Spatial econometric analysis is one approach presented. The most recent spatial methods seek to maximize the information potential of explicitly spatial data. Economists have developed conceptual frameworks that attempt to address the spatial characteristics of benefits and costs of land use changes in tandem with the natural scientists, who develop spatial models of resource systems but also a variety of new methodologies to analyze spatially explicit data. A second approach is simulation, including spatial-equilibrium and agent-based methods. A third approach is inferential and experimental, using reduced-form and structural econometric models, to better understand the drivers of land behavior, tease out causation, and predict hidden policy impacts.

The initial, synthetic chapter of this section, by Irwin and Wrenn, provides an overview and assessment of the main methods used to model spatially explicit data on land use and land use change. The chapter offers a valuable comparison of reduced-form and structural econometric models. It also compares spatial-equilibrium and agent-based simulation. Irwin and Wrenn provide a critical assessment of three important questions: what are the advantages and disadvantages of these various empirical approaches to modeling land use and land use change? Which questions are best suited to be answered using one versus the other approach? And, where are the gaps in the current literature? Chapters about specific modeling approaches follow this overview.

4.1 Spatial Econometric Methods in Land Use

During the past two decades, spatial econometric methods have matured into a formal, insightful, and widely used method for assessing land use and land policy. Cho, Kim, and Roberts, in Chapter 17, provide an overview of the state-of-art spatial econometric methods and a comparison of different approaches. The chapter offers an application for predicting development rates in Nashville-Davidson County, Tennessee.

Chapter 14, by Klaiber and Kuminoff, provides a comprehensive treatment of the equilibrium sorting methodology. It clarifies the relationship between an equilibrium sorting model, in which households make location decisions as well as being spatially explicit and characterizing household preferences, and a reduced-form hedonic model that does not involve sorting. The chapter presents a detailed description of the econometric procedures for estimating equilibrium sorting models and the simulation procedures for policy evaluation.

4.2 Simulation Methods in Land Use

Two chapters describe simulation methods. Plantinga and Lewis, in Chapter 15, describe econometric-based landscape simulation models for policy evaluation in a spatially heterogeneous landscape. They identify modeling challenges such as capturing the variation in private returns to land use at the right analytical level and the private information landowners possess about these returns. Plantinga and Lewis also present an application that connects land use (shoreline development in Wisconsin) with habitat provision (green frog population).

In Chapter 16, Parker offers a very different simulation method: agent-based modeling. In a spatially explicit virtual landscape, these models capture the decisions and interactions of economic agents. Parker reviews this approach in terms of model attributes, computational issues, and the questions the models can answer. The models are well positioned to address, jointly, spatial and agent heterogeneity.

4.3 Experimental Methods in Land Use

Two chapters describe experimental methods, both of which can inform the likely effectiveness of land policies without necessarily having to evaluate an existing policy in a specific location. In Chapter 18, Towe, Lewis, and Lynch, discuss the methods and challenges of quasi-experimental econometric estimation for evaluating land policies. It has long been recognized that selection issues confound inference of policy impacts; simply, land outcomes cannot be modeled as a result of a policy because these policy treatments were not randomly assigned. But methods for addressing selection problems have continually advanced. Towe et al. describe these inferential problems and how one approach, the propensity score matching method, can solve them. Advantages of, challenges with, and steps to be taken when employing the propensity score matching method are explained. The chapter also provides a detailed application that analyzes how a smart growth policy affects land development outcomes in Maryland.

In Chapter 19, Messer, Duke, and Lynch present recent uses of laboratory and field experiments to inform land use and policy problems. The authors develop a framework to understand the tradeoffs in experimental control, problem context, and the representativeness of the participants to actual land decision makers. An application investigates the impact of different types of information on the performance of reverse auctions for ecosystem services. The results suggest that different levels of public information affect sellers' bidding behavior as well as auction competitiveness. Overbidding and too little market competition leads to significant auction efficiency loss.

5. The Economics of Land Use Law and Policy

Land use provides many economic benefits and costs that are not figured into the private landowner's decisions. These externalities lead to an inefficient allocation of land uses. Land market inefficiencies take diverse forms on the ground. For instance, developers may not bear all the environmental and infrastructural costs generated by their projects. Natural land owners do not enjoy all the social benefits they supply. Owners of small urban parcels hold out, thereby preventing optimally sized redevelopments and driving economic activity to the suburbs. Other market failures also characterize land markets—for instance, given that location makes many land uses perfectly heterogeneous, imperfect competition may arise.

Politicians, legal scholars, planners, policy makers, and the general public have long understood the problems associated with these land market failures—even though efficient resource allocation is probably not driving their thinking—because these failures often mirror readily understood notions of appropriate neighborly behavior and the interdependencies of modern life. In other words, people often believe that neighbors act inappropriately when they make decisions with negative externalities, foisting unwanted costs on them. Of course, Coase (1960) reframed the way economists think about causation in externalities, providing a recognition that two parties are competing for use of the same resource (see Duke 2004). But part of the innovation of Coase (1960) was to help economists recognize that the conventional explanation of external costs was incomplete.

The conventional story of land use conflict persists in the public imagination, despite Coase's (1960) efforts and those of the economists who followed. Residential voters and their representatives will support local zoning, recognizing that external costs of mixing commercial and residential land uses hurts their property values. Similarly, many will support revitalization of an urban brownfield, not to prevent "sprawl" and conversion of greenfields, but instead because they envision a future in which the local urban economy is revitalized and land is "clean." Policies to promote provision of positive land use externalities may be more recent, but preservation and conservation seem to "make sense" to many members of society. The alignment of economic rationale and the way the general public thinks about its well-being has likely led to the developed world's long history of land use policy.

Duke and Lynch (2006) derive a framework to explain the different forms land controls may take in the context of land retention. Some controls are regulatory, such as zoning. Other controls are incentive-based, such as an impact fee (tax) on new residential development to fund sewers. Techniques such as conservation easements are best framed as participatory, rather than incentive-based, because the public or private demander secures positive externalities by triggering demand in a market for a less-than-fee right in land (say, a negative easement). In other words, the easement market always existed, but it was the newly created demand from government or a private group that created the viability of this "new" market for conservation. A final set of controls is a hybrid of two of the preceding; for instance, a transferable development right program is part regulatory (the cap) and part incentive-based (the trading).

The aforementioned types of land use control, in effect, establish the specific markets for land. Framed differently, any land unit may be sold into various overlapping and/or mutually exclusive land use markets. For instance, one parcel of farmland may be supplied in agricultural land use markets and conservation markets, but that same parcel may not be supplied in preservation and developed use markets. Institutions establish the property rights that define markets (Schmid 1999). Resource allocation efficiency is a function of the prevailing institutional arrangements (Bromley 1989, chapter 5). Once rights are established, each policy can be assessed for its potential efficiency implications. Note also that all rights associated with land are not assigned, and remaining externality conflicts arise from the absence of rights (Duke 2004).

Legislatures and quasi-judicial bodies create these land markets, and courts sanction and refine the allocation of rights. As this section clarifies, land economists have participated in the land use policy debate in several ways. The unifying theme, however, is that work in this area tends to be applied. Economists' applications focus on specific policies (conservation easements, zoning, etc.) or specific areas of law (regulatory takings, eminent domain, etc.). A common result is that there are unintended consequences; seeking to solve one failure can trigger substantial welfare losses in the form of higher housing prices, smaller houses, and inefficient land use patterns (Cheshire and Sheppard 2002; Hascic and Wu 2012).

Most economic attention falls on incentive-based and participatory policies because these policies are new and match most economists' underlying aversion to inflexible regulations of any type. The incentive-based and participatory approaches seemingly have many advantages over direct regulatory land use control. A development impact fee can be used to achieve both the optimal pace and pattern of land development, a shortcoming of zoning regulations (Wu and Irwin 2008). However, zoning may be preferred from a practical viewpoint, as well as in cases in which the environmental costs of land conversion are highly uncertain. Zoning may also be preferable when one also considers the costs of implementing policies because regulations are less expensive than many participatory policies (Johnston and Duke 2007). In situations in which the natural and human systems interact in complex ways, thresholds and nonlinear dynamics are likely to exist, and the environmental costs could be very high and sensitive to land development. In such cases, zoning may be preferred. The policy challenge, however, is to know when the system is in the neighborhood of such thresholds.

Although federal spending on land-related conservation programs, such as the Conservation Reserve Program (CRP) and the Wetland Reserve Program (WRP), has increased substantially over the past 25 years, the federal government has yet to articulate a clear vision of how land use should be managed. Most land use controls are in the hands of local governments, and the level of government involvement in land use planning and regulation varies considerably across counties and municipalities in the United States. Some local governments have few land use controls, whereas others are actively involved in land use planning and regulation.

The forces of urbanization have motivated many local governments to impose strict land use control. Economists research whether these policies achieve their goals and how they impact associated markets. Evidence suggests that some of the efforts have successfully slowed development. For example, Wu and Cho (2007) found that local land use regulations reduced the total supply of developed land by 10% in the five western states between 1982 and 1997, with the largest percent reduction in Washington (13.0%), followed by Oregon (12.6%), California (9.5%), Idaho (4.7%), and Nevada (2.8%). Yet a predictable but unintended consequence of land use regulation is higher housing prices, which make housing less affordable to middle- and low-income households (Glaeser and Gyourko 2002; Cho et al. 2003; Glaeser and Ward 2006).

Private trusts and nonprofit organizations play an increasingly important, albeit uncoordinated, role in the mix of local and federal land use through their efforts to promote land conservation. For example, the Nature Conservancy (2013) has helped to protect approximately 15 million acres of ecologically important lands in the United States. However, some have questioned whether private conservation efforts crowd out or complement public efforts for land conservation (Albers et al. 2008).

Most land use controls prove contentious, especially in areas facing rapid urbanization. The simplistic view on land use control does not capture the complex motivations driving the decisions of the public and government. In this view, proponents envision protection of farmland, forests, water quality, open space, and wildlife habitat. They anticipate increases in property values and human health. Opponents argue that urban development is an orderly market process that allocates land from agriculture to urban use and that governments tend to overregulate because they rarely bear the costs of regulation (Hascic and Wu 2012).

A more complex perspective recognizes that land use controls generate both benefits and costs, and, in most cases, create both winners and losers, at least, in the short term. Each side attempts to marshall the forces of "good" (clean environment, job creation, good schools, health, etc.) against the other side's "evil" (pollution, job destruction, crime, etc.). Both sides recognize that any policy measures that aim at curbing urban development will ultimately affect a key element of the traditional "good" life—such as the ability to consume a large amount of living space at affordable prices.

Economists have much to contribute to the debate. Social welfare accrues from many sources, so the grip of advocacy need not necessarily determine the outcomes of the analysis. Conflict arises from poorly designed incentives and an absence of markets. Information asymmetry is rampant, driving many conflicts, and a poorly designed policy does not overcome this challenge. Policy makers ought to resist the temptation to attribute all "irregular" land use patterns to market failures and impose stringent land use regulations that may hinder the function of market forces. They should try to identify and understand the sources of market failures—such as those that cause "excessive development"—and address problems at their roots.

Part IV of this handbook presents seven chapters that analyze the economics of land use law and policy. The first four chapters disentangle the economics of land conservation and preservation, which has emerged as an increasingly important tool in the past several decades as land use regulations have waned. Chapter 20, by Gnedenko and Heffley, presents a rich open-city model of the tax, spending, and land use zoning policies of local government and applies the model to analyze the impact of open space preservation on local land use and community characteristics. The chapter provides an applied analysis, suggesting that policies that seemingly promote open space may in fact work against that goal.

In Chapters 21–23, land conservation policies in the United States and the European Union are explained and compared. Ferris and Lynch, in Chapter 21, categorize US conservation policies into the four-part scheme of Duke and Lynch (2006)—the categorization described earlier. The authors use this categorization to organize the economics literature on US conservation and derive synthetic results on the effectiveness of each approach. Hodge, in Chapter 22, conducts an assessment of European agri-environmental policies, focusing on the voluntary contracts in place since the mid-1980s under the Common Agricultural Policy. Hodge's analysis considers policy challenges with asymmetric information and transaction costs, and he concludes that future policy will need to enhance payment targeting, competition among suppliers, coordination, and security of the environmental benefits obtained. Chapter 23, by Claassen et al. complements Chapters 21 and 22 with a systematic comparison of US and EU agri-environmental policies. In both locations, these policies began in earnest in the 1980s, and both employ a mix of three types of policies: incentive-based, regulatory, and cross-compliance. Although the policies have similarities, most economists tend to focus their research on a policy in one location or the other. The chapter focuses on a comparison of the economic research results on the effectiveness of these policies and the data used by economists in these studies.

Chapters 24–26 turn to the economic analysis of the legal institutions of land use. These chapters focus on law and economic problems about the limits of permissible government control of land in the US context. In Chapter 24, Eisen reviews the broader context of "brownfields" redevelopment in urban areas, analyzes developers' brownfields development decisions, and assesses how state and federal laws affect the decisions. Contamination imposes a stigma on these sites, and stigma is affected by the cleanup policies employed. Information problems are highlighted, as are novel incentives to overcome stigma, including voluntary programs, public input, and the lifecycle impacts of remediation.

Chapters 25 and 26 investigate takings, both regulatory and eminent domain. Miceli and Segerson in Chapter 25 explain the legal and economic theories determining when a regulation crosses the compensation threshold, thus becoming a compensable taking. They explain the seminal Blume, Rubinfeld, and Shapiro (1984) model of takings, the connection to regulatory takings, and the surprising result of efficient zero compensation. Then Miceli and Segerson interpret and expand this model with a review of decades of subsequent work. Collectively, their chapter clarifies the efficiency implications of various compensation rules.

In Chapter 26, Duke assesses the economic literature on eminent domain, focusing solely on physical appropriations as opposed to the nonpossessory actions described in Chapter 25. Rather than assessing efficient compensation—which is well covered in Chapter 25—Duke examines two other themes in the economic literature on eminent domain. First, eminent domain solves inefficiencies in land assembly: holdouts and the provision of inefficiently low levels of public goods from urban redevelopment. The chapter builds a model of information asymmetry in assembly markets, then compares the conditions under which eminent domain does and does not enhance efficiency relative to market assembly.

6. Future Research Directions

This handbook concludes with a synthetic chapter (Chapter 27) on future research directions in land economics. All the chapters offer assessments of where research is going—or should be going—in the areas covered. Duke and Wu assimilate these suggestions and predictions into five general directions for future work.

The first direction involves spatially explicit structural modeling. The interdependence of land use patterns and economic growth highlights the need for spatially explicit structural modeling. Such a modeling approach better explains economic performance, the distribution of economic activity in a region, the impact of shocks, and poverty. Although economists are accustomed to structural models, a great deal of the current empirical work relies on reduced-form models. Irwin et al. (2009) call for structural modeling to better identify the potential causal linkages among the many interdependent processes that affect urban-rural growth.

The second direction is toward greater integrated economic and ecological modeling. Integrated modeling gives economists a way to increase explanatory power by linking economic models with quantitative modeling efforts in different economic fields and in noneconomic disciplines. Integration may include linking land use and development or linking land use and ecosystem services. Increasingly, economists' research interests are aligned with questions from other scientists. For instance, the linkage of economic and ecological systems offers great promise, with many economists interested in research questions that build on or are nested with models traditionally addressed by ecologists, hydrologists, and other natural scientists.

Advancing methods to understand and uncover agents' behavior offers a third direction. The methods chapters cover spatial, econometric, simulation, and experimental approaches. Most of these methods have been developed to better understand selection issues. In other words, the methods allow economists to understand agents' interactions and decisions without necessarily observing, in a given location, a real-world policy or a real-world market. Inferences can be made without bias. Collectively, economists are becoming better able to understand land use behavior and phenomena.

A fourth direction involves land economists' efforts to build models that best employ newly abundant spatial and other land data. Many chapters highlight new sources of data on land prices, uses, and services. Despite their increasing abundance, these data are often incomplete and inconsistent. There are many suggestions for how to use these data, but the chapter authors also identify areas in which some measures need to be developed, where data need to be collected, and where datasets ought to be linked.

The fifth and final direction concerns economists' efforts to overcome information challenges in policy design. Not surprisingly, economists see spatial analysis playing a key role in future analyses. Many chapters suggest moving toward more structural modeling or various experimental methods to draw more broadly applicable results on land use policy. Several of the chapters also suggest increasingly sophisticated approaches to the underlying information problems that prevent the creation of first-best policies. In large part, information problems in land manifest as incentive problems in voluntary policies—especially in agri-environmental policies. Land economists see great opportunities to improve policy performance with respect to additionality, leakage/slippage, and other incentive problems. Some chapters recommend that economists take a step back from the focus on solving these problems and, instead, encourage research about how multiple policies interact and how policy/market complexities affect performance.

7. Conclusion

This handbook is framed with the idea that an integrated approach to land use economics is needed. Why is this approach needed? First, partial equilibrium analysis is not always adequate to examine the questions society needs answered. Second, land economic problem settings are often too fluid to warrant the simplification economists seek to derive tight and tractable results, ready lab experiments, and empirically testable theoretically derived results. Third, integrated work may help prevent unexpected suboptimal recommendations.

Integration can occur within economics, but across fields. Or, it can occur between economic and noneconomic models. Even within the discipline, greater recognition and integration stimulates cross-fertilization between the fields of land economics research. By providing a comprehensive survey of land-related work in several economics fields, we hope this handbook will provide the basic tools needed for new and established land economists to redefine the scope and focus of their work, to better incorporate the contemporary thinking from other fields, and to push out the frontiers of land economics in the areas identified.

References

Albers, H. J., A. W. Ando, and M. Batz. 2008. Equilibrium patterns of land conservation:Crowding in/out, agglomeration, and policy. *Resources and Energy Economics* 30(4): 492–508.

Attavanich, W., B. S. Rashford, R. M. Adams, and B. A. McCarl. 2014. Land use, climate change, and ecosystem services. In *The Oxford handbook of land economics*, eds. J. M. Duke and J. Wu, 255–280. New York: Oxford University Press.

Barbier, E. B. 2014. Land use and sustainable economic development: developing world. In *The Oxford handbook of land economics*, eds. J. M. Duke and J. Wu, 139–159. New York: Oxford University Press.

Blume, L., D. Rubinfeld, and P. Shapiro. 1984. The taking of land: When should compensation be paid? *Quarterly Journal of Economics* 99: 71–92.

Bromley, D. W. 1989. *Economic interests and institutions: The conceptual foundations of public policy*. Oxford: Basil Blackwell.

Cheshire, P., and S. Sheppard. 2002. The welfare economics of land use planning. *Journal of Urban Economics* 52: 242–269.

Cho, S.-H., S. G. Kim, and R. K. Roberts. 2014. Spatial econometric modeling of land use change. In *The Oxford handbook of land economics*, eds. J. M. Duke and J. Wu, 430–451. New York: Oxford University Press.

Cho, S.-H., J. Wu, and W. G. Boggess. 2003. Measuring interactions among urbanization, land use regulations, and public finance. *American Journal of Agricultural Economics* 85: 988–999.

Claassen, R., J. Cooper, C. Salvioni, and M. Veronesi. 2014. Agri-environmental policies: A comparison of US and EU experiences. In *The Oxford handbook of land economics*, eds. J. M. Duke and J. Wu, 648–667. New York: Oxford University Press.

Coase, R. H. 1960. The problem of social cost. *Journal of Law and Economics* 3:1–44.

Czech, B., P. R. Krausman, and P. K. Devers. 2000. Economic associations among causes of species endangerment in the United States. *BioScience* 50: 593–601.

Duke, J. M. 2004. Institutions and land-use conflicts: Harm, dispute processing, and transactions. *Journal of Economic Issues* 38(1): 227–252.

Duke, J. M. 2014. Eminent domain and the land assembly problem. In *The Oxford handbook of land economics*, eds. J. M. Duke and J. Wu, 723–735. New York: Oxford University Press.

Duke, J. M., and L. Lynch. 2006. Four classes of farmland retention techniques: Comparative evaluation and property rights implications. *Land Economics* 82(2): 189–213.

Duke, J. M., and J. Wu. 2014. Future research directions in land economics. In *The Oxford handbook of land economics*, eds. J. M. Duke and J. Wu. New York: Oxford University Press.

Eisen, J. B. 2014. Stigmatized sites and urban brownfield redevelopment. In *The Oxford handbook of land economics*, eds. J. M. Duke and J. Wu, 668–697. New York: Oxford University Press.

Ferris, J., and L. Lynch. 2014. Land conservation in the United States. In *The Oxford handbook of land economics*, eds. J. M. Duke and J. Wu, 583–611. New York: Oxford University Press.

Food and Agriculture Organization (FAO). 2004. Statistics from www.faostat.fao.org, updated February 2004.

Glaeser, E. L., and J. Gyourko. 2002. The impact of zoning on housing affordability. Harvard Institute of Economic Research, Discussion Paper Number 1948. Accessed November 19, 2007. http://post.economics.harvard.edu/hier/2002papers/HIER1948.pdf

Glaeser, E. L., and B. A. Ward. 2006. The causes and consequences of land use regulation: Evidence from greater Boston. Harvard Institute of Economic Research, Discussion Paper Number 2140. Accessed November 19, 2007. http://www.economics.harvard.edu/hier/2006papers/HIER2124.pdf

Gnedenko, E., and D. Heffley. 2014. Open space preservation: Direct controls and fiscal incentives. In *The Oxford handbook of land economics*, eds. J. M. Duke and J. Wu, 547–582. New York: Oxford University Press.

Hascic, I., and J. Wu. 2012. The cost of land use regulation versus the value of individual exemption: Oregon's measures 37 and 49. *Contemporary Economic Policy* 30: 159–214.

Hobsbawm, E. 1962. *The age of revolution: 1789–1848*. London: Weidenfeld & Nicolson.

Hodge, I. 2014. European agri-environmental policy: The conservation and re-creation of cultural landscapes. In *The Oxford handbook of land economics*, eds. J. M. Duke and J. Wu, 612–647. New York: Oxford University Press.

Irwin, E. G., and D. Wrenn. 2014. An assessment of empirical methods for modeling land use. In *The Oxford handbook of land economics*, eds. J. M. Duke and J. Wu, 327–351. New York: Oxford University Press.

Irwin, E., K. P. Bell, N. E. Bockstael, D. Newburn, M. D. Partridge, and J. Wu. 2009. The economics of urban-rural space." *Annual Review of Resource Economics* 1(October): 1–26.

Johnston, R. J., and J. M. Duke. 2007. Willingness to pay for agricultural land preservation and policy process attributes: Does the method matter? *American Journal of Agricultural Economics* 89(4): 1098–1115.

Johnston, R. J., S. K. Swallow, D. M. Bauer, E. Uchida, and C. M. Anderson. 2014. Connecting ecosystem services to land use: Implications for valuation and policy. In *The Oxford handbook of land economics*, eds. J. M. Duke and J. Wu, 196–225. New York: Oxford University Press.

Khanna, M., D. Zilberman, and C. L. Crago. 2014. Modeling the land use change with biofuels. In *The Oxford handbook of land economics*, eds. J. M. Duke and J. Wu, 85–110. New York: Oxford University Press.

Kirwan, B., R. N. Lubowski, and M. J. Roberts. 2005. How cost-effective are land retirement auctions? Estimating the difference between payments and willingness to accept in the Conservation Reserve Program. *American Journal of Agricultural Economics* 87(5): 1239–1247.

Klaiber, H. A., and N. V. Kuminoff. 2014. Equilibrium sorting models of land use and residential choice. In *The Oxford handbook of land economics*, eds. J. M. Duke and J. Wu, 352–379. New York: Oxford University Press.

Lewis, D. J., and E. Nelson. 2014. The economics of wildlife conservation. In *The Oxford handbook of land economics*, eds. J. M. Duke and J. Wu, 163–195. New York: Oxford University Press.

Larson, J., J. Findeis, and S. Smith. 2001. Agricultural adaptation to urbanization in southeastern Pennsylvania. *Agricultural and Resource Economics Review* 30: 32–43.

Lisansky, J. 1986. Farming in an urbanizing environment: Agricultural land use conflicts and rights to farm. *Human Organization* 45: 363–371.

Lockeretz, W. 1988. Urban influences on the amount and structure of agriculture in the north-eastern United States. *Landscape and Urban Planning* 16: 229–244.

Lopez, R. A., A. O. Adelaja, and M. S. Andrews. 1988. The effects of suburbanization on agriculture. *American Journal of Agricultural Economics* 70: 346–358.

Lynch, L., and J. Carpenter. 2003. Is there evidence of a critical mass in the mid-Atlantic agricultural sector between 1949 and 1997? *Agricultural and Resource Economics Review* 32: 116–128.

Marland G., R. A. Pielke, M. Apps, R. Avissar, R. A. Betts, K. J. Davis, P. C. Frumhoff, S. T. Jackson, L. A. Joyce, P. Kauppi, J. Katzenberger, K. G. MacDicken, R. P. Neilson, J. O. Niles, D. S. Niyogi, R. J. Norby, N. Pena, N. Sampson, and Y. Xue. 2003. The climatic impacts of land surface change and carbon management, and the implications for climate-change mitigation policy. *Climate Policy* 3:149–157.

McCarl, B. A., W. Attavanich, M. Musumba, J. E. Mu, and R. Aisabokhae. 2014. Land use and climate change. In *The Oxford handbook of land economics*, eds. J. M. Duke and J. Wu, 226–254. New York: Oxford University Press.

Messer, K. D., J. M. Duke, and L. Lynch. 2014. Applying experiments to land economics: Public information and auction efficiency in ecosystem service markets. In *The Oxford handbook of land economics*, eds. J. M. Duke and J. Wu, 481–546. New York: Oxford University Press.

Miceli, T. J., and K. Segerson. 2014. Regulatory takings. In *The Oxford handbook of land economics*, eds. J. M. Duke and J. Wu, 698–722. New York: Oxford University Press.

Mills, E. S. 2014. Are large metropolitan areas still viable? In *The Oxford handbook of land economics*, eds. J. M. Duke and J. Wu, 74–84. New York: Oxford University Press.

Montgomery, C. A. 2014. Fire: An agent and a consequence of land use change. In *The Oxford handbook of land economics*, eds. J. M. Duke and J. Wu, 281–301. New York: Oxford University Press.

The Nature Conservancy. 2013. Private lands conservation. Accessed January 31, 2013. http://www.nature.org/about-us/private-lands-conservation/index.htm

Nickerson, C. J., and W. Zhang. 2014. Modeling the determinants of farmland values in the United States. In *The Oxford handbook of land economics*, eds. J. M. Duke and J. Wu, 111–138. New York: Oxford University Press.

Parker, D. C. 2014. An economic perspective on agent-based models of land use and land cover change. In *The Oxford handbook of land economics*, eds. J. M. Duke and J. Wu, 402–429. New York: Oxford University Press.

Partridge, M. D., and D. S. Rickman. 2014. Integrating economic development analysis and land use economics. In *The Oxford handbook of land economics*, eds. J. M. Duke and J. Wu, 23–51. New York: Oxford University Press.

Plantinga, A. J., and D. J. Lewis. 2014. Landscape simulations with econometric-based land use models. In *The Oxford handbook of land economics*, eds. J. M. Duke and J. Wu, 380–401. New York: Oxford University Press.

Nechyba, T. J., and R. P. Walsh. 2004. Urban sprawl. *Journal of Economic Perspectives* 18: 177–200.

Schmid, A. A. 1999. Government, property, markets... In that order... Not government versus markets. In *The fundamental interrelationships between government and property*, ed. N. Mercuro and W. J. Samuels. Greenwich, CT: JAI Press, 237–242.

Smith, R. B. W. 1995. The conservation reserve program as a least-cost land retirement mechanism. *American Journal of Agricultural Economics* 77 (1995): 93–105.

Soulé, M. E. 1991. Conservation: Tactics for a constant crisis. *Science* 253: 744–750.

Stone, E., and J. Wu. 2014. Land use and municipal profiles. In *The Oxford handbook of land economics*, eds. J. M. Duke and J. Wu, 302–324. New York: Oxford University Press.

Towe, C., R. Lewis, and L. Lynch. 2014. Using quasi-experimental methods to evaluate land policies: Application to Maryland's priority funding legislation. In *The Oxford handbook of land economics*, eds. J. M. Duke and J. Wu, 452–480. New York: Oxford University Press.

US Department of Housing and Urban Development (USDHUD). 2000. *The state of the cities 2000*. Washington, DC: US Department of Housing and Urban Development.

Wu, J. 2006. Environmental amenities, urban sprawl, and community characteristics. *Journal of Environmental Economics and Management* 52: 527–547.

Wu, J. 2010. Economic fundamentals and urban-suburban disparities. *Journal of Regional Science* 50: 570–591.

Wu, J., and B. A. Babcock. 1996. Contract design for the purchase of environmental goods from agriculture. *American Journal of Agricultural Economics* 78: 935–945.

Wu, J., P. W. Barkley, and B. A. Weber, eds. 2008. *Frontiers in resource and rural economics*. Washington DC: Resources for the Future.

Wu, J., and S. Cho. 2007. The effect of local land use regulations on urban development in the western United States. *Regional Science and Urban Economics* 37: 69–86.

Wu, J., M. Fisher, and U. Pascual. 2011. Urbanization and the viability of local agricultural economies. *Land Economics* 87: 109–125.

Wu, J., and E. Irwin. 2008. Optimal land development with endogenous environmental amenities. *American Journal of Agricultural Economics* 90: 232–248.

Zilberman, D., M. Khanna, S. Kaplan, and E. Kim. 2014. Technology adoption and land use. In *The Oxford handbook of land economics*, eds. J. M. Duke and J. Wu, 52–73. New York: Oxford University Press.

PART I

DETERMINANTS AND DRIVERS OF LAND USE CHANGE

CHAPTER 1

INTEGRATING REGIONAL ECONOMIC DEVELOPMENT ANALYSIS AND LAND USE ECONOMICS

MARK D. PARTRIDGE AND DAN S. RICKMAN

Academic economists historically separated issues related to land use from those related to regional economic development. One reason is that land use studies typically do not consider the connectedness of firm and household location decisions, whereas regional economic development studies rarely account for land (McDonald, 2001). Moreover, it appears that land use researchers think more at the microscale of neighborhoods (or intraregional), whereas economic-development researchers think more at the macroscale (or interregional).

The division between the two fields does not reflect how local economic development policy is undertaken. Economic development is inherently about land because it is about activity in a place or on a specific land area. Local governments compete with one another in trying to attract households and firms to their *place*.

Land use and economic development, then, are inherently linked through zoning, transportation, infrastructure, sprawl, and environmental attributes that jointly affect firm productivity and household utility. Because local policy is about place, land economics is linked to economic development policy through competition for new development. This raises further questions about governance and local government effectiveness in delivering public services that underlie development through Tiebout (1956) sorting and spatial equilibrium processes generally.

In this chapter, we attempt to tie together the two separate literatures. We stress the economic development literature in regional and urban economics that most closely relates to land economics. An implicit theme is that land economic studies should pay closer attention to joint firm/household location decisions, whereas the regional economic development literature should pay closer attention to land as it defines the place

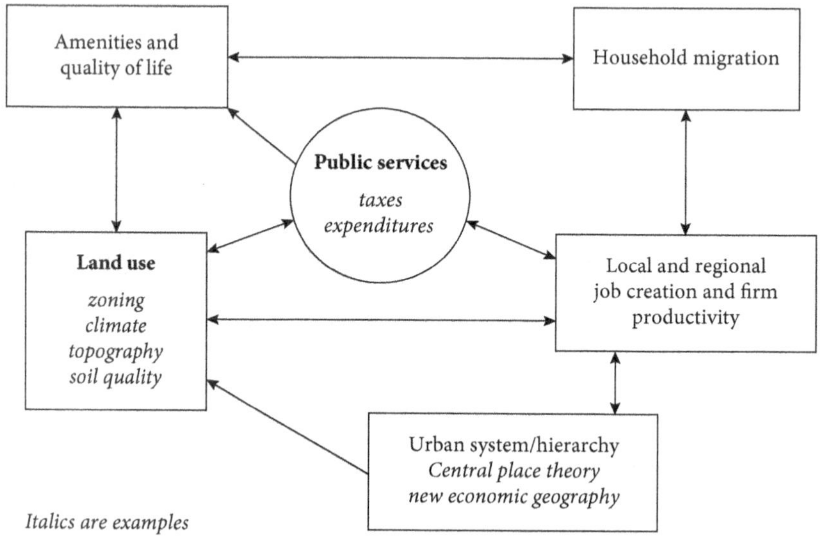

FIGURE 1.1 Model of regional economic development with land use.

that the activity occurs. Likewise, another theme is that research should focus more on the regional interaction of activity across space. Models and empirical approaches are needed that recognize regions as complex systems, fully understanding and modeling the interplay between land use and economic development, including the linkages between the intraregion distribution of economic activity and overall regional economic performance.

Figure 1.1 shows the interdependence of local and regional economic development (depicted as job creation and firm productivity) with several key factors including land use, amenities and quality of life, household migration, public services, and the urban system. Italics indicate some examples of these factors. The figure reflects the key role of land use in directly affecting economic development and, in turn, being directly affected by economic development. Land use also indirectly influences economic development through its interactions with the other factors. These interactions also illustrate the difficulties of identification of causality in empirical analysis. The chapter will outline these direct and indirect effects that land use and economic development have with each other, illustrating the central connections between land economics and regional and urban economics.

Before describing the contents of the chapter, we note that some important topics are given brief treatment or omitted because of space limitations. Examples include public infrastructure, tax competition, urban amenities, and spatial econometrics. Section 1 outlines the basic spatial equilibrium approach used in modern regional economic development studies and outlines ways to include land. Section 2 describes the natural link between land economics and economic development through proximity to urban centers. Economic activity across space is strongly affected by access to agglomeration economies that influences economic location both within and across regions, with the latter being our focus. Section 3 describes how land use affects the provision of natural and urban amenities that influence whether households and businesses want to locate in a particular place. We focus on the common features in the two literatures in which the land use literature focuses on microscale amenities such as open space, whereas the economic development literature focuses more on amenities at the regional scale that affect regional economic growth.

Section 4 provides a brief introduction to government policy aimed to improve land use and increase economic activity. This literature is extensive and we can only provide a cursory treatment. Section 5 describes some of the empirical approaches used in the economic development literature, focusing on the quasi-experimental and structural approaches that currently predominate. We note that both have advantages for empirical assessment but they suffer from shortcomings. The unifying theme is that studies using either approach need to more rigorously assess the legitimacy of their identifying assumptions and check robustness. Section 6 briefly highlights areas ripe for future research while Section 7 presents our conclusions.

1. Land Use in Regional Economic Development Analysis

Despite its central role in firm and household location decisions and regional economic activity generally, land routinely is omitted in regional economic development analysis. In part, this results from the traditional tools used in economic development analysis, which often are chosen for convenience rather than demonstrated accuracy (Partridge and Rickman, 1998, 2010). In studies where land use is the focus, regional economic development considerations often are ignored or are of secondary importance. Nevertheless, there is growing recognition of the central role of land use in regional economic development.

Land is completely removed from consideration in economic impact analysis that involves application of an input–output model because of its implicit assumption of perfectly elastic supply. Factors of production implicitly are assumed in excess supply in short-run analysis or perfectly mobile in long-run analysis. As a fixed factor, often in limited supply, the implicit omission of land from consideration questions the routine use of input–output models in regional economic development analysis. This omission likely leads to highly inaccurate impact assessments when land prices are highly responsive to economic development or when there is intraregional heterogeneity in how land prices respond.

Computable general equilibrium (CGE) models incorporate factor supply constraints, making them more general than input–output models (Partridge and Rickman, 1998). Although CGE models potentially are more accurate in a wide range of applications, this depends critically on the formulation of the CGE models. For example, McGregor, Swales, and Yin (1996) formulate a CGE model with short-run labor supply and capital adjustment constraints. They relax the constraints in the long run in demonstrating how the CGE model then functions as an input–output model. Partridge and Rickman (2010) argue that the traditional method of formulating regional CGE models limits their applicability for regional economic development analysis; rather than patterning regional CGE models after their national counterparts, they should be based on spatial equilibrium theory, including explicitly incorporating land.

Rickman (1992) incorporates fixed land and imperfectly mobile capital and labor in a regional CGE model, demonstrating how this produces dramatically smaller economic multipliers than what is obtained by assuming factors of production are elastically supplied. Fixity of land drives up its price when exports increase, crowding out other production (the model did not separately consider residential land though). The CGE multiplier effects then greatly depend on the elasticity of substitution between land and the mobile factors.

Despite von Thünen's (1966) model of land use and the general importance of land in location theory, land has largely been ignored in the increasing-returns literature (Combes, Duranton, and Overman 2005). Helpman (1998) added a nontradeable housing sector to the New Economic Geography (NEG) model to introduce congestion costs, though land use is not explicitly modeled. Pflüger and Tabuchi (2010) incorporate land used in housing and in production by an increasing returns sector in a general equilibrium model, which produces a differing pattern of economic development than if land is only used in housing.

McDonald (2001) effectively argues for connecting regional economic development policies to both labor and land markets. Land markets not only affect predicted outcomes, but also may be a source of economic development gains. Consistent with Bartik (1991), benefits of regional economic development policies that allocate land to industrial uses include employment of previously unemployed or underemployed members of the labor force and higher land values. Welfare gains to original residents of the area from economic development are enhanced to the extent land is owned by residents (Morgan, Mutti, and Rickman 1996).

Burnett, Cutler, and Thresher (2007) incorporate land in a CGE model of Fort Collins, Colorado to examine potential crowding out effects on other industries from increased tourist activity and to assess whether tourism is an optimal land use. The supply of land is specified as price elastic for both commercial and residential uses. They found land used in tourism as having the largest per-acre effect on gross city product and real household income. A notable feature of the model is the connection between sectoral land use, direct job creation, in-migration, and residential land use. Tourism reduced in-migration and hence less residential demand for land. Using the same framework, Cutler and Davies (2007) report that sectors primarily employing low-skilled labor generally reduce in-migration and demand for residential land use compared to high-skilled sectors, producing a larger per acre contribution of gross product and income. Kim and Ju (2003) integrate an urban land supply module with a CGE model for Seoul in examining the impacts on gross regional product, welfare, and income distribution from converting industrial land and green space into residential use.

Another long-standing omission in the regional economic development literature is the positive role land plays as a natural amenity. Land used for public parks, or left as open space, for example, create recreational opportunities and provide attractive vistas, increasing the local quality of life. Higher quality of life increases retiree and labor force migration, stimulating regional growth.

Land's contribution to the local quality of life then provides another feedback loop in a regional economy. Changes in land use that enhance quality of life increase in-migration and growth (Rickman and Rickman 2011). Regional economic development analyses then must not only consider the relative direct benefits of alternative commercial or residential uses, they also should consider the effects on local quality of life.

Thus, we advocate that regional economic development analysis be conducted using a modeling framework broadly capable of capturing important feedback loops within a regional economy. One such framework is the widely used spatial equilibrium approach (Roback 1982; Beeson and Eberts 1989). The spatial equilibrium approach is sufficiently flexible to reflect an array of quality of life and firm agglomeration considerations (Tabuchi and Thisse 2006).

In the spatial equilibrium approach, households geographically locate so as to maximize utility, whereas firms maximize profits in their location. Central to both decisions are nominal wage rates and land costs, as well as perfect mobility. Higher wages, adjusted for land costs, attract households. Lower wage rates and land costs attract firms. In addition, the framework incorporates site specific characteristics, reflecting the quality of life and quality of the business environment. Quality of life includes benefits households derive from land use beyond those obtained from residential housing. In equilibrium, the values of site-specific characteristics are capitalized into wages and land costs. The approach can be formulated in growth terms by assuming that economies transition across spatial equilibria as exogenous conditions change (Dumais et al. 2002). Besides predictive equations for wages and land costs, equations can be derived from a spatial equilibrium model for growth in employment, gross regional product, investment, and population (Brown, Hayes, and Taylor 2003; Partridge and Rickman 2003; Brown and Taylor 2006).

Both traded and nontraded goods can be included in the model, in which the traded good can be specified with varying elasticity of demand.[1] Alternative theories of agglomeration economies can be captured in the approach, ranging from NEG (Ottaviano and Pinelli 2006) to urbanization economies, and those related to Central Place Theory

[1] The traditional approach assumes that firms producing a traded good are price takers. Alternatively, traded goods can be modeled using the Armington assumption, in which there is imperfect substitution between traded goods of differing origins (Partridge and Rickman 2010). McDonald (2001) examines the significance of alternative assumptions on the elasticity of demand for export goods in assessing regional economic development policies.

(Partridge, Ali, and Olfert 2010). Quality of life includes exogenous attributes such as weather, proximity to oceans or freshwater, or mountains. Other natural amenity attributes may be endogenous, being affected by local economic activity, including, air and water quality, forests, open space, attractive vistas. Endogenous quality of life attributes also include manmade amenities such as public infrastructure.

In the traditional spatial equilibrium framework, regions are assumed to have uniform land use policies. However, within a growth context, Glaeser and Tobio (2008) extend the model to allow for the effects of differential changes in land use and housing policies. They find that in former Confederate states, policies favorable to housing development were more likely responsible for strong population growth near the end of the 20th century than favorable weather.

Along these lines, Rappaport (2009) numerically simulates a structural spatial equilibrium model to produce a series of equilibriums in examining US metropolitan population growth. The model's sole congestion force is land, which is used to produce both a traded good and residential housing. Simulated feedback effects include population growth effects on area amenity attractiveness and the effects of increased population density on productivity.

2. Economic Development: Distance and Proximity

Land economics and economic development are linked through the location of households and firms. Although urban economists often emphasize the location of households and businesses within a given urban or metropolitan area, regional economists tend to focus on the relative differences across space, that is, comparing outcomes *across* economic regions that could be metropolitan, nonmetropolitan, or some combination. Because *intra*metropolitan area location patterns are discussed elsewhere, we only briefly highlight them, instead emphasizing broader regional patterns.

2.1 Distance and Regional Economic Development

Both land use and economic development are tied to a given place with its economic activity closely tied to proximity within the urban system. A first effort was Von Thünen's (1966) classic model of land use surrounding a single urban center on a featureless plane (Hite 1997). He shows that high-value-added products with high transportation costs locate closest to the urban center. The missing feature is it does not reflect the interaction of cities and regions across an urban system.

Central Place Theory (CPT) represented the first formal effort to model the urban system (Christaller 1933; Lösch 1940). Under assumptions including a featureless plane,

CPT shows how a multitiered urban system could develop in which the type of services determine the size and location of urban center—for example, the top of the urban system has all higher-ordered services such as patent attorneys, whereas the very bottom has basic services such as convenience stores.[2] CPT is adept at predicting the location of cities within urban systems, particularly in areas such as the North American Great Plains with traditionally high farm intensities (Fox and Kumar 1965; Wensley and Stabler 1998; Olfert and Stabler 1999). CPT is useful in predicting the location of actual business and consumer services and their population thresholds. A primary critique of CPT is its static nature. It is usually necessary to impose ad hoc assumptions regarding changes in technology and transport costs to describe an evolving urban system.

Nevertheless, CPT is still quite useful in understanding the organic process of how urban-centered regions have expanded since the 1950s (Irwin et al. 2010). This process is driven by many factors such as labor saving productivity gains in the primary sector that released labor for urban employment, further facilitated by the rising use of automobiles that aid long-distance rural–urban commuting. Increasing population thresholds for public and private services also led more services to be provided from a central location. The inherent spillovers as economies began to regionalize have long led to calls for government consolidation and regional collaboration around the functional economic regions delineated from CPT (Fox and Kumar 1965; Tweeten and Brinkman 1976). Increasing agglomeration economies imply that growth prospects are better in regions with critical mass (Portnov and Schwartz 2009). Conversely, promoting growth in small communities in isolation would be ineffective because they lack the agglomeration economies necessary to generate endogenous growth (Fox and Kumar 1965; Berry 1970).

The question whether urban-centered growth helps the surrounding hinterlands spawned a regional version of the spread and backwash literature that originated in international development,[3] namely, does prosperity in urban growth centers "spread" into the countryside and create economic opportunities, primarily through commuting, or does it create a "backwash" where urban growth pulls rural workers and capital into cities? United States results suggest urban growth spreads into the countryside (Hughes and Holland 1994; Barkley, Henry, and Bao 1996; Henry et al. 1997), while spreading up to 200 kilometers in Canada (Partridge et al. 2007). Yet, urban spread is more likely when rural communities have sufficient quality of life and services to support a commuting residential population (Henry et al. 1997; Kahn, Orazem, and Otto 2001; Partridge, Ali, and Olfert 2010). Likewise, Ke and Feser (2010) found that spread effects predominate in China, though Chen and Partridge (2011) find that growth in the three Chinese mega cities (Beijing, Shanghai, Guangzhou) creates widescale backwash.

[2] See Mulligan (1984) for a review of the CPT literature.

[3] See Myrdal (1957) for early applications and reviews by Richardson (1976) and Gaile (1980).

A key economic development question then is whether urban-led growth can reduce rural unemployment. There are reasons for pessimism. Renkow (2003) found that about 60% of the adjustment to local nonmetropolitan employment growth is accommodated through changes in commuting flows and another 30% is through changes in migration—that is, employment growth is only partially met through increases in *local* labor-force participation.

Although CPT inspired a large economic development literature, CPT theoretical research waned after the 1980s. One reason is that CPT was rather mature, and enthusiasm shifted to NEG. Another is that Geographical Information System (GIS) technology was not sufficiently developed to produce reliable empirical measures. Not until Partridge et al. (2008*a*, 2008*b*) was there a full test of CPT across a broad landscape. They used US county data to consider hundreds of metropolitan areas that are typically separated by rural space, forming a perfect setting for assessing the urban hierarchy's intervening effects on job and population growth. They employed detailed measures of access to the five nearest higher-ordered tiers in the urban hierarchy. Their results show that urban proximity has strong intervening effects that act through access to all the nearest higher-tiered urban areas.[4] Partridge et al. (2008*b*) also investigated the so-called "distance is dead" hypothesis that enhanced information technology and transportation had slayed the "tyranny of distance." They found that not only is distance *not* dead, but its effects are actually becoming stronger over time, most likely due to spatial transactions costs (e.g., face-to-face contact) in the expanding service sector. If distance is *more* problematic for rural areas and small cities, there are policy implications for the provision of broadband, transportation, business development, and regional governance.

Hedonic studies further support the notion that distance is a key factor behind spatial variation in wages and housing costs—which ultimately reflects how remoteness affects productivity and quality of life. Defining remoteness as being nonadjacent to a metropolitan area, Wu and Gopinath (2008) find that remoteness accounts for 76% of the expected differences in average wages between the highest and lowest US county quintiles, exceeding the importance of other factors such as amenities and human capital. Partridge et al. (2009, 2010) further confirm that remoteness is a key factor behind wages and housing prices. Partridge et al. (2010) find that most of the distance effects relate to productivity disadvantages (not household effects) and that these disadvantages are rising over time even with new technologies.

NEG models generated significant enthusiasm after Krugman's (1991) seminal work. They capture agglomeration economies and product variety (both as inputs to firms and

[4] Partridge et al. (2008*b*) find that distance from the nearest metropolitan area of at least 50,000 population leads to an economic penalty. If the nearest metropolitan area is not at least 1.5 million people, there are added penalties for the distance to reach metropolitan areas of at least 250,000 people, to reach metropolitan areas of at least 500,000 people, and to reach metropolitan areas of at least 1.5 million. For a clever application of the attenuation of agglomeration economies *within metropolitan areas*, see Rosenthal and Strange (2008). For applications of how the CPT urban hierarchy affects locale industry composition, see Wensley and Stabler (1998) and Polèse and Shearmur (2004).

to consumers) that can lead to core-periphery patterns (Brakman, Garretsen, and van Marrewijk 2009*a*). Economists are attracted to NEG models because they have explicit microfoundations, are analytically tractable, and they can explain uneven regional development (World Bank 2009). For example, Fujita, Krugman, and Mori (1999) show how a CPT urban hierarchy could initially form and Tabuchi and Thisse (2011) show how shocks affect the hierarchy. There are relative few empirical NEG applications, but examples include Brülhart and Koenig (2006) (transition economies), Volpe-Martincus (2010) (Brazil); Redding and Sturm (2008) (Postwar Germany); Brakman et al. (2009*b*) (European Union); and Hering and Poncet (2010) (China).

NEG has been used to inform regional development policy, often suggesting that traditional place-based policy to support lagging regions is misguided. The World Bank (2009) uses NEG to support its contention that regional policy should be spatially neutral because excessive support of peripheral regions shifts resources from central regions, leading to lower aggregate growth due to lost agglomeration economies. Likewise, providing infrastructure to peripheral regions could actually hurt them because it lowers transportation costs from central regions, allowing central firms to supply peripheral regions, further taking advantage of their agglomeration economies (Puga 1999). NEG frameworks have also been used to argue that large cities can have higher tax rates, allowing them to capture some of the "agglomeration rents" they provide businesses (Baldwin and Krugman 2004).

Despite their mathematical elegance, NEG models are criticized for lacking relevance for economic development policymaking. Several strict assumptions are typically employed to make these models solvable including a simplistic production function, iceberg transportation costs, little consideration of institutional factors, and household location preferences that are crude (Partridge 2010). NEG models often produce knife-edge results in which small parameter changes generate unstable outcomes. Partridge (2010) argues that the patterns uncovered in NEG models have limited applicability in North America, especially when compared to factors such as amenities and human capital. Partridge et al. (2008*b*, 2009, 2010) find that standard CPT significantly outperforms NEG in explaining US population movement, wages, and land costs. Krugman even notes that NEG models better described American development at the dawn of the 20th century, not the dawn of the 21st century, though he argues that contemporary China is a better setting.

2.2 Land Economics and Intrametropolitan-Area Economic Development

There are two workhorse models that economists use to describe urban location theory. First is the Alonso, Mills, Muth Monocentric City Model (MCM) (Alonso 1964; Mills 1967; Muth 1969). The MCM postulates an inverse relationship between land prices and distance to the central business district to compensate for longer commutes, though the rise of polycentric cities has reduced some of its applicability (McDonald and McMillen

2000). Yet, in an MCM framework, lower transport costs and higher incomes imply an expanding city footprint—or sprawl (Glaeser and Kahn 2004; Nechyba and Walsh, 2004; Wu 2010). Although sprawl has ambiguous impacts on social welfare (Glaeser and Kahn 2004), Fallah, Partridge, and Olfert (2011) find that sprawl is associated with decreased firm productivity, presumably due to diminished agglomeration economies, suggesting businesses are less competitive in sprawling cities.

The Tiebout (1956) model is the second major model describing *intra*-urban location. People "vote with their feet" by sorting to places that offer higher utility on the basis of economic and noneconomic factors. Quality of life and environmental services could be one factor that induces self-sorting within metropolitan areas (Banzhaf and Walsh, 2008). Public finance applications stress intrametropolitan differences in public services and their tax price.

Self-sorting in the Tiebout model gives communities incentives to use exclusionary zoning to attract the type of residents who will positively contribute toward public service provision. This could lead to equity and efficiency concerns if there is spatial mismatch between the location of workers and jobs (Kain 1968; Ihlanfeldt and Sjoquist 1998; Houston 2005). For example, zoning (and segregation) may limit affordable housing for lower skilled workers to the central cities, but firms that employ low-skilled workers relocate in the suburbs (Martin 2004; Stoll 2006). Blumenberg and Shiki (2004) argue that spatial mismatch may even be more severe in remote rural areas because thin labor markets and longer distances could further reduce employment access for specific skill groups.

Raphael and Stoll (2002) provide evidence that job accessibility for minority workers remains problematic, though it improved during the 1990s. Partridge and Rickman (2008) report indirect evidence that job accessibility is one reason for high poverty in central cities by showing that job growth has a stronger inverse association with lower poverty in central counties. Conversely, sorting of residents with weak labor market attachment into central cities would have suggested a smaller job growth-poverty linkage. Providing low-skilled households better employment access through providing cars or public transit and finding ways to relocate households closer to employment seems to be sensible as this benefits the workers *and* the employers. Yet, the notion of Tiebout sorting and exclusionary practices by local governments may limit the effectiveness of such policies.

3. Land Use, Quality of Life, and Regional Economic Development

The quality of life afforded by natural amenities has long been recognized as a critical factor in regional growth. An area with high quality of life attracts both working-age adults and retirees (Vias 1999; Deller et al. 2001; Gunderson, Pinto, and Williams 2008; Whisler et al. 2008). In-migration of working-age adults shifts labor supply and the demand for land outward, reducing the real-wage rate through lower nominal wages and/or higher land prices. Firms also may consider the amenity attractiveness of an area in their location decision in order to attract skilled workers (Gottlieb 1995), and because of preferences of managers or owners for amenity consumption. Retiree in-migration and new firms shift labor demand outward, particularly for workers employed in local service sectors, and increase land prices. Natural amenities especially may attract those with greater human capital, further boosting employment (Shapiro 2006; McGranahan and Wojan, 2007), wages, and land prices. Whether nominal wages are lower in areas with a high quality of life depends on the balance of these forces in addition to a number of structural characteristics of the local economy (Rappaport 2008).[5]

As a normal good, the demand for amenities in the United States increased in the 20th century with rising income (Costa and Kahn 2003; Rappaport 2007). In fact, argued to be fueled by rising income, increased wealth, and an aging population, Partridge (2010) reports natural amenities as dominating other theories, such as NEG, as the primary reason for US regional growth differentials in the latter half of the 20th century.[6] However, although increased demand for amenities increases household willingness to pay higher land prices, the extent that it leads to in-migration depends on amenity consumption's elasticity of substitution with nonamenity goods and services; a lower elasticity leads to greater in-migration (Rappaport 2009).

There are limits to the growth that can be attained in areas with high levels of natural amenities. For one, as amenities become capitalized into wages and land prices, household utility advantages in the region are reduced, causing growth to become more spatially equalized (Partridge et al. 2008*a*). Even with continued rising income, forward-looking households can lead to capitalization of amenities in the near term, shutting off growth.

Inelastic land supply is one reason for many cities having faster housing price growth and an increasingly right-skewed distribution of income (Gyourko, Mayer, and Sinai 2006). These cities often have limited land supply because of geographical barriers such as coastlines and mountains, and often enact policies that limit the development of new housing. Many also are places with perceived high levels of natural amenities (Rappaport 2009).

Yet, if regional policies allow growth to diminish quality of life (Gabriel, Mattey, and Wascher 2003), negative feedback effects on growth will occur (Chen, Irwin, and Jayaprakash 2009). Rickman and Rickman (2011) find evidence of within-Census region deterioration of quality of life in nonmetropolitan areas possessing high levels of natural amenities during the 1990s. They conclude that localities should manage

[5] Rappaport's (2008) model predicts that high quality of life is capitalized much more into land prices than wages. Empirically, Wu and Gopinath (2008) and Rickman and Rickman (2011) find that natural amenities are capitalized much more into housing prices than wages.

[6] See Partridge (2010) for discussion of amenity migration studies for other countries.

growth in ways to reduce negative amenity effects lest both the quality of life and growth be diminished.

Land use affects an area's quality of life through several channels, which is a consideration particularly critical for areas primarily dependent on quality of life for economic growth. Unmanaged growth in high-amenity areas can lead to sprawl, and the associated traffic congestion and pollution (Hansen et al. 2002). There also may be development-related losses in valued attributes such as open space (Vias and Carruthers 2005; Cho, Poudyal, and Roberts 2008), wildlife and its diversity (Hansen et al. 2002), the quantity or quality of vegetation and forests (Cho et al. 2009), and scenic views (Benson et al. 1998).

Proximate public lands, land owned by nonprofit organizations, and restrictive zoning may contribute to an area's amenity attractiveness and its economy in some ways, but also may inhibit the economy in other ways (McGranahan 2008). Henderson and McDaniel (2005) suggest that restrictive zoning in high-amenity areas may be one reason why they found manufacturing growth lagging that of other sectors. Yet, Rickman and Rickman (2011) did not find evidence of changes in land use regulations or reduced productivity affecting population growth in high amenity nonmetropolitan areas during the 1990s.

Lewis, Hunt, and Plantinga (2002) find slightly higher net migration rates for counties with more conservation land in the US Northern Forest region but no differences in employment growth. In an evaluation of the Northwest Forest Plan by the US Forest Service, Eichman et al. (2010) found negative employment effects from reduced timber use that are only slightly offset by positive effects of increased in-migration, which contrasts with findings reported in other studies. They attributed the difference in findings in part to the productiveness of the timberland withdrawn from production in the northwest. Rosenberger, Sperow, and English (2008) concluded that official wilderness designation did not greatly affect the transition of Appalachian Region counties from being primarily dependent on natural-resource and manufacturing activity to primary dependence on nonlabor sources of income and services. In a review of studies on wilderness designation and local growth, Rosenberger and English (2005) concluded that the link depends on the structure of the local economy and its longer-term trend.

Land use in cities also may adversely affect their environmental quality and feedback negatively on growth. City size can be associated with increases in various congestion forces such as crowded roads and increased pollution. Not only city size but also the degree of urban sprawl has often been identified as having a number of adverse environmental impacts (Johnson 2001; Hasse and Lathrop 2003; Nechyba and Walsh 2004). Stone (2008) found sprawl to be associated with the number of times monitored ozone concentrations exceeded the National Ambient Air Quality Standards across 45 US cities. Other impacts include loss of open space, reduced diversity of wildlife species, increased water pollution, and emission of particulates, significant losses of native vegetation and forests, loss of natural wetlands, blocking of mountain views, and ecosystem fragmentation.

Some studies question the perceived negative relationship between sprawl and environmental quality. Despite growing numbers of higher-income households living in suburbs and commuting to work, Kahn and Schwartz (2008) found reduced air pollution in California cities, which they attributed to technological improvements in auto emissions. Although Kahn (2001) found evidence of reduced quality of life in fast-growth California cities, he did not attribute this to air pollution because it had decreased, which suggested other causes such as increased traffic congestion. In surveying research on the dynamics of urban growth and ecological systems in the western world, Czamanski et al. (2008) concluded that "peri-urban" areas associated with sprawl provide ecosystem benefits because of their position between developed urban areas and agricultural lands. In an analysis of the impact on ecosystem services from urban sprawl in San Antonio Texas from 1976 to 1991, Kreuter et al. (2001) found that despite a dramatic increase in the area of urban land use and reduction in the size of rangelands, the shift of rangelands to woodlands greatly helped limit the loss of ecosystem services. Wu (2006) demonstrates how spatial variation in environmental amenities themselves can contribute to what is perceived as sprawl.

Therefore, an assessment of what constitutes sprawl and how it affects the quality of life is critical for sustainable regional economic development. More research is needed to assess the channels through which land use, growth, and environmental impacts interrelate. How these environmental changes affect perceived quality of life also require further investigation along the lines of hedonic studies of regional differences in quality of life.

4. Fiscal Federalism, Land Use, and Regional Economic Development

The spatial location of economic activity and land use also are affected by regional fiscal and land use policies. Both fiscal and land use policies can affect sprawl and regional economic development. The complexity of regional economies also makes the policies interdependent, both within and across jurisdictions.

Within the spatial equilibrium framework, variation in state and local fiscal policies has been found to be as important as individual characteristics in explaining wage differentials across US metropolitan areas and to matter as much for metropolitan quality of life as natural amenities (Gyourko and Tracy 1989, 1991). They also have been found to be important in explaining US nonmetropolitan county wage and land rent differentials, in which some policies primarily affect quality of life, whereas others affect the business climate (Yu and Rickman 2011). State and local fiscal policies directly affect quality of life through the taxes that households pay and government services they receive. Likewise, firm profits are affected by taxes and government services. Indirectly, however, local fiscal policies may have spillover effects, affecting economic activity and land use in neighboring jurisdictions.

High taxes and inadequate services in central cities can push economic activity outward into the suburbs and beyond, creating sprawl. Although there are potential social welfare gains from Tiebout-sorting of individuals according to their preferences for government services, the deconcentration of local government can affect the relative efficiency of the provision of government services, and hence the quality of life and productivity (Mattoon 1995; Innes and Booher, 1999). Public infrastructure exhibiting economies of scale or network effects (Dalenberg, Partridge, and Rickman, 1998) may be underprovided in a deconcentrated environment.

In reviewing the literature, Mattoon (1995) lists water and sewerage disposal as most efficiently provided by centralized metropolitan governments, whereas services such as education are reported as better provided with decentralized government. As discussed earlier in the chapter, increased sprawl can affect the amenity attractiveness in the broader metropolitan area such as through increased air and water pollution. Increased traffic congestion associated with sprawl can affect firm productivity. Therefore, the relative centralization and coordination of local fiscal policies can affect land use and economic development of the broader region.

Using state level data, Akai and Sakata (2002) find measures of local government expenditures and revenue relative to those for the state to be positively related to growth. In an examination of all US metropolitan areas, Stansel (2005) reports that decentralization increased growth (though state fixed effects are not accounted for and state laws and constitutions set the framework for local governments). In a related study, he found that the negative effect was weaker in the largest 100 metropolitan areas (Stansel 2002). Hammond and Tosun (2011) examined all US counties and found that decentralization in metropolitan areas, as measured by increased fragmentation of single-purpose governments, increased employment growth, whereas reduced revenue centralization increased income growth. In contrast, they found that general purpose government fragmentation reduced population and employment growth in nonmetropolitan counties. They concluded that their varied results suggest that general claims could not be made regarding fiscal deconcentration and regional growth.

Deconcentration also may occur in land use regulations. Jurisdictions in metropolitan areas with tighter controls push building activity into neighboring jurisdictions possessing fewer controls, which often are positioned at the periphery of the metropolitan area and beyond, creating sprawl (Carruthers 2003). Mills (2006) argued that Tiebout competition increases jurisdictional competition and reduces inefficient low-density development, a point disputed by Vigdor (2006). Brueckner (2000) argued that urban expansion reflects consumer demands for larger houses and yards, as well as proximity to consumer amenities. If these suburban options are unavailable, this could reduce a metropolitan area's attractiveness to households. Lax land use regulations and an absence of charging for social costs of development such as damage to ecosystem services also can lead to rural sprawl (Weiler 2003), which may feed back negatively on growth.

So-called "smart-growth" policies have been widely enacted to promote sustainable development (Wu 2006; Braun and Scott 2007) through increased efficiency of government services and added environmental protection. Yin and Sun (2007) report that metropolitan smart-growth policies increased the population share living in dense areas in the 1990s, whereas state-level smart-growth policies did not. Wu and Cho (2007) found that local and state land use restrictions reduced land development in five western states. Boyle and Mohamed (2007) concluded that state, regional, and local attempts to limit urban sprawl in Michigan largely failed. Kline and Alig (1999) concluded that Oregon's land use planning program concentrated development within urban growth boundaries, but the effect on land use in forest and farm land use zones was uncertain. In comparing Portland, Oregon; Orange County, Florida; and Montgomery County, Maryland, Song (2005) reported a long-term increase in population density in residential neighborhoods, which is partly attributed to growth management policies. Yet, reduced external connectivity and a lack of mixed land use are bemoaned, including low access to mass transit.

Glaeser and Kahn (2010) considered the effect on national carbon emissions associated with transportation, home heating and cooling, and electricity use, from spatial variation in local land use restrictions. They suggest that strict land use restrictions in lower emissions areas might cause their economic activity to shift to areas with high emissions. A potential policy recommendation would be to impose federal fees on development in high emission areas.

Overall, a complex relationship exists between fiscal federalism, land use decisions, and economic development. Sustainable economic development at all levels of spatial aggregation requires conceptualizing local and regional economies as complex systems, including land use and economic development policy interactions (Innes and Booher 1999). The extent of externalities across jurisdictions in a region, state, or nation suggests a need for some government coordination and more government involvement. Considerably more research on the complexity of interactions is needed to inform policymakers regarding government's proper role.

5. Empirically Assessing Economic Development

When assessing economic development, one needs to consider several issues such as (a) firm and household self-sorting; (b) the endogeneity of public policy (e.g., roads are built where policymakers expect future growth or maybe where they do not expect future growth); (c) unobservable factors that are correlated with both the dependent and independent variables that cause endogeneity and omitted variable bias; and (d) sample heterogeneity. The four main approaches in assessing economic development are CGE models; simulations of theoretical models; instrumental variable

(IV)/quasi-experimental approaches; and structural models.[7] CGE models have already been discussed. Brakman, Garretsen, and Marrewijk (2009*a*) describe NEG simulations, whereas other simulation approaches are covered elsewhere. Thus, we outline the latter two econometric approaches.[8]

Ordinary least squares (OLS) consists of regressing the dependent variable y (e.g., population growth) on several explanatory variables **X** (e.g., job growth, taxes).

$$y = \beta X + e \tag{1}$$

in which e is the residual. A key assumption is Cov(e, X)= 0, or there is no endogeneity bias. Endogeneity bias can arise from direct reverse causality—for example, regressing population growth on average wages—which is less of a problem in contemporary work because of improved research design. The more likely cause is omitted variables (unobservables) that are correlated with some of the X—for example, persistent factors such as a good harbor that is correlated with job growth in the population model.

A Hausman test can be used to determine the existence of statistical endogeneity in Equation (1), which requires instrument(s) Z that predicts the potentially endogenous explanatory variable(s) X_1, but Z cannot have a causal relationship with y (Cov(e, Z) = 0)–that is, the exclusion restriction. In other words, Z only influences y *indirectly* through how it affects X_1. It is essential that Z be "strong" (Stock and Watson 2007), or does a good job of predicting X_1 in the first stage. Strong economic rationale and institutional features often are used to find Z. For example, a good instrument for interstate highway mileage is how many miles were in the original World War II era military plan for the interstate system (Duranton and Turner 2011). In a population growth model, a good instrument for job growth is the predicted job growth if all of the local area's industries grew at the national rate—that is, from shift-share analysis (Bartik 1991). A related question is deciding which variables should be tested for endogeneity. Local economies are general equilibrium systems in which feedback loops are endemic. Good judgment needs to distinguish between statistical endogeneity that biases the coefficients in an economically meaningful way from trivial "endogeneity" that can arise from almost all any variable.

The primary solution for endogeneity is the IV approach (Stock and Watson 2007). In a careful study of how roads influence driving, Duranton and Turner (2011) use the IV

[7] Holmes (2010) also labels reduced-form and descriptive exercises as another approach, noting its limitations for establishing causality. However, Angrist and Pischke (2009, 213) describe the inherent value of reduced-form models for careful empirical analysis. We do not separately consider descriptive approaches because the dividing line between IV and reduced-form approaches has greatly blurred.

[8] See Holmes (2010), Angrist and Pischke (2009), and Stock and Watson (2007) for more econometric details. We do not describe spatial econometric methods because they are well known. In addition, their value has recently been questioned due to specification issues including a lack of theoretical motivation for their use and identification problems. See Overman and Gibbons (2010), McMillen (2010), and Pinske and Slade (2010) for recent critiques.

approach. Building a good economic case for their use, "clever" instruments are developed for contemporary interstate highway mileage: military road plans, early explorer routes, and late 1890s railroad mileage. Further, they test for the strength of these instruments and illustrate that an instrument can be conditionally valid after accounting for other control variables.[9] Alternative models such as limited information maximum likelihood estimators are used as robustness checks for weak instruments (see Angrist and Pischke 2009 for related discussion).

Random experiments are the gold standard of empirical assessment, but rarely exist in economic development practice (Holmes 2010). Quasi-experimental (QE) approaches are used to approximate this setting (Card 1990). Holmes' (1998) study of business climate is one example. He examined the influence of state business climate on manufacturing employment growth in the border counties between US states with and without right-to-work union laws. The key identifying assumption is that productivity would be the same at the border, in which state policy would be the main factor that causes employment growth to vary. Of course, there could be many other factors that could influence productivity such as historic location of cities. Holmes spent considerable effort in controlling for these persistent factors to strengthen identification.

Another QE approach is the difference-in-difference approach (DID) (Stock and Watson 2007, Chapter 13). One example is Funderberg et al.'s (2010) examination of 1990s-era highway expansions in California. They examined population and employment growth in the immediate surrounding census tracts around selected highway projects, comparing this to growth in nearby control tracts. Essentially, in the treatment tracts, they differenced growth in the years after the completion of the road from growth in the years immediately preceding completion. They did the same for the control tracts that did not receive a new project. If the treatment experienced significantly higher growth *after* the project, then the DID would be positive.[10] The identifying assumption is that the main factor affecting trend differences between the two groups is the road construction, a strong assumption. Funderberg et al. (2010) control for other factors that could account for different growth rates between the groups to strengthen their identification. A possible research design weakness is that the control tracts were very close to the treatment tracts. The new roads could shift growth from the treatment to the control tracts, positively biasing the impact of the road construction, which needs to be considered in research design.

[9] Duranton and Turner (2011) argue that 19th-century railroads were built for short-term profits and indirectly affect population today by affecting historic population. Thus, controlling for historic population from the early-20th century would remove any correlation of the instrument with the residual—that is, $\text{Cov}(Z, \varepsilon \mid X) = 0$.

[10] Suppose that the DID window was five years before (period 0) and after (period 1) for employment growth. Then the difference across the two periods for the treated region: $\Delta T = \text{EmpGrowth}_1 - \text{EmpGrowth}_0$. The analogous can be written for the control region ΔC. The DID estimator is $\Delta T - \Delta C$.

Greenstone, Hornbeck, and Moretti (2010) (GHM) is an example of the advantages and potential pitfalls of QE design. They examined how large plant openings affect total factor productivity (TFP) of *other manufacturers* in the county with the opening. Greenstone, Hornbeck, and Moretti argued that comparing winning county TFP to that in all other counties would produce biased results due to unobservables.[11] To develop a counterfactual, they compare "winner" county TFP to the runner up or "loser" county's TFP. Loser counties are identified in a monthly article in the trade publication *Site Selection Magazine,* which reported location announcements of large plants. The article lists the "loser" counties that GHM contend "narrowly" lost the competition. Greenstone, Hornbeck, and Moretti's identifying assumption is that the loser county is like the winner county in every economically consequential way, forming a good counterfactual. They employed best-practice DID methodology augmented by time trends, industry dummies, and other plant-specific inputs to account for other factors associated with that plant's TFP.

Greenstone, Hornbeck, and Moretti found that the winner's TFP growth averaged 5% to 12% more than in losing counties. Such strong agglomeration economies far exceed the typical estimates from the agglomeration literature (Rosenthal and Strange 2004). Greenstone, Hornbeck, and Moretti concluded that these spillovers justify the generous tax incentives offered by local governments to new firms. Yet, in an odd result, when they compared winner TFP to all US counties, they found that all counties had TFP growth that was about 5% greater than the winners, suggesting that either their complete set of DID controls were ineffective (which seems unlikely) or their identifying assumption is suspect.

Greenstone, Hornbeck, and Moretti's identifying assumption does not square with the institutional features of local governments bidding for firms. Profit-maximizing firms would not engage in a publically announced bidding war to establish counterfactuals for researchers, but to strategically affect the bidding, thereby possibly creating endogeneity. Take GHM's example of Greenville, SC beating Omaha, NE for a large Mercedes plant in the 1990s. Is Omaha a true counterfactual? It is located far from ports and far from markets and auto suppliers. Indeed, despite "narrowly" losing to Greensville for Mercedes, Omaha has never landed an auto assembly plant. Was Mercedes simply using Omaha to sweeten their deal from Greensville—that is, "losers" may be more willing to offer large tax incentives to help their economy. Wouldn't a better true counterfactual have been in the Southeast with similar market attributes and low union densities as Greensville? The point is QE studies should engage in robustness checks to assess their experiment. For GHM, a good robustness check would use matching or propensity score approaches.

[11] Although GHM did not predict the sign of this bias, it seems reasonable that comparing the winning county's TFP to all counties would overstate the TFP effects of a large plant opening because the firm would likely locate in counties with underlying factors that would raise TFP for all firms.

Another econometric problem is unobservable variables. This is especially problematic when there are unobserved location-specific factors that are correlated with the *X* variables, producing omitted variable bias. If a researcher has pooled-time-series data, they can control for location fixed effects that account for persistent factors associated with the place. When including fixed effects, all cross-sectional differences are in the location fixed effects, meaning that only within-location time-series variation in the variables is identifying the coefficients.

Including fixed effects, however, does not account for unobserved time-varying effects for the location. Also, if there is measurement error in the *X* variables, then the time-series variation will be increasingly dominated by noise, substantially biasing the coefficients toward zero. Finally, fixed effect models incorporate the very strong assumption that the X_t variables and the residuals are not only contemporaneously uncorrelated, but X_t has to be uncorrelated with the residuals across *all* time periods (Wooldridge 2002). Conversely, first-difference models that net out location fixed effects do not need this strong assumption.

Heterogeneous responses can greatly alter the interpretation of the results. In such cases, locally weighted regression (LWR) approaches (or geographically weighted regression) can estimate different regression coefficients β_i that vary across locations.[12] Locally weighted regression typically requires a separate regression for each observation on a sample of neighboring observations that is usually determined by proximity. Locally weighted regressions have gained prominence and have been used to examine factors such as employment density (McMillen 2004), housing prices (McMillen and Redfearn 2010; Redfearn 2009), population growth (Ali, Partridge, and Olfert 2007), and environmental hazards (Carruthers and Clark 2010). Ali et al. (2007) and Carruthers and Clark (2010) show how to decompose the variance of the predicted effects into that due to variation in the *X* variables and that due to spatial variation in the regression coefficients.

Structural models use theory to derive identifying restrictions to help establish causality when there are heterogeneous agents (Keane 2010). Yet, they have only been used at the edge of the economic development literature with most applications occurring in the fields of environmental economics or public finance (see Holmes 2010; Kuminoff, Smith, and Timmins 2010; "An Assessment of Empirical Methods for Modeling Land Use" by Irwin and Wrenn and "Equilibrium Sorting Models of Land Use and Residential Choice" by Klaiber and Kuminoff for reviews). If the correct theoretical model is employed, then structural models better inform policy because the underlying causal mechanisms are uncovered. Moreover, they are useful for evaluating nonmarginal changes in policies or amenities.

The disadvantage of structural approaches is that the results can be sensitive to the underlying model or functional form of, say, the utility function (Kuminoff and Jarrah 2010). Others criticize them for imposing too much structure and not "letting the data

[12] See McMillen (1996) and Fotheringham, Brunsdon, and Charlton (2002) for details.

speak" (Angrist and Pischke 2010), though structural proponents argue they are more upfront about explicitly stating the model's assumptions (Keane 2010). Angrist and Pischke (2010) convincingly argue that another shortcoming is that authors do not subject structural models to sufficient robustness tests of their assumptions.

Structural models require further advances to capture the multiple dimensions of modeling economic development and land use. Modeling of forward-looking household behavior and place of work/place of residence behavior are in its infancy (Kuminoff, Smith, and Timmins 2010) and both of these are key features of economic development and land use processes. Likewise, modeling firm behavior is still emerging; thus, the *joint* firm/household decision making that characterizes the special equilibrium approach is another area needing further research for developing structural models.

6. Conclusion and Future Research

The primary theme of this chapter is the need to fully integrate land use in economic development analysis. The complexity of regional economies combined with data and methodological limitations have too often led to piecemeal analysis of regional economic development and land use. Unfortunately, this has resulted in widely varying findings and an incomplete understanding of key issues. Too little is known about the interconnectedness of regional economic development and land use.

We outlined some areas for future research in the chapter, but there are other possibilities that warrant mention. We have already noted that sprawl studies typically do not assess the interrelation between land use, regional economic growth, and environmental quality. Likewise, firm location and workplace decisions are understudied within this context. Modeling metropolitan areas or functional economic regions in isolation of the interaction of cities across the entire hierarchy may produce misleading findings as shown by Polèse and Shearmur (2004) and by Partridge et al. (2008*a*, 2008*b*, 2009). Likewise, we know little about how structural shocks such as energy shocks, housing bubbles/busts, and economic recessions such as the Great Recession alter the course of land use and local economic development trajectories. The CGE model is one tool that can be further utilized to structurally assess these complex interactions with studies by Burnett et al. (2007) and Cutler and Davies (2007) representing a good first step.

With income inequality reaching very high levels in the United States and elsewhere (Atkinson, Piketty, and Saez 2011), another topic warranting more attention is how land use and its interrelation with economic development affect poverty rates and income inequality. The spatial mismatch literature shows that housing availability and employment access can affect employment outcomes for low-income households. Likewise, land use decisions affect housing costs, which further affect income inequality.

Examining these issues requires better data. More work has been done with micro geo-coded housing data using GIS than with geo-coded firm-level data, although Greenstone, Hornbeck, and Moretti (2010) demonstrate the possibilities. Very little research brings both geo-coded firm and household data together, although the planning literature is one exception (e.g., Funderberg et al. 2010).

Combined with the increased availability of GIS and microdata, and improved methods of empirical estimation and modeling, the spatial equilibrium approach offers significant promise for increasing our understanding of the relationship between regional economic development and land use issues. Without a greater understanding of the connection between the two, regional economic development and land use policies may prove to be ineffective or harmful.

References

Akai, N., and M. Sakata. 2002. Fiscal decentralization contributes to economic growth: Evidence from state-level cross section data for the United States. *Journal of Urban Economics* 52: 93–108.

Ali, K., M. D. Partridge, and M. R. Olfert. 2007. Can geographically weighted regressions improve regional analysis and policymaking? *International Regional Science Review* 30: 300–329.

Alonso, W. 1964. *Location and land use.* Cambridge, MA: Harvard University Press.

Angrist, J. D., and J. Pischke. 2009. *Mostly harmless economics: An empiricist's companion.* Princeton, NJ: Princeton University Press.

Angrist, J. D., and J. Pischke. 2010. The credibility revolution in empirical economics: How better research design is taking the con out of econometrics. *Journal of Economic Perspectives* 24: 3–30.

Atkinson, A. B., T. Piketty, and E. Saez. 2011. Top incomes in the long run of history. *Journal of Economic Literature* 49: 3–71.

Baldwin, R. E., and P. Krugman. 2004. Agglomeration, integration and tax harmonisation. *European Economic Review* 48: 1–23.

Banzhaf, H. S., and R. P. Walsh. 2008. Do people vote with their feet? An empirical test of Tiebout's mechanism. *American Economic Review* 98: 843–863.

Barkley, D. L., M. S. Henry, and S. Shuming Bao. 1996. Identifying "spread" versus "backwash" effects in regional economic areas: A density functions approach. *Land Economics* 72(3): 336–357.

Bartik, T. J. 1991. *Who benefits from state and local economic development policies?* Kalamazoo, MI: W. E. Upjohn Institute.

Beeson, P. E., and R. W. Eberts. 1989. Identifying productivity and amenity effects in interurban wage differentials. *Review of Economics and Statistics* 71(3): 443–452.

Benson, E. D., J. L. Hansen, A. L. Schwartz, and G. T. Smersh. 1998. Pricing residential amenities: The value of a view. *Journal of Real Estate Finance and Economics* 16(1): 55–73.

Berry, B. J. L. 1970. Labor market participation and regional potential. *Growth and Change* 1: 3–10.

Blumenberg, E., and K. Shiki. 2004. Spatial mismatch outside of large urban areas: An analysis of welfare recipients in Fresno County, California. *Environment and Planning C: Government and Policy* 22: 401–421.

Boyle, R., and R. Mohamed. 2007. State growth management, smart growth and urban containment: A review of the US and a study of the heartland. *Journal of Environmental Planning and Management* 50(5): 677–697.

Brakman, S., H. Garretsen, and C. van Marrewijk. 2009*a*. *The introduction to geographical economics.* Cambridge, UK: Cambridge University Press.

Brakman, S., H. Garretsen, and C. van Marrewijk. 2009*b*. Economic geography within and between European nations: The role of market potential and density across space and time. *Journal of Regional Science* 49: 777–800.

Braun, G. O., and J. W. Scott. 2007. Smart growth as new metropolitan governance: Observations on U.S. experience. In *The international handbook of urban policy: Contentious global issues*, Vol. 1, ed. H. S. Geyer, 213–223. Cheltenham, UK: Edward Elgar.

Brown, S. P. A., and L. L. Taylor. 2006. The private sector impact of state and local government. *Contemporary Economic Policy* 24(4): 548–562.

Brown, S. P. A., K. J. Hayes, and L. L. Taylor. 2003. State and local policy, factor markets and regional growth. *Review of Regional Studies* 33(1): 40–60.

Brueckner, J. K. 2000. Urban sprawl: Diagnosis and remedies. *International Regional Science Review* 23(2): 160–171.

Brülhart, M., and P. Koenig. 2006. New economic geography meets Comecon. *Economics of Transition* 14: 245–267.

Burnett, P., H. Cutler, and R. Thresher. 2007. The impact of tourism for a small city: A CGE approach. *Journal of Regional Analysis and Policy* 37(3): 233–242.

Card, D. 1990. The impact of the Mariel boatlift on the Miami labor market. *Industrial and Labor Relations Review* 43: 245–257.

Carruthers, J. I. 2003. Growth at the fringe: The influence of political fragmentation in United States metropolitan areas. *Papers in Regional Science* 82: 475–499.

Carruthers, J. I., and D. E. Clark. 2010. Valuing environmental quality: A space-based strategy. *Journal of Regional Science* 50: 801–832.

Chen, A., and M. D. Partridge. 2011. When are cities engines of growth? Spread and backwash effects across the Chinese urban hierarchy. *Regional Studies* doi:10.1080/00343404.2011.589831.

Chen, Y., E. G. Irwin, and C. Jayaprakash. 2009. Dynamic modeling of environmental amenity-driven migration with ecological feedbacks. *Ecological Economics* 68: 2498–2510.

Cho, S-H., N. C. Poudyal, and R. K. Roberts. 2008. Spatial analysis of the amenity value of green open space. *Ecological Economics* 66(2–3): 403–416.

Cho, S-H., Kim, R. K. Roberts, and S. Jung. 2009. Amenity values of spatial configurations of forest landscapes over space and time in the southern Appalachian highlands. *Ecological Economics* 68(10): 2646–2657.

Christaller, W. 1933. *Die zentralen Orte in Süddeutschland.* Jena: Gustav Fischer. (Partial English translation: 1966. *Central places in southern Germany*. Prentice Hall.)

Combes, P-P., G. Gilles Duranton, and H. G. Overman. 2005. Agglomeration and the adjustment of the spatial economy. *Papers in Regional Science* 84: 311–349.

Costa, D. L., and M. E. Kahn. 2003. The rising price of nonmarket goods. *American Economic Review* 93(2): 227–232.

Cutler, H., and S. Davies. 2007. The impact of specific-sector changes in employment on economic growth, labor market performance and migration. *Journal of Regional Science* 47(5): 935–963.

Czamanski, D., I. Benenson, D. Malkinson, M. Marinov, R. Roth, and L. Wittenberg. 2008. Urban sprawl and ecosystems—can nature survive? *International Review of Environmental and Resource Economics* 2(4): 321–366.

Dalenberg, D. R., M. D. Partridge, and D. S. Rickman. 1998. Public infrastructure: Pork or jobs creator? *Public Finance Review* 26(1): 24–52.

Deller, S., T-H. Tsai, D. Marcouiller, and D. English. 2001. The role of amenities and quality of life in rural economic growth. *American Journal of Agricultural Economics* 83(2): 352–365.

Dumais, G., G. Ellison, and E. Glaeser. 2002. Geographic concentration as a dynamic process. *Review of Economics and Statistics* 84: 193–204.

Duranton, G., and M. A. Turner. 2011. The fundamental law of road congestion: Evidence from US cities. *American Economic Review* 101(6): 2616–2652.

Eichman, H., G. L. Hunt, J. Kerkvliet, and A. J. Plantinga. 2010. Local employment growth, migration, and public land policy: Evidence from the northwest forest plan. *Journal of Agricultural and Resource Economics* 35(2): 316–333.

Fallah, B., M. D. Partridge, and M. R. Olfert. 2011. Urban sprawl and productivity: Evidence from U.S. metropolitan areas. *Papers in Regional Science* 90(3): 451–472.

Fotheringham, S., C. Brunsdon, and M. Charlton. 2002. *Geographically weighted regression: The analysis of spatially varying relationships*. Chichester, UK: John Wiley & Sons.

Fox, K. A., and T. K. Kumar. 1965. The functional economic area: Delineation and implications for economic analysis and policy. *Papers of the Regional Science Association* 15: 57–85.

Fujita, M., P. Krugman, and T. Mori. 1999. On the evolution of hierarchical urban systems. *European Economic Review* 43: 209–251.

Funderberg, R. G., H. Nixon, M. G. Boarnet, and G. Ferguson. 2010. New highways and land use change: Results from a quasi-experimental research design. *Transportation Research Part A* 44: 76–98.

Gabriel, S. A., J. P. Mattey, and W. L. Wascher. 2003. Compensating differentials and evolution in the quality of life among U.S. states. *Regional Science and Urban Economics* 33: 619–649.

Gaile, G. L. 1980. The spread-backwash concept. *Regional Studies* 14(1): 15–25.

Glaeser, E. L., and M. E. Kahn. 2004. Sprawl and urban growth. In *Handbook of regional and urban economics*, Vol. 4, eds. V. Henderson and J. F. Thisse, 2481–2527. Amsterdam: North-Holland.

Glaeser, E. L., and M. E. Kahn. 2010. The greenness of cities: Carbon dioxide emissions and urban development. *Journal of Urban Economics* 67: 404–418.

Glaeser, E. L., and K. Tobio. 2008. The rise of the sunbelt. *Southern Economic Journal* 74(3): 610–643.

Gottlieb, P. D. 1995. Residential amenities, firm location and economic development. *Urban Studies* 32(9): 1413–1436.

Greenstone, M., R. Hornbeck, and E. Enrico Moretti. 2010. Identifying agglomeration spillovers: Evidence from million dollar plants. *Journal of Political Economy* 118: 536–598.

Gunderson, R. J., J. V. Pinto, and R. H. Williams. 2008. Economic or amenity driven migration? A cluster-based analysis of county migration in the four corners states. *Journal of Regional Analysis and Policy* 38(3): 243–254.

Gyourko, J., C. Mayer, and T. Sinai. 2006. Superstar cities. NBER Working Paper 12355.

Gyourko, J., and J. Tracy. 1989. The importance of local fiscal conditions in analyzing local labor markets. *Journal of Political Economy* 97(5): 1208–1231.

Gyourko, J., and J. Tracy. 1991. The structure of local public finance and the quality of life. *Journal of Political Economy* 99(4): 774–806.

Hammond, G., and T. Mehmet. 2011. The impact of decentralization on economic growth: Evidence from U.S. counties. *Journal of Regional Science* 51(1): 47–64.

Hansen, A. J., R. Rasker, B. Maxwell, J. J. Rotella, J. D. Johnson, A. Wright Parmenter, U. Ute Langner, W. B. Cohen, R. L. Lawrence, and M. P. V. Kraska. 2002. Ecological causes and consequences of demographic change in the new west. *BioScience* 52(2): 151–162.

Hasse, J. E., and R. G. Lathrop. 2003. Land resource impact indicators of urban sprawl. *Applied Geography* 23: 159–175.

Helpman, E. 1998. The size of regions. In *Topics in public economics*, eds. D. Pines, E. Sadka, and I. Zilcha. Cambridge, MA: Belknap Press.

Henderson, J. R., and K. McDaniel. 2005. Natural amenities and rural employment growth: A sector analysis. *The Review of Regional Studies* 35(1): 80–96.

Henry, M. S., D. L. Barkley, and S. Bao. 1997. The hinterland's stake in metropolitan area growth. *Journal of Regional Science* 37: 479–501.

Hering, L., and S. Poncet. 2010. Market access and individual wages: Evidence from China. *Review of Economics and Statistics* 92: 145–159.

Hite, J. 1997. The Thunen model and the new economic geography as a paradigm for rural development policy. *Review of Agricultural Economics* 19: 230–240.

Holmes, T. J. 1998. The effect of state policies on the location of manufacturing: Evidence from state borders. *Journal of Political Economy* 106: 667–705.

Holmes, T. J. 2010. Structural, experimentalist, and descriptive approaches to empirical work in regional economics. *Journal of Regional Science* 50: 5–22.

Houston, D. 2005. Methods to test the spatial mismatch hypothesis. *Economic Geography* 81(4): 407–434.

Hughes, D. W., and D. W. Holland. 1994. Core-periphery economic linkage: A measure of spread and possible backwash effects for the Washington economy. *Land Economics* 70: 364–377.

Ihlanfeldt, K. R., and D. L. Sjoquist. 1998. The spatial mismatch hypothesis: A review of recent studies and their implications for welfare reform. *Housing Policy Debate* 9: 849–892.

Innes, J. E., and D. E. Booher. 1999. Metropolitan development as a complex system: A new approach to sustainability. *Economic Development Quarterly* 13: 141–156.

Irwin, E. G., A. M. Isserman, M. Kilkenny, and M. D. Partridge. 2010. A century of research on rural development and regional issues. *American Journal of Agricultural Economics* 92(2): 522–553.

Johnson, M. P. 2001. Environmental impacts of urban sprawl: A survey of the literature and proposed research agenda. *Environment and Planning A* 33: 717–735.

Kahn, M. E. 2001. City quality-of-life dynamics: Measuring the costs of growth. *Journal of Real Estate Finance and Economics* 22(2/3): 339–352.

Kahn, M. E., and J. Schwartz. 2008. Urban air pollution progress despite sprawl: The 'greening' of the vehicle fleet. *Journal of Urban Economics* 63: 775–787.

Kahn, R., P. F. Orazem, and D. M. Otto. 2001. Deriving empirical definitions of spatial labor markets: The roles of competing versus complementary growth. *Journal of Regional Science* 41: 735–756.

Kain, J. 1968. Housing segregation, negro employment, and metropolitan decentralization. *Quarterly Journal of Economics* 82: 175–183.

Ke, S., and E. Feser, 2010. Count on the growth pole strategy for regional economic growth? Spread-backwash effects in Greater Central China. *Regional Studies* 44: 1131–1147.

Keane, M. P. 2010. Structural vs. atheoretic approaches to econometrics. *Journal of Econometrics* 156: 3–20.

Kim, E., and J. Ju. 2003. Growth and distributional impacts of urban housing supply: An application of urban land use and a CGE model for Seoul. *Review of Urban and Regional Development Studies* 15(1): 66–81.

Kline, J. D., and R. J. Alig. 1999. Does land use planning slow the conversion of forest and agricultural land? *Growth and Change* 30(1): 3–22.

Kreuter, U. P., H. G. Harris, M. D. Matlock, and R. E. Lacey. 2001. Change in ecosystem service values in the San Antonio area, Texas. *Ecological Economics* 39: 333–346.

Krugman, P. 1991. Increasing returns and economic geography. *Journal of Political Economy* 99(3): 483–499.

Krugman, P. 2010. The new economic geography, now middle aged. Paper prepared for presentation to the Association of American Geographers Meetings, Washington, DC, April 16, 2010. http://www.princeton.edu/~pkrugman/aag.pdf

Kuminoff, N. V., and A. S. Jarrah. 2010. A new approach to computing hedonic equilibria and investigating the properties of locational sorting models. *Journal of Urban Economics* 67: 322–335.

Kuminoff, N. V., V. K. Smith, and C. Timmins. 2010. The new economics of equilibrium sorting and its transformational role for policy evaluation. NBER Working Paper 16349.

Lewis, D., G. Hunt, and A. Plantinga. 2002. Public conservation land and employment growth in the Northern Forest Region. *Land Economics* 78(2): 245–259.

Lösch, A. 1940. *Die räumliche Ordnung der Wirtschaft*. Jena: G. Fischer. English translation (of the 2nd rev. ed.): *The Economics of Location*. New Haven, CT: Yale University Press, 1954.

Martin, R. W. 2004. Spatial mismatch and the structure of American metropolitan areas, 1970–2000. *Journal of Regional Science* 44: 467–488.

Mattoon, R. H. 1995. Can alternative forms of governance help metropolitan areas? *Economic Perspectives* (Federal Reserve Bank of Chicago) 19(6): 20–32.

McDonald, J. F. 2001. Cost-benefit analysis of local land use allocation decisions. *Journal of Regional Science* 41(2): 277–299.

McDonald, J. F., and D. P. McMillen. 2000. Employment subcenters and subsequent real estate development in suburban Chicago. *Journal of Urban Economics* 48: 135–157.

McGranahan, D. A. 2008. Landscape influence on recent rural migration in the U.S. *Landscape and Urban Planning* 85: 228–240.

McGranahan, D. A., and T. R. Wojan. 2007. Recasting the creative class to examine growth processes in rural and urban counties. *Regional Studies* 41(2): 197–216.

McGregor, P. G., J. K. Swales, and Y. P. Yin. 1996. A long-run interpretation of regional input-output analysis. *Journal of Regional Science* 36(3): 479–501.

McMillen, D. P. 1996. One-hundred fifty years of land values in Chicago: A nonparametric approach. *Journal of Urban Economics* 40: 100–124.

McMillen, D. P. 2004. Employment densities, spatial autocorrelation, and subcenters in large metropolitan areas. *Journal of Regional Science* 44: 224–243.

McMillen, D. P. 2010. Issues in spatial data analysis. *Journal of Regional Science* 50: 119–141.

McMillen, D. P., and C. L. Redfearn. 2010. Estimation and hypothesis testing for nonparametric hedonic house price functions. *Journal of Regional Science* 50: 712–733.

Mills, E. S. 1967. An aggregative model of resource allocation in a metropolitan area. *American Economic Review* 57(2): 197–210.

Mills, E. S. 2006. Sprawl and jurisdictional fragmentation. *Brookings-Wharton Papers on Urban Affairs*, 231–256.

Morgan, W., J. Mutti, and D. Rickman. 1996. Tax exporting, regional economic growth, and welfare. *Journal of Urban Economics* 39: 131–159.

Mulligan, G. F. 1984. Agglomeration and central place theory: A review of the literature. *International Regional Science Review* 9: 1–42.

Muth, R. 1969. *Cities and housing.* Chicago: University of Chicago Press.

Myrdal, G. 1957. *Economic theory and underdeveloped regions.* London: G. Duckworth.

Nechyba, T. J., and R. P. Walsh. 2004. Urban sprawl. *Journal of Economic Perspectives* 18(4): 177–200.

Olfert, M. R., and J. C. Stabler. 1999. Multipliers in a central place hierarchy. *Growth and Change* 30: 288–302.

Ottaviano, G., and D. Pinelli. 2006. Market potential and productivity: Evidence from Finnish regions. *Regional Science and Urban Economics* 36: 636–657.

Overman, H., and S. Gibbons. 2010. Mostly pointless spatial econometrics? Unpublished manuscript, London School of Economics.

Partridge, M. D. 2010. The duelling models: NEG vs amenity migration in explaining US engines of growth. *Papers in Regional Science* 89(3): 513–536.

Partridge, M. D., K. Ali, and M. R. Olfert. 2010. Rural-to-urban commuting: Three degrees of integration. *Growth and Change* 41: 303–335.

Partridge, M. D., R. Bollman, M. R. Olfert, and A. Alasia. 2007. Riding the wave of urban growth in the countryside: Spread, backwash, or stagnation. *Land Economics* 83: 128–152.

Partridge, M. D., and D. S. Rickman. 1998. Regional computable general equilibrium modeling: A survey and critical appraisal. *International Regional Science Review* 21: 205–248.

Partridge, M. D., and D. S. Rickman. 2003. Do we know economic development when we see it? *Review of Regional Studies* 33(1): 17–39.

Partridge, M. D., and D. S. Rickman. 2008. Does a rising tide lift all boats? Assessing employment-poverty dynamics by metropolitan size and county type. *Growth and Change* 39: 283–312.

Partridge, M. D., and D. S. Rickman. 2010. CGE modelling for regional economic development analysis. *Regional Studies* 44(10): 1311–1328.

Partridge, M. D., D. S. Rickman, K. Ali, and M. R. Olfert. 2008*a*. Employment growth in the American urban hierarchy: Long live distance. *B.E. Journal of Macroeconomics: Contributions* 8(1): 1–36.

Partridge, M. D., D. S. Rickman, K. Ali, and M. R. Olfert. 2008*b*. Lost in space: Population dynamics in the American hinterlands and small cities. *Journal of Economic Geography* 8: 727–757.

Partridge, M. D., D. S. Rickman, K. Ali, and M. R. Olfert. 2009. Agglomeration spillovers and wage and housing cost gradients across the urban hierarchy. *Journal of International Economics* 78: 126–140.

Partridge, M. D., D. S. Rickman, K. Ali, and M. R. Olfert. 2010. Recent spatial growth dynamics in wages and housing costs: Proximity to urban production externalities and consumer amenities. *Regional Science and Urban Economics* 40(6): 440–452.

Pflüger, M., and T. Tabuchi. 2010. The size of regions with land use for production. *Regional Science and Urban Economics* 40: 481–489.

Pinske, J., and M. E. Slade. 2010. The future of spatial econometrics. *Journal of Regional Science* 50: 103–117.

Polèse, M., and R. Shearmur. 2004. Is distance really dead? Comparing industrial location over time in Canada. *International Regional Science Review* 27: 431–457.

Portnov, B. A., and M. Schwartz. 2009. Urban clusters as growth foci. *Journal of Regional Science* 49: 287–310.

Puga, D. 1999. The rise and fall of regional inequalities. *European Economic Review* 43: 303–334.

Raphael, S., and M. A. Stoll. 2002. *Modest progress: The narrowing spatial mismatch between blacks and jobs in the 1990s*. Washington, DC: The Brookings Institution.

Rappaport, J. 2007. Moving to nice weather. *Regional Science and Urban Economics* 37(3): 375–398.

Rappaport, J. 2008. Consumption amenities and city population density. *Regional Science and Urban Economics* 38: 533–552.

Rappaport, J. 2009. The increasing importance of quality of life. *Journal of Economic Geography* 9: 779–804.

Redding, S. J., and D. M. Sturm. 2008. The costs of remoteness: Evidence from German division and reunification. *American Economic Review* 98: 1766–1797.

Redfearn, C. L. 2009. How informative are average effects? Hedonic regression and amenity capitalization in complex urban housing markets. *Regional Science and Urban Economics* 39: 297–306.

Renkow, M. 2003. Employment growth, worker mobility, and rural economic development. *American Journal of Agricultural Economics* 85: 503–513.

Richardson, H. W. 1976. Growth pole spillover: The dynamics of backwash and spread. *Regional Studies* 5: 1–9.

Rickman, D. S. 1992. Estimating the impacts of regional business assistance programs: Alternative closures in a computable general equilibrium model. *Papers in Regional Science* 71(4): 421–435.

Rickman, D. S., and S. D. Rickman. 2011. Population growth in high-amenity nonmetropolitan areas: What's the prognosis? *Journal of Regional Science* 51(5): 863–879.

Roback, J. 1982. Wages, rents, and the quality of life. *Journal of Political Economy* 90: 1257–1278.

Rosenberger, R. S., and D. B. K. English. 2005. Impacts of wilderness on local economic development. In *The multiple values of wilderness*, eds. H. K. Cordell, J. C. Bergstrom, and J. M. Bowker, 181–204. State College, PA: Venture Publishing.

Rosenberger, R. S., M. Sperow, and D. B. K. English. 2008. Economies in transition and public land use policy: Discrete duration models of eastern wilderness designation. *Land Economics* 84(2): 267–281.

Rosenthal, S. S., and W. C. Strange. 2004. Evidence on the nature and sources of agglomeration economies. In *Handbook of regional and urban economics*, Vol. 4, eds. V. Henderson and J. F. Thisse, 2119–2171. Amsterdam: North-Holland.

Rosenthal, S. S., and W. C. Strange. 2008. The attenuation of human capital spillovers. *Journal of Urban Economics* 41: 373–389.

Shapiro, J. M. 2006. Smart cities: Quality of life, productivity, and the growth effects of human capital. *Review of Economics and Statistics* 88(2): 324–335.

Song, Y. 2005. Smart growth and urban development pattern: A comparative study. *International Regional Science Review* 28(2): 239–265.

Stansel, D. 2002. Interjurisdictional competition and local economic performance: A cross-sectional examination of US metropolitan areas. In George Mason University Working Papers in Economics, 02.16. (www.gmu.edu/departments/economics/working/directory.html).

Stansel, D. 2005. Local decentralization and local economic growth: A cross-sectional examination of US metropolitan areas. *Journal of Urban Economics* 57: 55–72.

Stock, J. H., and M. W. Watson. 2007. *Introduction to econometrics*, 2nd ed. Boston: Pearson.

Stoll, M. A. 2006. Job sprawl, spatial mismatch and black employment disadvantage. *Journal Policy Analysis and Management* 25: 827–854.

Stone, B, Jr. 2008. Urban sprawl and air quality in large US cities. *Journal of Environmental Management* 86: 688–698.

Tabuchi, T., and J. F. Thisse. 2006. Regional specialization, urban hierarchy, and commuting costs. *International Economic Review* 47: 1295–1317.

Tabuchi, T., and J. F. Thisse. 2011. A new economic geography model of central places. *Journal of Urban Economics* 69: 240–252.

Tiebout, C. M. 1956. A pure theory of local expenditures. *Journal of Political Economy* 64: 416–424.

Tweeten, L. G., and G. L. Brinkman. 1976. *Micropolitan development: Theory and practice of greater rural development.* Ames: Iowa State University Press.

Vias, A C. 1999. Jobs follow people in the rural Rocky Mountain west. *Rural Development Perspectives* 14(2): 14–23.

Vias, A. C., and J. I. Carruthers. 2005. Regional development and land use change in the Rocky Mountain west, 1982–1997. *Growth and Change* 36(2): 244–272.

Vigdor, J. L. 2006. Comment on Mills, sprawl and jurisdictional fragmentation. Brookings-Wharton Papers on Urban Affairs, 231–256.

Volpe-Martincus, C. 2010. Spatial effects of trade policy: Evidence from Brazil. *Journal of Regional Science* 50: 541–569.

Von Thünen, J. H. 1966. *Von Thünen's isolated state: An English edition of "Der Isolierte Staat."* In C. M. Wartenberg (trans.), P. Hall (ed.). New York: Pergamon (Published in German in 1826.)

Weiler, S. 2003. Pioneers of rural sprawl in the Rocky Mountain west. *The Review of Regional Studies* 33(3): 264–283.

Wensley, R. D. M., and J. C. Stabler. 1998. Demand-threshold estimation for business activities in rural Saskatchewan. *Journal of Regional Science* 38: 155–177.

Whisler, R. L., B. S. Waldorf, G. F. Mulligan, and D. A. Plane. 2008. Quality of life and the migration of the college educated. *Growth and Change* 39(1): 58–94.

Wooldridge, J. M. 2002. *Econometric analysis of cross section and panel data.* Cambridge, MA: MIT Press.

World Bank. 2009. *World development report reshaping economic geography.* Washington, DC: The World Bank.

Wu, J. 2006. Environmental amenities, urban sprawl, and community characteristics. *Journal of Environmental Economics and Management* 52: 527–547.

Wu, J., and S-H. Cho. 2007. The effect of local land use regulations on urban development in the western United States. *Regional Science and Urban Economics* 37: 69–86.

Wu, J., and M. Gopinath. 2008. What causes spatial variations in economic development in the United States? *American Journal of Agricultural Economics* 90: 392–408.

Wu, J. 2010. Economic fundamentals and urban-suburban disparities. *Journal of Regional Science* 50: 570–591.

Yin, M., and J. Sun. 2007. The impact of state growth management programs on urban sprawl in the 1990s. *Journal of Urban Affairs* 29(2): 149–179.

Yu, Y., and D. S. Rickman. 2011. U.S. state and local fiscal policies and nonmetropolitan area economic performance: A spatial equilibrium analysis. *Papers in Regional Science* doi:10.1111/j.1435-5957.2012.00423.x.

CHAPTER 2

TECHNOLOGY ADOPTION AND LAND USE

DAVID ZILBERMAN, MADHU KHANNA, SCOTT KAPLAN, AND EUNICE KIM

THE adoption of new technologies in agriculture (such as new irrigation technologies, crops for new biofuels, high-yielding seed varieties, etc.) have been crucial contributors to technological change. Innovations have enabled support for a growing global population, which has increased sevenfold from 1 billion in 1800, while increasing acreage by only 150%. Adoption of new technologies has transformed agriculture from a labor- to a capital-intensive industry in the developed world, and it is crucial for the progress of agriculture in the developing world. It has also expanded the range of goods produced in agriculture, going beyond food and fiber to include biofuel and fine chemicals. Much of the economic literature on adoption and diffusion originated from research on adoption of technologies in agriculture, be it hybrid corn in the United States or Green Revolution varieties (varieties discovered and implemented during the Green Revolution) throughout the world.

The adoption of these innovations has drastically affected land use and land values. Much of the adoption of innovations has been embodied in changes in land use. For example, adoption may result in the growth of new varieties and crops, as well as in the installation of new irrigation equipment. In turn, much of the literature on adoption (Feder et al. 1985), to a large extent, models adoption decisions as land use choices. Adoption of new innovations in certain locations will affect outputs and costs and, thus, spatial patterns of land prices. Thus, understanding the economics of adoption of new technologies and innovation in agriculture is important in studying agriculture land use and its value.

This chapter first presents the basic theories of adoption. Then, it identifies how patterns of adoption vary depending on the characteristics of these technologies. Next, it assesses how various economic and noneconomic factors affect patterns of adoption. And, finally, it considers how technology adoption and its economic implications are evolving in a modern world with an integrated supply chain and contracting.

1. Adoption and Diffusion

Adoption and diffusion are two processes that affect the introduction of technological innovations. *Adoption* represents individual decisions regarding the technology and is measured as a discrete choice; that is, whether or not a technology was adopted by a farmer or used on a piece of land. But it may also be accompanied by measures of intensity; that is, the extent to which adoption occurs (degree of land share devoted to new varieties). When new technologies have multiple components, they may be adopted jointly or sequentially (Khanna 2001). For example, adoption of Green Revolution varieties is also associated with choice of complementary inputs, such as fertilizer. In this case, both land share of the new technology and the extent of fertilizer use are measures of adoption.

Diffusion represents aggregate adoption. One measure of diffusion is the fraction of farmers who adopt a new technology, whereas another measure is the fraction of the land that is switched to using the new technology. When new technologies are embodied in capital goods, they are often rented, and purchase decisions are only made after sufficient experiences are accumulated. In these cases, diffusion is measured by the use of new technology rather than the ownership of equipment.

Early empirical studies of diffusion were conducted by sociologists, such as Rogers (2003), who collected data on aggregate adoption of different technologies and found that diffusion was an S-shaped function of time, reflecting slow initial diffusion, then a period of takeoff, and then an eventual tapering off. Rogers established the imitation model, and, assuming homogeneity among farmers, he was able to model the spread of a technological innovation as a process of imitation, which is similar to the spread of an epidemic. In particular, if $p(t)$ is the land share of the new technology over time, then $P(t)=\dfrac{K}{1+e^{-(\alpha+\beta t)}}$, where K is the maximum diffusion rate, α is a measure of the initial rate of adoption, and β is the measure of the speed of adoption. Griliches (1957) expanded the Rogers model by suggesting that the relative profitability of new technologies affects the speed of imitation. The more profitable the new technology, the faster the imitation, the steeper the slope of the S-shaped curve (higher β), and the larger the value of the maximum adoption, K.

David (1975) and Feder, Just, and Zilberman (1985) argue that the imitation model does not include an explicit economic decision-making model, and so David introduced the threshold model. The threshold model incorporates three major components. First, farmers consider multiple factors in making economic decisions, including profit, utility, risk, and other criteria. Second, it takes into consideration heterogeneity of farm size, human capital, and/or land quality. Third, it is a dynamic model. Frequently, studies have assumed static profit maximization or expected utility maximization by the decision maker. Recent studies have assumed dynamic optimization, with the timing of adoption being determined by considering the tradeoff of benefits from use in the present with reduced prices as production expands in the future (McWilliams and Zilberman 1996). Sometimes, the dynamic processes that affect returns or costs are stochastic, such as additive and multiplicative random walk. In these cases, decision makers are taking a real option approach; thus, timing of adoption is selected so that marginal benefit overcomes marginal cost plus the hurdle rates that increase with uncertainty (Khanna et al. 2000; Seo et al. 2008). The threshold model emphasizes the importance of the effective rollout of a technology, as well as its introduction in locations with the highest returns and willingness to experiment with the product. People who adopt early are those who have the most favorable conditions. But, over time, a new technology may become more attractive because of learning by doing (i.e., knowledge acquisition from experience in production of a product), learning by using (i.e., learning through use of a technology), or network externalities, causing more adopters to join in. When there is partial adoption, increase in adoption over time may be both at the intensive and extensive margins. For example, over time, the adoption of Green Revolution varieties may expand because adopters increase the relative land share used by the technology (intensive margin) and because nonadopters enter and allocate land to the technology (extensive margin). In the case of mechanical innovation, larger scale farmers will adopt first, but as a technology becomes cheaper and custom services are developed, smaller farmers will adopt the technology (Sunding and Zilberman 2001). In the case of drip irrigation, the sources of heterogeneity are represented by the differences in water-holding capacity of the soil, and adoption occurs on land that previously utilized traditional technologies, as well as on land with low water holding capacity that was unable to be used previously. Adoption of technologies such as drip irrigation and pesticides tends to increase the acreage of usable agricultural land by adding land that could not be utilized previously because of water or pest constraints. With adoption, the value of this land increases as a result of its new use.

The threshold model emphasizes the importance of heterogeneity among farmers and has been applied using data on technology, as well as on land use choices at the plot or the farm level. Discrete-choice econometric approaches (using a probit or logit model) are used to explain factors that affect the selection of specific divisible technologies by farmers (e.g., whether a farmer uses a tractor), whereas the use of the Tobit model allows for the investigation of situations in which adoption is partial. This can be seen when farmers allocate some of their land to Green Revolution technologies as opposed to traditional technologies. Panel data on changes in technology choice and land use over time, at the plot or farm level, identify sources of heterogeneity, as well as the patterns of the evolution of diffusion and adoption (Sunding and Zilberman 2001). Studies have also used treatment effect models to analyze the effects of adoption on land use or input use (Khanna 2001).

2. Technology Characteristics

The threshold model emphasizes the importance of heterogeneity in the adoption process, and the characteristics of the technology determine the source of heterogeneity and its impacts on land use and other key factors. Several characteristics of special importance are described in the following sections.

2.1 Divisibility

Some technologies are embodied in indivisible equipment—like tractors or combines—whereas others, like new seed varieties, are divisible. When an indivisible technology has to be purchased, scale becomes the dominant source of heterogeneity. If a technology that requires a fixed annual cost of F_t dollars and increases profit per acre in period t by $\Delta\pi_t$, then profit-maximizing firms of farm size $L_t = F_t / \Delta\pi_t$ greater than the critical farm size will adopt the technology at time t, showing farm size as a source of heterogeneity. The dynamics of diffusion will be affected by the distribution of both farm size and critical size. Learning by doing, which acts to reduce F_t, and learning by using, which acts to increase $\Delta\pi_t$, will reduce L_t and drive diffusion. We plausibly assume that the farm size distribution is unimodal and the diffusion curve is S-shaped (Sunding and Zilberman 2001). Farm size distributions can be altered, and when technologies are indivisible, owners of small farms have to expand the size of their operation to make adoption profitable.

Thus, the distribution of land among farms may affect the timing and dynamics of diffusion, and the introduction of new technologies may alter farm size distribution. The introduction of indivisible technologies may have contributed to increases in average farm size in the United States and other Organisation for Economic Co-operation and Development (OECD) countries. One mechanism that enables smaller farmers to benefit from large, nondivisible machinery has been the introduction of custom service provision. In locations where there are fewer barriers to the establishment of such services, farmers can benefit from the technology without buying it, and the diffusion rates measured by percentage of land used with machinery are much higher. Furthermore, when farmers are uncertain about benefits of a technology, the introduction of rental services allows them to gain experience with the technology prior to purchasing it.

In the case of divisible technologies, adoption may be partial. Farmers may adopt new crop varieties or a pest control treatment on part of their land first, and then vary the land share over time. Even in cases of technologies that are seemingly divisible, like new seed varieties, farmers have fixed costs of learning and adjustment. Thus, a certain amount of scale is needed to adopt some of these technologies, especially early in the innovation process, in order to cover these fixed costs.

2.2 Impact on Input Use Efficiency

Technologies vary in the efficiency of the use of variable inputs, such as water or fertilizer. Caswell and Zilberman (1986) distinguished between applied and effective input and mention that the ratio of applied to effective input is input use efficiency. Input use efficiency varies across locations and among technologies. For example, traditional irrigation, such as furrow irrigation, may have an input use efficiency of 0.6 in relatively heavy soil and 0.1 in sandy soil, whereas the efficiency of drip irrigation may be 0.95 in heavy soil and 0.85 in sandy soil. The residual input (irrigation water runoff or pesticide residue) is frequently a pollutant, and adoption of technologies that increase input use efficiency leads to improved pollution control.

Input use efficiency augmenting technologies include improved pesticides and chemical application and fuel efficiency, and their adoption may be induced by higher input prices or environmental regulations (Khanna and Zilberman 1997). They tend to require higher fixed cost per unit of land but often increase operational profits (revenue minus variable costs per acre). Related technology types include damage control agents (e.g., various forms of disease and pest controls; Lichtenberg and Zilberman 1986), soil erosion control technologies (Ervin and Ervin 1982), and input augmenting technologies, notably the introduction of irrigation to augment rainfall or the use of synthetic fertilizers.

Technologies that augment input use efficiency enable farmers to overcome the limitations imposed by low land qualities. These technologies tend to be adopted first on locations of lower land quality, which is measured by the input use efficiency while using the traditional technology. They also tend to affect land prices significantly. In particular, they may lead to reductions in the premium for land of higher quality, as is demonstrated in Figure 2.1. The traditional technology has higher profits on high-quality lands because it does not require the extra fixed costs associated with the new technology, so the gain from the modern technology is relatively small. Before the introduction of the modern technology, all of the land with qualities in the range B–D utilized traditional technology, whereas the lower quality lands did not. After the introduction of the modern technology, lands in the range B–C were switched from using the traditional technology to using the modern technology, and land in the range A–B was added to production. Before the introduction of the modern technology, profit per acre, which represents land rent, was denoted by the curve BF. After the introduction, the rent per acre is denoted by the curve AEF, which reflects higher premiums for lower quality land. If adoption of new technologies increases supply and reduces output price, then low-quality land that enters production tends to gain from the technology and high-quality lands tend to lose. Thus, a decline in the land quality premium is evident. The survey of Schoengold and Zilberman (2007) confirms that adoption of water conserving technologies (e.g., drip irrigation) increases input use efficiency, tends to increase yield, leads to reduced drainage, and, in some cases, water use per acre decreases. Ward and Pulido-Velazquez (2008) showed that the expansion in acreage may increase water use after adoption of modern irrigation technologies despite a reduction in per-acre use.

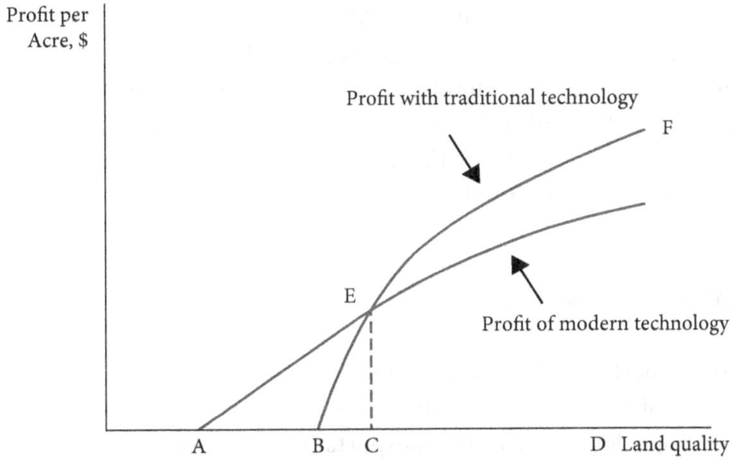

FIGURE 2.1 The effect of technology adoption on land use.

Introduction of new technologies alters the relative value of land and may lead to expansion of farmland into areas that weren't previously utilized; this expansion is called the *extensive margin effect of adoption*. An example of increasing returns to scale due to the extensive margin effect of adoption is seen with the invention of pumps. Before the invention of pumps, areas located below rivers were considered superior to areas located above rivers because canals could irrigate them, but pumps raised the value of land located above rivers and expanded farming to these areas. Drip irrigation increased the relative value of sandy soil that has low water-holding capacity and led to farming in areas that were previously deserted (Caswell and Zilberman 1986).

Each of these technology categories must overcome constraints but may lead to the expansion of agricultural land, change the relative prices of land, and may actually turn inferior land into superior land (as is the case in the introduction of irrigation to California's central valley).

2.3 Impact on Risk

Agriculture is subject to a high degree of variability. When farmers are risk averse, they will pay high premiums to avoid it and, in turn, evaluate technologies by not only their impact on average profit but by their riskiness as well. Just and Pope introduced the Just-Pope production function, $y = f(x) + g(x)\varepsilon$, where y is output and x is input, ε is a random variable with a mean of 0, $f(x)$ denotes impact of input on average output, and $g(x)$ is impact on risk. If $g(x)$ is positive, then the technology is risk-enhancing. The adoption of risk-reducing innovations or crop insurance programs was modeled using a portfolio in which land and other inputs are allocated among risky alternatives. Some technologies, including Green Revolution varieties that both enhance average profit and risk, were selected by risk-averse farmers to diversify their land portfolio among varieties in order to balance overall risk with expected gain. One of the advantages of irrigation is that it both increases yield and reduces risk, so if the adoption cost is sufficiently low, then irrigation technologies stochastically dominate dry farming. One advantage of genetically modified (GM) cotton is that it both increases yield and reduces risk, and the fixed cost associated with adoption is more than recovered in regions with sufficient pest damage (NRC 2010).

2.4 Transport Cost Intensity

The von Thunen model established the importance of transportation cost consideration in the allocation of agricultural activities. When farmers adopt technologies at a given location, they consider the price of transportation costs for both outputs and inputs. Thus, the adoption of technologies that reduce transportation costs may contribute to changes in land use patterns and the introduction of new practices where they didn't exist before. Both the railroad and steamships allowed expansion of grain production in the Midwest. The introduction of refrigerated trucks helped shift the production of fruit and vegetables to California. The introduction of refrigerated air-freight facilitated the adoption of intensive cash crops in various parts of Africa. Adoption of improved transportation technologies outside of the farm affects land use and land value within farming regions.

2.5 Complementary Technologies

Production may consist of several complementary processes, which include pest control, irrigation, and fertilization. Namely, a reduction in pest damage will increase the value of fertilization or irrigation. Precision farming involves a bundle of technologies, such as soil testing, variable rate fertilizer application, and yield monitoring. In some cases, adoption of technologies that affect one process of production may not be profitable, but adoption of a package of complementary components may be profitable. The Green Revolution consisted of many technology packages that combined new varieties with modern inputs like fertilizer and irrigation. However, the various components may be sold individually or as a combined package. Not all farmers will adopt all components of the package at once (Byerlee and de Polanco 1986), and, in fact, farmers often prefer to adopt technologies sequentially based on risk considerations, supply constraints, and due to a lack of knowledge. Khanna (2001) found that although adoption of soil testing for fertilizer requirements of the land was scale neutral, the subsequent adoption of variable-rate fertilizer applicators was more likely to take place with larger, more experienced and innovative farmers with greater human capital skills. Some technology packages combine improved modes of transportation with higher value crops, and together they increase land values in remote regions. For example, the adoption of air-freight for high value cash crops was essential to the adoption of such crops in Africa.

2.6 Economies of Scale and Scope

Industries characterized by decreasing returns to scale lead to competitive market outcomes, whereas those characterized by increasing returns to scale favor oligopolistic structures (Arthur 1994). Notably, technologies with increasing return to scale have completely different patterns of evolution and adoption than do traditional technologies with increasing marginal cost. Most crop production technologies have decreasing returns to scale, which has led to a primarily competitive structure. But the minimum cost associated with crop production has increased over time, leading to increased farm size and a decline in the number of farms. In some sectors of animal agriculture, the least-cost scale grew immensely, leading to concentration and emergence of an oligopolistic industrial structure. The high cost of investment in livestock resulted in institutional innovations in management and finance, as well as in the emergence of industrial agriculture (Boehlje 1999).

3. Economic Considerations Affecting Adoption

Technology adoption decisions are basically investment decisions. Assume that a new technology requires an investment of I dollars and has a life horizon of T years. At the beginning of each year, the farmer has to allocate his or her land ($\bar{L}$ between the traditional L_{0t} and the modern technology L_{1t}). The modern technology is also likely to change output (Δy_t) as well as input use (Δx_t) and pollution (Δz_t), but these impacts are uncertain. The prices of output, input, and pollution at time t are p_t, w_t, and v_t, respectively. The change in profit at period t is $\Delta\pi_t = (p_t\Delta y_t - w_t\Delta x_t - v_t\Delta z_t)L_{1t}$. Basic modeling suggests that a risk-neutral farmer will adopt the technology if its net present value $\left(\sum_{t=0}^{T}\frac{\Delta\pi_t}{(1+r)^t} - I\right)$ is positive. This model suggests that the likelihood of adoption increases; as the discount rate and initial investment for the farmer become lower, the planning horizon, the price of output (if the technology increases yield), the price of input (if the technology saves input), and the pollution penalty (if the technology reduces pollution) become higher. The analysis suggests that larger farms are more likely to adopt the technology and that larger initial investments, as well as higher discount rates, increase the critical farm size for adoption.

The net present value approach emphasizes the role of financial incentives in inducing adoption. Linn (2008) showed that financial incentives have a positive effect on adoption of energy-conserving technology, but the elasticity of adoption in response to financial incentives is low. Thus, financial incentives alone are not significant in determining the feasibility of adoption, which points to the need to incorporate other considerations that may affect adoption choices. These considerations may include imperfect capital markets, risk aversion, and government policies, which are discussed in detail in the next sections.

3.1 Credit Constraints

Potential adopters may need to finance the high up-front costs of new technology, as well be willing to burden negative income streams associated with the establishment phase of adoption of these technologies. The ability to finance investment in new technologies is constrained and is highly correlated to both a borrower's wealth and the capacity to pledge assets as collateral (Foster and Rosenzweig 2010*b*). Both transaction costs and asymmetric information have been major causes of credit constraints in which farmers are unable to get loans that can repay themselves, including for adoption of innovations (Stiglitz and Weiss 1981). Credit provision and even subsidies have been crucial for small farmers to adopt new technologies, particularly during the initial stage of the Green Revolution in the late 1960s and 1970s (Fan et al. 2008). Credit can be attained by the use of collateral, and, frequently, land is used for this purpose. Thus, higher prices of land expand credit availability and may facilitate adoption of new technologies that, in turn, may raise land value even further (Hochman et al. 1977).

3.2 Risk Consideration

An extensive literature shows that risk considerations affect the technology adoption decision, and differences in risk preferences and attitudes across individuals also lead to heterogeneity in the adoption decision. Early studies of adoption under risk apply safety rules, including the safety-first rule, which suggests that farmers and other land users will select technologies that minimize the probability of a disaster—defined as a situation in which their income falls below a subsistence level. The safety first rule was used by Roumasset (1976) to explain why farmers in certain parts of Asia did not adopt Green Revolution rice varieties.

The second, more widely used framework is based on the expected utility model, which assumes that farmers are aware of the riskiness of different technologies and account for it in calculating expected benefits. Frequently, adoption choices are analyzed as optimal land portfolio management. Applications are based on the assumption that farmers value higher profits but associate negative benefits to the riskiness (frequently measured by variance) of those profits. Risk has been a major cause for diversification of land among divisible technologies. Let L_1 be the land area allocated to the modern technology of farm size $\bar{L}$ and μ_0, $\sigma_0{}^2$, μ_1, $\sigma_1{}^2$ the mean and variance of profits per acre of the traditional and modern technologies, respectively, and σ_{12} the correlation between the profits per acre for the two technologies. Just and Zilberman (1983) found that the area allocated to the modern technology is

$$L_1 = \frac{\mu_1 - \mu_0}{\phi(\sigma_1^2 - \sigma_0^2 + 2\sigma_{12})} - \frac{\sigma_{12} - \sigma_0^2}{(\sigma_1^2 - \sigma_0^2 + 2\sigma_{12})}\bar{L}, \tag{1}$$

where ϕ is the measure of risk aversion, assuming that the modern technology has higher mean and variance of profits. Equation (1) suggests that more land will be allocated to the new technology the higher the yield gain is from this technology, the smaller the risk aversion of this new technology, and the riskier the traditional technology is relative to the new technology. The equation emphasizes the role of correlation in land allocation; adoption of the new technology will increase as the correlation between the traditional and new technology becomes smaller.

There is heterogeneity in the degree of risk aversion and loss aversion across farm sizes and farmer wealth. Studies have found that larger and richer farmers tend to allocate more acreage to a modern technology, but, in some cases, the land share of modern technology is higher on smaller farms. For example, Marra and Carlson (1990) show that the pattern of adoption of double cropping soybeans with wheat in the United States is consistent with risk aversion and the covariance of returns between the old and new technologies. In making decisions about allocating land for crops or other products, farmers have to consider a number of risks, such as variability in yields due to weather, difficulties in establishing the crop, and volatility in prices because of variable demand and supply. High returns from other possible uses of the land may also play a primary role in the farmers' willingness to adopt a given technology.

A third approach is based on prospect theory (Kahneman and Tversky 1979) and has more predictive power than expected utility theory in explaining decisions to adopt new technologies, under certain conditions (Zellner and Zilberman 2011). The three key features of prospect theory are (1) loss aversion, which implies that farmers are more sensitive to losses below a reference; (2) framing of alternatives, namely specific simplification of risky alternatives considered in adoption choices; and (3) the difference in perceived risk used for decision making and the actual associated risks. An empirical study conducted by Malawi, Smale et al. (1994) shows that land use allocations between new and old crops are explained by risk management strategies that combine portfolio diversification, safety-first rules, and experimentation. Similarly, Huang and Liu (2013) showed that both risk and loss aversion may delay the adoption of GM cotton in China.

A fourth approach to include risk in technology adoption is the real option approach developed by Dixit, Pindyk, and Davis (1994). Whereas the other three approaches are based on static analysis, Dixit, Pindyk, and Davis view adoption as a dynamic investment decision but also suggest that, instead of using net present value to decide whether or not to adopt a technology at a given time, decision makers have another degree of freedom—they can also determine the timing of the adoption. For example, if there is uncertainty in the properties of the technologies or the behavior of prices in the future, there may be gains (option-value) from taking advantage of waiting until uncertainties are clarified. McWilliams and Zilberman (1996) showed that when prices of new technologies tend to decline over time, seen in the case of adoption of computers, optimal timing balanced the gains from the decline of prices versus the loss of the services of the new technology. Carey and Zilberman (2002) show that when considering adoption of new irrigation technologies when water pricing is fluctuating, the critical price of water that triggers adoption is the critical price under certainty plus a "hurdle rate" that takes into account the fluctuation of water prices. Greiner, Patterson, and Miller (2009) combined option-value consideration and risk aversion to explain barriers of adoption of conservation technologies in Australia. Khanna et al. (2000) and Isik et al. (2001) show that uncertainty about output prices and expectations of declining fixed costs of adoption can create incentives to delay investment in precision technologies, particularly on components that have relatively high fixed costs. This is particularly the case on land parcels with low soil quality and low variability in soil quality, where the benefits of adopting these technologies are relatively small. Thus, one venue through which risk and uncertainty affect land use and land values is through their impact on technology adoption. Risk consideration will affect adoption, and, at the same time, adoption of new technologies will affect the magnitude of risk.

3.3 Information and Learning

The uncertainty about new technologies declines over time as farmers acquire knowledge on their own and from others. A recent study by Conley and Udry (2010) suggests that individuals tend to learn from the experience of members of the community and adopt the practices used by successful individuals. As agriculture modernizes, farmers become more specialized and information increases immensely, causing farmers to rely on various sources for their decision making. For example, when it comes to information on new technologies, farmers reported that the most important sources of information were the agricultural media, informal sources (other farmers), extension, and commercial vendors (Wolf et al. 2001). Although much of the information on new technologies is provided by formal networks, Just et al. (2002) estimated that roughly 50% of the information farmers used for economic decision making comes through informal networks that are often perceived to be less reliable than formal networks. Expansion of formal networks associated with the increased information provided through the Internet is likely to increase adoption. Internet-based information and e-commerce are also improving the quality of information available to places farther from the urban center, thus reducing the distance barrier to adoption.

Adoption of information technologies themselves are motivated by the benefits of the network externalities they create (Shapiro and Varian 1999). These technologies enable farmers to develop virtual networks of buyers and sellers that allow them to negotiate volume discounts and obtain better prices for their output, sometimes using e-marketing (Schmitz et al. 2005).

4. Sectoral Policies and Institutions

The agricultural sector has historically been characterized by institutional arrangements to reduce risk, as well as by government policies to stabilize farm income. Several different policies play a big role in the adoption of new land use technologies.

4.1 Crop Insurance

Crop insurance tends to increase adoption and even intensify adoption of high-yield, high-risk varieties because it reduces risk while at the same time increases mean yield (Just and Zilberman 1988). Farmers are more willing to incorporate additional land with insurance programs because it provides a safety net for the risk involved in marginal land use. Empirically, there is some evidence linking crop insurance to adoption. The study by Christiaensen and Dercon (2010) found that lack of insurance and ability to smooth consumption discouraged adoption of fertilizer by farmers in Ethiopia.

4.2 Price Insurance Scheme

The low elasticity of agricultural demand combined with variability in supplies leads to significant price fluctuations (Gardner 1987). Several institutional mechanisms reduce price risks and future markets, which are markets where farmers can sell a contract of a given level of output at a particular price. Theoretically, reduced risk will enhance adoption, but more empirical evidence is needed. Price support policies provide a floor on the price received by farmers. Price supports both increase the average price expected by farmers and reduce risk of adoption of technologies by risk-averse farmers. Availability of price insurance schemes tends to increase land values, and that may increase adoption through availability of credit. Several studies have suggested that expansion of agricultural supply through adoption and land use intensification over the years was related to price support programs that reduce risk and increase average profit (Gardner 1987).

4.3 Decoupled Income Support

Farmers place increasing reliance on "decoupled" payments; namely, payments that assure a certain income regardless of actual production choices and yields. These payments assure a certain income based on historical planting decisions or regional income average and are independent of actual choices. Under risk neutrality, decoupled support is neutral in its impact on crop choices, so the way land is allocated to different crops is unaffected. However, it can affect a farmer's decision to remain in agriculture or use the land for nonagricultural activities. Serra et al. (2005, 2006) show that decoupled policies reduce farmers' aversion to risk through the wealth effect and contribute to the intensification of farming.

4.4 Credit Subsidies

Lack of credit has been documented as a major constraint on adoption, especially by small farmers. Governments established policies to overcome credit constraints. Giné and Yang (2009) show that credit subsidies enhance the adoption of modern corn technologies in Malawi. Hochman et al. (1977) suggest that credit supports enable further adoption of waste management technologies in the context of animal waste in California.

4.5 International Trade Policies

Tariffs and export subsidies, foreign exchange insurance, and exchange rates have significantly affected the evolution of global agriculture (Schuh 1974). Government policy may enhance adoption that expands supply of exporting industries by instituting export subsidies, as well as by policies and regulation to reduce transportation costs. Trade barriers on imports may lead to expansion of domestic industries to enhance input substitution. Foreign direct investment has been associated with the introduction of new technologies, especially in developing countries, but there has been concern about foreign ownership of land, especially in Africa, and the tradeoff between increased development and "neo-colonialism" (Cotula et al. 2009).

4.6 Regulations

Firms and farms are subject to various regulations, including worker safety regulations, environmental regulations, and the like that can affect the costs and returns to alternative technologies. Regulations can increase the net gains from adopting environmentally friendly technologies, rewarding farmers for reducing externalities associated with land use. Some regulations are performance based, a criterion that may constrain the outcomes of economic activity (e.g., upper bounds on concentration of chemicals in water disposed by farms), whereas other regulations are practice based, which limit or even ban specific practices. Lichtenberg (2002) documents how environmental regulations (water quality regulations, runoff controls, pesticide residue regulations) led to adoption of conservation and precision technologies. Casey et al. (1999) describe the role that regulations have played in inducing adoption or disadoption of technologies. Khanna et al. (2002) show that cost share subsidies and input reduction subsidies can induce greater adoption of modern irrigation technologies than pollution taxes that achieve the same level of pollution abatement.

4.7 Supply Chains and Contracting

The work by James Jr. et al. (2011) suggests that farmers in the United States and globally are relying less on cash transactions and more on contractual relationships and vertical integration for managing exchange. According to MacDonald and Korb (2008), 40% of the value of US agricultural production is sold through contractual arrangements. The deployment of contracting and vertical integration varies by crops and activities, but it affects technology adoption, land allocation, and land value. It is also useful to distinguish between marketing and production contracts. Marketing contracts specify the price and/or quantity of the product sold by the farmer, as well as the condition of delivery. In production contracts, the contractor owns the commodity when it is being produced by the farmer and pays the farmer for services provided.

There are divisions of responsibilities between the farmer and contractor. For example, the contractor may provide genetic materials and specialized inputs (feed for livestock), whereas the farmer may own specialized capital (farm, structures, land) and conduct production activities subject to specified conditions from the contractors. The farmer is paid a fee for services provided, rather than the market value of the output produced, although this fee may depend on the output's market value.

MacDonald and Korb (2011) suggest that the nature of the product and the technology used determine the use of contracting or vertical integration. For example, in 2008, around a quarter of the total corn crop, 90% of sugar beets, and 68% of hogs were produced under production contracts. MacDonald and Korb (2011) show that contracting enabled producers to assume more debts and that the use of contracting varies among regions. James Jr. et al. (2011) suggest that establishment of contractual relationships, as well as vertical integration, is associated with multiprocess production systems, where each stage requires specialized capital. Thus, the introduction of contractual relationships affects patterns of technology choice and land use. There is not much research explicitly addressing the design of contracts as part of a technology diffusion process. However, the literature on contracts (Alexander et al. 2011) emphasizes that they have to be flexible enough to accommodate heterogeneity among farmers, which will lead to variations in the responses to contracts by farmers. Barry et al. (1992) suggest that the institutional designs for agricultural production systems have to take into account financial considerations. Contractual arrangements are likely to increase the ability to borrow, as well as affect the scale of operation of a system. James Jr. et al. (2011) suggest that marketing contracts are associated with modification of existing production systems, whereas production contracts and vertical integration are associated with the introduction of new production systems. For example, the introduction and adoption of new crops (e.g., kiwi fruit) or new products (e.g., broilers) occurred under vertical integration or production contracts.

The deployment of contract farming has been increasing globally, and the terms of these contracts are shaped by the conditions of the country and the product (Rehber 1998). In many developing countries, the introduction of contracts was part of the introduction of new products or new production systems that aimed at improving product quality. This improved quality allowed market expansion of various products such as fresh fruit, vegetables, and meats and the introduction of new technologies, such as the enclosed industrial systems for producing poultry. In the developing world, contracts are used as coordination mechanisms in terms of quality, quantity, and time, and they provide incentives for performance, as well as provide protection against financial risks. The growing importance of an integrated supply chain in agriculture suggests that more emphasis should be placed on studying technology adoption and land use choices under contracts and vertical integration.

5. Noneconomic Factors

There is growing evidence that adoption choices depend not only on monetary benefits, but also on nonpecuniary benefits as well. The household production function literature spawned by Becker (1965) and Lancaster (1966) has shown that households make choices that consider both market and nonmarket goods and consider factors such as leisure, health, aesthetic beauty, and lifestyle in allocating resources, including technology adoption. Marra and Piggot (2006) document that one major reason that farmers have adopted GMO varieties in the United States, sometimes in spite of low-yield gains, is that they entail less health risk, environmental damages, and effort than traditional varieties.

The *theory of planned behavior* (Ajzen 1991) has been used to understand decision making by agricultural producers. This theory considers attitudes, subjective norms, and perceived behavioral controls to be the primary determinants of behavioral intentions, and it seeks to understand the factors that determine these behaviors.

5.1 Attitudes

There is not much quantitative assessment on the impact of attitude on adoption. Positive attitudes among farmers toward environmentally friendly practices have led to the adoption of crop rotations, sustainable agriculture, soil conservation practices, and best management practices in dairy farms (Villamil et al. 2008).

5.2 Social Perception

Positive attitudes toward the adoption of a practice may not always be sufficient to induce adoption. Perceived inability to successfully adopt the practice and social pressures from important reference groups were major factors contributing to the inability of farmers to convert positive attitudes into adoption of a technology. The effect of social norms regarding visual appearance of a crop is an indicator of the success of a farmer and may affect technology choices (Villamil et al. 2008). Social perception and attitudes may trigger adoption of technologies that will benefit the community as a whole, which may result in an increase in the value of land in the community.

6. Demographic and Socioeconomic Characteristics

Farmer demographic and socioeconomic characteristics are expected to influence technology adoption for a number of reasons. First, they are an indicator of heterogeneity among adopters that may affect the economic gains and costs of adoption. Following the threshold model of adoption, these characteristics could influence the dynamics of the diffusion process. Second, these characteristics can be correlated with farmer attitudes, and knowing the extent to which those attitudes influence intentions (following the theory of planned behavior), they could affect adoption decisions. Some of the key demographic and socioeconomic factors that affect adoption are described here.

6.1 Human Capital

Nobel laureate Theodore Schultz distinguished between two types of human capital: "worker ability," which is the capacity to perform hard manual tasks, and "allocative ability," or the "ability to deal with disequilibrium," namely, the ability to assess problems, make rational choices, and adjust to change (Schultz 2003). The adoption of more advanced technologies and their effects on land use is clearly related to allocative ability; however, this ability is not easily observable. One good proxy is education. The literature on adoption of various technologies—computers, new seed varieties, machinery, and better management systems—shows that more educated farmers are early adopters (Sunding and Zilberman 2001). On the other hand, some innovations, such as pesticides and management consulting, are human capital augmenting technologies and are more likely to be adopted by human capital-challenged or less educated farmers. New seed varieties, like GM varieties that reduce the complexity of pest control, may also have special appeal for less educated individuals.

6.2 Wealth

This factor contributes to adoption in a variety of ways. Wealthier individuals face less credit and other financial constraints that may hinder adoption, and they are often less averse to risk; thus, they are more likely to invest in high-risk, high-return technologies. Higher wealth may also lead to riskier decisions in terms of how to use land. Finally, early adoption of some new and advanced technologies (tractors, computers, etc.) is often prestigious, and a wealthier individual can more easily afford it. To the extent that wealth contributes to adoption of technologies or crop varieties that increase the average profitability of farmers, it also serves as a mechanism to further increase the value of land in wealthier regions.

6.3 Scale

A large body of evidence suggests that several dimensions of operational scale contribute to adoption. Larger farm size is likely to enhance the adoption of technologies that are either indivisible or have economics of scale. Size is likely to reduce risk aversion and thus enhance adoption of high-risk, high-return technologies. Scale allows farmers to buy inputs, including both physical (farm machinery, e.g., combines) and human (expert advice) capital, which reduces the per-unit costs of these inputs and enhances the utilization of these assets. A stronger capital asset base reduces the cost of adoption of technologies that use these assets as complementary inputs. Foster and Rosenzweig (2010*a*) argue that, in addition to being a catalyst for adoption of technologies in developing countries, size is a major contributor to increased productivity. The notion of "small farms" varies by crop and activity. For example, a five-acre wheat farm will be minuscule whereas a nursery of the same size will be a viable business.

6.4 Health

The intellectual capacity that is crucial for allocative ability also depends on health status and good nutrition. The study by Croppenstedt and Muller (2000) documents that improved nutritional status improves productivity, presumably through improved allocation and technology choices.

6.5 Age

Several studies have found that age affects adoption choices. Younger farmers are more knowledgeable about new practices and may be more willing to bear risk and invest in new technologies (Gould et al. 1989; Polson and Spencer 1991; Adesina and Zinnah 1993). The major reason that younger agents are more likely to adopt new technologies is that they have a longer planning horizon and are thus likely to get more use from the technology over their lifetime. Some authors find positive correlation between age and adoption (Hussain et al. 1994). Older farmers may be more likely to adopt technologies with shorter repayment periods that may reduce effort and allow improved lifestyle.

6.6 Location

The early studies of adoption emphasized the role of location in explaining diffusion. Distance and access to markets and experts can have significant impacts on adoption. Villages farther away from centers of commerce were less likely to adopt technologies such as hybrid corn (Rogers 2003). Key factors like climate and soil quality also influence the profitability of adoption and depend on location of the farmer.

7. Conclusion

Allocation of land for different activities is affected by adoption of new technologies. The adoption process is gradual and depends on economic incentives, technological incentives, policies, and regulation. The threshold model of adoption suggests that the rate of adoption is affected by the heterogeneity of potential adopters and by dynamic processes, including technological improvements and knowledge acquisition, that increase the relative advantage of new technologies over time. Adoption of new technologies may expand utilized land and introduce agriculture to regions that were previously unable to be farmed. It also may change the relative value of various types of land. Adoption behavior is frequently an investment and is subject to uncertainties, thus crop-sharing institutions and various insurance mechanisms can affect the rate of adoption and the spread of the technology. Government may encourage adoption by providing financial incentives, but also by enhancing research and extension activities, as well as by establishing mechanisms for expanding knowledge among farmers. Enhanced profitability is a major motivation behind adoption, but adoption may be motivated by nonpecuniary factors, such improved convenience and increased safety. Environmental regulation may also serve as a major mechanism for inducing adoption and introducing technological change. Investment in research and activities that enhance productivity of farming systems may contribute in reducing pressure on land resources and slowing processes of deforestation by accelerating the adoption of technologies that intensify agricultural production, thus leading to more output per unit of land.

Acknowledgments

The research leading to this chapter was supported by the Energy Biosciences Institute, U.C. Berkeley and BP Environmental Science Challenge Project.

References

Adesina, A., and M. Zinnah. 1993. Technology characteristics, farmers' perceptions and adoption decisions: A Tobit model application in Sierra Leone. *Agricultural Economics* 9(4): 297–311.

Ajzen, I. 1991. The theory of planned behavior. *Organizational Behavior and Human Decision Processes* 50:179–211.

Alexander, C., R. Ivanic, S. Rosch, W. Tyner, S. Y. Wu, and J. R. Yoder. 2012. Contract theory and implications for perennial energy crop contracting. *Energy Economics* 34(4): 970–979.

Arthur, W. B. 1994. *Increasing returns and path dependence in the economy*. Ann Arbor: University of Michigan Press.

Barry, P. J., S. T. Sonka, and K. Lajili. 1992. Vertical coordination, financial structure, and the changing theory of the firm. *American Journal of Agricultural Economics* 74(5): 1219–1225.

Becker, G. S. 1965. A theory of the allocation of time. *Economic Journal* 75(299): 493–517.

Boehlje, M. A. 1999. Structural changes in the agricultural industries: How do we measure, analyze and understand them? *American Journal of Agricultural Economics* 81(5): 1028–1041.

Byerlee, D., and E. H. de Polanco. 1986. Farmers' stepwise adoption of technological packages: Evidence from the Mexican Altiplano. *American Journal of Agricultural Economics* 68(3): 519–527.

Carey, J., and D. Zilberman. 2002. A model of investment under uncertainty: Modern irrigation technology and emerging markets in water *American Journal of Agricultural Economics* 84(1): 171–183.

Casey, F., A. Schmitz, S. Swinton, and D. Zilberman. 1999. *Flexible incentives for the adoption of environmental technologies in agriculture*. Norwell, MA: Kluwer Academic Publishers.

Caswell, M. F., and D. Zilberman. 1986. The effects of well depth and land quality on the choice of irrigation technology. *American Journal of Agricultural Economics* 68(4): 798–811.

Conley, T. G., and C. R. Udry. 2010. Learning about a new technology: Pineapple in Ghana. *American Economic Review* 100(1): 35–69.

Cotula, L., S. Vermeulen, L. Leonard, and J. Keeley. 2009. Land grab or development opportunity? Agricultural investment and international land deals in Africa. Report to the International Institute for Environment and Development, London.

Croppenstedt, A., and C. Muller. 2000. The impact of farmers' health and nutritional status on their productivity and efficiency: Evidence from Ethiopia. *Economic Development and Cultural Change* 48(3): 475–502.

David, P. 1975. *Technical choice, innovation and economic growth*. Cambridge, UK: Cambridge University Press.

Dercon, S., and L. Christiaensen. 2010. Consumption risk, technology adoption and poverty traps: Evidence from Ethiopia. *Journal of Development Economics* 96(2): 159–173

Dixit, A. K., R. S. Pindyck, and G. A. Davis. 1994. *Investment under uncertainty*. Princeton, NJ: Princeton University Press.

Ervin, C. A., and D. E. Ervin. 1982. Factors affecting the use of soil conservation practices: Hypotheses, evidence, and policy implications. *Land Economics* 58(3): 277–292.

Fan, S., Gulati, A. and S. Thorat, S. 2008. Investment, subsidies, and pro-poor growth in rural India *Agricultural Economics* 39(2): 163–170.

Feder, G., R. E. Just, and D. Zilberman. 1985. Adoption of agricultural innovations in developing countries: A survey. *Economic Development and Cultural Change* 33(2): 255–298.

Foster, A., and M. Rosenzweig. 2010*a*. Barriers to farm profitability in India: Mechanization, scale, and credit markets. Paper presented at World Bank-UC Berkeley Conference on Agriculture for Development, Berkeley, CA.

Foster, A. D., and M. R. Rosenzweig. 2010*b*. Microeconomics of technology adoption. *Annual Review of Economics* 2(1): 395–424.

Gardner, B. L. 1987. *The economics of agricultural policies*. New York: Macmillan.

Giné, X., and D. Yang. 2009. Insurance, credit, and technology adoption: Field experimental evidence from Malawi. *Journal of Development Economics* 89(1): 1–11.

Gould, B. W., W. E. Saupe, and R. M. Klemme. 1989. Conservation tillage: The role of farm and operator characteristics and the perception of soil erosion. *Land Economics* 65(2): 167–182.

Greiner, R., Patterson, L., and Miller, O. 2009. Motivations, risk perceptions and adoption of conservation practices by farmers. *Agricultural Systems* 99: 86–104.

Griliches, Z. 1957. Hybrid corn: An exploration in the economics of technological change. *Econometrica, Journal of the Econometric Society* 25(4): 501–522.

Hochman, E., D. Zilberman, and R. E. Just. 1977. Two-goal regional environmental policy: The case of the Santa Ana river basin. *Journal of Environmental Economics and Management* 4(1): 25–39.

Huang, J., and E. M. Liu. 2013. Risk preferences and pesticide use by cotton farmers in China. *Journal of Development Economics* 103: 202–215.

Hussain, S. S., D. Byerlee, and P. W. Heisey. 1994. Impacts of the training and visit extension system on farmers' knowledge and adoption of technology: Evidence from Pakistan. *Agricultural Economics* 10(1): 39–47.

Isik, M., M. Khanna, and A. Winter-Nelson. 2001. Sequential investment in site-specific crop management under output price uncertainty. *Journal of Agricultural and Resource Economics* 26(1): 212–229.

James Jr., H. S., P. G. Klein, and M. E. Sykuta. 2011. The adoption, diffusion, and evolution of organizational form: Insights from the agrifood sector. *Managerial and Decision Economics* 32(4): 243–259.

Just, D. R., S. A. Wolf, S. Wu, and D. Zilberman. 2002. Consumption of economic information in agriculture. *American Journal of Agricultural Economics* 84(1): 39–52.

Just, R. E., and D. Zilberman. 1983. Stochastic structure, farm size and technology adoption in developing agriculture. *Oxford Economic Papers* 35(2): 307–328.

Just, R. E., and D. Zilberman. 1988. The effects of agricultural development policies on income distribution and technological change in agriculture. *Journal of Development Economics* 28(2): 193–216.

Kahneman, D., and A. Tversky. 1979. Prospect theory: An analysis of decision under risk. *Econometrica: Journal of the Econometric Society* 47(2): 263–291.

Khanna, M. 2001. Sequential adoption of site-specific technologies and its implications for nitrogen productivity: A double selectivity model. *American Journal of Agricultural Economics* 83: 35–51.

Khanna, M., M. Isik, and A. Winter-Nelson. 2000. Investment in site-specific crop management under uncertainty: Implications for nitrate pollution control and environmental policy. *Agricultural Economics* 24(1): 9–21.

Khanna, M., M. Isik, and D. Zilberman. 2002. Cost-Effectiveness of alternative green payment policies for conservation technology adoption with heterogeneous land quality. *Agricultural Economics* 21(2): 157–174.

Khanna, M., and D. Zilberman. 1997. Incentives, precision technology, and environmental quality. *Ecological Economics* 23: 25–43.

Lancaster, K. J. 1966. A new approach to consumer theory. *Journal of Political Economy* 74(2): 132–157.

Lichtenberg, E., and D. Zilberman. 1986. The econometrics of damage control: Why specification matters. *American Journal of Agricultural Economics* 68(2): 261–273.

Lichtenberg, E. 2002. Agriculture and the environment. In *Handbook of agricultural economics*, Vol. 21, eds. B. Gardner and G. Rausser, 249–1313. Amsterdam: Elsevier.

Linn, J. 2008. Energy prices and the adoption of energy-saving technology. *Economic Journal* 118(553): 1986–2012.

MacDonald, J. M., and P. Korb. 2008. *Agricultural contracting update*. Washington, DC: USDA Economic Research Service.

MacDonald, J. M., and P. Korb. 2011. Agricultural contracting update: Contracts in 2008. *Economic Information Bulletin 72*. Washington, DC: U.S. Department of Agriculture.

Marra, M. C., and G. A. Carlson. 1990. The decision to double crop: An application of expected utility theory using Stein's theorem. *American Journal of Agricultural Economics* 72(2): 337–345.

Marra, M., and N. Piggott. 2006. The value of non-pecuniary characteristics of crop biotechnologies: A new look at the evidence. *Regulating Agricultural Biotechnology: Economics and Policy. Natural Resource Management and Policy* 30(1): 145–177.

McWilliams, B., and D. Zilberman. 1996. Time of technology adoption and learning by using. *Economics of Innovation and New Technology* 4(2): 139–154.

NRC. 2010. *Impact of genetically engineered crops on farm sustainability in the U.S.* Washington, DC: National Academies Press.

Polson, R. A., and D. S. C. Spencer. 1991. The technology adoption process in subsistence agriculture: The case of cassava in southwestern Nigeria. *Agricultural Systems* 36(1): 65–78.

Rehber, E. 1998. *Vertical integration in agriculture and contract farming*. Food Marketing Policy Center, University of Connecticut.

Rogers, E. M. 2003. *Diffusion of innovations*, 5th ed. New York: Free Press.

Roumasset, J. A. 1976. *Rice and risk: Decision making among low-income farmers*. Amsterdam and New York: Elsevier.

Schmitz, T. G., C. B. Moss, A. Schmitz, A. Kagan, and B. Babcock. 2005. *E-Commerce in Agribusiness*. Longboat Key, FL: Florida Science Source.

Schuh, E. 1974. The exchange rate and US agriculture *American Journal of Agricultural Economics* 56: 1–13.

Schoengold, K., and D. Zilberman. 2007. The economics of water, irrigation, and development. In *Agricultural development: Farmers, farm production and farm markets*, 2940–2966,

Handbook of agricultural economics, Vol. 3, eds. Robert E. Evenson, Prabhu Pingali, and T. Paul Schultz. Amsterdam: Elsevier.

Schultz, T. P. 2003. Human capital, schooling and health. *Economics & Human Biology* 1(2): 207–221.

Seo, S., Segarrab, E., Mitchell, P., and Leathamd, D. 2008. Irrigation technology adoption and its implication for water conservation in the Texas High Plains: A real options approach. *Agricultural Economics* 38: 47–55.

Serra, T., D. Zilberman, B. K. Goodwin, and A. Featherstone. 2006. Effects of decoupling on the mean and variability of output. *European Review of Agricultural Economics* 33(3): 269.

Serra, T., D. Zilberman, B. K. Goodwin, and K. Hyvonen. 2005. Replacement of agricultural price supports by area payments in the European Union and the effects on pesticide use. *American Journal of Agricultural Economics* 87(4): 870.

Shapiro, C., and H. R. Varian. 1999. *Information rules: A strategic guide to the network economy*. Cambridge, MA: Harvard Business School Press.

Smale, M., R. E. Just, and H. D. Leathers. 1994. Land allocation in HYV adoption models: An investigation of alternative explanations. *American Journal of Agricultural Economics* 76(3): 535–546.

Stiglitz, J. E., and A. Weiss. 1981. Credit rationing in markets with imperfect information. *American Economic Review* 71(3): 393–410.

Sunding, D., and D. Zilberman. 2001. The agricultural innovation process: Research and technology adoption in a changing agricultural sector. In *Handbook of agricultural economics*, Vol. 1, eds. B. L. Gardner and G. C. Rausser, 207–261. Amsterdam: Elsevier.

Villamil, M. B., A. H. Silvis, and G. A. Bollero. 2008. Potential for miscanthus' adoption in Illinois: Information needs and preferred information channels. *Biomass and Bioenergy* 32: 1338–1348.

Ward, F. A., and M. Pulido-Velazquez. 2008. Water conservation in irrigation can increase water use. *Proceedings of the National Academy of Sciences of the USA* 105(47): 18215–18220.

Wolf, S., D. Just, and D. Zilberman. 2001. Between data and decisions: The organization of agricultural economic information systems. *Research Policy* 30(1): 121–141.

Zellner, A. and D. Zilberman. 2011. The economics and econometrics of risk: An introduction to the special issue. *Journal of Econometrics* 162(1): 1–5.

CHAPTER 3

ARE LARGE METROPOLITAN AREAS STILL VIABLE?

EDWIN S. MILLS

THIS chapter[1] concerns the functions of and prospects for large metropolitan areas. In the United States, the federal government recently revised and expanded its metropolitan concepts[2]. In 2004, there were 375 generic metropolitan areas (MAs) that contained 80% of the US population. Since MAs consist of entire counties, they contain much rural land, perhaps 25–40% of total MA land areas. One result is that 2–5% of metropolitan residents are rural. Since only 2–3% of US workers are employed on farms, the vast majority of rural workers are engaged in the same work that urban residents do. In fact, a substantial number of US rural residents work in urban or metro areas, assisted by our superb interstate highway system that enables rural residents to commute long distances to urban jobs.

International comparisons of MAs are approximate. Nearly all governments define a metropolitan concept, but not in quite the same way. By any reasonable definition, Tokyo is the world's largest metropolitan area, with about 25 million people, or 20% of the Japanese population. Mexico City may be the world's second largest MA, although it is difficult to decide where the MA ends. In the United States, New York (18 million people), Los Angeles (13 million people), and Chicago (9 millions people) have for decades been ranked in that order as the three largest MAs.

Most high-income countries are 60–85% urban. Middle-income countries are mostly 40–60% urban. Low-income countries are mostly in the 20–40% range. Good cocktail party conversation can be made of the fact that two countries that are popularly thought

[1] This chapter is a substantial revision and updating of Mills (1992*b*).

[2] See Gacquin and DeBrandt (eds.) (2006, 774, 775) for concise definitions. This annual 1,200-page volume contains by far the best summary of US data for states, metropolitan areas, counties, and cities. The statistics in this section are from it and recent issues of the World Development Report.

of as agricultural are among the most highly urbanized countries in the world: Israel and New Zealand are 91% and 86% urban, respectively.

Although most MAs in the world have been suburbanizing during the post–World War II period, the process has gone much further in the United States than in most countries. Beyond 1–5 miles from the city center, population and employment densities do not vary systematically with distance from US MA centers. The result is that US suburbs are extremely low density by comparison with those in almost any other country. More cocktail party conversation: one MA, Cheyenne, has a lower MA population density than the entire 48 contiguous states.

Why do MAs exist? They exist because they perform functions that cannot be performed as well by any other form of spatial organization. In the United States, an acre of prime downtown land in a large MA might sell for upward of $50 million, whereas an acre of prime agricultural land 50 miles away might sell for $5,000–10,000, making downtown land 5,000–10,000 times as valuable as nearby farmland. In large European and Asian MAs, comparisons are equally dramatic. There is hardly any comparably dramatic social comparison. The comparison suggests that MA land is extremely productive. People pay so much more for downtown land only because it provides commensurate benefits.

1. Functions of Metropolitan Areas

The literature on the functions of large MAs is confused and emotional, but the truth is prosaic. MAs provide no technology and no form of social or business organization that is not available elsewhere. The only characteristic that is unique to large MAs is proximity among tens of thousands of businesses and households within a few miles.

Why is proximity so valuable that it may drive up the price of land that provides the best access by a factor of 5,000–10,000? The reason, of course, is that proximity economizes on transportation and communication costs. Transportation and communication are expensive. A downtown location is worth more than a suburban location to a highly paid professional who must meet frequently with other similar professionals. The travel times to such meetings are much shorter downtown even if travel speeds are faster at suburban locations but travel distances are greater. Also, the cost of moving people is much greater than the costs of moving commodities, and, as people costs have risen relative to commodity costs, commodity production has almost completely moved away from central locations in large MAs.

The high cost of transporting people and goods is a necessary but not sufficient condition for MAs. If all commodities and services could be produced as cheaply at small volume as in large volume, most transportation costs could be avoided if small businesses located very close to each other, to their customers and employees, and to their material suppliers. But it is uneconomical to produce cars, education, or almost anything else in facilities that supply only a few consumers. Economies of scale require that production be on a substantial scale if it is to be at low cost. Economies of scope make it advantageous to produce a variety of related commodities and/or services that are related in production and/or marketing in a single facility. It is thus economical to produce commodities and services in large volume and for consumers and producers to locate close to each other if transportation and communication among them are necessary.

The final factor, which finishes the story and permits high-density MAs, is the technical ability to substitute structures for land where land is expensive. Offices and dwellings permit such substitution most easily. For given costs of land and construction, it is hardly more expensive per square foot of usable space to produce office or residential space in a 100-story building than in a 10-story building. Substitution of structures for land is much more difficult for manufacturing plants and warehouses and somewhat more difficult for retail establishments. An important reason is the high cost of moving commodities among floors. Vertical transportation of people is also expensive, and that requires a balancing of costs of horizontal and vertical transportation in choosing office and residential heights.[3]

This analysis applies to MAs of all sizes; indeed, to the smallest agricultural market town. Small towns exist because of scale and scope economies in processing agricultural products and in providing commodities and services to the townspeople and to the surrounding rural population. Nevertheless, Peoria is different from Chicago. The number and variety of commodities and services produced is much greater in large than in small MAs or in small towns. Most of the world's large MAs are on navigable waterways that provide access to the oceans. The exceptions are a few national capitals, such as Brasilia, Delhi, Mexico City, Paris, Seoul, and Washington. They are large because they produce government services rather than commodities or services for export. Their locations were chosen for political, not economic, reasons. (Most such capitals are locations of centralized and intrusive governments.) These days, road and air transportation are at least as important as water and rail transportation. Of course, large MAs are well served by roads and airports, but that is both cause and effect. Roads and airports are built where large MAs are, but they also promote MA growth. Sorting out cause and effect is difficult.

In recent decades some large MAs, but not the largest, have become centers for scientific research, development, and innovation. Route 128 near Boston was an early postwar example. Silicon Valley near San Francisco; Research Triangle in North Carolina; Austin, Texas; and, more recently, Bangalore in India are other examples. Undoubtedly, proximity among such activities facilitates exchange of people and ideas. (See Jaffe, Trajtenberg, and Henderson in Henderson 2005.) All are on the fringe of large MAs and are close to one or more research universities.

[3] Substantial opinion among real estate professionals holds that the tallest recently constructed office towers are excessively tall. Even in the early days of New York's World Trade Center, the top floors were more difficult to rent than lower floors. It is perhaps indicative that most of the world's recently built towers, including the World Trade Center, were built by governments or with large government subsidies. The top floors of such structures are sometimes referred to as "vanity floors."

2. Growth and Sizes of Large Metropolitan Areas

There is enormous stability in the relative population sizes of MAs within a country, although the MAs that occupy particular ranks change from time to time (see Gabaix in Henderson 2005). New York has been the country's largest MA since the first census in 1790. The same MAs have occupied each of the top 5 size ranks since 1970. Over a longer period, Los Angeles has risen and Baltimore has fallen in rank.

Throughout the post–World War II period, the largest MAs have grown relatively slowly. Of the 10 largest MAs in 2004, only Atlanta and Dallas were among the 10 fastest growing MAs from 2000 to 2004. Among the 10 fastest growing MAs from 2000 to 2004, all were in the Sunbelt except Sacramento. The fastest growing, Las Vegas, grew 3.4 times as fast as the average US MA. (That the largest MAs grow more slowly than smaller MAs does not mean that MA sizes are converging. Just because tall parents tend to have children who are shorter than their parents, and short parents tend to have children who are taller than their parents does not mean people are converging to a uniform height.) Five US MAs had annual growth rates in excess of 10% from 2000 to 2004. Such growth rates rival those of the most rapidly growing third-world MAs. (The data in this paragraph are from DeBrandt and Gaquin 2006, 774.)

What limits the sizes of the largest MAs? First is the size and geography of the country. Only countries with large populations have large MAs. No MA with more than about 8 million population is in a country with fewer than 50 million people. Large MAs tend to be distant from each other. Bombay and Calcutta are on the opposite coasts of India, as are New York and Los Angeles in the United States. In many countries, the best natural harbor is also the site of the largest metropolitan area: New York, Tokyo, Mumbai, Manila, and London (World Bank, various issues).

Second, and most fundamentally, are limits to the demand for commodities and services produced in the MA. Every MA "exports" some commodities and services to buyers outside the MA; nearly all commodities manufactured in an MA are sold outside the MA. (Similar comments apply to material inputs purchased from outside the MA.) Many services also are sold outside the MA where they are produced, perhaps as many as one-third. Patients come from great distances to the Johns Hopkins Hospital in Baltimore, as do students to the major universities. Many of the sales on financial exchanges in MAs are among buyers and sellers located outside the MA. As international trade has increased in recent decades, foreign demand has added to the growth of large MAs in some countries, including New York, London, Los Angeles, and Mumbai.

Because of lower transportation and communication costs, the cost of an MA's export tends to increase as a function of distance. Far away customers not only will be served at greater cost, but the competition from other MAs will increase as well. Many studies have shown that foreign demand cannot be explained by distance; presumably, the same holds for MA exports. Large MAs often export commodities and services, sometimes at great distance, that are not produced by smaller MAs. New York has the highest quality maritime attorneys in the country, and Chicago has the most sophisticated commodities exchanges.

The final factor related to MA exports relates to costs. As noted earlier, land values increase with MA size. Rents, wages, and other input prices are raised accordingly, making large MAs expensive places to produce. In the final analysis this is the signal that the MA is as big as it should be. In recent years, both workers and businesses have discovered that Southern California is an expensive place to work or to locate a business. The same appears to be true in many Asian MAs, such as Mumbai.

To this point, no mention has been made in this chapter of congestion and pollution, factors many believe are limits to the size of large MAs. Absent remedial measures, both problems tend to become worse as the size of an MA increases. Nevertheless, both can be alleviated by government and private expenditures. Transportation facilities can be built and improved. Sewage treatment facilities can be built and upgraded, and emission standards can be upgraded. The additional costs are a logical cost of large MAs. In the United States, the federal government intervenes extensively, for example by financing MA public transit construction with nationally raised taxes. The result is to understate the true costs of large MAs to people and businesses in the MA. Such monies could be raised by MA governments, with oversight by state governments. Then, the costs of the MA would be reflected in prices that would be charged for commodities and services produced in the MA. Thus, congestion and pollution can be alleviated by appropriate expenditures, and such expenditures are a logical part of the cost of living and doing business in the large MAs. If this cost is reflected in prices of commodities and services produced in large MAs, markets will get the right signals about appropriate MA sizes.

The final issue discussed here pertains to crime, homelessness, poverty, illegitimacy, racial tensions, and other forms of alienation that increase with MA size and tend to limit size. With poverty, the claim is demonstrably false. The incidence of poverty is lower in MAs than elsewhere and does not increase with MA size. There is some evidence that welfare-prone people are attracted to MAs with unusually generous welfare programs and that large MAs have more generous welfare programs than small MAs. The appropriate measure is welfare payments relative to living costs, and "real" welfare payments hardly rise with MA size. In any case, such effects are small, and the claims are often thinly disguised forms of racism.

Street crime rates also rise with MA size, but, again, the correlation is not strong. One key observation is that large MAs are more impersonal and consequently less civil than towns or small MAs. No one who has lived in both a small town and a large city can doubt this, but it is difficult to imagine that impersonal relations increase significantly in places with more than 1 or 2 million people. Such MAs are already impersonal.

3. Suburbanization

As previously noted, US MAs have suburbanized more than those in almost any other country. Carefully documented reasons include falling transportation costs and rising incomes. The more up-scale housing preferred by higher income people generally can be provided most economically in suburbs, where land values are lower.

Less well studied, but probably important, is the interaction between suburbanization of employment and housing. Manufacturing has long dispersed from central cities and has been moving to distant edges of MAs and beyond since the 1950s.This stems from technical progress that has reduced labor inputs even as manufacturing output has grown. In addition, our superb interstate highway system enables many workers to commute from MA suburbs to manufacturing jobs even well outside the MA. Factories line the interstates leading from the Chicago MA. Many services, including finance, insurance, real estate, retailing, and healthcare have moved to the suburbs massively in recent decades, perhaps following their employees and customers as much as leading them.

Finally, increasingly stringent land use controls, especially since the mid-1970s, have limited population densities to below competitive levels in both central cities and suburbs, especially in large MAs. Chicago illustrates typical effects of suburbanization. From 1980 to 2003, the urban population of the Chicago MA increased less than 30%, but the land area increased more than 40% (see DeBrandt and Gaquin 2006). Two-thirds of the population and 60% of employment are located in near-by suburbs.

Costs of moving people and commodities fall gradually, but costs of processing and transporting information fall much more rapidly. Estimates are that the real cost of doing a given arithmetic operation has fallen at a compound annual rate of 10–20% during the last quarter or third of a century. Experts assert that no end of this technical revolution is in sight. During the 1970s and 1980s, the costs of moving information—anything that can be put on paper—fell dramatically. The cost of data transmission over long distances has fallen because of improved small computers, fax machines, e-mail, cheaper long distance telephone service, and computers especially designed to network.

Although careful studies do not exist, this revolution must have promoted growth of the suburbs and development of edge cities. There is as yet little evidence of dispersion of service sector employment away from substantial centers, either downtown or in suburbs. That suggests that access—inexpensive face-to-face contacts among people—has been the driving force. My hypothesis is that subcenter development is proceeding much the same way and for much the same reasons that downtown development proceeded in earlier years. The difference is that cluster development is proceeding faster outside of downtown areas in large MAs than in small MAs. Businesses in suburban subcenters appear to interact little with downtown businesses. Naperville, nearly 30 miles west of downtown, is the quintessential edge city in the Chicago MA. It is an edge city of 140 thousand residents in 2004, having more than tripled since 1980, and is a thriving and independent community. In 2000, 65,000 jobs were located there, but not everyone who worked there lived there, and everyone who lived there did not also work there.

The rapid and extensive growth of the suburbs increasingly blurs the distinction between metropolitan and rural. People who work in Naperville or who sell commodities and/or services there can easily live 20–40 miles west of Naperville, placing them well beyond the limits of the Chicago MA. As edge cities become larger and more self-contained, exurban locations become increasingly attractive. Indeed, in some places an exurban location, say, no more than 50 miles from an MA downtown, may be little farther from the downtowns of one or two other MAs. Are such locations rural or metropolitan? The name is not crucial, but the effects may be very important. Twenty years ago, these would have been distant rural areas. For many small towns and rural places that have become edge cities or have come to have easy access to edge cities, such developments have provided increased employment and large capital gains on farmland. For others, such developments have brought unwelcome newcomers and lifestyle changes.

4. The Future of Large Metropolitan Areas

I conclude with speculations about the future of large MAs. The only safe statement is that the largest 5–10 US MAs in 2000 are almost certain to grow at slower rates than the US population in coming decades. It would physically difficult for these 5–10 largest MAs to grow much because they are located near other MAs. In 2004, the five largest MAs contained 52.6 million people, 17.9% of the total US population and 22.4% of the MA population.

I expect the MA share of total population to increase about 1 percentage point during the decade or so after 2004. However, the MA share of total population is unlikely to rise as far as 85% during the first few decades of the 21st century. The five largest MAs are likely to grow slowly and to fall slightly as a share of total MA population.

This forecast is a conservative extrapolation of trends during the past 20 years. Why might it be wrong? One common conjecture is that large MAs are increasingly unpleasant places to live and do business and that people prefer small MAs anyway. I do not believe that is a significant argument. For decades, people have told pollsters that they prefer to live and work in small urban areas; 50,000–100,000 people is the most common range. Whatever such polls tell us, they do not forecast behavior. Population and employment have continued to grow throughout the MA size distribution, and small MAs have not grown much faster than middle-size MAs.

Living and working are not unpleasant in MAs; they are, to some extent, unpleasant in some large MA cities. Population fell slowly in many large MA cities for several decades, but the trend reversed slowly toward the end of the 1990s. Growth has focused in suburbs, and nearly two-thirds of the MA population now lives in suburbs. As noted earlier, many large suburban communities now have most of the advantages of central cities: cultural, recreational, and the like. The polls tell us that many MAs are of the sizes where many people like to live. Many suburban residents think that large suburban communities are developing some of the disadvantages of central cities: traffic congestion and crime, specifically. Because land use controls are, or can be, effective in keeping out low-income people, and because traffic investments can be made, I do not think the danger is great. In sum, I do not believe quality of life issues will cause people and jobs to flee large MAs.

Suburbs have grown relative to large or inner cities for a variety of reasons. The result, however, is clear: suburbanites have higher incomes and greater educational attainment than inner-city residents. Inner cities have a greater mixture of racial and ethnic minorities and an appalling concentration of alienated and poor black residents.

Studies indicate that school performance, illegitimacy, and crime all improve if low-income minorities are somewhat dispersed instead of living together in low-income neighborhoods. Role models appear to be the key causal factor. Large MAs have larger fractions of their middle and upper middle-income populations living in exclusionary suburbs than have small MAs. The ratio of suburban to central city income increases with MA size. The result is more segregation of large groups of low-income minorities in inner cities and greater alienation in large than in small MAs. An important part of the solution of this peculiarly US inner-city problem is reduced government density controls in both inner cities and suburbs, but it is not essentially a problem of MA size.

Why have poor minorities not followed jobs to suburbs? The answers are complex and poorly understood. But one partial answer revealed by studies is government density controls. The poor are effectively zoned out of many suburbs. How many more low-income and minority residents would live in suburbs, and how many would perform better there, if land use controls were less of a barrier is impossible to know. However, some simple calculations in Mills (1985) indicate that central cities would contain more white residents, more residents altogether, and more jobs if low-income and minority people were more evenly spread out among MA suburbs. The reason is that, to some extent, high-income people locate in suburbs to avoid the "blight" that results from the concentration of low-income and minority residents in central cities. If it were easier for low-income and minority residents to disperse from the inner cities, there would be less real or perceived inner city blight. In sum, there would be fewer places for higher income people to go and less to escape from (also see also Mills 2005).

Therefore, movement of upper income residents to the suburbs and the use of police power to keep low-income people out of suburbs have caused movement to the suburbs to be more extreme than it would be otherwise, and neither the private nor government sectors in the inner cities perform as well as they are capable of performing.

More difficult to deal with is the second common conjecture: computerization. It is certain that the compilation, analysis, and transmission of data over long distances will become increasingly cheap and common in the coming years. Some conjecture this will destroy the rationale for large collections of office-type activity. If information can be transmitted electronically, why locate in an office center where land is many times as expensive as it would be at a more isolated location?

The key issue is whether computers will destroy the need for face-to-face contact in business communication. Inexpensive long distance electronic transmission of information has been available for some years. It has long been possible to fly diskettes across the country overnight by express delivery services, and fax messages and e-mail have been widely used for more than two decades. Videophones and low long distance phone rates have long been available as well. These innovations seem to have had almost no effect in dispersing business activity beyond MA boundaries. During the 70s and 80s, suburbanization probably was faster because of these technologies, but this seems to have been caused more from gradually falling costs of moving people and goods rather than from rapidly falling costs of moving data. Technology will soon be available that will permit instantaneous interaction by voice, video, and printed documents over great distances and at low cost, permitting meetings among people separated by long distances. They will be able to see and hear one another and transmit documents to each other quickly and cheaply.

I have maintained that access to large numbers of businesses and households is the essence of large MAs. If face-to-face meetings became obsolete, beyond a doubt, large MAs would shrink dramatically within a decade or so. I have grave doubts whether that will happen, but I have no crystal ball and I offer the following with an unusual dose of humility.

I do not believe electronics will make face-to-face meetings obsolete. Anything that can be spoken can be transmitted electronically. The issue is the benefits versus the costs of electronic transmission as compared to face-to-face transmission. In Mills (1992*a*), I distinguished between unambiguous and ambiguous information. Ambiguous information is what is transmitted in early meetings between potential vendors and buyers of a new product. Each side wants to explore the other side's needs, wishes, abilities, reliability, willingness-to-pay, and likely costs and speed of production and delivery. It is what is transmitted when opposing attorneys in a case meet to discuss possible settlement out of court. It is what is transmitted when members of a profession meet for lunch. They all know they are competitors, and they all want to get more valuable information than they give about technology, market trends, product innovations, and the like. Yet they all know that they must give some information in order to get some. Quintessentially, it is what is transmitted in an academic seminar. The essence of a research seminar is that a group of people with a common vocabulary and body of expertise come together to listen to a colleague discuss a half-baked idea. The result is akin to a controlled free association exchange, the essence of the creative process.

My claim is that the exchange of ambiguous information is what face-to-face communication has always been about and that electronic communication is a poor substitute. In such exchanges, it is disadvantageous to write too much down. In addition, each participant wants to iterate in the information exchange. Finally, participants frequently want to "feel each other out" prior to providing unambiguous information. The exchange proceeds in ways that depend on the information set that participants bring to the meeting and are willing to communicate. Such information can be known only approximately prior to the meeting.

Experiments and scientific (mostly by sociologists and management specialists) observations of electronic meetings confirm the above conjectures. Electronic meetings induce people to bring prepared statements and take positions they then find it awkward to modify or abandon. Those with supervisory responsibility may not be able to manage those who are long-winded or get sidetracked. Closely related, those with managerial responsibility find it difficult to monitor the productivity of their supervisees when they are not on the same site. That has limited the spread of work-at-home jobs. If it were not so, supervisees would be paid piece rates. Finally, work on a common site stimulates employees by creating a competitive atmosphere. This extends to schools and universities. An important advantage of a common site for education is the stimulation, exchanges, and competition that students provide for each other.

Academics should consider the possibility of an electronic university. It is now technically possible for me to live in Buena Vista, Colorado and to lecture, with voice, visual, and written communications, students who are dispersed around the country or the world. Communication can easily be interactive. Indeed, my research can be done the same way. It is possible to bring on my computer screen any book or article that is in the university library now, or, indeed, any data set stored in some central location. My working papers can be distributed to a worldwide audience, and seminars can be held using the same computer network. My paycheck can, of course, be sent to me or my bank. Approximations to such electronic universities already exist but show little sign of substituting for high-quality research institutions. And deans have shown little enthusiasm for sending paychecks to distant bank accounts.

Electronic communication certainly has had, and will continue to have, important effects. It permits increased specialization, downsizing, and efficiency among institutions. To take one example, each large bank, until recently, had its own economics department that did forecasting and market analysis for bank management. Now, it is possible to buy higher quality forecasts and analysis than the bank can undertake itself. Such information can be transmitted electronically to any place in the world. That and similar examples are, I believe, at the core of downsizing that has been and is under way throughout the US economy. Entire layers of middle level employees who formerly compiled, analyzed, and transmitted data are being replaced by electronic systems that do the work, both domestically and internationally.

Electronics already has and will continue to facilitate suburbanization. Face-to-face meetings have come to be needed less frequently, but they are still required. That process permits businesses to be located in more distant suburbs than was previously economical. But it does not permit universities, law office, or similar organizations offices to be dispersed among Chicago, Buena Vista, or Baja, California.

In conclusion, my forecast for the next 10–20 years is the continued rapid growth of suburbs. I believe also there will be growth, but slower growth, of the large MAs than for the population as a whole.

References

DeBrandt, K. A., and D. A. Gaquin (eds.). 2006. *2006 County and city extra*. World Development. Lanham, MD: Bernan Press.

Henderson, J. V. (ed.). 2005. *New economic geography*. Northampton, MA: Edward Elgar.

Mills, E. 1985. Open housing laws as stimulus to central city employment. *Journal of Urban Economics* 17(2): 184–188.

Mills, E. 1992*a*. Sectoral clustering and metropolitan development. In *Sources of metropolitan growth*, eds. Edwin S. Mills and John F. McDonald (3–18). New Brunswick, NJ: Center for Urban Policy Research.

Mills, E. 1992*b*. Large metropolitan areas: Their function and prospects. *National Rural Studies Committee, a Proceeding*, 94–100. Corvalis, OR: Oregon State University.

Mills, E. 2005. Why do we have urban density controls? *Real Estate Economics* 3(3): 571–585.

CHAPTER 4

MODELING THE LAND USE CHANGE WITH BIOFUELS

MADHU KHANNA, DAVID ZILBERMAN, AND CHRISTINE L. CRAGO

There is growing interest in increasing reliance on biofuels to reduce dependence on foreign oil, mitigate climate change and stimulate rural economic development. Increased biofuel production can change land use directly by diverting land away from agricultural production and indirectly by affecting crop prices. Changes in crop prices can create incentives to intensify agricultural production (by increasing yields per acre) and to expand agricultural acreage. Land use changes due to an increase in biofuel production in one country can affect land use throughout the globe, and have implications for food security and greenhouse gas emissions (Rajagopal and Zilberman 2007; Searchinger et al. 2008; Khanna and Crago 2012).

Although first-generation biofuels are being produced primarily from food-based crops and sugarcane, there is considerable policy support and research to develop advanced or second-generation biofuels from cellulosic feedstocks, such as crop and forest residues and dedicated energy crops. These biofuels typically have lower life-cycle greenhouse gas (GHG) intensity compared to food-crop-based biofuels and would divert less productive land from food production per unit of fuel produced since they could be produced either from crop by-products or from energy crops that can potentially be grown productively on low-quality land that is marginal for food crop production. There is considerable variability in the land requirements, GHG intensity, and costs of production among the different pathways for second-generation biofuels (Huang et al. 2013).

The United States US and European Union (EU) are relying on mandates, tax credits, and import tariffs to stimulate biofuel production. The advent of biofuels has raised several research and policy questions: How much land will be required to meet the various mandates for biofuels? How much of the additional demand for land for biofuels will be met by changes at the intensive margin versus the extensive margin? Which feedstocks are likely to be used for biofuel production? What economic, technological, and biophysical factors are likely to significantly influence land use choices to support biofuel production? How does the land use effect of biofuels differ with various policy choices? A number of economic models are being used to answer these questions. The purpose of this paper is to examine the key assumptions and synthesize the major findings of these models to develop an understanding of the drivers of land use change and the land availability constraints for biofuel expansion.

Land use changes are outcomes of decisions affected by returns to land under alternative activities. Collectively, these microlevel decisions affect the aggregate supply and costs of food and fuel. In turn, macrolevel variables, like demand, prices and energy and climate policies influence decisions at the microlevel. Major economic theories and concepts have been introduced to explain land use decisions, patterns of trade, and the value of land and the economic benefits and ecosystem services it provides. These include the classic von Thünen (1966) model of regional land allocation, which laid the foundation of "Urban Economics," David Ricardo's (1891) theory of trade and the notion of rent, and John Krutilla's (1967) "Conservation Reconsidered" that emphasized the economic importance of ecological services. These bodies of literature provide the foundation for the development of models to study the drivers of land use change for biofuels. Section 1 of this chapter provides a background on the land economics literature and key principles that have emerged from it for understanding land use changes induced by biofuels.

The recent development of biofuels has integrated the energy and the agricultural sectors. Prior to biofuels, energy prices have affected the supply side of agricultural production, since energy is a key input. Now energy prices are also affecting the demand for land and crops (used for biofuels). The nexus between energy markets and land use has required adaptation of existing models and development of new models of agricultural markets. These models tend to emphasize the heterogeneity in land and to link biophysical models of biofuel feedstocks with economic models. They differ in their structure, assumptions, data used, and the mix of biofuel feedstocks and policy choices considered. Section 2 of this chapter describes the impacts of introducing biofuels on models used to analyze the agricultural sector, followed by a description of the elements of an ideal model for analyzing the implications of biofuels.

Section 3 of this chapter presents a description of different types of models being used to study the implications of biofuel policies for land use, and classifies them into: static partial equilibrium models, dynamic partial equilibrium models, and general equilibrium models. It examines how the differences in model structure affect outcomes. Section 4 of this chapter discusses the key drivers of land use change due to biofuels, and

Section 5 discusses ways to deal with multiple models. Section 6 presents the main findings that emerge from these models and Section 7 concludes.

1. Overview of the Land Economics Literature

There are several strands of economics literature relevant to understanding the impacts of biofuel on land use changes. Some are conceptual models that recognize that land is heterogeneous and that differences among parcels of land will affect their use and value. von Thünen (1966) established a major principle that land will be used in the activity in which it generates the most value. His work suggests that land use choices will differ across locations and will change over time as technology and the climate change. This literature provides insights that are useful for determining the location of biofuel feedstock production and refineries for biofuels.

Ricardo (1891) introduced the notion of rent, which is the residual left to landowners after selling the output and paying for all inputs. When each landowner selects the most profitable activity, rents and land use patterns can be derived given prices and technological coefficients at each location. Since agricultural products are frequently traded, with free trade, land use patterns will adjust to take advantage of distribution of resources across locations (Heckscher and Ohlin 1991).

Another relevant literature expands the Hotelling approach of dynamic modeling of utilization and pricing of nonrenewable resources over time to examine the effects of introducing renewable energy as a backstop. Chakravorty, Magne, and Moreaux (2008) use the Ricardian-Hotelling framework to analyze the dynamics of land allocation decisions for food and fuel production as available energy resources become scarce. Xabadia, Goetz, and Zilberman (2006) developed a conceptual framework for optimal allocation of resources over space and time. Tsur and Zemel (2005) incorporated research and development (R&D) of alternative technologies in dynamic models analyzing nonrenewable resources.

The existing literature identifies the following factors as being important in driving land use change in agriculture.

Technological Change and Innovation: R&D processes produce new innovations that are adopted first at locations where they provide the most value (Sunding and Zilberman 2001) and may lead to expansion of farmland to areas that have not been previously utilized (the extensive margin effect of adoption). Adoption of new technologies can also increase yield per unit of land (the intensive margin effect), thus decreasing the land requirement per unit of output (Gardner 1992). Thus, the net effect of technological changes on land use in agriculture is an empirical question. The changes in output in the extensive and intensive margins will affect the amount of land required to accommodate increased crop production due to biofuels.

Risk: Producers are frequently averse to risk, and their land allocation choices among crops and, in particular, adoption choices are affected by uncertainty about yields and other variables (Feder, Just, and Zilberman 1985). Introduction of insurance policies that reduce risk or institutions like futures markets or contracts may lead to increased acreage of high-risk–high-reward activities. Risk would be a major factor influencing land allocation to second-generation biofuel feedstocks.

Institutions and Policies: The perfectly competitive model does not fully capture the institutions and policies that affect land use patterns. Feder and Feeny (1991) argue that introduction of land titles removes uncertainty about landownership and tends to increase investment in agricultural production and land productivity. Commodity-support programs in the United States and Europe as well as building of transport infrastructure have expanded agricultural acreage (Anderson et al. 2001). Similarly, water use and energy subsidies have led to expansion of irrigated agriculture (Schoengold and Zilberman 2007).

Environmental Considerations: Existence of externalities like pollution provides justification for government intervention such as taxation and zoning. Externality issues are not restricted to pollution problems; land and nature provide valued ecosystem services and consumers benefit from open space (Krutilla, 1967). Policies (zoning, permits, and conservation preserve programs) have been introduced to protect these environmental services. Irwin et al. (2009) demonstrate that environmental regulation indeed affects land use and location of crops.

Changes in Consumer Preferences and Economic Growth: Demand for food is dependent on food prices as well as on income. Poor individuals may consume mostly grains, while higher income households may consume more meat. Since meat production requires more land per calorie, economic growth in developing countries will increase agricultural acreage. On the other hand, shifts away from a meat-rich diet in other parts of the world may have the opposite effect.

Population Growth and Demographics: Population growth is likely to increase demand, but the pattern of increased demand for food depends on where and when these changes occur. Migration, especially from rural to urban areas, also affects land use patterns. A shift from production for self-consumption in rural areas to production for export to urban centers affects the composition of food portfolios, energy intensity of food production, and productivity.

Renewable and Nonrenewable Resources: Agricultural productivity is dependent on natural resources like water and soil quality, whose stocks may vary over time. The depletion of groundwater or increase in cost of pumping strongly affects patterns of land use (Schoengold and Zilberman 2007). Similarly, processes of soil erosion may also affect what and how much can be grown at different locations. Finally, climate change will affect land use patterns through its effect on precipitation, temperature, and sunlight, among others (Mendelsohn and Dinar 2009).

2. Implication of Biofuels for Land Use Analysis

The introduction of biofuel to agriculture has led to a new reality that challenged the way agriculture and land use are analyzed and modeled. The agricultural sector was traditionally quite isolated, produced mostly food/feed products and was affected by sectoral policies. Studies analyzing the sector used specialized models that could focus on the agricultural sector by itself. The introduction of biofuel has expanded the range of activities conducted and the policies that affect the agricultural sector, and expanded the importance of environmental issues in management and modeling of agriculture, as discussed in more detail below.

First, biofuels have integrated the agricultural, livestock, and energy markets. Biofuels have added a new demand to agricultural activities; this has led to diversion of land from production of food to fuel (Rajagopal et al. 2007). Modeling of farmers' choices now has to take into account not only relative food prices and traditional agricultural policies, but energy prices and biofuel policies. Moreover, biofuels have linked energy markets and livestock markets since some of the co-products of biofuels are substitutes for traditional feed for livestock. Furthermore, biofuels have expanded the range of spatial considerations in modeling farmers' choices. The selection of where to allocate land for food or fuel is affected not only by relative prices, but by the biophysical suitability of locations to produce biofuel crops and distance to refineries and end users. Distance from a refinery and from livestock facilities will affect markets for corn and the by-products of corn ethanol, which is used as animal feed and, therefore, land use choices. Incorporating biofuels in land use models also links transportation choice decisions with fuel choices and has implications for feedstock production and land use. Since demand for biofuels is a derived demand, it depends on the demand for vehicle kilometers traveled and on the substitutability between biofuels and gasoline (Khanna, Ando, and Taheripour, 2008). With biofuels, land use choices are affected by vehicle fleet structure, development of biofuel supply chain, and development of biofuel conversion technologies. Moreover, these land use choices now impact fuel markets because biofuel production displaces gasoline and can affect gasoline prices with consequent feedback effects on demand for biofuels and costs of energy for the agricultural sector. Modeling the implications of biofuels, therefore, requires determining market clearing prices in the food and fuel sectors simultaneously (Khanna et al. 2011).

Second, different biofuel feedstocks expand the types of land that could be displaced by biofuel production. Both corn and sugarcane ethanol, for the most part, requires diversion of existing land in commodity production to production of crops for fuel. On the other hand, introduction of new second-generation energy crops that can be grown on marginal land may require conversion of land that is under pasture or forests into agricultural production. This requires further modeling efforts to identify regions with good potential to grow these crops.

Third, biofuel expands the range of policies that affect agriculture and land use. These include agricultural policies as well as climate and energy policies. Policies such as biofuel mandates, subsidies, and import tariffs on biofuels affect demand for biofuels and, therefore, land use allocation and crop prices. Similarly, climate policies will not only affect energy prices and the cost of agricultural inputs but will also affect demand for biofuels and, therefore, crop prices and land use. These biofuel and climate policies affect not only domestic land use but have indirect impacts on global land use because they affect the prices of globally traded crops. The diversion of globally traded food/feed crops for biofuel production and the competition for cropland induced by biofuel production has the inevitable impact of raising world prices of biofuel feedstocks and other crops that compete for land resources. The increase in world prices could induce crop acreage expansion on native vegetation and forested land leading to indirect land use changes that also contribute to greenhouse gas emissions (Khanna and Crago 2012).

Fourth, biofuels have expanded the type of technical change that affects land use. In addition to changes in agricultural technologies that affect the productivity of biofuel and related crops, technical change in the biofuel processing industry will also affect land use. Technological breakthroughs that lower the cost of producing advanced biofuels from cellulosic feedstocks will affect the mix of biofuels and the amount and type of land diverted from food and feed production to fuel production.

The introduction of biofuel and biofuel policies, thus, require significant additions to existing ways of modeling agricultural markets. The linkage between agricultural and energy markets imply the need for an integrated model of the food, feed, and fuel markets that endogenously determines food and fuel prices and their feedback effects on demand for biofuels and allocation of land for food and fuel crops. Models that seek to quantify the land use implications of biofuels and simulate the effects of biofuel policies need to integrate across many different scales. A global representation of relevant markets is needed to capture the effect of biofuel-induced changes in land use and prices on international trade and land use in other countries. At the same time, the assessment of biofuel impacts requires a high degree of spatial resolution to account for heterogeneous land qualities, climate, land availability and ease of its conversion from one use to another. These assessments need to be based not only on models that capture economic behavior but also on models that incorporate crop production technologies, biophysical factors that affect crop productivity, and land suitability and availability constraints. Finally, models should also take into account the market structure of the energy markets. The market imperfection in the oil market due to the presence of an oil cartel such as OPEC could impact the change in fuel prices that results from the displacement of gasoline with biofuel, and it could have feedback effects on the demand for biofuels (Hochman, Rajagopal, and Zilberman 2010).

The production of biofuel has both direct and indirect land use impacts as shown in Figure 4.1. The pathway by which biofuel production affects land use is described in the upper set of boxes. The determinants of the magnitude of these effects are listed in the lower set of boxes and discussed in Section 4. The direct land requirements for biofuel production are simply the land on which biofuel feedstocks are grown and could be simply

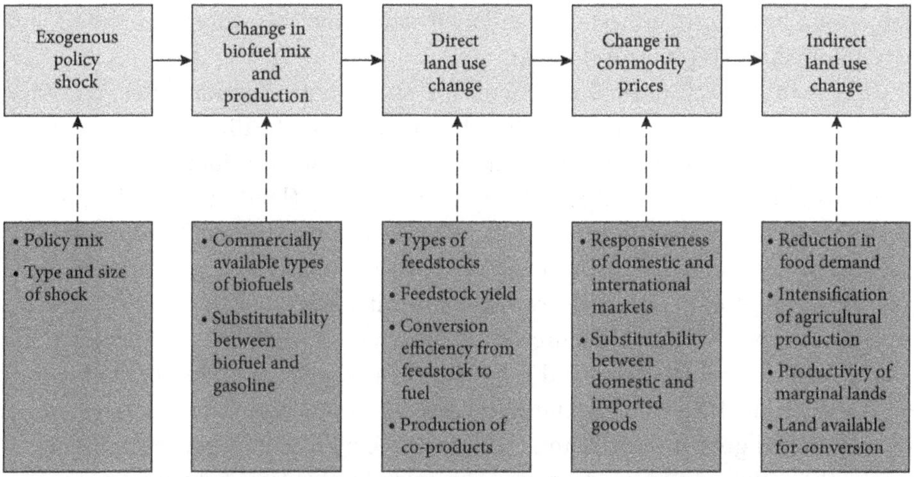

FIGURE 4.1 Pathway of land use changes due to biofuels.

measured by [biofuel quantity/(conversion efficiency of feedstock to fuel times the crop yield)]. The magnitude of this direct land requirement is, therefore, critically dependent on the yield of biofuel crops per unit of land and the conversion efficiency of feedstock to fuel. This will depend on the type of feedstock that is being used and the technology for converting it to biofuel. However, this is not the amount of additional land required due to biofuel production, since some biofuels (like corn ethanol) produce co-products that can replace other products that require land for their production. Biofuels also affect land use indirectly because they increase competition for land and affect the price of land and all land-using activities. In the case of biofuel crops that are tradable, the production of biofuels reduces exports and increases both domestic and world price of biofuel crops. This increase in prices for biofuel crops has four types of effects both domestically and in the rest of the world. First, it can affect crop yields by inducing crop producers to adopt improved technologies and management practices; these changes increase the intensity of crop production and reduce the demand for additional land due to biofuel production. Second, it can increase the value of land under biofuel crops and make it profitable for landowners to substitute land from other crops to biofuel crops. This will reduce production of substitute crops and increase their prices as well as those of biofuel crops. Third, the increase in crop prices for tradable commodities leads to an increase in cultivated land both domestically and in other regions of the world (extensive margin effect). This increase could occur on land under grasses or on forestland and bring marginal/noncropland into production. The expansion of biofuel crops to other cropland or to noncropland could lower yields per hectare and increase the land required to meet demand for biofuel crops; this will, at least partly, offset the intensive margin effect that raises crop yields. These indirect land use changes have the potential to lead to the release of carbon stored in those ecosystems and negate some of the greenhouse gas benefit of biofuels. Lastly, the increase in price of biofuel crops and substitute crops will reduce demand for these commodities both domestically and internationally. This will reduce the additional land required due to biofuel production.

Thus, the net land use requirement for biofuel production after considering co-products and indirect effects is likely to be smaller than the direct effect. For example Hertel et al. (2010) show that the land required to meet the 57 million-liter corn-ethanol mandate would naively be 15 million hectares if resources (land, labor, and capital) were in perfectly elastic supply and there was no price response at all. The finite availability of suitable land induces a price increase, which will lead to a reduction in demand for food and nonfood (forestry) products and intensification of livestock, crop, and forest-product production. The use of co-products of corn-ethanol production for livestock feed also reduces demand for corn. As a result, the additional land requirement is reduced to 4.4 million hectares. It is further reduced to 3.8 million hectares due to price-induced growth in baseline yields in the United States; however, this is offset partly by the expansion of production on less productive land, which lowers yield. As a result, the net increase in cropland conversion is estimated to be 4.2 million hectares, which implies that each gross hectare of corn diverted to fuel use results in 0.28 hectares of net land conversion for corn production.

Isolating the extent to which biofuel production affects land use is complicated and difficult because it is likely to be distributed across multiple regions by global trade and occur with significant time lags. This makes it difficult to separate the causal impact of biofuels on ILUC from all the other factors affecting observed land use changes. With multiple uses of land and possibilities for crop substitutions and displacements occurring simultaneously, the only way to isolate land use changes due to biofuels is by using regional or global models of agricultural markets that simulate the effect of an incremental exogenous shock to biofuel production from some baseline level on equilibrium prices and land use. These are compared, in a comparative static sense, to land requirements in a baseline or counterfactual state in the absence of biofuels to examine the direct and indirect land use effects of biofuels.

3. Existing Models Being Used for Analyzing the Impact of Biofuels

Various types of economic models are being used to examine the impact of biofuels. These models can be classified broadly into partial equilibrium and general equilibrium models. Each of these two types can be further classified into models that are static versus dynamic. Some of these models are global and can analyze both domestic and international land use changes, whereas others only analyze domestic land use changes in the country producing biofuels. We describe a few examples of each of these types of models in the next section, although there are many other models that are being used to analyze the land use implications of biofuels (see reviews in Edwards, Mulligan, and Marelli 2010; Prins et al. 2010).

Additionally, several biophysical models are being used to study the land use impacts of biofuels. These models can provide the foundation for determining where certain crops can be grown subject to biophysical constraints. They have been used to examine the technical potential for biofuel production given land availability (see, for example, Cai, Zhang, and Wang, 2011). We do not describe these biophysical models here in the interest of brevity. Only some of the economic models below rely explicitly on biophysical models for modeling heterogeneity in land suitability and crop productivity across locations.

3.1 Partial Equilibrium Models

Partial equilibrium models focus on a few sectors of the economy that are most closely associated with biofuel production, namely the agricultural, forestry and fuel sectors. Prices, production, and land allocation within these sectors are determined within the model, and it is assumed that conditions in the rest of the economy remain unchanged with biofuel production.

Static Equilibrium Models: These models include multiple markets represented by demand and supply conditions; these markets are linked to each other by considering own- and cross-price effects. A shock to demand or price in one market, for example due to a biofuel policy, perturbs the market equilibrium and leads to changes in all markets to establish an instantaneous new equilibrium. Multimarket models usually do not explicitly include a constraint on land availability.

The Food and Agricultural Policy Research Institute (FAPRI-CARD) model, developed at Iowa State University's Center for Agricultural and Rural Development (CARD) is a widely used multimarket model for analyzing the land use impact of biofuels (Fabiosa et al. 2010). It includes world agricultural, food, livestock, fiber, and bioenergy crop markets but does not explicitly include land constraints. The model currently only considers corn ethanol as the source of biofuel. It also does not include a gasoline sector; a reduced form relationship is used to incorporate a feedback effect of biofuel production on oil prices. Crop yields are responsive to prices over time both in the United States and internationally. This price-induced yield increase is partially offset by the reduced yields that result from expanding on to new crop acres. All non-US countries are analyzed at the national level, with the exception of Brazil. The FAPRI-CARD model is linked with the Brazilian Land Use Model (BLUM) to compute the impacts of sugarcane ethanol exports to the United States on land use and GHG emissions. BLUM is developed by Brazil's Institute for International Trade Negotiations (ICONE, 2011). Land use change in BLUM occurs due to two effects: competition and scale. Different activities compete for a given amount of land based on their net returns per acre and at the same time returns to land determine the need for expansion of agricultural area over natural vegetation (Gouvello 2010).

Dynamic Programming Models: Unlike static multimarket models that are reduced form models of supply and demand, dynamic programming models are structural models that represent the behavior of utility maximizing consumers and profit maximizing producers. They typically include fairly detailed biophysical data to model the dynamics of crop yields, soil carbon changes, and GHG emissions. A programming model can be a one-period or multiperiod model. These models use nonlinear programming methods to determine land allocation, equilibrium production, and prices that maximize the discounted sum of consumer and producer surplus (net of externality costs) subject to constraints on land, technology, and various material balances, and solves for endogenous output and factor prices. Landowners are assumed to choose allocation of land among alternatives based on the net present value of the future returns, subject to calibration constraints that prevent large deviations from historical land use patterns.'Land can shift from cropland to pasture based on relative returns, and equilibrium land prices can vary across regions. In contrast to these intertemporal models, dynamic-recursive models calculate results one period at a time. In all these models, traded and domestically produced goods are treated as homogenous and net trade flows are endogenously determined as the difference between demand and supply.

Multiperiod models include the Forestry and Agricultural Sector Optimization Model (FASOM), the Global Biomass Optimization Model (GLOBIOM) and the Biofuel and Environmental Policy Analysis Model (BEPAM), which have a similar structure but differ in terms of the sectors included, their geographic scope, the degree of spatial heterogeneity and the time horizon considered. FASOM, developed at Texas A&M University is a US-based model of the agricultural and forestry sectors (Adams et al. 2005; Beach et al. 2009; Beach, Zhang, and McCarl 2012). The production activities incorporated include crop and livestock production and processing, bioenergy production, and forest product production and processing. Biofuels can be produced from several types of first-and second-generation feedstocks. In addition to biofuels, FASOM contains a set of activities for replacing coal with biomass in electricity production. Agricultural land can move between cropland pasture (marginal land) and cropland by incurring conversion costs that are equal to the difference in land rental rates between alternative uses based on the assumption of equilibrium in land markets. The model assumes perfect foresight over a 100-year time horizon, and expected future prices are identical to prices realized in the future. Technological change in crop production and in biofuel conversion, which reduces biofuel production costs, is assumed to be exogenously given over time. FASOM also includes a comprehensive set of GHG mitigation options, including biological sequestration of carbon in agricultural soils and forest stands, alternative crop and livestock production practices to reduce emissions, and bioenergy feedstock substitutes for fossil fuels (McCarl and Schneider 2001). The model has recently been used to analyze the effect of biomass-storage costs for the mix of feedstocks used to produce second-generation biofuels and the land use changes due to biofuel and carbon policies in the United States (Beach, Zhang, and McCarl 2012).

GLOBIOM, developed at the International Institute for Applied Systems Analysis is similar to FASOM but models global agricultural, bioenergy, and forestry sectors

(Havlík et al. 2011). Although the regions are fairly aggregated, land use decisions are examined at a much finer spatial resolution. The availability of land resources and their productivity are determined using a biophysical model EPIC (Environmental Policy Integrated Climate Model) and detailed geospatial data on soil, climate, and topography, which is used to define homogenous simulation units at fine spatial scale. The model assumes there is zero technological progress in crop improvement. Like FASOM, this model also accounts for the major GHG emissions/sinks related to agriculture and forestry. In GLOBIOM, ethanol is produced from corn and sugarcane, and biodiesel from rapeseed and soybeans. Second-generation biofuels use forest products as feedstock. Bioenergy can also be used to generate heat and power. Demand for biofuels and the share of first- and second-generation biofuels are fixed at exogenously given levels. Unlike FASOM and BEPAM, which are US-based models, GLOBIOM examines land use changes globally and it can, therefore, determine both domestic and international land use changes due to biofuel production.

BEPAM, developed at the Energy Biosciences Institute at the University of Illinois Urbana-Champaign differs from FASOM and GLOBIOM in that it integrates the agricultural and fuel sectors (Chen, Huang, and Khanna 2011; Khanna et al. 2011; Chen et al. 2012). Demand for gasoline and biofuels is derived from the demand for vehicle miles traveled. The vehicle fleet structure is explicitly included and influences the extent and type of biofuels that can be consumed. The model includes various first- and second-generation biofuels, including from corn and imported sugarcane ethanol, crop and forest residues, and perennial herbaceous grasses for biofuel production. It includes the use of forest biomass residues but not the use of highly valued forest products as biofuel feedstocks. The mix of feedstocks used to produce biofuels and the share of first-generation to second-generation biofuels is endogenously determined subject to the restrictions and incentives provided by various biofuel and climate policies. The model also distinguishes between domestically produced gasoline and imported gasoline. The imports and the price of gasoline in the United States is determined endogenously; this allows for biofuel production in the United States to affect the world price of gasoline and generate a feedback effect on the demand for biofuels in the United States. The model incorporates spatial heterogeneity in yields and returns to land by considering decision making at a crop reporting district level. BEPAM includes life-cycle GHG emissions from gasoline, diesel, and biofuel production and from all crop production activities. Instead of assuming perfect foresight and extremely long time horizons for decision making, BEPAM considers a 10-year rolling horizon for decision making based on expectations about prices and land availability. These expectations are updated annually (for the following 10 years) after equilibrium market outcomes are realized each year (see Chen et al. 2012). FASOM relies on historical crop mixes to generate results that are consistent with farmers' planting history, and allows crop acreage to deviate 10% from observed historical mixes to accommodate new bioenergy crops and unprecedented changes in future crop prices. BEPAM, instead uses the estimated own- and cross-price crop elasticities to limit the flexibility of crop-acreage changes. Crop yields grow at an exogenous rate over time and are also price responsive and thus partly determined endogenously by the model. Another distinguishing feature of BEPAM is that it incorporates an experience curve for each type of biofuel, which allows for the costs of processing feedstocks into biofuel to be endogenously determined based on the cumulative production levels of the biofuel. Unlike other models, that consider cost-reducing technological change to be entirely determined by the passage of time, this approach incorporates the possibility of learning by doing and endogenous technological change. As a result, policies that differ in their effect on the volume and mix of biofuels lead to varying levels of cost-reducing technological change in biofuel production.

The AGLINK-COSIMO model, used by the Organisation for Economic Co-operation and Development and the Food and Agriculture Organisation is a dynamic-recursive partial equilibrium model of world agricultural markets (OECD 2008). The model treats most OECD member countries and their main trading partners as individual supplying and demanding regions. The model considers fossil energy prices as exogenously fixed. It includes first- and second-generation biofuels; the former is modeled endogenously, whereas the latter is treated as exogenous and is assumed to have no land use implications. AGLINK-COSIMO does not simulate land use effects in Indonesia and Malaysia; therefore, any land use impact resulting from land expansion is not included in the quantified global arable land use change (Fonseca et al. 2010). Exogenous rates of technical progress are assumed for first-generation biofuels and their by-products and for crop-yield growth, based on past trends. Yields of major crops are price endogenous, as in BEPAM. Land use constraints are not modeled explicitly but the implicit assumption is that total agricultural land is fixed.

Dynamic programming models include more spatial detail and explicit land availability constraints compared to static multi-market models; the latter, however, are easily modified to consider noncompetitive behavior, and usually include many sectors and cover a larger geographical area. The main appeal of both static and dynamic programming partial equilibrium models is that they are generally well contained, and results are easy to interpret and very intuitive. However, the main flaw of these models is that they do not include some of the major feedbacks that are caused by changes in income because of changes in commodity prices, which may in turn affect demand for commodities in other markets. To address these issues one needs a more inclusive model that goes beyond the small number of sectors incorporated in partial equilibrium analysis.

3.2 Computable General Equilibrium Models

Unlike partial equilibrium models, computable general equilibrium (CGE) models simulate economy-wide effects of a biofuels shock and include intersectoral linkages and constraints on labor and capital and determine all prices and incomes in the economy simultaneously. These models are global in scope, represent multiple economic sectors in each region, and include factor markets for labor and capital. They consider some of the feedbacks that biofuel policy may have through its costs to the taxpayer and through the employment possibilities that are generated through the supply chain as a result of biofuel production. CGE models are especially suited to address a globally common problem like climate change. Although broad in geographic and sectoral scope, many CGE models have limited spatial resolution and usually partition the world into a few large homogenous regions called agro-ecological zones (AEZs). Each region has a regional representative household that allocates resources domestically and a representative producer that produces goods and services using consumer-owned endowments as primary inputs. Each region interacts with other regions through trade. Consumers maximize utility and producers maximize profits in a perfectly competitive market setting, leading to endogenously determined prices and quantities of goods and factors of production. These models typically limit the number of agricultural products considered by categorizing individual commodities into large groups (e.g., all coarse grains) and imposing the same behavioral and market assumptions on the individual components.

CGE models analyzing the effect of biofuel production on land use include the Global Trade Analysis Project (GTAP), the Integrated Global System Model (IGSM), and the Modeling International Relationships in Applied General Equilibrium (MIRAGE) model. The three models are similar in that they are global in scope, and are multiregional, multisectoral, and multifactoral models. All three models are using essentially the same database developed by GTAP but differ in the base year used for calibration. IGSM and MIRAGE are both dynamic models, with varying time-steps and time horizons, whereas the GTAP is an intrinsically static model (CARB 2009; Hertel et al. 2010). IGSM and MIRAGE are different from GTAP, which considers only managed land, in that they model the conversion of natural forests and grasslands into cropland or pasture land.

In CGE models, land conversion occurs within an agro-ecological zone (AEZ) or grid cell. The easier it is for land to be converted from one use to another, the greater the potential is for biofuel production and land use change. In GTAP and MIRAGE, the ease of land conversion from one use to another is governed by a Constant Elasticity of Transformation (CET) frontier. The CET frontier is used to determine the supply of particular types of land (pasture, cropland, forest) given total availability of land. It is based on the assumption that a landowner allocates land to different uses in order to maximize the total rents. The responsiveness of land in a particular use to a change in the land rent influences the ease with which land is transformed from one use to another.[1] The greater the elasticity of transformation parameter, the easier it is for land to be converted from one use to another. IGSM uses a number of techniques to model land conversion, including an "observed land supply response" approach—which is similar to the CET method described earlier. Other approaches, such as the "pure conversion

[1] The absolute value of the CET parameter depends on the elasticity of supply of land to a given use of land in response to a change in its rental rate and the share of revenue from that land use in the total revenue for all land. The value of CET ranges between 0 and 1. The more dominant a given use in total land revenue is, the smaller the value of CET (since the potential for further changes in the amount of land in that use are small, even if land rents increase).

cost response" are also used. In this case, land conversion occurs as long as the cost of conversion is less than returns from clearing land for production. The advantage of the latter approach is that it allows land rents to equalize across all uses and is, therefore, consistent with long run equilibrium behavior.

The GTAP model, developed at Purdue University's Center for Global Trade Analysis considers first-generation biofuels from coarse grains (ethanol), edible oils (biodiesel), and sugarcane (ethanol) (Golub et al. 2010). It uses difference in land rental rates within each AEZ between cropland, pasture, and forests to determine which land will be converted to cropland as a result of increasing biofuel demand. For modeling the competition between livestock and crop sectors, it uses the average coarse-grain yield in each AEZ as representative of pasture land yields. Unmanaged land such as shrubland, savanna, and grassland, is not allowed to be brought into productive use (EPA 2010).

The IGSM is developed by the Massachusetts Institute of Technology Joint Program for the Science and Policy of Global Change (Gurgel, Reilly, and Peltsev 2007; Melillo et al. 2009). The model integrates three components, a dynamic recursive CGE model (Emissions Prediction and Policy Analysis or EPPA), a climate model and a land ecosystems model (Terrestrial Ecosystem Model). The IGSM framework has the most sophisticated emissions modeling, as it features full dynamic accounting of carbon fluxes in vegetation and soils. In contrast, GTAP and MIRAGE use constant factor intensities of conversion from one land use to another. However, the modeling of biofuel production pathways is relatively coarse in the IGSM, whereas GTAP and MIRAGE have fairly detailed modeling of first-generation biofuel-production pathways, including co-products and interaction with the livestock industry. One of the distinguishing features of IGSM and MIRAGE is that they incorporate both managed and unmanaged land unlike GTAP, which includes only managed land. Another advantage of IGSM is that it also considers feedback effects between the climate and the economy, and can examine the land use effects of various climate stabilization policies.

The MIRAGE model developed at the International Food and Policy Research Institute is a dynamic recursive CGE model that considers two main biofuel sectors, ethanol and biodiesel from first-generation feedstocks (Al-Riffai, Dimaranan, and Laborde 2010; Laborde 2011). Feedstocks for ethanol include wheat, sugarcane, sugar beet, and maize, and those for biodiesel include palm oil, soybean oil, sunflower oil and rapeseed oil. It combines a bottom-up approach for the biofuel sector to include production costs and volume, by-products and input requirements. It improves on the GTAP model, which only includes values and not physical quantities, by linking land value and volume. It allows for intensive margin effects, through increased use of fertilizers to increase crop yields, exogenous technical change and endogenous factor based intensification (land combined with more labor and capital). Extensive margin effects are considered by differentiating between different types of AEZs and allowing for substitution of land among different crops and expansion of arable land using different land-responsiveness coefficients in different AEZs. Allocation of land expansion among different types of unmanaged land (grasslands, shrublands, etc.) is based mostly on historical data and on remote sensing data for some countries.

4. Drivers of Land Use Change in Economic Models of Biofuels

Based on the models discussed in the previous section, we identify several demand and supply side factors that affect the estimated land use change impact of biofuels.

4.1 Demand-Side Determinants of Land Use Change

Ease of Substitution Between Liquid Fossil Fuels and Biofuels: The most important demand side considerations are the technological constraints to substitution of biofuels for gasoline (that is the blend wall), the substitution of one type of biofuel for another type and the price of substitute goods (namely, liquid fossil fuels). In addition to the vehicle fleet, the infrastructure for distributing ethanol and blending it could also be a constraint to its usage. Models differ in the way they incorporate demand for ethanol. The partial equilibrium models, with the exception of BEPAM and the FAPRI-CARD model consider ethanol and gasoline to be perfect substitutes. Unlike BEPAM, other models such as FASOM and the FAPRI-CARD model represent demand for biofuels either as a mandated quantity or as a result of an oil price shock (which creates demand for its substitute good, ethanol). CGE models include an elasticity of substitution between biofuels and gasoline and between different types of biofuels but differ in the extent to which they consider these fuels to be substitutes. Earlier versions of FAPRI-CARD ignored the effect of biofuels on global petroleum markets and its feedback effect on the demand for biofuels and other bottlenecks to consume biofuels. As a result, the oil-price shock considered by Searchinger et al. (2008) led to a much greater increase in biofuel production and indirect land use change than it would if these bottlenecks are considered (as discussed in Dumortier et al. 2011). The analysis using BEPAM shows that increasing the elasticity of substitution between biofuels and gasoline in the presence of volumetric tax credits for biofuels leads to a significant increase in biofuel production.

Size and Type of Policy Shock: Biofuel production can be induced by various policies, such as technology mandates and subsidies as well as by climate policies like a Low Carbon Fuel Standard or carbon cap and trade policy. The type of policy stimulus as well as the magnitude of the stimulus will affect the demand for biofuels and the mix of first- and second-generation biofuels induced and, thus, the direct and indirect land use changes. Studies differ in their assumptions about the nature and magnitude of the policy shock considered. The size of the policy shock matters because the relationship between land use change and biofuel production is nonlinear. An increase in the volume of biofuel increases land requirements more than proportionately. This is because greater pressure for biofuel production from a higher target results in increasing use of less efficiently produced feedstock. Similarly the adverse effect on indirect land use changes increases nonlinearly with an increase in biofuel production. Chen et al. (2012) also show that a carbon tax policy will lead to a modest increase in corn ethanol consumption at low carbon prices and will not induce any second-generation ethanol production. Carbon prices that are over $150 per ton of CO2 will be needed to induce production of second-generation biofuels. The extent to which price-based policies like a carbon tax or a biofuel subsidy will induce demand for biofuels depends on the responsiveness of demand for fuel or of vehicle kilometers traveled to its price.

Mix of Policies: Countries are typically using multiple policy instruments to support biofuels. Chen et al. (2012) and Khanna et al. (2011) show (using BEPAM) that the land use impacts of the Renewable Fuel Standard (RFS), can be significantly modified by accompanying tax credits for second-generation biofuels that can increase their competitiveness relative to corn ethanol. Since these second-generation biofuels have higher yields per unit of land, this policy induced shift in the mix of biofuels lowers the demand for corn and the land needed to meet the RFS. Moreover, it has implications for the type of land used for biofuel production: the use of noncropland for second-generation biofuels increases, whereas the use of cropland for corn production decreases.

Land use is also sensitive to trade barriers. The US import tariff on biofuels reduces the competitiveness of sugarcane ethanol and increases the land use impact of the RFS. Trade liberalization would increase the volume of sugarcane ethanol used to meet the mandate and lower the pressure on diversion of land to biofuel production domestically in the United States. Using BEPAM, Chen and Khanna (2012) show that the removal of the tax credit for ethanol and the tariff on imports of sugarcane ethanol to the United States could significantly alter the mix of biofuels and increase reliance on sugarcane ethanol to meet the RFS with implications for land use under corn and sugarcane in the United States and Brazil, respectively.

Al-Riffai, Dimaranan, and Laborde (2010) consider the implications of the EU Renewable Energy Directive (RED) with and without trade liberalization in the EU and find that trade liberalization significantly changes the impact on biofuel production in the EU. They find that the removal of tariffs on ethanol would lead to a surge in European imports of sugarcane ethanol. In 2020 ethanol production would increase by 157% in the EU under the EU RED in the absence of trade liberalization, whereas it would decrease by 48% in the event of the full liberalization scenario because of increased imports from Brazil.

4.2 Supply-Side Determinants of Land Use Change

Conversion Efficiencies and Co-Products: Conversion efficiencies differ across feedstocks (Huang et al. 2013) with some energy crops yielding more than twice as many liters of biofuels per hectare as corn ethanol. Therefore, a change in the mix of biofuels toward sugarcane or high-yielding energy crops would significantly lower the land use impact of biofuels.

The land requirements for biofuels also depend on their co-products, which can replace other products in the market place, reducing the net quantity of food or feed displaced. Thus, the amount of additional or net land required to produce these biofuels is less than the total amount of land on which the biofuel crop is produced. Most first-generation biofuels produce co-products that substitute for products that would otherwise require land. This is particularly the case for corn ethanol, which produces DDGS that can substitute for corn meal and soymeal used for animal feed. Taheripour et al (2010) introduced by-products in the GTAP model and showed that it reduced the need for cropland conversion due to US and EU biofuel mandates by 27%.

Land Productivity in Intensive and Extensive Margins: Assumptions about the rate of growth of crop productivity affect the land use impact of biofuels. Yield increases through the application of nonland inputs on currently utilized land will lower the rate of land conversion to cropland. Most models specify an exogenous rate of growth for yields for crops and conversion efficiency. Some models, such as BEPAM, GTAP and MIRAGE, allow for the possibility of price-induced yield growth. The effect of a policy shock on land use also depends on differences in yields between land under crop production and marginal land. Keeney (2010) reports that estimates of the ratio of marginal to average land productivity range from 0.47 to 0.9 in the literature. MIRAGE assumes that the productivity of marginal land is half of the average productivity in existing cropland for all regions, except in Brazil where the value is 0.75 (Laborde 2011). GTAP assumes this ratio is 0.66 globally (Hertel et al. 2010). Data on the productivity of marginal land, particularly in developing countries is limited, and much more research is needed in this area. There is some evidence that yields may not be much lower on newly converted lands on the agricultural frontier; Babcock and Carriquiry (2010) found that regions in Brazil experiencing faster expansion of soybeans did not have lower soybean yields or yield growth.

Ease of Substitution of Land from one use to Another: As prices change, profit-maximizing producers change the mix of crops they produce and may bring noncropland into crop production. However, land use changes are costly. For example, former pasture or forestland is expected to be less productive for crop production compared to existing cropland. Models like GTAP and MIRAGE have reflected the cost of converting land from one use to another by specifying a CET value that represents the ease of substitutability between crops and other uses. This approach introduces nonlinearity in the ease of conversion of land with the implicit costs of conversion increasing as more land is converted. This creates greater pressure at the extensive margin to expand cropland as the demand for land for biofuels increases. A similar mechanism applies to pasture and forestland that is converted to cropland. Substitution possibilities are limited and nonlinear due to the CET effect.

In other models, land conversion is based on the net returns to land and a conversion cost that is incurred by converting unmanaged land to managed land. This may lead to a lower elasticity of transformation across land uses in the short run but a larger elasticity of transformation in the long run. The advantage of the approach based on net returns and conversion cost is that it allows rents to equalize across all uses and is, therefore, consistent with long-run equilibrium. Using IGSM, Gurgel, Reilly, and Paltsev (2007) show that global bioenergy production is 10–20% greater when land conversion is based only on net returns as compared to when it is based on the elasticity of transformation, which tends to limit market response to follow observed historical trends. Chen, Huang, and Khanna (2011) show that limits on the amount of idle/marginal land that can be converted to energy crops in BEPAM can raise the costs of producing energy crops while reducing the ease of conversion of land across different conventional crops can raise the costs of producing corn ethanol.

Technological Factors: Technological change in the biofuel industry will be a significant driver of land use change. The cost-effectiveness of second-generation biofuels and the type of technological development that occurs for conversion of feedstocks to liquid fuel will influence the amount of land that is converted to energy crops. High initial costs of producing advanced biofuels and low learning rates will reduce their competitiveness relative to first-generation biofuels and require larger diversion of land from food to fuel production to meet given biofuel targets. Development of new technologies for harvesting biomass, for collecting crop residues in one pass over the field and methods for establishing energy crops (using seeds or rhizomes) can have a significant effect on the mix of feedstocks that are produced and land required to produce them (Chen et al. 2012). There are very few studies that analyze the implications of varying levels of technological development and costs of new biofuel technologies on land use. Using BEPAM, Chen et al. (2012) show that higher processing cost for cellulosic biofuels and low learning rates relative to the benchmark case would significantly affect the mix of biofuels and reduce land under energy crops while increasing acreage under corn for ethanol and total land under crop production. Beach, Zhang, and McCarl (2012) show that high storage costs for feedstocks like crop residues and energy crops can reduce their competitiveness relative to corn, which has a well-developed and low-cost infrastructure for storage and marketing.

Ease of Transmission of Price Shocks in World Markets: The impact of increased biofuel production on land use changes in the rest of the world depends on the ease with which price shocks are transmitted from domestic markets to the rest of the world. This, in turn, depends on assumptions about the ease with which goods can be traded across countries. Two approaches are currently used in the models described here—the Armington approach, used in GTAP and MIRAGE, differentiates otherwise homogenous goods by country of origin. In contrast, the Integrated World Model (IWM) used in IGSM[2] and in Searchinger et al. (2008) assume that there is one world price for homogenous goods and goods will be produced where it is least costly to do so. IWM allows for an easier transmission of a shock throughout the world economy. However, Golub et al. (2010) note that using the IWM could result in "unrealistic" trade patterns. For example in Searchinger et al. (2008), a lot of agricultural production and land conversion occur in

[2] The IGSM model uses a Heckscher-Ohlin model for biofuels, which is similar to IWM, and it uses Armington for other goods.

India due to favorable growing conditions, even though historically, India has not been a major exporter of agricultural commodities. The Armington approach leads to results that follow observed trade patterns. Countries or regions first decide on the sources of their imports, and then, based on the composite import price, decide on the allocation between domestic production and imports. A potential pitfall of this approach is that it allows price differentials for homogenous goods, such as imported ethanol and domestic ethanol, to persist.

5. How to Deal with Multiple Models

Having multiple models may be a source of confusion, but also a source of extra insight and increased reliability for policy design. Different models are introduced for different purposes or built under different assumptions, but when they address similar phenomena they can provide a range of answers and a complementary insight that will allow better decision making. The outcome of these models may differ due to differences in model specifications, the counterfactual baseline considered, the policy scenarios analyzed the sectoral and geographic scope included. The results of these models should be used to determine directions and ranges for outcomes and orders of magnitudes for effects.

There are several approaches to deal with multiple models. Policy analysis can use triangulation to synthesize the results from several models. When several models address the same phenomenon, they provide a distribution of estimates. These distributions can provide either a range of values that determine the impact or yield a weighted statistical estimate based on all the studies that may contain much more information. The second approach for researchers that are choosing which model to use is nesting two or more models or linking them off-line. The same problem may have many dimensions that have to be addressed at different degrees of detail. For example, when assessing the impact of introducing a new feed crop in a certain region, a good understanding of where the new crop can be produced and reliable parameters of the distribution of yield and cost, are needed. Obtaining this information may require a very detailed biophysical model. The information that this model generates can be used as an input in an economic model that can allocate land use over space and time based on economic criteria. A third approach is modularity that takes the nesting approach much further and involves incorporating subroutines of one model in another model. Developing a network of models that can be linked with each other is quite challenging because different models use different softwares, operate on different time and geographical scales, and so forth. However, a system of models that speak to one another can allow us to take advantage of all the different components so that the total will be bigger than the sum of the parts.

6. Key Findings on Land Use Impacts of Biofuels

6.1 Land Requirement for Biofuels

In the near term, Hertel et al. (2010) find that 3.5 million hectares of land is needed to meet the US corn ethanol mandate. This estimate depends on the baseline used, and assumptions about growth in yield and population. Chen et al. (2011) find that 12 million hectares are required in the United States to meet the total RFS, of which about 4.7 million hectares is the additional land needed to produce corn to meet the RFS. Using MIRAGE, Laborde (2011) finds that the EU RED is expected to increase total cropland globally by 1.73 million hectares without trade liberalization and 1.83 with trade liberalization. The additional cropland comes primarily from pasture and managed forests, with 80% of the land use change taking place on managed land.

The preceding estimates are for total land requirement, which includes direct and indirect land use changes. Some studies specifically focus on estimating the indirect land use change associated with biofuels. Khanna and Crago (2012) review these studies and find that estimates for corn ethanol in the United States range from 20 to 430 hectares per million liters. These estimates are sensitive to the scale of biofuel production, to the counterfactual baseline, to the mix of policies and biofuels considered, and to variations in the parametric assumptions of the models.

In general, these studies show that the additional area planted to biofuel feedstocks will come from a reduction in cropland and pasture area, as well as some conversion of idle or natural areas to agricultural production. The results from the different models suggest that some competition with agricultural production is inevitable, even if there is greater production of second-generation biofuels that rely on crop residues or energy crops that can be grown on marginal land (Chen, Huang, and Khanna 2011). In addition, conversion of forests to cropland is also to be expected. The impact of biofuel feedstock production on deforestation and competition for land could be minimized by increasing biomass yields and conversion efficiencies of biomass to liquid fuel. Encouraging biofuels that have lower land requirements will also ease the pressure on land supply.

6.2 Location of Biofuel Production

Most of the studies reviewed point to significant feedstock production in Latin America, specifically Brazil, and Africa. The greater feedstock productivity and land availability in these regions have the potential to make them the largest producers of biofuels in the world in the long run. The United States is likely to be the third largest producer of biofuels (Reilly, Gurgel, and Paltsev 2008). Analysis of the EU RED using AGLINK-COSIMO shows that RED requirements are met by significant increases in biofuels from Brazil and Southeast Asia (Fonseca et al. 2010). In contrast, the analysis by Laborde (2011) using MIRAGE shows significant land use change in sub-Saharan Africa. Within Brazil, studies suggest that expansion is expected to occur in the center-south region where sugarcane production has been traditionally grown (de Souza Ferreira Filho and Horridge 2011; ICONE 2011). Models of land use change in Brazil show that an increase in sugarcane production leads to land use change, but these changes are mostly due to conversion of other cropland to sugarcane production. Deforestation occurs due to the expansion of the agricultural frontier, but the land use change due to deforestation is minimal. In the study by de Souza Ferreira Filho and Horridge (2011), deforestation accounts for less than 3% of land expansion associated with increased biofuel production from 2006–2020; the majority comes from a reduction in pasture and forest plantations. They estimate the ILUC effect to be 8%, that is, 0.08 hectare is deforested per 1 hectare increase in sugarcane production. The results for biofuel production are mixed for China and India. The production of biofuel feedstocks in these countries will depend on the growth of domestic demand for food, which competes with biomass production for land resources, and on government policy about enforcing mandates and providing economic incentives for biofuel production. In the case of India, a 20% blend mandate could be met by diverting about 1 million hectare (< 1% of cropland) from food crops to sugarcane production without significant impact on the production of other crops (Khanna et al. 2013).

The findings here are based on the assumption that production will occur in areas with land availability as well as low cost of land and production. However, these models do not account for other factors such as political stability that may deter production in the African region. In addition to production cost, the exchange rates between biofuel exporting and importing countries will also be an important determinant of biofuels trade and production location (Crago et al. 2010).

6.3 Mix of Feedstocks

If biomass is to be produced on a grand scale without compromising food supply, feedstock from nonfood sources like crop and forest residues, woody biomass, and dedicated energy crops will dominate the biomass supply landscape in the coming decades. Among energy crops, the incentives to use switchgrass and miscanthus for producing second-generation biofuels have been analyzed in considerable detail using FASOMGHG and BEPAM. The relative yields per hectare and conversion efficiency of feedstock to liquid fuel differ considerably among these feedstocks and are crucial determinants of which specific feedstocks will be used (EPA 2010; Beach, Zhang, and McCarl 2012; Chen et al. 2012; Huang et al. 2013) Miscanthus has a much higher biomass yield per hectare of land than switchgrass or corn stover. Using BEPAM, which includes miscanthus as a feedstock option, Chen et al. (2011) find that miscanthus has a significant potential as a feedstock compared to other feedstocks due to its superior yields, longer lifetime, and low input requirements. Earlier versions of FASOM, without miscanthus as an energy crop, predicted that corn stover and switchgrass will be the main feedstocks used to meet the RFS (EPA 2010). Recent analysis that includes miscanthus as a feedstock option in FASOM also find that miscanthus is the dominant feedstock to produce second-generation biofuels (Beach, Zhang, and McCarl 2012). Biofuel subsidy policies that are typically paid per unit of volume or per ton of biomass also encourage high yielding feedstocks and would create further incentives to increase acreage under the higher yielding miscanthus as compared to switchgrass in the United States (Khanna et al. 2011).

7. Summary and Implications

This chapter presents an overview of alternative modeling approaches to assess the factors that will determine land use changes associated with the introduction of biofuel and their implications for the location of land use changes and the types of land that will be converted to biofuel production. Numerical models used to predict land use changes simulate future scenarios of biofuel production using economic parameters on market behavior, in particular elasticities of demand and supply in relevant markets, biophysical data on land characteristics and suitability, as well as projections about future biofuel technologies. These models vary in their scope of operation: some are regional or national and others are global. They also vary in their assessment of the feedbacks associated with the introduction of biofuels through the agricultural and fuel markets. Nevertheless, the general qualitative findings of various models are consistent, although there is a high degree of variability in the numerical outcomes reflecting differences in assumptions regarding the behavior of economic agents, features of the technology, model structure and policy scenarios. These studies show that biofuels have the potential to meet a significant percentage of liquid fuel demand and demand for renewable electricity in the future and that current targets being set in the United States and EU for renewable fuels are feasible with moderate increases in crop prices. To reach these targets, however, requires the use of a diverse portfolio of biofuel feedstocks that includes first-generation feedstocks, in particular, corn and sugarcane, second-generation feedstocks like miscanthus and switchgrass, and multiple forest products and crop residues. High-yielding feedstocks are more likely to be economically viable and are critical to achieve policy targets with minimal adverse impacts on crop prices and indirect land use change.

Model results also show that large-scale production of bioenergy will entail some trade-offs. Because biomass production competes with agricultural production for land, crop prices will increase, although the effect is likely to be modest if the biomass is produced from crop/forest residues and from dedicated energy crops. These crops are more likely to be economically viable on marginal land. Thus, expansion of second-generation biofuels is likely to result in expansion of agricultural land for biofuel production as fallow and low-quality pasture land is brought into production. This could reduce some areas under native grasses or permanent pastureland unless regulated by policy. Some policies, such as large tax credits for second-generation biofuels, may even make energy crops competitive on cropland. In this case the substitution between food and fuel cannot be completely avoided, but the price effects are likely to be smaller because the amount of land that will need to be diverted to meet given biofuel targets will be smaller than with first-generation biofuels. Moreover, the productivity of both traditional agricultural crops as well as of biofuel feedstock will crucially determine the linkage between food and fuel production and prices, and will have implications for land use changes. Higher productivity of traditional crops and biofuel crops reduces the conflict between biofuel and food production and the adverse impact of biofuel production on deforestation and GHG emissions. Increasing biomass yields and conversion efficiencies will lower the land requirement for biofuel production. Intensifying livestock production could also ease the competition for land.

Acknowledgments

The authors are grateful for funding provided by the BP Environmental Sustainability Challenge Project and the Energy Biosciences Institute, University of California, Berkeley, for this research.

References

Adams, D., R. Alig, B. McCarl, and B. C. Murray. 2005. FASOMGHG conceptual structure, and specification: Documentation. http://agecon2.tamu.edu/people/faculty/mccarl-bruce/FASOM.html.

Al-Riffai, P., B. Dimaranan, and D. Laborde. 2010. Global trade and environmental impact study of the EU Biofuels Mandate. International Food Policy Research Institute Report for the Directorate General for Trade of the European Commission, Washington, DC.

Anderson, K., B. Dimaranan, J. Francois, T. Hertel, B. Hoekman, and W. Martin. 2001. The cost of rich (and poor) country protection to developing countries. *Journal of African Economies* 10: 227–257.

Babcock, B., and M. Carriquiry, M. 2010. An exploration of certain aspects of Carb's approach to modeling indirect land use from expanded biodiesel production. Center for Agricultural and Rural Development. Ames: Iowa State University.

Beach, R. H., A. J. Daigneault, B. A. McCarl, and S. Rose. 2009. Modeling alternative policies for forestry and agricultural bioenergy production and GHG mitigation. Paper presented at the Association of Environmental and Resource Economists Workshop. Energy and the Environment, June 18–20, 2009, Washington, DC.

Beach, R. H., Y. W. Zhang, and B. A. McCarl. 2012. Modeling bioenergy, land use, and GHG emissions with FASOMGHG: Model overview and analysis of storage cost implications. *Climate Change Economics* 3(3): 1250012.

Cai, X., X. Zhang, and D. Wang. 2011. Land availability for biofuels. *Environmental Science and Technology* 45: 334–339.

California Air Resources Board (CARB). 2009. *Proposed regulation to implement the low carbon fuel standard*, Vol. I. California Environmental Protection Agency Air Resources Board. http://www.arb.ca.gov/fuels/lcfs/030409lcfs_isor_vol1.pdf.

Chakravorty, U., B. Magne, and M. Moreaux. 2008. A dynamic model of food and clean energy. *Journal of Economic Dynamics and Control* 32: 1181–1203.

Chen, X., H. Huang, and M. Khanna. 2011. Land use and greenhouse gas implications of biofuels: Role of technology and policy. *Climate Change Economics* 3(3): 1250013.

Chen, X., H. Huang, M. Khanna, and H. Onal. 2012. Meeting the mandate for biofuels: Implications for land use and food and fuel prices. In *The intended and unintended effects of U.S. agricultural and biotechnology policies*, eds. J. G. Zivin and J. Perloff. Chicago: University of Chicago Press.

Chen, X. and M. Khanna. 2013. Food vs. fuel: Role of biofuel policies. *American Journal of Agricultural Economics* 95(2): 289–295.

Crago, C., M. Khanna, J. Barton, E. Giuliani, and W. Amaral. 2010. Competitiveness of Brazilian sugarcane ethanol compared to US corn ethanol. *Energy Policy* 38: 7404–7415.

De Souza Ferreira Filho, J. B., and M. Horridge. 2011. *Ethanol expansion and indirect land use change in Brazil*. Clayton, Australia: Centre of Policy Studies, Monash University.

Dumortier, J., D. J. Hayes, M. A. Carriquiry, F. Dong, X. Du, A. Elobeid, J. Fabiosa, and S. Tokgoz. 2011. Sensitivity of carbon emission estimates from indirect land-use change. *Applied Economic Perspectives and Policy* 33: 428–448.

Edwards, R., D. Mulligan, and L. Marelli. 2010. Indirect land use change from increased biofuels demand. *JRC Scientific and Technical Reports JRC* 59771.

EPA. 2010. *Renewable fuel standard program regulatory impact analysis*. Washington, DC: Assessment and Standards Division, Office of Transportation and Air Quality, U.S. Environmental Protection Agency.

Fabiosa, J. F., J. C. Beghin, F. Dong, A. Elobeid, S. Tokgöz, and T. Yu. 2010. Land allocation effects of the global ethanol surge: Predictions from the International FAPRI Model. *Land Economics* 86: 687–706.

Feder, G., and D. Feeny. 1991. Land tenure and property rights: Theory and implications for development policy. *The World Bank Economic Review* 5: 135–153.

Feder, G., R. E. Just, and D. Zilberman. 1985. Adoption of agricultural innovations in developing countries: A survey. *Economic Development and Cultural Change* 32: 255–298.

Fonseca, M., A. Burrell, H. Gay, M. Henseler, A. Kavallari, R. M'barek, I. Domínguez, and A. Tonini. 2010. Impacts of the EU biofuel target on agricultural markets and land use: A comparative modelling assessment. European Commission Joint Research Centre, Institute for Prospective Technological Studies. http://ftp.jrc.es/EURdoc/JRC58484.pdf.

Gardner, B. L. 1992. Changing economic perspectives on the farm problem. *Journal of Economic Literature* 30: 62–101.

Golub, A., T. Hertel, F. Taheripour, and W. Tyner. 2010. Modeling biofuels policies in general equilibrium: Insights, pitfalls, and opportunities. In *New developments in computable general equilibrium analysis for trade policy* (Frontiers of Economics and Globalization, Vol. 7), 153–187. Bingley, UK: Emerald Group Publishing.

Gouvello, C. 2010. Brazil low-carbon country case study: The World Bank Group. Washington, DC: The International Bank for Reconstruction and Development, The World Bank.

Gurgel, A., J. Reilly, and S. Paltsev. 2007. Potential land use implications of a global biofuels industry. *Journal of Agricultural and Food Industrial Organization Special Issue: Explorations in Biofuels Economics, Policy and History* 5(2), Article 9.

Havlík, P., U. A. Schneider, E. Schmid, H. Böttcher, S. Fritz, R. Skalský, K. Aoki, S. D. Cara, G. Kindermann, F. Kraxner, S. Leduc, L. Mccallum, A. Mosnier, T. Sauer, and M. Obersteiner. 2011. Global land-use implications of first and second generation biofuel targets. *Energy Policy* 39: 5690–5702.

Heckscher, E. F., and B. Ohlin. 1991. *Heckscher-Ohlin trade theory*, eds. Harry Flam and M. June Flanders. Cambridge, MA: MIT Press.

Hertel, T. W., A. A. Golub, A. D. Jones, M. O'Hare, R. J. Plevin, and D. M. Kammen. 2010. Effects of US maize ethanol on global land use and greenhouse gas emissions: Estimating market-mediated responses. *BioScience* 60(3): 223–231.

Hochman, G., D. Rajagopal, and D. Zilberman. 2010. The effect of biofuels on crude oil markets. *AgBioForum* 13: 112–118.

Huang, H., M. Khanna, H. Onal, and X. Chen. 2013. Stacking low carbon policies on the renewable fuel standard: Economic and greenhouse gas implications. *Energy Policy* 56: 5–15.

Instituto de Estudos do Comércio e Negociações Internacionais (ICONE). 2011. Simulating land use and agriculture expansion in Brazil: Food, energy, agroindustrial and environmental impacts. Internal report, ICONE, Brazil. http://www.iconebrasil.org.br/arquivos/noticia/2258.pdf.

Irwin, E., K. Bell, N. Bockstael, D. Newburn, M. Partridge, and J. Wu. 2009. The economics of urban-rural space. *Annual Review of Resource Economics* 1: 435–459.

Keeney, R. 2010. Yield response and biofuels: Issues and evidence on the extensive margin. Paper presented at the World Congress of Environmental and Resource Economists. June 28–July 2, 2010, Montreal.

Khanna, M., A. W. Ando, and F. Taheripour. 2008. Welfare effects and unintended consequences of ethanol subsidies. *Applied Economic Perspectives and Policy* 30: 411–421.

Khanna, M., X. Chen, H. Huang, and H. Önal. 2011. Land use and greenhouse gas mitigation: Effects of biofuel policies. *University of Illinois Law Review* 2: 549–588.

Khanna, M., and C. L.Crago. 2012. Measuring indirect land use change with biofuels: Implications for policy. *Annual Review of Resource Economics* 4: 161–184.

Khanna, M., H. Onal, C. L. Crago, and K. Mino. 2013. Can India meet biofuel policy targets? Implications for food and fuel prices. *American Journal of Agricultural Economics* 95(2): 296–302.

Krutilla, J. V. 1967. Conservation reconsidered. *The American Economic Review* 57: 777–786.

Laborde, D. 2011. Assessing the land use consequences of EU biofuel policies. Specific Contract No SI2. 580403 implementing Framework Contract No. TRADE/07/A2. Final Report for ATLASS Consortium. http://www.ifpri.org/sites/default/files/publications/biofuelsreportec2011.pdf.

McCarl, B. A., and U. A. Schneider. 2001. Greenhouse gas mitigation in U.S. agriculture and forestry. *Science* 294: 2481–2482.

Melillo, J. M., J. M. Reilly, D. W. Kicklighter, A. C. Gurgel, T. W. Cronin, S. Paltsev, B. S. Felzer, X. Wang, A. P. Sokolov, and C. A. Schlosser. 2009. Indirect emissions from biofuels: How important? *Science* 326: 1397–1399.

Mendelsohn, R., and A. Dinar. 2009. Land use and climate change interactions. *Annual Review of Resource Economics* 1: 309–332.

OECD. 2008. *Biofuel support policies: An economic assessment.* Organisation for Economic Co-operation and Development.

Prins, A., E. Stehfest, K. Overmars, and J. Ros. 2010. Are models suitable for determining ILUC factors? Netherlands Environmental Assessment Agency (PBL) 12. http://www.pbl.nl/en/publications/2010/Are-models-suitable-for-determining-ILUC-factors.html

Rajagopal, D., S. E. Sexton, D. Roland-Holst, and D. Zilberman. 2007. Challenge of biofuel: Filling the tank without emptying the stomach? *Environmental Research Letters* 2, 044004.

Rajagopal, D., and D. Zilberman. 2007. Review of environmental, economic and policy aspects of biofuels. Policy Research Working Paper Series: 4341. Washington, DC: The World Bank.

Reilly, J., A. Gurgel, and S. Paltsev. 2008. Biofuels and land use change. In Proceedings of *Farm Foundation Conference: Transition to a bioeconomy: Environmental and rural development impacts*, eds. M. Khanna, October 15–16, 2008, St. Louis, MO, 1–17.

Ricardo, D. 1891. *Principles of political economy and taxation*. London: G. Bell and Sons.

Schoengold, K., and D. Zilberman. 2007. The economics of water, irrigation, and development. In *Handbook of agricultural economics*, Vol. 3, eds. R. Evenson and P. Pingali, 2933–2977. Amsterdam: Elsevier.

Searchinger, T., R. Heimlich, R. A. Houghton, F. Dong, A. Elobeid, J. Fabiosa, S. Tokgoz, D. Hayes, and T.-H. Yu. 2008. Use of U.S. croplands for biofuels increases greenhouse gases through emissions from land-use change. *Science* 319: 1238–1240.

Searchinger, T. D. 2010. Biofuels and the need for additional carbon. *Environmental Research Letters* 5.

Sunding, D., and D. Zilberman. 2001. The agricultural innovation process: Research and technology adoption in a changing agricultural sector. In *Handbook of agricultural economics*, Vol. 1. eds. B. L. Gardner and G. C. Rausser, 207–261. North-Holland, Amsterdam: Elsevier.

Taheripour, F., T. Hertel, W. Tyner, J., Beckman, and D. Birur. 2010. Biofuels and their by-products: Global economic and environmental implications. *Biomass and Bioenergy* 34: 278–289.

Tsur, Y., and A. Zemel. 2005. Scarcity, growth and Rand. *Journal of Environmental Economics and Management* 49: 484–499.

Von Thünen, J. 1966. *Isolated state: An English edition of Der Isolierte Staat by C.M. Wartenberg*, ed. P. Hall. Oxford: Pergamon Press.

Xabadia, À., R. U. Goetz, and D. Zilberman. 2006. Control of accumulating stock pollution by heterogeneous producers. *Journal of Economic Dynamics and Control* 30: 1105–1130.

CHAPTER 5

MODELING THE DETERMINANTS OF FARMLAND VALUES IN THE UNITED STATES

CYNTHIA J. NICKERSON AND
WENDONG ZHANG

ALTHOUGH once distributed for free to the earliest settlers in the United States, land has long been traded in private markets. For most of the past 100 years, real estate (land and structures) has comprised a significant portion of the wealth of many landowners. This is particularly true for the farming sector, which also is a major user of land—51% of the US land base in 2007 was in agricultural use (Nickerson et al. 2012). Valued at $1.85 trillion in 2010, farm real estate accounted for 85% of total US farm assets (US Department of Agriculture, Economic Research Service [USDA-ERS] 2012). Because it comprises such a significant portion of the balance sheet of US farms, changes in the value of farm real estate have an important bearing on the farm sector's financial performance. Farm real estate also represents the largest single investment item in a typical farmer's investment portfolio; as a principal source of collateral for farm loans and a key component of many farmers' retirement funds, changes in its value can affect the financial well-being of landowners.

Because of the longstanding significance of land values to both the farming sector and landowners, understanding the determinants of farmland values has been the subject of a great deal of economic research. Although the earliest studies date back well more than 100 years, most methodological and empirical advances in the study of farmland values have occurred more recently. The farmland valuation models developed and tested in the ensuing decades have generally evolved to help explain changes in farmland values that began to diverge from trends in returns to farming. The foci of the research have shifted over time partly due to recognition that existing models were not very well explaining significant swings in farmland values observed both at national and regional levels. The direction of research has also been influenced by the types of data available for empirical analysis, with the availability of increasingly detailed data spawning new opportunities to explain the determinants of farmland values and changes in those values.

In this chapter, we provide a comprehensive overview of significant developments in modeling farmland values. In doing so, we cover a wide variety of models and give particular attention to methodological challenges and recent modeling innovations. We begin by outlining the capitalization model, which has been—and continues to be—widely used as the theoretical basis in economic studies on this topic. We next discuss modeling efforts to address perceived shortcomings of this basic model in the context of farmland values. Dynamic modeling approaches using aggregate data to explain changes in farmland values have been heavily used for this purpose. We then turn attention to cross-sectional hedonic models that use spatially disaggregate or parcel-level data to examine the influence of particular determinants on farmland values, which in recent decades have become the mainstay of modeling techniques in the farmland values literature. We describe estimation issues that arise in hedonic modeling of farmland values, devoting most attention to those methodological issues that deserve special consideration in the context of farmland values, including spatial dependence and sample selection bias. In the course of doing so, we focus less on the specific findings of the studies (of which there are many) and more on the models themselves.

Because many of the advances in the study of farmland values occurred due to changes in farmland markets over time and to the applications of new modeling techniques, it is instructive to proceed in a more or less linear fashion, beginning with the earliest models, and describe the conditions that induced changes in modeling. We conclude with the most recent advances in modeling the determinants of farmland values and a discussion of what we perceive to be promising future research directions.

1. The Basic Capitalization Model

David Ricardo's (1817) formulation of an economic theory of rent, which was originally developed in the context of the value of farmland, is an important theoretical cornerstone in the basic model of land rents and land values. Ricardo's key insight was that land that differs in quality and is limited in supply generates rents that arise from the productive differences in land quality or from differences in location. Ricardo's work and that of others (e.g., Malthus' concept of residual surplus and von Thünen's theory of rent differentials arising from distance from a central market) form the basis of our modern understanding of land rents and land values (Barlowe 1986).

In the basic model, farmland is recognized as a fixed factor of production. Farmland prices are comprised of the discounted stream of economic returns generated by the land, where returns are defined as the return above all variable factors of production. Formally, the model is written as

$$P_t = \int_{t=0}^{\infty} A_i(t)e^{-rt}\,dt \qquad (1)$$

where P_t is the price of farmland in period t, A_i is annual net returns from farming, and r is the discount rate. The use of this basic model underlies not only farmland values research but also is used to model landowner decisions about land use choices.

Throughout the early decades of the 1900s, even though commodity prices experienced both rapid increases and significant declines, farmland prices and net returns remained relatively closely correlated. Farmland values began diverging from net returns in the 1950s, with farmland values increasing fourfold relative to farm income between 1952 and 1964 (Chryst 1965). Around this time, several studies attempted to model farmland values in a simultaneous equations framework (e.g., Herdt and Cochrane 1966; Tweeten and Martin 1966). However, this direction of research was short-lived, due primarily to concerns about identifying classic supply equations in a market with inelastic farmland quantities (e.g., Falk 1991), and subsequent research that determined the ability of these models to explain changes in farmland prices was very sensitive to the time period of the data (Pope et al. 1979).

2. Developments Using Time Series Models and Aggregate Data

Dramatic changes in farmland prices occurred in the following decades, with rapid appreciation in the 1970s followed by large declines in the 1980s. These changes raised a number of questions about the usefulness of the basic capitalization model in explaining changes in farmland values. In addition to assuming that land is valued only for its economic returns (which are known with certainty), the model assumes a constant discount rate, risk neutrality, and no effects from capital gains, inflation, transaction costs, and taxes. These issues lend themselves to examination using dynamic approaches, and many of the ensuing studies used time series techniques used to study stock price movements to test empirically these and other assumptions. These studies also used highly aggregated data in most cases—often state-level averages—due at least in part to a lack of more disaggregated, high-quality data for farmland.

An issue receiving early attention was the specification of A, net returns. Melichar (1979) pointed out that net farm income may not be the best measure of returns because it includes returns to all productive assets, labor, and management time. As a result, many subsequent papers used net rents instead of net farm income as the measure of returns. However, other studies support the use of imputed returns (Mishra et al. 2004).

2.1 Distributed Lag and Vector Autoregressive Models

Several time-series studies used distributed lag models to test the relative effects of returns and inflation on farmland price movements. Because returns anticipated in the future are not observable, these models used observed returns in previous years to proxy for expected returns. The models placed less weight on returns earned in the most recent years than in earlier years, reasoning that changes are capitalized into land values only if they persist. Using different specifications of distributed lags with different aggregated data, both Alston (1986) and Burt (1986) found returns to be the major explanation of land prices and the effects of inflation to be small at most. Alston's study used data from eight US Midwestern states between 1963 and 1982, whereas Burt used data from Illinois over a similar time period. A study by Moss (1997) suggested that the relative effects of returns and inflation vary by region, with returns providing more explanatory power in regions relying more heavily on government payments.

Vector autoregressive (VAR) techniques were also used to test the basic capitalization model. These models capture interdependencies by defining an equation for each variable that is based on own-value lags, as well as on lags of the other variables in the model. An often cited study is that by Featherstone and Baker (1987), who simultaneously estimated equations for farmland values, returns, and interest rates to examine the time path of farmland value adjustments to changes in returns and interest rates. Using annual data on US farmland values for 1910–1985, their results suggest that speculative factors seem important: that is, farmland values overreact to shocks in values, real returns, or interest rates, and the reaction lasts for up to six years. Others have used VAR methods to test whether the discount rate in the capitalization model was time-varying (e.g., Falk 1992). Assuming the trend series was difference-stationary rather than stationary, Falk and Lee (1998) used VAR and Iowa data from 1922–1994 and concluded that the capitalization model explained farmland price movements in the long run; in the short run, however, they concluded that overreactions to temporary shocks caused deviations between prices and predictions of the capitalization model.

2.2 Cointegration Analysis

Advances in the study of time series data led to challenges of the stationarity assumptions used in traditional time series representations. A number of ensuing studies were influenced by the work of Campbell and Shiller (1987), which showed that if the PV model were to hold, (1) land prices and rents must both have the same time-series properties, and (2) certain restrictions were required on the VAR representation of the changes in rents and the spread between rents and land prices (see Falk 1991, 3–4). These studies used cointegration analysis to overcome spurious results that could occur when using traditional time series approaches with data characterized by nonstationarity and unit roots. A number of these studies reject the present value model on the basis of an inability to find that farmland prices and rents are cointegrated (e.g., Falk 1991; Clark et al. 1993; Tegene and Kuchler 1993). However, Gutierrez et al. (2007) argue that this lack of support may be due to previous studies' not taking into account structural breaks and also assuming that states' data are independent of each other—which they point out is unlikely to hold, given the common boom-bust cycles in the data typically employed. Using recent advances in modeling nonstationary panel data and data from 31 US states over 1960–2000, they find that, by controlling for structural breaks, they cannot reject the present value model. Using a cointegration approach and error-correction models, Erickson, Mishra, and Moss (2003) also found support for the present value model, but note that the results are sensitive to the specification of the economic returns to land.

Cointegration analysis has also been used to examine whether discount rates vary by income source. Weersink et al. (1999) found government payments tended to be discounted less than market-based returns in Ontario. Schmitz (1995) found the opposite in Saskatchewan, which Weersink et al. (1999) posit is a result of farmers viewing government payment programs in the former province as a more stable source of income than the ad hoc transfers that are more characteristic of payments in the latter.

2.3 Structural Models

The conflicting evidence these studies find on the role of expectations, inflation, time-varying discount rates, and other factors is attributed by some to the use of econometric approaches that examine possible influences in isolation and which use specifications that are not based on economic theory (e.g., Just and Miranowski 1993; Chavas and Thomas 1999; Weersink et al. 1999). In a seminal paper, Just and Miranowski (1993) developed a comprehensive structural model to examine the multidimensional effects of inflation on capital and savings-return erosion and real debt reduction, as well as of changes in the opportunity cost of capital, while accounting for risk preferences and transaction costs. Using state-level pooled cross section data from 1963–1986, they found increased returns to farming, inflation, and opportunity cost were major explanations of the large increases in farmland prices in the 1970s, whereas only the latter two factors primarily explained subsequent large declines in the 1980s. Their results also suggest that inflation and opportunity cost explained the tendency of changes in land prices to exceed changes in rents (Featherstone and Baker 1987; Falk 1991). They did not find the results were sensitive to the expectations regime used. Although the study did not account for nonstationarity of the data as pointed out by Lence (2001), a subsequent study that did and which used very similar data found similar results (Awokuse and Duke 2006).

In another particularly notable paper, Chavas and Thomas (1999) developed a model at the microeconomic level that incorporates risk aversion, transaction costs, and dynamic preferences. Recognizing that time series data have been available almost exclusively only at an aggregate level, they described the conditions necessary for maintaining consistency between microlevel decision rules and aggregate price data—and the particular challenges for empirical modeling of the role of transaction costs. Using data on US farmland values over 1950–1996, they found that both risk aversion and transaction costs affected land prices and helped explain the inadequacies of the static present value model.

2.4 Other Dynamic Modeling Approaches

Other dynamic modeling approaches have been employed in the farmland value literature, although they have not been adopted as widely as the models just discussed.[1] Several of these techniques were utilized to specifically examine the influence of government payments. Because agricultural payment programs in the United States have been in place since the Agricultural Adjustment Act of 1933, several studies using dynamic modeling approaches considered the impact of government payments on changes in farmland values. Several studies found that US government payments had little effect on annual changes in farmland prices in the United States (e.g., Just and Miranowski 1993; Gardner 2003), attributing the findings of limited impacts on price fluctuations to the stabilizing effects of the payments. Studies using cointegration techniques suggest the relative responsiveness of land values to changes in government payments in Canada may depend on the proportion of government payments to total income (Weersink et al. 1999).

Estimating the impacts of government programs with precision in a dynamic modeling framework is challenging because these programs have been subject to change during the course of Farm Bill reauthorizations that occur approximately every five years, and the complexity of farm policies has increased over time. For many years, payments were tied to production or market conditions, so payment amounts could vary substantially across Farm Bill periods. Changes in the programs also mean that estimated effects of past farm programs may not be representative of effects of current farm programs. In particular, through 1950, commodity programs provided relatively little support, but during the next 15 years or so new programs were introduced that provided more support (Gardner 2003). Farm legislation in the 1980s and 1990s shifted away from market-distorting policies, with the addition of income-supporting (as opposed to price-supporting) commodity loan programs in 1985 and the introduction of planting flexibility on acres qualifying for commodity program payments in 1990. The Federal Agricultural Improvement and Reform Act of 1996 (i.e., the 1996 Farm Bill) eliminated

[1] For example, see papers included in Moss and Schmitz, eds. (2003).

all cropping restrictions; commodity payments previously tied to current planting decisions were decoupled from current production decisions and replaced with payments based on historical production choices (Nelson and Schertz 1996).

A few studies accommodated these program complexities by using different empirical techniques to model explicitly whether the land value effects of US commodity payment programs have varied across Farm Bill periods. Gardner (2003) used pooled county-level data between 1950 and 1992 and found only weak evidence that the rate of growth in farmland values in counties with substantial amounts of program crops was higher than it would have been in the absence of commodity programs (i.e., compared to "non-program crop" counties). Gardner (2003) posits that the evidence was not stronger because farmland may benefit more uniformly from the existence of commodity programs (i.e., if farms are not enrolled, the value attached to the option to enroll would be capitalized into the value of the land). Also, although payment impacts may be evident in the short run, the effect could be dampened in the long run if a larger share of program benefits goes to commodity buyers.

Using a recursive model to account for identification issues arising from the counter-cyclical nature of some farm program payments, Shaik et al. (2005) find that farm program payments may have increased farmland values by as much as 30–40% during 1940–1980, but that the effect declined to 15–20% during 1980–2002. Mishra et al. (2011) used an information measure and found that impacts on land value changed after passage of the 1996 Farm Bill, noting less divergence between the distributions of farmland values and government payments in the post-1996 Bill period. Nonetheless, a challenge continues to be that modeling the impacts of government payments with aggregate data is problematic. That, coupled with the recognition that government payments are likely to also affect input and output markets, helps explain a shift in modeling the incidence of policies away from the effects on prices (Sumner et al. 2010).

Collectively, studies employing dynamic modeling techniques demonstrate that these approaches offer several benefits in the context of modeling farmland values. Among the most important are that these models inform on the relative importance of macroeconomic factors, such as interest rates and inflation, whose identification requires temporal variation. The contributions they provide to informing farmland value forecasting models are also important (Erickson et al. 2003). Criticisms include a lack of a behavioral basis, as well as the potential for aggregation bias; a continuing challenge is obtaining consistent results. Although recent advances in nonstationary panel techniques may help improve consistency or the identification of some impacts (e.g., Gutierrez et al. 2007), and extensions that incorporate demands for land in alternative uses could be useful (Moss and Katchova 2005; Shaik et al. 2005), they may not fully address the criticisms noted above.

3. Developments Using Cross-Sectional Models and Spatially Explicit Data

In more recent decades, the increasing availability of cross-sectional and spatially disaggregated data provided new opportunities to model the determinants of farmland values with data at a scale that more closely matched economic behavioral decisions (Irwin et al. 2010). A strain of farmland values literature evolved that exploited these increasingly disaggregate data and adapted property value modeling approaches that were common in the urban economics literature. In particular, application of these techniques to farmland markets in urbanizing areas became widespread. This occurred in part due to the recognition that, in many regions, farmland can earn returns not just from agricultural production and government payments, but also from "nonfarm" sources. Principal among the nonfarm sources of returns first considered was the expected future rent increases arising from returns from future development for residential or commercial uses for farmland in close proximity to urban areas. Capozza and Helsley's (1989) seminal work laid the theoretical foundation for this literature and showed how the value of expected future rent increases could be quite large, especially in rapidly growing cities. That is, in such areas, farmland values are represented by (setting aside uncertainty):

$$P_t = \int_{t=0}^{u} A_i(x_i, t)e^{-rt}dt + R_i(x_i, u)e^{-ru} \tag{2}$$

where P_t is the price of farmland in period t, A_i is annual net returns from farming, R_i is the one-time net returns from converting the land to an urban use at the optimal conversion time u, x_i is a vector of exogenous parcel characteristics, and r is the discount rate. In this specification, farming returns are no longer earned once time u arrives. The returns to conversion are represented as a one-time payment to reflect the typical lump sum payment that landowners receive when land is converted to an urban use. This model could also be expanded to include other sources of nonfarm income—income from hunting leases, for example—that generate a stream of payments that are earned in addition to farming returns.

Hedonic models quickly became the most widely used property value model in the study of the determinants of farmland values. Because of its extensive use, we provide an overview of the basic model and issues that require attention when estimating the model. We note that hedonic models are not the only models used to explain nonfarm influences. For example, Hardie et al. (2001) adapt an urban growth model and used a simultaneous equations approach with county-level data to explain residential and farm real estate prices. Others used ordinary least squares (OLS) regressions with farm-level survey data to study the impacts of both various forms of government payments (disaggregated by program type) and potential returns from future development (Goodwin et al. 2003*a*, 2003*b*).

3.1 Hedonic Models: Conceptual Approach

Hedonic models are a revealed preference technique based on the notion that the price of a good observed in the marketplace is a function of its attributes or characteristics. A seminal article by Rosen (1974) developed the model for differentiated consumer products (as noted by Palmquist [1989]; Freeman [1974] also developed a similar model). These models provide the theoretical underpinnings for empirical models that estimate marginal prices for a product's characteristics. The theory of hedonic property value models is thoroughly described in Freeman (1993) and in Palmquist (2006); however, those models were confined to residential properties. Under the assumption of perfect competition, the hedonic price function represents an equilibrium price schedule that is comprised of the market-clearing bid-and-offer curves of heterogeneous agents (Rosen 1974). This equilibrium price of a property is a function of property attributes and location characteristics, and each characteristic is valued by its implicit price. Although studies have shown that these implicit prices could be used to identify marginal willingness-to-pay (MWTP) functions in the second stage estimation of hedonic models (e.g., Freeman 1993), most current studies only focus on the first stage estimation of implicit prices due to potential endogeneity concerns (Bartik 1987; Epple 1987; Bishop and Timmins 2011).

The equilibrium conditions of the hedonic model have been criticized because they require instantaneous adjustment in demand or supply. In particular, when market forces are moving continuously in one direction (or are expected to move in one direction), the imperfect adjustments of the market to changing conditions of supply and demand might introduce bias in the estimates of MWTP using observed implicit prices from hedonic regressions (Freeman 1993). As a result, researchers should be especially cautious in applying hedonic models when markets are changing rapidly. However, in most circumstances, divergence from hedonic equilibrium will only introduce random errors, and, even in cases of rapidly changing markets, hedonic estimates could still serve as the upper (or lower) bound of the MWTP estimates and provide useful information to infer the direction of biases.

In a seminal paper, Palmquist (1989) adapted the model for differentiated factors of production and applied it in the context of farmland rental markets. That paper assumes farmland owners and buyers are profit-maximizing farmers who own and buy land strictly for its productive capacity. Palmquist and Danielson (1989) discussed modifications needed in models using farmland sales as opposed to rent data but did not explicitly model them. Specifically, they note that the interpretation of the coefficients can differ depending on whether rents or sales prices are used in the hedonic model. Differences can arise when the marginal value of a characteristic differs in a short amount of time (within the length of the rental lease) relative to a longer period that would be capitalized into the value of the land. For example, being adjacent to a national park might reduce the rental price of farmland due to potential wildlife damage of crops but could increase the sales price if close proximity is expected to provide positive benefits in the more distant future.

The Palmquist and Danielson framework also does not account for the fact that, for many farm parcels, the land provides benefits beyond the net returns earned from farming, such as the value associated with the option to convert the land to residential use at some point in the future as modeled in (2) above, and benefits from close proximity to open space or other natural amenities that do not contribute specifically to the land's productive capacity. Indeed, US Department of Agriculture data reveal that most farmland owners in 1999 (the most recent data available on farmland ownership) did not operate farms as their primary business (US Department of Agriculture, National Agricultural Statistics Service [USDA-NASS] 2001). Some farmland owners farm on a part-time basis, but about 25% of farmland in 2007 was farmed by operators who were retired or operated a farm primarily for residential or lifestyle reasons (Hoppe and Banker 2010). The point that farmland has value both as a factor of production and as a consumption good has been recognized by some (e.g., Henneberry and Barrows 1990; Ma and Swinton 2012), although it appears that most researchers who estimate hedonic models in all but the most rural areas cite Rosen's theory related to consumer goods.

Many of the early applications of hedonic models to farmland markets used the approach to estimate the marginal value of both farm and nonfarm characteristics of farmland in urbanizing areas. One of the earliest and most well-cited papers is Chicoine (1981), who used sales data on unimproved farmland parcels in Will County, Illinois and found that the influence of factors affecting potential development returns R were far greater than soil productivity, the sole characteristic included in A as a proxy for farm returns. Numerous subsequent studies have also modeled the impact of urban proximity on farmland values; in areas that are more urbanized or have rapid population growth, these studies find that the demand for land for urban uses is the most significant nonfarm factor affecting farmland values (e.g., Shi et al. 1997; Plantinga et al. 2002; Huang et al. 2006; Guiling et al. 2009).

Hedonic models have also been used to examine the role of environmental factors and recreational opportunities on farmland prices. In response to concerns about farmland erosion resulting from the 1970s agricultural export boom and increases in nonpoint water pollution, a number of studies during the 1980s examined the effect of soil erodibility, as well as drainage, on farmland values (e.g., Miranowski and Hammes 1984; Ervin and Mill 1985; Gardner and Barrows 1985; Palmquist and Danielson 1989). Ervin and Mill (1985) also noted that such studies are useful for identifying the extent to which private markets capture the value of changes in a land characteristic that have implications for both on-site productivity and off-site environmental quality. Other studies examined the impact of wildlife recreation opportunities (e.g., Henderson and Moore 2006) and other amenities (see Bergstrom and Ready 2009 for a review), as well as the impact of restrictions on land uses, such as zoning (e.g., Chicoine 1981; Henneberry and

Barrows 1990), agricultural district and greenbelt designation (Vitaliano and Hill 1994; Deaton and Vyn 2010), and farmland protection easements (e.g., Nickerson and Lynch 2001; Lynch et al. 2007). Several recent studies have considered the impact of bioenergy policies by analyzing the impact of proximity to ethanol plants on farmland values (e.g., Henderson and Gloy 2009; Blomendahl et al. 2011; Zhang et al. 2012).

3.2 Empirical Issues in Hedonic Modeling of Farmland Prices

A number of well-known econometric problems may arise when estimating hedonic models. One issue that has particular significance in the context of farmland markets relates to the geographic extent of the market. A key assumption of the equilibrium hedonic price schedule is that sales transactions are drawn from a single market. This assumption is particularly restrictive in studies using farmland price data, since the historical thinness of the market limits the number of transactions within narrowly defined geographic areas. Indeed, recent surveys reveal that less than 2% of farmland is sold annually (Sherrick and Barry 2003; Duffy 2011). Previous studies have utilized transactions data at various levels, from a single county (e.g., Chicoine 1981; Henneberry and Barrows 1990), to a single state (e.g., Guiling et al. 2009), and to entire regions (e.g., Barnard et al. 1997; Roka and Palmquist 1997). However, the appropriate size will likely vary depending on the topic of the study. Studies on the value of farmland in urbanizing areas could arguably have markets covering a much smaller geographic area compared to studies on farmland values in rural areas, for example.

The historical thinness of farmland markets also raises two other important issues unique to farmland values studies. The first is about the construction of the dependent variable, given the fact that sales prices reflect the value of both land and structures in the presence of farm structures, residential dwellings, or both. Previous researchers have included a dummy variable indicating the presence of structures (e.g., Palmquist and Danielson 1989), subtracted the value of improvements from the total sales price (e.g., Guiling et al. 2009; Zhang et al. 2012), or simply excluded the parcels with structures (e.g., Chicoine 1981). Although information on the attributes or even presence of farm buildings is rarely available, including the value of structures in the dependent variable is not inconsistent with theory (Freeman 1993). The other issue relates to the choice of the data source. Whereas use of survey data (e.g., Roka and Palmquist 1997; Henderson and Gloy 2009) can yield more observations than microlevel sales transaction data, it raises a question about how well survey respondents' assessments of farmland values represent true market prices.[2]

A particularly important empirical issue that requires consideration in farmland value hedonic studies is omitted variable bias, in which the correlation of observed

[2] Ma and Swinton (2012) found tax assessor estimates of farmland values were particularly likely to underestimate the value of surrounding natural amenities.

variables and unobserved attributes lead to biased estimates of the implicit prices of characteristics of a property, a land parcel, or a product (Palmquist 2006). Bias resulting from spatial dependence and sample selection due to observables and unobservables are two distinct types of omitted variable bias that researchers have begun address in recent farmland value studies. Agricultural land parcels are essentially spatially ordered data, and achieving unbiased and efficient estimates requires addressing the inherent spatial dependence (Anselin 1988). This dependence has long been recognized in the areas of regional science and geography and was nicely summarized in Tobler's (1970, 236) *First Law of Geography*—"everything is related to everything else, but near things are more related than distant things." In the presence of spatial dependence, the standard OLS assumptions of uncorrelated error terms and independent observations are violated, and thus the parameter estimates from the standard hedonic regressions will be biased and inefficient. A sample selection problem occurs when a nonrandomly selected sample used to estimate behavioral relationships is not representative of the desired population (Heckman 1979), which could arise from selection on the unobservables (Heckman 1979) or on the observed characteristics (Heckman and Robb 1985). If left uncontrolled, the sample selection problem may result in biased parameter estimates of the hedonic models.

Two other well-known problems that may affect any hedonic study are the functional form of the empirical model and multicollinearity. Although the choice of functional form can affect both the magnitude and significance of coefficients, as noted by many studies, economic theory offers little guidance regarding model specification and restrictions on functional form. In practice, data availability and the goodness of fit often dictate the choice among different functional forms; farmland value studies have used a variety of forms, including transcendental, linear, semi-log, and double-log; some researchers prefer the flexibility afforded by the Box-Cox functional form, which lets the data determine the appropriate form (Palmquist and Danielson 1989; Roka and Palmquist 1997; Nivens et al. 2002). Another key specification issue in hedonic models is the multicollinearity that often arises from the attempt to control for all relevant characteristics of the land. This problem arises at least in part from difficulties in obtaining enough data for ideal model specifications, which is challenging given the thinness of farmland markets. As noted by Freeman (1993), including collinear variables increases the variance of coefficient estimates and affects inference.

Substantial research effort has been devoted to alleviating all of these econometric problems imbedded in hedonic models. In the context of research on farmland values, recent econometric developments have largely been focused on addressing biases arising from spatial dependence and addressing sample selection bias due to observables and unobservables. Our discussion of these techniques in the following sections describes these developments. We also draw on the wider hedonics literature, in which several developments are sufficiently recent that they have not been often embraced in models of farmland values.

3.3 Recent Developments in Addressing Spatial Autocorrelation and Spatial Heterogeneity

To account for spatial dependence in hedonic models of farmland values, two parametric spatial econometric models are primarily applied: spatial lag (spatial autoregressive) models and spatial error (spatial autocorrelation) models. Spatial lag dependence means the dependent variable in one location is affected by independent variables in that location and other locations. The standard spatial lag model solves this problem by adding a weighted average of nearby values of the dependent variable as an additional set of explanatory variables, which instead of the traditional model $y = X\beta + u$ yields

$$\begin{aligned} y &= \rho W y + X\beta + u = (I - \rho W)^{-1}(X\beta + u) \\ &= (I + \rho W + \rho^2 W^2 + \cdots)(X\beta + u) \end{aligned} \tag{3}$$

where W is an $n \times n$ spatial weight matrix, and the scalar ρ is the spatial coefficient.

As can be seen in the last equation of (3), the Leontief inverse reduced form, spatial lag of the dependent variable implies a spatial diffusion process or a so-called "spatial multiplier" effect, in which each observation is potentially influenced by all other observations (Anselin 2001), and such influence decays with the increase in distance between observations.

Spatial error dependence or spatial autocorrelation, in which the correlation of error terms is across different spatial units, is typically caused by measurement error or omitted spatial variables, or by a modifiable areal unit problem (i.e., results differ when the data are aggregated in different ways) (Griffith 2009). In contrast with the spatial lag model, in which the spatial interaction is the process of interest, the spatial error model offers a more common and direct treatment of the spatial dependence among error terms of the observations, in which the spatial dependence is a nuisance:

$$\begin{aligned} &y = X\beta + u, \textit{ with } u = \theta W u + e \\ &y = X\beta + (I - \theta W)^{-1} e \end{aligned} \tag{4}$$

where W is an $n \times n$ spatial weight matrix, and the scalar is the spatial coefficient.

Opportunities to account explicitly for spatial dependence among observations in farmland values studies have grown in recent years, due to increased availability of spatially explicit data on farmland, the explosive diffusion of Geographic Information System software, and the dramatic increase in the ability of statistical packages to handle large spatial matrices. Using county-level data in the Corn Belt, Benirschka and Binkley (1994) offer one of the first treatments of spatial autocorrelation in studies of the relationship between agricultural land price variations and distances to markets, in which the spatial correlation of error terms across counties was represented by a standard spatial error model specification, with W being a simple binary continuity matrix. In a spatial lag, serially correlated hedonic pricing framework, Huang et al. (2006) further controlled for serial correlation using a first-order autoregressive process along with the assumed time-invariant spatial lag dependence using a Kronecker product of the spatial matrix W and a $T \times T$ identity matrix. A similar spatiotemporal weight matrix is also used by Maddison (2009). In a study of effects of natural amenities on Michigan farmland values, Ma and Swinton (2012) used a spatial error specification to account for spatial dependence, in which the spatial weights matrix was defined using the inverse distance formula with a cutoff distance of 600 meters from the parcel centroids beyond which no correlation is assumed. The spatial error model structure was determined through diagnosis and tests of the structure of spatial correlation.

Due to improved computational speed and functional simplicity, spatial lag and spatial error models have become routine fixes for nearly any model misspecification related to space (McMillen 2012). However, these standard spatial econometric models are far from problem-free. In particular, most spatial econometric models face an ironic paradox that their very use is an admission that the true model structure is unknown, yet the common estimation technique of maximum likelihood relies heavily on knowing the true structure in advance (McMillen 2010). Other criticisms include identification problems and usually exogenously imposed spatial weights matrix, which can result in biased parameter estimates if misspecified.[3]

As emphasized by McMillen (2010, 2012), standard spatial econometric models are simply another form of spatial smoothing, and they should be viewed as additional statistical tools for model specification tests and convenient robustness checks, rather than as the primary means of analyzing spatial data. In general, applications of spatial models should be guided by economic theory (e.g., Brueckner 2006) and by actual empirical questions (Pinkse and Slade 2010). Instead of focusing solely on spatial lag and spatial error models, researchers have advocated alternatives, such as semiparametric and nonparametric approaches (McMillen 2010), and "experimentalist paradigm" approaches, such as instrumental variables (IV) and spatial differencing (Gibbons and Overman 2012).

These alternative approaches have gained popularity in residential real estate valuation studies, for which spatially explicit data has traditionally been more readily available than farmland data. Two recent studies using these approaches are worth noting. The first is a nonparametric analysis of capitalization of proximity to rapid transit lines in residential house prices in Chicago, in which McMillen and Redfearn (2010) illustrate that, unlike standard parametric spatial models, nonparametric estimators control for spatial variations in marginal effects and spatial autocorrelation while using highly flexible functional forms, without imposing an arbitrary weight matrix. The second is a study that identifies the influence of spatial land use spillovers on housing values.

[3] See Pinkse and Slade (2010), McMillen (2010, 2012), Gibbons and Overman (2012), and Brady and Irwin (2012) for further discussions of the criticisms of standard spatial econometrics models.

Carrión-Flores and Irwin (2010) exploited a natural discontinuity in the data and show that a partial population identification strategy solves the endogeneity problem and is a superior alternative to the common spatial error model for eliminating spatial error autocorrelation and identifying spatial interactions.

Some progress in addressing spatial autocorrelation and spatial heterogeneity has also been made in studies of farmland values beyond the spatial lag and error models. Cotteleer et al. (2011) tried to resolve specification uncertainty in selecting explanatory variables and weighting matrices in parametric spatial econometric models by employing Bayesian Model Averaging in combination with Markov chain, Monte Carlo model composition. In this framework, no single correct model specification is assumed and learning from the data is allowed, but prior information is needed. Using parcel-level data in Northern Ireland, Kostov (2009) generalized the linear spatial lag model by employing a flexible, semiparametric IV quantile regression approach, which not only allowed for varying effects of the hedonic attributes, but also varying degrees of spatial dependence. In two similar Northern Ireland studies, Kostov et al. (2008) and Kostov (2010) employed two different nonparametric approaches and found that buyer characteristics and personal relationships exert nonuniform and nonlinear effects on the implicit prices of farmland characteristics. Using intramunicipal-level French data, Geniaux et al. (2011) extended Capozza and Helsley's (1989) model to account for uncertainty in future land use zoning and used mixed geographically weighted regression estimations of a spatial hedonic model to recover intramunicipally heterogeneous impacts of land use conversion anticipation on farmland prices.

3.4 Recent Developments in Addressing Sample Selection Bias

Sample selection problems may arise from a variety of selection mechanisms, including self-selection by the data units (Heckman 1979) and the so-called incidental truncation problem, in which data on a key variable are available only for a clearly defined subset (Wooldridge 2002); for example, farmland rental rates can only observed for those land that are actually rented. In such cases, unobserved factors determining inclusion in the subsample are correlated with unobservables influencing the variable of primary interest, leading to biased parameter estimates of the hedonic models.

Heckman's 1979 seminal paper offers the first and the most widely applied correction model of sample selection (or selectivity) bias. The sample selection problem is characterized by two latent variable equations, the selection or participation equation and the outcome equation, which are allowed to have correlated errors. Correction of the sample selection bias is commonly achieved through a limited-information two-step estimation procedure (Greene 2012), in which the inverse Mills ratios are formulated from the estimated parameters of the first-stage probit selection equation to control for selectivity bias. This Heckman-style selection model has become a standard solution to the sample selection problem in various fields of economics, especially in the literature of program evaluation. In the context of research on land values, especially farmland values, this model is also widely applied. In a study of residential land value functions in which land use is determined by zoning, McMillen and McDonald (1989) find evidence of selectivity bias for undeveloped and multifamily residential land uses in which the "self-selectivity" arises when local governments use land values to guide zoning decisions. However, in the context of farmland markets, sample selection was not detected in two recent studies that addressed it using a Heckman selection model (Nickerson and Lynch 2001; Kirwan 2009).

The Heckman selection models address selection on the unobservables; however, in a broader sense, sample selection could also occur when the unobserved disturbance in the outcome function is correlated with the observed explanatory variables in the selection model, which is introduced as "selection on the observables" by Heckman and Robb (1985). As a result, when estimating the average treatment effect, the assumptions about the distributional equality of the covariates across the treatment and control subsamples imposed by hedonic regressions could be problematic, and the differences between covariates among treatment and control units may need to be adjusted for (Imbens and Wooldridge 2009). Matching offers a straightforward and effective way to balance these differences, which facilitates the identification of the causal treatment effect. Intuitively, matching solves the sample selection on the observables by selecting treated observations and comparison observations with similar characteristics, by covariates X (e.g., Rubin 1980), or by propensity score p (e.g., Rosenbaum and Rubin 1983).

In this section, we focus on propensity score matching (PSM) methods, which use propensity scores (the probability of selection into treatment conditional on covariates) in matching, because these methods are most commonly used and have been shown to be reliable under certain regularity conditions (Todd 2007). PSM presents several key advantages over the least squares hedonic approach. Most importantly, PSM does not require a parametric model linking outcomes and program participation (Dehajia and Wahba 2002; Smith and Todd 2005; Ravallion 2007). In addition, unlike standard regression methods, PSM ensures that observations in treatment and control groups share the common support (Ravallion 2007), and, finally, unlike Heckman selection model, PSM does not assume a particular functional form for the price equation (Heckman and Navarro 2004). Matching estimators such as PSM are justified if the selection is only on the observables (Imbens and Wooldridge 2009), and the performance of PSM depends crucially on the set of covariates included in the estimation (Heckman et al. 1998; Todd 2007). However, instead of elaborating on the methodological and implementation details on PSM, we aim to highlight specific applications of PSM in farmland values. The reader is referred to Caliendo and Kopeinig (2005), Smith and Todd (2005), Todd (2007), Zhao (2004), and Towe, Lewis, and Lynch in this handbook (Chapter 18) for detailed discussions on the matching methods.

PSM has become a popular approach to estimate causal treatment effects and has been used in some recent studies of farmland values. In an analysis of the selection problem due to the voluntary nature of farmland easement programs analyzed also in Nickerson and Lynch (2001), Lynch et al. (2007) used a PSM approach in which observed variables closely related to the future development option values, and variables affecting eligibility or probability of program participation are included as conditioning variables. Specifically, in contrast with results from hedonic models but consistent with findings by Nickerson and Lynch (2001), they find little evidence that preserved parcels sell for a significantly lower price than nearby unrestricted land. Using a sample of UK cereal farms, Sauer et al. (2012) incorporated the PSM approach with a production theory based multi-output, multi-input directional distance function framework and find that different agri-environmental schemes significantly affect production behavior at farm level.

However, systematic differences in unobservables may still bias these PSM estimators. Various extensions have been proposed as a response, including combining PSM and linear regression (Imbens and Wooldridge 2009), allowing for selection on unobservables by imposing a factor structure on the errors and estimating the distribution of unobserved errors (e.g., Carneiro et al. 2003), and controlling for time-invariant unobserved heterogeneity using a difference-in-difference (DID) matching estimator as defined in Heckman et al. (1997). Here, we focus on the DID PSM estimator, which has attracted more interest in the farmland value literature. When estimating average treatment effect, the conditional DID PSM estimator compares the conditional before-after outcomes of treated units with those of nontreated units. This DID PSM estimator is attractive because it permits selection to be based on potential program outcomes and allows for selection on unobservables (Heckman et al. 1997). A study by Ciaian et al. (2011) is worth mentioning because, rather than using the conventional binary PSM estimator to identify the effects of European Union government programs, it employed a generalized propensity score (GPS) method proposed by Hirano and Imbens (2005), which allows for estimation of the capitalization rates into farmland values for different levels of government payments as multivalued, continuous treatments. Two very recent farmland value studies have used a DID PSM estimator to identify the impact of an expanding ethanol market. Using a panel dataset of US farmland parcels from 2001 to 2007, Towe and Tra (2013) investigated the differential impacts of the construction of new ethanol facilities before and after the Renewable Fuel Standard legislation passed. Their results suggest that the RFS created expectations of higher returns to agriculture, beyond those derived from higher commodity prices. Zhang et al. (2012) instead combined the regular binary PSM estimator with DID regressions and applied them on parcel-level agricultural land sales data in Ohio 2001–2010 and find evidence of a structural change in the marginal value of the proximity to ethanol plants induced by the 2007 residential housing market bust and concurrent expansion of ethanol facilities.

3.5 Addressing Omitted Variable Bias Using Instrumental Variables Approach

To address the omitted variable bias and endogeneity concerns other than sample selection bias, some recent studies have employed the standard instrumental variables (IV) approach to identify the impact of governmental subsidies. Although land studies in this area are all on farmland rental rates, the techniques are very amenable to examining the impact of government payments in the context of farmland value studies. Using US farm-level data, Kirwan (2009) designed an IV strategy to overcome the attenuation bias induced by the expectation error, which is the difference between actual agricultural subsidies and expected subsidies. Specifically, he instrumented the 1992–1997 subsidy change using the post-FAIR Act 1997 subsidy level and addressed the measurement error problem with a second instrument, the county-level average subsidy per acre. Following Lence and Mishra (2003) and using data in Northern Ireland, Patton et al. (2008) adopted an IV strategy combined with GMM technique to recognize the fact that payments are not known when rental contracts are determined and therefore instruments using lagged realizations of the "pre-2002 SAP" payments are needed in the presence of expectation error. Using a rich dataset of pooled cross-sections at the farm level, Goodwin et al. (2010) instrumented the expected payment benefits using a four-year historical average of real payments per farm acre in the county where the farm is located. They argued that this measure better represents the long-run potential benefits associated with agricultural policy, whereas the common measure, realized payments, may, in contrast, reflect individual policy choices and characteristics of the farms.

4. Conclusion and Future Research Directions

The continued significance of farmland values to both the farm sector and to many farm households means that understanding the key determinants of farmland prices will remain of perennial interest. In this chapter, we have sought to identify major modeling approaches used to model farmland values and to describe recent innovations. As this chapter highlights, both dynamic time series and static cross-sectional approaches have been utilized by a large number of studies, with each contributing unique insights. In this section, we identify several areas in which future research may yield the highest return both in terms of advances in modeling and in terms of topics of interest to policy makers.

Dynamic models reveal important information about macroeconomic factors affecting rates of change in farmland values. However, criticisms of *ad hoc* econometric specifications that could contribute to misleading results have plagued many of these studies. A natural direction for these studies would be to utilize some of the more recent advances in time series techniques in ways that are supported by an underlying structural model that is both consistent with individual behavior and that captures critical market relationships (along the lines of Just and Miranowski 1993). In particular, a better (or at least more current) understanding is needed of how expectations by landowners are formed over prices, costs, and other key variables. Also, how changes in determinants are transmitted through expectations as suggested by Just and Miranowski (1993) could be useful, especially if the studies can illuminate how quickly farmland values react to changes in its determinants.

Furthering our understanding of the dynamics of farmland markets in these ways seem useful for at least three reasons. First, the rapid onset of and large (double-digit) annual increases in farmland values that we have witnessed in recent years is occurring under different conditions than increases that occurred in the 1970s, so the primary drivers of change are different. In particular, studies that consider the formation and role of price expectations, market relationships, and incidence may help inform decision makers about how quickly high farmland values could erode (or could be further enhanced) due to policy changes under their control (e.g., government farm program payments, bioenergy policies that increase demand for biofuel crops like corn and soybean, and macroeconomic policies such as interest rates). Second, nonfarm influences on farmland are growing, and models that incorporate these influences can help inform on how changes in related land markets are influencing farmland values.[4] Finally, advances in these areas could help inform efforts to link farmland value models and models of land use and land use change. We return to this last point below.

In terms of future directions in cross-sectional hedonic studies, we note several compelling opportunities to better address omitted variable bias—which is arguably among the most important econometric issues requiring treatment in farmland value studies using disaggregated, parcel-level data. Exploiting the ever-widening range of new spatially explicit modeling approaches allows researchers to reveal the rich spatial heterogeneity of the influences of determinants of farmland values with fewer restrictive assumptions. These approaches include the nonparametric approaches, quasi-experimental (QE) designs, and structural econometric models, many of which we mentioned in Section 4 in this chapter. In the following sections, we highlight some examples relevant for farmland values research.

Minimizing the bias and inefficiency caused by untreated spatial dependence in cross-sectional studies has spurred the adoption of a variety of techniques in land values studies. Although largely applied in land markets in or near urbanizing areas, the inherent spatially correlated processes underlying many farmland value determinants means the results of farmland valuation studies that do not consider spatial dependence are likely to be suspect. Standard spatial lag and spatial error models have yielded insights regarding the magnitude of the bias that can result if spatial dependence is left untreated. However, future research using spatially ordered farmland transactions data would likely benefit by embracing newer techniques that avoid the restrictive assumptions of these models. In particular, these newer techniques enable researchers to control for spatial dependence without imposing a certain spatial structure a priori. Approaches such as those relying on quasi-randomness, such as the "partial population identifier"

[4] We also note that the increasing influence of urban demands on farmland raises questions about whether time series properties differ between farmland subject to urban influence and farmland that is not.

used in Carrión-Flores and Irwin (2010), and semiparametric and nonparametric approaches employed by McMillen and Redfearn (2010) seem particularly fruitful in this regard. However, the standard spatial econometric models still serve as a useful toolbox for model specification tests and robustness checks, and a spatial lag model is still justified if the objective is to identify the effects of neighboring values on the dependent variable and the empirical model rests on economic theory (McMillen 2010).

In contrast with the standard hedonic models, QE designs popular in labor and regional economics, such as matching approaches and regression discontinuity design (RDD), present some interesting alternatives. By controlling for observable covariate differences and time-invariant unobserved heterogeneity, the DID PSM estimators illustrated in Section 4.4 can yield more plausible results than traditional hedonic estimators, if correctly implemented. Researchers may also benefit by using matching estimators other than PSM. A good candidate is covariate matching, including the common Mahalanobis metric (e.g., Rubin 1980), or the recently developed genetic matching method (Diamond and Sekhon 2013).

Although, to our knowledge, RDD has not yet been applied in the studies of farmland values, it has been enthusiastically embraced in the literatures of political science, epidemiology, and other fields of economics, such as real estate studies.[5] Future farmland values studies could benefit by explicitly considering RDD, especially when estimating the impact of state or local governmental programs and the effects of strict agricultural zoning policies. However, caution must be exercised regarding the potential spatial spillover problems when geographic borders are used in RDD, in which case a robustness check using matching estimators may be helpful.

The importance of addressing sample selection is a well-known empirical issue in the farmland values literature. Given that a wide array of government policies and programs support the agricultural sector and the increasing reliance on mechanisms with voluntary participation, advances in addressing this issue could be particularly fruitful. However, current applications of Heckman selection models in farmland values research are limited to the original Heckman (1979) model, which has a rather limited structure and is highly parameterized (Vella 1998). Besides the aforementioned QE approaches, future research may adopt a broader view and consider more generalized selection models with less restrictive modeling assumptions, such as those used by Lee (1982, 1983), Heckman and Robb (1985), and Puhani (2000). Other methods, such as control functions, could also prove to be beneficial in certain circumstances (e.g., Heckman and Navarro 2004; Imbens and Wooldridge 2007; Navarro 2008).

As we mentioned earlier in this section, more work can be done in the farmland values literature to inform on efforts to uncover the structural parameters of the demand and supply of farmland, which helps link changes in farmland values with land use change

[5] The reader is referred to van der Klaauw (2008), Imbens and Lemieux (2008), and Lee and Lemieux (2010) for excellent reviews of RDD, and to Black (1999), Chay and Greenstone (2005), Greenstone and Gallagher (2008), and Grout et al. (2011) for applications of RDD in urban housing market studies.

models described (see, for instance, Chapter 13 by Irwin and Wrenn in this handbook). Modeling dynamic aspects that take into account the formulation of expectations by farmland owners over prices, costs, and other key variables is crucial to estimating the supply of farmland and necessitates a dynamic modeling approach for the structural estimation of farmland supply. Current reduced-form models, such as hedonics and QE designs, are static, and they do not take these dynamics into account. However, as illustrated in Chapter 13 by Irwin and Wrenn in this handbook, the complexity of dynamic discrete choice models makes it sometimes infeasible empirically. Nevertheless, incorporating feedback or forward-looking expectations in structural hedonic models of farmland markets remains a crucial unsolved issue. In the hedonics literature, some notable advances have been made to identify the marginal willingness-to-pay functions, including the IV approach by Ekeland et al. (2004), the new econometric inversion estimation by Bishop and Timmins (2011), and the dynamic hedonic model by Bishop and Murphy (2011), which allows for forward-looking behavior of decision-makers. However, as mentioned in Section 4, researchers need to be cautious about using hedonic approaches when market forces are changing rapidly (Freeman 1993).

The ability of researchers to move forward on many of these fronts will be contingent on the increasing availability of spatially disaggregated data. Previous studies on agricultural land values that have employed aggregate data often mask important differences in the spatially disaggregated determinants of farmland values, such as distance from urban centers and proximity to agricultural delivery points like ethanol plants, grain elevators, and agricultural terminals. Aggregate data also hinder the application of new modeling approaches from related fields such as residential land/housing values research to studies on farmland values. A data challenge will continue to be the cost of developing parcel-level panel datasets via surveys and the thinness of farmland markets of developing pooled parcel-level sales data over time. Nonetheless, with more spatially explicit data available and techniques like nonparametric approaches and panel data analysis, researchers will have improved opportunities to analyze spatial variation as well as potential structural changes in certain determinants of farmland values.

Acknowledgments

The authors wish to thank Elena G. Irwin for insightful comments and a critical review of an earlier draft. The views in this chapter are attributable to the authors and not to the USDA.

References

Alston, J. M. 1986. An analysis of growth of U.S. farmland prices, 1963–82. *American Journal of Agricultural Economics* 68(1):1–9.

Anselin, L. 1988. *Spatial econometrics: Methods and models*. Dordrecht: Kluwer Academic.

Anselin, L. 2001. Spatial Econometrics. In *A companion to theoretical econometrics*, ed. B. H. Baltagi, 310–330. Malden, MA: Blackwell.

Awokuse, T. O., and J. M. Duke. 2006. The causal structure of land price determinants. *Canadian Journal of Agricultural Economics* 54:227–245.

Barlowe, R. 1986. *Land resource economics: The economics of real estate*, 4th ed. Upper Saddle River, NJ: Prentice Hall.

Barnard, C. H., G. Whittaker, D. Westenbarger, and M. Ahearn. 1997. Evidence of capitalization of direct government payments into US cropland values. *American Journal of Agricultural Economics* 79(5): 1642–1650.

Bartik, T. J. 1987. The estimation of demand parameters in hedonic price models. *Journal of Political Economy* 95(1): 81–88.

Benirschka, M., and J. Binkley. 1994. Land price volatility in a geographically dispersed market. *American Journal of Agricultural Economics* 76: 185–195.

Bergstrom, J. C. and R. C. Ready. 2009. What have we learned from over twenty years of farmland amenity valuation research in North America? *Review of Agricultural Economics* 31(1): 21–49.

Bishop, K. C., and A. D. Murphy. 2011. Estimating the willingness to pay to avoid violent crime: A dynamic approach. *American Economic Review* 101(3): 625–629.

Bishop, K. C., and C. Timmins. 2011. Hedonic prices and implicit markets: Estimating marginal willingness to pay for differentiated products without instrumental variables. NBER Working Paper No. 17611.

Black, S. 1999. Do better schools matter? Parental valuation of elementary education. *Quarterly Journal of Economics* 114: 577–599.

Blomendahl, B. H., R. K. Perrin, and B. B. Johnson. 2011. The impact of ethanol plants on surrounding farmland values: A case study. *Land Economics* 87(2): 223–232.

Brady, M., and E. G. Irwin. 2011. Accounting for spatial effects in economic models of land use: Recent developments and challenges ahead. *Environmental Resource Economics* 48: 487–509.

Brueckner, J. K. 2006. Strategic interactions among governments. In *A companion to urban economics*, eds. R. J. Arnott and D. P. McMillen, 332–347. Malden, MA: Blackwell.

Burt, O. R. 1986. Econometric modeling of the capitalization formula for farmland prices. *American Journal of Agricultural Economics* 68(1): 10–26.

Caliendo, M., and S. Kopeinig. 2005. Some practical guidance for the implementation of propensity score matching. IZA Discussion Paper No. 1588.

Campbell, J. Y., and R. J. Shiller. 1987. Cointegration and tests of present value models. *Journal of Political Economy* 95(4):1062–1088.

Capozza, D. R., and R. W. Helsley. 1989. The fundamentals of land prices and urban growth. *Journal of Urban Economics* 26: 295–306.

Carneiro, P., K. T. Hansen, and J. J. Heckman. 2003. Estimating distributions of treatment effects with an application to the returns to schooling and measurement of the effects of uncertainty on college choice. *International Economic Review* 44(2): 361–422

Carrión-Flores, C., and E. G. Irwin. 2010. Identifying spatial interactions in the presence of spatial autocorrelation: An application to land use spillovers. *Resource and Energy Economics* 32: 135–153.

Chavas, J.-P., and A. Thomas. 1999. A dynamic analysis of land prices. *American Journal of Agricultural Economics* 81(4): 772–784.

Chay, K., and M. Greenstone. 2005. Does air quality matter: Evidence from the housing market. *Journal of Political Economy* 113: 376–424.

Chicoine, D. L. 1981. Farmland values at the urban fringe: An analysis of sale prices. *Land Economics* 57(3): 353–362.

Chryst, W. E. 1965. Land values and agricultural income: A paradox. *Journal of Farm Economics* 47(5): 1265–1273.

Ciaian, P., A. Kancs, and J. Michalek. 2011. SPS capitalization into land values: Generalized propensity score evidence from the EU. LICOS Discussion Paper No. 293.

Clark, J. S., M. Fulton, and J. T. Scott, Jr. 1993. The inconsistency of land values, land rents, and capitalization formulas. *American Journal of Agricultural Economics* 75(1):147–155.

Cotteleer, G., T. Stobbe, and G. C. van Kooten. 2011. Bayesian model averaging in the context of spatial hedonic pricing: An application to farmland values. *Journal of Regional Science* 52(2): 172–191.

Deaton, B. J., and R. J. Vyn. 2010. The effect of strict agricultural zoning on agricultural land values: The case of Ontario's greenbelt. *American Journal of Agricultural Economics* 92(4): 941–955.

Dehajia, R. H., and S. Wahba. 2002. Propensity score-matching methods for nonexperimental causal studies. *The Review of Economics and Statistics* 84(1): 151–161.

Diamond, A., and J. S. Sekhon. 2013. Genetic matching for estimating causal effects: A general multivariate matching method for achieving balance in observational studies. *The Review of Economics and Statistics* 95(3): 932–945.

Duffy, M. 2011. The current situation on farmland values and ownership. *Choices* 26(2). http://www.choicesmagazine.org/magazine/pdf/cmsarticle_24.pdf

Ekeland, I., J. J. Heckman, and L. Nesheim.2004. Identification and estimation of hedonic models. *Journal of Political Economy* 112(1): S60–S109.

Epple, D. 1987. Hedonic prices and implicit markets: Estimating demand and supply functions for differentiated products. *Journal of Political Economy* 95: 59–80.

Erickson, K., A. K. Mishra, and C. B. Moss. 2003. Cash rents, imputed returns, and the valuation of farmland revisited. In *Government policy and farmland markets: The maintenance of farmer wealth*, eds. C. B. Moss and A. Schmitz, 223–235. Ames: Iowa State University Press.

Ervin, D., and J. Mill. 1985. Agricultural land markets and soil erosion: Policy relevance and conceptual issues. *American Journal of Agricultural Economics* 67: 938–942.

Falk, B. 1991. Formally testing the present value model of farmland prices. *American Journal of Agricultural Economics* 73(1): 1–10.

Falk, B. 1992. Predictable excess returns in real estate markets: A study of Iowa farmland values. *Journal of Housing Economics* 2: 84–105.

Falk, B., and B. -S. Lee. 1998. Fads versus fundamentals in farmland prices. *American Journal of Agricultural Economics* 80(4): 696–707.

Featherstone, A. M., and T. O. Baker. 1987. An examination of farm sector real estate dynamics: 1910–85. *American Journal of Agricultural Economics* 69(3): 532–546.

Freeman, A. M., III. 1974. On estimating air pollution control benefits from land value studies. *Journal of Environmental Economics and Management* 1: 74–83.

Freeman, A. M., III. 1993. *The measurement of environmental and resource values: Theory and methods*. Washington, DC: Resources for the Future.

Gardner, B. 2003. US commodity policies and farmland values. In *Government policy and farmland markets: The maintenance of farmer wealth*, eds. C. B. Moss and A. Schmitz, 81–96. Ames: Iowa State Press.

Gardner, K., and R. Barrows. 1985. The impact of soil conservation investments on land prices. *American Journal of Agricultural Economics* 67(5): 943–947.

Geniaux, G., J.-S. Ay, and C. Napoléone. 2011. A spatial hedonic approach on land use change anticipations. *Journal of Regional Science* 61 (5): 967–986.

Gibbons, S., and H. G. Overman. 2012. Mostly pointless spatial econometrics? *Journal of Regional Science* 52(2): 172–191.

Goodwin, B. K., A. K. Mishra, and F. N. Ortalo-Magnè. 2003*a*. What's wrong with our models of agricultural land values? *American Journal of Agricultural Economics* 85: 744–752.

Goodwin, B. K., A. K. Mishra, and F. N. Ortalo-Magnè. 2003*b*. Explaining regional differences in the capitalization of policy benefits into agricultural land values. In *Government policy and farmland markets: The maintenance of farmer wealth*, eds. C. B. Moss and A. Schmitz, 97–114. Ames: Iowa State University Press.

Goodwin, B. K., A. K. Mishra, and F. Ortalo-Magnè. 2010. The buck stops where? The distribution of agricultural subsidies. NBER Working Paper No. 16693.

Greene, W. H. 2012. *Econometric analysis*. 7th ed. Upper Saddle River, NJ: Prentice Hall.

Greenstone, M., and J. Gallagher. 2008. Does hazardous waste matter? Evidence from the housing market and the Superfund Program. *Quarterly Journal of Economics* 123(3): 951–1003.

Griffith, D. A. 2009. Spatial autocorrelation. Unpublished. http://www.elsevierdirect.com/brochures/hugy/SampleContent/Spatial-Autocorrelation.pdf

Grout, C. A., W. K. Jaeger, and A. J. Plantinga. 2011. Land-use regulations and property values in Portland, Oregon: A regression discontinuity design approach. *Regional Science and Urban Economics* 41: 98–107.

Guiling, P., B. W. Brorsen, and D. Doye. 2009. Effect of urban proximity on agricultural land values. *Land Economics* 85(2): 252–264.

Gutierrez, L., J. Westerlund, and K. Erickson. 2007. Farmland prices, structural breaks and panel data. *European Review of Agricultural Economics* 34(2): 161–179.

Hardie, I. W., T. A. Narayan, and B. L. Gardner. 2001. The joint influence of agricultural and nonfarm factors on real estate values: An application to the Mid-Atlantic region. *American Journal of Agricultural Economics* 83(1):120–132.

Heckman, J. J. 1979. Sample selection bias as a specification error. *Econometrica* 47(1): 153–161.

Heckman, J. J., H. Ichimura, J. A. Smith, and P. E. Todd. 1998. Characterizing selection bias using experimental data. *Econometrica* 66(5): 1017–1098.

Heckman, J. J., H. Ichimura, and P. E. Todd. 1997. Matching as an econometric evaluation estimator: Evidence from evaluating a job training programme. *Review of Economic Studies* 64(4): 605–654.

Heckman, J. J., and S. Navarro. 2004. Using matching, instrumental variables and control functions to estimate economic choice models. *Review of Economics and Statistics* 86(1): 30–57.

Heckman, J. J., and R. Robb. 1985. Alternative methods for evaluation the impact of interventions. *Journal of Econometrics* 30: 239–267.

Henderson, J., and B. A. Gloy. 2009. The impact of ethanol plants on cropland values in the Great Plains. *Agricultural Financial Review* 69: 36–48.

Henderson, J., and S. Moore. 2006. The capitalization of wildlife recreation income into farmland values. *Journal of Agricultural and Applied Economics* 38(3): 597–610.

Henneberry, D. M., and R. L. Barrows. 1990. Capitalization of exclusive agricultural zoning into farmland prices. *Land Economics* 66: 249–258.

Herdt, R. W., and W. W. Cochrane. 1966. Farmland prices and technological advance. *Journal of Farm Economics* 48: 243–263.

Hirano, K., and G. W. Imbens. 2005. The propensity score with continuous treatments. In *Applied Bayesian modeling and causal inference from incomplete-data perspectives: An essential journey with Donald Rubin's statistical family*, eds. A. Gelman and X.-L. Meng, 73–84. Chichester, UK: John Wiley & Sons.

Hoppe, R. A., and D. E. Banker. 2010. *Structure and finances of US family farms: Family Farm Report, 2010 Edition*. EIB-66, USDA-Economic Research Service, July.

Huang, H., G. Y. Miller, B. J. Sherrick, and M. I. Gomez. 2006. Factors influencing Illinois farmland values. *American Journal of Agricultural Economics*, 88(2): 458–470.

Imbens, G. W., and T. Lemieux. 2008. Regression discontinuity designs: A guide to practice. *Journal of Econometrics* 142(2): 615–635.

Imbens, G. W., and J. M. Wooldridge. 2007. Control function and related methods. In NBER Summer Institute *What's new in econometrics?* Lecture 6. http://www.nber.org/WNE/lect_6_controlfuncs.pdf

Imbens, G. W., and J. M. Wooldridge. 2009. Recent developments in the econometrics of program evaluation. *Journal of Economic Literature* 47(1): 5–86.

Irwin, E. G., A. M. Isserman, M. Kilkenny, and M. Partridge. 2010. A century of research on rural development and regional issues. *American Journal of Agricultural Economics* 92(2): 522–553.

Irwin, E. G., and D. Wrenn. 2014. An assessment of empirical methods for modeling land use. In *The Oxford handbook of land economics*, eds. J. M. Duke and J. Wu, 327–351. New York: Oxford University Press.

Just, R. E., and J. A. Miranowski. 1993. Understanding farmland price changes. *American Journal of Agricultural Economics* 75(1): 156–168.

Kirwan, B. E. 2009. The incidence of US agricultural subsidies on farmland rental rates. *Journal of Political Economy* 117(1): 138–164.

Kostov, P. 2009. A spatial quantile regression hedonic model of agricultural land prices. *Spatial Economic Analysis* 4(1): 53–70.

Kostov, P. 2010. Do buyers' characteristics and personal relationships affect agricultural land prices? *American Journal of Agricultural Economics* 86(1): 48–65.

Kostov, P., M. Patton, and S. McErlean. 2008. Non-parametric analysis of the influence of buyers' characteristics and personal relationships on agricultural land prices. *Agribusiness* 24 (2): 161–176.

Lee, L. F. 1982. Some approaches to the correction of sample selection bias. *Review of Economic Studies* 49(3): 355–372.

Lee, L. F. 1983. Generalized econometric models with selectivity. *Econometrica* 51(2): 507–512.

Lee, D. S., and T. Lemieux. 2010. Regression discontinuity designs in economics. *Journal of Economic Literatures* 48: 281–355.

Lence, S. 2001. Farmland prices in the presence of transaction costs: A cautionary note. *American Journal of Agricultural Economics* 83: 985–992.

Lence, S. H., and A. K. Mishra. 2003. The impacts of different farm programs on cash rents. *American Journal of Agricultural Economics* 85: 753–761.

Lynch, L., W. Gray, and J. Geoghegan. 2007. Are farmland preservation program easement restrictions capitalized into farmland prices? What can propensity score matching tell us? *Review of Agricultural Economics* 29: 502–509.

Ma, S., and S. M. Swinton. 2012. Hedonic valuation of farmland using sale prices versus appraised values. *Land Economics* 88(1): 1–15.

Maddison, D. 2009. A spatio-temporal model of farmland values. *Journal of Agricultural Economics* 60(1): 171–189.

Melichar, E. 1979. Capital gains versus current income in the farming sector. *American Journal of Agricultural Economics* 61(5): 1085–1092.
McMillen, D. P. 2010. Issues in spatial data analysis. *Journal of Regional Science* 50: 119–141.
McMillen, D. P. 2012. Perspectives on spatial econometrics. *Journal of Regional Science* 52(2): 192–209.
McMillen, D. P., and J. E. McDonald. 1989. Selectivity bias in urban land value functions. *Land Economics* 65: 341–351.
McMillen, D. P., and C. Redfearn. 2010. Estimation and hypothesis testing for nonparametric hedonic house price functions. *Journal of Regional Science* 50: 712–733.
Miranowski, J. A., and B. D. Hammes. 1984. Implicit prices of soil characteristics for farmland in Iowa. *American Journal of Agricultural Economics* 66(4): 745–749.
Mishra, A. K., C. B. Moss, and K. E. Erickson. 2004. Valuing farmland with multiple quasi-fixed inputs. *Applied Economics* 36: 1669–1675.
Mishra, A. K., G. T. Livanis, and C. B. Moss. 2011. Did the Federal Agriculture Improvement and Reform Act of 1996 affect farmland values? *Entropy* 13: 668–682.
Moss, C. B. 1997. Returns, interest rates, and inflation: How they explain changes in farmland values. *American Journal of Agricultural Economics* 79(4): 1311–1318.
Moss, C. B., and A. Schmitz, eds. 2003. *Government policy and farmland markets: The maintenance of farmer wealth*. Ames: Iowa State Press.
Moss, C. B., and A. L. Katchova. 2005. Farmland values and asset performance. *Agricultural Finance Review* 65(2): 119–130.
Navarro, S. 2008. Control function. In *The new Palgrave dictionary of economics*, 2nd eds., eds. S. N. Durlauf and L. E. Blume, 208–212. London: Palgrave Macmillan Press.
Nelson, F. J., and L. P. Schertz. 1996. Provisions of the Federal Agriculture Improvement and Reform Act of 1996. AIB-729, USDA-Economic Research Service.
Nickerson, C. J., and L. Lynch. 2001. The effect of farmland preservation programs on farmland prices. *American Journal of Agricultural Economics* 83(2): 341–351.
Nickerson, C. J., M. Morehart, T. Kuethe, J. Beckman, J. Ifft, and R. Williams. 2012. Trends in farmland values and ownership. EIB-92, USDA-Economic Research Service, February.
Nivens, H. D., T. L. Kastens, K. C. Dhuyvetter, and A. M. Featherstone. 2002. Using satellite imagery in predicting Kansas farmland values. *Journal of Agricultural and Resource Economics* 27(2): 464–480.
Palmquist, R. 1989. Land as a differentiated factor of production: A hedonic model and its implications for welfare measurement. *Land Economics* 65(1):23–28.
Palmquist, R. B. 2006. Property value models. In *Handbook of environmental economics*, Vol. 2, eds. K. G. Mäler and J. R. Vincent, 763–819. North Holland: Elsevier.
Palmquist, R. B., and L. E. Danielson. 1989. A hedonic study of the effects of erosion control and drainage on farmland values. *American Journal of Agricultural Economics* 71: 55–62.
Patton, M., P. Kostov, S. McErlean, and J. Moss. 2008. Assessing the influence of direct payments on the rental value of agricultural land. *Food Policy* 33: 397–405.
Pinkse, J., and M. E. Slade. 2010. The future of spatial econometrics. *Journal of Regional Science* 50: 103–117.
Plantinga, A. J., R. N. Lubowski, and R. N. Stavins. 2002. The effects of potential land development on agricultural land prices. *Journal of Urban Economics* 52 (3): 561–581.
Pope, R., R. A. Kramer, R. D. Green, and D. B. Gardner. 1979. An evaluation of econometric models of US farmland prices. *Western Journal of Agricultural Economics* 4(1):107–118.

Puhani, P. A. 2000. The Heckman correction for sample selection and its critique. *Journal of Economic Surveys* 14(1): 53–68.

Ravallion, M. 2007. Evaluating anti-poverty programs. In *Handbook of development economics*, Vol. 4, eds. T. Schultz and J. Strauss, 3787–3846. North-Holland: Elsevier.

Ricardo, D. 1996. *The principles of political economy and taxation*. Amherst, NY: Prometheus Books [originally published in 1817].

Roka, F. M., and R. B. Plamquist. 1997. Examining the use of national databases in a hedonic analysis of regional farmland values. *American Journal of Agricultural Economics* 79: 1651–1656.

Rosen, S. 1974. Hedonic prices and implicit markets: Product differentiation in pure competition. *Journal of Political Economy* 82(1): 34–55.

Rosenbaum, P. R., and D. B. Rubin. 1983. The central role of the propensity score in observational studies for causal effects. *Biometrika* 70: 41–55.

Rubin, D. B. 1980. Bias reduction using Mahalanobis-metric matching. *Biometrics* 36: 293–298.

Sauer, J., J. Walsh, and D. Zilberman. 2012. Producer behaviour and agri-environmental policies: A directional distance based matching approach. Selected paper prepared for presentation at the 2012 Agricultural & Applied Economics Association Annual Meeting, Seattle, WA, August 12–14, 2012.

Schmitz, A. 1995. Boom-bust cycles and Ricardian rents. *American Journal of Agricultural Economics* 77(5): 1110–1125.

Shaik, S., G. A. Helmers, and J. A. Atwood. 2005. The evolution of farm programs and their contribution to agricultural land values. *American Journal of Agricultural Economics* 87(5): 1190–1197.

Sherrick, B. J., and P. J. Barry. 2003. Farmland markets: Historical perspectives and contemporary issues. In *Government policy and farmland markets: The maintenance of farmer wealth*, eds. C. B. Moss and A. Schmitz, 27–52. Ames: Iowa State Press.

Shi, Y. J., T. T. Phipps, and D. Colyer. 1997. Agricultural land values under urbanizing influence. *Land Economics* 73(February): 90–100.

Smith, J. A., and P. E. Todd. 2005. Does matching overcome LaLonde's critique of nonexperimental estimators? *Journal of Econometrics* 125: 305–353.

Sumner, D. A., J. M. Alston, and J. W. Glauber. 2010. Evolution of the economics of agricultural policy. *American Journal of Agricultural Economics* 92(2): 403–423.

Tegene, A., and F. Kuchler. 1993. A regression test of the present value model of US farmland. *Journal of Agricultural Economics* 44(1): 135–143.

Tobler, W. 1970. A computer movie simulating urban growth in the Detroit region. *Economic Geography* 46(2): 234–240.

Todd, P. E. 2007. Evaluating social programs with endogenous program placement and selection of the treated. In *Handbook of development economics*, Vol. 4, eds. T. P. Schultz and J. Strauss, 3847–3894. North-Holland: Elsevier.

Towe, C., R. Lewis, and L. Lynch. 2014. Applying experiments to land economics: Public information and auction efficiency in ecosystem service markets. In *The Oxford handbook of land economics*, eds. J. M. Duke and J. Wu, 481–510. New York: Oxford University Press.

Towe, C., and C. I. Tra. 2013. 'Vegetable spirits' and energy policy. *American Journal of Agricultural Economics* 95(1): 1–16.

Tweeten, L. T., and J. E. Martin. 1966. A methodology for predicting US farm real estate price variation. *Journal of Farm Economics* 48(2):378–393.

U.S. Department of Agriculture, Economic Research Service. 2012. Balance sheet of the farming sector, 2008–2012F. USDA-ERS Farm Income and Wealth Statistics Topic Page. http://www.ers.usda.gov/data-products/farm-income-and-wealth-statistics.aspx

U.S. Department of Agriculture, National Agricultural Statistics Service. 2001. 1997 Census of Agriculture. vol. 3, Special Studies; Part IV: Agricultural and Land Economics Ownership Survey. AC97-SP-4. December.

Vitaliano, D. F., and C. Hill. 1994. Agricultural districts and farmland prices. *Journal of Real Estate Finance and Economics* 8(3): 213–223.

van der Klaauw, W. 2008. Regression-discontinuity analysis: A survey of recent developments in economics. *Labour* 22(2): 219–245.

Vella, F. 1998. Estimating models with sample selection bias: A survey. *Journal of Human Resources* 33(1): 127–169.

Weersink, A., S. Clark, C. G. Turvey, and R. Sarker. 1999. The effect of agricultural policy on farmland values. *Land Economics* 75(3): 425–439.

Wooldridge, J. M. 2002. *Econometric analysis of cross section and panel data*. Cambridge, MA: MIT Press.

Zhang, W., E. G. Irwin, and C. J. Nickerson. 2012. The expanding ethanol market and farmland values: Identifying the changing influence of proximity to agricultural delivery points. Selected paper prepared for presentation at the 2012 Agricultural & Applied Economics Association Annual Meeting, Seattle, WA, August 12–14, 2012.

Zhao, Z. 2004. Using matching to estimate treatment effects: Data requirements, matching metrics, and Monte Carlo evidence. *The Review of Economics and Statistics* 86(1): 91–107.

CHAPTER 6

LAND USE AND SUSTAINABLE ECONOMIC DEVELOPMENT

Developing World

EDWARD B. BARBIER

Land use change in developing countries is critically bound up with the pattern of economic development in these countries. Most developing economies, and certainly the majority of the populations living within them, depend directly on natural resources. For many of these economies, primary product exports account for the vast majority of their export earnings, and one or two primary commodities make up the bulk of exports (Barbier 2005*b*, chapter 1). Agricultural value added accounts for an average of 40% of GDP, and nearly 80% of the labor force is engaged in agricultural or resource-based activities (World Bank 2008). Further adding to these disparities, by 2025, the rural population of the developing world will have increased to almost 3.2 billion, placing increasing pressure on a declining resource base (Population Division of the United Nations 2008).

Over the past 50 years, the pattern of land use change in developing as opposed to developed economies has been dramatically different (Fischer and Heilig 1997; Ramankutty and Foley 1999; FAO 2006; World Bank 2008; Barbier 2011). In developed countries, cropland area slowed its growth, eventually stabilized, and is now declining. As a result, the decline of forest and woodland has halted in developed countries in aggregate, and since 1990, total forest area has increased (FAO 2006). Not only has primary forest area recovered but also the growth in plantations has been strong. In contrast, in developing economies, cropland area has continued to expand. In the developing regions of Africa, Asia, and Latin America, tropical forests were the primary sources of new agricultural land in the 1980s and 1990s (Gibbs et al. 2010). Almost one-fifth of new crop production in developing countries from 1990 to 2050 is expected to rely on expanding cultivated area, and two-thirds of this new land will come from conversion of forests and wetlands (Fischer and Heilig 1997). In some regions, such as tropical Latin America, livestock grazing is also projected to cause extensive deforestation in the near future (Wassenaar et al. 2007).

However, although historically such land use changes leading to cropland expansion may have been associated with successful resource-based development, this is less likely for most developing countries today (Barbier 2011). The main purpose of this chapter is to offer an economic explanation about why this might be the case. That is, development in low and middle-income economies is accompanied by substantial resource conversion, especially the expansion of the agricultural land base through the conversion of forests, wetlands and other natural habitat, but this pattern of land use is generating less economy-wide benefits than in previous eras. The main reason is that the current process of land use and expansion has two unique structural features.

First, considerable land expansion in ecologically fragile areas is serving mainly as an outlet for the subsistence and near-subsistence needs of the rural poor (Barbier 2005*b*, 2010). A substantial proportion of the population in low and middle-income countries is concentrated in marginal areas and on ecologically fragile land, such as converted forest frontier areas, poor quality uplands, converted wetlands, and so forth (Comprehensive Assessment of Water Management in Agriculture 2007; World Bank 2003). Households on these lands not only face problems of land degradation and low productivity but also tend to be some of the poorest in the world. Yet, population increases and other economic pressures are driving many of the rural poor to bring yet more marginal land into production (Chen and Ravillion 2007; Population Division of the United Nations 2008). The result is that such marginal land expansion continues to be the main basis for absorbing the growing number of the rural poor in developing economies (Pichón 1997; Coxhead et al. 2002; Carr 2009; Barbier 2011).

Second, marginal land expansion may be an important outlet for the rural poor, but it may not be the main cause of overall land conversion and use in developing countries. Recent evidence suggests that commercially oriented economic activities are responsible for much of the land expansion that is occurring in low- and middle-income economies. For example, the main "agents of deforestation" globally are now plantation owners, large-scale farmers, ranchers, and timber and mining operations, assisted by government policies (FAO 2001, 2003, 2006; Chomitz et al. 2007; Rudel 2007; DeFries et al. 2010; Boucher et al. 2011). Large-scale capital investments, which include plantation agriculture, ranching, forestry and mining activities, often result in export-oriented extractive enclaves with little or no forward and backward linkages to the rest of the economy (Bridge 2008; Barbier 2005*b*, 2011; van der Ploeg 2011). The result is that development in low- and middle-income economies is accompanied by substantial resource conversion, especially the expansion of the agricultural land base through the conversion of forests, wetlands, and other natural habitat. At the same time, most developing economies remain highly dependent on the exploitation of natural resources and are unable to diversify.

The consequence of these two structural features of land use and expansion in developing economies is that they are symptomatic of a *dualistic frontier economy*. The classic definition of a *frontier* is "a geographic region adjacent to the unsettled portions of the continent in which a low man/land ratio and unusually abundant, unexploited, natural resources provide an exceptional opportunity for social and economic betterment" (Billington 1966, 25). To exploit these resources, processes of *frontier expansion* or *frontier-based development* are "characterized by the initial existence of abundant land, mostly unoccupied, and by a substantial migration of capital and people" (di Tella 1982, 212). For heavily resource-dependent developing economies, that is, those that have 75% or more of primary production to total exports, such a process of frontier-based development may characterize nearly the entire economy. For other low and middle-income economies, in addition to the frontier economy, there may also be burgeoning industrial and service sectors.

However, the main structural feature of the frontier economy in most developing countries is that it is inherently *dualistic*. The frontier economy contains both a traditional sector that converts and exploits available land to produce a nontraded agricultural output, and a fully developed, commercially oriented sector that converts and exploits available land and natural resources for a variety of traded outputs. The latter could include plantation agriculture, ranching, forestry and mining activities. In addition, the traditional agricultural sector is dominated by farm holdings that occupy marginal or ecologically fragile land with poor land quality and productivity potential. Although these two types of economic activities differ significantly and may also be geographically separated, they are linked by labor use, as the rural poor on marginal land form a large pool of surplus unskilled labor that can be employed in commercial frontier activities. This linkage is important not only to the dynamics of land expansion and use within developing economies but also to the pattern of overall economic development (Hansen 1979; Píchón 1997; Coxhead et al. 2002; Barbier 2005*a*; Maertens et al. 2006; Carr 2009).

To set the stage, this chapter first describes in more detail the dualistic frontier economy and processes of land expansion that typify many developing economies. A model of the dualistic frontier economy is then developed to explore its main economic implications for economic development in many low- and middle-income countries today. These implications lie at the core of why land use and expansion in developing economies may not be generating greater economy-wide benefits.

To summarize the key results, in the dual frontier economy, because there are no diminishing returns to labor in the use of marginal land for agricultural production, real wages are invariant to rural employment. As long as there remains abundant marginal land to absorb more farmers and employment, the use of land relative to labor on this land will determine nominal wages throughout the dual frontier economy. The implication is that, with given international prices for the marketed-oriented activities, the real wage and thus the amount of unskilled labor employed by these activities will be fully determined. The pool of surplus labor on marginal lands is essentially a barometer of frontier-based development. As long as there are abundant marginal lands for cultivation, they serve to absorb rural migrants, population increases, and displaced unskilled labor from elsewhere in the economy. On the other hand, expanding commercial activities that exploit more resources and land on the frontier will absorb more workers from the pool of surplus labor existing on marginal frontier lands. Although the latter outcome may seem beneficial, it has the tendency to promote *boom and bust cycles* of economic development (Wunder 2003, 2005; Barbier 2005*a*, 2005*b*, 2007, 2011; Ha and Shively 2008; Agergaard et al. 2009; Barney 2009; Rodrigues et al. 2009; Hall 2011; Knudsen and Folds 2011). Such cycles are reinforced by a policy environment that, on the one hand, encourages frontier commercial activities to remain as isolated enclaves and, on the other, fails to ensure that the resource rents generated by these activities lead to greater economic diversification (Barbier 2005*b*, 2007).

1. Land Use and the Dualistic Frontier Economy

Since 1950, many economies with abundant endowments of land, mineral and fossil fuel resources have had difficulty in achieving successful resource-based development (Barbier 2005*b*, 2011; van der Ploeg 2011). For example, Gylfason (2001) has examined the long-run growth performance of 85 resource-rich developing economies since 1965. Only Botswana, Malaysia, and Thailand managed to achieve a long-term investment rate exceeding 25% of GDP and long-run average annual growth rates exceeding 4%, which is a performance comparable to that of high income economies. Malaysia and Thailand have also managed successfully to diversify their economies through re-investing the financial gains from primary production for export. Botswana has yet to diversify its economy significantly but has developed favorable institutions and policies for managing its natural wealth and primary production for extensive economy-wide benefits. Although many other developing countries still depend on finding new reserves of land and other natural resources to exploit, very few appear to have benefited from such resource-based development. This poses an intriguing paradox: Why should economic dependence on natural resource exploitation and land expansion be associated with "unsustainable" resource-based development in many low and middle-income countries today, especially because historically this has not always been the case?

One reason is that the unique pattern of frontier land expansion emerging in developing economies appears to be inimical to successful economy-wide development. An early criticism of this pattern was the *hollow frontier hypothesis*, which James (1969) first used to describe the expansion of the coffee frontier in southern and central Brazil during the mid-20th century. Although these areas were originally settled by smallholders, they were later displaced to more remote regions by wealthy landowners through property aggregation, which lead to a relatively depopulated and "hollow" frontier. Evidence of this process has been found in the Brazilian Amazon not only for coffee but also for ranching and other forms of large-scale commercial agriculture (Casetti and Gauthier 1977; Wood 1983; Aldrich et al. 2006; Morton et al. 2006; Browder et al. 2008).

In addition, if institutions and economic policies encourage large profits from frontier expansion, then "well-capitalized interests, including land speculators and ranchers, consolidate the properties of subsistence farmers through market transactions or outright expulsions" (Aldrich et al. 2006, 272). However, such large-scale capital investments, which include plantation agriculture, ranching, forestry and mining activities, often result in export-oriented extractive enclaves with little or no forward and backward linkages to the rest of the economy (Barbier 2005*b*, 2011; Bridge 2008). As pointed out by Bunker (1989, 607): "Overconfidence in the linkage potential of extractive economies can lead directly to public investments aimed at capturing the linkages near the mouth of the mine when in fact the locational disadvantages are so great that only under extraordinary circumstances would these investments be competitive." The result is a vicious cycle, whereby policies and institutions continue to favor, subsidize, and support capital investments to create abnormal profits for mineral and large-scale agricultural projects in the frontier, yet the lack of linkages to the rest of the economy simply reinforce the tendency of these investments to create commercially oriented extractive enclaves (Barbier 2005*b*, 2011). These enclaves are more tied to the "global production network" that focuses on exploitation of agricultural and mineral resources for the world market or domestic consumption in urban and industrial centers (Bridge 2008).

Government policies have actively promoted capital investment in commercially oriented frontier agricultural and extractive activities. For example, in the Brazilian Amazon, "spatial differentiation in the pattern of development would be largely influenced by the State, in its infrastructure investment decisions (e.g., roads and utility extensions into the frontier) and in fiscal incentive policies targeted to specific regions that would invite capital investment there" (Browder et al. 2008, 1472). State programs to improve property rights and the efficiency of land markets increase land values and attract additional frontier investments. As Gould et al. (2006) illustrate with a case study of the Petén, Guatemala, such land administration and privatization policies can have the unintended consequence of increasing the incentive for land speculation rather than investment in productive agricultural activities. Similarly, Bromley (2008, 561) shows that, in Africa, "an exclusive focus on the property relations of isolated villages and their commons will necessarily fail if development programs ignore the institutional architecture of markets and market processes throughout the entirety of a nation."

Government policies have supported the expansion of large-scale soybean cultivation and mechanized agriculture in Amazonia (Hecht 2005; Bulte et al. 2007; Killeen et al. 2007; Carr 2009; Walker et al. 2009); oil palm, coffee, and other cash crops in Asia (Coxhead et al. 2002; Agergaard et al. 2009; Barney 2009; Curry and Koczberski 2009; Hirsch 2009; McCarthy and Cramb 2009); cocoa, cotton, and other cash crop frontiers in Africa (Mosley 2005; Bromley 2008; Knudsen and Fold 2011); ranching in Latin America (Walker 2003; Bulte et al. 2007; Killeen et al. 2007; Wassenaar et al. 2007; Caviglia-Harris and Harris 2008; Schmook and Vance 2009; Walker et al. 2009); and extractive frontiers globally (Hyndman 1994; Wunder 2003, 2005; Akpalu and Parks 2007; Bridge 2008; Campbell 2009).

Frontiers are also the means for *marginal land expansion* as a "safety valve" outlet for the rural poor. As noted by Coxhead et al. (2002, 345), "the land frontier has long served as the employer of last resort for underemployed, unskilled labor." This process was fostered by colonial policies in many developing regions yet has continued unabated since the 1950s (James 1969; Hansen 1979; Foweraker 1981; Bunker 1984; Williamson 2002, 2006; Austin 2007; Etter et al. 2008; Barbier 2011). The result has been a large concentration of the rural poor on low quality land for agriculture, characterized by traditional farming methods with negligible marginal productivity, zero land rents or profits, and informal or nonexistent land-tenure arrangements, inadequate transport and infrastructure, and other market imperfections (Mueller 1997; Coxhead et al. 2003; Barbier 2005*b*; Gould et al. 2006; Jepson 2006; Maertens et al. 2006; Carr 2009; Schmook and Vance 2009).

In sum, long-term land use trends and economic development in many low and middle income countries has evolved a *dualistic* frontier economy. This outcome was first highlighted by Hansen (1979) to describe colonial land use in developing regions, and then by Wood (1983, 259) to characterize frontier development in Amazonia: "A central feature of the contemporary settlement of the Brazilian Amazon is the simultaneous expansion into the region of capitalist enterprises and peasant farmers. The dual character of the frontier is, to a large extent, a consequence of the development policies adopted by the state." As noted by Aldrich et al. (2006, 72) the outcome of this dualistic process of frontier expansion is often *frontier stratification*: "Although the smallholders who initiate frontier settlement are poor, they share their poverty in relative equality until the aggregation of property causes the distribution of land to be skewed and drives social stratification."

The result is an inherently dualistic economy. Coexisting in most frontiers are highly developed, modern, and profitable commercial economic activities along with more traditional, relatively poor agricultural activities on marginal lands. That is, "according to the dualist model the frontier is comprised of two different economies: the traditional, non-capitalist sector, which is subsistence-oriented and has minimal ties to the marketplace; and the modern, capitalist sector, which is market-oriented and follows the logic of profit maximization" (Wood 1983, 263). Although these two types of economic activities differ significantly and may also be geographically separated, they are linked by labor use. This linkage is important to the dynamics of frontier expansion, because it means that rural poor on marginal land form a large pool of surplus unskilled labor that can be employed in commercial frontier activities (Hansen 1979; Píchón 1997; Coxhead et al. 2002; Barbier 2005*a*; Maertens et al. 2006; Carr 2009).

The dualistic frontier economy has important implications for economic development in many low- and middle-income countries today. To explore these implications more fully, it is useful to develop a model depicting land use and labor allocation in the dualistic frontier economy.

2. A Model of the Dualistic Frontier Economy

Following the discussion above, it is assumed that the dualistic frontier economy comprises two sectors: (1) a fully developed, commercially oriented sector that converts and exploits available land and natural resources for a variety of traded outputs, and (2) a traditional sector that converts and exploits available land to produce a nontraded agricultural output, which is dominated by farm holdings that occupy marginal or ecologically fragile land with poor land quality and productivity potential. Although these two sectors comprising the frontier economy differ significantly and may also be geographically separated, they are linked by labor use. That is, the rural poor on marginal land form a large pool of surplus unskilled labor that can be employed in commercial frontier activities, and the wage rate is determined by the dynamics of land expansion within the frontier economy (Hansen 1979; Píchón 1997; Coxhead et al. 2002; Barbier 2005*a*; Maertens et al. 2006; Carr 2009).

For heavily resource-dependent economies (i.e., those that have 75% or more of primary production to total exports), the commercial and traditional frontier sectors may comprise nearly the entire economy. For other low- and middle-income economies, there may also be a burgeoning industrial and/or service sectors. For the purposes of the model, it does not matter whether the dualistic frontier is an enclave within a larger developing economy or whether it comprises the entire economy.

2.1 Sector 1: Commercial Primary Production

Production of the traded primary product (plantation crops, timber, beef, mineral, etc.) is modeled in a similar way as in Findlay and Lundahl (1994). Primary production depends directly on inputs of land and/or natural resources (N_1)and labor (L_1), and indirectly on capital (K_1). The sector imports capital from either the rest of the economy or abroad, and this capital consists of both reproducible capital (machines, equipment, tools, etc.) and the skilled labor, or human capital, required to maintain and run such durable goods. As domestic and foreign claims on capital are perfect substitutes as stores of wealth, and the open economy is small in relation to the world economy, capital is available in perfectly elastic supply at the international interest rate, r (Barro and Sala-I-Martin 2004). Thus, the accumulation of capital in the commercial activity sector has a negligible impact on the interest rate, which can be treated as exogenous.

Primary production, Q_1, is determined by a function with the normal concave properties and is homogeneous of degree one

$$Q_1 = f(N_1, L_1),\ f_i > 0,\ f_{ii} < 0,\ i = N, L \tag{1}$$

The commercial activity can obtain more land or natural resources (hereafter referred to as "resources") for primary production, but only by employing and allocating more capital for this purpose. It is assumed that increasing N_1 incurs a rising input of K_1

$$K_1 = c(N_1), c' > 0, c'' > 0 \tag{2}$$

where $c'(N_1)$ is the marginal capital requirement of obtaining and transforming a unit of the resource input, which is a convex function of the amount of N_1 appropriated. As $c'(N_1)$ represents the "marginal cost" of obtaining land and resources, $c''>0$ implies that these costs are rising as more appropriation occurs.

Letting p_1 be the price of primary production output, r the interest rate, and w the wage rate, it follows that total profits are

$$\pi = L_1 p_1 f(n_1) - rc(N_1) - wL_1 n_1 = N_1 / L_1 \tag{3}$$

Profit-maximizing leads to

$$f(n_1) - f_N n_1 = \frac{w}{p_1} \tag{4}$$

$$\frac{p_1 f_N(n_1)}{c'} = r \tag{5}$$

Condition (4) is the normal value marginal product conditions for use of labor in production. Condition (5) determines the optimal use of natural resources, and indicates that the rate of return from appropriating N_1 for primary production must be equal to the interest rate. The rate of return consists of the marginal rent per unit of N_1 divided by the marginal cost of converting it for use in primary production.

2.2 Sector 2: Traditional Agriculture on Marginal Land

Production of nontraded agricultural output involves two inputs, land (N_2) and labor (L_2); any capital input is fixed and fully funded out of normal profits. Both land and labor are required for traditional agricultural production, Q_2, which is determined by a function with the normal concave properties and is homogeneous of degree one

$$Q_2 = g(N_2, L_2), g_i \geq 0, g_{ii} < 0, i = N, L \tag{6}$$

Note that the marginal productivity of land is not necessarily positive. This Ricardian surplus-land condition follows from the assumption that poor quality marginal land is unproductive in cultivation (Hansen 1979). That is, for traditional agriculture on marginal land, $g_N = 0$ and, thus, equilibrium is determined by

$$g'(n_2) = 0, \ g(n_2) = \frac{w}{p_2}, \ n_2 = n_2^m = \frac{N_2^m}{L_2^m} \tag{7}$$

The result of this outcome is that there are no diminishing returns to labor in the use of marginal land for agricultural production. Real wages are invariant to rural employment (the number of farmers and/or labor input on marginal land) and determined by the average product of labor. Moreover, the condition of zero marginal productivity fixes the land/labor ratio on marginal land, which can be designated as n_2^m. Finally, given the average product of labor relationship in Equation (7), the fixed land/labor ratio will determine the nominal wage rate w for any predetermined output price p_2. Thus, the best that farmers and their families on marginal land can do is either sell their labor to each other and obtain an equilibrium real wage w/p_2, or alternatively, farm their own plots of land and earn the same real wage. Since there is little advantage in selling their labor, farmers will tend to use their and family labor to farm their own land. Hence, under this marginal land condition, small family farms will predominate. Unless the population increases, no more land will be brought into production and there will be surplus land.[1]

Finally, the total labor force in the frontier economy is given, and is

$$L = L_1 + L_2^m \tag{8}$$

2.3 Equilibrium

Because the fixed land/labor ratio on marginal land determines the nominal wage rate, the model of the frontier economy is fully recursive. With w determined, condition (4) indicates that to each value of p_1 there corresponds a unique value of the resource/labor ratio n_1 in commercial primary production. As r is also given, Equation (5) can now be solved for the equilibrium amount of natural resources appropriated and used N_1. With n_1 and N_1 known, L_1 follows. Finally, Q_1 can be determined from Equation (1) for primary production.

[1] Although the agricultural production of the traditional sector is a nontraded good, any surplus produced in excess of subsistence consumption is likely to be sold in competitive local markets. The standard assumption is that the resulting output price p_2 is predetermined in such markets, which is the general observation for traditional agriculture in frontier economies, whether its output is wholly consumed for subsistence or any surplus is locally traded (see Hansen 1979; Mueller 1997; Píchón 1997; Coxhead et al. 2002; Barbier 2005*a*; Maertens et al. 2006).

With L_1 known, $L^m{}_2$ can be found as a residual from Equation (8). As the fixed land/labor ratio $n^m{}_2$ is already known, $N^m{}_2$ follows. From Equation (6) it is now possible to determine traditional agricultural production $Q^m{}_2$ from marginal land.

From Equation (4) and the concavity conditions of Equation (1), it follows that $\frac{dn_1}{dp_1} = \frac{w}{p_1^2 n f''} < 0$ and thus

$$n_1 = n_1(p_1), n_1' < 0 \tag{9}$$

As a rise in p_1 leads to a fall in n_1, the numerator of Equation (5) will increase. Given that $c''> 0$, then N_1 must rise in order for equilibrium condition (5) to continue to hold. Consequently,

$$N_1 = N_1(p_1), n_1' > 0 \tag{10}$$

It follows from Equations (2) and (10) that $K = c^{-1}\ (N_1(p_1))$ and $K' > 0$. Also, from Equations (9), (10) and (1),

$$L_1 = L_1(p_1), L_1' > 0, Q_1 = Q_1(p_1), Q_1' > 0 \tag{11}$$

Aggregate supply of primary products from the frontier is positively sloped.

From condition (7) on marginal lands, all output is consumed $wL_2^m = p_2 Q_2^m$. However, the outputs, Q_1, from primary production are traded goods that are exported to the rest of the economy or abroad. It follows that total income, Y, in the frontier economy, excluding subsistence income from marginal land, is determined by p_1

$$Y = wL_1 + rK + p_1 f_N(n_1) \tag{12}$$

Assuming that consumers have identical and homothetic preferences, define the demand function for primary products as

$$Q_1^D = Q_1^D(p_1, Y), \ \frac{\partial Q_1^D}{\partial p_1} < 0, \ \frac{\partial Q_1^D}{\partial Y} > 0 \tag{13}$$

From Equations (11) and (13), the excess supply function for primary products is, therefore,

$$EQ_1(p_1) = Q_1(p_1) - Q_1 D(p_1) > 0, \quad EQ_1' > 0 \tag{14}$$

Because primary products are traded, the excess supply is used to import goods and services, either from the rest of the economy or abroad; that is,

$$E_{Q_1}(p_1) = M\left(\frac{1}{p_1}\right), \quad M' < 0 \tag{15}$$

2.4 An Increase in Population

An increase in population is tantamount to the increase in the total labor force L in Equation (8). However, because neither nominal nor real wages change, the increase in population must occur solely on marginal land. In order for the land/labor ratio n_2^m to remain fixed, there must be an equal increase in N_2^m to absorb the rise in L_2^m. The demand for labor from converting and cultivating marginal land is almost infinitely elastic. Because n_2^m is unchanged, nominal and real wages remain the same. Consequently, the effect of an increase in population is to increase labor use, cultivated area, and, thus, aggregate agricultural output Q_2^m on marginal land.

As total and rural population has increased in developing countries, marginal lands have served as an important outlet. In 1950, the rural areas of the developing world contained 1.8 billion people, which, by 2005, had almost doubled to 3.4 billion. From 1950 to 1975, annual rural population growth in these regions was 1.8%, and from 1975 to 2007 it was just over 1.0% (Population Division of the United Nations 2008). Since 1950, the number of people on marginal land in developing economies has doubled, reaching nearly 1.3 billion today (World Bank 2003). The result is that marginal land expansion, especially in frontier areas, continues to be the main basis for absorbing the growing number of the rural poor in developing economies (Pichón 1997; Coxhead et al. 2002; Carr 2009; Barbier 2011).

2.5 An Increase in the Price of Primary Products

If p_1 rises, then real wages in this sector w/p_1 fall. The result is to increase the demand for labor L_1 used in primary production. Also, from (9) and (10), it follows that the resource/labor ratio for primary production will decline, and resource inputs will rise. More resource conversion will in turn attract additional capital to the sector. Condition (5) confirms that resource use must rise in primary production. The fall in the resource/labor ratio causes marginal rent $p_1 f_N$, which is the numerator of condition (5), to rise. Because the interest rate is unchanged, N_1 must rise to increase c' and maintain condition (5) in equilibrium.

In order for n_1 to fall, the rise in L_1 must exceed the increase in N_1. Given Equation (8), the increase in L_1 must come from reducing labor on marginal land L_2^m. The fall in L_2^m must be accompanied by an equivalent decline in N_2^m in order to keep the fixed land/labor ratio on marginal land. Thus, the increase in employment, capital, resource use, and output in the primary production sector in response to the rise in p_1 will reduce labor, cultivation, and production on marginal land. As Equation (14) indicates, excess supply of primary production increases, and the resulting exports allow more goods and services to be imported to the frontier.

Of course, if the price of primary products from the frontier falls, the opposite occurs. The export-oriented primary sector contracts, and the resulting surplus labor is absorbed on marginal land. The result is more land conversion and a larger share of the population cultivating less favorable land. Rural poverty invariably increases as a result.

These effects of price increases have been observed for coffee, ranching, large-scale commercial agriculture in the Brazilian Amazon (Casetti and Gauthier 1977; Wood 1983; Aldrich et al. 2006; Morton et al. 2006; Browder et al. 2008; Rodrigues et al. 2009), as well as for cocoa, coffee, oil palm, and shrimp in Southeast Asia and Africa (Ha and Shively 2008; Agergaard et al. 2009; Barney 2009; Hall 2011; Knudsen and Folds 2011). Oil price booms have interacted with agricultural expansion and deforestation in a range of tropical countries, but with only short-lived economy-wide gains (Wunder 2003, 2005). As will be discussed later, as price rises for primary products are often short-lived, they tend to promote "boom and bust" cycles of economic development in many frontier areas of developing countries.

2.6 An Increase in the Price of Traditional Agricultural Products

Because real wages are invariant to the number of farmers or workers employed on marginal land, an increase in p_2 must translate into a proportional increase in money wages w. That is, the land/labor ratio must stay fixed at n_2^m, and so despite the rise in agricultural prices, the real wage remains constant at w/p_2. However, with the rise in w, real wages in primary production w/p_1 go up. As a result, the amount of labor employed in this sector L_1 declines. The resource/labor ratio increases, but this causes marginal rents to fall. As the interest rate in Equation (5) is unchanged, N_1 must also decrease to maintain the equilibrium. In order for n_1 to increase, L_1 must decline more than N_1.

The unemployed labor on the frontier has to be absorbed through additional conversion of marginal land. As L_2^m increases, N_2^m must rise proportionately in order to keep the land/labor ratio fixed. Thus, the effect of the price rise is to expand cultivation and production on marginal land, whereas the export-oriented primary production sector on the frontier contracts. A fall in p_2 would have the opposite outcome. Some evidence of these effects of changes in the price of traditional products on marginal land expansion is available for the uplands in Southeast Asia (Coxhead et al. 2002; Maertens et al. 2005; Ha and Shively 2008).

2.7 An Increase in the Interest Rate

If the interest rises, then the rate of return from appropriating N_1 for primary production, the left-hand side of Equation (5), must also increase. However, since real wages in primary production w/p_1 are unchanged, the resource/labor ratio and, thus, marginal rent $p_1 f_N$ remain the same. Thus, only the denominator c' in Equation (5) can fall, and this means that fewer resources N_1 are converted and used for primary production. This is the expected outcome. An increase in the interest rate raises the cost of employing capital to obtain more resources for primary production.

In order for n_1 to remain constant, the contraction in N_1 must be accompanied by a proportionate decline in L_1. This displaced labor from primary production must find employment through additional conversion of marginal land. Once again, the increase in L_2^m occurs with a proportionate rise in N_2^m to keep n_2^m constant.

In sum, a rise in the interest rate causes a reduction in the capital employed in the primary production sector. Resource use, employment, and output decline in this sector, and excess supply for export also falls. The unemployed labor will be absorbed through expanded marginal land cultivation. In contrast, a fall in the interest rate will lead to a contraction in marginal land use and an expansion of the export-oriented primary production sector. Unfortunately, there appear to be little empirical evidence of the effects of an increase of interest rate on dualistic frontier economic conditions.

2.8 Technical Progress on Marginal Land

The introduction of new inputs, such as fertilizers or improved varieties, and other technical improvements on marginal land may be neutral, or biased in favor of either land or labor. However, if any such technical progress fails to affect the zero marginal productivity condition indicated in Equation (7), then the land/labor ratio for production on marginal land must, thereby, remain the same. However, the average productivity of labor ($n^m{}_2$) can rise as a result of technical improvements on marginal land, and if that is the case, real wages w/p_2 will increase. Since p_2 is fixed, this implies a rise in the nominal wage.

The rise in the nominal wage leads to an increase in real wages w/p_1 in commercial primary production activities. Labor employment L_1 declines and the resource/labor ratio increases. Marginal rents fall, but as the interest rate in (5) is fixed, N_1 must also decrease to maintain the equilibrium. In order for n_1 to rise, L_1 must decline more than N_1. Thus, the effect of technical progress on marginal land is a contraction in export-oriented primary production. The resulting unemployed labor must be absorbed through greater cultivation of marginal land. As L_2^m increases, N_2^m must rise proportionately in order to keep the land/labor ratio fixed.

Note, though, that this outcome hinges critically on the assumption that any technical progress on marginal land *does not* alter the zero marginal productivity condition in Equation

(7). In contrast, empirical evidence of technical change and public investments in frontier economies indicates that any resulting land improvements that do increase the value of homesteads can have a positive effect on both land rents and reducing agricultural expansion (Coxhead et al. 2002; Maertens et al. 2006; Sills and Caviglia-Harris 2008; Dercon et al. 2009).

3. Conclusion: Implications for Economic Development

In the dual frontier economy found in many developing countries, real wages are invariant to rural employment, because there are no diminishing returns to labor in the use of marginal land for agricultural production. As long as there remains abundant marginal land to absorb more farmers and employment, the use of land relative to labor on this land will determine nominal wages throughout the dual frontier economy. The implication is that, with given international prices for the marketed-oriented activities, the real wage and thus the amount of unskilled labor employed by these activities will be fully determined. The pool of surplus labor on marginal lands is essentially a barometer of frontier-based development. As long as there are abundant marginal lands for cultivation, they serve to absorb rural migrants, population increases, and displaced unskilled labor from elsewhere in the economy. On the other hand, expanding commercial activities that exploit more resources and land on the frontier will absorb more workers from the pool of surplus labor existing on marginal frontier lands.

Since 1950, the estimated population in developing economies on "fragile lands" has doubled (World Bank 2003). These fragile environments are prone to land degradation, and consist of upland areas, forest systems and drylands that suffer from low agricultural productivity, and areas that present significant constraints for intensive agriculture. Today, nearly 1.3 billion people—almost a fifth of the world's population—live in such areas in developing regions (Barbier 2011, Table 9.10). Almost half the people in these fragile environments (631 million) consist of the rural poor, who, throughout the developing world, outnumber the poor living on favored lands by 2 to 1 (Comprehensive Assessment of Water Management in Agriculture 2007, Table 15.1).

The result is that marginal land expansion in frontier areas continues to be the main basis of absorbing numbers of rural poor, whether they are displaced from more favorable lands or simply growing in number (Pichón 1997; Carr 2009; Barbier 2011). This process is described eloquently by Pichón (1997, 707–708) for "marginal farmers" in the Ecuadorian Amazon: "Most forest intervention in the region has come at the hands of colonist farmers attempting to establish land claims along transport routes originally constructed to aid in petroleum exploration and exploitation. These are farmers who formerly have made a living in long-established farmlands and who, for various reasons (population pressures, pervasive poverty, maldistribution of farmland, lack of inputs for intensive cultivation, lack of nonagrarian livelihood opportunities, and generally inadequate rural development) have been increasingly squeezed out of their homelands. A marginal person by virtue of his low socioeconomic and political status, the farmer often perceives no way to sustain his family other than by seeking a livelihood on the marginal environments of tropical rain forests."

Equally, the poor on marginal lands serve as a pool of surplus low-wage labor for commercial activities, including those in frontier regions. For example, in Southeast Asia, agricultural and extractive activities in the lowlands rely on labor from marginal uplands, and thus technological and economic changes in lowland agriculture significantly impacts agricultural expansion and deforestation in the uplands (Coxhead et al. 2002; Maertens et al. 2006; Barney 2009). Oil palm expansion on the Malaysian and Indonesian frontiers has depended on off-farm labor provided by agricultural smallholders and poor migrants (McCarthy and Cramb 2009). If such employment opportunities are sufficiently large and sustained, they can actually reduce long-term marginal land expansion. For example, in Colombia, since 1970 high-input, intensified, highly mechanized cropping on the most suitable land, as well expansion in cattle grazing has drawn labor from more traditional agriculture, so that "areas of marginal land are slowly being abandoned and left to revegetate (Etter et al. 2008, 17).

However, the continuing encouragement of commercial activities to exploit frontier land and natural resources is impacting environmental change, especially deforestation. For example, the main "agents of deforestation" globally are now plantation owners, large scale farmers, ranchers and timber and mining operations, assisted by government policies (FAO 2001, 2003; Chomitz et al. 2007; Rudel 2007; DeFries et al. 2010; Boucher et al. 2011). For example, according to Rudel (2007, 40), "to facilitate their plans for expansion, large landowners lobbied for the construction of improved and expanded networks of roads. Local politicians and bankers joined the landowners to form 'growth coalitions' that lobbied federal and provincial governments for improved infrastructure." These governments were soon "won over by powerful interest groups of landowners whose agendas involved agricultural expansion at the expense of forests."

There are nevertheless important regional differences (FAO 2001). In Africa, much deforestation (around 60%) is due to the conversion of forest for the establishment of small-scale permanent agriculture, whereas direct conversion of forest cover to large-scale agriculture, including raising livestock, predominates in Latin America and Asia (48% and 30%, respectively). As well as directly causing forest degradation and loss, many large-scale resource-extractive activities, such as timber harvesting, mining, ranching, and plantations, initially open up previously inaccessible forested frontier areas to permanent agricultural conversion (Wunder 2003, 2005; Barbier 2005*b*; Wassenaar et al. 2007). Small-scale farmers usually follow because forest and other land are now available and more accessible for conversion (Walker 2003; Verburg et al. 2004).[2]

[2] Wassenaar et al. (2007, 101) note that "Amazonian cropland expansion hot spots in Brazil and Bolivia for example are adjacent to current large soybean production zones, the creation of which,

Dualistic frontier expansion also promotes boom and bust cycles of economic development (Wunder 2003, 2005; Barbier 2005*a*, 2005*b*, 2007 and 2011; Ha and Shively 2008; Agergaard et al. 2009; Barney 2009; Rodrigues et al. 2009; Hall 2011; Knudsen and Folds 2011). State-sponsored promotion of commercial activities often ensures that frontier expansion occurs rapidly and generates growth in marketable outputs. However, this initial "economic boom" is invariably short-lived. Once the frontier is "closed" and the valuable land and natural resources have been fully exploited or converted, some economic retrenchment is inevitable. Under certain conditions, the "bust" may start even before profitable frontier opportunities are exhausted.[3] Such boom and bust cycles associated with rapid frontier expansion are further exacerbated if the commercial activities are isolated enclaves, as any production and profits generated will have limited impacts on economy-wide investment, innovation and growth. The short-term windfall benefits of a commodity price rise will further reinforce this outcome. In addition, during the expansion phase, commercial activities may generate employment opportunities for unskilled labor and off-farm work on the frontier, but with the inevitable bust and contraction, marginal land expansion once again becomes the main outlet for absorbing the rural poor. As cultivation of such lands generates little rents and productivity gains, economic livelihoods and incomes are not improved significantly in the long run.

Such boom and bust patterns of frontier expansion have occurred for cocoa, coffee, oil palm and shrimp in Southeast Asia and Africa (Ha and Shively 2008; Agergaard et al. 2009; Barney 2009; Hall 2011; Knudsen and Folds 2011). Oil price booms have interacted with agricultural expansion and deforestation in a range of tropical countries, but with only short-lived economy-wide gains (Wunder 2003, 2005). Long-run agricultural land expansion and oil and natural gas proved that reserve expansion appear to be associated with boom and bust cycles in a number of low- and middle-income countries (Barbier 2007). Finally, a study of 286 municipalities in the Brazilian Amazon found a consistent boom and bust pattern in levels of human development (Rodrigues et al. 2009). Relative standards of living, literacy, and life expectancy increase initially as forest conversion for cattle ranching, logging, and agriculture proceed. However, these improvements appear to be transitory; development levels decline in the postfrontier municipalities to levels similar to those in prefrontier municipalities. As the authors conclude, "this 'bust' is likely to reflect the exhaustion of the natural resources that supported the initial 'boom', compounded by the increasing human population. Accordingly, per capita timber,

largely driven by increasing animal feed needs, has caused large scale deforestation in the recent past." Walker (2003) describes a similar process linking the road building by loggers in the Brazilian Amazon and the subsequent "infilling" of the landscape by smallholder migrants. Barbier (2005*b*) and Wunder (2003, 2005) provide numerous case studies of the links between mineral, energy, and timber developments across the tropics and initially opening inaccessible frontier areas for subsequent agricultural conversion.

[3] For an economic model of such a boom and bust pattern of economic development in a resource-dependent small open economy, see Barbier (2005*a*, 2005*b*).

cattle and crop production also exhibit boom-and-bust patterns across the deforestation frontier" (Rodrigues et al. 2009, 1436).

A number of important research issues emerge from this review of land use and dualistic frontier economic conditions in developing countries. First, this chapter points to the need for better data on the geographical location of the rural poor. We require more reliable data on the distribution of populations and poor households in least favored and ecologically fragile areas in developing countries and more long-term monitoring of the economic livelihoods of such populations. Second, such evidence would assist greatly in testing two important hypotheses that emerges from this review: first, whether the pool of surplus labor on marginal lands is essentially a barometer of frontier-based development in low- and middle-income economies, and second, whether dualistic frontier expansion leads to boom and bust cycles of economic development. Finally, this chapter has also shown that patterns of land use change in developing countries are fundamental to their overall economic development. Yet, very few studies examine this link more closely. Hopefully, future economics research will take more seriously how land use change may influence sustainable economic development in low- and middle-income economies.

ACKNOWLEDGMENTS

I am grateful for comments by JunJie Wu on an earlier draft of this chapter.

REFERENCES

Agergaard, J., N. Fold, and K. Gough. 2009. Global-local interactions: Socioeconomic and spatial dynamics in Vietnam's coffee frontier. *The Geographical Journal* 175: 133–145.

Akpalu, W., and P. Parks. 2007. Natural resource use conflict: Gold mining in tropical rainforest in Ghana. *Environment and Development Economics* 12: 55–72.

Aldrich, S., R. Walker, E. Arima, and M. Caldas. 2006. Land-cover and land-use change in the Brazlian Amazon: Smallholders, ranchers, and frontier stratification. *Economic Geography* 82: 265–288.

Austin, G. 2007. Resources, techniques, and strategies south of the Sahara: Revising the factor endowments perspective on African economic development, 1500–2000. *Economic History Review* 1–38.

Barbier, E. 2005*a*. Frontier expansion and economic development. *Contemporary Economic Policy* 23(2): 286–303.

Barbier, E. B. 2005*b*. *Natural resources and economic development*. Cambridge, UK: Cambridge University Press.

Barbier, E. B. 2007. Frontiers and sustainable economic development. *Environmental and Resource Economics* 37: 271–295.

Barbier, E. B. 2010. Poverty, development and environment. *Environment and Development Economics* 15: 635–660.

Barbier, E. B. 2011. *Scarcity and frontiers: How economies have developed through natural resource exploitation*. Cambridge, UK: Cambridge University Press.

Barney, K. 2009. Laos and the making of a 'relational' resource frontier. *The Geographical Journal* 175: 146–159.

Barro, R. J., and X. Sala-I. Martin. 2004. *Economic growth*, 2nd ed. Cambridge, MA: MIT Press.

Billington, R. 1966. *America's frontier heritage*. New York: Holt, Rinehart and Winston.

Boucher, D., P. Elias, K. Lininger, C. May-Tobin, S. Roquemore, and E. Saxon. 2011. *The root of the problem: What's driving tropical deforestation today?* Cambridge, MA: Union of Concerned Scientists.

Bridge, G. 2008. Global production networks and the extractive sector: Governing resource-based development. *Journal of Economic Geography* 8: 389–419.

Browder, J., M. Pedlowski, R. Walker, R. Wynne, P. Summers, A. Abad, et al. 2008. Revisiting theories of frontier expansion in the Brazilian Amazon: A survey of colonist farming population in Rondônia's post-frontier, 1992–2002. *World Development* 36: 1469–1492.

Bromley, D. 2008. Resource degradation in the African commons: Accounting for institutional decay. *Environment and Development Economics* 13: 539–563.

Bulte, E., R. Damania, and R. López. 2007. On the gains of committing to inefficiency: Corruption, deforestation and low land productivity in Latin America. *Journal of Environmental Economics and Management* 54: 277–295.

Bunker, S. 1984. Modes of extraction, unequal exchange, and the progressive underdevelopment of an extreme periphery: The Brazilian Amazon, 1600–1980. *American Journal of Sociology* 89: 1017–1064.

Bunker, S. 1989. Staples, links, and poles in the construction of regional development theories. *Sociological Forum* 4: 589–610.

Campbell, B. (ed.) 2009, *Mining in Africa: Regulation and development*. London: Pluto Press.

Carr, D. 2009. Population and deforestation: Why rural migration matters. *Progress in Human Geography* 33: 355–378.

Casetti, E., and H. Guathier. 1977. A formalization and test of the "hollow frontier" hypothesis. *Economic Geography* 53: 70–78.

Caviglia-Harris, J., and D. Harris. 2008. Integrating survey and remote sensing data to analyze land use scale: Insights from agricultural households in the Brazilian Amazon *International Regional Science Review* 31: 115–137.

Chen, S., and M. Ravallion. 2007. Absolute poverty measures for the developing world, 1981–2004. *Proceedings of the National Academy of Sciences of the USA* 104(43): 16757–16762.

Chomitz, K., P. Buys, G. De Luca, T. Thomas, and S. Wertz-Kanounnikoff. 2007. *At loggerheads? agricultural expansion, poverty reduction, and environment in the tropical forests*. Washington, DC: The World Bank.

Comprehensive Assessment of Water Management in Agriculture. 2007. *Water for food, water for life: A comprehensive assessment of water management in agriculture*. London: Earthscan and International Water Management Institute, Colombo, Sri Lanka.

Coxhead, I., G. Shively, G. Shuai, and X. Shuai. 2002. Development policies, resource constraints, and agricultural expansion on the Philippine land frontier. *Environment and Development Economics* 7: 341–363.

Curry, G., and G. Koczberski. 2009. Finding common ground: Relational concepts of land tenure and economy in the oil palm frontier of Papua New Guinea. *Geographical Journal* 175: 98–111.

DeFries, R., T. Rudel, M. Uriarte, and M. Hansen. 2010. Deforestation driven by urban population growth and agricultural trade in the twenty-first century. *Nature Geoscience* 3: 178–801.

Dercon, S., D. O. Gilligan, J. Hoddinott, and T. Woldehanna. 2009. The impact of agricultural extension and roads on poverty and consumption growth in fifteen Ethiopian villages. *American Journal of Agricultural Economics* 91: 1007–1021.

di Tella, G. 1982. The economics of the frontier. In *Economics in the long view* , eds. C. Kindleberger and G. di Tella, 210–227. London: Macmillan.

Etter, A., C. McAlpine, and H. Possingham. 2008. Historical patterns and drivers of landscape change in Colombia since 1500: A regionalized spatial approach. *Annals of the Association of American Geographers* 98: 2–23.

Findlay, R., and M. Lundahl. 1994. Natural resources, "vent-for-surplus," and the staples theory. In *From classical economics to development economics: Essays in honor of Hla Myint*, ed. G. Meier, 68–93. New York: St. Martin's Press.

Fischer, G., and G. K. Heilig. 1997. Population momentum and the demand on land and water resources. *Philosophical Transactions of the Royal Society Series B* 352(1356): 869–889.

FAO. 2001. *Forest resources assessment 2000: Main report*. FAO Forestry Paper 140. Rome: Food and Agricultural Organization.

FAO. 2003. *State of the world's forests 2003*. Rome: Food and Agricultural Organization.

FAO. 2006, *Global forest resources assessment 2005, main report. Progress towards sustainable forest management*. FAO Forestry Paper 147. Rome: Food and Agricultural Organization.

Foweraker, J. 1981. *The struggle for land: A political economy of the pioneer frontier in Brazil from 1930 to the present day*. Cambridge, UK: Cambridge University Press.

Gibbs, H. K., A. S. Ruesch, F. Achard, M. K. Clayton, P. Holmgren, N. Ramankutty, and J. A. Foley. 2010. Tropical forests were the primary sources of new agricultural lands in the 1980s and 1990s. *Proceedings of the National Academy of Sciences of the USA* 107: 16732–16737.

Gould, K., D. Carter, and R. Shrestha. 2006. Extra-legal land market dynamics on a Guatemalan agricultural frontier: Implications for neoliberal policies. *Land Use Policy* 23: 408–420.

Gylfason, T. 2001. Nature, power, and growth. *Scottish Journal of Political Economy* 48: 558–588.

Ha, D., and G. Shively. 2008. Coffee boom, coffee bust and smallholder response in Vietnam's central highlands. *Review of Development Economics* 12: 312–326.

Hall, D. 2011. Land control, land grabs, and Southeast Asian crop booms. *Journal of Peasant Studies* 38: 837–857.

Hansen, B. 1979. Colonial economic development with unlimited supply of land: A Ricardian case. *Economic Development and Cultural Change* 27(4): 611–627.

Hecht, S. 2005. Soybeans, development and conservation on the Amazon frontier. *Development and Change* 36: 375–404.

Hirsch, P. 2009. Revisiting frontiers as transitional spaces in Thailand. *Geographical Journal* 175: 124–132.

Hyndman, D. 1994. A sacred mountain of gold: The creation of a mining resource frontier in Papua New Guinea. *Journal of Pacific History* 29: 203–221.
James, P. 1969. *Latin America*, 4th ed. New York: Odyssey Press.
Jepson, W. 2006. Producing a modern agricultural frontier: Firms and cooperatives in eastern Mato Grasso, Brazil. *Economic Geography* 82: 289–316.
Killeen, T., V. Calderon, L. Soria, B. Quezada, M. Steininger, G. Harper, et al. 2007. Thirty years of land-cover change in Bolivia. *Ambio* 36: 600–606.
Knudsen, M., and N. Folds. 2011. Land distribution and acquisition practices in Ghana's cocoa frontier: The impact of a state-regulated marketing system. *Land Use Policy* 28: 378–387.
Maertens, M., M. Zeller, and R. Birner. 2006. Sustainable agricultural intensification in forest frontier areas. *Agricultural Economics* 34: 197–206.
McCarthy, J., and R. Cramb. 2009. Policy narratives, landholder engagement, and oil palm expansion on the Malaysian and Indonesia frontiers. *Geographical Journal* 175: 112–123.
Morton, D. C., R. S. DeFries, Y. E. Shimabukuro, L. O. Anderson, E. Arai, F. del Bon Espirito-Santo, et al. 2006. Cropland expansion changes deforestation dynamics in the southern Brazilian Amazon. *Proceedings of the National Academy of Sciences of the USA* 103: 14637–14641.
Mosley, W. 2005. Global cotton and local environmental management: The political ecology of rich and poor small-holder farmers in southern Mali. *Geographical Journal* 171: 36–55.
Mueller, B. 1997. Property rights and the evolution of the frontier. *Land Economics* 73: 42–57.
Pichón, F. 1997. Colonist land-allocation decisions, land use, and deforestation in the Ecuadorian frontier. *Economic Development and Cultural Change* 45: 707–744.
Population Division of the United Nations Secretariat. 2008. *World urbanization prospects: The 2007 revision: Executive summary.* New York: United Nations.
Ramankutty, N., and J. A. Foley. 1999. Estimating historical changes in global land cover: Croplands from 1700 to 1992. *Global Biogeochemical Cycles* 13: 997–1027.
Rodrigues, A., R. Ewers, L. Parry, C. Souza, A. Verissimo, and A. Balmford. 2009. Boom-and-bust development patterns across the Amazonian deforestation frontier. *Science* 324: 1435–1437.
Rudel, T. 2007. Changing agents of deforestation: From state-initiated to enterprise driven process, 1970–2000. *Land Use Policy* 24: 35–41.
Schmook, B., and C. Vance. 2009, Agricultural policy, market barriers, and deforestation: The case of Mexico's southern Yucatán. *World Development* 37: 1015–1025.
Sills, E., and J. Caviglia-Harris. 2008. Evolution of the Amazonian frontier: Land values in Rondônia, Brazil. *Land Use Policy* 26: 55–67.
van der Ploeg, R. 2011. Natural resources: Curse or blessing? *Journal of Economic Literature* 49: 366–420.
Verburg, P., K. Overmers, and N. Witte. 2004. Accessibility and land-use patterns at the forest fringe in the northeastern part of the Philippines. *Geographical Journal,* 170: 238–255.
Walker, R. 2003. Mapping process to pattern in the landscape change of the Amazonian frontier. *Annals of the Association of American Geographers* 93: 376–398.
Walker, R., J. Browder, E. Arima, C. Simmons, R. Pereira, M. Caldas, et al. 2009. Ranching and the new global range: Amazônia in the 21st century. *Geoforum* 40: 732–745.
Wassenaar, T., P. Gerber, P. H. Verburg, M. Rosales, M. Ibrahim, and H. Steinfeld. 2007. Projecting land use changes in the neotropics: The geography of pasture expansion into forest. *Global Environmental Change* 17: 86–104.
Williamson, J. 2002. Land, labor and globalization in the Third World, 1870–1914. *Journal of Economic History* 62: 55–85.

Williamson, J. 2006. *Globalization and the poor periphery before 1950.* Cambridge, MA: MIT Press.

Wood, C. H. 1983. Peasant and capitalist production in the Brazilian Amazon: A conceptual framework for the study of frontier expansion. In *The dilemma of Amazonian development,* ed. E. F. Moran, 259–277. Boulder, CO: Westview Press.

World Bank. 2003. *World development report 2003.* Washington, DC: The World Bank.

World Bank. 2008. *Word development indicators 2008.* Washington, DC: The World Bank.

Wunder, S. 2003. *Oil wealth and the fate of the forest: A comparative study of eight tropical countries.* London: Routledge.

Wunder, S. 2005. Macroeconomic change, competitiveness and timber production: A five-country comparison. *World Development* 33: 65–86.

PART II

ENVIRONMENTAL AND SOCIOECONOMIC CONSEQUENCES OF LAND USE AND LAND USE CHANGE

CHAPTER 7

THE ECONOMICS OF WILDLIFE CONSERVATION

DAVID J. LEWIS AND ERIK NELSON

Wildlife populations have been adversely impacted by a multitude of human activities, although most ecologists argue that the clearing of forests and grasslands for urban areas and agriculture has had the greatest impact (Sala et al. 2000; Wilcove et al. 2000; Millennium Ecosystem Assessment [MEA] 2005). The economic argument for conserving wildlife is largely a public goods argument. A private landowner lacks the incentive to provide adequate habitat for wildlife species because much of the use value (hunting, bird-watching, ecosystem service regulation, etc.) and nonuse value (existence of species) produced on the landowner-provided habitat will accrue to other people. Therefore, government policies or nongovernmental organization (NGO) programs that encourage the conservation of wildlife habitat may improve the efficiency of land use patterns on landscapes.

This chapter covers several economic issues pertinent to wildlife conservation efforts. Wildlife conservation activities include climate change mitigation, limits on freshwater withdrawals from watersheds, and efforts to reduce the spread of invasive species. However, the dominant wildlife conservation activity undertaken globally is the setting aside of land to provide wildlife habitat. Here, we focus on unresolved economic issues related to the three primary means of establishing habitat set-asides: government regulation, direct appropriation or purchase of habitat by governments or NGOs, and payments to landowners for voluntarily altering land use activities to be more wildlife friendly. Rather than provide a comprehensive literature review, our approach is to provide an in-depth discussion of representative economic research related to these three habitat conservation approaches. The research we review is selected to highlight what we believe are some of the outstanding economic issues in wildlife conservation that deserve future research attention. Our main arguments are illustrated with several simple extensions to prior studies.

Government regulation is one approach to conserving habitat and is typified by the US Endangered Species Act (ESA). Under the ESA, a species determined to be at risk of extinction is listed and afforded regulatory protection. For example, the ESA generally gives the US government the authority to regulate timber harvesting if it is expected that unmitigated harvest activity would threaten the persistence or habitat of a listed species. We provide a simple extension to previous theoretical models to show that regulatory designs similar to the ESA can drive a wedge between privately and socially preferred behavior. Furthermore, it can create cases in which society in general prefers harming wildlife populations. Effective regulatory design must address the tensions that approaches like the ESA can create between societal wildlife goals and individual preferences. To that end, the ESA must integrate rigorous ex post evaluations of conservation outcomes, and regulators must be willing to act on uncovered shortcomings.[1]

The direct purchase of habitat by governments and conservation organizations is an alternative to government regulation of wildlife populations. The purchase of habitat for set-asides can take several forms. For example, Norway has bought and retired Peruvian government debt in exchange for the establishment of a reserve area in Peru (Hansen 1999). In fiscal year 2010, The Nature Conservancy spent $204 million on the purchases of conservation land and easements across the globe (The Nature Conservancy [TNC] 2010). At the heart of direct purchase programs is the problem of selecting which land to purchase when conservation funds are scarce and not all desirable habitat can be protected. The literature devoted to finding the best use of funds for some biological objective has been termed "reserve-site selection (RSS)" or "systematic conservation planning (SCP)" and has been developed by both economists and conservation biologists. Recent efforts to more accurately measure the biological benefit created by reserve networks have been dubbed return-on-investment (ROI) for conservation. We develop a new US-wide reserve selection model and use it to argue that existing reserve selection approaches must (1) properly specify the conservation benefits from a reserve system and (2) incorporate realistic expectations of landscape dynamics outside of the selected network.

The final approach to setting aside habitat is to offer voluntary payments to landowners to alter their land use practices. This approach is typified by Costa Rica's 1996 national forest law and the US Wildlife Habitat Incentives Program, both of which pay landowners directly for improved habitat provision. Two dynamics make efficient design of voluntary payment programs difficult: landowners' willingness to accept (WTA) payments is private information, and habitat benefits are spatially dependent, meaning benefits are a function of the spatial pattern of conservation across large landscapes of multiple landowners. The configuration of conservation across a landscape is difficult for agencies to control when WTA information is private because it is unclear *ex ante* which landowners will accept payments. Furthermore, when benefits of habitat conservation are spatially dependent, it is difficult for agencies to identify *ex ante* the benefits that

[1] Here we ignore another major type of government regulation associated with wildlife conservation, the direct appropriation of land. For example, in 1982 the Uganda government evicted approximately 4,500 families from land that became Lake Mburo National Park (Emerton 1999).

will result from a particular payment program. As such, we develop a simple example to argue that efficient conservation of wildlife with incentives must overcome the problem of eliciting private information on landowners' WTA. New empirical evidence from the state of Oregon is used to illuminate the importance of WTA information and to illustrate the large efficiency gains from solving this information problem.

1. Command-and-Control Approach and the US Endangered Species Act

The original version of the ESA, passed in 1973, prohibited an individual, corporation, or government agency from killing or destroying the habitat of a species listed under the Act (a "taking").[2] According to the law's original language, the imperative of saving endangered public goods trumped the private economic interests of landowners (McAnaney 2006). Therefore, just like the original versions of the US Clean Air and Clean Water Acts, the initial version of the ESA was a command-and-control policy with little regulatory flexibility and no compensation for landowner economic losses due to regulatory actions. Since 1978, however, the ESA has been amended several times and has become a more flexible or permissive policy than its original incarnation, especially when dealing with habitat on private land (Scott et al. 2006).

The ESA's private land policies are vital to the success and cost of the Act because data suggests that more than half of all listed species have at least 80% of their habitat on private property (Innes and Frisvold 2009). One example of this increased regulatory flexibility is the availability of permits that allow landowners or developers to destroy listed species or its habitat as long as the applicant can convince the permitting wildlife agency that the "take" will not appreciably reduce the species' likelihood of recovery. In many cases, incidental take permits are only granted if the applicant agrees to install conservation measures somewhere on their land or contribute to a general conservation fund (Thompson 2006). Landowner activities necessary to acquire an incidental take permit are laid out in a Habitat Conservation Plan (HCP).

In Section 1.1, we extend Polasky and Doremus's (1998) model of landowner-wildlife agency relationships to consider incidental take permits and HCPs and we argue that command-and-control regulation for wildlife conservation can create situations in which both individuals and society prefer harming wildlife populations. In Section 1.2, we review evidence of the effectiveness of the ESA and argue that it is reasonable for society to expect robust and recovering wildlife populations to result from

[2] An area is defined as habitat for a species if the species has been observed feeding or breeding on that land in the immediate past (Lueck and Michael 2003).

command-and-control regulation, given the well-documented welfare losses associated with such policy approaches. Unfortunately, evidence of the efficacy of the ESA is mixed.

1.1 Landowner–Wildlife Agency Relationships Under the ESA

Polasky and Doremus (1998) model the interplay between a landowner who is contemplating developing her land and an endangered species regulating agency, in which the agency is uncertain whether the landowner's plot contains listed species or their habitats. Although Polasky and Doremus consider several potential relationships between the landowner and agency, including payments for conservation, here we mention the two cases that most resemble the relationship under the current version of the ESA. In one case, the agency forces a landowner to set aside his or her land for conservation if the agency can prove that the value to society of this action, given by S, is greater than the private economic value that will accrue to the landowner after development, given by D (land development costs are netted out of D). Assume S falls to 0 if the land is developed (we will relax this assumption in a modification of the Polasky and Doremus model below) and U indicates private returns from conservation (if any) where $D > U$. In this case, the burden of determining S lies with the regulating agency. Assuming S can only be calculated by inspection of the land and that private property holders have the right to prevent any inspections, the landowner has no incentive to allow agency representatives on his land. This blanket refusal of inspection, although always privately optimal given that $D > U$, may be inefficient from society's perspective. Before development, a survey would be warranted from society's perspective if the expected net social benefit generated by paying for information on S exceeds the social benefits generated without the information,

$$(1-p)(S+U)+pD-C>D \Rightarrow \tag{1}$$

$$(1-p)(S+U-D)>C, \tag{2}$$

where $1-p$ is the probability that the survey will find $S \geq D$ and C indicates the cost of the survey.

Under another relevant landowner-agency relationship framework explored by Polasky and Doremus, the landowner must prove $D > S$ before he or she can develop, or otherwise pay a development fine F where $F > D$. First, the landowner will never develop without a survey, otherwise private net returns will be negative ($D–F < 0$). Therefore, a utility-maximizing landowner will commission a survey before development if the expected net private benefit of doing so outweighs the private benefit of not doing so,

$$pD+(1-p)U-C>U \Rightarrow \tag{3}$$

$$p(D-U)>C, \tag{4}$$

where p is the probability that the survey will find $D > S$. However, from society's perspective, a survey is only welfare enhancing if it is expected to reveal that D is significantly larger than S,

$$pD+(1-p)(S+U)-C>S+U \Rightarrow \tag{5}$$

$$p(D-S-U)>C. \tag{6}$$

According to inequalities (4) and (6), the landowner is more likely to find it in his best interest to survey than society would.[3] In both of these cases, a wedge exists between private and socially preferred behavior.

1.1.1 Landowner-Wildlife Agency Relationships with a Habitat Conservation Plan (HCP)

The current version of the ESA differs from the species conservation policies considered by Polasky and Doremus in several ways (also see Innes and Frisvold [2009] for a revision of the Polasky and Doremus model). First, a finding of a listed species or its habitat on a parcel does not mean it cannot be developed; instead, it may only mean a restriction on certain development activities in the parcel. Second, regulators are supposed to limit habitat destruction on a parcel no matter the expected social value of the conservation behavior. Finally, a landowner can choose to limit some species harm and/or habitat damage when developing in exchange for an incidental take permit.

We modify the Polasky and Doremus model to reflect the current agency-landowner relationship. We assume a landowner knows that her land contains listed species or its habitat but the agency does not necessarily know this. She can choose to fully develop the land and risk regulatory penalties, take the steps necessary to gain an incidental take permit, or not develop. *Ex ante* the private economic value generated by a developed parcel with an incidental take permit is uncertain because the landowner does not know what the regulating agency will require in exchange for a permit. An incidental take permit will require the landowner to institute some conservation action or implement a land use that results in less value than unfettered development. In addition, the landowner will incur some HCP negotiation and implementation costs. Let 0 to N indicate the range of private economic value generated on the parcel with a permit, less private permit transaction costs, where $N < D$. Let n indicate the expected private value of the developed parcel with an incidental take permit. Further, let t and w indicate the expected public and

[3] Specifically, D has to be $C/p + U$ units greater than S for private and social incentives to align.

private conservation value, respectively, generated by an HCP on the parcel. Because an HCP allows for some development the conservation or nonmarket value of a parcel with an HCP is not as great as the nonmarket values on an undeveloped parcel: $t < S$ and $w < U$.

By seeking an incidental take permit the landowner signals to the regulator that she has a listed species or habitat on her land. Even if the landowner does not signal the presence of a listed species or its habitat, development action by a landowner could trigger regulatory scrutiny and a judgment of a taking. Let p_S indicate the probability that the agency will become aware that a listed species does use or has used the parcel or the parcel does contain or did contain a listed species' habitat during parcel development. In this initial setup, we will assume that p_S is known to the parcel owner and it cannot be affected by parcel owner behavior. In other words, p_S will be determined by habitat distribution across space and the regulating agency's competence, budget, and other factors.[4] Again, let D indicate the private economic value of parcel development, where any land development costs are netted out.

If the parcel owner develops and the agency becomes aware of a taking, then fine F is levied and we assume the agency will enforce a redevelopment plan similar to the one that would have been generated under an incidental take permit negotiation process. Therefore, the profit-maximizing landowner chooses his development path according to the following,

$$\max\{(1-p_S)D + p_S(n+w-F), n+w, U\}. \tag{7}$$

where the first term is the expected net private economic value associated with not approaching the agency to cooperate on an HCP, [5] the second term is the expected net private economic value of approaching the agency to cooperate on an HCP, and the third term is the nonmarket return to the landowner from not developing her land (we assume the private economic value of undeveloped land is 0). The utility-maximizing landowner will approach the agency to cooperate on the design of an HCP if,

$$n \geq D - w - \left(\frac{p_S}{1-p_S}\right)F \tag{8}$$

and

$$n \geq U - w. \tag{9}$$

[4] There is some question as to how aggressively the ESA actually enforces takings on private land. In reality, p_S may essentially be 0 for many private landowners.

[5] We assume that w can be reached on a piece of land that was developed but then was forced to institute some conservation due to the discovery of a taking. In reality, the private nonmarket benefit on a parcel that was caught in a taking may not be reasonably restored to a nonmarket benefit level associated with the use of an HCP from the beginning.

In words, equation (8) indicates the landowner will only come forward to develop an HCP in conjunction with the agency if p_S and F are large enough to bridge the gap between D (the value of unfettered development) and n (the value of development with an HCP). Monetary compensation for cooperating landowners would enter inequality (8) on the left-hand side, making cooperation on an HCP more likely. For simplicity, we assume from here on out that n is always larger than $U{-}w$, or the expected value of development with an HCP is greater than the incremental private nonmarket value from no development versus development with an HCP.

Conversely, landowner initiative on an HCP is socially efficient only if the social returns of this decision are greater than expected social benefits of unfettered development,

$$n+t+w-C \geq (1-p_S)D+p_S(n+t+w-C) \Rightarrow, \tag{10}$$

$$n \geq D-t-w+C, \tag{11}$$

and the social benefits of nondevelopment,

$$n+t+w-C \geq S+U \Rightarrow, \tag{12}$$

$$n \geq S+U-t-w+C, \tag{13}$$

where C is the regulatory agency's HCP finding, planning, and implementation costs.[6] For simplicity, we assume from here on out that n is always larger than the incremental benefit of not developing at all, plus the regulatory agency's HCP planning and implementation costs (i.e., $n > S + U - t - w + C$). Therefore, social and landowner incentives on landowner initiated

HCPs are aligned when $t-C=\left(\frac{p_S}{1-p_S}\right)F$. Otherwise, if $t-C>(<)\left(\frac{p_S}{1-p_S}\right)F$, then society is more likely (less likely) to prefer landowner initiative on HCPs than the private landowner.

[6] Development fine F is not a social cost, just a redistribution of funds. We assume that t can be reached on a piece of land that was developed but then was forced to institute some conservation due to the discovery of a taking. In reality, the public nonmarket value created by a parcel that was caught in a taking may not be reasonably restored to a nonmarket value level associated with the use of an HCP from the beginning.

1.1.2 The "Shoot, Shovel, and Shut Up" Incentive

As Polasky (2001), Lueck and Michael (2003), and others have pointed out, the probability of the regulatory agency detecting a taking can be lower than p_S for several reasons. For example, the parcel owner can attempt to prevent the wildlife agency from gleaning information about his land prior to development by blocking access, or he can destroy or alter potential habitat on his land ("shoot, shovel, and shut up") prior to regulatory attention. Specifically, let $\overline{p}_S$ be the landowner-influenced probability that the wildlife agency will become aware of listed species or its habitat on the parcel in the process of development, and $c(p_s, \overline{p}_s)$ indicates the landowner's cost of obtaining $\overline{p}_s$ where $\overline{p}_s \leq p_s, c(p_s, \overline{p}_s) = 0$ if $\overline{p}_s = p_s$, and $c(p_s, \overline{p}_s)$ increases as the landowner reduces $\overline{p}_s$. Let $\overline{p}_s^*$ indicate the $\overline{p}_s$ that maximizes the expected value of full development on the plot. Now the landowner's problem is the same as (7) except the first term in (7) is subtracted by $c(p_s, \overline{p}_s)$ and the landowner determines the optimal "shoot, shovel up, and shot up" behavior before solving the maximization function. The landowner will approach the agency to design an HCP if,

$$n \geq D - w + \left(\frac{\overline{p}_S^*}{1 - \overline{p}_S^*} \right) F - \frac{c(p_S, \overline{p}_S^*)}{1 - \overline{p}_S^*}. \tag{14}$$

Because of lower odds of a takings discovery, the fine F that may have been large enough to convince the landowner to seek an HCP with exogenous p_s (inequality [8]) may not be high enough to engender the same reaction with endogenous $\overline{p}_s^*$; it will depend on the size of $\frac{c(p_S, \overline{p}_S^*)}{1 - \overline{p}_S^*}$. Again, the inclusion of landowner compensation in an HCP would make conservation cooperation much more likely because the left-hand side of inequality (14) would be larger.

Finally, we can show that, under certain conditions, privately optimal "shoot, shovel, and shut up" behavior under the ESA, given by $\overline{p}_s^*$, can generate higher net social benefits than when the landowner does not influence p_S. *Ex ante* society will prefer "shoot, shovel up, and shut up" behavior on the part of the landowner if it is expected to generate more in net social benefits than not engaging in it,

$$(1 - \overline{p}_S^*)D + \overline{p}_S^*(n + t + w - C) - c(p_S, \overline{p}_S^*) \geq \mathbf{L} \times \begin{bmatrix} (1 - p_S)D + p_S(n + t + w - C) \\ n + t + w - C \\ S + U \end{bmatrix} \tag{15}$$

where L is a 1 x 3 vector that has a value of 1 in the first element if the solution to problem (7) is development, has a value of 1 in the second element if the solution to problem (7) is an HCP, or has a value of 1 in the third element if the solution to problem (7) is no development. Further, the two elements that are not equal to 1 are equal to 0. If,

$$(1 - \overline{p}_S^*)D + \overline{p}_S^*(n + t + w - C) - U - S \geq c(p_S, \overline{p}_S^*), \tag{16}$$

then inequality (15) holds for all permutations of vector L and "shoot, shovel up, and shut up" behavior unconditionally generates higher net social benefits than having the landowner not influence P_S.[7] In other words, the lower that $\bar{p}_S^*$ can be driven at a reasonable cost, and the higher that the unfettered development value is compared to the social returns from an HCP, the more likely it is that optimal "shoot, shovel, and shut up" behavior is preferred by both the landowner and society in general.

To summarize, there are two main points from this section. First, under the current version of the ESA, the regulating agency can encourage conservation cooperation by levying high fines for a taking by the landowner (or compensating landowners for lost private economic value). However, there is a point at which the fine becomes too large from society's point of view because it encourages the development of an HCP that generates less in expected net social benefit than an uncooperative landowner. Second, because the social benefits of an HCP can be small compared to the value of development, net social benefits can be higher when the landowner reduces the odds of finding an HCP optimal or being punished for avoiding one ("shoot, shovel, and shut up"). The fact that net social benefits can be higher with such perverse landowner behavior than without it highlights the misalignment of private, social, and regulatory incentives under the current version of the ESA.

1.2 How Effective Is the ESA?

Despite these incentive compatibility issues on private land, whether the Act as currently constituted is, as a whole, creating more societal benefit than social cost is an open question and can only be determined by adding up all the market and nonmarket values created by the regulation and comparing these to the sum of the opportunity costs generated by the Act's restrictions (Rachlinski 1997). However, this monumental cost-benefit analysis (CBA) has not yet been undertaken by researchers. Given the difficulty in accurately monetizing nonmarket benefits, a CBA of the entire ESA may be impossible. An alternative measure of regulatory success is given by progress on regulatory goals. And, in cases where cost of achieving these goals can be monitized, cost-effective goal achievement would mean meeting goals at least cost (Shogren et al. 1999; Naidoo et al. 2006).

The goal of ESA regulators is to list species that might go extinct without intervention and then take actions such that these species can eventually be taken off the list due to sufficiently reduced extinction probabilities. Up to now, the ESA has failed miserably

[7] There are other contingent cases in which it is socially preferable for the landowner to engage in "shoot, shovel up, and shut up" behavior. Inequality Equation (15) also always holds if unfettered development or an HCP solves problem (7) and $(1-\bar{p}_S^*)(D+C-n-t-w) > c(p_S, \bar{p}_S^*)$. Inequality (15) also holds if an HCP solves problem (7)and $(p_S-\bar{p}_S^*)(D+C-n-t-w) > c(p_S, \bar{p}_S^*)$. Contact author Nelson at enelson2@bowdoin.edu or http://www.bowdoin.edu/faculty/e/enelson/ for a more detailed proof.

on this goal. As of June 2012, 2,000 animals and plant species[8] were listed as endangered or threatened (607 of these species inhabit ranges completely outside of US territories). Since 1973, only 21 species have been delisted due to recovery (US Fish and Wildlife Service [FWS] 2009).

Of course, the lack of recovered species does not mean that the Act has not had beneficial effect. Some have argued that many more listed species would have gone extinct without regulatory coverage (e.g., Schwartz 1999). It could also be that recovery sufficient for a delisting takes several generations of regulatory attention. If so, short-term progress toward delisting could be measured by change in the status of species over time, a metric tracked by the US Fish and Wildlife Service (FWS) (Rachlinski 1997; Male and Bean 2005; Kerkvliet and Langpap 2007). If we assign a 1 to species whose population is in decline, a 2 to species whose population is stable, and a 3 to species whose population is improving or recovered, then the average status score across 255 listed vertebrates was 1.71 in 1990, 1.74 in 1994, 1.75 in 1998, and 1.68 in 2002 (Kerkvliet and Langpap 2007). This trend seems to suggest that ESA protection has done little to improve the overall status of these 255 species.

Other than some landowners having incentive to reduce the persistence probabilities of listed species (see argument in Section 1.1), scarce progress on delisting could also be explained by too little spending on listed species' recovery activities (Miller et al. 2002). There is evidence that increased spending on listed species' recovery activities does promote progress toward delisting. For example, Kerkvliet and Langpap (2007) find that increased spending on a species is correlated with a lower likelihood that the FWS will classify that species' status as extinct or declining. However, the direction of causality is unclear: does increased spending lower the risk of extinction, or is more money being directed to species that are less likely to go extinct? Taylor et al. (2005) argue that increased recovery spending is likely to promote delisting because the activities that they found most explain species' progress towards delisting—published recovery plans, designated critical habitat, length of time listed, and the like—are positively correlated with more recovery spending, all else equal. Further, Ferraro et al. (2007) find that, on average, the conservation status of listed species with substantial recovery funding has improved over time compared to the contemporaneous conservation status of species with similar characteristics that are only candidates for listing and therefore are not subject to ESA protections and recovery funding. Provocatively, Ferraro et al. also find that the average conservation status of listed species with little or no recovery funding has deteriorated overall compared to the average status of similar candidate species. Why unfunded regulatory protection could lead to worse outcomes than no protection at all is still a matter of conjecture. Some argue that this trend can in part be explained by the incentives that private landowners have to engage in "shoot, shovel, and shut up" behavior (Ruhl 1998).

[8] Some listed species are actually subspecies, whereas others are distinct populations of species (e.g., gray wolf populations in the northern Rockies versus Great Lakes). Here, we refer to all listed entities as "species."

If it is true that "shoot, shovel, and shut up" behavior mainly impacts lightly funded species then then this would suggest that better funded species are more closely monitored and tracked on private land and this deters landowners from destroying the habitat of the better funded species.

Presuming ESA funding will never be great enough to implement all or even most recommended listed species' recovery activities, an endangered species-regulating agency has two reasonable constrained maximization objectives to choose from. One approach would be to spend recovery funds to maximize the number of species that are delisted (Mann and Plummer 1995). In this case, recovery funds would be directed toward species that could conceivably recover enough for delisting with limited funding. This choice likely would leave little money for other listed species and, therefore, could lead to an increased listed species extinction rate. An alternative approach would be to distribute recovery funds such that the sum of increase in persistence probabilities across all listed species is maximized. For many researchers, this is the definition of cost-effective biological conservation (e.g., Possingham et al. 2002; Polasky et al. 2008). Although this approach may not lead to many delistings, it should limit the number of extinctions. Figure 7.1 illustrates both approaches.

Is there any evidence to suggest that either of these two constrained maximization objectives have been adopted by the FWS and other ESA regulatory agencies? Recovery funding is unequally distributed across listed species (see Figure 7.2), so there does appear to be some pattern to funding. Cash (2001) does find that species that are considered by scientists more likely to recover have received more in recovery funding, all else equal. If we assume that these types of species are like species A in Figure 7.1—recovery curves that increase rapidly and meet the delisting criteria with limited funding—then this observed funding pattern supports an effort to prioritize delisting of a few species. However, at the same time, Cash (2001) also finds that species whose recovery is more likely to cause conflict with economic development goals have received more in funding, all else equal. Such a funding pattern is at odds with the basic tenants of cost-effective goal achievement. Metrick and Weitzman (1998) suggest that there is a strong preference among regulatory agencies for funding the recovery of charismatic species above and beyond what is warranted by recovery science. Such a funding pattern is consistent with the political economy story that regulators attempt to curry emotional support for the Act from the US public rather than demonstrate efficiency. In addition, the allocation of up to 75% in recovery funds has been dictated by line items in appropriations legislation from Congress (Miller et al. 2002), and listed species' funding has been shown to depend on whether their geographic range falls within political districts represented by Congressional representatives on the Department of Interior Subcommittees (Cash 2001; DeShazo and Freeman 2003, 2006).

1.3 Discussion

Forty years after its passage, opinion on the effectiveness and the net returns created by the ESA vary greatly. In 2003, then Assistant Secretary of the US Department of the

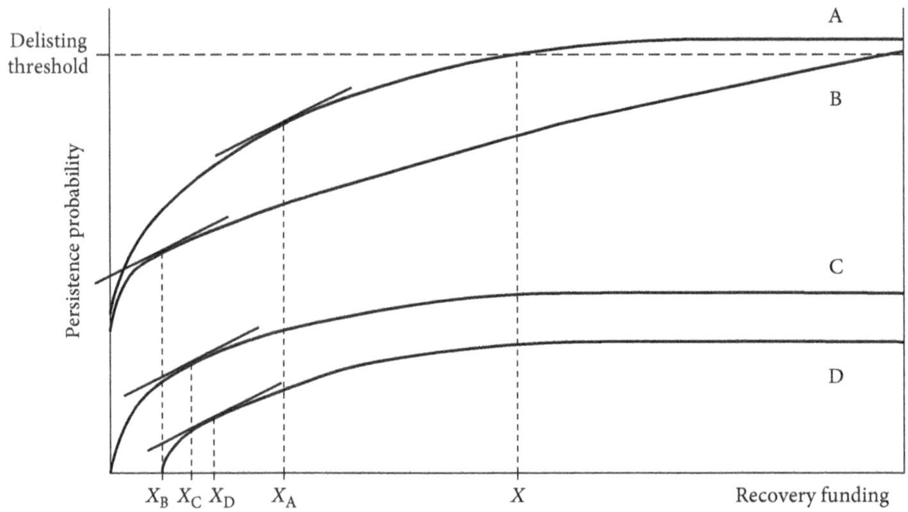

FIGURE 7.1 Potential recovery funding distribution strategies across listed species. Assume there are four listed species, named A, B, C, and D. Each curve represents how a species responds to recovery funding where the height of the curve indicates the species' indefinite persistence probability. In this case, the marginal persistence value of recovery funding is diminishing across the entire range of funding. (In some conservation contexts, the persistence probability curves may initially increase in recovery funding and, after some threshold, begin to decrease in recovery funding; see Lamberson et al. 1992 and Wu et al. 2000.) When persistence probability becomes high enough, a species is delisted. In this case, even with an unlimited budget, the agency could only fund the delisting of two species, A and B. Here, assume the wildlife agency only has X dollars to spend on listed species recovery activities. Suppose X, if entirely spent on species A's recovery, would be just enough to fund its delisting. If the agency's objective is to maximize the number of species delisted, it will provide X in recovery spending for species A. If the agency's objective is to fund as much of an increase in aggregate persistence probability as possible, it will give to species such that the marginal persistence value for each species is the same and the budget is exhausted. In this illustrative example, this occurs at the funding levels x_A, x_B, x_C, and x_D, where $x_A + x_B + x_C + x_D = X$.

Interior Craig Manson "said the 30-year-old environmental law is 'broken' and should no longer be used to give endangered plants and animals priority over human needs."[9] Manson argues that the Act does not give regulators enough flexibility to balance economic and environmental tradeoffs. In addition, the listing process has been embroiled in lawsuits over the past decade. Environmental groups that have brought the lawsuits argue that the US government is not fulfilling its regulatory obligation to list all

[9] Julie Cart, "Species protection act 'broken': A top interior officer says the law should be revised to give economic and other interests equal footing with endangered animals and plants," *L.A. Times*, November 14, 2003.

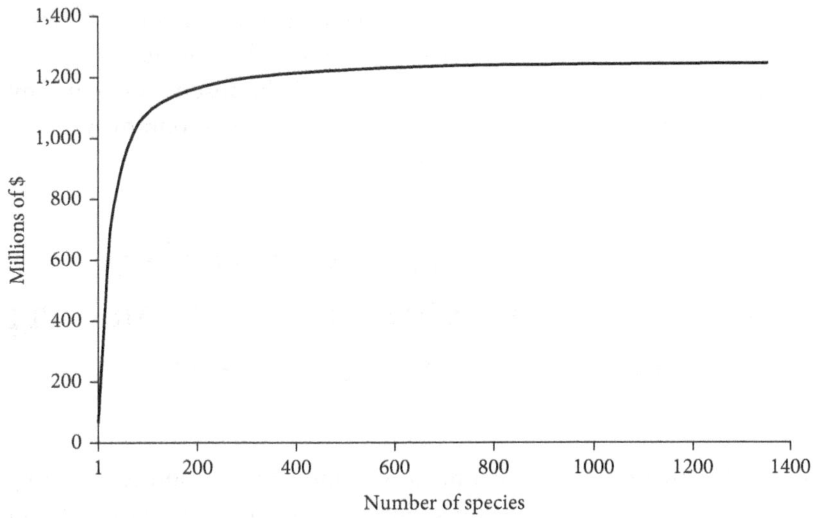

FIGURE 7.2 Cumulative recovery funding by US federal and state agencies across listed species in fiscal year 2009 (not including land acquisition costs). Listed species are arraigned on the x-axis in order of recovery funding. The top 10 and 50 listed species in terms of fiscal year 2009 recovery funding received 34% and 85%, respectively, of all spending that year (US FWS 2009).

endangered species. Recently, the US government has, in response to environmental group pressure, agreed to decide whether listing is appropriate for 757 additional species by 2018 (pending approval by a federal judge).[10] Advocates of the Act, such as the Center for Biological Diversity, argue that the Act is essential and deserves strengthening.

Recent estimates indicate that US urban area will increase by 33 million hectares from 2001 to 2052 (Radeloff et al. 2012). Climate models predict accelerated climate change in the lower 48 states, which has the potential to drastically alter habitat and species geographic ranges on a large scale (Lawler et al. 2009). Whether the ESA—and similar command-and-control regulatory approaches to species protection—can be effective in a rapidly developing and evolving landscape is questionable. To work, the ESA will need to provide landowners with a stronger incentive to conserve habitat than what is currently in place. We show that a landowner compensation system (or strongly enforced fine system) is one approach to providing this incentive under the ESA's current incidental take system. However, the more incentive that landowners are given to cooperate with authorities on listed species conservation, the more likely that net benefits to society will decrease if the decision to regulate private land activities is not a function of the opportunity cost of conservation. Our second argument is that any wildlife conservation program like the ESA must be subject to some type of ex post evaluation and adjustment

10 Matthew Brown, "Deal struck to protect imperiled plants, animals," July 12, 2011, Associated Press.

to compensate for some of the efficiency losses generated by a command-and-control policy. Such a process, however, requires researchers to develop appropriate counterfactual scenarios regarding how a species would fare in the absence of being covered in a conservation program. The recent econometric literature on program evaluation (e.g., Ferraro et al. 2007) has potential in this regard.

2. Purchasing Habitat for Conservation with Complete Information: Reserve-Site Selection

An alternative to government regulation of wildlife conservation is the purchase of existing habitat from private landowners. For a government or conservation organization involved in buying habitat, a basic question is which land should be purchased when conservation funds and/or available land is scarce. In this section, we present the basic reserve site selection (RSS) problem and highlight two largely unresolved issues of economic importance: (1) specifying a quantitative environmental benefit function and (2) how to incorporate baseline outcomes in the absence of reserve siting. We highlight these issues with a ROI approach using conservation siting across the United States.

Whereas species form the set of the decision units under the ESA, selecting a set of undeveloped sites for habitat protection is the focus of RSS problems (RSS is often referred to as *systematic conservation planning* in the conservation biology literature; see Margules and Pressey 2000). In the rudimentary RSS problem, the social planner selects a set of undeveloped sites to purchase such that the network of selected sites will provide additional habitat for as many species as possible, given an area or habitat protection cost constraint (Ando et al. 1998).

$$\max_{s_j} \sum_i \sum_j s_j x_{ij} \tag{17}$$

Subject to

$$\sum_j c_j s_j \leq B \tag{18}$$

$$s_j \in \{0, 1\} \tag{19}$$

where s_j equals 1 if site j is selected for habitat protection and equals 0 otherwise, j indexes all sites on the landscape, x_{ij} equals 1 if species i is known to use site j for breeding or feeding activities, c_j is the area of site j or cost of purchasing and maintaining or establishing habitat on site j, and B is the social planner's areal or monetary budget. If site j that contains species x is selected, then the species is considered "covered" or represented by the selected reserve network, and the objective function value increases by one. Solutions to (17)–(19) typically include sites that are strongly complementary with one another in terms of species composition, not necessarily the sites that contain the most species (e.g., two neighboring sites that contain many species may contain the same species, making the selection of only one of the sites optimal). Because solving binary integer problems over a large choice set can be computationally difficult, heuristic methods for solving (17)–(19) and related problems have been developed. For example, a simulated annealing heuristic that can approximate solutions to a problem like (17)–(19) has been codified in a software package called MARXAN (Ball et al. 2009). MARXAN is a widely used in the conservation planning community.

Early work on RSS formulated (17)–(19) as an area-constrained problem in which the planner was constrained by total land area rather than budget (Camm et al. 1996; Church et al. 1996; Dobson et al. 1997). Ando et al. (1998) relax the implicit assumption of uniform costs in the area-constrained problem and show that by setting c_j equal to the expected cost of purchasing an acre of habitat in county j and B equal to a conservation budget, the same number of species can be covered for less aggregate cost than Dobson et al.'s area-constrained solution to (17)–(19).

2.1 Issues in Reserve-Site Selection

Dobson et al. (1997) and Ando et al. (1998) assume that all species found in a selected county would benefit from a representative protected area within the county. However, this is unrealistic, given the size of counties and the disparate habitat preferences of species located within a county. Therefore, over time, the rudimentary RSS problem (17)–(19) has seen substantial refinement in representing the conservation benefits gained by selecting a site. One approach is to reduce the size of potential sites j so that each site contains uniform habitat (Haight et al. 2005; Polasky et al. 2008). Alternatively, the objective function (17) can be respecified such that additional habitat contributes to a more biologically complex metric. These more complex metrics include the sum of individual species persistence probabilities (Polasky et al. 2008) and some variant of the well-known biological species-area relationship (SAR) from the discipline of conservation biology (Rosenzweig 1995). Common across all of these approaches is that the biological score is more than just a sum of species covered by habitat area. Furthermore, in many second-generation RSS problems, the biological metric is also a function of the portions of the landscape that are not protected.[11]

Although all RSS problems assume that more habitat on a landscape increases the value of the objective function, the rate and shape of objective value increase can vary substantially across second-generation RSS problems. For example, Wu and Boggess (1999) and Wu and Skelton-Groth (2002) argue that returns to resource conservation (e.g., improving water quality for recreational purposes, adding habitat to the landscape to increase biodiversity persistence) tend to display a "ʃ"-shape. Under such an assumption, rapid increases in the benefits provided by additional resource conservation only occur once a threshold of minimum conservation has been reached; prior to that point, resource conservation only has a small effect on objective. Polasky et al. (2008) use such a "ʃ"-shape when explaining species' persistence probabilities across the Willamette Basin of Oregon. Eventually, species response to additional habitat becomes saturated. At fairly high levels of habitat on the landscape, additional habitat is relatively worthless. Conversely, the SAR, which specifies the number of species found on the landscape (richness) as a function of habitat provision, is strictly convex in conservation. In SAR-based RSS, the first few units of habitat on the landscape add the most to the biodiversity objective maximization. Therefore, using a "ʃ"-shape objective function versus a SAR curve in an RSS problem over the same landscape with the same policy parameters can generate fairly different outcomes and/or solutions. In some cases, the same pattern of habitat conservation is selected by both types of objective functions, but the gain in the relevant biodiversity score will be much more impressive with the SAR objective function. Or, in other cases, the threshold effect in "ʃ"-shaped objective functions will mean very different patterns of habitat conservation when compared to the SAR-generated landscape. For example, the threshold for rapid increases in species persistence is reached more quickly in Polasky et al. (2008) if the initial habitat is clumped spatially on the landscape due to spatial dependencies in habitat value. A SAR-based analysis of the same landscape would not necessarily reward habitat clumping to the same degree.

Another issue that has seen recent attention is uncertainty across the RSS's parameters. For example, Haight et al. (2005) maximized expected species coverage given probabilistic geographic range maps. Such an approach can account for probabilistic shifts in species' range due to ongoing climate change (Araújo et al. 2004; Pyke and Fischer 2005; Ando and Mallory 2012). In addition to biological uncertainty, some recent analyses have accounted for uncertain opportunity costs of conservation (e.g., Nelson et al.

[11] See Margules and Pressey (2000), Cabeza and Moilanen (2003), Moilanen et al. (2005), and Newbold and Siikamaki (2009) for other examples of RSS problems with more biologically meaningful objective functions.

2008; Carwardine et al. 2010; Lewis et al. 2011) and uncertainty in which habitat sites are actually available for purchase.

Landscape dynamics have also been incorporated in RSS problems. Much of the RSS literature assumes that sites not selected for protection will be lost to development. Although this may be true in the long run, it is not true in the short run: valuable habitat not selected for protection can persist indefinitely if current market conditions do not give the site's owner incentive to develop. In fact, optimal dynamic RSS analyses have shown efficiency gains by purchasing habitat sites that are immediately threatened by development, even if they are not as biologically valuable as less threatened sites (Costello and Polasky 2004). Conversely, biologically valuable highly unlikely to be developed in the near future may be best left unprotected indefinitely since there is limited expected value in protecting them immediately.[12]

2.2 An Empirical Illustration Using the Return on Investment (ROI) Approach

Recently, biological conservation journals have published a number of articles on the so-called ROI problem (e.g., Murdoch et al. 2007). The objective of the ROI problem is generally the same as the RSS problem: maximize the return (in biological terms) per unit investment (generally a conservation budget). However, ROI improves on several features of the fundamental RSS problem. First, ROI is more explicit in incorporating baseline or business-as-usual threats to undeveloped area over time. Second, to make this approach applicable to conservation organizations and their rapid funding cycles, ROI approaches may select the sites that are expected to generate the greatest ROI at each decision time step and not the trajectory of site selection that will maximize ROI over the problem's entire time frame. Third, in addition to habitat purchases, ROI approaches can allocate effort across other conservation actions that can increase species persistence in an area (e.g., invasive species removal, fire suppression, fuel reduction, etc.; Murdoch et al. 2007). Finally, the ROI approach acknowledges some of the realities in conservation implementation, including the risk that purchased protected areas and the species they host may be lost due to unforeseen events, species extinction may reduce the biological value of a protected site in the future, conservation organizations with different objectives compete for the same sites (Bode et al. 2011), and that funds are not fully fungible across regions.

In this section, we present an illustrative application that combines some of the conservation complications addressed in the dynamic RSS and ROI approaches with the traditional RSS problem given by (17)–(19). Similar to the early work of Ando et al.

[12] Examples of stochastic dynamic RSS are found in Costello and Polasky (2004), Snyder et al. (2005), and Haight et al. (2005).

(1998), we solve equations (17)–(19) using the set of US counties for the establishment of 1,000-hectare conservation reserves. Our dataset includes 1,066 vertebrate species in the continuous US, with detailed range maps. The data used are fully described in Withey et al. (2012). Finally, like most ROI literature, we assume the biological objective is convex in habitat.

Our goal is to illustrate the effects of (1) diminishing "biological returns" to conserving land, (2) a baseline or business-as-usual future in which not all land is at risk of development immediately, and (3) incorporating scale into a measure of biological benefits on solutions to the rudimentary RSS problem. First, we incorporate diminishing returns by favoring the selection of counties with less land already protected as of the late 2000s (The Conservation Biology Institute [CBI] 2010). Define P_j as one plus the proportion of county j protected, where higher P_j indicates greater existing protection (a completely unprotected county would have a score of 1 and a completely protected county would have a sore of 2). Second, the degree to which habitat is threatened is accounted for by targeting counties with higher rates of expected future habitat losses. Let T_j be a metric equal to one minus the proportion of natural land cover in county j developed between 1992 and 2001 (Fry et al. 2009). Therefore, T_j varies between 0 and 1, where a lower value means that development of habitat has been rapid in the immediate past and presumably will continue to be intense in the near future. Finally, given the large size of US counties, we account for the fact that a 1,000-hectare reserve is unlikely to cover the range of relevant habitats within each county. We address this scale issue by selecting counties that have relatively more homogeneous land cover. Define D_j to range from 1 (high diversity of natural land cover types in county j) to 2 (no diversity of natural land cover types in county j) as of 2001 (Comer et al. 2003).

There are several ways we could add these selection criteria to the traditional RSS problem. For example, weight w_i could be added to objective function (17), $\max_{s_j} \sum_i \sum_j w_{ij} s_j x_{ij}$, such that species that range over counties with lower P, lower T, and higher D values have higher w. Instead, our approach is to simply add constraints to the RSS problem such that the selected network has average P and T values equal to or less than 30th percentile values for P and T across all counties (1.0013 and 0.9748, respectively) and an average D value equal to or greater than the 70th percentile value for D across all counties (0.8460). This means selected networks will have very little protected area already, are expected to experience significant development pressure in the immediate future, and will have much less natural land cover diversity than other counties. The more we lower average P and T and increase average D in the selected network, the more consistent the network is with ROI principles. The budget constraint is given by,

$$\sum_{j=1}^{j} s_j A_j C_j \leq B, \tag{20}$$

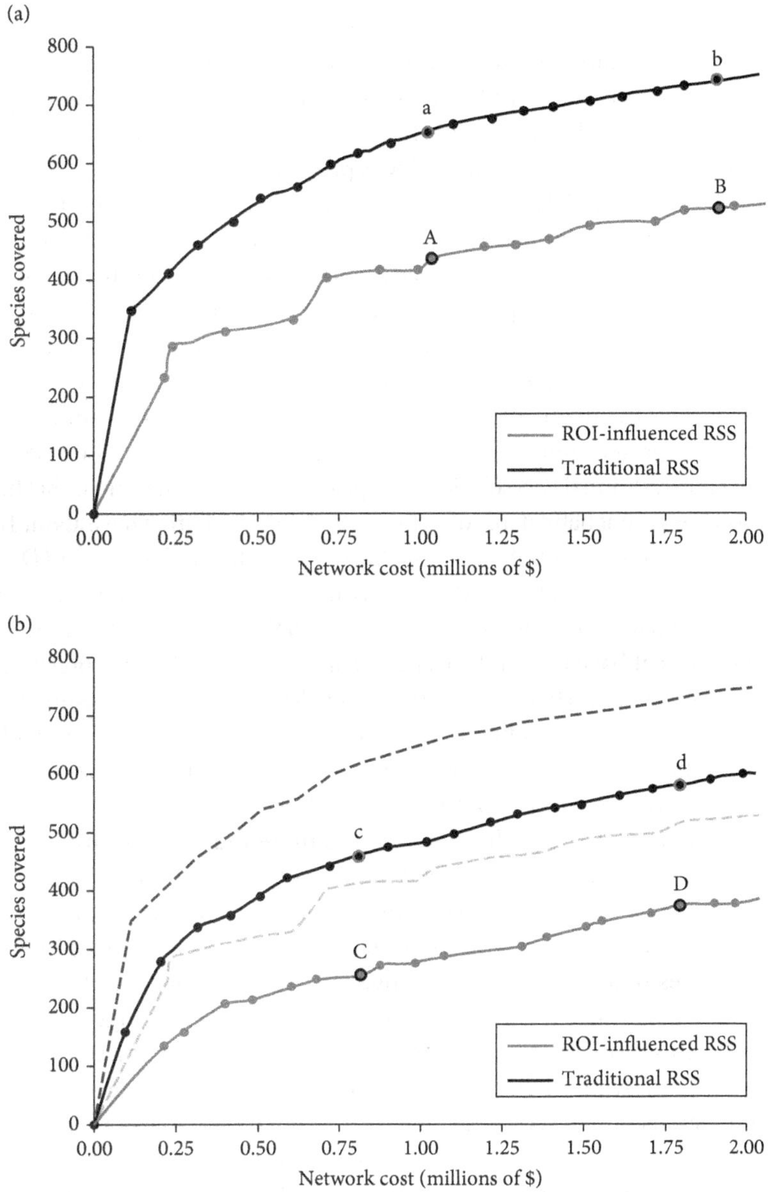

FIGURE 7.3 Species covered in networks selected by a traditional and ROI-influenced RSS problem at various budget levels. In Figure (a), a species is considered covered by a network if a 1,000-hectare site is selected in at least one county that the species is known to range in. The traditional RSS networks represented by the frontier in Figure (a) were found by solving problem (17)–(19). The ROI-influenced networks represented by the frontier in Figure (a) were found by solving the problem (17)–(19) with additional constraints that increase the network's ROI. In Figure (b), a species is considered covered by a network if a 1,000-hectare site is selected in at least two counties that the species is known to range in (unless the species is endemic to a county, then it is covered if its home county is selected). Otherwise, the traditional and ROI-influenced networks are selected in the same way as before. The dashed lines in Figure (b) are the frontier solutions from Figure (a).

where $s_j = 1$ if area in county j is selected and equals 0 otherwise, A_j is the area selected in j for protection and is equal to 1,000 ha for all j in this case, C_j is the average per hectare cost of undeveloped land in j as of 2001 (Withey et al. 2012), and B is the budget. For comparison, we also solve the traditional RSS problem (17)–(19).

In Figure 7.3 and Table 7.1, we present the comparison for various budget levels. If the networks that form the traditional RSS curve score poorly on average P, T, and D values that are associated with high ROI, then the vertical gap between the ROI-influenced and traditional RSS curves can be interpreted as a measure of untenable species protection if one assumes that the ROI-influenced RSS networks are much more likely to increase the persistence probabilities of the covered species than those species covered by the traditional RSS networks. Consider the highlighted points in Figure 7.3(a). Points "A" and "a" on the two graphed curves represent reserve networks that cost approximately \$1,025,000. Table 7.1 indicates that the traditional RSS solution ("a") places conservation in areas that have experienced, on average, recent habitat loss of less than 1% ($T = 0.994$), that have about 10% of their land already protected ($P = 1.098$), and that have a fairly diverse land cover ($D = 0.634$). In contrast, the ROI-influenced RSS ("A") places conservation in areas that have experienced, on average, recent habitat loss of more than 3% ($T = 0.969$), that have no existing protected land ($P = 1$), and that have less land cover diversity ($D = 0.85$). An interpretation is that by misspecifying conservation benefits, the traditional RSS drastically overestimates the number of "protected species" by failing to account for diminishing returns and a baseline in which much of the unprotected habitat remains on the landscape for the indefinite future.

An additional issue in specifying conservation benefits is the fact that effective coverage of species on a landscape is likely to require more than one additional habitat site. This is similar to Wu and Boggess's (1999) argument that returns to resource conservation tend to display a "∫" shape. To begin to explore the ramifications of requiring more sites for species coverage, we rerun the ROI-influenced and traditional RSS problems in which a species that has geographic range over two or more counties needs to have range in at least two selected counties to be considered covered. Figure 7.3(b) gives the cost curves for this more restrictive approach. The requirement of a second site reduces the species covered by one-half to a third across the modeled budget levels. Requiring two counties versus one for coverage does little to change the overall characteristics of counties selected for protection at various budget levels (compare the average values of D, P, and T between solutions "A" and "C", "a" and "c", "B" and "D", and "b" and "d" in Table 7.1). As with the one-county problem, the traditional RSS networks score poorly on the diminishing returns, threat, and natural land cover indices that indicate strong ROI. Therefore, the gap between the two frontiers in Figure 7.3(b) is likely to be indicative of overestimated species protection under the traditional RSS networks.

2.3 Discussion

The problem of where to site nature reserves under a budget constraint has become a classic economic problem. In this section, we optimally locate reserves across US counties to

Table 7.1 Selected solutions to the two versions of the RSS problem. See Figure 7.3 for the location of the selected reserve networks ('A', 'a', 'B', 'b', etc.) on the various frontiers

Reserve network	No. of species covered	Cost	No. of counties w/ a site	Average *D*	Average *P*	Average *T*
One-county cover						
A	439	1,034,800	5	0.850	1.000	0.969
a	656	1,022,429	6	0.634	1.098	0.994
B	522	1,913,140	8	0.861	1.001	0.971
b	743	1,909,807	9	0.545	1.141	0.993
Two-county cover						
C	255	821,313	6	0.858	1.000	0.977
c	461	814,650	8	0.514	1.090	0.993
D	376	1,799,383	9	0.850	1.001	0.976
d	583	1,799,004	11	0.579	1.137	0.993
All US counties	NA	NA	Mean	0.658	1.039	0.979
			Std. dev.	0.231	0.081	0.026

highlight two important features of the RSS problem that deserve further research attention. First, the solution of where to site reserves is greatly influenced by the specification of conservation benefits. Although ecologists understand many principles about desirable wildlife habitat, much work remains on understanding how the conservation benefits of reserve creation are influenced by factors such as diminishing returns, spatial dependencies in habitat value, and species range considerations (the benefits of reserve creation become even more difficult to model if it is assumed that returns to habitat provision are increasing over one range of provision and decreasing over another). Second, reserve siting is greatly influenced by how the analyst treats baseline outcomes in the absence of reserve siting. Many regions are likely to see little loss of habitat in the absence of reserve creation, and so siting reserves in such areas is likely to be inefficient in the usual case of a scarce conservation budget. Continued emphasis on modeling and incorporating baseline landscape dynamics into RSS would generate substantial research value.

3. Conserving Wildlife with Voluntary Incentive-Based Payments

Many countries and government entities attempt to conserve wildlife and other ecosystem services through nonregulatory means, with voluntary payment programs (often termed payments for ecosystem services) being among the most popular approaches. In the United States the multibillion dollar annual budget of the

Conservation Reserve Program is an example, whereby owners of agricultural land are offered voluntary payments to undertake conservation activities on their land. The efficient design of voluntary payments for wildlife conservation must overcome two principal challenges. First, a landscape's ability to provide the habitat resources necessary to sustain a wildlife population is likely dependent on the spatial configuration of that habitat across many independent landowners. Second, landowners have private information regarding their willingness to accept (WTA) payments in exchange for adopting conservation measures on their land, and profit-maximizing landowners typically have no incentive to truthfully reveal their WTA to a conservation agency. It is the combination of spatial dependencies and private WTA information that makes designing efficient payment programs challenging and will be the focus of this section. The underlying argument of this section is that efficient design of voluntary incentives for wildlife conservation is essentially a problem of obtaining private information on landowners' WTA.

3.1 A Simple Example with Spatial Dependencies

A 1 × 4 parcel landscape is used to demonstrate the challenges of designing an efficient payment program with spatial dependencies in conservation benefits and private WTA information. Figure 7.4 illustrates this landscape. The WTA of each landowner to place his or her parcel in conservation is indicated at the top of the parcel, whereas the wildlife benefit in biophysical units of conservation is indicated along the bottom. The first number is the benefit when the parcel is conserved but no adjacent neighbor is conserved. The second number is the benefit when the parcel is conserved and one adjacent neighbor is conserved as well. The third number is the benefit when the parcel is conserved and two adjacent neighbors is conserved as well.. Each parcel is assumed to generate biological benefits of zero if not conserved. On this landscape, wildlife benefits exhibit spatial dependencies, and conservation costs are heterogeneous.

Conservation costs may be heterogeneous because land quality varies across parcels or because landowners' WTA reflects different land management skills or other attributes associated with how they value their land. Wildlife benefits are heterogeneous across parcels because natural habitat may vary across the landscape, the ability to restore natural habitat may vary across the landscape, or the geographic range of some species may only comprise a subset of the four parcels. Finally, wildlife benefits exhibit spatial dependencies. In other words, benefits are increasing in the number of conserved neighbors. In general, species prefer larger contiguous patches of habitat than isolated, smaller patches.

If we assume that the value of biophysical benefits is $1/unit, the conserved landscape that maximizes net benefits can be determined by enumerating the total net benefits from all possible configurations. The maximum net benefit generated by parcel conservation on this landscape is $2, and it arises when adjacent parcels A, B, and C are conserved ($8 + $9 + $5 – $5 – $8 – $7). The marginal benefit of conservation generated by

Parcel A	Parcel B	Parcel C	Parcel D
\$5 6 8	\$8 4 6 9	\$7 4 5 6	\$8 4 6

FIGURE 7.4 An example landscape with costs (top number in \$) and biophysical benefits that depend on having zero, one, or two conserved neighbors (bottom numbers, in biophysical units).

parcel *i* in the optimal landscape configuration can be determined by calculating the total benefit from optimal conservation less the total benefit without parcel *i* in the conservation network. For example, the total benefit of conserving parcels A, B, and C (the optimal network) is \$22, whereas the total benefit would only be \$14 (\$8 + \$6) if parcel C were not conserved. Therefore, the marginal benefit of conserving parcel C is equal to \$8 (\$22 – \$14), which is larger than parcel C's opportunity cost of \$7. Parcel C is optimally conserved. If we measured parcel C's marginal benefit outside of the optimal network, for example a network in which only parcels B and C are conserved, then C's marginal benefit in conservation has decreased to \$7 (\$11 – \$4 = \$7). In this particular case, society is now indifferent to conserving C because its marginal benefit equals its WTA. When benefits are spatially dependent, the full marginal benefit of a conserved parcel can only be determined once the optimal landscape is known.

If the price of biophysical benefits is not known, an alternative formulation of the conservation problem would be to maximize biophysical benefits under a cost constraint. For example, all four parcels in Figure 7.4 would be optimally conserved under a cost constraint of \$28. In the cost-constrained formulation of the problem, the marginal benefit of an optimally conserved parcel is a function of the cost constraint. For example, the marginal benefit of parcel C is 8 biophysical units under a cost constraint of \$20 (8 + 9 + 5 – 8 – 6)[13] and 11 units under a cost constraint of \$28 (8 + 9 + 6 + 6 – 8 – 6 – 4).

Regardless of whether the problem is formulated as a net-benefit maximization or cost-constrained optimization problem, an important conservation question is how to implement the optimal landscape with voluntary payments when WTA is known by the landowners but not by the conservation agency. As we have just seen, under the net-benefit maximization problem, the optimal pattern is to conserve parcels A, B, and C. Let us say a uniform payment of \$8 was offered to parcel owners on the landscape in order to entice the owner of parcels A, B, and C to conserve his land. However, a payment of \$8 could also induce parcel D to enroll, which is not optimal. As an alternative to a uniform payment program, an "agglomeration bonus" has been proposed (Parkhurst et al. 2002; Parkhurst and Shogren 2007) as a means of giving a bonus payment to those landowners who jointly conserve their land along with a neighbor. However, the

[13] Biophysical benefits are maximized at a budget of \$20 when conserving adjacent parcels A, B, and C.

optimal size of the "bonus" would have to vary when marginal benefits from conserved land are heterogeneous across the landscape, as they are in the illustrative example here. In such cases, an agglomeration bonus program would require offering a menu of contracts in which each landowner's bonus would depend on the exact configuration of the landscape. As an example of how complex the menu could get even with small landscapes, a 4 × 4 landscape has 65,535 possible conservation configurations. A Piguovian subsidy is a third implementation strategy. If the price of biophysical services is $1/unit, a Pigouvian approach would entail offering landowners payments equal to their land's marginal benefit from conservation. If there were no spatial dependencies, each parcel would be offered a monetary payment equal to the first number in the row of numbers that indicate the parcel's benefit in conservation. Only parcel A would accept this payment, and the optimal landscape in the absence of spatial dependencies could be conserved. However, this approach doesn't work with spatial dependencies: without information about landowners' WTA, which we had in our illustrative examples, the regulator cannot solve the optimal landscape and determine each parcel's marginal benefit in equilibrium.

3.2 Empirical Analysis of Incentive Policies Under Spatial Dependencies and Asymmetric Information

We use data from a real landscape and extend the empirical analysis by Lewis et al. (2011) to illustrate two points discussed in Section 3.1. First, we show how sensitive spatially dependent marginal benefits can be to changes in the optimal landscape. Second, we illustrate the importance of WTA information by examining the poor performance of second-best conservation policies. The recent study by Lewis et al. provides an empirical analysis of the efficiency of a series of second-best policies that operate when private WTA information is combined with spatially dependent benefits of conservation. The authors combine econometrically generated distributions of landowners' WTA with biological models of species persistence. The WTA distributions are estimated from observed plot-level land use decisions over a 15-year period in the Willamette Basin of Oregon (Figure 7.5). The estimated WTA distributions are used to simulate landowner responses to a variety of incentive policies, whereby landowners know their WTA, but the conservation agency does not. The biological model uses spatial landscape patterns generated by the econometric models and information on species' range and habitat compatibility as inputs and returns the sum of estimated persistence probabilities across a set of 24 terrestrial species of conservation concern (the landscape's biological score is normalized on a 0–100 scale, where 100 means all species have a persistence probability of 100). In this application, the response of species persistence probabilities to additional conservation on the landscape is "ʃ"-shaped. The authors are able to compare outcomes from second-best policies with a first-best optimal policy. The optimal policy is estimated within a simulation by taking a random draw from the WTA distributions from each parcel, treating the draw as a known WTA value, and then selecting the

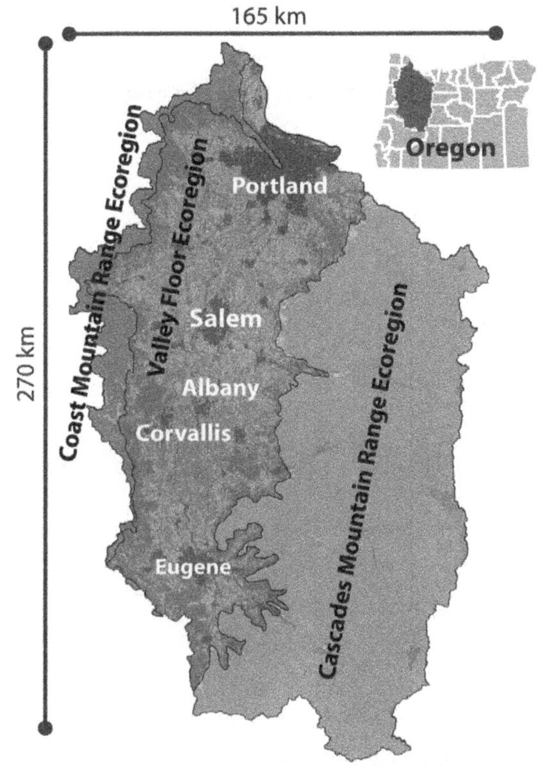

FIGURE 7.5 **The Willamette Basin of Oregon.**

conservation pattern that maximizes the biological score for a given level of opportunity cost. The opportunity cost constraint is treated as the sum of WTA across all conserved parcels.

The top row of maps in Figure 7.6 presents the landscapes that maximize the biological score for a given opportunity cost. The conservation budget sums the WTA for each conserved parcel, where the landscape of random draws from the estimated WTA distributions for each parcel is held fixed. The five landscapes differ in terms of their conservation budget. As seen in the maps of Figure 7.6, small changes in the budget constraint can imply fairly large changes in the optimal conservation pattern, whereby parcels are both added and subtracted from the optimal conservation pattern as the budget constraint is relaxed. These results are driven by the spatial dependencies in the biology model and the particular landscape of WTA values. Different draws from the WTA distribution would also change the optimal conservation pattern.

Figure 7.7 presents marginal benefits (expressed as marginal biological scores) for a select set of 16 parcels that are included in one or more of the optimal landscapes from Figure 7.6. As in the simple example in Section 3.1, the marginal benefits of conservation for optimally conserved parcel i can be evaluated by examining the optimal biology score minus the landscape score without parcel i being conserved. The main point to

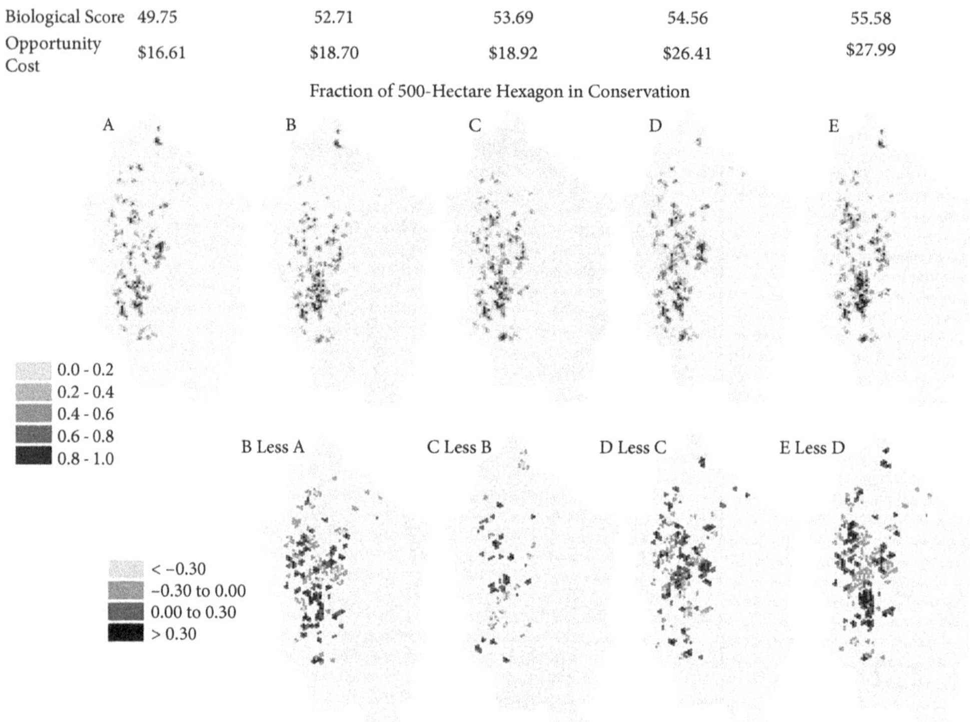

FIGURE 7.6 Optimal conservation for the Willamette Basin. The top row gives conservation patterns that maximize the biology score (scaled from 0–100) for a given opportunity cost budget. Each mapped unit is a 500-hectare hexagon and is comprised of nonuniform parcels. The darker the shade of a hexagon in the top row of maps, the greater the fraction of the parcel space in the hexagon that is conserved. The bottom row of maps is the difference between two maps; map B less map A, etc., which shows how the distribution of conserved area changes from one landscape to the next. Areas with the two lightest shade of gray represent hexagons that lost conserved area vis-à-vis the previous landscape, and hexagons with the two darkest shade of gray have gained more conserved area. For example, if a hexagon has a score of –0.31, its fraction of conserved area has fallen by 0.31; in other words it has lost 0.31 × 500 = 155 hectares of conserved area (the greatest decline is 99%; the greatest increase is 98%).

be taken from Figure 7.7 is the fact that marginal benefits greatly depend on the optimal landscape and so will differ as the budget constraint is changed. The other striking feature of Figure 7.7 is the magnitude of changes in marginal benefits that result from seemingly small changes in the conservation budget. This result falls from the highly nonlinear nature of the spatially dependent biological benefit function ("ʃ"-shaped persistence probability function) and the potential of turning a fairly fragmented network of conservation sites into a much more connected network by strategically placing a few more conserved parcels on the landscape. All of this is indicative of the complexity of examining optimal landscapes for wildlife conservation.

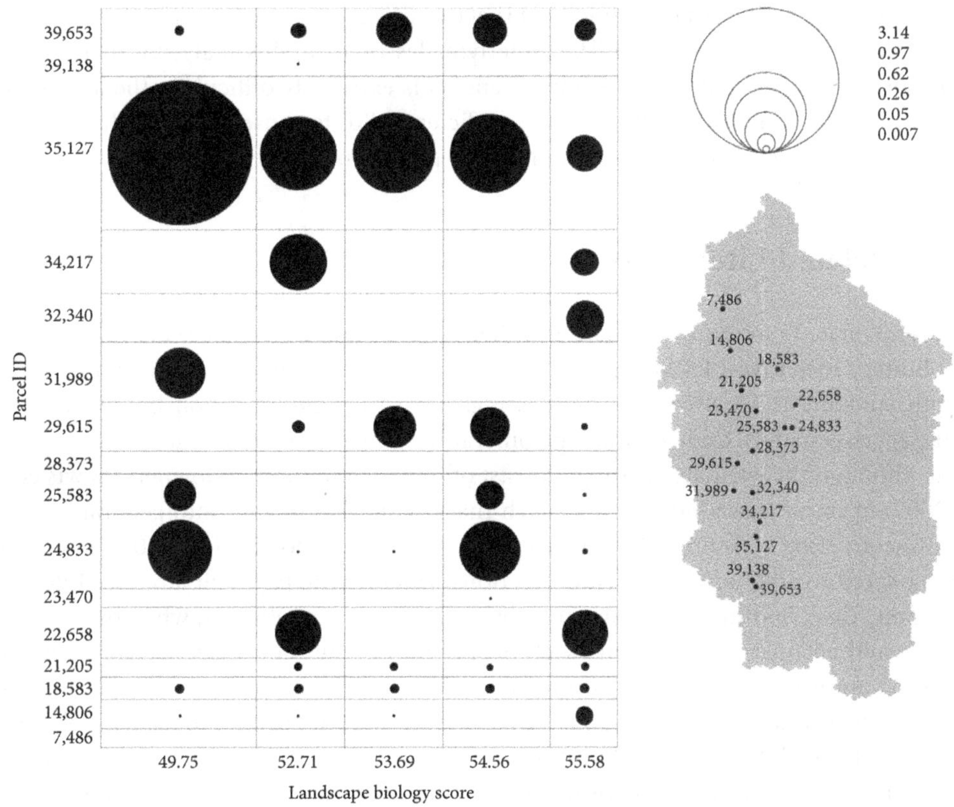

FIGURE 7.7 Marginal benefits for a select set of optimally conserved parcels. Each column of bubbles gives the parcel's marginal biological score on a given optimal landscape (indicated by the biology score at the bottom of the figure). Blank cells either mean that the parcel was not part of the landscape's conservation network or its marginal biodiversity score was so small that it cannot even be represented by a visible point. The map on the right of the bubble diagram indicates each parcel's location on the landscape.

Using the optimal landscape biology scores as a benchmark, Lewis et al. (2011) examine the performance of several alternative policy designs in which landowner WTA is assumed unknown by the regulator. First, a set of "least-cost" policies are evaluated in which uniform per-acre payments are offered to all landowners who meet particular eligibility requirements based on habitat type and size characteristics and are offered an agglomeration bonus. Relative to a baseline, none of the policies achieved even 25% (55%) of the optimal increase in the biology score at low budget levels (high budget levels). Second, a set of "benefit-cost" policies are evaluated, in which "benefit" indices were constructed using the same set of habitat type/size and agglomeration characteristics just considered. Although none of the "benefit-cost" policies achieved even 28% of the optimal increase in the biology score at low budget levels, the best-performing policy did achieve a more respectable 87% of the optimal increase at very high budget levels. Of course, it must be pointed out that one can conserve all available land as habitat if the budget is high enough. The underlying lesson from this analysis is that efficient conservation with spatially dependent benefits is extremely difficult in the absence of information on landowner WTA, and so efficient wildlife conservation with voluntary incentives should be treated as an information problem.

3.3 Related Literature

Several related literatures evaluate and shed light on issues in conserving wildlife with voluntary incentives. Parkhurst and Shogren (2002, 2007) use experimental methods with students to examine possibilities regarding the agglomeration bonus. This set of papers generally finds that an agglomeration bonus can encourage clustered habitat, although the evaluated settings consist of only two to four landowners. Lewis et al. (2009) examine a second-best approach that divides landscapes into geographic sections consisting of multiple landowners each, whereby uniform afforestation payments are offered to all landowners within sections, whereas the payment amount differs by section. Their findings emphasize the optimality of *corner solutions*, whereby it is optimal to either conserve all land in a section or none. Finally, there is a related literature on conservation auctions (Latacz-Lohmann and Van der Hamsvoort 1997; Stoneham et al. 2003; Cason and Gangadharan 2004; Kirwan et al. 2005; Schillizzi and Latacz-Lohmann 2007). Although this auction literature focuses on information asymmetry issues with conservation programs, none of the auction designs examined is aimed at achieving truthful revelation of landowner WTA. In a new paper, Polasky et al. (2013) develop an auction mechanism that pays a landowner the full marginal benefit generated by conserving their land and provides incentives for landowners to truthfully reveal cost information. This auction is unique in the literature it that it allows the conservation agency to implement the optimal provision of spatially-dependent ecosystem services under asymmetric information.

4. Conclusion

Slowing the rate of decline in wildlife populations presents a significant public goods provision challenge to economists. The benefits from wildlife are generally nonmarket and largely accrue to individuals who do not own land that contains habitat. Governments and NGOs have addressed the conservation of wildlife habitat largely through land use regulation, habitat purchases, and payments for voluntary conservation. This chapter synthesizes a set of outstanding economic issues that are necessary to understand the efficient design of wildlife conservation. Although we highlight many of the issues that have been the focus in the literature over the past 15 years, we argue that many important issues remain to be explored in the economics literature. First, land use regulatory design must provide direct conservation incentives for landowners or habitat destruction can be socially preferable, and researchers need to develop better methods for empirically evaluating regulatory outcomes and appropriately adjusting policy to partially compensate for the efficiency costs of regulation. Second, solving the problem of spending scarce conservation dollars on habitat purchases must devote more attention to the specification of a conservation benefit function and the specification of baseline landscape outcomes in the absence of habitat reserves. Finally, the efficient design of voluntary conservation payments must solve the problem of how to elicit landowner opportunity costs of conservation because there are no current auction methods that have been successfully developed for this problem.

Acknowledgments

The authors acknowledge funding from the National Science Foundation's Collaborative Research Grants No. 0814424 (Lewis) and No. 0814628 (Nelson). Senior authorship is shared.

References

Ando, A., J. Camm, S. Polasky, and A. Solow. 1998. Species distributions, land values, and efficient conservation. *Science* 279: 2126–2128.

Ando, A. W., and M. L. Mallory. 2012. Optimal portfolio design to reduce climate-related conservation uncertainty in the Prairie Pothole Region. *PNAS* published ahead of print March 26, 2012. doi: 10.1073/pnas.1114653109.

Araújo, M. B., M. Cabeza, W. Thuiller, L. Hannah, and P. H. Williams. 2004. Would climate change drive species out of reserves? An assessment of existing reserve-selection methods. *Global Change Biology* 10: 1618–1626.

Ball, I. R., H. P. Possingham, and M. Watts. 2009. Marxan and relatives: Software for spatial conservation prioritisation. In *Spatial conservation prioritisation: Quantitative methods and computational tools*, eds. A. Moilanen, A., K. A. Wilson, and H. P. Possingham, 185–195. Oxford: Oxford University Press.

Bode, M., W. Probert, W. R. Turner, K. A. Wilson, and O. Venter. 2011. Conservation planning with multiple organizations and objectives. *Conservation Biology* 25: 295–304.

Cabeza, M., and A. Moilanen. 2003. Site-selection algorithms and habitat loss. *Conservation Biology* 17: 1402–1413.

Camm, J. D., S. Polasky, A. Solow, and B. Csuti. 1996. A note on optimal algorithms for reserve site selection. *Biological Conservation* 78: 353–355.

Carwardine, J., K. A. Wilson, S. A. Hajkowicz, R. J. Smith, C. J. Klein, M. Watts, and H. P. Possingham. 2010. Conservation planning when costs are uncertain. *Conservation Biology* 24: 1529–1537.

Cash, D. W. 2001. Beyond cute and fuzzy: Science and politics in the US Endangered Species Act. In *Protecting endangered species in the United States. Biological needs, political realities, economic choices*, eds. J. F. Shogren and J Tschirhart, 106–137. New York: Cambridge University Press.

Cason, T., and L. Gangadharan. 2004. Auction design for voluntary conservation programs. *American Journal of Agricultural Economics* 86(5): 1211–1217.

Church, R. L., D. M. Stoms, and F. W. Davis. 1996. Reserve selection as a maximal coverage problem. *Biological Conservation* 76: 105–112.

The Conservation Biology Institute (CBI). 2010. PAD-US 1.1 (CBI Edition). Corvallis, OR. http://consbio.org/products/projects/pad-us-cbi-edition

Comer, P., D. Faber-Langendoen, R. Evans, S. Gawler, C. Josse, G. Kittel, S. Menard, M. Pyne, M. Reid, K. Schulz, K. Snow, and J. Teague. 2003. *Ecological systems of the United States: A working classification of US terrestrial systems*. Arlington, VA: NatureServe.

Costello, C., and S. Polasky. 2004. Dynamic reserve site selection. *Resource and Energy Economics* 26: 157–174.

DeShazo, J. R., and J. Freeman. 2003. The congressional competition to control delegated power. *Texas Law Review* 81: 1443–1520.

DeShazo, J. R., and J. Freeman. 2006. Congressional politics. In *The Endangered Species Act at thirty. Renewing the conservation promise*, Vol. 1, eds. D. D. Goble, J. M. Scott, and R. W. Davis, 68–71. Washington, DC: Island Press.

Dobson, A. P., J. P. Rodriguez, W. M. Roberts, and D. S. Wilcove. 1997. Geographic distribution of endangered species in the United States. *Science*, 275(5299): 550–553.

Emerton, L. 1999. Balancing the opportunity costs of wildlife conservation for communities around Lake Mburo National Park, Uganda. Evaluating Eden Series discussion paper No. 5. The International Institute for Environment and Development (IIED). http://pubs.iied.org/pdfs/7798IIED.pdf.

Ferraro, P. J., C. McIntosh, and M. Ospina. 2007. The effectiveness of the US Endangered Species Act: An econometric analysis using matching methods. *Journal of Environmental Economics and Management* 54: 245–261.

Fry, J. A., M. J. Coan, C. G. Homer, D. K. Meyer, and J. D. Wickham. 2009. Completion of the National Land Cover Database (NLCD) 1992–2001 Land Cover Change Retrofit product. U. S. Geological Survey Open-File Report 2008–1379.

Haight, R. G., S. A. Snyder, and C. S. Revelle. 2005. Metropolitan open-space protection with uncertain site availability. *Conservation Biology* 19: 327–337.

Hansen, S. 1999. Debt for nature swaps—Overview and discussion of key issues. *Ecological Economics* 1: 77–93.

Innes, R., and G. Frisvold. 2009. The economics of endangered species. *Annual Review of Resource Economics* 1: 485–512.

Kerkvliet, J., and C. Langpap. 2007. Learning from endangered and threatened species recovery programs: A case study using US *Endangered Species Act recovery scores. Ecological Economics* 63: 499–510.

Kirwan, B., R. N. Lubowski, and M. J. Roberts. 2005. How cost-effective are land retirement auctions? Estimating the difference between payments and willingness to accept in the Conservation Reserve Program. *American Journal of Agricultural Economics* 87: 1239–1247.

Lamberson, R. H., R. McKelvey, B. R. Noon, and C. Voss. 1992. A dynamic analysis of Northern Spotted Owl viability in a fragmented forest landscape. *Conservation Biology* 6(4): 505–512.

Latacz-Lohmann, U., and C. Van der Hamsvoort. 1997. Auctioning conservation contracts: A theoretical analysis and application. *American Journal of Agricultural Economics* 79(2): 407–418.

Lawler, J. J., S. L. Shafer, D. White, P. Kareiva, E. P. Maurer, A. R. Blaustein, and P. J. Bartlein. 2009. Projected climate-induced faunal change in the western hemisphere. *Ecology* 90: 588–597.

Lewis, D. J., A. J. Plantinga, E. Nelson, and S. Polasky. 2011. The efficiency of voluntary incentive policies for preventing biodiversity loss. *Resource and Energy Economics*, 33(1): 192–211.

Lewis, D. J., A. J. Plantinga, and J. Wu. 2009. Targeting incentives to reduce habitat fragmentation. *American Journal of Agricultural Economics* 91(4): 1080–1096.

Lueck, D., and J. A. Michael. 2003. Preemptive habitat destruction under the Endangered Species Act. *Journal of Law and Economics* 46: 27–60.

Male, T. D., and M. J. Bean. 2005. Measuring progress in US endangered species conservation. *Ecology Letters* 8: 986–992.

Mann, C., and M. Plummer. 1995. *Noah's choice*. New York: Alfred A. Knopf.

Margules, C. R., and R. L. Pressey. 2000. Systematic conservation planning. *Nature* 405: 243–253.

McAnaney, A. P. 2006. Remembering the spirit of the Endangered Species Act: A case for narrowing agency discretion to interpret 'significant portion' of a species' range. *Golden Gate University Law Review* 36: 6. http://digitalcommons.law.ggu.edu/ggulrev/vol36/iss3/6.

Metrick, A., and M. L. Weitzman. 1998. Conflicts and choices in biodiversity preservation. *The Journal of Economic Perspectives* 12: 21–34.

Millennium Ecosystem Assessment (MEA). 2005. *Living beyond our means: Natural assets and human well-being*. Washington, DC: Island Press.

Miller, J. K., J. M. Scott, C. R. Miller, and L. P. Waits. 2002. The Endangered Species Act: Dollars and sense? *BioScience* 52: 163–168.

Moilanen, A., A. M. A. Franco, R. I. Early, R. Fox, B. Wintle, and C. D. Thomas. 2005. Prioritizing multiple-use landscapes for conservation: Methods for large multi-species planning problems. *Proceedings of the Royal Society: Biological Sciences* 272: 1885–1891.

Murdoch, W., S. Polasky, K. A. Wilson, H. P. Possingham, P. Kareiva, and R. Shaw. 2007. Maximizing return on investment in conservation. *Biological Conservation* 139: 375–388.

Naidoo, R., A. Balmford, P. J. Ferraro, S. Polasky, T. H. Ricketts, and M. Rouget. 2006. Integrating economic costs into conservation planning. *Trends in Ecology & Evolution* 21: 681–687.

Nelson, E., S. Polasky, D. Lewis, A. Plantinga, E. Lonsdorf, D. White, D. Bael and J. Lawler. 2008. Efficiency of incentives to jointly increase carbon sequestration and species conservation on a landscape. *Proceedings of the National Academy of Sciences of the USA* 105(28): 9471–9476.

Newbold, S. C., and J. Siikamaki. 2009. Prioritizing conservation activities using reserve site selection methods and population viability analysis. *Ecological Applications* 19: 1774–1790.

Parkhurst, G. M., and J. F. Shogren. 2007. Spatial incentives to coordinate contiguous habitat. *Ecological Economics* 64: 344–355.

Parkhurst, G. M., J. F. Shogren, C. Bastian, P. Kivi, J. Donner, and R. B. W. Smith. 2002. Agglomeration bonus: An incentive mechanism to reunite fragmented habitat for biodiversity conservation. *Ecological Economics* 41: 305–328.

Polasky, S. 2001. Investment, information collection, and endangered species conservation on private land. In *Protecting endangered species in the United States. Biological needs, political realities, economic choices*, eds. J. F. Shogren and J. Tschirhart, 312–325. New York: Cambridge University Press.

Polasky, S., and H. Doremus. 1998. When the truth hurts: Endangered species policy on private land with imperfect information. *Journal of Environmental Economics and Management* 35: 22–47

Polasky, S., D. J Lewis, A. J. Plantinga, and E. Nelson. 2013. Implementing the Optimal Provision of Ecosystem Services. Economics Department Working Paper Series. Paper 10. http://digitalcommons.bowdoin.edu/econpapers/10.

Polasky, S., Erik Nelson, Jeff Camm, Blair Csuti, Paul Fackler, Eric Lonsdorf, Claire Montgomery, Denis White, Jeff Arthur, Brian Garber-Yonts, Robert Haight, Jimmy Kagan, Anthony Starfield, and Claudine Tobalske. 2008. Where to put things? Spatial land management to sustain biodiversity and economic returns. *Biological Conservation* 141: 1505–1524.

Possingham, Hugh P., Sandy J. Andelman, Mark A. Burgman, Rodrigo A. Medellin, Larry L. Master, David A. Keith. 2002. Limits to the use of threatened species lists. *Trends in Ecology & Evolution* 17: 503–507.

Pyke, C. R., and D. T. Fischer. 2005. Selection of bioclimatically representative biological reserve systems under climate change. *Biological Conservation* 121: 429–441.

Rachlinski, J. J. 1997. Noah by the numbers: an empirical evaluation of the Endangered Species Act. *Cornell Law Review* 82: 356–389.

Radeloff, V. C., E. Nelson, A. J. Plantinga, D. J. Lewis, D. Helmers, J. J. Lawler, J. C. Withey, F. Beaudry, S. Martinuzzi, V. Butsic, E. Lonsdorf, D. White, and S. Polasky. 2012. Economic-based projections of future land use in the conterminous United States under alternative policy scenarios. *Ecological Applications* 22: 1036–1049.

Rosenzweig, M. L. 1995. *Species diversity in space and time*. New York: Cambridge University Press.

Ruhl, J. B. 1998. The Endangered Species Act and private property: A matter of timing and location. *Cornell Journal of Law and Public Policy* 8: 37–53.

Sala, O. E., F. S. Chapin, III, J. J. Armesto, E. Berlow, J. Bloomfield, R. Dirzo, E. Huber-Sanwald, L. F. Huenneke, R. B. Jackson, A. Kinzig, R. Leemans, D. M. Lodge, H. A. Mooney, M. Oesterheld, N. L. Poff, M. T. Sykes, B. H. Walker, M. Walker, and D. H. Wall. 2000. Global biodiversity scenarios in the Year 2100. *Science* 287: 1770–1774.

Schillizzi, S., and U. Latacz-Lohmann. 2007. Assessing the performance of conservation auctions: An experimental study. *Land Economics* 83(4): 497–515.

Schwartz, M. W. 1999. Choosing the appropriate scale of reserves for conservation. *Annual Review of Ecology and Systematics* 30: 83–108.

Scott, J. M., D. D. Goble, and F. W. Davis. 2006. Introduction. In *The Endangered Species Act at thirty: Renewing the conservation promise*, Vol. 1, eds. D. D. Goble, J. M. Scott, and R. W. Davis, 3–15. Washington, DC: Island Press.

Shogren, J. F., J. Tschirhart, T. Anderson, A. W. Ando, S. R. Beissinger, D. Brookshire, G. M. Brown Jr., D. Coursey, R. Innes, S. M. Meyer, and S. Polasky, 1999. Why economics matters for endangered species protection. *Conservation Biology* 13: 1257–1261.

Snyder, S., R. Haight, and C. ReVelle. 2005. A scenario optimization model for dynamic reserve site selection. *Environmental Modeling and Assessment* 9: 179–187.

Stoneham, G., V. Chaudri, A. Ha, and L. Strappazzon. 2003. Auctions for conservation contracts: An empirical examination of Victoria's Bush Tender Trial. *The Australian Journal of Agricultural and Resource Economics* 47(4): 477–500.

Taylor, M. F. J., K. F. Suckling, and J. J. Rachkinski. 2005. The effectiveness of the Endangered Species Act: A quantitative analysis. *BioScience* 55: 360–367

The Nature Conservancy (TNC). 2010 Annual report: Roots of innovation. http://www.nature.org/aboutus/ouraccountability/annualreport/index.htm.

Thompson, B. H., Jr. 2006. Managing the working landscape. In *The Endangered Species Act at thirty. Renewing the conservation promise*, Vol. 1, eds. D. D. Goble, J. M. Scott, and R. W. Davis, 101–126. Washington, DC: Island Press.

US Fish and Wildlife Service (FWS). 2009. 2009 Expenditure report. http://www.fws.gov/endangered/esa-library/index.html.

Wilcove, D. S., D. Rothstein, J. Dubow, A. Phillips, and E. Losos. 2000. Leading threats to biodiversity: What's imperiling US species. In *Precious heritage: The status of biodiversity in the United States*, eds. B. A. Stein, L. S. Kutner, and J. S. Adams, 239–254. Oxford: Oxford University Press.

Withey, J. C., J. J. Lawler, S. Polasky, A. J. Plantinga, E. Nelson, P. Kareiva, C. B. Wilsey, C. A. Schloss, T. M. Nogeire, A. Ruesch, J. Ramos Jr., and W. Reid. 2012. Maximizing return on conservation investment in the conterminous USA. *Ecology Letters* 15: 1249–1256.

Wu, J., R. M. Adams, and W. G. Boggess. 2000. Cumulative effects and optimal targeting of conservation efforts: Steelhead trout habitat enhancement in Oregon. *American Journal of Agricultural Economics* 82(2): 400–413.

Wu, J., and W. G. Boggess. 1999. The optimal allocation of conservation funds. *Journal of Environmental Economics and Management* 38: 302–321.

Wu, J., and K. Skelton-Groth. 2002. Targeting conservation efforts in the presence of threshold effects and ecosystem linkages. *Ecological Economics* 42: 313–331.

CHAPTER 8

CONNECTING ECOSYSTEM SERVICES TO LAND USE

Implications for Valuation and Policy

ROBERT J. JOHNSTON, STEPHEN K. SWALLOW, DANA MARIE BAUER, EMI UCHIDA, AND CHRISTOPHER M. ANDERSON

ECOSYSTEM goods and services (henceforth, "services")[1] may be defined as the outputs of natural systems that benefit society (Daily 1997; Millennium Ecosystem Assessment 2005) or "the flows from an ecosystem that are of relatively immediate benefit to humans and occur naturally" (Brown et al. 2007, 334). Although economists have long sought to quantify the market and nonmarket benefits humans derive from natural systems, the concept of ecosystem services has gained recent attention among natural scientists, policy makers, and advocacy groups. Among the factors that distinguish this work from traditional economic analysis, at least in principle, is a more fundamental multidisciplinary focus, including an emphasis on both ecological production[2] and economic value.

Much of the recent research and policy emphasis on ecosystem services has targeted those services linked in some way to land use and cover (henceforth, "use"), including those flowing from agriculture, forests, wetlands, rangelands, and other terrestrial systems (Bauer and Johnston 2013). Changes in land use can affect multiple ecosystem services, many of which are not traded in markets and hence lack direct signals of value (Polasky et al. 2011). Among the primary motivations for research in this area is the provision of information to quantify tradeoffs and promote optimal, or socially efficient,

[1] We define ecosystem services to include both goods and services provided directly by ecosystems, including nonmarket goods that are often titled "cultural" or "social" benefits by the ecosystem services literature (Brown et al. 2007; Bateman et al. 2011). These may include aesthetic benefits.

[2] Bioeconomic researchers have long been concerned with ecological production functions (Clark 1976; Wilen 1985; Conrad and Clark 1987).

management. Within agricultural policy, for example, the nonmarket and often unrecognized value of ecosystem services and disservices is recognized as among the primary causes of market failure (Dale and Polasky 2007; Kroeger and Casey 2007; National Research Council 2010; Ribaudo et al. 2010). Many decisions are potentially informed by quantification and valuation of ecosystem services, including those related to restoration programs, land set-asides, and conservation easements or purchases; assessments of the equivalency of market credits or habitat mitigation; development of regulatory or incentive programs to motivate changes in agricultural or land use practices; and development of ecosystem service markets (Johnston and Duke 2007; Swinton et al. 2007; Swallow et al. 2008; Duke and Johnston 2010; Wainger et al. 2010).

Examples of the many conceptual, theoretical, and empirical publications linking ecosystem services to land use include Bateman et al. (2011), Dale and Polasky (2007), Heal and Small (2002), Johnston et al. (2002*a*, 2002*b*), Nelson et al. (2009), Polasky et al. (2011), Priess et al. (2007), Ricketts et al. (2004), Swinton et al. (2007), and Wainger et al. (2010). Although categorizations of ecosystem services vary and often double count contributions to welfare (Fisher et al. 2009), commonly cited services include the production of flora, fauna, and natural (bio)diversity; provision of water (quantity and quality); regulation of climate (e.g., through carbon sequestration or microclimate, such as through shading or heat islands in absence of shading); regulation of hazards (e.g., flood and erosion mitigation); breakdown and detoxification of waste; purification processes (e.g., of air and water); and the generation and maintenance of socially valued places and landscapes (Hanley and Barbier 2009; Balmford et al. 2011; Bateman et al. 2011; Polasky et al. 2011). Beyond the provision of food, fiber, and fuel, often cited examples of services related specifically to agricultural land use include nutrient cycling, pollination, wildlife habitat, biodiversity, carbon sequestration, aesthetic services, and recreational services (Millennium Ecosystem Assessment 2005; Swinton et al. 2007; Fisher et al. 2009); these can include services *received by* or that benefit agriculture (e.g., pollination services), services *provided by* agricultural land uses (e.g., open-space aesthetics), and *ecosystem disservices* or decreases in ecosystem services caused by agricultural production (e.g., animal waste generating odors or fostering insect pests) (Johnston et al. 2001; Ready and Abdalla 2005; Zhang et al. 2007).

Despite the relevance of ecosystem services for policy and recent enthusiasm for the concept, "there have been relatively few attempts to define the concept clearly to make it operational" (Fisher et al. 2008, 2051; 2009). "[W]hile progress is being made in the integration of economics and ecological sciences for understanding ecosystem services, this is a field still in its nascent stage" (Fisher et al. 2011, 152). The literature is dominated by works proposing frameworks, typologies, and perspectives. At the same time, researchers seeking to evaluate ecosystem services and link them to land use changes face empirical challenges (Bateman et al. 2011). Within this context, the validity and precision of ecosystem service evaluations (including quantification, prediction, and valuation) are largely determined by three overarching factors: (1) *what services are evaluated*—the conceptual and theoretical foundations of ecosystem service analysis and how these relate to the specific set of ecosystem conditions, functions, and outcomes chosen for analysis; (2) *how services are evaluated*—the validity and precision of the economic and ecological methods used to quantify and value selected services; and (3) *at which scopes and scales are services evaluated*—the magnitude of changes considered and the geographic scale over which evaluations are conducted.

This chapter describes methods, challenges, and prospects involved in linkages between ecosystem services and land use. We begin with a discussion of the current state of the literature devoted to land use–related ecosystem services. This is followed by a review of relationships between methods used for ecosystem service evaluations and the accuracy and precision of empirical results. We conclude with illustrative applications that elucidate some of the challenges faced when linking ecosystem services to land use, as well as the use of resulting information to guide policy.

1. Ecosystem Services and Land Use

The idea that ecological processes provide outputs valued by human society or that these outputs extend beyond direct products typically sold in markets is not new (Krutilla 1967; Daily et al. 2009). Many of the precepts of nonmarket valuation are grounded in this idea, extending back more than four decades (Champ et al. 2003; Freeman 2003). The capacity of land to provide market and nonmarket benefits—including those related to ecological composition, structure, and function—has long been a part of economic analysis and discourse related to land use policy (Swallow 1996*b*; Johnston and Swallo 2006; Bergstrom and Ready 2009). Valuation of ecosystem services is grounded in the theoretical structure that underpins all economic welfare analysis (Freeman 2003; Just et al. 2004), although many empirical applications apply methods that violate economic theory required for valid welfare estimation (see discussions in Toman 1998; Bockstael et al. 2000; Tallis and Polasky 2009, 268–269; Bateman et al. 2011, particularly 188–196). Valuation methods applicable to ecosystem services are summarized by numerous works, including those by Holland et al. (2010), Bateman et al. (2011), US Environmental Protection Agency (US EPA 2009), Swinton et al. (2007), and Hanley and Barbier (2009). Depending on the type of services involved and mechanisms through which they enhance welfare, options for valuation can include factor input methods, ecological productivity methods, and a wide range of nonmarket revealed and stated preference methods.

Recognizing these foundations, research linking ecosystem services to land use is most appropriately considered an application of existing methods rather than a novel methodological approach (Daily et al. 2009). Within agricultural policy for example, Gardner's 1977 *American Journal of Agricultural Economics* article elucidated the economic justification for public investment in farmland protection. The provision and preservation of nonmarket environmental amenities—many akin to what we now call ecosystem services—were among the primary motivations. Bergstrom and Ready (2009) review two decades of research estimating the value of agricultural amenity benefits in the United States, many of these related to what would now be labeled ecosystem services. Similarly, the multifunctional agriculture movement in the United States and Europe has at its core a recognition that agriculture provides nonmarket benefits beyond traditional food and fiber, including those related to the ecological functions of agro-ecosystems (Josling 2002; Batie 2003; Boody et al. 2005; Duke and Johnston 2010; National Research Council 2010). Similar themes appear in research related to the preservation of nonagricultural lands (Johnston and Swallow 2006).

Among the main distinguishing features of the ecosystem services movement is greater attention to the formal linkages between ecology and economics necessary to provide valid estimates of the human benefits. This includes an emphasis on the benefits of ecosystem structure and function realized through ecological production functions, rather than solely on the end products that influence welfare (Daily et al. 2009; cf., Collins et al. 2010). In the case of valuation, although the economic valuation *methods* are often identical, the *emphasis* is on the values provided directly or indirectly by ecosystem functions, rather than on the values provided by market or nonmarket goods. As noted below, this shift in emphasis—although perhaps subtle—can lead to nontrivial empirical challenges. These include steps required to account for, quantify, or appropriately disentangle multiple interacting services provided jointly by a single set of ecosystem functions (Nelson et al. 2009; Johnston and Russell 2011; Polasky et al. 2011).

Accordingly, and unlike some of the past research in nonmarket valuation, the literature linking ecosystem services to land use includes substantial participation of the natural science community. Models are often characterized by heavy use of geographic information systems (GIS) and attention to ecological modeling, although the characterization of ecological production relationships is one of the areas in which empirical results are often lacking (Bateman et al. 2011; Polasky et al. 2011). Empirical examples are diverse, with applications to such issues as nationwide agriculture (Bateman et al. 2011), statewide land use (Polasky et al. 2011), mangroves (Hanley and Barbier 2009), wetlands and intertidal habitats (Johnston et al. 2002*a*, 2002*b*; Boyer and Polasky 2004), carbon sequestration and species conservation (Nelson et al. 2009), biodiversity (Naidoo and Ricketts 2006), deforestation and pollination (Priess et al. 2007), invasive species (Wainger et al. 2010), and deforestation (Tallis and Polasky 2009).

Despite the diversity of empirical applications and divergent terminology applied across the ecosystem services literature, most research connecting ecosystem services to land use relies on a similar underlying conceptual framework, summarized in Figure 8.1.[3] This figure adapts and coordinates concepts found in works such as Brown et al. (2007), Fisher et al. (2009), Dale and Polasky (2007), and Johnston and Russell (2011). Within this framework, ecosystem properties, including structure and function at various trophic levels, contribute to biophysical outputs, which directly enhance the welfare

[3] Collins et al. (2010) provide an analogous framework that is more comprehensive with respect to social sciences other than economics.

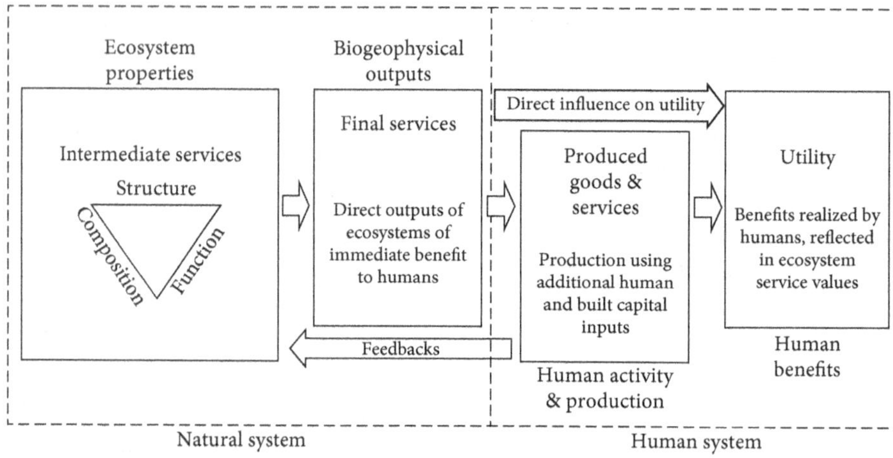

FIGURE 8.1 General linkages among ecosystem properties, ecosystem services, human production, and benefits.

of at least one human beneficiary (Johnston and Russell 2011). These outputs are defined as final ecosystem services (Boyd and Banzhaf 2007; Brown et al. 2007; Turner and Daily 2008; Fisher et al. 2009; Johnston and Russell 2011). Intermediate services, in contrast, are ecological conditions or processes that only benefit humans through effects on other, final services. These may be viewed as inputs into the production of final services. The status of an ecological condition or process as a final versus intermediate service may vary across beneficiaries (Johnston and Russell 2011).

As shown in Figure 8.1 (and discussed by Brown et al. [2007], Bateman et al. [2011], Fisher et al. [2009], and Johnston and Russell [2011]), ecosystem services only sometimes influence human welfare directly. An example would be nonuse benefits flowing directly from the provision of a biophysical output, such as wildlife abundance or diversity. However, more commonly, benefits are "generated by ecosystem services *in combination with* other forms of capital like people, knowledge, or equipment, e.g., hydroelectric power utilizes water regulation services of nature but also needs human engineering, concrete, etc." (Fisher et al. 2008, 2052). Once human labor or capital is applied to transform a biophysical output into something else, the result is no longer an ecosystem service but rather the result of human production (Johnston and Russell 2011); this is reflected by the "Produced Goods & Services" box in Figure 8.1. Most, if not all, agricultural commodities, for example, fall into this category. Human activities such as agricultural production, however, often jointly produce feedbacks that affect the ecosystem structures and functions that provide the initial ecosystem services (Zhang et al. 2007).

Based on this model, it is clear that valuation of market commodities produced using ecosystem services is not the same as valuation of ecosystem services (Bateman et al. 2011; Johnston and Russell 2011). In many cases, the final product sold in a market, and hence most easily valued, does not represent an ecosystem service. Rather, these services serve as inputs to market production. Although this distinction may render valuation of the ecosystem services themselves more difficult, it is required to consistently evaluate the benefits humans derive from ecosystems and distinguish these from the benefits that people obtain from human production (Johnston and Russell 2011).

For reasons such as this, it may sometimes be counterproductive to insist on separate and distinct values for ecosystem services. Land use and land use change affect ecosystem structure and function, intentionally and unintentionally. Swallow (1996*a*) places this observation within the context of basic economic theories of resource use, noting that the role of land in ecosystem production, both in its developed state, as well as in its "natural" (or undeveloped) state, affects its net value (cf., Swallow [1994] for an application). Often, land use change is focused on human-produced goods, some of which may be built on intermediate inputs or goods provided by ecosystems. The inseparability of human-produced values from at least some ecosystem-produced values recommends a careful understanding of derived demand and the view of ecosystems as one critical contributor to overall human well-being, but one that may not operate alone, in the absence of human ingenuity and productivity.

Beyond the general conceptual approach outlined in Figure 8.1, there have been many proposed typologies of ecosystem services; these seek to provide templates that may be used to identify and categorize services across applications (e.g., de Groot et al. 2002; Millennium Ecosystem Assessment 2005; Wallace 2007; Balmford et al. 2011). The relevance of such taxonomies, however, is limited. As noted by Fisher et al. (2008, 2051), for example, "while [the typology in the Millennium Ecosystem Assessment] is useful as a heuristic tool, it can lead to confusion when trying to assign economic values to ecosystem services."[4] Numerous authors have highlighted the double counting implicit in many typologies (Wallace 2007; Fisher et al. 2008, 2009; Johnston and Russell 2011), and Johnston and Russell (2011) note the impossibility of a universal typology that applies to all beneficiaries.

The ubiquity of frameworks and typologies within the literature may also obscure the multiple valid approaches that one may take toward quantification and valuation. Many market and nonmarket goods are joint products of multiple components of ecosystem structure and function. Within this context, the analyst should exercise caution before concluding that there is a single, proper point at which to conduct quantification and valuation. As discussed later in this chapter, there are many advantages to valuation focused on end products (e.g., final goods). However, there may be instances in which—for policy or analytical purposes—valuation of intermediate products might be desirable (Johnston et al. 2011).[5] In cases where values of intermediate outcomes

[4] Indeed, the category of "supporting services" is nearly tailor-made to induce double counting (Johnston et al. 2011). The concept seems closely associated with the standard economic concept of derived demand (see Swallow 1997); the careless analyst might forget that the value of inputs (ecological structures and functions) that "support" production of ecosystem service outputs of direct relevance to human well-being is fully incorporated (already) upon measuring the value of final services.

[5] For example, in some instances final welfare-producing products may be unobservable to the analyst or difficult to quantify, whereas intermediate outcomes may be more easily quantified or observed.

are estimated, the analyst may face increased risk of double counting or omission of welfare-relevant outcomes, particularly when a comprehensive understanding of relationships between intermediate and final services is unavailable. Although welfare theory enables valuation of either intermediate or final outcomes, there can be empirical challenges to both.

In summary, despite the foundation of contemporary ecosystem services research and the recent explosion of publications seeking to link land use to ecosystem service provision and value, this area of study remains immature. Improved methods—or at least a more transparent delineation of assumptions, caveats, and implications—are required if information on ecosystem services is to be used broadly to guide land use policy (Bauer and Johnston 2013). Challenges are particularly evident in empirical work.

2. The Validity and Precision of Research Linking Ecosystem Services to Land Use

The characteristics and quality of empirical methods within the ecosystem services literature vary. Despite this heterogeneity, the validity and precision of empirical ecosystem services research is strongly related to three often interlinked factors. These include (1) what services are evaluated, (2) how these services are evaluated, and (3) at which scopes and scales evaluations are conducted.[6]

2.1 The Conceptual Basis for Ecosystem Service Values: What Services Are Evaluated?

Consistent estimates of ecosystem service values require careful definition of the specific services under consideration and how these contribute to human welfare. Differentiation of intermediate ecosystem functions from final ecosystem services, where feasible, also ensures that the benefit of each distinct ecosystem condition or process, to each human beneficiary,[7] is counted once and only once (Fisher et al. 2008; US EPA 2009; Johnston and Russell 2011). The distinction between intermediate and final ecosystem services may be defined within the framework described by Boyd and Krupnick (2013), Fisher et al. (2009), Turner and Daily (2008), and Johnston and Russell

[6] In addition, many ecological studies advance the frontiers of ecological knowledge but miss opportunities to publish quantitative models to which economists could attach their own models. The corollary is also true, with economists' disciplinary focus failing to facilitate connections for ecologists.

[7] Following Johnston and Russell (2011), we define a "beneficiary" as a person or group operating in a particular role (e.g., bird watcher, farmer) whose welfare in that role is improved by a particular ecosystem service and is therefore willing to pay for improvement or to avoid reduction in the service.

(2011), among others, which characterizes the provision of natural outputs (goods and services) in terms of systems of ecological production. The final outputs of these systems—final ecosystem services—are biophysical outcomes that directly enhance the welfare of at least one human beneficiary.[8] Intermediate services are conditions or processes that only benefit humans through effects on other, final services.

Failure to recognize the value of intermediate ecosystem services encourages actions that lead to suboptimal provision of these services. Conversely, summation of values for both intermediate and final services is also misleading because it double counts the contribution of the intermediate services to welfare, which also promotes suboptimal provision relative to human welfare. Such double counting is common (Johnston and Russell 2011).

As a purely conceptual matter, valuation of intermediate services is straightforward. Within economic theory, one can value either changes in inputs or the corresponding change in the final output; the value of the change in output reflects the sum of the value of changes in all inputs used in production. However, in the context of ecosystem services, valuing changes in intermediate services often presents empirical challenges (Johnston et al. 2011). What is often missing is a quantifiable linkage between changes in ecosystem structure or function, implying changes in intermediate services, and how such changes affect the value of final services.

For example, revealed preference analyses rarely account for the influence of intermediate ecological inputs on final ecosystem goods and services that (directly) influence observed behaviors. Hence, revealed preference analyses generally provide values for final ecosystem services only.[9] Additional biophysical information is required to estimate values for associated intermediate services, such as water filtration services of undeveloped land; this is often unavailable (Johnston et al. 2011). Stated preference (SP) research has also given little attention to distinctions between intermediate and final services, or more broadly to the definition of ecosystem services, leading to the potential for welfare biases (Fisher et al. 2009; Johnston et al. 2011; Boyd and Krupnick 2013).

Existing works in the economics literature have sought to clarify the challenge and provide solutions (Boyd and Banzhaf 2007; Brown et al. 2007; Wallace 2007; Fisher and Turner 2008; Fisher et al. 2009; Boyd and Krupnick 2013). Solutions suggested by these works, however, have yet to gain broad adoption outside of the economics literature. Johnston and Russell (2011) argue that the emphasis of the ecosystem services literature on complex "one size fits all" classifications exacerbates the confusion over final versus intermediate services. In response, they propose a set of guidelines that can be used to clarify the set of final ecosystem services that benefit any given beneficiary and distinguish these from intermediate services.

[8] Boyd and Krupnick (2013) define a closely related concept of ecological endpoints.

[9] An exception is ecological productivity methods, in which empirical welfare estimates are grounded in an explicit model of ecological production (e.g., Johnston et al. 2002*b*).

Even given such guidelines, cataloguing of ecosystem services may prove difficult, because it often requires the analyst to characterize complex, dynamic, and interrelated processes responsible for the production of final ecosystem goods and services. These services may be subject to unknowns concerning both ecological and household production functions. Indeed, in a world of joint production (by ecosystems and by households using ecosystems), a set of separate and distinct service values and value estimates may prove impossible without potentially arbitrary allocation rules.[10] Here, the most critical need is often not for a complete cataloguing of intermediate and final services for any beneficiary but rather a consistent framework to ensure that double counting is mitigated. Some have also argued that the valuation of jointly produced ecosystem services is best accomplished within a general equilibrium framework (National Research Council 2005; Carbone and Smith 2008, 2010).[11]

Regardless of the specific mechanisms applied, research evaluating ecosystem services from land use requires careful attention to consistency and theoretical validity, including methods to identify the ecosystem services to be valued (Fisher et al. 2008; Bauer and Johnston 2013). These concerns are particularly relevant for broad-scale analyses that attempt to simultaneously quantify values for multiple, often interrelated or bundled ecosystem services, particularly when aggregated benefits from these models are used to inform land use policy.

2.2 The Methodological Basis for Ecosystem Service Values: How Are Services Evaluated?

Although methodological advances have been made in research linking ecosystem services to land use and quantifying associated values, required "[i]nterdisciplinary research, combining economics and other social sciences with the natural sciences... remains a relatively immature area of study" (Bateman et al. 2011, 209). Among "the most serious problems facing the effective and robust valuation of ecosystem services are gaps in our understanding of the underpinning science relating those services to the production of goods and the paucity of valuation studies and available data regarding the values of these goods" (Bateman et al. 2011, 193). Research linking ecosystem services to land use not infrequently incorporates substandard economic or ecological methods or unrealistic assumptions; "most modeling to date has been unavoidably

[10] For example, some authors characterize agricultural production as a final ecosystem service because the growth of crops is largely an ecological process (Fisher et al. 2009). Others characterize agricultural production as the result of a combination of human labor and capital with ecosystem services—such that the agricultural production itself is not a final ecosystem service (Brown et al. 2007; Johnston and Russell 2011). Neither perspective is incorrect; they merely reflect subtly different definitions of a final ecosystem service. What is most important is transparency and consistency in whatever classifications are applied.

[11] Finnoff et al. (2008) and Finnoff and Tschirhart (2008) illustrate a provocative approach.

simplistic" (Balmford et al. 2011). This simplicity arises, in part, because disciplinary segregation may not lead ecologists to produce quantitative models of links between drivers and outputs of relevance to human welfare and may not lead economists to produce models with sufficient foundation in ecological production processes.

Johnston et al. (2012), for example, detail ecological shortcomings of SP analyses of ecosystem service values, including the tendency of the literature to quantify values for "ecosystem services" that have no precise ecological definition. Simpson (1998) details similar shortcomings applicable to economists' treatment of ecology more broadly. Swallow (1996*b*) demonstrates that the dynamic ecological context of habitat development can invalidate standard economic intuition regarding the ranking of social value from new development in a heterogeneous, ecologically dynamic landscape.

At the same time, there are gaps in the underlying natural science knowledge necessary to link changes in ecosystem structure and function to effects on quantifiable ecosystem services (Bateman et al. 2011); we are often unable to predict, for example, how the flow of services will be affected by changes in land use or management (Daily et al. 2009; Polasky et al. 2011). Although large-scale, data-intensive models such as InVEST (Integrated Valuation of Ecosystem Services and Tradeoffs) have been developed to model the production and value of ecosystem services, these models generally operate over large scales, exceeding the scale of common decisions on land use or land development (Nelson et al. 2009; Tallis and Polasky 2009; Polasky et al. 2011). The ability of such tools to quantify changes in ecosystem service flows and values related to land use also depends on the validity of the underlying ecological and economic models and the coherence with which these models are combined.

Although established methods are available to quantify ecosystem service values linked to land use, many commonly cited analyses are grounded in economic methods that "generate misleading and potentially biased results" (Balmford et al. 2011, 167). Frequent shortcomings include (1) extrapolating from a small number of unrepresentative studies to entire biomes (Bockstael et al. 2000; Balmford et al. 2011); (2) the common use of economic measures, such as replacement costs that "bear little resemblance to the values they [are used to] approximate" (Bockstael et al. 2000; Holland et al. 2010; Bateman et al. 2011, p. 191); (3) overlooking the dependence of economic values on policy scope and scale (see discussion in Section 3 below), including analyses that attempt to value entire ecosystems rather than marginal changes and that ignore concepts such as diminishing marginal utility (Toman 1998; Bockstael et al. 2000; Fisher et al. 2008; Rolfe et al. 2011); and (4) the use of simplistic unit-value benefit transfers and other approaches that fail to meet minimal standards (Johnston and Rosenberger 2010; Bateman et al. 2011).

Whether these issues are of concern for policy applications depends on the level of validity and accuracy deemed necessary in particular policy contexts (Navrud and Pruckner 1997). As many of these shortcomings lead to quantitative value estimates that have little basis in economic theory (reducing or eliminating validity) and incorporate errors of unknown sign and magnitude (undermining credibility), economists tend to view resulting estimates with skepticism. The challenge for the field moving forward is to progress beyond illustrative analyses with fundamental economic or ecological flaws to empirical works grounded in a more rigorous coordination of natural and social sciences.

2.3 Recognizing Marginality: At What Scopes and Scales Are Ecosystem Services Evaluated?

For the sake of clarity, we here define *scope* as the quantity or quality of an ecosystem service under consideration, whereas *scale* is defined as the geographic area over which an analysis is conducted. Ecosystem service assessments are often conducted at large scopes and scales; for example, for many ecosystem services, over large geographical areas, often concerning nonmarginal changes or total values (Fisher et al. 2008). This is distinct from much of the prior nonmarket valuation literature, which tends to address resources at smaller scopes and scales.

The archetypal example is Costanza et al. (1997), which seeks to quantify and value ecosystem services at a planetary scale. Unfortunately, "there is little that can be usefully done with a serious underestimate of infinity" (Toman 1998, 58). Moreover,

> One needs a specified baseline, a specified measure of changes, and a set of criteria for evaluating and comparing these changes. A simple point aggregation of "everything,"...give[s] no insights into either the directions of current changes in ecosystems and their services or the relative urgency of different changes.
>
> (Toman 1998, 58)

Statewide and nationwide analyses are also common (Nelson et al. 2009; Bateman et al. 2011; Polasky et al. 2011), reflecting a tendency of the ecosystem services literature to seek results relevant to large scopes and scales (Turner and Daily 2008; Daily et al. 2009). Although the grounding of analyses in economic theory and measurable ecosystem service changes may ameliorate some of the concerns with these models, the concerns of Toman (1998) remain relevant.

In contrast, the most precise empirical assessments in both economics and ecology tend to involve evaluations at small scopes and scales. These address a few ecosystem services, over small geographical areas, for marginal changes. The divergence between the smaller scopes or scales at which research is most precise and the larger scopes or scales at which ecosystem service information is often requested has contributed to evaluations that have applied questionable, or at best oversimplified, methods to provide results over large scopes and scales (Toman 1998; Bockstael et al. 2000; Fisher et al. 2008; Rolfe et al. 2011). This emphasis on large scale, nonmarginal changes is often puzzling to economists because the role of such information in policy formation is questionable and analytical results may fail validity criteria (Toman 1998; Fisher et al. 2008). Large-scale analyses may motivate an attitude change among political forces, potentially fueling rhetoric for advocacy, but fail to provide insight necessary for better decisions or to establish priorities for action requiring policy-scale input.

Many of the challenges identified in the preceding sections of this chapter are related, at least indirectly, to the preoccupation of the ecosystem services literature on large scopes and scales. Valid economic valuation methods, for example, quantify values for clearly specified marginal changes (Bockstael et al. 2000; Fisher et al. 2008), thus meeting Toman's (1998) standard to work from a specified baseline and specified change. Among other advantages, the evaluation over small, marginal changes allows the use of partial equilibrium analyses that hold most factors in the outside world constant, beyond those closely related to the change being valued (Just et al. 2004). As the defined margin becomes larger, the accuracy of economic forecasts often declines (Fisher et al. 2008). Similarly, nonlinearities in ecological relationships can have important implications for ecosystem service value. The effects of these nonlinearities on ecosystem service values are often more difficult to model and predict for nonmarginal ecological changes, particularly in the presence of complicating factors such as ecological resilience and thresholds (Hanley and Barbier 2009; Bateman et al. 2011).

Attempts to link ecosystem services to land use over large scopes and scales has also contributed to a tendency to overlook heterogeneity in ecosystems, populations, and policy contexts and to apply often rudimentary benefit transfers that overlook the critical influences of these differences on values (Bateman et al. 2011; Rolfe et al. 2011). For example, the value of wetlands in filtering excess nutrients may be substantial when located upstream of a source water reservoir, but may be inconsequential—or at least valued for different reasons—in an area remote from human population centers. Recent applications linking ecosystem services to land use have attempted to use somewhat more advanced benefit transfer approaches that, in coordination with GIS and other spatial tools, enable at least somewhat improved adjustments for differences in ecosystems, populations, and policy contexts when conducting large-scale analyses (Bateman et al. 2011; Polasky et al. 2011). However, even these analyses require strong assumptions.

The perspective of marginality is often criticized for failing to recognize that nonlinearities may manifest as thresholds, thus creating potential shifts in ecological structure and function. Even in such situations, the disciplined analyst still establishes a clearly defined baseline from which change might occur, assessing the value of potential changes from that baseline. An analysis tailored to the level of the marginal decision can be organized within an economic framework to facilitate informed decision making, even if results of the decision cross nonmarginal thresholds within the ecological sphere.

3. Connecting Ecosystem Services to Land Use in Practice

Various analytical frameworks may be applied when evaluating ecosystem services. One of the most obvious is valuation; this is often the ideal if science (ecology and economics) can adequately support needed models. However, the data and modeling requirements for valuation can sometimes be prohibitive. Moreover, in some instances, valuation is not necessary to improve policy; what is needed instead is insight into relationships between ecosystem structures and functions and desired ecosystem outputs, whether or not these outputs have quantified values (Wainger and Mazzotta 2011). This leads to alternative approaches to research that link ecosystem services to land use.

This section attempts to present illustrative points, not necessarily endpoints, on a continuum of approaches that link ecosystem services to land use. The illustrated case studies purposefully involve nonvaluation frameworks that often receive less attention in the ecosystem services literature. The first application outlines the use of a bioeconomic model to land use controls. This approach occurs in the absence of quantified knowledge about values a community might hold for ecosystem services, proceeding on the presumption that the community has already established, perhaps through a collective process, a desire to preserve particular services. Here, the crucial question is not whether to preserve services or to what extent they are valued, but how preservation is best accomplished. The second application illustrates potential ways to incorporate ecosystem service values into landowner choices. This case illustrates the potential to move beyond valuation into market creation.

Returning to the three factors detailed in Section 2 (i.e., what services are evaluated, how services are evaluated, and the scopes and scales at which services are evaluated), the two case studies are explicit in terms of the outcomes that are evaluated (amphibian metapopulations; hayfields supporting bobolink nesting), the ways in which outcomes are evaluated (bioeconomic models, experimental markets), and the (small) scopes and scales at which evaluations are implemented (amphibian metapopulations within wetland patches in Richmond, Rhode Island; specific agricultural fields in Jamestown, Rhode Island). The case studies do not, however, specify the full set of linkages through which these specific ecological outcomes support different intermediate and final ecosystem services.

This potential shortcoming warrants additional emphasis—when is it necessary clarify all linkages between intermediate and final services? Among the primary reasons to clarify these linkages is the mitigation of double counting and development of comprehensive welfare estimates. As a result, clarification of these linkages is critical when welfare estimation (i.e., valuation) is the primary goal. In the case studies illustrated here, however, welfare estimation is not the goal. Hence, whether the ecological outcomes in question reflect intermediate or final ecosystem services, or both, for particular beneficiary groups is irrelevant to the research questions at hand—such information would not directly enhance the relevance or validity of the research results.

This distinction highlights a critical point in analyses that link ecosystem services to land use. That is, the variation in possible research and policy contexts implies that any set of unyielding guidelines for analysis, including some of those presented earlier, may have exceptions. What is most crucial in these heterogeneous contexts is the application of methods that are transparent and valid from the perspective of the underlying natural and social sciences. The case study examples here are meant to illustrate different, nonvaluation ways in which rigorous insight can be provided on ecosystem services connected to land use without sacrificing the validity of the underlying economics or ecology.

3.1 A Bioeconomic Modeling Approach

Bauer et al.'s (2010*a*, 2010*b*) work assesses whether familiar approaches to wetland conservation, based on treating wetland patches as sacrosanct, achieves the highest level of ecosystem services for a given set of development restrictions. Using an indicator species of amphibians, the work shows that integration of opportunity costs into policy design might either enable a higher level of ecosystem services at a given social cost or enable a lower cost to achieve a targeted level of ecosystem services. Related approaches are illustrated by Jiang et al. (2007), Montgomery et al. (1994), and Nalle et al. (2004).

Wetland policy is often based on regulations that restrict development of habitat patches, perhaps including a buffer zone, while leaving few restrictions on upland development. Recent work in conservation biology questions the wisdom of this approach, with authors such as Semlitsch (1998, 2007) and Semlitsch and Bodie (1998) raising questions within the context of a patch-corridor model motivated by metapopulation dynamics and concern for amphibian species that depend on seasonal wetlands. Species that depend on dispersed habitat patches, such as a network of wetlands, may exhibit a metapopulation structure whereby the subpopulations occupying different patches (at least for breeding) depend on connectivity between patches to enable long-term survival of the overall population; this connectivity enables patches to serve as sources of colonists should environmental uncertainty cause extinction of a subpopulation. The collection of such subpopulations comprises the metapopulation.

Bauer et al. (2010*a*, 2010*b*) develop a baseline landscape modeled from the town of Richmond, Rhode Island, drawing parameters to model a metapopulation of amphibians both from ecological data from the study area and from the literature more broadly. Hereafter, we will refer to the Bauer et al. papers as the BSP case study. The case study area is approximately 100 km^2 of predominantly mixed deciduous forest interspersed with residential development and small village centers. The actual town is 24% developed land, 33% protected, and 43% undeveloped and unprotected, incorporating 214 biologically distinct vernal pool clusters (or seasonal wetland ponds). For the case study, 30 existing zoning districts were condensed to 16 neighborhoods, each one zoned for one of five land uses (high, medium, and low density residential use; commercial and industrial land; and agricultural land).

This context presumes that the community, albeit through a state-level statute, has expressed a desire to maintain an ecologically viable network of wetlands capable of maintaining species dependent on vernal pools (fish-free, seasonal ponds). The existence of wetland protection laws constitutes an institutional or legal reaction to a community value for and desire to maintain ecosystem services.[12]

Within this context, the BSP case study was designed to assess how wetland policy might better reflect the role of both protected and developed land in landscape structure and function. BSP use a metapopulation model inspired by Hanski (1994) and co-authors (e.g., Moilanen and Hanski 1998; Hanski and Ovaskainen 2000; Ovaskainen and Hanski 2001) to measure ecosystem health using the landscape's metapopulation size, an analog to ecological carrying capacity based on the average probability that a habitat patch is occupied by amphibians in a steady state. With this measure of ecosystem quality, BSP assess the value of development that must be foregone to maintain a targeted level of ecosystem quality. This approach enables a consideration of the ecological and economic heterogeneity of the study area, thereby evaluating how flexibility in wetland policy might improve the cost-effective provision of ecosystem services, measured using amphibians' metapopulation capacity as an indicator.

Summarized in conceptual equations outlined below, the approach models ecosystem connections across land parcels and how the intensity of development alters these connections, thereby diminishing potential ecosystem health. The model's output then traces the link between ecosystem health and costs measured as the monetary value of lost development opportunities. Such information enables a community to evaluate its own values (subjectively) for ecosystem health relative to the costs of alternative sets of land use restrictions that it might adopt. These costs are measured using current (2005) real estate values and against a defined baseline, such as the maximum extent of development permitted under current wetland and land use regulations.

3.1.1 Conceptual Model

The model includes details of the structural and functional roles served by land in habitat patches and the land intervening between these patches, where the latter is described as *dispersal matrix*, which determines connectivity between patches. The analyst first identifies the effective area g_i of habitat patch i as a function of the patch size A_i (acres); its quality H_i, as indicated by field measurements and modeling of existing breeding populations at patch i (e.g., Eagan and Paton 2004); and the quantity of development Q_{Ai} within the patch (which cannot exceed patch size):

$$g_i = g(A_i, H_i, Q_{Ai}). \tag{1}$$

[12] The specific services desired by the community may be defined with varying levels of precision. Stated preference work in this community and others within Rhode Island shows that the residents are motivated by the maintenance of biodiversity; quality of surface and ground waters, with purposes including outdoor recreation; sustaining open space; and preserving the rural character of their community (Johnston et al. 1999, 2002*c*, 2002*d*, 2003).

Larger area, higher quality, and less development increases the effective area of a habitat patch. Connectivity between patches is critical to metapopulation survival and is influenced by the distance d_{in} between patch i and any other patch n; the amount d_{jin} of that distance that crosses matrix unit j; and the size Z_j of dispersal matrix j. Along with the quantity Q_{Zj0} of existing development, these factors establish the baseline conditions for the extent to which the landscape presents amphibians with barriers between patches i and n, and, in turn, these barriers are enhanced (dispersal matrix land is degraded) by any additional quantity Q_{Zj} of development. Thus, connectivity between patches i and n, f_{in}, depends on the permeability of the intervening matrix lands, which may be shared across several land management units in the overall dispersal matrix, such that

$$f_{in} = f(B_{in}, d_{in}), \tag{2a}$$

with

$$B_{in} = b(d_{ijn} / d_{in}, Q_{Zj0}, Z_j). \tag{2b}$$

This does not imply that absolute barriers exist, but rather that the model captures the degree to which the passage through matrix land is impermeable to migrating juvenile amphibians; in this model, more development implies a lower rate of successful dispersals. Connectivity is greater for lower distance between patches, with that distance passing through matrix land that is more permeable to migrants; permeability decreases (barriers increase) when migrants must cross more hostile segments of dispersal matrix, which occurs with more existing or new development as a proportion of total land within a management-unit j of dispersal matrix land of area Z_j. A mathematical matrix quantifying landscape structure brings the components of the metapopulation model together. This mathematical landscape structure matrix includes elements m_{in} that capture the impact of habitat patch n as a contributor of immigrants to patch i when patch i is empty. This is based on species-specific immigration and emigration rate parameters applied to the effective areas of both patches, g_i and g_n, and the connectivity measure f_{in}:

$$m_{in} = m(g_i, g_n, f_{in}). \tag{3}$$

Here, patches of larger effective area produce more emigrants, receive more immigrants, and support a larger subpopulation which, in turn, reduces the probability that the subpopulation goes (temporarily) extinct. The metapopulation model supports estimation of metapopulation size, S_m, under alternative configurations of development, particularly new development, in patches (Q_{Ai}) and dispersal matrix units (Q_{Zj}):

$$S_m = s(Q_{Ai}, Q_{Zj}, g_i, g_n, f_{in}) \tag{4}$$

where this representation places the emphasis on the management controls of allowing or limiting development within patches and dispersal matrix land units.

The challenge for managers is to identify restrictions that minimize the loss of development opportunities while sustaining the ecosystem services of interest, as measured via (or indexed by) metapopulation size. The decision maker minimizes the cost of allocating land (perhaps through regulatory control, rather than purchase) to preservation, considering both habitat patches and matrix lands:

$$\min \text{Opportunity Cost} = \sum_{i=1,N} R_{Ai}\, Q_{Ai} + \sum_{j=1,J} R_{Zj}\, Q_{Zj}, \tag{5}$$

where R_{Ai} and R_{Zj} represent the potential Ricardian rent or land value that a developer could realize by conversion of a unit within habitat patches i and dispersal matrix units j, respectively; and Q_{Ai} and Q_{Zi} represent the quantity of land chosen to be protected within these patches and matrix units. Within the zoning context, land protection would occur as a proportion of the respective undeveloped lands available, so that the sum of existing and new development plus protection does not exceed the total area available in a patch (A_i) or dispersal matrix unit. In this model, development is distributed evenly within a habitat patch or matrix unit, but spatial identity is maintained across these units.

3.1.2 Evaluating Results for Policy Application

By minimizing opportunity costs in (5), subject to establishing a minimum level of ecosystem health via a minimum metapopulation size $S_m{}^0$ using (4), this approach traces out a minimum cost in relation to alternative metapopulation sizes. Figure 8.2 provides a stylized illustration of the key results; the figure is illustrative and not quantitatively definitive. In Figure 8.2, each point on the curve represents the minimum cost (vertical axis) of providing for a given metapopulation size. Point A (Figure 8.2) represents the metapopulation size that would exist if Richmond developed every legally allowed parcel under 2005 zoning, keeping in mind that development in Richmond generally maintains a wooded landscape, albeit with increased fragmentation, but sustaining some connectivity and permeability to migrating amphibians. The model places metapopulation size at 0.804 under this "full build-out" scenario, interpreted as an 80% chance that a habitat patch is occupied in steady state, with an opportunity cost of zero (since the baseline of "full build-out" would imply no new protection).

Model results suggest that a steep increase in costs occurs at approximately a 0.95 value of metapopulation size, reflecting the challenge of mitigating development impacts when pristine conditions no longer apply. Nonetheless, a political or social decision process might establish a much more stringent level of metapopulation capacity, compared to 0.804 achieved under full build out. The common approach to protection of wetlands treats all wetlands the same, setting an across-the-board standard. In the present model, one such standard would be to establish a 165 m buffer around each

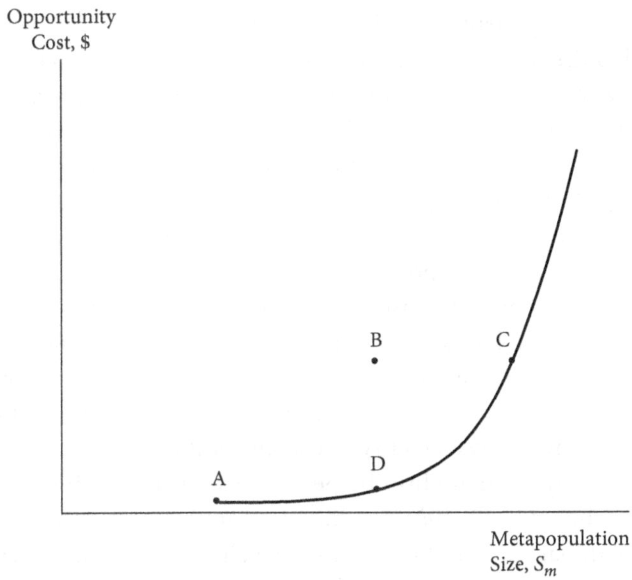

FIGURE 8.2 Stylized results of bioeconomic model estimating the opportunity cost of achieving a given metapopulation size. Bauer et al. (2010*b*) provide an empirical example of this concept diagram, whereas Bauer et al. (2010*a*) provide estimated traces of the opportunity cost curve under various policy assumptions.

wetland and protect all land within that buffer from any further development, consistent with biological delineation of key habitat, for example, following Semlitsch (1998). Such a policy would leave aside the issue of development in matrix lands. Bauer et al. (2010*b*) calculate the implications of such a policy (derived without consideration of economic factors), obtaining a result analogous to point B in Figure 8.2, which would achieve a metapopulation size of 0.924 at an opportunity cost of around $101 million. The key observation of the analysis is that a point such as B leaves at least two ways to do better for human well-being and ecosystems: (1) one may achieve the same 0.924 ecological quality at substantially lower cost of foregone development benefits (perhaps just 10% of $101 million), moving to a point like D in Figure 8.2; or (2) one may achieve greater ecological quality if the community chooses to endure the given cost, moving to a point like C in Figure 8.2, perhaps approaching the limit of 0.979 under a policy of fully protecting all remaining patch and matrix lands (Bauer et al. 2010*b*).[13]

Moving down and to the right, toward the minimum cost curve between C and D (Figure 8.2) would improve in both dimensions of cost and metapopulation size. However, it is also important to recognize that the model could allow a zoning constraint to be established either separately for matrix lands and land in habitat patches (as defined by a buffer zone) across the board or separately for patches and matrix land

[13] Estimated to incur an opportunity cost of $463 million (Bauer et al. 2010*b*).

within different management units. For example, Bauer et al. (2010*a*, 805–806) show that, compared to the full build-out (no protection) scenario, protecting 50% of habitat patches (within a 165 m buffer around vernal pools) would achieve a higher metapopulation size (nearly 0.90 versus about 0.87) at lower opportunity cost (about $50 million vs. more than $100 million) as compared to protecting 25% of undeveloped dispersal matrix (recognizing that total land area in the matrix is larger than total land in these patches). The model allows assessment of further tradeoffs between protecting land in different roles. For example, protecting 25% of both patch and matrix land yields a metapopulation size of 0.922 at a cost of $163 million; moving from that base position to 100% protection of patch lands along with 25% of matrix lands increases metapopulation size by 0.036 to 0.958 at an *additional* cost of $95 million. In comparison, moving to 100% protection of dispersal land while remaining with 25% protection of patch land raises metapopulation size by 0.044 to 0.966 at an additional cost of $395 million.

Such examples may oversimplify the perspective of human benefits from environmental quality. Bauer et al. (2010*b*) provide an example in which a metapopulation size of 0.95 occurs with partial or full protection of a cluster of habitat patches in the center of Richmond, leaving the vast majority of Richmond in 15 other zones (outside this core area) with little or no additional land conservation over current policy; they provide a modified model establishing a metapopulation constraint separately for five subsections of the town in an effort to assess alternatives across the town's landscape. Adding these additional constraints raises the cost-minimizing options at each metapopulation size (from around $12 million to approaching $50 million at S_m of 0.95), but if the community establishes goals to assure a broad, geographic distribution of opportunities for residents to live within a landscape that produces ecosystem services at a minimal level, these higher costs might prove acceptable.

Throughout this example, the specific ecosystem services provided are those associated with land conservation that promotes the longevity of amphibian metapopulations. The ecosystem service benefits, however, include many beyond those associated solely with amphibians. These may include services associated with a lower density of development and broader geographic distribution of undeveloped lands. Benefits may also include provision of habitat for a variety of other species, including birds or wildlife that cohabitate the forested patches and undeveloped matrix, or conservation of groundwater recharge through preserved wetlands, among others. A full catalogue of these services would improve the information base for land use decisions. Yet, even without this information, the bioeconomic model illustrates opportunities to enhance both the economic and ecological outcomes of land preservation as realized through the provision of ecosystem health and services.

3.2 Beyond Valuation, Toward Markets for Ecosystem Services

Beyond the valuation of ecosystem services, there is increasing interest in ways to integrate these values directly into the economy through markets, regulatory means, or other mechanisms. Indeed, society as a whole spends little time seeking to quantify the value of market goods because markets automatically establish prices effectively, even in the presence of variation in local supply and demand. If policy innovation could establish similar markets for currently nonmarket ecosystem services, many of the challenges of valuation might vanish; society could make more efficient decisions about ecosystem services if markets more fully incorporated ecosystem service values. The second application illustrates research that addresses this market challenge.

Swallow et al. (2008) describe experimental work that uses incentive mechanisms and rules of exchange to generate revenues for ecosystem services specifically linked to the management of farm hayfields as nesting bird habitat. Their application concerns the conflict between the nesting season for bobolinks (*Dolichonyx oryzivorus*), a neotropical migrant, and the peak nutritional value of hay as feed for livestock in northeastern US farms. In this study, the investigators served as brokers between farmers in Jamestown, Rhode Island, and nonfarm households in this rural fringe community. They established contracts through which farmers would agree to modify their harvest during late May to early July in order to avoid impacts on bobolink nesting. Farmers would give up at least one hay harvest so that nests in that field could produce fledglings. Harvesting during nesting and prior to fledging of young birds has been shown to generate nest mortality rates of nearly 100% (e.g., Bollinger et al. 1990). In turn, the investigators asked Jamestown residents to pay for these contracts. The study assigned groups of households to a particular hayfield. Within each group, the independent decisions of members regarding whether to buy into the contract determined whether the farmer for that field was paid for bobolink management or whether the contract was dropped, allowing the farmer to proceed with his or her normal harvesting plans.

The study thus implemented a voluntary market exchange. The researchers served the role of brokers, raised revenues from town residents, and paid farmers for bird-friendly hayfield management. In practice, such an exchange might be developed through independent private action, by a for-profit or not-for-profit broker, or it could be aided by a government subsidy providing a share of costs for a contract but requiring the remaining share to be generated from revenues contributed by local residents. An exchange such as this could reveal at least some of the value for ecosystem services. Even with imperfect rules of exchange and incentives (e.g., that allow some beneficiaries to free ride), the approach begins to develop market mechanisms for ecosystem services in a way that improves human welfare.

Within this study, marketing materials placed the habitat services of a 10-acre hayfield during a single season for nesting bobolinks as the focal point, including the slogan "Their home, your hometown." Marketing materials also noted the potential of hayfields to maintain agrarian heritage or open-field views, as well as noting potential linkages to water quality and carbon sequestration, and some Jamestown residents may have considered these or other aspects of ecosystem services. However, what is clear is that households were asked to contribute toward the specific action of bird-friendly management of a specified size hayfield. A strength of this example is that the hayfield contracts represent a specific action, or good, that households could consider buying into for the provision of ecosystem services linked to a particular land use; the change was clearly defined. The ability to at least partially capture resident's willingness to pay (WTP)—and thereby improve socially valuable outcomes—does not necessarily require analysts to define beforehand the particular ecosystem services or quantities of these services potentially affected, although the failure to do so may influence the ability of the market-maker to identify an optimal level of provision.

The research was designed to identify the value of bobolink contracts to residents of Jamestown and to identify a set of rules of exchange that might lead residents to offer a higher percentage of their full value as a financial contribution to support a contract with a farmer. Drawing on the experimental economics literature, the bobolink contracts were presented under a variety of provision point mechanisms (Poe et al. 2002; Spencer et al. 2009). In contrast to a pure, open-ended donations approach used by charitable organizations, provision point mechanisms establish a minimum, target level of aggregate funding that must be achieved before provision of a unit of the public good is assured. In this study, the unit was a 10-acre hayfield contracted for bird-friendly management during a single summer nesting season. If individuals from a group of households failed to make aggregate contributions that meet or exceed the cost of the farm contract[14] (the provision point), the farm field would be released from the contract, and all contributions would be refunded to the households providing the funds. Rondeau et al. (1999, 2005; cf., Poe et al. 2002) show that the provision point reduces incentives to free-ride[15] by establishing a rudimentary threat of nonprovision, as well as by assuring that contributions pay for a specified unit of the good; Swallow et al. (2008) implemented this provision point by defining a finite group of households to determine the outcome for each field.

The experimental market also incorporated marginal incentives to reduce the advantages of free-riding. A primary example is a proportional rebate method tested in laboratory experiments by Marks and Croson (1998; Spencer et al. 2009). The experimental market tested other rules of exchange, all involving a provision point, but each differing in the marginal incentives created by their rebate rule. Other rebate rules established a "price cap" or uniform price that was endogenously determined by aggregate contributions within a group as the lowest amount that could be used as maximum charge while still meeting the provision point, such that individuals making high offers would receive a rebate of money offered above the price cap. The proportional rebate and uniform price mechanisms were intended to raise revenues for actual provision of hayfields by private entrepreneurs. An alternative mechanism, the "pivotal mechanism," was not designed to raise revenues but rather to estimate the potential willingness to pay of participants.[16]

[14] In the experiments of Swallow et al. (2008), the actual provision points in some cases reflected a subsidy from funds obtained outside of the contributions of households. However, those subsidies were determined prior to solicitations to households, and the provision point reflected the net cost of the farm contract after any subsidy.

[15] Under a free-riding strategy, the beneficiary contributes zero or "cheap rides" by contributing less than their full value in an effort to benefit from the contributions that others make to facilitate provision of a public good, such as habitat services from hayfields.

[16] The mechanism is in a class that is weakly incentive compatible. Kawogoe and Mori (2001) note the advantages and disadvantages of this class of mechanisms.

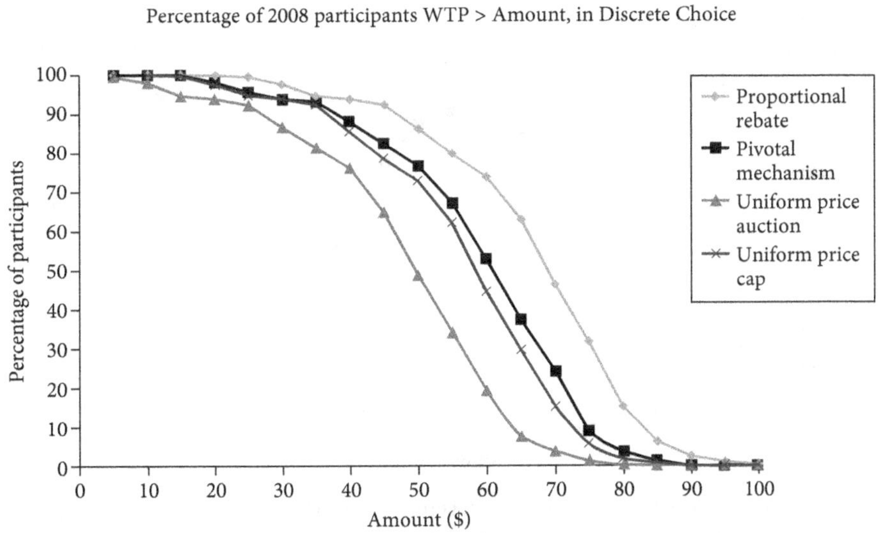

FIGURE 8.3 Proportion (%) of participants willing to offer a fixed amount for a 10-acre hayfield to be managed for one nesting season (unpublished data and analysis of S. Swallow, C. Anderson, and E. Uchida).

Figure 8.3 shows the proportion of participants in the Jamestown bobolink experiment who might be willing to offer a specified amount of money to support a single hayfield for one nesting season. Each of these "willingness to offer" curves corresponds to one of the rebate rules being tested in the experiment. Although these curves are based on an econometric model, their distribution may not necessarily prove to be statistically different. Therefore, Figure 8.3 should be considered illustrative rather than definitive. In this context, a participant is an individual who responded with a definitive answer to a direct mail solicitation; about 10–12% of Jamestown residents responded, with about two-thirds of participants making a particular offer amount via personal check or credit card authorization. Here, depending on the marginal incentives presented to a participant, 70% of participants appear to be willing to offer between \$52 and \$62 to support the seasonal contract under the best performing marginal incentives (about \$43 under the worst performing marginal incentives).

Figure 8.4 shows how these results might translate to revenue for an entrepreneur attempting to optimize her price point. These results suggest that price points of between \$50 and \$62 might generate the highest level of revenue for a hayfield, accounting for the number of participants who might decline to pay that amount but who may have paid a lower amount if given the opportunity. Based on these data, approximately 125 to 150 participants could cover the provision point on the marginal farm contract in Jamestown (requiring a revenue of about \$5,000 if unsubsidized), whereas in other farm communities, such as in upstate New York or in Vermont, these provision points might be substantially lower based on land use allocations and alternative availability of feedstock.

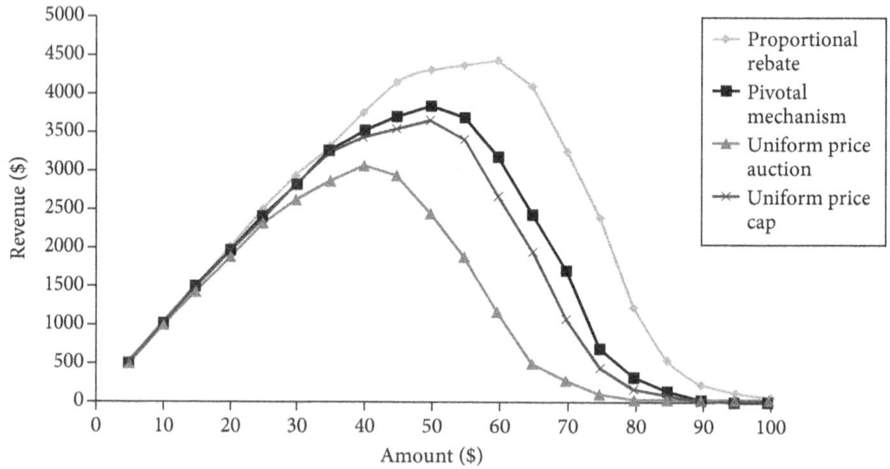

FIGURE 8.4 Point estimates of projected revenue from 100 participants in the Jamestown bobolink experiment versus a given fixed amount requested from all participants (unpublished data and analysis of S. Swallow, C. Anderson, and E. Uchida).

This illustration demonstrates ways in which one might potentially capitalize on economic insights and methods to improve the efficiency of ecosystem service provision without the need to necessarily quantify, value, or categorize the specific ecosystem services. It shows an example, more at the extreme end of the continuum of market approaches, that attempts to develop revenue-generating methods for ecosystem services. Services such as these are traditionally (under)provided either as the fortuitous by-products of normal land use, through government regulatory action, or perhaps through government incentive programs such as the USDA's conservation reserve program payments. In contrast to approaches that depend on centralized decisions or generic ties between consumer decisions and ecosystem outcomes, such as through eco-certification programs for traditional market goods, the market approach represented here has the advantage of linking consumer values and payment to specific actions.

Successful approaches to marketing ecosystem services could obviate much of the need for valuation of ecosystem services, thus leveraging entrepreneurial action to more completely recognize the contribution of ecosystems to human welfare. Unfortunately, this avenue of research faces its own challenge, including that of overcoming the incentives that beneficiaries have to free-ride on the contributions of others. Those incentives form a classic basis for market failure, which itself has spawned the need for valuation research. As noted by Kroeger and Casey (2007), ecosystem services related to land use often lack characteristics necessary for markets to assign prices linked to social benefits. Experience with markets and payments for these services provides has yet to provide clear evidence that such approaches can enhance ecosystem service provision on a broad scale, beyond services that would have been provided in the absence of these programs (Kroeger and Casey 2007; Claassen et al. 2008, Bauer and Johnston 2013).

4. Conclusion

The topics presented in this chapter may be consolidated into two broad themes. First, the ecosystem services perspective and associated research can provide significant insight to inform land use and policy. Ecosystem services research is grounded in decades of work by economists, ecologists, and others seeking to model interactions between humans and ecosystems. Much of the best ecosystem services research can be considered a well-grounded evolution of these existing methods. From this perspective, the validity of the underlying methods has already been established, and the key challenge is the recasting of results within an ecosystem services framework.

The second theme is that the integration of economics and ecology required by the ecosystem services framework can impose nontrivial challenges. These challenges expand as one moves beyond well-defined, marginal analyses to more revolutionary attempts to characterize all services, linkages, and values in large-scale systems. Even though the underlying economics and ecology may be well-developed, the integration and scale of these models can require methodological sacrifices that threaten validity.

Given such tradeoffs, an ecosystem services framework may not always be the most informative. Analysts must consider when and where the framework is appropriate versus those cases in which alternative methods are sufficient. The theoretical sections of this chapter have sought to identify some key considerations in the validity of ecosystem services research as a means to help answer these questions. Ecosystem services perspectives should be used when they can enhance the guidance that economists and others can provide to the policy process. When this is not the case, these perspectives may be unnecessary or even counterproductive. There are many cases in which careful use of integrated economic and ecological thinking alone can improve the foundation for decisions or in which market-based solutions can ameliorate society's undervaluation of ecosystems, even in the absence of operational ecosystem service frameworks.

Grounded in these themes, the two case studies illustrate both the insights provided by, as well as the empirical challenges of, research linking ecosystem services to land use. These illustrations reflect evolutionary rather than revolutionary work; for example, the case studies fall short of providing a comprehensive linkage among land use, ecosystem services, and human welfare. Such patterns are common in contemporary research that seeks to establish linkages between ecosystem services and land use; a substantial proportion of research in the field is best characterized as "proof of concept." Among the initial challenges in improving on research "still in its nascent stage" (Fisher et al. 2011) is the establishment of improved coordination across the natural and social sciences, from project initiation to completion, to promote empirical work widely accepted as both valid and relevant (Bauer and Johnston 2013). We also purposefully avoid illustrations focused on explicit valuation, instead illustrating alternative research paradigms through which linkages between ecosystem services and land use may be used to inform policy.

Moving forward, it is critical to acknowledge both the challenges and benefits of research linking ecosystem services to land use. Recognizing Toman's (1998) admonition, a willingness to sacrifice scientific rigor in an effort to demonstrate that all of nature is valuable risks the provision of useless or misleading information. In contrast, well-conceptualized ecosystem services analysis—whether through valuation or other perspectives—can help clarify tradeoffs necessary to enhance the benefits that humans realize from ecosystems and motivate concomitant policies. These tradeoffs may involve those aspects of nature whose degradation enhances human welfare, as well as those for which the benefits of nature's services warrant greater conservation. We recognize that limitations of the scientific state-of-the-art for ecosystem services research may leave some researchers desirous of a more complete set of revolutionary analytical tools. Despite these temptations, we urge greater efforts in the careful evolutionary development and evaluation of these tools, focusing on validity and provision of information relevant to decisions at hand.

ACKNOWLEDGMENTS

This chapter draws on work that was originally supported by the EPA STAR Decision Making and Valuation for Environmental Policy grant (R829384) and STAR Graduate Fellowship; USDA/CSREES/NRI Grant 2002-35401-11657 and USDA/NIFA/AFRI grants 2009-55401-05038 and 2011-67023-30378, a USDA/NRCS Conservation Innovation Grant, and the URI and UConn Agricultural Experiment Stations.

REFERENCES

Balmford, A., B. Fisher, R. E. Green, R. Naidoo, B. Strassburg, R. K. Turner and A. S. L. Rodrigues. 2011. Bringing ecosystem services into the real world: An operational framework for assessing the economics consequences of losing wild nature. *Environmental and Resource Economics* 48(2): 161–175.

Bateman, I. J., G. M. Mace, C. Fezzi, G. Atkinson, and K. Turner. 2011. Economic analysis for ecosystem service assessments. *Environmental and Resource Economics* 48(2): 177–218.

Batie, S. S. 2003. The multifunctional attributes of northeastern agriculture: A research agenda. *Agricultural and Resource Economics Review* 32(1): 1–8.

Bauer, D. M. and R. J. Johnston. 2013. The economics of rural and agricultural ecosystem services: Purism versus practicality. *Agricultural and Resource Economics Review* 42 (1): iii–xv.

Bauer, D. M., P. W. C. Paton, and S. K. Swallow. 2010*a*. Are wetland regulations cost effective for species protection? A case study of amphibian metapopulations. *Ecological Applications* 20 (3): 798–815.

Bauer, D. M., S. K. Swallow, and P. W. C. Paton. 2010*b*. Cost-effective species conservation in exurban communities: A spatial analysis. *Resource and Energy Economics* 32:180–202.

Bergstrom, J. C., and R. C. Ready. 2009. What have we learned from over 20 years of farmland amenity valuation research in North America? *Review of Agricultural Economics* 31(1): 21–49.

Bockstael, N. E., A. M. Freeman, R. J. Kopp, P. R. Portney, and V. K. Smith. 2000. On measuring economic values for nature. *Environmental Science and Technology* 34(8): 1384–1389.

Bollinger, E. K., P. B. Bollinger, and T. A. Gavin. 1990. Effects of hay-cropping of eastern populations of the bobolink. *Wildlife Society Bulletin* 18: 143–150.

Boody, G., B. Vondracek, D. A. Andow, M. Krinke, J. Westra, J. Zimmerman, and P. Welle. 2005. Multifunctional agriculture in the United States. *BioScience* 55: 27–38.

Boyd, J., and S. Banzhaf. 2007. What are ecosystem services? The need for standardized environmental accounting units. *Ecological Economics* 63(2–3): 616–626.

Boyd, J., and A. Krupnick. 2013. Using ecological production theory to define and select environmental commodities for nonmarket valuation. *Agricultural and Resource Economics Review* 42(1): 1–32.

Boyer, T., and S. Polasky. 2004. Valuing urban wetlands: A review of nonmarket valuation studies. *Wetlands* 24(4): 744–755.

Brown, T. C., J. C. Bergstrom, and J. B. Loomis. 2007. Defining, valuing and providing ecosystem goods and services. *Natural Resources Journal* 47(2): 329–376.

Carbone, J. C., and V. K. Smith. 2008. Evaluating policy interventions with general equilibrium externalities. *Journal of Public Economics* 92(5–6): 1254–1274.

Carbone, J. C., and V. K. Smith. 2010. Valuing ecosystem services in general equilibrium. NBER Working Paper No. w15844.

Champ, P. A., K. J. Boyle, and T. C. Brown, eds. 2003. *A primer on nonmarket valuation*. Dordrecht, The Netherlands: Kluwer Academic.

Clark, C. W. 1976. *Mathematical bioeconomics: The optimal management of renewable resources*. New York: John Wiley & Sons.

Claassen, R., A. Cattaneo, and R. Johansson. 2008. Cost-effective design of agri-environmental payment programs: U. S. experience in theory and practice. *Ecological Economics* 65: 737–752.

Collins, S. L., S. R. Carpenter, S. M. Swinton, D. E. Orenstein, D. L. Childers, T. L. Gragson, N. B. Grimm, J. M. Grove, S. L. Harlan, J. P. Kaye, A. K. Knapp, G. P. Kofina, J. J. Magnuson, W. H. McDowell, J. M. Melack, L. A. Ogden, G. P. Robertson, M. D. Smith, and A. C. Whitmer. 2010. An integrated conceptual framework for long-term social-ecological research. *Frontiers in Ecology and the Environment* doi:10.1890/100068.

Conrad, J. M. and C. W. Clark. 1987. *Natural resource economics: Notes and problems*. Cambridge, UK: Cambridge University Press.

Costanza, R., R. d'Arge, R. de Groot, S. Farber, M. Grasso, B. Hannon, K. Limburg, S. Naeem, R. V. O'Neill, J. Paruelo, R. G. Raskin, P. Sutton, and M. van den Belt. 1997. The value of the world's ecosystem services and natural capital. *Nature* 387 (May): 253–260.

Daily, G. C. 1997. *Nature's services*. Covelo, CA: Island Press.

Daily, G. C., S. Polasky, J. Goldstein, P. M. Kareiva, H. A. Mooney, L. Pejchar, T. H. Ricketts, J. Salzman, and R. Shallenberger. 2009. Ecosystem services in decision making: Time to deliver. *Frontiers in Ecology and Environment* 7(1): 21–28.

Dale, V. H., and S. Polasky. 2007. Measures of the effects of agricultural practices on ecosystem services. *Ecological Economics* 64: 286–296.

de Groot, R. S., M. A. Wilson, and R. M. J. Boumans. 2002. A typology for the classification, description and valuation of ecosystem functions, goods and services. *Ecological Economics* 41(3): 393–408.

Duke, J. M., and R. J. Johnston. 2010. Nonmarket valuation of multifunctional farm and forest preservation. In *New perspectives on agri-environmental policies: A multidisciplinary and transatlantic approach*, eds. S. J. Goetz and F. Brouwer, 124–142. Oxford: Routledge.

Eagan, R. S., and P. W. C. Paton. 2004. Within-pond parameters affecting oviposition by wood frogs and spotted salamanders. *Wetlands* 24:1–13.

Finnoff, D., A. Strong, and J. Tschirhart. 2008. Stocking regulations and the spread of invasive species. *American Journal of Agricultural Economics* 90(4):1074–1084.

Finnoff, D., and J. Tschirhart. 2008. Linking dynamic ecological and economic general equilibrium models. *Resource and Energy Economics* 30(2):91–114.

Fisher, B., S. Polasky, and T. Sterner. 2011. Conservation and human welfare: Economic analysis of ecosystem services. *Environmental and Resource Economics* 48(2): 151–159.

Fisher, B., K. Turner, M. Zylstra, R. Brouwer, R. de Groot, S. Farber, P. Ferraro, R. Green, D. Hadley, J. Harlow, P. Jefferiss, C. Kirkby, P. Morling, S. Mowatt, R. Naidoo, J. Paavola, B. Strassburg, D. Yu, and A. Balmford. 2008. Ecosystem services and economic theory: Integration for policy relevant research. *Ecological Applications* 18(8): 2050–2067.

Fisher, B., R. K. Turner, and P. Morling. 2009. Defining and classifying ecosystem services for decision making. *Ecological Economics* 68(3): 643–653.

Freeman, A. M. III. 2003. *The measurement of environmental and resource values: Theory and methods*. Washington, DC: Resources for the Future.

Gardner, B. D. 1977. The economics of agricultural land preservation. *American Journal of Agricultural Economics* 59(5): 1027–1036.

Hanley, N., and E. B. Barbier. 2009. *Pricing nature: Cost benefit analysis and environmental policy*. Cheltenham, UK: Edward Elgar.

Hanski, I. 1994. A practical model of metapopulation dynamics. *Journal of Animal Ecology* 63: 151–162.

Hanski, I., and O. Ovaskainen. 2000. The metapopulation capacity of a fragmented landscape. *Nature* 404: 755–758.

Heal, G. M., and A. A. Small. 2002. Agriculture and ecosystem services. In *Handbook of agricultural economics*, eds. B. L. Gardner and G. C. Rausser. Amsterdam: Elsevier.

Holland, D. S., J. Sanchirico, R. J. Johnston, and D. Joglekar. 2010. *Economic analysis for ecosystem based management: Applications to marine and coastal environments*. Washington, DC: RFF Press.

Jiang, Y., S. K. Swallow, and P. W. C. Paton. 2007. Designing a spatially-explicit nature reserve network based on ecological functions: An integer programming approach. *Biological Conservation* 140: 236–249.

Johnston, R. J., D. M. Bauer, and S. K. Swallow. 2002*c*. Spatial factors and stated preference values for public goods: Considerations for rural land use. *Land Economics* 78(4): 481–500.

Johnston, R. J., and J. M. Duke. 2007. Willingness to pay for agricultural land preservation and policy process attributes: Does the method matter? *American Journal of Agricultural Economics* 89(4): 1098–1115.

Johnston, R. J., T. A. Grigalunas, J. J. Opaluch, J. Diamantedes, and M. Mazzotta. 2002*b*. Valuing estuarine resource services using economic and ecological models: The Peconic estuary system study. *Coastal Management* 30(1): 47–66.

Johnston, R. J., J. J. Opaluch, T. A. Grigalunas, and M. J. Mazzotta. 2001. Estimating amenity benefits of coastal farmland. *Growth and Change* 32(3): 305–325.

Johnston, R. J., G. Magnusson, M. Mazzotta, and J. J. Opaluch. 2002*a*. Combining economic and ecological indicators to prioritize salt marsh restoration actions. *American Journal of Agricultural Economics* 84(5): 1362–1370.

Johnston, R. J., and R. S. Rosenberger. 2010. Methods, trends and controversies in contemporary benefit transfer. *Journal of Economic Surveys* 24(3): 479–510.

Johnston, R. J., and M. Russell. 2011. An operational structure for clarity in ecosystem service values. *Ecological Economics* 70(12): 2243–2249.

Johnston, R. J., Schultz, E. T., Segerson, K., Besedin, E. Y., and Ramachandran, M. 2012. Enhancing the content validity of stated preference valuation: The structure and function of ecological indicators. *Land Economics* 88(1): 102–120.

Johnston, R. J., K. Segerson, E. T. Schultz, E. Y. Besedin, and M. Ramachandran. 2011. Indices of biotic integrity in stated preference valuation of aquatic ecosystem services. *Ecological Economics* 70(11): 1946–1956.

Johnston, R. J., and S. K. Swallow, eds. 2006. *Economics and contemporary land use policy: Development and conservation at the rural-urban fringe.* Washington, DC: RFF Press.

Johnston, R. J., S. K. Swallow, C. W. Allen, and L. A. Smith. 2002*d*. Designing multidimensional environmental programs: Assessing tradeoffs and substitution in watershed management plans. *Water Resources Research* 38(7): IV 1–13.

Johnston, R. J., S. K. Swallow, D. M. Bauer, and C. M. Anderson. 2003. Preferences for residential development attributes and support for the policy process: Implications for management and conservation of rural landscapes. *Agricultural and Resource Economics Review* 32(1): 65–82.

Johnston, R. J., S. K. Swallow, and T. F. Weaver. 1999. Estimating willingness to pay and resource trade-offs with different payment mechanisms: An evaluation of a funding guarantee for watershed management. *Journal of Environmental Economics and Management* 38(1): 97–120.

Josling, T. 2002. Competing paradigms in the OECD and their Impact on the WTO agriculture talks. In *Agricultural Policy for the 21st Century*, eds. L. Tweeten and S. R. Thompson, 245–264. Ames: Iowa State University Press.

Just, R. E., D. L. Hueth, and A. Schmitz. 2004. *The welfare economics of public policy: A practical approach to project and policy evaluation*. Cheltenham, UK: Edward Elgar.

Kawagoe, T., and T. Mori. 2001. Can the pivotal mechanism induce truth-telling? An Experimental study. *Public Choice* 108: 331–354.

Kroeger, T., and F. Casey. 2007. An assessment of market-based approaches to providing ecosystem service on agricultural lands. *Ecological Economics* 64: 321–332.

Krutilla, J. V. 1967. Conservation reconsidered. *American Economic Review* 57(4): 777–786.

Marks, M., and R. Croson. 1998. Alternative rebate rules in the provision of a threshold public good: An experimental investigation. *Journal of Public Economics* 67(2): 195–220.

Moilanen, A., and I. Hanski. 1998. Metapopulation dynamics: Effects of habitat quality and landscape structure. *Ecology* 79: 2503–2515.

Millennium Ecosystem Assessment. 2005. *Ecosystems and human well-being: Synthesis.* Washington, DC: Island Press.

Montgomery, C. A., G. M. Brown Jr., and D. M. Adams. 1994. The marginal cost of species preservation: The northern spotted owl. *Journal of Environmental Economics and Management* 26: 111–128.

Naidoo, R., and T. H. Ricketts. 2006. Mapping the economic costs and benefits of conservation. *PLoS Biology* 4(11): E360. doi: 10.1371/journal.pbio.0040360.

Nalle, D. J., C. A. Montgomery, J. L. Arthur, N. H. Schumaker, and S. Polasky. 2004. Modeling joint production of wildlife and timber in forests. *Journal of Environmental Economics and Management* 48(3): 997–1017.

National Research Council. 2005. *Valuing ecosystem services: Towards better environmental decision-making.* Washington, DC: National Academies Press.

National Research Council. 2010. *Toward sustainable agricultural systems in the 21st century.* Washington, DC: National Academies Press.

Navrud, S., and G. J. Pruckner. 1997. Environmental valuation—to use or not to use? A comparative study of the United States and Europe. *Environmental and Resource Economics* 10(1): 1–26.

Nelson, E., G. Mendoza, J. Regetz, S. Polasky, H. Tallis, D. R. Cameron, K. M. Chan, G. C. Daily, J. Goldstein, P. M. Kareiva, E. Lonsdorf, R. Naidoo, T. H. Ricketts, and M. R. Shaw. 2009. Modeling multiple ecosystem services, biodiversity conservation, commodity production, and tradeoffs at landscape scales. *Frontiers in Ecology and Environment* 7: 4–11.

Ovaskainen, O., and I. Hanski. 2001. Spatially structured metapopulation modes: Global and local assessment of metapopulation capacity. *Theoretical Population Biology* 60: 281–302.

Poe, G. L., J. E. Clark, D. Rondeau, and W. D. Schulze. 2002. Provision point mechanisms and field validity tests of contingent valuation. *Environmental and Resource Economics* 23(1): 105–131.

Polasky, S. E. Nelson, D. Pennington, and K. A. Johnson. 2011. The impact of land-use change on ecosystem services: A case study in the state of minnesota. *Environmental and Resource Economics* 48(2): 219–242.

Priess, J. A., M. Mimler, A.-M. Klein, S. Schwartze, T. Tscharntke, and I. Steffan-Dewenter. 2007. Linking deforestation scenarios to pollination services and economic returns in coffee agroforestry systems. *Ecological Applications* 17(2): 407–417.

Ready, R. C., and C. Abdalla. 2005. The amenity and disamenity impacts of agriculture: Estimates from a hedonic pricing model. *American Journal of Agricultural Economics* 87(2): 314–326.

Ribaudo, M., C. Greene, L. Hansen, and D. Hellerstein. 2010. Ecosystem services from agriculture: Steps for expanding markets. *Ecological Economics* 69: 2085–2092.

Ricketts, T. H., G. C. Daily, P. R. Ehrlich, and C. D. Michener. 2004. Economic value of tropical forest to coffee production. *Proceedings of the National Academy of Sciences of the USA* 101: 12579–12582.

Rolfe, J., J. Bennett, R. Johnston and G. Kerr. 2011. *Using benefit transfer to inform environmental policy making.* Environmental Economics Research Hub Policy Brief. Crawford School of Economics and Government, Australian National University.

Rondeau, D., G. L. Poe, and W. D. Schulze. 2005. VCM or PPM? A comparison of the performance of two voluntary public good mechanisms. *Journal of Public Economics* 89(8):1581–1592; doi: 10.1016/j.jpubeco.2004.06.014.

Rondeau, D., W. D. Schulze, and G. L. Poe. 1999. Voluntary revelation of the demand for public goods using a provision point mechanism. *Journal of Public Economics* 72(3): 455–470.

Semlitsch, R. D. 1998. Biological delineation of terrestrial buffer zones for pond-breeding amphibians. *Conservation Biology* 12: 1113–1119.

Semlitsch, R. D. 2007. Differentiating migration and dispersal processes for pond-breeding amphibians. *Journal of Wildlife Management* 72: 260–267.

Semlitsch, R. D., and J. R. Bodie. 1998. Are small, isolated wetlands expendable? *Conservation Biology* 12: 1129–1133.

Simpson, R. D. 1998. Economic analysis and ecosystems: Some concepts and issues. *Ecological Applications* 8: 342–349.

Spencer, M. A., S. K. Swallow, J. F. Shogren, and J. A. List. 2009. Rebate rules in threshold public good provision. *Journal of Public Economics* 93: 798–806; doi:10.1016/J.jpubeco.2009.01.005.

Swallow, S. K. 1994. Renewable and nonrenewable resource theory applied to coastal agricultural, forest, wetland, and fishery linkages. *Marine Resource Economics* 9: 291–310.

Swallow, S. K. 1996*a*. Resource capital theory and ecosystem economics: Developing nonrenewable habitats of heterogeneous quality. *Southern Economic Journal* 6(1): 106–123.

Swallow, S. K. 1996*b*. Economic issues in ecosystem management: An introduction and overview. *Agricultural and Resource Economics Review* 25(2): 83–100.

Swallow, S. K. 1997. Biodiversity loss: Economic and ecological issues, eds. C. Perrings, K. -G. Mäler, C. Folke, C. S. Holling, and B.-O. Jansson. Cambridge: Cambridge University Press, 1995, *ix*, 332. *Southern Economic Journal* 64(1): 368–369.

Swallow, S. K., E. C. Smith, E. Uchida, and C. Anderson. 2008. Ecosystem services beyond valuation, regulation and philanthropy: Integrating consumer values into the economy. *Choices* 23(2): 47–52.

Swinton, S. M., F. Lupi, G. P. Robertson, and S. K. Hamilton. 2007. Ecosystem services and agriculture: Cultivating agricultural ecosystems for diverse benefits. *Ecological Economics* 64: 245–262.

Tallis, H., and S. Polasky. 2009. Mapping and valuing ecosystem services as an approach for conservation and natural resource management. *Annals of the N. Y. Academy of Sciences* 1162: 265–283.

Toman, M. 1998. Why not to calculate the value of the world's ecosystem services and natural capital. *Ecological Economics* 25: 57–60.

Turner, R. K., and G. C. Daily. 2008. The ecosystem services framework and natural capital conservation. *Environmental and Resource Economics* 39(1): 25–35.

U. S. Environmental Protection Agency (EPA). 2009. *Valuing the protection of ecological systems and services: A report of the EPA science advisory board*. Washington, DC: Author.

Wainger, L. A., D. M. King, R. N. Mack, E. W. Price, and T. Maslin. 2010. Can the concept of ecosystem services be practically applied to improve natural resource management decisions? *Ecological Economics* 69(5): 978–987.

Wainger, L., and M. Mazzotta. 2011. Realizing the potential of ecosystem services: A framework for relating ecological changes to economic benefits. *Environmental Management* 48 (4): 710–733.

Wallace, K. J. 2007. Classification of ecosystem services: Problems and solutions. *Biological Conservation* 139(3–4): 235–246.

Wilen, J. E. 1985. Bioeconomics of renewable resource use. In *Handbook of natural resource and energy economics*, Vol. I, eds. A. V. Kneese and J. L. Sweeney, 61–124. Amsterdam: North-Holland, 1985.

Zhang, W., T. H. Ricketts, C. Kremen, K. Carney, and S. M. Swinton. 2007. Ecosystem services and disservices to agriculture. *Ecological Economics* 64: 253–260.

CHAPTER 9

LAND USE AND CLIMATE CHANGE

BRUCE A. MCCARL, WITSANU ATTAVANICH, MARK MUSUMBA, JIANHONG E. MU, AND RUTH AISABOKHAE

THE climate change issue raises a number of risks and decision-making opportunities. The decision/risk space involves three dimensions: (1) societal vulnerability, in which the effects of climate change influence current and future productivity; (2) societal adaptation, in which adaptive actions are pursued to reduce the productivity effects of climate change; these actions involve changes in operations accompanied by investments of resources; and (3) societal mitigation, in which actions are undertaken to reduce the net emissions of greenhouse gases (GHGs) with the aim of reducing future atmospheric concentrations of GHGs and their consequent effects on climate change. This also involves modification in operations plus potential investments.

Land use is heavily involved with these climate change concerns. Land productivity, land use, and land management (LPLULM) decisions are relevant. Land productivity is affected by climate change, which, in turn, alters the returns to enterprises using land (representing vulnerability to climate change). Also, LPLULM decisions can alter net GHG emissions and contribute to reducing the future extent of climate change (mitigation). Finally, LPLULM provides possible mechanisms for altering management or changing enterprise mix to enhance productivity in the face of climate change (pursuing adaptation).

In this chapter, we discuss and review interrelationships among the vulnerability, adaptation, and mitigation aspects of land use and climate change. We do this based on the literature. A number of studies have addressed such issues and contained findings that apply to vulnerability, mitigation, and adaptation. We review key research on climate change issues regarding LPLULM, identifying key findings, pointing out research needs, and raising economic questions to ponder. In doing this, we go beyond previous reviews and simultaneously treat the troika of vulnerability, mitigation, and adaptation aspects of the issue. Hopefully, this will provide readers with a more comprehensive, multifaceted grasp of the spectrum of current issues regarding LPLULM and climate change.

1. Land Use and Climate Change Interrelationships

LPLULM is involved with all three aspects of the climate change issue. In terms of vulnerability, LPLULM productivity is sensitive to changes in climate. The Intergovernmental Panel on Climate Change (IPCC) (2007*a*) documents that the climate is changing by presenting data on increases in temperature, extreme events, heat waves, droughts, and alterations in rainfall incidence intensity. In addition, hydrological cycles, incidence of pests and diseases, and forest fires are also being affected.

In terms of mitigation, land cover change has been a major historical contributor to atmospheric GHG accumulation and is potentially reversible. Houghton (2003) and Golub et al. (2009) estimate that, since 1850, a third of the total anthropogenic emissions of carbon have come from land use change. In contemporary terms, the IPCC (2000) finds the current share of total anthropogenic emissions from LPLULM-related sources to be 18% from forestry and 14% from agriculture. These emissions are mainly from deforestation, in which forests are converted into cropland, pasture land, and developed uses; and grassland conversion, in which land use is changed into cropland from pasture or range. Furthermore, agriculture is estimated to account for 52% and 84% of global anthropogenic methane and nitrous oxide emissions, respectively (IPCC 2000; WRI 2005; Smith et al. 2007*a*). These emissions are mainly from land-based crop and livestock production. In the face of this, authors such as Lal, Follett, and Kimble (2003), Smith et al. (2007*a*, 2007*b*), and Fri et al. (2010) argue that LPLULM actions may enhance sequestration or reduce emissions, thus reducing future atmospheric concentrations.

LPLULM can also be used to adapt to a changing climate. Land use can be shifted among enterprises by changing crops, tree, or livestock species and also by changing uses between cropping, pasture, grazing, and forests to exploit relative changes in productivity. One can also alter land management involving practices for crops, livestock, and forest production to better accommodate a changed climate. Now, given this overview, we delve into the individual vulnerability, mitigation, and adaptation topics.

1.1 Climate Change Vulnerability and Land Use Change

Agriculture and forestry (AF) are decidedly vulnerable to climate change. Land use economists have widely addressed this vulnerability by examining effects on direct AF productivity, disturbances, land values, and water resources.

1.2 Climate Change and AF Productivity

The IPCC (2007*b*) indicates that we have observed increases in temperature, changes in rainfall patterns, increased climate variability, and a greater frequency of extreme events. These effects will differentially alter productivity across various types of crops, livestock, and trees and across regions. In addition, atmospheric carbon dioxide (CO_2) concentration increases enhance yields of some crops, grasses, and tree species. Findings on implications for major categories are reviewed later. Here, we limit coverage to findings using observed data but not that IPCC (2007*b*) reviewed studies using simulation models.

1.2.1 Observed Crop Yields

A wide variety of studies have addressed climate change effects on crop yields. Deschenes and Greenstone (2007) find that yields of corn and soybeans are negatively correlated to growing degree days. Schlenker and Roberts (2009) and Huang and Khanna (2010) find similar results and reveal a nonlinear effect of temperature on yields of corn and soybeans. Attavanich and McCarl (2011) and McCarl, Villavicencio, and Wu (2008) find that the effect of temperature on US state yields depends on location, with beneficial consequences to colder (northern) areas and detrimental outcomes to the hotter (southern) areas. Collectively, these and other studies show that climate change will likely reduce yields in areas where heat stress is a factor and increase them in areas where cold is a key factor.

Regarding the effect of precipitation, Chen, McCarl, and Schimmelpfennig (2004), Isik and Devadoss (2006), and McCarl, Villavicencio, and Wu (2008) find that increased precipitation enhances yields of corn, cotton, soybeans, wheat, and sorghum while having a negative impact on wheat. An inverted U-shaped relationship between corn and soybean yields and precipitation is found in Schlenker and Roberts (2009) and Huang and Khanna (2010). Attavanich and McCarl (2011) show heterogeneity in projected climate change effects, identifying negative effects over the currently wetter US Central and Northeast regions and positive effects for the drier North Plains regions, where precipitation gains are projected.

Climate variability and extreme events are addressed in a number of studies. McCarl, Villavicencio, and Wu (2008) find that increased temperature variation negatively impacts yields of all crops, and Huang and Khanna (2010) also find this result for corn and soybeans. McCarl, Villavicencio, and Wu (2008) and Attavanich and McCarl (2011) find that an increase in precipitation intensity reduces crop yields, whereas an increase in the Palmer drought index has a differential effect across crops. Chen and McCarl (2009) examine the effects of hurricane incidence and find yield reductions ranging from 0.20% to 12.90%, with the US Gulf Coast and the southern Atlantic coastal regions being the most vulnerable areas.

Crop yields are also affected by atmospheric CO_2 concentration. C3 crops are found to be more responsive to CO_2 than are C4 crops under the ample water conditions (Ainsworth and Long 2005; Kimball 2006 Long et al. 2006; Attavanich and McCarl

2011).[1] Leakey (2009) finds that C4 crops only benefit from elevated CO_2 in times and places of drought stress, as do Attavanich and McCarl (2011). Farmers in developing countries have been found to be highly vulnerable to climate change. Butt et al. (2005) combine biophysical and economic models to investigate implications of climate change in Mali. They find that, under climate change, crop farmers are severely affected, and overall food insecurity almost doubles.

1.2.2 Forests

Boisvenue and Running (2006) review previous literature related to climate change impacts on forest productivity. They find that climatic change has a generally positive impact on forest productivity when water is not limiting. McMahon, Parker, and Miller (2010) estimate that the Northeast US forest is growing at a much faster rate than expected and attribute this to rising levels of atmospheric CO_2, higher temperatures, and a longer growing seasons. Foster et al. (2010) argue to the contrary that past tree mortality could explain the difference in rates. Recent studies from the free-air CO_2 enrichment (FACE) experiments[2] suggest that direct CO_2 effects on tree growth may need to be revised downward (Norby et al. 2005; Karnosky and Pregitzer 2006; McCarthy et al. 2010). Allen et al. (2010) review studies and indicate that climate change may enhance tree mortality due to drought and heat in forests worldwide. Sohngen et al. (1999), in their global study on forest effects, find a market- and productivity-induced shift to subtropical areas.

1.2.3 Grasslands

Changes in rainfall, temperature, and CO_2 concentrations affect the productivity of grasslands, an important fodder source for livestock production. The IPCC (2007*a*) indicates projected declines in rainfall in some major grassland and rangeland areas (e.g., South America, South and North Africa, western Asia, Australia, and southern Europe). They state that grass production tends to increase in humid temperate regions but that it would likely see decreases in arid and semiarid regions (IPCC 2007*b*). In Australia, Cullen et al. (2009) predict an increase in grass production in subtropical and subhumid regions of eastern Australia, whereas in southern Australia they predict slight increases as of 2030 but decreases of up to 19% in 2070.

[1] All plants must convert sunlight to energy by "fixing" carbon as part of photosynthesis. C3 crops are crops in which the CO_2 is first fixed into a compound containing three carbon atoms, whereas C4 crops are crops in which the CO_2 is first fixed into a compound containing four carbon atoms before entering the Cavin cycle of photosynthesis. In brief, C4 crops are better adapted than C3 crops in an environment with high daytime temperatures, intense sunlight, drought, or nitrogen or CO_2 limitation. Examples of C3 crops include soybeans, wheat, and cotton; examples of C4 crops are corn and sorghum.

[2] In these experiments, air enriched with CO_2 is blown into the rings where crops are grown in a real field (not in a chamber). Then, a computer-control system uses the wind speed and CO_2 concentration information to adjust the CO_2 flow rates to maintain the desired CO_2 concentration. Finally, crop yield in the elevated CO_2 rings are compared to that in the control rings with nonelevated CO_2 environment.

Wang et al. (2007*a*) project that the net primary productivity of grasslands[3] in China will increase 7–21% under 2.7–3.9°C increases in temperature and 10% increases in precipitation coupled with doubled CO_2. However, they predict a drop of 24% when there are only increases in temperature. Mu et al. (2013) find in many regions land use shifts from cropland use to grasslands under predicted climate change. The IPCC (2007*b*) indicates that CO_2 fertilization enhances grass growth, with C3 pasture grasses and legumes positively responding and exhibiting about 10% and 20% productivity increases, respectively (Nowak et al. 2004; Ainsworth and Long 2005). Shifts in forage quality are also expected (Polley et al. 2012).

1.2.4 Livestock

Climate change affects livestock productivity. Warming climates can increase thermal stress reducing livestock productivity, conception rates, and survival rates. Increased climate variability and droughts may lead to livestock production reductions (IPCC 2007*b*; Thornton et al. 2009). Stocking rates may also decline as gross growth is reduced. For example, Mu et al. (2013) find an inverted U shape between summer precipitation and US cattle stocking rates and that cattle stocking rates decrease with increases in the summer temperature and humidity index (THI). Mader et al. (2009) find that under increased CO_2 concentration scenarios, the west side of the US Corn Belt encounters productivity losses for swine of as much as 22.4%, whereas on the east side, losses of over 70% occur. For beef, they find increasing temperature is beneficial to beef producers in the western Corn Belt but not in the northwest and southeast regions. Finally, dairy production is projected to decrease from 1.0 to 7.2, depending on location.

Livestock in developing countries are highly vulnerable. Sirohi and Michaelowa (2007) state that the livestock impacts could be large and devastating for low-income rural areas. Seo and Mendelsohn (2008*a*) find that net revenue for beef cattle is lower in warmer places, but sheep net revenue is lower in wetter places. They also indicate the expected profit from African livestock management will fall as early as 2020. Moreover, they show that climate change as predicted would cause considerable reductions in the net incomes of large livestock farms. Seo et al. (2009) find that a hot and dry climate results in a greater incidence of livestock compared to crop production. Butt et al. (2005) indicate that under climate change, livestock weights are projected to decrease by 14–16%.

1.3 Disturbances

Climate change can increase disturbances in the form of increased incidence of pest and diseases and fires. Numerous studies find that increases in temperature affect pest

[3] The Leymus chinensis meadow steppe is widely distributed in the east of the Eurasian region, and more than half of the steppe is located in China, especially in the northeastern China Plain and Inner Mongolian Plateau (Wang et al. 2007).

populations and migrations. Rising temperatures are also predicted to increase forest pests, crop pesticide usage costs, and wildfire risk (e.g., Chen and McCarl 2001; Williams and Liebhold 2002; Gan 2004, 2005; Taylor et al. 2007; Hicke and Jenkins 2008; Walther et al. 2009; Robinet and Roques 2010).

In a review of forestry studies, Taylor et al. (2007) find that the current outbreak of the mountain pine beetle in British Columbia is an order of magnitude larger in area and severity than all previous recorded outbreaks. Williams and Liebhold (2002) project that outbreak areas for southern pine beetles increase with higher temperatures and generally shift northward, whereas the projected outbreak areas for mountain pine beetle shifts toward higher elevations. Hicke and Jenkins (2008) map climate change effects on lodgepole pine stand susceptibility to mountain pine beetle attack, concluding that forests in the southern Rocky Mountains have the highest level of susceptibility.

Patriquin, Wellstead, and White (2007) find negative long-term economic implications of mountain pine beetle infestations in British Columbia. Schwab et al. (2009) predict a significant medium-term timber supply shortage, reduced stumpage revenues, and increased cost competition among primary wood products manufacturers. Williams et al. (2010) estimate that about 7.6% of US southwestern forest and woodland area experienced mortality associated with pine bark beetles between 1997 and 2008.

In terms of agriculture, crops are negatively affected by insect and disease pest outbreaks. Chen and McCarl (2001) find that increases in rainfall raise pesticide usage costs for corn, cotton, potatoes, soybeans, and wheat, whereas hotter weather increases pesticide costs for all crops except wheat. Rosenzweig et al. (2001) review studies on agricultural chemical use and conclude that, in a warmer climate, pests may become more active and may expand their geographical range, resulting in increased use of pesticides with accompanying health, ecological, and economic costs. Shakhramanyan, Schneider, and McCarl (2013) find that climate change causes significant increases in pesticide use and external costs.

For animal diseases, Purse et al. (2005) explore climate-induced shifts in bluetongue virus incidence in Europe and find that strains have spread across 12 countries and 800 kilometers further north due to climate change since 1998. Saegerman, Berkvens, and Mellor (2008) find similar results. Mu, McCarl, and Wu (2011) show that climate change may have caused part of the current increase in avian influenza incidence and is likely to further stimulate disease spread in the future.

Climate change also affects fire risk. Westerling et al. (2006) argue that climate change has caused wildfire risk to increase particularly since the mid-1980s, with the greatest increases occurred in mid-elevation Northern Rockies forests. Williams et al. (2010) find that about 2.7% of US southwestern forest and woodland area experienced substantial mortality due to wildfires between 1984 and 2006. Moriondo et al. (2006) find an increase in fire risk in the EU Mediterranean countries, especially in the Alps region of Italy, the Pyrenees of Spain, and the Balkan mountains. Brown, Hall, and Westerling (2004) argue that climate change will exacerbate forest fires and that new fire and fuels management strategies may be needed. Chapter 11 by Montgomery in this handbook provides additional material on fire and land use change.

1.4 Land Values

Climate change affects LPLULM, which in turn impacts land values. Overall, the effect is mixed in developed countries, but negative in developing countries. Mendelsohn, Nordhaus, and Shaw (1994) find that higher temperatures in all seasons except autumn reduce average US farm values, whereas more precipitation outside of autumn increases farm values. They estimate a climate change-induced loss in US farmland value ranging from –$141 to $34.8 billion. Schlenker, Hanemann, and Fisher (2005) do a similar study and find an annual loss in US farmland value in the range of $5–5.3 billion for dryland nonurban counties. Mendelsohn and Reinsborogh (2007) find that US farms are much more sensitive to higher temperature than Canadian farms, but are less sensitive to precipitation increases. Deschenes and Greenstone (2007) find that climate change will lead to a long-run increase of $1.3 billion (in 2002 dollars) in agricultural land values. They indicate that land values in California, Nebraska, and North Carolina will be lowered substantially by climate change, whereas South Dakota and Georgia will have the biggest increases.

For developing countries, Seo and Mendelsohn (2008*b*) find that, in South America, climate change will decrease farmland values except for irrigated farms. Moreover, they find small farms are more vulnerable to the increase in temperature, whereas large farms are more vulnerable to increases in precipitation. Mendelsohn, Arellano-Gonzalez, and Christensen (2010) project that, on average, higher temperatures decrease Mexican land values by 4,000–6,000 pesos per degree Celsius, amounting to cropland value reductions of 42–54% by 2100. Wang et al. (2009) find that, in China, an increase in temperature is likely to harm rain-fed farms but benefit irrigated farms. A small value loss is found in Southeast China farms, whereas the largest damage is discovered in farms in the Northeast and Northwest (Wang et al. 2009).

1.5 Water Supply

Climate change has important consequences for the hydrological cycle and water availability (IPCC 2007*b*; Bates et al. 2008). Land use patterns are affected by this change via the availability of irrigation water and the suitability of land for rain-fed production.

Regions where the majority of water supply comes from snow or glaciers are vulnerable to climate change because higher temperatures cause a reduction in mountain storage of water and seasonality of water availability (Gleick and Adams 2000; Barnett et al. 2005). Such regions include South American river basins along the Andes, the Greater Himalayas, and much of the US West, including California (Coudrian et al. 2005; Xu et al. 2009).

Climate change also poses water supply threats in Africa because much of the population relies on local rivers. De Wit and Stankiewicz (2006) project that a 10% decrease in precipitation in regions receiving about 1 meter of precipitation per year could reduce runoff into rivers by 17%, whereas in regions receiving 0.5 meters, that runoff could be reduced by 50%. Furthermore, they predict that, by the end of this century, surface water access will be reduced across 25% of Africa. Paeth et al. (2009) find climate change would cause a weakening of the hydrological cycle over most of tropical Africa, resulting in enhanced heat stress and extended dry spells. Additionally, on a global basis, the Mediterranean Basin, Central America, and sub-tropical Australia are projected to encounter declines in water availability (Bates et al. 2008) as is the Southwestern United States (Seager et al. 2007).

In the United States, climate change is projected to reduce California snow accumulation (Cayan et al. 2008). Barnett and Pierce (2009) find that climate change makes current levels of Colorado River water deliveries unsustainable into the future. Reilly et al. (2003) find that US irrigated agriculture needs for water are likely to decline approximately 5–10% and 30–40% for 2030 and 2090 due to increased precipitation and shortened crop-growing periods. McCarl (2008) finds that the US Pacific Southwest gains the most under the climate change scenarios studied, whereas the US South encounters the largest losses.

1.6 Vulnerability Research Needs

Although many research studies have focused on the vulnerability of AF land use to climate change, there are a number of pressing research needs. First, most studies have focused on developed countries. Thus, there is a need for future research in developing country settings, particularly those with the greatest projected climate change levels. Second, a number of issues related to LPLULM require more thorough research, including (1) increased incidence of extreme events including droughts, floods, and tropical storms; (2) analysis of multiple drivers acting at once, including water supply/demand, pests, diseases, fires, sea level rise, and extremes; (3) effects of shifts in risks in terms of, for example, yield variability, pest outbreaks, droughts, and market prices; and (4) analysis of longer term decision making under uncertainty regarding long-term phenomena like choice of tree species in the face of climate change uncertainty.

2. Mitigation and Land Use Change

LPLULM can alter net fluxes to the atmosphere through increases in sequestration or reductions in emissions (McCarl and Schneider 2001). Sequestration in the ecosystem can be increased through means like afforestation, forest management, grassland expansion, biochar, and reduced tillage intensity. Emissions can be limited through changes in land management and enterprise choice by means such as reducing fertilization, altering livestock feeding and numbers, providing less intensive emitting products like bioenergy, and reducing rice acreage. Here, we elaborate, discussing forestry and agriculture separately.

2.1 Forestry-Based Mitigation

Forestry mitigation includes means such as (1) reduction in emissions from deforestation and degradation[4] (REDD as discussed in Miles and Kapos 2008); (2) increasing forest carbon density through management; (3) afforestation (increasing forested land area); and (4) provision of substitutes for emission-intensive products, particularly replacing fossil fuels, but also cement, steel, and other items (McCarl and Schneider 2000; Canadell and Raupach 2008).

Deforestation creates an estimated net emission of 1.5 billion tons of carbon per year (Pg C $year^{-1}$) when carbon in standing trees, understory, and soils is released upon harvest and subsequent land use change (Canadell et al. 2007). The IPCC estimates that 17% of emissions come from forestry sources, largely from deforestation (IPCC 2001). Gullison et al. (2007) estimate that by reducing deforestation by 50% by 2050 and maintaining this level until 2100; society can avoid emissions equivalent to 50 billion tons of carbon.

Forest management offers another possibility for mitigation. Carbon density can be increased by thinning, protecting against disturbances (fires, diseases, pests), changing species mix, lengthening rotations, reducing harvest damage, accelerating replanting rates, and lengthening use life of harvested projects (Nabuurs et al. 2007). Afforestation can further reduce the net emissions. For example, in China, 24 million hectares of new forest were afforested to offset 21% of China's fossil fuel emissions in 2000 (Wang et al. 2007; Candell and Raupach 2008). Murray et al. (2005) show afforestation to be one of the large possible strategies for AF to participate in mitigation.

Bioenergy is commonly discussed as a means to mitigate climate change. In forestry, various trees species plus logging residues and forest byproducts have been proposed for use as feedstocks for bioenergy to replace fossil fuels, and many of these use short rotation trees (Cerri et al. 2004; Dias de Oliviera et al. 2005; Smith et al. 2008). Kaul et al. (2010) show that significant carbon benefits can be obtained in the long run by using land for short rotation energy crops and substituting biomass for fossil fuels.

Finally, in terms of forestry, there is a dynamic issue involved when temporary/impermanent carbon sequestration and permanent emissions reductions are considered. In

[4] The Reducing Emissions from Deforestation and Forest Degradation (REDD) is an initiative process to consider policy that reduces emission from deforestation and forest degradation initiated at the Eleventh Session of Conference Parties (COP 11) to the United Nations Framework Convention on Climate Change (UNFCC).

particular, the amount of carbon stock increase is limited by an approach to equilibrium. That is, as the tree grows to maturity and is subject to harvest, it reaches a point at which carbon quantity reaches an equilibrium state with no further meaningful gains possible under a given management system (Birdsey 1996; Kim et al. 2008). Furthermore, the sequestration in forestry can be reversed in the future by changing practices, forest or other forces. In the face of this, suppliers often propose to lease carbon sequestration in forests only for a limited time. This reduces the ultimate value of the carbon credits generated (Kim et al. 2008).

2.2 Agricultural-Based Emissions

Agriculture is a major emitter of GHGs but also has high potential to mitigate emissions using current technologies, many of which can be implemented immediately. Mitigation options in agriculture mainly include (1) enhancing carbon sequestration, (2) intensification and extensification in agricultural production and livestock management, and (3) substituting low-emission products for higher emission products (bioenergy) and reducing emissions (McCarl and Schneider 2000; Clemens and Ahlgrimm 2001; Schneider and Kumar 2008; Smith et al. 2008).

Carbon sequestration enhancement involves increasing carbon stored in the ecosystem (Cacho et al. 2003; Richard and Stokes 2004; Mendelsohn and Dinar 2009). This is accomplished by some combination of increasing carbon inputs to the soil or reducing carbon decomposition. Reductions in tillage intensity embody a reduction in soil disturbance that, in turn, limits exposure of carbon to the atmosphere and the amount of its oxidation and increases sequestration (Cerri et al. 2004; Smith et al. 2008). Conversion of croplands to grasslands, forests, and perennials also reduces disturbance, which leads to increased carbon in roots and in the soil. Global estimates have indicated that conversion of all cropland to conservation tillage could sequester 25 billion tons of carbon over the next 50 years (Pacala and Socolow 2004).

In terms of tillage or land use changes, one should note that the amount of carbon increase is limited by an approach to equilibrium, as discussed in the forestry section. Namely, as the carbon quantity increases, so does the decomposition rate and, at a point, the soil becomes saturated, with no further meaningful gains possible under a given management system (West and Six 2007; Kim et al. 2008). Furthermore, that can occur in as few as 10 years (West and Post 2002).

Emissions can be reduced by lowering the use of inputs like fertilizer, pesticides, and fossil fuels. In particular, reduced nitrogen fertilizer use limits N_2O emissions and also reduces the CO_2 involved in nitrogen fertilizer manufacturing (Schlesinger 1999). Deintensification of tillage also reduces fossil fuel usage, as does changes in other energy-intensive operations like drying and irrigation (McCarl and Schneider 2000). Improved rice management can reduce methane emissions (Aulakh et al. 2001; Yan et al. 2003; Smith and Cohen 2004; Smith et al. 2008).

Livestock are emissions sources through enteric fermentation and manure-related emissions. Managing livestock using improved diets and feed additives aimed at suppressing methanogens have been proposed to reduce emissions from enteric fermentation (Smith et al. 2007, 2008; Thornton and Geber 2010). Anaerobic digestion of animal wastes reduces methane emissions while producing biogas (Monteny et al. 2006; Gerber et al. 2008). Lowering the number of animals can also reduce emissions. For example, a change in human diet from beef to plant based protein would likely reduce herd size and total methane emissions, along with cropland needs and associated emissions (Schneider and Kumar 2008). Management changes, feed additives, and animal breeding that raises animal growth and spreads energy costs of maintenance across greater feed intake may reduce the methane output per kilogram of animal product (Boadi et al. 2004; Smith et al. 2008).

Mitigation can be achieved by substituting products that replace fossil fuels. In agriculture, production of bioenergy feedstocks may help achieve this. For example, an estimate of the percentage reduction in net GHG emissions by using corn-based ethanol is 17% relative to using gasoline (McCarl and Reilly 2007; McCarl 2008). However, one must be careful of market effects that may simulate land use change elsewhere because this can increase emissions (Murray et al. 2004; Fargione et al. 2008; Searchinger et al. 2008).

2.3 Role of Markets and Policies in Climate Change Mitigation

Cap-and-trade approaches have been implemented or contemplated as means of increasing mitigation by providing economic incentives. The Kyoto Protocol suggests such trading, and trading has been implemented in several forms and places such as in Europe (Foxon 2010) and California. Theory indicates that market-based incentives like carbon taxes or cap-and-trade are more economically efficient than are regulatory approaches in controlling GHGs and are favored by most economists (Metcalf and Reilly 2008; Raymond and Shively 2008).

There are implementation issues concerning the wide range of GHGs and the global nature of climate change. Implementation issues mainly arise from differential characteristics of additionality, permanence, uncertainty and leakage; transactions costs, including measurement and monitoring costs; and property rights. Each is discussed in the following sections.

2.3.1 Leakage

Leakage is a major mitigation concern in that practices may reduce net emissions in one region but lead to increased emissions elsewhere due to reduced supplies and market price signals. In particular, actions that divert production in the mitigating area may well cause increases in production elsewhere, with accompanying emissions increases (Murray et al. 2004). A number of authors have cautioned that this could well happen with expansion of biofuels or afforestation because such activities compete with traditional cropland and forest land. This can result in reduced production and increased market prices, thus stimulating other areas to expand production and, in turn, emissions (Murray et al. 2004; Fargione et al. 2008; Searchinger et al. 2008; Mendelson and Dinar 2009).

2.3.2 Additionality

Ideally, policy desires to only pay for "additional" GHG net emission avoidance, not that which would have occurred under business as usual. This raises the issue of baseline establishment, in which a without-policy baseline is compared to a with-policy alternative; ideally, only the additional contribution above the baseline would be eligible for market trading (Smith et al. 2007). Baseline projection is difficult and also implies that programs must be designed to anticipate future actions and not pay for actions that have not occurred under current circumstances but that are projected to occur in the future, in the absence of carbon markets. For example, consider deforestation: most studies use the assumption that deforestation will continue (IPCC 2007*b*), but the extent of this is uncertain, and there may be some changes in trends that portend less future deforestation (reductions in population growth and an increasingly renewable timber industry), as argued in Sohngen et al. (1999) and Mendelsohn and Dinar (2009). Policy makers may subsidize landholders to hold land in forests, but the question remains: would that forest have been cut down in the absence of policy, and might we be paying for something that never would have happened?

2.3.3 Permanence

Permanence is another major issue, particularly with carbon sequestration strategies, in that carbon credits and offsets are not necessarily stored permanently or sold on a forever basis (Murray et al. 2004; Sands and McCarl 2005; Smith et al. 2007). The problem is that carbon may not be stored permanently (permanence) due to such things as possible future LPLULM changes, limited time of guaranteed storage (leasing), needs for maintenance fees, approach to equilibrium, fires, or extreme events. In turn, this can lead to the release of sequestered carbon and may merit significant price discounts accounting for its nonpermanent nature (Kim et al. 2008).

2.3.4 Uncertainty

Uncertainty is a complex implementation issue. Agriculture and forestry, by their very nature, are affected by climate; thus, both emissions reductions and sequestration amounts will be affected and uncertain from year to year and over time. Uncertainty in estimating the magnitude of GHG emissions and sequestration rates has inhibited implementation of mitigation options in the AF sectors, causing some to argue against inclusion of AF sequestration in trading schemes. There are also variations and correlations among years, seasons, and locations that make estimation of the sequestration volume difficult. Kim and McCarl (2009) present a discounting procedure for taking this into account in trading, whereas Mooney et al. (2004, 2007) dimension the size of the error and a sampling scheme.

2.3.5 *Transactions Costs*

Conveyance of carbon credits in markets will likely result in cost wedges between buyers and sellers due to transaction costs. Kim (2011) separates such costs into a number of components as discussed below.

2.3.5.1 *Assembly Costs*

Carbon market purchases would likely need large quantities of offsets (with, for example, emissions of large power conglomerates in the hundreds of millions of tons) compared to what a land user could produce. Typically, it would not be economical for an offset purchaser in quest of 100,000 tons to deal with a single land user. An offset of 100,000 tons at an average sequestration rate of 0.25 tons of carbon per acre (and average rate from West and Post 2002) would require 400,000 acres. Considering a rough average farm size of 400 acres (the average US farm was 418 acres in 2007), this offset would involve nearly 1,000 farmers. Thus, there would be a role for brokers or aggregators to assemble groups to create marketable quantities. Costs arise in such a process. Also, there will be costs involved in keeping the group of farmers together and dispersing payments. The crop insurance case is one such scheme, and there transactions costs are about 25% for brokers.

2.3.5.2 *Measurement, Monitoring, and Certification*

Market trading will also require measurement and monitoring to establish that offsets are being produced and continue to be produced. This requires the development of low-cost measurement and monitoring approaches based on sampling, with an integration of field level measurement, computer simulation, and remote sensing data (Mooney et al. 2004, 2007).

There may also be a need for certain bodies to certify offset quantity estimates or the effectiveness of practices and then monitor that the practice continues. For example, under the Clean Development Mechanism (CDM), rules were established that indicate the number of offset credits from various practices. Such certification again introduces transactions costs.

2.3.5.3 *Shortfalls, Enforcement, and Liability*

Compliance with carbon contracts will not always happen, and an enforcement or liability mechanism may be needed. This may involve the setup and operation of shortfall insurance, an enforcement entity, or a liability imposition mechanism. This again will introduce transactions costs.

2.3.5.4 *Additional Adoption Cost Incentives*

Market participation may involve education and training of agricultural producers on how to alter their practices so that they produce emission offsets most efficiently. Costs may be borne by agencies, and this may also involve transactions costs.

2.3.6 *Property Rights*

A final issue involved in market design involves property rights. As argued in McCarl and Schneider (2001), embarking on the road toward enhanced carbon sequestration poses policy questions regarding private property rights. For example, if carbon programs involve land use conversion, there may be a need to ensure that these movements are not offset by countervailing movements, and this may limit the property rights of a number of land owners.

2.4 Mitigation Research Needs

A wide literature focuses on mitigation issues, but there are still pending unresolved questions. Raymond and Shively (2008) pose these questions: Which methods are best used, given transactions costs, regional variations, and uncertainties? Which strategies should not be adopted by agriculture? In addition to these questions, we pose the following: how does one design mitigation strategies to address leakage, additionality, uncertainty, and permanence, all of which have been major obstacles? How do we expand coverage to an international setting to avoid leakage and unnecessary shifts in comparative advantage? What are the tradeoffs and synergies between sustainable development and mitigation? How can one design incentives to practically harness the implementation of AF mitigation?

3. Adaptation and Land Use Change

Adaptation is the least explored economic area to date. Climate is expected to change agricultural productivity and shift ecosystems over space (Zilberman et al. 2004; Mendelsohn and Dinar 2009). Adaptation involves the purposeful manipulation of LPLULM to increase productivity in the face of such shifts.

There are two types of adaptation: actions undertaken by private decision makers in their own best interests (autonomous adaptation) and actions undertaken by the public sectors in the name of society (IPCC 2007*b*). Prior authors have called the latter "planned adaptation," but we prefer "public adaptation" because it generally addresses the public goods characteristics of underinvestment in certain adaptation actions.

3.1 A Conceptual View of Adaptation

Following Zilberman et al. (2004) and Mendelsohn and Dinar (2009), a theoretical view of adaptation through AF land use change is illustrated in Figure 9.1. There, suppose L depicts the total land available, which is assumed fixed. From right to left, the horizontal

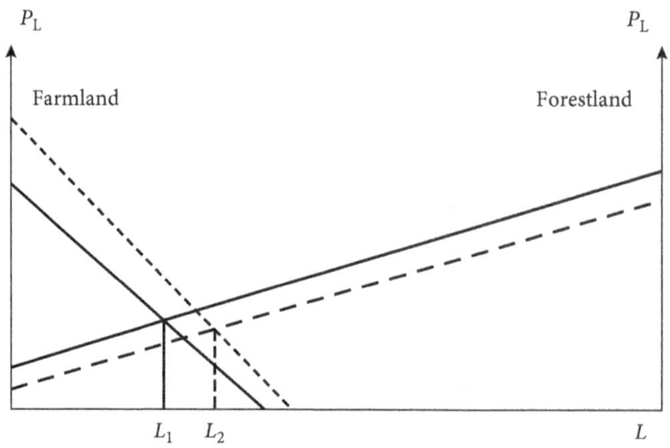

FIGURE 9.1 Theoretical model of land use change under climate change.

axis shows the land allocated to agriculture; from left to right, it shows land used for forest. The two sloped lines are the marginal returns to land allocated to agriculture and forestry. P_L is the land price. L_1 is current land allocated to agriculture. $L-L_1$ is current land allocated to forest. With climate change, the returns to agriculture and forest shift and are represented as dashed lines. The revised land allocation is then L_2, and $L-L_2$.

This reflects substitution to adapt to climate change-induced increases in productivity. The framework shows that users will autonomously adapt to improve their situation in response to climate change (Mendelsohn and Dinar 2009). However, public investments may be needed to either make alternative actions available, such as making crop varieties more heat tolerant, adapting infrastructure (changing the stock of roads, bridges, processing locations etc.), or providing information on heretofore unknown adaptation possibilities.

3.2 LPLULM Adaptation Options

A number of potential LPLULM adaptation options are available. These are often variations of existing climate risk management strategies (Howden et al. 2007) including changes in enterprise choice, crop, or livestock mix; moisture management; irrigation, soil, and water conservation; and management of natural areas, among others (McCarl 2007).

A number of authors have examined observed or potential adaptations in the AF sector. In national studies, Adams et al. (1990), and Reilly et al. (2003) examine changes in crop acreage and find northward shifts in crop mixes. Mu et al. (2013) examine the ways climate change induced land use adaptation between crop and pasture in the US and find that climate change causes shifts in land from crop to pasture and a lower stocking rate. They estimate that projected climate change will decrease cropland by

6% and increase pasture land by 33% by the end of this century. Seo (2010) finds that, in Africa, a hotter and wetter climate causes a shift from crops toward animals. In addition, Reilly et al. (2003) examine how crops have shifted over time by constructing the geographic centroid of production for corn and soybeans and find that, between the early and later 1900s, both US corn and soybean production shifted northward by about 120 miles. Attavanich et al. (2013) update this, finding that US corn and soybean production has shifted northward, ranging from 100–150 miles between 1950 and 2010.

Studies also have shown that cropping system management adjustments can be used to adapt (Adams et al. 2003; Easterling et al. 2003; Butt et al. 2005; Travasso et al. 2006; Challinor et al. 2007). Reilly et al. (2003) show considerable potential to varietal adaptation, but Schlenker and Roberts (2009) suggest limited historical adaptation of seed varieties or management practices to warmer temperatures. Jin et al. (1994) find that using new rice cultivars and changing planting dates in southern China can substantially adapt to climate change and increase rice yields. Kurukulasuriya and Mendelsohn (2008*a*, 2008*b*) find that, in Africa, farmers adapt by shifting toward more heat-tolerant crops as temperatures rises and farmers will also shift toward more heat-tolerant and water-loving crops. In Greece, Kapetanaki and Rosenzweig (1997) find that changing planting dates and varieties of corn can increase yields by 10%. In Spain, Iglesias et al. (2000) find that hybrid seeds and altered sowing dates can allow for double cropping of wheat and corn, thus increasing yields and reducing water use.

Within livestock systems, many adaptation options are connected with maintaining the availability of fodder and feed and reducing heat stress from animal housing (McCarl 2007; Parry et al. 2009). McCarl and Reilly (2008) estimate changes in the size of the US livestock herd under 2030 climate scenarios and find increased sheep, cow calf, dairy, turkey, hog, and broiler numbers with less feedlot beef animals. In South America, Seo et al. (2010) discover that livestock increase with warming climate but decrease when it becomes too wet. In Africa, Seo and Mendelsohn (2008*a*) find that a warming climate is harmful to commercial livestock but is beneficial to small landowners. Seo et al. (2009) find climate change will likely decrease African dairy cattle but increase sheep and chickens, although adaptation measures vary across agro-ecological zones.

Farmers can adapt to climate change by adjusting livestock numbers and species. Mu et al. (2013) find that adaptation involves reductions in cattle stocking rates under projected climate change. Alternatively, farmers could switch breeds so that livestock can adapt to a warmer temperature and changes in precipitation. Zhang et al. (2013) examine breed choices among cattle in Texas and find that heat-tolerant breeds like Brangus cattle are used as an adaptation strategy in a hot and humid environment.

Climate change is projected to have far-reaching impacts on ecosystems and supported species (Chopra et al. 2005; Lemieux and Scott 2005). Adaptation of managed forests could involve changes in tree species, harvesting patterns, pest control, and location of managed woodland (McCarl 2007). Ecological models have predicted that forests will expand globally and become somewhat more productive and also that forest ecosystems would shift poleward and to higher elevations (Zilberman et al. 2004; Mendelsohn and Dinar 2009). Howden et al. (2007) argue that the forest sector can plant better adapted tree species and can reduce disturbance losses by harvesting high-risk stocks before they can be destroyed. Mendelsohn and Dinar (2009) indicate that climate change will alter land allocation between forest and wild lands. Sohngen and Mendelsohn (2003), Mendelsohn and Dinar (2009) and Sohngen et al. (2010) show that forest adaptation is a dynamic process involving staged harvest decisions, thus limiting the ability to change large forest stocks quickly.

Parry et al. (2009) argue that complementary relationships between adaptation and mitigation can be exploited because adaptation actions can have positive or negative mitigation effects and vice versa. In the forest sector, afforestation of degraded hill slopes is an example of a mitigation action with a positive adaptation effect that would not only sequester carbon, but also control soil erosion (IPCC 2007*b*).

3.3 Completeness of Adaptation

Adaptation has been found to improve welfare, so it is therefore very likely that people will autonomously adapt (Butt et al. 2005; Mendelsohn and Dinar 2009). However, most impacts due to climate change are projected to continue to increase for some time (IPCC 2007*b*), implying a need for continuing adaptation. Furthermore, some adaptation actions may not be practical due to costs or barriers. Therefore, it is likely that some climate change impacts are unavoidable (Parry et al. 2009) and the resolution of who is going to pay for adaptation is also a major issue.

3.4 Adaptation and Development

Social-economic development and adaptation are intimately linked (Parry et al. 2009). Technological sophistication and progress are important determinants of farm productivity and adaptation potential and also influence adaptation demand. In particular, if technological progress lags behind population growth, there will be increased competition among land uses, including those for adaptation and mitigation (Mendelsohn and Dinar 2009; McCarl et al. 2012). Lobell et al. (2008) indicate that South Asia and Southern Africa are regions that, without sufficient adaptation measures, will likely suffer negative impacts on several crops, which are important to large, food-insecure human populations.

It is not clear what level of adaptation investment is appropriate because we have limited knowledge of climate change impacts, as well as limited studies on the effectiveness and optimal level of adaptation (Parry et al. 2009). The United Nations Framework Convention on Climate Change (UNFCCC) has estimated that the annual cost of AF adaptation ranged between $11.3 to $ 12.6 billion for 2030, with developing contries needing $7 billion dollars (McCarl 2007). With such levels of adaptation, about 80% of the costs of potential impacts might be avoided, but about 20% might not (Parry et al. 2009), and cost of adaptation may rise steeply after 2030 (IPCC 2007*b*).

3.5 Adaptation Research Needs

The choice of optimal adaptation levels is uncertain because information about future potential impacts and adaptation effectiveness is scarce (Parry et al. 2009), and this delays adaptation. Research efforts to narrow this uncertainty and identify robust adaptation are needed.

In addition, incorporating adaptation into integrated assessment models is needed, as is the inclusion of information on both autonomous and public adaptation cost. Although global estimates of adaptation cost have emerged (e.g., UNFCCC 2007; Nelson et al. 2009; Parry et al. 2009; and McCarl 2007 in a LPLULM sense), costs of adapting to varying levels of climate change need analysis, to provide a choice range for the level of adaptation investment. There is also a need to analyze the unavoidable impacts and the resulting damage costs that we need to anticipate (Parry et al. 2009).

Adaptation plans may suffer from maladaptation or leakage problems (Smith et al. 2000; Sathaye and Andrasko 2007; Sohngen and Brown 2008), in which actions in one region cause lower net adaptation in other locations. Furthermore, the roles of many nonclimatic factors, such as changes of commodity prices, population growth, economy development, or farm programs, and the like that interact with climatic stimuli in influencing LPLULM adaptation decision making are rarely substantively examined (Kandlikar and Risbey 2000; Schneider et al. 2000).

4. Interrelationships among Climate Change Effects, Mitigation, and Adaptation

The total burden of climate change consists of three elements: the costs of mitigation (reducing the extent of climate change), the costs of adaptation (reducing the impact of change), and the residual impacts that can be neither mitigated nor adapted to (Parry et al. 2009). Mitigation and adaptation both avoid climate change but are fundamentally different in timing, with adaptation providing an immediate avoidance and mitigation a long-term reduction in extent. Some studies have attempted to understand the interplay among impacts, adaptation, and mitigation. Yet there are still many unanswered questions.

Bosello et al. (2009) indicate that welfare is greater when adaptation and mitigation are implemented jointly and both contribute to better control of climate damages. Estimations considering only single mitigation or adaptation actions are therefore likely to yield biased results.

The major climate change policy question is: "What combination of emissions reduction and adaptation is appropriate in offsetting the impacts of climate change?" In addressing this question, one must realize that adaptation and mitigation can be both complementary and substitutes. The IPCC (2007*b*) reviews four major types of interrelationships between adaptation and mitigation: (1) adaptation actions that have consequences for mitigation, (2) mitigation actions that have consequences for adaptation, (3) decisions that include trade-offs or synergies between adaptation and mitigation, and (4) processes that have consequences for both adaptation and mitigation.

Important implications arise from the interdependence between mitigation and adaptation. Lecocq and Shalizi (2007) point out the need for mitigation and adaptation policies to be analyzed and implemented jointly, not separately. Mata and Budhooram (2007) state that, in a hypothetical world where all net costs are borne by a single global entity, choices would probably be driven by total cost minimization rather than by aversion to "dangerous anthropogenic interference with the climate system." However, the complexities of costs and benefits and their widespread distribution make these assumptions implausible (Mata and Budhooram 2007). Rather, society is saddled with the burden of optimally allocating resources subject to budget constraints and uncertainties. In addition, action should incorporate learning and irreversibility.

Some studies have tried to assess the optimal policy balance of mitigation and adaptation using cost-benefit frameworks based on integrated assessment models (IAMs) (IPCC 2007*b*). Temporal investment allocation results obtained using IAMs in de Bruin et al. (2009) and in Wang and McCarl (2013) show that both adaptation and mitigation are simultaneously employed, with adaptation prevailing initially then mitigation investment taking over in the long run as the damages from GHG emissions increase.

4.1 Research Needs

Most studies on climate change responses focus on single aspects of the adaptation-mitigation nexus, without considering their interplay. Hence, substantial research needs to address the optimal portfolio of adaptation and mitigation, along with practical inquiries into the extent to which climate change vulnerability can be addressed. The IPCC (2007*c*) indicates that the relationship between development paths and adaptation-mitigation interrelationships requires further research. This is particularly important in developing country settings.

5. Conclusion

LPLULM decision making is certainly affected by climate change and climate policy. Actions can address adaptation or mitigation, and there will be climate change-induced damages that are not mitigated or adapted to. In the future, we think substantial research will need to be devoted to determine how land use decisions can facilitate adaptation and mitigation, as well as the degree of vulnerability under alternative levels of action. We only hope that this review will inform researchers about past efforts and potential productive future ones.

Acknowledgments

We thank the editors for comments. Seniority of authorship is shared among authors.

References

Adams, R. M., C. Rosenzweig, R. M. Peart, J. T. Ritchie, B. A. McCarl, J. D. Glyer, R. B. Curry, J. W. Jones, K. J. Boote, and L. H. Allen, Jr. 1990. Global climate change and U.S. agriculture *Nature* 345: 219–224.

Adams R. M, B. A. McCarl, and L. O. Mearns. 2003. The effects of spatial scale of climate scenarios on economic assessments: An example from U.S. agriculture. *Climatic Change* 60:131–148.

Ainsworth, E. A., and S. P. Long. 2005. What have we learned from 15 years of free-air CO2 enrichment (FACE)? A meta-analytic review of the responses of photosynthesis, canopy properties and plant production to rising CO_2. *New Phytologist* 165(2): 351–372.

Allen, C. D., A. K. Macalady, H. Chenchouni, D. Bachelet, N. McDowell, M. Vennetier, T. Kitzberger, A. Rigling, D. D. Breshears, and E. H. Hogg. 2010. A global overview of drought and heat-induced tree mortality reveals emerging climate change risks for forests. *Forest Ecology and Management* 259(4): 660–684.

Attavanich, W., and B. A. McCarl. 2011. The effect of climate change, CO2 fertilization, and crop production technology on crop yields and its economic implications on market outcomes and welfare distribution. Paper presented at 2011 AAEA & NAREA Joint Annual Meeting, July 24–26, Pittsburgh, Pennsylvania.

Attavanich, W., B. A. McCarl, Z. Ahmedov. S. W. Fuller, and D. V. Vedenov. 2013. Effects of climate change on US grain transport. *Nature Climate Change* 3:638–643 doi:10.1038/nclimate1892

Aulakh, M. S., R. Wassmann, C. Bueno, and H. Rennenberg. 2001. Impact of root exudates of different cultivars and plant development stages of rice (Oryza sativa L.) on methane production in a paddy soil. *Plant Soil* 230: 77–86.

Barnett, T. P., J. C. Adam, and D. P. Lettenmaier. 2005. Potential impacts of a warming climate on water availability in snow-dominated regions. *Nature* 438(7066): 303–309.

Barnett, T. P., and D. W. Pierce. 2009. Sustainable water deliveries from the Colorado River in a changing climate. *Proceedings of the National Academy of Sciences of the USA* 106(18): 7334.

Bates, B., Z. W. Kundzewicz, S. Wu, and J. Palutikof, eds. 2008. Climate change and water. Technical Paper of the Intergovernmental Panel on Climate Change, IPCC Secretariat. Geneva.

Birdsey, R. A. 1996. Carbon storage for major forest types and regions in the conterminous United States. *Forests and Global Phange*, 2, 1-25.

Boadi, D., C. Benchaar, J. Chiquette, and D. Masse. 2004. Mitigation strategies to reduce enteric methane emissions from dairy cows: Update review. *Canadian Journal Animal Science* 84: 319–335.

Boisvenue, C. É. L., and S. W. Running. 2006. Impacts of climate change on natural forest productivity–evidence since the middle of the 20th century. *Global Change Biology* 12(5): 862–882.

Bosello, F., C. Carraro and E. De Cian. 2009. An analysis of adaptation as a response to climate change. University Ca'Foscari of Venice, Dept. of Economics Research Paper Series, (26_09).

Brown, T. J., B. L. Hall, and A. L. Westerling. 2004. The impact of twenty-first century climate change on wildland fire danger in the western United States: An applications perspective. *Climatic Change* 62(1): 365–388.

Butt, T. A., B. A. McCarl, J. Angerer, P. T. Dyke, and J. W. Stuth. 2005. The economic and food security implications of climate change in Mali. *Climatic Change* 68(3): 355–378.

Cacho, O. J., R. L. Hean, and R. Wise. 2003. Carbon-accounting methods and reforestation incentives. *Australian Journal of Agricultural and Resource Economics* 47: 153–179.

Canadell, J. G., C. L.Qu´er´e, M. R. Raupach, C. B. Field, E. T. Buitenhuis, P. Ciais, T. J. Conway, N. P. Gillett, R. A. Houghton, and G. Marlandi. 2007. Contributions to accelerating atmospheric CO2 growth from economic activity, carbon intensity, and efficiency of natural sinks. *Proceedings of the National Academy of Sciences of the USA* 104(47): 18866–18870.

Canadell, J. G., and M. R. Raupach. 2008. Managing forests for climate change mitigation. *Science* 320: 1456–1457.

Cayan, D. R., E. P. Maurer, M. D. Dettinger, M. Tyree, and K. Hayhoe. 2008. Climate change scenarios for the California region. *Climatic Change* 87: 21–42.

Cerri, C. C., M. Bernoux, C. E. P. Cerri, and C. Feller. 2004. Carbon cycling and sequestration opportunities in South America: The case of Brazil. *Soil Use Management* 20: 248–254.

Challinor, A., T. Wheeler, P. Craufurd, C. Ferro, and D. Stephenson. 2007. Adaptation of crops to climate change through genotypic responses to mean and extreme temperatures. *Agriculture, Ecosystems and Environment* 119: 190–204.

Chen, C. C., and B. A. McCarl. 2001. An investigation of the relationship between pesticide usage and climate change. *Climatic Change* 50(4): 475–487.

Chen, C. C., B. A. McCarl, and D. E. Schimmelpfennig. 2004. Yield variability as influenced by climate: A statistical investigation. *Climatic Change* 66(1): 239–261.

Chen, C. C., and B. A. McCarl. 2009. Hurricanes and possible intensity increases: Effects on and reactions from U.S. *agriculture. Journal of Agricultural and Applied Economics* 41(1): 125–144.

Chopra, K., R. Leemans, P. Kumar, and H. Simons. 2005. *Ecosystems and human well-being: Policy Responses*. Washington, DC: Island Press.

Clemens, J., and H. J. Ahlgrimm. 2001. Greenhouse gases from animal husbandry: Mitigation options. *Nutrient Cycling in Agroecosystems* 60: 287–300.

Coudrain, A., B. Francou, and Z. W. Kundzewicz. 2005. Glacier shrinkage in the Andes and consequences for water resources. *Hydrological Sciences Journal* 50(6): 925–932.

Cullen, B. R., I. R. Johnson, R. J. Eckard, G. M. Lodge, R. G. Walker, R. P. Rawnsley, and M. R. McCaskill. 2009. Climate change effects on pasture systems in south-eastern Australia. *Crop and Pasture Science* 60(10): 933–942.

De Bruin, K. C., R. B. Dellink, and R. S. J. Tol. 2009. AD-DICE: An implementation of adaptation in the DICE model. *Climatic Change* 95: 63–81.

De Wit, M., and J. Stankiewicz. 2006. Changes in surface water supply across Africa with predicted climate change. *Science* 311(5769): 1917–21.

Deschenes, O., and M. Greenstone. 2007. The economic impacts of climate change: Evidence from agricultural output and random fluctuations in weather. *American Economic Review* 97(1): 354–385.

Dias de Oliveira, M. E., B. E. Vaughan, and E. J. Rykiel, Jr. 2005. Ethanol as fuel: Energy, carbon dioxide balances, and ecological footprint. *BioScience* 55: 593–602.

Easterling, W. E., N. Chhetri, and X. Niu 2003. Improving the realism of modeling agronomic adaptation to climate change: Simulating technological substitution. In *Issues in the impacts of climate variability and change on agriculture—Applications to the southeastern United States*, ed. L. O. Mearns, 149–173. Dordrecht: Kluwer Academic.

FAO. 2010. Managing forests for climate change. http://www.fao.org/docrep/013/i1960e/i1960e00.pdf

Fargione, J., J. Hill, D. Tilman, S. Polasky, and P. Hawthorne. 2008. Land clearing and the biofuel carbon debt. *Science* 319(5867): 1235–1238.

Foster, J. R., J. I. Burton, J. A. Forrester, F. Liu, J. D. Muss, F. M. Sabatini, R. M. Scheller, and D. J. Mladenoff. 2010. Evidence for a recent increase in forest growth is questionable. *Proceedings of the National Academy of Sciences of the USA* 107(21): E86.

Foxon, T. J. 2010. Climate change mitigation policy: An overview of opportunities and challenges. In *Changing climates, earth systems and society*, eds. E. F. J. Nulder, and J. Dowson, 231–241. Netherlands: Springer.

Gan, J. 2004. Risk and damage of southern pine beetle outbreaks under global climate change. *Forest Ecology and Management* 191: 61–71.

Gan, J. 2005. Incorporating human and natural adaptations in assessing climate change impacts on wildfire occurrence. In *New research on forest ecosystems*, ed. A. R. Burk, 61–73. Hauppauge, NY: Nova Science.

Gerber P., N. Key, F. Portet, and H. Steinfeld. 2010. Policy options in addressing livestock's contribution to climate change. *Animal* 4: 393–406.

Gleick, P. H., and D. B. Adams. 2000. Water: The potential consequences of climate variability and change. A report of the National Water Assessment Group, U.S. Global Change Research Program, U.S. Geological Survey, U.S. Department of the Interior and the Pacific Institute for Studies in Development, Environment, and Security, Oakland, California.

Golub, A., T. Hertel, H. Lee, S. Rose, and B. Sohngen. 2009. The opportunity cost of land use and the global potential for greenhouse gas mitigation in agriculture and forestry. *Resource and Energy Economics* 31: 299–319.

Gullison, R. E., P. C. Frumhoff, J. G. Canadell, C. B. Field, D. C. Nepstad, K. Hayhoe, R. Avissar, L. M. Curran, P. Friedlingstein, C. D. Jones, and C. Nobre.2007. Tropical forests and climate policy. *Science* 316: 985–986.

Hicke, J. A., and J. C. Jenkins. 2008. Mapping lodgepole pine stand structure susceptibility to mountain pine beetle attack across the western United States. *Forest Ecology and Management* 255(5–6): 1536–1547.

Houghton, R. A. 2003. Revised estimates of the annual net flux of carbon to the atmosphere from changes in land use and land management: 1850–2000. *Tellus Series B: Chemical and Physical Meteorology* 55(2): 378–390.

Howden, S. M., J. F. Soussana, F. N. Tubiello, N. Chhetri, M. Dunlop, and H. Meinke. 2007. Adapting agriculture to climate change. *Proceedings of the National Academy of Sciences of the USA* 104(50): 19691–19696.

Huang, H., and M. Khanna. 2010. An econometric analysis of U.S. crop yield and cropland acreage: Implications for the impact of climate change. Paper presented at 2010 AAEA, CAES, & WAEA Joint Annual Meeting, Denver, Colorado.

Iglesias, A., C. Rosenzweig, and D. Pereira. 2000. Agricultural impacts of climate change in Spain: Developing tools for a spatial analysis. *Global Environment Change* 10: 69–80.

IPCC. 2000. *IPCC Special Report: Land use, land-use change, and forestry*, eds. T. W. Robert., I. R. Noble, B. Bolin, N. H. Ravindranath, D. J. Verardo, and D. J. Dokken. Cambridge, UK: Cambridge University Press.

IPCC. 2007*a*. *Climate change 2007: The physical science basis*. Contribution of working group I to the fourth assessment report of the Intergovernmental Panel on Climate Change, eds. S. Solomon, D. Qin, M. Manning, Z. Chen, M. Marquis, K. B. Averyt, M. Tignor, and H. L. Miller. Cambridge, UK: Cambridge University Press.

IPCC. 2007*b*. *Climate change 2007: Impacts, adaptation and vulnerability*. Contribution of working group II to the fourth assessment report of the Intergovernmental Panel on Climate Change, eds. M. L. Parry, O. F. Canziani, P. J. Palutikof, P. J. van der Linden, and C. E. Hanson. Cambridge, UK: Cambridge University Press.

IPCC. 2007*c*. *Climate change 2007: Mitigation of climate change*. Contribution of working group III to the fourth assessment report of the Intergovernmental Panel on Climate Change, eds. B. Metz, O. R. Davidson, P. R. Bosch, R. Dave, and L. A. Meyer. Cambridge, UK: Cambridge University Press.

Isik, M., and S. Devadoss. 2006. An analysis of the impact of climate change on crop yields and yield variability. *Applied Economics* 38(7): 835–844.

Jin, Z., D. Ge, H. Chen, and J. Fang. 1994. Effects of climate change on rice production and strategies for adaptation in southern China. In *Implications of climate change for international agriculture: Crop modeling study*, eds. C. Rosenzweig, and A. Iglesias, 1–24. Washington, DC: U.S. Environmental Protection Agency.

Kandlikar, M., and J. Risbey. 2000. Agricultural impacts of climate change: If adaptation is the answer, what is the question? *Climatic Change* 45: 529–539.

Kapetanaki, G., and C. Rosenzweig. 1997. Impact of climate change on maize yield in central and northern Greece: A simulation study with CERES-Maize. *Mitigation Adaptation Strategies for Global Change* 1: 251–271.

Karnosky, D. F., K. S. Pregitzer, J. Nosberger, S. P. Long, R. J. Norby, et al. 2006. Impacts of elevated atmospheric [CO2] and [O3] on northern temperate forest ecosystems: results from the Aspen FACE Experiment. In *Managed ecosystems and CO2: Case studies, processes,and perspectives*, eds. J. Nosberger, S. P. Long, R. J. Norby, M. Stitt, G. R. Hendrey, and H. Blum, 213–229. Berlin, Germany.: Springer-Verlag.

Kaul, M., G. M. J. Mohren, and V. K. Dadhwal. 2010. Carbon storage versus fossil fuel substitution: A climate change mitigation option for two different land use categories based on short and long rotation. *Mitigation Adaptation Strategies for Global Change* 15: 395–409.

Kelly, D. L., C. D. Kolstad, and G. T. Mitchell. 2005. Adjustment costs from environmental change. *Journal of Environmental Economics and Management* 50: 468–495.

Kim, M-K., B. A. McCarl, and B. C. Murray. 2008. Permanence discounting for land-based carbon sequestration. *Ecological Economics* 64(4): 763–769.

Kim, M-K., and B. A. McCarl. 2009. Uncertainty discounting for land-based carbon sequestration. *Journal of Agricultural and Applied Economics* 41(1): 1–11.

Kim, S. 2011. The effect of transactions costs on GHG emission mitigation for agriculture and forestry. Ph.D. dissertation, Texas A&M University.

Kimball, B. A. 2006. The effects of free-air [CO2] enrichment of cotton, wheat, and sorghum. In *Managed ecosystems and CO2*, 47–70. Berlin and Heidelberg: Springer.

Kurukulasuriya, P. and R. Mendelsohn. 2008*a*. A Ricardian analysis of the impact of climate change on African cropland. *African Journal Agriculture and Resource Economics* 2:1–23.

Kurukulasuriya, P., and R. Mendelsohn. 2008*b*. Crop switching as an adaptation strategy to climate change. *African Journal Agriculture and Resource Economics* 2: 105–126.

Lal, R., R. F. Follett, and J. M. Kimble. 2003. Achieving soil carbon sequestration in the United States: A challenge to the policy makers. *Soil Science* 168: 827–845.

Leakey, A. D. B. 2009. Rising atmospheric carbon dioxide concentration and the future of C4 crops for food and fuel. *Proceedings of the Royal Society B: Biological Sciences* 276(1666): 2333.

Lecocq, F., and Z. Shalizi. 2007. Balancing expenditures on mitigation of and adaptation to climate change: An exploration of Issues relevant to developing countries. Policy Research Working Paper Series 4299. Washington, DC: The World Bank.

Lemieux, C. J., and D. J. Scott. 2005. Climate change, biodiversity conservation and protected areas planning in Canada. *The Canadian Geographer* 49(4): 384–399.

Lobell, D. B., M. B. Burke, C. Tebaldi, M. D. Mastrandrea, W. P. Falcon., and R. L. Naylor. 2008. Prioritizing climate change adaptation needs for food security in 2030. *Science* 319: 607–610.

Long, S. P., E. A. Ainsworth, A. D. B. Leakey, J. Nösberger, and D. R. Ort. 2006. Food for thought: Lower-than-expected crop yield stimulation with rising CO2 concentrations. *Science* 312(5782): 1918–21.

Mader, T. L., K. L. Frank, J. A. Harrington, G. L. Hahn, and J. A. Nienaber. 2009. Potential climate change effects on warm-season livestock production in the Great Plains. *Climatic Change* 97(3): 529–541.

Mata, L. J., and J. Budhooram. 2007. Complementarity between mitigation and adaptation: the water sector. *Mitigation and Adaptation Strategies for Global Change* 12: 799–807, doi:10.1007/s11027-007-9100-y.

McCarl, B. A., and U. A. Schneider. 2001. Greenhouse gas mitigation in U.S. agriculture and forestry. *Science* 294: 2481–2482.

McCarl, B. A. 2007. Adaptation options for agriculture, forestry and fisheries. A report to the UNFCCC Secretariat Financial and Technical Support Division. http://agecon2.tamu.edu/people/faculty/mccarl-bruce/papers/1467mccarl.pdf

McCarl, B. A., and J. M. Reilly. 2007. Agriculture in the climate change and energy price squeeze: Part 2: Mitigation opportunities. Department of Agricultural Economics, Texas A&M University. http://agecon2.tamu.edu/people/faculty/mccarl-bruce/papers/1322agin climate2mitigation2.doc.

McCarl, B. A. 2008. Bioenergy in a greenhouse mitigating world. *Choices* 23(1): 31–33.

McCarl, B. A., and J. M. Reilly. 2008. U.S. agriculture in the climate change squeeze: Part 1: Sectoral sensitivity and vulnerability. Report to the National Environmental Trust. http://agecon2.tamu.edu/people/faculty/mccarl-bruce/689cc/topic5b_Agriculture%20in%20the%20climate%20change%20squeez1.pdf

McCarl, B. A., X. Villavicencio, and X. Wu. 2008. Climate change and future analysis: Is stationarity dying? *American Journal of Agricultural Economics* 90(5): 1241–1247.

McCarthy, H. R., R. Oren, K. H. Johnsen, A. Gallet-Budynek, S. G. Pritchard, C. W. Cook, S. L. LaDeau, R. B. Jackson, and A. C. Finzi. 2010. Re-assessment of plant carbon dynamics at the duke free-air CO_2 enrichment site: Interactions of atmospheric CO_2 with nitrogen and water availability over stand development. *New Phytologist* 185(2): 514–528.

McCarl, B. A., X. Villavicencio, X. M. Wu, and W. E. Huffman. 2013. Climate change influences on agricultural research productivity. *Climatic Change* 19: 815–824

McMahon, S. M., G. G. Parker, and D. R. Miller. 2010. Evidence for a recent increase in forest growth. *Proceedings of the National Academy of Sciences of the USA* 107(8): 3611–3615.

Mendelsohn, R., W. D. Nordhaus, and D. Shaw. 1994. The impact of global warming on agriculture: A Ricardian analysis. *American Economic Review* 84: 753–771.

Mendelsohn, R., and M. Reinsborough. 2007. A Ricardian analysis of U.S. and Canadian farmland. *Climatic Change* 81(1): 9–17.

Mendelsohn, R., and A. Dinar. 2009. Land use and climate change interactions. *Annual Review of Resource Economics* 1: 309–332.

Mendelsohn, R., J. Arellano-Gonzalez, and P. Christensen. 2010. A Ricardian analysis of Mexican farms. *Environment and Development Economics* 15(2): 153–171.

Metcalf, G. E., and J. M. Reilly. 2008. Policy options for controlling greenhouse gas emissions: Implications for agriculture. *Choices* 23(1): 34–37.

Miles. L., and V. Kapos. 2008. Reducing greenhouse gas emissions from deforestation and forest degradation: Global land-use implications. *Science* 13: 1454–1455.

Monteny, G. J., A. Bannink, and D. Chadwick. 2006. Greenhouse gas abatement strategies for animal husbandry. *Agriculture Ecosystems and Environment* 112: 163–170.

Montgomery, C. A. 2014. Fire: An agent and a consequence of land use change. In *The Oxford handbook of land economics*, eds. J. M. Duke and J. Wu, 281–301. New York: Oxford University Press.

Mooney, S., J. M. Antle, S. M. Capalbo, and K. Paustian. 2004. Influence of project scale on the costs of measuring soil sequestration. *Environmental Management* 33(S1): S252–263.

Mooney, S., K. Gerow, J. M. Antle, S. M. Capalbo, and K. Paustian. 2007. Reducing standard errors by incorporating spatial autocorrelation into a measurement scheme for soil carbon credits. *Climatic Change* 80:55–72.

Moriondo, M., P. Good, R. Durao, M. Bindi, C. Giannakopoulos, and J. Corte-Real. 2006. Potential impact of climate change on fire risk in the Mediterranean area. *Climate Research* 31(1): 85–95.

Mu, J. E., B. A. McCarl, and X. M. Wu. 2011. Climate change influences on the risk of avian influenza outbreaks and associated economic losses. Paper presented at the 2011 AAEA AND NAREA Joint Annual Meeting, July 24–26, Pittsburgh, Pennsylvania.

Mu, J. E., B. A. McCarl, and A. Wein. 2013. Adaptation to climate change: Changes in farmland use and stocking rate in the U.S. *Mitigation and Adaptation Strategies for Global Change.* 18: 713–730. doi: 10.1007/s11027-012-9384-4.

Murray, B. C., B. A. McCarl, and H. C. Lee. 2004. Estimating leakage from forest carbon sequestration programs. *Land Economics* 80: 109–124.

Murray, B. C., B. L. Sohngen, A. J. Sommer, B. M. Depro, K. M. Jones, B. A. McCarl, D. Gillig, B. DeAngelo, and K. Andrasko. 2005. *Greenhouse gas mitigation potential in U.S. forestry and agriculture, EPA-R-05-006.* Washington, DC: U. S. Environmental Protection Agency, Office of Atmospheric Programs, Washington, D.C.

Nabuurs, G. J., O. Masera, K. Andrasko, P. Benitez-Ponce, R. Boer, M. Dutschke, E. Elsiddig, J. Ford-Robertson, P. Frumhoff, T. Karjalainen, O. Krankina, W. A. Kurz, M. Matsumoto,

W. Oyhantcabal, N. H. Ravindranath, M. J. Sanz Sanchez, and X. Zhang, 2007: Forestry. In *Climate Change 2007: Mitigation.* Contribution of Working Group III to the Fourth Assessment Report of the Intergovernmental Panel on Climate Change, eds. B. Metz, O. R. Davidson, P. R. Bosch, R. Dave, L. A. Meyer. Cambridge, UK and New York, NY, USA: Cambridge University Press.

Nelson, G. C., M. W. Rosegrant, J. Koo, R. Robertson, T. Sulser, T. Zhu, C. Ringler, S. Msangi, A. Palazzo, M. Batka, M. Magalhaes, R. Valmonte-Santos, M. Ewing, and D. Lee. 2009. Impact on agriculture and costs of adaptation. International Food Policy Research Institute (IFPRI). http://ccsl.iccip.net/impact_agri.pdf

Norby, R. J., E. H. DeLucia, B. Gielen, C. Calfapietra, C. P. Giardina, J. S. King, J. Ledford, H. R. McCarthy, D. J. P. Moore, and R. Ceulemans. 2005. Forest response to elevated CO2 is conserved across a broad range of productivity. *Proceedings of the National Academy of Sciences of the USA* 102(50): 18052–18056..

Nowak, R. S., D. S. Ellsworth, and S. D. Smith. 2004. Functional responses of plants to elevated atmospheric CO2–Do photosynthetic and productivity data from FACE experiments support early predictions? *New Phytologist* 162: 253–280.

Pacala, S., and R. Socolow. 2004. Stabilization wedges: Solving the climate problem for the next 50 years with current technologies. *Science* 305: 968–972.

Paeth, H., K. Born, R. Girmes, R. Podzun, and D. Jacob. 2009. Regional climate change in tropical and northern Africa due to greenhouse forcing and land use changes. *Journal of Climate* 22(1): 114–132.

Parry, M., N. Arnell, P. Berry, D. Dodman, S. Fankhauser, C. Hope, S. Kovats, R. Nicolls, D. Sattherwaite, R. Tiffen, and T. Wheeler. 2009. *Assessing the costs of adaptation to climate change: A critique of the UNFCCC estimates.* London: International Institute for Environment and Development and Grantham Institute for Climate Change.

Patriquin, M. N., A. M. Wellstead, and W. A. White. 2007. Beetles, trees, and people: Regional economic impact sensitivity and policy considerations related to the mountain pine beetle infestation in British Columbia, Canada. *Forest Policy and Economics* 9(8): 938–946.

Polley, H. W., D. D. Briske, J. A. Morgan, K. Wolter, D. W. Bailey, and J. R. Brown. 2012. Climate change and North American rangelands: Evidence, trends, and implications. Commissioned paper under submission to Rangeland Ecology and Management.

Purse, B. V., P. S. Mellor, D. J. Rogers, A. R. Samuel, P. P. C. Mertens, and M. Baylis. 2005. Climate change and the recent emergence of bluetongue in Europe. *Nature Reviews Microbiology* 3(2): 171–181.

Raymond, L., and G. Shively. 2008. Market-based approaches to CO_2 emissions reductions. *Choices* 23(1):38–40.

Reilly, J. M. (ed.). 2002. *Agriculture: The potential consequences of climate variability and change for the United States.* New York: Cambridge University Press. http://www.usgcrp.gov/usgcrp/Library/nationalassessment/Agriculture.pdf

Reilly, J., F. Tubiello, B. A. McCarl, D. Abler, R. Darwin, K. Fuglie, S. Hollinger, C. Izaurralde, S. Jagtap, and J. Jones. 2003. U.S. agriculture and climate change: New results. *Climatic Change* 57: 43–67.

Richards, K., and C. Stokes. 2004. A review of forest carbon sequestration cost studies: A dozen years of research. *Climatic Change* 63: 1–46.

Robinet, C., and A. Roques. 2010. Direct impacts of recent climate warming on insect populations. *Integrative Zoology* 5(2): 132–142.

Rosenzweig, C., A. Iglesias, X. B. Yang, P. R. Epstein, and E. Chivian. 2001. Climate change and extreme weather events: Implications for food production, plant diseases, and pests. *Global Change and Human Health* 2(2): 90–104.

Saegerman, C., D. Berkvens, and P. S. Mellor. 2008. Bluetongue epidemiology in the European Union. *Emerging Infectious Diseases* 14(4): 539–544 539.

Sands, R. D. and B. A. McCarl, 2005: Competitiveness of terrestrial greenhouse gas offsets: are they a bridge to the future? In Abstracts of USDA Symposium on Greenhouse Gases and Carbon Sequestration in Agriculture and Forestry, March 22–24, Baltimore: USDA.

Sathaye, J. A., and K. Andrasko. 2007. Special issue on estimation of baselines and leakage in carbon mitigation forestry projects. *Mitigation Adaptation Strategies for Global Change* 12: 963–970.

Schlenker, W., W. M. Hanemann, and A. C. Fisher. 2005. Will U.S. agriculture really benefit from global warming? Accounting for irrigation in the hedonic approach. *American Economic Review* 95(1): 395–406.

Schlenker, W., and M. J. Roberts. 2009. Nonlinear temperature effects indicate severe damages to U.S. crop yields under climate change. *Proceedings of the National Academy of Sciences of the USA* 106(37): 15594–15598.

Schlesinger, W. H. 1999. Carbon sequestration in soils. *Science* 286: 2095.

Schneider, S. H., W. E. Easterling, and L. O. Mearns. 2000. Adaptation: Sensitivity to natural variability, agent assumptions and dynamic climate changes. *Climatic Change* 45: 203–221.

Schneider, U. A., and P. Kumar. 2008. Greenhouse gas mitigation through agriculture. *Choices* 23(1):19–23.

Schwab, O., T. Maness, G. Bull, and D. Roberts. 2009. Modeling the effect of changing market conditions on mountain pine beetle salvage harvesting and structural changes in the British Columbia forest products industry. *Canadian Journal of Forest Research* 39(10): 1806–1820.

Seager, R., M. F. Ting, I. M. Held, Y. Kushnir, J. Lu, G. Vecchi, H. P. Huang, N. Harnik, A. Leetmaa, N. C. Lau, C. Li, J. Velez, and N. Naik. 2007. Model projections of an imminent transition to a more arid climate in southwestern North America. *Science* 316: 1181–1184.

Searchinger T., R. Heimlich, R. A. Houghton, F. Dong, A. Elobeid, J. Fabiosa, S. Tokgoz, D. Hayes, and T. -H. Yu. 2008. Use of U.S. croplands for biofuels increases greenhouse gases through emissions from land-use change. *Science* 319: 1238–1240.

Seo, S. N., and R. Mendelsohn. 2008*a*. Measuring impacts and adaptations to climate change: a structural Ricardian model of African livestock management. *Agricultural Economics* 38: 151–165.

Seo, S. N., and R. Mendelsohn. 2008*b*. An analysis of crop choice: Adapting to climate change in Latin American farms. *Ecological Economics* 67: 109–116.

Seo, S. N., R. Mendelsohn, A. Dinar, R. Hassan, and P. Kurukulasuriya. 2009. A Ricardian analysis of the distribution of climate change impacts on agriculture across agro-ecological zones. *Africa Environmental and Resource Economics* 43: 313–332.

Seo, S. N. 2010. Managing forests, livestock, and crops under global warming: A microeconometric analysis of land use changes in Africa. *Australian Journal of Agricultural and Resource Economics* 54: 239–258.

Seo, S. N., B. A. McCarl, and R. Mendelsohn. 2010. From beef cattle to sheep under global warming? An analysis of adaptation by livestock species choice in South America. *Ecological Economics* 69: 2486–2494.

Shakhramanyan, N. G., U. A. Schneider, and B. A. McCarl. 2013. U.S. agricultural sector analysis on pesticide externalities—The impact of climate change and a Pigovian tax. *Climatic Change* 1–13.

Sirohi, S., and A. Michaelowa. 2007. Sufferer and cause: Indian livestock and climate change. *Climatic Change* 85(3): 285–298.

Smith, B., I. Burton, R. J. T. Klein, and J. Wandel. 2000. An anatomy of adaptation to climate change and variability. *Climatic Change* 45(1): 223–251.

Smith, P. 2004*b*. Engineered biological sinks on land. In *The global carbon cycle: Integrating humans, climate, and the natural world*, eds. Field, C. B., and M. R. Raupach, 479-491. Washington, DC: Island Press.

Smith, P., D. Martino, Z. Cai, D. Gwary, H. Janzen, P. Kumar, B. A. McCarl, S. Ogle, F. O'Mara, C. Rice, B. Scholes, and O. Sirotenko. 2007*a*. Agriculture. In *Climate change 2007: Mitigation.* Contribution of working group III to the fourth assessment report of the Intergovernmental Panel on Climate Change, eds. B. Metz., O. R. Davidson, P. R. Bosch, R. Dave, and L. A. Meyer. Cambridge, UK and New York: Cambridge University Press.

Smith, P. D. Martino, Z. Cai, D. Gwary, H. Janzen, P. Kumar, B. A. McCarl, S. Ogle, F. O'Mara, C. Rice, B. Scholes, O. Sirotenko, M. Howden, T. McAllister, G. Pan, V. Romanenkov, U. Schneider, and S. Towprayoon. 2007*b*. Policy and technological constraints to implementation of greenhouse gas mitigation options in agriculture. *Agriculture Ecosystems and Environment* 118: 6–28.

Smith, G. A., B. A. McCarl, C. S. Li, J. H. Reynolds, R. Hammerschlag, R. L. Sass, W. J. Parton, S. M. Ogle, K. Paustian, J. A. Holtkamp, and W. Barbour. 2007*c*. *Harnessing farms and forests in the low-carbon economy: How to create, measure, and verify greenhouse gas offsets*, eds. Zach Willey and Bill Chameides, Durham, NC: Duke University Press.

Sohngen, B., R. Mendelsohn, and R. Sedjo. 1999. Forest management, conservation and global timber markets. *American Journal of Agricultural Economics* 81:1–13.

Sohngen B., and R. Mendelsohn. 2003. An optimal control model of forest carbon sequestration. *American Journal of Agricultural Economics* 85:448–457.

Sohngen, B., and S. Brown. 2008. Extending timber rotations: Carbon and cost implications. *Climate Policy* 8: 435–451.

Sohngen, B., R. Alig, and B. Solberg. 2010. The forest sector, climate change, and the global carbon cycle–Environmental and economic implications. *Technical Coordinator* 37. http://www.arlis.org/docs/vol1/C/693780362.pdf#page=45

Stern, N. 2007. *The economics of climate change—The Stern review.* Cambridge, UK: Cambridge University Press.

Strassburg, B. B. N., A. S. L. Rodrigues, M. Gusti, A. Balmford, S. Fritz, M. Obersteiner, R. K. Turner, and T. M. Brooks. 2012. Impacts of incentives to reduce emissions from deforestation on global species extinctions. *Nature Climate Change* 2: 350–355.

Taylor, S. W., A. L. Carroll, R.I. Alfaro, L. Safranyik, and B. Wilson, B. (2007). Forest, climate and mountain pine beetle outbreak dynamics in Western Canada. The mountain pine beetle: a synthesis of biology, management and impacts on lodgepole pine, 67-94.

Thomson, A. M., K. V. Calvin, L. P. Chini, G. Hurtt, J. A. Edmonds, B. Bond-Lamberty, S. Frolking, M. A. Wise, and A. C. Janetos. 2010. Climate mitigation and the future of tropical landscapes. *Proceedings of National Academy of Science* 107:19633–19638.

Thornton, P. K., J. Van de Steeg, A. Notenbaert, and M. Herrero. 2009. The impacts of climate change on livestock and livestock systems in developing countries: A review of what we know and what we need to know. *Agricultural Systems* 101(3): 113–127.

Thornton, P. K., and P. Gerber. 2010. Climate change and the growth of the livestock sector in developing countries. *Mitigation Adaptation Strategies for Global Change* 15: 169–184.

Travasso, M., G. Magrin, W. Baethgen, J. Castaño, G. Rodriguez, J. Pires, A. Gimenez, G. Cunha, and M. Fernandes. 2006. Adaptation measures for maize and soybean in South Eastern South America. AIACC working paper No. 28. Washington, DC: AIACC.

Walther, G. R., A. Roques, P. E. Hulme, M. T. Sykes, P. Pysek, I. Kuhn, M. Zobel, S. Bacher, Z. Botta-Dukát, and H. Bugmann. 2009. Alien species in a warmer world: Risks and opportunities. *Trends in Ecology and Evolution* 24(12): 686–693.

Wang, W., and B. A. McCarl. 2013. Temporal investment in climate change adaptation and mitigation. *Climate Change Economics* DOI: 10.1142/S2010007813500097

Wang, P., R. Sun, J. Hu, Q. Zhu, Y. Zhou, L. Li, and J. M. Chen. 2007*a*. Measurements and simulation of forest leaf area index and net primary productivity in northern China. *Journal of Environmental Management* 85: 607–615.

Wang, Y., G. Zhou, and Y. Wang. 2007*b*. Modeling responses of the meadow steppe dominated by Leymus chinensis to climate change. *Climatic Change* 82(3): 437–452.

Wang, J., R. Mendelsohn, A. Dinar, J. Huang, S. Rozelle, and L. Zhang. 2009. The impact of climate change on China's agriculture. *Agricultural Economics* 40(3): 323–337.

West, T. O., and W. M. Post. 2002. Soil organic carbon sequestration by tillage and crop rotation: A global data analysis. *Soil Science Society of America Journal* 66: 1930–1946.

West, T. O., and J. Six. 2007. Considering the influence of sequestration duration and carbon saturation on estimates of soil carbon capacity. *Climatic Change* 80: 25–41.

Westerling, A. L., H. G. Hidalgo, D. R. Cayan, and T. W. Swetnam. 2006. Warming and earlier spring increase western U.S. forest wildfire activity. *Science* 313(5789): 940–943.

Williams, D. W., and A. M. Liebhold. 2002. Climate change and the outbreak ranges of two North American bark beetles. *Agricultural and Forest Entomology* 4: 87–99.

Williams, A. P., C. D. Allen, C. I. Millar, T. W. Swetnam, J. Michaelsen, C. J. Still, and S. W. Leavitt. 2010. Forest responses to increasing aridity and warmth in the southwestern United States. *Proceedings of the National Academy of Sciences of the USA* 107: 21289–21294

World Resources Institute. (WRI). 2005. Navigating the numbers, greenhouse gas data and international climate policy. http://www.wri.org/publication/navigating-the-numbers/

Xu, J., R. E. Grumbine, A. Shrestha, M. Eriksson, X. Yang, Y. Wang, and A. Wilkes. 2009. The melting Himalayas: Cascading effects of climate change on water, biodiversity, and livelihoods. *Conservation Biology* 23(3): 520–530.

Yan, X., T. Ohara, and H. Akimoto. 2003. Development of region-specific emission factors and estimation of methane emission from rice field in East, Southeast and South Asian countries. *Global Change Biology* 9: 237–254.

Zhang, Y. W., A. D. Hagerman, and B. A. McCarl. 2013. How climate factors influence the spatial distribution of Texas cattle breeds. *Climatic Change* 118(2):183–195.

Zilberman, D., X. Liu, D. Roland-Holst, and D. Sunding. 2004. The economics of climate change in agriculture. *Mitigation and Adaptation Strategies for Global Change* 9: 365–382.

CHAPTER 10

LAND USE, CLIMATE CHANGE, AND ECOSYSTEM SERVICES

WITSANU ATTAVANICH, BENJAMIN S. RASHFORD, RICHARD M. ADAMS, AND BRUCE A. MCCARL

RECENT studies, including those by the Intergovernmental Panel on Climate Change (IPCC 2001*a*, 2001*b*, 2007*a*, 2007*b*), indicate that greenhouse gas (GHG) emissions and resultant atmospheric concentrations have led to changes in the world's climate, including increases in temperatures, extreme temperatures, heat waves, droughts, and rainfall intensity. Such changes are expected to continue, with substantial impacts on a range of land uses. Agriculture is potentially the most sensitive economic sector to climate change, given that agricultural production is highly influenced by climatic conditions. Changes in climate can have direct effects on crop yields and production costs, as well as indirect effects on relative crop prices. Each effect can drive changes in cropping patterns.

In view of its importance to economic well-being, effects of climate change on agriculture have been well researched and documented, dating back at least 25 years (see Adams et al. 1990; Zilberman et al. 2004; and various IPCC reports). A recent review of climate change and agricultural effects and adaptations, including land use, is found in Chapter 9 by McCarl et al. (this volume). This chapter differs from Chapter 9 by McCarl et al. in that we discuss and provide an empirical application demonstrating the linkages among agricultural land use, climate change, and ecosystem services.

Adaptation, in the form of changes in crops and their locations, is the most likely immediate reaction of agricultural producers to climate changes. Crop production, for example, is expected to increase in high latitudes and decline in low latitudes (see Adams et al. 1990; Zilberman et al. 2004; IPCC 2007*b*; 2007*c*; and Chapter 9 by McCarl et al.). Research generally suggests that current zones where crops are suitable may shift more than 100 miles northward. In the US, northward shifts in the crop production mix have already been observed. Southern sections of traditional wheat-producing regions are now northern sections of corn-producing regions, as is already being observed in North Dakota (Upper Great Plains Transportation Institute 2011).

The combination of changes in rainfall, temperature, and carbon dioxide (CO_2) concentrations can also affect the productivity of pasture and rangelands, which are an important input for livestock production and an important source of wildlife habitat. Pasture production tends to increase in humid temperate grasslands, but is likely to decrease in arid and semiarid regions (IPCC 2007*b*), although climate change may decrease stocking rates. The combination of a northward shift in crop production and decreasing productivity of pasture and rangeland could lead to substantial conversion of land from low-intensity agricultural uses to intensive crop production. Conversion of grassland systems (i.e., pasture and rangeland) to crop production is associated with losses of grassland-dependent species (Green et al. 2005), releases of sequestered carbon (Foley et al. 2005), decreases in water quality (Moss 2008), and increases in soil erosion (Montgomery 2007). Shifts in crop production have been hypothesized to have important environmental and ecological consequences. These include increases in air and water pollution as land is converted to more intensive cropping systems and the reduction of ecological diversity provided by these altered landscapes. These various environmental and ecological effects are discussed in IPCC (2007*b*).

The purpose of this chapter is to discuss the linkages between climate change, changes in agricultural land use patterns, and the ecological performance of these altered landscapes. The chapter first reviews the literature on the relationships among these topics, including studies assessing farmers' adaptations to a changing climate, and possible changes in flora and fauna triggered by land use changes. This is followed by an empirical study directed at one important consequence of such behavior—the effects of changes in agriculture land use on the ecological performance of wetlands in the Prairie Pothole Region of North America (PPR), as measured by wetland and waterfowl abundance.

The PPR is a useful case study area because it is experiencing the effects of climate change and rapid changes in cropping patterns. The PPR is characterized by highly productive agricultural land, producing coarse and small grains, legumes, and livestock, interspersed with millions of prairie pothole wetlands. Although many of the historical wetland-grassland complexes in the PPR have been previously altered by agriculture (Tiner 1984; Kantrud et al. 1989), the region remains the most productive waterfowl breeding area in North America (Batt et al. 1989). Climate change has the potential to significantly alter the productivity of the PPR for waterfowl, both through direct effects on wetlands (e.g., fewer wetland due to increased drought frequency) and through the indirect effects of human response (i.e., land use change). Thus, this region offers an excellent case study for understanding the interplay among climate change, human response, and ecological outcomes.

1. Literature Review

This section first reviews the existing literature on potential climate change impacts on land use in US agriculture and associated adaptive response, with specific focus on changes in crop production patterns. This is followed by a review of ecological effects that may arise from the interplay of climate change and agricultural land use changes. Finally, we review previous studies related to the response of waterfowl to climate change and land use.

1.1 Change in US Crop Production Pattern as an Adaptive Response to Climate Change

There are a number of ways that land use can be affected by climate change. For example, climate change, through changes in temperature, precipitation, extreme events, and snow cover, can induce changes in land values and land productivity through changes in water supply; increased fire risks; productivity of crops, forests, pastures, and livestock; and spatial and temporal distribution/proliferation of pests and diseases (see Chapter 9 by McCarl et al.).

Change in crop production patterns is one immediate adaptive response of agricultural producers to changes in land value and land productivity. Crop production is expected to increase in high latitudes and decline in low latitudes since increases in precipitation are likely in the high latitudes, whereas decreases in rainfall and increased risk of drought are likely in most subtropical regions. Reilly et al. (2003) constructed the geographic centroid of production for maize and soybeans and plotted its movement from 1870 (1930 for soybeans) to 1990. They find that both US maize and soybean production shift northward by about 120 miles. Similar results for corn and soybeans is shown in Beach et al. (2009) and Attavanich et al. (2011). For example, Attavanich et al. (2011) find that the production-weighted latitude and longitude of national production trended northwest from 1950 to 2010 by approximately 100 and 138 miles for corn and soybeans, respectively.

Most studies conclude that changes in crop yields and relative crop prices induced by climate change will result in northward shifts in cultivated land (see, e.g., Adams et al. 1990; Attavanich et al. 2011). The Lake states, Mountain states, and Pacific region show gains in production; the Southeast, the Delta, the Southern Plains, and Appalachia generally lose. Results in the Corn Belt are generally positive. Results in other regions are mixed, depending on the climate scenario and time period. Attavanich and McCarl (2011) find that percentage of planted acreage of corn, sorghum, soybeans, cotton, and winter wheat increases the most in Appalachia, Corn Belt, Mountains, and Pacific regions, respectively. Their results indicate that more cropland would shift to pasture/grazing land under climate change.

1.2 Effects of Land Use Changes on Ecological Performance

The extant literature on agricultural effects and adaptations clearly demonstrates that changes in the agricultural landscape are likely to occur as a result of climate change. How these changes translate into changes in ecological performance requires information from the natural sciences. A substantial literature exists on potential effects of climate change on the environment (i.e., air and water), as well as ecological effects on flora and fauna. Some of this literature deals only with the physical and biological basis of such effects. Other studies tie these effects to economic outcomes, such as the costs of mitigating climate effects on environmental quality or ecological services. Still another set of studies include the relationship between climate and economic drivers of land use (e.g., changes in forest or agricultural landscapes arising from changes in temperature or precipitation or changes in crop prices) on these environmental and ecological outcomes.

A comprehensive summary of these effects is beyond the scope of this chapter. Various IPCC reports summarize possible environmental and ecological effects (IPCC 2007*b*). What is clear is that climate change is expected to adversely affect a range of plant and animal species. For example, Hoegh-Guldberg et al. (2007) review previous studies and conclude that if atmospheric CO_2 is stabilized at 380 part per million (ppm), coral reefs will continue to change but will remain coral dominated and carbonate accreting in most areas of their current distribution. However, if atmospheric CO_2 is between 450 and 500 ppm, the density and diversity of corals on reefs are likely to decline, which could lead to largely reduced habitat complexity and loss of biodiversity, including losses of coral-associated fish and invertebrates.

Sekercioglu et al. (2008) assess risks of bird extinctions caused by climate change. They reveal that for land birds, approximately 400–500 bird extinctions by 2100 are projected under intermediate scenarios (surface warming 2.8°C by 2100 with 50% of lowland bird species assumed to adjust their geographical and topographic distributions in response to warming), whereas up to 2,498 extinctions (30% of all land birds) are forecasted under extreme scenarios (surface warming 6.4°C by 2100 with all species assumed to adjust their distributions). In another study addressing avian species, Jetz et al. (2007) estimate projected impacts of climate change and land use change on the global diversity of birds. They predict that 11–21% of land bird species in the world could be endangered by climate change and land conversion by 2100 under the four Millennium Ecosystem Assessment (MA) global scenarios. They also suggest that land conversion (e.g., deforestation and conversion of grasslands to croplands) could have a much larger effect on species that inhabit the tropics.

Effects on mammalian species are also noted. For example, Welbergen et al. (2008) study the effects of temperature extremes on behavior and demography of Australian flying-foxes. They find that on January 12, 2002 in New South Wales, Australia temperatures exceeding 42.8°C killed at least 3,679 individuals in nine mixed-species colonies. The impacts of these temperatures had differential effects across subspecies, with the tropical black flying fox experiencing a greater mortality rate than the temperate grey-headed flying fox.

Reptiles and amphibians are also likely to be affected by climate change. During field-level monitoring of nests at an alpine site in southern Australia for the period 1997–2006, Telemeco et al. (2009) found that lizards (*Bassiana duperreyi*, Scincidae) responded to rising ambient temperatures by increasing their nest depth and increasingly early oviposition; however, they were unable to adjust themselves entirely to climate change. They reveal that rising ambient temperatures is likely to affect their hatchling sex ratio.

Finally, numerous studies have documented a wide range of effects of climate change on plants, both naturally occurring and managed, such as forest and agriculture. For example, Feeley and Silman (2010) report the effects of land use and climate change on population size and extinction risk of Andean plants. They find that plant species from high Andean forests may benefit from climate change and expand their population under a scenario that beneficial land use change practices are adapted and deforestation is halted (best-case scenario). On the other hand, if the pace of future climate change exceeds their abilities to migrate (worst-case scenario), all of these Andean species are projected to experience large population losses and consequently face risk of extinction. Moreover, all species are projected to experience large population losses regardless of potential migration rates under a business-as-usual land use scenario.

An example of a study explicitly linking landscapes to climate change and plant species is by Lawson et al. (2010). This study links a spatially explicit stochastic population model to dynamic bioclimate envelopes to investigate cumulative effects of land use, changed fire regime, and climate change on persistence of a rare, fire-dependent plant species (*Ceanothus verrucosus*) of southern California. They reveal that climate change is the most serious factor determining the reduction of this plant species' population. Interactions of climate change with changes in fire regime and land use change could increase risk to these species.

1.3 Integrated Assessments of Climate Change, Land Use, and Ecological Performance

As noted, numerous studies over the past two decades have linked economic behavior, changes in land use patterns and climate change. Most of these relate to agricultural and forest landscapes. A subset of this literature has looked at the co-effects of land use changes on ecological services and environmental quality, with climate change either directly or implicitly assumed. These studies have examined the economic impacts of land use changes or the cost of mitigating for these changes on the ecological or environmental metrics of interest. Although a variety of methods are used to link land use to ecological performance, two general approaches are most common. The first treats land use as an exogenous input to ecological models that then predict the ecological performance of alternative land use configurations (e.g., Lenzen et al. 2008; Polasky et al. 2008). This approach cannot meaningfully inform consequences and policy implication of climate changes because the feedback among climate, land use response, and ecological outcomes is incomplete. The second approach explicitly nests land use change models within ecological models (e.g., Lewis and Plantinga 2006; Langpap and Wu 2008). This approach typically maintains the modeling feedback loops necessary to understand the joint effects of exogenous shocks (e.g., climate change) and land use response on ecological performance. Some representative studies related to climate change are discussed later.

Wu et al. (2004) explored the influence of cropping pattern changes in the Midwest United States on regional water quality and, ultimately, on hypoxia potential in the Gulf of Mexico. They found that changes in cropping patterns (e.g., more corn, less pasture) and practices (e.g., minimum tillage) affected the run-off and erosion levels within the region. Although climate change was not explicitly examined, the underlying modeling included the influence of differences in weather variables. A number of studies have addressed the relationship among forest cover, riparian zone health, and water quality. For example, Watanabe et al. (2006) examined such relationships in the Pacific Northwest. The water quality parameters of interest were stream temperatures that, if elevated, can adversely affect cold water species, such as salmonids. The study noted that even active management of the landscape, such as tree planting or riparian zone protection, have limited potential to reduce water temperatures to desired levels. Other studies, such those by as Langpap et al. (2011) and Seedang et al. (2008), also note the difficulty (high costs) of obtaining reductions in water temperature through forest and riparian mitigation activities when landscapes have been extensively altered by human activities.

Pattanayak et al. (2005) performed an analysis of water quality co-effects associated with greenhouse gas mitigation activities on agricultural lands in the United States. As with other studies examining carbon sequestration on agricultural lands, they found substantial carbon sequestration potential from use of alternative cropping practices on agricultural lands. However, the study also found that such sequestration had an ancillary effect on national water quality. Specifically, overall water quality increased by 2% as a result of the sequestration practices. In another study of co-effects (co-benefits) of climate change mitigation policies, Plantinga and Wu (2003) assess the potential positive externalities of afforestation to sequester carbon. The authors find substantial benefits in terms of improved water quality (reduced soil erosion) and increased wildlife habitat from an afforestation policy.

In discussing effects of land use changes on ecological or environmental services, it is important to note that climate change is also expected to have impacts on both the participation patterns of recreationists and their willingness to pay to experience recreation activities. As climate change affects wetland resources and their productivity and snowpack patterns, and redistributes wildlife habitat, the intensity and spatial distribution of associated recreation activities (e.g., fishing, skiing, wildlife watching and hunting) are also likely to change. In addition, it is expected that recreationists' willingness to pay for preservation of environmental services (use and nonuse values) will be affected. Loomis and Crespi (1999) review the recreation literature regarding climate change and conclude that climate change will increase both participation rates and willingness to pay. Loomis and Richardson (2006) also confirm the effects of climate change on willingness to pay for ecological services. In general, warmer temperatures, earlier springs, and longer lasting summers are expected to increase the demand and willingness to pay for a variety of recreation activities. Few studies, however, consider both the direct and indirect (e.g., land use) effects of climate on recreation. Thus, although climate change may increase the demand and willingness to pay for outdoor recreation and ecosystem services, it remains to be seen whether climate-induced land use change will expand or restrict the supply of recreation opportunities and ecosystem services.

1.4 Response of Waterfowl to Climate Change and Land Use

Waterfowl production in the PPR is highly dependent on the quantity and quality of wetlands and on the suitability of upland land cover for nesting. Thus, a robust body of research has examined the relationship between wetland and grassland habitats and waterfowl production (see, e.g., Batt et al. 1989). In general, waterfowl populations are highly correlated with the number of wet basins, which generates the historic boom-and-bust cycle in waterfowl populations (Baldassare and Bolen 1994). Additionally, upland land cover, which provides critical waterfowl nesting habitat, can mitigate or exacerbate the effects of pond numbers. Waterfowl nest success is generally higher in large blocks of native grassland (see, e.g., Stephens et al. 2008) and lowest when wetland complexes are surrounded by intensive crops (Cowardin et al. 1983). Although waterfowl can adapt and persist in the margins of cropland (given sufficient wetlands), population growth rates tend to decrease significantly in highly fragmented landscapes (Klett et al. 1988).

Given the importance of both wetlands and upland land use, climate change has the potential to substantially affect waterfowl productivity in the PPR. Some research has explicitly considered the effect of climate change on wetland functions in the PPR (Poiani et al. 1996; Johnson et al. 2004, 2005, 2010). In general, this research concludes that the increases in temperature predicted for the PPR will result in shorter hydro periods and less dynamic wetlands. With sufficient warming (e.g., + 4°C) much of the PPR will lack wetland conditions necessary to support waterfowl nesting. The effects of climate change on wetland productivity, however, are heterogeneously distributed across space, with optimal conditions shifting east as climate warms (Johnson et al. 2010).

Other research has demonstrated that the effects of climate change on wetland productivity depend on upland land use (Voldseth et al. 2007). Upland land uses affects hydrological processes and vegetation dynamics and therefore influences downstream prairie wetlands. Some wetland characteristics improve when uplands are in managed cover (e.g., managed grassland or crops) because these covers increase water delivery to wetlands. Voldseth et al. (2009) explicitly found that managed covers could partially mitigate climate effects on wetland function; however, the authors note that although the wetland may appear more dynamic when surrounded by managed covers, waterfowl production would be limited due to a lack of adequate nesting habitat.

The research on climate impacts on wetlands and land use impacts on waterfowl suggests that climate change could dramatically reduce waterfowl production in the PPR. Research using historical climate and land use patterns indicates that conversion of grassland to crops in the Canadian prairies exacerbated the effects of low water years (Bethke and Nudds 1995). Additionally, Sorenson et al. (1998) found a strong correlation between drought indices and waterfowl populations in the US PPR and predict that climate change could reduce waterfowl population by as much as 70% compared to historical levels. Their analysis, however, did not include the possible effects of changes in upland land use. Although the past literature establishes the importance of both climate and land use, none of the previously developed models is capable of predicting the joint effect of climate change and the resulting land use response on waterfowl production in the PPR.

2. Model Components, Data, and Process Overview

Changes in temperature and precipitation can directly affect waterfowl production by impacting the quantity and quality of wetlands and can also indirectly influence waterfowl production through shifts in upland land use. We use three models to account for the direct and indirect effects of climate change on waterfowl. In this section, we provide a detailed description of the two component modeling systems, data used, and then discuss the model that links the two.

2.1 Model Components and Data

This section provides a detailed description of the two modeling systems (Agricultural Sector Model [ASM] and Wetland and Waterfowl Model [WWM]) and data we use to analyze the impact of climate change and land use on waterfowl production. Model components and process overview are summarized in Figure 10.1.

2.1.1 Agriculture Sector Model

We use an ASM to analyze the complex market mechanism that would occur in the agricultural sector as a result of climate change. The ASM has been developed on the basis of past work by McCarl and colleagues (McCarl and Spreen 1980; McCarl 1982; Schneider et al. 2007). It has been used in climate change-related studies for the IPCC,

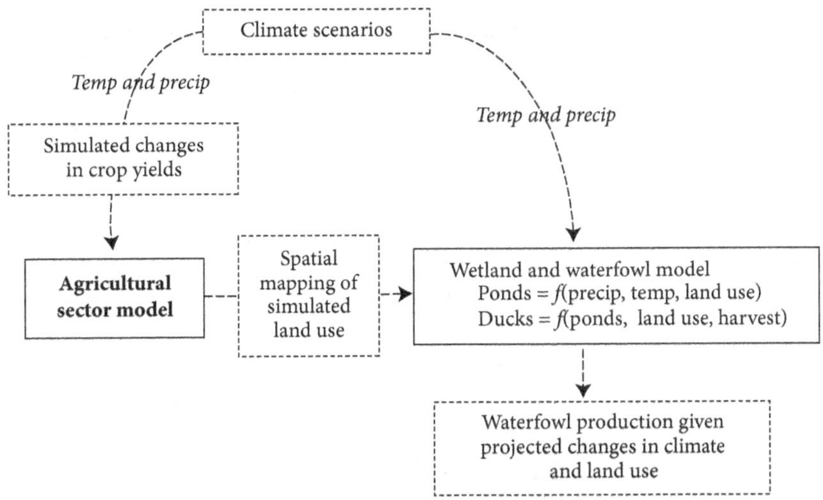

FIGURE **10.1** Waterfowl survey strata in the US Prairie Pothole Region.

Environmental Protection Agency (EPA), and United States Department of Agriculture (USDA).

In brief, the ASM model is a price endogenous, spatial equilibrium mathematical programming model of the agricultural sector in the United States. It includes all states in the conterminous United States, broken into 63 agricultural production subregions and 10 market regions (Table 10.1). It also captures land transfers and other resource allocations within the US agricultural sectors.

Simulated changes of crop yields under climate change scenarios are vital for this study since climate change affects crop yields, which influences the relative profitability of alternative land uses. We obtain simulated changes of crop yields from Beach et al. (2009). They use a modified version of the Environmental Policy Integrated Climate (EPIC) model, which was first developed by Williams et al. (1984), to simulate yield changes of 14 crops.[1] The authors use projected climate scenarios from four global circulation models (GCMs)[2] used in the 2007 IPCC assessment report with the IPCC SRES scenario A1B, which is characterized by a high rate of growth in CO_2 emissions. The scenarios are derived from:

- GFDL-CM 2.0, GFDL-CM 2.1 models developed by the Geophysical Fluid Dynamics Laboratory (GFDL), United States;
- Meteorological Research Institute Coupled Atmosphere-Ocean General Circulation Model (MRI-CGCM 2.2) developed by the Meteorological Research Institute and Meteorological Agency, Japan; and

[1] Their studied crops are barley, corn, cotton, forage production, oats, peanuts, potatoes, rice, rye, sorghum, soybeans, sugarbeets, tomatoes, and wheat.

[2] It is common practice in climate change analysis to use several GCM projections to reflect the uncertainty inherent in such projections.

Table 10.1 Agricultural Sector Model (ASM) regions and subregions

Market region	Production region (states/subregions)
Northeast (NE)	Connecticut, Delaware, Maine, Maryland, Massachusetts, New Hampshire, New Jersey, New York, Pennsylvania, Rhode Island, Vermont, West Virginia
Lake States (LS)	Michigan, Minnesota, Wisconsin
Corn Belt (CB)	All regions in Illinois, Indiana, Iowa, Missouri, Ohio (IllinoisN, IllinoisS, IndianaN, IndianaS, IowaW, IowaCent, IowaNE, IowaS, OhioNW, OhioS, OhioNE)
Great Plains (GP)	Kansas, Nebraska, North Dakota, South Dakota
Southeast (SE)	Virginia, North Carolina, South Carolina, Georgia, Florida
South Central (SC)	Alabama, Arkansas, Kentucky, Louisiana, Mississippi, Tennessee, Eastern Texas
Southwest (SW)	Oklahoma, All of Texas but the Eastern Part (Texas High Plains, Texas Rolling Plains, Texas Central Blacklands, Texas Edwards Plateau, Texas Coastal Bend, Texas South, Texas Trans Pecos)
Rocky Mountains (RM)	Arizona, Colorado, Idaho, Montana, Nevada, New Mexico, Utah, Wyoming
Pacific Southwest (PSW)	All regions in California (CaliforniaN, CaliforniaS)
Pacific Northwest (PNW)	Oregon and Washington, east of the Cascade mountain range

Source: Attavanich and McCarl, 2011

- Coupled Global Climate Model (CGCM) 3.1 developed by the Canadian Centre for Climate Modeling and Analysis, Canada.

We use these simulated yields results as an input in the ASM to simulate changes in land use. We first estimate the base scenario (without climate change) and then compare baseline results to results under climate change simulated from GCMs in 2050, which reflect the change in crop yields and shifts of crop production patterns as a result of climate change. Due to the uncertainty of factors in the future, we fix all supply-side factors to their current level in the base year and only allow the effect of the northward shift of crop production patterns and the change in crop yields. The introduction of change in crop yields and possibility of northward migration of crops causes ASM to change its equilibrium allocation of land use, crop mix, trade flows, commodity prices, production, and consumption. Changes in crop acreage are then used to model the resulting response of wetlands and waterfowl in the PPR.

2.1.2 *Wetland and Waterfowl Model*

We use a simple regression approach to understand the potential effect of climate and land use change on wetlands and waterfowl in the PPR. Our approach is similar in spirit to past models, which have been successfully used to understand the relationship among wetland numbers, weather characteristics, land use, and waterfowl populations (see Johnson and Shaffer 1987; Bethke and Nudds 1995; Sorenson et al. 1998). Specifically, we estimate two regression models using historical data. The first model relates pond numbers to climate and land use characteristics:

$$\text{Ponds} = f(\text{precipitation, temperature, land use}) \tag{1}$$

The number of waterfowl that settle in the PPR to breed is largely determined by the availability of wetland habitat. Thus, climate or land use change that affects wetland availability is expected to influence breeding waterfowl populations in the PPR. Previous research has demonstrated the important role of both land use and climate on wetlands in the PPR (see, e.g., Voldseth et al. 2007; Johnson et al. 2010).

The second model relates waterfowl populations to pond numbers, land use, and harvest:

$$\text{Ducks} = f(\text{ponds, land use, harvest}) \tag{2}$$

Although ponds largely influence where waterfowl settle in the PPR, upland land use can reallocate birds on the landscape because females also select landscapes based on the availability of nesting cover. Harvest during the previous hunting season could also influence the number birds in the northward migration and thus the number of birds that settle in the PPR. This simple set of regression models allows us to relate changes in climate and land use to changes in waterfowl breeding populations. Estimates of breeding population are the primary determinant of waterfowl hunting regulations and are thus one indicator of the potential social impacts of climate-induced changes in waterfowl populations.

We use data from a variety of sources to estimate (1) and (2). Pond and waterfowl numbers are from the US Fish and Wildlife Service (USFWS) Waterfowl Breeding Population and Habitat Survey (USFWS 2009). The survey is one of the most extensive, both in time and space, wildlife population and habitat surveys in the world. Since 1955, the USFWS has used aerial surveys to estimate annual pond and waterfowl numbers within temporally consistent survey strata. Six survey strata (41, 45–49) overlap the US PPR (Figure 10.2). We therefore use pond and waterfowl estimates from these six strata to estimate the regression models. For the waterfowl estimates, we use the total count of dabbling ducks, which constitute the largest subgroup of waterfowl that breed in the PPR and the bulk of the US harvest.

Historical land use data are from the National Agricultural Statistics Service (NASS 2010). We aggregate annual county-level estimates of area by crop to the strata level. To be consistent with the ASM model, we focus on the primary field crops in the PPR (e.g., corn, soybeans, barley, oats, potatoes, sugar beets, and wheat). Additionally, since all field crops have similar effects on wetlands and waterfowl nesting habitat, we convert individual crop area to strata-level shares by dividing the total crop area (sum over individual crops) by the total area in each survey strata.

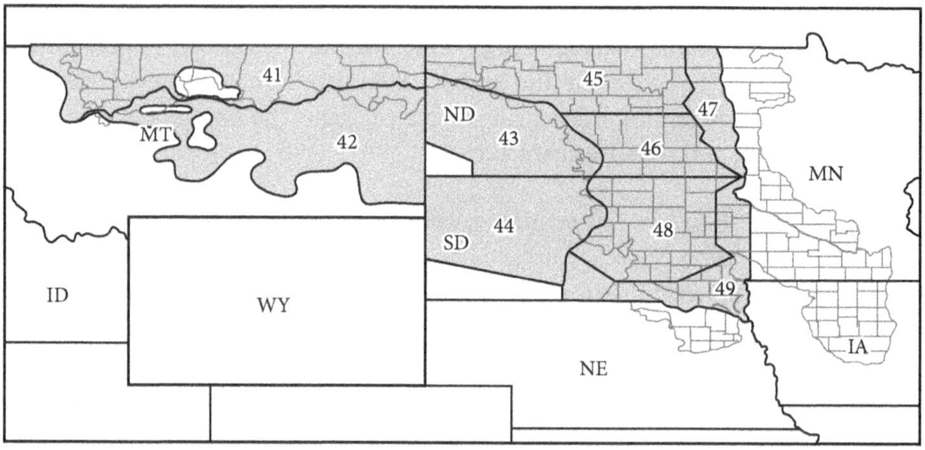

FIGURE 10.2 Model components and process overview.

We collect historical precipitation and temperature data from the National Climate Data Center (NOAA 2011). We use data from weather stations distributed across each waterfowl survey strata to estimate average precipitation and temperature at the strata level. Last, harvest data comes from the Flyways.us website (http://www.flyways.us/), which is a collaborative effort between waterfowl management agencies to organize data on North American waterfowl. Harvest data are reported annually at the flyway level for the period 1961–2009; we therefore use the total harvest for the Central flyway to capture potential harvest impacts on waterfowl breeding populations.

2.2 Linking Changes in Cropland Use to Waterfowl Recruitment

To link the effect of climate change on the agricultural sector to waterfowl response, we use the ASM simulated changes in production of crops as inputs in the regression models described in Section 2.1. The change in crop production reflects agricultural reaction to future climate conditions, given market mechanisms. This study compares "baseline" scenario in 2007[3] (current condition) with four climate change scenarios in 2050, as discussed in Section 2.1.

We first use the ASM to predict regional shifts in cropping patterns due to climate change using the yield effects simulated during 2045–2055 provided in Beach et al. (2009) for 63 regions in the United States. Although this is a fairly fine level of spatial detail for economic analysis, it is not sufficiently detailed for waterfowl response

[3] We adjust the base year used in ASM from 2005 to 2007 to reflect empirical evidences from the latest Agricultural Census.

modeling. Therefore, we used an auxiliary model to downscale ASM results for use in the waterfowl model. Development of a county-level counterpart to the ASM crop mix would not be necessary if we could use county as the ASM spatial specification. However, not only would such a model be very large, but developing/maintaining production budget, crop mix, and resource data for such a scale is daunting. Thus, we run ASM at a more aggregate level and reduce the solution crop mixes to the county level.

We disaggregate the ASM solution of crop acreage to the county level using a county-level multiobjective mathematical programming model developed by Attwood et al. (2000), and used in Pattanayak et al. (2005). The Attwood et al. (2000) model was later modified by Attavanich (2011) to better reflect the possibility of crop expansion into new production areas under climate change scenarios. The regionalizing downscaling of Atwood et al. (2000) disaggregates the crop mixes and crop acreage solutions from the sector model to the county-level by fixing the solutions close to the county-level historical crop mix. This process cannot fully account for factors that fall significantly outside the range of historical observation. The modified model uses the area of a particular crop allocated to an irrigation status in each county as the primary choice variable. This choice variable is constrained so it matches the land area shift in the ASM but minimally deviates from the Census of Agriculture, US Bureau of Census, USDA National Resource Inventory (NRI), and USDA county crops data, after accounting for crop migration due to climate change.

The ASM results provide county-level estimates of crop area, temperature, and precipitation. For projected climate data, we also obtains IPCC SRES scenario A1B[4]'s projected agricultural district level mean temperature and precipitation in the PPR from four GCMs, as previously discussed. We then use estimated crop area, temperature, and precipitation to simulate wetland and waterfowl numbers under each climate scenario by (1) aggregating county crop area to waterfowl strata level and calculating crop shares, (2) aggregating mean temperature and precipitation predictions under each climate scenario to waterfowl strata using simple averages, and (3) using the land use and climate data in the estimated pond and duck equations (e.g., [1] and [2]). We use predicted 2007 pond and duck numbers as the baseline for comparison and assume that waterfowl harvest remains constant on average. For the change in the land use share in the baseline, we use change in average crop share between the 1900s and 2000s. Since we do not know how yield levels are likely to change, and since the yield impact is relatively small, we fix yields at the 2000–2009 average for all simulations. Also, since the climate

[4] Scenario A1B most closely reproduces the actual emissions trajectories during the period since the SRES scenarios were completed (2000–2008). It is reasonable to focus on A1B scenario group versus those in the B1 and B2 scenario groups that have lower emissions projections because in recent years actual emissions have been above the A1B scenario projections. At the same time, there has been considerable interest and policy development to encourage nonfossil fuel energy, which is consistent with the A1B scenario vs. A1F1 or A2 that assume a heavier future reliance on fossil fuels (Beach et al. 2009).

predictions represent the decadal average predicted for 2045–2055, we use the same predicted average temperature and precipitation for all lagged values (i.e., the two-year lagged precipitation and the one-year lagged precipitation are both the predicted average precipitation for each climate scenario). Hence, our predicted changes in pond and duck numbers should be interpreted as averages over the decade not values for any individual future year.

3. Model Results

This section reports our empirical findings from the three models. We first provide the ASM results of projected changes in cropland use. We then report the regression results of the effect of changes in climate and cropland use on wetland and waterfowl production obtained from the wetland and waterfowl model. Finally, we report the simulated results of the responses of waterfowl populations to changes in climate and land use in the PPR. Overall, we find that cropland in the PPR is likely to increase. Moreover, lower pond numbers and higher crop shares are correlated with lower duck numbers. Thus, ignoring land use change would lead to a significant underestimate of the impacts of climate change on duck populations by as much as 10% or nearly 300,000 birds. Under alternative climate scenarios, pond and wetland numbers decrease substantially, and land use response to climate change generally exacerbates the negative effects of climate change on duck populations.

3.1 Results from ASM and Its Spatial Mapping

Table 10.2 shows acreage of major crops in the PPR under climate change projected from the IPCC scenarios compared to the base scenario. Overall, cropland in the PPR is likely to increase. Considering major crop acreage, corn, soybeans, and hay are projected to increase by 15%, 39%, and 19%, respectively, whereas acreage of other remaining major crops tends to decrease, with wheat projected to have the largest acreage reduction.

Because climate-induced shifts in crop production patterns are expected to significantly influence the productivity of the PPR for waterfowl, understanding changes in the movements and distributions of cropland under climate change is important. Our study provides such information. Figure 10.3 shows the estimated percent change of county-level crop shares from the base scenario given climate change in 2050 from four GCM scenarios. We calculate crop share by dividing the county-level acreage of all major crops (i.e., barley, corn, oats, wheat, hay, silage, soybeans, and sugar beets, which accounted for 95% of total crop acreage in the PPR in 2007) by the total land area in that county. In all scenarios, small percent changes in crop share are found in almost all Iowa counties. Across GCMs, results generally suggest that areas in the eastern section of North Dakota, the western section of South Dakota, and the central to northern

Table 10.2 Acreage of major cropland use (1,000 acres) in the Prairie Pothole Region (PPR) under climate change

	Base	MRI-CGCM 2.2	GFDL 2.0	GFDL 2.1	CGCM 3.1
Major cropland[a] (1000 acres)					
Barley	2,216	1,438	1,557	1,544	1,510
Corn	19,085	19,961	22,040	21,904	20,614
Oats	513	372	438	371	383
Wheat	14,336	10,517	9,945	10,384	10,492
Hay	5,104	7,119	6,925	6,821	6,885
Silage	800	751	742	1,275	795
Soybeans	15,346	18,275	16,657	15,715	17,652
Sugar beets	710	398	437	404	436

Note: A Crop acreage in the PPR is calculated by breaking down results of ASM crop acreage into the county level and reaggregating to the PPR level using spatial mapping approach discussed in section 3.2.

section of Minnesota will have a large increase in crop share, which potentially reduces waterfowl productivity. Increases in crop share are generally associated with conversion of grassland to intensive cropland, which reduces quantity and quality of wetlands and the suitability of upland land cover for waterfowl nesting. On the other hand, we predict a large reduction of crop share in the southern section of Minnesota and the central to southern part of South Dakota, which could benefit waterfowl if cropland is replaced by land covers suitable to waterfowl production (e.g., grassland).

3.2 Results from the Wetland and Waterfowl Models

We use the data described in Section 2.1.2 to estimate (1) and (2). For each equation, we use a log-linear specification and a one-way fixed effects model to capture unobserved cross-sectional heterogeneity. We experimented with running the model as a system and with correcting for autocorrelation and heteroscedasticity (i.e., Parks method). Since our primary purpose is prediction and none of the alternative regression approaches produced meaningfully different predictions, we report and use estimates from the simple model.

In the pond equation (1), we include temperature (T), one- and two-year lags for precipitation (P) because prairie wetlands are dependent on accumulated soil moisture (Sorenson et al. 1998), and the change in the crop share (ΔCS) because changes in crop area better capture potential wetland loss. In the duck equation (2), we include the current year and one-year lag of ponds, the crop share, and the lagged harvest (H) since birds are harvested in the fall and thus affect the following spring migration. The regressions fit the data well with R^2 of 0.75 and 0.83 for the pond and waterfowl models,

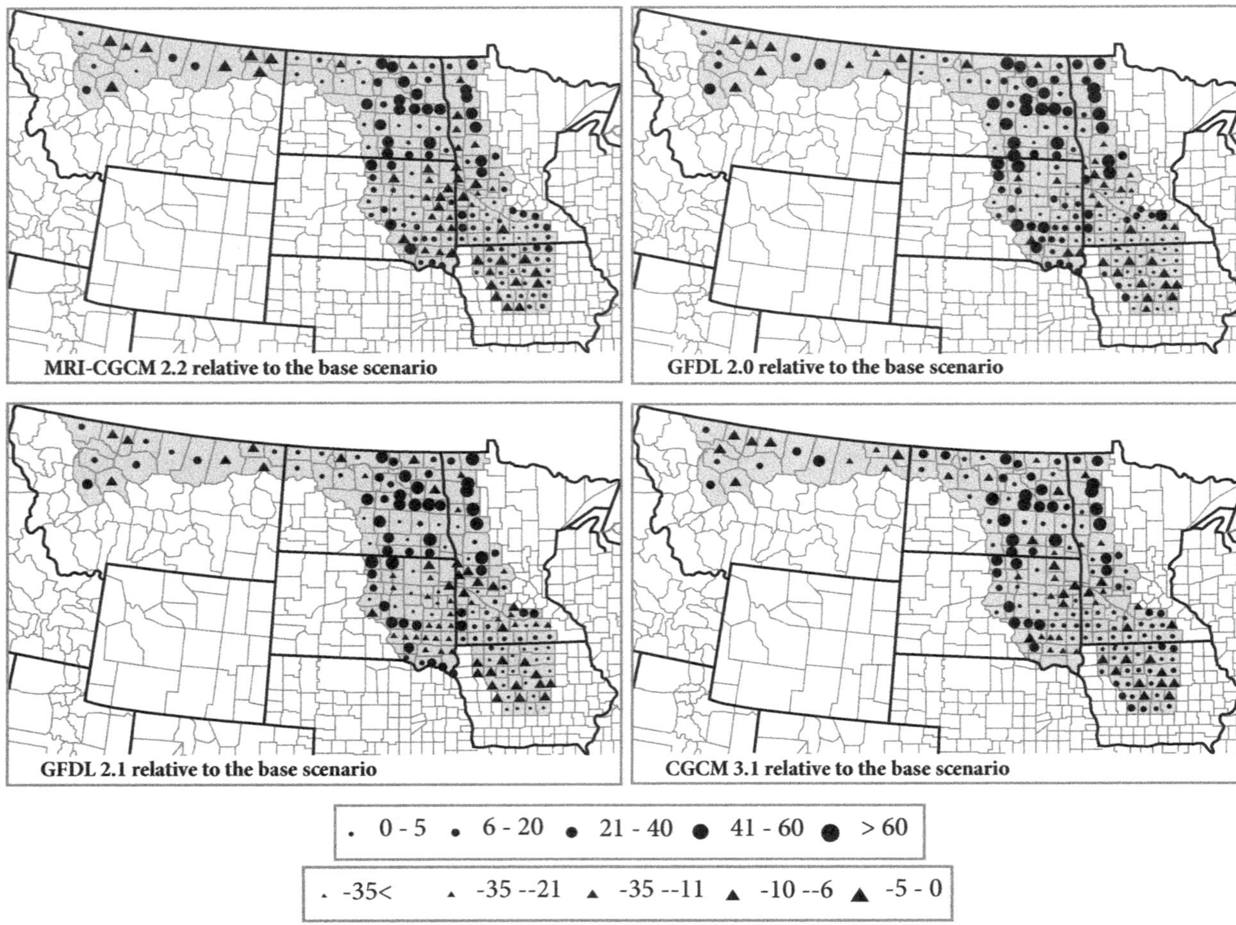

FIGURE **10.3** Estimated percent change of county-level crop share from the base scenario under climate change in 2050 from GCM scenarios in the Prairie Pothole Region.

respectively, and highly significant F-statistics. The estimated equations, with fixed effects omitted for simplicity and p-values in parentheses, are:

$$\begin{aligned} ln(\text{Ponds}) &= 13.76 - 0.04 \times T + 0.01 \times P + 0.09 \times P_{t-1} + 0.14 \times P_{t-2} - 1.49 \times \Delta\text{CS} \\ &\quad (<0.0001)(0.01) \quad (0.85) \quad (0.018) \quad (0.0001) \quad (0.06) \end{aligned} \tag{3}$$

$$\begin{aligned} ln(\text{Ducks}) &= 12.25 + 0.000003 \times \text{Ponds} + 0.000001 \times \text{Ponds}_{t-1} - 1.34 \times \text{CS} + 0.00000008 \times \text{H} \\ &\quad (<0.0001)(<0.0001) \quad (0.013) \quad (0.048) \quad (0.073) \end{aligned} \tag{4}$$

Parameter estimates generally have the expected sign and reasonable magnitudes. Higher average temperatures, lower average precipitation, and higher shares of land in crops decrease pond numbers. Similarly, higher pond numbers and lower crops shares are correlated with high duck numbers. Harvest has a very small and positive effect on duck numbers. This seemingly counterintuitive result is consistent with the theory that harvest is compensatory (i.e., increased survival rates for birds not harvested compensate for the loss of harvested birds—thus, the total population is no smaller than it would have been in the absence of harvest). The estimate on harvest essentially implies that every harvested duck is perfectly compensated for through increased production. The estimated models allow us to predict impacts on waterfowl, given a climate scenario and predicted land use from the ASM model.

3.3 Effects of Climate and Land Use Change on Waterfowl Populations in the PPR

Our results suggest that climate change and its induced land use changes will have dramatic impacts on waterfowl in the PPR; however, the impacts vary substantially by climate scenario. To highlight the total impacts and variability across climate scenarios, we calculate the change in pond and duck numbers (i.e., predicted ducks|baseline—predicted ducks|climate change), expressed as a percentage, using each GCM (Figure 10.4). Under three of the four climate scenarios, pond and wetland numbers decrease substantially, with a worst-case scenario reduction in duck numbers of 25% from the 2007 baseline. For the GFDL 2.0 climate scenario, however, our results suggest an increase in ponds (9%) and thus duck populations (4%).

Differences across scenarios are largely explained by differences in temperature and precipitation predictions. The GFDL 2.0 scenario includes minor increases in temperature accompanied by significant increases in precipitation (by 1 inch, or approximately 25% on average across strata). The increases in precipitation are sufficient to offset any negative impacts of temperature or land use change on pond numbers. The GFDL 2.1 scenario also has increased precipitation (0.2 inch on average); however, the increase

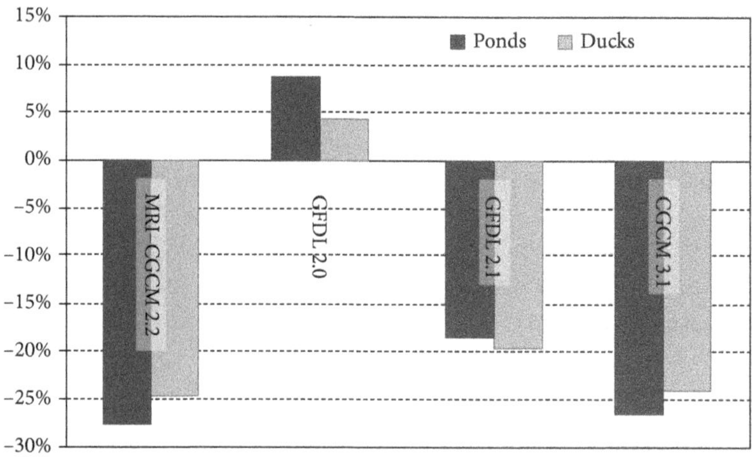

FIGURE 10.4 Percent change in pond and duck numbers relative to 2007 baseline under four alternative climate scenarios.

in temperature predicted in this scenario (2.3°F on average) is sufficient to cause large decreases in pond and duck numbers. The most extreme scenarios, CGCM 3.1 and MRI-CGCM 2.2, predict small decreases in precipitation combined with increases in temperature (2–3°F on average). This combination results in substantial reduction in pond and duck numbers.

The impacts of climate change on pond and duck numbers, however, are not completely explained by precipitation and temperature. Land use change plays an important role. The ASM model generally predicts an increase in corn and soybeans acreage and a decrease in wheat acreage in the PPR. The reduction in wheat and other minor crops can be accompanied by increases in pasture or other major crops, especially corn and soybeans. Although increases in pasture, which can be suitable waterfowl habitat, should be positive for waterfowl, the net effect of land use change implies an increase in the share of land in crops in most waterfowl strata under most climate scenarios. Land use response to climate change therefore generally exacerbates the negative effects of climate change on duck populations.

The extent of land use change impacts is best demonstrated by considering temperature and precipitation impacts absent of land use change. We therefore predict pond and duck numbers assuming that crop shares remain at baseline levels. For the three scenarios under which climate change reduces pond and duck numbers, ignoring land use change would lead to a significant underestimate of climate change impacts (Table 10.3). Not accounting for land use response leads to underestimating ponds and ducks by as much as 14% and 10%, respectively. This implies underestimating the effect of climate change on duck populations by nearly 300,000 birds, approximately 10% of the average current harvest.

Table 10.3 Comparison of pond and duck prediction under climate change, with and without land use response

	Percent change from baseline			
	With land use change		Without land use change	
	Ponds	Ducks	Ponds	Ducks
MRI-CGCM 2.2	−28%	−25%	−17%	−15%
GFDL 2.1	−19%	−20%	−5%	−16%
CssGCM 3.1	−26%	−24%	−16%	−22%

Although climate change and the associated land use response are likely to have significant impacts on ducks in the PPR, the impacts are not uniformly distributed over space. Predicted temperatures and precipitation under alternative climate scenarios differ by waterfowl strata. Thus, even with our highly aggregated strata-level data, land use response and the ultimate impact on ponds and ducks have spatial variations that could be important for targeting programs to mitigate climate impacts.

Regardless of climate scenario, the Montana portion of the PPR (strata 41) is predicted to gain ducks with climate change. This region has historically been a relatively low duck production area because it receives less rainfall than regions to the east and south. It also has the lowest crop share of any strata. With climate change, the region is predicted to gain precipitation and have relatively little change in the share of land in crops. Thus, the region could see increased pond numbers with little loss in waterfowl nesting habitat (Figure 10.5).

The central portion of the PPR is predicted to see the largest negative impacts to duck populations. In all climate scenarios, the strata in eastern North and South Dakota lose significant portions of their current duck populations. These strata currently produce the most ducks (78%) because they have relatively high pond numbers and, related, significant land area not in crop production (>50%). With climate change, these strata are predicted to experience small to no increase in precipitation, significant temperature increases, and the largest relative increases in crop land area. As a result, this traditionally productive waterfowl region will have fewer ponds, less nesting habitat, and, as a result, significantly fewer ducks.

In contrast, the strata in eastern and southern North and South Dakota are predicted to have very modest gains or losses in duck populations across climate scenarios. Here, the explanation is largely unrelated to climate change factors. These regions are currently dominated by intensive crop production (>60%), and, as a result, have relatively low pond numbers. They therefore have not attracted many breeding ducks in recent history. The changes in temperature, precipitation, and land use predicted under alternative climate scenarios are not substantial enough to significantly change, in either direction, the waterfowl potential of these regions.

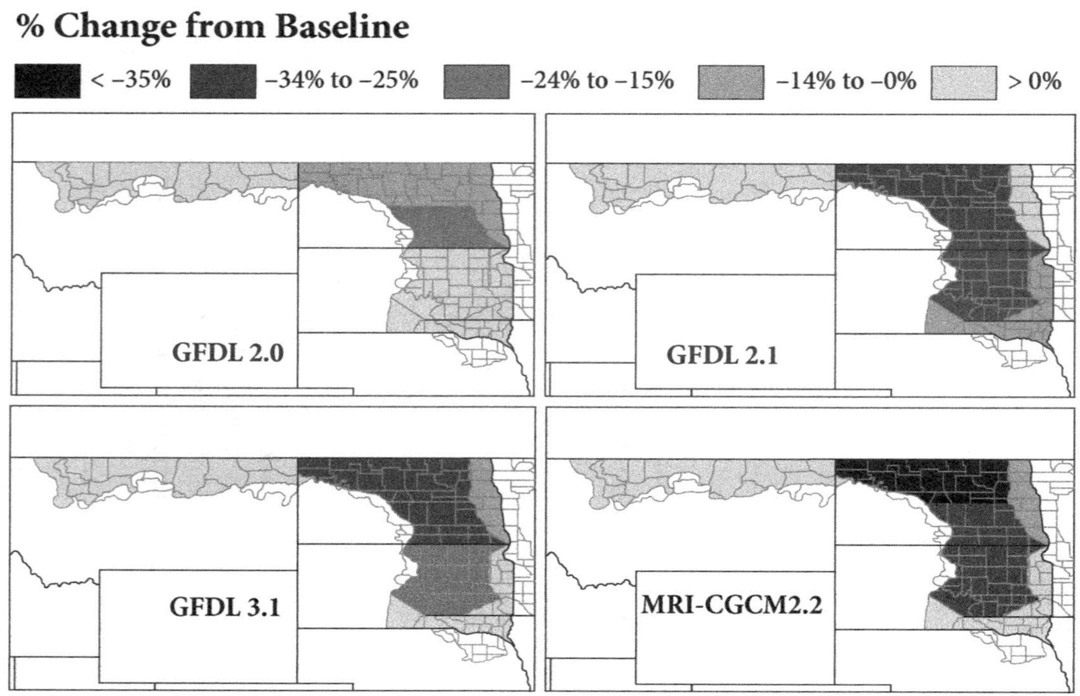

FIGURE 10.5 Percent change in duck populations from baseline by waterfowl survey strata under alternative climate scenarios.

4. Conclusion

This application examines the joint effect of climate change and the resulting land use response on waterfowl production in the PPR by linking a model of land use changes induced by climate change with a wildlife habitat and productivity model. Our results reveal that overall cropland in the PPR is likely to increase, but changes vary spatially across the region. In all the climate scenarios, small percent changes in crop share are found in almost all of counties in the Iowa part of the PPR. A majority of climate scenarios project that areas in the eastern section of North Dakota, the western section of South Dakota, and the central to northern section of Minnesota are generally predicted to have a large increase in crop share. On the other hand, a large reduction of crop share is likely detected in the southern section of Minnesota and the central to southern part of South Dakota.

Using the estimates from the climate, wetlands, and waterfowl productivity models, we also find that (1) higher average temperatures, lower average precipitation, and higher shares of land in crops relative to pasture decrease pond numbers; (2) lower pond numbers and higher crop shares are correlated with lower duck numbers; and (3) yield increase have a very small and positive effect on duck numbers. In addition, when we include alternative climate scenarios and their effects on crop mixes, we find that pond and wetland numbers decrease substantially, with a worst-case scenario reduction in duck numbers of 25% from the 2007 baseline. For the GFDL 2.0 climate scenario, however, our results suggest an increase in ponds (9%) and thus duck populations (4%). The study also finds that land use response to climate change generally exacerbates the negative effects of climate change on duck populations.

The spatial heterogeneity in climate effects could pose serious challenges to waterfowl conservation efforts targeted toward climate mitigation. Investments could, for example, be targeted toward securing habitat in Montana. These investments could further bolster the predicted increases in duck production, given climate change. The Montana region, however, has historically produced a very small proportion of the region's ducks. Moreover, even with the predicted improvements with climate change, this region does not produce sufficient additional ducks to offset those lost in other regions. In the three climate scenarios that reduce duck populations, for example, removing all land from crop production in the Montana portion of the PPR only offsets 5% of the duck losses in the rest of the PPR.

This suggests that conservation investments will have to be focused in the central or eastern portion of the PPR to have any chance of significantly mitigating climate effects. These regions, however, have high historic shares of land in crops and/or are predicted to gain significant crop shares under alternative climate scenarios. Land in these regions is therefore likely to be more highly valued. Thus, conservation efforts will have to compete with agriculture to secure wetland and nesting habitat. Given the duck deficits predicted under several climate scenarios, limited conservation budgets will likely be challenged to conserve the amount of area required to mitigate climate change impacts. Conservation programs will therefore need to be strategically targeted to maximize cost effectiveness (see, e.g., Rashford and Adams 2007).

The findings and conclusions reported in this section also have implications for the general literature on land use and ecosystems services reviewed earlier in this chapter. Specifically, deriving policy-relevant conclusions about complex ecological systems is only possible by integrating models from multiple disciplines. Moreover, models must contain the linkages between the economic forces that drive human processes (e.g., land use decisions) and the ecological performance supported by those same processes (e.g., landscapes). The analysis developed here is only possible because of considerable investment in an ecosystem-based land use model that was developed with input from multiple disciplines. Although the need for an interdisciplinary approach is intuitive and has been discussed in the environmental economics literature for decades, in practice, one finds relatively few empirical applications that are sufficiently integrated to be useful in assessing the efficacy of alternative policies.

One reason for the lack of empirical applications has been normal tension between disciplines and the lack of incentives to perform such assessments. In our opinion, this reluctance or hesitancy to pursue truly integrated analyses is diminishing, due to enhanced funding opportunities and the broadened curricula of graduate programs in resource economics and in the natural sciences, which encourages an interdisciplinary "mindset" in new graduates. Studies of the type we report here demonstrate the potential utility of investments in interdisciplinary team and model building.

References

Adams, R. M., C. Rosenzweig, J. Ritchie, P. Peart, J. D. Glyer, B. A. McCarl, B. Curry, and J. Jones. 1990. Global climate change and agriculture. *Nature* 345: 219–224.

Attavanich, W. 2011. Essays on the effect of climate change on agriculture and agricultural transportation. Ph.D. Dissertation. Texas A&M University.

Attavanich, W., and B. A. McCarl. 2011. The effect of climate change, CO_2 fertilization, and crop production technology on crop yields and its economic implications on market outcomes and welfare distribution. Paper presented at 2011 AAEA & NAREA Joint Annual Meeting, Pittsburgh, PA.

Attavanich, W., B. A. McCarl, S. W. Fuller, D. V. Vedenov, and Z. Ahmedov. 2011. The effect of climate change on transportation flows and inland waterways due to climate-induced shifts in crop production patterns. Paper presented at 2011 AAEA & NAREA Joint Annual Meeting, July 24–26, 2011, Pittsburgh, PA.

Attwood, J. D., B. A. McCarl, C. C. Chen, B. R. Eddleman, B. Nayda, and R. Srinivasan. 2000. Assessing regional impacts of change: Linking economic and environmental models. *Agricultural Systems* 63(3): 147–159.

Baldassare, G. A., and E. G. Bolen. 1994. *Waterfowl ecology and management*. New York: John Wiley & Sons.

Batt, B. D. J., M. G. Anderson, C. D. Anderson, and F. D. Caswell. 1989. The use of prairie potholes by North American ducks. In *Northern prairie wetlands*, ed. A. van der Valk, 204–227. Ames: Iowa State University Press.

Beach, R. H., C. Zhen, A. Thomson, R. M. Rejesus, P. Sinha, A. W. Lentz, D. V. Vedenov, and B. A. McCarl. 2009. *Climate change impacts on crop insurance*. Contract AG-645S-C-08-0025. Final Report. Research Triangle Park, NC: RTI International. Prepared for USDA Risk Management Agency.

Bethke, R. W., and T. D. Nudds. 1995. Effects of climate change and land use on duck abundance in Canadian Prairie-Parklands. *Ecological Applications* 5(3): 588–600.

Cowardin, L. M., A. B. Sargeant, and H. F. Duebbert 1983. Problems and potentials for prairie ducks. *Naturalist* 34(4): 4–11.

Feeley, K. J., and M. R. Silman. 2010. Land-use and climate change effects on population size and extinction risk of Andean plants. *Global Change Biology* 16(12): 3215–3222.

Foley, J. A., R. DeFries, G. P. Asner, C. Barford, G. Bonan, S. R. Carpenter, F. S. Chapin, M. T. Coe, G. C. Daily, and H. K. Gibbs. 2005. Global consequences of land use. *Science* 309: 570–574.

Green, R. E., S. J. Cornell, J. P. W. Scharlemann, and A. Balmford. 2005. Farming and the fate of wild nature. *Science* 307: 550–555.

Hoegh-Guldberg, O., P. J. Mumby, A. J. Hooten, R. S. Steneck, P. Greenfield, E. Gomez, C. D. Harvell, P. F. Sale, A. J. Edwards, and K. Caldeira. 2007. Coral reefs under rapid climate change and ocean acidification. *Science* 318 (5857): 1737.

IPCC. 2001*a*. *Climate change 2001: The scientific basis*. Contribution of Working Group I to the Third Assessment Report of the Intergovernmental Panel on Climate Change, eds. J. T. Houghton, Y. Ding, D. J. Griggs, M. Noguer, P. J. van der Linden, X. Dai, K. Maskell and C. A. Johnson. Cambridge, UK: Cambridge University Press.

IPCC. 2001*b*. *Climate change 2001: Impacts, adaptation, and vulnerability*. Contribution of Working Group II to the Third Assessment Report of the Intergovernmental Panel on Climate Change, eds. J. J. McCarthy, O. F. Canziani, N. A. Leary, D. J. Dokken and K. S. White. Cambridge, UK: Cambridge University Press

IPCC. 2007*a*. *Climate change 2007: The physical science basis*. Contribution of Working Group I to the Fourth Assessment Report of the Intergovernmental Panel on Climate Change, eds. S. Solomon, D. Qin, M. Manning, Z. Chen, M. Marquis, K. B. Averyt, M. Tignor and H. L. Miller. Cambridge, UK: Cambridge University Press.

IPCC. 2007*b*. *Climate change 2007: Impacts, adaptation and vulnerability*. Contribution of Working Group II to the Fourth Assessment Report of the Intergovernmental Panel on Climate Change, eds. M. L. Parry, O. F. Canziani, P. J. Palutikof, P. J. van der Linden and C. E. Hanson. Cambridge, UK: Cambridge University Press.

IPCC. 2007*c*. *Climate change 2007: Mitigation of climate change*. Contribution of Working Group III to the Fourth Assessment Report of the Intergovernmental Panel on Climate Change, eds. B. Metz, O. R. Davidson, P. R. Bosch, R. Dave and L. A. Meyer. Cambridge, UK: Cambridge University Press.

Jetz, W, D. S. Wilcove, and A. P. Dobson 2007. Projected impacts of climate and land-use change on the global diversity of birds. *PLoS Biology* 5(6): E157. doi:10.1371/journal.pbio.0050157

Johnson, D. H., and T. L. Shaffer. 1987. Are mallards declining in North America? *Wildlife Society Bulletin* 15: 340–345.

Johnson, W. C., S. E. Boettcher, K. A. Poiani, and G. Guntenspergen. 2004. Influence of weather extremes on the water levels of glaciated prairie wetlands. *Wetlands* 24: 385–398.

Johnson, W. C., B. V. Millett, T. Gilmonov, R. A. Voldseth, G. R. Guntenspergen, and D. E. Naugle. 2005. Vulnerability of northern prairie wetlands to climate change. *BioScience* 55: 863–872.

Johnson, W. C., B. Werner, G. R. Guntenspergen, R. A. Voldseth, B. Millett, D. E. Naugle, M. Tulbure, R. W. H. Carroll, J. Tracy, and C. Olawsky. 2010. Prairie wetland complexes as landscape functional units in a changing climate. *BioScience* 60: 128–140.

Kantrud, H. A., G. L. Krapu, and G. A. Swanson. 1989. Prairie basin wetlands of the Dakotas: A community profile. Biological Report 85, U. S. Department of the Interior, U. S. Fish and Wildlife Service, Jamestown, ND.

Klett, A. T., T. L. Shaffer, and D. H. Johnson. 1988. Duck nest success in the prairie pothole region. *Journal of Wildlife Management*, 52(3): 431–440.

Langpap, C., and J. Wu. 2008. Predicting the effect of land-use policies on wildlife habitat abundance. *Canadian Journal of Agricultural Economics* 56: 195–217.

Huang, B, C. Langpap, and R. M. Adams. 2012. The value of in-stream water temperature forecasts for fisheries management. *Contemporary Economic Policy* 30 (2): 247–261.

Lawson, D. M., H. M. Regan, P. H. Zedler, and J. Franklin. 2010. Cumulative effects of land use, altered fire regime and climate change on persistence of Ceanothus verrucosus, a rare, fire-dependent plant species. *Global Change Biology* 16 (9): 2518–2529.

Lenzen. M., A. Lane, A. Widmer-Cooper, and M. Williams. 2008. Effects of land use on threatened species. *Conservation Biology* 23(2): 294–306.

Lewis, D. L., and A. J. Plantinga. 2006. Policies for habitat fragmentation: Combining econometric models with GIS-based landscape simulations. *Land Economics* 83: 109–127.

Loomis, J., and J. Crespi. 1999. Estimated effects of climate change on selected outdoor recreation activities in the United States. In *The impact of climate change on the United States economy*, eds. R. Mendelsohn and J. Neumann, Chapter 11. Cambridge, UK: Cambridge University Press.

Loomis, J., and R. Richardson. 2006. An external validity test of intended behavior: Comparing revealed preference and intended visitation in response to climate change. *Journal of Environmental Planning and Management* 49(4): 621–630.

McCarl, B. A., W. Attavanich, M. Musumba, J. E. Mu, and R. Aisabokhae. 2014. Land use and climate change. In *The Oxford handbook of land economics*, eds. J. M. Duke and J. Wu, 226–254. New York: Oxford University Press.

McCarl, B. A., and T. H. Spreen. 1980. Price endogenous mathematical programming as a tool for sector analysis. *American Journal of Agricultural Economics* 62(1): 87–102.

McCarl, B. A. 1982. Cropping activities in agricultural sector models: A methodological proposal. *American Journal of Agricultural Economics* 64(4): 768–772.

Montgomery, D. R. 2007. Soil erosion and agricultural sustainability. *Proceedings of the National Academy of Sciences of the USA* 104: 13268–13272.

Moss, B. 2008. Water pollution by agriculture. *Philosophical Transactions of the Royal Society of London, Series B* 363: 659–666.

National Agricultural Statistics Service (NASS). 2010. County estimates. http://www.nass.usda.gov/.

National Oceanographic and Atmospheric Administration (NOAA). 2011. National Climatic Data Center. http://www.ncdc.noaa.gov/oa/ncdc.html.

Pattanayak, S. K., B. A. McCarl, A. J. Sommer, B. C. Murray, T. Bondelid, D. Gillig, and B. DeAngelo. 2005. Water quality co-effects of greenhouse gas mitigation in US agriculture. *Climatic Change* 71 (3): 341–372.

Plantinga, A. J., and J. Wu. 2003. Co-benefits from carbon sequestration in forests: Evaluating reductions in agricultural externalities from an afforestation policy in Wisconsin. *Land Economics* 79(1): 74–85.

Poiani, K. A., W. C. Johnson, G. A. Swanson, and T. C. Winter. 1996. Climate change and northern prairie wetlands: Simulation of long-term dynamics. *Limnology and Oceanography* 41: 871–881.

Polasky, S. E., E. Nelson, J. Camm, B. Csuti, P. Fackler, E. Lonsdorf, C. Montgomery, D. White, J. Arthur, B. Garber-Yonts, R. Haight, J. Kagan, A. Starfield, and C. Tobalske. 2008. Where to put things? Spatial land management to sustain biodiversity and economic returns. *Biological Conservation* 141:1505–1524.

Rashford, B. S., and R. M. Adams. 2007. Improving the cost-effectiveness of ecosystem management: An application to waterfowl production. *American Journal of Agricultural Economics* 89(3): 755–768.

Reilly, J., F. Tubiello, B. A. McCarl, D. Abler, R. Darwin, K. Fuglie, S. Hollinger, C. Izaurralde, S. Jagtap, and J. Jones. 2003. US agriculture and climate change: New results. *Climatic Change* 57 (1): 43–67.

Schneider, U. A., B. A. McCarl, and E. Schmid. 2007. Agricultural sector analysis on greenhouse gas mitigation in US agriculture and forestry. *Agricultural Systems* 94(2): 128–140.

Seedang, S., S. Fernald, R. M. Adams, and D. L. Landers. 2008. Economic analysis of water temperature reductions practices in a large river flood plain. *River Research and Applications* 24: 941–959.

Sekercioglu, C., S. Schneider, J. Fay, and S. Loarie. 2008. Climate change, elevational range shifts, and bird extinctions. *Conservation Biology* 22 (1): 140–150.

Sorenson, L. G., R. Goldberg, T. L. Root, and M. G. Anderson. 1998. Potential effects of global warming on waterfowl populations breeding in the Northern Great Plains. *Climatic Change* 40: 343–369.

Stephens, S. E., J. A. Walker, D. R. Blunck, A. Jayaraman, D. E. Naugle, J. K. Ringleman, and A. J. Smith. 2008. Predicting risk of habitat conversion in native temperate grasslands. *Conservation Biology* 22: 1320–1330.

Telemeco, R. S., M. J. Elphick, and R. Shine. 2009. Nesting lizards (Bassiana duperreyi) compensate partly, but not completely, for climate change. *Ecology* 90(1): 17–22.

Tiner, R. W. 1984. *Wetlands of the United States: Current status and recent trends.* Cambridge, Washington, DC: US Fish and Wildlife Service, US Government Printing Office.

Upper Great Plains Transportation Institute. 2011. *Road investment needs to support agricultural logistics and economic development in North Dakota.* Agricultural Roads Study, North Dakota State University.

USFWS. 2009. Waterfowl Breeding Population and Habitat Survey. U. S. Department of the Interior, https://migbirdapps.fws.gov/mbdc/databases/db_selection.html.

Voldseth, R. A., W. C. Johnson, T. Gilmanov, G. R. Guntenspergen, and B. V. Millett. 2007. Model estimation of land-use effects on water levels of northern prairie wetlands. *Ecological Applications* 17: 527–540.

Voldseth, R. A., W. C. Johnson, G. R. Guntenspergen, T. Gilmanov, and B. V. Millett. 2009. Adaptation of farming practices could buffer effects of climate change on northern prairie wetlands. *Wetlands* 29: 635–647.

Watanabe, M., R. M. Adams, and J. Wu. 2006. The economics of environmental management in a spatially heterogeneous river basin. *American Journal of Agricultural Economics.* 88(3): 617–631.

Welbergen, J. A., S. M. Klose, N. Markus, and P. Eby. 2008. Climate change and the effects of temperature extremes on Australian flying-foxes. *Proceedings of the Royal Society B: Biological Sciences* 275(1633): 419–425.

Williams, J. R., C. A. Jones, and P. T. Dyke. 1984. A modeling approach to determining the relationship between erosion and soil productivity. *Transactions of the American Society of Agricultural Engineers* 27(1): 129–144.

Wu, J., R. M. Adams, C. Kling, and K. Tanaka. 2004. From micro-level decisions to landscape changes: An assessment of agricultural conservation policies. *American Journal of Agricultural Economics* 86(1): 26–41.

Zilberman, D., X. Liu, D. Roland-Holst, and D. Sunding. 2004. The economics of climate change in agriculture, mitigation and adaptation strategies. *Global Change* 9: 365–382.

CHAPTER 11

FIRE

An Agent and a Consequence of Land Use Change

CLAIRE A. MONTGOMERY

As long as people and fire have coexisted on this planet, fire has been both purposefully used as an agent and subsequently experienced as a consequence of land use change. In fact, our ability to manipulate the landscape to our own purpose is fundamentally dependent on our ability to use fire. This chapter begins with a history how people have used fire as an agent of land use change over many millennia, how attitudes toward fires have evolved over time, how fire policy has developed in the United States over the last century, and what challenges for fire policy are emerging now. That is followed by a description of three core themes that appear in the literature on the economics of fire: spatial externalities, incentives, and risk-based decision analysis. The chapter closes with a discussion of how future economics research might best contribute to the design of efficient and effective fire policy for the future.

1. People and Fire

In the suite of books that comprise his Cycle of Fire and his subsequent synopsis, "Fire: A Brief History" (Pyne 2001), Stephen Pyne, fire historian, describes three great stages in the relationship between people, fire, and land use.

First, there was aboriginal fire. The colonization of vast areas by people was only possible with fire as a tool. Prior to the capture of fire by humans, most places were inhospitable for human habitation. People occupied only a small part of the landscape. However, once people could carry fire, they took it everywhere. As they colonized new places, they used fire to transform the landscape into, and maintain it as, a place suitable for people to live in. Every major migration can be tracked in the geologic record by a layer of charcoal that was left when the existing biota was burned and replaced with more fire-friendly ecosystems in which fuel was regenerated and made available for repeated burning. People brought more regularity to the fire regime than had existed when fire occurrence depended on the coincidence of lightning, burnable fuel, and dry weather, and most places burned more frequently than before.

Regular use of fire altered ecosystems; it changed travel patterns of wildlife, moisture regimes, and even entire microclimates. Vegetation and wildlife adapted to its regular presence. It is usually this systematic and repeated use of fire by aboriginal people that we really mean when we talk about "natural" fire regimes.

In this first stage, fire was used as a tool to convert large areas for humans to live in, to hunt, to forage for food, and to protect villagers from predation, from warfare, and, ironically, to protect from uncontrolled wildfire. Perhaps most importantly, fire nurtured a sustainable supply of combustible fuel to be used for cooking, heating, and as the center of village life. Without anthropogenic fire, many areas would revert to closed canopy forest, impenetrable by light and fire and hostile to human presence.

Aboriginal fire was followed by agricultural fire. Large areas of existing vegetation had to be cleared for farming, and fire was an invaluable tool for that purpose. Fire released nutrients from existing vegetation and, often, the period immediately following the first burning was an enormously productive one. In some places, fire was then used to beat back the encroaching vegetation and maintain the land in its agricultural use. Once farming was established, fire could be part of a cycle of periodic renewal that sustained continued productivity of a site; this included the burning of fields to stimulate sprouting of forage for livestock whose manure replenished soil nutrients; it also included postharvest field burning to release nutrients from the remaining vegetation, to prepare the field for replanting, and to purge the soil of disease and pests. In places where nutrients are so easily leached from soil that they are mostly held in biomass, fire was part of the longer cycle of shifting agriculture. Fields were cleared and nutrients released from the existing vegetation by fire. Farming continued until the soil was depleted. Then new sites were cleared by fire and old sites were left for long periods of time in which the forest vegetation regrew and restocked with nutrients.

Little remains of aboriginal fire; because it is free-ranging, it poses a threat in a densely populated world. However, agricultural fire remains an important component of life. For example, 1.2 million hectares of cropland is burned annually in the contiguous United States alone (McCarty et al. 2009). Broadcast burning after clear-cut logging is a common practice to prepare logged sites for forest regeneration (Van Lear and Waldrup 1991). Shifting agriculture is estimated to support up to 500 million people, mainly in the tropics (Kleinman, Pimentel, and Bryant 1995). Biomass continues to be removed from forests to provide fuel for the home; currently, fuelwood comprises nearly half of global wood consumption (FAO 2011).

Now, most of the developed world is either in, or in transition to, the third stage in which agricultural fire is supplanted by industrial fire. The nature of the relationship between fire, people, and land use is, again, changing dramatically. Industrial fire is combustion that is confined to engineered containers such as the engines of automobiles, the boilers that produce steam heat, and the plants that burn coal to generate electricity to power the appliances in urban homes. Industrial fire is ubiquitous in our lives and yet we rarely see its flame. It is mostly fueled by fossilized biomass rather than living biomass. It replaces agricultural fire with petrochemicals that enrich soil and kill pests—chemicals that are produced elsewhere using industrial fire. Industrial fire doesn't happen on the landscape, but its implications for land use change are vast.

First, as living biomass is replaced with fossilized biomass to fuel combustion, people are no longer altering only the landscape through fire; they are also altering the atmosphere through the release of carbon from its geologic cache. The economics of carbon and global climate change are addressed elsewhere in this book. Suffice it to say here that climate change is a direct consequence of how the relationship between fire, people, and land use is changing.

Second, the spread of industrial fire happened alongside urbanization. The combined effect of these two trends is that people tend to see fire less as an integral part of their homes and daily lives and more as a threat to both. People rarely see fire's open flame and, when they do, it is often in the form of wild and uncontrolled fire that destroys and kills. Moreover, people who live primarily in the built environment tend to see the countryside less as a resource to be managed for use and more as a resource to be preserved to provide refuge from the city and reserves for vegetation and wildlife. This urge to "protect nature" is having unintended consequences, at least with respect to wildfire. One policy outcome has been the banishment of anthropogenic fire from most places. On the other hand, policy for natural fire has been somewhat contradictory. In many places, such as the western United States, fire is treated as a threat. It is aggressively suppressed with the discipline and ardor of military action. In a few places where fire is recognized as a natural ecological process, there have been experimental attempts to let wildfire burn unhampered. For example, the National Park Service in the United States began to reintroduce wildfire in the national parks in the 1950s and has largely held to that policy in spite of a few spectacular fires, such as the fire that burned 320,000 hectares in Yellowstone National Park in 1988, which have stirred public controversy (Carle 2002; Omi 2005).

Indigenous people of the United States used fire for a variety of purposes, typically burning in the spring and fall. Documented uses include driving game animals to places where they were easier to hunt, encouraging sprouting of green forage for game, favoring fire-adapted edible plants such as yucca, berries, camas, providing fire protection by burning areas around settlements, controlling flies and mosquitoes, opening spaces for easy travel, reducing fuels so that summer fires are less severe, and punishing and harassing enemies (Williams 2000). Burning was not completely controlled, and there were likely many escaped fires. Most areas appear to have been burned frequently—sometimes every 1–3 years. The overall effect was that when European immigrants ventured west, they found broad expanses of tall grass prairie, oak savanna, or chaparral, particularly in river basins.

By the time European settlement of the west occurred, indigenous populations had been decimated by disease and conquest; they and their fires were, for the most part, removed from the landscape. Encroachment of forest on the valleys and plains was well underway. For example, in the Willamette Valley of Oregon, early logging towns were located high in the Coast Range or the foothills of the Cascades because that was where the interface between oak savanna and Douglas fir forest was. Now the forest has crept up to the Willamette River except where it has been blocked by agriculture and urban development.

The elimination of frequent burning led to a build-up of fuels so that when fire did occur, either from lightning strikes or escaped anthropogenic fire, it was more likely to be large and catastrophic. For example, in 1871, the Peshtigo fire burned 500,000 hectares in Wisconsin and Michigan and killed at least 1,250 people. The Yacolt fire in Washington burned about 400,000 hectares and killed 38 people in 1902. The Great Fire of 1910 burned 1.2 million hectares in Washington, Idaho, and Montana killing over 85 people (Omi 2005).

This set the stage for federal fire policy in the 20th century. When the United States National Forest Reserve system (later to become the USDA Forest Service) was established in 1891, its first responsibility was to protect the forests from fire. Debate raged about whether all wildfire should be suppressed or whether wildfire could be controlled and used for beneficial purposes (Carle 2002). However, the great fires that were occurring across the continent dampened the debate and a policy of aggressive fire suppression was adopted. The 1908 Forest Fires Emergency Act authorized unlimited spending to fight wildfire (Omi 2005) effectively eliminating fiscal responsibility. In 1935, federal forest fire policy became formalized in the so-called "10:00 A.M. policy," the goal of which was to contain every wildfire by 10:00 A.M. the day after it was reported. Bambi and Smokey the Bear brought a message to the public that forest fire is an enemy to be vanquished.

The suppression policy was successful in reducing the extent of wildfire for a while, but by the 1970s, it was becoming apparent to fire ecologists and forest managers that a policy of aggressive suppression could not be sustained (Biswell 1980). Fire exclusion was driving forest conditions well outside the range of variation that had prevailed in the forests of the western United States for millennia. Forest fire fuels were accumulating in the form of downed woody debris and dead standing trees. Without fire to cleanse the forest of weak and diseased trees, whole forests were swept by insect infestations, adding even more to fuel loads. Ingrowth of seedlings that would have been eliminated by a light burning developed into ladder fuels capable of carrying fire into the forest canopy where it is far more deadly. When wildfire occurred, it was becoming far more difficult and costly to contain.

Recognizing the beneficial effects of light fire, federal land management agencies began to revise fire policy to encourage preventative measures, such as mechanical fuel removal, prescribed burning, and restoration thinning. The most recent guidelines allow all fires, including human-caused or unplanned fires, to be used to achieve management and resource goals (Lasko 2010). This means that both anthropogenic fire (prescribed burning) and cautious use of wildfire are now considered viable management tools.

However, change has been slow to arrive. Although current policy allows for wildfire use, less than 0.5% of wildfires originating on federal land were allowed to burn between 1998 and 2008 (NIFC 2011). Wildland fire activity in the western United States continues to increase in the 2000s, and fire suppression expenditures continue to escalate (Calkin et al. 2005; NIFC 2011). Even though the 1908 Forest Fires Emergency Act was repealed in 1978, Congress continues to reimburse the agencies for fire suppression costs. The USDA Forest Service, which is responsible for approximately 70% of all wildland fire expenditures in the United States, tripled its annual expenditure on fire suppression in the 2000's over the levels of the previous three decades (Abt, Prestemon, and Gebert, 2009).

At the same time, the aging of the baby-boom generation, increasing wealth, and technological change that allows people to interact with one another at a distance are fueling a wave of low density housing development along the edge of, and intermixed with, wildland that has forest fire fuels. The extent of area that can be classified as wildland-urban interface (WUI) has increased by over 50% since the 1970s and is expected to increase by another 10% by 2030. Nearly 90% of the WUI in the 11 western states of the United States can be classified as a high wildfire-hazard type (Theobald and Romme 2007). People are drawn to the WUI because they want the amenities of a forest or wildland setting. However, they also want the benefits of urban life, including protection of lives and property from fire. This phenomenon of WUI development is challenging to wildland managers because it imposes conflicting management mandates—to manipulate vegetation to block fire from destroying residences while, at the same time, managing vegetation and wildlife in its natural state—of which fire is a component.

Although the details of fire policy and forest ecology described here are specific to the United States, the general pattern—ecosystems adapted to frequent burning by indigenous people, subsequent banishment of anthropogenic fire with industrialization and urbanization, massive fuel accumulation, escalating wildfire severity and cost—is not (Pyne 1995). In the Russian taiga, fire suppression was as aggressively military during the Cold War as it was in the United States. Anthropogenic fire was totally banned during the Brezhnev years. Now, with the resulting fuel accumulation, combined with the collapse of the Soviet Union, the number of wildfires is fairly steady, but area burned and expenditure to control fire are exploding. On the Iberian peninsula, fuel loading was controlled more by intense grazing than by anthropogenic fire, but with the shift from rural to urban life, grazing diminished, fuels built up, and wildfire became more frequent and more damaging. The authoritarian regimes of Salazar in Portugal and Franco in Spain took up the charge to suppress wildfire with the same military vigor as in the United States. Similar patterns appear in Brazil, Sweden (a country thought to be named after its long practice of slash and burn, or *svedje*, agriculture), Canada (Martell 2011), and elsewhere.

2. Economics of Fire

Economists have only recently turned to these issues, but three themes appear to be emerging in the economics literature: inefficiency in the face of the spatial externalities associated with fire, the influence of institutional incentives (e.g., liability rules, insurance, and regulations) on private landowners' and public land managers' decisions about fire risk management, and the development of tools to guide fire and fuel management decisions.

2.1 Spatial Externalities

Spatial externalities arise because fire spreads. Any fuel management, timber harvest, or fire that occurs on one unit of land affects the probability of fire reaching adjacent units and, hence, fire risk on those units.

Konoshima et al. (2008, 2010) formulated the spatial problem for timberland as a stochastic dynamic programming problem in which a single landowner chooses the spatial configuration of fuel treatment and timber harvest in each time period to maximize the expected net present value of timber production over two periods, assuming Faustmann rotation age and no fire beyond the time horizon. The spatial spread of fire was explicitly modeled using the equations that drive fire spread in widely used fire simulation models, such as FARSITE (Rothermel 1972; Finney 1998) in order to estimate transition probabilities. Fuel treatment reduces fire spread rate across the landscape; timber harvest generates revenue but leaves flammable fuel on-the-ground and a new stand through which fire moves relatively quickly. Ignoring the spatial externality, fire risk acts as an increase in the discount rate and *reduces* optimal timber harvest age (Reed 1984). When the spatial externality is taken into account, however, it acts to *increase* optimal harvest age, because timber harvest speeds the spread of fire through the harvested unit to adjacent units. Hence, there is a trade-off between harvesting earlier to protect on-site timber value and harvesting later to protect adjacent timber value. Which effect dominates for a particular unit depends on timber value on site, timber value on adjacent units, and the location of the unit with respect to topography and prevailing wind. As formulated, this model is relevant primarily for industrial timberland owners.

Crowley et al. (2009) extended the problem by modeling two adjacent timberland owners, each choosing timber and fuel management to maximize the expected net present value of timber production and amenities on their respective properties. Fire suppression effort, when fire occurs, is determined (and its cost is born by) an external government agency and depends on fuel and timber value. The problem was formulated as a game and was solved for three cases:

1. Landowners understand the effect of fuel treatment on adjacent properties on their own fire risk. They do timber and fuel management.

2. Landowners ignore the spatial fuel treatment externality. They do timber and fuel management.
3. Landowners do timber management and no fuel treatment. This model is equivalent to Reed (1984) in which an isolated timber landowner responds to fire risk by harvesting earlier.

The solutions were compared to a "socially optimal" baseline in which fuel and timber management decisions are made by a single agent to maximize expected net present value of timber and amenities on both units. The results demonstrate the potential for inefficient fuel management choices. Landowners do too little fuel treatment for two reasons: they don't bear fire suppression costs, which depend on fuel loads, and they try to free-ride on their neighbors' fuel treatment. In numerical simulations, it appears that the suppression cost externality is a far greater problem than the spatial fuel treatment externality. As formulated, this model is relevant primarily for small private timber landowners such as those that dominate the landscape in the southern and southeastern United States and in Scandinavia.

Busby, Albers, and Montgomery (2012) took the problem into the WUI where private owners choose fuel management to protect their own buildings and the stream of amenity values generated on their own and adjacent units that accrue to them. Public land managers choose fuel management to protect public goods such as aesthetics, wildlife, and ecosystem health. Because nontimber values dominate in the WUI, timber was not included in this model. Fuel treatment reduces fire severity and, hence, extent of damage on the treated unit and adjacent units. However, landowners ignore the effect of their fuel treatment on fire spread. Fire suppression is exogenous and not part of the landowners' decision process. This is approximately true in the WUI where any wildfire brings on a full (and expensive) fire-suppression effort.

The authors were particularly interested in the effect of the spatial pattern of ownerships (public and private) on the extent of inefficiency arising from spatial externalities in both fire risk and amenity value. They formulated the problem as a game in which one player represents a coordinated private landowner and the other player represents the public-land-management agency. The game was solved for each of five spatial patterns of ownership ranging from two adjacent blocks of public and private land to a nine-square checkerboard of public and private ownership. The following cases were modeled: spatial externality from fire spread only; spatial externalities from both fire spread and amenity values; and three forms of response of fire severity to fuel treatment. The results suggest that the spatial pattern of ownership in the WUI matters; increasing fragmentation decreases efficiency as landowners free-ride on the fuel treatment effort of adjacent landowners. That inefficiency is offset somewhat by the presence of off-site amenities as landowners increase fuel treatment in order to provide protection for amenities generated on adjacent units. The results also suggest that nonlinear response functions for fire severity give rise to strategic behavior as landowners choose their own fuel treatment levels to influence fuel treatment on adjacent units. Evidence from an empirical analysis of homeowners' fuel treatment choices in the WUI in Colorado

(Shafran 2008) indicates that landowners are indeed influenced by their neighbors' fuel treatment choices and that it matters whether adjacent property is publicly or privately owned. These models are particularly relevant for understanding how optimal policy might differ between the two main categories of WUI: the interface where residential development presses up against wildland and the intermix where residential development is dispersed throughout the wildland.

2.2 Incentives Matter

Fire management in and around the WUI is further complicated by the fact that both private homeowners and agency fire managers face a complex mix of incentives for managing fire risk.

Private homeowners may engage in risk averting activities and/or they may purchase insurance. However, the efficiency of insurance and real estate markets depends on the availability of accurate information about wildfire hazard. The state of California, where structure values in the WUI are high, has implemented a natural hazards disclosure law (AB 1195) that requires homeowners to inform potential buyers of hazard ratings for an array of hazards, including wildfire, when they sell their homes. Troy and Romm (2007) used hedonic pricing to explore how house prices were affected by implementation of the law, but their results were mixed. Troy (2007) speculated that other fire insurance laws may have actually promoted development in the WUI in California by subsidizing insurance in high hazard zones for people who otherwise could not obtain it.

To the extent that fire reduces both market (e.g., structures) and nonmarket values (e.g., amenities), insurance can only partially compensate a loss. Therefore, there is reason for homeowners to avert risk even when full market insurance is available and risks are accurately known. In fact, Talberth et al. (2006) analyzed experimental and survey data and found that most households choose to purchase a mix of insurance and averting activities and that households that rated amenity values as high devote relatively more of their budget to averting risk than those who do not.

Ehrlich and Becker (1972), in a theoretical analysis of the demand for insurance, defined two types of risk-averting actions: "Self-insurance" reduces the size of a loss when a hazardous event occurs and "self-protection" reduces the probability of a hazardous event occurring. Fuel treatment by individual households is most effective as self-insurance; homeowners treat fuel around their homes to reduce the intensity of any fire that occurs and/or to create "defensible space" immediately around the structure. Self-protection requires that fuel treatment be broad enough in scale to slow or block the spread of fire across the landscape, increasing the likelihood that fire will be contained before it reaches residential developments. Private landowners are unlikely to undertake treatment at such a scale because it requires coordination among landowners and because the large expanse of forest where fire often originates is mostly public in the western United States. Hence, investment in self-protection is largely the responsibility of public-land-management agencies.

Fire managers in public agencies face a bewildering mix of conflicting incentives. Decisions regarding management for fire prevention and fire suppression are related and they should be made simultaneously to maximize the expected net value of the landscape or, equivalently, to minimize the expected value of all fire-related costs including the net value change of the forest resulting from fire. The optimal fire-management problem was first formulated as the "least-cost-plus-loss" model (Sparhawk 1925) in which fire managers choose the optimal level of suppression effort to minimize suppression cost plus loss to fire. The formulation was later modified to incorporate preventative measures and beneficial effects of wildfire (Althaus and Mills 1982) so that fire managers choose the optimal level of suppression and prevention to minimize treatment and suppression cost plus net value change of the forest when the benefit of fire is accounted for as well as the loss. However, under current policy, suppression and prevention decisions are disconnected. Because forest wildfire continues to be treated as an emergency, there is no effective budget limit on suppression. Suppression cost savings that might result from preventative fuel treatment do not accrue to the agencies making fuel-treatment decisions. Donovan and Brown (2005) suggested adjusting the incentives faced by fire managers by allotting them a joint budget for prevention and suppression, but in the absence of such a measure, the current structure of incentives gives rise to an array of inefficiencies. Public agencies will spend too much on fire suppression and will be unlikely to allow wildfire to burn even if it seems that it would be beneficial to do so.

There is substantial evidence that fire managers in public agencies have attitudes toward risk that reinforce the problem. Wilson et al. (2011) used a web-based survey instrument to explore whether risk biases are held by USDA Forest Service personnel responsible for decisions regarding wildfire and, if so, how such biases affect the decisions they make. Their survey results revealed that fire managers do exhibit risk-based biases. They display an aversion to loss; they prefer long-term to short-term risk; and they tend to rely on "status quo" rather than sophisticated risk-assessment tools when faced with complexity and uncertainty. In another recent survey, fire managers indicated that they tend to choose high-cost suppression strategies even though they say they would prefer to choose more cost-effective strategies (Calkin et al. 2012). Berry (2007) hypothesized that social and political pressures contribute to suboptimal suppression decisions and, indeed, Donovan, Prestemon, and Gebert (2011) included an array of variables representing newspaper coverage and political influence in a regression analysis of suppression costs for large fires, and they found empirical evidence to support that notion.

With a virtually unlimited fire-suppression budget, not only is there little incentive to control fire-suppression costs, but there is little incentive to invest efficiently in fire-hazard reduction. The analysis reported in Crowley et al. (2009), described earlier, demonstrates the potential for too little investment in fuel treatment when the suppression cost savings that result are externalities. In an innovative approach to the problem, Thompson et al. (2013) propose a method to provide feedback between suppression expenditures and the general management budget at the national forest level within the USDA Forest Service. They suggest establishing an insurance pool to finance wildfire-suppression expenditures. Each national forest would pay a premium into the pool based on past suppression expenditures, the level of fire risk, and management to reduce that risk via preventative measures such as fuel treatment and beneficial use of wildfire. Premiums would be adjusted regularly to reflect changes in risk status and suppression cost containment. This structure would provide incentives to reduce risk through fuel treatment, to place firebreaks around high-valued resources, and to use cost-effective suppression strategies.

Furthermore, resources that are allocated to fuel treatment may not be applied cost-effectively. Although the Healthy Forests Restoration Act directs that priority be given to fuel treatment in and around the WUI (HFRA 2003, Sec. 103), that may not be the strategy that most effectively protects private property values. Ager, Vaillant, and Finney (2010) used repeated simulation of fire on a landscape in northeast Oregon to generate burn probability profiles under two fuel-treatment strategies: one in which areas with the greatest fuel accumulations were prioritized for treatment and one in which areas in and near the WUI were prioritized for treatment. Their results suggest that a strategy of treating relatively remote areas with the greatest fuel accumulations could substantially reduce fire risk in the WUI. That is because fires that ignite in remote places will spread more slowly and thus be less likely to reach the WUI (providing self-protection) than when treatment is concentrated in the WUI (providing self-insurance).

The least costly method of fuel treatment, prescribed burning, is likely to be underutilized due to concerns about liability. Prescribed burning reduces the risk associated with wildfire by reducing fuel loads on the landscape, but it can escape prescription to wreak havoc on nearby property. For example, the 2000 Cerro Grande fire was a prescribed fire that escaped and burned 18,000 hectares and destroyed 235 homes in Los Alamos, New Mexico.

Yoder et al. (2003) and Yoder (2004) developed an analytical model of prescribed burning and ran simulations to explore the interaction of three related decisions under different forms of liability rules. Landowners who benefit from burning choose when to use prescribed burning and they choose the level of precaution to take against its escape. Adjacent homeowners choose the level of self-insurance undertaken (fuel treatment on their own property and creation of defensible space around their homes). Yoder's model indicates that there is a trade-off between risk from escaped prescribed fire while treating fuels and risk from wildfire if fuels are not treated. To the extent that liability rules apply only to damage from escaped prescribed fire, prescribed burning for fuel treatment purposes is underutilized. Strict liability (where the burner is liable for damage regardless of precautionary measures taken) is likely to result in too little use of prescribed burning for any purpose. However, most states have some form of negligence rule that frees the burner from liability unless it can be shown that he or she was negligent in some way. Negligence rules may be designed to encourage the efficient level of precaution on the part of the burner, but the decision about when and how much to burn will still be distorted by the failure to impose liability for the wildfire hazard arising from the presence of untreated fuels. The homeowners will also make suboptimal fire-risk-management decisions. To the extent that the burner is liable for damage from escaped prescribed fire, homeowners will undertake too little self-insurance.

Although the federal government is not directly liable under state law for damage from prescribed fire, it may be sued under the Federal Tort Claims Act if it or its employees can be shown to be negligent according to the laws of the place where the action occurred (U.S.C. Title 28, 1346(b)). Hence, the incentives facing public fire managers will also likely lead to overly cautious use of prescribed fire. There is a movement to balance liability for prescribed fire with liability for wildfire spreading from national forests that have an abnormal accumulation of forest fire fuels. See, for example, the proposed Enhanced Safety from Wildfire Act introduced in 2003 (USGPO 2003). These efforts, if successful, could tilt the scale back toward fuel treatment.

2.3 Decision Support Tools

It may be possible to mitigate the effect of risk attitudes by developing risk-based decision support tools—at least for the agencies responsible for fire management on public land. Because these tools process complex information systematically, they have the potential to both inform risky decisions when they are being made and to provide a vehicle for explaining these decisions after the fact. They also provide means for exploring outcomes from policy alternatives via simulations. In this section, two approaches to decision support tools are described: risk assessment and optimization under risk. There are significant research efforts currently underway to develop tools under each approach.

Risk assessments integrate information about risk (the likelihood of an event occurring and the outcome if it does) in order to inform decision making. Thompson and Calkin (2011) provide an excellent summary of current research and the challenges in applying it to forest wildfire. They note that there are several sources of uncertainty that must be accounted for in risk assessment. First, the location and timing of fire events and the weather in which it occurs are inherently unpredictable. We do know something about probability distributions from historical frequencies, but we can predict only patterns of events and not any particular event. There is also uncertainty due to large gaps in our knowledge about how to model fire behavior, the response of fire to various treatments and actions that might be taken, the effect of fire on resources, and the relative values that people place on those resources. This uncertainty can be reduced via research in the appropriate disciplinary fields. The latter, valuation, falls in the realm of economics. Many, if not most, of the values that may be affected by fire are not easily monetized because they are not conducive to market exchange (e.g., endangered species habitat, visual amenities, air and water quality, carbon sequestration, cultural heritage, and more). Nonmarket valuation techniques, including stated preference methods such as contingent valuation and choice modeling, are developed and applied by environmental economists in an array of resource contexts. Because fire-risk assessment may pose some special challenges, this is a knowledge gap that is unlikely to be closed any time soon. Venn and Calkin (2011) acknowledge these challenges and propose an economics research agenda to address them.

Optimization takes risk assessment one step further by attempting to identify actions and strategies that optimally achieve management objectives. All of the modeling challenges that must be addressed in fire-risk assessment must also be addressed in optimization. The main challenge in moving beyond simulation-based risk assessment to optimization is computational.

Optimization has a long history in forestry (Montgomery and Adams 1995). The stand-level problem of how long to hold a tree before harvesting was first posed over 150 years ago by a German forester named Faustmann (1968) and confirmed just 35 years ago by Samuelson (1976). The problem is easy to solve numerically if the timber-stand volume function is known. Economists have since extended the basic analytical model to include the flow of ecosystem services dependent on attributes of standing timber (Hartman 1976; Strang 1983). The Faustmann model was extended to include fire by Reed (1984), who demonstrated that the optimal response to fire risk is to harvest timber at a younger age.

The Faustmann model applies to a single isolated stand of trees. However, foresters don't manage stands; they manage forests composed of many stands of different ages. Regulations on forest practices impose an array of spatial constraints, such as maximum clear-cut size and limits on activities on adjacent stands because many of the benefits from ecosystem services depend on the spatial pattern of vegetation, such as wildlife habitat contiguity and connectivity.

When a problem is spatial, it is combinatorial and generally involves integer decision variables. For some problems, there may be no exact solution algorithm; for others, the size of the problem quickly outgrows available computational resources (Bettinger, Sessions, and Boston 2009) because the decision space grows exponentially with the number of management units. Because of this so-called "curse of dimensionality," approximate methods such as genetic algorithms, simulated annealing, and Tabu search (Reeves 1993) are used in forestry where they have found some degree of acceptance (for example, Yoshimoto, Brodie, and Sessions 1994; Lichtenstein and Montgomery 2003; Nalle et al. 2004; and Hummel and Calkin 2005).

Adding a large-scale stochastic disturbance, such as fire, to the mix complicates the problem enormously. Fire is spatial and temporal because its spread across the landscape depends on the spatial configuration of fuels, wildlife and other forest values at risk from fire depend on the spatial configuration of vegetation, and both vegetation and fuels evolve over time depending on the spatial configuration and timing of management activities. The fire problem is stochastic and dynamic because the optimality of decisions made now depends on future fire events that cannot be predicted with any certainty and for which possible outcomes are wildly diverse. Decisions in future periods will surely depend on the occurrence of fire events in the interim. Adaptation to new information as it arrives must be accounted for in the current decision.

The problem can be formulated as a stochastic dynamic programming problem in which, in each period, the fire manager chooses a spatial vector of timber and fuel management activities and a suppression response to fire, when it occurs, to maximize the expected net present value of actions in the current period, assuming value-maximizing decisions in all future periods once the outcomes from stochastic fire events in the interim are known.

Most previous attempts to optimize fuel management on the forested landscape are static. That is, they model the potential of the landscape to burn, given a post-treatment configuration of fuel on the landscape. For example, Finney (2007) developed an algorithm for identifying the pattern of fuel treatments that maximized the minimum time it takes for a fire to spread across a particular landscape under typical high fire-severity weather conditions (e.g.; wind direction and speed, relative humidity, temperature). In Wei, Rideout, and Kirsch (2008) and Jones et al. (2010), the placement of fuel treatments is optimized to minimize the expected value loss from the next fire. The burn probability profile for the untreated landscape was estimated using repeated simulations with random ignition points, assuming typical severe fire weather. Wei, Rideout, and Kirsch (2008) simplified the computational aspect of the problem by decomposing the burn probabilities for each unit into ignition and spread probabilities and assuming a structure for the effect of fuel treatment on spread probability. They solved the problem using integer programming. Jones et al. tried to make the problem intertemporal by using simulated annealing to schedule timber and fuel management over a 5-period time horizon, assuming fire doesn't actually occur. They used repeated fire simulations to evaluate the effect of fuel treatments on the burn probabilities and, hence, expected loss to the next fire. Vegetation is updated in each period using a forest vegetation simulation model (Crookston and Dixon 2005) but it is not burned.

Konoshima et al. (2008, 2010) is the first attempt that this author is aware of to formulate and solve the fuel treatment and timber management problem simultaneously as a stochastic dynamic programming problem. They solved the problem exactly for a very stylized landscape of 7 management units over 2 time periods with 4 possible management activities. They simulated the spread of fire from 7 possible fire-ignition locations and 2 possible weather conditions, using fire-spread equations (Rothermel 1972) to estimate transition probabilities for each possible configuration of post-treatment vegetation and fuels. They solved the problem using complete enumeration for each possible initial configuration of vegetation and fuels on the landscape.

There are at least two problems with these analyses. First, in order for any bioeconomic model of forest and fire management to provide useful guidance for resource managers, it must capture important elements of the decision process itself and, at the same time, it must represent the resource and management actions with sufficient realism so that solutions can be translated into feasible actions on the ground. Fire ecologists and forest planners tend to favor simulation approaches that are relatively rich in details of the landscape, fire behavior, and vegetation development. They simplify the decision process, however, by ignoring its dynamic aspect. Economists favor analytical approaches that represent the important elements of the decision process but, in order to find solutions, the biological setting and processes are so stylized as to be practically irrelevant.

The second problem is that once the spatial aspect of a resource-management problem is accounted for, it is very difficult to draw any general inference from the results. Detailed models yield results that are specific to a particular landscape and cannot be applied elsewhere, but even the more stylized models of economists can be hard to interpret. In fact, general tendencies in the Konoshima results were identified by visual examination of the solutions—of which there were many.

3. Fire Economics Research in the Future

Because fire is just now attracting the attention of economists, economic analysis of fire is relatively rare in both the economics literature and the fire literature. However, the consequences of ignoring fire or of prolonging the status quo of aggressive fire suppression and banishment of anthropogenic fire could be costly. Economists can make an important contribution to the design of efficient and effective fire policy for the future. In this concluding section, I suggest several paths that could advance existing research in ways that may be especially relevant for pressing policy concerns. I close the section by speculating about the role of economics in the broader context of the complex ecosystems of which fire is an important component.

Existing studies of fire-risk management in the WUI take the current configuration of land ownership and residential development as given. They focus on how households choose to invest in risk-averting activities to protect private property values. The interaction between private landowners and public-land managers should continue to be explored using game theory in order to learn more about the potential to reduce the negative effects of spatial externalities via insurance, liability rules, cost-sharing, and coordinating groups such as homeowners' associations and cooperatives. However, the larger question of whether there is too much residential development in fire-prone forests has yet to be addressed. Does the fact that the federal government bears the cost of forest-fire suppression, and some of the liability for the damage that wildfire causes, create moral hazard? This question might be addressed by modeling land use change and amenity migration. And, if the answer is yes, those models might be used to explore means of internalizing wildfire risk in the decision to locate in the WUI.

The existing literature identifies several cases in which incentives that public-agency fire managers face do not lead to socially optimal choices. The most important sources of inefficiency appear to be (1) the lack of feedback between fire hazard reduction (e.g., fuel treatment) and fire suppression decisions, and (2) the absence of any effective budget limit for suppression. The incentives for individual managers within the agencies that are responsible for fire suppression, and also for managing large expanses of public land where fuel accumulation is most severe, are seriously misaligned with overall agency objectives. This is an opportunity for the economics of public choice. There is much to be gained by exploring what motivates the interactions between three sets of actors: individuals within the agencies, elected officials who determine policy and allocate funding, and the voting individuals who elect them. Analysis could focus on realigning budgets so that suppression and prevention are endogenous, developing performance measures for fire managers that truly reflect desired outcomes, linking budgets to outcomes, and lessening the effect of risk aversion on suppression decisions. Thompson et al.'s (2013) proposal to establish an insurance pool to pay for fire suppression is one example of what might come out of this line of research.

One limiting factor in extending risk assessment to the optimization of fire and fuel management is the computational difficulty of the problem. The challenge is twofold: first, to solve the computational problem, and then to interpret the results once it is solved. The appropriate decision framework for fire is stochastic dynamic programming. Because fire is spatial, however, any specification of the problem that is realistic enough to be informative to policy makers and land managers, and large enough in scale to capture important fire behavior, will not be amenable to analytical methods and will be too large to solve using exact methods. The approximate optimization methods currently used in forestry are useful for large problems that involve spatial interactions, but they are not dynamic and, hence, not adequate for modeling policy in the context of large-scale stochastic disturbance, such as fire.

There is hope. New methods in operations research and computer science are being developed and evaluated. One, in particular, approximate dynamic programming (ADP), also known as reinforcement learning (Powell 2009), may prove useful for the fire problem. The policy iteration version of ADP is intriguing because, instead of producing a specific plan for a landscape, it produces a "rule" that recommends an action based on attributes of the state (vegetation and fuels) and attributes of the stochastic event (ignition and weather) that are known at the time of the decision. The basic idea of ADP with policy iteration is to "learn" an optimal policy by iteratively solving a deterministic problem for each of a large number of individual Monte Carlo simulations of future time paths of random events (e.g., ignitions and weather). The solutions provide data for estimating a policy rule using regression. The process is repeated until the policy rule stabilizes. The policy rule, thus derived, would be applicable only to the landscape on which it was developed. However, it may be possible to apply techniques of machine learning to derive more general results by systematically "tweaking" the attributes of the landscape in order "learn" a more general model for fire management. The coefficients of the resulting policy rule are simple to interpret because they reveal how optimal choices adjust to changing external conditions. In ongoing research, we are attempting to apply ADP to the problem of when it is optimal to allow a wildfire to burn, and we hope to extend it to the optimal placement of fuel treatments on a landscape.

Finally (and in a necessarily speculative vein), the relationship between fire, people, and land use is just one small aspect of the larger question of how we live on our planet in a sustainable manner. Fire is an ecological process that plays an important role in the functioning of complex ecosystems. Its exclusion has ramifications well beyond the immediate impacts to people of increasing suppression costs and loss of property and lives. Complex ecosystems often exhibit cycles of conservation and renewal that are triggered by disturbances such as fires and hurricanes (Holling 1995). These cycles and interactions occur at many scales in time and space.

In the Oregon Coast Range (for example), the natural disturbance regime appears to be infrequent large-scale catastrophic fire events every 100–400 years. These fires play a critical role in the renewal of the aquatic ecosystems that support salmon populations. Without fire to kill large trees and trigger landslides, the stream systems become starved of large woody debris and sediment. Over time, the complexity and quality of freshwater salmon habitat declines and populations collapse (Reeves et al. 1995). Currently, several evolutionarily significant units of Pacific salmon and distinct populations segments of steelhead in the Pacific Northwest are listed as endangered under the Endangered Species Act (NOAA 2011). Degradation of freshwater habitat that results from exclusion of catastrophic disturbance from watersheds in coastal forests is one contributing factor. Reeves and Duncan (2009) argue that disturbance is crucial to the maintenance of salmon habitat and, since reintroduction of catastrophic fire is unlikely to be socially acceptable, forested watersheds should be managed to mimic its effect. Instead, however, these watersheds are managed to maintain steady conditions over time and across space so that habitat is moderately degraded everywhere and high-quality habitat exists nowhere (Reeves, Burnett, and Gregory 2002).

C. S. Holling, one of the early contributors to the field of ecological economics, describes case after case in which people who are uncomfortable with uncertainty attempt to bring order to chaos, protect resources, and ensure a predictable supply of ecosystem services by regulating ecosystems to uniform standards in order to dampen disturbance cycles. There is no place for wildfire in these managed ecosystems. Natural cycles of conservation, disruption, and renewal are interrupted so that, over time, ecosystems become "brittle," that is, less resilient and more vulnerable to collapse when disturbance does occur (Holling 1995).

People are comforted by stability and it can be argued that one legitimate role of government is to reduce uncertainty, limit fluctuations, and maintain a stable economy. However, as Holling notes, in ecological systems there is a trade-off between local stability and global stability. The challenge for economists is to inform the design of land use policy so that it finds a balance between social acceptability and ecological resilience, allowing for disturbance at local temporal and spatial scales in the interest of sustaining stability at larger and longer scales. In the traditional regulatory approach to resource policy, the standards that are imposed must be enforceable. For regulations to be enforceable, they must be applied uniformly to outcomes that can be observed and measured. Regulations that are too complicated and allow variability may be perceived as arbitrary and unfair.

What can economics bring to this dilemma? In recent decades, there has been a growing interest in the application of the science of complexity to economic systems (Rosser 1999). One working definition of complexity from Durlauf (1998) states, "[A] system is said to be complex when it exhibits some type of order as a result of the interactions of many heterogeneous objects." It has long been recognized that economic systems are complex by that definition. Because the aggregate economy is the result of many agents, all with different histories, endowments and objectives, interacting with one another in markets, it is fundamentally complex (Colander 2009).

The emerging discipline of complexity economics is developing in many directions. However, there do appear to be some common themes that are relevant for resource policy for complex ecosystems. One is that, when systems are complex, we can never know enough about each of its elements to allow us to predict specific outcomes. We can only predict general patterns that may occur (Hayek 1999). The idea that there exists a steady state for the economy is replaced with the notion that economic systems evolve over time and the path of that evolution cannot be predicted because it depends on a legacy of past events (path dependency) and also on chance (Colander 2009). There appears to be a sense that the most robust systems are those that are self-regulating. In other words, if regulations that must be strictly defined and enforced can be replaced with an institutional environment in which incentives are designed to lead individual agents to make choices that are consistent with the overall objective, the outcome may be an environment more tolerant of local variation and, hopefully, more stable in the long run.

As promised, this section is mostly speculative. The discipline of complexity economics is in its infancy and it is not clear what it will yield. My thinking about its potential application to land use and resource policy when disturbance is important for ecosystem health is, likewise, in its infancy, and it is not clear what that will yield. However, my hope is that this avenue of research will provide new and useful insights for future resource management and policy—particularly with respect to fire.

References

Abt, K. L., J. P. Prestemon, and K. M. Gebert. 2009. Wildfire suppression cost forecasts for the U.S. Forest Service. *Journal of Forestry* 107(4): 173–178.

Ager, A. A., N. M. Vaillant, and M. A. Finney. 2010. A comparison of landscape fuel treatment strategies to mitigate wildland fire risk in the urban interface and preserve old forest Structure. *Forest Ecology and Management* 259(8):1556–1570.

Althaus, I. A., and T. J. Mills. 1982. *Resource values in analyzing fire management programs for economic efficiency*. General Technical Report PSW-57. Berkeley, CA: U.S. Department of Agriculture Forest Service, Pacific Southwest Forest and Range Experiment Station.

Berry, A. 2007. Forest policy up in smoke: Fire suppression in the United States. Bozeman, MT: Property and Environment Research Center. http://www.law1.northwestern.edu/searlecenter/papers/Berry_forest_policy.pdf.

Bettinger, P., J. Sessions, and K. Boston. 2009. A review of the status and use of validation procedures for heuristics used in forest planning. *International Journal of Mathematical and Computational Forestry & Natural Resource Sciences* 1(1): 26–37.

Biswell, H. 1980. Fire ecology: Past, present, and future. Keynote speech presented at annual meeting of the American Association for the Advancement of Science, Davis, CA, June 22–27.

Busby, G. M., H. J. Albers, and C. A. Montgomery. 2012. Wildfire risk management in a landscape with fragmented ownership and spatial interactions. *Land Economics* 88: 496–517.

Calkin, D. E., K. M. Gebert, J. G. Jones, and R. P. Neilson. 2005. Forest service large fire area burned and suppression expenditure trends: 1970–2002. *Journal of Forestry* 103: 179–183.

Calkin, D. E., T. J. Venn, M. J. Wibbenmeyer, and M. P. Thompson. 2012. Estimating U.S. federal wildland fire managers' preferences toward competing strategic suppression objectives. *International Journal of Wildfire Research* 22: 212–222.

Carle, D. 2002. *Burning questions: America's fight with nature's fire.* Westport, CT: Praeger.

Colander, D. 2009. Complexity and the history of economic thought. In *Handbook of research on complexity*, eds. J. Barkley Rosser Jr. and Kirby L. Cramer, 409–426. Northampton, MA: Edward Elgar.

Crookston, N. L., and G. E. Dixon. 2005. The forest vegetation simulator: A review of its structure, content, and applications. *Computers and Electronics in Agriculture* 49(1): 60–80.

Crowley, C. S. L., A. S. Malik, G. S. Amacher, and R. G. Haight. 2009. Adjacency externalities and forest fire prevention. *Land Economics* 85(1): 162–185.

Donovan, G. H., and T. C. Brown. 2005. An alternative incentive structure for wildfire management on national forest land. *Forest Science* 51(5): 387–395.

Donovan, G., J. P. Prestemon, and K. M. Gebert. 2011. The effect of newspaper coverage and political pressure on wildfire suppression costs. *Society & Natural Resources* 24(8): 785–798.

Durlauf, S. N. 1998. What should policymakers know about economic complexity? *The Washington Quarterly* 21(1): 155–165.

Ehrlich, I., and G. S. Becker. 1972. Market insurance, self-insurance, and self-protection. *The Journal of Political Economy* 80(4): 623–648.

Faustmann, M. 1968. Calculation of the value which forest land and immature stands possess for forestry. In *Martin Faustmann and the evolution of discounted cash flow*, ed. M. Gane, 27–55. Oxford: University of Oxford Commonwealth Forestry Institute. (Originally published in 1849.)

Finney, M. A. 1998. *FARSITE: Fire area simulator—Model development and evaluation.* Research Paper RMRS-4. Missoula, MT: U. S. Department of Agriculture Forest Service, Rocky Mountain Research Station.

Finney, M. A. 2007. A computational method for optimizing fuel treatment locations. *International Journal of Wildland Fire* 16: 702–711.

FAO. 2011. State of the world's forests, 2011. Rome: Food and Agriculture Organization.

Hartman, R. 1976. The harvesting decision when a standing forest has value. *Economic Inquiry* 14: 52–68.

Hayek, F. A. 1999. The theory of complex phenomena. In *Critical approaches to science and philosophy*, ed. M. Bunge, 332–349. New Brunswick, NJ: Transaction Publishers. (Originally published in 1964 by The Free Press.)

HFRA. 2003. Healthy Forests Restoration Act of 2003. http://ag.senate.gov/Legislation/Compilations/Forests/healthy.pdf

Holling, C. S. 1995. What barriers? What bridges? In *Barriers and bridges to the renewal of ecosystems and institutions*, eds. L. H. Gunderson, C. S. Holling, and S. S. Light, 3–37. New York: Columbia University Press.

Hummel, S. S., and D. E. Calkin. 2005. Costs of landscape silviculture for fire and habitat management. *Forest Ecology and Management* 207(3): 385–404.

Jones, G. J., W. Chung, C. Seielstad, J. Sullivan, and K. Krueger. 2010. *Optimizing spatial and temporal treatments to maintain effective fire and non-fire fuels treatments at landscape scales.* Final Report FJSP Project 06-3-3-14. U.S. Department of Agriculture/U.S. Department of the Interior, Joint Fire Science Program. http://www.fs.fed.us/rm/pubs_other/rmrs_2010_jones_g002.pdf.

Kleinman, P. J. A., D. Pimentel, and R. B. Bryant. 1995. The ecological sustainability of slash-and-burn agriculture. *Agriculture Ecosystems & Environment* 52: 235–249.

Konoshima, M., C. A. Montgomery, H. J. Albers, and J. L. Arthur. 2008. Spatial endogenous fire risk and efficient fuel management and timber harvest. *Land Economics* 84(3): 449–468.

Konoshima, M., H. J. Albers, C. A. Montgomery, and J. L. Arthur. 2010. Optimal spatial patterns of fuel management and timber harvest with fire risk. *Canadian Journal of Forest Research* 40(1): 95–108.

Lasko, R. 2010. Implementing federal wildland fire policy—Responding to change. *Fire Management Today* 70(1): 5–7.

Lichtenstein, M. E., and C. A. Montgomery. 2003. Biodiversity and timber in the coast range of Oregon: Inside the production possibility frontier. *Land Economics* 79(1): 56–73.

Martell, D. 2011. The development and implementation of forest fire management decision support systems in Ontario, Canada: Personal reflections on past practices and emerging challenges. *International Journal of Mathematical and Computational Forestry & Natural Resource Sciences* 3(1): 18–26.

McCarty, J. L., S. Korontzi, C. O. Justice, and T. Loboda. 2009. The spatial and temporal distribution of crop residue burning in the contiguous United States. *Science of the Total Environment* 407: 5701–5712.

Montgomery, C. A., and D. M. Adams. 1995. Optimal timber management. In *Handbook of environmental economics*, ed. D. W. Bromley, 379–404. Oxford: Basil Blackwell.

Nalle, D. J., C. A. Montgomery, J. L. Arthur, N. H. Schumaker, and S. Polasky. 2004. Modeling joint production of wildlife and timber in forests. *Journal of Environmental Economics and Management* 48(3): 997–1017.

NIFC (National Interagency Fire Center). 2011. Wildland fire statistics. http://www.nifc.gov

NOAA (National Oceanic and Atmospheric Administration). 2011. ESA salmon listings. http://www.nwr.noaa.gov/ESA-Salmon-Listings

Omi, P. N. 2005. *Forest fires: A reference handbook.* Santa Barbara, CA: ABC-CLIO.

Powell, W. B. 2009. What you should know about approximate dynamic programming. *Naval Research Logistics* 56: 239–249.

Pyne, S. J. 1995. *World fire: The culture of fire on earth.* New York: Holt.

Pyne, S. J. 2001. *Fire: A brief history*. Seattle, WA: University of Washington Press.

Reed, W. J. 1984. The effects of the risk on the optimal rotation of a forest. *Journal of Environmental Economics and Management* 11: 180–190.

Reeves, C. R. 1993. *Modern heuristic techniques for combinatorial problems.* New York: John Wiley & Sons.

Reeves, G. H., L. Benda, K. M. Burnett, P. A. Bisson, and J. R. Sedell. 1995. A disturbance-based ecosystem approach to maintaining and restoring freshwater habitats of evolutionarily significant units of anadromous salmonids in the Pacific Northwest. *American Fisheries Society Symposium* 17: 334–349.

Reeves, G. H., K. M. Burnett, and S. V. Gregory. 2002. Fish and aquatic ecosystems of the Oregon coast range. In *Forest and stream management in the Oregon coast range*, ed. S. D. Hobbs, J. P. Hayes, R. L. Johnson, G. H. Reeves, T. A. Spies, J. C. Tappeiner II, and G. E. Wells, 68–98. Corvallis: Oregon State University Press.

Reeves, G. H., and S. L. Duncan. 2009. Ecological history vs. social expectations: Managing aquatic ecosystems. *Ecology and Society* 14(2): 8. www.ecologyandsociety.org/vol14/iss2/art8/

Rosser J. B., Jr. 1999. On the complexities of complex economic dynamics. *Journal of Economic Perspectives* 13(4): 169–192.

Rothermel, R. C. 1972. *A mathematical model for predicting fire spread in wildland fuels*. Research Paper INT-115. Ogden, UT: U.S. Department of Agriculture Forest Service, Intermountain Forest and Range Experiment Station.

Samuelson, P. A. 1976. Economics of forestry in an evolving society. *Economic Inquiry* 14: 466–492.

Shafran, A. P. 2008. Risk externalities and the problem of wildfire risk. *Journal of Urban Economics* 64: 488–495.

Sparhawk, W. N. 1925. The use of liability ratings in planning forest fire protection. *Journal of Agricultural Research* 30: 693–761.

Strang, W. J. 1983. On the optimal forest harvesting decision. *Economic Inquiry* 21: 576–583.

Talberth, J., R. P. Berrens, M. McKee, and M. Jones. 2006. Averting and insurance decisions In the wildland-urban interface: Implications of survey and experimental data for wildfire risk reduction policy. *Contemporary Economic Policy* 24(2): 203–223.

Theobald, D. M., and W. H. Romme. 2007. Expansion of the U.S. wildland–urban interface. *Landscape and Urban Planning* 83: 340–354.

Thompson, M. P., and D. E. Calkin. 2011. Uncertainty and risk in wildland fire management: A review. *Journal of Environmental Management* 92: 1895–1909.

Thompson, M. P., D. E. Calkin, M. A. Finney, and K. G. Gebert. 2013. A risk-based premium approach to wildland fire finance and planning. *Forest Science* 59: 63–77.

Troy, A. 2007. A tale of two policies: California programs that unintentionally promote development in wildland fire hazard zones. In *Advances in the economics of environmental resources*, Vol. 6, eds. A. Troy and R. G. Kennedy, 127–140. Oxford: Elsevier JAI Press.

Troy, A. and J. Romm. 2007. The effects of wildfire disclosure and occurrence on property markets in California. In *Advances in the economics of environmental resources*, Vol. 6, eds. A. Troy and R. G. Kennedy, 101–119. Oxford: Elsevier JAI Press.

USGPO (United States Government Printing Office). 2003. H.R. 2551 Summary. http://www.gpo.gov/fdsys/pkg/BILLS-108hr2551ih/pdf/BILLS-108hr2551ih.pdf.

Van Lear, D. H., and T. A. Waldrop. 1991. Prescribed burning in regeneration. In *Forest regeneration manual*, eds. M. L. Duryea and P. M. Dougherty, 235–250. Dordrecht, Netherlands: Kluwer Academic.

Venn, T. J., and D. E. Calkin. 2011. Accommodating non-market values in evaluation of wildfire management in the United States: Challenges and opportunities. *International Journal of Wildland Fire* 20: 327–339.

Wei, Y., D. Rideout, and A. Kirsch. 2008. An optimization model for locating fuel treatments across a landscape to reduce expected fire losses. *Canadian Journal of Forest Research* 38: 868–877.

Williams, G. W. 2000. Introduction to aboriginal fire use in North America. *Fire Management Today* 60(3): 8–12.

Wilson, R. S., P. L. Winter, L. A. Maguire, and T. Ascher. 2011. Managing wildfire events: Risk-based decision making among a group of federal fire managers. *Risk Analysis* 31(5): 805–818.

Yoder, J., M. Tilley, D. Engle, and S. Fuhlendorf. 2003. Economics and prescribed fire law in the United States. *Review of Agricultural Economics* 25(1): 218–233.

Yoder, J. 2004. Playing with fire: Endogenous risk in resource management. *American Journal of Agricultural Economics* 86(4): 933–948.

Yoshimoto, A., J. D. Brodie, and J. Sessions. 1994. A new heuristic to solve spatially constrained long-term harvest scheduling problems. *Forest Science* 40(3): 365–396.

CHAPTER 12

LAND USE AND MUNICIPAL PROFILES

EDWARD STONE AND JUNJIE WU

LAND is a fundamental resource, and the character of the landscape influences quality of life in significant ways. "Land use" refers to more than simply the pattern of different land covers (e.g., cropland, forests, urban) in space. Rather, land use is "the total of arrangements, activities, and inputs that people undertake in a certain land cover type to produce, change, or maintain it" (FAO/UNEP 1999). In other words, land use for a particular parcel encompasses land cover, as well as management intensity and practices. Changing land use could mean changing land cover, or it could mean maintaining the same land cover while altering management. Land use determines the availability of primary inputs including food, fiber, building materials, and even developable land. If the consequences of individual land use decisions were to fall entirely on individual landowners, markets for these inputs should result in an efficient allocation of land uses. However, individual land use decisions—and the resulting land use patterns—may generate environmental and social externalities.

First, the decision to extract ecosystem goods and services from the landscape may generate an environmental externality. Removing ecosystem goods or managing land to enhance the production of these goods may have indirect consequences on flows of supporting ecosystem services, such as freshwater storage and release, soil formation and fertility, biodiversity, and climate regulation (DeFries et al. 2004). Typically, land use activities involve making natural resources available for human consumption at some cost to environmental quality. This is the case for farming or forestry, as well as for urban development (Foley et al. 2005).

Second, land use decisions and the resulting patterns may give rise to social externalities, including the impacts on local public finance and school quality. Collective land use decisions shape community well-being in ways beyond market and environmental impacts. The link between land use and various indicators of environmental quality has been the subject of much research. This chapter explores the social implications of land use, which have been less well-studied. Collectively, the socially relevant features of a city or a neighborhood may be termed its "municipal profile." Relevant features include local taxes and public services, public safety and health, open-space provision and natural amenities, income distribution, housing prices, development densities, demographic composition and distribution, and transit and congestion.

Land use patterns affect municipal profiles. For example, urban sprawl has been linked to obesity, congestion, and open-space loss (see, e.g., Nechyba and Walsh 2004; Plantinga and Bernell 2007). Suburbanization is often associated with income stratification and concentrated poverty, with their inherent fiscal and social implications (e.g., Mieszkowski and Mills 1993). Municipal profiles in turn affect land use patterns. The expression "flight from blight" refers to falling incomes and deteriorating public safety and services causing high-income households to relocate from city centers to suburbs and thus contributing to suburbanization and sprawl. Conversely, high-income communities may enact zoning and tax regimes that affect land use patterns by attracting new residents and/or restricting the pattern of development.

In many cases—and in many economic models (e.g., Wu 2007)—the interaction between land use and municipal profiles is self-reinforcing. "Flight from blight" further diminishes central city incomes and tax revenues, leading to deteriorating public services and safety and thus more flight. High-income suburbs with high tax revenue and high levels of services attract more high-income households. Other urban development phenomena are also self-reinforcing, including gentrification and urban revitalization.

Historically, urban expansion has been accompanied by the rise of the automobile and patterns of suburbanization. This is markedly true in the United States but holds internationally as well (Mieszkowski and Mills 1993). This much-lamented tendency has been associated with social and environmental costs. Many households continue to locate in the urban fringe. Despite social and environmental externalities, households enjoy substantial private benefits from consuming more land and housing. Sprawl and other "undesirable" development patterns leave many households better off. That is not to say that such land use patterns are efficient. Indeed, they have given rise to regulations and incentive-based policies aimed at correcting perceived inefficiencies associated with "excessive sprawl," including urban growth boundaries, zoning protections for open space, and impact fees for new development.

The aggregate location decisions of firms and households are the drivers behind both land use and municipal profile change. Two primary bodies of economic literature attempt to explain historical development patterns through the lens of household locational choice. The contemporary urban economics literature dates back to the monocentric city model, with early incarnations by Alonso (1964), Mills (1967), and Muth (1969). This approach explains historical patterns of suburbanization in terms of rising incomes, falling commuting costs, and newer housing on the periphery. In contrast, the local public finance approach explains development patterns in terms of preferences for alternative bundles of local taxes and public goods and services. This body of literature expands on Tiebout's (1956) household sorting model.

Although urban economics models capture the primary drivers of urban expansion, they do not account for other factors that influence household locational choice within a metropolitan area, including amenities and public finances (Nechyba and Walsh 2004). Local public finance models include these factors and better explain why many households moving to the suburbs prefer to form homogeneous groups, but these models are typically aspatial. Due to data limitations, the bulk of empirical research in this area has focused on changes at the county or city level, although many relevant decisions are made at a smaller scale. Recent developments in computing, especially Geographic Information System (GIS) software, facilitate observation and analysis within metropolitan areas.

The purpose of this chapter is twofold: first, to survey the most significant developments in theory and analyses that explore the interactions among household location decisions, land use patterns, and municipal profiles; and, second, based on the survey, to explore strategies to model these interactions using a case study from Portland, Oregon.

The remainder of this chapter is organized as follows. Section 1 reviews the literature in urban economics and local public finance that focuses on various links between land use and municipal profiles. Section 2 illustrates the role of emerging data and information technologies in modeling household location choice within a metropolitan area, as opposed to at the county or city level. Section 2 also discusses appropriate estimation strategies. Section 3 provides a conclusion.

1. Literature Review

Household preferences and collective location decisions determine land use patterns and neighborhood characteristics.[1] This section first reviews the literature on household location decisions and then focuses on the interactions between location decisions and municipal profiles.

1.1 Household Location Decisions

Suburbanization has been a dominant trend in aggregate household location decisions and urban spatial development in the modern era, particularly in the United States. As previously mentioned, economists offer two main classes of theory explaining household residential location choices: urban economics and local public finance. The monocentric city model is a basic formalized model of the urban economics approach. In

[1] Strictly speaking, land use and thus municipal profiles are determined by the collective location decisions of both households and firms. Although an in-depth investigation of firm location decisions is beyond the scope of this chapter, there is a rich literature in this area. One fundamental question is whether jobs follow people or people follow jobs. For example, Muth (1971) finds that jobs primarily follow people. Carlino and Mills (1987) find that people primarily follow jobs. By focusing on households, the framework presented in this chapter implicitly assumes that jobs follow people.

early incarnations of the monocentric city model (e.g., Alonso 1964; Mills 1967; Muth 1969), all employment lies within the central business district (CBD), households are differentiated by income, and the key difference between alternative household locations is distance to the CBD. Since housing closer to the employment center requires less commuting, it is more desirable and therefore more expensive. Thus, households face a tradeoff between commuting time and housing price. Those who choose to live farther away incur higher commuting costs but face lower housing prices and can thus afford to consume more housing. The primary driver behind suburbanization and modern urban spatial expansion has been falling commuting cost due to the proliferation of the automobile and the development of highway systems. Simple CBD models account for this driver and correctly predict expanding urban footprints in the face of decreasing transportation costs. However, simple CBD models do not account for a number of other relevant factors—including alternative transportation modes, locational amenities, and age of the housing stock—nor do they predict multicentric metropolitan areas and various observed historical development patterns. A number of researchers have relaxed assumptions and generalized CBD models to address these concerns.

LeRoy and Sonstelie (1983) incorporate two alternative transport modes—one fast and one slow—and demonstrate that when the rich are better able to afford the faster mode, they will tend to suburbanize more rapidly than others. They argue that this was the case early on with the automobile. However, as the cost of the faster mode falls (the vast majority of American households can now afford car-commuting), the rich lose this comparative advantage for suburbanizing. In fact, since wages—and thus opportunity cost of time—are higher for high earners, LeRoy and Sonstelie predict gentrification by the rich as commuting costs fall and the poor suburbanize. According to this model, when the rich and poor use the same transport mode, the rich will tend to locate in the city center.

Brueckner, Thisse, and Zenou (1999) add natural and historical amenities to explain alternative income distributions across different cities. They observe the stark difference between most American cities, where high-income households tend to live in the suburbs, and many European cities, where the wealthy occupy the central city.[2] Their model explains these differences in terms of differing levels of natural and historical amenities across cities. As with classic CBD models, the rich are pulled to the suburbs by their preference for more housing, which is available more cheaply on the periphery; simultaneously, they are pulled into the center by their high time-cost of commuting. However, this model also allows for heterogeneous levels of natural and historical amenities between the center and the suburbs. When the central city, such as Paris, has high levels of amenities, these constitute an additional attraction for the wealthy. On balance, the time-cost effect and the amenity effect outweigh the housing price effect,

[2] The simple CBD model is consistent both with the rich locating in the center (the ratio of commuting cost per mile to housing consumption increases with income) and with the rich locating in the suburbs (opposite). However, it seems implausible that the behavior of this ratio across countries

and the wealthy locate in the center. When the central city has low or even negative amenity value, as in Detroit, the housing price effect dominates, and the wealthy locate in the suburbs. A key assumption of this model is that preferences for amenities rise with income.

Wu (2006) incorporates amenities in a different fashion. Distinguishing between exogenous amenities (natural and historical features) and endogenous amenities (e.g., local public services), this study incorporates exogenous amenities in a modified CBD model. Alternative locations within the city differ in terms of the distance to the employment center and the level of local amenities. In contrast to the Brueckner-Thisse-Zenou model, spatially heterogeneous amenities in this model attract households to various suburbs. With this spatial heterogeneity in amenities, households may be willing to pay more for a nice location than for a short commute; thus, housing prices may not fall uniformly as distance from the center increases. At a given distance from the center, higher income households will choose locations with better amenities. This model is consistent with noncontiguous development patterns and non–distance-based patterns of income segregation. Wu (2006) includes a model incorporating endogenous amenities as well, discussed in Section 1.2, with local public finance models.

Brueckner and Rosenthal (2009) posit that age of the housing stock is an important determinant of the location of high- and low-income households. The resulting model is consistent with both suburbanization and gentrification. In addition to short commutes and low housing prices, high-income households prefer newer housing. Commuting concerns pull households inward; housing price concerns pull them outward. The location of new housing determines the direction of the housing age effect. As a city grows, new housing is always available on the periphery. Some new housing is also available in the interior—more so during periods of rapid redevelopment. If new housing is abundant in the interior city, it exerts an additional pull, causing some high-income households to locate in the center. Holding housing age constant, this model predicts a negative relationship between income and distance—the rich prefer to live in the center. This is in contrast with the traditional CBD model, in which suburbanization by the rich implies a positive relationship between income and distance.

CBD models, including those just discussed, assume monocentricity—that is, all firms (and thus all employment) locate in the CBD. Whereas household location is determined endogenously within the model, firm location is exogenously given. Ogawa and Fujita (1980) and Fujita and Ogawa (1982) relax this assumption and explore the conditions under which a nonmonocentric city is the equilibrium urban spatial configuration. In addition to commuting cost, these models include a transaction cost parameter, which measures the benefits of spatial clustering for firms. When transaction costs are high relative to marginal commuting costs, the incentive for firms to cluster outweighs the incentive for households to locate close to work. A monocentric city is the

differs enough to fully explain differences in spatial income distribution. See Brueckner, Thisse, and Zenou (1999) for a more complete discussion.

equilibrium spatial arrangement. Higher relative marginal commuting costs give rise to multiple dispersed employment centers because households have increasingly strong incentives to minimize commuting distance. In the extreme case, in which firms do not benefit from spatial proximity, the equilibrium spatial arrangement is a fully mixed city with firms and residences dispersed throughout.

1.2 Interactions Between Residential Location Choices and Municipal Profiles

Local public finance models offer an alternative lens through which to examine household locational choice. Even broadened to include amenities, housing age, and transit considerations, CBD models do not fully capture the role of community characteristics. Dating back to Tiebout (1956), local public finance models endogenize the provision of public services. In other words, these models account for the interaction between household locational choice and the levels of local taxes and public services. Households choose a location based, in part, on their preferences for various bundles of local taxes and public services at the community scale. They "vote with their feet." Simultaneously, households influence the level of taxes and services in a community through the representative process and through peer and local public finance externalities. A brief discussion of the link between household locational choice and community characteristics follows.

A household chooses a home based on income/wealth, own preferences, home characteristics, and community characteristics. Based on their finances, families choose a preferred option from available house-community combinations. The role of community characteristics in this process is clear: families like nice, safe neighborhoods and good school districts. The link between household location decisions and community characteristics is more involved. Relevant community characteristics include tax rates and the levels of amenities and public services. Some community characteristics are exogenous; they are not affected by household location decisions. Consider natural features, such as a hill, lake or river, or a well-established man-made attraction, for example. These types of sites exist prior to any location decisions and will persist regardless of those decisions. Other community characteristics are endogenous; they are affected by household location decisions.

Collective location decisions—and the preferences and characteristics of the resulting population—affect these endogenous community characteristics in three ways: voting, local public finance externalities, and peer externalities. Spatial context also matters. First, community residents vote for their preferred bundle of taxes and services. As the voter base changes due to household relocations, the results of these votes may change. Voting determines the local tax rate directly, but relocation decisions can alter the size of the tax base, thus indirectly affecting local public service provision.

Second, if high-income households move out of central cities and into suburbs in classic "flight-from-blight," this results in an erosion of the city tax base and a strengthening of the suburban tax base, leading to deteriorating public services in the center and enhanced services in the suburbs. This is the local public finance externality. Collective location decisions that shift income distributions affect the ability of jurisdictions to provide services.

Third, peer externalities also affect the level or quality of services independently of finance. Consider public education, for example. Funding affects school quality, and wealthier school districts tend to be better-funded—the local public finance externality. Highly involved parents may also affect school quality. So, two comparably funded districts with different levels of parental engagement might expect different results. Peer externalities are present when the level of the public services provided depends on the characteristics of the population being served, as well as on the level of funding. Interestingly, peer externalities may preclude the possibility of leveling the playing field by increasing funding to lagging communities. Depending on the scale of spillovers, economists may alternatively term these effects family or neighborhood externalities. A desire to take advantage of perceived peer externalities may influence location decision and has been put forth as an explanation for the formation of homogeneous suburbs (Nechyba and Walsh 2004).

Of course, some community characteristics defy identification as purely endogenous or exogenous. The presence of a previously existing park or open space is exogenous. However, the quality of experience in the park may be endogenous and subject to change due to voting, local public finance externalities, peer externalities, and spatial context. The community could vote to cut or boost maintenance funding. A weakening tax base could force maintenance reductions via local public finance externalities. Citizen-use levels and participation in volunteer maintenance could affect quality of experience, which are examples of peer externalities. Finally, spatial context matters; a well-maintained park in a high-income neighborhood provides amenities to local residents and increases values of nearby properties, whereas an under-maintained park that serves as a focal point for criminal behavior is much less valuable to local residents and could potentially be viewed as a disamenity (Anderson and West 2006; Troy and Grove 2008). Home buyers value nearby shopping and transit access but may prefer not to live adjacent to a shopping center or highway. More space is devoted in later sections to spatial context in the discussion of the home price hedonics literature.

By incorporating interaction between community characteristics and household location decisions, local public finance models go beyond their CBD counterparts. Following Tiebout's 1956 seminal paper, other researchers expand on Teibout's general equilibrium model. Ellickson (1971) derives the single-crossing property, a necessary condition for equilibrium characterized by income stratification. Epple, Filimon, and Romer (1984) incorporate housing markets. Epple and Sieg (1999) develop a general method for estimating equilibrium models of local jurisdictions. Although these papers generate strong predictions of characteristics of communities in equilibrium—including income stratification across communities or, more generally, income stratification across communities by preference—they ignore location.

Wu (2006) incorporates distance and exogenous amenities in a hybrid of CBD and local public finance models. The first model from this paper, mentioned earlier, simply adds exogenous amenities to a CBD model. A second model, however, includes both exogenously determined amenities and endogenously determined taxes and public services, not to mention location. This model predicts income stratification by amenity level for a given distance from the city center.

In addition to urban economics and local public finance, papers from several economic subgenres inform this investigation of the link between land use and municipal profiles. Hedonic home pricing offers insight into the preferences driving household location choice, which, in turn, drives land use change. Oates (1969) introduces hedonic modeling to test Tiebout's hypothesis, and a wide range of empirical studies use hedonics to estimate the value of community characteristics (both positive and negative) as capitalized in home sale prices (e.g., Bowes and Ihlanfeldt 2001; Irwin 2002; Anderson and West 2006; Cohen and Coughlin 2008; Troy and Grove 2008).

One clear message emerges from this literature: when estimating the effect of amenities (or disamenities) on home prices, spatial context matters. For example, Cohen and Coughlin (2008) find that the effect of proximity to the airport varies with distance. If you are too close, airport noise drives down home prices; sufficiently far away to mitigate noise, proximity to the airport drives up home prices. There are many examples from the literature on the amenity value of open space. Troy and Grove (2008), mentioned earlier, find that parks in high-crime areas may be disamenities. Other studies have found that the amenity value of open space varies widely with distance from the city center (Geoghegan et al. 1997), whether the site is permanently designated as open space (Irwin and Bockstael 2001), type and proximity of open space (e.g., Smith et al 2002; Anderson and West 2006), and income and age structure of the neighborhood (Anderson and West 2006), to name a few. Investigating how households value particular community characteristics—and how those values vary depending on context—enhances understanding of household location decisions.

A number of related papers focus on urban sprawl. The term "sprawl" has negative connotations and is often cited as an example of a land use pattern with negative social implications. Nechyba and Walsh (2004) provide a comprehensive review of the literature on sprawl. They argue that, despite its negative reputation, sprawl occurs because individual households are happier with the larger homes and lots that it offers. However, they do identify four costs: road congestion, vehicle pollution, loss of open space, and unequal service and public good provision across metro areas due to self-segregation and associated pockets of affluence and poverty. Lopez (2004) and Plantinga and Bernell (2007) investigate the link between obesity and urban sprawl. These papers and most of the related literature focus on concrete sprawl impacts: weight, emissions, and income distribution. Brueckner and Largey (2008) notably depart from this trend and focus on sprawl and the reduction of social interaction. They investigate the premise that low-density living reduces social interaction to the detriment of society as a whole.

Having reviewed the economic literature on the interaction between land use and municipal profiles, an illustrative example follows. Specifically, in the next section, a case study from the Northwest United States illustrates how researchers might go about modeling these relationships. Whereas much of the economic literature investigates household locational choice and land use change at a county or city level, emerging data and information technology facilitate investigation within a metropolitan area.

2. Case Study

Household locational choice is a central driver of land use and municipal profile change. Individually, households relocate based on a variety of factors. Family, career, or other factors often determine the city, although municipal profile may play a role. Households then choose a home within that city or metropolitan area based on the households' characteristics (preferences, income, wealth), home characteristics (price, size, etc.), and municipal profile (regulations, public goods, demographics, etc.). Relevant regulations include taxes and land use regulations. Relevant public goods or amenities include school quality, public safety, transit access, environmental quality, access to parks and open space, and social amenities like shopping, dining, and culture. With these theoretical relationships in mind, how can researchers go about modeling this process? How can researchers take advantage of emerging information technology and rapidly improving data availability? The following case study details the data collection and processing used to model the link between household locational choice and municipal profiles in the Portland, Oregon, and Vancouver, Washington, metropolitan area. A discussion of alternative estimating strategies follows. Although the data collection and processing described here are specific to this case study, the approach described is adaptable to a variety of geographic areas and research questions, contingent on the availability of appropriate GIS data.

2.1 Data Processing

GIS data differ from conventional data in that they are spatially explicit. Although conventional data may contain variables describing spatial relationships, such as distance from each observation to a park, they do not preserve the underlying spatial arrangement of different features. A GIS dataset or layer includes the location (and shape) of each feature and can therefore be represented as a map. Also associated with each layer is a table containing one or more variables. Data layers differ in terms of their spatial resolution; for the same geographic area, a high-resolution layer will contain more observations than will a low-resolution layer. GIS software facilitates the use of multiple, overlapping data layers.

The Portland, Oregon, and Vancouver, Washington, metropolitan area—specifically Clackamas, Multnomah, and Washington Counties in Oregon and Clark County in Washington—makes an excellent laboratory. Abundant GIS data are available for the

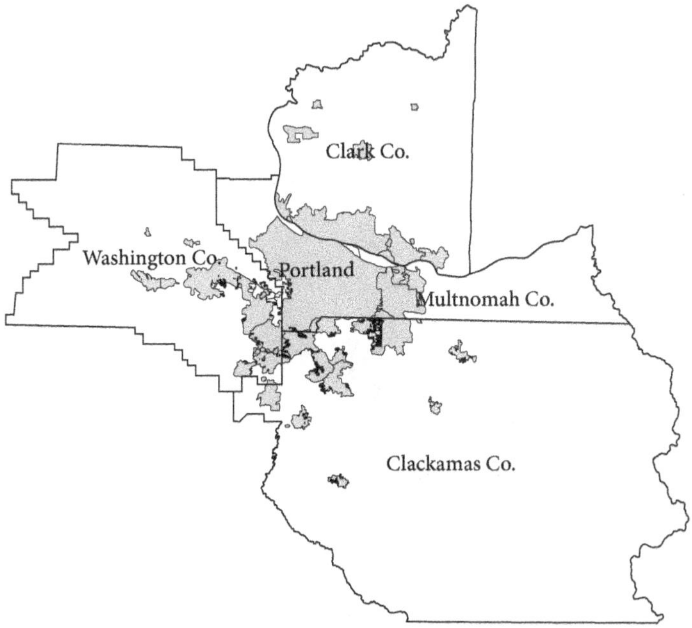

FIGURE 12.1 The study region.

area from a variety of sources, often at quite high spatial resolution. In addition to rich data, the region consists of multiple jurisdictions—more than 40 incorporated towns and cities in four counties and two states (see Figure 12.1) These jurisdictions differ significantly in regulatory regimes, which should influence locational choice. Combined, the four counties have an area of 3,727 square miles and a 2000 population of 1.79 million, which grew to 2.07 million in 2010 (15.5% decennial growth).

Several issues must be addressed to move from a theoretical concept of household locational choice to an empirical model of the effect of municipal profiles. First, a dependent variable, some measure of household choice, is needed. Second, data quantifying local municipal profiles are required. Third, the researcher must select a unit of observation. Finally, GIS is used to process information from the underlying layers and construct a dataset for estimating a model of the effects of municipal profiles on household location choice.

The data described here for the Portland, Oregon, and Vancouver, Washington, metropolitan area do not include information on individual household location choices, but they do include a measure of a direct consequence of these choices; that is, population change at the US Census block level. The metropolitan area as a whole grew rapidly, but certainly some areas grew more rapidly than others. Population change is a feasible dependent variable. The resulting model would aim to explain variations in population change within the region using variables describing the local municipal profile. Of course, some elements of municipal profile are exogenous, including natural amenities such as lakes, rivers, and other topographical features, whereas other elements of

2000 Land use: Parks and open space

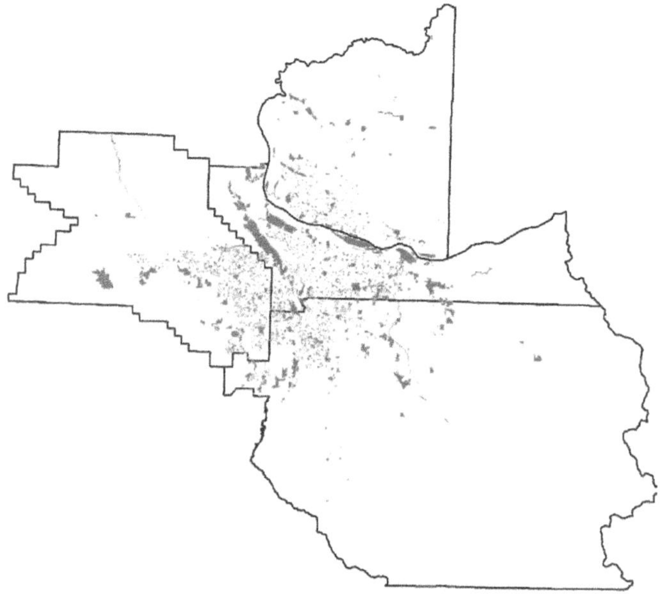

FIGURE 12.2 The distribution of parks and designated open space.

municipal profile are endogenous to population change, including parks and designated open space (see Figure 12.2) and public goods such as school quality (see Figure 12.3).

For the dependent variable, GIS-compatible population data are available at the Census block level from both the 2000 and the 2010 US Census. Data relevant to local municipal profiles are available from a variety of sources, most importantly the US Census and local governments.

The 2000 US Census includes a number of potentially relevant demographic variables, including age and race/ethnicity at the block level. Data on education, income, housing characteristics, and more are available at the block group level. To give an idea of scale, in 2000, the study area contained 34,178 census blocks and 1,160 block groups.

For the three counties in Oregon, the elected regional government, METRO, maintains the Regional Land Information System (RLIS), a high-quality GIS database with a variety of data layers. Potentially relevant layers for quantifying local municipal profiles include zoning, water features, parks and designated open space, mass transit, and taxlots, which includes parcel-level data on land use and home characteristics (for residential properties). The Clark County, Washington, Assessor also offers similarly detailed GIS data. Although similar, these datasets are not identical, and substantial care is necessary to ensure consistency when merging data across states. The end result is a single map covering the entire study area for each relevant layer.

For some layers, including school districts, these GIS data contained maps but no relevant variables. If available, the relevant data are easily incorporated into GIS. In the case of school districts, an index of school quality is constructed using test score data

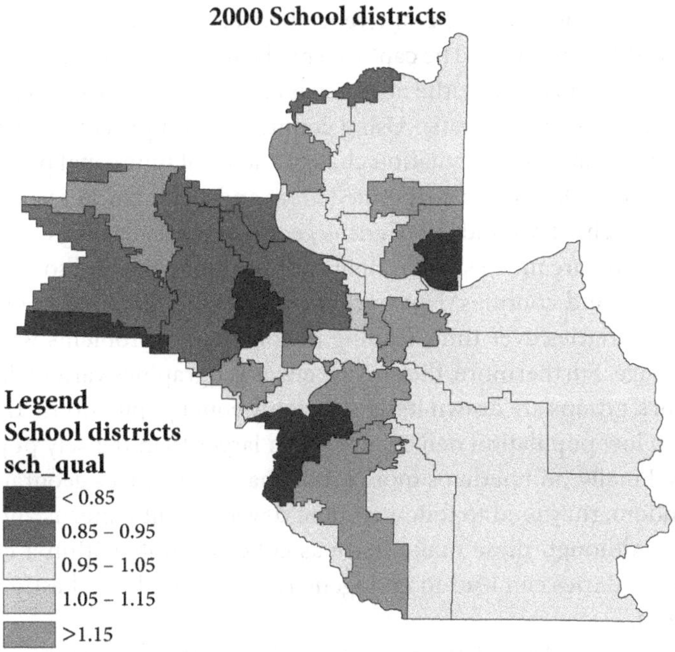

FIGURE 12.3 School quality measured by an index of test scores relative to state averages.

available from Oregon and Washington state departments of education. In each case, reading and math test scores are reported for multiple grade levels. A composite score is a viable option to compare districts across multiple grades and subjects. However, because data and testing vary across the two states, composite scores from Oregon and Washington are not comparable. This is resolved by normalizing using state averages.

For Washington, 2000 district-level reading and math scores for the 4th, 7th, and 10th grades are reported as percentages. Each score is divided by the corresponding state-level score, converting scores from percentages to shares of the state average. These shares are then averaged across subjects and grade levels with equal weight. The result is an index measuring district-level test score performance relative to the state average.

For Oregon, reading and math test results are reported at the 3rd-, 5th-, 8th-, and 10th-grade levels. Instead of percentages, the share of students who do not meet, meet, or exceed performance standards is reported. In addition, data are at the individual school level, and the number of students taking each test is known. First, a single score for each subject and grade level at each school is constructed. This score is the share of students who meet the standard plus two times the share of students who exceed the standard. At this point, each score is normalized using the corresponding state score, then averaged across subjects, grade levels, and schools. Additionally, for Oregon, these averages are weighted based on the number of students taking each test. The result is a single value, which again measures district test performance relative to the state average, making it comparable to the Washington index. However, normalizing by state averages implicitly assumes little systematic difference between Oregon and Washington. Any such systematic difference would be captured by the intercept in estimation.

With underlying data in place, the next step is choosing units of observation. Existing geographies tend to be problematic. Using counties would provide only four observations and ignore variation in population change and local municipal profiles within the counties. Using cities drops unincorporated areas and again ignores variation, particularly in the largest city, Portland. US Census geographies, including census blocks and census block groups, are much smaller than counties and cities and so can capture variation within cities and counties. However, a considerable proportion of census geographies shift boundaries over time, leading to consistency problems when measuring population change. Furthermore, the size of census geographies varies widely, as census blocks and block groups are drawn to have roughly equal populations. Thus, rural census blocks with low population density are much larger than densely populated urban census blocks. Finally, and perhaps more problematically, census geographic boundaries are not random; they tend to follow evident development patterns and form homogeneous units. Although these make sense as cohesive units within a city or county, nonrandom boundaries can lead to endogeneity issues and biased estimates (Banzhaf and Walsh 2008).

Researchers can avoid problems associated with existing geographies by constructing new units of observation in GIS. For this case study, a grid of two-mile diameter circles is overlaid on the study area, and those circles not completely within the study area are dropped. These circles do not represent cohesive communities in any traditional sense.[3] Rather, this method constitutes an effective sampling methodology that allows us to take advantage of high-resolution spatial data. Of course, a grid of two-mile circles is not the only option. Alternative diameters, shifting the grid incrementally, and random locations as opposed to a grid are possible. Indeed, comparing alternative units is a good strategy for testing the sensitivity of coefficient estimates. This approach has been used by Banzhaf and Walsh (2008) to test the Tiebout hypothesis that "people vote with their feet."

GIS software and data are used to quantify variables measuring population change (see Figure 12.4) and municipal profiles for each circular "community" or observation. This procedure varies depending on the data in question. Some GIS layers cover the entire study area, such as census geographies, tax lots, zoning, and school districts. These layers each contain one or more potential explanatory variables. For each layer, a GIS script aggregates the variables of interest from the underlying geometry to the circular observations. A number of variables relevant to municipal profile are constructed in this fashion, including median household income (Figure 12.5) and home value (Figure 12.6).

[3] Indeed, because the four counties in the study area include rural areas devoted to forestry (including State and National Forests) and agriculture, there are 178 out of 844 (21%) observations with zero population, as noted in Table 12.1. Clearly, these observations are not communities.

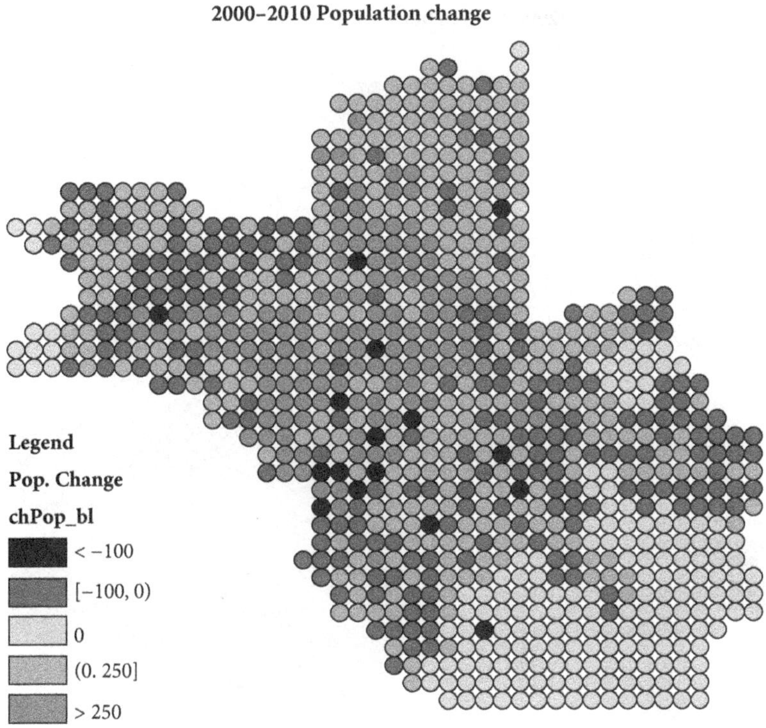

FIGURE 12.4 Population change between 2000 and 2010.

For other GIS layers that do not fully cover the study area, such as bus stops and parks, the appropriate measure is less clear. The bus stop layer contains only points, so an appropriate measure might be the number of bus stops in a circular observation. One can measure access to parks and open space in a variety of ways: park acreage within the observation, distance to the nearest park, and number or acreage of parks within some distance, among others. One can differentiate parks by type from the data as well. Also, one recalls that the hedonics literature reveals variations in amenity values of open space depending on many factors including income, proximity, type of open space, age, urban density, and crime. Interaction terms allow models to capture differential effects. For example, a community park located in a low-income, high-crime neighborhood may not be valued as much as a park located in a high-income, low-crime neighborhood. A model specification including interactions between crime or income and park proximity variables might pick up this effect whereas an alternative specification would not. Anderson and West (2006) provide a good discussion of interaction terms in this context, in addition to a hedonic model with multiple types of open space and multiple interaction terms. Table 12.1 provides summary statistics of some of the constructed variables.

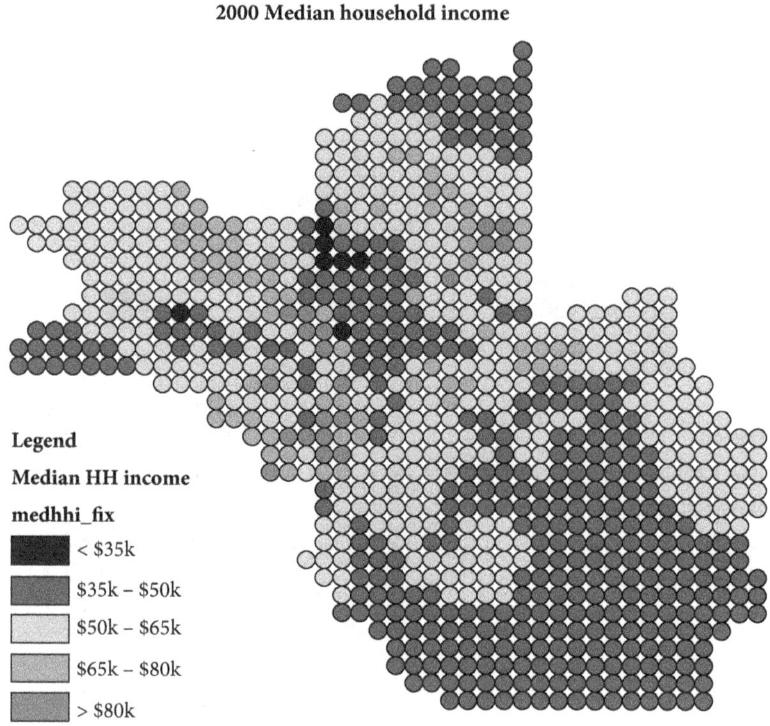

FIGURE 12.5 Median household income in 2000.

2.2 Model Specification and Estimation

This case study explored underlying data collection, construction of units of observation, and quantification of variables. Although specific, the process described is applicable to other regions and research questions. The data clearly indicate correlations between land use and municipal profiles (Table 12.2). The challenge is to specify an appropriate model to identify the causal relationships among the dependent variable, population change, and the independent variables, which quantify various aspects of local municipal profile. Several estimation strategies are available to the researcher investigating household locational choice and municipal profiles. The appropriate estimation strategy depends on the precise research question. In all cases, an appropriate estimation strategy must account for the fact that some variables measuring local municipal profiles are exogenous, whereas others are endogenous. Examples of exogenous variables include natural features and historical development patterns. Examples of endogenous variables include median household income, school quality, and property tax rate. In the absence of endogeneity, the researcher could simply regress population change on variables quantifying municipal profile. Due to endogeneity, this simple approach would yield biased estimates. Because some of the explanatory variables are

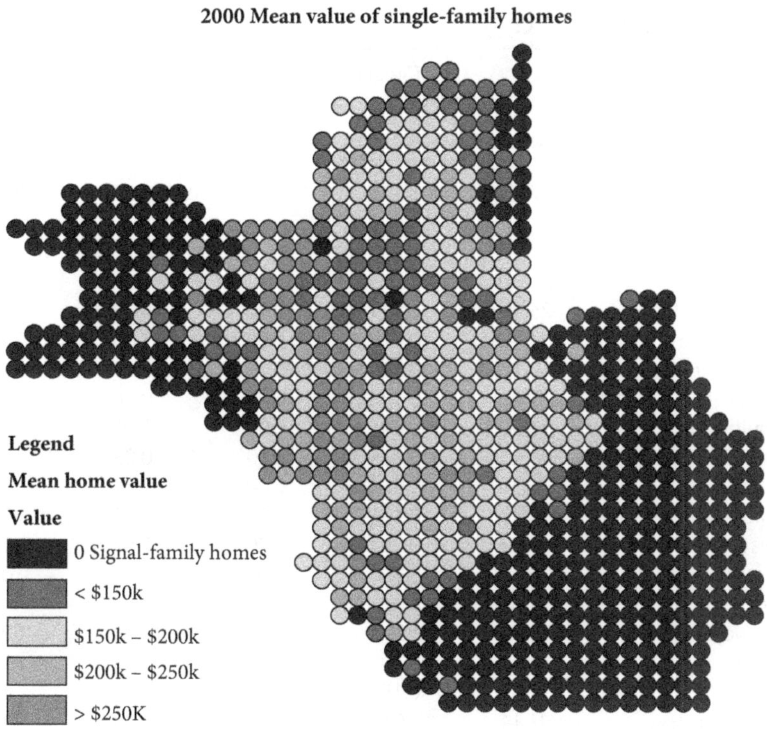

FIGURE 12.6 The mean value of single-family homes in 2000.

affected by the dependent variable and thus correlated with the error term, the model becomes a system of simultaneous equations. In structural form, the model looks like:

$$Y = X_n\beta_n + X_s\beta_s + \varepsilon_y, \tag{1}$$

$$X_s^i = Y\gamma_y^i + X_n\gamma_n^i + Z^i\gamma_z + \varepsilon_x^i, \quad i = 1, 2, \ldots, n \tag{2}$$

where Y is the population change vector, X_n is exogenous municipal profile variables, $X_s = (X_s^1, X_s^2, \ldots, X_s^n)$ is the endogenous municipal profile variables, Z^i is a vector of variables that affect endogenous profile variable i, but do not affect household location choices directly, the β's and γ's are the respective coefficients, and the ε's are the error terms. The structural model can be estimated in different ways, depending on the availability of appropriate instrumental variables and data.

If variables Z^i can be identified for each endogenous profile variable, and data on Z^i are available, then $(Z^1, Z^2, \ldots, Z^n)$ can serve as a set of instrumental variables because they are correlated with the endogenous explanatory variable and uncorrelated with the error term (i.e., causally unrelated to the dependent variable). In this case, the structural model

Table 12.1 Summary statistics

	Circular observations				Study area
Variable	Mean	Std. Err.	Min	Max	Total change (%)
Change in population	267.25	800.80	−809.25	9,206.78	276,942 (15.5%)
					Mean/Study Area
Distance to city center	25.45	12.62	0.00	56.36	
Share of forest land	0.49	0.41	0.00	1.00	0.50
Share of agricultural land	0.12	0.23	0.00	0.97	0.12
Share of single-family home	0.12	0.19	0.00	0.76	0.12
Share of multi-family home	0.00	0.01	0.00	0.10	0.00
Share of commercial land	0.01	0.03	0.00	0.23	0.01
Share of industrial land	0.01	0.05	0.00	0.74	0.01
Share of national forests	0.26	0.43	0.00	1.00	0.46
Share of water	0.02	0.06	0.00	0.59	0.02
Share of park and designated open space	0.03	0.07	0.00	0.80	0.03
Mean home value ($)	197,135	92,901	0.00	1,351,806	182,131
Mean lot size	1.81	8.30	0.00	170.17	0.63
School quality	1.04	0.15	0.75	1.53	1.05
2000 property tax levy	11.14	2.05	8.08	19.92	14.02
Population share in poverty	0.09	0.06	0.00	0.28	0.09
Urban population share	0.24	0.38	0.00	1.00	0.90

* Observations with zero population ($n = 178$) dropped from mean and standard deviation calculations.

can be estimated using two or three-stage least squares or partial or full information maximum likelihood estimation methods. For example, using two-stage least squares, first regress each endogenous variable in X_s on all exogenous variables in the model ($Z^1, Z^2, \ldots, Z^n$ and X_n) and obtain fitted values, $\widetilde{X}_s$. Then replace endogenous variables with fitted values in (1) in the second-stage regression.

$$Y = X_n\beta_n + \widetilde{X}_s\beta_s + \varepsilon_y \tag{3}$$

Estimates derived from instrumental variables and two-stage least squares are only as reliable as the instruments. If the chosen instruments are correlated with the error term, the bias problems encountered in the structural form remain unresolved. If the chosen instruments are poor (weakly correlated with the endogenous variables they are replacing), the result is poorly fitted values with little variation generated in the first stage. For this case study, appropriate instruments would need to be correlated with endogenous

Table 12.2 Correlation coefficients

	Mean home value	Medium household income	School quality	Property tax levy
Share of forest land	−0.47*	−0.14*	0.13*	−0.52*
Share of agricultural land	0.15*	0.10*	−0.01	0.00
Share of single-family home	0.33*	0.11*	−0.07	0.45*
Share of multi-family home	0.16*	−0.15*	−0.15*	0.28*
Share of commercial land	0.22*	−0.15*	−0.08*	0.26*
Share of industrial land	0.18*	−0.17*	−0.06	0.31*
Share of park and designated open space	0.30*	0.15*	−0.13*	0.36*

* Significant at the 5% level
Observations with no population in 2000 and in 2010 are dropped (n = 666).

amenities, uncorrelated with the error term, and not included in the set of explanatory exogenous amenities. It can be challenging to identify such variables.

When appropriate instruments cannot found, researchers may resort to estimating the reduced form of the structural model to uncover useful information about the effect of amenities on location choices. Solving for Y and $X_s = (X_s^1, X_s^2, \ldots, X_s^n)$, one can derive each of these endogenous variables as a function of X_n and perhaps $(Z^1, Z^2, \ldots, Z^n)$. These reduced-form equations can then be estimated using an appropriate method. The related literature strongly suggests that exogenous natural amenities influence development patterns, and these development patterns in turn affect the level of endogenous social amenities (see, e.g., Wu 2006). Thus, exogenous amenity variables can be used to explain endogenous amenity variables. The reduced form approach has a major drawback: estimation does not identify the structural coefficients found in (1). So, although estimating the reduced form in this case sheds light on how natural amenities affect the level of social amenities, it does not reveal the effects of various elements of municipal profile on population change.

The model specification in (1) potentially includes multiple endogenous covariates, for example, tax rate, school quality, and park access. This case study has a broad research question. How do elements of municipal profile affect population change? By narrowing the research question to focus on a single endogenous covariate, asking instead how property tax rate affects population change, a number of other estimation strategies from the treatment effects literature become available. Ordinary least squares

(OLS) estimation of treatment effects is typically biased because treatment effectiveness depends on factors that determine whether an observation gets treated. In a medical context, the effectiveness of medical intervention depends on the characteristics of the patient. At the same time, the characteristics of the patient determine whether the patient receives the treatment. Although a full discussion of treatment effects is beyond the scope of this chapter, a number of measures developed for nonexperimental settings in the medical field are increasingly being adopted by economists.

Two relevant estimation strategies from this literature are propensity score matching and difference-in-difference estimators, both described later in the context of property taxes. Propensity score matching could be used to evaluate the effect of differential tax rates on population growth. Propensity score matching estimates the treatment effect by systematically comparing pairs of observations from the treatment and nontreatment groups that are otherwise alike. This method first estimates a model predicting likelihood of treatment and pairs observations for comparison based on the resulting fitted values. For property taxes, this would involve identifying low- and high-tax observations, regressing tax rate on variables thought to influence tax rate (e.g., income distribution, demographics), and calculating predicted tax rates using the estimated coefficients. Each low-tax observation is paired with the high-tax observation with the closest predicted tax rate. By controlling across a number of relevant covariates, propensity score matching improves the likelihood that observed differences in population change are, in fact, the result of different tax rates.

Difference-in-difference methods, conversely, measure the effect of a treatment at a given point in time. The idea behind this method is to compare the treated group to itself before treatment, as well as to some other untreated control group. Simply evaluating treated observations relative to themselves before treatment does not account for events or trends that occur during treatment and affect the entire treatment group. If the researcher fails to include a nontreatment control group, then changes attributable to trends affecting the general population will be attributed inappropriately to treatment. In the property tax context, local population changes should not be attributed to changes in local tax rates without first accounting for the population change trends in the region. If the region as a whole is growing, then it is likely misleading to attribute local population growth entirely to local changes in tax rate. The researcher can net out the regional trend by comparing the treated group to an untreated control group.

The preceding case study details the data collection and processing used to construct a model of household locational choice (population change) in the Portland, Oregon metropolitan area. GIS software facilitate creative solutions for data at different resolutions. Still, substantial care is necessary in model specification and estimation to avoid the pitfalls associated with interactions and endogeneity.

In fact, the organization of the case study, particularly the model estimation section, closely follows the authors' efforts to take advantage of rich data for the study area while avoiding the aforementioned pitfalls. Although detailed presentation of results is beyond the scope of this chapter, a brief discussion of the empirical work that provides the basis for the case study follows.

The initial focus of this research was causal links between municipal profile and land use change, broadly, and, specifically, the effect of natural and social amenities on household location choice. The inclusion of a broad set of municipal attributes, some of which are undoubtedly endogenous, precludes unbiased OLS estimation. Broad controls also render instrumental variable estimation infeasible in practice due to the difficulties of identifying appropriate instruments. Without sacrificing broad controls, a reduced form model explaining endogenous municipal attributes in terms of exogenous attributes remains a feasible option. In this case, reduced-form estimation reveals that exogenous natural and historical amenities do indeed influence the level of endogenous municipal characteristics, including population change and density, median income, school quality, property taxes, and home values. Results indicate how natural characteristics (e.g., slope, elevation) and proximity to different natural amenities (e.g., water bodies, parks by type) influence endogenous characteristics. Of course, reduced-form estimation does not shed light on the underlying relationships between location choice and endogenous municipal characteristics. Furthermore, although they illustrate preferences, reduced-form results may have little policy relevance since natural features are difficult to change.

To quantify the underlying relationships in the absence of appropriate instruments, one alternative approach is to abandon broad controls and focus on a single municipal feature. In this case, although biased, preliminary OLS estimates highlight the impact of race/ethnicity on population change. Neighborhoods with high concentrations of black residents tended to shrink. Other minority neighborhoods grew fast, especially Asian neighborhoods, whereas majority neighborhoods grew modestly. These observations gave rise to a more focused research question: how do minority concentrations affect local municipal profile or neighborhood quality?

Simple correlations reveal that high minority concentrations are associated with lower school quality and higher crime. However, this approach ignores systematic differences between minority and majority groups, for example, in terms of income and educational attainment. To isolate the effect of minority concentration from the effect of these systematic differences, a more sophisticated method is required. In this case, treatment effects methods, specifically propensity score matching, are appropriate. Under propensity score matching, pairs of observations that differ in terms of minority concentration but that are similar in other dimensions of municipal profile are compared. In this context, that means a higher minority concentration community compared to a lower minority concentration community with the most similar other characteristics. Controlling for other dimensions of municipal profile can yield results that differ strikingly from simple correlations. For example, once other relevant municipal attributes were controlled for, communities with higher concentrations of black residents exhibited significantly lower crime rates than communities with black resident concentrations closer to the study area mean.

This case study provides a fairly specific example of data collection and processing. It also provides a general guide to estimation procedures and several descriptions of empirical applications. The fundamental challenge of modeling the relationships between land use and municipal profiles is the interconnected nature of individual location decisions and outcomes at the neighborhood, city, or regional scale. Quality data do not preclude the fundamental challenges of identification in the presence of endogeneity.

3. Conclusion

Land use and quality of life are inextricably linked. Collective household location decisions affect local municipal profiles, the character of cities, and landscapes. Shifting populations affect municipal profiles through voting, local public finance externalities, and peer externalities. At the same time, local municipal profiles affect location decisions because households choose the bundle of regulations and public goods they prefer. Understanding these effects and interactions is central to managing development and land use change in the future.

Several bodies of work within the economics literature shed light on household location decisions. Urban economics models identify the primary drivers behind observed suburbanization trends: rising incomes and falling commuting costs. However, these models tend to ignore many regulations, public goods, and amenities that affect household location choice. Local public finance models include preferences for these alternative bundles, but many such models are aspatial.

Emerging GIS software and rapidly improving data availability facilitate analysis within metropolitan areas, as opposed to at the county or city level. Although this approach is promising, the sound judgment of the researcher remains necessary. In particular, the researcher must construct relevant measures of local municipal profiles, often from a profusion of underlying GIS data. Some choice between alternative empirical measures of the same theoretical variable may be necessary. A significant effect may only appear with properly specified interaction terms. An inappropriate estimation strategy can bias results.

One additional obstacle facing researchers in this area is measuring endogenous social amenities. How do researchers measure the intangible desirability of neighborhoods and districts? For example, shopping is an amenity, but it is difficult to quantify. Even data on the location of retail stores are insufficient because big-box suburban shopping centers are qualitatively different from walkable urban shopping districts. Although measures of some social amenities are hard to come by, spatial analysis and the increasing profusion of GIS data present a wider array of potential measures than has previously existed. Although interactions between land use and municipal profiles are complex and may be difficult to measure, the tools available to address this issue have never been better.

Acknowledgments

This material is based on work supported by the US Forest Service Pacific Northwest Research Station under JVA No. 11-JV-11261985-073. Any opinions, findings, and conclusions or recommendations expressed in this material are those of the author(s) and do not necessarily reflect the views of the US Forest Service.

References

Alonso, W. 1964. *Location and land use*. Cambridge: Harvard University Press.

Anderson, S. T., and S. E. West. 2006. Open space, residential property values, and spatial context. *Regional Science and Urban Economics* 36(6): 773–789.

Banzhaf, H. S., and R. P. Walsh. 2008. Do people vote with their feet? An empirical test of Tiebout. *American Economic Review* 98(3), 843–863.

Bowes, D. R., and K. R. Ihlanfeldt. 2001. Identifying the impacts of rail transit stations on residential property values. *Journal of Urban Economics* 50(1): 1–25.

Brueckner, J. K., J. F. Thisse, and Y. Zenou. 1999. Why is central Paris rich and downtown Detroit poor? *European Economic Review* 43(1): 91–107.

Brueckner, J. K., and A. G. Largey. 2008. Social interaction and urban sprawl. *Journal of Urban Economics* 64(1): 18–34.

Brueckner, J. K., and S. S. Rosenthal. 2009. Gentrification and neighborhood housing cycles: Will America's future downtowns be rich? *Review of Economics and Statistics* 91(4): 725–743.

Carlino, G. A., and E. S. Mills. 1987. The determinants of county growth. *Journal of Regional Science* 27: 29–54.

Cohen, J. P., and C. C. Coughlin. 2008. Spatial hedonic models of airport noise, proximity, and housing price. *Journal of Regional Science* 48(5): 859–878.

DeFries, R. S., J. A. Foley, and G. P. Asner. 2004. Land-use choices: Balancing human needs and ecosystem function. *Frontiers in Ecology and the Environment* 2(5): 249–257.

Ellickson, B. 1971. Jurisdictional fragmentation and residential choice. *American Economic Review* 61(2): 334–339.

Epple, D., R. Filimon, and T. Romer. 1984. Equilibrium among jurisdictions: Toward an integrated treatment of voting and residential choice. *Journal of Public Economics* 24(3): 281–308.

Epple, D., and H. Sieg. 1999. Estimating equilibrium models of local jurisdictions. *Journal of Political Economy* 107(4): 645–681.

FAO/UNEP. 1999. *Terminology for integrated resources planning and management*. Rome, Italy and Nairobi, Kenya: Food and Agriculture Organization/United Nations Environmental Programme.

Foley, J. A. et al. 2005. Global consequences of land use. *Science* 309(5734): 570–574.

Fujita, M., and H. Ogawa. 1982. Multiple equilibria and structural transition of non-monocentric urban configurations. *Regional Science and Urban Economics* 12(2): 161–196.

Geoghegan, J., L. A. Wainger, and N. E. Bockstael. 1997. Spatial landscape indices in a hedonic framework. *Ecological Economics* 23(3): 251–264.

Irwin, E. G., and N. E. Bockstael. 2001. The problem of identifying land use spillovers: Measuring the effects of open space on residential property values. *American Journal of Agricultural Economics* 83(3): 698–704.

Irwin, E. G. 2002. The effects of open space on residential property values. *Land Economics* 78(4): 465–480.

LeRoy, S. F., and J. Sonstelie. 1983. Paradise lost and regained: Transportation innovation, income, and residential location. *Journal of Urban Economics* 13(1): 67–89.

Lopez, R. 2004. Urban sprawl and the risk for being overweight or obese. *American Journal of Public Health* 94: 1574–1579.

Mieszkowski, P., and E. S. Mills. 1993. The causes of metropolitan suburbanization. *Journal of Economic Perspectives* 7(3): 135–147.

Mills, E. S. 1967. An aggregative model of resource allocation in a metropolitan area. *American Economic Review* 57: 197–210.

Muth, R. F. 1969. *Cities and housing*. Chicago: University of Chicago Press.

Muth, R. F. 1971. Migration: Chicken or egg? *Southern Economic Journal* 37(3): 295–306.

Nechyba, T. J., and R. P. Walsh. 2004. Urban sprawl. *Journal of Economic Perspectives* 18(4): 177–200.

Oates, W. E. 1969. The effects of property taxes and local public spending on property values: An empirical study of tax capitalization and the Tiebout hypothesis. *Journal of Political Economy* 77(6): 957–971.

Ogawa, H., and M. Fujita. 1980. Equilibrium land use patterns in a non-monocentric city. *Journal of Regional Science* 20(4): 455–475.

Plantinga, A. J., and S. Bernell. 2007. The association between urban sprawl and obesity: Is it a two-way street? *Journal of Regional Science* 47(5): 857–879.

Smith, V. K., C. Poulos, and H. Kim. 2002. Treating open space as an urban amenity. *Resource and Energy Economics* 24(1): 107–129.

Tiebout, C. M. 1956. A pure theory of local expenditure. *Journal of Political Economy* 64(5): 416–424.

Troy, A., and J. M. Grove. 2008. Property values, parks, and crime. *Landscape and Urban Planning* 87(3): 233–245

Wu, J. 2006. Environmental amenities, urban sprawl, and community characteristics. *Journal of Environmental Economics and Management* 52(2): 527–547.

Wu, J. 2007. How does suburbanization affect local public finance and communities? *Review of Agricultural Economics* 29(Fall 2007): 564–571.

PART III

METHODOLOGICAL DEVELOPMENTS

CHAPTER 13

AN ASSESSMENT OF EMPIRICAL METHODS FOR MODELING LAND USE

ELENA G. IRWIN AND DOUGLAS H. WRENN

Many of society's most pressing socioeconomic and environmental issues relate in some way to land use and land use change. Environmental problems such as carbon cycling (Post et al. 1982; Schimel 1995), terrestrial water cycles (Vorosmarty and Sahagian 2000), loss of biodiversity (Sala et al. 2000), and climate change (Vitousek et al. 1997) are directly or indirectly impacted by anthropogenic land use decisions. From a socioeconomic perspective, issues such as sprawl and suburbanization, congestion, public service provisioning, and segregation are fundamentally related to land use change and land use policies (Anas et al. 1998; Glaeser anf Kahn 2004; Nechyba and Walsh 2004).

The wide-ranging issues surrounding land use have led policy makers and researchers alike to develop land use models as a means of better understanding policy and other effects. A variety of empirical land use modeling approaches is evident across multiple academic disciplines. These approaches often have been distinguished by a key difference in research focus: identification of specific parameters of the underlying process versus spatial prediction of land use patterns. Economists typically have focused on causal *identification* of the underlying economic processes that generate land use outcomes and patterns using reduced-form models to identify one or more key parameter values. For example, hedonic models of land values are common in which the research question is to identify the influence of a specific landscape feature or spatially articulated policy on equilibrium land prices. The advantage of this approach is that consistent and unbiased parameter estimates can be recovered to infer something about the effect of a marginal change on the equilibrium. This approach is limited for spatial prediction or counterfactual policy simulation, however, since the focus is on explaining the observed price equilibrium, and the underlying structural parameters of demand and supply are not recovered. Geographers and others outside of economics typically have focused on empirical prediction of land use patterns and changes, for example, by calibrating model parameters to derive transition rules that describe the evolution of land use or land cover over space and time. Although these models are useful for description and perhaps for the very short-run prediction of patterns, they provide little insight into the underlying economic and other processes that generate these patterns. Thus, they also cannot be used for counterfactual policy simulation or any spatial prediction with nonmarginal changes. More recently, these disciplinary distinctions have blurred. Geographers have sought to develop agent-based models that provide a process-based approach to land use modeling, and economists have pursued structural econometric models that can be used to predict large-scale changes over time and space.

The purpose of this chapter is to provide an overview and assessment of the main methods used to model land use and land use change, with a focus on newer methods. We focus on empirical models, which we define broadly as models that use data on land use and the underlying demand and supply processes to specify model parameters in some way. We array these models along two dimensions: first, models that are structural versus reduced-form and second, econometric models versus other empirical approaches that are used to specify parameter values. Rather than providing an in-depth primer on these modeling techniques, our goal is to present a general overview and a targeted assessment. The key questions we seek to address are (1) what are the advantages and disadvantages of these various empirical approaches to modeling land use and land use change, (2) which questions are best suited to be answered using one versus the other approach, and (3) where are the gaps in the current literature?

The remainder of the chapter is organized as follows. Following a general discussion of modeling approaches, we turn to the particular case of modeling land use and land use change. We ask what makes modeling land use and land use change special and how the various modeling approaches stack up with respect to these key considerations. We provide a discussion of each of the main modeling approaches, highlighting strengths and weaknesses and illustrating with a few recent examples from the literature. We conclude with some thoughts about the existing gaps in the literature and future research needs.

1. An Overview of Modeling Methods

Any economic model begins with a structural model of the underlying economic processes, for example, supply and demand equations, indirect utility function (household side), or cost function (firm side), that are hypothesized to generate an observed market equilibrium. Most economists would consider a structural econometric model to be the gold standard for empirically modeling this process. Put simply, this approach uses econometric methods to recover the full set of parameters of the underlying structural model by making explicit assumptions about what is and is not observed (Timmins and Schlenker 2009). For example, in a model of land development, the underlying structural parameters of a land developers' profit or cost functions would be recovered using econometric methods given a series of assumptions about functional form, choice sets, equilibrium in the market, and the distribution of the unobservables. The advantage of a structural econometric approach is that by modeling these processes explicitly, it is possible to account for the endogeneity of prices and other market-level or nonmarket feedbacks that determine the equilibrium. A structural modeling approach is necessary for counterfactual policy simulation, in which the goal is to evaluate the impacts of a nonmarginal policy change on land use outcomes.[1] This is particularly important when modeling complex processes such as land use in which nonmarginal feedbacks can arise from interactions within and between the socioeconomic and biophysical systems.

Although we consider structural econometric modeling to be the benchmark, the type of model implemented is ultimately determined by the particular research question, limitations of theory and data, and the willingness of the researcher to make certain assumptions. One of the main disadvantages of structural econometric modeling is that the researcher must be willing to make certain modeling assumptions regarding the distributions of unobserved variables, the choice sets, the equilibrium relationship in the market, and the functional forms that represent the behavioral equations. Theoretical models often provide key insights into the processes at work—for example, utility maximization or cost minimization—but they rarely provide an explicit functional form for the objective functions, a specific distribution for the error structure, or guidance on specification of choice sets or how to best define equilibrium in the market. In addition, even if a robust empirical specification can be established, it still may be difficult to gather data on all of the processes deemed important in answering a particular research question. This is especially true in the area of land use modeling, given the complexity of interactions across multiple spatial and temporal scales.

Given the challenges involved in fully estimating structural models, alternative approaches are often pursued. One alternative is to retain a structural modeling approach, but to take a less rigorous approach to parameter specification. Rather than estimating the structural parameters in a manner that is fully consistent with the observed data, a more ad hoc econometric strategy may be pursued or a combination of empirical approaches used. For example, utility or cost parameters may be estimated using multiple datasets taken from different sources or settings, or key parameter values may simply be taken from the results of other studies reported in the literature (e.g., such as a demand or supply elasticity). A limitation of this approach is that the parameters may reflect different underlying conditions of demand and supply that are not

[1] Although it is not always obvious what constitutes a marginal versus nonmarginal change, the intent is to distinguish marginal changes as small changes that do not shift the underlying equilibrium and nonmarginal changes as those that are large enough that they could. For example, a major downzoning, in which the maximum allowable number of lots decreases from one house per acre to one house per 50 acres would be likely to shift residential land supply and induce a demand response and therefore is nonmarginal. Conversely, an incremental change in a local jurisdiction's budget for farmland preservation is unlikely to generate a large shift in the demand or supply of land preservation and is therefore marginal.

consistent with any single equilibrium. The advantage is that it may be easier to parameterize a structural model using some combination of empirical methods and data or, in cases in which econometric estimation of the structural model is infeasible, this may be the only possible means to parameterize a structural model.

In other cases, when model intractability or data limitations prevent structural econometric estimation of the model, a reduced-form model is estimated instead. Reduced-form models are models of an equilibrium outcome (e.g., land use, land use change, or land or housing prices) derived from an underlying structural model of demand and supply and expressed in terms of the simultaneous equilibrium relationship. Unless further structure is imposed, the explanatory variables included in a reduced-form equation cannot be attributed to a specific underlying structural process but instead reflect the net effects of these variables on the equilibrium outcome. In most cases, this implies that parameter estimates cannot be used to simulate the impacts of a nonmarginal change on land use outcomes.

In many reduced-form models of land use and land use change, the model may not be fully reduced to only exogenous variables—that is, the model may include one or more endogenous explanatory variables that are determined by the same equilibrium process as the dependent variable. This is particularly true for land use models in which local interactions imply that many of the variables are jointly determined by the same equilibrium process. For example, in the case of open space spillovers that influence the amenity value of a location, the spatial distribution of open space is usually endogenous to the land market, implying that the spatial patterns of residential and open space are jointly determined. If the endogeneity is properly dealt with, then the estimation will yield a consistent estimate of the reduced-form parameters, which can then be used in hypothesis testing or for simulation of marginal changes. The results can only be interpreted as representing the effect of a marginal change and are conditional on the assumption that the equilibrium is unchanged.

In some cases, a reduced-form model is preferred when the research is focused on the identification of one or several key reduced-form parameters rather than on recovering the underlying structure. As discussed in depth in Chapter 18 by Towe, Lewis, and Lynch in this handbook, this is the case with reduced-form models used in quasi-experimental designs in which the structural system has been fully solved so that the dependent variable is defined only in terms of exogenous variables. This approach is touted as being free of functional form assumptions and, assuming that the covariates are indeed exogenous, provides a transparent identification strategy. It should be noted, however, that reduced-form models are not free from assumptions, and it is best to begin any modeling exercise with a review of the relevant theoretical literature. Keane (2010) points out that even in the case of the most clever instrument or quasi-experimental setting, if the initial modeling exercise is not based on some economic model, then it is impossible to assign meaning to the output.

2. What Is Special About Modeling Land Use?

We do not consider the approach to modeling land use or land markets to be any different from the basic approach used in economics to model any behavioral process. Land development outcomes, for example, are determined by the constrained utility-maximizing location decisions of households based on their preferences over parcel, neighborhood, and regional characteristics, and the supply decisions of developers and landowners are based on expectations of profits and costs subject to technological and regulatory constraints. However, there are several features of land and related markets (e.g., housing) that deserve special attention because of their importance in determining market equilibrium and the spatial distribution of land use and land use change.

First, land is an extremely *heterogeneous* good over which individuals have heterogeneous preferences and heterogeneous expectations about the future. Each of these sources of heterogeneity is hypothesized to influence land use outcomes. The evolution of leapfrog development, for example, has been alternatively explained as the result of heterogeneous land quality (Harvey and Clark 1965), heterogeneous preferences over large exurban lots (Newburn and Berck 2011), or heterogeneous expectations by land developers (Mills 1981).

Second, land use and land use changes are the outcomes of market interactions among many heterogeneous individuals, which generate market and nonmarket feedbacks that also influence these land use outcomes. These feedbacks may exist at multiple spatial and temporal scales. For example, individual households may buy and sell houses depending on their own agreed-upon terms of trade, which are influenced by the number of other buyers and sellers of similar houses on the market and by nonmarket feedbacks, such as congestion externalities or agglomeration benefits. The implication for modeling is that many so-called explanatory variables are likely to be endogenous in a model of land use or land use change and that relevant feedbacks may exist at multiple scales, which introduces additional challenges for empirical modeling.

Third, both the causes and impacts of land use change are cumulative and often irreversible, implying that dynamics over time are important. Economists typically use the word "dynamics" to mean forward-looking behavior, whereas most noneconomists use it to mean changes in state variables over time without regard to expectations. Both types of dynamics are important in the land use modeling context. Forward-looking behavior is a critical element of many economic land use models—for example, farmers who make current planting decisions based on anticipated future prices of agricultural commodities and forest managers who make optimal harvesting decisions based on expected growth rates and future prices. Accounting for changes in land use over time is an equally important modeling goal and one that is particularly important for policy evaluation and scenarios.

3. A Comparison of Approaches

The complexities involved in modeling land use and land use change prevent any single model from accounting for all the aspects of land use and land use change. Here we summarize three main approaches to modeling land use and land use change: reduced-form econometric models, structural econometric models and, for lack of a better term, other spatial simulation models. We provide a synthesis of their strengths and weaknesses particularly as they relate to the ability of the modeling approach to capture the critical aspects of land use modeling discussed above: heterogeneity, interactions, and dynamics. Our interest is in models that are able to account for spatial heterogeneity and interactions and therefore we focus on models that are able to capture heterogeneity and interactions at either a parcel or neighborhood scales.

3.1 Reduced-Form Econometric Models of Land Use Change

Because land use is most often characterized as a categorical variable, estimation of land use and land use change models using spatially disaggregated data requires a discrete choice framework. The earliest reduced-form models of land use and land use change focused on binary or multinomial discrete choice models of discrete land use or land cover categories (e.g., Bockstael 1996; Nelson and Hellerstein 1997; Bockstael 1996). Recognizing the importance of intertemporal decision making by landowners, the next generation of spatially disaggregate models of land use focused on the optimal timing decision of conversion at the parcel level (Irwin and Bockstael 2002; Newburn and Berck 2006; Towe et al. 2008). More recently, researchers have incorporated both discrete and continuous change aspects of land use (Lewis et al. 2009; Lewis 2010; Wrenn 2012). For example, conditional on the decision to convert a parcel to a residential subdivision, the parcel owner must make a decision about the optimal number of buildable lots to create. The outcome of both the discrete land use change and the density of development, which is a continuous variable, have important impacts on many issues directly related to land use and its spatial configuration, including ecosystem fragmentation and loss of farmland, urban sprawl, and optimal zoning and regulatory policy.

There are a number of reasons why researchers are only beginning to model these joint decisions. First, modeling timing and intensity require a modeling technique that can jointly model the two decisions and account for the necessary correlations between them. Although multistage econometric models have existed for some time, land use researchers are just beginning to adapt these to the particular behavioral processes unique to land use change.

Second, much of the theory in the real options investment literature that has been used to motivate econometric land use change models (Capozza and Helsley 1990; Dixit and Pindyck 1994) is focused on the timing decision and does not account for variation in parcel sizes, regulatory structures, or the potential for intensity differences between parcels. Versions of the real options model that do account for timing, intensity, and space provide theoretical predictions and testable hypotheses for both the timing and intensity decisions, but those models have only recently been adapted to land use questions.

And finally, a lack of data on the original decision-making parcel has made the second-stage intensity decision irrelevant. Although geographic information system (GIS) parcel-level data are used extensively in reduced-form models, researchers usually only have data on individual lots (children) and not on the original parcel (parent) from which they were formed. In order to model this parent-child process, it is necessary to combine individual parcels into their original parent parcel; this is particularly important in the case of residential subdivision development where hundreds of small lots can be produced from a single agriculture parcel. As a solution to this problem, researchers have combined plat maps with GIS parcel data as a means of determining the parent-child process. Using these new parcel-level panel datasets, models of the optimal timing and intensity decision can be estimated.

Two recent papers provide good examples of how these new datasets can be combined with joint econometric models to evaluate important land use policy questions. In a model of land use and ecosystem change, Lewis (2010) combines a spatial-temporal dataset of land use change with a Probit-Poisson model to estimate an econometric model of timing and intensity. Using the coefficient values from the model, Lewis (2010) generates land use change simulations that are then combined with an ecological model to determine how current land use configurations and policies are impacting the likelihood of extinction of green frogs. Because the survival rate of green frogs is determined not just by the timing and location of development, but also by the intensity of development, it is imperative that the second-stage intensity decision be modeled in the analysis of this question. In his simulation model, Lewis shows that intensity indeed plays an important role in determining the future probability of extinction for green frogs (see also Chapter 15 by Plantinga and Lewis in this handbook).

In a Probit-Poisson model of residential subdivision development, Wrenn (2012) combines historical subdivision data with data on regulatory delay over space and time to evaluate the role of spatiotemporal heterogeneity in explaining fragmentation and sprawl in an urbanizing Maryland county. Real options theory predicts that delay in costs can impact both the timing and intensity of an investment decision if the owner of the real option has control over both the timing and the size of the project. In the land use context, this implies that it is important to account for the effect of cost or regulatory delay on both the timing and intensity decision. He finds that delay indeed impacts both decisions, reducing both the probability of development and the optimal number of lots created. The simulations also provide evidence that policy-induced differences in regulatory cost are contributing to increased sprawl and fragmentation of the landscape.

These models provide improvements over previous reduced-form models, but still have a number of limitations. First, although they do a good job of accounting for parcel heterogeneity, they do not explicitly account for agent heterogeneity because the agent's characteristics are not modeled separately from those of the parcel. In the case of panel data, individual random effects are used to account for some of this unobserved heterogeneity, but this technique does not explicitly separate out the individual characteristics. Second, because the models are reduced-form in nature, they are not able to capture general equilibrium feedbacks. As a result, endogeneity issues are dealt with using traditional econometric techniques, and analysis and simulation studies are confined to marginal changes. Third, the models can account for out-of-sample predictions of land use change by using the coefficient values from the models to simulate alternate landscapes over time. However, these predictions are limited to marginal changes because the model does not account for feedbacks or forward-looking expectations during the estimation process.[2]

To account for feedback effects and agent heterogeneity as well as model nonmarginal changes in policy instruments, researchers have begun to apply structural models to model the underlying demand and supply processes of land use.

3.2 Structural Econometric Models of Land and Housing Markets

Structural models of land use include models of the demand or supply of land itself or of output markets in which the derived demand for land as an input is modeled. For example, models of agricultural production that consider land as a derived input generate predictions of agricultural land use as the result of farmers' optimal cropping decisions. Empirical structural models of land use are not new; structural agricultural production models that posited land use as the result of optimal decision making by a representative farmer and are estimated using county-level data have a long tradition in agricultural economics (e.g., Lichtenberg 1989; Wu and Segerson 1995; Plantinga 1996). However, when richer models were made possible by the availability of spatially disaggregated microdata (e.g., at the parcel level), new identification challenges were also introduced (e.g., due to heterogeneity and selection effects) that made structural econometric modeling more challenging. This led to a focus on reduced-form models with clear identification strategies. Nonetheless, some progress in estimating structural econometric models with microdata has been made, most notably with models of household demand for residential housing[3] and, to a lesser extent, models of land and housing supply. These

[2] Although reduced-form models do not model dynamics in the traditional sense, with forward-looking agents forming expectations and maximizing discounted present values of uncertain future payoffs (e.g., Rust 1987), some researchers have built individual predictions of future economic variables into their models using time-series techniques to capture the dynamics (Cunningham 2007; Bulan et al. 2009).

[3] For a full review of equilibrium sorting models and their connection to hedonic models and models of differentiated products, see Chapter 14 in this handbook by Klaiber and Kuminoff and reviews by Klaiber and Smith (2011) and Kuminoff, Smith, and Timmins (2012).

models have been usefully applied to simulate policies or the effect of other hypothetical nonmarginal changes that may push the system to a new equilibrium. Here we focus our discussion on structural modeling of urban land and housing markets with an emphasis on how these models account for endogenous price and other market and equilibrium feedbacks.

The basic assumption of all structural models is that the land and housing markets are in a spatial equilibrium. Spatial equilibrium conditions differ depending on the model assumptions. For example, in a residential land use model with homogeneous households, such as the canonical monocentric model, spatial equilibrium is characterized by equal utility across space since any advantage or disadvantage of a location is capitalized into its price. Given heterogeneity in preferences or incomes, as is the case with household sorting models, spatial equilibrium in the residential land market is characterized by each household having made an optimal decision, given the location and supply decisions of all other agents. In other words, it is not possible for any agent to make himself better off by making a different choice. As with the homogeneous case, the equilibrating element of this process is price. The resulting spatial equilibrium is often characterized by a hedonic function that is comprised of the market-clearing bid and offer curves of heterogeneous agents (Rosen 1974). Although Rosen (1974) provides a thorough description of how the hedonic equilibrium is achieved, he does not make explicit how these bids and offers lead to a spatial equilibrium. Tiebout (1956) was the first to observe that it is the process of heterogeneous agents sorting themselves across differentiated neighborhoods that determines the spatial equilibrium. In this model, the larger region is subdivided into many heterogeneous or differentiated locations; as agents sort, they bid on different neighborhoods, and prices are determined by the intersection of the bid and offer curves of the agents moving to each neighborhood. Households choose a neighborhood, conditional on their budgets, to maximize utility, and developers provide housing, given technological and regulatory constraints, to maximize profits. The sorting process continues until no one has the incentive to move and the region reaches a spatial equilibrium.

It is the application of the Tiebout (1956) theory to housing markets that allows researchers to specify and estimate equilibrium sorting models. By combining the information provided by the hedonic equilibrium (Rosen 1974; Ekeland et al. 2004) with a description of the choice process that leads heterogeneous agents to sort (McFadden 1974; Berry et al. 1995), researchers are able to estimate the structural parameters of the model; that is, it is the information revealed by households about their preferences for different neighborhoods that allow researchers to specify and estimate the structural parameters of the equilibrium sorting model and to characterize the heterogeneity of preferences for local public goods and amenities. The equilibrium sorting framework combines a mixture of discrete (neighborhood) choices with continuous choices (characteristics of the houses). The approach makes explicit how preference-induced sorting can lead to endogenous feedbacks that make it very challenging to use estimates from reduced-form land use models to determine amenity values (Epple and Sieg 1999; Bayer and Timmins 2005).

In some cases, the supply of amenities can be taken as exogenous, and households sort to take advantage of these amenities. Often, however, the amenities in a particular area are either completely determined by the sorting process or significantly affected by it. As an example, one neighborhood may have a particularly nice open space area. As households move to this area, they bid up the price. If higher house prices result in greater tax revenues for schools, then the attraction of the open space area can lead to increased school quality, which leads to additional feedbacks. As more people move in, it can also lead to a reduction in the quality of the open space areas as they become congested or as the actions of residents degrade the quality of them. Thus, even if the original amenity was exogenous, its future value and the values of other public goods may be determined by the sorting process.

Because many environmental amenities are not explicitly traded, researchers have used the theory and econometrics of hedonic and discrete-choice models of differentiated product markets to uncover willingness to pay (WTP) for various amenities from local housing values. The theory of capitalization (Oates 1969) provides evidence that house prices will reflect the value of both the structural characteristics of the house as well as the local public goods and amenities in the house's neighborhood. By observing the outcome of the sorting process and the resulting prices of houses sold across different neighborhoods, researchers can estimate values of households' WTP for the public goods and environmental amenities in those neighborhoods.[4] Because the models are structural, they can also be used to simulate counterfactual policy analysis to analyze the costs and benefits of alternative policies.

Given the clear advantages of this equilibrium sorting framework, it is important to highlight both what these models do well and what they do not do so well in terms of land use modeling. Unlike reduced-form models, structural models capture agent heterogeneity (separate from neighborhood heterogeneity) by including information on income, household composition, education, and other demographic factors that are hypothesized to affect preferences. These data are interacted with neighborhood-level amenity values, which allows the value placed on local public goods and amenities to vary with the characteristics of the individual household. One disadvantage, however, is that because structural models must be estimated at the neighborhood level, they miss much of the spatial heterogeneity at the parcel level that is captured in reduced-form models.[5]

[4] This outcome relies on a number of assumptions that may not hold in every context, such as being able to capture and measure all the relevant amenities as well as find suitable instruments that can control for the unobservable amenities that cannot be measured.

[5] To achieve consistency and efficiency in equilibrium sorting models, the number of households or decisions makers must rise faster than the number of choices (Berry et al. 2004). Thus, the choice set in these models includes neighborhoods, which are geographically aggregated areas that have been constructed to be internally homogeneous but differentiated relative to other locations. Even assuming consistent segregation of the study area into neighborhoods, it is still not possible, for technical reasons, to estimate these models at the parcel level.

Another advantage of these models is their ability to account for market and non-market feedbacks. Researchers first specify a utility or indirect utility function that reflects the fundamental preference relationships from microeconomic theory (i.e., monotonic and convex preferences). Then, using data on the individual characteristics of the agents and their respective choices, they estimate the structural parameters of the function. Because these estimates reflect the underlying preference structure of the agents and how they respond to changes in market fundamentals, the model can be used to examine counterfactual policy scenarios in which large-scale nonmarginal changes occur, which cause a resorting of agents and a shift the market equilibrium. Although this is a clear advantage from the policy analysis perspective, these feedbacks and their predictions for land use change are only conducted at the neighborhood scale or higher. In most cases, this is sufficient, but smaller scale analysis of feedbacks and land use change may be necessary for certain research questions, such as those related to land fragmentation, loss of biodiversity, and the impact of land use change on ecosystems.

In addition to their lack of spatial disaggregation, another disadvantage of current structural models is that they are largely static. By static, we mean that they do not account for the formation of expectations by the agents about future house price values and local neighborhood amenities and how individual decisions affect those values.

A variety of papers apply equilibrium sorting models to policy questions, but only a few look explicitly at issues of land use. We highlight two of the most recent examples: Walsh (2007) and Klaiber and Phaneuf (2010). Both of these papers deal with the issue of open space allocation and valuation but use different modeling techniques. We explain the key differences between the two and highlight their key findings.

Walsh (2007) applies a vertical or "pure characteristics" sorting model (Epple and Sieg 1999) to the question of the equilibrium impacts of open space protection and growth control policies. As is the case with all equilibrium sorting models, the larger region is delineated into exhaustive and mutually exclusive neighborhoods. The vertical sorting model assumes that all households place equal weight on the value rank of the neighborhoods but have heterogeneous preferences for those neighborhoods as a result of differences in personal characteristics. The main implication of this vertical specification is that households, when they substitute, only consider those neighborhoods that are directly adjacent to them in preference and income space.

Using this model, Walsh (2007) evaluates open space policy with an approach that incorporates the endogenous formation of private open space and residential land. Each neighborhood has two types of open space—public open space, which he assumes is exogenously provided, and private open space, which is provided as a result of the development decisions of households and land developers. Households value their relative location to the public open space and trade off this type of open space with private open space relative to their distance from it. The key finding of this paper is that if one allows for the endogenous adjustment of private open space, then an increase in public open space can actually lead to a reduction in overall open space in the region. This results stems from the fact that as public open space in a neighborhood increases, it both increases the demand for the location and reduces the amount of private open space needed as households have better access to the public amenity. The result is an overall reduction in land that is preserved by a policy that was designed to do just the opposite.

Klaiber and Phaneuf (2010) apply a random-utility, horizontal sorting model (Bayer et al. 2004) to a similar research question related to open space valuation and protection but allow the preference structure and types of open space to be more flexible. Unlike the vertical sorting model, horizontal models allow preferences for alternatives, as well as the weights of the individual rankings of those alternatives, to vary. For example, in the vertical model, all households would assign the same neighborhood ranking to good school districts regardless of the characteristics of the household, and household-specific preferences would determine their actual choice. In the horizontal model, the relative ranking of each choice is not the same for all households and instead depends on the characteristics of the household. For example, households with young children are likely to rank neighborhoods with good schools higher than would senior citizens.

The innovation of the Klaiber and Phaneuf model, in terms of land use and open space nonmarket valuation and allocation, is to allow not only the preferences and ranking of neighborhood alternatives to vary by household type, but also to allow open space amenities to be disaggregated into multiple categories. The paper also uses data that allows for higher spatial resolution than past work. This paper provides several important findings. First, they find that distinguishing among different types of open space is critical in determining the tradeoffs people make during the sorting process. They find that different types of open space amenities are valued differently depending on the characteristics of the household. Second, they find that as the scale of the open space policy increases, the welfare estimates between partial and general equilibrium models diverge.[6] Finally, they show that localized and targeted open space policies are more likely to be efficient than region-wide policies that do not account for household heterogeneity. This result follows from the fact that the interactions between household characteristics and different types of open space provide drastically different WTP values.

Like the reduced-form models reviewed in the previous sections, most equilibrium sorting models to-date are static in the sense that they do not take into account the formation of expectations by the agents in terms of prices, costs, and other amenity variables. However, given that location choice and land use conversion are either irreversible or difficult to reverse, this implies that agents, when choosing to relocate (demand) or develop (supply), consider not just current market conditions, but also take into account the current and expected future value of all state variables. For example, conventional static sorting models assume that agents move freely between locations without regard for technological, institutional, or social constraints. In the real world, however, agents

[6] This finding is particularly important in the analysis of land use policy. For marginal land use policy changes, it indicates that partial equilibrium or reduced-form analysis may be sufficient to provide insight into marginal willingness to pay values of the policy. However, when policy changes are such that they induce a resorting of households, then it is likely that reduced-form analysis will not provide accurate welfare measure.

consider moving costs, wealth constraints resulting from changes in home equity values, and social ties to current locations when deciding to move from one place to another. These constraints influence the sorting equilibrium and the estimation of household demand for locational attributes. Bayer et al. (2009), for example, show the importance of accounting for moving costs in estimating households' demand for air quality.

Unlike static choice models, dynamic discrete choice models take account of both the evolution of the model's state variables and how agents form expectations about future values of these variables. They may also account explicitly for the interactions between agents. The parameters are estimated in these dynamic models by nesting a Bellman-style optimization equation in an empirical optimization technique. The results of these models describe agent's preferences and beliefs about technological and intuitional constraints as they evolve over time. One of the main issues with these models is the curse of dimensionality and the fact that the complexity of the estimation techniques required to solve these models increases rapidly with the number of state variables or interactions among agents (Aguirregabiria and Mira 2010). Each state variable is endogenously determined within the dynamic optimization framework, and agents are assumed to form expectations over each of these variables in each period. Thus, as the size of the state space increases so does the complexity of the empirical estimation process, making large state space models over many periods empirically infeasible.

Two recent papers have attempted to estimate structural models with forward-looking expectations. Bayer et al. (2011) extend the structural household sorting model to include the formation of expectations about prices and local amenities and show that including these in the model has a substantial effect on the marginal WTP values relative to those computed using the static model.[7] They find a significant divergence between the predictions of the dynamic model from those of the static sorting model. The main factor driving the wedge between the values in the two models is the introduction of moving costs and of wealth formation from capital gains in house values, which impact the budget constraint apart from income.

Murphy (2013) estimates a dynamic model of housing supply that takes into account both variable and fixed costs, as well as uncertainty over future land use regulations. It is has been shown by a number of authors (Mayer and Somerville 2000; Glaeser et al. 2005) that land use regulations, when they translate into a reduction in the elasticity of housing supply, can lead to significant increases in home prices. In this paper, Murphy captures local cost uncertainties in the development process using a dynamic fixed effects technique and finds that the majority of the rise in home prices in the San Francisco Bay area over his study period could be attributed to regulatory effects that reduce the ability of the supply side of the market to respond to demand. This result has

[7] They give the example of a neighborhood in which the change in environmental quality or crime is expected to be drastic in the future. As a result, households may be more willing to purchase in these neighborhoods at a lower price if the future expected improvements mean larger expected capital gains.

important implications for policy in the area of housing supply and provides further evidence of the impact of land use regulations on home prices and supply responses to demand.

3.3 Other Spatial Simulation Models of Land Use Change

Because of data demands, necessary assumptions, and complexity of the modeling techniques that are typically needed, it is not always be possible to estimate a structural econometric model. This is particularly true when the interest is in accounting for the sequencing of land use changes over time, for example, due to growing population in a region. In such cases, a static spatial equilibrium assumption is problematic since the long-run spatial equilibrium land use pattern is assumed to be instantaneously reached, and the sequencing over time or space of individual agents' decisions is not determined (Chen et al. 2011).

Spatial simulation models have emerged as a means of representing land markets in a spatially explicit framework that can better capture changes in land use patterns over time. Although a variety of approaches to spatial simulation exist, these models have in common the approach of a spatially explicit framework in which changes in land use patterns over time are simulated as the result of individual-level decisions regarding land use or location. Many different types of land use models may be adapted to a spatial simulation framework. For example, as discussed in Chapter 15 by Plantinga and Lewis in this handbook, coefficients from land use models estimated with aspatial plot-level data on land use, land characteristics and net returns have been used to simulate predicted spatial patterns of land use under alternative policy scenarios by applying these estimates to spatially disaggregated land use data. And, as we have already discussed and is further detailed in Chapter 14 by Klaiber and Kuminoff in this handbook, structural econometric models can be used to simulate changes in residential location and land use at a neighborhood scale. Because these empirical simulation methods are discussed in detail in these other chapters, here we focus on two other types of spatial models that are used in simulation: (1) spatial equilibrium models that account for dynamics by incorporating some exogenous change over time, such as population or income growth and (2) agent-based models that focus on individual market trades in the absence of an overall market equilibrium assumption.

Although the strength of these types of spatial simulation models is in representing spatial heterogeneity and capturing some forms of dynamics, their weakness is in model specification. In the absence of a fully structural econometric estimation approach, empirical specification of a spatial simulation model may proceed in various ways. For example, reduced-form parameters may be estimated using datasets taken from different sources or settings. Secondary data on observable outcomes, including land use, prices, and other variables that influence land or housing markets, or primary data collected from surveys or lab or field experiments may be used. In other cases, estimates reported in the literature may be used to specify key parameters or reasonable ranges of these parameters, for example, demand or supply elasticities. Once specified, simulation of these spatial simulation models can proceed in an analogous fashion to that of structural econometric models by using the empirically specified structural equations to predict land use outcomes, given a policy shift or other changes. A limitation of this approach to empirical specification is that the parameters may reflect different underlying conditions of demand and supply that are inconsistent with any single equilibrium (or, more generally, with any single observable outcome). Unobserved differences in macroeconomic variables or other constraints that differ across different regions, scales, or time periods, for example, can cause differences in the underlying demand and supply processes.

Spatial equilibrium simulation models are based on an assumption of instantaneous adjustment of prices to a spatial equilibrium. Spatial equilibrium prices evolve over time, given exogenous changes in population, income, or some other variable. Agents may be myopic, in which case the equilibrium is conditional on current levels, or forward-looking, in which case spatial equilibrium is determined by agents' expectations over future growth. The model may account for market frictions, such as informational asymmetry, credit constraints, construction lags, search costs, which may prevent instantaneous adjustment to the long-run spatial equilibrium. Thus, it is possible to draw a distinction between a short-run equilibrium, in which market frictions create a binding constraint, and an unconstrained long-run equilibrium. Given an analytical expression for price as a function of heterogeneous space and specified parameter values, simulation methods can be used to predict how growth over time generates changes in spatial equilibrium land use patterns.

Although there are very good examples of structural spatial simulation models that consider how spatially heterogeneous costs or amenities influence land use patterns, many are static and describe only the long-run spatial equilibrium in the absence of growth (e.g., Wu and Plantinga 2003; Tajibaeva et al. 2008). The canonical urban economic model with growth is Capozza and Helsley (1989), in which the influence of deterministic population growth on the land value gradient is considered in a one-dimensional monocentric model. However, because their interest is in characterizing how growth influences land values, the authors do not consider changes in the land development pattern over time. Instead they solve for an analytical expression of long run spatial equilibrium land prices to show how the market value of developed and agricultural land depends on the growth rate. Newburn and Berck (2011) extend this model by simulating it across time for a stylized exurban region with population growth. Their model provides a good example of how a spatial equilibrium model, which is dynamic in terms of how population growth influences land rents and development decisions, can be simulated and made to "step through time" to generate spatial predictions of land use change over time. Household behavior is specified by a Cobb-Douglas utility function in which households are assumed to trade-off a composite good and lot size. Lots may be either small (suburban) or large (exurban) and household preferences over these lot sizes are heterogeneous. Deterministic population growth is capitalized into land rents and leads to a contiguous expansion of suburban development over time. However, given differences in the development costs of suburban versus exurban lots and preference heterogeneity in which some households have a greater preference for large lots, leapfrog development can emerge in the exurban region located beyond the suburban fringe. The resulting spatial equilibrium land rents and other model outputs, which include each household type's optimal location choice, the rate of suburban expansion, and the conditions for exurban leapfrog development, are expressed analytically. The model is then simulated to explore the magnitude of the effects of sewer and commuting costs on suburban development and how city size influences the extent of exurban leapfrog development. The simulations are performed in discrete time, with an exogenously determined population growth rate for each household type. An iterative approach is used to solve for equilibrium in each time period in both the suburban and exurban land markets. In each period, for a given level of population of each household type, initial values of the proportion of suburban and exurban land at each distance are assumed. The model equations that characterize the spatial equilibrium are then used to iterate between prices and these relative proportions until the predicted boundary of the suburban area converges to a constant value.

The clear strength of this approach—simulation of spatial equilibrium models with some source of exogenous growth—is that these are structural models of the land market in which prices are modeled in a theoretically consistent manner that reflects both individual-level preferences and constraints and market-level conditions. A primary limitation of this approach is that the degree of spatial dynamics or agent and spatial heterogeneity that can be considered is limited since an analytical expression for spatial equilibrium prices is usually necessary to close the model.

The second approach, agent-based modeling,[8] does not impose spatial equilibrium and instead focuses on individual trades in the absence of this assumption. The essential features of these models are typically heterogeneous agents, defined by a set of behavioral rules and their interactions that evolve the system over time. Given a set of detailed initial conditions (e.g., that fully specify the institutional arrangements, initial number and types of consumers and firms, endowments, decision-making and trading rules, geography), agents carry out production, pricing, and trade activities that generate feedbacks (e.g., profits, utility, learning) that determine future decisions. A key departure is the lack of an equilibrium constraint: given the initial specifications of the economic system, the dynamics are driven solely by agent trading that is typically not subject to a market-level equilibrium condition.

The primary advantage of agent-based modeling is that many more details can be incorporated into the model, such as greater spatial disaggregation and heterogeneity at an individual agent and parcel scale. However, because the equilibrium assumption is dropped, these advantages come at the expense of additional model complexity that

[8] See the Chapter 16 by Parker in this handbook for a much more in-depth discussion and for many examples of this modeling approach. See Parker and Filatova (2008) and Chen et al. (2011) for further discussion of agent-based models of land markets and Irwin (2010) for further comparison of agent-based and other economic modeling approaches.

is necessary to specify the bidding and market interaction processes. More importantly, this approach is not consistent with the basic spatial equilibrium theory of land markets and as a result, represent market feedbacks in an *ad hoc* manner.

Filatova, Parker, and van der Veen (2009*a*) and Magliocca et al. (2012) provide good examples of how agent interactions can be modeled in an agent-based framework by specifying household offer bids, seller ask bids, and the interactions between individual buyers and sellers. Filatova et al. (2009*a*) specify the household's WTP as a function of income net of transportation costs and expenditures on a composite good, household utility, and the price of the composite good. The functional form used to specify the WTP function is ad hoc but reflects standard demand relationships, such as increasing WTP with income. The landowner's willingness to accept (WTA) is given by the reservation rent, assumed to be equal to agricultural land rents. Buyers and sellers interact via a specified sequence of events that includes sellers announcing their WTA bids and buyers searching for the location that generates the largest surplus. To account for market feedbacks, they adapt an approach used in agent-based finance models (LeBaron 2006), in which the individual WTP and WTA bids are adjusted by a multiplicative factor $(1 + \varepsilon)$, where $\varepsilon = (NB - NS)/(NB + NS)$, NB = number of buyers and NS = number of sellers. This is admittedly ad hoc, but allows bidding to be adjusted based on agent perceptions of market conditions. Given positive gains from trade, then the transaction price is set assuming that the buyer and seller divide these gains equally.

Although this model and related work by Filatova and Parker (e.g., Parker and Filatova 2008; Filatova et al. 2009*b*) is innovative, a limitation of this approach is that the bids are not explicitly derived from a specific utility maximization model and, as a result, assumptions about the microeconomic foundations of the model, including the substitutability between location and the composite good, are not made explicit. Magliocca et al. (2012) improve on this by deriving the household's WTP function from a Cobb-Douglas utility function and the developer's derived demand for land from an expected profit function. In addition, they separately model land and housing markets, an innovation that is not usually done, and consider other sources of heterogeneity, including multiple housing types, variable minimum lot zoning, and heterogeneous expectations among landowners. However, they use the same ad hoc adjustment procedure as Filatova et al. (2009*a*) to account for market competition in which the WTP and WTA bids are adjusted based on the relative number of buyers and sellers.

Several papers have combined agent-based modeling with an equilibrium assumption at each point in time as a means of incorporating spatial equilibrium into an agent-based framework. For example, Caruso et al. (2007) consider the emergence of different forms of residential sprawl as the result of endogenous neighborhood amenities in a two-dimensional urban economic model. Two types of neighborhood amenities are considered, both of which are locally defined as a function of the neighborhood land use pattern at a given location: open space amenities, which decrease with the amount of nearby development, and social amenities, which increase with nearby development. Households make optimal location decisions by trading off these competing neighborhood amenities with the travel costs associated with a given location. When the benefits of surrounding open space outweigh the costs of travel and lower social amenities, households will find it optimal to locate away from the urban fringe and in so doing generate sprawl. Given homogeneous households that are myopic (i.e., they do not anticipate population growth), short run equilibrium land rents are determined by the equalization of utility across space in a given time period and are conditional on the population level in each time period. Land rents are bid up over time as additional households enter the region and reach a long run spatial equilibrium when utility inside and outside the region are equalized.

Chen et al. (2013) follow a similar approach to incorporating population growth into a model of leapfrog development, but use a different approach to modeling household bidding. They begin with a Cobb-Douglas model of utility with households that are heterogeneous in income and a highly stylized landscape that is distinguished by distance from the urban center. The main innovation of this paper is that the household's optimal bidding function is derived as a function of preferences, income, and the expected number of competing bidders relative to supply using an auction model. Specifically, a first-price, sealed auction model is used to derive an analytical expression for the agent's optimal bid for location, which maximizes the household's expected surplus associated with a given location (defined as the difference between its maximum WTP and its actual bid) multiplied by the probability of winning. This approach incorporates key market conditions, namely the number of households in the region, the distribution of income and supply of land at each location, that, along with travel costs, determine the competitive level of bidding for each land parcel. Landowners determine market land rents by selecting the highest bid and development occurs if this bid exceeds the landowners' opportunity cost. Given heterogeneous households that are myopic, the short run equilibrium is defined by the optimal choice of each household and landowner, the lack of incentive for agents to renegotiate, and the current population and income distribution. Market conditions change over space due to income differences and over time as additional households enter the region, which increases competition and bids away the surplus that a household can attain at any given location. Changes in surplus permit the model to "step through time" by providing a temporal and spatial ordering of the location choices of heterogeneous households based on their utility-maximizing location decisions. The model is implemented using simulation methods that allow each household type and location to be explicitly considered in the bidding process, and therefore agent and spatial heterogeneity can readily be incorporated. Given this specification of the bidding process, Chen et al. (2013) hypothesize that leapfrog development can emerge if households are able to retain a larger surplus at more remote locations due to fewer bidders and a greater supply of substitutable land at these distances. The main result of the paper confirms this hypothesis. However, leapfrog development is ultimately a short-run property of the model since, over time, as more households move into the exurban region, the spatial differences in surplus are gradually bid away.

Like the assumption of a spatial equilibrium, the assumptions about price formation and market interactions that are necessary for agent-based modeling of land and housing markets are maintained assumptions. Unlike spatial equilibrium models, however, they usually omit any kind of equilibrium constraint and thus are inconsistent with a standard microeconomic model of behavior. In addition, although assumptions may be motivated by stylized facts about the trading process, they are often difficult to test empirically. The perceived lack of a stronger theoretical or empirical basis for modeling price formation has generated skepticism among some economists regarding the efficacy of agent-based modeling for modeling markets. However, as the advances in modeling just noted illustrate, it is possible to develop agent-based models that are derived from microeconomic foundations and that incorporate some notion of a spatial equilibrium. Although unsolved challenges regarding questions of dynamics and spatial equilibrium remain, we believe that recent work in both agent-based modeling and in other simulation models that are more prevalent in economics are pushing these modeling methods closer together. This is a point that we discuss in the Section 4.

4. Conclusion

In this chapter, we have sought to provide an overview and assessment of empirical methods for modeling land use by addressing the following questions: (1) what are the advantages and disadvantages of these various empirical approaches to modeling land use and land use change; (2) which questions are best suited to be answered using one versus the other approach, and (3) where are the gaps in the current literature? In drawing conclusions, we reiterate that there is no single "right" modeling method and that, instead, the appropriate method depends on the research question, modeling goals, and available data. Although in many cases a specific modeling method is appropriate and will suffice, we are also encouraged by the complementarities that may be possible by using a combination of methods. Here, we see at least three compelling opportunities. First, it may be possible to usefully combine reduced-form parameter estimates with a structural econometric model. For example, Chetty (2009) uses a structural model to derive expressions for the welfare consequences of various policies that are functions only of high-level elasticities, which can be estimated with reduced-form models. He then combines these reduced-form parameter estimates with a structural model to conduct counterfactual policy simulations. Whereas Chetty is focused on the welfare effects of policies, it may also be possible to use an analogous approach to modeling land markets if it is possible to use the structural model to identify opportunities for simplifying the number of structural parameters that must be estimated and instead estimate one or more reduced-form parameters. This approach could be useful for estimating the parameters of aggregate-level demand and supply relationships, for example, at the neighborhood, county, or metropolitan scales.

Second, we see complementarities between the structural spatial equilibrium models, including the structural econometric models and other types of spatial equilibrium simulation models, and agent-based models. In some ways, these methods are converging as more microeconomic foundations are included in agent-based models and as more heterogeneity, disaggregation, and dynamics are introduced into spatial equilibrium models. There are clear gains to be had from continuing to work toward narrowing the gap between these two approaches. An eventual goal is a modeling framework that includes the disaggregation and dynamics of the agent-based models and a theoretically consistent specification of spatial equilibrium and market feedbacks from the economic structural models. In addition, because of their added flexibility, agent-based models may be useful in testing the maintained assumptions of economic structural models, such as comparing model predictions from long-run spatial equilibrium with short-run equilibrium.

Third, we see complementarities between the spatial modeling approaches that we have focused on here and general equilibrium models in which other sectors of the economy are considered. Most models of housing or land markets ignore other input or output markets and thus are limited to considering partial equilibrium effects on land or housing rents or land use outcomes. However, recent work illustrates the importance of accounting for feedbacks from related markets. Kuminoff (2008) accounts for the jointness of households' residential location and employment decisions in an integrated model of housing and labor markets. Desmet and Rossi-Hansberg (2010) illustrate how feedbacks across multiple input and output markets matter for regional spatial dynamics and growth. Combes et al. (2005) account for feedbacks across multiple input and output markets and demonstrate the importance of accounting for these multiple channels of adjustments for policy analysis.

Although we are encouraged by this work that integrates multiple models or modeling approaches to address current research gaps, other critical gaps in modeling also need attention. First, there is a pressing need for empirical testing of the many maintained assumptions that must be made to make models tractable. As data and computational power increase, so does the scope, complexity, and number of maintained assumptions of our models. Kuminoff (2009) provides an example of testing the implications of maintained assumptions of functional form, preference distributions, and neighborhood delineation for identification and welfare measurement in structural models of household locational choice. He also shows how uncertainty regarding functional form and distributional assumptions can be measured and assessed. More work along these lines is needed. This need applies equally to structural econometric and other structural empirical models, as well as to agent-based models that rely on a number of maintained assumptions about the agent bidding and market interactions processes.

Second, incorporating dynamics into location and land use choice models remains a substantial challenge. The curse of dimensionality presents a key challenge since the complexity of the model increases as the number of state variables or interactions among agents increases, and estimation of large state space models over many periods is empirically infeasible. Spatial simulation techniques can fill this gap. Because spatial simulation models are not limited by the same estimation constraints, they can allow researchers to build land use models that are based on theory and that allow for more complex interactions and dynamic feedbacks by accounting for more state variables. If this translates into a more realistic model of real-world outcomes, then there is a clear advantage in using these models in modeling dynamic land use outcomes provided that the parameter and functional form assumptions can be empirically verified.

Finally, one of the ultimate tests of any modeling approach is how useful it is for policy. As applied researchers, we often conclude with the policy implications of our findings. However, the number of times that academic articles actually have an impact on the policy process is limited at best. Policy makers operate under substantial time and resource constraints and are usually looking for a quick approximate answer rather than a precise estimate that takes time to produce. Even when we design our models to run policy scenarios, we may not capture the realities of the political or policy process that determines the feasibility of a particular policy or policy change. The criteria by which the usefulness of our models are judged for real-time policy decisions are different from the criteria we would choose for their academic evaluation, but yet the optimal tradeoff between academic rigor and real-world practicality is uncertain. Certainly, rigorous policy analysis requires more than models that just generate pattern predictions, which implies that some representation of agents' demand and supply decisions is needed. However, the tradeoffs among models that are fully structural, incorporate dynamics and multiple feedbacks, and account for interactions across multiple scales remain uncertain. Much more work is needed to assess the relative costs and benefits of different modeling approaches for policy analysis and the relative gains from added model complexity versus the time and opportunity costs that these innovations require. Unfortunately, such questions have received scant attention in the literature—in large part due to publishing incentives that academic economists face that reward novel results and methods far more than replication or model comparison. Replication and cross-site comparisons are emphasized much more in other scientific disciplines. We see value in encouraging this kind of research in land economics that could synthesize and assess model results and modeling methods in a way that is useful for non-Ph.D. economists and policy makers.

Acknowledgments

We would like to thank Josh Duke for very helpful feedback on an earlier draft of this chapter. Support from the National Science Foundation (DEB LTER-1027188, WSC-1058059, GSS-1127044), the U.S. Forest Service's Northern Research Station, and the James S. McDonnell Foundation is gratefully acknowledged.

References

Aguirregabiria, V., and P. Mira. 2010. Dynamic discrete choice structural models: A survey. *Journal of Econometrics* 156: 38–67.

Anas, A., A. R. Arnott, and Small, K. 1998. Urban spatial structure. *Journal of Economic Literature* 36: 1426–1464.

Bayer, P., R. McMillan, and K. Reuben. 2004. What drives spatial segregation? New evidence using census microdata. *Journal of Urban Economics* 56: 514–535.

Bayer, P., N. Keohane, and C. Timmins. 2009. Migration and hedonic valuation: The case of air quality. *Journal of Environmental Economics and Management* 58(1): 1–14.

Bayer, P., R. McMillan, A. Murphy, and C. Timmins. 2011. A dynamic model of demand for houses and neighborhoods. Unpublished manuscript available upon request from authors.

Bayer, P., and C. Timmins. 2005. On the equilibrium properties of locational sorting models. *Journal of Urban Economics* 57, 462–477.

Berry, S., J. Levinsohn, and A. Pakes. 1995. Automobile prices in market equilibrium. *Econometrica* 63: 280–296.

Berry, S. T., O. Linton, and A. Pakes. 2004. Limit theorems for estimating the parameters of differentiated product demand systems. *Review of Economic Studies* 71: 613–654.

Bockstael, N. 1996. Modeling economics and ecology: The importance of a spatial perspective. *American Journal of Agricultural Economics*, 785: 1168–1180.

Bulan, L., C. Mayer, and C. Somerville. 2009. Irreversible investment, real options, and competition: Evidence from real estate development. *Journal of Urban Economics* 65: 237–251.

Capozza, D., and R. Helsley. 1989. The fundamentals of land prices and urban growth. *Journal of Urban Economics* 26: 295–306.

Capozza, D., and R. Helsley. 1990. The stochastic city. *Journal of Urban Economics* 28: 187–203.

Caruso, G., D. Peeters, J. Cavailhes, and M. Rounsevell. 2007. Spatial configurations in a periurban city: A cellular Automata-based microeconomic model. *Regional Science and Urban Economics* 37(5): 542–567.

Chen, Y., E. G. Irwin, and C. Jayaprakash. 2011. Incorporating spatial complexity into economic models of land markets and land use change. *Agricultural and Resource Economics Review* 40(3): 321–340.

Chen, Y., E. G. Irwin, and C. Jayaprakash. 2013. Thin markets and leapfrog development. Unpublished manuscript available upon request from authors.

Chetty, R. 2009. Sufficient statistics for welfare analysis: A bridge between structural and reduced-form methods. *Annual Review of Economics* 1: 451–488.

Combes, P. P., G. Duranton, and H. G. Overman. 2005. Agglomeration and the adjustment of the spatial economy. *Papers in Regional Science* 84(3): 311–349.

Cunningham, C. 2007. Growth controls, real options, and land development. *The Review of Economics and Statistics* 89: 343–358.

Desmet, K., and E. Rossi-Hansberg. 2010. On spatial dynamics. *Journal of Regional Science* 50(1): 43–63.

Dixit, A., and R. Pindyck. 1994. *Investment under uncertainty*. Princeton, NJ: Princeton University Press.

Ekeland, I., J. Heckman, and L. Nesheim. 2004. Identification and estimation of hedonic models. *Journal of Political Economy* 112: S60–S109.

Epple, D., and H. Sieg 1999. Estimating equilibrium models of local jurisdictions. *Journal of Political Economy* 107: 645–681.

Filatova, T., D. P. Parker, and A. van der Veen. (2009*a*). Land market interactions between heterogeneous agents in a heterogeneous landscape: Tracing the macro-scale effects of individual trade-offs between environmental amenities and disamenities. *Canadian Journal of Agricultural Economics* 57(4): 431–457.

Filatova, T., Parker, D., and A. van der Veen. (2009*b*). Agent-based urban land markets: Agent's pricing behavior, land prices and urban land use change. *Journal of Artificial Societies and Social Simulation*, 12(1) http://jasss.soc.surrey.ac.uk/12/1/3.html

Glaeser, E., J. Gyourko, and R. Saks. 2005. Why is Manhattan so expensive? *Journal of Law and Economics* 48: 331–370.

Glaeser, E., and M. Kahn. 2004. Sprawl and urban growth. In *Handbook of regional and urban economics*, Vol. 4, eds. J. V. Henderson and J.-F. Thisse, 2481–2527. Amsterdam: Elsevier.

Harvey, E. O., and W. Clark 1965. The nature and economics of urban sprawl. *Land Economics* 41: 1–9.

Irwin, E. G. 2010. New directions for urban economic models of land use change: Incorporating spatial dynamics and heterogeneity. *Journal of Regional Science* 50: 65–91.

Irwin, E., and N. Bockstael. 2002. Interacting agents, spatial externalities and the endogenous evolution of residential land use patterns. *Journal of Economic Geography* 2: 31–54.

Keane, M.P. 2010. Structural vs. atheoretic approaches to econometrics. *Journal of Econometrics* 156:3–20.

Klaiber, H. A., and D. Phaneuf. 2010. Valuing open space in a residential sorting model of the twin cities. *Journal of Environmental Economics and Management* 60: 57–77.

Klaiber, H. A., and N. V. Kuminoff. 2014. Equilibrium sorting models of land use and residential location. In *The Oxford handbook of land economics*, eds. J. M. Duke and J. Wu, 352–379 New York: Oxford University Press.

Klaiber, H. A., and V. K. Smith. 2011. Preference heterogeneity and non-market benefits: the roles of structural hedonic and sorting models. In *International handbook on non-market environmental valuation*, ed. J. Bennett, 222–253. Edward Elgar. Massachusetts.

Kuminoff, N. 2008. *Partial identification of preferences in a dual-market locational equilibrium*. Working Paper.

Kuminoff, N. 2009. Decomposing the structural identification of non-market values. *Journal of Environmental Economics and Management* 57(2): 123–129.

Kuminoff, N. V., V. K. Smith, and C. Timmins. 2012. The new economics of equilibrium sorting and policy evaluation using housing markets. Forthcoming: *Journal of Economic Literature*.

LeBaron, B. 2006. Agent-Based Computational Finance. In K. L. Judd & L. Tesfatsion (eds.), *Handbook of computational economics*, Vol. 2 *Agent-based computational economics* (pp. 1187–1233): Elsevier B.V.

Lewis, D. 2010. An economic framework for forecasting land-use and ecosystem change. *Resource and Energy Economics* 32: 98–116.

Lewis, D., B. Provencher, and V. Butsic. 2009. The dynamic effects of open-space conservation policies on residential development density. *Journal of Environmental Economics and Management*, 57: 239–252.

Lichtenberg, E. 1989. Land quality, irrigation development, and cropping patterns in the northern high plains. *American Journal of Agricultural Economics* 71: 187–194.

Magliocca, N., V. McConnell, M. Walls, and E. Safirova. 2012. Zoning on the urban fringe: Results from a new approach to modeling land and housing markets. *Regional Science and Urban Economics* 42(1–2): 198–210.

Mayer, C., and C. Somerville. 2000. Residential construction: Using the urban growth model to estimate housing supply. *Journal of Urban Economics* 48: 85–109.

McFadden, D. 1974. Conditional logit analysis of qualitative choice behavior. In Frontiers in Econometrics. ed. P. Zarembka, 105–142. New York: Academic Press.

Mills, D. 1981. Growth, speculation, and sprawl in a monocentric city. *Journal of Urban Economics* 10: 201–226.

Murphy, A. 2013. A dynamic model of housing supply. Unpublished manuscript available upon request from author.

Nechyba, T., and R. Walsh. 2004. Urban sprawl. *Journal of Economic Perspectives* 18: 177–200.

Nelson, G., and D. Hellerstein. 1997. Do roads cause deforestation? Using satellite images in econometric analysis of land use. *American Journal of Agricultural Economics* 79: 80–88.

Newburn, D., and P. Berck. 2006. Modeling suburban and rural-residential development beyond the urban fringe. *Land Economics* 82: 481–499.

Newburn, D., and P. Berck. 2011. Exurban development. *Journal of Environmental Economics and Management* 62: 323–336.

Oates, W. 1969. The effects of property taxes and local public spending on property values: An empirical study of tax capitalization and the Tiebout hypothesis. *The Journal of Political Economy* 77: 957–971.

Parker, D. 2013. An economic perspective on agent-based models of land-use and land-cover change. In *The Oxford handbook of land economics*, eds. J. M. Duke and J. Wu, 402–429. New York: Oxford University Press.

Parker, D., and T. Filatova. 2008. A conceptual design for a bilateral agent-based land market with heterogeneous economic agents. *Computers, Environment and Urban Systems* 32: 454–463.

Plantinga, A. 1996. The effect of agricultural policies on land use and environmental quality. *American Journal of Agricultural Economics* 78: 1082–1091.

Plantinga, A., and D. Lewis. 2014. Landscape simulations with econometric-based land use models. In *The Oxford handbook of land economics*, eds. J. M. Duke and J. Wu, 380–401. New York: Oxford University Press.

Post, W., W. Emauel, P. Zinke, and A. Stangenberger. 1982. Soil carbon pools and world life zones. *Nature* 298: 156–159.

Rosen, S. 1974. Hedonic prices and implicit markets: Product differentiation in pure competition. *Journal of Political Economy* 82: 34–55.

Rust, J. 1987. Optimal replacement of GMC bus engines: An empirical model of Harold Zurcher. *Econometrica* 55: 999–1033.

Sala, O., F. S. Chapin, III, J. Armesto, E. Berlow, J. Bloomfield, R. Dirzo, E. Huber-Sanwals, L. F. Huenneke, R. B. Jackson, A. Kinzig, R. Leemans, D. Lodge, H. A. Mooney, M. Oesterheld., N. L. Poff, M. T. Sykes, B. H. Walker, and D. H. Wall. 2000. Global biodiversity scenarios in the year 2100. *Science* 287: 1770–1774.

Schimel, D. 1995. Terrestrial ecosystems and the carbon cycle. *Global Change Biology* 1: 77–91.

Tajibaeva, L., R. Haight, and S. Polasky. 2008. A discrete-space urban model with environmental amenities. *Resource and Energy Economics* 30(2): 170–196.

Tiebout, C. 1956. A pure theory of local expenditures. *The Journal of Political Economy* 64: 416–424.

Timmins, C., and W. Schlenker. 2009. Reduced-form versus structural modeling in environmental and resource economics. *Annual Review of Resource Economics* 1: 351–380.

Towe, C., C. Nickerson, and N. Bockstael. 2008. An empirical examination of the timing of land conversions in the presence of farmland preservation programs. *American Journal of Agricultural Economics* 90: 613–626.

Towe, C., R. Lewis, and L. Lynch. 2014. Using quasi-experimental methods to evaluate land policies: Application to Maryland's priority funding legislation. In *The Oxford handbook of land economics*, eds. J. M. Duke and J. Wu, 452–480. New York: Oxford University Press.

Vitousek, P., H. Mooney, J. Lubchenco, and J. Melillo, 1997. Human dominance of earth's ecosystems. *Science* 277: 494–499.

Vorosmarty, C., and D. Sahagian. 2000. Anthropogenic disturbance of the terrestrial water cycle. *BioScience* 50: 753–765.

Walsh, R. 2007. Endogenous open space amenities in a locational equilibrium. *Journal of Urban Economics* 61: 319–344.

Wrenn, D. 2012. Time is money: An empirical examination of the dynamic effects of regulatory uncertainty on residential subdivision development. PhD Dissertation. The Ohio State University.

Wu, J., and K. Segerson. 1995. The impact of policies and land characteristics on potential groundwater pollution in Wisconsin. *American Journal of Agricultural Economics* 77(4): 1033–1047.

Wu, J., and A. Plantinga. 2003. The influence of public open space on urban spatial structure. *Journal of Environmental Economics and Management* 46: 288–309.

CHAPTER 14

EQUILIBRIUM SORTING MODELS OF LAND USE AND RESIDENTIAL CHOICE

H. ALLEN KLAIBER AND NICOLAI V. KUMINOFF

> Far better an approximate answer to the *right* question, which is often vague, than an *exact* answer to the wrong question, which can always be made precise.
>
> —John Tukey (1962)

AMERICANS are remarkably mobile. Since World War II, 18% of the US population has moved to a new residence every year, on average. As Charles Tiebout (1956) famously observed, these movers face a public goods counterpart to the private market shopping trip. They choose among residential communities that differ in their housing prices and in their provision of amenities, such as local public goods, urban attractions, and environmental services. The location choices that they make reveal features of their preferences. As heterogeneous households sort themselves across the urban landscape, their collective location choices will influence housing prices as well as the supply of amenities through a combination of voting, social interaction, and feedback effects. To better understand this two-way interaction between people and their surrounding environment, economists have developed equilibrium models of the sorting process.

Equilibrium sorting models begin with a formal description for the spatial landscape and the structure of household preferences. Utility-maximizing location choices are expressed as a function of the observable characteristics of households, houses, and communities, as well as of structural parameters describing latent preferences. This functional relationship is then inverted, using the logic of revealed preferences to characterize the distribution of preferences in the population of households. Estimation results are used to calculate the willingness to pay for large-scale changes in landscape amenities. Sorting models can also be used to simulate how people and markets will adjust to unexpected events and make predictions for "general equilibrium" benefit measures and future land use trends. This is a new and exciting framework for policy evaluation that offers the potential to improve our understanding of land economics.

Compared to the standard quasi-experimental framework for describing how landscape changes affect housing prices, the development and estimation of a structural sorting model can seem intimidating. The analyst must be willing to collect additional data and think deeply about the economic forces that underlie market equilibria. Econometric identification may seem less transparent. It may be necessary to code the estimator from scratch, and the results may be viewed with skepticism by critics who dislike structural modeling. Despite these challenges, the potential insights from formulating, estimating, and interpreting an equilibrium sorting model far outweigh the learning costs. Put simply, the equilibrium sorting methodology allows us to provide approximate answers to the right questions about the relationships among land use, residential choice, and public policy.

This chapter summarizes the equilibrium sorting methodology. We have two main objectives. First, we intend to make the empirical models accessible to economists who are new to the literature. Thus, we provide more detail about datasets and estimators than one finds in the typical journal article. Our second objective is to clarify the relationship between the newer structural models of the sorting process and the older reduced-form models of hedonic equilibria that have long served as workhorses for economic analysis of land use and household location choice. We argue that the two frameworks are inseparable. Hedonic price functions describe sorting equilibria, and what we learn about the sorting process influences how we interpret hedonic price functions.

We intend this chapter to be more pragmatic than previous efforts to characterize the literature. Considerable space is devoted to (1) empirical descriptions for the spatial landscape and household preferences, (2) econometric procedures for estimating structural preference parameters, and (3) procedures for simulating how markets adjust to unexpected events. This leaves us with less space to cover historical background, systematically catalog empirical results, or recommend directions for future research. Readers interested in these topics are directed to Palmquist (2005); Klaiber and Smith (2011); Epple, Gordon, and Sieg (2010); and Kuminoff, Smith, and Timmins (2013).

The chapter proceeds as follows. Section 1 begins with a general description for the spatial landscape that nests empirical hedonic and sorting models. Then we define the household's location choice problem, characterize a sorting equilibrium, and briefly summarize results on existence and uniqueness. In Section 2, we move from theory to practice. Focusing on the two predominant microeconometric frameworks—the "pure characteristics model" (Epple and Sieg 1999) and the "random utility model" (Bayer et al. 2004)—we explain how to build an empirical sorting model and estimate structural parameters. Datasets, modeling assumptions, and econometric procedures are covered. Section 3 explains how the estimation results can be used to simulate how people and markets would adjust to an unexpected event. Many of the insights gleaned from the estimation and simulation of sorting models also have important implications for hedonic estimation. Section 4 summarizes insights on the causes and consequences of omitted variable bias, benefit measurement, and the interpretation of land value capitalization effects. Finally, Section 5 concludes.

1. Conceptual Framework

1.1 The Spatial Landscape

Consider a metropolitan region comprised of $j = 1, \ldots, J$ housing communities, each of which contains N_j houses.[1] The region is assumed to be sufficiently small that most working households could relocate anywhere in the region without having to move to a different job. At the same time, the region is assumed to be self-contained in the sense that few households would consider living outside the region. Some regions that meet these criteria may be small and isolated, such as the Grand Junction metro area in western Colorado. Others may be large and integrated, such as the San Francisco-Oakland-San Jose consolidated metropolitan statistical area, containing more than 4 million people spread out over several interconnected cities and suburbs.

Within the region, each housing community provides a unique bundle of amenities, g_j. "Amenities" are defined broadly to include any nonmarketed goods and services that matter to households. Examples include local public goods produced from property tax revenue (public education, police and fire protection), environmental services (air quality, microclimate), proximity to urban attractions (central business district, shopping, dining), and the demographic composition of the community (race, age, wealth). Within a community, individual houses differ in their structural characteristics. The vector h_{n_j} will be used to describe the physical attributes of a particular house, n, located in community j. Examples include the square footage of the house, the number of bedrooms, and the quality of building materials.

Households are heterogeneous. They differ in terms of their incomes (y), preferences (α), and demographic characteristics (d). Each household will maximize its utility by choosing a specific house in its preferred community. We use n_j to denote the household's simultaneous choice of a community and a house within that community:

$$\max_{n_j} U_i(g_j, h_{n_j}, b, \alpha_i) \text{ subject to } y_i = b + P_{n_j}. \tag{1}$$

In the budget constraint, the price of the numeraire commodity (b) is normalized to 1 and P_{n_j} represents the annualized after-tax price of housing.

The collective location choices made by the population of households may influence the spatial distribution of amenities. For example, as open space gets converted to urban development, new opportunities for dining and nightlife may emerge, along with increased

[1] The terms "community" and "neighborhood" are used interchangeably in the literature.

traffic and air pollution. Homeowners may be asked to vote on assessments to fund the preservation of remaining open space or to support public schools. The academic performance of students in those schools may depend on the incomes and education levels of their parents. Although we do not model these mechanisms formally, it is important to keep them in mind because they create a need for instruments in econometric estimation.

Finally, three assumptions are typically maintained to reduce the amount of friction in the market. First, everyone is assumed to have perfect information about the spatial landscape. Second, everyone is assumed to face the same schedule of prices. Finally, households are assumed to be freely mobile.

1.2 Characterizing a Sorting Equilibrium

In a sorting equilibrium, prices, physical housing characteristics, amenities, and location choices are all defined such that no household could improve its utility by moving, and each household occupies exactly one house. Equation (2) provides a formal statement of this condition.

$$U_i(g_j, h_{n_j}, y_i - P_{n_j}, \alpha_i) \geq U_i(g_k, h_{m_k}, y_i - P_{m_k}, \alpha_i), \quad \forall \quad i, m, k \quad : \quad P_{m_k} < y_i,$$
$$\text{and} \sum_{n_j} A_{i,n_j} = 1, \forall\, i,_j, \tag{2}$$

where A_{i,n_j} is an indicator variable that equals 1 *if and only if* household i occupies house n in community j. Although we suppress temporal subscripts, equation (2) is best viewed as a single-period snapshot of market outcomes. It may or may not be a long-run steady state. Current incomes and preferences may reflect temporary factors. Credit may be unusually easy (or difficult) to obtain. The average household may be unusually optimistic (or pessimistic) about the future asset value of housing. Budget constraints may reflect other transitory macroeconomic or microeconomic shocks. As these factors change over time, so will the features of the sorting equilibrium.

With a few mild restrictions on preferences, the market outcomes from a sorting equilibrium can be described by a hedonic price function. If $U_i(g_j, h_{n_j}, b, \alpha_i)$ is continuously differentiable, monotonically increasing in the numeraire, and Lipschitz continuous, then theorem 1 from Bajari and Benkard (2005) can be invoked to prove that equilibrium prices must be functionally related to housing characteristics and amenities, $P_{n_j} = P(g_j, h_{n_j})$.[2] This result places less discipline on the price function than Rosen's (1974) hedonic model. Households are not assumed to be free to choose continuous quantities of each amenity. Nor is the market assumed to be perfectly competitive. In

[2] Although Bajari and Benkard (2005) treat nonprice attributes as exogenous, it is straightforward to extend their result to the case of endogenous amenities by assuming that households ignore their own contributions to each amenity.

fact, Bajari and Benkard demonstrate that no assumptions about the supply side of the market are needed to prove that equilibrium can be described by a price function.

Relaxing the assumptions of Rosen's model has costs and benefits. The main benefit is a more realistic description of the spatial landscape. Although households may be able to purchase approximately continuous quantities of physical housing characteristics, the same is not true for landscape amenities. Air quality changes discretely from air basin to air basin; test scores change discretely from school district to school district; and some communities are adjacent to open space, whereas others are not. The cost of relaxing Rosen's continuity assumption is that we lose the ability to translate the price function gradient into measures of the marginal willingness to pay (MWTP) for amenities. Nevertheless, we shall see that the price function still plays an important role in estimation.

A second, stronger, restriction that has proven useful in characterizing sorting equilibria is the single-crossing condition. Single crossing helps to characterize the ways in which households sort themselves across locations according to their heterogeneous incomes and preferences. To see the intuition, consider the simplest form of preference heterogeneity—vertical differentiation. In a "vertical" model, households differ only in their preferences for housing "quality" relative to the numeraire. They are assumed to agree on a ranking of locations by overall quality, $q = f(g,h)$. Given this assumption, equation (3) defines the slope of an indirect indifference curve in (q, p) space.

$$M(q, p, \alpha, y) = \left\langle \frac{dp}{dq} \mid V = \bar{V} \right\rangle. \tag{3}$$

If M is monotonically increasing in $(y \mid \alpha)$ and $(\alpha \mid y)$, then indifference curves in the (q, p) plane will satisfy single crossing in y and α. Under this condition, any sorting equilibrium must satisfy three properties: *boundary indifference, increasing bundles*, and *stratification*.[3]

To interpret the three properties, it is useful to first order locations by quality. Without loss of generality, let the ordering be defined such that $q_1 < \cdots < q_R$. The *increasing bundles* property requires that households must pay for the amenities provided by higher ranked locations through higher housing prices: $P_1 < \cdots < P_R$. *Stratification* requires that households are stratified across the R locations by $(\alpha \mid y)$ and $(y \mid \alpha)$. In other words, all else constant, households in higher ranked locations will have higher income and stronger preferences for amenities. Finally, *boundary indifference* defines the set of values for (α, y) that would make a household exactly indifferent between locations r and $r + 1$.

Figure 14.1 provides a simple illustration of a sorting equilibrium that satisfies the three properties. Consistent with increasing bundles, the price ranking of communities

[3] For additional background on the role of single-crossing conditions in equilibrium sorting models see Epple and Romer (1991); Epple and Sieg (1999); and Kuminoff, Smith, and Timmins (2013).

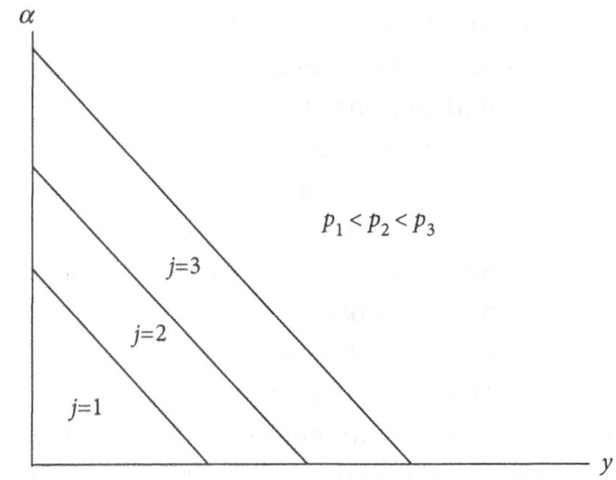

FIGURE 14.1 Partition of households into communities by preferences and income.

matches the ranking by overall amenity provision. The figure partitions (α, y) space into three cells corresponding to (α, y) combinations that rationalize the choice of each community. For example, community 1 would maximize utility for any household with values for income and preferences in the lower left cell of the partition. The boundaries between adjacent cells define the (α, y) combinations that would make a household exactly indifferent between the corresponding communities. To see how households are stratified across communities notice that, conditional on preferences, wealthier households choose communities with more public goods. Likewise, conditional on income, households with stronger preferences choose communities with more public goods. This two-dimensional stratification is consistent with Tiebout's (1956) reasoning and helps to explain why we sometimes observe low-income households living in high-amenity communities and high-income households living in low-amenity communities.

Stratification, increasing bundles, and boundary indifference are particularly helpful in estimating the class of pure characteristics models covered in Section 2.2. The single-crossing condition is sufficient, but not necessary, to guarantee that a sorting equilibrium will satisfy these properties. In addition to providing a simple characterization of equilibrium, the single-crossing condition can help to guarantee that equilibria exist.

1.3 Existence and Uniqueness

General proofs of existence and uniqueness require fairly strong restrictions on preferences and amenities. One strategy is to assume that households have identical preferences ($\alpha_i = \alpha, \forall i$), so they differ only in their incomes. In this case, the single-crossing condition makes it possible to prove existence in the presence of an endogenously determined amenity (Ellickson 1971; Westoff 1977). Another strategy is to allow preference heterogeneity but rule out social interactions (Nechyba 1997). Bayer and Timmins (2005) develop a third approach. They smooth the preference function by adding an idiosyncratic iid shock to utility. This allows them to prove existence in a setting where households with heterogeneous preferences for exogenous amenities share a common marginal utility for a single endogenous amenity. Whether the equilibrium is unique depends on whether marginal utility is positive or negative.

In the presence of more complex preference structures, analysts have used numerical simulations to demonstrate that equilibria *may* exist (Epple and Platt 1998; Sieg et al. 2004; Walsh 2007; Klaiber and Phaneuf 2010; Kuminoff and Jarrah 2010; Kuminoff 2011). Despite the lack of general proofs for existence and uniqueness, the empirical literature has moved forward with preference structures that allow considerable heterogeneity and acknowledge the potential endogeneity of amenities. Analysts simply assume that the available data reflect an equilibrium. Then they write down a utility function and estimate values for the structural parameters that justify those data as an equilibrium.

2. Estimation

Moving from theory to estimation requires three sources of information: (1) a definition for the choice set, (2) a parametric representation of the preference function, and (3) assumptions for the statistical distributions used to characterize sources of unobserved heterogeneity. Although specific modeling choices differ from study to study, most applications can be grouped into two broad frameworks: random utility models (RUM) based on Bayer, McMillan, and Reuben (2004) and pure characteristics models (PCM) based on Epple and Sieg (1999).[4]

The RUM and PCM frameworks provide alternative characterizations of the same sorting equilibrium. They require data on the same core variables: prices, housing characteristics, household demographics, and spatially delineated amenities. Data sources vary. Housing prices and structural characteristics are typically drawn from the same sources as the hedonic literature—assessor databases or the US Census of Housing. Data on consumer demographics are typically drawn from the Census of Population. Data on amenities have been drawn from a variety of federal and state government agencies. Although it is possible to calibrate empirical models using aggregate data, the rule of thumb is to use the highest resolution microdata that are available.[5]

[4] Ferreyra (2007) proposed a third "general equilibrium" approach building on earlier work by Nechyba (1997, 1999, 2000).

[5] Sieg et al. (2004); Bayer, Ferreira, and McMillan (2007); and Klaiber and Phaneuf (2010) provide particularly detailed descriptions of how their datasets were assembled.

2.1 The Random Utility Framework

The random utility framework builds on McFadden's (1974) seminal discrete choice model. Bayer, McMillan, and Reuben (2004) developed the first application to residential sorting, using data from the San Francisco area. A key feature of their application is the recognition that both housing prices *and* amenities may be endogenous in the estimation process. Consider housing prices. Unobserved attributes of communities that make them more desirable also increase the demand to locate there. *Ceteris paribus*, equilibrium prices must be higher in more desirable communities. The implication of this logic is the need to use instrumental variables to disentangle the correlation between equilibrium housing prices and unobserved amenities. A similar argument applies to amenities that are endogenously determined through the sorting process. Bayer, McMillan, and Reuben (2004) show that the structure of the sorting model itself can help to overcome these econometric challenges.

Subsequent applications refined the RUM framework and used it to estimate preferences for school quality (Bayer et al. 2007), land use (Klaiber and Phaneuf 2010), and air quality (Tra 2010). A distinguishing characteristic of these applications is the way they define locations as particular "types" of housing. For example, Klaiber and Phaneuf define a housing type as a unique (house size, time period, community) rather than an individual house. This aggregation follows from Berry, Linton, and Pakes (2004) who demonstrate that consistent estimation for this class of RUM model requires the number of consumers to exceed the number of choice alternatives. Bayer, Ferreira, and McMillan (2007) use micro-census data on individual houses, whereas Tra uses information on sampled houses contained within Census public use microdata areas (PUMAs) grouped by common housing characteristics. Each of these approaches either implicitly or explicitly aggregates individual houses into "housing types within communities" that form the choice set.

2.1.1 *Parameterization of the Model*

Parameterization of the model begins by dividing utility into observed and unobserved components. A location-specific unobservable, ξ, is used to represent housing characteristics and amenities that are observed by households, but not the analyst. Additionally, an "error" term, ε, is added, recognizing that households may have idiosyncratic preferences for each location.

The utility a household receives from choosing a particular housing type, t, in community j, is usually expressed as a linear function of its attributes,

$$V_{t_j}^i = \alpha_h^i h_{t_j} + \alpha_g^i g_j + \alpha_p^i p_{t_j} + \xi_{t_j} + \varepsilon_{y_j}^i. \tag{4}$$

The way that communities are subdivided into housing types varies from study to study. At one extreme, a type could be defined as precisely as an individual house. At the opposite extreme, a type could be defined as coarsely as the mean or median house in a particular community. Most studies use definitions between these extremes for reasons that we discuss in the context of the mechanics of the estimator. Meanwhile, communities are often defined using Census aggregates, such as PUMAs, tracts, or block groups.

Three features of (4) are worth noting. First, the i superscripts on α allow households to differ in their relative preferences for different attributes. This generalizes the "vertical" preference structure introduced earlier and is often referred to as "horizontal" differentiation.[6] Second, the marginal utility of income is implicitly assumed to be constant. It is suppressed in (4), as is the custom in random utility models.[7] Last, although the choice of a location is deterministic from the perspective of each household, assuming a statistical distribution for the idiosyncratic term, $\varepsilon^i_{t_j}$, makes it possible to derive a closed-form expression for the share of households who choose each housing type.

Assuming $\varepsilon^i_{t_j}$ is distributed according to an iid type I extreme value distribution produces a familiar logit expression for the probability that household i chooses each housing type,

$$Pr^i_{t_j} = \frac{\exp(\alpha^i_h h_{t_j} + \alpha^i_g g_j + \alpha^i_p p_{t_j} + \xi_{t_j})}{\sum_{s,k} \exp(\alpha^i_h h_{s_k} + \alpha^i_g g_k + \alpha^i_p p_{s_k} + \xi_{s_k})}. \tag{5}$$

Aggregating (5) over $i = 1, \ldots I$ households generates the expected share of households choosing a particular housing type,

$$\sigma_{t_j} = \frac{1}{I}\sum_i pr^i_{t_j}. \tag{6}$$

This share forms the foundation for market clearing in the model. There is no direct assignment of individual households to specific housing types. Instead, equilibrium is characterized using the predicted share of households selecting each housing type.

Ensuring market clearing requires that the predicted share of households choosing each housing type must be identical to the observed share for that type. In other words, housing supply must equal housing demand. This condition is satisfied by the inclusion of the alternative specific unobservables, ξ_{t_j}. Given a distributional assumption for $\varepsilon^i_{t_j}$, Berry (1994) demonstrates that including a complete set of alternative specific unobservables results in predicted and observed market shares coinciding as a necessary condition for maximum likelihood estimation.[8]

6 The "vertical" and "horizontal" terminology is adapted from Lancaster (1979).

7 Tra (2010) includes a nonlinear income term of $\ln(y^i - p_h)$, which preserves the budget constraint but presents difficulties for welfare measurement (Herriges and Kling 1999; McFadden 1999).

8 This property holds for the linear exponential family of models that includes conditional logit.

2.1.2 *Estimation Procedures*

Recall that the specification for utility in (4) allows for horizontal preference heterogeneity. Past applications have taken advantage of this flexibility by decomposing each preference parameter, α^i, into the sum of a constant component and a component that varies along observable demographic characteristics of households:

$$\alpha^i = \alpha^0 + \alpha^1 d^i. \tag{7}$$

Using this decomposition, the utility function can be expanded as (8).

$$V_{t_j}^i = \alpha_h^0 h_{t_j} + \alpha_h^1 d^i h_{t_j} + \alpha_g^0 g_j + \alpha_g^1 d^i g_j + \alpha_p^0 p_{t_j} + \alpha_p^1 d^i p_{t_j} + \xi_{t_j} + \varepsilon_{t_j}^i. \tag{8}$$

All of the structural parameters in (8) can be recovered using a two-stage approach to estimation.

The first stage recovers parameters that vary with household demographic characteristics (α_h^1, α_g^1, α_p^1), as well as the mean indirect utility for each alternative (θ_{t_j}). The second stage uses the first-stage estimate for mean indirect utility to recover preference parameters common to all households (α_h^0, α_g^0, α_p^0). This partitioning is shown in equations (9a) and (9b)

$$V_{t_j}^i = \alpha_h^1 d^i h_{t_j} + \alpha_g^1 d^1 g_j + \alpha_p^1 d^i p_{t_j} + \theta_{t_j} + \varepsilon_{t_j}^i \tag{9a}$$

$$\hat{\theta}_{t_j} = \alpha + \alpha_h^0 h_{t_j} + \alpha_g^0 g_j + \alpha_p^0 p_{t_j} + \xi_{t_j}, \tag{9b}$$

using the script-free α term in (9b) to represent an intercept.[9]

In principle, the parameters in (9a) could be estimated using a standard conditional logit model. For many applications, however, the number of housing types is large, making gradient-based maximum likelihood estimation burdensome due to the propagation of mean indirect utility parameters. To reduce this computational burden, past studies have relied on the results from Berry (1994). Specifically, a contraction mapping algorithm enables recovery of estimates for each mean indirect utility parameter ($\widehat{\theta}_{t_j}$) without using gradient-based searches. This computational "trick" speeds model convergence significantly.[10]

[9] An intercept is included to account for the normalization that occurs in first-stage estimation. Evaluating differences in utility prevents recovery of the full $j = 1 \ldots J$ mean indirect utility parameters. In practice, researchers often normalize by setting the first mean indirect utility parameter equal to zero and estimate the remaining J - 1 parameters.

[10] The standard contraction mapping routine is: $\theta_{t_j}^{s+1} = \theta_{t_j}^s - \ln\left(\sum_i \frac{pr_{t_j}^i}{\sigma_{t_j}}\right)$, where s indexes the iteration of the contraction mapping routine.

Second stage estimation of (9b) raises several econometric issues. First, because the dependent variable consists of *estimated* mean indirect utilities from (9a), some additional criteria must be satisfied to establish consistency and asymptotic normality (Berry et al. 2004). Let $T = \sum_{t,j} t_j$ represent the total number of distinct housing types. Consistency and asymptotic normality are defined as $T \rightarrow \infty$. To guarantee consistency, the number of households must grow large relative to the number of types: $\frac{T \log T}{I} \rightarrow 0$. Asymptotic normality requires the additional restriction that $\frac{T^2}{I}$ is bounded. These two requirements help motivate the characterization of housing types.

Consistency cannot be established if t is defined as an individual house because this results in $T = I$. At the same time, it seems important to recognize that the prices and structural characteristics of houses vary within the Census aggregates used to define housing communities. Empirical studies have sought a middle ground that addresses both issues. For example, Klaiber and Phaneuf (2010) use square footage to divide the houses in each Census block group into "small," "medium," and "large" terciles. Then they define housing types using the median values of structural housing characteristics, amenities, and prices for the houses in each block group and size category.

Another econometric issue is that prices, and potentially amenities, are likely correlated with the error term in (9b), confounding ordinary least squares (OLS) estimation. A popular instrumentation strategy is to exploit the logic of the sorting process to form an "optimal" instrument (Bayer and Timmins 2007). The insight behind the IV strategy explained by Bayer and Timmins is to utilize the variation in prices that reflects exogenous characteristics of distant locations. Such instruments are relevant because the equilibrium levels of endogenous attributes at each location are influenced by the attributes of all other locations through the sorting equilibrium. Their validity relies on the assumption that the analyst can identify "exogenous" attributes at distant locations that are uncorrelated with ξ_{t_j}.

If we treat amenities as exogenous and employ the Bayer-Timmins instrument for price, Klaiber and Phaneuf (2010) demonstrate that the two-step estimator can proceed as follows:

Step 1. Estimate (9a) to obtain parameter estimates.
Step 2. Make a guess for the coefficient on price, α_p^{0*}.
Step 3. Move the term $\alpha_p^{0*} p_{t_j}$ in (9b) to the left hand side and add additional control variables (denoted by tildes) formed within rings around each choice, alternative to the right hand side of the modified (9b).
Step 4. Estimate the modified (9b) from step 2 via OLS and set the residual to zero.
Step 5. Calculate the mean indirect utility implied by step 3, denoting it by $\tilde{\theta}_{t_j}$.

Step 6. Use the first stage estimates from step 0 along with the initial guess for the coefficient on price and the estimates obtained in step 4 to solve for the set of prices, ρ_h^{iv} such that aggregate predicted shares exactly equal observed shares of each alternative t_j.

Step 7. Perform IV estimation of (9b) using $p_{t_j}^{IV}$ as an instrument.

Step 8. Use the estimate of α_p^0 from step 7 to iterate starting at step 1 until the estimate of α_p^0 converges.

2.2 The Pure Characteristics Framework

Most of the recent empirical models developed within the pure characteristics framework build on earlier work by Dennis Epple and his co-authors (e.g., Epple et al. 1984, 1993; Epple and Romer 1991). These studies introduced a constant elasticity of substitution (CES) specification for preferences as an example. Epple and Platt (1998) calibrated the CES function to data on housing market outcomes, and Epple and Sieg (1999) developed a structural estimator. Their approach to estimation was refined in subsequent work by Sieg et al. (2002, 2004). The PCM framework has since been used to investigate the benefits of numerous amenities, including landscape attributes in Portland, Oregon (Wu and Cho 2003), air quality in Southern California (Smith et al. 2004) and Northern California (Kuminoff 2009), open space in the Raleigh-Durham area of North Carolina (Walsh 2007), and school quality in Phoenix, Arizona (Klaiber and Smith 2012).

2.2.1 Parameterization of the Model

One of the distinguishing features of the PCM framework is a mixed discrete-continuous depiction of the choice set. Households are assumed to be free to choose continuous quantities of physical housing characteristics in each of a discrete number of residential communities. Under this assumption, the location choice process can be characterized by the choice of a community. Conditional on that choice, a household will select a house with the optimal combination of physical characteristics.

Sieg et al. (2002) illustrate how the discrete-continuous representation for the choice set influences how we define the "price of housing" in an indirect utility function. They demonstrate that as long as h_{n_j} enters utility through a separable subfunction that is homogeneous of degree 1, housing expenditures can be expressed as the product of a price index and a quantity index, $P_{n_j} = q(h_{n_j}) \cdot p(g_j)$. In this case, $p_j = p(g_j)$ replaces P_{n_j} in the indirect utility function. Equation (10) steps through this logic.

$$\begin{aligned} &U[g_j, h_{n_j}(g_j, P_{n_j}, \alpha_i, y_i), y_i - P_{n_j}(g_j, h_{n_j}), \alpha_i] \\ &= U[g_j, h_{n_j}(g_j, q(h_{n_j}) \cdot p_j(g_j), \alpha_i, y_i), y_i - q(h_{n_j}) \cdot p_j(g_j), \alpha_i] \\ &= V(g_j, p_j, \alpha_i, y_i). \end{aligned} \tag{10}$$

The first equality follows from Sieg et al. (2002). The second equality simply rewrites utility in indirect terms. The "price of housing" in each community, p_j, represents the implicit price (per unit of q) to consume the bundle of nonmarket amenities provided by that community.

The same assumptions that allow Sieg et al. (2002) to factor housing expenditures into price and quantity indices also support a strategy to estimate $p_1,\ldots,p_J$ from a hedonic regression. Taking logs of the expenditure function yields a general expression for an estimable hedonic model,

$$\ln(P_{n_j}) = \ln[q(h_{n_j})] + \ln[p_j(g_j)]. \tag{11}$$

Given an assumption for the functional form of the quantity index, microdata on housing sales can be used to recover $\hat{p}_1,\ldots,\hat{p}_J$ as community-specific fixed effects in a regression of log sale prices on housing characteristics.[11] Normalizing the smallest fixed effect to equal one produces the prices that enter the discrete-choice model of community selection.

Equation (12) illustrates the CES specification for preferences. It describes the utility that household i obtains from living in community j.

$$V_{i,j} = \left\{ \alpha_i \left(G_j\right)^{\rho} + \left[\exp\left(\frac{\left(y_i\right)^{1-\nu} - 1}{1-\nu} \right) \exp\left(-\frac{\beta P_j^{\eta+1} - 1}{1+\eta} \right) \right]^{\rho} \right\}^{\frac{1}{\rho}}, \tag{12}$$

where $G_j = \gamma_1 g_{1,j} + \cdots + \gamma_{R-1} g_{R-1,j} + \xi_j$, and $F(\alpha, y) \sim$ *lognormal*.

This indirect utility function does not correspond to any closed-form expression for direct utility, but it has several useful properties. It recognizes that physical housing characteristics may not be perfect substitutes for amenities. It also generates a convenient Cobb-Douglas specification for the demand for housing.[12] Finally, the CES specification maps directly into the underlying theory from Section 1. It yields parametric expressions for boundary indifference, stratification, and increasing bundles that serve as the basis for the estimation algorithm.[13]

The first term inside the CES nest represents utility from amenities. Households obtain utility from a linear index of amenities provided by each community. They are assumed to agree on a common set of weights for the amenities in the index $(\gamma_1,\ldots,\gamma_{R-1})$, but

[11] For example, if the quantity index is assumed to be multiplicative, then the regression is a simple linear-in-logs specification with fixed effects for communities. Data on the transaction prices of actual housing sales are converted to annualized values by adapting the formula from Poterba (1992).

[12] This follows from the exponential form of the term in square brackets.

[13] For additional discussion of the properties of CES specifications for utility in sorting model see Epple, Filimon, and Romer (1984, 1993); Epple and Romer (1991); Epple and Platt (1998); Epple and Sieg (1999); and Sieg et al. (2002).

they differ in their overall preferences for amenities relative to the private good component of housing and the numeraire (α_i). Of the R amenities in the index, $R-1$ are observable. $g_{R,j} = \xi_j$ represents the composite effect of community-specific attributes that are observed by households but not the analyst. As in the RUM model, ξ varies across choices but is restricted to be the same for every household.[14] This is an example of what Berry and Pakes (2007) label the "pure characteristics" approach to modeling choice among differentiated objects. Utility is defined purely over the characteristics of communities; there is no idiosyncratic location-household-specific ε_{ij} shock.

The second term inside the CES nest represents utility from the private good component of housing. Households are assumed to share the same elasticity of substitution between amenities and private goods (ρ) and the same demand parameters for the private good component of housing: price elasticity (η), income elasticity (v), and demand intercept (β). Applying Roy's Identity to (12) yields a simple expression for the demand for housing,

$$q_i = \beta p_j^{\eta} y_i^{v}. \tag{13}$$

Although households share a common set of demand parameters, notice that individual demand varies with income.

A key feature of the CES specification in (12) is that preferences are vertical. Since households have identical relative preferences for $g_1, \ldots, g_R$, they agree on the ranking of communities by the G index. Given the expected signs for the housing demand parameters ($\beta > 0, \eta < 0, v > 0$), preferences satisfy single crossing if $\rho < 0$.[15] This makes it possible to describe how households sort themselves across communities in equilibrium. To see this, first order communities by price: $p_1 < p_2 < \cdots < p_J$. *Increasing bundles* implies $G_1 < G_2 < \cdots < G_J$. Equation (14) uses *boundary indifference* to implicitly define the (α, y) combinations that make a household exactly indifferent between j and $j + 1$.

$$\ln(\alpha_i) - \rho\left(\frac{y_i^{1-v} - 1}{1-v}\right) = \ln\left(\frac{Q_{j+1} - Q_j}{G_j^{\rho} - G_{j+1}^{\rho}}\right) = B_{j,j+1}, \text{ where } Q_j = \exp\left[-\frac{\rho}{1+\eta}\left(\beta p_j^{\eta+1} - 1\right)\right] \tag{14}$$

Notice that all of the heterogeneity in income and preferences appears to the left of the equality. The *stratification* property implies that any household with income and preference such that: $\ln(\alpha_i) - \rho[(y_i^{1-v} - 1)/1 - v] < B_{j,j+1}$ will prefer community j to every higher ranked community: $j + 1, j + 2, \ldots, J$. Therefore, the left side of (14) can be used to

14 Although the RUM and PCM frameworks both use ξ to represent choice-specific unobserved attributes, they will generally recover different estimates for ξ due to the different spatial scales at which they define the variable and due to their different specifications for preferences.

15 Empirical studies have been unanimous in confirming the expected signs of these four parameters.

characterize the sorting of households into communities. This result plays an important role in the mechanics of the estimator.

2.2.2 *Estimation Procedures*

Estimation procedures vary slightly from study to study. Here we describe the simulated GMM approach developed by Sieg et al. (2004). Treating the first-stage estimates for housing prices as known constants, the GMM estimator can be used to recover all of the structural parameters. Let θ represent a vector of these parameters, $\theta=[\beta,\eta,\nu,\rho,\mu_{\alpha},\mu_{y},\sigma_{\alpha},\sigma_{y},\lambda,G_1,\gamma_1,\dots,\gamma_{R-1}]$. Equation (15) defines the GMM objective function, where is a set of instruments, represents the moment conditions, and A is the covariance matrix of moments.

$$\theta=\arg\min_{\theta\in\Theta}\left\{\frac{1}{J}\sum_{j=1}^{J}z_j m_j(\theta)\right\}' A^{-1}\left\{\frac{1}{J}\sum_{j=1}^{J}z_j m_j(\theta)\right\} \tag{15}$$

Sieg et al. demonstrate that the seven moment conditions in (16) can be used to identify all the parameters in θ.[16]

$$m_j(\theta)=\left\{\begin{array}{c} \tilde{G}_j-\gamma_1 g_{1,1}-\cdots-\gamma_{R-1}\cdot g_{R-1,j} \\ y_j^{25}-\tilde{y}_j^{25} \\ y_j^{50}-\tilde{y}_j^{50} \\ y_j^{75}-\tilde{y}_j^{75} \\ \ln P_{n\in j}^{25}-\ln\beta-(\eta+1)\ln p_j-\nu\ln\tilde{y}_j^{25} \\ \ln P_{n\in j}^{50}-\ln\beta-(\eta+1)\ln p_j-\nu\ln\tilde{y}_j^{50} \\ \ln P_{n\in j}^{75}-\ln\beta-(\eta+1)\ln p_j-\nu\ln\tilde{y}_j^{75} \end{array}\right\}. \tag{16}$$

The first moment condition is based on the level of amenity provision. Given a value for overall provision of amenities in the cheapest community, G_1, the sorting behavior implied by vertical differentiation allows $G_2,\dots,G_J$ to be defined recursively. The predictions for $G_2,\dots,G_J$ are then used to identify the (constant) weights in the amenity index. The residual to the moment condition defines the composite unobserved amenity in each community $(\xi_1,\dots,\xi_J)$.

[16] The particular moment conditions selected by Sieg et al. are somewhat arbitrary. In principle, one could use fewer moment conditions and additional instruments. Alternatively, one could develop moment conditions based on different quantiles of the distributions of income and housing expenditures.

The next three moment conditions are based on the model's prediction for the distribution of income. Under the maintained assumptions on preferences, the information in θ can be used to simulate community-specific income distributions. Three of the moment conditions match the 25th, 50th, and 75th quantiles from the simulated distributions of income in each community $(\tilde{y}_j^{25}, \tilde{y}_j^{50}, \tilde{y}_j^{75})$ to their empirical counterparts $(y_j^{25}, y_j^{50}, y_j^{75})$.

The last three moment conditions use the simulated income distributions to match predicted and observed quantiles from the distribution of housing expenditures in each community. The expenditure moments are obtained by multiplying (13) by price and taking logs.

Instruments are required to address endogeneity in the moment condition based on provision of amenities. The problem is that observed and unobserved amenities may be correlated. If households sort themselves across communities according to their income and preferences for a seemingly exogenous amenity—air quality, for example—their location choices may influence the levels of other endogenous amenities, such as public school quality, inducing correlation between them. PCM applications have followed Epple and Sieg (1999) in developing instruments from monotonic functions of each community's rank in the price index. These instruments will be valid as long as unobserved amenities are of second-order importance; that is, if they affect households' location choices without affecting the price rank of a community. The relevance of the instruments stems from the expectation that communities with higher levels of observed amenities will tend to be higher in the price ranking.

The mechanics of the simulated GMM estimator are straightforward. It can be implemented using a Nelder-Mead algorithm that iterates over the following steps.

Step 1. Select a starting value for $\theta = \left[\beta, \eta, \nu, \rho, \mu_\alpha, \mu_y, \sigma_\alpha, \sigma_y, \lambda, G_1, \gamma_1, \ldots, \gamma_{R-1}\right]$

Step 2. Draw I "households" from $F(\alpha, y) \sim$ *lognormal*. In some applications, I is set to the actual population of the study region. In other cases, it is scaled down by an order of magnitude to reduce computational demands.

Step 3. Calculate $K_i = \ln(\alpha_i) - \rho\left(\frac{y_i^{1-\nu} - 1}{1-\nu}\right)$ for all $i = 1, \ldots, I$ and use it to sort households in ascending order. Epple and Sieg (1999) demonstrate that the vertical model implies that, in any equilibrium, households will sort themselves across communities according to K_i, such that households with higher values for K_i will always locate in higher ranked communities.

Step 4. Sort households across communities. Let $S_1, \ldots, S_J$ represent the observed population counts of each community such that $\sum_j S_j = I$. Starting with the lowest K_i, assign the first S_1 households to community 1. Then assign the next S_2 households to community 2, and so on.

Step 5. Given G_1, solve for G_2 to make the boundary person between communities 1 and 2 indifferent between them. Then given G_2, solve for G_3, and so on....

Step 6. Calculate $\hat{y}_j^{25}, \hat{y}_j^{50}, \hat{y}_j^{75}$ for each community.

Step 7. Use $\hat{y}_j^{25}, \hat{y}_j^{50}, \hat{y}_j^{75}$, and $G_2(\hat{\theta}),\ldots,G_J(\hat{\theta})$ and $\hat{\theta}$ to evaluate the GMM objective function (15). If the minimization criteria of the numerical algorithm are satisfied, stop. If not, update θ and return to step 2.

2.3 Comparing the RUM and PCM Frameworks

The RUM and PCM frameworks are each capable of explaining a given dataset as a sorting equilibrium. This makes it difficult to compare the two models based on in-sample performance. In our opinion, neither model is strictly preferred to the other. Each has some features that seem flexible and others that seem restrictive.

PCM models provide a relatively flexible preference function, recognizing that public and private goods are not perfect substitutes. They also embed a budget constraint. The identifying assumption is that each household is able to afford a subset of houses in the community where it actually locates and in the communities that are adjacent in the price ranking. In contrast, the PCM maintains a relatively strong assumption about the importance of unobserved amenities. Unobserved amenities that influence the price ranking of communities threaten the validity of the rank-based instruments.

Advantages of the RUM model include its relatively flexible characterization of the choice set. It recognizes that zoning regulations may prevent home buyers from choosing continuous quantities of housing characteristics. Moreover, the instruments proposed by Bayer and Timmins (2007) are robust to the presence of unobserved amenities that influence the price ranking of communities. Yet, the RUM model also makes strong assumptions. The linear specification for utility assumes amenities and structural housing characteristics are perfect substitutes. Likewise, every household is assumed to be capable of purchasing every house.

Both frameworks maintain strong assumptions about preference heterogeneity. The PCM's vertical characterization fails to recognize that households are likely to differ in their relative preferences for landscape amenities. Households with young children may be primarily concerned about public school quality, for example, whereas retirees may place more weight on proximity to golf courses. RUM models are capable of recognizing these tradeoffs. However, that flexibility comes at a cost. The RUM model's flexible treatment of preference heterogeneity is enabled by its strong assumption that every household's preferences for the unobserved attributes of every house happen to be drawn from the same iid type I extreme value distribution. Kuminoff (2009) illustrates how the two frameworks present a bias-variance tradeoff. By restricting the extent of preference heterogeneity, the PCM introduces some bias. The RUM framework relaxes the restriction that causes the bias, but it does so in a way that increases the scope for distributional assumptions to influence the results.

It is important to keep in mind that the "flexible" and "restrictive" assumptions of RUM and PCM models are not inexorably linked to either framework. They reflect modeling decisions embedded in the original estimators developed by Epple and Sieg (1999) and Bayer, McMillen, and Reuben (2004). A clever econometrician could mix, match, and alter the features of the two models to develop new estimators. That said, no amount of econometric cleverness can ever identify the true behavioral model with absolute certainty. Perhaps the best way to evaluate the validity of a sorting model is to test its out-of-sample predictions for how people and markets will adjust to unexpected changes in the spatial landscape.

3. Evaluating the Benefits of Large-Scale Changes in the Spatial Landscape

Estimates for the structural parameters of a RUM or PCM model can be used to develop theoretically consistent predictions for the distribution of benefits from large-scale changes in the spatial distribution of prices or amenities. One can easily calculate partial equilibrium measures of willingness to pay (WTP) for a prospective policy change. The model can also be used to simulate the transition to the new equilibrium that would follow the introduction of the policy. Comparing the ex ante and ex post equilibria makes it possible to predict migration patterns, capitalization effects, changes in the levels of endogenous amenities, and the corresponding "general equilibrium" measures of WTP. In this section, we define "partial" and "general" equilibrium benefit measures and then discuss how to close the model and solve for a new equilibrium.

3.1 Benefit Measurement

Consider a policy that changes the supply of a single amenity in community j from g_{j1} to $\overset{*}{g}_{j1}$. A partial equilibrium measure of the willingness to pay for this change, WTP_{PE}, holds constant all other features of the equilibrium.[17] In contrast, a general equilibrium measure, WTP_{GE}, accounts for potential changes in housing prices, location choices, and the levels of other endogenous amenities. Equations (17a) and (17b) formalize this distinction,

$$V\left(\alpha_i, y_i - WTP_{PE}, \overset{*}{g}_{j1}, g_{j\sim1}, h_{n_j}, P_{n_j}\right) = V(\alpha_i, y_i, g_{j1}, g_{j\sim1}, h_{n_j}, P_{n_j}) \tag{17a}$$

$$V\left(\alpha_i, y_i - WTP_{GE}, \overset{*}{g}_{k1}, \overset{*}{g}_{k\sim1}, h_{m_k}, \overset{*}{P}_{m_k}\right) = V(\alpha_i, y_i, g_{j1}, g_{j\sim1}, h_{n_j}, P_{n_j}), \tag{17b}$$

[17] Calculation of partial equilibrium benefit measures differs between the PCM and RUM frameworks. In the PCM (17a) is inverted to calculate WTP directly. In the RUM, the idiosyncratic error term means that WTP must be defined as an expected value using a version of the usual log-sum rule.

where $g_j = [g_{j1}, g_{j-1}]$. In (17b) the change in subscripts from n_j to m_k recognizes that households may respond to the change by moving to a new location. The asterisk superscripts on g^*_{k-1} and $P^*_{m_k}$ recognize that, as people resort, their behavior may affect the levels of other endogenous amenities, and prices may need to adjust to clear the market. As $\Delta g_j = g_j - g_j$ grows or impacts a larger number of households, it becomes increasingly important to model general equilibrium feedback effects. Overall, the richness in this characterization for how people interact with their surrounding environment makes the general equilibrium sorting model a powerful framework for policy evaluation.

3.2 Closing the Model

The RUM and PCM estimators essentially characterize housing demand, treating the supply of housing as fixed. However, solving for a new equilibrium requires characterizing both supply and demand, as well as any sources of friction in the market. Thus, to close the model, the analyst must define the supply of housing, formalize their assumptions about moving costs, write down production functions for endogenous amenities, and clarify whether households are treated as owners or renters. The way that each of these issues is treated varies from application to application. However, three general trends are worth discussing.

First, land use policies often play dual roles. They simultaneously enhance open space amenities and they restrict urban development. As such, a new land use policy targeting the current supply of an amenity may also influence the future supply of housing. Although equilibrium sorting models are capable of modeling this connection, few applications have done so. Instead, the supply of housing is usually treated as fixed or defined by a constant-elasticity assumption (e.g., Sieg et al. 2004; Smith et al. 2004; Klaiber and Phaneuf 2010; Kuminoff 2011). This approach simplifies computation of the new equilibrium, but risks overlooking important policy implications. Future research that models the impacts of land use policies on both amenities and housing supply would be a welcome addition to the literature. Walsh (2007) provides an initial example of how this can be done.

Second, the initial general equilibrium applications have mostly treated households as being freely mobile. In our experience, this assumption tends to produce a good deal of consternation among seminar audiences. Anyone who has gone through the process of moving to a new house is all too familiar with the costs involved: physical costs, search costs, time costs, borrowing costs, and the psychological cost of adjusting to a new environment. The good news is that the structure of a sorting model makes it straightforward to utilize prior information about moving costs (Kuminoff 2009). For example, Kuminoff (2011) models the changes in commuting costs and wage rates that occur when working households alter their job and/or house locations. Likewise, Bayer, Keohane, and Timmins (2009) demonstrate that some moving costs can be estimated using related information, such as the location of an individual's hometown.

Finally, all of the applications we discuss in this chapter treat households as renters. Capital gains from housing sales are assumed to be captured by absentee landowners. This approach simplifies computation of the new equilibrium, but abstracts from issues that matter to policy makers. Many policies are effectively enacted on the owners of capital, especially policies influencing individual tax treatment. With this in mind, future research that builds changes in assets into the budget constraint would be another useful addition to the literature.

3.3 Solving for a New Equilibrium in a Random Utility Model

Solving for a new equilibrium in the RUM framework requires calculating housing prices, location choices, and the levels of endogenous amenities such that housing supply and housing demand equate in all locations. Klaiber and Phaneuf (2010) describe the solution process for the special case where amenities are exogenous. The basic idea is to iterate over price changes until the predicted market shares for each housing type equal the supply of housing for that type. The steps are as follows:

Step 1. Given the new spatial distribution of amenities, use the estimated preference parameters to calculate the aggregate demand for each housing type, $\sigma_{t_j}^{d,0}$, where d stands for "demand" and 0 indicates that this is the initial iteration of the algorithm.

Step 2. Determine whether excess demand ($\sigma_{t_j}^{d,0} > \sigma_{t_j}^{s}$) or excess supply ($\sigma_{t_j}^{d,0} < \sigma_{t_j}^{s}$) exists for each housing type.

Step 3. For types with excess demand, increase prices by a small percentage. Decrease prices by a small percentage for types with excess supply.[18]

Step 4. Using the new prices, recalculate the aggregate housing demand for each type, $\sigma_{t_j}^{d,1}$.

Step 5. Continue iterating over steps 2–4 until $\sigma_{t_j}^{d} = \sigma_{t_j}^{s}$ for every type.

3.4 Solving for a New Equilibrium in the Pure Characteristics Model

As in the RUM framework, it is straightforward to solve for a new PCM equilibrium in the special case where amenities are exogenous. The "vertical" restriction on preference heterogeneity allows the problem to be formulated as a one-dimensional root-finding problem. To see this, first recall that communities will always be ordered by

[18] A weighted average of previous and new prices can help to prevent oscillation in convergence. The magnitude of price changes can be weighted to be proportional to the difference in observed shares to speed convergence.

their equilibrium housing prices and provisions of public goods: $p_1 < p_2 < \cdots < p_J$ and $G_1 < G_2 < \cdots < G_J$. Following a shock to public goods, the new equilibrium price ranking must be identical to the new ranking by G. Using this fact, the solution algorithm proceeds as follows:

Step 1. Make a guess for the new price of housing in the cheapest community, p_1^*.
Step 2. Use the left side of (14) to sort households into community 1 until total housing demand equals supply, aggregating over (13) to calculate demand.
Step 3. Use the last household sorted into community 1 to solve for the value of p_2^* that satisfies (14).
Step 4. Repeat steps 2–3 for communities 2 through J, or until all households are assigned to communities.
Step 5. If there is excess housing supply in community J, increase p_1^* and return to step 2. If there is excess demand, decrease p_1^* and return to step 2.

This recursive structure effectively reduces the simulation to a one-dimensional problem where the new equilibrium price of housing in community 1 is adjusted until the market clears in community J.

3.5 Endogenous Amenities

RUM and PCM solution algorithms can be modified to recognize that, as households resort, their behavior can affect the supply of endogenous amenities. The way this is modeled is context-specific. We briefly describe three examples, each of which finds that endogenous adjustment of amenities is important for characterizing the impacts of a prospective policy.

Klaiber and Smith (2012) use a PCM to evaluate the general equilibrium implications of reductions in teaching staff in Maricopa County (Arizona) school districts. School quality is measured using the student/teacher ratio. Mandated reductions in teaching staff reduce school quality, inducing some households to move. As households with school-aged children move, the number of students in each school district changes, which feeds back into the student/teacher ratio, inducing additional households to move.... and so on until prices, location choices, and the student/teacher ratio all converge in equilibrium.

Walsh (2007) uses a PCM to investigate the impact of public open space preservation on households and urbanization in Wake County, North Carolina. He endogenizes the supply of housing by recognizing that privately owned farmland will tend to be developed as the demand for housing increases. As a result, land preservation polices can have unintended consequences. Suppose that public funds are used to purchase a small amount of scenic open space near a residential neighborhood. If the amenities associated with the preserved parcels increase the demand for housing in the neighborhood, it may actually accelerate the rate at which the remaining privately owned open space is developed.

Finally, Bayer and McMillan (2005) use a RUM to assess the role of households' preferences for several amenities, including the demographics of their neighbors. Measures of demographic composition, such as average income, average education, and neighborhood population shares by race, are directly determined by the sorting process. As a result, a public policy that influences an exogenous amenity is shown to be capable of altering neighborhood demographic composition.

4. Implications for Hedonic Estimation

Since hedonic and sorting models describe the same underlying equilibrium, advances in the sorting literature also improve our understanding of the challenges associated with using reduced-form hedonic regressions to evaluate the benefits of prospective changes in the spatial landscape. We briefly summarize three ways in which the theory, estimation, and simulation of sorting models has clarified the challenges with hedonic estimation.

4.1 The Economics of Omitted Variable Bias

Omitted variables systematically confound the identification of conventional hedonic regressions. This stylized fact has motivated an entire subliterature on quasi-experimental approaches to estimation (Parmeter and Pope 2013). The experimentalist perspective is that the analyst never observes all of the landscape amenities that are correlated with the amenity of interest. Breaking the correlation requires instruments that effectively randomize the amenity "treatment." The equilibrium sorting literature complements the experimentalist perspective by providing an explanation for omitted variable bias and suggesting further implications for benefit measurement.

If people choose where to live based, in part, on their heterogeneous incomes and preferences for amenities, then their location choices will influence the long run levels of endogenous amenities (Ferreyra 2007; Walsh 2007; Epple and Ferreyra 2008; Bayer and McMillan 2010). Under single-crossing restrictions on preferences, it is natural to expect multiple amenities to be spatially correlated. As wealthier households move to areas with nice microclimates and low crime rates, for example, they may vote to pass special assessments that enhance local public education. If data on microclimates and crime rates are unavailable, then conventional hedonic estimates of the MWTP for school quality will tend to be biased upward. This logic helps to explain why quasi-experimental estimates of the MWTP for school quality are typically less than half the size of estimates from conventional hedonic regressions (Black 1999; Bayer et al. 2007; Kuminoff and Pope 2014).

Endogenous amenities present an additional challenge for benefit measurement. A public policy that alters the spatial distribution of one amenity may influence the long-run levels of other endogenous amenities. In this case, hedonic price functions do not provide enough information to evaluate the welfare implications of the policy.

4.2 Benefit Measurement and Policy Evaluation

The empirical hedonic literature is mostly limited to estimating the willingness to pay for marginal changes in amenities.[19] However, estimates for average MWTP are often used to approximate the benefits from prospective policies that would produce nonmarginal changes. Sorting models underscore the limitations of this strategy and provide a means to address them.

Hedonic and sorting models tend to generate similar estimates for average MWTP. For example, Sieg et al. (2004) find that the average MWTP for reduced ozone concentrations is approximately \$67 (1990 dollars) per household in the Los Angeles metro area. This figure is well within the range of estimates from comparable hedonic studies (\$8–\$181).[20] Bayer, Ferreira, and McMillan (2007) provide a more refined comparison. Using the same data and the same quasi-experimental identification strategy, they find that hedonic and RUM estimates of the average MWTP for school quality differ by less than 14%. However, average MWTP is rarely a sufficient statistic for policy evaluation. Policy makers care about distributional implications. Moreover, developing credible benefit measures requires recognizing the demand is less than perfectly elastic and that people may react to the policy by adjusting their behavior.

Heterogeneity in preferences and the supply of amenities can lead to wide benefit distributions. For example, Sieg et al. (2004) find that the average *marginal* WTP for air quality in Los Angeles County is twice as large as in neighboring Ventura County. When they evaluate the *nonmarginal* ozone reductions that actually occurred between 1990 and 1995, the difference in WTP between Los Angeles and Ventura increases to 800%! This difference arises from a combination of lower baseline levels of ozone in Ventura, a smaller reduction in Ventura between 1990 and 1995, and heterogeneity in preferences and income. Predicted adjustments to housing prices and location choices also have

19 Rosen's (1974) original vision for hedonic demand estimation remains unfulfilled due to the difficulty with identifying demand curves (Bartik 1987; Epple 1987).

20 Klaiber and Phaneuf (2010) provide a more detailed comparison. Using the same dataset (but different controls for omitted variables), they find that hedonic and sorting models produce very similar estimates of MWTP for some types of open space (\$30 vs. \$28 for a 1% increase in local parks) and very different estimates for other types of open space (–\$277 vs. \$618 for a 1% increase in agricultural preserves).

significant welfare implications. Partial and general equilibrium benefit measures differ by over 100% for the average Ventura household.

4.3 The Wedge Between Capitalization Effects and Benefit Measures

Public policies or unexpected events that shock the spatial distribution of an amenity can also be used to identify the rate at which that amenity is capitalized into property values. The quasi-experimental branch of the hedonic literature has focused on developing clever research designs for identifying these "capitalization effects" (see Parmeter and Pope [2013] for examples). These studies typically reformulate the price function within a panel data framework, using first differences, fixed effects, or difference-in-difference estimators. The resulting estimates for capitalization effects are interesting, but they cannot be interpreted as benefit measures unless we are prepared to make a series of heroic assumptions about people and markets.

One of the key maintained assumptions that make it possible to interpret marginal capitalization effects as measures of MWTP is that the gradient of the hedonic price function is constant over the duration of the study. This assumption effectively requires demand curves for the amenity to be perfectly elastic. If demand is downward sloping, the adjustment to a new sorting equilibrium will generally produce a wedge between the marginal capitalization effect and the MWTP. The size of the wedge will depend on the distribution of income and preferences, the supply response, and concomitant changes to the landscape over the duration of the study.

The wedge between capitalization and willingness to pay can be very large. Kuminoff and Pope (2014) find that capitalization effects for reported changes in public school quality tendto differ from quasi-experimental measures of ex ante and ex post MWTP by more than 100%. Likewise, Klaiber and Smith (2013) find it difficult to predict the size or the direction of the bias in using capitalization effects to approximate the benefits of nonmarginal changes. These findings reinforce the earlier theoretical results of Lind (1973) and Starrett (1981), as well as simulation results from Sieg et al. (2004) and Smith et al. (2004), where predicted changes in housing prices bear little resemblance to predicted changes in benefits. Thus, the collective evidence from the sorting literature suggests that capitalization effects for amenities are best interpreted literally, as a statistical description of changes in housing asset values.

5. Conclusion

Equilibrium sorting models provide a powerful framework for modeling the two-way interaction between people and their surrounding environment. They have tremendous potential for policy evaluation. The Clean Air Act, the Clean Water Act, and the Superfund program are examples of major public policies designed to produce large-scale changes in the spatial distribution of nonmarket amenities. We would like to understand their distributional implications and be able to predict how new policies will affect consumer welfare and market outcomes. Equilibrium sorting models are the first revealed preference framework capable of meeting this task while recognizing that people adapt to changes in their surrounding environment.

Like every revealed preference framework, sorting models rely on maintained assumptions about the structure of consumer preferences. This means their predictions for benefit measures, housing market outcomes, and the evolution of the surrounding landscape are best viewed as approximations. How accurate are these approximations? The ability to answer this question is one of the novelties of the literature. Sorting models make testable predictions for market and nonmarket outcomes! Thus, the same types of natural experiments and policy discontinuities that have been used to develop instruments for reduced-form hedonic models could also be used to test a sorting model's predictions for property value capitalization effects and migration patterns. Future evidence on external validity would help to refine the current generation of estimators and continue to advance the literature.

Finally, our objective has been to provide an introductory guide to sorting models for empirical analysts. We have tried to be clear about the subtleties of the microeconometric models and the mechanics of estimation and simulation procedures. Nevertheless, our own experience has been that the most effective way to learn a sorting model is to "get your hands dirty." Readers who are up to the challenge can find examples of data and code on our webpages.

Acknowledgments

Our research on equilibrium sorting has benefited from collaborations and conversations with several colleagues. We thank without implicating Pat Bayer, Spencer Banzhaf, Antonio Bento, Amy Binner, Kelly Bishop, Keith Evans, Paul Fackler, Michael Hanemann, Abdul Jarrah, Alvin Murphy, Ray Palmquist, Chris Parmeter, Dan Phaneuf, Jaren Pope, V. Kerry Smith, Chris Timmins, Roger von Haefen, Randy Walsh, and Kent Zhao. We also thank JunJie Wu for helpful comments on an earlier draft of this chapter.

References

Bajari, P., and C. L. Benkard. 2005. Demand estimation with heterogeneous consumers and unobserved product characteristics: A hedonic approach. *Journal of Political Economy* 113(6): 1239–1276.

Bartik, T. J. 1987. The estimation of demand parameters in hedonic price models. *Journal of Political Economy* 95(1): 81–88.

Bayer, P., F. Ferreira, and R. McMillan. 2007. A unified framework for measuring preferences for schools and neighborhoods. *Journal of Political Economy* 115(4): 588–638.

Bayer, P., N. Keohane, and C. Timmins. 2009. Migration and hedonic valuation: The case of air quality. *Journal of Environmental Economics and Management* 58(1): 1–14.

Bayer, P., and R. McMillan. 2005. Racial sorting and neighborhood quality. NBER Working Paper No. 11813.

Bayer, P., and R. McMillan. 2010. Tiebout sorting and neighborhood stratification. ERID Working Paper 49.

Bayer, P., R. McMillan, and K. Reuben. 2004. An equilibrium model of sorting in an urban housing market. NBER Working Paper No. 10865.

Bayer, P., and C. Timmins. 2005. On the equilibrium properties of locational sorting models. *Journal of Urban Economics* 57(3): 462–477.

Bayer, P., and C. Timmins. 2007. Estimating equilibrium models of sorting across locations. *The Economic Journal* 117(518): 353–374.

Berry, S. 1994. Estimating discrete-choice models of product differentiation. *The RAND Journal of Economics* 25(2): 242–262.

Berry, S., O. B. Linton, and A. Pakes. 2004. Limit theorems for estimating the parameters of differentiated product demand systems. *Review of Economic Studies* 71(3): 613–654.

Berry, S., and A. Pakes. 2007. The pure characteristics demand model. *International Economic Review* 48(4): 1193–1225.

Black, S. E. 1999. Do better schools matter? Parental valuation of elementary education. *Quarterly Journal of Economics* 114(2): 577–599.

Ellickson, B. 1971. Jurisdictional fragmentation and residential choice. *American Economic Review* 61(2): 334–339.

Epple, D. 1987. Hedonic prices and implicit markets: Estimating demand and supply functions for differentiated products. *Journal of Political Economy* 95(1): 59–80.

Epple, D., and M. M. Ferreyra. 2008. School finance reform: Assessing general equilibrium effects. *Journal of Public Economics* 92(5–6): 1328–1351.

Epple, D., R. Filimon, and T. Romer. 1984. Equilibrium among local jurisdictions: Toward an integrated treatment of voting and residential choice. *Journal of Public Economics* 24(3): 281–308.

Epple, D., R. Filimon, and T. Romer. 1993. Existence of voting and housing equilibria in a system of communities with property taxes. *Regional Science and Urban Economics* 23(5): 585–610.

Epple, D., and G. J. Platt. 1998. Equilibrium and local redistribution in an urban economy when households differ in both preferences and incomes. *Journal of Urban Economics* 43(1): 23–51.

Epple, D., B. Gordon, and H. Sieg. 2010. Drs. Muth and Mills meet Dr. Tiebout: Integrating location-specific amenities into multi-community equilibrium models. *Journal of Regional Science* 50(1): 381–400.

Epple, D., and T. Romer. 1991. Mobility and redistribution. *Journal of Political Economy* 99(4): 828–858.

Epple, D., and H. Sieg. 1999. Estimating equilibrium models of local jurisdiction. *Journal of Political Economy* 107(4): 645–681.

Ferreyra, M. M. 2007. Estimating the effects of private school vouchers in multi-district economies. *American Economic Review* 97(3): 789–817.

Herriges, J., and C. Kling. 1999. Nonlinear income effects in random utility models. *Review of Economics and Statistics* 81(1): 62–72.

Klaiber, H. A., and D. J. Phaneuf. 2010. Valuing open space in a residential sorting model of the Twin Cities. *Journal of Environmental Economics and Management* 60(2): 57–77.

Klaiber, H. A., and V. K. Smith. 2011. Preference heterogeneity and non-market benefits: The roles of structural hedonics and sorting models. *International handbook on non-market environmental valuation*, ed. J. Bennet, 222–253. Northampton, MA: Edward Elgar.

Klaiber, H. A., and V. K. Smith. 2012. Developing general equilibrium benefit analyses for social programs: An introduction and example. *Journal of Benefit-Cost Analysis* 3(2).

Klaiber, H. A., and V. K. Smith. 2013. Quasi experiments, hedonic models, and estimating tradeoffs for local amenities. *Land Economics* 89: 413–431.

Kuminoff, N. V. 2009. Decomposing the structural identification of nonmarket values. *Journal of Environmental Economics and Management* 57(2): 123–139.

Kuminoff, N. V. 2011. An intraregional model of housing and labor markets for estimating the general equilibrium benefits of large changes in public goods. AERE 2011 Summer Conference Sponsored Session Paper. http://www.webmeets.com/aere/2011/Prog/viewpaper.asp?pid=487.

Kuminoff, N. V., and A. S. Jarrah. 2010. A new approach to computing hedonic equilibria and investigating the properties of locational sorting models. *Journal of Urban Economics* 67(3): 322–335.

Kuminoff, N. V., and J. C. Pope. 2014. Do 'capitalization effects' for public goods reveal the public's willingness to pay? *International Economic Review*, in press.

Kuminoff, N. V., V. K. Smith, and C. Timmins. In press. The new economics of equilibrium sorting and its transformational role for policy evaluation. *Journal of Economic Literature* 51(4): 1007–1062.

Lancaster, K. J. 1979. *Variety, equity, and efficiency*. New York: Columbia University Press.

Lind, R. C. 1973. Spatial equilibrium, the theory of rents, and the measurement of benefits from public programs. *Quarterly Journal of Economics* 87(2): 188–207.

McFadden, D. 1974. Conditional logit analysis of qualitative choice behavior. In *Frontiers in econometrics*, ed. Paul Zarembka, 105–142. New York: Academic Press:

McFadden, D. 1999. Computing willingness-to-pay in random utility models. In *Trade, theory and econometrics: Essays in honor of John S. Chipman*, eds. J. Moore, R. Riezman, and J. Melvin, 253–274. London: Routledge.

Nechyba, T. J. 1997. Existence of equilibrium and stratification in local and hierarchical Tiebout economies with property taxes and voting. *Economic Theory* 10(2): 277–304.

Palmquist, R. B. 2005. Property value models. In *Handbook of environmental economics*, Vol. 2, eds. Karl-Göran Mäler and Jeffery Vincent, 763–820. Amsterdam: North Holland Press:

Parmeter, C. F., and J. C. Pope. 2013. Quasi-experiments and hedonic property value methods. In *Handbook on experimental economics and the environment*, eds. John List and Michael Price. Northampton, MA: Edward Elgar.

Poterba, J. M. 1992. Housing and taxation: Old questions, new answers. *American Economic Review* 82: 237–242.

Rosen, S. 1974. Hedonic prices and implicit markets: Product differentiation in pure competition. *Journal of Political Economy* 82(1): 34–55.

Sieg, H., V. K. Smith, H. S. Banzhaf, and R. Walsh. 2002. Interjurisdictional housing prices in location equilibrium. *Journal of Urban Economics* 52(1): 131–153.

Sieg, H., V. K. Smith, H. S. Banzhaf, and R. Walsh. 2004. Estimating the general equilibrium benefits of large changes in spatially delineated public goods. *International Economic Review* 45(4): 1047–1077.

Smith, V. K., H. Sieg, H. S. Banzhaf, and R. Walsh. 2004. General equilibrium benefits for environmental improvements: Projected ozone reductions under EPA's prospective analysis for the Los Angeles air basin. *Journal of Environmental Economics and Management* 47(3): 559–584.

Starrett, D. A. 1981. Land value capitalization in local public finance. *Journal of Political Economy* 89(2): 306–327.

Tiebout, C. M. 1956. A pure theory of local expenditures. *Journal of Political Economy* 64(5): 416–424.

Tra, C. I. 2010. A discrete choice equilibrium approach to valuing large environmental changes. *Journal of Public Economics* 94 (1–2): 183–196.

Tukey, J. W. 1962. The future of data analysis. *Annals of Mathematical Statistics* 33(1): 1–67.

Walsh, R. L. 2007. Endogenous open space amenities in a locational equilibrium. *Journal of Urban Economics* 61(2): 319–344.

Westoff, F. 1977. Existence of equilibria in economies with a local public good. *Journal of Economic Theory* 14(1): 84–112.

Wu, J., and S-H. Cho. 2003. Estimating households' preferences for environmental amenities using equilibrium models of local jurisdictions. *Scottish Journal of Political Economy* 50(2): 198–206.

CHAPTER 15

LANDSCAPE SIMULATIONS WITH ECONOMETRIC-BASED LAND USE MODELS

ANDREW J. PLANTINGA AND DAVID J. LEWIS

THE spatial configuration of land use and land cover has important influences on populations of birds (Askins 2002; Faaborg 2002) and amphibians (Kolozsvary and Swihart 1999; deMaynadier and Hunter 2000), the health of riverine systems (Gergel et al. 2002) and estuaries (Hale et al. 2004), human perceptions of scenic quality (Palmer 2004), and the extent of urban sprawl (Carrion-Flores and Irwin 2004). Land use change results in changes in the spatial pattern of land use, often in ways that diminish environmental quality. For example, habitat fragmentation can occur when changes in land use transform a contiguous habitat patch into disjunct patches. Many species of conservation interest are sensitive to habitat fragmentation, including birds (Askins 2002; Faaborg 2002), amphibians (Kolozsvary and Swihart 1999; Lehtinen et al. 2003), and large mammals (Costa et al. 2005; Noss et al. 2006). Land use change is the leading driver of biodiversity loss in terrestrial ecosystems and is expected to remain so in the future (Sala et al. 2000; Wilcove et al. 2000; Millennium Ecosystem Assessment 2005).

Much of the habitat important for biodiversity conservation occurs on privately owned land. One study found that 70% of species listed under the U.S. Endangered Species Act (ESA) depend on nonfederal land, most of which is privately owned, for the majority of their habitat (Natural Heritage Data Center Network 1993). In landscapes dominated by private ownership, landowners lack the incentive to coordinate decisions to influence the spatial land use pattern and the environmental outcomes that depend on it. Econometric-based landscape simulation models have been developed to understand the nature and extent of this market failure problem and to identify and quantify the effects of corrective land use policies. A landscape simulation begins with a spatial representation of the landscape, such as a land use map in which the unit of analysis is a land parcel, and simulates changes in the landscape through the use of rules applied at the unit scale. An econometric-based simulation model uses rules derived from econometric estimation. For example, Lewis and Plantinga (2007) estimate an econometric model that relates observed land use changes to economic returns to alternatives uses. The econometric results are then incorporated into a landscape simulation model used to study how forest fragmentation is affected by incentive-based policies that modify the relative returns to different uses. Lewis, Plantinga, and Wu (2009) analyze the spatial targeting of incentives to increase contiguous forest habitat, and Lewis et al. (2011) consider the relative efficiency of voluntary incentive-based policies in achieving biodiversity conservation objectives. The latter analysis combines an econometric land use model, landscape simulations, and a biological model of biodiversity that depends on the spatial pattern of land use.

The development of econometric-based simulations for landscapes dominated by private ownership presents four basic challenges. The first is to represent variation in the private economic returns to land at the same scale at which land use varies. Hedonic price studies reveal that returns to urban land uses vary considerably at fine spatial scales. Housing prices, for example, are affected by proximity to the central business district, roads, and amenities (Wu et al. 2004), as well as by spatial interactions with neighboring parcels (Irwin and Bockstael 2002). Returns to rural land uses, such as cropland and forests, typically exhibit little variation at this scale because output and input prices for land-based commodities are relatively constant over space. Factors that can cause varation in rural land returns include soil quality, which affects crop and timber yields, and access to markets. Land use regulations, such as zoning restrictions, can also have important effects on economic returns (Grout et al. 2011).

The second challenge is to model the private information that landowners possess about the returns to their land. Researchers have incomplete information about private returns because of unobservable parcel attributes, landowner characteristics such as managerial expertise, and private nonmarket benefits (e.g., recreation) associated with particular uses of the land. The random utility framework is a common way to accommodate the incomplete information. The returns to land are represented by a deterministic component and a random error observed only by the landowner. This gives rise to a probabilistic model of land use change, as in Lubowski, Plantinga, and Stavins (2006). Lewis et al. (2011) estimate a mixed logit model that includes random parameters to account for spatial and temporal correlation in land use decisions. Their results indicate a significant degree of unobserved heterogeneity in returns to land.

The third challenge is how to best account for land use intensity. In addition to choosing the use of their land, landowners must decide on the intensity of use. For example, once the landowner has chosen to develop her land, she must also decide on how many housing lots to build per acre or how many floors to add to a commercial building. Likewise, a farmer who allocates his land to crops must decide which crops to produce and how intensively to cultivate them. Finally, the forest owner must choose species and rotation length, among other management decisions. Land use intensity is, thus, the set of secondary choices faced by a landowner once the land use decision has been made. Land use intensity has important implications for econometric land use models because it affects the economic return to the chosen use. In many previous studies, land use intensity is implicitly assumed in the measurement of net returns to each use (e.g., Stavins and Jaffe 1990; Plantinga 1996; Lubowski et al. 2006).[1] Lewis, Provencher, and Butsic (2009) and Lewis (2010), however, model land intensity as a joint decision with land use. Explicit representation of land use intensity may be warranted if differences in intensity are important for the landscape-level processes of interest. For example, in the application presented here, the intensity of development—measured as the number of shoreline housing lots—has important effects on the green frog population we study.

The fourth challenge arises from the probabilistic nature of the land use transition rules derived from econometric analysis (Bockstael 1996). The researcher can determine whether a particular parcel is more likely to convert than another parcel but not that any particular parcel will convert with certainty. Some analysts present maps showing the spatial distribution of the estimated probabilities (Bockstael 1996; Cropper et al. 2001), whereas others form deterministic rules from probabilistic ones (e.g., Chomitz and Gray 1996; Irwin and Bockstael 2002). A problem with the latter approach is that a given deterministic rule is only one of many possible rules. Thus, the simulation produces a single landscape that represents only one of what is typically a very large number of potential landscapes. An alternative is to generate a large number of different landscapes conforming to the underlying probabilistic rules. However, one must then summarize this information in a way that effectively conveys the range of potential outcomes.

This chapter discusses landscape simulations based on econometric land use models, emphasizing ways to overcome the four challenges just mentioned. Section 1 reviews the related literature. Section 2 presents the basic methodology for econometric modeling of private land use decisions, and Section 3 describes the use of these models in landscape simulations. An application of the methods is provided in section 4, and a final section considers directions for future research.

1. Previous Literature

Numerous studies in the economics literature seek to explain observed land use decisions in terms of profit-maximizing behavior. Early studies employed aggregate (typically county-level) data on land use (Stavins and Jaffe 1990; Plantinga 1996; Hardie and Parks 1997), whereas more recent analyses have used plot-level data (Lubowski et al. 2006; Lewis et al. 2011) and spatially explicit land use or land cover data (Bockstael 1996; Cropper et al. 2001; Nelson et al. 2001; Irwin and Bockstael 2002, 2004; Carrion-Flores and Irwin 2004). An advantage of spatial data is that they allow spatial processes to be modeled explicitly. For example, Bockstael (1996) uses a

[1] Lubowski, Plantinga, and Stavins (2006), for example, construct net returns to forest by assuming that landowners choose the existing mix of forest species in their county and follow the Faustmann rule in determining the rotation length.

hedonic function of residential development value to predict the potential developed value of agricultural parcels. The hedonic function includes measures of distances to cities, water access, and neighborhood characteristics. The potential development values are used, along with other controls, in a probit model of land conversion estimated with spatially explicit data.

The results of econometric estimation provide a set of rules governing parcel-level changes in land use. By combining econometric results with a geographic information system (GIS)-based landscape representation, Lewis and Plantinga (2007), Lewis, Plantinga, and Wu (2009), Nelson et al. (2008), and Lewis et al. (2011) simulate future land use patterns under alternative biodiversity conservation policy scenarios. Their simulations account for land conversion into urban use, as well as exchanges between rural uses (e.g., cropland to forest), which have important implications for species habitat. Many earlier landscape simulation studies focused on urbanization (e.g., Bockstael 1996; Carrion-Flores and Irwin 2004) or deforestation (e.g., Nelson et al. 2001). Researchers in other disciplines, notably geography, have also made important contributions to the development of spatial models of landscape change (Clarke and Gaydos 1998; Wu 1998, 2002; Li and Gar-On Yeh 2000 Allen and Lu 2003; Guzy et al. 2008). A criticism of the models in the geography literature is that the transition rules represent human decisions yet typically are not based on well-specified and empirically validated models of human behavior (Wu and Webster 2000).

The literature on systematic conservation planning (SCP) is also concerned with characterizing future landscapes (Margules and Pressey 2000). In contrast to the simulation approach just discussed, SCP uses optimization methods to identify sites for conservation. In the basic formulation of the problem, sites are chosen to maximize species conservation, subject to a constraint on the total area conserved or total conservation budget allotted (e.g., Kirkpatrick 1983; Vane-Wright et al. 1991; Camm et al. 1996; Church et al. 1996; Csuti et al. 1997). Extensions of the basic optimization problem incorporate land costs (e.g., Ando et al. 1998; Balmford et al. 2000; Polasky et al. 2001), considerations of compactness or contiguity (e.g., Fischer and Church 2003; Onal and Briers 2003), and dynamics (e.g., Costello and Polasky 2004; Meir et al. 2004; Newburn et al. 2006; Strange et al. 2006). More recent studies in the SCP literature have analyzed complex spatial patterns that affect species persistence, including habitat fragmentation and dispersal ability (e.g., Cabeza and Moilanen 2003; Nalle et al. 2004; Moilanen et al. 2005; Polasky et al. 2005, 2008; Nicholson et al. 2006; Jiang et al. 2007).

2. Econometric Models

The results of econometric estimation provide a set of rules governing land use change in landscape simulations. In this section, we present a general framework for specifying and estimating econometric land use models with parcel-scale data. We also discuss strategies to address the first three challenges described: how to represent variation in the private economic returns to land at the same scale at which land use varies, how to model the private information that landowners possess about the returns to their land, and how to account for land use intensity.

2.1 Model Specification

Landowners are assumed to allocate a land parcel of uniform quality to the use that maximizes the present discounted value of expected net revenues minus conversion costs. It is convenient to assume that landowners form static expectations. That is, landowners consider currently available information and form an expectation about the future annual return to their land that is constant (although can be updated as new information becomes available). The assumption of static expectations yields a simple decision rule under which the use generating the greatest annualized net revenues net of conversion costs is chosen (Plantinga 1996). The problem with relaxing this assumption is that the land use decision then depends on the future sequence of net returns, and one must apply Bellman's equation to find the optimal solution. This complicates the estimation problem considerably, although previous authors have estimated structural models of dynamic decision making (e.g., Rust 1989; Provencher 1995). An interesting application of these methods would be to the land use decision problem.

Assuming static expectations, the landowner compares the annualized net return to alternative uses and allocates her parcel to the use providing the greatest return. The net return (NR_{ikt}) equals the annual net revenues generated from parcel (R_{ikt}) less annualized conversion costs (C_{ijkt}), where i indexes the parcel, k the chosen use, j the initial use, and t the time. In general, the researcher cannot observe all of the factors that determine net returns to the landowner, motivating a specification of net returns that includes deterministic and random components, such as:

$$NR_{ikt} = \beta_{0jk} + \beta_{1jk} R_{ikt} + \beta_{2jk} C_{ijkt} + \mu_{ijkt}, \tag{1}$$

where $(\beta_{0jk}, \beta_{1jk}, \beta_{2jk})$ are parameters specific to the j-to-k transition and μ_{ijkt} is a random error term.

Lewis et al. (2011) adopt the following specification of net returns, which is a special case of (1):

$$NR_{ikt} = \beta_{0jk} + \beta_{1jk} R_{c(i)kt} + \beta_{2jk} LCC_i R_{c(i)kt} + \mu_{ijkt}, \tag{2}$$

where $R_{c(i)kt}$ is the average net revenue from use k at time t in county $c(i)$ where parcel i is located and LCC_i indicates the productivity, as measured by the Land Capability Class (LCC) rating, of parcel i. The LCC system assigns a rating of I through VIII to a land parcel, where lower numbers indicate higher productivity for agricultural crops. The interaction of $R_{c(i)kt}$ and LCC_i allows the net revenue for parcel i to deviate from the county average net revenue due to observable land quality. The effects of annualized conversion costs are assumed to be constant across parcels and time and are measured implicitly by β_{0jk}. Similar specifications are used in Lubowski et al. (2006) and Lewis and Plantinga (2007).

The three studies mentioned earlier meet the first modeling challenge—representing variation in the private economic returns to land at the same scale at which land use varies—using the interaction of the county average net return and parcel-level land quality. An alternative approach is to use parcel-level data to estimate separate hedonic price models for the net returns to each use. These models can incorporate spatial variables, such as distances to urban centers and features of the surrounding landscape, and be used to predict net returns for the unselected land uses in the choice set. In this fashion, Bockstael (1996) estimates a hedonic price model of the value of land in residential housing. Parcel-level predictions of the value of land in residential use are then incorporated into a probit model to explain development of agricultural land. Carrion-Flores and Irwin (2004) and Newburn, Berck, and Merenlender (2006) enter the determinants of net returns (e.g., slope, elevation, soil characteristics, distances to cities, zoning, and neighboring land uses) directly into the land use change model. The disadvantage of this reduced-form approach is that one loses economic information—specifically, the relationship between land use decisions and net returns—that can be used in simulations of incentive-based policies, such as subsidies for land conversion.

The random utility framework, adopted for all of the econometric land use models discussed in this section, addresses the second challenge—modeling the private information that landowners possess about the returns to their land. In (1), the deterministic component of net returns, $\beta_{0jk} + \beta_{1jk}R_{ikt} + \beta_{2jk}C_{ijkt}$, is assumed to be common knowledge, whereas the random error μ_{ijkt} is observed by the landowner, but not by the researcher. The average net revenues from crop production in a county, R_{ijkt}, are typically observable, but the researcher is unlikely to observe deviations from the mean return due to landowner-specific skills, knowledge, and other individual attributes. These deviations are captured in μ_{ijkt} and represent a landowner's private information about her returns. In all but one of the studies mentioned, researchers impose assumptions on the distribution of μ_{ijkt} that yield probit or multinomial logit models. Lewis et al. (2011) have panel data on land use change and thus can use a more flexible random parameters specification:

$$\mu_{ijkt} = \sigma_{1jk}\varpi_{1c(i)jk} + \sigma_{2jk}\varpi_{2ijk} + \varepsilon_{ijkt}, \quad (3)$$

where $(\varepsilon_{ijkt}, \varpi_{1c(i)jk}, \varpi_{2ijk})$ are random variables and $(\sigma_{1jk}, \sigma_{2jk})$ are parameters. The random parameters allow for spatial correlation ($\sigma_{1jk}\varpi_{1c(i)jk}$ takes the same value for all parcels within a county) and temporal correlation ($\sigma_{1jk}\varpi_{2ijk}$ takes the same value for a given parcel in all time periods).[2]

A useful property of random utility models is that they define a distribution over—in the land use context—the maximum net return from each land parcel. Given the starting use *j*, and *K* possible land use choices, the maximum net return derived from parcel *i* in time *t* is:

$$R_{ijt}^{*} = \max\{\beta_{0jk} + \beta_{1jk}R_{ikt} + \beta_{2jk}C_{ijkt} + \mu_{ijkt}\}_{k=1}^{K}. \tag{4}$$

The assumption that μ_{ijkt} is distributed type I extreme value allows (4) to be rewritten:

$$R_{ijt}^{*} = \frac{1}{\xi_j}\left(\ln\left[\sum_k \exp(\beta_{0jk} + \beta_{1jk}R_{ikt} + \beta_{2jk}C_{ijkt})\right] - \gamma\right) + v_{ijt}, \tag{5}$$

where γ is Euler's constant and v_{ijt} is distributed type I extreme value with location parameter equal to zero and scale parameter ξ_j (Ben-Akiva and Lerman 1985). Equation (5) can be used in landscape simulations to introduce land uses other than those in the original choice set, as long as one can assume that landowners will accept the maximum net return from their parcel as compensation for adopting the new use. Lewis et al. (2011) use this approach to model habitat conservation on private land. In this context, equation (5) defines a distribution over landowners' willingness to accept conservation payments.

This discussion assumes that the net returns in (1) are fixed. In most cases, however, the net return is chosen by the landowner when she selects the land use intensity. The appropriate way to model this is the third challenge discussed earlier. Formally, for parcel *i*, use *k*, and time *t*, the landowner chooses the intensity *m* to solve:

$$NR_{ikt} = \max_m \left\{NR_{ikt,m}\right\}_{m=1}^{M_k}, \tag{6}$$

where M_k is the number of intensity choices associated with use *k*. The simplest approach is for the researcher to assume she knows the solution to (6) (or at least the deterministic component of the solution). Provided that one can observe the choice of intensity, a

[2] Many econometric challenges arise with the estimation of econometric land use models, particularly when spatial processes are an important feature of land use decisions. See Brady and Irwin (2011) for discussion of these issues.

more flexible approach is to model the intensity decision explicitly. A natural extension of the random utility models discussed here is to model intensity as a nested choice conditional on land use. In this formulation, the landowner is assumed to simultaneously choose land use and intensity, conditional on the net returns to each use-intensity combination. Lewis, Provencher, and Butsic (2009) estimate a probit model of the binary development decision jointly with a count model of the number of housing lots. They address the sample selection problem inherent to their data; namely, that the number of housing lots are observed only for developed parcels. Landscape simulations are normally concerned with the population of land parcels, which argues for the use of econometric methods that can mitigate sample selection bias.

3. Landscape Simulations

The results from the estimation of econometric land use models translate into a set of rules governing land use change. In the case of random utility models, specifically, the researcher obtains a $K \times K$ matrix of land use transition probabilities for each parcel:

$$P_{ijkt} = F(\mathbf{X}_{it}' \hat{\beta}_{jk}), \tag{7}$$

where $\mathbf{X}_{it}$ is a vector of explanatory variables for parcel i in time t (e.g., the net returns to each of the alternative uses) and $\hat{\beta}_{jk}$ is the vector of estimated parameters associated with the use j-to-k transition. The transition matrices are then matched to parcels in a GIS using the variables in $\mathbf{X}_{it}$. Figure 15.1 illustrates how this is done for the model specification in (2). One obtains GIS layers on land ownership, political boundaries, soil quality, and initial land cover and overlays them to define distinct parcels on the landscape. Each parcel corresponds to a set of transition probabilities defined in (7). The land ownership layer is needed to eliminate public land parcels since the econometric model applies only to private lands. The county and soil quality layers indicate the values of $R_{c(i)kt}$ and LCC_i to use in applying (7), and the land cover layer indicates the initial set of estimated parameters to use. If j is the initial land use of the parcel, then the relevant parameter set is $\hat{\beta}_{jk}$, $k = 1,\ldots, K$. In a similar fashion, one can associate a maximum net return distribution with each parcel in the GIS.

Once this matching exercise is complete, Monte Carlo methods are used to simulate future changes in the landscape. To begin, suppose that parcel i is initially in crop use and, according to the matched set of transition probabilities for the parcel, will remain in crops with a 70% probability and change to pasture, forest, and urban use, each with a 10% probability. A random draw from a specified distribution, such as a U(0,1), determines whether the parcel remain in crops (e.g., if the random draw is between 0 and 0.70), changes to pasture (between 0.70 and 0.80), and so on. This procedure is repeated for every parcel and results in a period t+1 landscape. The transition probabilities are then updated for each

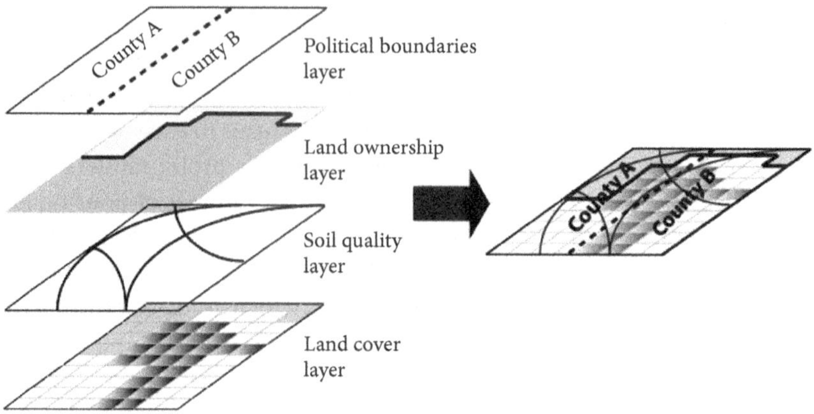

FIGURE 15.1 Matching land use transition matrices to parcels in a geographic information system (GIS).

parcel on the $t+1$ landscape. For example, if parcel i changed to pasture use, then transition probabilities for this parcel must be computed with a different parameter set. Or, net returns may be different in period $t+1$ due, for example, to endogenous price feedbacks. This process is repeated until a landscape representation is obtained for the future period of interest.

Of course, the simulated landscape is only one of many possible landscapes consistent with the underlying transition rules. Some earlier authors have used the transition probabilities to form a deterministic rule for land use change (Chomitz and Gray 1996; Irwin and Bockstael 2002). For example, Nelson and Hellerstein (1997) and Nelson et al. (2001) assume that each parcel will be put to the use with the highest estimated transition probability. This practice, however, is at odds with the random utility framework underlying the econometric model. Because of the unobserved component of net returns, the researcher does not have the information needed to predict changes in land use with certainty. Only probabilistic statements about land use changes can be made. To characterize the range of potential outcomes, one can repeat the process described here many times to generate a large number of future landscapes, each of which is consistent with the probabilistic transition rules. This, however, raises our fourth modeling challenge: how does one summarize this information in a way that effectively conveys the range of potential outcomes?

Lewis and Plantinga (2007) solve this informational challenge with landscape metrics that summarize the spatial pattern of land use. The focus of their study is forest fragmentation, and so, for each landscape, they compute the average forest patch size and the area of core forest (forest parcels that are completely surrounded by other forest parcels). This defines a distribution over the landscape metrics. In a similar fashion, Lewis et al. (2011) convert each landscape into a biodiversity score using a biological model that combines simulated landscapes with information on species and habitats. They summarize the results by computing the mean biodiversity score.

An important question that arises in Monte Carlo analysis is how many repetitions are enough? In the context of our problem, how many landscapes need to be simulated? In most cases, the number of possible landscapes will be astronomically large. For instance, there are 5×10^{47} possible ways to arrange three land uses on a 100-parcel landscape. Fortunately, the researcher is interested not in describing all possible landscapes, but rather with characterizing the distribution over the outcome of interest, such as a fragmentation metric or a biodiversity score. Stability in the outcome distribution is likely to be achieved after a relatively small number of simulations. The ideal approach would be to implement a convergence rule that would end the simulations when additional landscapes change the outcome distribution in a sufficiently small way, although this may not be feasible if multiple computer programs are in use. In his study of forest fragmentation, Lewis (2005) found that the first three moments of the distributions defined over five fragmentation indices changed very little once 500 landscapes had been simulated. As a further test, Lewis generated two samples of 500 landscapes and tested for differences in the sample moments across the two samples. Of course, these tests need to be done for each application to ensure the stability of the outcome distributions.

The power of econometric-based landscape simulations lies with their use for investigating effects of land use policies on landscape-scale environmental outcomes. If $\mathbf{X}_{it}$ includes measures of net returns, then one can simulate the effects of incentive-based policies, such as subsidies for afforestation or habitat conservation. Lewis et al. (2011) evaluate a suite of conservation policies, ranging from a simple per-acre subsidy applied uniformly across the landscape to targeted policies that account for biological characteristics of land parcels. The authors generate landscapes for each policy scenario, comparing the mean biodiversity score in each case to the mean score obtained under a reference scenario with no policy.

4. Application

In this section, we present an application of an econometric-based landscape simulation model based on Lewis et al. (2009) and Lewis (2010). A model of shoreline development along 140 lakes in northern Wisconsin is described. The model represents both the decision to develop and the development intensity, where the unit of observation is a parcel of land. The model is used in a landscape simulation and coupled with a previously published regression model of green frog populations expressed as a function of a lake's development density (Woodford and Meyer 2003).

4.1 Econometric Specification

A landowner is assumed to make a binary decision to develop shoreline parcel i or leave it undeveloped. Denoting development by $k = 1$ and the current undeveloped use by $k = 0$, conversion is optimal if the net value of conversion (NVC) is positive:

$$NR_{i1t} - NR_{i0t} = NVC_{it} = U(\mathbf{X}_{it}) + \mu_l > 0, \tag{8}$$

where NVC is measured as a reduced-form function of observable parcel attributes $\mathbf{X}_{it}$ (e.g., soil quality, distance to town centers) and an unobservable μ_l specific to lake l (e.g., the scenic beauty of the lake). NVC is an indirect function of the land use intensity decision upon conversion to the developed use. Formally, the value of choosing density m (i.e., m housing lots) is given by:

$$V_{1m}(\mathbf{X}_{it}) + \varphi_{i1m} + \varepsilon_{i1t}, \tag{9}$$

where V_{im} is a density-specific function of observable variables $\mathbf{X}_{it}$, φ_{i1m} is a time-invariant density-specific unobservable for development, and ε_{i1t} is an unobservable for developed use in time t that is independent of density. The optimally chosen density is, then:

$$m^*_{it}(X_{it}, \omega_i) = \underset{m}{\text{argmax}}\{V_{1m}(\mathbf{X}_{it}) + \varphi_{i1m}\}_{m=1}^{M_1} \tag{10}$$

and the net return to developed use is given by:

$$NR_{i1t} = V_{1m^*}(\mathbf{X}_{it}) + \varphi_{i1m^*} + \varepsilon_{i1t}. \tag{11}$$

The net return to developed use is a random variable because it is derived by maximizing over a set of random variables.

A logical modeling approach would be to estimate an econometric model of expected land use intensity Em^*_{it} as a function of a set of observable variables $\mathbf{X}_{it}$. However, since both Em^*_{it} and the net value of conversion NVC_{it} are derived from operations on the same set of random variables φ_{ilm}, there necessarily exists a sample selection problem in estimation of Em^*_{it}: the analyst only observes the intensity decision for those parcels converted to the developed use. We assume that we can represent (10) as a Poisson process, where Em^*_{it} depends on $\mathbf{X}_{it}$ and the random variable ω_i, where ω_i reinforces that the optimal density choice in (10) is a random variable generated by an operation on the set of random variables φ_{ilm}. The probability that $m_{it}^{*} = m, m = 1, 2, \ldots, M_1$ follows a zero-truncated Poisson distribution:

$$\Pr[m_{it}^{*} = m \mid \mathbf{X}_{it}, \gamma_i] = \frac{\exp[-\exp(\theta \mathbf{X}_{it} + \sigma_2 \gamma_i)][\exp(\theta \mathbf{X}_{it} + \sigma_2 \gamma_i)]^m}{m!(1 - \exp[-\exp(\theta \mathbf{X}_{it} + \sigma_2 \gamma_i)])}, \tag{12}$$

where $\omega_i = \sigma_2 \gamma_i$ is a normally distributed random variable with standard deviation σ_2, implying that λ_i is a standard normal random variable, and θ is a parameter vector.

To account for the sample selection problem discussed earlier, we assume that the net value of conversion depends on the unobservable ε_{i1t} that is correlated with γ_i, specifically:

$$NVC_{it} = U(\mathbf{X}_{it}) + \mu_l = \delta \mathbf{X}_{it} + \mu_l + \varepsilon_{i1t}. \tag{13}$$

In sum, the binary decision to develop is determined by (13), which features, first, spatial correlation in the unobservables induced by the presence of a common unobservable (μ_l) for all parcels on lake l, and, second, an unobservable (ε_{i1t}) that is correlated with the unobservables in the land use intensity decision (γ_i). If we make the assumption that ε_{i1t} is a standard normal, then the conditional probability of development ($d_{it} = 1$) is given by,

$$\Pr(d_{it} = 1 \mid \mathbf{X}_{it}, \mu_l) = \Phi(\delta \mathbf{X}_{it} + \mu_l). \tag{14}$$

And, if we assume that ε_{i1t} and γ_i are joint standard normal with correlation coefficient ρ, then using the properties of the joint normal distribution (Greene 2012), we obtain:

$$\Pr(d_{it} = 1 \mid \mathbf{X}_{it}, \mu_l, \gamma_i) = \Phi\left([\delta \mathbf{X}_{it} + \mu_l + \rho \gamma_i] / \sqrt{1 - \rho^2}\right). \tag{15}$$

Conditioning the probability in (15) only on observables $\mathbf{X}_{it}$ requires integrating out μ_l and γ_i:

$$\Pr(d_{it} = 1 \mid \mathbf{X}_{it}) = \iint \Pr[m_{it}^{*} = m \mid \mathbf{X}_{it}, \gamma_i][\Pr(d_{it} = 1 \mid \mathbf{X}_{it}, \mu_l, \gamma_i)] \phi(\gamma_i) \phi(\mu_l) d\gamma_i d\mu_l, \tag{16}$$

where ϕ is the standard normal density function. Thus, the probability of the observed behavior (d_{it}, m_{it}) on parcel i at time t is,

$$\Pr(d_{it}, m_{it} \mid \mathbf{X}_{it}) = \iint [(1 - d_{it}) + d_{it} \Pr[m_{it}^{*} = m_{it} \mid \mathbf{X}_{it}, \gamma_i]] \times [\Phi((2d_{it} - 1)(\delta \mathbf{X}_{it} + \mu_l + \rho \gamma_i] / \sqrt{1 - \rho^2})] \phi(\gamma_i) \phi(\mu_l) d\gamma_i d\mu_l. \tag{17}$$

Of particular importance in this model is the lack of statistical independence across parcel decisions, as γ_i captures parcel-specific and time-invariant unobservables whereas μ_l captures lake-specific and time-invariant unobservables. Thus, this specification includes both temporal and spatial correlation in the unobservables.

Lewis et al. (2009) estimate (17) by maximum simulated likelihood, where D_l denotes the full set of development and intensity decisions on lake l. Conditional on a draw of γ_i and μ_l, the probability of D_l is,

$$\Pr(D_l) = \prod_i \prod_t [(1-d_{it}) + d_{it} \Pr[m_{it}^* = m_{it} \mid \mathbf{X}_{it}, \gamma_i]] \\ \times [\Phi((2d_{it}-1)(\delta \mathbf{X}_{it} + \mu_l + \rho\gamma_i]/\sqrt{1-\rho^2})]. \tag{18}$$

Taking R sets of draws of γ_i and μ_l, the simulated approximation to the likelihood function is,

$$\Pr^{Sim}(D_l) = R^{-1} \sum_{r=1}^{R} \Pr(D_l^r). \tag{19}$$

The econometric model is applied to legally subdividable lakeshore parcels across 140 lakes in Vilas County, a popular vacation destination in northern Wisconsin. The panel data were derived from a number of sources, including a GIS parcel database, the Wisconsin Department of Natural Resources (WI DNR), US Department of Agriculture (USDA) soil surveys, and town governments in Vilas County. The GIS parcel database was constructed from county tax parcel data and historic plat maps and consists of complete spatial coverage of all parcel boundaries in 4-year intervals from 1974 through 1998. The set of independent variables used to estimate (19) consists of parcel characteristics (size, soil restrictions, distance to town, zoning), lake characteristics (water clarity, lake size and depth, shoreline open-space), and time-period dummy variables. There were 335 individual subdivisions that occurred between 1974 and 1998 on a landscape that began with 1,310 legally subdividable shoreline parcels. The lakeshore development process was dominated by fairly small developments because 82% of recorded subdivisions generated fewer than six new parcels each. More details on the model, in addition to estimation results and treatment of potentially endogenous variables, are found in Lewis et al. (2009).

4.2 Simulation Model and Results

Here, we illustrate two important simulation issues. First, we show how to include both categorical land use change and land use intensity measures within a landscape simulation. Second, we demonstrate how an econometric land use model can be coupled with an ecological model as a solution to the problem of summarizing information from a large number of simulated landscapes. We draw on Lewis's (2010) simulation study of shoreline land development in northern Wisconsin. The econometric model in this chapter treats the net returns to land as a reduced-form expression of a set of soil characteristics, lake characteristics (water clarity, lake size, etc.), and a zoning policy variable indicating the minimum shoreline frontage for new residential lots. Output from the econometric model includes parcel-specific estimates of the probability of subdivision (a Probit model) and the expected number of new lots upon subdivision (a Poisson model). Importantly, the Poisson model of the expected number of lots can also be used to estimate the probability of each possible choice of density (one new lot, two new lots, etc.).

The development and intensity probabilities are functions of the set of independent variables, enabling Lewis (2010) to use the model to simulate the landscape effects of changes to shoreline zoning policies. The use of a joint model of categorical land use change and land use intensity raises the challenge of using two probability models (with correlation across the models) for the simulation. The following steps were used in the simulation:

1. Following the Krinsky and Robb method (1986), draw a parameter vector from the econometrically estimated distribution to calculate the estimated Probit and Poisson probabilities for each parcel.[3]
2. Standard normal random draws are multiplied by the corresponding standard deviations from step 1 to generate a draw from the estimated random parameter distributions.
3. A complete time path ($t = 1 \ldots T$) of development is estimated for each lake.
   - Draw a $U \sim [0,1]$ random number r_1 for each parcel, where development occurs if r_1 is less than or equal to the estimated subdivision probability; otherwise, the parcel is assumed to remain in its current state.
   - If developed, use the estimated Poisson probability, $\Pr[m^* = m]$, of the number of new lots m as follows: Draw a $U \sim [0,1]$ random number r_2; one new lot is created if $r_2 \le \Pr[m^* = 1]$, two new lots are created if $\Pr[m^* = 1] < r_2 \le \Pr[m^* = 2]$, and so forth until m^* is equal to the maximum number of lots allowable under zoning.
   - Repeat these two steps until $t = T$.
4. Steps 1–3 are repeated to produce a large number of simulated landscapes.

[3] A simulated parameter vector is equal to $\psi_s = \hat{\psi} + C'\lambda_K$, where $\hat{\psi}$ is the estimated parameter vector, C is the $K \times K$ Cholesky decomposition of the estimated variance-covariance matrix, and λ_K is a K-dimensional vector of draws from a standard normal distribution.

This simulation procedure accounts for variation in the estimated model parameters and the random error terms. Furthermore, since step 1 uses the covariance matrix of parameters from the joint estimation of the Probit and Poisson models, the simulation accounts for the estimated unobserved correlation between land development and land intensity and implicitly addresses the sample selection problem discussed earlier.

Each simulated landscape is evaluated in terms of habitat for green frog populations. The coupled economic-ecological model exploits the predictions from the econometric model of landscape pattern, which are then used as input to the ecological model. Lewis (2010) predicts shoreline development across each of 140 lakes, and shoreline development density is used to predict the population of green frogs. The green frog population model is a regression model developed by Woodford and Meyer (2003) that includes shoreline development density as an independent variable.[4] Notably, the Woodford and Meyer (2003) model was estimated with green frog data from lakes in our study region in northern Wisconsin. The spatial scale of the model is a lake (i.e., each lake is a habitat patch), which nicely fits the scale of Lewis's (2010) simulations, which provide lake-level estimates of development density. Since development density is the driver of green frog populations, this model also illustrates the value of modeling a land use intensity choice rather than just land use categories.

Figure 15.2 illustrates a 20-year forecast from the econometric model as an empirical distribution of the number of lots on a select lake in northern Wisconsin. As expected, elimination of the zoning policy increases the likelihood of a larger number of lots being built. The coupling of the econometric model with the ecological model is performed by using the predicted shoreline development density for each simulation as an input into the ecological model to generate a predicted probability of extinction for green frogs.[5] Figure 15.2 illustrates how relaxing the zoning constraint along the lakes translates into a greater probability of extinction for green frog populations. The results in Figure 15.2 draw on a large number of probabilistic landscape simulations, each of which is consistent with the underlying econometric models. Thus, the results are represented in terms of empirical distributions of development densities and extinction probabilities. By modifying an independent variable in the econometric model, we see how these empirical distributions change as a function of a policy change.

[4] The regression model from Woodford and Meyer (2003) is very simple and is estimated as $E(Frogs \mid Lots) = 2.537 - 1.189 \times Lots$, where *Frogs* is the number of Frogs per 100 m shoreline and *Lots* is the number of developed lots per 100 m shoreline. This function is slightly revised from the original published version that was sent directly to us by James Woodford. See the original paper, Woodford and Meyer (2003), for additional information. The *Lots* variable is generated during each iteration of the simulation and plugged into this function to get a *Frogs* measure. More complex ecological models can be coupled to the economic model provided that the ecological outcomes of interest can be related to the predicted landscapes. See Lewis et al. (2011) for an example involving a larger set of species.

[5] Rather than use the expected number of green frogs, we use the properties of the simple regression function to generate extinction probabilities. The regression function from Woodford and Meyer has an

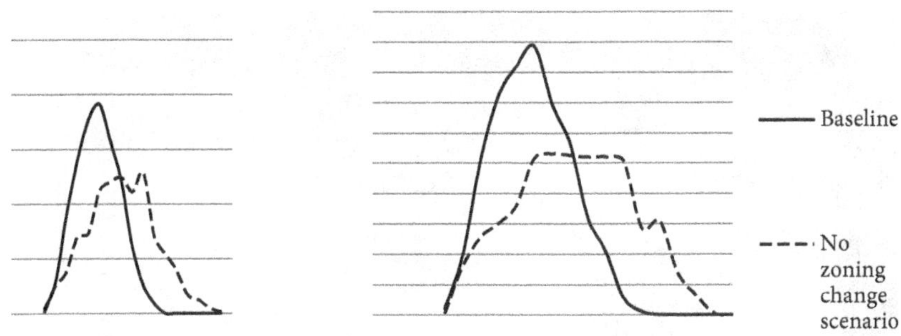

FIGURE 15.2 Coupling a landscape simulation with an ecological model for a select lake—two frequency plots.

5. Future Research

In landscapes dominated by private ownership, landowners lack the incentive to coordinate decisions to influence the spatial land use pattern and the environmental outcomes that depend on it. Econometric-based landscape simulation models have been developed to understand the nature and extent of this market failure problem and to identify and quantify the effects of corrective land use policies. In this chapter, we have discussed—and suggested solutions to—four challenges that arise with econometric-based landscape simulations: (1) representing variation in the private economic returns to land at the same scale at which land use varies, (2) modeling the private information that landowners possess about the returns to their land, (3) accounting for land use intensity as part of the land use decision process, and (4) recognizing the probabilistic nature of the land use transition rules derived from econometric analysis.

Further challenges remain, including what we term the "salt-and-pepper" effect. To illustrate this, we present a simulated future landscape for the area surrounding Madison, Wisconsin (Figure 15.3). The simulation was done using land use transition probabilities of the form in (7) applied to 30-meter pixels.[6] The existing urban areas are the large black shapes, and most of the small black dots are projected future urban land. Clearly, the degree to which future urban land is scattered across the landscape is unrealistic. One would expect most future urban land to be added near existing

estimated mean number of green frogs per 100 m of $E(Frogs \mid Lots) = 2.537 - 1.189 \times Lots$. Also, using the sum of squared residuals, the model has an estimate of $\sigma = 1.48$. The probability of extinction is calculated at each simulation iteration by plugging the predicted *Lots* into the regression function and using the cumulative normal distribution function with mean $E(Frogs \mid Lots)$ and $\sigma = 1.48$ to find the probability that fewer than zero frogs occur on each lake.

[6] In particular, each $K \times K$ set of transition probabilities varies only by soil quality and county.

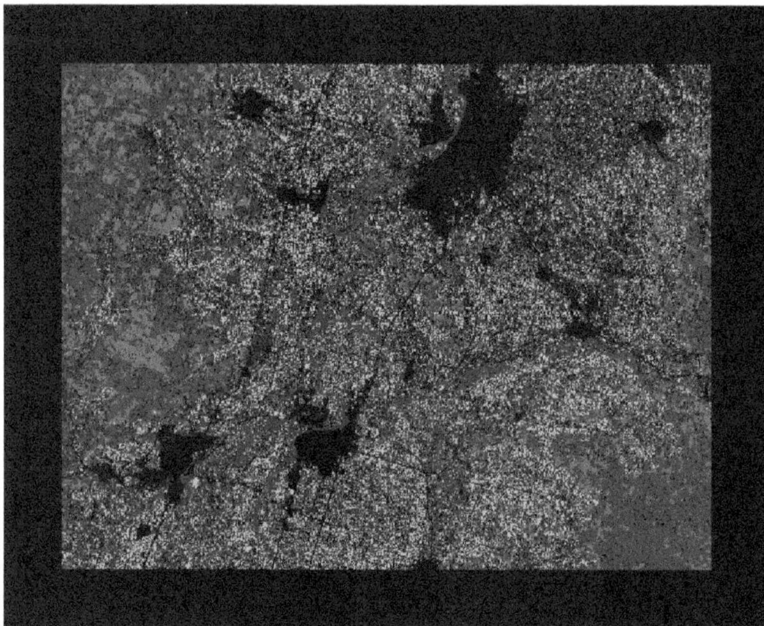

FIGURE 15.3 The salt-and-pepper effect (urban land is shown in black).

urban areas and along transportation corridors. One of the reasons for this result is the decision-making scale. We assumed in this simulation that a land use decision is made at the scale of each pixel on the landscape, which produces implausibly small areas (dots) of urban land. But, what is the right decision-making scale? This is a question critical to land use modeling,[7] but not one that can be easily answered in practice. One approach would be to assume that ownership determines the scale at which land use decisions are made. That is, each landowner could be assumed to allocate her parcel to a single use. But, clearly, there are many exceptions to this, as in the case of a diversified farm with land in crops, pasture, and forests. In the case of rented land, the use—and, particularly, the intensity—decision may be made by somebody other than the owner. And, finally, ownership can involve complicated legal arrangements that make it difficult to establish the actual owner of a particular parcel of land. In their simulation analysis, Lewis and Plantinga (2007) defined decision-making units in terms of contiguous blocks of land allocated to single uses. This mitigated the salt-and-pepper effect, but likely had other shortcomings.

[7] In addition to affecting simulated landscape patterns, as demonstrated in Figure 15.3, the decision-making scale can have important influences on land use decisions if scale economies are present.

The salt-and-pepper effect also can occur if the econometric land use model fails to account for important spatial processes. For example, urban development is often more likely to occur near roads. Ignoring this dependency in the econometric model will carry through to landscape simulations and likely produce a scattered pattern of future urbanization. The remedy is to estimate spatially explicit econometric models of land use, which we regard to be the most important next step in the development of econometric-based landscape simulations. The earlier work in this chapter focused on the linkage between the spatial pattern of land use at the landscape scale and ecological outcomes but did not emphasize the spatial relationships that affect land use decisions. To represent these spatial processes, one needs high-quality spatial data to use in the estimation of econometric land use models. These data are increasingly available, but their use gives rise to a number of additional econometric challenges. We conclude this chapter by emphasizing the importance of economic theory in guiding the development of spatial econometric models to be used for landscape simulations. Readers are referred to Brady and Irwin (2011) for a more complete discussion.

There are surely important spatial processes that affect land use decisions, but what are they exactly? Why is urban development more likely to occur near to existing urban land (one can imagine negative externalities pushing development farther away)? If a person's land borders a farm, are they more likely to choose an agricultural use and, if so, why? These are examples of theoretical questions that should motivate the specification of spatial econometric models. One finds theoretically grounded spatial land use models in Irwin and Bockstael (2002) and Lewis et al. (2011). Irwin and Bockstael (2002) conjecture that residential development creates a negative spatial externality that affects land use decisions on neighboring land parcels. Their empirical analysis is motivated by and finds support for the underlying theory. Lewis et al. (2011) model the growth in organic dairy farms in Wisconsin, accounting for a positive spatial externality that reduces the fixed costs of learning. In these studies, the underlying theory makes clear that neighboring land uses are determined endogenously, requiring the use of instrumental variables, as in Irwin (2002), or of panel data methods, as in Lewis et al. (2011). The combination of economic theory and appropriate econometric procedures is critical if the intent is to use the econometric results in a landscape simulation. In this case, the underlying spatial process is identified explicitly and thus can be reproduced in the simulation.

References

Allen, J., and K. Lu. 2003. Modeling and prediction of future urban growth in the Charleston Region of South Carolina: A GIS-based integrated approach. *Conservation Ecology* 8(2): 2.

Ando, A., J. Camm, S. Polasky, and A. Solow. 1998. Species distributions, land values, and efficient conservation. *Science* 279: 2126–2128.

Askins, R. A. 2002. *Restoring North America's birds: Lessons from landscape ecology*, 2nd ed. New Haven, CT: Yale University Press.

Balmford, A., K. J. Gaston, A. S. L. Rodrigues, and A. James. 2000. Integrating conservation costs into international priority setting. *Conservation Biology* 11: 597–605.

Ben-Akiva, M., and S. Lerman. 1985. *Discrete choice analysis*. Cambridge, MA: MIT Press.

Bockstael, N. E. 1996. Modeling economics and ecology: The importance of a spatial perspective. *American Journal of Agricultural Economics* 78(5): 1168–1180.

Brady, M., and E. Irwin. 2011. Accounting for spatial effect in economic models of land use: Recent developments and challenges ahead. *Environmental and Resource Economics* 48(3): 487–509.

Cabeza, M., and A. Moilanen. 2003. Site-selection algorithms and habitat loss. *Conservation Biology* 17: 1402–1413.

Camm, J. D., S. Polasky, A. Solow, and B. Csuti. 1996. A note on optimal algorithms for reserve site selection. *Biological Conservation* 78: 353–355.

Carrion-Flores, C., and E. G. Irwin. 2004. Determinants of residential land-use conversion and sprawl at the rural-urban fringe. *American Journal of Agricultural Economics* 86(4): 889–904.

Chomitz, K. M., and D. A. Gray. 1996. Roads, land use, and deforestation: A spatial model applied to Belize. *The World Bank Economic Review* 10(3): 487–512.

Church, R. L., D. M. Stoms, and F. W. Davis. 1996. Reserve selection as a maximal coverage problem. *Biological Conservation* 76: 105–112.

Clarke, K. C., and L. J. Gaydos. 1998. Loose-coupling a cellular automaton model and GIS: Long-term urban growth prediction for San Francisco and Washington/Baltimore. *International Journal of Geographic Information Science* 12(7): 699–714.

Costa, L. P., Leite, Y. L. R., Mendes, S. L., and A. D. Ditchfield. 2005. Mammal conservation in Brazil. *Conservation Biology* 19(3): 672–679.

Costello, C., and S. Polasky. 2004. Dynamic reserve site selection. *Resource and Energy Economics* 26: 157–174.

Cropper, M., J. Puri, and C. Griffiths. 2001. Predicting the location of deforestation: The role of roads and protected areas in North Thailand. *Land Economics* 77(2): 172–186.

Csuti, B., S. Polasky, P. H. Williams, R. L. Pressey, J. D. Camm, M. Kershaw, A. R. Kiester, B. Downs, R. Hamilton, M. Huso, and K. Sahr. 1997. A comparison of reserve selection algorithms using data on terrestrial vertebrates in Oregon. *Biological Conservation* 80: 83–97.

deMaynadier, P. G., and M. L. Hunter. 2000. Road effects on amphibian movements in a forested landscape. *Natural Areas Journal* 20: 56–65.

Faaborg, J. 2002. *Saving migrant birds: Developing strategies for the future*. Austin, TX: University of Texas Press.

Fischer, D. T., and R. L. Church. 2003. Clustering and compactness in reserve site selection: An extension of the biodiversity management area selection model. *Forest Science* 49(4): 555–565.

Gergel, S. E., E. H. Stanley, M. G. Turner, J. R. Miller, and J. M. Melack. 2002. Landscape indicators of human impacts to riverine systems. *Aquatic Sciences* 64(2): 118–128.

Greene, W. H. 2012. *Econometric analysis*, 7th ed. Upper Saddle River, NJ: Prentice Hall.

Grout, C. A., W. K. Jaeger, and A. J. Plantinga. 2011. Land-use regulations and property values in Portland, Oregon: A regression discontinuity design approach. *Regional Science and Urban Economics* 41: 98–107.

Guzy, M. R., C. L. Smith, J. P. Bolte, D. W. Hulse, and S. V. Gregory. 2008. Policy research using agent-based modeling to assess future impacts of urban expansion into farmlands and forests. *Ecology and Society* 13(1): 37.

Hale, S. S., J. F. Paul, and J. F. Heltshe. 2004. Watershed landscape indicators of estuarine benthic condition. *Estuaries* 27(2): 283–295.

Hardie, I. W., and P. J. Parks. 1997. Land use with heterogeneous land quality: An application of an area base model. *American Journal of Agricultural Economics* 79: 299–310.

Irwin, E., and N. E. Bockstael. 2002. Interacting agents, spatial externalities and the evolution of residential land use patterns. *Journal of Economic Geography* 2: 331–354.

Irwin, E. G., and N. E. Bockstael. 2004. Land use externalities, open space preservation, and urban sprawl. *Regional Science and Urban Economics* 34: 705–725.

Jiang, Y., S. K. Swallow, and P. W. C. Paton. 2007. Designing a spatially-explicit nature reserve network based on ecological functions: An integer programming approach. *Biological Conservation* 140: 236–249.

Kirkpatrick, J. B. 1983. An iterative method for establishing priorities for the selection of nature reserves: An example from Tasmania. *Biological Conservation* 25(2): 127–134.

Kolozsvary, M. B., and R. K. Swihart. 1999. Habitat fragmentation and the distribution of amphibians: Patch and landscape correlates in farmland. *Canadian Journal of Zoology* 77(8): 1288–1299.

Krinsky, I., and A. Robb. 1986. On approximating the statistical properties of elasticities. *The Review of Economics and Statistics* 86: 715–719.

Lehtinen, R. M., J. B. Ramanamanjato, and J. G. Raveloarison. 2003. Edge effects and extinction proneness in a herpetofauna from Madagascar. *Biodiversity and Conservation* 12(7): 1357–1370.

Lewis, D. J. 2005. Managing the spatial configuration of land: The economics of land use and habitat fragmentation. Unpublished PhD dissertation, Department of Agricultural and Resource Economics, Oregon State University.

Lewis, D. J. 2010. An economic framework for forecasting land use and ecosystem change. *Resource and Energy Economics* 32(2): 98–116.

Lewis, D. J., and A. J. Plantinga. 2007. Policies for habitat fragmentation: Combining econometrics with GIS-based landscape simulations. *Land Economics* 83(2): 109–127.

Lewis, D. J., A. J. Plantinga, and J. Wu. 2009. Targeting incentives to reduce habitat fragmentation. *American Journal of Agricultural Economics* 91(4): 1080–1096.

Lewis, D. J., B. Provencher, and V. Butsic. 2009. The dynamic effects of open-space conservation policies on residential development density. *Journal of Environmental Economics and Management* 57(3): 239–252.

Lewis, D. J., A. J. Plantinga, E. Nelson, and S. Polasky. 2011. The efficiency of voluntary incentive policies for preventing biodiversity loss. *Resource and Energy Economics* 33(1): 192–211.

Li, X., and A. Gar-On Yeh. 2000. Modeling sustainable urban development by the integration of constrained cellular automata and GIS. *International Journal of Geographic Information Science* 14(2): 131–152.

Lubowski, R. N., A. J. Plantinga, and R. N. Stavins. 2006. Land-use change and carbon sinks: Econometric estimation of the carbon sequestration supply function. *Journal of Environmental Economics and Management* 51(2): 135–152.

Margules, C. R. and R. L. Pressey. 2000. Systematic conservation planning. *Nature* 405: 242–253.

Meir, E., S. Andelman, and H. P. Possingham. 2004. Does conservation planning matter in a dynamic and uncertain world? *Ecology Letters* 7: 615–622.

Millennium Ecosystem Assessment. 2005. *Living beyond our means: Natural assets and human well-being*. Washington, DC: Island Press.

Moilanen, A., A. M. A. Franco, R. I. Early, R. Fox, B. White, and C. D. Thomas. 2005. Prioritizing multiple-use landscapes for conservation: Methods for large multi-species planning problems. *Proceedings of the Royal Society, Series B* 272: 1885–1891.

Nalle, D. J., C. A. Montgomery, J. L. Arthur, S. Polasky, and N. H. Schumaker. 2004. Modeling joint production of wildlife and timber. *Journal of Environmental Economics and Management* 48(3): 997–1017.

Natural Heritage Data Center Network. 1993. *Perspectives on species imperilment: A report from the Natural Heritage Data Center Network*. Arlington, VA: The Nature Conservancy.

Nelson, G. C., and D. Hellerstein. 1997. Do roads cause deforestation? Using satellite images in econometric analysis of land use. *American Journal of Agricultural Economics* 79: 80–88.

Nelson, G. C., V. Harris, and S. W. Stone. 2001. Deforestation, land use, and property rights: Empirical evidence from Darien, Panama. *Land Economics* 77(2): 187–205.

Nelson, E., S. Polasky, D. J. Lewis, A. J. Plantinga, E. Lonsdorf, D. White, D. Bael, and J. J. Lawler. 2008. Efficiency of incentives to jointly increase carbon sequestration and species conservation on a landscape. *Proceedings of the National Academy of Sciences of the USA* 105(28): 9471–9476.

Newburn, D. A., P. Berck, and A. M. Merenlender. 2006. Habitat and open space at risk of land-use conversion: Targeting strategies for land conservation. *American Journal of Agricultural Economics* 88(1): 28–42.

Nicholson, E., M. I. Westphal, K. Frank, W. A. Rochester, R. L. Pressey, D. B. Lindenmayer, and H. P. Possingham. 2006. A new method for conservation planning for the persistence of multiple species. *Ecology Letters* 9: 1049–1060.

Noss, R., B. Csuti, and M.J. Groom. 2006. P. 213–251. Habitat fragmentation. In *Principles of conservation biology*, 3E. eds. M.J. Groom, G. K. Meffe and C. R. Carrol. Sunderland, MA: Sinauer Associates.

Onal, H., and R. A. Briers. 2003. Selection of a minimum boundary reserve network using integer programming. *Proceedings of the Royal Society of London B*, 270: 1487–1491.

Palmer, J. F. 2004. Using spatial metrics to predict scenic perception in a changing landscape: Dennis, Massachusetts. *Landscape and Urban Planning* 69(2–3): 201–218.

Plantinga, A. J. 1996. The effect of agricultural policies on land use and environmental quality. *American Journal of Agricultural Economics* 78: 1082–1091.

Polasky, S., J. D. Camm, and B. Garber-Yonts. 2001. Selecting biological reserves cost-effectively: An application to terrestrial vertebrate conservation in Oregon. *Land Economics* 77(1): 68–78.

Polasky, S., E. Nelson, E. Lonsdorf, P. Fackler, and A. Starfield. 2005. Conserving species in a working landscape: Land use with biological and economic objectives. *Ecological Applications* 15: 1387–1401.

Polasky, S., E. Nelson, J. Camm, B. Csuti, P. Fackler, E. Lonsdorf, D. White, J. Arthur, B. Garber-Yonts, R. Haight, J. Kagan, C. Montgomery, A. Starfield, and C. Tobalske. 2008. Where to put things? Spatial land management to sustain biodiversity and economic production. *Biological Conservation* 141(6): 1505–1524.

Provencher, B. 1995. Structural estimation of the stochastic dynamic decision problems of resource users: An application to the timber harvest decision. *Journal of Environmental Economics and Management* 29: 321–338.

Rust, J. 1989. Optimal replacement of GMC bus engines: An empirical model of Harold Zurcher. *Econometrica* 55(5): 999–1033.

Sala, O. E., F. S. Chapin, III, J. J. Armesto, E. Berlow, J. Bloomfield, R. Dirzo, E. Huber-Sanwald, L. F. Huenneke, R. B. Jackson, A. Kinzig, R. Leemans, D. M. Lodge, H. A. Mooney,

M. Oesterheld, N. L. Poff, M. T. Sykes, B. H. Walker, M. Walker, and D. H. Wall. 2000. Global biodiversity scenarios in the year 2100. *Science* 287: 1770–1774.

Stavins, R. N., and A. B. Jaffe. 1990. Unintended impacts of public investments on private decisions: The depletion of forested wetlands. *American Economic Review* 80(3): 337–352.

Strange, N., B. J. Thorsen, and J. Bladt. 2006. Optimal reserve selection in a dynamic world. *Biological Conservation* 131: 33–41.

Vane-Wright, R. I., C. J. Humphries, and P. H. Williams. 1991. What to protect? Systematics and the agony of choice. *Biological Conservation* 55(3): 235–254.

Wilcove, D. S., D. Rothstein, J. Dubow, A. Phillips, and E. Losos. 2000. Leading threats to biodiversity: What's imperiling U.S. species. In *Precious heritage: The status of biodiversity in the United States*, eds. B. A. Stein, L. S. Kutner, and J. S. Adams, 239–254. Oxford, UK: Oxford University Press.

Woodford, J. E., and M. W. Meyer. 2003. Impact of lakeshore development on green frog abundance. *Biological Conservation* 110: 277–284.

Wu, F. 1998. SimLand: A prototype to simulate land conversion through the integrated GIS and CA with AHP-derived transition rules. *International Journal of Geographic Information Science* 12(1): 63–82.

Wu, F. 2002. Calibration of stochastic cellular automata: The application to rural-urban land conversions. *International Journal of Geographic Information Science* 16(8): 795–818.

Wu, F., and C. J. Webster. 2000. Simulating artificial cities in a GIS environment: Urban growth under alternative regulation regimes. *International Journal of Geographic Information Science* 14(7): 625–648.

Wu, J., R. M. Adams, and A. J. Plantinga. 2004. Amenities in an urban equilibrium model: Residential development in Portland, Oregon. *Land Economics* 80(1): 19–32.

CHAPTER 16

AN ECONOMIC PERSPECTIVE ON AGENT-BASED MODELS OF LAND USE AND LAND COVER CHANGE

DAWN CASSANDRA PARKER

WITH the advent of high-performance computing and increased availability of spatial data, interest is increasing in the development of spatially explicit models across a wide range of scientific disciplines. These models are being developed to address a host of growing management challenges related to diverse problems such as urban sprawl, the decline of former industrial cities, the challenge of ecosystem service preservation in human-impacted landscapes, containment of invasive species, and emerging global trends in agricultural production, such as biofuel production, yield gaps, and management of genetically modified crops. A variety of new methods for spatial analysis and modeling have developed in response to these opportunities and challenges. This chapter reviews one family of such new models: agent-based models of land use and land cover change (ABM/LUCC). ABM/LUCC are computational simulation models that operate at the scale of real-world decision making and directly represent the decisions and interactions of economic agents at that scale, over a spatially explicit and dynamic virtual landscape. The goal of this chapter is not to replicate recent excellent reviews of agent-based land use models, but rather to provide practical guidance and context for land economists who wish to understand, evaluate, and construct agent-based land use models. The chapter strives to answer the following questions, with an economist's perspective in mind:

- What are agent-based land use models?
- How are they structured, how does their structure relate to standard theoretical and statistical models in economics, and how does this structure facilitate investigation of novel economic questions?

- What novel issues need to be considered for their construction and execution, relative to standard economic models?
- What complementarities exist between these models and other economic modeling and analysis methods?
- What are important future research directions for this field?

1. What Are Agent-Based Models of Land Use Change?

Agent-based modeling (ABM) is a simulation methodology that is increasingly used throughout the social sciences (Berry et al. 2002; Hernandez et al. 2008; Waldrop 2009). ABMs have been applied to a variety of economic questions (Tesfatsion and Judd 2006), with some of the most visible work in the area of agent-based financial markets (LeBaron 2006; Anufriev and Branch 2009). ABMs often represent heterogeneous decision-making entities and their interactions with their social and physical environment (Parker et al. 2003; Irwin 2010). In contrast to mathematical or computational techniques traditionally used in economics, ABMs are simulation-based, not equilibrium-based. Although models may reach equilibrium, the equilibrium results from interactions between lower-level entities. Thus, they are suitable for modeling domains in which the complex relationships between agent heterogeneity, interactions, and cross-scale feedbacks render traditional equilibrium-based models analytically intractable. They are also often applied to explore the out-of-equilibrium dynamics of an economic system (Arthur 2006). ABMs can be used as computational laboratories to explore future status quo trajectories for systems of interest, as well as to explore how modified economic incentives can alter system outcomes (Tesfatsion 2006).

ABM/LUCC combine an ABM of land use change with a spatially explicit landscape, modeling land use, conversion, management, and exchange events. Some (perhaps all) of the agents in ABM/LUCC make decisions regarding these events in the modeled landscape. Although some ABM/LUCC, including Schelling's famous model of residential segregation (Schelling 1971) were developed before the advent of the high-performance computing and geographic information systems (GIS), a significant number of scientific applications began to develop during the 1990s (Kohler 2000; Gimblett 2002; Bousquet and Le Page 2004), in parallel with major advances in high-performance computing, object-oriented programming, and GIS. (Interestingly, the development of ABM/LUCC has lagged, to some extent, the development of conceptually parallel individual-based models in ecology; see Grimm and Railsback [2006]). Following the 2001 workshop on ABM/LUCC (Parker et al. 2002), the number of scientific publications on this topic has increased exponentially (Polhill et al. 2011). Several excellent review articles summarize the contributions of specific models over the past decade, including coupled natural and human systems models (Parker et al. 2003; Matthews et al. 2007), agricultural models (Schreinemachers et al. 2010), agent-based land market models (Parker and Filatova 2008), and urban land use change models (Benenson and Torrens 2004; Irwin 2010).

2. Structure, Function, and Relationship to Standard Economic Models

Analytical equilibrium-based and econometric economic models have been used to shed light on a variety of important economic problems. For example, the declines in fuel consumption and the value of outlying properties predicted by traditional modeling approaches are robustly observed as fuel prices increase. However, the application of such models often requires a large number of simplifying assumptions. ABMs are generally implemented in situations where the research question under study requires the modeler to relax simplifying assumptions designed to maintain analytical tractability and closed-form solutions. A more general, flexible model structure is possible because ABMs use a simulation approach, rather than imposing equilibrium conditions. This simulation approach, including its technical implications, is discussed in greater details in Section 3. In this section, the general structure of ABM/LUCC is discussed, highlighting the ways in which this structure can parallel, but also generalize, traditional microeconomic models.

2.1 Bringing the "Invisible Hand" to Life: An Illustrative Example

Figure 16.1(a-b) (Nolan et al. 2009) illustrates basic conceptual differences between the two model types. Traditional models (Panel a) analytically aggregate firm supply and consumer demand curves (often making simplifying assumptions to ensure continuous and monotonic functions) into market supply and demand curves. A set of equilibrium conditions is then imposed and solved. From this solution, market prices and quantities and corresponding welfare and income measures are derived.

Panel b illustrates a potential spatial agent-based market. As with the traditional approach, each producer and consumer will have some rule set (which may be a boundedly rational form of a traditional supply or demand curve) that links current economic conditions to selling and buying decisions. However, the representation of each decision function remains an active aspect of the model, rather than being aggregated into supply and demand curves. In short, ABMs strive to represent decision making at the scale at which it occurs in the real world. Each firm and consumer will also have a fixed location in space—and therefore a fixed spatial relationship to other economic actors, and their decisions may be influenced by spatial factors that would be difficult to include at a microscale in traditional models. For example, Panel b might represent a local market for residential landscaping plants. Greenhouse firms located in the exurban environment supply plants for residential landscaping, which consumers buy to landscape their yards. Firm 1 may decide to adopt a new integrated pest management strategy after learning, through social interactions and observation, that firm 2 has had success with this strategy. Firm 3, being located close to firm 1, may price certain products a bit below Firm 1 in the hopes of gaining their potential customer base (a strategic interaction). Alternatively, Firm 3 may offer a product not offered by Firm 1, in the hopes of capturing additional dollars from potential shoppers. On the residential side, neighbors may imitate the landscaping decisions they find attractive, potentially also transferring plant starts between themselves. Further, their landscaping decisions may be strongly influenced by social norms within the neighborhood that dictate that only certain landscaping practices are acceptable.

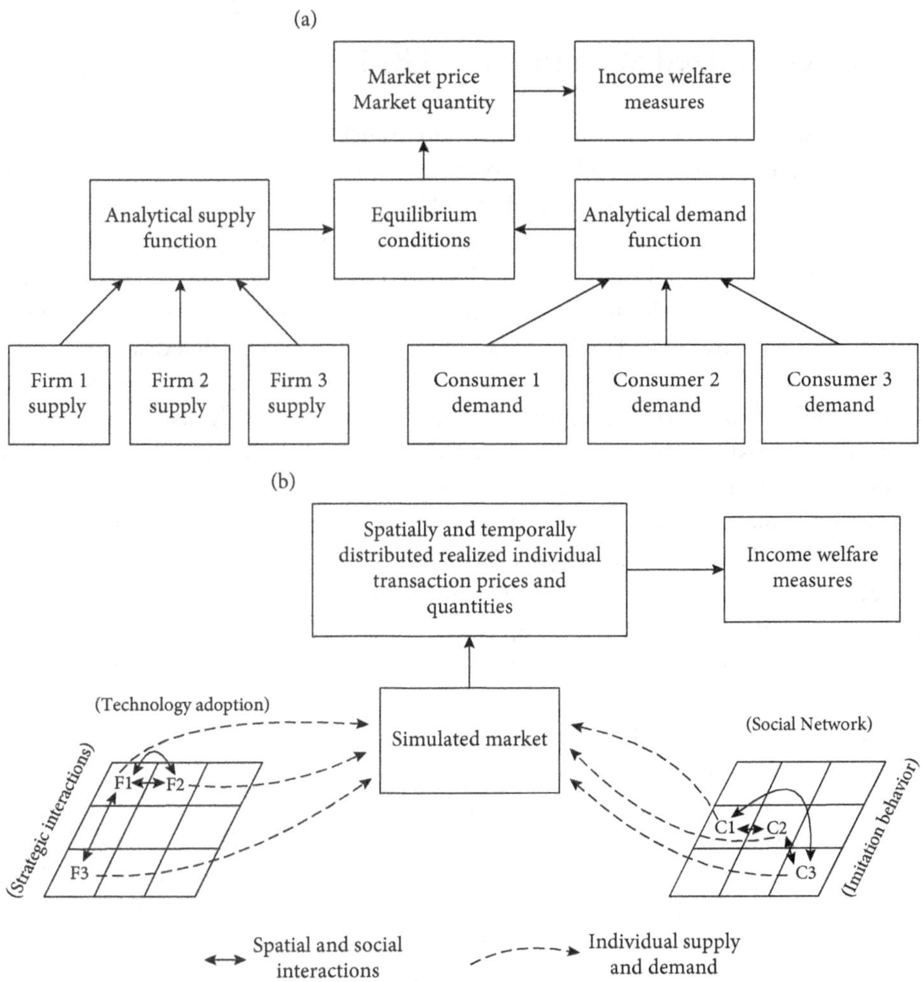

FIGURE 16.1 Comparison of the structure of traditional economic and spatial agent-based models (Nolan et al. 2009).

Next, rather than aggregating individual supply and demand functions to obtain a market clearing price and quantity, actual bilateral market interactions may be simulated. In this simple example, residents will likely purchase plants from greenhouse suppliers at a fixed price. In other spatial markets—for example, land or labor markets—bargaining may occur between buyers and sellers over a final transaction price. Buyers may also conduct an incomplete product search. For example, a buyer's decision regarding which landscaping firm to stop at may depend on a stochastic travel route through the countryside. Although this simple example may not seem particularly significant from an economic perspective at first glance, if landscaping plant purchases are tied, for example, to the spread of an invasive pest, the spatial dynamics described in this example could be critical to understanding the circumstances under which the pest could spread and cause significant economic damage.

2.2 A Generalized Structure for ABM/LUCC

The previous section discussed essential differences between a traditional microeconomic model and ABM/LUCC from an economic lens. To provide a more general overview of the structure of ABM/LUCC, the next section uses the MR POTATOHEAD (Model Representing Potential Objects That Appear in The Ontology of Human-Environmental Actions & Decisions) framework (Parker, Brown, et al. 2008; Parker, Entwisle, et al. 2008) to demonstrate how ABM/LUCC can generalize economic land use models. MR POTATOHEAD is a hierarchical ontology that describes and categorizes the key components of ABM/LUCC. Such an ontology is needed for ABMs because their model structure cannot be described completely using mathematical equations or statistical algorithms, as is possible for most economic models. The ontology describes model elements and their relationship to one another, but does not give details on specific functions, causal linkages, and algorithms present in models.

MR POTATOHEAD was developed with several goals in mind. The first is to describe the key components of an ABM/LUCC—an answer to the question, "What elements need to be specified in order to develop a functional ABM/LUCC?" To this end, Parker, Brown et al. (2008) identify which elements of the ontology are essential. The second goal of MR POTATOHEAD is to provide a template that can be used to describe the structure of a given ABM/LUCC, either for the purposes of assisting model development or as a means of documenting existing models. In Parker, Brown et al. (2008), five separately developed models are described using MR POTATOHEAD. Once disparate models are described using the same ontology, MR POTATOHEAD facilitates model comparison, as demonstrated in Parker, Entwisle et al. (2008). An extended goal of the project is to use the MR POTATOHEAD template as part of a graphical modeling language, so that nonprogrammers can easily develop, run, and analyze ABM/LUCC. MR POTATOHEAD has been implemented in OWL (Web Ontology Language) using the Protégé/OWL software (Stanford Center for Biomedical Informatics Research 2007). For the purposes of this chapter, the main classes and select elements (the *Landscape*

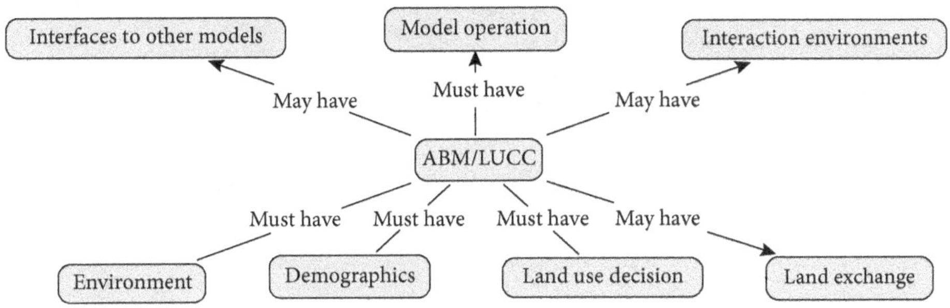

FIGURE **16.2** Key top-level class elements of an agent-based models of land use change (ABM/LUCC).

element of the *Environment* class, the *Demographic* class, the *Land use Decision* class, and the *Land Exchange* class) are discussed in detail and are illustrated using the CMAP software (Institute for Human and Machine Cognition 2011), which allows creation of nested graphics. Readers are referred to previous publications for complete details of the ontology, including examples of how different models implement the various elements.

MR POTATOHEAD contains seven main classes (Figure 16.2). The *Interfaces to Other Models, Model Operation*, and *Interaction Environments* classes are not discussed in detail here, although event-sequencing mechanisms are discussed later. A more detailed discussion of the other elements follows.

The *Environment* class (Figure 16.3) specifies the spatial and socioeconomic elements that influence land use decisions. It contains several elements: *Landscape, Other Spatial Elements* (spatial network and neighborhood models), *Non-spatial networks* (social, trade, and affiliation), *Institutional/Political Rules and Constraints, Economic Structures* (local markets and economic parameters), *Potential Land Uses*, and *Factors Affecting Land Productivity*. As discussed earlier, many of these elements, such as networks and neighborhood relationships, are rarely included in traditional economics models. The *Landscape* class (Figure 16.3) is used to describe the spatial structure over which the model operates. Its elements essentially describe the spatial environment in GIS terms. Although many economists now use data generated through GIS as inputs to empirical models (Bockstael 1996; Nelson and Geoghegan 2002), few economists run spatial simulation models over a dynamic spatial landscape (Irwin 2010).

However input data are generated, implementation of an ABM/LUCC requires the modeler to make key decisions about the spatial structure of the simulation environment. The *Landscape* class contains two elements: *GIS (spatial data) Layers*, and *Spatial Data Structure*. It asks the modeler to specify whether the model is empirical or abstract, the nature of agent-parcel relationships (one-to-one or many-to one, from both sides), whether parcels can contain multiple management units, whether the data structure is vector or raster, and whether parcel boundaries are fixed or vary as the simulation runs. These details highlight the additional spatial structural detail that is possible in ABM/LUCC relative to traditional economic models. Although some two-dimensional spatial analytical models have been developed, to the author's knowledge, they either operate

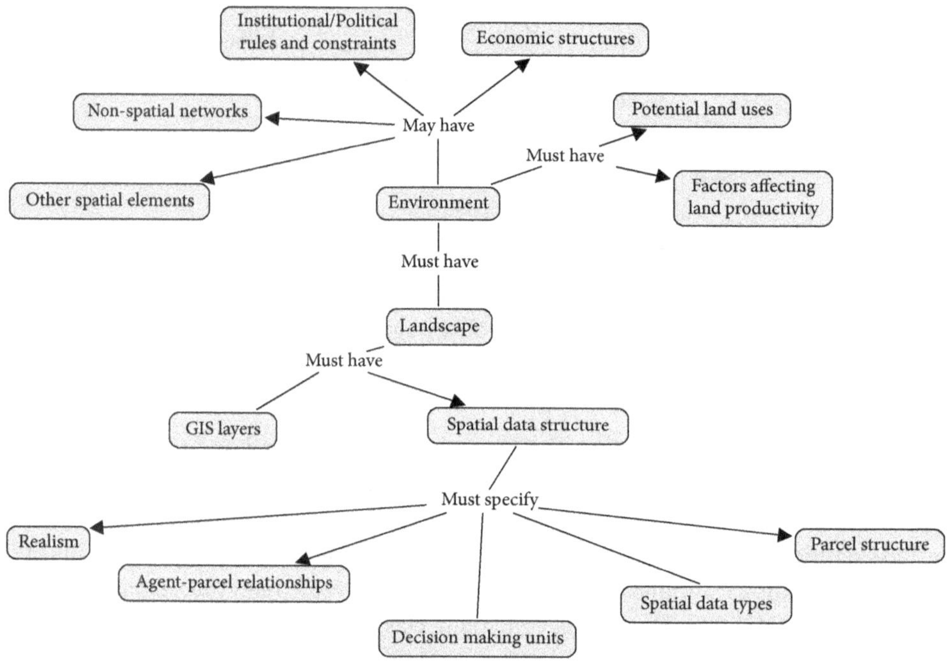

FIGURE 16.3 The *Environment* class of agent-based models of land use change (ABM/LUCC), with detail for *Landscape* and *Spatial Data Structure* elements.

over a limited number of cells or represent locations as dimensionless points under continuous space. (See Albers et al. [2010] and Horan and Lupi [2010] for recent examples of novel economic spatial models.) Although the flexible spatial structures of ABM/LUCC create many technical challenges (discussed later), they facilitate exploration of a wide range of questions, such as urban gentrification and densification (Diappi and Bolchi 2008; Jackson et al. 2008), effects of parcel size zoning on exurban development (Robinson and Brown 2009), and effects of market forces and incentive policies on agricultural land consolidation (Happe et al. 2008; Angel et al. 2011).

ABM/LUCC may contain a wide variety of decision-making agents. For example, urban land use change models may represent residential buyers and sellers, businesses, developers, and zoning boards. Agricultural models may represent many types of farming households, large commercial farming operations, input suppliers, purchasers of agricultural outputs, extension agents, and regulatory agents. The *Demographic* class (Figure 16.4) describes the characteristics of the population of agents active in the models, their demographic dynamics, and the decision-making model of each agent type. For each agent type, the *Agent* class (Figure 16.4) describes the *Agent Decision Model* (which should minimally include a decision about land use and/or land management), their *Internal Characteristics*, and their *External Resources*. Each of these elements could be designed to mirror a very traditional microeconomic model. For example, the *Agent Decision Model* should specify how agents *Calculate Payoffs* for each land use or

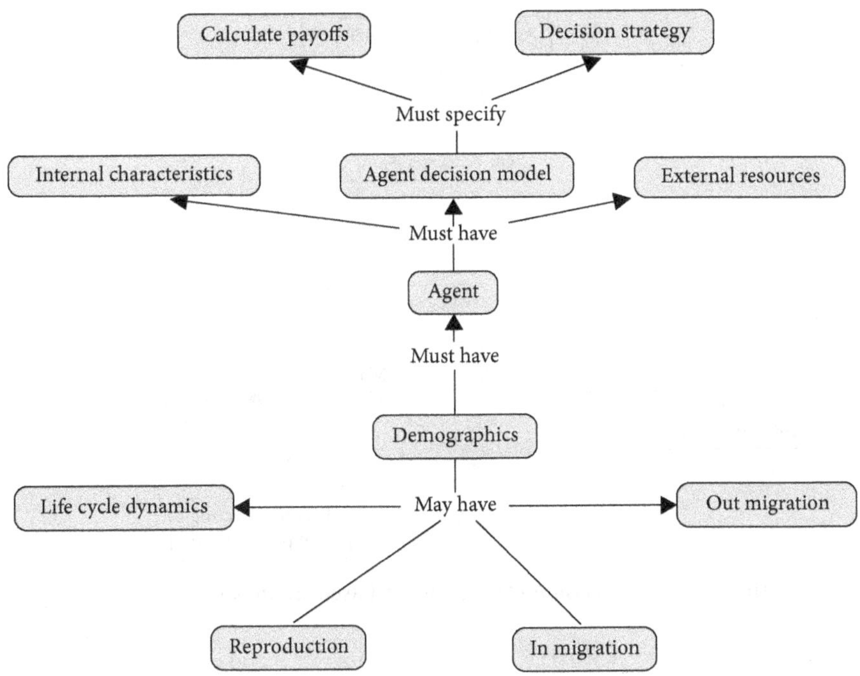

FIGURE 16.4 The *Agent* and *Demographic* classes of agent-based models of land use change (ABM/LUCC).

management strategy, as well as the *Decision Strategy* they would use. Consistent with a traditional economic approach, payoffs could be calculated through expected profit or utility, and boundedly rational profit or utility maximization could be used as a decision strategy. However, alternative models, such as imitation and satisficing, can also be implemented. Agent's *Internal Characteristics* can include factors standard to economics models, such as human capital, time horizon, discount rate, and risk preference. They can also include noneconomic factors, such as household age and composition, cultural preferences, satisfaction thresholds, and propensity to imitate neighbors. *External Resources* can also be standard economic factors, such as household labor, physical, and financial capital, but also noneconomic factors such as status in a social network.

Moving beyond traditional models, ABM/LUCC often embed agent decision models within a dynamic model of demographic change. In short, models are initialized with a certain population of agents, and those agents may have demographic rules governing their growth and decline. Models may have exogenously set rates of in-and-out-migration. They may also have endogenous reproduction, birth, and death, and household division, governed by aging and marriage or partnership. Such dynamics may be important for models of residential location and for models of agricultural household decision making. (See, for example, Jackson et al. [2008] and Torrens [2007] for urban land use change examples, and Parker, Entwisle et al. [2008] for examples related to land use change in frontier regions.)

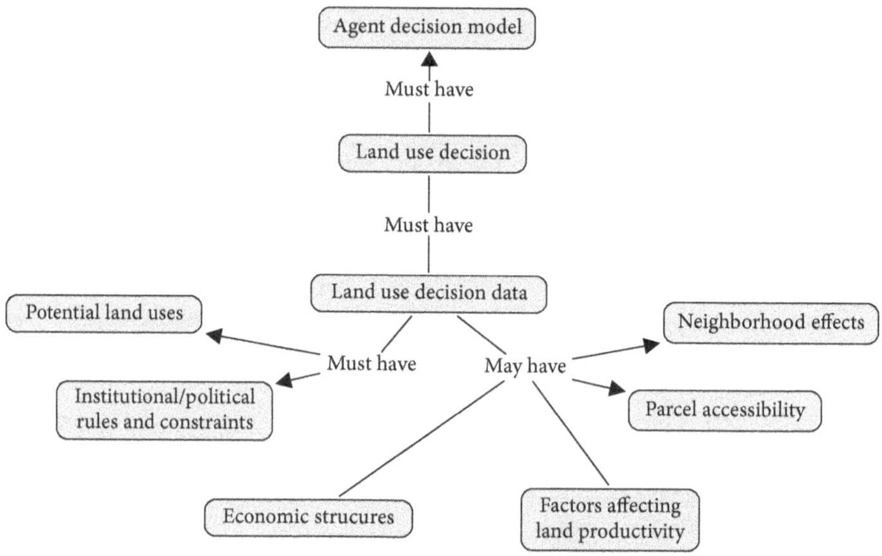

FIGURE 16.5 The *Land Use Decision* class of agent-based models of land use change (ABM/LUCC).

In economic models of the land system, two important events are generally modeled, sometimes independently and sometimes together: a land use decision and land exchange. In MR POTATOHEAD, the *Land Use Decision* class (Figure 16.5) basically serves to identify the spatial and social factors that feed into the land use/land management decision component of the *Agent Decision Model.* These factors include standard drivers of land use change, consistent with the von Thünen and Ricardian conceptual models of land allocation, including parcel accessibility, other market influences, and biophysical suitability. However, they can also include nonmarket factors such as neighborhood effects and institutional rules and constraints.

ABM/LUCC can include representations of *Land Exchange* (Figure 16.6) that include, but also go beyond, land markets. This explicit modeling of land exchange dynamics sets ABM/LUCC aside from standard economic models. MR POTATOHEAD characterizes land exchange as having three main elements: *Suppliers of Land, Acquirers of Land*, and *Exchange rules.*

Suppliers of Land have a *Motivation for Supply*, a specification of *Parcels Supplied*, and *Terms Offered* for land exchange. These can be purely economic. For example, farmers may offer particular parcels for rent, at a minimum price of the shadow value of land, as a result of constrained profit maximization (Berger 2001). Or, developers may offer residential parcels for sale at a profit-maximizing expected price based on recent comparable sales (Magliocca et al. 2011). Alternatively, out-migrating bankrupt household agents may abandon land, making it available for acquisition without cost (see Parker, Entwisle et al. [2008] for examples).

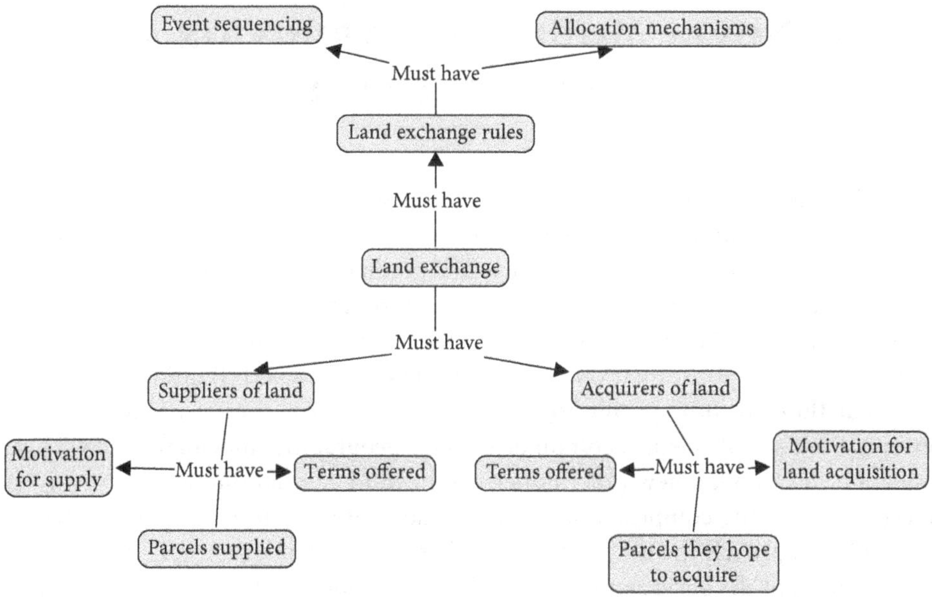

FIGURE 16.6 The *Land Exchange* class of agent-based models of land use change (ABM/LUCC).

In parallel, *Acquirers of Land* have a *Motivation for Land Acquisition*, a set of *Parcels they hope to Acquire*, and *Terms Offered* for parcel acquisition. Again, these can be purely economic: a developer offering a bid for an agricultural parcel based on expectation of profits from the subsequent sale of residences (Magliocca et al. 2011) or a resident offering a budget-constrained bid on her highest utility residential parcel (Filatova, Parker, and van der Veen 2009; Filatova, van der Veen, and Parker 2009). However, land acquisition can also be based on in-migration or the need to maintain household subsistence (see Parker, Entwisle et al. [2008] for examples).

Exchange Rules consist of both *Event Sequencing* (triggers for land transfer) and *Allocation Mechanisms*. In a land market model, buyers and sellers may be allocated into the market by the modeler, either as a one-time allocation (Filatova, Parker, and van der Veen 2009) or as a dynamic flow representing in-migration (Robinson and Brown 2009; Ettema 2010). Alternatively, they may put their house up for sale and seek a new residence when a dissatisfaction threshold is reached (Benenson and Torrens 2004), or they may offer a parcel up for sale when profit expectations exceed a certain threshold (Magliocca et al. 2011). In ABM/LUCC, alternative triggers for land supply and demand may also be implemented, such as inheritance or a bequest to a newly split household (Parker, Entwisle, et al. 2008). In a land market model, the *Allocation Mechanism* is likely to include a bilateral trade or auction mechanism. However, allocation can also occur through an agent simply occupying a chosen parcel (in a frontier setting, for instance), through bequest, negotiation, or even takings.

3. Novel Model Construction and Analysis Issues

Standard methodologies for the most commonly used modeling methods in economics are very well developed, and, in general, textbooks and courses detailing these methods are available at both the undergraduate and graduate levels. In contrast, agent-based social science models are sufficiently new that standard methodological templates are not available, and these models are covered only in a small number of specialized graduate classes. Supporting texts are just now being developed (Railsback and Grimm 2012), but they are not specific to economic applications. Because ABM combines concepts from social science, computer science, geographic information science, and simulation modeling, a new practitioner will need to gain familiarity with many new concepts. Due to the complex systems foundations of these models, practitioners will also need to approach the modeling of familiar social science concepts in novel ways. In short, many of the basic assumptions related to economic dynamics are modified in ABM/LUCC, and these modifications have implications for model design and operation. Furthermore, practitioners will need to learn and apply new concepts from computer science and simulation. In the following section, this set of novel issues is briefly reviewed, with each concept supported through specific examples related to the economics of land use change.

3.1 Model Design

3.1.1 Simulating Landscape Structure

As discussed earlier, ABM/LUCC can, in principle, be designed with complex and dynamic spatial structures (vector landscapes, network and neighborhood effects, compound agent-parcel relationships, and parcel structures that evolve dynamically). In practice, several practical challenges arise when building ABM/LUCC. The first is integrating GIS functionality with the ABM. Options are discussed in detail in Parker (2005) and Castle and Crooks (2006). In general, models that incorporate GIS functionality as part of the ABM have been more successful in terms of speed, performance, and robustness than models that attempt to build an ABM within a commercial GIS. A second challenge relates to generation of simulated model landscapes whose properties structurally resemble real-world landscapes. Many abstract ABMs operate over fixed, raster-based landscapes, with cells of uniform size and shape. In the real world, the size and distribution of parcel sizes is rarely uniform, and irregularities in structure can be very important—for instance, when examining the effects of scale economies in agriculture or the increasing gradient of parcel sizes in residential landscapes. Some exciting new methods are evolving to generate simulated landscapes with specific distributional properties. Morgan and O'Sullivan (2009) use quad-tree algorithms to generate simulated urban landscapes whose parcel size distribution follows empirically observed fractal or power-law urban land use distributions. Le Ber et al. (2009) use both Voronoi and rectangular tessellations to simulate parcel boundaries in agricultural landscapes, comparing the empirical performance of each against real-world landscapes. The most difficult outstanding spatial modeling challenge in ABM/LUCC is the modeling of parcel division and agglomeration. Each requires a model of how a developer or zoning board might combine, divide, and redesign a parcelized landscape. Although some promising work has been done in this area (Alexandridis and Pijanowski 2007), much more work is needed.

3.1.2 Characterizing Agent Heterogeneity

As mentioned earlier, the ability to represent multiple sources of heterogeneity and interactions in a single model is a driving motivation for the construction of ABM/LUCC. Referring again to Figure 16.4, agents can be heterogeneous at the class level (implying a unique set of values for any or all of the key elements: decision model, internal characteristics, or external resources), or they can be of the same class but simply have variations along a distribution for any of these elements. Ideally, the sources of agent heterogeneity that are included in an ABM/LUCC will be motivated by the research application and corresponding research questions. However, even when these are identified, questions remain as to how to represent and measure agent heterogeneity. Theoretically, agent heterogeneity can be instantiated through a set of discretely different agent types, drawing on the concept of classes and subclasses from computer science. For example, Berger (2001) differentiates between large commercial and smallholder household farmers. In models of residential land markets, following Schelling (1971), agents are often endowed with different ethnicities (Benenson and Torrens 2004). Land developers can also be modeled as specializing in particular residential development product types (Robinson and Brown 2009). Often these agent types are identified empirically by applying cluster or principal components analysis or econometric methods (Valbuena et al. 2008; Schreinemachers et al. 2009). Alternatively, agent heterogeneity can be implemented by specifying continuous stochastic distributions for particular agent properties. For example, Filatova et al. (2011) explore the effects of risk perceptions using both theoretical stochastic distributions and empirical risk perception distributions from survey data. Happe et al. (2008) initialize their model with a population of representative farms whose characteristics are derived from census data. Robinson et al. (2007) review additional methods for developing empirically based agent decision rules, which could also be applied to measure agent heterogeneity.

3.1.3 Characterizing Agent Interaction

The ability to model agent-agent interaction is another prime motivation for ABM/LUCC (Polhill et al. 2011). Agent-agent interactions can be either direct or indirect. Direct modeling of land market interactions is a primary innovation for ABM/LUCC (Parker and

Filatova 2008).[1] Several excellent agricultural production applications include models of land rental markets (Balmann and Happe 2000; Berger 2001; Happe et al. 2008). Markets for land services can also be represented. For example, Mathevet et al. (2003) model markets for duck hunting rights on agricultural landscapes. Although an obvious potential application, to the author's knowledge, no ABM/LUCC with strong economic foundations include endogenously priced local commodity markets. Other direct interactions can include information transfer (Berger 2001) and imitation of successful agricultural strategies (Polhill et al. 2001). Indirect interactions can generally be understood as externalities. Distance-dependent spatial externalities are a classic example (Parker and Meretsky 2004). Others might be characterized as pecuniary externalities. For example, when market price expectations are based on previous recent sales, a particularly high bid by a single agent can raise prevailing market prices for all other potential buyers (Magliocca et al. 2011).

Agent-agent interactions are simple to conceive and characterize, but much more difficult to implement empirically. For example, although transaction price data representing the final result of bargaining between potential buyers and sellers can often be obtained, it is almost impossible to obtain data on the initial bid and ask prices of buyers and sellers. Contingent valuation or experimental methods can be used to estimate willingness to pay (WTP) and willingness to accept (WTA) functions for buyers and sellers (Plantinga and Lewis, Chapter 15; Cho et al., Chapter 17; Messer et al., Chapter 19). Effects of spatial externalities can also be measured using spatial hedonic methods or direct production function methods in the case of agricultural externalities. The structure and effects of social networks and the ways in which they transmit information has traditionally been more difficult to measure, although standard surveys can be very useful in this respect. However, with the prevalence of social media, cell phones, and voluntary participatory information websites, new avenues are opening for data collection (Batty et al. 2010; Onnela and Reed-Tsochase 2010).

3.1.4 Event Sequencing

With some exceptions (e.g., game theoretic or experimental models that might have a first and second mover, individual models of optimal timing decisions, and statistical duration or hazard models), the sequence of action of agents is not explicitly represented in economic models. In contrast, in ABMs, the modeler must make deliberate decisions as to how the sequence of agent action will or might unfold. These rules are called *event sequencing mechanisms*.

Event sequencing mechanisms can be predetermined, meaning that the timing of agent actions and interactions are specified through a set of fixed rules by the modeler. Predetermined event sequencing mechanisms can be synchronous (all agents

[1] Although many economists might argue that standard economic approaches already model market interactions, as illustrated in Figure 16.1, they do not—rather they model an equilibrium based on the assumption that trades are occurring. ABMs often model the trades themselves, producing outcomes that differ from those that would be obtained through indirect, equilibrium approaches (Gode and Sunder 1993; Filatova, Parker, and van der Veen 2009).

are assumed to make simultaneous decisions in each time period) or asynchronous (only a portion of agents are allowed to be active in a given time period). In a land use change context, Filatova, Parker et al. (2009) model synchronous bidding, in which all active buyers simultaneously examine market conditions and place a bid on their highest utility parcel. In the next time period, all sellers simultaneously examine bid offers and accept the highest bid, if it exceeds their WTA. In contrast, Parker and Meretsky (2004) implement an asynchronous event sequencing mechanism, in which land manager agents make a land allocation decision every other time period in a checkerboard pattern. Because payoffs to land uses in this model depend on the actions of nearest neighbors, this event sequencing mechanism avoids economically irrational oscillation of land uses. Event sequencing mechanisms can also occur according to some stochastic distribution, for example the "Poisson alarm clock," in which any agent has a fixed probability of being active in a given time period. For example, in a housing market model, a resident might evaluate the utility of her current residence in relation to alternatives according to this random process.

For predetermined event sequencing mechanisms, there is a tradeoff between the degree of structure/predictability of the mechanism and the degree of path dependence introduced. Path dependence refers to sensitivity of model outcomes to initial conditions and/or stochastic elements. A synchronous event sequencing mechanism, since it has no additional stochastic elements, introduces no path dependence. However, if agents and their decision environment are highly homogeneous, and if agents are not modeled as forward looking, this can introduce economically irrational behavior, such as too-frequent switching of strategies, oscillation, and cyclical behavior. (Consider for example the classic cobweb model of agricultural supply.) Although a completely stochastic event sequencing mechanism, with a reasonably small number of agents active in each time period, can resolve this economic irrationality, it introduces a high degree of path dependence, especially if agents and their decision environment are highly heterogeneous. As an example, consider the case of technology adoption discussed in Parker et al. (2003). If technology adoption follows a bandwagon model in which certain groups adopt only if they observe a given proportion of other agent adopting, the presence of an early adopter is required to trigger a cascade of technology adoption. In a highly stochastic model, that early adopter may appear early on in some runs, later in others, and not at all in still others, leading to a path-dependent variety of outcomes. In such cases, a high number of model runs may be necessary to map out the complete potential output space of the model.

The alternative to predetermined event sequencing mechanisms is an event-driven model. In such models, agents become active decision makers only when internal or external conditions meet a given threshold. For example, agricultural producers may decide to sell land when they hit a solvency constraint (Polhill et al. 2008*b*) or when a family farmer dies or retires (Lynch and Lovell 2003). An urban resident may decide to relocate when household family structure changes due to demographic transitions or when the household becomes unsatisfied due to the demographic or income composition of the neighborhood (Benenson and Torrens 2004). Event-driven mechanisms can obviously introduce a higher degree of path dependence into ABM/LUCC. However, their advantage is that they can mirror real-world structure and dynamics, which are often central to the research questions of interest. For example, event-driven models have been used to examine agricultural land consolidation (Happe et al. 2008; Angel et al. 2011), the emergence of spatial segregation (Benenson and Torrens 2004), and urban gentrification (Diappi and Bolchi 2008; Jackson et al. 2008).

3.1.5 *Representing Boundedly Rational Optimization*

ABMs are generally applied to systems that do not have closed-form mathematical solutions, implying that the modeler herself has incomplete information, before models are run, regarding the path and final state of price and quantity outcomes (Anufriev and Branch 2009; Nolan et al. 2009). Because of the degree of interdependencies built into these models, agents' decisions are contingent on the path of previous agents' decisions, due to stochastic initial conditions and event sequencing mechanisms. These issues are present even for short-run equilibrium problems but are exacerbated for dynamic problems. Even in nonstochastic environments, mapping out the state space of possible outcomes and their best responses may be computationally intractable. (Consider, for example, the limitations of computerized chess programs.) Thus, agents in ABMs practically must be modeled as having incomplete information—putting them into the class of bounded rationality, as discussed by Simon (1996).[2]

Within this limited information context, however, agents can be modeled as optimizers. In short, some model of learning or expectations formation must be formally included in models in order to acquire an estimate of uncertain future parameters. This mandate for boundedly rational agents is clearly illustrated through alternative approaches to modeling residential land markets. Traditional closed-form models use simplifying assumptions (equal utility for homogeneous agents or equal utility to an exogenous, outside housing option) to identify housing prices, so that buyers' bid prices can be derived through budget-constrained utility maximization. In ABM land market models, since both buyers and the spatial goods being traded are heterogeneous, it is analytically impossible for a given buyer to exactly anticipate the cost of housing as a function of its characteristics. Thus, the utility maximization problem cannot be directly solved. One alternative (as proposed by Parker and Filatova [2008]) is to develop inductive models of price expectation formation and to use these expected prices to solve for a formal demand function. Both Ettema (2010) and Magliocca et al. (2011) have developed alternative price expectation formation models that could be used for this purpose, modeling a role that, in the real world, is provided by real estate agents or information sites such as Zillow. Inductive price expectation models could also be applied to estimate future agricultural commodity input and output prices. Again, this strategy would parallel the real world because actual agricultural supply decisions are based

[2] Other sources of bounded rationality can and have been represented in ABMs; for example, satisficing behavior (Gotts et al. 2003).

on incomplete estimates of future costs and prices. Although some related work has been done for financial markets, much more research is needed to understand which models are, in fact, consistent with how real-world agents form price expectations, how much real-world variation there is in expectations formation mechanisms, and how alternative models interact to influence actual market prices. Experimental economic approaches can help to fill in this gap.

3.1.6 Modeling Learning

ABMs (and the parallel individual-based models in ecology; see Grimm [2006] for an overview) often incorporate models of learning and adaptation—about the agent's environment, about the behavior of other agents, or about the success of various strategies. As can be seen from the discussion in Section 3.1.5, price expectation formation can be a key example of such learning in ABM/LUCC. Ettema (2010) and Magliocca et al. (2011), for example, both model price expectation formation in residential land markets, for developers, rural sellers, and residential buyers, respectively. Agricultural agents may also learn about the relative success of production options through both experimentation and imitation (Gotts et al. 2003; Polhill et al. 2008*b*), about the cost of compliance with pest control regulations (Carrasco et al. 2012), and about anticipated value of rental land and the optimal bidding strategies on the land market (Kellermann and Balmann 2006).

3.1.7 Equilibrium

The review of these design issues highlights the dynamic, evolutionary nature of most ABM/LUCC. These evolutionary dynamics may be inconsistent with the concept of economic equilibrium (Arthur 2006; Parker and Filatova 2008). In fact, some authors argue that economic systems, and land markets in particular, should be characterized and studied as nonequilibrium systems. Even for equilibrium models, ABMs allow more exploration of the path toward equilibrium than do traditional models (Nolan et al. 2009). However, in some cases, a researcher may construct an ABM/LUCC with the specific goal of extending an analytical equilibrium model, in which case the equilibrium properties of the extended model may be of interest (Caruso et al. 2007; Filatova, Parker, and van der Veen 2009; Filatova, van der Veen, and Parker 2009, 2011; Parker and Meretsky 2004). In such models, equilibrium can be achieved by holding the number of active agents in the model fixed in a given time period and instituting a stopping rule when no further trades occur. This rule is consistent with the standard concept of a short-run economic equilibrium—no additional economic activities for which gains from trade are positive are possible for active agents. In a residential housing or agricultural commodity market context, such a short-run equilibrium is consistent with a seasonal market. (Note that agents participating in such markets may use temporally dynamic, forward-looking models to assess future payoffs to land use.)

ABM/LUCCs generally become dynamic when the population of active agents changes over time. For example, Robinson and Brown (2009) and Magliocca (2011) assume growing populations of buyers in order to model expanding urban areas. For land markets, even if net population is fixed, some exogenous entry and exit to markets may be needed if endogenous land supply decisions are modeled. In short, since a relocating buyer may need to sell his or her current property before entering the market, an active relocation market requires that some properties be on the market at any given time. Ettema (2010) resolves this issue by modeling exogenous entry and exit but keeps the total population of agents fixed. In principle, if agent population characteristics were fixed over time, such a residential land market could reach a steady state in which rates of exit and entry were equal, and no agents currently in the market had an incentive to relocate, given current market opportunities. Similarly, an agricultural market could be viewed as being in a long-run equilibrium if no agents had an incentive to change their production decisions or buy or sell land. Whether markets such as these exist in the real world is an open question.

3.2 Experimental Design

3.2.1 Pseudo-Inductive Modeling

In most economic analysis, theoretical and empirical modeling are distinct (although potentially logically connected) activities, and models are constructed, presented, and analyzed separately. Theoretical models are derived deductively, with a set of assumptions regarding model structure leading mathematically or logically to a set of equilibrium conditions and a corresponding set of comparative static or dynamic propositions. The derivation of a supply curve from profit maximization is a classic example. Empirical models are generally inductive, distilling patterns or trends from real-world data. Econometric modeling can be considered inductive because it essentially is a pattern analysis technique that calibrates a set of best-fit coefficients to an assumed set of mathematical relationships. For example, supply curves may be estimated econometrically, with the expectation (derived from the theoretical model) that the coefficient on price should be positive. Some exceptions to these generalities exist. For example, mathematical programming (MP) models are often parameterized with a set of empirically derived coefficients, while basing their mathematical structure on theory. Computable general equilibrium (CGE) models also start with a mathematical structure based on theory, but then calibrate a set of coefficients that best fit real-world outcome data.

As with MP and CGE models and their theoretical antecedents, ABM/LUCC models can be purely theoretical or highly empirical. However, it is generally acknowledged that ABMs cannot be classified as purely inductive or purely deductive (Axelrod 1997). Essentially, these models begin with a set of structural assumptions, per a deductive approach. However, rather than generating a set of equilibrium conditions, theoretical propositions, or axioms, as would an analytical or logical model, model runs generally generate multiple data observations—often with a structure that parallels the real-world data that would be used to calibrate an econometric or CGE model. Such generated data can then be analyzed inductively to search for regular patterns that can form the analog of the theoretical propositions produced by a closed-form model.

For example, ABM land market models are built on traditional (but boundedly rational) models of land supply and demand. These models generate a spatial and temporal landscape of successful transactions, as well as of unsuccessful land bids and sales attempts. Each data point has associated spatial (property and accessibility) characteristics, as well as associated characteristics and behaviors of economic agents (information often not available in real-world data). These data can be analyzed using statistical methods to estimate a hedonic land rent function, in parallel to real-world econometric models (Filatova et al. 2009). Alternatively, econometric modeling that examines the relationship between input parameters and macroscale outcomes of interest can be used to conduct model sensitivity analysis (Happe et al. 2006). When a theoretical model is applied in this context, the inductive model's results can, in principle, play a similar role to comparative statics and dynamics, producing a set of testable hypotheses that are embedded in the estimated coefficients. For example, a negative estimated coefficient on distance in a hedonic land rent function estimated from computational data parallels the theoretical downward-sloping land rent gradient derived in the traditional analytical von Thünen/Alonzo model. (However, as discussed further later, particular issues related to complex systems data—nonlinearities, thresholds, and endogeneity between micro- and macroscale elements—can render traditional statistical approaches inappropriate, leading to a new set of outstanding challenges.) When an empirically parameterized model is applied in this context, the estimated model provides a direct target for empirical model validation (testing to see whether the outputs of the model have a reasonable correspondence to their real-world analogs). (See Fagiolo, Birchenhall et al. [2007] and Fagiolo, Moneta et al. [2007] for more extensive discussion of validation in ABMs, and Verburg et al. [2006] for an overview of validation in land use models.)

3.3 Model Construction, Execution, and Analysis

3.3.1 Software Choices and Resources

One current challenge for developers of ABM/LUCC is that no standard software exists for ABM in the social sciences that is appropriate for large-scale scientific modeling analysis and that does not require a high level of programming ability. These issues, and some current popular programming environments, are discussed in more detail in Parker et al. (2002), Nolan et al. (2009), and Castle and Crooks (2006). The models discussed in this chapter have been programmed in a variety of environments, including Swarm, C++, RePast (Java libraries for ABM), Netlogo, and Matlab. Little or no code sharing occurs between research groups, in spite of openness to making code available and a consensus that code sharing might bring efficiency gains. Several factors likely contribute to this situation. First, although funding for the development of ABM/LUCC has increased markedly in the past decade, especially in the United States and the European Union, it is difficult to obtain funding to develop a general code base, especially one that brings together code from separately funded projects. At the same time, the user base is too small to support the development of commercial ABM software. Furthermore, a wide variety of modeling approaches exist concurrently (Parker et al. 2003; Richiardi et al. 2006; Fagiolo et al. 2007), meaning that it might not be clear what set of standard models should be included in the core of a community modeling library or a commercial software product. Finally, models are often developed for different purposes and to address different questions, thus reducing the amount of potential shared code. Yet, other fields have successfully developed community modeling libraries that support multiple research endeavors (Krieger 2006; Gent et al. 2011), and this author hopes that similar standard libraries will be developed for ABM/LUCC (Parker, Brown, et al. 2008). These would potentially substantially lower model development costs and reduce barriers to entry to the field.

3.3.2 Communicating Model Structure and Results

As discussed extensively in other publications (Allesa et al. 2006; Richiardi et al. 2006; Parker, Brown, et al. 2008), because ABM/LUCC cannot be expressed solely in terms of mathematical equations or statistical algorithms, communication of model rules, structure, and function can be a major challenge. Modelers are encouraged to publish model code or executables along with research findings. A growing number of journals are providing archival links to code along with electronic publication, and the Open ABM website (openABM.org) has also been established as a model code archive for ABMs of coupled human-natural systems. However, perusing model code is a highly inefficient way to discern model structure, especially as the same model can be implemented in many alternative software libraries. Current alternative model communication protocols include the MR POTATOHEAD framework developed specifically for ABM/LUCC, demonstrated here, and the ODD protocol and its extensions, developed for any individual or ABM (Grimm et al. 2010; Groeneveld et al. 2012). These two protocols have been applied to the same subset of ABM/LUCC (Parker, Brown, et al. 2008; Polhill et al. 2008*a*). Many computational modelers, including this author, however, imagine a future in which readers will not only be able to understand model rules, but will be able to directly interact with models, including not only examining multiple output visualizations from the published experiments, but also running alternative models and analyzing their output, without having to modify programming code—and ideally without having to download models. An extensive set of programming libraries that would support such modeling is described by Parker, Brown et al. (2008), and a supporting a new format for research publication is described in detail by Mesirov (2010).

3.3.3 Generating Data

As with any simulation model that has a stochastic element, multiple model runs are often required for ABM/LUCC, even for a fixed set of parameters. In short, stochasticity can enter models both through differing initial conditions, through event sequencing, and through any other stochastic element, such as a demographic event, an exogenous price, or a biophysical condition whose value might depend on a stochastic draw. Ideally, Monte Carlo model runs should be conducted to completely map outcomes for any parameter set. Often, to further complicate matters, a modeler may want to run models for multiple parameter values, to perform sensitivity or scenario analysis. Thus, a distribution of model outcomes will exist for each parameter set, and a parameter sweep will consist of a large collection of output distributions, resulting in a large output database whose generation is not conceptually complex but is computationally intensive.

3.3.4 Analyzing Generated Data

A major outstanding challenge for ABM/LUCC lies in how to effectively analyze this wealth of generated data in order to answer research questions of interest. In theory, by following the steps given in the preceding sections (building a theoretical model and generating a database of outcomes under an appropriate range of initial conditions, random variations, and model parameters), the modeler should produce a collection of simulated data similar to what he or she might have access to in the real world. This should be, in principle, an opportunity and not a problem, especially for economists. Economists love data, and most have years of rigorous academic training in statistical data analysis methods. The problem lies in the structure of the models that generated the data, which itself dictates the structure of the data. Complex systems are characterized by nonlinear, nonmonontic, nonstationary relationships; non-Gaussian (power law) distributions; and feedbacks across scales. This implies that the relationships between model parameters and model outputs are not likely to be additive, linear, and monotonic, and input data are not likely to be normally distributed (Fagiolo, Birchenhall, and Windrum 2007; Fagiolo, Moneta, and Windrum 2007). The majority of econometric methods are developed for data that are separable, monotonic, and stationary. Therefore, new data analysis methods need to be developed. Again, some promising work in this area is under way, especially related to examination of the joint influence of changes in multiple model parameters on model outputs. Happe et al. (2006) conduct regression-based meta-modeling using a design of experiments approach to examine the sensitivity of agricultural structural change to agricultural household level drivers. Gimona et al. (2011) use regression tree analysis to analyze potentially nonlinear relationships between multiple land preservation incentives and species diversity in an ABM/LUCC. Ligmann-Zielinska and Sun (2010) use time-dependent global sensitivity analysis to separate independent and interaction effects of behavioral parameters on the time-path of fragmentation in residential landscapes, including analyzing thresholds and regime shifts. Yet again, much more basic work is needed in this area, and, given economists' tremendous skill and experience in statistical data analysis for social systems, their potential contributions to the effort are substantial (Nolan et al. 2009).

4. Conclusion

With the perspective of an economist new to ABMs of land use change in mind, this chapter has defined and described this class of models and has offered a detailed technical discussion of potential novel issues that an economist might face in their design, construction, and analysis. Numerous examples of existing ABM/LUCC have been used for illustration purposes, thus providing a technically focused review of current work in the field. To conclude the chapter, some thoughts on promising future research directions and a call for bold forward movement are offered.

4.1 Complementarities with Other Economic Modeling Methods

As illustrated through the many examples cited in this chapter, ABMs are often used to expand the range of research questions that can be addressed using economic modeling, and, in these cases, the ABM approach can serve as a substitute for more traditional approaches. Yet the development of ABMs often takes advantage of other modeling approaches that complement ABM. For example, simple versions of ABMs are often developed to replicate well-established theoretical analytical models, in order to provide structural validation for the ABMs. Econometric methods can also be used to empirically test the hypotheses generated by theoretical ABMs. Both econometric and experimental approaches are essential in helping to develop decision models for empirically grounded ABMs. Thus, the development of economically based ABM/LUCC provides a new opportunity for collaborative research and knowledge sharing with better-established economic modeling methods.

4.2 Future Research Directions: Cross-Scale Modeling

The ABM/LUCC cited in this chapter operate at a single scale—generally a land parcel (spatial scale) or a land manager managing multiple parcels (behavioral/institutional scale). These models have made important methodological advances and have been used to answer novel research questions. Yet many of the most interesting research questions related to the operation of spatial markets require models that operate across scales (Irwin 2010; Chen et al. 2011).

For example, to understand the patterns of growth and decline of residential land markets within cities, the relationship between employment centers and residential locations must be understood. This relationship operates at a neighborhood, rather than a parcel scale. At a regional scale, some understanding of the local economy is also required: what jobs will be created and lost, who will migrate into and out of the urban area as a result, and what will be their demographic and socioeconomic characteristics? This requires models that at least interface with regional and national scale models.

A second example relates to regional and global commodity production—for example, understanding the effects of new demand for biofuels on food commodity production. At a local scale, agricultural production decisions are shaped by both parcel- and household-level characteristics, such as biophysical suitability and household knowledge and resources, and by the incentives provided by potential sales prices for commodities in external markets. These factors have been effectively modeled using ABM/LUCC. However, at a regional, national, and global scale, local production decisions will modify external prices. These feedbacks have not been effectively modeled using ABM/LUCC. Furthermore, regional and global commodity supply models generally fail to account for the impacts of local spatial and agent-level heterogeneity on commodity production. The two modeling scales need to be brought together. In particular, work needs to be done to explore the extent to which ABM/LUCC agricultural production models can be integrated with higher scale computable general equilibrium models. These efforts could potentially be informed by ongoing efforts to link integrated assessment models with lower scale supply and demand models and examples of coupled models from other domains (Energy Modeling Forum 2012; Rausch and Mowers 2012).

Finally, tradable permit models for the preservation of ecosystem services have received much attention, both from a theoretical and applied policy perspective (Tietenberg 2005). However, such models rarely account for important sources of spatial heterogeneity in potential markets. Carbon markets are a potentially promising application area. Currently, markets for carbon sequestration are a patchwork of regional and national policies, with little coordination and uniformity of structure and regulatory level. ABM/LUCC could potentially be used to explore how these markets might function together if global standards were implemented, but local programs were allowed to be maintained to meet standards, thus exploring how patterns of carbon emissions and trading would change if markets were integrated. Models could also track the development of pollution hot spots and patterns of other ecosystem service generation (e.g., biodiversity preservation). However, again, higher scale market models would need to be developed to track permit trades and market clearing at a regional scale.

4.3 A Call for Innovation

Economics tends to be a methodologically conservative discipline. This conservatism certainly has its benefits: highly technical standards for academic training, detailed technical scrutiny of new methods, and rigorous peer review for published work. Yet, in a world where policy challenges are emerging at a rapid rate and unexpected global and environmental crises are capable of destabilizing global commerce, a portfolio of technical approaches to economic analysis is needed—some standard and codified by years of use, others novel, innovative, and even risky. It can be quite difficult for an economist using novel methods to succeed in a purely economic academic context due to a high degree of challenge involved in publishing analysis based on nontraditional methods in economics journals, navigating the review and promotion process, and obtaining grant funding from traditional sources (although new funding initiatives by the US National Science Foundation have relaxed this last constraint).

There is wide consensus in the economics profession that economics is not a particular method but rather more generally the science of the study of scarce resources. A wide variety of models have been used for this purpose, with new methods emerging, proving their utility, and gaining broader acceptance. I encourage the economics community to give reasonable consideration to any new methods that logically and rigorously study this allocation. Given the global-scale challenges we face and the need to quickly develop novel responses, I issue a call to the economics profession to consider, evaluate, and test these new methods with a moderately higher degree of tolerance for risk and uncertainly than is the norm in the profession. In fact, a more diverse portfolio of research approaches could be seen as an economically rational response to new challenges and the uncertainty they entail. The rewards for the profession—and more importantly, for policy analysis—could be huge. As pointed out by Nolan et al. (2009), econometric methods were once new, also, but have provided proven utility for the profession over time (Messer et al., Chapter 19, this volume.). Experimental methods are even newer but have also proven their utility. Much of the work cited in this chapter represents careful, economically grounded work by classically trained urban, environmental, resource, and agricultural economists. A subset of that work has been successfully published in economics journals. Hopefully, these works have broken the ground for the next generation of agent-based land use models to find a home within the economics literature.

Acknowledgments

This project has benefited from funding from and extensive discussions with the SLUCE2 project team (funding by US NSF CNH-0813799) related to this concept of static versus dynamic equilibrium in land markets. The manuscript content has also benefited from discussion with many participants at Waterloo Institute for Complexity and Innovation (WICI.CA) seminar and workshop participants.

References

Albers, H. J., A. Ando, and J. F. Shogren. 2010. Introduction to spatial natural resource and environmental economics. *Resource and Energy Economics* 32(2): 93–7.

Alexandridis, K., and B. C. Pijanowski. 2007. Assessing multiagent parcelization performance in the MABEL simulation model using Monte Carlo replication experiments. *Environment and Planning B* 34(2): 223–244.

Allesa, L. N., M. Laituri, and M. Barton. 2006. An "all hands" call to the social science community: Establishing a community framework for complexity modeling using agent based models and cyberinfrastructure. *Journal of Artificial Societies and Social Simulation* (4), http://jasss.soc.surrey.ac.uk/9/4/6.html.

Angel, N., M. North, E. Tatara, C. E. Laciana, E. Weber, and F. Ruiz Toranzo. 2011. An agent based model to simulate structural and land use changes in agricultural systems of the argentine pampas. *Ecological Modelling* 222(19): 3486–3499.

Anufriev, M., and W. A. Branch. 2009. Introduction to special issue on complexity in economics and finance. *Journal of Economic Dynamics and Control* 33(5): 1019–1022.

Arthur, W. B. 2006. Out-of-equilibrium economics and agent-based modeling. In *Handbook of computational economics*, Vol. 2 *Agent-based computational economics*, eds. L. Tesfatsion and K. L. Judd. Amsterdam: Elsevier B.V., 1551–1564.

Axelrod, R. 1997. Advancing the art of simulation in the social sciences. In *Simulating social phenomena*, eds. R. Conte, R. Hegselmann, and P. Terna. Berlin: Springer, 21–40.

Balmann, A., and K. Happe. 2000. Applying parallel genetic algorithms to economic problems: The case of agricultural land markets. Paper read at "Microbehavior and Macroresults," IIFET 2000 Proceedings, at Corvallis, Oregon USA.

Batty, M., A. Hudson-Smith, R. Milton, and A. T. Crooks. 2010. Map mashups, Web 2.0 and the GIS revolution. *Annals of GIS* 16(1): 1–13.

Benenson, I., and P. Torrens. 2004. *Geosimulation: Automata-based modeling of urban phenomena*. London: John Wiley & Sons.

Berger, T. 2001. Agent-based spatial models applied to agriculture: A simulation tool for technology diffusion, resource use changes, and policy analysis. *Agricultural Economics* 25(2–3): 245–260.

Berry, B. J. L., L. D. Kiel, and E. Elliot. 2002. Adaptive agents, intelligence, and emergent human organization: Capturing complexity through agent-based modeling. *Proceedings of the National Academy of Sciences of the USA* 99(Supplement 3): 7178–7188.

Bockstael, N. E. 1996. Modeling economics and ecology: The importance of a spatial perspective. *American Journal of Agricultural Economics* 78: 1168–1180.

Bousquet, F., and C. Le Page. 2004. Multi-agent simulations and ecosystem management: A review. *Ecological Modelling* 76(3–4): 313–332.

Carrasco, L. R., D. Cook, R. Baker, A. MacLeod, J. D. Knight, and J. D. Mumford. 2012. Towards the integration of spread and economic impacts of biological invasions in a landscape of learning and imitating agents. *Ecological Economics* 76: 95–103.

Caruso, G., D. Peeters, J. Cavailhes, and M. Rounsevell. 2007. Spatial configurations in a peri-urban city: A cellular automata-based microeconomic model. *Regional Science and Urban Economics* 37(5): 542–567.

Castle, C., and A. T. Crooks. 2006. Principles and concepts of agent-based modelling for developing geospatial simulations. In *CASA working paper series*. London: Center for Advanced Spatial Analysis. Report number 110, http://www.casa.ucl.ac.uk/publications/workingPaperDetail.asp?ID=110.

Chen, Y., E. G. Irwin, and C. Jayaprakash. 2011. Incorporating spatial complexity into economic models of land markets and land use change. *Agricultural and Resource Economics Review* 40(3): 1–10.

Cho, S-H. Hoon, S. G. Kim, and R. K. Roberts. 2014. Spatial econometric modeling of land use change. In *Oxford handbooks of land economics*, eds. J. M. Duke and J. Wu, 430–451. New York: Oxford University Press.

Diappi, L., and P. Bolchi. 2008. Smith's rent gap theory and local real estate dynamics: A multi-agent model. *Computers, Environment, and Urban Systems* 32(1): 6–18.

Energy Modeling Forum. 2012. Snowmass conferences: Climate change impacts and integrated assessment (CCI/IA). Stanford University 2012. Available from http://emf.stanford.edu/research/snowmass/.

Ettema, D. 2010. A multi-agent model of urban processes: Modelling relocation processes and price setting in housing markets. *Computers, Environment, and Urban Systems* 35(1): 1–11.

Fagiolo, G., C. Birchenhall, and P. Windrum. 2007. Empirical validation in agent-based models: Introduction to the special issue. *Computational Economics* 30(3): 189–194.

Fagiolo, G., A. Moneta, and P. Windrum. 2007. A critical guide to empirical validation of agent-based models in economics: Methodologies, procedures, and open problems. *Computational Economics* 30(3): 195–226.

Filatova, T., D. C. Parker, and A. van der Veen. 2009. Agent-based urban land markets: Agent's pricing behavior, land prices and urban land use change. *Journal of Artificial Societies and Social Simulation* 12(1): 3.

Filatova, T., A. van der Veen, and D. C. Parker. 2009. Land market interactions between heterogeneous agents in a heterogeneous landscape: Tracing the macro-scale effects of individual trade-offs between environmental amenities and disamenities. *Canadian Journal of Agricultural Economics* 57(4): 431–445.

Filatova, T., A. van der Veen, and D. C. Parker. 2011. The implications of skewed risk perception for a Dutch coastal land market: Insights from an agent-based computational economics model. *Agricultural and Resource Economics Review* 40(3): 405–423.

Gent, P., G. Danabasoglu, L. Donner, M. Holland, E. Hunke, S. Jayne, D. Lawrence, R. Neale, P. Rasch, M. Vertenstein, P. Worley, Z-L. Yang, and M. Zhang. 2011. The community climate system model Version 4. *Journal of Climate* 24(19): 4973–4991.

Gimblett, H. R. (ed.). 2002. *Integrating geographic information systems and agent-based modeling techniques for simulating social and ecological processes*. Oxford: Oxford University Press.

Gimona, A., and J. G. Polhill. 2011. Exploring robustness of biodiversity policy with a coupled metacommunity and agent-based model. *Journal of Land Use Science* 6(2–3): 175–93.

Gode, D., and S. Sunder. 1993. Allocative efficiency of markets with zero-intelligence traders: Market as a partial substitute for individual rationality. *Journal of Political Economy* 101(1): 119–137.

Gotts, N. M., J. G. Polhill, and A. N. R. Law. 2003. Aspiration levels in a land use simulation. *Cybernetics and Systems* 34: 663–683.

Grimm, V., and S. F. Railsback. 2006. Chapter 1: Introduction. In *Individual-based modeling and ecology*, eds. V. Grimm and S. F. Railsback. Princeton, NJ: Princeton University Press, 2–20.

Grimm, V., U. Berger, D. L. DeAngelis, J. G. P., J. Giske, and S. F. Railsback. 2010. The ODD protocol: A review and first update. *Ecological Modelling* 221(23): 2760–2768

Groeneveld, J., B. Müller, F. Angermüller, R. Drees, G. Dreßler, C. Klassert, J. Schulze, H. Weise, and N. Schwarz. 2012. Good modelling practice: Expanding the ODD model description protocol for socioenvironmental agent based models. Paper read at Proceedings of the 2012 International Congress on Environmental Modelling and Software: Managing Resources of a Limited Planet., July 2–5, Leipzig, Germany.

Happe, K., K. Kellermann, and A. Balmann. 2006. Agent-based analysis of agricultural policies: An illustration of the agricultural policy simulator AgriPoliS, its adaptation and behavior. *Ecology and Society* 11(1): 49.

Happe, K., A. Balmann, K. Kellermann, and C. Sahrbacher. 2008. Does structure matter? The impact of switching the agricultural policy regime on farm structures. *Journal of Economic Behavior & Organization* 67(2): 431–444.

Hernandez, C., K. Troitzsch, and B. Edmonds (eds.). 2008. *Social simulation technologies: Advances and new discoveries*. Hershey, PA: Information Science Reference.

Horan, R. D., and F. Lupi. 2010. The economics of invasive species control and management: The complex road ahead. *Resource and Energy Economics* 32(4): 477–482.

Institute for Human and Machine Cognition. 2011. Cmap Tools knowledge modeling toolkit. Available from http://cmap.ihmc.us/.

Irwin, E. G. 2010. New directions for urban economic models of land use change: Incorporating spatial dynamics and heterogeneity. *Journal of Regional Science* 50(1): 65–91.

Jackson, J., B. Forest, and R. Sengupta. 2008. Agent-based simulation of urban residential dynamics and land rent change in a gentrifying area of Boston. *Transactions in GIS* 12(4): 475–491.

Kellermann, K., and A. Balmann. 2006. How smart should farms be modeled? Behavioral foundation of bidding strategies in agent-based land market models. Paper read at 2006 Annual Meeting, Queensland, Australia.

Kohler, T. A. 2000. *Dynamics in human and primate societies*. New York and Oxford: Oxford University Press.

Krieger, K. 2006. Life in silico: A different kind of intelligent design. *Science* 312(14): 188–190.

LeBaron, B. 2006. Agent-based computational finance. In *Handbook of computational economics*, Vol. 2 *Agent-based computational economics*, eds. L. Tesfatsion and K. L. Judd, 1187–1233. Amsterdam: Elsevier B.V.

Le Ber, F., C. Lavigne, K. Adamczyk, F. Angevin, N. Colbach, J. –F. Mari, and H. Monod. 2009. Neutral modelling of agricultural landscapes by tessellation methods: Application for gene flow simulation. *Ecological Modelling* 220(24): 3536–3545.

Ligmann-Zielinska, A., and L. Sun. 2010. Applying time-dependent variance-based global sensitivity analysis to represent the dynamics of an agent-based model of land use change. *International Journal of Information Science* 24(12): 1829–1850.

Lynch, L., and S. Lovell. 2003. Combining spatial and survey data to explain participation in agricultural land preservation programs. *Land Economics* 79(2): 259–276.

Magliocca, N., E. Safirova, V. McConnell, and M. Walls. 2011. An economic agent-based model of coupled housing and land markets (CHALMS). *Computers, Environment and Urban Systems* 35(3): 183–191.

Mathevet, R., F. Bousquet, C. Le Page, and M. Antona. 2003. Agent-based simulations of interactions between duck population, farming decisions and leasing of hunting rights in the camargue (southern France). *Ecological Modelling* 165: 107–126.

Matthews, R. B., N. G. Gilbert, A. Roach, J. G. Polhill, and N. M. Gotts. 2007. Agent-based land-use models: a review of applications. *Landscape Ecology* 22(10): 1447–1459.

Mesirov, J. P. 2010. Accessible reproducible research. *Science* 327: 415–416.

Messer, K. D., J. M. Duke, and L. Lynch. 2014. Applying experiments to land economics: Public information and auction efficiency in ecosystem service markets. In *Oxford handbook of land economics*, eds. J. Duke and J. Wu, 481–546 New York: Oxford University Press.

Morgan, F., and D. O'Sullivan. 2009. Using binary space partitioning to generate urban spatial patterns. *4th International Conference on Computers in Urban Planning and Urban Management*, 1–16.

Nelson, G., and J. Geoghegan. 2002. Introduction to the special issue on spatial analysis for agricultural economists. *Agricultural Economics* 27(3): 197–200.

Nolan, J., D. C. Parker, and G. Cornelis van Kooten. 2009. An overview of computational modeling in agricultural and resource economics. *Canadian Journal of Agricultural Economics* 57(4): 417–429.

Onnela, J-P., and F. Reed-Tsochase. 2010. Spontaneous emergence of social influence in online systems. *Proceedings of the National Academy of Sciences* of the USA 107(43): 18375–18380.

Parker, D. C., T. Berger, and S. M. Manson, eds. 2002. *Agent-based models of land-use and land-cover change: Report and review of an international workshop*, October 4–7, 2001. Vol. 6, LUCC report series. Bloomington: LUCC Focus 1 office.

Parker, D. C., S. M. Manson, M. A. Janssen, M. Hoffmann, and P. Deadman. 2003. Multi-agent systems for the simulation of land-use and land-cover change: A review. *Annals of the Association of American Geographers* 93(2): 314–337.

Parker, D. C., and V. Meretsky. 2004. Measuring pattern outcomes in an agent-based model of edge-effect externalities using spatial metrics. *Agriculture, Ecosystems and Environment* 101: 233–250.

Parker, D. C. 2005. Integration of geographic information systems and agent-based models of land use: Challenges and prospects. In *GIS, Spatial Analysis and Modeling*, eds. D. J. Maguire, M. F. Goodchild, and M. Batty. Redlands, CA: ESRI Press, 403–422.

Parker, D. C., D. Brown, J. G. Polhill, S. M. Manson, and P. Deadman. 2008. Illustrating a new "conceptual design pattern" for agent-based models and land use via five case studies: The MR POTATOHEAD framework. In *Agent-based modelling in natural resource management*, eds. A. L. Paredes and C. H. Iglesias. Valladolid, Spain: Universidad de Valladolid, 29–62.

Parker, D. C., B. Entwisle, E. Moran, R. Rindfuss, L. Van Wey, S. Manson, L. Ahn, P. Deadman, T. Evans, M. Linderman, S. M. M. Rizi, and G. Malanson. 2008. Case studies, cross-site comparisons, and the challenge of generalization: Comparing agent-based models of land-use change in frontier regions. *Journal of Land Use Science* 3(1): 41–72.

Parker, D. C., and T. Filatova. 2008. A theoretical design for a bilateral agent-based land market with heterogeneous economic agents. *Computers, Environment, and Urban Systems* 32(6): 454–463.

Plantinga, A. J., and D. J. Lewis. 2014. Landscape simulations with econometric-based land-use models. In *Oxford handbook of land economics*, eds. J. M. Duke and J. Wu, 380–401. New York: Oxford University Press.

Polhill, J. G., N. M. Gotts, and A. N. R. Law. 2001. Imitative versus nonimitative strategies in a land use simulation. *Cybernetics and Systems* 32(1–2): 285–307.

Polhill, J. G., D. C. Parker, D. Brown, and V. Grimm. 2008*a*. Using the ODD protocol for describing three agent-based social simulation models of land-use change. *Journal of Artificial Societies and Social Simulation* 11(2–3). http://jasss.soc.surrey.ac.uk/11/2/3.html

Polhill, J. G., D. C. Parker, and N. M. Gotts. 2008*b*. Effects of land markets on competition between innovators and imitators in land use: Results from FEARLUS-ELMM. In *Social simulation technologies: Advances and new discoveries*, eds. C. Hernandez, K. Troitzsch and B. Edmonds. Hershey, PA: Information Science Reference.

Polhill, J. G., A. Gimona, and R. J. Aspinall. 2011. Agent-based modelling of land use effects on ecosystem processes and services. *Journal of Land Use Science* 6(2–3): 75–81.

Railsback, S. F., and V. Grimm. 2012. *Agent-based and individual-based modeling: A practical introduction*. Princeton, NJ: Princeton University Press.

Rausch, S., and M. Mowers. 2012. Distributional and efficiency impacts of clean and renewable energy standards for electricity. In *Joint program report series*. Boston: MIT Joint Program on the science and policy of global change.

Richiardi, M., R. Leombruni, N. Saam, and M. Sonnessa. 2006. A common protocol for agent-based social simulation. *Journal of Artificial Societies and Social Simulation* (1), http://jasss.soc.surrey.ac.uk/9/1/15.html. http://globalchange.mit.edu/files/document/MITJPSPGC_Rpt225.pdf Report number 225, 48 pp.

Robinson, D. T., and D. G. Brown. 2009. Evaluating the effects of land-use development policies on ex-urban forest cover: An integrated agent-based GIS approach. *International Journal of Geographic Information Science* 23(9): 1211–1232.

Robinson, D. T., D. G. Brown, D. C. Parker, P. Schreinemachers, M. A. Janssen, M. Huigen, H. Wittmer, N. Gotts, P. Promburom, E. Irwin, T. B., F. Gatzweiler, and C. Barnaud. 2007. Comparison of empirical methods for building agent-based models in land use science. *Journal of Land-Use Science* 2 (1): 31–55.

Schelling, T. 1971. Dynamic models of segregation. *Journal of Mathematical Sociology* 1: 143–186.

Schreinemachers, P., T. Berger, A. Sirijinda, and S. Praneetvatakul. 2009. The diffusion of greenhouse agriculture in northern Thailand: Combining econometrics and agent-based modeling. *Canadian Journal of Agricultural Economics* 57(4): 513–536.

Schreinemachers, P., C. Potchanasin, T. Berger, and S. Roygrong. 2010. Agent-based modeling for ex ante assessment of tree crop innovations: Litchis in northern Thailand. *Agricultural Economics* 41(6): 519–536.

Simon, H. 1996. *The sciences of the artificial*. Cambridge, MA: MIT Press.

Stanford Center for Biomedical Informatics Research. 2007. Protege OWL 2007. Available from http://protege.stanford.edu.

Tesfatsion, L. 2006. Agent-based computational economics: A constructive approach to economic theory. In *Handbook of computational economics* Vol. 2: *Agent-based computational economics*, eds. L. Tesfatsion and K. L. Judd, 831–880. Amsterdam: Elsevier B.V.

Tesfatsion, L., and Kenneth L. Judd. 2006. *Handbook of computational economics, Volume 2: Agent-based computational economics*. Amsterdam: Elsevier B.V.

Tietenberg, T. 2005. Economic instruments for environmental regulation. In *Economics of the environment: Selected readings*, ed. R. Stavins, 277–301. New York: W. W. Norton.

Torrens, P. M. 2007. A geographic automata model of residential mobility. *Environment and Planning B: Planning and Design* 34: 200–222.

Valbuena, D., P. Verburg, and A. K. Bregt. 2008. A method to define a typology for agent-based analysis in regional land-use research. *Agriculture, Ecosystems and Environment* 128(1–2): 27–36.

Verburg, P., K. Kok, R. G. Pontius, A. Veldkamp, A. Angelsen, B. Eickhout, T. Kram, A. J. Walsh, D. C. Parker, K. Clarke, D. Brown, and K. Overmars. 2006. Modelling land-use and land-cover change. In *Land-use and land-cover change: Local processes, global impacts*, eds. E. Lambin and H. Geist, 117–131. New York: Springer Berlin Heidelberg.

Waldrop, M. 2009. A model approach. *Nature* 460: 667.

CHAPTER 17

SPATIAL ECONOMETRIC MODELING OF LAND USE CHANGE

SEONG-HOON CHO, SEUNG GYU KIM, AND ROLAND K. ROBERTS

LAND is used by humans and other living creatures and involves complex human-environment interactions. Land uses may be broadly classified for forest, agriculture, and urban uses, and their uses may be altered by land users' purposes. Understanding land use change is essential because it occurs to generate desirable and undesirable impacts on the environment and human welfare. Theoretical and empirical modeling approaches have been developed to examine the drivers, processes, and implications of changes in land use.

Theories of land use change conceptualize the frameworks describing changes from one type of use to another and explain why, when, how, and where land use changes occur under the frameworks of disciplines studying economic, environmental, and spatial changes. Microeconomic theory-based approaches have adopted von Thunen's agricultural rent theory (Thünen and Heinrich 1966), Alonso's (1972) urban land market theory, and agent-based theories of urban and regional spatial structure (Schaffer 1999). Von Thunen's agricultural rent theory covers location theory and the urban and regional spatial structure of a wide range of spatial scales and provides the foundations for Alonso's urban land market theory. Alonso's theory derives individual equilibria for households based on bid-rent functions and a market clearing mechanism. The agent-based theoretical approaches accommodate the endogeneity of the spatial distribution of agents and of their associated activities.

Empirical modeling of land use change emphasizes discrete land use decisions at the parcel or plot scale (e.g., develop or not). The discrete land use decisions conceptualize landowners choosing to develop land if the present value of the future stream of net returns from development is greater than the present value of the future stream of net returns from the land remaining in its current nonurban use (Bockstael 1996). The main objective of this chapter is to provide a comprehensive review and critique of the literature of empirical modeling of land use decisions, focusing particularly on the strengths and weaknesses of different spatial econometric modeling approaches and important future research directions. To accomplish the objective, (1) a comprehensive review of the literature on spatial econometric modeling of land use decisions is presented, (2) a case study to illustrate one of the approaches is developed, (3) an overall assessment of different approaches is provided, and (4) important directions and challenges for future research are presented.

1. Literature Review

Empirical specifications typically use binary probit or logit regression models in which conversion from nonurban to urban use is explained by rents derived from different land uses, such as rents derived from forest or farmland (White and Fleming 1980; Alig 1986; Alig et al. 1988; Lichtenberg 1989; Parks and Murray 1994; Hardie and Parks 1997; Kline and Alig 1999; Plantinga et al. 1999), distances to commodity markets and amenity areas (Chomitz and Gray 1996; Turner et al. 1996; Nelson and Hellerstein 1997; Cropper et al. 1999; Cho and Newman 2005), and land use regulations (Irwin and Bockstael 2002; Irwin et al. 2003; Libby and Sharp 2003; Miller and Vaske 2003).

A major challenge with econometric specification of discrete land use decisions is that land conversion decisions may be co-determined through neighborhood spillover effects. Neighbors share common characteristics, hence their decisions exhibit high dependence among the error terms in land conversion models (Irwin and Bockstael 2001; Carrión-Flores and Irwin 2004; Cho and Newman 2005; Irwin et al. 2006). Spatial dependence can occur due to spatially correlated land use decisions or as a consequence of residual correlation caused by unobserved factors that are spatially dependent. Like any other statistical problem caused by the lack of independence of the errors, the presence of spatial dependence of the errors (referred to as "spatial error autocorrelation") in the econometric specification of discrete land use decisions causes parameter estimates to be inconsistent and inefficient (Carrión-Flores and Irwin 2004).

The application of spatial econometrics to discrete dependent variable models, such as binary probit and logit models, is comparatively less developed than for models with continuous dependent variables. Discrete spatial process models that accommodate spatial error autocorrelation typically are based on the maximum likelihood estimation (MLE) method (Case 1992), the linearized version of the generalized method of moments (GMM) (Pinske and Slade 1998; Fleming 2004; Klier and McMillen 2008), the spatial general linear model (GLM) method (Schabenberger and Pierce 2002), the nonparameteric probit geographically weighted regression (GWR) model approach (LeSage 1999; Páez 2006), or the nonparametric GMM model method (Conley 1999; Conley and Dupor 2003).

Case (1992) assumed a block-diagonal matrix of spatial weights by taking a common spatial component for all observations within a given boundary using the MLE for the spatial probit model. This restrictive specification has been criticized for not accounting for distance-decay effects. The GMM estimator with a spatial autoregressive term proposed by Kelejian and Prucha (1999) is considered better than MLE mainly because (1) the number of integrals in the likelihood function equals the sample size, which is computationally intractable when the sample size is large; and (2) MLE requires full distributional assumptions, which can affect parameter estimation and the accuracy of spatial predictions when the error distribution asssumption is incorrect, whereas GMM has no such requirement.

Páez (2006) presented a nonparametric probit GWR with heteroscedastic error terms to analyze land development by generating parameter estimates for every regression point to highlight spatial variation. Despite the benefits of the probit GWR, the literature using GWR identifies potentially serious problems with the approach such as (1) spatial error dependence (Leung et al. 2000; Fotheringham et al. 2002), (2) potential multicollinearity among local regression coefficients (Wheeler and Tiefelsdorf 2005), and (3) extreme coefficients, including sign reversals (Farber and Páez 2007). Alternatively, nonparametric GMM models that allow for spatial dependence generate consistent covariance-matrix estimators regardless of sample size (e.g., Grenander and Rosenblatt 1957; Hall et al. 1994; Hall and Patil 1994; Conley 1999; Conley and Dupor 2003) (Grenander and Rosenblatt 1957; Hall, Fisher, and Hoffmann 1994; Hall and Patil 1994). (Grenander and Rosenblatt 1957; Hall, Fisher, and Hoffmann 1994; Hall and Patil 1994; Conley 1999; Conley and Dupor 2003).

2. Case Study

This section showcases a case study of applying the nonparametric GMM model to discrete land use decisions with 12,375 observations using a consistent covariance matrix for the GMM estimator in the presence of spatial error autocorrelation. The case study uses the model to evaluate maximum lot coverage as a potential policy tool for mitigating urban sprawl.[1] Maximum lot coverage is the maximum percentage of impervious surface allowed on any given lot. Lot coverage is calculated as the total amount of impervious surface on the lot divided by the total lot area. For example, if the maximum lot coverage of 20% were assigned to a residential lot, the area of the lot could not be covered by impervious surface of more than 20%, leaving the remaining uncovered portion as private open space. Maximum lot coverage restrictions have been implemented (1) to maintain a consistent and compatible land use pattern for residential neighborhoods

[1] The word "sprawl" first appeared in print in 1955, in the context of low-density and leapfrogging development (Evans 1999; Rybczynski 2005). Despite divergent viewpoints on the definition of urban

and (2) to prevent excessive impervious surfaces and thus reduce the risk of drainage and flooding problems (Pierson 2002; City of Redmond 2011). Maximum lot coverage was chosen as a potential policy tool for mitigating urban sprawl because it explicitly utilizes the tradeoff between lot size and public open space, ensures the provision of open space, and can curb urban sprawl (Lichtenberg and Hardie 2007; Lichtenberg et al. 2007). To examine the effects of maximum lot coverage on urban sprawl, landowners' development decisions for new residential housing at the parcel level are empirically estimated in a land conversion model based on the conceptual framework developed in Section 2.1.

Once estimates are acquired from the land conversion model, the impacts of changes in maximum lot coverage on development patterns are evaluated by ex ante simulations of development patterns inside and outside the developed area that existed prior to the emergence of urban sprawl. The ex ante simulations forecast development rates under observed status quo and hypothetical maximum lot coverage scenarios. The ex ante simulations suggest that an increase in maximum lot coverage encourages increased development inside the area of non-disconnected, preexisting development that existed prior to the emergence of urban sprawl (referred to as "preexisting development"), relative to the area outside preexisting development. With an increase in maximum lot coverage, a greater development rate inside the area of preexisting development than outside this area effectively serves to mitigate sprawl by encouraging development close to preexisting development and discouraging fragmented sprawl development farther from preexisting development.

2.1 Conceptual Framework

Household location choices are modeled by extending the work of Brueckner (1987), Fujita (1990), Fujita and Thisse (2002), Wu (2006), and Glaeser et al. (2008). Households are assumed to choose consumption bundle (q, s, o) to maximize utility subject to a budget constraint:

$$\begin{aligned} &\max_{q,s} U(q,s,o) \\ &s.t.\, pq + s = y \end{aligned} \tag{1}$$

where $U(\cdot)$ is a differentiable utility function, q is the size of residential space (feet^2), s is the consumption of a composite numéraire nonhousing good, o is the size of neighboring open space surrounding the residential location, p is the housing price per unit

sprawl, there is consensus that urban sprawl is well-described as the leapfrogging of development beyond the city's outer boundary into smaller rural settlements (Hanham and Spiker 2005). An area of leapfrogging or fragmented development is considered an area of urban sprawl when development occurs disjoint from existing development (Isberg 1973; Ewing 1994; Wu and Plantinga 2003; Wu 2006).

(\$/feet^2), and y is gross household income. The indirect utility function can be implicitly defined from the maximization problem in equation (1):

$$V(p,y,o) = U(q^*, y - pq^*, o) = V^o, \tag{2}$$

where $q^* = \arg\max_q U(q, y - pq, o)$ is the demand function for housing. In equilibrium, each household has the same level of utility V^o, which is independent of its location. V^o is also exogenous from the perspective of a single "open city," because in- and out-migration will equate household utility across cities (Wu 2006).

Assumptions about q are posed to analyze the effect of the policy variable, maximum lot coverage:

$$q = q(l,m), \tag{3}$$

where l is the lot size for a residential house and m is the maximum lot coverage imposed by zoning. The size of residential space q is expected to be positively related with lot size l and maximum lot coverage m because both larger lot size and maximum lot coverage provide more residential space. Also, m is expected to be smaller in areas with more neighboring open space; that is, $m = m(o)$ and $\partial m/\partial o < 0$, because maximum lot coverage intends to preclude excessive structure development on each parcel and is relatively stricter in low-density developed areas (e.g., agriculturally zoned districts) than in densely designed areas (e.g., multifamily districts) (Johnston and Madison 1997; Harrison County 2009; New York City 2009). By substituting equation (3) into (2), equation (3) can be rewritten as:

$$V(p,y,o) = U(q^*(l,m(o)), y - pq^*(l,m(o),o)) = V^o. \tag{4}$$

Equation (4) implicitly defines a market-level inverse demand function ($p^* = p(\cdot)$):

$$p^* = p(y,o,V^o), \tag{5}$$

where $o = o^{-1}(m)$. To see the impact of maximum lot coverage on housing demand, we apply the implicit function theorem to equation (5):

$$\frac{\partial p^*}{\partial m} = -\frac{\frac{\partial V}{\partial m}}{\frac{\partial V}{\partial p^*}} = \frac{\partial p^*}{\partial o^{-1}(m)} \cdot \frac{\partial o^{-1}(m)}{\partial m}. \tag{6}$$

The first ratio on the right-hand side of equation (6) is typically positive because neighboring open space provides a positive amenity to households. The second ratio is positive if private open space is perceived as a substitute for neighboring open space because higher maximum lot coverage reduces private open space, and larger neighboring open space substitutes for the reduced private open space.[2] Consequently, the sign of equation (6), the effect of maximum lot coverage on housing demand reflected in the housing price (p^*), is positive. Thus, an increase in m (i.e., less stringent maximum lot coverage) increases housing demand.

The supply side of the housing market is specified in terms of maximum lot coverage by assuming a competitive industry with constant return to scale production technology (Wu 2006). The developers choose the density of development to maximize profit π:

$$\max_{d} \pi(d) = p^* d - r - c(d), \tag{7}$$

where d is the development density represented by the structure/lot size ratio, r is site-specific land cost, and $c(d)$ is material-labor-capital cost. The first-order condition, $p^* - c'(d) = 0$, implicitly defines the optimal development density d^*:

$$d^* = c'^{-1}(p^*), \tag{8}$$

where $c'^{-1}(\cdot)$ is the inverse of the marginal cost function. Developers are forced to face two possible alternatives for the residential development decision:

$$\begin{array}{ll} \textit{developable}, & \textit{if } d^* \leq m \\ \textit{undevelopable}, & \textit{if } d^* > m, \end{array} \tag{9}$$

which shows that developers would develop a residential house when their optimal choice of development density is not bound by the maximum lot coverage regulation; that is, $d^* \leq m$. A lower m sets a more stringent bar for development. Thus, the probability of development would be lower if m were lower (i.e., more stringent regulation of maximum lot coverage). Because a decrease in m decreases the probability of development and consequently decreases the supply of new housing, a decrease in m reduces housing levels in equilibrium because both supply of new housing and demand

[2] Thorsnes (2002) found that that larger residential lot sizes are viewed as a substitute for forest open space to some extent. Cho and Roberts (2007) found different degrees of willingness to trade between neighborhood density (representing open space availability) and lot size. Likewise, Kopits, McConnell, and Walls (2007) found that in the urban-rural fringe, owning a private lot was preferrable to public open space with low willingness to trade between the two. Cho et al. (2009) recently found that substitutability between open space and lot size exists inside the city boundary.

for housing are lower if private open space is perceived as a substitute for neighboring open space.

Because the stock of housing depends on the urban population, according to urban spatial theory, observed land development decisions are regarded as an equilibrium point at which supply of housing service meets consumer demand (Dipasquale 1999). To examine the effect of maximum lot coverage on the equilibrium housing level, land development decisions by landowners for new residential housing at the parcel level are empirically estimated. Equilibrium housing levels are observed as land development decisions under the observed status quo maximum lot coverage. A parcel-based land development model (e.g., Bockstael 1996; Bockstael and Bell 1998; Nickerson and Lynch 2001; Bell and Irwin 2002; Irwin and Bockstael 2002, 2004; Irwin et al. 2003; Cho and Newman 2005) and ex ante simulations measure deviations from equilibrium housing levels following implementation of alternative hypothetical maximum lot coverage scenarios.

2.2 Spatial Binary Model Applying a Nonparametric Estimator

Let $\mathbf{Y}_i$ denote a binary indicator of the choice for observation i of whether or not to develop a parcel for a single family house. Then a probit model is defined as:

$$P(\mathbf{Y}_i = 1 \mid \mathbf{X}_i) = \Phi(\mathbf{X}'_i \beta), \tag{10}$$

where Φ is the cumulative distribution function for the standard normal distribution; $\mathbf{X}_i$ is a $(k+1)\times 1$ vector of explanatory variables including parcel information such as parcel size, socioeconomic and environmental variables associated with the parcel's location, and zoning regulations (i.e., maximum lot coverage); and β is a $(k+1)\times 1$ vector of parameters including an intercept.

The parameters in equation (10) were estimated by nonparametric methods that allow for spatial dependence. The methods are capable of generating consistent covariance-matrix estimators regardless of sample size. Heteroscedasticity-consistent standard errors were estimated to remove residual spatial autocorrelation caused by codetermined development decisions (e.g., clustered residential developments within subdivisions). The covariance-matrix estimators were modified to allow regression disturbance terms to be correlated across neighborhood parcels as a general function of their Euclidean distances.

By assuming stationarity in $\mathbf{X}$, which enables the joint distribution of $\mathbf{X}$ for any location to be invariant to shifts in the entire set of locations, the covariance of two observations is measured by a function of Euclidian distances without directional information (Conley 1995).

$$\text{cov}(\mathbf{X}_{S_i}, \mathbf{X}_{S_j}) = f(\| s_i - s_j \|), \tag{11}$$

where x_{s_i} and x_{s_j} are vectors of explanatory variables of observations located in s_i and s_j within a Euclidean space (Conley and Topa 1999).

The spatial autocovariance at distance (δ) is estimated by applying the nonparametric estimator of the spatial autocovariance function proposed by Hall, Fisher, and Hoffmann (1994):

$$f(\delta)=\sum_{i=1}^{n}\sum_{j=1}^{n}\mathbf{W}_n[|\delta-\|s_i-s_j\||](\mathbf{X}_{S_i}-\bar{\mathbf{X}})(\mathbf{X}_{S_j}-\bar{\mathbf{X}}), \tag{12}$$

where $\bar{\mathbf{X}}$ is the sample mean and $\mathrm{W_n}[\cdot]$ is a function of the sample size that concentrates its mass at zero as the sample becomes arbitrarily large at an appropriate rate defined by Conley and Topa (1999). The spatial covariance was estimated by an average of cross-products between the vectors $(\mathbf{X}_{S_i}-\bar{\mathbf{X}})$ and $(\mathbf{X}_{S_j}-\bar{\mathbf{X}})$ within a given distance δ. By employing the nonparametric estimator of the spatial autocovariance function in the spatial GMM approach, the error term is permitted to be conditionally heteroskedastic and spatially correlated across parcels. Once the parameters are estimated in equation (10), for example, the marginal effect for X_k (kth explanatory variable) is calculated by $\partial\, Prob(Y_i=1\,|\,X_i)/\partial X_k=\Phi(X_i'\,\beta)\beta_k$, where β_k is the kth parameter estimated.

The predicted values for the GMM approach of the spatial probit model facilitate ex ante comparisons between predicted probabilities generated under the observed status quo maximum lot coverage and two hypothetical maximum lot coverage scenarios; that is, plus and minus 10% of the status quo. In a binary model like the spatial probit model, unequal frequencies of the two outcomes always lead to lower estimated prediction probabilities for the less frequent outcome than for the more frequent outcome (Cramer 1999). Cramer (1999) suggested the average occurrence rate of the two outcomes as a cutoff value, which has been used as the alternative cutoff value for the binary model in previous empirical studies (McPherson et al. 2004; Liu et al. 2005). In this study, the average occurrence rate of development ($\mathrm{Y}_i = 1$) and no development ($\mathrm{Y}_i = 0$) was calculated as the average predicted probability of development and used as a cutoff value for the prediction of development in the spatial probit model. The use of this occurrence rate, instead of the conventional threshold of 0.5, accounts for unequal frequencies in our dataset (to be presented later).

2.3 Identifying the Area of Preexisting Development

Identifying areas of preexisting development for the purpose of dividing the areas that existed prior to and after the emergence of urban sprawl to measure the impact of maximum lot coverage on development pattern is not straightforward. The areas of preexisting development should reflect the areas of clustered development prior to the emergence of urban sprawl, whereas the area outside of preexisting development should represent the area of sprawl. A spatial break dividing these two areas is not clear because cumulative growth of a city is done through additions to its periphery over the course of many years.

One tentative way is simply to identify areas of parcels that were developed prior to the duration of the model period as preexisting development. Although this makes sense if sprawl development did not exist prior to the sample period used for model development, measuring and comparing development rates within and outside of preexisting development prior to and after the sample period may not be appropriate because areas that were developed prior to the sample period may include areas with sprawl development patterns. Under this definition, the areas of preexisting development are probably not free from sprawl, and thus comparisons of development patterns between these two areas may not accurately reflect the degree of sprawl.

Alternatively, a two-step approach was designed to systematically identify preexisting development clusters and thus draw the spatial break. In the first step, local indicators of spatial association (LISA) for the built years of parcel data were estimated. LISA values of built years of parcel data indicate the extent of spatial autocorrelation between the built year of a particular parcel and the built years of the parcels around it. Through inference analysis, spatial clusters of old-built parcels (old-built parcels surrounded by old-built parcels) were identified as clusters developed prior to the emergence of urban sprawl. The LISA values of built years of parcel data served well for the purpose of identifying spatial breaks in the built years of parcel data.

Disjoint areas among the spatial clusters of old-built parcels identified from the first step were removed from preexisting development in the second step. Joint spatial clusters of old-built parcels were difficult to verify because continuous clusters of old-built parcels may still have gaps (e.g., roads, industrial and commercial development, and unusable land). Thus, buffer polygons of a specified distance around the old-built parcels were created using a buffer tool in ArcMap 9.3 (Environmental Systems Research Institute 2009). The buffers were used to merge the continuous buffer areas. The buffers of old-built parcels that were joined in continuous buffer areas were assumed to be areas of preexisting development, and those areas that were not joined in continuous buffer areas were assumed to be disjoint from the spatial clusters of old-built parcels.

The buffer size needed to distinguish the parcels that were inside and outside preexisting development was initially unclear. Thus, the second step was repeated with buffer polygons of different distances around the old-built parcels (i.e., 0.1- to 1-mile radii with 0.1-mile increments). After a number of trials of the procedure with different distances, 0.5 mile was chosen as the threshold. Buffer polygons of 0.5 mile were merged into a single spatial cluster containing 95% of the clusters of old-built parcels identified using LISA in the first step.

2.4 Study Area and Data

This study used four primary geographic information system (GIS) datasets: individual parcel data, census-block group data, boundary data, and environmental feature data from Nashville-Davidson County, Tennessee. The individual parcel data were obtained from the Metro Planning Department, Nashville-Davidson County (MPD 2009) and the Davidson County Tax Assessor's Office. Information from 467 census-block groups was used to reflect the socioeconomic status of neighborhoods, such as per capita income and unemployment rate for parcels located within the boundaries of the census-block groups. The average size of a census-block group was 721 acres, with a standard deviation of 1,588 acres. Boundary data (e.g., high school districts and jurisdiction boundaries) were also obtained from the Metro Planning Department, Nashville-Davidson County (MPD 2009). Environmental feature data (e.g., water bodies and golf courses) were collected from Environmental Systems Research Institute Data and Maps 2004 (Environmental Systems Research Institute 2004). Other environmental feature data (e.g., shape files for railroads and parks) were also acquired from MPD. Definitions and simple descriptive statistics of the variables used in the regressions are listed in Table 17.1.

Developed parcels used for the dependent variable in the spatial probit model were defined as single-family houses that were built in 2007. At the start of 2007, the number of vacant parcels in Nashville-Davidson County was 20,990. Only single-family housing development in residentially zoned districts was considered in the model because the development decision processes for other land uses (e.g., multifamily housing, commercial, and industrial land uses) are influenced by different development factors and property characteristics. Of the 12,375 parcels in residentially zoned districts, 1,603 parcels (or 13.0%) were developed for single-family housing in 2007. The average size of undeveloped parcels was 1.8 acres, whereas the average size of parcels developed for single-family housing was 0.3 acres.[3] Distances between any two closest neighboring parcels among the 12,375 observations ranged from 10 feet to 8,231 feet. The average distance of 236 feet was used as the cutoff value for spatial correlation. Maximum lot coverage regulated by Nashville-Davidson County ranged from 0.2 to 0.6.[4]

2.5 Empirical Results

The overall percentage of correct predictions was 78%, using the average probability of development of 0.13 from the data. The rates of correct prediction were 80% for developed parcels and 65% for undeveloped parcels. The marginal effects calculated based on the parameter estimates of the GMM spatial probit model are presented in Table 17.2.

[3] We treat the lot size as a lagged exogenous variable and thus face no endogeneity problem because all information available for decision makers, including lot size, at the time of development is collected prior to the duration of development in 2007.

[4] Developers were not allowed to cover more than 20% (0.2 maximum lot coverage), 30% (0.3 maximum lot coverage), 35% (0.35 maximum lot coverage), 40% (0.4 maximum lot coverage), 45% (0.45 maximum lot coverage), 50% (0.5 maximum lot coverage), and 60% (0.6 maximum lot coverage) for Zoning Districts of AG, AR2a, RS80, and R80; RS40 and R40; RS20, R20, RS15, R15, and RM2; RS10, R10, and RM4; R8 and RS7.5; R6, RS5, RM6, RM9, and RM15; and RS3.75, OR40, RM20, OR20, RM40, RM60, and I, respectively.

Table 17.1 Variable names, definitions, and descriptive statistics

Variables	Description	Mean (Std. Dev.)
Develop	Dummy variable for development in 2007 (1 if a single family house was built in 2007, 0 otherwise)	0.130 (0.336)
Lot size	Lot size in thousand square feet	78.485 (388.639)
Lot value per acre	Assessed land value in $1,000 per acre in 2007	46.299 (85.743)
Per capita income	Per capita income in $1,000 for census-block group in 2000	23.027 (11.127)
Housing density	Housing density (the number of houses per acre) for census-block group in 2000	1.323 (1.284)
Travel time to work	Average travel time (minutes) to work for census-block group in 2000	23.734 (4.358)
Unemployment rate	Unemployment rate for census-block group in 2000	0.051 (0.045)
Vacancy	Vacancy rate for census-block group in 2000	0.067 (0.041)
ACT	Average composite score of American College Test by high school district in 2007	17.819 (1.358)
Water	Distance in 1,000 feet to the nearest water body	6.671 (4.623)
Park	Distance in 1,000 feet to the nearest park	6.283 (4.276)
Park size	Size of nearest park in 1,000 square feet	5,598.627 (12,711.409)
Golf	Distance in 1,000 feet to the nearest golf course	21.002 (12.782)
CBD	Distance in 1,000 feet to the central business district	40.093 (20.345)
Greenway	Distance in 1,000 feet to the nearest greenway	11.003 (7.886)
Rail	Distance in 1,000 feet to the nearest railroad	7.822 (6.901)
Interstate	Distance in 1,000 feet to the nearest interstate highway	8.808 (6.565)
Slope	Slope in degrees where the parcel is located	4.756 (3.991)
Maximum lot coverage	Maximum lot coverage assigned by zoning regulation	0.406 (0.073)
Number of observation		12,375

The discussion here is limited to the variables that are statistically significant at the 5% level. The marginal effects of per capita income, unemployment rate, vacancy rate, and housing density were found to be significant. These four variables capture the socio-economic status of neighborhoods at the census-block group level: an increase in per capita income by $1,000 decreases the probability of development by 0.01. The negative effect of income on development may be explained by greater supply of land that can be developed in lower income areas. A decrease in the unemployment rate by 1 percentage point increases the probability of development by 0.31. A decrease in the vacancy rate by 1 percentage point increases the probability of development by 0.16. The negative effects of the unemployment and vacancy rates indicate that the economic status of the neighborhood at the census-block group level is an important factor affecting the dynamics of housing development. A decrease in housing density by 1 house per acre increases

Table 17.2 Estimated marginal effects from the land development model

Variable	Marginal effect	Spatial standard error
Lot size	0.002***	0.000
Lot value per acre	0.132***	0.005
Per capita income	−0.009**	0.004
Housing density	−0.010***	0.003
Travel time to work	0.001	0.001
Unemployment rate	−0.314***	0.081
Vacancy rate	−0.163**	0.068
ACT	−0.001	0.002
Water	−0.005	0.003
Park	0.038***	0.005
Park size	−0.001**	0.000
Golf	0.005**	0.002
CBD	−0.002	0.002
Greenway	0.012***	0.002
Rail	0.008***	0.002
Interstate	0.004	0.002
Slope	−0.002***	0.001
Maximum lot coverage	0.203***	0.036

** and *** indicate statistical significance at the 5% and 1% levels.

the probability of development by 0.01. The greater probability of development in lower density housing areas reflects a pattern of urban sprawl.

Similarly, variables reflecting the properties of the parcel itself (i.e., size, value, and proximities to local parks, golf courses, and greenway, slope) were significant. A lot size increase of 1,000 feet^2 (or 0.023 acres) increases the probability of development by 0.002. A $1,000 per acre increase in lot value increases the probability of development by 0.13. The positive effect of lot value per acre on development reflects higher development pressure for land with higher value (Brueckner and Kim 2003; Cho et al. 2010). A 1,000-foot (or 0.19 miles) increase in distance to the nearest local park increases the probability of development by 0.038. A 1,000-foot increase in distance to the nearest golf course increases the probability of development by 0.01. The negative effects of proximity to local parks and golf courses may be explained by the crowding of preexisting residential development closer to local parks and golf courses that occurred prior to 2007. A 1,000-foot increase in distance to the nearest greenway increases the probability of development by 0.01. The negative effect of proximity to a greenway may be explained by greenways being built in mature residential neighborhoods; thus, new development occurs farther away from greenways. A decrease in the slope of a parcel by 1 degree increases the probability of development by 0.002, implying the importance of flatness of land for residential development.

Given this context, an increase in maximum lot coverage by 1 percentage point increases the probability of development by 0.20. This finding indicates that higher maximum lot coverage (or less stringent maximum lot coverage) increases the probability of development. This empirical result confirms the theoretical expectations that less stringent regulation on maximum lot coverage increases both housing supply and demand, thus increasing the probability of development. Thus, maximum lot coverage plays a significant role in land development decisions.

The development rates (i.e., number of parcels predicted to be developed in each area divided by the number of parcels predicted to be developed in the entire county) and development occurrence rates (i.e., number of parcels predicted to be developed in each area divided by the number of vacant parcels in the residentially zoned districts in each area) inside and outside the area of preexisting development under the observed status quo maximum lot coverage and the two hypothetical maximum lot coverage scenarios are reported in Table 17.3. Under the current maximum lot coverage, 59% of parcels (3,963 of 6,725 parcels) are predicted to be developed in the area outside of preexisting development. In contrast, only 19% of parcels (1,068 of 5,650 parcels) are predicted to be developed inside the area of preexisting development. Thus, 21% (1,068 of 5,031) of the parcels that were predicted to be developed occurred inside the area of preexisting development, whereas 79% (3,963 of 5,031) occurred outside the area of preexisting

Table 17.3 Development rates and development occurrence rates under the observed status quo maximum lot coverage and two hypothetical maximum lot coverage scenarios

	Development rates [a]		Development occurrence rates [b]		
Maximum lot coverage scenarios	Inside the area of preexisting development	Outside the area of preexisting development	Inside the area of preexisting development	Outside the area of preexisting development	Entire county
Current maximum lot coverage	21% (1068/5031)	79% (3963/5031)	19% (1068/5650)	59% (3963/6725)	41% (5031/12375)
10% lower hypothetical maximum lot coverage	18% (845/4644)	82% (3799/4644)	15% (845/5650)	57% (3799/6725)	38% (4644/12,375)
10% higher hypothetical maximum lot coverage	25% (1349/5439)	75% (4090/5439)	24% (1349/5650)	61% (4090/6725)	44% (5439/12375)

[a] Number of parcels predicted to be developed in each area/Number of parcels predicted to be developed in the entire county.

[b] Number of parcels predicted to be developed in each area/Number of vacant parcels in the residentially zoned districts in each area.

development. The considerably higher frequency of predicted development outside the area of preexisting development implies a pattern of urban sprawl.

The predicted development rate for the entire county falls from 41% (or 5,031 of 12,375 parcels) under the current maximum lot coverage to 38% (or 4,644 of 12,375 parcels) under the 10% lower hypothetical maximum lot coverage scenario (more stringent maximum lot coverage). The decline in the development rate due to lower maximum lot coverage occurs both inside and outside of the preexisting development area (i.e., 19% to 15% in the preexisting development area and 59% to 57% outside of the preexisting development area). Among the 4,644 parcels that are predicted to be developed in the overall area under the 10% lower hypothetical maximum lot coverage scenario, 845 parcels (or 18%) occur inside the area of preexisting development, whereas 3,799 parcels (or 82%) occur outside the area of preexisting development. These results indicate a 3 percentage point decrease in the predicted development rate inside the area of preexisting development and a 2 percentage point increase in the development rate outside of the area, suggesting that more stringent maximum lot coverage limits overall development but constrains development more inside relative to outside the area of preexisting development.

The predicted development rate for the entire county rises from 41% (or 5,031 of 12,375 parcels) under the status quo maximum lot coverage to 44% (or 5,439 of 12,375 parcels) under the scenario with 10% higher hypothetical maximum lot coverage (less stringent maximum lot coverage). The rise in the development rate due to higher maximum lot coverage occurs both inside and outside of the area of preexisting development area (i.e., 19% to 24% in the preexisting development area and 59% to 61% outside of the preexisting development area). Among the 5,439 parcels that are predicted to be developed under the scenario with 10% higher hypothetical maximum lot coverage, 1,349 parcels (or 25%) occurred inside the area of preexisting development, whereas 4,090 parcels (or 75%) occurred outside the area of preexisting development. These results indicate a 4 percentage point increase and a 4 percentage point decrease in the development rates inside and outside the area of preexisting development, respectively, compared to current maximum lot coverage. The evidence suggests that less stringent maximum lot coverage encourages overall development but provides greater encouragement for development inside relative to outside the area of preexisting development.

The empirical results from the spatial probit model for land development confirm that more stringent regulation of maximum lot coverage (lower maximum lot coverage) decreases the probability of development over the entire metropolitan county while it results in a larger decrease in the development rate inside relative to outside the area of preexisting development. In contrast, less stringent regulation of maximum lot coverage (higher maximum lot coverage) increases the probability of development over the entire county but the development rate increases less outside relative to inside the area of preexisting development. Thus, less stringent maximum lot coverage encourages overall development but provides greater incentive for development inside relative to outside the area of preexisting development.

Greater responses in the probability of development to changes in maximum lot coverage inside relative to outside the area of preexisting development suggest that changes in maximum lot coverage regulations create more profound deviations from equilibrium housing levels inside relative to outside the area of preexisting development. These results imply that equivalent changes in maximum lot coverage cause greater changes in housing demand and supply inside relative to outside the area of preexisting development. A further implication is that the positive amenity of neighboring open space (first ratio on the right-hand side of equation [6]) and the substitutability between private open space and neighboring open space (second ratio on the right-hand side of equation [6]) are larger inside relative to outside the area of preexisting development. Hence, results imply that the optimal choice of development density (equation [1]) is more likely bound by regulation of maximum lot coverage inside relative to outside the area of preexisting development.

Modifying site-specific maximum lot coverage based on predicted development rates inside and outside the area of preexisting development under different maximum lot coverage scenarios provides policy makers with additional information for designing or updating site-specific maximum lot coverage policies in their efforts to moderate urban sprawl. For example, if local policy makers and planners wished to curb sprawl development and revitalize the inner city, they could impose zoning regulations that increase maximum lot coverage in the inner city and simultaneously lower maximum lot coverage outside the inner city. Results from this case study suggest that local policy makers and planners should weigh differences in the spatial effects of zoning regulations when considering maximum lot coverage as a policy tool for curbing urban sprawl.

3. Conclusion

This chapter contributes to the general understanding of spatial econometric modeling as a tool for evaluating policies designed to influence land development patterns. The evaluation of land use policies involves a complex process driven by spatial interactions between changes in land use and the policies being considered (Irwin and Geoghegan 2001). Land use management practices without consideration of these interactions do not respond to the system dynamics caused by spatial interactions. Advances in spatial econometric modeling, including the nonparametric methods used in the case study, allow policy makers to design land use management practices that are more effective in stimulating the desired response from a system characterized by spatial interactions.

The econometric specification of discrete land use decisions is useful in the sense that underlying spatial dynamic processes of land use decisions are modeled explicitly, which allows linking the land use models with GIS characterizing the spatial pattern of land use (e.g., land use dynamics and landscape change patterns). Plot- and parcel-level data, such as those used in the case study, have been applied to the aforementioned framework and much effort has been focused on high spatial dependence among the error terms in models for land use decisions (e.g., develop or not), which makes standard probit estimation inconsistent. Methods such as MLE, GMM, GLM, probit GWR, and nonparametric GMM are among the potential econometric techniques that accommodate spatial error autocorrelation in the discrete spatial process model.

The spatial probit model used in the case study to model discrete land use decisions has typically not been estimated with MLE methods mainly due to the computational intensity of the iterative techniques that control for both heteroscedastic and spatially correlated errors (Carrión-Flores and Irwin 2004). For instance, Carrión-Flores and Irwin (2004) explicitly avoided using a spatial binary model, because the iterative techniques were impractical for the large sample size (9,760 observations).

Responding to this very issue, Klier and McMillen (2008) proposed a computationally feasible estimator for spatial discrete-choice models. Their estimator is a linearized version of the GMM estimator proposed by Pinske and Slade (1998), and it extends the literature on spatial modeling by allowing a spatially weighted dependent variable to be estimated in a discrete-choice framework. The benefits of linearization are that it allows the model to be estimated with large sample sizes because no matrix needs to be inverted, and estimation requires only standard probit or logit models. The approach produces a practical estimation method with a few approximations of sample-based moments. The shortcoming of this type of GMM estimator is that the asymptotic properties of the GMM do not hold, so that it is biased (Smirnov 2010).

Alternatively, nonparametric GMM models have been applied to discrete land use decisions, as shown in the case study. Because nonparametric GMM models investigate the impact of spatial error autocorrelation based on the estimators of the asymptotic variance of the sample average, the asymptotic covariance matrix estimators derived from large-sample approximation do not suffer from the issue of computational intensity associated with MLE for the spatial probit model. In additon, nonparametric GMM provides consistency and asymptotic normality of the GMM estimator (Conley 1995).

As shown in the case study, spatial econometric estimates of the land use change model can be used to simulate changes in landscapes, and simulation results can reveal different effects of land use policies on not only individual development decisions but also on overall landscape patterns. For example, Carrión-Flores and Irwin (2004) developed a two-step approach that combines a parcel-level, discrete land use decision model and ex ante simulations of the discrete-choice model with and without land use policies using spatial landscape pattern metrics. This kind of a two-step approach, which was adopted in the case study, has the advantage of being able to link between econometric modeling and landscape patterns. Such a modeling approach also allows simulation of the aggregate effects of landscape transition probabilities resulting from land use policy (Newburn et al. 2006; Lewis and Plantinga 2007; Langpap et al. 2008).

Future research in spatial econometric modeling of land use decisions needs to focus on spatiotemporal modeling. Knowing the spatial structure of land use decisions is essential to making informed policy and planning decisions, as shown in the case study presented in this chapter. Likewise, enhanced understanding of the temporal dynamics of land use decisions is important. A better model would be a spatial-dynamic model based on a time series of actual land cover changes with the appropriate time-varying explanatory variables under the framework of spatial econometric modeling (Geoghegan et al. 2010). For example, three levels of land use change processes are essential for spatial-dynamic modeling: (1) the slow processes of industrial, residential, and transport construction; (2) the medium processes of economic, demographic, and technological changes; and (3) the fast processes of mobility of labor, goods, and information (Wegener 1994). These temporal processes are to be incorporated in the spatial model.

An attempt at spatial-dynamic modeling could be framed as a spatial panel data model, which is an emerging topic within the spatial econometrics literature (e.g., Baltagi et al. 2003; Elhorst 2003; Baltagi, Egger, and Pfaffermayr 2007; Baltagi, Kelejian, and Prucha 2007; Kapoor et al. 2007; Anselin et al. 2008; Baltagi and Liu 2008; Baltagi et al. 2009; Elhorst 2009; Millo and Piras 2009; Lee and Yu 2010*b*; 2010*a*, Lee and Yu 2010*c*; Pesaran and Tosetti 2011; Millo and Piras 2012). A rare application in modeling discrete land use decisions is the panel data spatial logistics regression model by Frazier and Kockelman (2005). Under their framework, both spatial autocorrelation and time adjustment are incorporated to simulate future changes in population and land cover. Forecasting based on simulation of land use changes is particularly useful in the framework of the panel data spatial model because the spatial panel model and its corresponding forecasts better fit with time series forecasting. The demand for panel data for use in spatial-dynamic modeling is expected to increase as demand for forecasts of future land use changes increases, particularly as interest increases in predicting the impact of climate change on land use.

Acknowledgments

The views expressed are those of the authors and cannot be attributed to University of Tennessee.

References

Alig, R. J. 1986. Econometric analysis of the factors influencing forest acreage trends in the southeast. *Forest Science* 32(1): 119–134.

Alig, R. J., F. C. White, and B. C. Murray. 1988. Economic factors influencing land use changes in the south-central United States. U.S. Department of Agriculture Forest Service, Southeastern Forest Experiment Station. Res. Pap. SE-272:23.

Alonso, W. 1972. A theory of the urban land market. In eds. M. Edel and J. Rothenberg, *Readings in urban economics*, 104–111. New York: Macmillan.

Anselin, L., J. Le Gallo, and H. Jayet. 2008. Spatial panel econometrics. In eds. L. Matyas and P. Sevestre, *The econometrics of panel data: Fundamentals and recent developments in theory and practice*, 3rd ed., 624–660. Berlin, Heidelberg, Germany: Springer-Verlag.

Baltagi, B. H., P. Egger, and M. Pfaffermayr. 2007. Estimating models of complex FDI: Are there third-country effects? *Journal of Econometrics* 140(1): 260–281.

Baltagi, B. H., P. Egger, and M. Pfaffermayr. 2009. *A generalized spatial panel data model with random effects*. CPR Working paper series.

Baltagi, B., H. H. Kelejian, and I. R. Prucha. 2007. Analysis of spatially dependent data. *Journal of Econometrics* 140(1): 1–4.

Baltagi, B. H., and L. Liu. 2008. Testing for random effects and spatial lag dependence in panel data models. *Statistics & Probability Letters* 78(18): 3304–3306.

Baltagi, B. H., S. Heun Song, B. Cheol Jung, and W. Koh. 2007. Testing for serial correlation, spatial autocorrelation and random effects using panel data. *Journal of Econometrics* 140(1): 5–51.

Baltagi, B., S. Song, and W. Koh. 2003. Testing panel data regression models with spatial error correlation. *Journal of Econometrics* 117: 123–150.

Bell, K. P., and E. G. Irwin. 2002. Spatially explicit micro-level modelling of land use change at the rural-urban interface. *Agricultural Economics* 27(3): 217–232.

Bockstael, N. E. 1996. Modeling economics and ecology: The importance of a spatial perspective. *American Journal of Agricultural Economics* 78(5): 1168–1180.

Bockstael, N. E., and K. P. Bell. 1998. Land use pattern, and water quality: The effect of differential land management controls. In R. Just, and S. Netanyahu, eds. *International water and resource economics consortium Conflict and cooperation on trans-boundary water resources*, 169–191. Dordrecht: Kluwer Academic.

Brueckner, J. K. 1987. The structure of urban equilibria: A unified treatment of the Muth-Mills model. In E. S. Mills, eds. *Handbook of regional and urban economics*, Vol. 2, 821–845. Amsterdam: NorthHolland.

Brueckner, J. K., and H. A. Kim. 2003. Urban sprawl and the property tax. *International Tax and Public Finance* 10(1): 5–23.

Carrión-Flores, C., and E. G. Irwin. 2004. Determinants of residential land-use conversion and sprawl at the rural-urban fringe. *American Journal of Agricultural Economics* 86(4): 889–904.

Case, A. 1992. Neighborhood influence and technological change. *Regional Science and Urban Economics* 22(3): 491–508.

Cho, S., C. D. Clark, W. M. Park, and S. G. Kim. 2009. Spatial and temporal variation in the housing market values of lot size and open space. *Land Economics* 85(1): 51–73.

Cho, S., D. M. Lambert, and R. K. Roberts. 2010. Forecasting open space with a two-rate property tax. *Land Economics* 86(2): 263–280.

Cho, S., and D. H. Newman. 2005. Spatial analysis of rural land development. *Forest Policy and Economics* 7(5): 732–744.

Cho, S., and R. K. Roberts. 2007. Cure for urban sprawl: Measuring the ratio of marginal implicit prices of density-to-lot-size. *Review of Agricultural Economics* 29(3): 572–579.

Chomitz, K. M., and D. A. Gray. 1996. Roads, land use, and deforestation: A spatial model applied to Belize. *The World Bank Economic Review* 10(3): 487–512.

City of Redmond. 2011. Site requirements for residential zones. http://www.codepublishing.com/WA/redmond/CDG/RCDG20C/RCDG20C3025.html.

Conley, T. G. 1995. Econometric modeling of cross-sectional dependence. PhD dissertation, University of Chicago.

Conley, T. G. 1999. GMM estimation with cross sectional dependence. *Journal of Econometrics* 92 (1):1–45.

Conley, T. G., and B. Dupor. 2003. A spatial analysis of sectoral complementarity. *Journal of Political Economy* 111(2): 311–352.

Conley, T. G., and G. Topa. 1999. *Socioeconomic distance and spatial patterns in unemployment.* C.V. Starr Center for Applied Economics, New York University.

Cramer, J. 1999. Predictive performance of the binary logit model in unbalanced samples. *Journal of the Royal Statistical Society. Series D (The Statistician)* 48(1): 85–94.

Cropper, M., C. Griffiths, and M. Mani. 1999. Roads, population pressures, and deforestation in Thailand, 1976–1989. *Land Economics* 75(1) 58–73.

Dipasquale, D. 1999. Why don't we know more about housing supply? *The Journal of Real Estate Finance and Economics* 18(1): 9–23.

Elhorst, J. P. 2003. Specification and estimation of spatial panel data models. *International Regional Science Review* 26(3): 244–268.

Elhorst, J. P. 2009. Spatial panel data models. In M. M. Fischer, and A. Getis, eds. *Handbook of applied spatial analysis*, 377–407. Berlin, Heidelberg, New York: Springer.

Environmental Systems Research Institute. 2004. *Data and maps 2004.* Redlands, CA: ESRI Inc.

Environmental Systems Research Institute. 2009. *Arcgis 9.3.* Redlands, CA: ESRI Inc.

Evans, A. 1999. The land market and government intervention. In eds. E. S. Mills, and P. C. Cheshire, *Handbook of regional and urban economics, 1637–1669.* The Netherlands: Elsevier.

Ewing, R. 1994. Characteristics, causes, and effects of sprawl: A literature review. *Environmental and Urban Issues* 21(2): 1–15.

Farber, S., and A. Páez. 2007. A systematic investigation of cross-validation in GWR model estimation: Empirical analysis and Monte Carlo simulations. *Journal of Geographical Systems* 9(4): 371–396.

Fleming, M. 2004. Techniques for estimating spatially dependent discrete choice models. In L. Anselin, R. J. G. M. Florax, and S. J. Rey, eds. *Advances in spatial econometrics*, 145–168. Heidelberg: Springer.

Fotheringham, A. S., C. Brunsdon, and M. Charlton. 2002. *Geographically weighted regression: The analysis of spatially varying relationships.* West Sussex, UK: John Wiley & Sons.

Frazier, C., and K. M. Kockelman. 2005. Spatial econometric models for panel data: Incorporating spatial and temporal data. *Transportation Research Record: Journal of the Transportation Research Board* 1902: 80–90.

Fujita, M. 1990. Spatial interactions and agglomeration in urban economics. In M. Chatterji, and R. E. Kunne, eds. *New frontiers in regional sciences*, 184–221. London: Macmillan.

Fujita, M., and J. Thisse. 2002. *Economics of agglomeration: Cities, industrial location, and regional growth.* Cambridge, UK: Cambridge University Press.

Geoghegan, J., D. Lawrence, L. C. Schneider, and K. Tully. 2010. Accounting for carbon stocks in models of land-use change: An application to southern Yucatan. *Regional Environmental Change* 10(3): 247–260.

Glaeser, E. L., M. E. Kahn, and J. Rappaport. 2008. Why do the poor live in cities the role of public transportation. *Journal of Urban Economics* 63(1): 1–24.

Grenander, U., and M. Rosenblatt. 1957. *Some problems in estimating the spectrum of a time series.* Berkeley: University of California Press.

Hall, P., N. Fisher, and B. Hoffmann. 1994. On the nonparametric estimation of covariance functions. *The Annals of Statistics* 22(4): 2115–2134.

Hall, P., and P. Patil. 1994. Properties of nonparametric estimators of autocovariance for stationary random fields. *Probability Theory and Related Fields* 99(3): 399–424.

Hanham, R., and J. S. Spiker. 2005. Urban sprawl detection using satellite imagery and geographically weighted regression. In R. Jensen, J. Gatrell, and D. McLean, eds. *Geo-spatial technologies in urban environments*, 137–151. Berlinthebe: Springer.

Hardie, I. W., and P. J. Parks. 1997. Land use with heterogeneous land quality: An application of an area base model. *American Journal of Agricultural Economics* 79(2): 299–310.

Harrison County. 2009. What is lot coverage? Http://Co.Harrison.Ms.Us/Downloads/Downloads%20by%20department/Zoning/Informational%20brochures/Lot%20coverage%20brochure%20final.Pdf).

Irwin, E. G., K. P. Bell, and J. Geoghegan. 2003. Modeling and managing urban growth at the rural-urban fringe: A parcel-level model of residential land use change. *Agricultural and Resource Economics Review* 32(1): 83–102.

Irwin, E. G., K. P. Bell, and J. Geoghegan 2006. Forecasting residential land use change. In eds. R. J. Johnston, and S. K. Swallow, *Economics and contemporary land use policy: Development and conservation at the urban-rural fringe*, 55–82. Washington, DC: Resources for the Future.

Irwin, E. G., and N. E. Bockstael. 2001. The problem of identifying land use spillovers: Measuring the effects of open space on residential property values. *American Journal of Agricultural Economics* 83(3): 698–704.

Irwin, E. G., and N. E. Bockstael. 2002. Interacting agents, spatial externalities and the evolution of residential land use patterns. *Journal of Economic Geography* 2(1): 31.

Irwin, E., and N. Bockstael. 2004. Land use externalities, open space preservation, and urban sprawl. *Regional Science and Urban Economics* 34(6): 705–725.

Irwin, E. G., and J. Geoghegan. 2001. Theory, data, methods: Developing spatially explicit economic models of land use change. *Agriculture, Ecosystems & Environment* 85(1–3): 7–24.

Isberg, G. 1973. Controlling growth in the urban fringe. *Journal of Soil and Water Conservation* 28(4): 155–161.

Johnston, R. A., and M. E. Madison. 1997. From landmarks to landscapes. *Journal of the American Planning Association* 63(3): 365.

Kapoor, M., H. H. Kelejian, and I. R. Prucha. 2007. Panel data models with spatially correlated error components. *Journal of Econometrics* 140(1): 97–130.

Kelejian, H. H., and I. R. Prucha. 1999. A generalized moments estimator for the autoregressive parameter in a spatial model. *International Economic Review* 40(2): 509–533.

Klier, T., and D. P. McMillen. 2008. Clustering of auto supplier plants in the United States: Generalized method of moments spatial logit for large samples. *Journal of Business and Economic Statistics* 26: 460–471.

Kline, J. D., and R. J. Alig. 1999. Does land use planning slow the conversion of forest and farmlands? *Growth and Change* 30(1): 3–22.

Kopits, E., V. McConnell, and M. Walls. 2007. The trade-off between private lots and public open space in subdivisions at the urban-rural fringe. *American Journal of Agricultural Economics* 89(5): 1191–1197.

Langpap, C., I. Hascic, and J. Wu. 2008. Protecting watershed ecosystems through targeted local land use policies. *American Journal of Agricultural Economics* 90(3): 684–700.

Lee, L., and J. Yu. 2010*a*. A unified estimation approach for spatial dynamic panel data models: Stability, spatial co-integration, and explosive roots. In A. Ullah and D. E. A. Giles, eds. *Handbook of empirical economics and finance*, 397. Chapman and Hall/CRC.

Lee, L., and J. Yu. 2010*b*. A spatial dynamic panel data model with both time and individual fixed effects. *Econometric Theory* 26(2): 564–597.

Lee, L., and J. Yu. 2010*c*. Estimation of spatial autoregressive panel data models with fixed effects. *Journal of Econometrics* 154(2):165–185.

LeSage, J. P. 1999. *Spatial econometrics*. Regional Research Institute, West Virginia University.

Leung, Y., C. L. Mei, and W. X. Zhang. 2000. Testing for spatial autocorrelation among the residuals of the geographically weighted regression. *Environment and Planning A* 32(5): 871–890.

Lewis, D. J., and A. J. Plantinga. 2007. Policies for habitat fragmentation: Combining econometrics with GIS-based landscape simulations. *Land Economics* 83(2): 109–127.

Libby, L. W., and J. S. Sharp. 2003. Land-use compatibility, change, and policy at the rural-urban fringe: Insights from social capital. *American Journal of Agricultural Economics* 85(5): 1194–1200.

Lichtenberg, E. 1989. Land quality, irrigation development, and cropping patterns in the Northern High Plains. *American Journal of Agricultural Economics* 71(1): 187–194.

Lichtenberg, E., and I. Hardie. 2007. Open space, forest conservation, and urban sprawl in Maryland suburban subdivisions. *American Journal of Agricultural Economics* 89(5): 1198–1204.

Lichtenberg, E., C. Tra, and I. Hardie. 2007. Land use regulation and the provision of open space in suburban residential subdivisions. *Journal of Environmental Economics and Management* 54(2): 199–213.

Liu, C., P. Berry, T. Dawson, and R. Pearson. 2005. Selecting thresholds of occurrence in the prediction of species distributions. *Ecography* 28(3): 385–393.

McPherson, J., W. Jetz, and D. Rogers. 2004. The effects of species' range sizes on the accuracy of distribution models: Ecological phenomenon or statistical artifact? *Journal of Ecology* 41(5): 811–823.

Miller, C., and J. Vaske. 2003. Individual and situational influences on declining hunter effort in Illinois. *Human Dimensions of Wildlife: An International Journal* 8(4): 263–276.

Millo, G., and G. Piras. 2009. *Implementation of ML estimation for spatial panels*. Unpublished, Regional Research Institute.

Millo, G., G. Piras. 2012. Splm: Spatial panel data models in R. *Journal of Statistical Software* 47(1): 1–38.

MPD. 2009. Metro planning department. Http://Www.Nashville.Gov/Mpc/.

Nelson, G. C., and D. Hellerstein. 1997. Do roads cause deforestation? Using satellite images in econometric analysis of land use. *American Journal of Agricultural Economics* 79(1): 80–88.

New York City. 2009. New York City zoning. Http://Www.Nyc.Gov/Html/Dcp/Html/Zone/Glossary.Shtml.

Newburn, D. A., P. Berck, and A. M. Merenlender. 2006. Habitat and open space at risk of land-use conversion: Targeting strategies for land conservation. *American Journal of Agricultural Economics Report* 88(1): 28–42.

Nickerson, C., and L. Lynch. 2001. The effect of farmland preservation programs on farmland prices. *American Journal of Agricultural Economics* 83(2): 341–351.

Páez, A. 2006. Exploring contextual variations in land use and transport analysis using a probit model with geographical weights. *Journal of Transport Geography* 14(3): 167–176.

Parks, P. J., and B. C. Murray. 1994. Land attributes and land allocation: Nonindustrial forest use in the Pacific Northwest. *Forest Science* 40(3): 558–575.

Pesaran, H., and E. Tosetti. 2011. Large panels with common factors and spatial correlations. *Journal of Econometrics* 161(2): 182–202.

Pierson, K. M. 2002. Livable communities toolkit: A best practices manual for metropolitan regions. http://www.crcog.org/community_dev/livable_toolkit.html.

Pinske, J., and M. E. Slade. 1998. Contracting in space. *Journal of Econometrics* 85(1): 125–154.

Plantinga, A. J., T. Mauldin, and R. Alig 1999. *Land use in Maine: Determinants of past trends and projections of future changes, 20*. Portland, OR: U.S. Department of Agriculture, Forest Service, Pacific Northwest Research Station.

Rybczynski, W. 2005. Suburban despair. Is urban sprawl really an American menace? *Slate*, November 7.

Schabenberger, O., and F. J. Pierce. 2002. *Contemporary statistical models for the plant and soil sciences*, xxii, 738. Boca Raton, FL: CRC Press.

Schaffer, W. 1999. *The web book of regional science*. Regional Research Institute, West Virginia University.

Smirnov, O. A. 2010. Modeling spatial discrete choice. *Regional Science and Urban Economics* 40(5): 292–298.

Thorsnes, P. 2002. The value of a suburban forest preserve: Estimates from sales of vacant residential building lots. *Land Economics* 78(3): 426–441.

Thünen, J. H., and J. Heinrich. 1966. *The isolated state*. Trans. Carla M. Wartenberg. Oxford: Pergamon.

Turner, M. G., D. N. Wear, and R. O. Flamm. 1996. Land ownership and land-cover change in the Southern Appalachian Highlands and the Olympic Peninsula. *Ecological Applications* 6(4): 1150–1172.

Wegener, M. 1994. Operational urban models: State of the art. *Journal of the American Planning Association* 60(1): 17–29.

Wheeler, D., and M. Tiefelsdorf. 2005. Multicollinearity and correlation among local regression coefficients in geographically weighted regression. *Journal of Geographical Systems* 7: 161–187.

White, F. C., and F. N. Fleming. 1980. An analysis of competing agricultural land uses. *Southern Journal of Agricultural Economics* 12(4): 99–103.

Wu, J. 2006. Environmental amenities, urban sprawl, and community characteristics. *Journal of Environmental Economics and Management* 52(2): 527–547.

Wu, J., and A. Plantinga. 2003. The influence of public open space on urban spatial structure. *Journal of Environmental Economics and Management* 46(2): 288–309.

CHAPTER 18

USING QUASI-EXPERIMENTAL METHODS TO EVALUATE LAND POLICIES

Application to Maryland's Priority Funding Legislation

CHARLES TOWE, REBECCA LEWIS, AND LORI LYNCH

STATES and local governments use a variety of instruments to direct the location, intensity, and timing of growth. In some cases, governmental entities desire growth to locate in area with existing infrastructure such as roads, sewer, and schools. In others, governmental entities cannot accommodate the number of housing structures being built and the population growth with existing resources. In hopes of retaining open space or a viable agricultural industry, governments may increase (decrease) or encourage (discourage) the density permitted within certain areas. However, even with ongoing planning and constant review of the instruments selected, concerns about land use continue. Establishing the effectiveness of the plethora of instruments has been plagued by the difficulty of establishing the causality of a particular policy related to encouraging and discouraging certain land use actions. Recently, researchers examining land use issues have begun to explore new methods to elicit the effectiveness of land-related policies and programs.

Empirical researchers need to establish a causal effect of programs or policies. This task is complicated by implicit or explicit selection and potential endogeneity on the part of land agents. In the past two decades, and especially in the field of labor economics, researchers have been focused on the econometrics and statistical analysis of causal effects (Imbens and Wooldridge 2009). To this end, researchers seek to evaluate how a program (or treatment) affects certain entities (individuals or parcels of land) given some desired outcome of interest. In the sciences, one randomly assigns an individual to receive the new drug or the placebo and then compares the outcome of individuals who were "treated"—that is, received the new drug—to those of the "control"—that is, those who received the placebo. Complications arise, however, when researchers are unable to design a study that implements random assignment, a virtual impossibility in the field of land economics and land use policy evaluation. Quasi-experimental methods are a class of models that utilize observational data and attempt to recreate the ideal of random assignment. Many models exist under this framework, including instrumental variables, regression discontinuity, various difference in difference type models, and propensity score matching (PSM).

In this chapter, we outline the land policy environment in Maryland and the issues that arise when trying to determine causality of a policy on outcomes. We describe the policy we use as an illustrative example. After discussing the challenges, we consider various econometric and statistical approaches, including PSM. We then demonstrate the strengths of the PSM method in the evaluation of this particular land use policy utilizing an extensive spatial microlevel dataset from the state. We discuss the potential areas of concern with PSM approach. We discuss the results of the analysis and their limitations. In the conclusion, we discuss some of the broader issues with quasi-experimental methods related to land use issues.

1. Policy Environment

Most, if not all, policy environments dealing with land use are not candidates for experimentation or random assignment, and, as such, basic regression-based modeling techniques are open to the critique of ignoring selection issues or functional form assumptions to construct counterfactuals. These methods often fail to detect small biases in the data between the so-called treated and untreated. Even among methods classified as quasi-experimental, such as instrumental variables, producing and observing "good" instruments are rare. Similarly with regression discontinuity approaches, clear and exogenous discontinuities often are not available. In the context of land use policy evaluation, PSMs main advantage is that it does not rely on exclusion restrictions (i.e., a variable that affects "treatment" status but does not affect the outcome of interest). In fact, all variables affecting both the treatment and the outcome should be included in the propensity score model. However, we do not need to specify exactly how the variables impact treatment or outcome. We choose to evaluate an actual policy in the state of Maryland to illustrate the use of the PSM approach most effectively. This policy focuses financial incentives for development in targeted geographic areas while leaving similar geographic areas without such incentives.

Generally speaking, quasi-experimental methods can be used to evaluate regulatory or voluntary programs in which decision makers can be individual landowners or renters, counties, states, regional entities, or any other geographic aggregation.[1] Treatments

[1] As long as the geographic aggregation is not confounded with the outcome measurement, as might be the case using census-defined boundaries.

could be any of the instruments or programs employed to alter the location, intensity, or timing of land use decisions. We will employ the matching technique with land units typically smaller than non-subdivided parcels being the implicit actors to analyze a spatially defined incentive-based land use policy.

In this application, Maryland's Smart Growth Program relies on financial incentives to direct growth to designated areas in an attempt to curb low-density (intensity) or sprawling development (location). Under Smart Growth, the state sought to stop "subsidizing sprawl" and direct its funding for infrastructure only to locally designated and state-approved Priority Funding Areas (PFAs). A county seeking state funds to finance infrastructure needed to designate and have approved such geographic areas or PFAs (or designated growth areas). The policy is similar to an urban growth boundary in design but lacks the "teeth" of regulatory policy, such as strong zoning changes to support it.

The PFA approach utilized a combination of planning and monetary incentives to direct housing development to these growth areas in order to make it relatively less profitable to convert land currently in an agricultural or resource use and to constrain urban expansion. These designated areas: (1) depict a physical line between urban and rural areas; (2) limit expansion of services such as water and sewer infrastructures by withholding state-level financial incentives outside PFAs; and (3) by providing infrastructure spending inside PFAs, lower the cost of housing construction. However, one questions whether the PFA approach has accomplished its goals. At the bottom line, one might ask: Have PFAs caused the redirection of the housing construction, or any subset of housing construction, within Maryland?

On the face of it, one could answer this question simply by comparing housing starts within the PFA to those outside the PFA. However, assessing the impact of the PFAs on housing starts is more challenging that it appears. The research question centers on comparing what would have happened to an individual land parcel in two scenarios; that is, one knows what has happened to housing starts for a land parcel within the PFA, but one would also like to know what would have happened to housing starts for the same land parcel if it had not been within a designated PFA. This land parcel within the PFA cannot be in two states simultaneously, nor can a researcher randomly assign which area is designated a PFA and which is not. This is the classic evaluation problem, which Holland (1986) defines as the fundamental problem of causal inference. Because we are analyzing data from a real-world policy (i.e., observational data rather than experimental data), we face challenges in estimating causal effects without making assumptions concerning unconfoundedness, exogeneity, ignorability, or selection on observables (Imbens and Wooldridge 2009). For example, if PFAs are only designated in areas where growth would otherwise have gone, the change in financial incentives could have been inconsequential, thus not affecting the timing or location of housing starts at all. As such, it would be an inefficient expenditure of scarce public funds. One would find growth dominates within the PFAs, but the causality may be spurious.

This type of endogeniety is not a new issue in econometrics. In fact, these issues have been well studied, particularly by labor econometricians. The common example in labor economics is that individuals choosing to participate in a training program may be fundamentally different from those who do not. If these differences affect the labor market outcome, such as the wage level, then the computed causal effects of the training may be invalid. Those who chose to not participate in the identical training program may not have the same outcome if they did. Similar concerns confront land program evaluations. The selection of the land parcels within a designated growth area can be influenced by factors including the political power of local communities, the open space inventory within a county, rising land values, and other development pressures. Landowners may only "permit" the PFA to include their land when they anticipate an increase in their land value. And landowners outside the PFA may fight to include their land within a PFA if they perceive their land value will decrease if placed outside the PFA due to fewer incentives for housing development.

Analogous to the training program example, the factors that cause certain parcels or areas to be inside or outside the PFA boundary (participate/not participate in training) will also affect the outcome—in our case, the probability of conversion to housing. If one estimates the impact of the PFA without considering the potential endogeneity of its boundaries, the impact of these other factors on the probability of housing starts within the PFA will also be included in the impact estimates of the PFA program and invalidate the causal implications of the analysis.

Endogeniety, measurement error, and omitted variables issues can result in included covariates being correlated with the error term in the regression. In these cases, the estimates in an ordinary least square (OLS) regression would be biased and inconsistent. To overcome such issues, researchers have resorted to a variety of econometric and statistical approaches. Land program evaluation may use an instrumental variable approach, which relies on the presence of an instrument, or several variables, that satisfy specific exogeneity and exclusion restrictions. As outlined in Angrist and Krueger (2001), Wright (1928) used curve shifters such as weather and price of substitute goods to estimate supply and demand curves. Theil (1953) introduced a two-stage approach to allow the inclusion of more than one instrument to predict the endogenous covariates. However, these necessary exogeneity and exclusion restrictions have often proved quite difficult to meet. An instrument must be correlated with the endogenous covariate but not be correlated with the error term. Discovering such an instrument can be problematic. For example, if the instrument is correlated with the error, estimators will remain inconsistent. Similarly, instrumental variable that have some association with omitted variables can result in biased estimators. In addition, weak instruments may result in predicted covariates with little variation and, as such, they do not have much explanatory ability in the regression equation (Angrist and Krueger 2001). Thus, one cannot interpret an insignificant estimator as evidence of the lack of causality because it could be that the instrument was too weak to elicit the causality effect.

When using standard regression methods that assume a linear approximation, researchers must also be aware that the average treatment effects estimated can be biased if the linear approximation in not accurate globally. Imbens and Rubin (forthcoming, as cited in Imbens and Wooldridge 2009, 24) suggest, "as a rule of thumb that with a normalized difference exceeding one quarter, linear regression methods tend to be sensitive to the specification." Imbens and Rubin (forthcoming, as cited in Imbens and Wooldridge 2009) suggest comparing the covariates of the treated and the control groups by computing the normalized differences. They believe normalized differences, which are not sensitive to sample size, are superior to comparing *t*-statistics. The problem of inference for the average treatment effect and thus credible results is also not inherently more difficult in larger samples as the *t*-test could suggest. In cases in which the normalized difference exceeding one-quarter, PSM, which does not rely on a linear approximation, provides a more viable approach to the analysis.

In some cases, researchers can utilize a regression discontinuity design if a common and exogenous border of some type can be identified such that the continuity can be exploited. Regression discontinuity can be used when one is designing an experiment but wants to ensure the treatment is received by those in most need (i.e., the sickest, poorest, the preferred growth area, or least educated for example) rather than randomly. Due to the observational quality of the data, a land policy evaluation is most likely to be used when the treated is geographically next to the control or untreated sample. One assumed in this case that the treated parcels along the cutoff point would be quite similar to the untreated parcel along the same point. As such, to employ the technique, the two samples must be ordered across space, with a clear cutoff point for inclusion in the treated or control group. One then can compare the outcomes of the treated parcel inside the cutoff with those outside the cutoff to determine if there is a difference. In some cases, however, one find a "fuzzy" discontinuity rather than a sharp cutoff point. In this case, the discontinuity may be highly correlated with the treatment. This could be due to geographic features in the land; path-dependency, such as previous land use decisions; or political pressure. This can create many of the same problems as faced by instrumental variables.

By design, regression discontinuity produces results along the cutoff point; that is, local average treatment effects. These results may not be generalizable to the whole population. Also, many regressions have fewer data points due to the necessity of being set along the cutoff point. There could also be fewer observations outside the cutoff area compared to more within the treated area. The lack of power may result in an insignificant estimator. Regression discontinuity estimates also suffer if misspecified; for example, functional forms that do not include existing nonlinear relationships result in biased results.

1.1 Advantages of the Propensity Score Matching Approach

In this analysis, we use a quasi-experimental approach, PSM (Rosenbaum and Rubin 1983), which implicitly assumes endogenous PFA boundaries. Our focus is on a binary treatment (in PFA/out of PFA), which is a common situation confronted by researchers addressing land issues.[2] In this case, we have a large and rich set of covariates that will impact both the treatment designation (PFA status) and influence the outcome variable of interest (number of housing starts). We employ the PSM method to evaluate the PFA program ability to shift the location of housing starts by comparing the outcome for the gridded landscape[3] of Maryland within the PFAs with observationally equivalent grids that are outside the PFAs (Kaza et al. 2011). The primary advantages of PSM under these circumstances are that (1) we do not need to specify how each variable will affect selection into treatment or control, (2) we do not need to specify how each variable affects the potential outcome, and (3) nor do we need to determine an exogenous variable to satisfy an exclusion restriction. The PSM method has several other benefits as well. First, the matching protocol ensures that the grids within the PFAs are matched to the grids outside the PFAs that are most similar to them in terms of observable characteristics. This provides a more transparent means to limit the influence of outliers and dissimilar grids. Second, because not all grids are equally likely to have been designated PFAs or have housing starts, this method incorporates pretreatment covariates that may influence the existence of a PFA designation ands housing starts into the propensity score calculation. Third, a linear functional form is not assumed for the outcome equation, the decision process, or the unobservable variables. As such, PSM requires fewer functional form and homogeneity assumptions. However, we do rely on the assumption of "selection on observables," which implies the data are rich enough to describe the selection process (Smith and Todd 2005). Because we have information on the outcome for treated and control land parcels both before and after the treatment, a difference-in-difference approach can be utilized, which should remove any selection issues derived from time-insensitive unobservable.

2. Analytical Method

We employ the PSM method developed by Rosenbaum and Rubin (1983). PSM has not been used to study land policy evaluation issues until recently. It is used to study the land market effects of zoning (McMillan and McDonald 2002), the land market effects of conservation easement restrictions (Lynch et al. 2007, 2009), land market effects of down-zoning (Liu and Lynch 2011*a*), the impact of farmland preservation programs on farmland loss (Liu and Lynch 2011*b*), the impact of designated preservation zones (i.e., Rural Legacy Areas [RLAs]) on rates of preservation (Lynch and Liu 2007), the impact of energy policy on farm prices (Towe and Tra 2013), and the impact of development

[2] Quasi-experimental methods have been extended recently to multivalued and continuous treatments (Imbens 2000; Gill and Robins 2001; Lechner 2001; Lechner and Miquel 2005).

[3] We grid the landscape at ¼-mile squares to allow for aggregation of data (e.g., housing starts) by an area not defined by the landscape, social or geographic, of existing houses, like Census designations.

moratoria on housing starts (Bento et al. 2007). Each of these studies performed useful analysis within its specific policy environments; however, the applicability of these finding to other policy environments may be limited; this is an empirical question that further PSM analysis will help researchers answer.

As mentioned earlier, assessing the impacts of PFAs on housing starts, like many other land policy evaluation, is difficult because of incomplete information. Although one can identify whether a grid is part of a PFA (is treated) or not (not treated/a control) and the outcome (number of housing starts or the difference in housing starts pre and post PFA) conditional on its treatment, one cannot observe the counterfactual—what would have happened if the grid was not part of the PFA. Thus, the fundamental problem in identifying the true causal effect is constructing the unobservable counterfactuals for treated observations.

At this point, some simple notion serves to demonstrate the issue, let Y_1 denote the outcome in the group of grids if treatment has occurred ($D = 1$), and Y_0 denote the outcome for the grids of control observations ($D = 0$). If one could observe the treated and the control states, the average treatment effect, τ, would equal $\overline{Y}_1 - \overline{Y}_0$ where $\overline{Y}_1$ equals the mean outcome of the treatment grids and $\overline{Y}_0$ of the control grids. Unfortunately, only $\overline{Y}_1$ or $\overline{Y}_0$ are observed for each observation. In a laboratory experiment, researchers solve this problem by randomly assigning subjects to be treated or not treated, and then they construct the unobserved counterfactual. In a natural setting, however, $\tau \neq \overline{Y}_1 - \overline{Y}_0$ because the treatment condition is not randomly assigned. The PSM method demonstrates that if data justify matching on some observable vector of covariates, X, then matching pairs on the estimated probability of selection into treatment or control groups based on X is also justified. In our case then, within land grids with the same propensity score, the land characteristics and other variables can be treated as independent of the treatment status. Therefore, the average treatment on the treated estimates for grids with the same propensity scores will not be biased and can be compared.

The PSM method relies on the assumption of conditional independence, which requires that there are no unobserved factors associated both with the treatment and the outcomes conditional on observed covariates. The PSM method, like other econometric and statistical approaches, suffers from the presence of unobservable covariates that may not be independent to the treatment assignment or to the treatment itself.

To satisfy the conditional independence assumption (CIA) and estimate an unbiased treatment effect, one must find a vector of covariates, X, such that $\overline{Y}_0 \perp D \mid X$; or $\overline{Y}_0 \perp D \mid P(D=1 \mid X)$ where $P(D=1 \mid X) \in (0,1)$ is the propensity score that an individual self-selects into treatment groups, and $\perp$ denotes independence. If CIA holds, Y_0, the outcome for the controls ($D = 0$), can be assigned to the corresponding treated observations ($D = 1$) as their unobserved counterfactuals using certain matching techniques. This assumption may fail if the "independent" variables, the parcel characteristics, are affected by the treatment as well. Wooldridge (2005) demonstrates that if treatment is randomized with respect to the counterfactual outcome but not with respect to the other variables, then CIA will be violated.

The CIA condition is quite strong. Therefore, we use the conditional mean independence (CMI) assumption (Heckman et al. 1998) that $E[Y_0 \mid D=1, X] = E[Y_0 \mid D=0, X] = E[Y_0 \mid X], P(D=1 \mid X) \in (0,1)$ to estimate the average treatment effect.

The average treatment effect on the treated sample is thus the expected difference in outcome Y between the PFA grids and their corresponding counterfactuals (non-PFA grids) constructed from the matched controls:

$$\Delta^{TT} = E(Y_1 \mid D=1) - E(Y_0 \mid D=1) = E(Y_1 \mid D=1) - E(Y_0 \mid D=0, P(X)) \quad (1)$$

For the weaker condition to hold, the set of X needs to include all of the variables that may affect the outcome (housing starts) and the selection into the treatment state (PFA status or not).

By using the matching algorithm, we are constructing a counterfactual pool of land grids equivalent in the covariates for the matched treatment and control observations, and we are controlling for the effect that these factors may have on the number of housing starts. In short, we are recreating a random experiment or, in this case, a quasi-random experiment. As such, we must also ensure that the samples "overlap." The treated areas must have control areas that are observationally equivalent, such that: $0 < pr(W_i = 1X_i = x) < 1, \textit{ for all } x$.

Thus, the support of the conditional distribution of X_i given $W_i = 0$ contains the conditional distribution of X_i given $W_i = 1$. If the covariates for the control observations (non-PFAs) do not overlap with the covariates for the treatment observations (PFAs), then we end up estimating an average impact only over the range where the overlap exists. The overlap is called the *common support*. The propensity scores can illuminate whether this assumption is satisfied. For example, if few or none of the non-PFA grids have a high probability of being a PFA, then those grids with a high probability of being a PFA will have few grids from which to make the counterfactual comparison(s). Similarly, if many of the grids have propensity scores close to zero, estimating the average effect of the treatment precisely becomes more difficult (Imbens and Wooldridge 2009). Problems are also likely to arise when some grids are almost certain to receive treatment. When the covariate distributions are different between the treatment and control grids, the propensity scores may approach zero and 1. This might produce different probabilities or propensity scores for logit and probit models, yet model choice in these cases are often ad hoc rather than well-motivated (Imbens and Wooldridge 2009).

Dehejia and Wahba (2002) suggest finding the smallest value of the estimated propensity score among the treated observations and dropping all control observations that have an estimated propensity score less than it. By setting the relevant sample to have common support, one eliminates those non-PFA grids that are so different from the PFA grids that they should not be compared. The results will be sensitive to the threshold chosen for the common support and, as such, some sensitivity analysis may be warranted. Heckman, Ichimura, and Todd (1997) and Heckman et al. (1998) use density functions to determine the set of treatment and control variables. Rubin

(2006) proposes using a matched sample by ordering the treated observations by their estimated propensity score and then matching them to the nearest control grid. If one matches without replacement, one will end up with an equal number of non-PFA and PFA grids. One does not need to use these pairs for estimating the average treatment on the treated—the impact results—but rather to determine an overlapping sample. This approach can also improve the balance between covariates.

2.1 Matching Methods and Bandwidth Selection

Matching estimators construct an estimate of the expected unobserved counterfactual for each treated observation by taking a weighted average of the outcomes of the control observations.[4] In our case, this would be an estimate of a PFA's housing starts if it was not a PFA based on the outcome of the non-PFAs grids. Several different matching methods are available. For example, nearest-neighbor-only uses the control grid with the closest propensity score to each treated grid. All matching estimators have the generic form for estimated counterfactuals:

$$(\hat{Y}_{io} \mid D_i = 1) = \left(\sum_{j \in \{D_j = 0\}} w(i, j) Y_{jo} \mid D_j = 0 \right),$$

where j is the index for control observations that are matched to the treated observation i based on estimated propensity scores ($j = 1, 2, \ldots J$). The matrix, $w(i, j)$, contains the weights assigned to the jth control observation that is matched to the ith treated observation. By using different weights in different matching estimators, one is implicitly making a tradeoff between efficiency and bias. All the estimators are asymptotically the same in large sample but might return different estimates in finite samples. Nearest-neighbor matching has each PFA grid paired with the control grid whose propensity score is closest in absolute value (Dehejia and Wahba 2002). Dehejia and Wahba (2002) and Rosenbaum (2002) both found that matching with replacement performs as well or better than matching without replacement (in part because it increases the number of possible matches and avoids the problem that the results are potentially sensitive to the order in which the treatment observations are matched). This may result in a control grid never being used to compute the average treatment effect if it is not the nearest neighbor to any treated PFA grid. This reduces possible bias but is not necessarily the most efficient.

Kernel and local linear matching techniques match each treated PFA grid with all control grids where the estimated propensity scores fall within a specified bandwidth. Uniform kernel, for example, gives equal weight to all control grids within the chosen

[4] This subsection follows the description provided by in Liu and Lynch (2011*b*).

bandwidth or for a wide variety of bandwidths if implemented via multiple nearest neighbors. The matched control grids are weighted according to the density function of the kernel type, but more control grids are used, which permits higher efficiency but potentially more bias. Bandwidths are centered on the estimated propensity score of the treated observation.

In some evaluation studies, the distribution of the control and treated propensity scores are not equivalent. For example, the estimated propensity scores for the control grids can be asymmetrically distributed with a large tail at zero. The estimated propensity scores for the treatment grids can be more evenly distributed or with a large tail at one. Kernel matching uses the additional data, where they exist, but excludes bad matches; thus, it can be a better choice when asymmetric distributions exist. McMillen and McDonald (2002) suggest that the local linear estimator is less sensitive to boundary effects (i.e., when many observations have a propensity score near one or zero).

The minimum mean square errors (MSE) for different matching methods and different bandwidth combinations can be used to pick the optimal bandwidth for each kernel type. Then, using the optimal bandwidth, one can select the optimal kernel type based on the minimum MSE for each matching method. Finally, one may compute which matching method to use based on the minimum MSE, given their optimal kernel type and bandwidth. One can also employ Racine and Li's (2004) leave-one-out validation mechanism to choose among the matching methods. The formula for calculation of treatment effect on treated thus is:

$$\Delta^{TT} = \frac{1}{N}\sum_{i=1}^{N}\left[Y_{i1} - \left(\hat{Y}_{io} \mid D_i = 1\right)\right] = \frac{1}{N}\sum_{i=1}^{N}\left[Y_{i1} - \left(\sum_{j\in\{D_j=0\}} w(i,j)Y_{jo} \mid D_j = 0\right)\right]$$

2.2 Balancing Test

Three types of balancing test methods exist in the empirical literature: standardized difference test, Hotelling T^2 for joint equality test, and a regression-based test. The Hotelling T^2 tests the joint null of equal means of all of the variables included in the matching between the treatment group and the matched control group. Smith and Todd (2005) found that, in some cases, Hotelling T^2 incorrectly treated matched weights as fixed rather than random. The standardized difference test uses a t-test for equality of the means for each covariate in the matched treated and control grids. The regression test estimates a regression of each covariate on polynomials of the estimated propensity scores, $[\hat{P}(X)]^l$ and the interaction of the polynomials with the treatment binary variable, $D * [\hat{P}(X)]^l$ (l, the order of the polynomial, equals 3). The treated PFA grids would not have a different regression line than the non-PFA control grids, and the balancing condition is satisfied if the estimated coefficients on the interaction terms are jointly equal to zero according to an F-test.

2.3 Difference in Difference

The effect of the PFA on the likelihood of new housing starts, controlling for the overall trend in housing starts over the relevant time period, is accomplished using the difference-in-difference approach or by simply replacing the outcome variable, housing starts in 2000–2003, with the difference in housing starts from 1994–1997 to 2000–2003. These years were selected because the legislation passed in 1997 and was implemented in the counties by 2000.

$$Y^{Post} = Y^{2003} + Y^{2002} + Y^{2001} + Y^{2000}$$

and

$$Y^{Pre} = Y^{1997} + Y^{1996} + Y^{1995} + Y^{1994}$$

So, $\Delta Y = Y^{Post} - Y^{Pre}$ is the outcome variable. This overall trend incorporates the market-level effects of housing demands and has the added advantage of controlling for time invariant and unobservable characteristics.

One may also conduct robustness tests by restricting to which control grids the treated grids can be compared. This can address possible unobservable characteristics of grids that vary spatially, by time period, or by governmental entities. For example, in this case, intuitively, the further away the PFA grids are from the grids that are not within the PFA, the more likely it is that their housing starts may be influenced by unobserved factors (e.g., different land markets). For example, the Chesapeake Bay Bridge may be a psychological barrier to many individuals who do not look beyond it to buy a home, irrespective of the time or distance of the commute. These types of unobserved factors may bias our estimates if we use all PFA and non-PFA grids when matching whether or not they are on the same side of the Chesapeake Bay Bridge. For robustness against possible unobservable factors, we restrict matches on three scales: (1) any PFA and non-PFA grid in the state (least restrictive); (2) any PFA grid and non-PFA grid within the same region as defined in Figure 18.1; and (3) any comparable PFA grid and non-PFA grid within the same county (most restrictive). We also limit our analysis to smaller geographic regions of the state: Western, Central 1 and Central 2, South, Upper Eastern Shore, and Lower Eastern Shore. See Figure 18.1 for the regional boundaries.

We first match the treatment and control observations without any restriction and calculate the overall treatment effect. Matching over the full sample has the advantage of providing better controls for treated grids than matching within the county where fewer non-PFA grids would be available. We also restrict matches to grids within the same region and county.

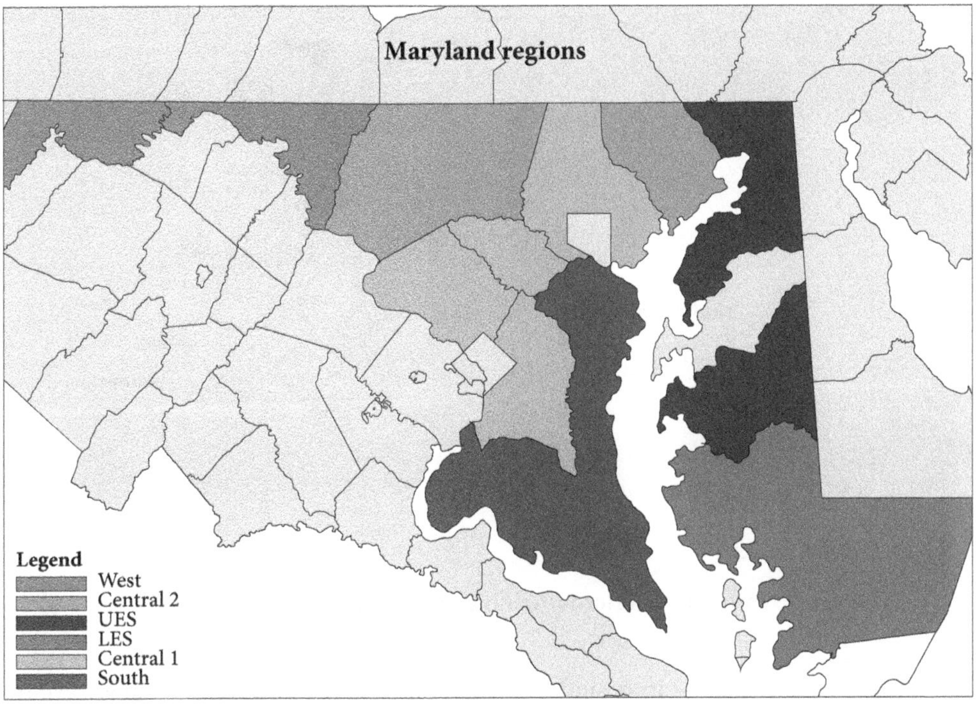

FIGURE 18.1 Maryland regions used in the propensity score analysis to limit grid matching to within same colored area.

In practice, we estimate the propensity score with the dichotomous dependent variable of being in a PFA equal to 1 and not in PFA as zero using a logit model with the variables outlined earlier and including county fixed effects. Subsequently, we implement nearest-neighbor matching based on the predicted value from the propensity score regression. The average treatment on the treated (ATT) is then calculated as the difference in means between the housing starts for the treatment grids, and the control grids. All standard errors are constructed via 1,000 replication bootstrap estimates of the ATT.

3. The Policy-Priority Funding Areas

The Smart Growth Areas Act passed in 1997 by Maryland required all counties to designate PFAs. The Maryland Department of Planning then reviewed and approved the areas. Unless an exception or exemption is granted, the state spends growth-related funds for new infrastructure and some revitalization and economic development programs only within the PFAs. PFAs automatically include certain areas of the state—Baltimore City, other incorporated municipalities, areas within the Baltimore and Washington Beltways, and designated neighborhoods, enterprise zones, and heritage

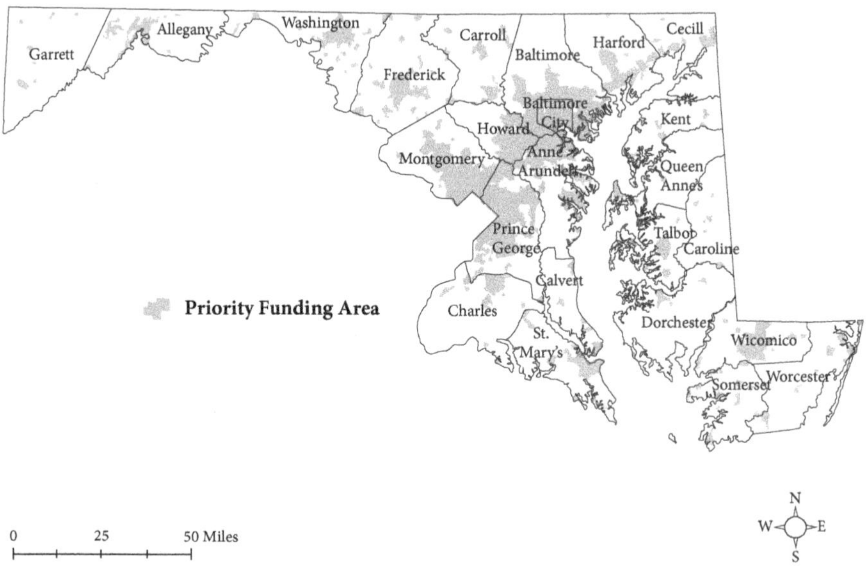

FIGURE 18.2 Priority funding areas within Maryland.

areas.[5] Local governments can designate additional areas as PFAs if they meet certain criteria, based on existing and planned densities and infrastructure (Maryland Code Annotated: State Finance & Procurement Article, §§ 5-7B-01 to -10, 2010; see appendix). A map of Maryland's PFAs is shown in Figure 18.2. Specific categories of spending for roads, housing programs, water and sewer infrastructure, state buildings, and certain economic development incentives are defined by the statute as "growth-related" (see appendix). Spending is constrained for certain types of projects for five agencies: Transportation, Housing and Community Development, Environment, General Services, and Business and Economic Development (Maryland Code Annotated: State Finance & Procurement Article, §§ 5-7B-01 to -10, 2010).

As a land use regulation in its relative infancy, empirical studies of PFA impact on housing starts have been limited. Using land use and land cover data, Shen, Liao, and Zhang (2005) and Shen and Zhang (2007) examined the effects of PFA and PFAs Smart Growth counterpart, RLAs, which seek to preserve resource and important ecological lands, on land conversion in Maryland from 1992 to 1997 and from 1997 to 2002. Using a logit model and land use land cover data, the authors found that urban development was more likely inside PFAs and less likely in RLAs, although the effects varied by county. These authors did not consider the endogeniety of the PFA or RLA designation. Therefore, although PFA areas were most likely to see growth, they may have been so even before the PFA designation. Because they did not consider the endogeneity, we

[5] These areas were not included as observations for our analysis.

question whether the PFA grids were compared to proper counterfactual grids similar across many attributes.

Hanlon, Howland, and McGuire (2009) examined the effects of PFAs on the probability of land development in Frederick County from 2000 to 2004. They also concluded that parcels inside PFAs were more likely to be developed than parcels outside. Lewis, Knaap, and Sohn (2009) evaluate implementation of the statutes and development outcomes before and after the designation of PFAs. Because state agency compliance with reporting requirements was lax, it was difficult to assess where and how much state funding was spent inside PFAs in accordance with the law. Using a *t*-test of means to conduct before and after analysis at the county, regional, and state level, Lewis, Knaap, and Sohn (2009) show that PFAs had little discernible impact on development patterns after the Act went into effect.

Howland and Sohn (2007) find investments in water and sewer infrastructure were more likely inside the PFAs than outside between 1997 and 2002. They found counties that received more state funding were more likely to invest in water and sewer infrastructure projects inside the PFA. However, they also found that investments in infrastructure continued outside PFAs, and some of this infrastructure received state funds. Since 1997, Maryland provides larger tax credits and less stringent criteria within PFAs for job creation than outside PFAs (Sohn and Knaap 2005). They also found that more jobs were created inside PFAs after 1997. The differential in job growth across the PFA, however, was small and occurred only in a few selected industries.

4. The Data

One of the most important decisions in this type of analysis is the choice of covariates, regardless of the analytical method used. Economic theory provides a starting point for what broad classes of data one should employ, but, as to the exact measurement or what specification to use, little guidance is provided. Imbens and Wooldridge (2009) suggest more research is needed to help choose which covariates to include from a large set of possible variables and what functional form should be employed. In this study, and in general, the quantity and quality of data necessary to satisfy the untestable assumption of CIA does not often include data from one source. We have collected and compiled data theorized to impact PFA selection and housing starts in Maryland from numerous sources. These included the Maryland Department of Planning, Maryland Department of Assessment and Taxation, US Geological Service, US Department of Agriculture Natural Resources Conservation Service (NRCS), Department of Transportation, and the National Center for Smart Growth at the University of Maryland. Significant effort has been made to attain and measure data for the relevant pre-PFA designation in 1997

Table 18.1 Number of grids within the sample, number of grids with perfect prediction of priority funding area (PFA) status, and number of grids used to estimate the model

	Total observations	Total number of grids in the priority funding areas
Full sample	169,773	27, 594
Excluded as perfect predictors*	20,983	14,088
Estimation sample	148,790	13,506

* Municipalities, high-density residential, commercial, and industrial zones are automatically included in the PFA and thus excluded from the choice set.

and in a format that is consistent across the counties in our study area.[6] For the outcome variable, the number of new homes constructed (i.e., housing starts), we chose to aggregate the underlying parcel and all independent variables into a ¼-square-mile grid cell on the landscape.

The estimation data correspond to many time invariant features of the grid, including soils, slopes, distances to the predominant central business districts of Baltimore or Washington, DC, distances to amenities (parks and water), and some time-variant features including land use, land cover,[7] density of housing, and number of landowners. These variables are calculated from the neighboring grids utilizing queen contiguity as the definition of neighbor. Tables 18.1 and 18.2 present the variables and summary statistics. These variables define the substitutable areas for development in the all areas of the state inside and outside the PFA. Variables are primarily measured as a percentage of the grid to account for higher home construction costs in these areas. These variables, drainage, slopes, flooding, and soils, are constructed using the Soil Survey Geographic Database (SURGO) classifications (Soil Survey Staff, Natural Resources Conservation Service 2011).

Land cover measures include water, agriculture, and forest, each with its own attracting and repelling effect on new housing starts. Distances to amenities, such parks, the ocean, or lakes, are included, as are distances to interstates and state highways (urban arterials). Other distance to amenity-based measures include an estimated travel time to various-size Census designated places[8] within an hour's drive proxy for the accessibility of any given grid cell. The Maryland Department of Planning's generalized zoning category variable is also included, ranging from the typical commercial, municipal, and

[6] All Maryland Counties except Queen Anne's County are included. Queen Anne's had incomplete and thus usable data.

[7] Measured as of 2002.

[8] Concentration of population identified by the US Census Bureau.

Table 18.2 Summary statistics for 148,790 grids included in the analysis

Variable	Mean	Std. Dev.	Max
prePFAresDev	0.087	0.368	5.088
averSalesPr_ByBG	6.879	5.739	13.815
numSales_ByBG	33.807	44.692	408.000
numOwners1997_bg	1.119	0.891	6.858
aw_slope	7.804	9.221	110.500
aw_runoff_high	0.061	0.141	1.000
aw_drain_vpd	0.063	0.188	1.000
aw_fldFreq_freq	0.056	0.153	1.000
aw_soils1_3	0.445	0.368	1.000
aw_fedland	0.027	0.150	0.998
park	0.054	0.140	0.998
aw02_lcAg	0.305	0.356	1.000
aw02_lcFor	0.396	0.376	1.000
aw02_lcWater	0.148	0.329	1.000
tt_min6	89.999	56.680	222.960
tt_num1_1hr	9.002	10.341	52.000
tt_num2_1hr	5.898	7.411	35.000
tt_num3_1hr	4.200	5.638	24.000
tt_num4_1hr	6.347	8.981	37.000
tt_num5_1hr	0.318	0.530	2.000
dist2Int	7.060	7.509	29.082
dist2Arterial	2.359	1.805	9.221
dist2ocean	10.332	13.225	50.330
dist2lake	6.132	4.055	18.336
s_prePFAresDev	0.145	0.357	4.080
s_numSales_ByBG	34.409	36.836	408.000
s_numOwners1997_bg	1.296	0.846	6.278
s_aw_slope	7.829	8.263	76.293
s_aw_runoff_high	0.061	0.108	0.928
s_aw_drain_vpd	0.062	0.137	1.000
s_aw_soils1_3	0.587	0.287	1.000
s_aw_fedland	0.027	0.129	0.998
s_park	0.054	0.111	0.990

industrial to a finer scale of least protected, moderately protected, and very-low-, low-, medium-, and high-density residential.[9] We also calculate the number of owners of the grid (*number of owners*) as a proxy for density and for the number of landowners (decision makers) in the area from whom a developer may purchase land. All of these variables describing the grids attempt to explain where housing is most demanded and most likely to occur either because of amenities, workplace commute, or cost of development.

[9] See www.mdp.state.md.us/OurWork/zoningtext.htm for exact definitions.

5. Results

The estimated coefficients using OLS are reported in Table 18.3 and the logit propensity score results in Table 18.4. The results of the balancing test using a *t*-test approach are presented in Table 18.5. The ATTs for the propensity score approach are reported in Tables 18.6 and 18.7. Both types of analysis find consistent evidence that PFAs have impacted the location of housing starts statewide. In the regression, PFAs are found to have 1.663 more housing starts than comparable non-PFA grids. Comparing the 131,401 non-PFA grids to the 12,451 PFA grids, we find when matching that PFA grids have an average housing start level of 2.75 compared to the most observationally equivalent non-PFAs' 1.71. All matching algorithms are implemented in Stata 11 using psmatch2 (Leuven and Sianesi 2003). The large sample sizes makes eliminating any statistical differences in means an insurmountable task; however, no statistical difference appears economically important. For example, when looking at the average sales price per square foot of house, we find PFA grids have a mean of 10.733 and those matched grids outside the PFA a mean of 10.359. These means are statistically different, but their absolute difference is small enough that we do not believe this will bias the average treatment effect on the treated. Similarly, the number of owners was 2.774 in 1997 within the PFA grids but only 2.53 within the non-PFA grids.

It is interesting to note the impact that the matching procedure has on the sample counterfactual group mean housing starts. The limited evidence from other studies compares the cumulative housing starts either in or out of the PFA and, as is obvious from the increase in matched controls from 0.28 to 1.71 housing starts, the algorithm does well to select more appropriate matches. The average treatment effect on the PFA designation is 1.04 more new homes within the PFAs grids than would have occurred otherwise. Similarly, when we use a difference-in-difference approach (pre-PFA housing starts to post-PFA housing starts), we find comparable results, with 1.05 new housing starts following the PFA designation. This suggests that the OLS method overestimates the impact of the PFA designation by treating it as if it is exogenous. One might view this as evidence of limited impact of unobservables on the estimates and as a robustness check of the main results.

This statewide matching approach allows matches across counties so, as an additional robustness check, we also restricted matches to grids within the same counties and found similar although slightly larger impacts. In this case, we lose both PFA and non-PFA observations due to the unavailability of "good" matches. Some PFA grids have no comparable matches (off the common support) and some non-PFA grids are very far in propensity score from any PFA grids (beyond the designated bandwidth). For the estimation, we had 130,330 non-PFA grids and 10,874 PFA grids. The average treatment effect was estimated to be 1.21 new housing starts within PFA grids and 1.39 for the difference measure. This restriction captures county-specific unobservables that were

Table 18.3 Estimated coefficients using ordinary least squares regression dependent variable: Number of housing starts

Variable	Coefficients	Variable	Coefficients
PFA	1.663***	tt_num3_1hr	0.0363**
	(0.0439)		(0.0143)
prePFAresDev	0.85***	tt_num4_1hr	0.499***
	(0.0314)		(0.0064)
averSalesPr_ByBG	0.0333	tt_num5_1hr	0.0363**
	(0.0027)		(0.0425)
numSales_ByBG	0.00049	dist2Int	−0.0228***
	(0.0005)		(0.0064)
numOwners1997_bg	−1.196***	dist2Arterial	−0.011
	(0.0217)		(0.0081)
aw_slope	0.00748***	dist2ocean	−0.0044
	(0.0027)		(0.0051)
aw_runoff_high	0.0229	dist2lake	0.0203***
	(0.1120)		(0.0056)
aw_drain_vpd	0.159*	s_prePFAresDev	0.00551***
	(0.0874)		(0.0374)
aw_fldFreq_freq	−0.321***	s_numSales_ByBG	−0.0878***
	(0.0775)		(0.0006)
aw_soils1_3	0.515***	s_numOwners1997_bg	1.369***
	(0.0500)		(0.0233)
aw_fedland	−1.023***	s_aw_slope	−0.0072**
	(0.1440)		(0.0035)
park	−0.361***	s_aw_runoff_high	−0.313*
	(0.0667)		(0.1600)
aw02_lcAg	−3.096***	s_aw_drain_vpd	0.231*
	(0.0597)		(0.1340)
aw02_lcFor	−2.815***	s_aw_soils1_3	−0.253***
	(0.0589)		(0.0682)
aw02_lcWater	−2.514***	s_aw_fedland	0.17
	(0.0727)		(0.1700)
tt_min6	0.00077*	s_park	0.272***
	(0.0004)		(0.0864)
tt_num1_1hr	−0.0065	County Fixed Effects	Yes
	(0.0078)		
tt_num2_1hr	−0.01	Constant	3.343***
	(0.0113)		(−0.218)
Observations	148,790	R^2	0.1000

Standard errors in parentheses
*** $p < 0.01$, ** $p < 0.05$, * $p < 0.1$

Table 18.4 Estimated coefficients for logit propensity score model dependent variable: Probability of a grid being within a priority funding area (PFA)

Variable	Coefficients	Variable	Coefficients
prePFAresDev	−0.043	tt_num4_1hr	0.0368***
	(0.0314)		(0.0086)
averSalesPr_ByBG	−0.0304***	tt_num5_1hr	0.16***
	(0.0043)		(0.0539)
numSales_ByBG	0.00686***	dist2Int	−0.0924***
	(0.0009)		(0.0126)
numOwners1997_bg	0.146***	dist2Arterial	−0.429***
	(0.0207)		(0.0153)
aw_slope	−0.00202	dist2ocean	−0.0328***
	(0.0047)		(0.0088)
aw_runoff_high	0.291**	dist2lake	0.0256***
	(0.1470)		(0.0089)
aw_drain_vpd	−0.692***	s_prePFAresDev	0.203***
	(0.1770)		(0.0323)
aw_fldFreq_freq	0.966***	s_numSales_ByBG	0.000521
	(0.1220)		(0.0006)
aw_soils1_3	−0.235***	s_numOwners1997_bg	1.457***
	(0.0747)		(0.0239)
aw_fedland	−0.107	s_aw_slope	−0.0658***
	(0.1960)		(0.0064)
park	−0.309***	s_aw_runoff_high	1.336***
	(0.0980)		(0.2180)
aw02_lcAg	−1.494***	s_aw_drain_vpd	−1.097***
	(0.0661)		(0.2840)
aw02_lcFor	−1.132***	s_aw_soils1_3	0.0575
	(0.0613)		(0.1210)
aw02_lcWater	−2.735***	s_aw_fedland	1.98***
	(0.1140)		(0.2310)
tt_min6	0.0113***	s_park	1.433***
	(0.0017)		(0.1320)
tt_num1_1hr	0.153***	County Fixed Effect	Yes
	(0.0103)		
tt_num2_1hr	−0.0337**	Constant	−2.754***
	(0.0134)		(−0.441)
tt_num3_1hr	−0.196***	Observations	148,790
	(0.0176)		

Standard errors in parentheses

*** $p < 0.01$, ** $p < 0.05$, * $p < 0.1$

Table 18.5 Balance test to ensure the priority funding area (PFA) grids are similar to the control grids using *t*-tests

Variable	Sample	Mean		*t*-test	$p > \|t\|$
		PFA Grids	Non-PFA		
prePFAresDev	Unmatched	2.2871	0.15977	70.08	0
	Matched	2.0271	2.434	−3.67	0
averSalesP~G	Unmatched	10.767	6.9688	69.35	0
	Matched	10.733	10.359	7.19	0
numSales_B~G	Unmatched	80.954	32.131	108.9	0
	Matched	80.497	83.477	−3	0.003
numOwners1~g	Unmatched	2.8553	1.0062	232.49	0
	Matched	2.7739	2.5284	12.27	0
aw_slope	Unmatched	7.0611	7.0165	0.54	0.587
	Matched	7.1325	7.2208	−1.2	0.229
aw_runoff_~h	Unmatched	0.08145	0.05466	19.98	0
	Matched	0.07736	0.08681	−4.66	0
aw_drain_vpd	Unmatched	0.01137	0.06738	−31.83	0
	Matched	0.01195	0.01229	−0.34	0.73
aw_fldFreq~q	Unmatched	0.04637	0.0478	−1.13	0.26
	Matched	0.04663	0.05492	−4.97	0
aw_soils1_3	Unmatched	0.58709	0.45339	37.22	0
	Matched	0.5939	0.55033	9.98	0
aw_fedland	Unmatched	0.0307	0.03112	−0.26	0.795
	Matched	0.03165	0.07783	−16.57	0
Park	Unmatched	0.08451	0.10951	−9.14	0
	Matched	0.08701	0.09458	−2.36	0.018
aw02_lcAg	Unmatched	0.10809	0.32988	−64.52	0
	Matched	0.11334	0.12494	−3.71	0
aw02_lcFor	Unmatched	0.26584	0.41699	−41.51	0
	Matched	0.27512	0.2864	−2.71	0.007
aw02_lcWater	Unmatched	0.01539	0.1263	−39.45	0
	Matched	0.01608	0.02017	−3.5	0
tt_min6	Unmatched	48.806	92.612	−77.56	0
	Matched	49.915	52.958	−4.95	0
tt_num1_1hr	Unmatched	22.669	9.2261	129.77	0
	Matched	22.255	22.044	1.27	0.204
tt_num2_1hr	Unmatched	15.731	6.0778	129.04	0
	Matched	15.433	15.432	0.01	0.995
tt_num3_1hr	Unmatched	11.514	4.3614	126.06	0
	Matched	11.309	11.313	−0.05	0.962
tt_num4_1hr	Unmatched	18.008	6.5809	125.14	0
	Matched	17.616	17.48	0.89	0.372
tt_num5_1hr	Unmatched	1.0101	0.31347	132	0
	Matched	0.98933	0.95179	3.8	0
dist2Int	Unmatched	3.3374	7.7556	−58.47	0
	Matched	3.4544	3.8915	−5.07	0
dist2Arter~l	Unmatched	0.60027	2.3651	−105.93	0
	Matched	0.61819	0.76512	−10.16	0
dist2ocean	Unmatched	7.0073	9.6718	−21.46	0
	Matched	7.0485	6.4794	6.37	0
dist2lake	Unmatched	4.4154	5.7588	−35.38	0
	Matched	4.4552	4.6129	−3.7	0

Table 18.6 Propensity score results for statewide comparisons, prior to 1997 and post 1997 and for within-county comparisons

	Observations on support			Mean housing starts by group			Statewide impact^
	Controls	PFA		Control	PFA	ATT	
Statewide model							
Off Support	3,884	1,054	Unmatched	2.65	0.28		
On Support	131,401	12,451	Matched	2.75	1.71	1.04**	8,546 units
Statewide model (difference in pre- and post-PFA housing starts as outcome, a difference-in-difference PSM)							
Off Support	3,884	1,054	Unmatched	2.25	0.22		
On Support	131,401	12,451	Matched	2.37	1.32	1.05**	8,628 units
Statewide model (matches are forced to be within same county)							
Off Support	4,955	2,631	Unmatched	2.4	0.3		
On Support	130,330	10,874	Matched	2.57	1.36	1.21**	8,684 units

*** $p < 0.01$, ** $p < 0.05$, * $p < 0.1$

^ adjusted for cells used multiple times as counterfactual by using only the best match

PFA, Priority Funding Area; PSM, propensity score matching

Table 18.7 **Propensity score results by region of the state**

	Observations on support			Mean housing starts by group			Statewide impact^
	Controls	PFA		Control	PFA	ATT	
West							
Off Support	–	48	Unmatched	0.35	0.18		
On Support	6,659	420	Matched	0.33	0.38	−0.05	(21) Units
Central 1							
Off Support	2,188	1,908	Unmatched	2.69	0.62		
On Support	15,239	4,653	Matched	3.36	1.74	1.62**	4,975 Units
Central 2							
Off Support	2,882	150	Unmatched	4.8	0.32		
On Support	18,763	1,712	Matched	4.39	1.66	2.73**	3,084 Units
South							
Off Support	792	121	Unmatched	2.41	0.54		
On Support	22,828	2,267	Matched	2.38	1.42	0.96**	1,436 Units
Upper Eastern Shore							
Off Support	3,765	31	Unmatched	1.69	0.21		
On Support	16,495	569	Matched	1.47	0.83	0.64**	121 Units
Lower Eastern Shore							
Off Support	5,031	58	Unmatched	1.44	0.097		
On Support	24,650	1,252	Matched	1.43	1.36	0.07	29 Units
							9,624 Units

*** $p < 0.01$, ** $p < 0.05$, * $p < 0.1$

^ adjusted for cells used multiple times as counterfactual ATT, average treatment on the treated; PFA, Priority Funding Area

not captured estimating the propensity score. However, it disregards the fact that developers face no restrictions to operate within county boundaries.

5.1 Regional Results

Although the state-level results were all statistically significant, ample evidence exists to suggest that growth pressures are not constant across the state. One way to investigate heterogeneity in the distribution of the outcome of interest is to estimate at a regional (multicounty) level of aggregation. In fact, we find significant heterogeneity across the regions of the state, with insignificant policy impacts for two (or three in the differenced outcome) of the geographic regions we examined. In both Western Maryland and the Lower Eastern Shore, we could not reject the null hypothesis that the PFA had no impact on housing starts. Both of these areas have a lower number of housing starts than the other regions and a lower demand for homes in general. In these areas, it is possible that the PFA is not redirecting growth because growth is not sizable enough to impact through state incentives. Perhaps, because both regions are more rural, people who move to these regions may prefer low-density housing, and, if they were willing to move to a denser area, would have chosen other counties or geographic regions.

However, in the Central Regions, the South, and the Upper Eastern Shore, PFAs were found to redirect housing. In the Central region I, the average treatment effect on the PFA grids was 1.62 housing starts. This region contains those counties under significant development pressure and also describes counties with many decades of strong land use planning regimes. In the Central II region, the average treatment effect was 2.73 housing starts. This region, in contrast to the Central I region, is largely rural with significantly less stringent land use regimes and more reliance on state funds. In terms of number of housing starts, the Central regions experience the largest shift of housing starts compared to other regions of the state. It is interesting to note a couple of points concerning the magnitudes of the differenced outcome versus the common cross-sectional post-PFA outcome measure. First, the magnitude of the average housing starts from the matched samples suggests there are ample grids developing in both time periods. Second, in some cases, the large differences between the cross-sectional and the differenced outcome illustrate the potential influence of unobservables missed in a standard PSM implementation premised on the selection of observables assumption.

In Southern Maryland, we also find that the PFA designation has influenced the location of housing starts, although the magnitude is smaller. The average treatment effect on the PFA grids was 0.96 housing starts. Similar to the Central II region, the South has experienced significant growth pressure in the last decade and is perhaps more responsive to state funding as well. The Eastern Shore had fewer housing starts overall but still an average treatment effect of 0.64, suggesting a modest shift to housing starts inside the PFA.

Given the current political and economic climate, it is highly unlikely that a regulatory approach to land development policy will continue to have broad enough support for implementation. Additionally, it is becoming clear that externalities associated with the timing and location of residential development is not fully captured at county boundaries.[10] Thus, inventive and incentive-based land use policies that cross jurisdictional boundaries, such as Maryland's statewide PFA policy, are likely instruments for the future of development controls. The question is whether these types of policies can effectively steer activity.

We find evidence that the PFA policy has effectively shifted development away from areas similar in characteristics to PFA areas but that have not been so designated. We should be clear that this does not suggest that the PFA has encouraged infill development or discouraged exurban expansion. Any analysis of the state housing starts will show exurban expansion continues to occur throughout the study period. This cannot be overstated; we have identified the impact of the PFA where the counterfactual is land similar to PFA-designated land that just happens to have been excluded from designation. In short, PSM as a policy analysis tool in this context can identify whether housing starts occurred in PFA-designated areas as opposed to comparable non-PFA areas. Econometrically, this is the appropriate comparison group, but it might not produce the measured treatment effect that most interests policy makers. Here, we find that, when faced with a development decision between identical lands, developers will focus on PFA lands. Whether this due to the availability of state funds or perhaps simply a signal that the state and the county have agreed this is a preferred location for housing is not clear and perhaps not relevant. As an evaluation tool, PSM is not a panacea, and one should be precise in what is identifiable compared to what is most desirable by the land use community. We believe this overlap is significant here.

For example, there may be lands near to existing urban or suburban communities that are not desirable for development from the societal view. Perhaps such lands have unique habitat or other ecosystem services that are currently without a market. These results suggest the PFA policy can effectively steer development away from those areas to more socially acceptable locations. This type of policy has the potential to steer near-term development at the fringe, and, used as such, it can potentially protect areas from development. Overall, our results suggest that between 8,500 and 9,500 homes have located inside the PFA that otherwise would have located outside the PFA during years immediately following implementation.[11]

6. Conclusion

In the context of land use policy, the use of the quasi-experimental method of PSM is still in its infancy; however, the method has gained broader appeal across other fields

[10] See "Bay on the Brink" report from the Maryland Journalism School for a classic example.

[11] Calculated using only the "best" match when a control is used multiple times.

of economics. The method is well suited for land use applications precisely because the vast majority of land use data is observational and there are rarely circumstances that produce clean instrumental variables. Land use evaluation and other applications do not fit well within basic regression-based modeling either. Those conducting land policy evaluations are in need of methods like PSM to address issues of selection and potential endogeneity.

It is critical that these policies are evaluated appropriately. Unlike many other policy evaluation environments, the land researcher is often dealing with policies that result in permanent adjustments to the landscape, such as the location of housing, commercial, or industrial activity. PSM's ability to use observational data while limiting the impacts of endogeneity and of functional form assumptions is a tremendous asset in the researchers' toolbox. On the other hand, one should note that the generalizability of results is difficult from PSM studies, as it is in many reduced form analyses. This chapter's results explore the effectiveness of an existing policy and inform practitioners of areas to focus on—or stay clear of—in the future. However, these results do not suggest an optimal policy or build on a literature moving toward discovery of an optimal policy if one exists.

Given the brief history of these methods in the land use literature, we believe many arenas exist in which these methods can provide insights. Furthermore, the shift from regulatory to incentive-based policies and the fiscal issues facing many state and local entities make any information regarding existing policy impacts necessary and relevant.

Appendix

A1. Statutory Context

PFAs are perhaps the centerpiece and the most innovative of the Maryland Smart Growth tools. Unlike urban growth boundaries in Oregon, which impose direct restrictions on urban development, the 1997 Smart Growth Areas Act merely restricts state spending on statutorily defined "growth-related" programs to areas designated for urban growth. According to the Maryland Department of Planning (MDP) website:

> The 1997 Priority Funding Areas Act capitalizes on the influence of State expenditures on economic growth and development. This legislation directs State spending to Priority Funding Areas. Priority Funding Areas are existing communities and places where local governments want State investment to support future growth.
>
> (Maryland Department of Planning, 2009*a*, http://planning.maryland.gov/ourproducts/pfamap.shtml)

A2. Geographic Scope

By statute, PFAs automatically include certain areas of the state: Baltimore City, incorporated municipalities, areas within the Baltimore and Washington beltways, and areas designated by the Department of Housing and Community Development for revitalization, enterprise zones, and heritage areas. In addition to areas designated as PFAs by statute, local governments can designate additional areas as PFAs if they meet certain criteria. (Maryland Code Annotated: State Finance & Procurement Article, §§ 5-7B-01 to -10, 2010; Lewis, R., Knaap, G.-J., and Sohn, J. [2009].)

Counties may designate additional areas as PFAs based on land use, developed density, zoned density, and water and sewer service criteria. Specifically, counties may include (a) areas inside locally designated growth areas zoned for industrial use by January 1, 1997, or served by public sewer; (b) employment areas inside locally designated growth areas served by or planned for water and sewer; (c) a community existing prior to 1997 that is located within a locally designated growth area, served by a public/community sewer or water system, and has an allowed, average residential density of ≥2.0 units per net acre; (d) an area outside the developed portion of an existing community, if the area has an allowed, average build-out density of ≥3.5 units per net acre; (e) areas beyond the periphery of the developed portion of existing development that are scheduled for public water and sewer service and have a permitted residential density of ≥3.5 units per net acre, and (f) rural villages included in the comprehensive plan before July 1, 1998 (Lewis et al. 2009).

Counties may designate "areas other than existing communities" as PFAs based on analyses of supply and demand. That is, counties must analyze land capacity and demand for the present and future, and PFAs must match the amount of land needed for a clearly defined planning horizon (Maryland Department of Planning, 1997). Although the statutes did not specify a particular planning horizon, MDP used a 20-year horizon as a standard benchmark.

Criteria for delineating PFAs are based on both actual and permitted densities. The density criteria established in the 1997 bill were the subject of much debate and have been the subject of criticism (Cohen 2002; Knaap and Frece 2007). The original version of the bill established a permitted density threshold at 5.0 units per net acre, but this was amended to a permitted density of 3.5 units per net acre with urging from the Maryland Association of Counties. The Smart Growth advocacy organization 1,000 Friends of Maryland argued that the threshold was too low, given that actual densities are often lower than permitted densities (Cohen 2002; Knaap and Frece 2007). Although the legislation contains language stating that land can be designated for inclusion in PFAs if "the design represents a long-term development policy for promoting the orderly expansion of urban growth and an efficient use of land and public services" (Maryland Code Annotated: State Finance & Procurement Article, §§

5-7B-01 to -10, 2010), the primary criteria for designating PFAs is based on existing or zoned densities and infrastructure capacity, rather than "orderly" plans for future urban growth.

A3. "Growth-Related" Expenditures

As mentioned, PFAs are intended to affect growth patterns by concentrating state spending on "growth-related" projects in PFAs. This "growth-related" spending consists of specific programs by Maryland Department of Environment (MDE), Department of Housing and Community Development (DHCD), Department of Business and Economic Development (DBED), and Maryland Department of Transportation (MDOT). By statute, a "growth-related" expenditure is "any form of assurance, guarantee, grant payment, credit, tax credit, or other assistance, including a loan, loan guarantee, or reduction in the principal obligation of, or rate of interest payable on, a loan or a portion of a loan" (Maryland Code Annotated: State Finance & Procurement Article, §§ 5-7B-01 to -10, 2010).

References

Angrist, J. D., and A. B. Krueger. 2001. Instrumental variables and the search for identification: From supply and demand to natural experiments. *Journal of Economic Perspectives* 15(4): 69–85.

Bento A., C. Towe, and J. Geoghegan 2007. The effects of moratoria on residential development: Evidence from a matching approach. *American Journal of Agricultural Economics* 89: 1211–1218.

Cohen, J. R. 2002. Maryland's smart growth: Using incentives to combat sprawl. In *Urban sprawl: Causes, consequences, and policy responses*, ed. G. D. Squires, 293–324. Washington, DC: Urban Institute.

DeGrove, J. M. 2005. *Planning policy and politics: Smart growth and the states*. Cambridge, MA: Lincoln Institute of Land Policy.

Dehejia, R., and S. Wahba. 2002. Propensity score matching methods for non-experimental causal studies. *Review of Economics and Statistics* 84(1): 151–161.

Gill, R. D., and J. M. Robins. 2001. Causal inference for complex longitudinal data: The continuous case, *Annals of Statistics* 29(6): 1785–1811.

Hanlon, B., M. Howland, and M. McGuire. 2009. Hotspots for growth: Land use change in a transitional county in the U.S. Unpublished manuscript, University of Maryland.

Heckman, J., H. Ichimura, and P. Todd. 1997. Matching as an econometric evaluation estimator: Evidence from evaluating a job training programme. *Review of Economic Studies* 64(4): 605–654.

Heckman, J., H. Ichimura, and P. Todd. 1998. Matching as an econometric evaluation estimator. *Review of Economic Studies* 65(2): 261–294.

Holland, P. W. 1986. Statistics and causal inference. *Journal of the American Statistical Association* 81: 945–970.

Howland, M. and J. Sohn. 2007. Will Maryland's Priority Funding Areas Initiative contain urban sprawl? *Land Use Policy* 24(1): 175–186.

Imbens, G. 2000. The role of the propensity score in estimating dose-response functions. *Biometrika* 87:706–710.

Imbens, G. W., and D. B. Rubin. Forthcoming. *Causal inference in statistics and the social sciences*. Cambridge and New York: Cambridge University Press.

Imbens, G. W., and J. M. Wooldridge. 2009. Recent developments in the econometrics of program evaluation. *Journal of Economic Literature* 47(1): 5–86.

Ingram, G. K., A. Carbonell, Y. -H. Hong, and A. Flint, A., eds. 2009. *Smart growth policies: An evaluation of programs and outcomes*. Cambridge, MA: Lincoln Institute for Land Policy.

Kaza, N., C. Towe, and X. Ye. 2011. A hybrid land conversion model incorporating multiple end uses. *Agricultural and Resource Economics Review* 40(3): 341–359.

Knaap, G. J., and J. Frece. 2007. Smart growth in Maryland: Looking forward and looking back. *Idaho Law Review* 43: 2.

Lechner, M. 2001. Identification and estimation of causal effects of multiple treatments under the conditional independence assumption. *Econometric Evaluation of Labour Market Policies. ZEW Economic Studies* 13: 43–58.

Lechner, M., and R. Miquel. 2005. Identification of the effects of dynamic treatments by sequential conditional independence assumptions. University of St. Gallen economics discussion paper No. 2005-17.

Leuven, E., and B. Sianesi. 2003. PSMATCH2: Stata module to perform full Mahalanobis and propensity score matching, common support graphing, and covariate imbalance testing. Software. http://ideas.repec.org/c/boc/bocode/s432001.html.

Lewis, R., G-J. Knaap, and J. Sohn, 2009. Managing growth with priority funding areas: A good idea whose time has yet to come. *Journal of the American Planning Association* 75(4): 457–478.

Liu, X., and L. Lynch. 2011*a*. Do zoning regulations rob rural landowners' equity? *American Journal of Agricultural Economics* 93(1): 1–25.

Liu, X., and L. Lynch. 2011*b*. Do agricultural land preservation programs reduce farmland loss? Evidence from a propensity score matching estimator. *Land Economics* 87(2): 183–201.

Lynch, L., W. Gray, and J. Geoghegan. 2007. Are farmland preservation programs easement restrictions capitalized into farmland prices? What can a propensity score matching analysis tell us? *Review of Agricultural Economics* 29(3): 502–509.

Lynch, L., and X. Liu. 2007. Impact of designated preservation areas on rate of preservation and rate of conversion: Preliminary evidence. *American Journal of Agricultural Economics* 89(5): 1205–1210.

Lynch, L., W. Gray, and J. Geoghegan, 2009. An evaluation of working land and open space preservation programs in Maryland: Are they paying too much? In *New perspectives on agri-environmental policies: A multidisciplinary and transatlantic approach*, eds. S. Goetz and F. Brouwer, 72–92. New York: Routledge.

Maryland Code Annotated, State Finance and Procurement Article, §§ 5-7B-01 to -10. 2010. LexisNexis.

Maryland Department of Planning. 2009. Smart Growth Priority Funding Areas Act of 1997. Retrieved January 5, 2009. http://www.mdp.state.md.us/fundingact.htm

McMillen, D. P., and J. F. McDonald. 2002. Land values in a newly zoned city. *Review of Economics and Statistics* 84(1): 62–72.

Racine, J. S, Q. Li. 2004. Nonparametric estimation of regression functions with both categorical and continuous data. *Journal of Econometrics* 119(1): 99–130.

Rosenbaum, P. R. 2002. *Observational Studies* (2nd ed.). New York: Springer-Verlag.

Rosenbaum, P., and D. Rubin. 1983. The central role of the propensity score in observational studies for causal effects. *Biometrika* 70:41–55.

Rubin, D. B. 2006. *Matched sampling for causal effects.* Cambridge, UK: Cambridge University Press.

Shen, Q., Liao, J., and Zhang, F. 2005. Changing urban growth patterns in a pro-smart growth state: The case of Maryland, 1973–2000. Working paper.

Shen, Q., and F. Zhang. 2007. Land use changes in a pro-smart growth state: Maryland, USA. *Environment and Planning A* 39(6): 1457–1477.

Smith, J., and P. Todd. 2005. Does matching overcome LaLonde's critique of nonexperimental estimators? *Journal of Econometrics* 125: 305–353.

Sohn, J., and G. J. Knaap. 2005. Does the job creation tax credit program in Maryland help concentrate employment growth? *Economic Development Quarterly* 19 (4), 313–326.

Soil Survey Staff, Natural Resources Conservation Service, United States Department of Agriculture. Soil Survey Geographic (SSURGO) Database for Maryland. http://soildatamart.nrcs.usda.gov

Theil, H. 1953. *Repeated least squares applied to complete equation systems.* The Hague: Central Planning Bureau.

Towe C., and C. Tra. 2013. Vegetable spirits and energy policy. *American Journal of Agricultural Economics* 95(1): 1–16.

Wooldridge, J. M. 2005. Violating ignorability of treatment by controlling for too many factors. *Econometric Theory* 21(5): 1026–1028.

Wright, Phillip G. 1928. *The tariff on animal and vegetable oils.* New York: Macmillan.

CHAPTER 19

APPLYING EXPERIMENTS TO LAND ECONOMICS

Public Information and Auction Efficiency in Ecosystem Service Markets

KENT D. MESSER, JOSHUA M. DUKE, AND LORI LYNCH

UNDERSTANDING how institutions affect resource allocation efficiency persists as a leading concern in land economics. A large body of research has been seeking to explain individual land use decisions under various policies while accounting for complications associated with information and heterogeneity. Empirical and theoretical approaches offer valuable insights but some questions remain difficult to answer. Economists have increasingly turned to experimental economics techniques in both the laboratory and the field because of the degree of control that the researcher can provide in the setting; their similarity to the natural-scientific process, including replicability; and the ability to use salient financial incentives that engage research participants in a manner that engenders greater credibility to their responses. Experiments thus are an essential tool for economists seeking to provide the most complete advice on how institutions affect land behavior.

This chapter has several objectives. The chapter introduces the methodological approach of experiments to land economists, who may be unfamiliar with the technique. Although many excellent primers exist to familiarize economists with experiments, this chapter focuses on the design issues associated with land markets and it also highlights the areas land economists have focused their research. Attention is given to research settings where experiments might best be employed either because experiments are well positioned to provide insight on land research questions or because experiments would likely fill gaps in knowledge about how policy interacts with land markets. Throughout this section, existing research findings in land economics are emphasized—especially relating to land conservation auctions because this area has attracted a great deal of recent land research—along with emerging topics. The second half of the chapter provides a more intensive understanding of economics experiments in land conservation by conveying the results of an original experiment. The experimental research examines how efficiently a conservation auction delivers ecosystem services under varying information structures.

1. The Experimental Economics Method for Land Economics

Over the past three decades, economists have increasingly turned to experimental methods—which provide replicability, laboratory controls, and the ability to create salient incentives—to explore important economic questions. Many initial applications were related to testing economic theories. The laboratory often provided an ideal location for investigation because researchers could "induce" research participants with values and use salient rewards to create incentive situations that mimicked the assumptions from theory. As challenges to traditional economic theory began to form and the field of behavioral economics rose in prominence, experiments became a critical research tool for testing and developing various theories of human economic behavior.

Modeling real world behavior comes with challenges, which are difficult to simplify in many settings—particularly when aspects of each individual decision are unknown to the researcher. With experiments, the researcher is exerting control over the environment, participants are getting paid according to the decisions they make, and deception is not permitted by the economic experimenters' social norms. Thus, participants are making real decisions that affect their payoffs and not hypothetical ones like in questionnaire-based research. In an uncontrolled environment, the researcher has difficulty explaining causality and cannot change a single condition (treatment) to determine its marginal impact on decision-making. However, within the laboratory setting, the investigator can design the institutional context, know the real monetary payoffs (i.e., the payment scheme), and examine the implications of changing one attribute (treatment) at a time. This allows for test-bedding policies at a fine scale, thereby suggesting the mix of institutions that will lead to the greatest social welfare in addition to identifying policy options that will likely lead to lower welfare.

Replicability offers another element adding to experimental methods popularity. Like other scientific disciplines, the ability to replicate one's own or another's results proves the robustness of a finding. Some investigators replicate the same experiment multiple times. This allows one to test the results with different sets of participants to determine similarities and differences for different pools and possibly for different social groups. It also allows one to collect enough data to estimate econometric models of behavior. By publishing the experimental instructions and protocols along with the research paper, other researchers can replicate the experiment to verify the results or to use the design to aid in university teaching.[1] Replicability is one advantage of laboratory experiments as compared to pure field experiments. While researchers may attempt to duplicate field experiments as well, their relatively more unconstrained environment may introduce changes that are unobservable between different locations and different time periods. While these issues of different locations and time periods can also pose problems in laboratory studies, they tend to be less of a concern as the researcher can use the controls of a laboratory to mitigate these factors. For instance, in a laboratory experiment the administrator can monitor all participants simultaneously and control the rules of communication. Thus, the researchers can limit the setting to having no communication amongst participants or to permit communication under certain established rules. They could also allow for free communication and simply record the communication for use in a subsequent analysis. In contrast, in a field experiment, the researcher has little to no ability to control or directly record the communication among participants and may only be able to gather information about the nature and amount of the communication by having participants complete self-reported, post-experiment surveys.

Friedman and Sunder (1994) outline the four types of records and documentation that experimental researchers should keep to ensure their experiments are replicable. One is written instructions for participants and the details of the recruitment process. Two, researchers should keep copies of the software and the hardware used (if applicable) and should make them available to other so that other researchers can replicate the experiment. Third, researchers should maintain documentation of the lab activities (a "log") that includes the date and times of experiments and other relevant facts as well as copies of the raw data. Finally, researchers should keep a record and copies of statistical programs and code used to analyze the data.

Recognizing that existing theory sometimes provides limited policy guidance—especially in complex settings—applied economists increasingly use experiments to search for insights to important questions. Shogren (2004, 1218) described the process as being "like a wind tunnel to test airplane design, lab experiments provide a testbed for what is called *economic design*—the process of constructing institutions and mechanisms to examine resource allocation." Experiments as a testbed are particularly useful in settings where implementation of a policy change would be difficult or costly; testing alternative policies in the laboratory first can be highly cost-effective.

Economists have also used the controls available in experiments to identify specific behaviors of interest, such as consumer responses to foods produced with different methods or producers' willingness to adopt new production technologies. Additionally,

[1] While the principle of replicability is a fundamental element of experimental economics, we recognize that publishing studies that simply replicate another experiment is difficult in economics. As authors who have also served as journal editors, we believe that this trend may be detrimental to the creation of knowledge because researchers should have incentives to confirm the results of other studies, ensuring proper checks and balances in our discipline's research process.

economists have found that results from experiments can be more compelling to industry leaders and policy makers as they learn about the methods and the research setting by participating directly in educational versions of these experiments.

Data collected on naturally occurring behavior often suffer from self-selection; those most likely to benefit from a behavior are the most likely to participate. As such, one has little information on the behavior of those individuals who did not participate. Experimental methods allow some control of this phenomenon. Often undergraduate students are recruited for experiments without knowing a priori about the experiment design or questions. Many experiments extrapolate from any real context entirely and are marketed generically as "research on economic decision making." In such cases, for instance, students more interested in land use are not the most likely to participate. Nor will students with little experience in making decisions in land markets decline to participate. How big an obstacle this recruitment is depends on the purposes of the study. If a goal of the study is to understand behavior of landowners with significant experience and interest in land use, then recruiting from a general population of undergraduates is less appropriate. However, if the research also wants to study the behavioral response for people who are not traditionally in the land market, people who have little interest or experience in land use decision-making such as heirs who recently inherited agricultural land, or people who are profit maximizing under several straightforward institutions, then perhaps a more general participant pool makes sense. As a general rule, researchers ought to think carefully about whether their approach to the selection of subjects matches the purposes of the study. For instance, when experimental studies look at consumers' willingness to pay for various foods, it makes sense to recruit household shoppers rather than undergraduates. However, if one wants to look at trends and responses to new music or electronics, then an undergraduate population may be more appropriate.

That said, many lab experiments do not address recruitment as systematically as traditional survey research. Like intercept surveys, experimental participant pools may be affected by a convenience bias. In addition, those who do not participate in lab experiments may systematically differ from participants, which is equivalent to nonresponse bias in survey research.

In the past, many experiments have recruited undergraduate students as participants in sessions conducted in rooms of computers equipped with privacy shields that serve as experimental laboratories in universities. Many researchers are now interested in whether college students respond similarly to other social groups. Laboratory experiments have been criticized as artificial and removed from the normal decision making situation. Many researchers now conduct experiments in the "field" with different participant groups to evaluate the generalizability of the students' results. As discussed in Harrison and List (2004), there also exists a spectrum of research settings between pure lab and pure field experiments that uses experimental techniques.

While some researchers value the seemingly higher representativeness and realism of field experiments and may shun the relatively artificial setting of undergraduate-student participants in a university experimental laboratory, we think that there is no simple "one-size-fits-all" rule when it comes to applying experiments to land economics. We try to illustrate in Figure 19.1, that each experimental design involves balancing of strengths and weaknesses upon three dimensions: *control*, *context*, and *representativeness*. Figure 19.1 provides an extension of the framing of Lusk and Shogren (2007, 15), who discuss the trade-offs between *control* and *context* in experimental designs for auctions. These authors define these terms as follows:

> "*Control* means the researcher has control over the environment such that no unmeasured external force drives choices. That is, confounding of cause and effect is eliminated." (p. 6)
>
> "*Context* implies that subjects have some contextual cues about why their decision might matter in a bigger world." (p. 15)

We build upon this description by adding the third dimension of *representativeness*, which examines the participant pool used in the experiments and assesses how similar the behavior of people in this pool is to the behavior of the people making the actual economic decisions related to land economics. While several studies have shown that, in some settings, the behavior of actual land market participants is similar to the behavior observed by undergraduate students, we do not believe that this will always be the case. Therefore, researchers should be aware of the inherent trade-offs among the different design elements as they seek to define causality, achieve external (face) validity, and test theories and policies related to land economics.

An examination of Figure 19.1 shows that on one extreme are experiments with low context and representativeness but high control. These experiments usually involve student participants (low representativeness) in a university laboratory with researcher-set induced values (high control) and context-neutral language (represented by Point 1). This control of participants' values may be particularly important when the experiments are designed to look at settings or behavior that are difficult to examine with actual data or when the values are formed with information generally hidden from an outside observer, such as rent seeking in auctions, adverse selection conservation auctions, or nonpoint source pollution behavior. These experiments also tend to be easiest and cheapest to conduct as the researcher can readily recruit participants from a large pool of undergraduate students (most often economics and business majors) and generally needs to offer these students relatively small financial incentives (approximately the regular hourly wage for student workers on campus) to get the students engaged in competitive behavior in a laboratory setting.

The framing of the instructions is also an important design consideration. Point 1 assumes that the instructions use context-neutral language. For instance, participants might be asked to sell "units" to a "buyer" given various market rules or to make different "production" decisions that lead to different "payoffs" and "costs" for themselves and others in their group. However, some researchers worry that these generic terms are difficult for participants to understand and therefore have preferred more context-specific language (represented by Point 2). For instance, participants might be asked to sell their "parcels of land" to the "government" or into a "conservation program" given various market rules. However, the introduction of specific land conservation terms may also

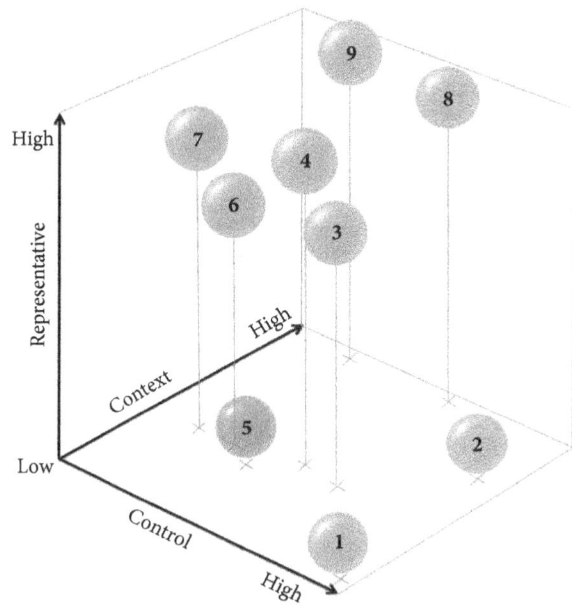

FIGURE 19.1 Tradeoffs in experimental control, context, and representativeness.

lead to problems if certain landowners are reluctant to sell their property to a government agency but would consider preserving their land with a local nongovernmental organization such as a land trust. Similarly, participants might make different "pollution abatement" decisions that lead to different "profits" and "taxes" for themselves and others in their group. While context specific language provides more reality to the experiment settings—which may help participants understand the situation and thereby lessen confusion and inadvertent error that leads to poor data—the researcher is likely also sacrificing some control of the induced values as participants bring other values into the research setting. For instance, some participants may view selling their parcels to the government or paying taxes to be highly objectionable due to their political beliefs or personal/family experiences, while others may view these terms positively. To help assess these types of concerns, post-experiment surveys can test for some of these potential factors and can control for them in subsequent data analysis. However, researchers should seek to recognize potential biases in the experimental choices through well-designed survey questions.

Points 3 and 4 on Figure 19.1 show how experiments that recruit actual landowners as participants can improve the representativeness of the study. While being harder to recruit and—costing more on a per-participant basis, landowners can be brought into the experiment laboratory at a university (Point 3) and participate in the same experimental market with context specific instructions.[2] Concerns that the landowners who

[2] Landowner participants could also participate in an experiment with neutrally framed instructions; however, it likely would be most helpful to provide these landowners directly with context specific language as this is the setting context that the researchers are likely most interested in studying their

would participate in a research study at university setting may be sufficiently different than other regional landowners might lead the researcher to use mobile equipment and set-up the experimental market in a setting that could attract a more representative sample of landowners such as a State Fair or a conference traditionally attended by landowners (Point 4).

Of course, any group of landowners may bring to the laboratory attitudes and social norms that the researcher is unaware of that may unexpectedly craft their behavior in the research setting. Therefore, the level of experimental control over the values truly being used by the participants is likely lower. An issue of greater concern is situations where landowners may be concerned that the results of the research will affect the policies and regulatory environment that affect them in future. In these cases, the participants may act strategically by behaving in a different manner in the experiment than they would when facing the actual decisions. For instance, the participants in an experiment, even with relatively high stakes, may behave in a more cooperative manner or voluntarily reduce agricultural production to demonstrate that government regulation is not necessary. In this case, the experiment's seemingly salient rewards fail to be the motivating factor in participants' decisions and the researcher may unknowingly lose control of their research setting.

Points 5, 6, and 7 on Figure 19.1 represent situations where markets are setup in the lab, but the researcher has no control of the values. The participants' values are endogenous (also referred to as "homegrown" values). For land economics, it is unusual for research budgets to allow for experiments that involve actual land transactions. Therefore, other lower-cost items can be used to study participant behavior. For instance, participants could be given or endowed with coffee mugs, bottles of wine, or plants where their values for the items are endogenous to the participants, and then trading could occur. In some settings, the values for these items may be observed directly through the use of auctions; however, in other settings knowing this true value for the item is not important. Generally, researchers trade off control for context with endogenous values. This type of research design may be especially helpful when looking at underlying behaviors. However, researchers may find that some research questions, such as studying problems with asymmetric information, may be difficult to answer when the values are endogenous and as such unknown. Additionally, without the control of induced values, researchers may need to collect more data (run more experiments or collected additional information on post-experiment surveys) to overcome the noisier data and to detect behavioral changes due to treatment effects.

While relatively expensive, research designs can be created where participants make actual land decisions in markets with rules established by the researcher (Point 8). These settings are clearly high in context and representativeness, though the amount of control may be limited by both the natural policy environment and by the amount of available

behavior. For simplicity, Figure 19.1 does not show all of the scenarios with regards to context specific and neutral instructions, but focuses on the most common.

research funding. From a policy perspective, research involving real landowners making decisions regarding their land given different settings is likely the most convincing form of external (face) validity. Given the likely costs associated with this research, it makes sense that this research should build upon previous findings from research conducted in simpler and less expensive settings such as those described above. A potential cost-saving (and data-increasing) technique is to use a lottery or competitive auction to reduce the number of accepted experimental contracts that actually are paid.

Finally, the extreme of induced-value, neutrally-framed, lab experiments with student participants at a university (Point 1) are natural experiments that arise due to random actions or heterogeneity in the policy environment (Point 9). While natural experiments provide a high level of context and representativeness, their level of control can be highly variable as the researcher is constrained ex post by the changes. Researchers are also confronted with participants self-selecting to participate based on the policies themselves.

1.1 Technology for Data Collection

Many of the initial applications of experimental techniques involved the experiment administrator collecting responses from participants with slips of paper and then concluding the session with a brief socioeconomic survey. While computers have generally become the tool of choice for experimental economists, the basic "pencil-and-paper" approach can still be quite successful, especially when conducting research in the field, such as a county fair or a developing country, where the advantages of computers are offset by the technical logistics of a more remote setting. Mobile computer devices bring more capabilities to remote settings and have grown more popular over time; however, there will remain groups of participants that find new technologies to be a barrier for participation, especially older populations and those people in developing countries who are unfamiliar with their use.

Along with the popularity of experimental methods has come specialized and easy-to-use computer software such as "z-Tree" (Fischbacher 2007), which is an open source program that already has been programmed in common experimental settings while still allowing for research manipulation of the experimental framework. Other research has used web-based programs for the use in the lab or created macros to link Excel spreadsheets and Access databases using Visual Basic with Applications. These computer programs allow experimenters to collect data in real time and can provide real-time feedback to participants. The internet has web-based survey and experimental tools to enable one to recruit large and potentially diverse participant pools for both simple and more complex experiments allowing people in multiple settings to participate simultaneously. While appealing in many ways, web-based experiments may limit some aspects of the control a researcher desires. For instance, the session administrator will be unable to observe and fully control the behavioral setting of the participants.

1.2 Experimental Design Issues

While others have already written at length about the proper design of economic experiments (see Davis and Holt 1993; Friedman and Sunder 1994; Lusk and Shogren 2007), there are some important issues in experimental design that are worth emphasizing as these are decisions that every research project needs to make prior to running sessions.

How much does one need to pay participants to ensure that they are motivated by the incentives offered in the experiment? This issue, frequently referred to as the saliency of the rewards, is critical as the administrator wants to use the controls in the laboratory to ensure that the marginal incentives are sufficient to overcome other factors, such as trying to select behaviors that they think will please the experiment administrator or trying to outcompete other participants but ignoring the fundamental financial incentives established by the experimental design. As a general rule, the higher the economic rewards, the more attention to detail you can expect from your participants. If the researcher sets the marginal incentives such that participants can gain significantly more money from "optimal" or "near optimal" choices compared to just "good" choices, then one could expect that participants will dedicate more cognitive effort in determining the true optimal choice. Salient rewards will be smaller for undergraduate students than for professionals. In our experiments, we have generally compensated undergraduate students an average $15 per hour while compensation for professional participants can be more than $50 per hour.[3] Taking into account each group's opportunity costs of time and proximity to the laboratory or field setting before setting compensation levels is important for encouraging broad participation in the experiments.

How does one set-up the laboratory controls to ensure that one is isolating the behavior that one is interested in? Does one also need to employ econometric controls to the experimental data? These issues are especially important if one is involving participants in repeated decisions because this can provide additional statistical power, but it also require proper statistical accounting for the treatments generating these observations.

How important is context to the research setting? Should the instructions be written with context-specific language or in a neutral tone? As mentioned above, an advantage of context-specific language is that participants may have an easier time understanding the experimental setting. However, terms such as "taxes," "pollution," "conservation," or even "government program" can often be value-laden for the participants. Therefore, participants may not consider the economic incentives offered in the experiment to be salient enough to overcome their attraction (or resistance) to behavior related to these terms.

Many of the issues related to proper experimental design can also help address potential concerns that may arise from the Institutional Review Board (IRB) at the researcher's

[3] Of course, the participant's choices and the general outcomes of the experiment either through group behavior or random outcomes determines the actual payoff of the participant.

institution. Our experience has been that IRBs appreciate the norm in experimental economics of not deceiving participants. Similarly, experiments can often be designed where participants are not identified by name, but instead simply by identification number. IRBs also tend to like that the choices in experiments are often confidential: single-blind (where the participants do not know the choices and payoffs of other participants) or double-blind (where neither the other participants nor the administrators in the session know the choices and payoffs).

The staffing of experiments also depends upon the research design. In settings involving double-blind confidentiality or multiple experiment sessions being conducted simultaneously, the research team may need to consist of three to four administrators. In market settings involving induced values, only one administrator may be necessary. Nevertheless, an extra administrator can be helpful in preparing for the experiment, distributing experiment instructions and materials, addressing questions that arise from participants, dealing with any computer problems, and assisting with the payment of participants at the conclusion of the session.

Emerging applications of experiments to land economics include risk attitudes of landowners, landowners' propensity to develop their land, institutions to reduce nonpoint source pollution in complicated geological and political situations, such as the Chesapeake Bay in the United States, agglomeration in conservation project selection, and the application of behavioral economics to encourage more socially beneficial land uses. The following section reviews recent research related to auctions, including discriminatory pricing versus uniform pricing, the effect of information sets on auction efficiency, and markets for ecosystem services.

2. The Experimental Economics Method: Applications to Land Conservation Auctions

Experiments related to land economics often seek to mimic real-world conservation auctions, and the Conservation Reserve Program (CRP) is one of the largest in the United States. The United States Department of Agriculture (USDA) runs the CRP auction in each state at various times during the year. This voluntary program for agricultural landowners is characterized by broad environmental objectives, and the requirement that funds be allocated on a competitive basis is satisfied with an auction. Under the CRP, a landowner submits an offer indicating the compensation that she would accept to enroll land in the program for ten to fifteen years. At the end of September 2011, the CRP had 417,386 farms with 31.2 million acres enrolled and was paying out $1.7 billion in rental payments annually (USDA 2011). According to USDAs Farm Service Agency (2006), CRP enrollment has led to the abatement of 450 million tons of erosion per year, the restoration of 2 million acres of wetlands and adjacent buffers, the reduction of 48 million metric tons of carbon dioxide emissions, and the protection of 170,000 stream miles. The CRP has also increased duck and quail populations, as well as other wildlife, by restoring habitat and corridors.

Conservation auctions are also used throughout the world, and the results generally suggest that auctions are more cost effective than alternate institutions for procuring conservation services. For instance, the CRP's structure was adopted by conservation agencies in Australia for the Bush Tender pilot trials (Stoneham et al. 2003) and the Auction for Landscape Recovery pilot program (Gole et al. 2005). Stoneham et al. (2003) concluded that the amount of biodiversity benefit gained through the first round of Bush Tender auctions in Victoria, Australia, would have cost the government seven times as much if a fixed payment had been used instead of an auction.

A reverse auction mechanism was used in Scotland under the Challenge Fund scheme, and research demonstrated that the total cost would have been 33% to 36% greater under a fixed payment (CJC Consulting 2004, 63). Connor et al. (2008) concluded that, under the same budget, a fixed payment plan would produce only 56% of the benefits achieved with auctions in the Catchment Care Australian conservation auction in 2004. In one of the few theoretical treatments of this issue, Latacz-Lohmann and Van der Hamsvoort (1997) found that total emission reduction gained by different formats of auctions ranges from 16% to 29% more than flat-rate offer system.

2.1 Conservation Auctions in the Laboratory

Lab experiments on conservation auctions investigate how much excess rent participants secure under different treatments as a measure of auction efficiency. The setting of many of these experiments is conservation auctions similar to those noted above. Cason and Gangadharan (2004) examined information effects in discriminatory and non-discriminatory pricing schemes, finding that more information available to sellers about the environmental benefits of their project led to more strategic behavior and greater rents. Schilizzi and Latacz-Lohmann (2007) found that both target- and budget-constrained auctions performed better than fixed payments in a single period. However, with repetition, the advantage of auctions quickly diminishes. Hellerstein and Higgins (2010) used the CRP as the basis for land conservation auction experiments. Their results showed that capping the maximum amount a landowner can receive in environmental markets may have intuitive appeal as a way of reducing government expenditures but the caps may actually lead to increases in expenditures. Hellerstein and Higgins (2010) argued that relaxing restrictions on maximum offers from landowners could yield better results, especially when one considers the quality of the land enrolled.

2.2 Discriminatory-Price Auctions versus Uniform-Price Auctions

There are several types of auctions, common auctions include the "call markets" and "double-sided auctions" used for stock markets with multiple buyers and sellers; ascending-price "English" auctions where there is one seller and multiple buyers; and descending-price "Dutch" auctions (see Davis and Holt [1993] and Kagel and Roth [1995] for details on auctions). For "reverse" auctions that involve multiple sellers and one buyer, common auctions include "discriminatory-price auctions" in which the buyer pays the winning sellers the amount of their offers and "uniform-price auctions," a type of Vickrey (1961) auction, in which the buyer pays all the winning sellers a single-price based on the either the highest-accepted offer or the lowest-rejected offer. Latacz-Lohmann and Schilizzi (2005) concluded from their theoretical analysis that the optimal strategy for landholders in a discriminatory-price auction is to inflate their offer above their real opportunity cost in order to secure information rents. Further, the authors found that the incentive to inflate offers is greatest among sellers whose costs are lowest—and therefore most likely to be successful—while high-cost sellers will tend to make offers that are closer to their true costs—but they are unlikely to be selected by the auction mechanism.

Cason and Gangadharan (2004) used a laboratory experiment in which landowners competed in sealed-offer auctions to obtain payments for reducing nonpoint source pollution from land activities. One treatment was a uniform-price auction where everyone was paid the amount of the lowest price rejected, and the other was a discriminatory-price auction. Offers in the uniform-price treatment were within 2% of owners' cost, while most offers in the discriminatory-price auction were at least 8% higher than owners' cost. However, because the discriminatory-price auction did not pay a single market-clearing price—rather it paid each successful seller a price equal to his or her offer—overall, it was more efficient.

2.3 Information and Conservation Auctions

The amount of information provided to landholders before they make offers can substantially influence the efficiency of an auction as the amount of information can influence whether sellers can make strategic offers in the search for higher rents. Banerjee et al. (2011) considered an iterative auction for selecting offers of projects adjacent to each other on a circular grid, finding auction performance was negatively affected by more information available to participants. Their paper shows that when participants had more information, the conservation program paid more for the conservation units.

Cason et al. (2003) used an experiment on landowner behavior in a nonpoint source pollution-reduction setting to test how information affected auction performance. They conceptualized information as whether or not participants knew the buyer's value for the landowner/participant's project. Their results show that participants tend to inflate offers more for projects with a high value to the buyer. Consequently, less information about buyer value may increase auction efficiency.[4] An auction would be efficient if sellers (landowners) offer their willingness to accept (reservation value) rather than garnering rents. This could be thought of as "procurement efficiency." Given the assumption of homogeneous acres, the optimal auction performance would result in the buyer obtaining the most acreage for the lowest expense. Clearly, auction efficiency is associated with buyers (often government) optimizing their budgets. Cason and Gangadharan (2004) reported similar results on information impacts to Cason et al. (2003).

In some settings, the provision of information also can undermine price-induced competitiveness traditionally assumed to occur in markets. Hong and Shum (2002) found that in a procurement auction format where individual participants have private and common value information, the average procurement cost can rise as the number of participants increases instead of participants making more conservative offers. While more information may improve seller certainty and increase competitive pressure—which would reduce rents—participants may be more strategic and request more rent (Rolfe et al. 2009).

2.4 Multiple Auction Rounds versus Single-Shot Auctions in Experiments

Most experimental studies of conservation programs frame the auctions as single independent rounds—where each round represents the beginning and end of the world. In cases of permanent land protection from a one-time program, that assumption is appropriate. However, single-shot auctions are not appropriate in all instances.

Opinions differ on the use of multiple rounds of offers versus a single round. Rolfe et al. (2009, 290) described three theoretical reasons that favor the single-shot approach: "Incentives to reveal true opportunity costs, avoiding strategic behavior, and minimizing administration and transaction costs." The aforementioned studies by Cason et al. (2003) and Cason and Gangadharan (2004) used multiple rounds with information treatments, finding that strategic bidding did occur and that multiple rounds can generate increased administration and transaction costs.

A number of studies have favored multi-round auctions, especially because multi-round auctions such as the CRP are the most common found in conservation settings. McAfee and McMillan (1996) argued that interdependencies among offers

[4] This result has important implications for ecosystem service markets as the buyer preferences, such as habitat for endangered species, are often well publicized. Additionally, priorities, such as only acquiring land that is adjacent to already protected land, may lead to higher offers from sellers to conservation programs.

or combinatorial benefits are introduced when there are multiple rounds. Information can be gained by sellers through multiple rounds about the suitability of their proposals (Rolfe et al. 2009). Klemperer (2002) reported that allowing sellers to learn about others' valuations through multiple rounds could make the sellers more comfortable with their own assessments and less cautious in making offers. Other arguments for repeat-auction designs are that participants need more than one round to understand the auction mechanism and how to offer true valuations, as well as to learn from market feedback (List and Shogren 1999). In contrast, Bernard (2005) argued that, in place of repeated trials, experiments employ single-shot auctions accompanied by in-depth instructions and practice.

Multi-round auctions may be associated with efficiency, particularly in initial rounds. Lusk et al. (2004) suggested that in a closed, multiple-bidding, second-price auction setting, offers for different quality goods will increase, and this will happen particularly between the first and second rounds. Rolfe et al. (2009, 292) suggested that the question of single-shot versus repeated rounds may need to be answered "on a case-by-case basis." Rolfe et al. (2009, 300) argues that multiple rounds tend to deliver auction efficiency when landowners are "unfamiliar with the provision of conservation actions" and "uncertain about the opportunity costs of providing actions." In recent experimental research, Fooks et al. (2012) show that participant behavior differs significantly if situations with identical incentives are structured to be either a single-shot or multiple-round setting.

3. Application: The Impact of Information on Auctions for Ecosystem Services

This section describes original research, using an experiment on conservation auctions. Governments increasingly use reverse auctions to procure ecosystem services generated from land use at the lowest cost possible. A popular mechanism is a discriminatory reverse auction where the government purchases services from willing sellers based on a process that selects the least expensive offers first. The price paid to each of the selected landowners is equal to the amount of the offers they submitted. In the simplest form, the government achieves procurement efficiency—and budgetary cost-effectiveness—from a discriminatory reverse auction because it benefits from the competition of the market as it selects and pays for the number of lowest-cost offers that exhaust the budget. Procurement efficiency occurs (when land is of homogeneous quality) when the government enrolls land from those landowners with the lowest opportunity cost; i.e., it obtains the ecosystem services desired with the least transfers and therefore the least potential distortion. In a similar sense, budgetary cost-effectiveness measures the amount the government is paying for these ecosystem services. A well-functioning auction will obtain the highest value in ecosystem services for each dollar of taxpayers' money. Ideally, this approach encourages competition and allows the government to "pick off" the supply curve, driving landowners to make offers that equal their opportunity costs—the minimum willingness-to-accept compensation—and thus maximizing the conservation services per budgetary dollar expended by the government.

However, there are several reasons to be skeptical that these auctions actually work as well as intended. A means for evaluating their performance is to measure the "rent premium" received by the landowners: the amount of excess profit they obtain if the government's payment exceeds the true opportunity cost. Kirwan et al. (2005) offered an empirical estimate of such rent premiums generated in the CRP, which uses a reverse auction. The authors estimated that between 10% and 40% of the program expenditures went to rent premiums. This estimate is consistent with the experimental results described earlier, and thus economists continue to study auction designs in laboratory experiments, which offer the means to test, in a controlled fashion, many design features. Three major lines of research have developed.

One line of inquiry focuses on selection under asymmetric information with parcel and landowner heterogeneity. Foundational theoretical work on this problem of adverse selection includes Wu and Babcock (1996) and Smith (1995). Recent work focused on auctions using economic experiments comes from Arnold et al. (2013). These papers show that the existence of heterogeneity generates a systematic tendency for landowners of lower-quality parcels to make low-priced offers, which are more likely to be selected. Even though these successful offers cost less, they still carry substantial information rent premiums.

A second area of economic-experimental investigation compares the performance of discriminatory auctions with fixed-price procurement. As discussed previously, discriminatory auctions have generally outperformed uniform-price auctions (Cason and Gangadharan 2004). Yet there is concern about the efficiency of this approach in energy markets where auctions often involving multiple rounds per day, auctions are information rich, and sellers have some market power that comes from withholding offers for some units from the market or for reducing supply capacity by putting down plants for "repairs" (Rassenti et al. 2003; Vossler et al. 2009).

A third area, and the focus of our research, is the role of public and private information in conservation auctions. Questions about how information impacts auction efficiency have naturally arisen from recent research on how participants learn through information provided (information quality) and auction repetition (experience). In a study addressed above, Cason et al. (2003) used experiments to examine the role of information quality and experience and found that (1) sellers' rents increase as they gain experience; and (2) sellers extract more rent when they know the benefit of their offer from the buyer's perspective (i.e., participants had more information about demand/benefit heterogeneity). Schilizzi and Latacz-Lohmann (2007) offered experimental economic evidence that auctions are generally more efficient than fixed-price procurement but that the advantage dissipates over time as participants gain experience. This result corresponds with an earlier, agent-based model by Hailu and Schilizzi (2004) that found that seller experience led to decreased auction efficiency.

Our work extends these papers by examining the effect of experience while controlling for a set of policy-relevant treatments based on three levels of information. Our conceptualization of information treatments involves market information and thus complements the information treatments in Cason et al. (2003) involving benefit heterogeneity. The research question addressed here is whether market information provided to sellers affects the efficiency of a discriminatory land conservation auction and, if so, whether the effect attenuates with experience.

3.1 Policy Setting

Government agencies that conduct conservation auctions provide various levels of information regarding past results of auctions to the public and to future auction participants. Our research has been influenced by an auction used yearly since the 1990s by the Delaware Agricultural Lands Preservation Foundation (DALPF) to secure conservation easements on agricultural land. The DALPF auction provides a detailed information set that includes the following data:

1. current period budget;
2. amount of program budgets in previous years;
3. number of offers received in previous years;
4. number of offers accepted in previous years;
5. highest accepted offer in previous years;
6. lowest accepted offer in previous years; and
7. average accepted offer in previous years.

Policy makers may feel that providing such information meets general goals of fairness to owners and openness and transparency in the fiscal conduct of a governmental program. It may also promote competition among owners, which would increase auction efficiency. Previous research has suggested, however, that such detailed public information is likely to decrease the auction's efficiency because potential applicants can use it to inflate their offers (Messer and Allen 2010).

In contrast to DALPF, other programs, such as the Maryland Agricultural Lands Preservation Foundation (MALPF), provide little detailed information to the public or to auction participants. In this case, offers to sell for the upcoming annual cycle are made before the previous year's results are announced. Horowitz et al. (2009), in their analysis of 19 years of MALPF program data, found evidence of inflated offers in this no-information setting.[5] They found that on average, bids are 5 to 15% above the

[5] Similarly, the Bush Tender project in Australia does not reveal information to landowner sellers about the environmental benefits in the biodiversity preservation auction, perhaps because auctions

underlying reservation value for a landowner and show that increased competition (in the form of lower budgets or more bidders) reduces this mark-up. They also find evidence that bidders adjust for a possible "winner's curse" by increasing their bids by 8 to 14%.[6]

Because actual auction processes offer various degrees of information in highly variable settings that are difficult to compare, systematically generated data are needed to understand the influence of information on auction efficiency. It could be that the answer is program-specific—that some information interacts with a program or locational characteristics in an unobserved or unobservable manner. The most efficient auction mechanism thus would be determined on a case-by-case basis. Or, it could be that auction efficiency depends, subtly, on exactly how much information is provided. The results of this research suggest that information and auction efficiency may be analogous to the classic children's story of Goldilocks and the Three Bears, where the program must identify the amount of public information that is neither "too little" nor "too much," but instead is "just right." Experimental economics provides an effective platform to test various types of information as treatments in a controlled setting.

3.2 Experimental Design

This research evaluates the impact of various levels of public information on (1) seller behavior in conservation auctions; and (2) the conservation program's overall effectiveness. It characterizes three information regimes, extending recent experimental conservation auction work by Messer et al. (2012). The experimental sessions were conducted at the University of Delaware's Laboratory for Experimental & Applied Economics. Ninety participants were recruited using email addresses from students in undergraduate courses in business and economics. Each experiment lasted approximately 90 minutes and average earnings were $25.

Each participant was randomly assigned to a group of ten participants. Each participant was assigned the role of a landholder, who owned one parcel and could sell or keep it. Participants were seated so that private decisions were made on individual laptop computers with privacy screens. Participants completed a consent form and then read

conducted annually in the same region could allow sellers to infer the regulator's private information regarding the benefits.

[6] Used first to discuss auctions for mineral rights such as oil reserves purchased from the government, a winner's curse phenomenon is predicted, in auctions where the buyers have actual values that are unknown to the either the other buyers or the seller (program administrator), but are correlated (common values). Buyers also tend to make bidding decisions based on estimated values (geological survey based) rather than market values. Theory suggests that the buyer who "wins" these type of auctions will have bid too highly in part because they over-estimate the value of the auction item. However, this phenomenon tends to be well-known and, as such, experienced buyers anticipate it and adjust their bids to compensate.

the written instructions provided (see the Appendix for the actual participant instructions used in the experiment). The administrator described the experiment verbally with the aid of presentation software to ensure consistency. No participant-to-participant communication was allowed.

As in several experiments described previously, each round represented a single-period game—the beginning and end of the world. The incentives in each round were thus described as net present values, meaning that ownership returns and offers reflected the future stream of benefits accruing from retaining or selling parcels. Consequently, there was no incentive to wait to sell because the budget was reset and the induced values were new in the next round. Thus, this setting did not allow for option value of information as each round constituted an independent observation on choice behavior in the group.[7]

The experiment used "induced values"[8] as the opportunity cost for the landowner, which was conceptualized as an "ownership return" for the participant for the 100-acre parcel of land. "Experimental dollars" (hereafter denominated "$") were designed to match the incentives real landowners would have in actual land markets. The exchange rate between experimental dollars and real dollars was provided to participants and used to calculate cash payments upon completion of the experiment. Ownership returns were randomly selected from a uniform distribution ranging from $2000 to $8000 per acre. The opportunity cost distribution was designed to mimic agricultural land markets in the mid-Atlantic and Northeast United States, the location of some of the largest and most active land conservation programs in the country and a market where land values vary substantially according to development pressure.

Participants decided whether to submit an offer to sell their parcel. If a participant chose not to submit an offer for the parcel, then the parcel was retained and the landowner received payment equal to the return on ownership for the parcel. The amount of each offer was confidential. If an offer was submitted, the participant incurred a nominal nonrefundable transaction cost ("submission fee") of $20. The submission fee was designed to reflect real-world conditions associated with landowners attempting to participate in conservation markets and also to prevent the choice of submitting any offer, even a very high one, from weakly dominating a strategy to submit "no offer" under all conditions. If the offer was accepted by the conservation program, the

[7] This statement does not assume that knowledge of the market was independent for each round. On the contrary, as will be discussed later, participants learned about the market quickly and incorporated this information into their selling decisions.

[8] Induced values are the monetary values or incentives that are set by the researcher and are not endogenously determined by the participants. Induced values have a long history of use in experimental economics as they allow the researchers to have greater control of the research settings as the values can be design to test behavioral hypotheses and theory (Davis and Holt 1993). This approach can be particularly helpful in situations where in real markets the values of individuals are hidden and participants have incentives not to truthfully reveal them.

participant received payment equal to the offer; if it was not accepted, the participant received payment equal to the return on ownership. Accepted offers for the conservation program were determined using a discriminatory auction in which the lab administrator computer (acting as the government) selected the least expensive offers in turn until there were no longer enough funds in the budget to buy the next least-expensive parcel.

The conservation budget ranged from \$2 million to \$6 million with an average of \$4 million. A random process using a uniform distribution determined the budget before each round.[9] While the dollar amount of each budget was selected randomly, the specific budget for each round was held constant in each experimental session. This enabled full control of the experience effect related to budgets and facilitated data analysis. Of course, the budget for each round was not known a priori to the participants in any of the treatments.

3.3 Information Treatments

Invariant information in the experiment includes the private induced value of a parcel. Prior to making a decision, each participant knew his or her opportunity cost of participating in the auction, i.e. the private value, mirroring the presumed private knowledge of an actual landholder. All participants knew the distribution from which private values (theirs and others) were drawn. Although the assumption of knowing the distribution is stronger than only knowing one's own private value, this setting captured the notion that some landowners would anticipate how readily other landowners in their region might choose to participate in conservation auctions. The experiment also was constructed so that all participants knew the distribution from which the program budget was drawn. This assumption captured the idea that, though program budgets may vary over time, landowners may have expectations about the range and relative likelihood of high, low, or average funding levels in any given period.

Other information in the experiment varied across treatments and is presented in Table 19.1. The information sets included:

(1) a "full" set of detailed public information that closely mimicked the seven types of information provided by the DALPF program;
(2) a "partial" set of public information that consisted of the previous and current program budget; and

[9] The choice to have the budgets randomly determined is consistent with the situation observed with the DALPF program and with other government programs, such as the USDA Forest Legacy Program, which tend to have a large variation in yearly budgets (Messer and Allen, 2010; Fooks and Messer, 2012). Of course, some conservation programs establish their budgets over longer time horizons and thus have far less year-to-year variability. Because the setting of this research builds upon the assumption that each round was the beginning and end of the world, using a random budget seems most appropriate.

Table 19.1 Definition of full-, partial-, and no-information treatments

Information	Full	Partial	No
Participants' private information			
Own WTA ("ownership return" for each parcel)	x	x	x
Previous history of sale for each own parcels	x	x	x
Public information			
Distribution of landowners ownership returns	x	x	x
Distribution of program budgets	x	x	x
Budgets from previous rounds	x	x	x
Budgets for current period	x	x	
Number of offers received from previous rounds	x		
Number of offers accepted from previous rounds	x		
Highest accepted offer from previous rounds	x		
Lowest accepted offer from previous rounds	x		
Average accepted offer from previous rounds	x		
Which owners sold parcels from previous rounds	x		

Note: Owners were identified only by number, not by name

(3) a treatment that provided "no" public information other than the budget for the previous round.

The three information treatments were implemented in sessions of 45 rounds. Each participant, and thus each group, participated in only one treatment so there was no need for treatment ordering. In any given treatment, all participants were supplied with the same information irrespective of their individual choices. Participants had private information about their past choices, and the participants' screens displayed historic information on their opportunity costs, and overall market information (if any).

3.4 Extent of the Market

The experiment consists of a policy intervention, where preservation necessarily affects the supply of land in preserved and unpreserved states. All else equal, greater levels of preservation raise the value of unpreserved land, thereby raising the opportunity cost of future preservation. One anticipates that these price effects will be more significant factors affecting behavior when budgets are larger and over time, as land increasingly migrates to a state of protection. These arguments may form the basis for future experimental work, but they do not affect the results of the experiment discussed in this chapter. First, this experiment was not dynamic—each decision period represented the stream of measureable benefits and costs accruing to the landowner and conservation buyer from the current moment through the foreseeable future. In other words, each round represented the "beginning" and "end" of the world from the perspective of both buyer and seller. Second, the participants were not informed whether intervention targeted a large portion of the landscape or was so small as to constitute a marginal change in land use allocations. In other words, this experiment could be viewed as a partial equilibrium analysis.

3.5 Experimental Data Analysis, Hypotheses, and Results

Panel data regression models can be used to assess the results of the experiment. In all treatments, the unit of analysis was the round and the dependent variable was the amount of rent (excess profits) captured by the sellers as the aggregate participant rent for the group. The rent premium was defined as the price received by a successful seller minus the induced value for the sold unit. A large rent meant that participants were able to secure returns that exceeded their opportunity costs; smaller rent corresponded to auction efficiency. Panels reflected the session in which the dependent variable was the aggregate group rent in each round for each of the nine groups.[10]

The independent variables captured the key design characteristics of the experiment. The primary design measures were *Full Info* and *No Info*, which reflected the full-information and no-information treatments, while the partial-information treatment was the reserve category in the regression. The variable of *Budget* controlled for the impact of different budget levels. Larger budgets should lead to greater rent premiums because there is less competition when the number of sellers and their opportunity costs are fixed and the budget is bigger. The variable of *Round* controlled for the round number. A positive parameter was expected because participants gained experience in each auction treatment and were therefore likely to make fewer mistakes by over-pricing offers and missing out on potentially profitable transactions in later rounds. In addition, the participants could extract higher rent premiums, especially from units with low ownership returns. Several interaction variables test for joint effects with *Round*. The information-treatment interactions with *Round* test whether the learning effect was magnified or attenuated in the full information and no information settings. Also, a budget interaction with *Round* controlled for any synergistic impact when the *Round* value and the budget were both large (providing especially large rent premium opportunities) and when they were both small (offering relatively low rent premium opportunities). The coefficients on the interaction variables shift the slope on learning.

Table 19.2 presents a panel data analysis of the experiment results. The total number of observations was 396, which reflects 44 observations (rounds) over nine sessions. The model estimation is statistically significant. The statistical results show that larger budgets lead to greater participant rents. On average, one extra dollar in budget delivered

[10] The first round was discarded for analysis because the participants at that point did not have any prior round result from which to gather information.

Table 19.2 Panel data analysis of group price premium (excess profit)

Variable	Coefficient (s.e.)
Full Info	306,895.6**
	(94,291.2)
No Info	306,915.6**
	(94,291.2)
Budget	0.3874**
	(0.0467)
Round	17,206.51**
	(6264.08)
Full Info * *Round*	-5616.68*
	(2799.00)
No Info * *Round*	-3582.35
	(2799.00)
Budget * *Round*	-0.0040*
	(0.0016)
Constant	-715,789.0**
	(190,676.9)
Observations	396
Wald chi²	345.0
Prob > chi²	0.000

Note: ** indicates statistical significance at the 1% level; * indicates statistical significance at the 5% level.

$0.39 in rent premium. This is a high efficiency cost and one that, by itself, calls into question whether auctions can efficiently deliver conservation services. The magnitude is similar to estimates from Kirwan et al. (2005) that between 10% and 40% of the CRP's budget were paid to landowners as information rent premiums. A second result is that the impact of budget size on rents attenuated slightly as participants gained more experience; that is, the *Budget*Round* interaction was negative. This means that, over time, greater competition drives down rents (although the effect is small).

Round had a positive impact on rents, showing that groups were able to obtain greater rent over time as they gained experience with the auction environment and the behavior of others in the group. Although it was critical to control this measure of learning in the lab environment, it is less clear how important this result is in real-world auctions. Specifically, the real-world analog would be a landholder who owns multiple units and sells them over time or takes multiple rounds to get his or her farm accepted by the program. Some landowners may reflect these characteristics but many would not. The results do not indicate whether landowners who closely observed but did not participate in early auctions would learn over time at the same rate as those who participated in the earlier auctions.

This study suggests that the partial-information case leads to the smallest degree of rent premiums, which implies that partial information provides the auctioneer with the most efficient discriminatory conservation auction. The full-information treatment and the no-information treatment inflate rents by an equivalent amount relative to the reserve category of partial information. The magnitude of the group's rent increase associated with the full-information and the no-information treatments was approximately \$307,000; the average budget was \$4 million, and the information effects are approximately 7.7% of the budget. Thus, those two treatments transferred public money to landowners, instead of using this money for protecting additional ecosystem services.

Interactions between the *Round* variable and the information treatments led to different results. In the full-information treatment, participants' experience led to a decrease in rents. Over time, conservation auctions with full information would likely become somewhat more competitive, and the largest rent premiums would be gained in the initial rounds. However, this effect was relatively small (coefficient of –5616.68), meaning the benefit to the sellers of having full information was not offset even at the conclusion of the experiment. In the no-information treatment, there was no statistical decline (or increase) in rents over time—i.e., the impact of experience captured by the *Round* coefficient was equal in the no-information and the partial-information treatments. In the absence of full information the entire benefit of experience is captured by the coefficient on *Round*—it measures only experience.

4. Conclusion

Experimental economics techniques have been applied to a variety of land economics questions. These techniques can be useful for land researchers as they allow for control of values for both buyers and sellers within the market, replicability among experimental events, examination of difference between the more controlled environment of the laboratory and the less artificial environment of the field. They permit a researcher to test theories about land markets, to analyze particular policies and institutional structures, to look at landowners' willingness to participate in different programs, to examine specific behaviors of interest, and as a method of educating the public and the policy makers. Of particular interest has been the efficiency of various auction mechanisms used for obtaining the ecosystem services generated by land use and how different forms of information alter outcomes for sellers and buyers. This chapter reviewed the relevant literature and reported the results of an original experiment that explores these issues in the context of markets for ecosystem service procurement.

Results of the experiment suggest that, for a discriminatory reverse auction, a limited-information setting may lead to greater market efficiency than either the no-information or the full-information setting tested in this research. In other words, this study suggests that just announcing the anticipated program budget before offers are submitted can lead to more land enrolled, i.e., more offers closer to the landowners' opportunity costs, from the perspective of the buyer. While these experiments did not test all of the possible variations of the information set to identify the optimal amount of public information, they do highlight how too much public information allows participants to "game" the auction by strategically raising their offers above their true reservation values. Furthermore, too little public information can lead participants to inflate their offers because market competition is not fully realized and prices are not forced to be close to the true opportunity cost. Although a limitation of this study is that opportunity costs are treated as exogenous and market prices are not permitted to adjust over time, the design isolates market experience and suggests that auction efficiency may decrease as the size of the procurement budget increases and decreases over time as sellers learn through their experience to elevate their offers strategically to secure greater rent premiums. If one assumes there is no systematic joint impact of experience and endogenous opportunity costs—a question for future experiments—then the evidence suggests that these factors lead to the conservation program paying more than it would otherwise have to and thereby reducing the provision of ecosystem services given the limits of governmental resources. These results contribute to the ongoing research in the area of ecosystem markets and illustrate how experiments can be applied to address important issues related to land economics.

Acknowledgments

Funding for this research was provided by the U.S. Department of Agriculture's Economic Research Service (ID#58-6000-7-0089). The authors appreciate Marca Weinberg and Dan Hellerstein for their support and feedback on earlier versions of this research. We also appreciate the research assistance from Robin Dillaway, Jacob Fooks, Jubo Yan, and Shang Wu from the University of Delaware.

References

Arnold, M., J. M. Duke, and K. Messer. 2013. "Adverse selection in reverse auctions for environmental services" *Land Economics* 89(3): 387-412.

Banerjee, Simanti, Shortle, James S., and Kwasnica, Anthony M., 2011. "An iterative auction for spatially contiguous land management: An experimental analysis," 2011 Annual Meeting, July 24-26, 2011, Pittsburgh, Pennsylvania 103220, Agricultural and Applied Economics Association.

Bernard, J. C. 2005. Evidence of affiliation of values in a repeated trial auction experiment. *Applied Economics Letters* 12: 687–691.

Cason, T. N., and L. Gangadharan. 2004. Auction design for voluntary conservation programs. *American Journal of Agricultural Economics* 86(5): 1211–1217.

Cason, T., Gangadharan, L., and Duke, C. 2003. A laboratory study of auctions for reducing non-point source pollution. *Journal of Environmental Economics and Management* 46: 446–471.

CJC Consulting. 2004. "*Economic Evaluation of the Central Scotland Forest and Grampian Challenge Funds*." Final report for Forestry Commission Scotland. www.forestry.gov.uk/pdf/FCchallenge.pdf/$FILE/FCchallenge.pdf

Connor, J. D., J. Ward, and B. A. Bryan. 2008. Exploring the cost effectiveness of land conservation auctions and payment policies. *The Australian Journal of Agricultural and Resource Economics*. 52(3): 303–319.

Davis, D. D. and C. A. Holt. 1993. *Experimental economics*. Princeton University Press, Princeton, New Jersey.

Fooks, J. R. and K. D. Messer. 2012. "Maximizing conservation and in-kind cost share: Applying goal programming to forest protection" *Forest Economics*. 18: 207–217.

Fooks, J., K. D. Messer and J. M. Duke. 2012. *Dynamic entry, reverse auctions, and the purchase of environmental services*. Manuscript: University of Delaware.

Fischbacher U. 2007. "z-Tree: Zurich toolbox for ready-made economic experiments," *Experimental Economics* 10(2), 171–178.

Friedman, D. and S. Sunder. 1994. *Experimental methods: a primer for economists*, New York: Cambridge University Press.

Gole, C., M. Burton, K. Williams, H. Clayton, D. P. Faith, B. White, A. Huggett, and C. Margules. 2005. *Auction for landscape recovery: Final report*. WWF-Australia, Perth.

Hailu, A. and S. Schilizzi. 2004. Are auctions more efficient than fixed price schemes when offerers learn? *Australian Journal of Management* 29(2): 147–168.

Harrison, G.W. and J.A. List. 2004. "Field experiments." *Journal of Economic Literature* XLII: 1009–1055.

Hellerstein D. and N. Higgins. 2010. The effective use of limited information: Do offer maximums reduce procurement costs in asymmetric auctions? *Agricultural and Resource Economics Review* 39(2): 288–304.

Hong, H. and M. Shum. 2002. Increasing competition and the winner's curse: Evidence from procurement. *Review of Economic Studies* 69: 871–898.

Horowitz J. K., L. Lynch, and Andrew Stocking, 2009. Competition-based environmental policy: An analysis of farmland preservation in Maryland. Land Economics, 85(4) 555–575.

Kagel J. H. and A. E. Roth. 1995. *The handbook of experimental economics*, Princeton, New Jersey: Princeton University Press.

Kirwan, B., R. N. Lubowski, and M. J. Roberts. 2005. How cost-effective are land retirement auctions? Estimating the difference between payments and willingness to accept in the Conservation Reserve Program. *American Journal of Agricultural Economics* 87(5): 1239–1247.

Klemperer, P. 2002. What really matters in auction design. *Journal of Economic Perspectives* 16 (1): 169–189.

Latacz-Lohmann, U. and S. Schilizzi. 2005. *Auctions for conservation contracts: A review of the theoretical and emprical literature*. Report to the Scottish Executive Environment and Rural Affairs Department. Project No: UKL/001/05.

Latacz-Lohmann, U., and C. Van der Hamsvoort. 1997. Auctioning conservation contracts: A theoretical analysis and an application. *American Journal of Agricultural Economics* 79 (2): 407–418.

List, J. A. and J. F. Shogren. 1999. Price information and bidding behavior in repeated second-price auctions. *American Journal of Agricultural Economics* 81: 942–949.

Lusk, J. L., T. Feldkamp and T. C. Schroeder. 2004. Experimental auction procedure: Impact on valuation of quality differentiated goods. *American Journal of Agricultural Economics* 86: 389–405.

Lusk, J. L. and J. F. Shogren. 2007. *Experimental auctions: Methods and applications in economic and marketing research*. New York: Cambridge University Press.

McAfee, R. P. and J. McMillan. 1996. Analyzing the airwaves auction. *Journal of Economic Perspectives* 10 (1): 159–175.

Messer, K. D. and W. L. Allen. 2010. Applying optimization and the analytic hierarchy process to enhance agricultural preservation strategies in the State of Delaware. *Agricultural and Resource Economics Review* 39(3): 442–456.

Messer, K. D., J. M. Duke, and L. Lynch. 2012. *When does public information undermine the effectiveness of reverse auctions for the purchase of ecosystem services?* Manuscript: University of Delaware.

Rassenti, S. J., Smith, V. L., and Wilson, B. J. (2003). Discriminatory price auctions in electricity markets: Low volatility at the expense of high price levels. *Journal of Regulatory Economics*, 23(2): 109–123.

Rolfe, J., Windle, J., and McCosker, J. 2009 Testing and implementing the use of multiple offering rounds in conservation auctions: a case study application. *Canadian Journal of Agricultural Economics* 57: 287–303.

Schilizzi, S. and U. Latacz-Lohmann. 2007. Assessing the performance of conservation auctions: an experimental study. *Land Economics* 83: 497–515.

Shogren, J. F. 2004. Incentive mechanism testbeds: Discussion. *American Journal of Agricultural Economics*. 86(2004): 1218–1219.

Smith, R. B. W. 1995. The conservation reserve program as a least-cost land retirement mechanism. *American Journal of Agricultural Economics* 77: (1995) 93–105.

Stoneham, G., V. Chaudri, A. Ha, and L. Strappazon. 2003. "Auctions for conservation contracts: An empirical examination of Victoria's bushtender trial." *Australian Journal of Agricultural and Resource Economics* 47 (4): 477–500.

United Stated Department of Agriculture. 2006. Conservation reserve programs: Largest Conservation Partnership on Private Land. Farm Service Agency. Accessed on January 17, 2012. http://www.fsa.usda.gov/Internet/FSA_File/crp20trifold.pdf

United Stated Department of Agriculture. 2011. CRP Enrollment as of September 2011 and October 2011 Rental Payments. Accessed January 17, 2012. www.fsa.usda.gov/Internet/FSA_File/apportstate091311.pdf

Vickrey, W. 1961. "Counterspeculation, auctions and competitive sealed tenders." *Journal of Finance* 16: 8–37.

Vossler, C. A., T. D. Mount, R. Thomas, and R. Zimmerman. 2009. An experimental investigation of soft price caps in uniform price auction markets for wholesale electricity. *Journal of Regulatory Economics* 36(1): 44–59.

Wu, J., and B. Babcock. Contract design for the purchase of environmental goods from agriculture. *American Journal of Agricultural Economics* 78 (1996) 935–945.

APPENDIX

A1. EXPERIMENT INSTRUCTIONS

Welcome to this experiment in the economics of decision making. In the course of the experiment, you will have opportunities to earn money. Any money earned is yours to keep. Therefore, please read these instructions carefully. Please do not communicate with other participants during the experiment.

In this experiment, you will participate in a series of market trading **rounds**. You and all of the other participants in the room will assume the role of landowners and you will be given the opportunity to sell a parcel of land. The administrator will be the buyer. In each round, you will need to decide whether you want to keep your parcel or try to sell it. If you decide to try to sell it, you will also need to decide the offer price for your parcel.

Below is a hypothetical example (see Figure 19.2), where three rounds have been completed and the fourth round is just about to begin. On your computer screen, you will note a variety of important information. Your parcel is assigned an Ownership Return per acre, which is the amount of money that will be added to your profit if the parcel is not sold in that round. The size of your parcel is 100 acres. In this hypothetical example, the ownership return for your parcel in the first round is $3000 per acre.

In general, your ownership returns may not be the same as those of other sellers and will change throughout the experiment. As shown in Figure 19.3, since the possible ownership returns were randomly determined from a uniform distribution that has a minimum value of $2000 per acre and a maximum value of $8000 per acre, the average ownership return can be expected to be $5000 per acre. Your ownership returns have been determined by random prior to the start of the experiment and you will know your ownership return at the start of each round.

	Round 1	*Round 2*	*Round 3*	*Round 4*
Ownership Return per acre:	$ 3,000	$ 6,000	$ 4,000	$ 5,000
Offer Price per acre:	$ 5,000	$ 8,000	$ -	$ -
Submission Cost per acre:	$ 20	$ 20	$ -	$ -
Number of Acres:	100	100	100	
Sold:	Yes	No	No	
	Submit	Submit	Submit	Submit
	Update	Update	Update	Update
Total Profit:	$ 498,000	$ 598,000	$ 400,000	$ -

FIGURE 19.2 Experimental interface for participants (screen shot).

FIGURE 19.3 Distribution of ownership return.

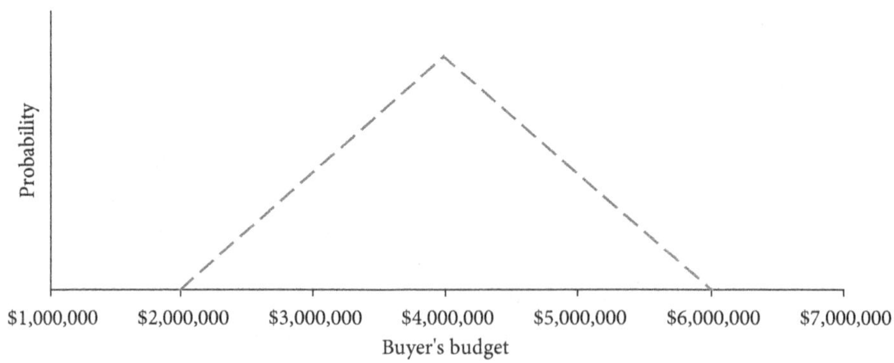

FIGURE 19.4 Distribution of budgets.

The buyer's budget will be announced before the start of each round. Like with the ownership returns, the budgets were randomly determined before the start of the experiment. The budgets were randomly determined from a triangle distribution that has a minimum value of $2 million, an average value of $4 million, and a maximum value of $6 million. As shown in Figure 19.4, the most likely budget will be $4 million. Values closer to $4 million are more likely than values further away from $4 million.

In each round, you must decide whether you want to sell your parcel and, if so, at what price you are willing to sell it. You will pay a submission cost of $20 per acre if you decide to submit an offer for your parcel. You can submit your offer price confidentially by entering it into the yellow box in your spreadsheet. Then, hit "Enter" on your keyboard, and click on the "Submit" button. In this example for Round 1, the seller submitted an offer price of $5000. If you elect not to submit an offer, such as in Round 3, just leave the yellow box blank and click the "Submit" button. In this case, you do not pay the submission cost.

After everyone has submitted their decision, the administrator will purchase as many parcels as possible starting from the lowest offer price and moving up until the available budget for that round is exhausted. For example, imagine that current round budget is $300 and eight offer prices were submitted—ranked from lowest to highest: [Offer Prices: $30, $40, $50, $60, $70, $80, $90, $100].

Parcels are purchased in order (from left to right) until the buyer does not have enough money to purchase another parcel. In the example, the five lowest offer prices ($30 + $40 + $50 + $60 + $70) are purchased for a total of $250. None of the last three offers are purchased, since even the lowest non-accepted offer of $80 would bring the total cost to $330 ($250 + $80) and therefore be higher than the buyer's budget.

A2. Determination of Profits

After all offer prices have been received, the auctioneer will determine which parcels were purchased. You will then click on the "Update" button. There are three possible profit scenarios:

1) Successful sellers will receive a price equal to their offer, and thus, their profits will be their offer price for that parcel minus the submission cost.
2) Participants that submit an offer for a parcel which is too high for the available budget will not receive their offer price, but instead their profits will be their ownership return for that parcel minus the submission cost.
3) Profits for participants who do not submit an offer for a parcel will be their ownership return for that parcel.

In Round 1 of the example below (see Figure 19.5), the participant earned a total profit of $498,000 by successfully selling the parcel for $5000 per acre and paying the submission cost of $20 per acre. In round 2, the participant earned $598,000 as they received their ownership return of $6000, acre when they did not successfully sell their unit, but still had to pay the submission cost of $20 per acre. Finally, in Round 3, the participant would earn $400,000 by receiving the ownership return of $4000 per acre and not paying the submission cost.

Your computer will calculate your profits for each parcel in each round and will keep track of your cumulative earnings. An exchange rate of 1,200,000 to 1 will be used to converts your earnings from experimental dollars to dollars. For example, if you earn 24,000,000 experimental dollars will have earned $20 US to take home today.

A3. Market Information

In addition to the information regarding your ownership returns and whether you sold your parcels, you will receive information regarding the market (as seen in the example) when you click on the "Update" button after each round:

		Round 1	Round 2	Round 3	Round 4
	Ownership Return per acre:	$ 3,000	$ 6,000	$ 4,000	$ 5,000
	Offer Price per acre:	$ 5,000	$ 8,000	$ -	$ -
	Submission Cost per acre:	$ 20	$ 20	$ -	$ -
	Number of Acres:	100	100	100	
	Sold:	Yes	No	No	
		Submit	Submit	Submit	Submit
		Update	Update	Update	Update
	Total Profit:	$ 498,000	$ 598,000	$ 400,000	$ -
	Next Round's Budget:	$ 2,200,000	$ 5,500,000	$ 6,000,000	
	This Round's Budget:	$ 2,800,000	$ 2,200,000	$ 5,500,000	
Part A (Profit):	Number of Offers Received:	8	6	9	
$ 1,496,000	Lowest Successful Offer:	$ 2,500	$ 2,000	$ 2,000	
	Highest Successful Offer:	$ 7,000	$ 5,500	$ 5,500	
Exchange Rate:	Average Successful Offer:	$ 5,000	$ 3,500	$ 3,500	
1,400,000	Seller ID Numbers:	1	2	1	
		2	4	2	
Part A (US$):		5	6	3	
$ 1.07		9	8	6	
		10		9	
				10	

FIGURE 19.5 Experimental interface for participants with information (screen shot).

Before each round, the administrator will announce:

- The buyer's budget for that round.

After each round, the administrator will announce:

- The number of offers submitted to the market,
- The price of the lowest successful offer,
- The price of the highest successful offer,
- The price of the average successful offer, and
- The computer identification numbers of participants that successfully sold their parcels.

PART IV

THE ECONOMICS OF LAND USE LAW AND POLICY

CHAPTER 20

OPEN SPACE PRESERVATION

Direct Controls and Fiscal Incentives

EKATERINA GNEDENKO AND DENNIS HEFFLEY

THE forces of urbanization and the quest for open space reflect a basic economic tradeoff. The benefits of agglomeration, communication, and exchange are well understood and have been explored in depth by Mills (1967), Fujita, Krugman, and Venables (1999), Glaeser (2008), and many other economists, geographers, planners, and sociologists. Yet, although humans seem willing to endure the negative aspects of crowded living to reap the economic and social benefits of cities, they also show a need, or at least a longing, for more "elbowroom."

Open space may include public lands such as parks, recreation areas, or national forests, as well as privately owned parcels: farms, golf courses, or even large residential lots. This "private open space" may limit public access yet still offer amenity benefits to owners and neighbors (Cheshire and Sheppard 2002). In this sense, private open space competes with public open space, both because it, too, provides externalities, but also because it reduces land available for public open space.

Open space preservation efforts are not new, but they have recently gained momentum, especially at the nonfederal level, where many states, counties, and towns actively seek to protect or expand open space. The popularity of such initiatives has prompted a large body of theoretical and applied research. Beyond reviewing some of the studies and the origins, rationale, and goals of preservation efforts, we offer a simple but adaptable model that highlights the need to consider the long-run effects of such programs. To illustrate the point, we focus on the use of state aid to local governments to alleviate fiscal pressure and facilitate open space zoning. We show, however, that well-intended policies can have unintended results when long-run adjustments occur in household behavior and local fiscal and zoning policies—a lesson that applies to many public efforts to shape land market outcomes.

1. Open Space Benefits and Preservation Programs

1.1 Origins and Directions

Despite the mixed success of past preservation efforts, there has been a visible upsurge in public desire to preserve open space. Our analysis focuses on the notion of an optimal amount of local open space and the role of intergovernmental revenue, particularly state aid to municipalities, as a potential way to encourage preservation. The analysis is especially relevant for the northeastern United States, where much of the land is privately owned, subject to local land use controls, "and pressures to develop the remaining rural land for residential and other uses are among the strongest in the country" (Parks and Schorr 1997, 85), but the questions and issues we address apply elsewhere as well.

Interest in open space is widespread and well established. Ancient societies understood the value of reserving areas for agriculture, public use, and even traditional ceremonies. Elizabeth I, in 1580, banned new construction within several miles of central London (Evans 1999), and, in a similar display of royal preference for more room (or perhaps a more secure buffer zone), picturesque landscapes and parks surrounded 17th-century Versailles and the 18th-century Pavlovsk Palace. But the demand for open space also has strong democratic roots: the US federal government first attempted to secure parklands for the nation's capital in 1791, Congress established Yellowstone National Park in 1872, and Cape Hatteras was designated the first National Seashore in 1937. In 1988, the governors of five New England states formally recognized open space as a key quality-of-life indicator and the foundation of a multibillion dollar tourist industry. Such acknowledgments of the economic and social benefits of open space, echoed more recently by many public officials, have signaled state and local efforts to preserve low-density land use patterns.

The recent *America's Great Outdoors* report (America's Great Outdoors [AGO] Initiative 2011), prepared by the US Departments of Interior and Agriculture and the Environmental Protection Agency, calls for support of a conservation agenda and emphasizes the joint efforts of federal, state, and local governments, but, for some observers, this agenda is long overdue. More than two decades ago, Anas (1988, 159) expressed concern that "the American wilderness within the public lands has shrunk to 2% of its original size, becoming a scarce, irreplaceable resource in need of efficient marginal pricing." Hollis and Fulton (2002, 5) similarly note that open space protection has lagged despite "the long list of federal policies that have promoted conservation of open space... [such as] the Land and Water Conservation Fund, the Endangered Species Act, the Clean Water and Safe Drinking Water Acts, the North American Wetland Conservation Act, and the National Environmental Policy Act." They attribute this ineffectiveness to the fact that: "In many cases, ... open space protection has been secondary to the environmental goals of these programs. Partly for this reason, most strategies to use open space to consciously shape metropolitan form have been initiated by states or localities."

Decentralization of land use policy and open space preservation has advantages and drawbacks. Given the range of geographic conditions, settlement patterns, and socioeconomic mix across states, counties, and municipalities, it is unlikely that a national "one-size-fits-all" approach would serve any state or community very well. Experimentation and a localized or "tailored" approach have some obvious advantages, allowing a better fit between individual preferences and the provision of open space, as described by Tiebout (1956) for local public goods in general. But Tiebout efficiency requires mobility—ample opportunities for households to seek out, identify, and occupy communities that best fit their preferences for open space, other local public goods, and taxes. Such "frictionless" conditions are more likely to prevail in the long run, when transaction costs hamper mobility less.

Decentralized provision of open space expands the menu of options and caters to local tastes, but it raises other problems, and some researchers still see a vital role for higher level or cooperative multilevel programs (Bates and Santerre 2001). One challenge in analyzing subnational preservation efforts is that "every state has its own unique governmental structure with varying degrees of involvement in parks, recreation, and conservation" (Betz and Cordell 1998, 9). Uncoordinated local initiatives also may face unfavorable spillovers and free-rider problems between jurisdictions (Loomis, 2000). Yet federal programs have their own shortcomings. In theory, they should provide a more consistent approach to preservation, but special interest legislation (Holcomber and Staley 2001) and budget fluctuations produce cross-sectional and intertemporal differences in federal efforts that may need to be "smoothed" or complemented by state and local programs.

This mixed approach may be messy, but it has strong supporters. Ostrom (2010) sees a need for "polycentric" governance systems to address public good and common pool resource problems, but she also stresses the importance of nongovernmental organizations and individuals in achieving successful outcomes. However, coordination is not easily achieved when governments and constituents are able to react to policy changes. Stavins (2011, 82) stresses the importance of formally considering responses to proposed policies, noting that although economic theory "has made major contributions to our understanding of commons problems and the development of prudent public policies,... government policies that have not accounted for economic responses have been excessively costly, often ineffective, and sometimes counterproductive."

McGonagle and Swallow (2005, 477) share this concern, noting that: "States and municipalities have committed over $24 billion in bond issues for land conservation in recent years, yet the structure of the land conservation industry and markets is poorly understood." Nelson (1998, 34) calls for systematic evaluation of farmland retention policies since "we actually do not know what the metropolitan regional landscape would be in the absence of externalities and market failure. Lacking this basic understanding, there is no way in which to compare farmland preservation techniques because there is no benchmark with which to compare them." Poe (1999, 589) further argues that land use policies need to shift from pure resource development to a cohesive land use/land preservation strategy that "may also require 'top-level' efforts to coordinate agency actions." Toward this end, Duke and Lynch (2006) offer a useful taxonomy and comparison of 28 farmland retention techniques, falling into four major categories: regulatory, incentive-based, governmental-participatory, and hybrid.

1.2 Hands Off or Hands On?

Support for preservation may be growing but is not universal, and even those who value open space may not see government intervention as essential. Some researchers suggest that market forces may suffice (Thorsnes and Simons 1999; Holcomber and Staley 2001; McConnell et al. 2003). Many years ago, Muth (1961) showed that even in the face of urban population and income growth, rural land conversion will be contained around urban areas that rely on local agricultural production, but not necessarily around those dependent on national food markets. As the urban population expands or income grows, cities supplied with food from local sources must bid land away from farmers, but the increase in demand for food also makes farmland more valuable, thus slowing the conversion of rural land to housing. More recently, Holcomber and Staley (2001, 3, 9) argue that market-oriented approaches tend to maximize the value of property and often address the loss of open space better than do zoning or other regulatory devices that may fall prey to special interests or compromise popular goals.

On the other hand, many researchers see a proper, if limited, role for government. Ladd (1980) cites several reasons for inefficient land use and underprovision of open space, including its public good attributes and external benefits, irreversibility of the development process, and "fewer benefits [from local public services] per dollar of market valuation to owners of agricultural or open space land than to other types of landowners." She concludes that: "some form of government action might be desirable to increase agricultural or open space land" (19). Even Gardner (1977), who expresses concerns about the use of "extra-market means" to preserve farmland (1028), sees that in "the case where market failure is most apparent—the creation of open space and environmental amenities... there may be some justification for social action to remedy this market failure" (1031). Wu and Irwin (2008, 233) note that private markets inefficiently convert too much undeveloped land to residential (and other) uses because they "fail to account for the environmental costs of land development, which include not only the standard environmental damages from pollution, but also a loss of flexibility in adjusting the future path of pollution due to the irreversibility of development."

Fundamental forces like population growth and rising incomes, which increase demands for residential and commercial land, are the major causes of open space loss and cannot be readily contained or avoided. Market failures associated with unfettered land development, including undervaluation of open-space amenities, unpriced traffic congestion, and underpriced infrastructure costs of new development, must be remedied by appropriate government policies (Brueckner 2000; Anas and Rhee 2006; Brueckner and

Helsley 2011). Plantinga and Ahn (2002, 128) suggest that: "One role of land-use policies is to narrow the divergence between privately and socially optimal land allocations by modifying the economic incentives faced by private landowners." McGuire and Sjoquist (2003, 8) reiterate the externality rationale for preservation by noting that "open space on the fringe of urban areas may have value beyond its private value."

Even opponents of publicly subsidized preservation programs endorse occasional intervention. Bae (2007, 39) believes that although "the macro argument is unconvincing, . . . at the micro (regional) level there may be instances where a plausible case for farmland preservation can be made." But microlevel land use policy also has its critics. Hollis and Fulton (2002, 46) claim that the United States' "decentralized system tends to encourage reactive or ad hoc open space protection at the local level and, in many cases, large-scale acquisitions based on different strategic objectives." They claim that local preservation is fragmented, and neither state nor local programs are well documented, making interjurisdictional comparisons difficult.

1.3 Preservation Strategies

Preservation strategies vary in their locus of control—national, state, local, or mixed—and their reliance on market-oriented versus nonmarket approaches. Other than outright public purchase of land, zoning is perhaps the most direct form of intervention in land markets to affect open space. In this regard, it is important to distinguish between *land use* zoning (or allowable-use zoning) and *density* zoning restrictions. Land use zoning essentially "carves up" an area into zones where certain activities, or combinations of activities, are permitted: residential, commercial, industrial, agriculture, mixed-use, and the like. Mixed-use zoning has enjoyed a US revival, but mixed uses often conflict with land use zoning objectives: separating "incompatible" uses to avoid negative externalities, restricting the local supply of certain types of land, and assigning particular activities to the "most suitable" sites.

If land use zoning is the planner's "macro" policy instrument, density zoning is the "micro" tool used to fine-tune land use. Land within a residential zone can be developed in many ways, but density zoning ordinances often set lower bounds on lot size, floor space, and set-back distances from roads and neighboring properties, as well as upper bounds on height and lot coverage. These provisions, individually or jointly, restrict development density and thus tend to (imprecisely) limit population, especially if constraints are binding.

With the two types of zoning, local authorities can preserve or even expand open space, primarily by using land use zoning to protect or enlarge such areas (which, absent annexation of unincorporated areas, will limit the size of the development zone) or by relaxing density zoning to increase the "holding capacity" of the development zone and thereby channel activity away from threatened areas. In this way, allowing smaller building lots, easing height limits, or permitting multifamily units within a residential zone can ease the pressure on open space.

Direct agricultural zoning prevents conversion of land to other uses, but it is a blunt instrument that may benefit the broader public at farmers' expense. Removing the right to develop farmland without compensating the owner may be difficult to justify. This has fostered "voluntary" approaches, including outright land purchase, purchase of development rights (PDR), and transferable development rights (TDR) programs.

Fee-simple public purchase of farmland or open space gives the fullest control of land use and ensures (barring public resale) long-term protection, but it also saddles the government with an asset that requires further maintenance or operating expenditures. Land donations to communities or private land trusts avoid the acquisition costs, but not the ongoing outlays, unless there are specific provisions made for those in the gift. Some of these maintenance costs to governments or land trusts can be reduced, or at least shifted, by compensating landowners to forego development, but development rights programs also have limitations.

PDR programs use public funds to purchase separable development rights from landowners who, if they accept the offer, agree to forego development in perpetuity or for a specific period. Here, since there is no well-developed market to price the development rights, the common problem is how to determine "fair" compensation: high enough to secure the rights, but not so high as to overpay landowners, offend taxpayers, and jeopardize the program. Wolfram (1981) also warns that costs of implementing and administering a PDR program may be too high to become an efficient means of providing open space. Analyzing survey opinion toward farmland preservation, Foltz and Larson (2002, 15) conclude that "because the public supports low cost PDR programs uniformly across geographic and socioeconomic boundaries, farmland preservation is an issue perhaps best engaged at the state rather than a local level." Lopez, Shah, and Altobello (1994, 61) compare the effects of, and farmland owners' support for, PDR and agricultural zoning programs and conclude that PDRs "can be effective in attaining a socially optimal allocation of land." Liu and Lynch (2011) find that such programs are effective in reducing the rate of farmland loss, but Nickerson and Hellerstein (2003) note that popularity of these programs with farmers has led to oversubscription and queuing. More public funding would ease the problem, but such programs must compete with other important public services.

TDR programs seek to address this chronic "underfunding" of public open space programs by creating a private demand for the development rights. Costonis (1973, 1975) proposed this approach to preserve historic buildings in Chicago, but the concept is readily applied to open space preservation (Barrows and Prenguber 1975; Field and Conrad 1975; Mills 1980; Thorsnes and Simons 1999). Rather than being paid by government, landowners in the "preservation area" who agree to forego development are issued TDRs, which can be sold for use in some "development area" to marginally increase development density (e.g., permission to build on a somewhat smaller lot than normal zoning would permit). Carpenter and Heffley (1982) show that getting a TDR market to form and behave as intended may not be trivial, possibly explaining why only about 140, mostly local, TDR programs exist throughout the United States (Walls and McConnell 2007, 8).

1.4 Effects of Preservation Policies on Land Values

Effects of preservation policies on the price of open space depend on the nature and permanence of the policy, as well as on the total area of the target region (Irwin 2002; Geoghegan et al. 2003). Some programs seek to preserve farmland by enhancing the income that can be derived from using, or even just holding, farmland. Just and Miranowski (1993) observe a positive capitalization effect of government agricultural support payments on farmland values for three states, whereas Weersink et al. (1999) find the same for Ontario, Canada. Wu and Lin (2010, 2) note that "the conventional wisdom is that because the supply of agricultural land is highly inelastic, government payments are largely capitalized in farmland values." Using 1997 county-level data, they show that the major US conservation program, the Conservation Reserve Program (CRP), "has a positive and statistically significant effect on farmland values in all regions" (11).

But if a program does more than simply augment the income of farmers or landowners, if it restricts actual or potential use of the land without sufficient compensation, the price impact is more typically negative, although not always significant; see, for example, Hascic and Wu (2012). Nickerson and Lynch (2001, 341) use hedonic methods to analyze Maryland's development restrictions, imposed by permanent easement acquisition, to show that "[a]lthough preserved parcels' actual land values are lower, the effect of the restrictions is not statistically significant." Using a similar approach to study a moratorium on urban development of agricultural land near Toronto, Deaton and Vyn (2010, 954) find that "[f]armland within the Greenbelt, and in close proximity to the Greater Toronto Area (GTA), experienced a statistically significant decline in property values. More specifically, the negative effect occurs mainly at the urban–rural boundary: i.e., farmland within 5 km of the GTA." Henneberry and Barrows (1990) find that exclusive agricultural zoning impacts farm values in even more complex ways that depend on property characteristics, whereas Hascic and Wu (2012) find evidence of land value impacts of zoning both inside and outside the zoned areas. They also note that "a zoning regulation may affect the value of a parcel both directly by restricting its use and indirectly by affecting land use in its surrounding areas" (199).

Adverse effects of restrictions on the price of open space itself may be offset by positive capitalization of the amenity effects on other properties (Correll et al. 1978; Katz and Rosen 1987; Do and Grudnitski 1995; Geoghegan et al. 1997; Mahan et al. 2000; Lutzenhiser and Netusil 2001; Shultz and King 2001; Smith et al. 2002; Geoghegan et al. 2003; Earnhart 2006; Wu and Lin 2010). This intralocal spillover may encourage communities to preserve open space to raise property values and reap tax benefits, but sluggish property markets may limit the approach. Geoghegan, Lynch, and Bucholtz (2003) offer empirical evidence that certain counties in Maryland show this capacity to self-finance preservation from the increase in property tax base due to the preserved open space. Weigher and Zerbst (1973) even cite examples where profit-seeking landowners offer part of their land for open space to enhance the overall value of their residential development. Bolitzer and Netusil (2000, 193) note that the "degree of open space self-financing... depends on many factors including the size of the open space, the number of homes in proximity to the open space, open-space amenities, and the local property tax structure." Jiang and Swallow (2006) use simulations to show that financing open space via amenity-induced property tax increments may be more feasible if open space is evenly distributed to benefit more homes, although presumably the amenities also can be spread "too thin." This tradeoff suggests the existence of an optimal spatial pattern of open space, a challenging topic that warrants more research. Finally, adding a healthy touch of reality to the lure of "self-financing" open space schemes, Wu, Xu, and Alig (2012) show that when preservation costs must be covered by property taxes, both higher tax rates and a lower level of public services may reduce property values.

2. A Model of Local Zoning for Open Space

2.1 Motivation

Many states have initiated preservation programs, ranging from outright land purchase and PDR programs to market-oriented TDR schemes that use private rather than public funds to compensate landowners who forego development. However, given the paucity of working TDR programs, state-level preservation efforts generally rely heavily on the public purse to acquire land or stockpile development rights.

Local governments also seek to preserve open space, typically via land use controls, but researchers have noted that fragmented local efforts can lead to suboptimal levels of open space (Hollis and Fulton 2002) and inefficient leapfrog development patterns (Wu and Plantinga 2003). Given the public good attributes and external benefits of open space, the state might seem to be the right level of government to provide this "transboundary public good" (Loomis 2000), but, in the United States, a common public-power split often impedes or distorts open space preservation.

With numerous tax instruments at their disposal (income, sales, excise, corporate, estate, and others), states can potentially finance preservation efforts more readily than localities, which rely heavily on property taxes and are often precluded from levying other taxes. In many states, though, zoning and other land use control powers have been legislatively ceded to counties, cities, or towns. Consequently, even where states could (in good economic times) devote resources to preservation, they may lack the legal authority or political will to actively move local landowners toward broad public goals.

Local governments, on the other hand, may be able to facilitate open space preservation through zoning changes, but if this requires extra spending or limits local revenue by thwarting economic development, necessary policy changes also may fail to occur at the local level. In sum, local governments often wield the direct instruments of land use control but lack the necessary resources, especially if landowners must be compensated to forego development; state governments, by contrast, may have the tax powers to finance preservation but often have yielded land use control powers to counties or towns. This awkward alignment of land use authority and fiscal powers may explain why public surveys point to a significant unmet demand, often expressed as a strong willingness to pay for various types of open space (Bergstrom et al. 1985; Kline and Wichelns 1994; Duke and Ilvento 2004; Gnedenko 2009). The strength of this demand for conservation, however, also depends on the policy mechanism or instrument (Johnston and Duke 2007).

The separation or imbalance of fiscal and zoning powers has led to suggestions that increased state aid to communities be used to encourage local governments to zone more land for open space. Ladd (1980) and Gottlieb (2006) discuss various aspects of such intergovernmental transfers, whereas Gnedenko (2009) offers an analytical framework for examining the optimal mix of open space and development and its response to state aid. On the surface, the argument for more state aid seems straightforward: it should reduce pressure for communities to accommodate new development as a necessary way to finance cash-starved schools and other essential public services. Consequently, this injection of revenue ought to make preservation economically feasible and politically more palatable for local governments.

It sounds simple enough, but the issue is more complex. More state aid likely affects the local government's fiscal decisions, allowing it to boost spending and/or lower its property tax rate while maintaining a balanced budget. Yet, if anything, such adjustments would make the community more attractive for households and firms, and this added development pressure could make it more, not less, difficult to preserve open space via land use (or allowable-use) zoning. Analysis of this unintended effect of state aid on local open space requires a model that fully endogenizes local tax, spending, and land use zoning decisions, as well as the behavior of households.

In this section we describe an extended open-city model that has these elements and allows us to consider the long-run effects of more state aid on a community's land use zoning (open-space vs. residential development) and fiscal mix (property tax rate and public spending), household consumption patterns (lot-size, structure, and other goods), land prices, aggregate land value, and population size. The model indicates that more state aid will not always promote additional open space, as illustrated by simulations of a calibrated version of the model and further supported by empirical analysis of town-level panel data for Connecticut.

2.2 Households

The representative household, with annual income y, selects a lot-size (x), an amount of structure or "floorspace" (k), and a numeraire consumption good (g), but it also derives utility (U) from local public expenditures (G) and local open space (X_0). Exogenous community features, such as its location relative to regional job centers or proximity to an important amenity, also affect household utility, but this vector of characteristics (C) can be deferred to the empirical analysis. Local open space is privately owned, but the amount within the community's bounded land area (L) is determined by the local government's land use zoning mix (X_o, L–X_o). X_o and G, as well as the local property tax rate (T), are exogenous to the household but endogenous within the extended model of government choice.

The household sees the local policy mix (X_o,G,T) and chooses (x, k, g) to maximize $U(x, k, g; G, X_o)$, subject to its budget constraint: $(1-a)y = (1 + T)(px + rk) + (1 + s)g$, where p and r are annual rental prices of residential land and structure, respectively; a is the average combined (state plus federal) income tax rate; T is the effective local property tax rate (expressed as a fraction of the annual rental value of land and structure); and s is the state sales tax rate on nonhousing consumption. We include income and sales tax parameters (a and s) for realism and better calibration of the model, rather than any attempt to fully capture higher level policy making, but these parameters do offer a link to other levels of government that could be exploited in a multilevel framework.

The household's constrained choice problem yields general-form demands for lot-size, structure, and other goods:

$$x^*(y,p,r,a,s,T,G,X_o), k^*(y,p,r,a,s,T,G,X_o), g^*(y,p,r,a,s,T,G,X_o), \quad (1)$$

and the corresponding indirect utility function gives the maximum attainable utility for a given set of parameters:

$$U^*(y,p,r,a,s,T,G,X_o). \quad (2)$$

If the typical household with income y can achieve a level of utility U_o in the "outside world" and is fully mobile in the long-run, and if the rental price (r) of structure is exogenously determined in a regional or national market, the endogenous price (p) of local developable land must adjust to ensure the local household can do just as well, or:

$$U^*(y,p,r,a,s,T,G,X_o) - U_o = 0. \quad (3)$$

Solving (3) implicitly for p gives the local equilibrium price of land (p^e):

$$p^e(y,r,a,s,T,G,X_0,U_o). \quad (4)$$

Substituting p^e back into the earlier demand for land (x^*) gives the equilibrium lot-size (x^e), or:

$$x^e(y,r,a,s,T,G,X_o,U_o), \quad (5)$$

and, if the community has zoned X_0 acres of its total land area (L) for open space and the remaining L-X_0 acres for residential use, land market clearance implies that the equilibrium number of households (n^e) is:

$$n^e = (L - X_0) / x^e, \tag{6}$$

where x^e is the expression in (5).

Some discussion of the asymmetric treatment of the prices of land and structure is needed. Many urban models merge the two inputs by assuming that households consume a composite good described as "housing services," and, in urban spatial equilibrium versions of such models, the price of housing services is endogenous and declines with distance from the urban center to compensate for commuting costs. Because we focus on the allocation of a town's land to residential use and open space, we see some advantage in separating land and structure. This, in turn, raises the question of how the price of each gets determined.

Casual observation and empirical evidence support the notion that land prices are more endogenous and subject to local variation than the price of structure. For example, even in a small state like Connecticut, it is difficult to explain the large variation in home prices across different towns in terms of building cost differences. Materials and labor costs differ, but usually not enough to account for the large differences in home prices between (or even within) towns. Land prices, on the other hand, are quite sensitive to location-specific attributes, including fiscal disparities and neighborhood effects. We think this approach—an endogenous price of land that serves as the open-city adjustment mechanism, coupled with an exogenous price of structure—works best within this model, but for an alternative approach, see Wu and Plantinga (2003), where housing prices are derived as a function of land prices.

For simplicity, we ignore commercial land use in this model, but for a similar model that examines the long-run effects of residential versus commercial zoning (but ignores open space), see Heffley and Hewitt (1988). Strong and Walsh (2008) offer a model of the local housing market that focuses on the private provision of open space by developers when there exist spatial spillovers, but abstracts from the local government's role in determining public open space and the fiscal mix.

2.3 Local Government

Households may regard local zoning and fiscal policies (X_o, G, T) as given, but, ultimately, we should allow these policies to respond to exogenous events, such as a change in state aid. In the "open-city" environment, where households may enter or exit the community, local officials can do little to permanently affect utility. Helpman and Pines (1977), Brueckner (1979, 1982, 1983), Yinger (1982), Ross and Yinger (1999), Scotchmer (2002), and many others have pointed out that this fluid environment may drive local authorities to maximize the value of local land, the fixed resource whose market price can be influenced by local zoning, spending, and tax policies. Casual observation of officials' concern about the impact of budget decisions and zoning changes (or variances) on local property values—their primary tax base as well as a common source of voter complaints—reinforces the validity of the "open-city" assumption of land value maximization as the driving force of local policy making. Fischel (1990) also points to the potential importance of aggregate land values in assessing the efficiency of zoning.

But our focus here is open space preservation. Why would a local government seeking to maximize aggregate land value ever zone *any* land for open space? Would not it be optimal to just let the market operate and freely determine the amount of open space by letting competition allocate land to its "highest and best use"? In a geographically unconstrained world, perhaps so, but when total area of the jurisdiction is fixed, it is easy to show why land use zoning is rational and why it is normally optimal to zone some land for open space, even if it has no amenity value for other residents. If spillovers do exist, the case for open space is simply strengthened.

To illustrate this point, before specifying a fuller model of local government behavior, suppose the Walrasian demands for developable land (X) and open space (X_o), respectively, are $p(X)$ and $m(X_o)$, where $p_X < 0$ and $m_{Xo} > 0$. Maximization of aggregate land value $[V(X, X_o) = p(X)X + m(X_o)X_o]$ in a community where land area (L) is fixed requires equality of the marginal value functions $[p(X) + Xp_X = m(X_o) + X_o m_{Xo}]$ and satisfaction of the land constraint ($L = X + X_o$). As shown in Figure 20.1, where demands and associated marginal value functions for the two land types are shown "face-to-face" to reflect the land constraint, V is *not* maximized by simply allowing the market to freely equate prices of the two land types. Maximization of $V(X, X_o)$ requires zoning X^* acres of land for development and $X_o^* = L\text{-}X^*$ acres of land for open space, where the marginal value functions intersect (point A). In most cases, this marginal condition implies *unequal* prices, $p(X^*) \neq m(X_o^*)$, as shown by points B and C.

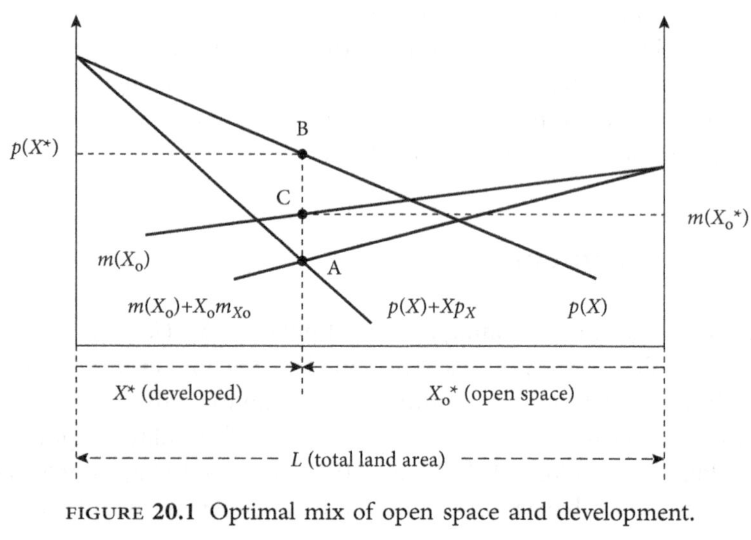

FIGURE 20.1 Optimal mix of open space and development.

This simple figure points to the economic value of having some open space in a community, even if it confers no external benefits to occupants of the developed area. Open space can increase aggregate land value within the bounded community by simply limiting the amount (and raising the price) of developable land. Note that even if $m(X_o)$ lies everywhere below $p(X)$ in Figure 20.1, X^* may still be less than L, providing an economic rationale for some open space (i.e., $X_o^* > 0$). Gnedenko (2009, 15) discusses this case in greater detail.

Alternatively, one can view land use zoning as a way to differentiate land and thereby generate higher land rents, in much the same way that product differentiation and unequal prices allow a seller to increase revenues. Density zoning instruments (minimum lot-size, minimum floor-area requirements, height limits, coverage and set-back restrictions, etc.) further expand the local government's capacity to differentiate land and boost aggregate rents. White (1975), Hamilton (1975, 1978), Grieson and White (1981), Miceli (1992*a*, 1992*b*), and others have seen zoning as the exercise of monopoly power by local governments. Empirical studies by Thorson (1996), Rose (1989), and Bates (1993) support this notion. Fischel (1978, 1980, 1985) stresses a property rights approach, whereas Wallace (1988) empirically tests the hypothesis that zoning policies simply tend to "follow the market." Yet, regardless of motive, zoning does not permanently protect open space; it "fails to establish a market price for the externality" (Wolfram 1981, 402) and may cause "development to be inefficiently dispersed" (Pollakowski and Wachter 1990, 324).

The simple view of open space as a way to differentiate local land and secure monopoly rents from development is obviously too narrow. Open space (X_o) may further boost local land values if it generates external benefits that enhance the market price of developed land; that is, if $p(X, X_o)$, where $p_X < 0$ and $p_{Xo} > 0$. Our extended open-city model, which incorporates the long-run behavior of households outlined earlier, not only allows for this externality effect, but also for the potential effects of endogenous local spending (G) and tax rate (T) decisions on the price of developable land ($p_G > 0, p_T < 0$).

The open-city model in Section 2.2 describes the equilibrium behavior of a representative household and yields an expression (4) for the equilibrium price of developed land. Households were assumed to view local public policies as given, but now we focus on how those policies (X_o, G, T) are established, conditional on household behavior. Again invoking the open-city assumption of land value maximization, we assume that local authorities understand the potential effects of their policy choices on the price of developed land, as embodied in equation (4), or $p^e(y, r, a, s, T, G, X_o, C, U_o)$. For simplicity, the price of open space is assumed to be constant, $m(X_o) = m > 0$, but this can be relaxed.

Excluding for now the vector of community characteristics (C) and assuming utility is Cobb-Douglas in form, $Ax^{\alpha}k^{\beta}g^{1-\alpha-\beta}G^{\gamma}X_o^{\delta}$, or equivalently:

$$U(x, k, g; G, X_o) = \ln A + \alpha \ln x + \beta \ln k + (1-\alpha-\beta) \ln g + \gamma \ln G + \delta \ln X_o, \quad (7)$$

where $A > 0$, $\alpha \in (0, 1)$, $\beta \in (0,1)$, $\gamma > 0$, and $\delta > 0$, the resulting household demands and indirect utility function are:

$$x^* = \alpha(1-a)y/(1+T)p \tag{8}$$

$$k^* = \beta(1-a)y/(1+T)r \tag{9}$$

$$g^* = (1-\alpha-\beta)(1-a)y/(1+s) \tag{10}$$

$$\begin{aligned} U^* = {} & \ln A + \alpha \ln[\alpha(1-a)y/(1+T)p] + \beta \ln[(1-a)y/(1+T)r] + (1-\alpha-\beta) \\ & \times \ln[(1-\alpha-\beta)(1-a)y/(1+s)] + \gamma \ln G + \delta \ln X_o \end{aligned} \tag{11}$$

Setting (11), a specific form of (2), equal to the outside level of utility (U_o) and solving for p gives the specific form of (3):

$$p^e = \alpha\{[A(1-a)y\beta^{\beta}(1-\alpha-\beta)^{(1-\alpha-\beta)}G^{\gamma}X_o^{\delta}]/[r^{\beta}(1+s)^{(1-\alpha-\beta)}(1+T)^{(\alpha+\beta)}e^{U_o}]\}^{1/\alpha}. \tag{12}$$

Increases in income (y), local public goods (G), and open space (X_o) boost the rental price of residential land (p^e), whereas increases in the income tax rate (a), sales tax rate (s), property tax rate (T), and the rental price of structure (r) reduce land rents. Substituting (12) for p in (8) also gives the equilibrium lot-size (x^e):

$$x^e = \{[r^{\beta}(1+s)^{(1-\alpha-\beta)}(1+T)^{\beta}e^{U_o}]/[A\{(1-a)y\}^{(1-\alpha)}\beta^{\beta}(1-\alpha-\beta)^{(1-\alpha-\beta)}G^{\gamma}X_o^{\delta}]\}^{1/\alpha}. \tag{13}$$

In the Cobb-Douglas case, demand for structure depends on its exogenous price (r), but is independent of the equilibrium price of land (p^e), so $k^e = k^*$, just as in (9).

With X_o acres of the community's total land area (L) zoned for open space, the equilibrium number of households (n^e) is:

$$n^e = (L-X_o)\{[A\{(1-a)y\}^{(1-\alpha)}\beta^{\beta}(1-\alpha-\beta)^{(1-\alpha-\beta)}G^{\gamma}X_o^{\delta}]/[r^{\beta}(1+s)^{(1-\alpha-\beta)}(1+T)^{\beta}e^{U_o}]^{1/\alpha}\}. \tag{14}$$

Note that open space appears twice in this expression and has an ambiguous long-run effect on population: increasing X_o reduces land for residential use ($L–X_o$), but the amenity effect of more open space allows residents to achieve the outside level of utility (U_o) with a smaller private lot (see [13] to verify $\delta x^e/\delta X_o < 0$), so the net effect on the number of households (n^e) is ambiguous.

This information about the long-run behavior of households can be imbedded in the choice problem facing local officials. Again, assuming that local government selects open space (X_o), public spending (G) and a property tax rate (T), levied on both types of land and residential structure, to maximize aggregate land value (V)—the rental value of residential land as well as open space—subject to a balanced-budget condition and an imbedded constraint on total land area, the constrained optimization problem can be expressed as:

$$\text{Max } v(X_o, G, T, \mu) = p^e(L - X_o) + mX_o + \mu\{R + T[p^e(L - X_o) + mX_o + n^e rk^e] - G\}, \tag{15}$$

where p^e and n^e contain the policy instruments (X_o, G, T), as shown in (12) and (14), and R is exogenous state aid to the local government. Back-substitution of the optimal policies (X_o*, G*, T*) into (12), (13), (14), and (15) also gives final values for the rental price of residential land, lot size, population, and aggregate rental land value in the community. The optimal value of the Lagrange variable (μ*) measures the per-dollar impact of state aid on the community's aggregate land value ($\delta V^*/\delta R$).

Even with the underlying Cobb-Douglas (or log) utility function, the first-order conditions for (15) are complex and do not yield reduced-form expressions for the three instruments. In view of our earlier discussion of proposals to stimulate local provision of open space by increasing state aid, our primary interest is in the sign of $\delta X_o^*/\delta R$. To examine this question, Section 3 gives some simulation results for the above model. The simulations, as well as an econometric analysis of town land use and fiscal patterns over multiple periods, counter the notion that steering more funds to local governments will encourage open space zoning by easing the fiscal pressures to allow more development.

3. Simulating the Effects of State Aid on Local Open Space

3.1 Purpose

This simulation illustrates that when the long-run responses of households and local governments are considered, simple prescriptions to encourage preservation may not only fail to deliver, but may even be counterproductive. One such proposal that has surfaced in the United States, with its division of state and local powers, is to use state aid to relieve local fiscal pressures. The underlying premise is that an exogenous inflow of revenue will ease the pressure on local governments to generate more property tax revenue from development. If so, localities may feel freer to maintain or even expand areas zoned for open space or lower density uses such as agriculture. Unfortunately, it is not clear that this transfer will have the desired effect on open space if we allow for endogenous changes in the local property tax rate, public spending, population, land prices, and household behavior prompted by the grant.

As noted before, despite many simplifications, the model of local fiscal and land use zoning policies, with an imbedded open-city model of household choice, does not give reduced-form expressions that can be directly analyzed for comparative static properties. Still, a plausibly calibrated version of the model serves to illustrate the potential effects of various policies, including the use of higher level grants to affect local land use and fiscal decisions. The calibration is far from exact, but relatively current data for Connecticut and its 169 townships are used to set plausible baseline parameter values that give "ballpark" initial outcomes. Exogenous changes in the state aid parameter (R) then induce changes in equilibrium household behavior, property values, town population, local land use and fiscal decisions, and aggregate land value.

3.2 Simulating the Open Space Response to State Aid

Connecticut is one of America's geographically smaller states (48th in land area), composed of 169 distinct townships that vary in area, population, and socioeconomic composition. Each town sets local zoning policies and relies primarily on local property taxes and state aid to finance public services, notably education. Our goal in the simulation is not to replicate this patchwork quilt of communities, but to show for a typical town how the model can be used to examine questions related to the provision of open space. Specifically, we focus on the long-run impacts of an exogenous increase in state aid (R), intended to relieve fiscal pressure and thereby allow towns to limit development and zone more land for open space. Given the "localization" of open space initiatives over the past decade or two, this seems a useful exercise, one that highlights the need to consider the ultimate impacts, not simply the stated intent, of such policies.

The notation, definition, units of measurement, and baseline parameter values are listed in Table 20.1, which also gives the notation, definition, and units of measurement for endogenous variables in the open-city household submodel and the model of local public choice.

We are interested in the response of endogenous elements of the model, particularly the amount of land zoned for open space (X_o), to exogenous changes in state aid (R). Using the open-city land value maximization model outlined earlier, with its nested submodel of household choice, and the parameter values in Table 20.1, *Mathematica*'s FindRoot procedure is used to compute a baseline numerical solution, shown in the middle row of Table 20.2. State aid (R) is then allowed to vary from its baseline value of \$17 million, upward and downward, by intervals of \$1 million. The effects of R on the local government's choice of an optimal property tax rate (T), level of local public spending (G), and the amount of land zoned for open space (X_o) are shown in the appropriate columns of Table 20.2. Table 20.2 also shows how other endogenous elements respond to the changes in state aid and the induced changes in local fiscal and zoning policies.

Recall that households in this model cannot choose the amount of open space zoned by local authorities (X_o), but they do derive utility from it. Because of such amenity effects, local officials wanting to maximize aggregate land value (V) might see an

Table 20.1 Notation and baseline parameters

Notation	Definition	Units	Baseline value
Parameters:			
L	Town land area	acres	19,000
m	Annual rental price of open space	\$/acre	500
r	Annual rental price of residential structure (floorspace)	\$/sq. ft.	5
y	Household income	\$/year	84,000
U_0	"Outside" level of household utility	constant	12
A	Utility function scalar	constant	1
α	Post-tax expenditure share on rental cost of residential land	fraction	1/9
β	Post-tax expenditure share on rental cost of housing structure	fraction	2/9
$1-\alpha-\beta$	Post-tax expenditure share on numeraire consumption good	fraction	2/3
γ	Preference weight on local public spending	fraction	0.10
δ	Preference weight on local land zoned for open space	fraction	0.15
s	State sales tax rate	fraction	0.06
a	Combined (state and federal) income tax rate	fraction	0.20
R	State aid to the local government	\$/year	17,000,000
Endogenous Variables:			
U	Household utility		
x	Residential land (lot-size)	acres	
k	Housing structure (floorspace)	sq. ft.	
g	Numeraire consumption good (price = 1)	\$/year	
p	Annual rental price of residential land	\$/acre	
n	Local population	households	
T	Local property tax rate (fraction of annual rental payments)	fraction	
G	Local public spending	\$/year	
X_0	Local land zoned for open space	acres	
$L-X_0$	Local land zoned for residential use	acres	
V	Aggregate land value (rental value of residential land and open space)	\$/year	
μ	Lagrange variable ($\delta V^*/\delta R$)		

increase in open space as a way to boost V, particularly if an external source provides additional revenue and thereby eases the local government's reliance on property tax revenue from development to finance public spending. As seen in Table 20.2, the increase in state aid ($\Delta R > 0$) does provide this fiscal relief, allowing town officials to reduce the tax rate ($\Delta T < 0$) and increase public spending ($\Delta G > 0$). But this policy response ultimately attracts more households ($\Delta n > 0$) and increases the equilibrium price of residential land ($\Delta p > 0$), resulting in more land being allocated to development ($\Delta(L-X_0) > 0$) and less to open space ($\Delta X_o < 0$). Despite the extra land for

Table 20.2 Simulating the effects of state aid

	R (state aid)*	U (utility)	x (lot-size)	k (floorspace)	g (numeraire)	p (land price)	n (households)	T (tax rate)	G (spending)*	X_o (open space)	L-X_o (developed)	V (agg. land value)*	μ (dV*/dR)
	7.0	12.0	1.240	2,228	42,285	4,492	6,294	0.339	44.545	11,195	7,805	40.661	2.541
	8.0	12.0	1.165	2,239	42,285	4,806	6,715	0.333	47.364	11,179	7,821	43.179	2.494
	9.0	12.0	1.099	2,249	42,285	5,114	7,128	0.327	50.125	11,165	7,835	45.652	2.452
	10.0	12.0	1.042	2,257	42,285	5,417	7,533	0.322	52.834	11,153	7,847	48.085	2.414
	11.0	12.0	0.991	2,265	42,285	5,716	7,930	0.317	55.495	11,142	7,858	50.482	2.380
	12.0	12.0	0.945	2,273	42,285	6,010	8,321	0.313	58.113	11,133	7,867	52.846	2.348
	13.0	12.0	0.905	2,280	42,285	6,300	8,706	0.309	60.693	11,124	7,876	55.179	2.319
	14.0	12.0	0.868	2,286	42,285	6,587	9,086	0.305	63.235	11,116	7,884	57.485	2.292
	15.0	12.0	0.834	2,292	42,285	6,870	9,460	0.302	65.744	11,109	7,891	59.765	2.267
	16.0	12.0	0.803	2,298	42,285	7,150	9,830	0.298	68.222	11,103	7,897	62.020	2.244
Baseline:	**17.0**	**12.0**	**0.775**	**2,303**	**42,285**	**7,428**	**10,195**	**0.295**	**70.671**	**11,097**	**7,903**	**64.254**	**2.223**
	18.0	12.0	0.749	2,308	42,285	7,703	10,557	0.293	73.093	11,091	7,909	66.466	2.202
	19.0	12.0	0.725	2,313	42,285	7,975	10,914	0.290	75.489	11,086	7,914	68.659	2.183
	20.0	12.0	0.703	2,318	42,285	8,245	11,268	0.287	77.861	11,081	7,919	70.833	2.165
	21.0	12.0	0.682	2,322	42,285	8,513	11,618	0.285	80.211	11,077	7,923	72.989	2.148
	22.0	12.0	0.663	2,327	42,285	8,779	11,965	0.282	82.538	11,073	7,927	75.129	2.132
	23.0	12.0	0.644	2,331	42,285	9,043	12,309	0.280	84.846	11,069	7,931	77.253	2.117
	24.0	12.0	0.627	2,334	42,285	9,304	12,650	0.278	87.134	11,065	7,935	79.363	2.102
	25.0	12.0	0.611	2,338	42,285	9,564	12,989	0.276	89.404	11,062	7,938	81.458	2.088
	26.0	12.0	0.590	2,342	42,285	9,823	13,325	0.274	91.656	11,058	7,942	83.539	2.075
	27.0	12.0	0.582	2,345	42,285	10,080	13,658	0.272	93.891	11,055	7,945	85.608	2.062

* $ millions

development, lot size shrinks ($\Delta x < 0$), but larger structures are built ($\Delta k > 0$). Given the underlying log (or Cobb-Douglas) utility function, numeraire consumption is unaffected ($\Delta g = 0$), but the utility gains from more structure and greater public spending compensate for the reductions in lot size and open space to provide the larger number of households the same ($\Delta u = 0$) "outside" level of utility (U_0) as before the increase in state aid.

The model has a variety of limitations, but it illustrates that simply channeling revenue from state to local governments, with the expectation that communities will rationally zone more land for open space, could actually result in less open space when long-run adjustments occur. Is there any evidence, though, that more state aid is associated with less open space? In the next section, we address this question by examining a unique multiperiod dataset for Connecticut's 169 towns.

4. Empirical Analysis

4.1 Specification

The government choice problem, expressed in equation (15) and simulated in Section 3, implies a set of general expressions for T^*, G^*, $X_0{}^*$, and μ^* that depend on the vector of exogenous elements ($y, C, L, R, U_0, A, \alpha, \beta, \gamma, \delta, s, a, r, m$). Some elements of the vector reflect the underlying model of the representative household and are either empirically unobservable or assumed to be roughly constant across communities. Income (y), a vector (C) of other community characteristics (suppressed in the earlier analytical model), total land area of the town (L), and state aid (R) are observable and vary considerably across towns and over time, so these are included in our empirical specification. But "outside" utility (U_0) is inherently unobservable and likely to be highly correlated with income. Parameters of the utility function ($A, \alpha, \beta, \gamma, \delta$) also might be income-sensitive, but again we have no systematic information about how these parameters vary spatially or over time, so we assume that the inclusion of income sufficiently captures latent differences in residents' preferences. The state's sales tax rate (s) is uniform across towns and has not varied much over the period of our panel data analysis; the combined state and federal average income tax rate (a) also is assumed to be time and town invariant. Residential land prices (p) vary considerably across towns and over time, but are endogenous in our model and imbedded in the local government's choice problem. The price of structure (r) and the price of open space (m) are more homogeneous and also likely to be correlated with some of the town characteristics included in C (e.g., location within the state). With these points in mind, our empirical specification of the three reduced-form policy expressions is:

$$T^*(y, C, L, R) \tag{16}$$

$$G^{*}(y, C, L, R) \tag{17}$$

$$X_{o}^{*}(y, C, L, R) \tag{18}$$

Equations (16)–(18) represent the town's land-value maximizing choice of a local property tax rate (T^*), level of public spending (G^*), and the area of town land zoned for open space ($X_o{}^*$), each expressed as a function of local per capita income (y); a vector of three town characteristics including the town's index crime rate (C_1) as a measure of general socioeconomic conditions, minimum distance from the town to New York or Boston (C_2), both important regional focal points on opposite sides of the state, and a dummy variable for shoreline towns (C_3) to capture an important amenity for New Englanders; total available land area of the town (L); and intergovernmental revenue (R), the focus of our analysis. To allow for the possibility of a delayed response to state aid, R is empirically specified as the average (R_{avg}) of current (R) and one-year lagged (R_{lag}) values of intergovernmental revenue.

4.2 Data

For the analysis, we use a unique dataset compiled by the Center for Land Use Education & Research (CLEAR) in the College of Agriculture and Natural Resources at the University of Connecticut. Using data generated from satellite imagery for five separate years (1985, 1990, 1995, 2002, 2006), CLEAR reports 12 categories of "land cover" for each of the state's 169 towns: (1) developed, (2) turf and grass, (3) other grass, (4) agricultural field, (5) deciduous forest, (6) coniferous forest, (7) water, (8) nonforested wetland, (9) forested wetland, (10) tidal wetland, (11) barren, and (12) utility corridors. The underlying model in Section 3 focuses on the allocation of local land to "development" and potentially usable "open space," so we exclude several categories that are not usable or readily subject to town control—water, various wetlands, and utility corridors (items 7–10 and 12)—and then define the remaining categories (items 1–6 and 11) as the total land area (L) available for either open space (X_o) or development ($L - X_o$). The first two categories (developed and turf grass) are generally regarded as "developed areas," so the other nonexcluded categories (other grass, agricultural field, deciduous forest, coniferous forest, and barren) are treated as "open space." Based on these definitions, Table 20.3 shows the state's overall pattern of land cover change, aggregated from town-level data, as well as the corresponding means of the town-level data, in each of the five available years.

Although Connecticut is the fourth most densely populated state, the table shows that the "developed" ($L - X_o$) area's share of "total available acres" (L) rose from just 24.30% in 1985 to 28.95% in 2006, an increase of 139,255 acres or more than 217 square miles. Similarly, the 169-town mean value of "percent developed" rose from 28.22% to 33.06% over the same period.

Table 20.3 Connecticut land cover, 1985–2006

		1985	1990	1995	2002	2006	chg 85 to 06	% chg 85 to 06
CONNECTICUT								
Open Space	X_o	2,205,118	2,158,576	2,138,506	2,103,539	2,079,420	−125,698	−5.7
Developed	$(L\text{-}X_o)$	708,030	760,465	785,394	822,607	847,285	139,255	19.7
Total Available Acres	L	2,913,148	2,919,041	2,923,900	2,926,146	2,926,705	13,557	0.5
Percent Open Space	$\% X_o$	75.70	73.95	73.14	71.89	71.05	−4.65	
Percent Developed	$\%(L\text{-}X_o)$	24.30	26.05	26.86	28.11	28.95	4.65	
169-TOWN MEANS								
Open Space	X_o	13048	12773	12654	12447	12304	−744	−5.7
Developed	$(L\text{-}X_o)$	4190	4500	4647	4867	5014	824	19.7
Total Available Acres	L	17238	17272	17301	17314	17318	80	0.5
Percent Open Space	$\% X_o$	71.78	69.94	69.07	67.78	66.94	−4.84	
Percent Developed	$\% (L\text{-}X_o)$	28.22	30.06	30.93	32.22	33.06	4.84	
DEFINITIONS		LAND COVER CATEGORIES						
Open Space	Xo	: other grass, agricultural field, deciduous forest, coniferous forest, barren						
Developed	$(L\text{-}Xo)$	: developed space, turf grass						
Total Available Acres	L	: developed space, turf grass, other grass, agricultural field, deciduous forest, coniferous forest, barren *Excluded*: water, nonforested wetland, tidal wetland, utility corridors						

Source: Based on satellite imagery data from the Center for Land Use Education and Research (CLEAR), College of Agriculture and Natural Resources, University of Connecticut, Storrs, CT.

Town-level fiscal data—effective property tax rate (equalized mill rate) and local public spending—are drawn from reports of the Connecticut Office of Policy and Management (OPM). Income figures are from US Census data, crime rates are from the Connecticut Department of Emergency Services and Public Protection, and the minimum driving distance from each town to either New York or Boston is generated by Google Maps.

Both the endogenous and exogenous variables in Table 20.3 show considerable variation among the 169 Connecticut towns in each of the five periods. For example, in the most recent year (2006), land cover identified as "open space" (X_o) ranges from 528 to 32,535 acres; government spending (G) varies from \$2.03 million to \$460.22 million; and the effective property tax rate (T) ranges from \$4.72 to \$27.89 per \$1,000 of market value. Among the explanatory variables, annual per capita income (y) ranges from \$15,739 to \$99,664, and the index crime rate per hundred persons (C_1) ranges from 0.19 to 8.32. Distance to the nearest major metropolitan center (C_2)—New York or Boston—ranges from 39.4 to 131.0 miles, and the shoreline dummy variable (C_3) assumes a value of zero for 145 of Connecticut's 169 towns and one for its 24 shoreline towns. Total available land area (L), as defined earlier in our discussion of the land cover data, varies from 3,187 to 38,136 acres. The average (R_{avg}) of current (R) and one-year lagged (R_{lag}) intergovernmental revenue (primarily state aid in most Connecticut towns) is used to capture the effect of grants on the amount of local open space. In 2006, the two-year average figure varies from \$154,175 to \$233.87 million. Despite its small size, Connecticut's towns show considerable diversity in land use patterns, fiscal policies, and underlying characteristics.

4.3 Results

Three reduced-form equations—for open space acreage (X_o), total town spending (G), and the effective property tax rate (T)—were estimated in *Stata* using generalized least squares regression to correct for heteroscedasticity. Table 20.5 gives the econometric results for the pooled five-year sample of all 169 Connecticut towns, with 1985 as the base year and dummy variables for the other four nonconsecutive years (D_{90}, D_{95}, D_{02}, D_{06}).

The adjusted R^2 for the first estimated reduced-form equation indicates that more than 92% of the town-level variation in open space (X_o), across 169 towns and over five discrete periods (N = 845), is explained by the joint effect of factors that closely mirror the structure of the theoretical model. The same set of explanatory variables account for more than 78% of the variation in local public spending (G) and about 55% of the variation in effective property tax rates (T).

Controlling for other factors, more affluent towns tend to have less open space ($\delta X_o/\delta y < 0$). Such towns may have more "private open space" in the form of larger residential lots, but since here the defined open space consists of the combined acreage of grassland, agricultural fields, deciduous forest, coniferous forest, and barren areas, X_o tends to decline with higher incomes (and the accompanying larger private lots). Higher

Table 20.4 Descriptive statistics, by year (1985, 1990, 1995, 2002, 2006) and pooled data

			1985	1990	1995	2002	2006	Pooled
DEPENDENT VARIABLES								
Open Space (undeveloped acres)	X_o^*	min	652	590	570	528	528	528
		max	32,750	32,661	32,664	32,614	32,535	32,750
		mean	13,048	12,773	12,654	12,447	12,304	12,645
Government Spending (dollars)	G^*	min	571,330	1,334,498	1,131,349	1,600,324	2,029,022	571,330
		max	203,793,895	338,885,879	398,180,852	423,442,000	460,218,044	460,218,044
		mean	18,910,771	31,488,593	38,481,369	50,782,061	61,499,178	40,232,394
Property Tax Rate ($ per $1000 market value)	T^*	min	6.80	5.30	8.84	7.70	4.72	4.72
		max	33.40	18.90	42.97	32.73	27.89	42.97
		mean	16.31	11.28	17.17	17.59	14.18	15.31
REGRESSORS								
Per Capita Income (dollars)	y	min	9,661	11,044	12,178	14,158	15,739	9,661
		max	42,697	52,063	65,344	87,519	99,664	99,664
		mean	16,825	21,270	25,572	32,560	36,398	26,525
Index Crime Rate (crimes per 100 persons)	C_1	min	0.53	0.90	0.68	0.13	0.19	0.13
		max	13.23	16.13	12.62	8.80	8.32	16.13
		mean	2.69	2.85	2.56	1.74	1.63	2.29
Min. Distance to NY or BOS (miles)	C_2	min	39.40	39.40	39.40	39.40	39.40	39.40
		max	131.00	131.00	131.00	131.00	131.00	131.00
		mean	93.72	93.72	93.72	93.72	93.72	93.72

(continued)

Table 20.4 (Continued)

			1985	1990	1995	2002	2006	Pooled
Shoreline Dummy (shore = 1)	C_3	min	0.00	0.00	0.00	0.00	0.00	0.00
		max	1.00	1.00	1.00	1.00	1.00	1.00
		mean	0.14	0.14	0.14	0.14	0.14	0.14
Total Available Acres (acres)	*L*	min	3,176	3,178	3,183	3,186	3,187	3,176
		max	38,027	38,083	38,107	38,121	38,136	38,136
		mean	17,238	17,272	17,301	17,314	17,318	17,289
Intergovernmental Revenue (dollars)	*R*	min	74,935	171,386	95,438	122,674	145,548	74,935
		max	92,107,359	150,644,618	207,770,194	242,028,000	242,112,000	242,112,000
		mean	4,648,419	8,913,625	10,796,759	14,395,113	15,534,999	10,857,783
Intergovernmental Revenue 1-year lagged (dollars)	*R*lag	min	75,183	149,684	93,821	117,745	162,802	75,183
		max	92,231,560	124,509,272	201,758,880	243,359,822	225,628,000	243,359,822
		mean	4,289,922	7,797,690	10,558,514	14,139,557	14,083,370	10,152,203
Intergovernmental Revenue 2-year average (dollars)	*R*avg	min	75,059	160,535	108,734	120,210	154,175	75,059
		max	92,169,459	137,576,945	204,764,537	242,693,911	233,870,000	242,693,911
		mean	4,485,818	8,362,935	10,703,497	14,267,335	14,823,794	10,504,993
	N	169	169	169	169	169	845	

per capita income also is associated with more government spending ($\delta G/\delta y > 0$) and a lower effective property tax rate ($\delta T/\delta y < 0$). The positive effect of income on G needs little explanation and is well documented in empirical studies. However, the negative relationship between a community's tax rate and its residents' average income, even though readily observed in the raw data before controlling for other influences, is a common source of public confusion. Because affluent communities often pay more property taxes per head, people assume they also face a higher *rate*, but this typically is not the case. Enjoying a larger property tax base per person, higher income communities can tax their residents at a lower rate and still generate enough revenue to outspend poorer towns.

Crime rates (C_1) are negatively related to open space ($\delta X_o/\delta C_1 < 0$) and positively related to both local spending ($\delta G/\delta C_1 > 0$) and tax rates ($\delta T/\delta C_1 > 0$). Like most urban areas, Connecticut cities tend to have higher crime rates, less open space, larger budgets, and higher tax rates than do suburban or rural towns, so these estimated coefficients, all quite significant, are consistent.

Towns further from New York or Boston (C_2) typically have more open space ($\delta X_o/\delta C_2 > 0$) and lower public spending ($\delta G/\delta C_2 < 0$), but also higher property tax rates ($\delta T/\delta C_2 > 0$) than towns closer to these regional centers. The first two results are self-explanatory. The third effect, less significant than the first two, reflects the fact that towns farther from one of the two regional economic centers tend to have lower property values (the effect of regional rent gradients), which must be taxed at a higher mill rate to support a desired level of public spending.

A similar logic applies to estimated coefficients for the shoreline dummy variable, but due to the way it is defined ($C_3 = 1$ for shoreline towns; 0 otherwise), the corresponding signs are reversed. Popular shoreline towns tend to be densely settled with limited open space ($\delta X_o/\delta C_3 < 0$), but have relatively high levels of public spending ($\delta G/\delta C_3 > 0$), perhaps needed to serve nonresident visitors as well as the "locals." Despite these higher public outlays, coastal amenities are capitalized into property values, allowing shoreline tax rates to be lower ($\delta T/\delta C_3 < 0$) than in an otherwise similar inland town. All three effects are statistically quite significant.

Controlling for other features, geographically larger towns tend to have more open space ($\delta X_o/\delta L > 0$); the marginal effect is large (0.856) and highly significant, with an elasticity of open space with respect to town area of 1.170 (using the estimated coefficient and pooled sample means of 12,645 acres for X_o and 17,289 acres for L). Bigger towns also face higher outlays ($\delta G/\delta L > 0$), reflecting the costlier delivery of many types of public services (utilities, school transportation costs, fire services, etc.) to more dispersed populations. The property tax rate is negatively related to town area ($\delta T/\delta L < 0$), but the implied elasticity is small (−0.08).

The effect of a change in intergovernmental revenue (R) on the amount of open space is of special interest. Once again, simulations in the preceding section show how an increase in R can decrease rather than increase the amount of land optimally allocated to open space (X_o). Using the average (R_{avg}) of current and one-year lagged values of R to allow for somewhat delayed or cumulative response of the local government to extra

Table 20.5 GLS estimates of open space, public spending, and property tax rates (five-year panel of 169 Connecticut towns)

		Open Space (Xo)	Spending (G)	Tax Rate (T)
REGRESSORS:				
Per Capita Income (dollars)	y	−56.5464 (-6.15)	774,236 (4.93)	−0.089723 (-7.48)
Index Crime Rate (crimes per 100 persons)	C_1	−796.639 (-8.73)	10,627,551 (4.27)	0.700663 (4.46)
Min. Distance to NY or BOS (miles)	C_2	32.7720 (7.37)	−422,810 (-5.60)	0.009548
Shoreline Dummy (shore = 1)	C_3	−1,366.11 (−5.72)	23,565,463 (5.68)	−1.66773
Total Available Acres (acres)	L	0.855556 (88.04)	630.517 (4.73)	−0.000068
Intergovernmental Revenue 2-year average (dollars)	$Ravg$	−0.000019 (-4.13)	1.33147 (4.75)	0.000000036 (2.96)
1990 Dummy	D_{90}	97.0425 (0.45)	5,472,765 (1.64)	−4.79105 (−13.73)
1995 Dummy	D_{95}	8.21837 (0.04)	9,172,473 (1.86)	1.61266 (3.89)
2002 Dummy	D_{02}	−396.281 (−1.54)	19,898,008 (2.35)	3.10217 (6.17)
2006 Dummy	D_{06}	−402.057 (−1.47)	28,097,687 (3.01)	0.094199 (0.19)
Intercept		−1,349.57 (−2.23)	−6,469,437 (−0.72)	16.1948 (17.57)
R^2		0.927	0.790	0.556
adj R^2		0.926	0.787	0.551
F		1,105.94	148.73	107.31
Root MSE		2,038.76	27,684,495	3.07
Log likelihood		−7,632.45	−15,673.71	−2,140.10
N		845	845	845

revenue, we find support for the negative relationship in the simulations ($\delta X_o/\delta R < 0$). A million-dollar increment in R_{avg} is associated with a 19-acre reduction in open space. The negative coefficient is significant at the 1% level, but the implied elasticity at sample means is quite small (−0.016). This finding suggests that increments in unrestricted state aid are more likely to slightly reduce, rather than increase, the amount of open space. Not surprisingly, additional state aid is strongly associated with higher local public spending ($\delta G/\delta R > 0$), and the calculated elasticity is much larger in magnitude (0.348). Contrary to simulation results, the estimated response of the property tax rate is positive ($\delta T/\delta R > 0$), but again the calculated elasticity is small (0.025).

Dummy variable estimates in the first regression generally reflect the secular loss of open space. Evidence of an upward drift in government spending, at least in nominal terms, is seen in the estimated dummy variable coefficients for the second regression, whereas the pattern is less distinct in the property tax rate regression. The negative and highly significant coefficient for D_{90} in the latter equation likely reflects a systematic reduction in effective property tax rates across many Connecticut towns in the late 1980s, when market values soared and effective tax rates fell.

The contrary empirical result for $\delta T/\delta R$ and the weaker fit of the tax rate equation point to a potential limitation in the present analysis. In both the underlying theoretical model and the empirical specification of reduced forms, we treat intergovernmental revenue (R) as exogenous and unrestricted. This simplifies the analysis but ignores the fact that, in Connecticut, and in most other states, transfers to local governments are potentially endogenous and sensitive to socioeconomic indicators such as crime rates or per capita income. Extending the model to incorporate a "typical" aid formula and refining the empirical analysis to allow for the potential endogeneity of R would be desirable. The question of how to treat R and the degree to which local public expenditures are fungible or constrained by conditional grants also raises the nagging "flypaper effect" issue, recently discussed again by Inman (2008). For these reasons, and probably others, our empirical results should be regarded as preliminary findings.

5. Conclusion and Research Agenda

Open space preservation programs in the United States, and perhaps in most countries, range from large-scale national initiatives to protect wilderness areas and unique natural resources, to smaller scale state and local efforts to preserve farmland, parks, and historic sites. Both types of programs play important social and economic roles, and it would be unwise to wholly abandon one approach for the other, but local preservation efforts are particularly important for two key reasons. First, as noted earlier, preferences for open space vary, just as they do for other public goods, and allowing local governments to "customize" their preservation policies to local conditions and preferences may enhance efficiency. Strong advocates of "regionalism" may find this notion unappealing, opting instead for more uniformity, consolidation, and presumed scale economies in the acquisition or management of open space, but many public finance economists recognize the potential benefits of a more decentralized approach. Second, local preservation programs are important simply because they are most prevalent in areas of relatively high density. In the United States, this means the northeastern states, coastal regions, and suburban areas surrounding larger cities—areas that account for a modest share of total land area but a large portion of the population. Consequently, these are precisely the areas where market pressure to convert farmland and open space to other uses is strongest. A large portion of the population will actively benefit from, and therefore support, open space initiatives only if they include visible state and local programs in higher density areas.

Given the fragmented nature of US open space preservation, the analytical and empirical results presented in this chapter offer a caution to policy makers, but the results should be qualified. The principal simulation results show that more intergovernmental aid, intended to facilitate open space preservation by reducing the fiscal incentive for local authorities to zone land for development, can produce just the opposite: more land zoned for development and less for open space. The result initially seems counterintuitive, but a closer look at the community-wide adjustments in the open-city model offers a plausible explanation. More state aid allows officials to simultaneously increase public spending and lower the property tax rate. Both adjustments make the community more attractive to potential entrants, and, as population expands, land rents are bid up, average lot size shrinks, and more households are accommodated. If officials seek to maximize the total value of land within the community, this increase in the market price of residential land, relative to that of open space, encourages them to zone more land for development and less for open space—not the intended outcome.

There are, as usual, variants or extensions of the model that could affect these results. First, in a less restrictive model in which the price of open space is not constant but is instead a decreasing function of the amount of land zoned for open space, $m(X_o)$, the simulated decline in open space in response to more state aid would be mitigated by an increase in its price, perhaps not reversing our finding, but likely choking it off sooner and damping the final effect.

A second extension of the model would relax the treatment of public goods and open space, which here are treated as pure public goods: each resident derives the full benefit of public spending (G) and local open space (X_o), independent of population (n). Borcherding and Deacon (1972), Santerre (1985), and others have relaxed this assumption to allow for "crowding" or congestion effects, in which individual consumption of the public good increases with spending (G) but decreases with the population (n) sharing the public good. Bates and Santerre (2001) use this approach in their study of the demand for locally owned open space and find it to be quite congestible. Given that G and n, as well as X_o, are endogenous in our model, extending it to allow for congestion in both public goods and open space would be useful.

Third, in the scenario described in our simulations, the lot size reduction that accommodates more households, may be limited by minimum lot size restrictions, absent in the present model. Incorporating both land use zoning and various forms of density zoning (minimum lot size, maximum height, etc.) would make the model even more applicable. Again, it is useful to think of these various zoning instruments as additional ways for a community to differentiate itself and better satisfy residents' preferences, thereby enhancing aggregate land value. Such restrictions, though, raise vital questions about the distributional impacts and exclusionary effects of zoning and other land use policies. For a contemporary analysis of the emergence of zoning and its welfare effects, see Calabrese, Epple, and Romano (2007).

A fourth feature of the model, its assumption of land value maximization as the public sector's only goal, ignores more subtle objectives, such as ecological sustainability, wildlife protection, encouragement of local food production, and the like. Open space affects household utility in the current model, so amenity benefits are considered, but broadening the public goal (land value maximization) to incorporate less tangible social returns, not fully capitalized in land values, could be beneficial.

Expanding the model to incorporate other types of agents, including farmers and nonagricultural firms, is a fifth extension that would generalize the model and allow researchers to address more questions. How does farmland preservation affect agricultural output and food prices? Are the costs of farmland preservation partly borne by businesses in the form of higher commercial land rents? What are the cheapest and least distortionary ways to finance open space preservation?

Finally, another possible extension of the model warrants special mention. Much within the present model is endogenous—household behavior, local fiscal and land use zoning decisions, land values, and population size—but linkages between the community and other localities (other than via the open-city condition), or between the community and higher level governments, are lacking. Households in the model face income and sales taxes, typically levied by federal or state governments, but these linkages take the form of exogenous parameters. For many areas, a model that details the interaction between the land use and fiscal policies of a higher level government and a local government, or a network of localities subject to policy spillover effects, would be useful in addressing policy coordination questions. Lenon, Chattopadhyay, and Heffley (1996) find empirical evidence of zoning and fiscal interdependencies between neighboring towns, and Brueckner (1998) documents similar interactions for growth controls, but further understanding how a network of communities also interacts with a higher level government to determine an equilibrium pattern of land use, fiscal mix, and community types would be valuable. Among other applications, it could be used to study the economic and land use impacts of statewide fees or taxes designed to finance preservation in selected subareas. A multilevel model also might be used to evaluate Briffault's (1996, 1115) call for "a 'mixed strategy' that would both reduce the significance of existing local boundaries and create elected regionally bounded governments to address matters of regional significance."

As in most areas of study, the range of interesting questions about open space preservation expands rapidly as simplifying assumptions are relaxed and new elements are added to the analysis. The present model may be a useful foundation for such extensions. As in the workhorse monocentric model of urban economics, land use is explicit and rents are endogenous. The monocentric model offers more spatial detail, in that users of land select both a lot size and location (distance from the urban center), but this model offers a simpler foundation for some of the extensions noted earlier, without abandoning the spatial dimension needed to study land use issues. Some of the suggested extensions are of technical interest, but others should help to inform land use policy making. Fortunately, open space preservation is an area of land economics in which researchers' enthusiasm is matched by public interest.

Much of the work on open space preservation has been empirical, and, as new data emerge and new analytical and empirical techniques are developed and applied, that work will continue to expand our understanding of how various conservation programs really work and the public's willingness to support them. Another development in this area of research and in other land use studies is the increasing availability of land cover data from satellite imagery, over sufficiently long periods of time to reveal measurable changes. We have used this type of data for Connecticut in the empirical section, but similar data for other states and other countries will become more commonplace. Marrying the data with site-specific information about zoning and other land use controls is a bigger task, but one that would greatly improve our understanding of the public sector's capacity to steer land use.

References

America's Great Outdoors Initiative. 2011. *America's great outdoors: A promise to future generations*. Washington, DC: United States Departments of Interior, United States Department of Agriculture, The Environmental Protection Agency.

Anas, A. 1988. Optimal preservation and pricing of natural public lands in general equilibrium. *Journal of Environmental Economics and Management* 15: 158–172.

Anas, A., and H. -J. Rhee. 2006. Curbing excess sprawl with congestion tolls and urban boundaries. *Regional Science and Urban Economics* 36: 510–541.

Bae, C. -J. 2007. Containing sprawl. In *Incentives, regulations and plans*, eds. G.-J. Knaap, H. K. Haccou, K. J. Clifton, and J. Frece, 36–53. Northampton, MA: Edward Elgar.

Barrows, R., and B. Prenguber. 1975. Transfer of development rights: An analysis of a new land use policy tool. *American Journal of Agricultural Economics* 57: 549–557.

Bates, L. 1993. Municipal monopoly power and the supply of residential development rights. *Eastern Economic Journal* 19: 173–184.

Bates, L., and R. Santerre. 2001. The public demand for open space: the case of Connecticut communities. *Journal of Urban Economics* 50: 97–111.

Bergstrom, J., B. Dillman, and J. Stoll. 1985. Public environmental amenity benefits of private land: the case of prime agricultural land. *Southern Journal of Agricultural Economics* 17: 139–149.

Betz, C., and H. K. Cordell. 1998. *Outdoor recreation supply in the United States: A description of the resources, data, and other information sources*. Athens, GA: USDA Forest Service, Southern Research Station.

Bolitzer, B., and N. Netusil. 2000. The impact of open spaces on property values in Portland, Oregon. *Journal of Environmental Management* 59: 185–193.

Borcherding, T., and R. Deacon. 1972. The demand for the services of non-federal governments. *American Economic Review* 62: 891–901.

Briffault, R. 1996. The local government boundary problem in metropolitan areas. *Stanford Law Review* 48: 1115–1171.

Brueckner, J. 1979. Property values, local public expenditure and economic efficiency. *Journal of Public Economics* 11: 223–245.

Brueckner, J. 1982. A test for allocative efficiency in the local public sector. *Journal of Public Economics* 19: 311–331.

Brueckner, J. 1983. Property value maximization and public sector efficiency. *Journal of Urban Economics* 14: 1–15.

Brueckner, J. 1998. Testing for strategic interaction among local governments: The case of growth controls. *Journal of Urban Economics* 44: 438–467.

Brueckner, J. 2000. Urban sprawl: Diagnosis and remedies. *International Regional Science Review* 23: 160–171.

Brueckner, J., and R. Helsley. 2011. Sprawl and blight. *Journal of Urban Economics* 69: 205–213.

Calabrese, S., D. Epple, and R. Romano. 2007. On the political economy of zoning. *Journal of Public Economics* 91: 25–49.

Carpenter, B., and D. Heffley. 1982. Spatial-equilibrium analysis of transferable development rights. *Journal of Urban Economics* 12: 238–261.

Cheshire, P., and S. Sheppard. 2002. The welfare economics of land use planning. *Journal of Urban Economics* 52: 242–269.

Correll, M., J. Lillydahl, and L. Singell. 1978. The effects of greenbelts on residential property values: Some findings on the political economy of open space. *Land Economics* 54: 207–217.

Costonis, J. 1973. Development rights transfer: An exploratory essay. *The Yale Law Journal* 83: 75–128.

Costonis, J. 1975. The unconstitutionality of transferable development rights. *The Yale Law Journal* 84: 1101–1122.

Deaton, B., and R. Vyn. 2010. The effect of strict agricultural zoning on agricultural land values: The case of Ontario's greenbelt. *American Journal of Agricultural Economics* 92: 941–955.

Do, A. Q., and G. Grudnitski. 1995. Golf courses and residential house prices: An empirical examination. *Journal of Real Estate Finance and Economics* 10: 261–270.

Duke, J., and T. Ilvento. 2004. A conjoint analysis of public preferences for agricultural land preservation. *Agricultural and Resource Economics Review* 33: 209–219.

Duke, J., and L. Lynch. 2006. Farmland retention techniques: property rights implications and comparative evaluation. *Land Economics* 82: 189–213.

Earnhart, D. 2006. Using contingent-pricing analysis to value open space and its duration at residential locations. *Land Economics* 82: 17–35.

Evans, A. 1999. The land market and government intervention. In *Applied urban economics*, eds. P. Chesire and E. Mills, 1637–1669. Amsterdam: Elsevier Science, North-Holland.

Field, B., and J. Conrad. 1975. Economic issues in programs of transferable development rights. *Land Economics* 51: 331–340.

Fischel, W. 1978. A property rights approach to municipal zoning. *Land Economics* 54: 64–81.

Fischel, W. 1980. Zoning and the exercise of monopoly power: a reevaluation. *Journal of Urban Economics* 8: 283–293.

Fischel, W. 1985. *The economics of zoning laws: A property rights approach to American land.* Baltimore: Johns Hopkins University Press.

Fischel, W. 1990. Introduction: Four maxims for research on land-use controls. *Land Economics* 66: 229–236.

Foltz, J., and B. Larson. 2002. Public support for farmland preservation programs: Empirical evidence from Connecticut. Paper presented at the Northeast Agricultural and Resource Economics Association (NAREA) Conference, Camp Hill, PA.

Fujita, M., P. Krugman, and A. Venables. 1999. *The spatial economy: Cities, regions, and international trade.* Cambridge, MA: MIT Press.

Gardner, B. D. 1977. The economics of agricultural land preservation. *American Journal of Agricultural Economics* 59: 1027–1036.

Geoghegan, J., L. Wainger, and N. Bockstael. 1997. Spatial landscape indices in a hedonic framework: An ecological economics analysis using GIS. *Ecological Economics* 23: 251–264.

Geoghegan, J., L. Lynch, and S. Bucholtz. 2003. Capitalization of open spaces into housing values and the residential property tax revenue impacts of agricultural easement programs. *Agricultural and Resource Economics Review* 32: 33–45.

Glaeser, E. 2008. *Cities, agglomeration and spatial equilibrium*. New York: Oxford University Press.

Gnedenko, E. 2009. Three essays on the economics of open space. Ph.D. dissertation, University of Connecticut.

Gottlieb, P. 2006. State-aid formulas and the local incentive to chase (or shun) ratables. *Urban Studies* 43: 1087–1103.

Grieson, R., and J. White. 1981. The effects of zoning on structure and land markets. *Journal of Urban Economics* 10: 271–285.

Hamilton, B. 1975. Zoning and property taxation in a system of local governments. *Urban Studies* 12: 205–211.

Hamilton, B. 1978. Zoning and the exercise of monopoly power. *Journal of Urban Economics* 5: 116–130.

Hascic, I., and J. Wu. 2012. The cost of land use regulation versus the value of individual exemption: Oregon's measures 37 and 49. *Contemporary Economic Policy* 30: 159–214.

Heffley, D., and D. Hewitt. 1988. Land-use zoning in a local economy with optimal property taxes and public expenditures. *Journal of Real Estate Finance and Economics* 1: 373–391.

Helpman, E., and D. Pines. 1977. Land and zoning in an urban economy: Further results. *American Economic Review* 67: 982–986.

Henneberry, D., and R. Barrows. 1990. Capitalization of exclusive agricultural zoning into farmland prices. *Land Economics* 66: 249–258.

Holcomber, R., and S. Staley. 2001. Land-use planning: An overview of the issues. In *Smarter growth: Market-Based Strategies for Land-Use Planning in the 21st century*, eds. R. Holcomber and S. Staley, 1–12. Westport, CT: Greenwood Press.

Hollis, L., and W. Fulton. 2002. *Open space protection: Conservation meets growth management*. Washington, DC: The Brookings Institution.

Inman, R. 2008. The flypaper effect. NBER working paper series, WP 14579. Cambridge, MA: National Bureau of Economic Research.

Irwin, E. 2002. The effects of open space on residential property values. *Land Economics* 78: 465–480.

Jiang, Y., and S. Swallow. 2006. Tax increment financing for optimal open space preservation: an economic inquiry. Paper presented at the American Agricultural Economics Association Annual Meeting, Long Beach, CA.

Johnston, R., and J. Duke. 2007. Willingness to pay for agricultural land preservation and policy process attributes: Does the method matter? *American Journal of Agricultural Economics* 89: 1098–1115.

Just, R., and J. Miranowski. 1993. Understanding farmland price changes. *American Journal of Agricultural Economics* 75: 156–168.

Katz, L., and K. Rosen. 1987. The interjurisdictional effects of growth controls on housing prices. *Journal of Law and Economics* 30: 149–160.

Kline, J., and D. Wichelns. 1994. Using referendum data to characterize public support for purchasing development rights to farmland. *Land Economics* 70: 223–233.

Ladd, H. 1980. Tax policy considerations underlying preferential tax treatment of open space and agricultural land. In *Property Tax Preferences for Agricultural Land*, eds. N. A. Roberts and H. J. Brown. Montclair, NJ: Allanheld, Osman & Co., Inc.

Lenon, M., S. Chattopadhyay, and D. Heffley. 1996. Zoning and fiscal interdependencies. *Journal of Real Estate Finance and Economics* 12: 221–234.

Liu, X., and L. Lynch. 2011. Do agricultural land preservation programs reduce farmland loss? Evidence from a propensity score matching estimator. *Land Economics* 87: 183–201.

Loomis, J. 2000. Vertically summing public good demand curves: an empirical comparison of economic versus political jurisdictions. *Land Economics* 76: 312–321.

Lopez, R., F. Shah, and M. Altobello. 1994. Amenity benefits and the optimal allocation of land. *Land Economics* 70: 53–62.

Lutzenhiser, M., and N. Netusil. 2001. The effect of open spaces on a home's sale price. *Contemporary Economic Policy* 19: 291–298.

Mahan, B., S. Polasky, and R. Adams. 2000. Valuing urban wetlands: A property price approach. *Land Economics* 76: 100–113.

McConnell, V., M. Walls, and E. Kopits. 2003. A market approach to land preservation. *Resources* 150: 15–18.

McGonagle, M., and S. Swallow. 2005. Open space and public access: A contingent choice application to coastal preservation. *Land Economics* 81: 477–495.

McGuire, T., and D. Sjoquist. 2003. Urban sprawl and the finances of state and local governments. In *State and local finances under pressure*, ed. D. Sjoquist. London: Edward Elgar.

Miceli, T. 1992*a*. Optimal fiscal zoning that distorts housing consumption. *Journal of Real Estate Finance and Economics* 5: 323–331.

Miceli, T. 1992*b*. Optimal fiscal zoning when the local government is a discriminating monopolist. *Regional Science and Urban Economics* 22: 579–596.

Mills, E. 1967. An aggregative model of resource allocation in a metropolitan area. *American Economic Review* 57: 197–210.

Mills, D. 1980. Transferable development rights markets. *Journal of Urban Economics* 7: 63–74.

Muth, R. 1961. Economic change and rural-urban land conversions. *Econometrica* 29: 1–23.

Nelson, A. 1998. Farmland preservation policies: What works, what doesn't and what we don't know. In *Proceedings—The performance of state programs for farmland retention, A national research conference*, 9–48. Columbus, OH.

Nickerson, C., and L. Lynch. 2001. The effect of farmland preservation programs on farmland prices. *American Journal of Agricultural Economics* 83: 341–351.

Nickerson, C., and D. Hellerstein. 2003. Protecting rural amenities through farmland preservation programs. *Agricultural and Resource Economics Review* 32: 129–144.

Ostrom, E. 2010. Beyond markets and states: Polycentric governance of complex economic systems. *American Economic Review* 100: 641–672.

Parks, P., and J. Schorr. 1997. Sustaining open space benefits in the Northeast: An evaluation of the Conservation Reserve Program. *Journal of Environmental Economics and Management* 32: 85–94.

Plantinga, A., and S. Ahn. 2002. Efficient policies for environmental protection: An econometric analysis of incentives for land conversion and retention. *Journal of Agricultural and Resource Economics* 27: 128–145.

Poe, G. 1999. Maximizing the environmental benefits per dollar expended: An economic interpretation and review of agricultural environmental benefits and costs. *Society & Natural Resources* 12: 571–598.

Pollakowski, H., and S. Wachter. 1990. The effects of land-use constraints on housing prices. *Land Economics* 66: 315–324.

Rose, L. 1989. Urban land supply: Natural and contrived restrictions. *Journal of Urban Economics* 25: 325–345.

Ross, S., and J. Yinger. 1999. Sorting and voting: a review of the literature on urban public finance. In *Handbook of regional and urban economics.* Vol. 3 of Applied urban economics, ed. P. Chesire and E. Mills, 2001–2060. Amsterdam: Elsevier Science, North-Holland.

Santerre, R. 1985. Spatial differences in the demands for local public goods. *Land Economics* 61: 119–228.

Scotchmer, S. 2002. Local public goods and clubs. In *Handbook of public economics.* Vol. 4, ed. A. J. Auerbach and M. Feldstein, 1998–2042. Amsterdam: Elsevier Science B.V.

Shultz, S., and D. King. 2001. The use of census data for hedonic price estimates of open-space amenities and land use. *Journal of Real Estate Finance and Economics* 22: 239–252.

Smith, K., C. Poulos, and H. Kim. 2002. Treating open space as an urban amenity. *Resource and Energy Economics* 24: 107–129.

Stavins, R. 2011. The problem of the commons: Still unsettled after 100 years. *American Economic Review* 101: 81–108.

Strong, A., and R. Walsh. 2008. Communities, competition, spillovers, and open space. *Land Economics* 84: 169–187.

Thorsnes, P., and G. Simons. 1999. Letting the market preserve land: The case for a market-driven transfer of development rights program. *Contemporary Economic Policy* 17: 256–266.

Thorson, J. 1996. An examination of the monopoly zoning hypothesis. *Land Economics* 72: 43–55.

Tiebout, C. 1956. A pure theory of local expenditures. *Journal of Political Economy* 64: 416–424.

Wallace, N. 1988. The markets effects of zoning undeveloped land: Does zoning follow the market? *Journal of Urban Economics* 23: 307–326.

Walls, M., and V. McConnell. 2007. *Transfer of development rights in U.S. communities: Evaluating program design, implementation, and outcomes.* Washington, DC: Resources for the Future.

Weersink, A., S. Clark, C. Turvey, and R. Sarker. 1999. The effect of agricultural policy on farmland values. *Land Economics* 75: 425–439.

Weigher, J., and R. Zerbst. 1973. The externalities of neighborhood parks: An empirical investigation. *Land Economics* 49: 99–105.

White, M. 1975. Fiscal zoning in fragmented metropolitan areas. In *Fiscal zoning and land use controls*, eds. E. Mills and W. Oates. Lexington, MA: Heath.

Wolfram, G. 1981. The sale of development rights and zoning in the preservation of open space: Lindahl equilibrium and a case study. *Land Economics* 57: 398–413.

Wu, J., and E. Irwin. 2008. Optimal land development with endogenous environmental amenities. *American Journal of Agricultural Economics* 90: 232–248.

Wu, J., and H. Lin. 2010. The effect of the Conservation Reserve Program on land values. *Land Economics* 86: 1–21.

Wu, J., and A. Plantinga. 2003. The influence of public open space on urban spatial structure. *Journal of Environmental Economics and Management* 46: 288–309.

Wu, J., W. Xu, and R. Alig. 2012. Optimal location and size of open space: How do they affect urban landscapes? Unpublished manuscript.

Yinger, J. 1982. Capitalization and the theory of local public finance. *Journal of Political Economy* 90: 917–943.

CHAPTER 21

LAND CONSERVATION IN THE UNITED STATES

JEFFREY FERRIS AND LORI LYNCH

1. Land Conservation: Examples from the United States

LAND conservation provides a plethora of environmental benefits: improving ecosystem function, increasing habitat to endangered or threatened species, greenhouse-gas sequestration, and more. In addition, land conservation provides concrete economic benefits. Conserved lands improve the productivity of farmland by reducing soil erosion and water contamination, as well as by improving overall soil quality. Furthermore, natural ecosystems and the species that populate these lands are directly valued by the general public through activities such as outdoor recreation.

Yet, in a market system, these benefits are public goods and often underprovided from a societal viewpoint. These public goods are difficult to value and sell within land markets because they exhibit nonexcludability (it is difficult or costly to exclude people from using the goods and services even if they have not paid for them) and nonrivalry (one person's use of the goods and services does not reduce another's use). As such, these goods and services tend to be difficult to purchase by individuals and, even when purchased, the market price underestimates individuals' willingness to pay (WTP). In markets without coordination and/or regulations, these low prices result in underprovision; that is, too little of the goods and services will be provided.

Underprovision of these goods can result in negative externalities on a spatial basis. For example, owners on adjacent parcels would prefer farmland and/or a conservation use on a neighboring parcel and have a positive WTP to keep it from converting. However, the landowner of the parcel in question does not observe this uncoordinated WTP for conservation. Rather, the landowner observes the developers offer to purchase the land to convert it to a residential use. Similarly, people may value having an old growth redwood forest or a rainforest remain intact even if they never intend to visit or see it, but uncoordinated markets make this difficult to fulfill through a market mechanism. Beyond the difficulties of market provision, the US government has pursued many policy interventions, such as transportation policies, educational policies, banking regulations, and crime prevention or lack there of, which all affect the individual's optimal land use choices. By affecting development patterns, these policies may also contribute to suboptimal levels of land conservation and the provision of ecosystem services.

Because private landowners often make decisions in their private best interest rather than to optimize society's welfare, governments as well as private nongovernmental organizations (NGOs) operate to address the resulting market failures and conserve land. Their conservation programs often seek to redirect private and public decisions to ensure society's welfare is considered. Several different types of policies can be used to aid in this redirection: regulatory, incentive-based, participatory, and hybrid policies of these three types (categorization from Duke and Lynch 2006). Regulatory techniques adjust existing markets or define new markets such that society's benefits from conservation are addressed. Incentive-based techniques adjust price in the existing market structure to encourage certain conservation practices or land uses through taxes (penalties) or subsidies (Conservation Reserve Program [CRP] rental payments). Governments, land trusts, and other nongovernmental entities use participatory techniques—buying or selling land parcels or land rights to redirect market activities to desired conservation goals. In some cases, these techniques are utilized together to accomplish conservation goals. Recently, US Department of Agriculture (USDA) programs have focused on conservation practices on working land that are designed to improve the environmental performance of cropped agricultural land. These are in addition to land retirement programs, which completely remove land from agricultural use.

On a governmental level, land conservation is promoted through use of participatory, incentive-based, and regulatory initiatives with a variety of outcomes. In this chapter, we provide an overview of contemporary programs for land conservation in the United States. This chapter includes a discussion of the diversity of objectives in land conservation, recent research, and experiences from these programs, as well as the future of land conservation in the United States. We first explore the types of conservation and the different objectives that are pursued. These include participatory conservation through the fee-simple purchase of land, as well as through land use regulations and incentive-based programs for both land retirement and working lands. Recent shifts, such as conservation on working lands due to economic development concerns of local communities, are considered. Private efforts at land conservation are also explored. Some of these employ a hybrid of techniques. For example, tax deductions are used as an incentive to motivate participatory-type easement donations to land trusts and governmental organizations. Financing of conservation efforts is explained. We then outline two different methods of accounting for the benefits of land conservation: ecosystem services and societal economic values for these services. We explore the most recent literature on land conservation evaluations to determine what research can tell us about the existing policies and approaches. Important questions include the effectiveness of the policies in terms of benefits provided, prevention of development and/or other unintended consequences from the conservation, impact on land values, and spatial patterns invoked. We then draw some conclusions.

2. Types and Objectives of Land Conservation

Land conservation is pursued by many government agencies and individuals with a range of desired objectives. At the public level, various federal, state, and local entities promote land conservation through a series of interconnected programs and initiatives. These programs range in size as well as scope and seek a diversity of conservation goals. Here, an overview of current programs related to land conservation is provided. These programs are broken out into five main categories (applying the Duke and Lynch 2006 classification): publicly protected land conservation (participatory), regulatory requirements, conservation easements (participatory), working land programs (incentive based), and private initiatives for land conservation (participatory and hybrid).

Conservation was not the foremost thought of the United States in its formative years. Following the founding of the nation, public policy focused on the conversion of forest and prairies into agricultural uses and, to a lesser extent, to urban uses rather than conservation. Beginning with the Homestead Act of 1862 until 1934, the government transferred 10% of the land within the US to private ownership. To obtain their deed, landowners had to demonstrate "improvement to the land" i.e., conversion to a productive use. In addition, land reclamation converted wetlands and deltas into high-quality agricultural lands. In Colonial America, the 48 contiguous United States contained an estimated 221 million acres of wetlands (Dahl 1990). Over a period of 200 years, the lower 48 states lost more than half (53%) of their original wetlands (Dahl 1990). Over time, individuals and then government entities began to realize that conservation of forest, prairies, wetlands, and high-quality soils may be beneficial to social welfare. Efforts toward conservation moved slowly in many cases but strengthened in the early 20th century.

3. Participatory Conservation

3.1 Publicly Protected Land

Perhaps the most visible publicly sponsored land conservation in the United States is the network of federal, state, and local protected lands that dot the US landscape. In 1864, advocates convinced the US government to designate Yosemite Valley a publicly protected area. Yellowstone Park soon followed, withdrawing more than 2 million acres from private hands to preserve forest, wildlife, and minerals from human use. But it was not until 1916 that Congress created a federal bureau, the National Park Service (NPS), to manage lands designated under the concept of large-scale natural preservation of areas for public enjoyment.

At the federal level, protected areas are divided into three main categories: wilderness areas, national parks and national forests.[1] Across the United States, there are a total of nearly 290 million acres[2] of federally protected land classified as wilderness area, national park, or national forest. These lands exist in all 50 US states, plus the District of Columbia, and represent approximately 17% of the total US land area. At the state level, more than 6,600 state parks cover approximately 14 million acres of land in the United States (Walls et al. 2009). No central database exists for information regarding local parks, but based on an annual survey conducted by the Trust for Public Land (2011), there are at least 22,493 individual parks covering an area of 1.5 million acres in the United States in 100 cities. More than half of these received 1 million visitors per year.

Publicly protected lands provide the best source of permanent and dedicated lands for ecosystems to flourish. These lands also provide a dual function as primary locations for outdoor recreation in the United States. Although publicly protected lands may be acquired through a variety of regulatory[3] and voluntary[4] methods, the vast majority of public resources are spent in maintaining and improving existing protected land. The authorized operating budget of the US National Parks Service alone was nearly $2.6 billion in 2012 (US Department of Interior, 2012).

3.2 Private Initiatives

Beyond government efforts at land conservation, many private NGOs pursue conservation objectives. Many of these are land trusts, which are nonprofit organizations that operate to conserve land through conservation easements or direct fee-simple acquisition. People organize them at the local, state, and national level. In 2010, 1,723 land trusts were active; 1,699 at the state and local level and 24 at the national level. Together, they conserved 47 million acres, an increase of 23 million acres in the past decade (Chang 2011). Because land trusts can act more quickly than governmental agencies, they often purchase land or the development rights that they can then convey to a governmental agency. Although all regions of the United States have land trusts, those in the Northeast

[1] Wilderness areas are afforded the highest level of protection and are designed to be completely untrammeled by humans. National parks are managed for ecosystem function, but also allow recreational access, and national forests are afforded the least protection and are managed primarily for sustainability.

[2] Wilderness areas encompass 109.7 million acres, national parks 79.7 million acres, and national forests 192.9 million acres

[3] Lands may be procured by the government through the right of eminent domain.

[4] Some governments also receive protected lands by donation or outright purchase.

have preserved almost twice as much land as land trusts in other regions. The 2010 National Land Trust Census Report suggests that almost half of the land trusts have now written project selection criteria to guide their selection of parcels, with important natural areas and wildlife habitat being the most important priorities (Chang 2011).

4. Regulatory Conservation Land Use Restrictions

Society seeks to alter the pace and/or pattern of land use for various reasons and, in some cases, has used regulatory mechanisms. Regulatory conservation methods are frequently utilized when either conservation objectives require a high degree of coordination or private citizens cannot be incentivized to preserve land of their own accord.

Some of the most readily used options for promoting regulatory conservation at the state and local level is through low-density or agricultural zoning and development restrictions. These measures include such policies as minimum lot size or clustering zoning restrictions, urban growth boundaries (UGBs), and adequate public facility ordinances (APFOs) (Irwin et al. 2005). These policies can be implemented simultaneously. Experience with conservation zoning has been mixed; while some communities aggressively pursue conservation zoning, others ignore it all together, which creates a patchy network of conservation zones for wildlife to utilize. Minimum lot zoning has also been criticized for encouraging the consumption of larger land parcels rather than for creating conservation zones.

At the federal level, the Endangered Species Act (ESA)[5] uses recovery plans that include regulatory measures to conserve species considered endangered or threatened. After a species receives ESA protection, the recovery plan is developed to prohibit the harvesting and hunting of the species and to establish a "critical habitat zone" with a habitat conservation plan. A critical habitat zone is a geographic area that is deemed necessary for the species' survival and may exist on either public or private lands. If a critical habitat zone intersects private land, development of this land is significantly constrained by regulation and requires an extensive permitting process for any additional construction, thus limiting human use. However, substantial political and bureaucratic hurdles must be surmounted before a species may be guaranteed protection by the ESA, thus limiting its application to large-scale conservation efforts.

Most recently, the Environmental Protection Agency (EPA) has been working to implement a regulatory scheme to enforce the Total Maximum Daily Loads (TMDL) requirements in cases in which water pollution problems endure. Although a cap-and-trade system has been proposed, the TMDL regulations require that all land

[5] http://www.epa.gov/lawsregs/laws/esa.html

users must reduce their nutrient pollution, in contrast with the USDA's incentive-based and largely voluntary programs.

5. Incentive-Based Conservation

5.1 Voluntary Land Retirement Programs

Voluntary incentive-based initiatives are another tool used for conservation—most often individuals are paid a subsidy to adopt a conservation practice on their land. In the early 1990s, about one-fifth of the US land area (382 million acres) was used for crop production and one-quarter of privately owned land for grazing land for livestock (525 million acres) (USDA National Resources Conservation Service [NRCS] 1996). The USDA Economic Research Service reported that 2007 cropland had increased to 408 million acres, with grassland pasture and rangeland at 614 million acres (both public and privately owned). Urban land occupied only 61 million acres (3%) (Nickerson et al. 2011). Given the large number of acres in agricultural landowners' hands, conservation efforts may be well directed to them. It was not until 1936 that the USDA established the first programs to pay farmers to use soil conserving practices. In part, these programs sought to support farm incomes by reducing surplus grain supplies and increasing commodity prices. Soil conservation programs were justified by "on farm" benefits like enhancing crop yields and preserving crop productivity. It was not until 50 years later that the 1985 Farm Bill radically altered the conservation agenda. In addition to addressing conservation in its own right, it expanded soil erosion control concerns, used "swampbuster" provisions to reverse USDA policies on draining wetlands, and employed land retirement policies to remove lands with most pressing erosion problems from production. In addition, the cross-compliance provision specifically linked commodity payments to conservation practices for farmers. Currently, the USDA has 20 conservation programs that can be split into five broad categories: land retirement programs (around 48% of the 2010 budget was spent on these); working land programs that provide cost-share or payments for conservation assistance (with 30% of the 2010 budget); conservation technical assistance (with 17.5% of the total); agricultural land preservation and rural development programs (with around 3.4%); and watershed structural activities like flood prevention work (with 1.4% of the total) (Pavelis et al. 2011).

In the United States, the CRP is by far the largest program for voluntary incentive-based conservation contracts between the government and willing landowners. Under CRP, farmers are paid an annual rent to remove land from agricultural production for a predetermined or occasionally indefinite period and adopt a conservation practice. Farmers often enroll low-productivity lands, which may be infrequently cropped to begin with, in hopes that government subsidies for conservation exceed the expected profit from agricultural production. In this way, farmers benefit by receiving fixed and guaranteed revenue from agricultural lands, and society benefits[6] from the ecological services provided and the improvements on these conserved lands.

CRP is administered by the US Farm Service Agency (FSA) and is broken up into a number of smaller programs.[7] "Annual signup" is the largest constituent program,[8] and it allows farmers to enroll land under contracts of 10–15 years in exchange for a predetermined annual payment. The other subprograms work similarly but focus on preserving high-priority conservation lands (Ferris and Siikamäki 2009). In 2010, CRP enrolled a total of 31.3 million acres, land area approximately equivalent to the size of the state of Mississippi, and made annual payments in excess of $1.6 billion.

In the 1700s, the 48 contiguous United States contained an estimated 221 million acres of wetlands (but lost 53% of them over the next 200 years; Dahl 1990). To slow the loss of wetlands on farms, the USDA also initiated the Wetland Reserve Program (WRP)[9] administered by the Natural Resource Conservation Service. In the WRP, the government purchases long-term or perpetual easements to restore, protect, and enhance wetlands that have been in agricultural production. The WRP enrolls only a fraction of the land[10] that is enrolled in CRP, but has also steadily grown in size in recent history, unlike the CRP.

5.2 Working Land Programs

The USDA, in cooperation with other government agencies, generates additional conservation benefits through use of various working land programs. Working land programs help to promote sustainability and engage farmers hesitant to adopt long-term land retirement. Under these programs, farmers are allowed to continue cropping agricultural lands while implementing conservation practices that generate substantial ecological benefits.

The USDA Natural Resources Conservation Service (NRCS) is responsible for managing a majority of the working land programs in the United States. The NRCS manages a network of "financial assistance programs";[11] among the largest and best studied are the Environmental Quality Incentives Program (EQIP) and the Conservation Stewardship Program (CSP). These programs promote a range of conservation goals

[6] Farmers may also derive environmental benefit from conservation easements, in the form of improved agricultural productivity of surrounding lands.

[7] Formally, CRP is composed of five subprograms with similar objectives: general signup, continuous signup, Conservation Reserve Enhancement Program (CREP), Farmable Wetland Program (FWP), and the Emergency Forest Conservation Reserve Program (EFCRP).

[8] More than 26.6 million acres are enrolled, and annual payments are in excess of $1.1 billion in 2010 (US Farm Service Agency 2011).

[9] http://www.nrcs.usda.gov/wps/portal/nrcs/main/national/programs/easements

[10] Slightly more than 200,000 acres were enrolled in 2011.

[11] A full list is available at http://www.nrcs.usda.gov/wps/portal/nrcs/main/national/programs/financial

through education, cost-sharing opportunities, and access to sustainable infrastructure development. Smaller programs include the Grassland Reserve Program (GRP), which is a voluntary conservation program that enhances plant and animal biodiversity on working grazing operations. Landowners agree to restrict future development and cropping uses of the land but can graze the land outside of the nesting seasons of declining bird species. The Farm and Ranch Land Protection Program (FRPP) works with existing farmland preservation programs by providing matching funds to help purchase development rights to retain farm and ranchland as working lands. Similarly, the Healthy Forests Reserve Program (HFRP) helps landowners restore and protect forests serving as habitat for endangered and threatened species, to improve diversity, and for carbon sequestration, either permanently or via 30-year contracts. The NRCS working land programs have the additional advantage of promoting conservation of high-quality, highly productive agricultural land. In this way, program administrators can help promote targeted and focused conservation goals when landowners wish to continue farming.

6. Land Conservation Financing

6.1 Tax Revenue Finances both Participatory and Incentive-Based Conservation

Many conservation programs on the federal and state level are financed through general income tax revenue. Other conservation has received public support through ballot-approved financings. Counties or states sell bonds and incur debt to finance land conservation today. These bonds are then repaid through local or state tax income over a 20- to 30-year period. People also have approved new taxes to pay for conservation. For example, communities may agree to a ½% increase in their sales tax or a 1% increase on their real estate transaction tax to finance the land conservation efforts. This money can be used for fee-simple land acquisition, conservation easement purchase, or to provide incentives to landowners to adopt conservation practices. Figure 21.1 demonstrates the steady increase in conservation funding initiatives until 2008, when more than $8 billion in conservation funding was approved through the ballot box. Since the economic downturn in 2008, this funding has declined.

Some programs benefit from dedicated funds. For example, if the general public has approved new taxes to pay for conservation, this extra sales tax or real estate transaction tax must be used for conservation purposes. Dedicated funds are not always sufficient to accomplish a program's goals. And if these dedicated conservation funds are connected to conversion of farmland, as is the case with Maryland's agricultural transfer tax, then conservation becomes linked to farmland exiting the industry. For example, Lynch et al. (2007) found that in Carroll County, the conversion of $60,051 worth of farmland—almost 12 acres—would be needed to conserve 1 acre of farmland in the county.

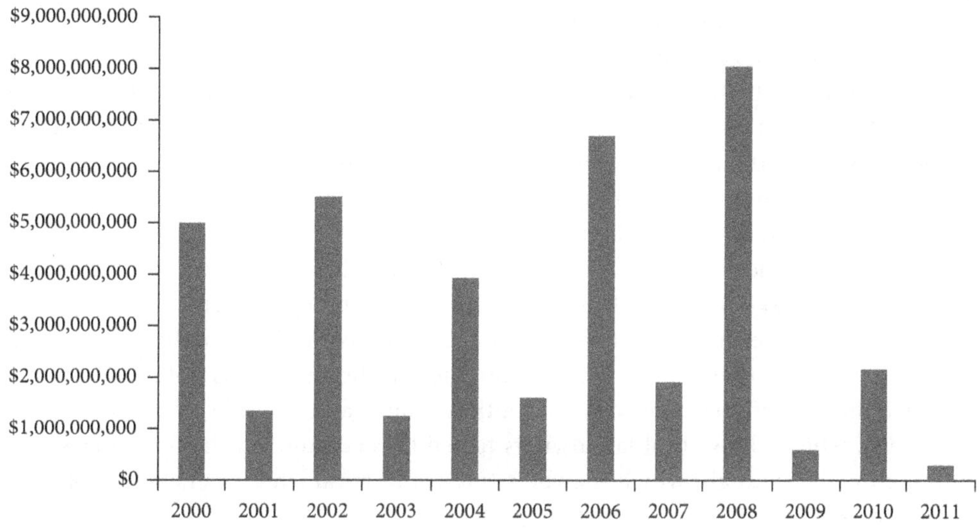

FIGURE 21.1 Conservation funds approved.

Similarly, in Baltimore County, the conversion of $76,352 or 9.6 acres would be needed to preserve 1 acre (Lynch et al. 2007). Thus, the funding and the goals of the program can work at cross purposes.

6.2 Tax Deductions Act as Incentive-Based Tools for Participatory Conservation

Both governmental programs and NGOs benefit from a 1976 special exception to the rule against deduction of partial interests in property. At the federal level, due to this exception, individual(s) who donates a conservation easement on all or part of their land are entitled to an income tax reduction (charitable deduction) equivalent to the fair market value of the donation,[12] subject to certain eligibility requirements,[13] even though they retain ownership of the land. The tax code allows landowners to deduct 30% of their adjusted gross income each year over a six-year period. Depending on the existing land conservation status and percentage of income derived from agriculture by the landowner, an individual may be eligible for additional income tax deductions (Internal Revenue Service [IRS] 2012). In the tax

[12] The difference between the value of their land before easement and the value of the land after easement.

[13] To be eligible for donation, the easement must be in perpetuity, be held by a valid nonprofit or government agency, and serve an approved conservation purpose. All further eligibility requirements are listed at http://www.irs.gov/businesses/small/article/0,,id=249135,00.html

years 2006–2011, these incentive-based tools were enhanced to allow landowners to take deductions of up to 50% of their adjusted gross income and expanded the carry-forward period to 15 years after the year of the first deduction. These enhancements allowed more individuals to utilize the deduction fully and appears to have encouraged additional conservation easement donations. The enhancement was allowed to expire at the end of 2011 but has recently been extended through 2013. Thus unless Congress extends the provisions again, this enhanced incentive will expire December 31, 2013.

In addition to the federal deduction, as of 2012, at least 16 states[14] provide some form of income tax credits for land donation or conservation easement (Land Trust Alliance 2012). For example, Maryland landowners receive a $5,000 credit on their state income taxes when they donate their development rights, as well as state property tax relief. Colorado, Georgia, New Mexico, South Carolina, and Virginia grant transferable tax credits, which allow rural landowners to sell these credits on the open market to high-income individuals, which may be attractive to rural landowners with relatively modest incomes and low tax brackets.

7. Conservation Benefits: Accounting and Economic Value

Land conservation generates benefits in two primary ways: ecosystem benefits from land preservation ("conservation benefit accounting") and societal benefits from preservation (the "economic value of conservation"). Although interrelated, researchers and policy makers distinguish between these two forms of conservation measurement. In the following section, an overview of policy and recent research is provided for both forms of conservation benefits in the context of prominent programs for land conservation in the United States.

7.1 Conservation Benefit Accounting

Conservation benefit accounting is an area of research that has undergone a rapid evolution in recent years. Owing to the complexities of ecosystem and wildlife dynamics, the task of determining the ecological benefits resulting from a particular land conservation program used to be insurmountable. However, as understanding of these complex ecosystem processes have improved, and as modeling efforts gain more computational

[14] These states include Arkansas, California, Colorado, Connecticut, Delaware, Florida, Georgia, Iowa, Maryland, Massachusetts, Mississippi, New Mexico, New York, North Carolina, South Carolina, and Virginia

power, contemporary models of ecosystem benefits resulting from land conservation provide us with more information.

In part because of the additional information, policy makers have changed the metrics by which they report ecosystem benefits and program successes and the design elements of conservation policy. Previously, the two most important metrics in conservation benefit accounting were program budget and total enrolled acres. However, ecosystem benefits accrue in different ways depending on the program design. Thus, an acre of land enrolled in a working land program, such as EQIP, is not equivalent to an acre enrolled in WRP, which is also different from an acre of national parks land. As a matter of procedure, government conservation programs increasingly and prominently report ecological benefits as a measure of programmatic success.

This focus on ecological benefits has an impact on conservation effectiveness as well. Given a specific conservation goal, such as reducing soil erosion, policy makers have an improved capacity to design programs that address this ecological issue. As a result, policy makers have begun to shift more conservation resources away from fee-simple land purchases toward targeted easement procurement and targeted working land programs. In a case study in Maryland, Messer (2006) found that the emphasis on fee-simple acquisition of highly ranked (and often expensive) land conservation overlooked the higher overall returns of purchasing lower ranked, lower cost land, as well as the benefits of using easements. Similarly, program designs that take into account threshold impacts of conservation function more effectively. Lynch and Liu (2007) found that the targeted preservation areas set by the Maryland Rural Legacy program attract additional preservation to these areas, thus achieving higher degrees of contiguity than would otherwise occur.

7.2 Economic Value of Conservation

In addition to providing important ecosystem benefits, conserved land also generates value to human society. Economic benefits from conservation may accrue in many ways, including through direct valuation of ecosystem services on these lands and indirect improvement in agricultural production, as well as through the value of outdoor recreation. Economists estimate the direct and indirect value of conservation to society and also seek to understand the dynamic response of large landowners, like farmers and other members of the public, to land conservation programs.

Conservation programs generate benefits in a number of ways, and economists help policy makers understand the value such programs add to society. Because many programs set multiple goals, researchers must consider not only the primary benefit but also the secondary benefits of conservation in their analysis, including unintended consequences. As an example, the CRP was originally established to help reduce farmland soil erosion, but, as a secondary benefit, it also provided significant income support to farmers with relatively marginal cropland. CRP has also realized numerous other conservation objectives, such as habitat restoration and additional space for recreation, as well as carbon sequestration, among others. The conservation value of the CRP program, then, is its direct benefit of primary conservation objectives, its secondary benefits to farmers, and its tertiary benefits to other conservation objectives.

Researchers have also improved their understanding of the dynamic interaction between human behavior and conservation outcomes. Even programs designed with the best intent can often lead to undesired consequences. For instance, the Endangered Species Act (ESA) prohibits the destruction of critical habitats of protected species. However, this Act may create incentives for landowners to speed up the extraction of resources from lands that they suspect might fall under ESA protection (Lueck and Michaels 2003). This "shoot, shovel, and shut up" behavior, also known as the 3-S treatment, may result in species and habitat destruction rather than species and habitat retention.

With dwindling resources for conservation, government agencies are forced to provide more societal benefits with less money. Increasingly, these government agencies are relying on researchers to help target resources that yield the greatest amount of benefit for the least amount of money. Experiences with program evaluations have been diverse. Government agencies have been gradually shifting away from broad national initiatives designed to protect the greatest amount of acres but that may not fit all locations and toward more locally defined initiatives in which local conditions can be best addressed. A more localized approach to conservation may increase the effectiveness of achieving specific conservation objectives, as well as engage the local population to achieve important community goals. However, this may come at the cost of missing low-cost, high-benefit conservation opportunities.

8. Participatory: Publicly Protected Lands

In many ways, assessing the ecological benefits from permanently protected lands is quite difficult. Although important for habitat maintenance and ecosystem services, much of this land has been protected for years. Some of these lands have never been developed or converted into nonconservation uses. As a result, researchers find it difficult to determine the counterfactual (i.e., "How would this land's use differ if not publicly protected?"). As a result, few assessments of the economic value of ecosystem services provided by protected land exist. However, a substantial volume of research seeks to evaluate the recreational value of protected areas.

Most research on the ecological impacts of protected areas has focused on the potential threat that residential development, particularly along the edges of the protected areas, poses (Table 21.1). Gude et al. (2007) studied the potential for exurban development in the neighborhood of Yellowstone National Park to undermine local habitats and biodiversity. On a national scale, Radeloff et al. (2010) and Wade et al. (2010, 2011) performed a multisystem assessment of threats to protected land from developmental

Table 21.1 Assessing threats to protected land from exurban development

Study	Study program	Focus	Study area	Findings
Gude et al. (2007)	National Parks	Rural development encroaching on critical habitats in publicly protected land	Yellowstone National Park	Measured biodiversity responses are likely to undergo between 5% and 40% conversion due to exurban development.
Radeloff et al. (2010)	Federally protected land	Housing growth near publicly protected land	Nationwide	Housing growth rates were 7% higher on lands within 1 km of protected areas than the national average during the 1990s. Potentially, another 17 million housing units will be built within 50 km of protected areas by 2030 (1 million within 1 km).
Wade and Theobald (2010)	Federally protected land	Housing growth near publicly protected land	Nationwide	Conservation buffer zones around publicly protected areas will have decreased by 12% from 1970 to 2030 as a result of development.
Wade et al. (2011)	Federally protected land	Assessing threats to US protected areas	Nationwide	At least 35% of currently protected land is at risk from external development. Only 20% of currently unprotected lands provide opportunities for future conservation.

encroachment on habitat buffer zones. Radeloff et al. (2010) found that housing growth rates were higher near protected lands. Wade and Theobald (2010) also found that buffers around the parks were decreasing quickly. Similarly, Wade et al. (2011) find that fully 35% of all protected land is threatened by external development, whereas only 20% of unprotected land could be conserved (Table 21.1). Collectively, findings by these researchers suggest that policy makers need to be proactive in ensuring that future development around existing protected areas does not undermine the conservation objectives of these preserved lands.

Table 21.2 Value of parks as an urban amenity

Study	Study program	Focus	Study area	Findings
Crompton (2007*a*)	Mostly urban parks	Assessment of impacts of parks on the tax-receipts from neighborhood homes	Aggregations of many studies and locations	Park-adjacent homes generate premiums of up to 20% in increased property value. When evaluated in aggregate, increased tax revenues from proximate homes may be enough to meet costs of developing and maintaining parks.
Crompton (2007*b*)	Mostly urban parks	Evaluating the effect of parks on attracting companies, labor supplies, and retirees to cities	Aggregations of many studies and areas	After reaching a certain income threshold, improvements in quality of life become more important than increases in income. Parks are key to improving lifestyle and attracting highly skilled employees and companies.
Ham et al. (2012)	National park	Ascertaining the proximate value of national forests to home-owners	Pike National Forest	A 1% decrease in mean distance to the Pike National Forest increases house prices by 6.4%.
Klaiber and Phaneuf (2009, 2010)	City parks	Modeling the hedonic value of parks under the assumption of population heterogeneity and sorting	Minneapolis-Saint Paul Metropolitan Area, Minnesota	A 12.5% increase in regional park area would result in a hedonic willingness to pay (WTP) per household of $30. When sorting and heterogeneity are taken into account, WTP is between $5.19 and $9.36.
Poudyal et al. (2009)	City parks	Performed a two-stage hedonic assessment of the value of urban parks based on local home prices	Roanoke, Virginia	A 20% increase in park size increased per-household consumer surplus by more than $160. Total consumer surplus was in excess of $6.5 million for all 50,000 homes located within a mile of each park.

Table 21.3 Recreational value of publicly protected lands

Study	Study program	Focus	Study area	Findings
Baerenklau et al. (2010)	National Forest Land	Developing a method to analyze the recreational value of forest cover	Southern California	Annual values range from $41 to $10,369 per hectare of forest land, depending on location and other characteristics of these lands.
Deisenroth, Loomis, and Bond (2009)	A variety of protected land classes	Estimating the nonmarket valuation of off-road recreation	Larimer County, Colorado	Mean per-person consumer surplus is estimated to be $78 per day. Every summer, each trail is expected to provide $219,467–$296,876, and off-roading provides $796,447-$1,077,367 to the entire county.
Siikamäki (2011)	State Park System	Valuing recreation generated at state parks around the nation based on the American Time Use Survey	Nationwide	State parks generate approximately 2.2 billion hours of nature recreation per year. In total, the value of recreation generated at all state parks is $14 billion.

Parkland is a valuable community resource impacting the health and well-being of many urban communities (Table 21.2). Home buyers seek proximity to parkland and are willing to pay, with such property values being upward of 20% higher than those farther away (Crompton 2007*a*). Using hedonic models, as well as other WTP approaches, other researchers have consistently shown a positive impact of park proximity on home-value, including Klaiber and Phaneuf (2009), Poudyal et al. (2009) and Ham et al. (2012). When evaluated at the social level, parkland has the highest valued land classifications per acre. Parkland has higher value as open space than as residential development. Crompton (2007*b*) argues that parks are also crucial to a community's ability to attract companies, new labor, and retirees. All these bolster a community's tax base and future growth prospects, thus stimulating long-term economic growth.

Local, state, and national parks are among the premier destinations in the United States for outdoor recreation. As such, research has been conducted to assess the value of these assets from a recreational standpoint (Table 21.3)[15] employing contingent WTP

[15] Walls, Darley, and Siikamäki (2009) provide a breakdown of multisystem benefits resulting from US city, state, and national parks.

surveys as well as revealed preference studies. In recent work, Baerenklau et al. (2010) and Deisenroth, Loomis, and Bond (2009) studied the recreational value of federally protected lands, finding ranges from $41 to almost $300,000 per hectare of forest land and trails within the various parks. At the state level, Siikamäki (2011) studied the value of state parks based on aggregate time-use trends from the American Time Use Survey taken from individuals sampled[16] across the United States. This research found that about 2.2 billion hours of nature recreation occurred at state parks each year. These studies demonstrate the high value of protected lands, providing millions of dollars each year in consumer surplus across the United States. From a public policy perspective, the use-value of protected land can be an overlooked component of conservation benefits. For many, their use of these parks for outdoor recreation explains a large part of their WTP for such areas.

9. Conservation Reserve Program and Wetland Reserve Program

Together, CRP and WRP have been among the most studied land conservation programs in the United States. Owing to their geographic expansiveness and the availability of data, researchers continue to improve their understanding of the benefits resulting from these programs. Although CRP and WRP have slightly differing conservation focuses, with CRP focusing on agricultural land and WRP focusing on wetlands, their similar organizational structure has led many researchers to group these two programs together. Research has evaluated the ecological benefits, estimated the economic value of these programs, and explored how farmers behave in response to CRP/WRP parameters.

Most researchers interested in the ecological benefits of CRP/WRP have conducted regional assessments of program benefits and environmental performance (Table 21.4). In a series of papers, Gleason et al. (2008, 2011) estimated the quantity of ecosystem services (decreased erosion, carbon sequestration, increased bird populations) provided by CRP and WRP in the Prairie Pothole Region[17] of the United States.[18] Wentworth, Brittingham, and Wilson (2010) utilized data from Pennsylvania farms to assess Conservation Reserve Enhancement Program (CREP) effect on grassland

[16] Individuals were sampled using the American Time Use Survey (ATUS), which offers detailed descriptions of the daily activities elicited from a rotating sample of individuals.

[17] A loosely defined region of the US Upper Midwest that includes areas of North Dakota, Minnesota, South Dakota, and Iowa, critically important for migratory bird nesting.

[18] They find that CRP/WRP conservation in these areas significantly decreases erosion (approximately 2.6 metric tons per acre enrolled) and carbon sequestration (1.05 metric tons per acre), in addition to significantly increasing migratory bird population, such as ducks.

Table 21.4 Ecosystem services provided by Conservation Reserve Program (CRP)/Wetland Reserve Program (WRP) lands

Study	Study program	Focus	Study area	Findings
Gleason et al. (2008, 2011)	CRP/WRP	Estimating the ecosystem services provided by CRP/WRP lands	The Prairie Pothole Region (PPR)	CRP/WRP conservation in these areas significantly decreases erosion (~2.6 metric tons per acre enrolled) and increases carbon sequestration (1.05 metric tons per acre). CRP/WRP also significantly increases migratory bird population, such as ducks.
Gallant et al. (2011)	CRP/WRP	Modeling historical land use patterns in the context of current CRP/WRP enrollment	Iowa	Researchers determined that most ecosystem losses in Iowa occurred in areas with a high concentration of wetlands, whereas CRP and WRP wetland improvements occurred in areas with historically few wetlands.
Wentworth et al. (2010)	CREP	Evaluating the effectiveness of CREP at maximizing programmatic benefits from enrolled lands	Pennsylvania	These researchers conclude that Conservation Reserve Enhancement Program (CREP) wildlife benefits could be maximized if CREP targeted large parcels of land or land adjacent to other grassland fields.

fauna.[19] Gallant et al. (2011) utilizes data regarding historical land use patterns in Iowa as a means of evaluating CRP and WRP program effectiveness in this region.[20] Research on CRP and WRP suggests that these programs provide a substantial amount of ecosystem services. However, researchers suggest that targeting and integrating CRP/WRP lands into the existing supply of conserved land could improve program performance.

Considerable attention has been given to evaluating the economic value of CRP conservation (Table 21.5). Hansen and Ribaudo (2008) provided one of the most comprehensive estimates of per-ton benefits from reduced soil erosion on CRP lands. They provide estimates for economic benefits resulting from a variety of conservation objectives[21] and conclude that, per ton of conserved soil, societal benefits for measured conservation objectives range between $0.83 and $26.40[22] per year. Wu and Lin (2010) analyzed the impact of CRP conservation on aggregate farmland values and found that, nationwide, CRP increased the value of farmland between $18 and $25 per acre (about 1.3–1.8% of the land value). Vukina et al. (2008) estimated the farmer's value of conservation based on the bids each made to enroll his land into available programs. They find that farmers with higher quality land submit higher bids. Secchi et al. (2009) evaluated the impact that continued ethanol subsidies could have on the supply of CRP lands and found that high corn prices and thus competition for land resources could hamper CRP conservation benefits.

Some researchers have analyzed CRP bid mechanisms to determine cost-benefit of the program. CRP initially focused on enrolling as much land as possible through least-cost enrollment: farmers who offered land below a threshold value were accepted into the program. However, starting in the 1990s, CRP has gradually shifted toward benefit-cost targeting, which scores a prospective parcel using an Environmental Benefit Index (EBI) and enrolls land that provides the most conservation benefit per value of contract until the budget is exhausted (Claassen et al. 2008). Changes in bidding structure and parcel "ranking" have increased the efficiency of CRP since the program's inception in the early 1980s (Ferraro 2008). However, Vukina et al. (2008) found that making these ranking criteria publicly available has resulted in farmers adjusting their bids based on the quality of their own land, which undermines the cost effectiveness of the auction mechanism.

[19] These researchers conclude that CREP wildlife benefits could be maximized if CREP targeted large parcels of land and/or land adjacent to other grassland fields.

[20] In the course of their research, they determined that most ecosystem losses in Iowa occurred in areas with a high concentration of wetlands, whereas CRP and WRP wetland improvements occurred in areas with historically few wetlands.

[21] These benefits result from reduced wind erosion, water treatment, soil productivity, reservoir services, fisheries, and recreation, among other categories.

[22] At these levels, total benefits from reduced soil erosion range between $182 million and $5,808 million per year.

Table 21.5 Economic analysis of Conservation Reserve Program (CRP)

Study	Study program	Focus	Study area	Findings
Hansen and Ribaudo (2008)	CRP	Estimating societal benefits from reduced soil erosion from CRP lands around the nation	Nationwide	Per-ton economic benefits are calculated across a variety of soil conservation objectives and regions. Over the entire United States, each ton of soil conserved results in \$0.83–\$26.40 worth of benefit per year, for a total societal benefit of \$182–\$5808 million per year.
Wu and Lin (2010)	CRP	Implementing a system of equations to ascertain the total effect of CRP on agricultural land values	Nationwide	CRP increases agricultural land values between \$18 and \$25 per acre (~1.3–1.8% of land value). The areas with the largest gains include Mountain, Southern Plains, and Northern Plains regions.
Vukina et al. (2008)	CRP	Assessing farmer value of conservation based on farmer bids to CRP	North Carolina and Georgia	Farmer CRP bids are relatively competitive, with average bids of ~\$42.70; the actual cost of conservation made up 99% of total bid (\$42.27) and only a \$0.43 premium. Furthermore, farmers condition bids based on the perceived quality of the land, with bids increasing by \$0.73 for each increase in Environmental Benefit Index (EBI) score.
Secchi et al. (2009)	CRP	Evaluating the potential impacts to the supply of CRP lands based on increases in total corn-based ethanol production	Iowa	At corn prices of \$196.84/ton per hectare, sediment losses increase from 0.1 tons/ha for the almost 700,000 hectare of CRP included in the EPIC analysis to almost 1.9 tons per hectare as almost 500,000 hectares of CRP land are put back into production.
Ferraro (2008)	Payment for Ecosystem Services	Asymmetric information and contract design for payments for environmental services	Nationwide	The EBI used by CRP to rank farmer bids creates competition and prioritizes funding to highly valued conservation targets. However, making this information public to landowners also may encourage rent-seeking behavior from farmers with highly sought-after land.
Claassen et al. (2008)	Payment for Ecosystem Services	Analyzing the literature on the effectiveness of benefit-cost targeting in CRP farmland bidding	Nationwide	Although research has shown that the EBI did increase the environmental benefits of the CRP, additional improvements in environmental cost-effectiveness of the CRP could be achieved by further shifting emphasis from soil productivity maintenance to enhancing water quality and wildlife habitat.

Program administrators have incorporated the research finding into program evaluations and made changes to improve the economic efficiency and achieve specific conservation objectives. Total enrolled land peaked in 2007 at 36.8 million acres and then decreased to a low of 31.3 million acres in 2010, the most recent year for which CRP data are available (US Farm Service Agency [FSA] 2011). The acreage decline results from lower budgets and nonrenewal of expiring CRP contracts. Although land enrolled in the general CRP signups has been decreasing, land enrolled in CREP and other subprograms has actually increased. CREP focuses on high-priority lands for conservation and uses much stricter guidelines for acceptance into the program than general signup (Ferris and Siikamäki 2009). Thus, although enrolled acres have decreased by more than 5 million acres, environmental benefits have declined at a much slower rate, and the environmental benefits per enrolled acre have actually increased. Figure 21.2 displays reduced nitrogen, phosphorus, and sequestered carbon dioxide per CRP acre per year[23] over the time frame 2004 to 2010, as well as total CRP land during this time.

10. Conservation Through Conversion Prevention

10.1 Regulatory Conservation Through Development Restrictions and Redirection

Since approximately the 1950s, commercial, industrial, and housing development has shifted from city centers to suburban and exurban communities nationwide. Brown et al. (2005) estimates that between 1950 and 2000, urban land area[24] has grown less than 1–2%, compared to 5–25% for exurban land[25] during this same time frame. In response to these rapid changes in land use patterns, state, county, and city governments implement a variety of initiatives to slow the development of resource land, shift the spatial patterns, and protect resource lands. These initiatives may be classified as developmental restriction (regulatory) and easement procurement (participatory). Researchers seek to assess the impact of conservation initiatives on communities, as well as understand the economic impact of these regulations. They have conducted both ex ante and ex post analyses of these development restrictions and easement programs.

Unlike other national-level policies, community-level conservation programs are not applied uniformly over a large geographic area and, as such, often provide researchers

[23] These figures are further scaled by the average reduction of each pollutant during this time for the sake of comparison.

[24] Less than one acre per dwelling.

[25] Between 1 and 40 acres per dwelling.

with natural experiments to exploit. In this way, program effectiveness may be ascertained by comparing communities with active conservation policies to neighboring communities without such policies in place. As a result, researchers have a possible counterfactual of how a community would have evolved if a conservation policy were not implemented.

Many local, regional, and state governments utilize developmental restrictions to conserve land in the short-term. A large variety of conservation initiatives exist throughout the United States, but the most intensely studied programs include low-density and minimum lot size zoning, UGBs, and APFOs. Irwin et al. (2009) provide a comprehensive overview of the economics of urban and rural space, including a discussion of policy options for community-led conservation initiatives. In general, research has found that development restrictions provoke mixed outcomes. Although effective in some instances, these policies may also have unexpected and unintended impacts.

Many researchers have found that properly implemented zoning restrictions can reduce the probability of land conversion and, as such, provide for land conservation. However, the end result of zoning regulations can be surprising. For instance, in an analysis of zoning and development patterns in Calvert County, Maryland, McConnell et al. (2006) found zoning regulations decreased the quantity of residential lots by 10% relative to what would have otherwise occurred. However, they also find that developmental patterns are affected by many factors other than zoning laws. Magliocca et al. (2012) apply an agent-based simulation model to study the effect of minimum lot zoning on exurban development. They find that whereas hypothetical two-acre minimum lot

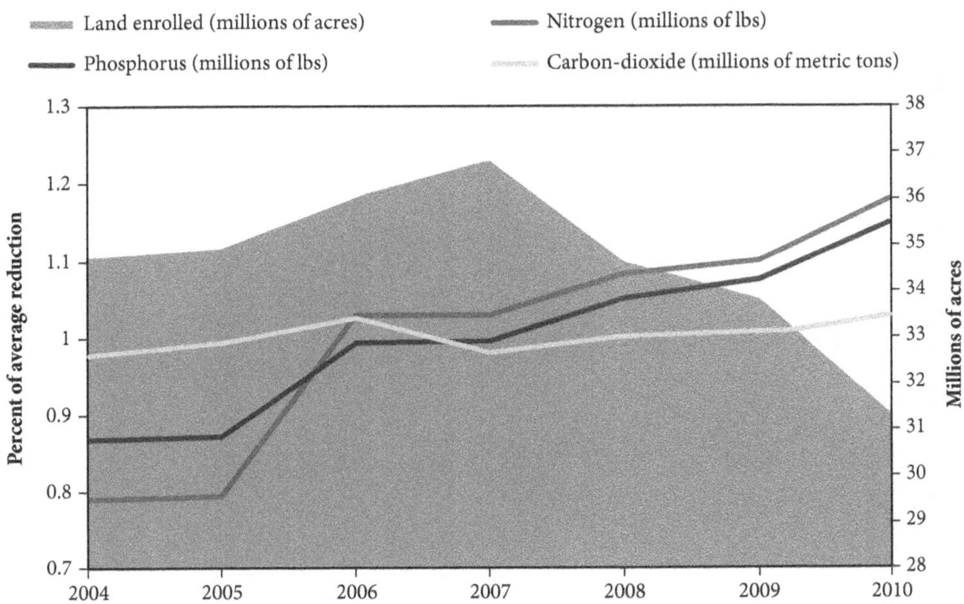

FIGURE **21.2** 2004–2010 Conservation Reserve Program ecosystem benefits per year (FSA 2007, 2011).

Table 21.6 Low-density zoning impact on development

Study	Study program	Focus	Study area	Findings
McConnell et al. (2006)	Low-density zoning, transfers of development rights (TDRs)	Estimating the impact of low-density zoning and TDRs on development trends	Calvert County, Maryland	Low-density zoning had a small, but non-negligible effect on development. If zoning restrictions were relaxed only a little, more than 10% more lots would have been added overall in subdivisions facing relatively low-density limits over the sample period.
Magliocca et al. (2012)	Minimum lot zoning	Simulating the development of a hypothetical mid-Atlantic community with an urban core, imposing zoning regulations and other heterogeneous conditions to monitor how development patterns adapt	Hypothetical Mid-Atlantic community	Urban sprawl may arise from any number of conditions, including variations in (i) agricultural productivity across the landscape, (ii) consumers' housing preferences, and (iii) how expectations of future prices are formed. Researchers found evidence of "leapfrogging" of urban development and preferences for large lots, implying relatively stringent minimum lot zoning in order to prevent subdivision.
Butsic et al. (2011)	Low-density zoning, tax credits for conservation	Analyzing the impact of low-density zoning restrictions of development, accounting for the endogeneity between development and zoning patterns	Columbia County, Wisconsin	After accounting for endogeneity, low-density zoning had no impact on development decisions, and Wisconsin's tax credit system had, at best, a weak impact on development decisions.
Gottlieb et al. (2009)	Minimum lot zoning	Studying the impact of large-lot zoning on rural communities	New Jersey	Large-lot zoning in excess of 4 acres actually encouraged more development by forcing more land into the market to accommodate the same number of people.
Lichtenberg (2011)	Minimum lot size zoning, Forest Conservation Act	Evaluating the impact of minimum lot size zoning on land use patterns	Baltimore-Washington corridor	A 1-acre increase in minimum lot size results in 0.83% increase in land area needed to accommodate the current population.

zoning restrictions have little effect on land development patterns, five-acre minimum lots significantly reduced the level of exurban development. These studies' results, as well as those of several others, are outlined in Table 21.6.

In many communities, zoning restrictions are criticized for failing to adequately protect land from conversion. Researchers contend that some communities implement overly generous or poorly planned zoning restrictions, which do little to actively protect land (see Table 21.7). Butsic et al. (2011) utilized a variety of econometric models to study the impact of low-density zoning in rural Wisconsin. They find that zoning restrictions did not influence landowners' decision to subdivide their property. Gottlieb et al. (2009) studied the impact of minimum-lot zoning and open space land preservation on development patterns in New Jersey and found that, at least in the short run, these policies may actually increase property subdivision. In Maryland, Lichtenberg (2011) studied the impact of minimum-lot regulations and local forest conservation laws on development patterns in the Baltimore-Washington metropolitan area. He finds that these policies contribute to more sprawl development as more land needs to be converted to accommodate the same number of households.

UGBs are also a popular policy option, whereby a community demarcates a compact urban development zone but imposes stringent zoning and infrastructure expansion laws outside this area. Overall, UGBs have had mixed impacts in the United States. Although these regulations may have some impact on development patterns, their effect is often not that anticipated by policy makers. For instance, Newburn and Berck (2006, 2011) studied residential land use change in Sonoma County, California, and found that, although the existing UGB constrained suburban development near the UGB, exurban development was largely unconstrained by these policies. Cunningham (2007) found that the UGB implemented by Seattle, Washington, lowered the probability of development for parcels outside the UGB by between 28% and 39%. Interestingly, the author finds that low-density development restrictions may decrease the price volatility of these lands, which in turn might speed up development, all else equal. Although the actual effect of UGBs on community development has been mixed, some communities have benefited from having clearly defined growth areas, while leaving more rural areas for conservation efforts.

Maryland has been one of the most proactive states at implementing land use tools to promote conservation. Priority Funding Areas (PFAs) are among the most prominent components of its 1997 Smart Growth legislation. As an incentive-based policy, the PFA legislation restricts state spending on growth-related programs to areas designated for urban growth (i.e., the PFAs); spending is permitted for infrastructure improvement to water and sewer, for example. Although not identical to UGBs, PFAs have a similar focus but use the carrot of state subsidization of infrastructure improvements rather than a regulatory approach. Hanlon, Howland, and McGuire (2010) analyze the effectiveness of Maryland's PFAs at reducing development on agricultural lands outside PFAs near Baltimore and Washington, DC. They find that development pressure can be high on the agricultural land outside the PFA areas, but that Maryland's PFA have been effective at reducing the probability of conversion of these resource

Table 21.7 Urban growth boundaries

Study	Study program	Focus	Study area	Findings
Newburn and Berck (2006, 2011)	Urban Growth Boundaries (UGB)	Estimating the impact of UGB on development in study region	Sonoma County, California	Sonoma's UGB was effective at reducing the probability of suburban development outside the ring region, but they find evidence of exurban development leapfrogging.
Cunningham (2007)	Urban Growth Boundaries	Evaluating the impact of Seattle's UGB on probability of development for properties outside the urban center	Seattle, Washington	Seattle's UGB was effective in lowering the probability of development of rural lands by between 28% and 39%, but it also reduced price volatility of these lands. This reduced the barriers to development.
Hanlon, Howland, and McGuire (2010)	Priority Funding Areas	Studying the impact of Maryland's PFA on a parcel's probability of future development	Frederick County, Maryland	They find that some of the areas with the greatest threat of development are outside Maryland's PFA and, although the program is not 100% effective at reducing development, it does affect a property's probability of development.
Lewis et al. (2009*b*)	Priority Funding Areas	Provides an overview of 10 years' experience with Maryland's PFA program, as well as some recommendations for improvement	State of Maryland	The PFA program has not entirely lived up to its potential, although it has had some effect on reducing development in rural areas; the research also provides several recommendation for program improvement.

lands. Lewis, Knaap, and Sohn (2009*b*) found that, despite some conceptual and practical limitations of the program, Maryland's PFAs did have limited success at deterring rural development. Towe, Lewis, and Lynch (Chapter 18 of this volume) find that PFAs have 1.04 more new homes within each ¼-square-mile PFA grid than would have occurred without the program. Similarly, using the difference-in-difference approach (pre-PFA housing starts to post-PFA housing starts), they find comparable results of an average of 1.05 new housing starts within the ¼-square-mile PFA grids compared to similar non-PFA grids (Table 21.8).

Both the public and policy makers are also concerned about the impact that development restrictions have on land values. Several teams of researchers have analyzed this issue, again finding mixed results. Although down-zoning restricts land use options, these restrictions may not be stringent enough to put any practical limitations on land use (i.e., they are nonbinding). Down-zoning rural lands may create positive amenities for neighboring lands, which causes difficulties in the analysis of the overall effect that zoning may have on property values. Dehring and Lind (2007) find that, depending on

Table 21.8 Impact of zoning on rural home values

Study	Study program	Focus	Study area	Findings
Dehring and Lind (2007)	Low-density zoning	Estimating the impact of down-zoning on rural home values	Dallas, Texas	Depending on the property type and regulation, zoning decreases land value by 0–21%.
Deaton and Vyn (2010)	Low-density zoning	Evaluating the impact of down-zoning across a variety of land classes and zoning restrictions	Toronto, Canada	Toronto-area properties were decreased in value by 20%, whereas more remote properties actually increased in value, although this result was statistically insignificant.
Liu and Lynch (2011*a*)	Low-density zoning	Studying the impact of down-zoning on property value, accounting for the interdependence between property value and probability of being down-zoned	Nine rural Maryland Counties	Resource-based, high-quality agricultural lands are unaffected by down-zoning, whereas non-resource based lands decrease in value by between 20% and 50%.

the stringency of regulation, down-zoning had a potentially negative impact on vacant lots in Dallas, Texas. On the other hand, Deaton and Vyn (2010) found that although down-zoning decreased property value for properties near Toronto, more remote areas actually increased in value. One major challenge to attributing the real effect of zoning is that the probability of a parcel being down-zoned is not independent of its property value. Thus, failure to account for this relationship (known as endogeneity) introduces bias into resulting estimations. Liu and Lynch (2011*b*) analyzed the impact of down-zoning on property values in several rural Maryland counties using both propensity score matching and instrumental variables techniques to control for endogeneity. They find that the overall impact is differentiated by land type, with resource-based agricultural and forest lands unaffected by down-zoning and other rural lands having decreases in property value. Overall, these results suggest that policy makers should be concerned about land values when designing zoning regulation that pursues desired conservation objectives.

Open space requirements are another popular regulatory method to encourage direct conservation of scarce resources. Interestingly, these requirements may also have unintended effects on the pace and pattern of land development and conservation. Local governments may also mandate conservation plans and enact buffer zones around sensitive resources. Sander and Polasky (2009), Bin, Landry, and Meyer (2009), and Ham et al. (2012) have confirmed that these open space requirements increase residential home value. Similarly, Bucholtz, Geoghegan, and Lynch (2003) find that permanently preserved land increases adjacent parcel's land values in most cases. However, because they provide amenity value, these open-space lands may act as a magnet for additional development. Lichtenberg, Tra, and Hardie (2007) and Lichtenberg (2011) studied the impact of the Maryland's Forest Conservation Act (FCA) open-space and tree retention requirements on development.[26] They find that FCA lands crowd out other sources of open space in Maryland and actually contribute to additional sprawl and conversion of resource lands. Similarly, Towe, Nickerson, and Bockstael (2008) find that permanent open space adjacent to a parcel increases its rate of conversion. However, the effect of open space on development may not be uniform across all areas. Lewis et al. (2009*a*) and Zipp et al. (2011) studied how an increase in open-space requirements (public beaches) around suburban Wisconsin area lakes actually decreased the likelihood of lakefront development. These results illustrate the need to design conservation policy specific to local conditions, incorporating many policy options to achieve desired objectives.

[26] In Maryland, the Forest Conservation Act (FCA) was enacted in 1991 and mandates that any new subdivisions or additional development of lands greater than approximately one acre must implement a forest conservation plan to either protect existing forest cover or reestablish equal or greater forest cover on other lands.

11. Participatory and Incentive-Based Programs for Conversion Prevention

Communities have many tools in their arsenal to promote conservation. Unlike regulatory approaches, participatory and incentive-based provisions provide guaranteed conservation (with monitoring). Because these are voluntary tools, county and local governments find them easier to implement to preserve land resources and often use them to complement existing developmental regulations as hybrids. As such, developmental restrictions and voluntary programs are often analyzed together at the local level (Table 21.9).

Local governments utilize agricultural and conservation easements to protect resource lands from conversion to development. Often referred to as Purchase of Development Rights (PDR) or Purchase of Agricultural Conservation Easements (PACE), these programs have increased in popularity because other developmental restrictions have not provided enough protection for resource lands from conversion to urban sprawl. PDR/PACE programs are effective in protecting land from development according to several recent studies. For example, using a hazard model, Towe, Nickerson, and Bockstael (2008) find that rural landowners delay the conversion of land by up to an additional six years, even if they do not enroll the land into the local PDR program. Liu and Lynch (2011*b*) implemented a propensity score matching method to determine the effectiveness of PDR programs across six Mid-Atlantic states. They found that counties with PDR/PACE programs had an average rate of agricultural land conversion 40–55% lower than similar counties without such a program. These results suggest that, where appropriate, PDR programs can be effective at incentivizing local resource landowners and lowering the rate of agricultural land conversion.

Transfers of development rights (TDR) were a popular conservation tool whereby communities allow resource properties to sell their development rights to developers to utilize to increase development densities elsewhere.[27] In theory, the social costs of a TDR program could be lower than a comparable PDR program by creating a competitive market for development rights.[28] Lynch and Musser (2001) found that TDR programs were less efficient in preserving parcels with the desired characteristics than were PDR programs. The TDR programs studied had based their allocation strategies primarily on acreage rather than on other parcel characteristics, such as prime soils or proximity to urban areas. Few TDR programs have been successful: nine programs have been revoked, 17 have protected no land, and only 12 programs have protected more than 1,000 acres of farmland (American Farmland Trust [AFT] 2008). However, the TDR

[27] As of 2008, at least 109 municipalities had active TDR programs in the United States (Kaplowitz et al. 2008).

[28] Kaplowitz et al. (2008) administered a mail-in survey of active TDR program directors that provided insight into the experiences of these programs.

Table 21.9 Land use easements

Study	Study program	Focus	Study area	Findings
Towe, Nickerson, and Bockstael (2008)	Purchase of Development Rights (PDR)	Examining the impact of farmland preservation programs on timing of development	Howard County, Maryland	The option to preserve farmland delays the timeframe of development by up to six years, a reduction of 12–43% of median conversion time.
Liu and Lynch (2011*b*)	Purchase of Development Rights	Evaluating the impact of PDR programs on reducing farmland conversion	Six Mid-Atlantic States	Having a PDR program decreases a county's rate of farmland loss by 40–55% and decreases farmland acres lost by 375 to 550 acres per year.
Horowitz, Lynch, and Stocking 2009)	Purchase of Development Rights	Analyzing the efficiency of competition-based PDR programs	Carroll County, Maryland	Competitive PDR programs enrolled as many as 3,000 acres (12%) more than a take-it-or-leave-it offer would have enrolled for the same budgetary cost. Each additional bidder competing for the same resources leads to a decreases in bid value of 0.1–1.4%
Crompton (2009)	Purchase of Development Rights	Examining state statues to understand the goals of these laws and effectiveness of these programs at promoting conservation	20 states with active PDR programs	Among the PDR state statutes, (i) almost all the language focused on agricultural interests; (ii) did not claim any open space benefits; and (iii) term and rescinding provisions were authorized, as well as in-perpetuity purposes, even though they offer no enduring public benefits.

programs inform the design of future PDR programs to increase efficiency and lower costs. By promoting competition among landowners, PDR programs may leverage their funding and preserve more acreage. In an analysis of the Maryland Agricultural Land Preservation Foundation (MALPF), Horowitz, Lynch, and Stocking (2009) found that each additional bidder decreased a farmer's bids between 0.1% and 1.4%. However, untargeted land use easements may not be as environmentally effective, which raises questions regarding the most critical conservation goals. Crompton (2009) analyzed 20 states' statutes regarding PDR programs, finding that these programs prioritized agricultural interests rather than conservation goals. Although PDR initiatives have been effective at promoting agricultural land conservation, similar programs have not been established to focus on other conservation priorities (Table 21.10).

12. Conclusion

Conservation tools have been successful in accomplishing many of the multitude of goals set by society and policy makers. While regulatory efforts continue, many participatory, incentive-based, and hybrid programs have surfaced in the United States in the past 30 years. The long-term impacts of these programs continue to be of interest. Overall, program evaluations continue to suggest that policy makers need to consider how to get the "biggest bang for the buck." Evaluations tend to focus more heavily on patterns of conservation and ecological and other benefit metrics than on the number of acres preserved or the number of dollars expended. Similarly, because of unintended impacts, including inducing development adjacent to conservation, further refinement may be required to existing programs to more effectively accomplish the objectives set by society. In addition, concerns about economic development have redirected some land conservation from land retirement (conservation practice or restoration on to a natural state) to working land conservation. These programs will need evaluation as well.

Similar to other resource and environmental policies, society is seeking land conservation programs that make appropriate tradeoffs between economic growth and environmental benefits. The United States has made this particularly important for agricultural lands from a desire to maintain a critical mass of farmland for strong local agricultural economies (Lynch and Carpenter, 2003). Resources have been shifting towards working land programs at the USDA as well. These programs have received less evaluation to date. A greater willingness to target land conservation to those areas or lands with the highest benefits has also emerged. This shift in policy has generated interest in both metrics to use for targeting and mechanisms to ensure voluntary programs incentivize targeted goals appropriately. Efforts continue on the development prevention front, attempting to prevent and redirect housing development as well as conserve land using programs like Maryland's Smart Growth Program.

On the research front, land conservation research has evolved dramatically with the advent of geographic information system (GIS) data of all kinds. These data have

Table 21.10 Open space requirements

Study	Study program	Focus	Study area	Findings
Sander and Polasky (2009)	NA	Studying the impact of views and open space on residential home value	Ramsey County, Minnesota	Starting at 1,000 m, the marginal implicit price for reducing the distance to the nearest lake by 100 m produces a $216 increase in home sale value.
Bin, Landry, and Meyer (2009)	Riparian Buffers	Evaluating the impact of proximity to riparian buffer on rural home value	Neuse River Basin in North Carolina	Proximity to riparian buffer raises the property value by 25.9%.
Lichtenberg, Tra, and Hardie (2007); Lichtenberg (2011)	Minimum lot size zoning, Forest Conservation Act	Evaluating the impact of FCA acreage on urban sprawl	Baltimore-Washington corridor	A one-acre increase in the required FCA land results in between 0.12 and 0.85 acres of additional open space, varying primarily based on the county and sewer access of the subdivision.
Lewis et al. (2009*a*)	Public protection of lake-front land	Determining the effect of open-space conservation policies on residential development density	Vilas County, Wisconsin	Researchers found evidence that public conservation land on lake shorelines can actually reduce the probability that privately owned residential parcels subdivide and develop.
Zipp et al. (2011)	Public protection land	Assessing the impact of open-space conservation on development decision	Door County, WI	Open space and private land are complements, and open space decreases the likelihood of development for land classes aside from agriculture.

allowed researchers to access more information on a spatial scale than previously available. This allows the land use models to expand beyond the Von Thunen/Mills variety by allowing heterogeneity to be included within the analysis. These spatially based data have been combined with US Census data—both population and agricultural—to utilize demographic and economic variables with physical factors to answer a wide range of questions. Researchers have also utilized the USDA NRCS's National Resource Inventory data to answer interesting questions about recent land use change (Karetnikov, 2012). Econometric and nonparametric models have also become more complex, allowing for incorporation of both time and spatial dimensions of land conservation. A duration analysis now can incorporate both timing and spatial variability into the approach. Similarly, genetic algorithms have allowed a seemingly infinite number of land use options to be computed more easily. As mentioned earlier, increased computational power has allowed further refinements to ecosystem models that permit the framing of optimal program design.

Although significant advances have been made, many challenges to evaluation and program design exist. Most land conservation programs have multiple goals and, often cannot accomplish them all simultaneously without multiple mechanisms. Yet these multiple mechanisms may interact in unexpected ways. In addition to many mechanisms, land conservation is inherently spatial and policy decisions must be conducted over multiple dimensions. Spillovers and other interdependencies will impact the outcomes in both the time and space dimensions. Each action impacts other actions and many other outcomes. This path dependency from both a time and space perspective can be quite difficult to resolve using many of the existing evaluation techniques. Similarly, program design becomes fraught with difficulties. To make matters more difficult, endogeneity of program selection and program outcomes can make causality and assignment of outcomes to a particular program mechanism difficult to determine.

However, researchers continue to make progress on these fronts. Ongoing studies about interactions between different programs and regulations continue to progress. Although not all of the unintended consequences of certain tools may be undesirable, knowing how programs interact on a spatial basis is crucial to designing and perfecting programs. Similarly, conservation costs have become an issue, especially when threshold impacts exist; therefore, further information on how financing mechanisms impact program outcomes would benefit policy makers. Heterogeneous landowners also affect the efficiency of a program, and thus determine how much information about landowners is needed. How information asymmetries impact conservation outcomes and how landowners' behavior correlates to publicly available data, such as land use and land cover, remain to be further considered. In the same vein, researchers often wish to connect GIS data with survey data and need to determine mechanisms to overcome confidentiality issues. Interdisciplinary studies that link economic and ecological benefits appropriately must also be pursued. Modeling ecological systems and determining benefits in a variety of locations is needed both to ensure targeting is well done and to evaluate if a program is accomplishing its goals.

References

American Farmland Trust (AFT). 2008. *Transfer of development rights fact sheet*. Northampton, MA: Farmland Information Center.

Baerenklau, K. A., A. Gonzalez-Caban, C. Paez, and E. Chavez. 2010. Spatial allocation of forest recreation value. *Journal of Forest Economics* 16(2): 113–126.

Bin, O., C. E. Landry, and G. E. Meyer. 2009. Riparian buffers and hedonic prices: A quasi-experimental analysis of residential property values in the Neuse River Basin. *American Journal of Agricultural Economics* 91(4): 1067–1079.

Brown, D. G., Johnson, K. M., Loveland, T. R., and Theobald, D. M. 2005. Rural land use change in the conterminous U.S., 1950–2000. *Ecological Applications*, 15(6): 1851–1863.

Bucholtz, S., J. Geoghegan, and L Lynch. 2003. Capitalization of open spaces into housing values and the residential property tax revenue impacts of agricultural easement programs. *Agricultural and Resource Economics Review* 32(1): April 33–45.

Butsic, V., D. J. Lewis, and L. Ludwig. 2011. An econometric analysis of land development with endogenous zoning. *Land Economics* 87(3): 412–432.

Chang, Katie. 2011. R. C. 2010 *National Land Trust CENSUS REPORT: A look at voluntary land conservation In America*, eds. R. Aldrich and C. Soto. Land Trust Alliance. Washington, DC.

Claassen, R., R. Cattaneo, and R. Johansson. 2008. Cost-effective design of agri-environmental payment programs: US experience in theory and practice. *Ecological Economics* 65: 738–753.

Crompton, J. L. 2009. How well do purchase of development rights programs contribute to park and open space goals in the United States? *World Leisure Journal* 51(1): 54–71.

Crompton, J. L. 2007*a*. The impact of parks and open spaces on property taxes. In *The economic benefits of land conservation*, ed. C. de Brun, 1–12. San Francisco: Trust for Public Land. http://cloud.tpl.org/pubs/benefits_econbenefits_landconserve.pdf.

Crompton, J. L. 2007*b*. Competitiveness: Parks and open space as factors shaping a location's success in attracting companies, labor supplies, and retirees. In *The economic benefits of land conservation*, ed. C. de Brun, 48–54. San Francisco: Trust for Public Land. http://cloud.tpl.org/pubs/benefits_econbenefits_landconserve.pdf.

Cunningham, C. 2007. Growth controls, real options, and land development. *Review of Economics and Statistics* 89(2): 343–358.

Dahl, Thomas E. 1990. Wetlands losses in the United States—1780s to 1980s (version July 16, 1997). Washington, DC: US Department of the Interior, Fish and Wildlife Service. Jamestown, ND: Northern Prairie Wildlife Research Center Online. http://www.npwrc.usgs.gov/resource/wetlands/wetloss/index.htm.

Deaton, J., and R. Vyn 2010. The effect of strict agricultural zoning on agricultural land values: The case of Ontario's greenbelt. *American Journal of Agricultural Economics* 92(4): 941–955.

Dehring, C., and M. Lind. 2007. Residential land-use controls and land values: Zoning and covenant interactions. *Land Economics* 83(4): 445–457.

Deisenroth, D., J. Loomis, and C. Bond. 2009. Non-market valuation of off-highway vehicle recreation in Larimer County, Colorado: Implications of trail closures. *Journal of Environmental Management* 11: 3490–3497.

Duke, J. M., and L. Lynch. 2006. Four classes of farmland retention techniques: Comparative evaluation and property rights implications. *Land Economics* 82(2):189–213.

Ferris, J., and J. V. Siikamäki. 2009. *Conservation reserve program and wetland reserve program: Primary land retirement programs for promoting farmland conservation*. Washington, DC: Resources for the Future.

Ferraro, P. J. 2008. Asymmetric information and contract design for payments for environmental services. *Ecological Economics* 65: 811–822.

Gallant, A. L., W. Sadinski, M. F. Roth, and C. A. Rewa. 2011. Changes in historical Iowa land cover as context for assessing the environmental benefits of current and future conservation efforts on agricultural lands. *Journal of Soil and Water Conservation* 66(3): 67–77.

Gleason, R. A., N. H. Euliss, Jr., B. A. Tangen, M. K. Laubhan, and B. A. Browne. 2011. USDA conservation program and practice effects on wetland ecosystem services in the Prairie Pothole Region. *Ecological Applications* 21(Supplement): S65–S81.

Gleason, R. A., M. K. Laubhan, and N. H. Euliss, Jr. (eds). 2008. Ecosystem services derived from wetland conservation practices in the United States prairie pothole region with an emphasis on the US Department of Agriculture conservation reserve and wetlands reserve programs. US Geological Survey Professional Paper 1745, Reston, Virginia, USA.

Gorte, R. W. 2012. *Wilderness laws: Statutory provisions and prohibited and permitted uses*. Washington, DC: Congressional Research Service.

Gottlieb, P. D., A. O'Donnell, T. Rudel, K. O'Neill, and M. McDermott. 2009. The impact of large-lot zoning and open space acquisition on home building in rural communities. 2009 Annual meeting of the Agricultural and Applied Economics Association, July 26–28, 2009, Milwaukee, WI.

Gude, P. H., A. J. Hansen, and D. A. Jones. 2007. Biodiversity consequences of alternative future land use scenarios in Greater Yellowstone. *Ecological Applications* 17: 1004–1018.

Ham, C., P. A. Champ, J. B. Loomis, and R. M. Reich, 2012. Accounting for heterogeneity of public lands in hedonic property models. *Land Economics* 88 (3): 444–456

Hanlon, B., M. Howland, and M. McGuire. 2010. Hotspots for growth: Land use change in a transitional county in the US. Unpublished manuscript, University of Maryland.

Hansen, L., and M. Ribaudo. 2008. *Economic measures of soil conservation benefits*. Technical Bulletin Number 1922. Washington, DC: United States Department of Agriculture.

Horowitz, J. K., L. Lynch, and A. Stocking. 2009. Competition-based environmental policy: An analysis of farmland preservation in Maryland. *Land Economics* 85(4): 555–575.

Internal Revenue Service. 2012. Conservation easements techniques guide. http://www.irs.gov/businesses/small/article/0,,id=249135,00.html.

Irwin, Elena G., Kathleen P. Bell, Nancy E. Bockstael, David A. Newburn, Mark D. Partridge, and JunJie Wu. 2009. The economics of urban-rural space. *Annual Review of Resource Economics* 1: 435–459.

Kaplowitz, M., P. Machemer, and R. Pruetz. 2008. Planners' experiences in managing growth using Transferable Development Rights (TDR) in the United States. *Land Use Policy* 25 (3): 378–387.

Karetnikov, D. A. 2012. Have the National Resources Inventories advanced conservation policy? Ph.D. Dissertation, University of Maryland.

Klaiber, H. A., and D. J. Phaneuf. 2009. Do sorting and heterogeneity matter for open space policy analysis? An empirical comparison of hedonic and sorting models. *American Journal of Agricultural Economics* 91(5): 1312–1318.

Klaiber, H. A., and D. J. Phaneuf. 2010. Valuing open space in a residential sorting model of the Twin Cities. *Journal of Environmental Economics and Management* 60(2): 57–77.

Land Trust Alliance Conservation Resource Center. 2007. *State conservation tax credits: Impact and analysis*. Boulder, CO: Land Trust Alliance. http://www.landtrustalliance.org/policy/documents/state-tax-credits-report.pdf/view

Lewis, D. J., B. Provencher, and V. Butsic. 2009*a*. The dynamic effects of open-space conservation policies on residential development density. *Journal of Environmental Economics and Management* 57(3): 239–252.

Lewis R., G. J. Knaap, and J. Sohn. 2009*b*. Managing growth with priority funding areas: A good idea whose time has yet to come. *Journal of the American Planning Association* 75:457–478.

Lichtenberg, E., C. Tra, and I. Hardie. 2007. Land use regulation and the provision of open space in suburban residential subdivisions. *Journal of Environmental Economics and Management* 54: 199–213.

Lichtenberg, E. 2011. Open space and urban sprawl: The effects of zoning and forest conservation regulations in Maryland. *Agricultural and Resource Economics Review* 40(3): 393–404.

Liu X. P., and L. Lynch. 2011*a*. Do zoning regulations rob rural landowners' equity? *American Journal of Agricultural Economics* 93: 1–25.

Liu, X., and L. Lynch. 2011*b*. Do agricultural land preservation programs reduce farmland loss? Evidence from a propensity score matching estimator. *Land Economics* 87: 183–201.

Lueck, D. L., and J. A. Michael. 2003. Preemptive habitat destruction under the Endangered Species Act. *Journal of Law and Economics* vol. XLVI (April): 27–60.

Lynch L. and J. Carpenter. 2003. Is there evidence of a critical mass in the Mid-Atlantic Agriculture sector between 1949 and 1997? *Agricultural and Resource Economics Review* 32(1)(April 2003): 116–128.

Lynch, L., and X. Liu. 2007. Impact of designated preservation areas on rate of preservation and rate of conversion: Preliminary evidence. *American Journal of Agricultural Economics* 89(5): 1205–1210.

Lynch, L. and W. N. Musser. 2001. A relative efficiency analysis of farmland preservation programs. *Land Economics* November 77 (4): 577–594.

Lynch, Lori, K. Palm, S. Lovell, and J. Harvard. 2007. *Expected cost of tripling Maryland's preserved acres: Using a hedonic price analysis on agricultural land values from 1997–2003*. Wye Mills, MD: Harry Hughes Center for Agroecology, University of Maryland.

Magliocca, N., V. McConnell, and M. Walls. 2012. Explaining sprawl with an agent-based model of exurban land and housing markets. RFF discussion paper No. DP 11–33, Washington, DC: Resources for the Future.

McConnell, V., M. Walls, and E. Kopits. 2006. Zoning, TDRs, and the density of development. *Journal of Urban Economics* 59: 440–457.

Messer, K. D. 2006. The conservation benefits of cost-effective land acquisition: A case study in Maryland. *Journal of Environmental Management* 79: 305–315.

Newburn, D. A., and P. Berck. 2006. Modeling suburban and rural residential development beyond the urban fringe. *Land Economics* 82(4): 481–499.

Newburn, D. A., and P. Berck. 2011. Growth management policies for exurban and suburban development: Theory and an application to Sonoma County, California. *Agricultural and Resource Economics Review* 40(3): 375–392.

Nickerson, C., R. Ebel, A. Borchers, and F. Carriazo. 2011. *Major uses of land in the United States, 2007*. Economic Information Bulletin No. (EIB-89). Washington, DC: US Department of Agriculture, Economic Research Service.

Pavelis, G. A., D. Helms, and S. Stalcup. 2011. *Soil and water conservation expenditures by USDA agencies, 1935–2010.* Washington, DC: Historical Insights. Natural Resources Conservation Service, Ecological Sciences Division.

Poudyal, N. C., D. G. Hodges, and C. D. Merrett. 2009. A hedonic analysis of the demand for and benefits of urban recreation parks. *Land Use Policy* 26: 975–983.

Radeloff, V. C., S. I. Stewart, T. J. Hawbaker, U. Gimmi, A. M. Pidgeon, C. H. Flather, R. B. Hammer, and D. Helmers. 2010. Housing growth in and near United States protected areas limits their conservation value. *Proceedings of the National Academy of Sciences of the USA* 107: 940–945.

Sander, H. A., and S. Polasky. 2009. The value of views and open space: Estimates from a hedonic pricing model for Ramsey County, Minnesota, USA. *Land Use Policy* 26(3): 837–845.

Secchi S., P. W. Gassman, J. R. Williams, and B. A. Babcock. 2009. Corn-based ethanol production and environmental quality: A case of Iowa and the conservation reserve program. *Environmental Management* 44: 732–744.

Siikamaki, J. 2011. Contributions of the US state park system to nature recreation. *Proceedings of the National Academy of Sciences of the USA* 108: 14031–14036.

Towe, C., R. Lewis, and L. Lynch. 2014. Using quasi-experimental methods to evaluate land policies: Application to Maryland's priority funding legislation. In *The Oxford handbook of land economics*, eds. J. M. Duke and J. Wu, 452–480. New York: Oxford University Press.

Towe, C., C. Nickerson, and N. E. Bockstael. 2008. An empirical examination of the timing of land conversions in the presence of farmland preservation programs. *American Journal of Agricultural Economics* 90(3): 613–626.

Trust for Public Land. Center for City Park Excellence. 2011. *City park facts.* San Francisco: Trust for Public Land.

USDA. 1982. A national program for soil and water conservation: 1982 final program report and environmental impact statement: Soil and Water Resources Conservation Act, p. 18.

USDA National Resources Conservation Service (NRCS). National conservation practice standards—NHCP | NRCS|National conservation practice standards—NHCP | NRCS. Accessed July 16, 2012. http://www.nrcs.usda.gov/wps/portal/nrcs/detailfull/national/technical/cp/ncps/?&cid=nrcs143_026849.

USDA National Resources Conservation Service (NRCS). 1996. America's private land, a geography of hope. http://www.nrcs.usda.gov/wps/portal/nrcs/detail/national/technical/nra/rca/?cid=nrcs143_014212

USDA National Resources Conservation Service. 2001. A Resources Conservation Act report: Interim appraisal and analysis of conservation alternatives. www.nhq.nrcs.usda.gov/land/pubs/rca_interim.html

USDA National Resources Conservation Service. 2012. Financial assistance. http://www.nrcs.usda.gov/wps/portal/nrcs/main/national/programs/financial

USDA National Resources Conservation Service. 2012. Wetland reserve program. http://www.nrcs.usda.gov/wps/portal/nrcs/main/national/programs/easements

US Department of the Interior. 2012. National Park Service: Budget and appropriations. http://www.doi.gov/budget/appropriations/2013/highlights/upload/BH071.pdf

US Environmental Protection Agency. 2012. Summary of the Endangered Species Act. http://www.epa.gov/lawsregs/laws/esa.html

US Farm Service Agency. 2007. Conservation reserve program: 2006 Annual summary and enrolment statistics. http://www.fsa.usda.gov/Internet/FSA_File/annual2006summary.pdf

Farm Service Agency. 2011. Conservation reserve program: 2010 Annual summary and enrolment statistics. http://www.fsa.usda.gov/Internet/FSA_File/annual2010summary.pdf

Vukina, T., X. Zheng, M. Marra, and A. Levy. 2008. Do farmers value the environment? Evidence from a conservation reserve program auction. *International Journal of Industrial Organization*, 26(6): 1323–1332.

Wade, A. A., and D. M. Theobald. 2010. Residential development encroachment on US protected areas. *Conservation Biology* 24: 151–161.

Wade, A. A., D. M. Theobald, and M. J. Laituri. 2011. A multi-scale assessment of local and contextual threats to existing and potential US protected areas. *Landscape and Urban Planning* 101(3): 215–227.

Walls, M., S. Darley, and J. Siikamäki. 2009. *The state of the great outdoors: America's parks, public lands, and recreational resources*. Washington, DC: Resources for the Future.

Wentworth, K. L., M. C. Brittingham, and A. M. Wilson. 2010. Conservation reserve enhancement program fields: Benefits for grassland and shrub-scrub species. *Journal of Soil and Water Conservation* 65: 50–60.

Wu, J., and H. Lin. 2010. The effect of the conservation reserve program on land values. *Land Economics* 86(1): 1–21.

Zipp, K., D. Lewis, and B. Provencher. 2011. Does open space conservation increase neighboring development? 2011 Association of Environmental and Resource Economics Presentation. http://www.webmeets.com/files/papers/AERE/2011/196/AERE_door_county_final_draft2.pdf

CHAPTER 22

EUROPEAN AGRI-ENVIRONMENTAL POLICY

The Conservation and Re-Creation of Cultural Landscapes

IAN HODGE

SINCE its introduction in the mid-1980s, agri-environmental policy has become a major component of agricultural policy in Europe. This chapter outlines the context of its introduction and its present position. It then reviews the research that has been undertaken, looking particularly at scheme characteristics and evaluation. A final section reflects on the prospects for agri-environment policy and raises some wider issues. The primary focus of the chapter is on agri-environmental policy operated within the European Union (EU). This is implemented as an obligatory part of the Second Pillar of the Common Agricultural Policy under the Rural Development Regulation. Similar policies and approaches have been implemented in other European Countries, particularly in Norway and Switzerland, and the literature reflects the wider coverage of these policies.

Government intervention in the management of rural land at a broad scale for the provision of public good environmental values represents a novel development in public policy, still in a relatively early stage in its implementation. It is now being pursued in many developed countries, and the approach is being further extended in payments for ecosystem services. The experience gained from the theoretical and empirical analysis discussed here provides insights both for the further development of agri-environment policy itself and for the design of payments for ecosystem services.

1. The Common Agricultural Policy and Land Use Change in Europe

Agri-environment schemes were introduced into European policy in the mid-1980s. This was a time of mounting agricultural surpluses, increasing concerns as to the budgetary costs of the Common Agricultural Policy (CAP), and an emerging recognition of the damage that agricultural intensification, stimulated by the incentives established under the CAP, was having on the environment (e.g., Shoard 1980; Bowers and Cheshire 1983). Around this same time, a coalition of interest began to emerge in place of what had previously been a clear conflict between the interests of farming and conservation (Lowe et al. 1986). Baldock and Lowe (1996, 12) comment: "Thus, some agricultural policy makers have responded to environmental concerns, not necessarily through any deep convictions, but because of a perceived coincidence between the aims of environmental improvement and the need to reduce agricultural output, thereby contributing to the alleviation of surplus and budgetary problems." This suggests that policies to pay farmers to reduce the level of their production intensity could have the triple benefits of protecting the environment, reducing levels of commodity production, and thus lowering the cost to government of dealing with commodity surpluses (Willis et al. 1988) and, perhaps, of offering a new justification for government payments to farmers.

After some initial trials of schemes in the United Kingdom and the Netherlands initiated under the Less Favoured Areas Directive (Countryside Commission 1984), Article 19 of the 1985 European Structures Regulation (797/85) allowed Member States to provide funding for schemes that contributed toward the introduction or continued use of agricultural production practices while being compatible with the requirements of conserving the natural habitat and ensuring an adequate income for farmers. This led, for instance, to the introduction of the Environmentally Sensitive Areas scheme in England following the implementation of the Agriculture Act 1986, as well as to schemes in other parts of the United Kingdom and other European Member States. It was generally not taken up by southern Member States. The Regulation did not provide for any financial support from the European Community budget, but this was changed in Regulation 1760/87, which provided for a maximum of 25% reimbursement from the European Agricultural Guidance and Guarantee Fund (FEOGA).

Although the focus of these schemes has been on influencing the way in which farm land is managed, schemes have had varying objectives across different countries and contexts (Baldock and Lowe 1996). In some cases, essentially on the extensive margin, the concern has been to maintain agricultural use and prevent abandonment of marginal areas. This has been a particular priority in parts of France, the Alpine countries, Scandinavia, and parts of southern Europe. In other locations, concern has been more to mitigate the effects of agricultural intensification, along the intensive margin, particularly of pollution associated with livestock wastes, inorganic fertilizers, and pesticides. But there are concerns, too, with intensification at the extensive margin where it threatens habitats and species that are associated with more extensive land uses. In the United Kingdom, the focus has been particularly on the protection and enhancement of landscapes and wildlife.

2. Rural Land Management in an Old World

Agri-environment schemes operate through environmental contracts under which government offers payments to farmers who agree to undertake or not to undertake certain farming practices or forms of management. Thus, the objective is to promote a rural environment that is farmed in a particular way, almost invariably in a way that reflects traditional and longstanding farming practices in that locality. This represents the predominant judgment that what is valued in the rural environment is a cultural landscape that is a product of particular forms of agricultural management. This is a feature of an "Old World," where, over long periods of time, agricultural practices, environmental habitats, and community arrangements have co-evolved to generate highly valued environments (Hodge 2000).

In this respect, the rationale for the approach is consistent with the Organisation for Economic Co-operation and Development (OECD) definition of multifunctionality. This is typically defined in terms of two criteria: (1) jointness between commodity and noncommodity outputs from agriculture and (2) the public good character of the noncommodity output (OECD 2001*a*). Jointness is defined by the OECD (2001*a*, 16) when a firm produces two or more outputs that are interlinked so that an increase or decrease in the supply of one output affects the levels of the others. This may arise (OECD 2001*a*, 30; see also Blandford and Boisvert 2005) when there are technical interdependencies in the production process, when outputs are produced from a nonallocable input, or when outputs compete for an allocable input that is fixed at the firm level. An alternative argument concentrates on costs, so that jointness arises from economies of scope when the costs of production are lower when two or more outputs are produced together by the same firm. Hagedorn (2004) refers to this as "institutional jointness." Publicness follows the standard assumptions of nonrivalry and nonexcludability, although, in practice, noncommodity outputs are generally not pure public goods (Cooper et al. 2009).

The justification for paying farmers for the improvement of the environment also makes an assumption about the allocation of property rights to the landholder. This is that landowners have a right to undertake agricultural production activities subject to any laws that regulate land uses relating to limits on pollution or activities that might impose costs on third parties. This defines a reference level of property rights (Hodge 1989; OECD 2001*b*) and a reference environmental standard that is associated with it. Thus, the provision of a higher environmental standard, beyond Good Farming Practice, represents a public good for which the supplier deserves payment. This thus applies the "provider gets principle" (OECD 1999), an inverse of the "polluter pays principle" in which landholders cause environmental impacts for which they do not hold property rights. These principles are set out by the European Commission as a basis for the implementation of agri-environment schemes in the European Union.[1]

3. Agri-Environment Schemes Operated in the European Union

Agri-environment schemes became mandatory on Member States in the European Union under a package of measures introduced in 1992 (Council Regulation 2078/92) accompanying the MacSharry CAP reforms. These reforms introduced partial decoupling through direct arable area and livestock headage payments. The schemes under this Regulation developed from the previous agri-environment initiatives but the Regulation made it obligatory for all Member States to implement a national agri-environment programme, including a range of measures to generate "positive effects on the environment and the countryside" (Regulation Article 2(1)). These included measures to reduce substantially the use of fertilizers and plant protection products, to change to more extensive forms of crop production, to reduce the numbers of sheep and cattle per forage area, to use other farming methods compatible with the requirement of the protection of the environment and natural resources, to rear animals of local breeds in danger of extinction, to ensure the upkeep of abandoned farmland or woodlands, to set aside farmland for at least 20 years, and to manage land for public access and leisure activities. Member States were expected to include all of these measures unless there was a clear reason why they should not apply. The hope was that the implementation of the Regulation would lead to a reduction in the intensity of agriculture over a significant area of land, thus helping to stabilize or reduce production and to ease the wider pressures on the CAP (Baldock and Lowe 1996). The rate of take up of measures under the Regulation differed widely between different Member States. Whitby (1996) reports data from 1995 on the % of Utilised Agricultural Area entered into schemes, varying between Austria at 91% and Netherlands at 3.3%. The majority of countries achieved between 12 and 25%.

Under the Agenda 2000 reforms of the CAP, provision for agri-environment schemes was included under the Rural Development Regulation as part of Pillar II of the CAP; Pillar I covering market support measures and direct aids, and Pillar II covering rural development. The arrangements for agri-environment schemes were set out initially for the period 2000–2006 in the Rural Development Regulation 1257/1999 and then,

[1] http://ec.europa.eu/agriculture/envir/cap/index_en.htm The legal obligations that form the reference level for the agri-environment measures are indicated in Article 39.3 of Regulation No 1698/2005 in terms of the relevant mandatory standards.

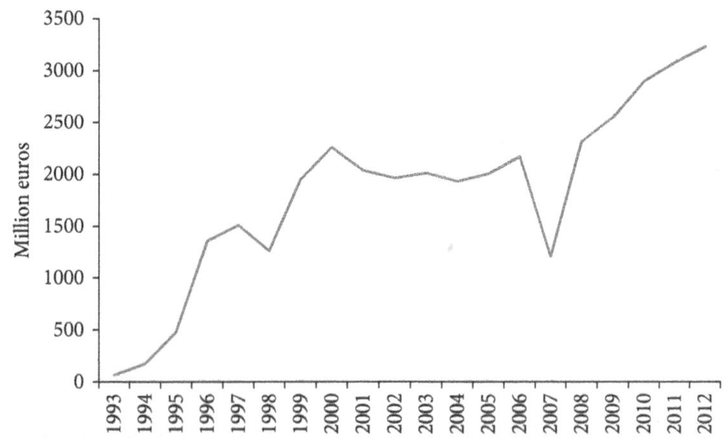

FIGURE 22.1 EU budget spending on agri-environment schemes 1993–2011.

Source: European Commission, Directorate General for Agriculture and Rural Development (2005) Agri-environment measures: Overview on General Principles, Types of Measures and Application. Unit G-4—Evaluation of Measures applied to Agriculture, Studies.

(*Initial source*: EAGGF Guarantee Section, budget execution), updated from Jukka Niemi (2012), personal communication.

subsequently for the period 2007–2013, under Regulation 1698/2005. Under these Regulations, Member States have been required to implement Rural Development Programmes approved by the European Commission. Figure 22.1 illustrates the growth of spending on agri-environment schemes in Member States between 1993 and 2011. This reflects the total spending across the numbers of Members States in the EU at any particular time. The rapid growth in 2008 reflects the increased variety of measures available in the current programming period.

Council Regulation 1698/2005 provided for support for rural development by the European Agricultural Fund for Rural Development (EAFRD) in order to promote sustainable rural development throughout the Community. Its approach should be complementary to the market and income support policies of the CAP. It established four Axes, representing coherent groups of measures with specific goals:

Axis 1: Improving competitiveness of the agricultural and forestry sector
Axis 2: Improving the environment and countryside
Axis 3: The quality of life in rural areas and diversification of the rural economy
Axis 4: Leader

The European Commission set rules as to the required balance in expenditure to be achieved between these goals. Leader represents area-based bottom-up local action projects and is an approach to be taken in the implementation of a proportion of projects under the first three Axes. At least 5% of total expenditure across all axes must be via Leader. Agri-environment schemes are included under Axis 2, which also includes other measures targeting the sustainable use of agricultural and forestry land, such as

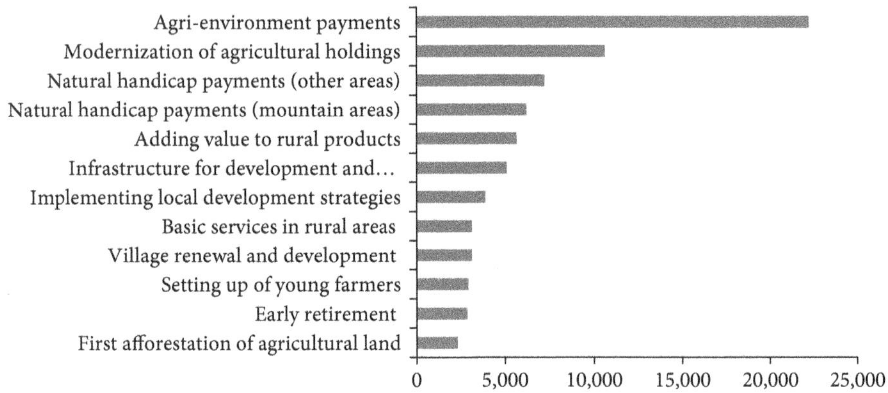

FIGURE 22.2 Planned EAFRD expenditure on main Rural Development measures in the European Union 2007–2013 (million €).

Source: European Commission (2010). Rural Development in the European Union—Statistical and Economic Information—Report 2010 Chapter 3. Overview of the EU Rural Development Policy 2007–2013, http://ec.europa.eu/agriculture/agrista/rurdev2010/ruraldev.htm

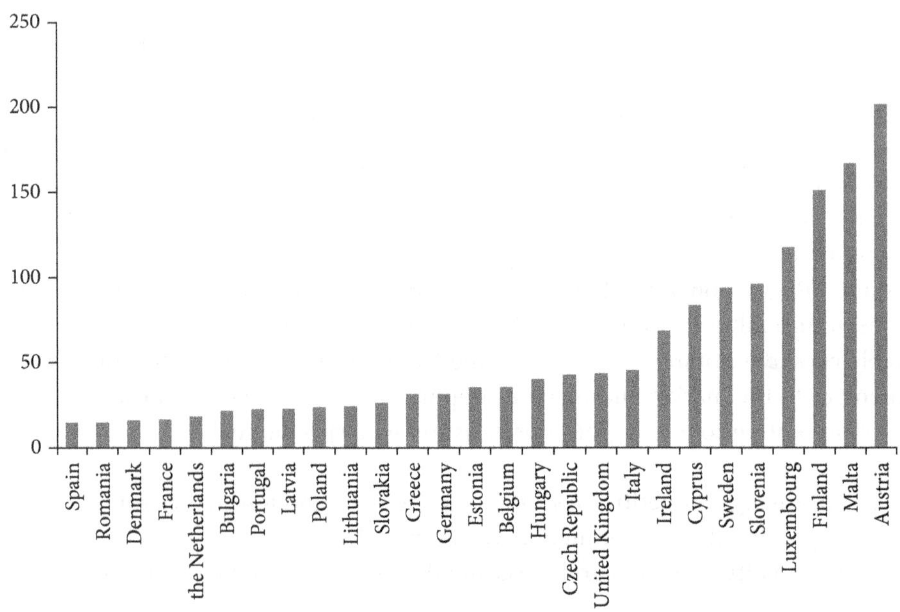

FIGURE 22.3 Total planned public expenditure on agri-environment measures 2007–2013. Mean expenditure in € per ha per annum over total Utilised Agricultural Area in 2007.

Source: European Commission (2010) Rural Development in the European Union—Statistical and Economic Information—Report 2010. ANNEX G—EAFRD—Overview of the financial plans. UAA from Eurostat Agricultural Statistics

payments in areas with natural handicaps, nature conservation areas, and animal welfare payments. At least 25% of the total contribution from EAFRD must be applied to Axis 2. The maximum contribution from EAFRD toward total expenditure on Axis 2 is 80% of eligible public expenditure in regions covered by the Convergence Objective, the least developed Member States and regions, and 55% in other regions. Agri-environment payments to farmers or other land managers are granted on a voluntary basis, covering only those commitments that go beyond the relevant mandatory standards and beyond minimum requirements for fertilizer and plant protection product use. Payments are granted annually, generally over periods of five to seven years, and covering additional costs and income foregone. Where necessary, they may also cover transactions costs. The Rural Development Regulation also states that, where appropriate, the beneficiaries may be selected on the basis of calls for tender, applying criteria of economic and environmental efficiency.

Planned expenditures over the 2007–13 programming period are published by the European Commission (2010). Total Community support planned for rural development across the 27 Member States between 2007–2013 amounted to some €96.3 billion, of which just under a quarter was allocated to agri-environment measures. The distribution amongst the major rural development measures is shown in Figure 22.2.

The level of agri-environment expenditure planned in Rural Development Programmes varies considerably between the Member States. Overall, just over half of expenditure (52%) on Axis 2 is directed to agri-environment payments, but the proportion ranges between, say, 86% in Belgium and 70% in the United Kingdom, as compared with 26% in Portugal or 28% in Slovakia. The intensity of expenditure per hectare on average across the total Utilised Agricultural Area is shown in Figure 22.3. This shows Austria at one extreme with over €200/ha and Spain and Romania at the other with about €15/ha.

Purvis et al. (2009) estimate that there are probably in excess of 355 EU-funded agri-environment schemes, varying widely in terms of structure, scope and focus. The issues covered fall predominantly across three general headings: natural resources, biodiversity and landscape quality. A fuller list of topics is shown in Table 22.1.

More details of the ways in which agri-environment schemes have been implemented can be illustrated through the experiences in Austria and England.

4. ÖPUL IN AUSTRIA

Austria has for a long while placed considerable emphasis on supporting land management by its farmers. Darnhofer and Schneeberger (2007) discuss the context and operation of agri-environment measures in Austria. Farms are generally small, with an average size of 17ha, and nearly 70% of the total agricultural area is located within the Less Favoured Area and more than half in mountainous areas. Darnhofer and

Table 22.1 Frequent topics covered in EU agri-environmental (AE) schemes

AE issue	Individual topics	% in sample of 244 schemes*
Natural Resources	Aspects of soil quality and stability Aspects of water quantity and quality Aspects of air quality	63%
Biodiversity	Conservation of wildlife species and habitats Protection and utilization of functional biodiversity within farming systems Maintenance of genetic diversity, particularly crop varieties and livestock breeds	73%
Landscape quality	Aesthetic appearance and cultural historic value of the countryside Multifunctional (amenity, recreational and educational) value and use of the countryside	50%
Other	Food quality and safety Public health and animal welfare Controlling natural hazards	12%

* Individual schemes target more than one issue and so total sums to more than 100%.
Source: Purvis et al. (2009).

Schneeberger (2007, 362) comment that "despite these unfavorable farming conditions, suitable management of Alpine grasslands is imperative; they contribute to the attractiveness of the mountainous areas and to their recreational value, which are crucial for the tourism industry. Their sensitive ecosystem harbors an endemic flora and fauna, which contributes to Europe's natural heritage, and plays an important role in the prevention of avalanches and landslides. Alpine agriculture is thus a typical example of 'multifunctional agriculture,' as its nonagricultural value in terms of environmental benefits and maintenance of the rural infrastructure may be higher than its agricultural production value." Environmental considerations gained importance for agricultural policy in the early 1970s and were a central issue in the negotiations for Austria to join the European Community in the early 1990s.

Since 1995, agri-environmental policy has been implemented through ÖPUL, the Austrian programme to promote agricultural production methods compatible with the requirements of the protection of the environment, extensive production and the maintenance of the countryside. Participation in ÖPUL is available on a voluntary basis to all privately owned farms with a minimum size of 2 ha. It includes measures that are available to all farmers and others that are offered within specific regions. Currently under the Austrian Rural Development Programme (Netzwerk Land 2011) the scheme has continued to cover a very high proportion of the total agricultural area, at around

90%, and includes over 70% (118,000) of all farms. The programme includes 29 measures supporting extensive and environmentally friendly management of the whole farm, cultivated landscape and nature conservation, and soil, climate and water protection. Expenditure on ÖPUL represents about 48% of total expenditure on Rural Development and 28% of total CAP expenditure in Austria. The average payment under ÖPUL amounts to some €220/ha/annum, of which about 50% of the funds come from the European Union.

ÖPUL may be expected to have a major impact on the rural environment. 17% of farmland is organic and 73% of the land is subject to reduction and prohibition of the use of yield increasing inputs (Puchta 2011). However measurement and evaluation of policy effects is difficult due to the problems in identifying causality between the specific policy and the environmental conditions. At the same time, ÖPUL represents an important source of income for Austrian farmers. Darnhofer and Schneeberger (2007) emphasize the importance of public support for proposed policies, what they term "political efficiency", and comment that this does not generally coincide with economic efficiency. The political process "was guided by the choice to keep the administration costs as low as possible, so that more funds would be available for farmers" (p. 373).

5. Environmental Stewardship in England

Agri-environment policy in the UK is operated through separate Rural Development Programmes in the areas of England, Scotland, Wales and Northern Ireland. Environmental Stewardship, the current scheme in England, was introduced in 2005. There have been some clear shifts in the orientation of agri-environment policy since its initial aim of restraining agricultural intensification to protect valued aspects of the rural environment. The first implementation in 1986 was in designated Environmentally Sensitive Areas (ESAs) whose objective was "to help conserve those areas of high landscape and/or wildlife value which are vulnerable to changes in farming practices by offering payments to farmers willing to maintain or introduce environmentally beneficial farming practices" (MAFF 1989). At that stage the focus was on avoiding change taking place, especially on areas of land being brought into more intensive production as a consequence of the support mechanisms offered under the CAP. ESAs were targeted as representing particularly significant landscape values and vulnerable habitats, such as wetlands and extensive grasslands. Agri-environment schemes extended the "voluntary principle" that had been implemented in UK policy for management agreements within Sites of Special Scientific Interest (SSSIs) under the Wildlife and Countryside Act 1981 and subsequently incorporated into European rules.

Over time the emphasis shifted from simply preventing change toward seeking environmental enhancement, especially to restore environmental values that had been lost as a consequence of agricultural intensification and technical change in the past. This development in policy was reflected in the introduction of the Countryside Stewardship Scheme (CSS), a selective scheme made available to land holders throughout the country at the start of the 1990s, and in the development of higher tier contracts to promote environmental enhancement within the ESAs.

Environmental Stewardship replaced previous schemes in 2005. It is comprised of two elements, Higher Level Stewardship (HLS) and Entry Level Stewardship (ELS). While HLS essentially continues with the CSS approach, ELS is a major innovation. ELS adopts a "broad and shallow" approach with the objective of enrolling the majority of agricultural land into the scheme. This may then be seen as a third phase in agri-environment policy that extends payments beyond the primary concentration on the extensive margin to include payments across all agricultural land areas to alter agricultural production intensity along the intensive margin (Hodge and Reader 2010). Under ELS, farmers can choose from a variety of land management options, such as hedge management or the introduction of buffer strips, for which they are awarded points. It is a whole farm scheme and, in lowland areas, farmers need to attain an equivalent of 30 points per hectare for the total area of the farm, for which they are paid £30 per hectare per annum. There is also an Organic Entry Level Stewardship (OELS) and an Uplands Entry Level Stewardship (UELS) for farms in Less Favoured Areas. Current take up of agri-environment schemes is shown in Table 22.2.

As a consequence of the introduction of ELS, over two thirds of agricultural land is now covered by agri-environment contracts. This does not mean that all of this land is subject to active agri-environmental management. Rather it represents the total areas of the farms that have been entered into the scheme on which some such management is being undertaken. However, it does mean that the managers of this area have had to

Table 22.2 Take up of agri-environment schemes in England, 2012

Scheme	Area (ha)	% of UAA	No. of agreements	Annual value of public expenditure £M	Payment £ per ha
CSS	169,805	1.8	6,025	37.9	223.2
ESA	339,382	3.7	5,700	28.4	83.7
ELS	5,332,639	57.4	39,455	152.9	28.7
OELS	343,483	3.7	2,367	27.6	80.4
HLS (Combined)	*821,331*		*7,898*	*137.5*	*167.4*
HLS (Standalone)	106,477	1.1	1,170	23.0	216.0
Total HLS	*927,808*		*9,068*	*160.5*	*173.0*
UELS	*825,058*		*5,503*	*68.3*	*82.8*
Overall total	6,291,785	67.7	54,717	407.3	64.7

Source: Natural England (2012) Land Management Update, April 2012.

consider how they manage the agri-environment on their farms and all of the environmental features on the farms have had to be recorded and must be protected.

6. The Characteristics of European Agri-environment Schemes

Agri-environment schemes have been developed around the world in a variety of forms. Similar concerns for the quality of the rural environment have been the focus for initiatives dating back to the mid 1980s. For instance the Food Security Act of 1985 in the United States authorized the Conservation Reserve Program, with a goal of retiring 45 million acres of highly erodible land. In Australia, within a very different agricultural policy context, the Landcare movement dates back to 1986. But a number of aspects of the approach that has been taken in Europe have been the particular subject of research. This section focuses on these aspects.

7. Jointness

As mentioned above, much of what is valued in the European rural environment is a product of specific agricultural systems and as such, policy is directed toward the encouragement of the particular forms of land management and agricultural practices that support these environmental values. In this respect the environmental values and agricultural commodities are treated as joint products. A detailed study by Wätzold et al. (2008) illustrates some common characteristics and challenges of European agri-environment measures. Their study aims to estimate an "optimal level of species conservation" for the Scarce Large Blue butterfly (*Maculinea teleius*), an endangered meadow-dwelling species, in Landau in Germany. The females lay their eggs on the Large Pimpernel (*Sanguisorba officialis*) plant. Caterpillars fall from the plant and are carried away by red ants to their nests where they are fed by the ants over winter. However, plant and ants require a particular mowing regime in order to survive and this is no longer practiced due to the introduction of modern agricultural machinery and simultaneous and regular mowing of the meadows. The optimal level of conservation depends both on the supply and demand for the species. The supply depends on the effect of changing the mowing regime on the performance of the butterfly population and the costs to the farm of changing practices. The level of costs incurred on any particular farm depends on the situations of its individual meadows and farm business. Demand is assessed in this study in terms of the willingness of the local population to pay for larger numbers of butterflies. The analysis is conducted at a field level to simulate cost-effective mowing regimes to deliver a given number of butterflies. The authors conclude that from amongst the range of mowing regimes studied, the regime generating the greatest number of butterflies was optimal. In this example, biodiversity conservation requires the maintenance of a particular agricultural system that retains meadows that are mowed at particular times. The biodiversity is thus jointly produced with the agricultural production. The presence of the species is specific to a particular locality and its value may be dependent on the preferences of a local population. The success of the species depends on the way in which decisions across different farms and fields are coordinated. The requirement for particular spatial configurations of agricultural activity is also illustrated by Bamière et al. (2011) who have developed a spatially explicit mathematical programming model for analysis of options for the conservation of the Little Bustard (*Tetrax tetrax*). This bird requires the presence of extensive temporary grasslands distributed throughout the landscape. This means that a least cost option that concentrates grassland on the least profitable farms would be unlikely to provide sufficiently disaggregated habitat.

Brunstad et al. (2005) model multifunctional agriculture in terms of its provision of public goods of food security and landscape. While it is recognized that in practice it is not possible to model all the attributes that enhance the value of the agricultural landscape, such as openness, variation, biodiversity and type of agricultural technique, the environmental benefit is assumed to be associated with the area of land under tillage. They conclude that agricultural production would be sub-optimal in the absence of policy toward the environment, although they judge that in practice the level of subsidy offered in Norway exceeds that required to optimize environmental output. Lankoski and Ollikainen (2003) model local land use with heterogeneous land qualities. They include three agri-environmental externalities: biodiversity, landscape diversity and nutrient run-off. Biodiversity is enhanced through the introduction of buffer strips around field boundaries, the aesthetic value of landscape is promoted through a diversity of land uses, and nutrient run-off depends on both fertilizer use and buffer strips. Thus, environmental benefits are attained through the promotion of a diversity of cropping and by means of buffer strips that reduce the area of land under production. Their preferred policy instruments are a fertilizer tax and a buffer strip subsidy, both of which reduce total agricultural production. The complexity of adjustments required in promoting environmental quality is recognized by Miettinen and Huhtala (2004) who model the relationship between cereal production and the numbers of grey partridges. They show that farmers should increase the area under rye, reduce the use of herbicides and limit the partridge hunting bag in recognition of the social benefits associated with partridge conservation, but that this reduces the private returns to farming.

Peerlings and Polman (2004) investigate the joint production of milk, wildlife and landscape services in Dutch dairy farming using a micro-econometric profit model. The output of wildlife and landscape services is represented by the revenue received from government and nature organizations for participation in agri-environment schemes. They find that wildlife and landscape services compete with milk and other outputs, i.e. producing more milk makes the production of wildlife and landscape services less attractive. They also conclude that economies of scope exist on a small proportion of farms, although in practice farms do not specialize, suggesting that there may be other factors that are not taken into account in the model. Havlik et al. (2005) consider both complementarity and competition between agricultural production and environmental goods. They note that with regard to grassland biodiversity, agricultural production and environmental goods can be complementary over a certain range but compete beyond this range and that this is the case in practice for pasture stocking intensity in the Pyrenees. They analyze the position in two Environmentally Sensitive Areas, one where the danger is of over-intensification and another at risk from land abandonment. The provision of environmental goods is modelled by introducing constraints into a mathematical programming model that represents the requirements of particular agri-environmental contracts, assuming that keeping to the conditions of the agri-environmental contracts will generate the specified environmental goods. The authors conclude that there is little justification for commodity-linked instruments, noting that both complementary and competing relationships were observed within even a relatively small region, so that commodity price increases would generate a loss of biodiversity in some contexts.

There has been some discussion of the interactions amongst public good outputs. Brunstad et al. (2005) consider both landscape preservation and food security and Lankoski and Ollikainen (2003) include both biodiversity and landscape. But there seems to have been little analysis that has modelled the complexities of the interactions between different environmental outputs, suggesting a need to clarify the circumstances under which environmental production takes place. More generally with regard to jointness, it is clear that there are complementarities between the production of agricultural commodities and environmental quality in certain circumstances but competition in others. It is not a simple relationship. These relationships vary between locations and agricultural systems and within systems at different levels of production. General support for the prices of agricultural commodities will be very unlikely to generate consistent environmental improvements. Rather, agri-environmental policies need to promote detailed changes in farm practices that are specific to local environmental objectives and farming practices.

8. Asymmetric Information

Much of the early analysis of agri-environmental schemes focussed on the issue of asymmetric information. Agri-environment schemes are generally implemented through voluntary environmental contracts between a government agency and a group of heterogeneous farmers and farms. In these circumstances, the farmer has more complete information about the opportunity costs of adopting the requirements of the contract and has the potential to hide actions as to whether or not the contract is being complied with. This gives rise to the problems of adverse selection and moral hazard. These issues have been extensively analyzed in the literature. Most of this work has been theoretical, often simulating plausible parameter values. Moxey et al. (1999), White (2002) and Ozanne and White (2007) have analyzed the incentive compatibility of alternative mechanism designs based on combinations of either input quotas or input charges and transfer payments. This work has been extended by Ozanne and White (2007) who demonstrate that the two approaches lead to identical outcomes in terms of abatement levels, compensation payments, monitoring costs, probabilities of detection and social welfare. Gren (2004) compares a uniform flat-rate agri-environment payment to all farmers with a differentiated payment under conditions of private information available to farmers' on their individual costs of providing and managing their land. This information is not available to the principal. Under the differentiated payments, payment level depends on the farmer's cost type. She concludes that the general analytical results are indeterminate in that the relative advantages of the two policy designs depend on second derivatives of environmental land provision cost and benefit functions. Canton et al. (2009) focus on the impact of spatial targeting and delegation in mechanism design on overall efficiency. Spatial targeting can improve the information available to the principal ex ante and so simplify the trade-off between allocative efficiency and information rents. Delegation can be seen as a means of improving the regulator's information because local institutions may have a better knowledge of a farmer's characteristics. Their approach emphasizes the redistributive effects of disaggregated information structures with the most efficient farmers being most likely to be negatively affected. One study that has analyzed a specific agri-environment scheme is Quillérou and Fraser's (2010) assessment of Higher Level Stewardship in England. They find that, at the regional level, the enrolment of more land from lower payment regions for a given budget constraint has reduced the adverse selection problem through contracting a greater overall area and thus providing higher overall environmental benefit. Further, the regulator's allocation appears to reflect differences in environmental benefits thereby also reducing the adverse selection problem.

Moral hazard and compliance monitoring have also been the subject of specific analysis. Ozanne et al. (2001) develop a model that demonstrates that if monitoring costs are negligible or fixed, or farmers are highly risk averse, the moral hazard problem can be eliminated. However, if monitoring costs depend on monitoring effort and the degree of risk aversion is low, only a second best solution can be obtained. Fraser (2004) has analyzed the use of targeting to reduce moral hazard. Hart and Latacz-Lohmann (2005) report observations that the predictions of models of moral hazard problems are not consistent with what limited observations of actual experience are available, where a combination of low fines, low rates of checking and relatively little cheating seems to be the norm. This might reflect farmers misjudging their subjective evaluations of small risks of detection, or else that some farmers are basically honest and simply do not consider cheating as an option. They adopt the latter as an assumption and develop a model that allows for a continuum of farmer compliance costs and in which they relax the assumption that all farmers are profit maximizers. They note that in practice, given multiple periods, the regulator has an opportunity to learn about the characteristics of farmers and adjust behavior accordingly. The authors also draw attention to the fact that in practice farmers are more likely to cheat at the margin rather than to blatantly not comply at all, i.e. they may not fulfil the conditions of the contract to the letter and the level of penalty will be graduated in relation to the offence. In these circumstances, even farmers who cheat marginally may contribute to the fulfilment of the environmental target. These circumstances make real world compliance monitoring more complex than recognized in most models and it might also be noted that in practice the costs of monitoring compliance vary between different contract requirements. For instance, it is simpler to monitor farmer record keeping than it is to monitor the actual adoption of land management practices in the field.

One approach toward the problem of asymmetric information lies in the use of auctions or tendering as a mechanism for creating competition amongst farmers and getting them to reveal information about their costs. In principle, auctions can reduce information rents accruing to farmers and increase the cost-effectiveness of public goods provision, although strategic bidding behavior and high transactions costs may reduce efficiency (Latacz-Lohmann and Van der Hamsvoort 1998). Experimental work suggests that conservation auctions outperform fixed price schemes in a one-shot setting, but that with repetition the auction loses its edge (Latacz-Lohmann and Schilizzi 2007). However, while tendering has been applied in the US and Australia, and despite the provision for the use of tendering in the European Regulation 1698/2005, there is little empirical experience in the context of European agri-environment policies.

9. Entry into Schemes

The theoretical models of mechanism design almost invariably assume that farmers will enter agri-environment schemes where the financial payment exceeds the opportunity cost. However, in practice adoption depends on a much wider variety of factors and these have been the focus of a large number of empirical studies (e.g.Wilson 1997; Wynn et al. 2001; Wilson and Hart 2001; Vanslembrouck et al. 2002; Dupraz et al. 2003; Wossink and van Wenum 2003; Defrancesco et al. 2008; Hynes and Garvey 2009). Analysis tends to be based on data collected in surveys of farmers enrolling into a particular scheme, sometimes including nonparticipants, and the analyses test relationships with a wide variety of potential influences, often in categories such as those adopted by Wynn et al. (2001): physical farm factors, farmer characteristics, business factors and situational factors. From amongst these, such factors as farm size, farmer age, information available, the ease with which the requirements of the scheme can be accommodated into the farming system, farmers' attitudes and experience with agri-environment schemes are commonly included. Some studies have focussed on particular aspects of the decision to enrol. Falconer (2000) has concentrated on the transactions costs facing farmers in joining an agri-environment scheme, while Polman and Slangen (2008) included variables representing trust in government and institutional design. Frondel et al. (2012) look at the provision of information, pointing out that while not having an unambiguous effect in either encouraging or discouraging entry, it may be expected to improve the quality of decisions and help to avoid mistakes. Various theoretical approaches have been applied, such as Morris et al. (2000) who apply innovation decision theory or Beedell and Rehman (2000) who apply the Theory of Planned Behaviour. It is clear that farmers' decisions are affected by a wide variety of factors and it has also been suggested that participants who are only motivated by financial incentives may be less effective environmental managers than other participants. Along similar lines, Stobbelaar et al. (2009) note the internal motivation of organic farmers for nature conservation who were more likely to internalize the goals of environmental policy schemes. This implies an objective to build up cultural and social capital (Burton and Paragahawewa 2011).

These studies of actual behavior ex post are limited in terms of the scheme options that can be considered. A small number of studies have used choice experiments in order to explore farmers' preferences for alternative scheme design (Ruto and Garrod 2009; Espinosa-Goded et al. 2010; Christensen et al. 2011). These studies illustrate the ways in which farmers are willing to trade the level of payment for particular scheme requirements and suggest levels of payment that may be required in order to attract farmers to adopt agri-environment measures.

10. Transactions Costs

Environmental policy analysis often concentrates solely on the direct or opportunity costs to the firm of undertaking the changes required by the policy. However, this neglects the transaction costs faced by government in identifying and selecting policy options, disseminating information to potential participants, negotiating and implementing contracts and monitoring and enforcing compliance. Transactions costs vary substantially depending on the type of policy being considered (Rørstad et al. 2007) and can represent a significant proportion of total policy costs. This is the case for agri-environment measures. However, they are difficult to measure and while there is often a lack of evidence relating to them, one study by Falconer and Whitby (1999) reported costs varying across a wide range of agri-environment measures in Europe of between 30% and 80% of the total policy cost.

Evidence indicates that the administrative costs when schemes are first implemented are initially high but that they fall steadily and significantly as schemes become more established. Statistical analysis of the administrative costs of the Environmentally Sensitive Areas in England (Falconer et al. 2001) also suggests administrative economies of size related to scheme participation. Mettepenningen et al. (2011) have analyzed transactions costs of agri-environment schemes in nine European countries based on stakeholders' perceptions. They conclude that the complexity of the schemes, the number of agri-environmental measures that need to be designed and the required precision of the measures are the major influences on costs. They also note that a number of stakeholders believed that high transactions costs do not correspond to their environmental benefits. Falconer and Whitby (1999) suggest that transaction costs could be reduced by extending the contract period, by unifying schemes, and by investigating alternative contract mechanisms such as auctions.

McCann et al. (2005) have identified a number of categories for the transactions costs of environmental policies: research and information, policy enactment, policy design and implementation, support and administration, contracting, compliance monitoring/detection, and prosecution/enforcement. The relatively high transactions costs in agri-environment schemes reflect asset specificity, such as the variation in the potential value of outputs between sites, dependence on specific inputs or the influence of the quality of the labor input from particular farmers; the relative infrequency of transactions and farmers' lack of familiarity with them; and the uncertainty in terms of what a farmer might be contracted to do and what the outcomes of those actions might be (Coggan et al. 2010). A general thrust in transaction cost economics is that the purpose of institutions is to minimize transactions costs (Williamson 1996). However, in designing agri-environment schemes it is clear that alternative contractual arrangements, and hence different levels of transactions costs, have important implications for the value of the public goods that are generated. What is important is not the absolute level of transaction costs, but rather the return that they bring in terms of enhanced value of environmental outputs.

The essence of transactions costs lies in the acquisition of information. In a market transaction, each party will assess the value of the transaction to them and negotiate a contract accordingly. In this context, there is effectively no "exchange" and government is acting on behalf of a wide range of potential beneficiaries who could benefit from changes in land management. Thus government needs information on the costs and the potential outcomes of the possible changes in management and the values attached to those outcomes by the general public. Information is required in order to be able to predict what value can be expected to be generated from any potential environmental contract, taking account of the particular nature of the land being managed, its spatial and management context, the relationships between management actions and environmental outcomes, and the spatial and temporal context within which those outcomes will arise. There is thus a significant information requirement for policy design and implementation, and there will still remain a high degree of uncertainty. A similar argument applies to the completeness of contracts. More complete contracts may provide more specific direction to land managers in particular circumstances, reducing uncertainty and increasing the expected value of the environmental outcome. However, the development and implementation of such contracts will, again, increase transactions costs.

There is thus a trade-off between the transactions costs of gaining better information and the capacity to design, implement and monitor higher value environmental contracts. In principle, the optimal level of transactions costs will be where the marginal cost of obtaining better information is equal to the marginal value of the environmental improvement attained, with respect to each of the categories of transaction cost noted above. In practice, measurement of both costs and benefits is challenging, but it is an important issue on which there has been rather little empirical research. There appears to have been no analysis that has attempted to identify the optimal level of transactions costs in agri-environment schemes.

11. Scheme Effectiveness and Evaluation

Assessment of agri-environment schemes is important in determining appropriate allocations of public finance and in guiding the developments in mechanism design over time. While noting progress in the development of agri-environment schemes, the European Court of Auditors (2011) has recently criticized schemes for a lack of clear objectives, insufficient differentiation of payments between farmers to reflect local conditions, and a lack of application of procedures to select projects that represent best environmental value for money. Evaluation faces many complex challenges, including a lack of clear stated objectives for the policy, the limited availability of data, the challenge of identifying causality, in defining a reliable counterfactual and in assessing additionality. Some analysis that has been undertaken focuses somewhat simplistically on the numbers of farmers participating in schemes and on the changes in farm management practices, without evidence as to the extent to which these changes do in practice deliver environmental benefits or the importance of these benefits. Assessment of the indirect effects of schemes represents a further challenge for analysis.

Much of the effort that has been made to assess the impacts of agri-environment schemes has concentrated on the effects on biodiversity and the evidence remains controversial. A paper by Kleijn et al. (2001) suggesting that some schemes simply do not achieve their objectives or possibly even have adverse ecological effects has been widely cited, although it was countered by Stoate and Parish (2001) and Carey (2001) who argued that there was other evidence that some schemes are successful. Some studies of initiatives for the conservation of particular species have demonstrated success, such as for the cirl bunting (Peach et al. 2001) or corn bunting (Perkins et al. 2011). Studies of schemes have demonstrated positive long-term impact in particular contexts (e.g. Taylor and Morecroft 2009). Kleijn and Sutherland (2003) reviewed the available evidence on European schemes and concluded that, while just over half of the studies found an increase in species richness or abundance, research design was often inadequate to provide reliable results so that they could not reach a general judgment on the effectiveness on agri-environment schemes. They did not assess potential benefits other than biodiversity, such as reduced emissions or landscape enhancement. Kleijn et al. (2006) reviewed agri-environmental schemes in five European countries concluding that in all countries agri-environment schemes had marginal to moderately positive effects on biodiversity but that rare species benefited less often. Most recently Batáry et al. (2011) have undertaken a meta-analysis of mostly European studies. They conclude that agri-environmental management effectively enhances species abundance in croplands, and enhances both species richness and abundance in grasslands, regardless of landscape context. Whittingham (2011, 509) has commented recently that

"European agri-environment schemes have so far delivered only moderate biodiversity gains." However, under a range of circumstances, they can achieve substantial benefit to both biodiversity and ecosystem services. He also observes differences in the efficacy of schemes depending on the species/taxon concerned: plants show the strongest positive responses, followed by invertebrates, with birds and mammals showing the lowest responses.

Burrell (2011) has recently provided a conceptual framework for the evaluation of agri-environment schemes, differentiating between administrative, scientific and economic approaches. Within the European Union, agri-environment schemes, as funded under the Rural Development Regulation, are required to be evaluated under the European Commission's framework for evaluating rural development policies (European Commission 2006). Höjgård and Rabinowicz (2011) have identified some weaknesses in the evaluation procedure and suggested potential improvements. Primdahl et al. (2010) have reviewed the use of impact models in supporting the design, implementation and evaluation of agri-environment schemes in the EU. Purvis et al. (2009) have proposed a standardized approach to evaluation in terms of an "Agri-environmental Footprint Index" (AFI). This establishes a common framework within which the characteristics of particular schemes may be identified. Stakeholders, experts and farmers may be involved in the identification of suitable indicator variables which are then standardized and weighted. The AFI score for a specified sample of farms is calculated by multiplying the indicator scores by the agreed weights. Such an approach faces challenges in terms of data availability, the subjectivity of the weighting, and in assessing the causality and additionality of the scheme incentives. However, it can offer a common framework within which to assess scheme performance and to aid improved understanding and wider debate about the implementation of agri-environment schemes within a particular context. Westbury et al. (2011) suggest that the same methodology could also be used for more routine monitoring of the environmental performance of farming systems.

Some methods have been developed in order to generate more reliable evaluations. In principle, a counterfactual might be based on the performance of a control group of farms that do not participate in the agri-environment scheme. However, in practice there will be selection effects in that the farms that do participate are not the same as the farms that do not. Thus any differences represent some combination of the causal effect of the programme and the selection effect. Pufahl and Weiss (2009) have used a semi-parametric propensity score matching estimator combined with a difference-in-difference approach to evaluate agri-environment programmes in Germany. They find a positive effect on the area in agricultural use and a reduction in chemical usage per hectare. Their analysis also shows differences amongst individual farms but these were not addressed in detail. Chabé-Ferret and Subervie (2011) have also used difference-in-difference analysis to estimate the causal effect of agri-environment programmes in France, finding that the windfall effects of the programmes depend on the specific requirements of the particular program. They then seek to integrate the results into a cost-benefit analysis.

A further complication in evaluation is that the value of changes on any particular farm may depend on its local landscape context and on the changes being made on other farms nearby (Concepción et al. 2008). Schouten et al. (2013) have developed a spatially explicit agent-based model for an area in the Netherlands. The agricultural landscape is modelled as an agent-based system, taking account of both the farmers' behavior and the spatial configuration of the landscape. Their results indicate that when policy makers want to achieve the highest contribution to the spatial habitat network they should consider spatially differentiated payments. They point out that their model does not take account of transactions costs, although suggest that an auction mechanism might provide a way of allocating payments on the basis of farm opportunity costs.

The environmental benefits arising from agri-environment schemes have been the focus for a substantial number of economic valuation studies. Valuation has had to rely largely on stated preference techniques, earlier studies using contingent valuation (Garrod et al. 1994, Garrod and Willis 1995), while more recently use has been made of choice experiments (Campbell 2007), sometimes comparing the two (Hanley et al. 1998). Hynes et al. (2011) compare a holistic valuation of landscape using contingent valuation with a valuation of landscape attributes using a choice experiment. They find an insignificant difference between the two approaches. Madureira et al. (2007) have reviewed valuation studies conducted in France, Germany and Portugal. They find a predominance of stated preference methods and a focus on a regional scale. However, they conclude that the information generated is not widely used by policy makers. Campbell et al. (2009) have conducted a choice experiment for the value of rural landscape in Ireland and then interpolated willingness to pay estimates (WTP) for the whole of the country. They find that WTP for rural landscape declines considerably from the rural west of Ireland to the more urbanized and modern farm landscapes of the east. They suggest that their results indicate that landscapes are valued primarily with regard to their active use rather than just for their existence. Garrod et al. (2012) used a choice experiment to assess whether individual preferences for the environmental benefits associated with Environmental Stewardship vary across landscape types. They find that there is spatial heterogeneity of preferences as well as a preference toward benefits delivered closest and most accessibly to where respondents live. They conclude that spatial targeting should also take account of the size of local populations. While considerable progress has been made in the methodological developments for valuation, less attention has been given to combining valuation studies with critical analyses of the issues of the counterfactuals and additionality of agri-environment schemes (Hodge and McNally 1998).

12. Prospects for Agri-environment Schemes

Agri-environment policy represents a new challenge to governments: to re-create or even create new actively managed rural landscapes that generate complex mixes of private and public goods. It takes environmental policy into a new era, beyond the regulation of environmental costs to the delivery of environmental benefits. It can be seen as the forerunner of the increasingly pervasive discussion of policies for the provision of payments for ecosystems services. Agri-environment policy has seen considerable development since its introduction some 25 years ago. The initial concentration on restraining pressures for agricultural intensification has moved on toward more general policies that aim to promote environmental enhancement. At the same time, following decoupling of the CAP in 2005, more effort will be required from agri-environment policy to hold land in production where the greater environmental threat is from land abandonment (Renwick et al. 2013). The longer term position will become clearer once the nature of the CAP to be implemented beyond 2013 is determined (European Commission 2011).

At the same time, there are likely to be increased pressures in the future on the management of rural land to mitigate and adapt to climate change and to do more to promote resource conservation. It seems reasonable to expect that the world will see generally higher and more variable commodity prices and that at the same time there will be increased pressures to reduce the levels of public expenditure. These circumstances set a number of challenges for the further development of agri-environment policy in that they extend the range of outcomes that will be sought, increase the opportunity costs of implementing policy and reduce the public resources available to support it. These conditions may become more apparent as the wider pressures and constraints bind more tightly. Indeed, it might be questioned whether the use of public funds at this scale to deliver rural public goods is to be a permanent feature of European rural policy.

There is then a clear logic for seeking both to increase the efficiency of agri-environment schemes while at the same time looking for alternative means by which the required environmental standards might be delivered. The issue of efficiency relates both to precision, in terms of the standard conditions for optimality (Vatn 2002), as well as to the optimal level of transactions costs. The evidence indicates that agri-environment schemes can have beneficial environmental impacts, but that they do not always do so. It is clearly important to do more to unravel which approaches are or are not successful, from both environmental and socioeconomic perspectives. Herzog (2005) discusses agri-environment schemes as landscape experiments, suggesting the potential for research based on more formal experimental designs to test the effects of alternative mechanisms. Whittingham (2011) argues for adaptive management, an iterative approach to decision-making that learns from the evidence that is accumulated over time. This might suggests more local approaches to governance through socioecological adaptive co-management (Hodge 2007). There is potential for institutional analysis of alternative arrangements whereby local communities may be able to deliver such management. Research has indicated potential ways in which efficiency might be increased, including clarifying objectives and focussing on what society judges to be the highest priorities, targeting schemes more directly, both in terms of specific public goods and in terms of specific locations and co-ordination across space, and introducing more competition in the allocation of contracts. Economic theory points to potential advantages from basing payments on results rather than on the costs of making standard changes to farming systems that are expected to generate the desired outcomes (Schwarz et al. 2008; Matzdorf and Lorenz 2010). This raises questions as to the identification appropriate indicators (Hasund 2013) and the treatment of risk. Burton and Schwarz (2013) argue that the novel risks associated with payments for the provision of environmental goods might promote cultural/social capital amongst farmers who develop new approaches and share knowledge about the ecological production function. There is potential to model many of these issues as a method of evaluating different policy approaches. In the pursuit of more effective policies, it will be important to do more work on the scale at which agri-environment contracts should be implemented, such as looking at the potential for closer cooperation both amongst farmers and between different interest groups, especially at a local scale (Franks 2010), and on the interactions and trade-offs among different ecosystems services. Emery and Franks (2012) and Franks and Emery (2013) have examined farmers' willingness in principle to collaborate in agri-environment schemes and the actual experience to date with the opportunities that are available in existing schemes.

The origins of agri-environmental policy have colored the way in which the policy has been developed. It has generally been viewed as an offshoot of agricultural policy, beginning with the farmer, rather than as a separate rural environmental policy, starting from the objective of achieving environmental change. Whether or not it is viewed suspiciously as a policy to disguise agricultural subsidies (Anderson 2000), support for farm businesses remains at least as an implicit objective. More analysis is required on the incidence and distribution of the costs of implementing agri-environment management at the farm level. Jointness is used as a rationale for the policy in general rather than being considered simply as an argument in favor of a particular approach to implementation in certain circumstances. An ecosystems services perspective might challenge some of the assumptions that have generally been accepted in designing policy approaches. This raises more general questions as to the sort of agricultural systems that can be most effective in delivering alternative combinations of ecosystem services and commodity outputs.

There are some limits that are fundamental to the use of environmental contracts in agri-environment schemes in their present form (Hodge 2001). These include: the problems in defining and measuring the outputs that are demanded, the near impossibility of defining farm practices that are best suited to the delivery of environmental benefits in individual farm circumstances, the subsequent problem of writing these as conditions into enforceable contracts, the inevitability of some degree of asymmetric information, and the problem that any fixed term contract will come to an end, with uncertainty as to how land management will change in the subsequent period (Whitby 2000). There is then an uncertainty as to the "ownership" of the environmental enhancements that have been achieved through the expenditure of public funds. Environmental contracts commoditize the provision of environmental services and hence may crowd out (Frey 1997) a culture of stewardship (Colman 1994) that might anyway have delivered at least some of the environmental benefits at zero public cost. This might make the introduction of agri-environmental payments effectively irreversible. These are questions for social and institutional analysis. Environmental contracts promote a culture of service delivery rather than entrepreneurship. Agri-environmental policy needs to be considered alongside other policy approaches of regulation, conservation covenants, land ownership and nonprofit and community organizations (Hodge 2001). These other approaches have their own strengths and weaknesses, but a comprehensive agri-environmental policy will draw from a wider range of policy mechanisms and resources than has been the case to date. These are areas for further work.

References

Anderson, K. 2000. Agriculture's "multifunctionality" and the WTO. *Australian Journal of Agricultural and Resource Economics* 44(3): 475–494.

Baldock, D., and P. Lowe. 1996. The development of European agri-environment policy. In *The European environment and CAP reform*, ed. M. Whitby, 8–25. Wallingford, UK: CAB International.

Bamiere, L., et al. 2011. Farming system modelling for agri-environmental policy design: The case of a spatially non-aggregated allocation of conservation measures. *Ecological Economics* 70: 891–899.

Batáry, P., A. Báldi, D. Kleijn, and T. Tscharntke. 2011. Landscape-moderated biodiversity effects of agri-environmental management: A meta-analysis. *Proceedings of the Royal Society of London B* 278(1713): 1894–1902.

Beedell, J., and T. Rehman. 2000. Using social-psychology models to understand farmers' conservation behaviour. *Journal of Rural Studies* 16: 117–127.

Blandford, D., and R. Boisvert. 2005. Non-trade concerns: Reconciling domestic policy objectives with trade liberalisation. *International Journal of Agricultural Resources Governance and Ecology* 4(3/4): 277–291.

Bowers, J., and P. Cheshire. 1983. *Agriculture, the countryside and land use: An economic critique*. London: Methuen.

Brunstad, R., I. Gaasland, and E. Vardal. 2005. Multifunctionality of agriculture: An inquiry into the complementarity between landscape preservation and food security. *European Review of Agricultural Economics* 32(4): 469–488.

Burrell, A. 2011. Evaluating policies for delivering agri-environmental public goods. Paper presented at OECD Workshop on the Evaluation of Agri-environmental Policies, Braunschweig, June 20–22.

Burton, R., and U. Paragahawewa. 2011. Creating culturally sustainable agri-environment schemes. *Journal of Rural Studies* 27: 95–104.

Burton, R., and G. Schwarz. 2013. Result-oriented agri-environmental schemes in Europe and their potential for promoting behavioural change. *Land Use Policy* 30: 628–641.

Campbell, D. 2007. Willingness to pay for rural landscape improvements: Combining mixed logit and random-effects models. *Journal of Agricultural Economics* 58(3): 467–483.

Campbell, D., W. Hutchinson, and R. Scarpa. 2009. Using choice experiments to explore the spatial distribution of willingness to pay for rural landscape improvements. *Environment and Planning A* 41: 97–111.

Canton, J., S. De Cara, and P-A. Jayet. 2009. Agri-environment schemes: Adverse selection, information structure and delegation. *Ecological Economics* 68: 2114–2121.

Carey, P. 2001. Schemes are monitored and effective in the UK. *Nature* 414: 687.

Chabé-Ferret, S., and J. Subervie. 2011. Estimating the causal effects of the French agri-environmental schemes on farmers' practices by difference in difference matching. Paper presented at OECD Workshop on the Evaluation of Agri-environmental Policies, Braunschweig, June 20–22.

Christensen, T., A. B. Pedersen, H. O. Nielsen, M. R. Mørkbak, B. Hasler, and S. Denver, S. 2011. Determinants of farmers' willingness to participate in subsidy schemes for pesticide-free buffer zones—A choice experiment study. *Ecological Economics* 70: 1558–1564.

Coggan, A., S. Whitten, and J. Bennett. 2010. Influences of transactions costs in environmental policy. *Ecological Economics* 69: 1777–1784.

Colman, D. 1994. Ethics and externalities: Agricultural stewardship and other behaviour. *Journal of Agricultural Economics* 45(3): 299–311.

Concepción, E., M. Diaz, and R. Baquero. 2008. Effects of landscape complexity on the ecological effectiveness of agri-environment schemes. *Landscape Ecology* 23: 135–148.

Cooper, T., K. Hart, and D. Baldock. 2009. *The provision of public goods through agriculture in the European Union*. Report prepared for DG Agriculture and Rural Development. Contract 30-CE-0233091/00-28, Institute for European Environmental Policy, London.

Countryside Commission. 1984. Application of the Less Favoured Areas (LFA) Directive in The Netherlands, CCP 167, Countryside Commission, Cheltenham.

Darnhofer, I., and W. Schneeberger. 2007. Impacts of voluntary agri-environmental measures on Austria's agriculture. *International Journal of Agricultural Resources, Governance and Ecology* 6(3): 360–377.

Defrancesco, E., P. Gatto, F. Runge, and S. Trestini. 2008. Factors affecting farmers' participation in agri-environmental measures: A northern Italian perspective. *Journal of Agricultural Economics* 59(1): 114–131.

Dupraz, P., D. Vermersch, B. Henry de Franham, and L. Delvaux. 2003. The environmental supply of farm households: A flexible willingness to accept model. *Environmental and Resource Economics* 25: 171–189.

Emery, S., and J. Franks. 2012. The potential for collaborative agri-environment schemes in England: Can a well-designed collaborative approach address farmers' concerns with current schemes? *Journal of Rural Studies* 28: 218–231.

Espinosa-Goded, M., J. Barreiro-Hurlé, and E. Ruto. 2010. What do farmers want from agri-environment scheme design? A choice experiment approach. *Journal of Agricultural Economics* 61(2): 259–273.

European Commission. 2006. *Handbook on common monitoring and evaluation framework*. Brussels: Directorate General for Agriculture and Rural Development.

European Commission. 2010. *Rural development in the European Union—Statistical and economic information—Report 2010*. http://ec.europa.eu/agriculture/agrista/rurdev2010/ruraldev.htm

European Commission. 2011. CAP Reform—an explanation of the main elements. MEMO/11/685.

European Court of Auditors. 2011. *Is agri-environment support well designed and managed?* Special Report No. 7, European Court of Auditors, Luxembourg.

Falconer, K., and M. Whitby. 1999. The invisible costs of scheme implementation and administration. In *Countryside Stewardship: Farmers, policies and markets*, eds. G. Van Huylenbroeck and M. Whitby, 67–88. Amsterdam: Pergamon.

Falconer, K. 2000. Farm-level constraints on agri-environmental scheme participation: A transactional perspective. *Journal of Rural Studies* 16: 379–394.

Falconer, K., P. Dupraz, and M. Whitby. 2001. An investigation of policy administrative costs using panel data for the English Environmentally Sensitive Areas. *Journal of Agricultural Economics* 52(1): 83–101.

Franks, J. 2010. Boundary organizations for sustainable land management: The example of Dutch environmental co-operatives. *Ecological Economics* 70: 283–295.

Franks, J., and Emery, S. 2013. Incentivising collaborative conservation: Lessons from existing Environmental Stewardship Scheme options. *Land Use Policy* 30: 847–862.

Fraser, R. 2004. On the use of targeting to reduce moral hazard in agri-environmental schemes. *Journal of Agricultural Economics* 55(3): 525–540.

Frey, B. 1997. *Not just for the money: An economic theory of personal motivation*. Cheltenham, UK: Edward Elgar.

Frondel, M., P. Lehmann, and F. Wätzold. 2012. The impact of information on landowners' participation in voluntary conservation program—Theoretical considerations and empirical evidence from an agri-environment program in Saxony, Germany. *Land Use Policy* 29: 388–394.

Garrod, G., K. Willis, and C. Saunders. 1994. The benefits and costs of the Somerset Levels and Moors ESA. *Journal of Rural Studies* 10(2): 131–145.

Garrod, G., and K. Willis. 1995. Valuing the benefits of the South Downs Environmentally Sensitive Area. *Journal of Agricultural Economics* 46(2): 160–173.

Garrod, G., E. Ruto, K. Willis, and N. Powe. 2012. Heterogeneity for the benefits of Environmental Stewardship: A latent-class approach. *Ecological Economics* 76: 104–111.

Gren, I-M. 2004. Uniform or discriminating payments for environmental production on arable land under asymmetric information. *European Review of Agricultural Economics* 31(1): 61–76.

Hagedorn, K. 2004. Multifunctional agriculture: An institutional interpretation. In Proceedings of the 90th EAAE seminar, *Multifunctional agriculture, policies and markets: Understanding the critical linkages*, Abstract, 17–20, Part 2, INRA, Rennes.

Hanley, N., D. MacMillan, R. Wright, C. Bullock, I. Simpson, D. Parsisson, and B. Crabtree. 1998. Contingent valuation versus choice experiments: Estimating the benefits of Environmentally Sensitive Areas in Scotland. *Journal of Agricultural Economics* 49: 1–15.

Hart, R., and U. Latcz-Lohmann. 2007. Combating moral hazard in agri-environmental schemes: A multi-agent approach. *European Review of Agricultural Economics* 32(1): 75–91.

Hasund, K. P. 2013. Indicator-based agri-environmental payments: A payment-by-result model for public goods with a Swedish application. *Land Use Policy* 30: 223–233.

Havlik, P., P. Veysset, J. M. Boisson, M. Lherm, and F. Jacquet. 2005. Joint production under uncertainty and multifunctionality of agriculture: Policy considerations and applied analysis. *European Review of Agricultural Economics* 32(4): 489–515.

Herzog, F. 2005. Agri-environment schemes as landscape experiments. *Agriculture, Ecosystems and Environment* 108: 175–177.

Hodge, I. 1989. Compensation for nature conservation. *Environment and Planning A* 21(8): 1027–1036.

Hodge, I., and S. McNally. 1998. Evaluating the Environmentally Sensitive Areas: The value of rural environments and policy relevance. *Journal of Rural Studies* 14(3): 357–367.

Hodge, I. 2000. Agri-environmental relationships and the choice of policy mechanism. *The World Economy* 23(2): 257–273.

Hodge, I. 2001. Beyond agri-environmental policy: Towards an alternative model of rural environmental governance. *Land Use Policy* 18: 99–111.

Hodge, I. 2007. The governance of rural land in a liberalised world. *Journal of Agricultural Economics* 58(3): 409–432.

Hodge, I., and M. Reader. 2010. The introduction of entry level stewardship in England: Extension or dilution in agri-environment policy? *Land Use Policy* 27(2): 270–282.

Höjgård, S., and E. Rabinowicz. 2011. Evidence based agri-environmental policies—Can institutionalized evaluation procedures provide useful input? The Swedish experience. Paper presented at OECD Workshop on the Evaluation of Agri-environmental Policies, Braunschweig, June 20–22.

Hynes, S., D. Campbell, and P. Howley. 2011. A holistic vs. an attribute-based approach to agri-environmental policy evaluation: Do welfare estimates differ? *Journal of Agricultural Economics* 62(2): 305–329.

Hynes, S., and E. Garvey. 2009. Modelling farmers' participation in an agri-environmental scheme using panel data: An application to the Rural Environmental Protection Scheme in Ireland. *Journal of Agricultural Economics* 60: 546–562.

Kleijn, D., F. Berendse, R. Smit, and N. Gilissen. 2001. Agri-environment schemes do not effectively protect biodiversity in Dutch agricultural landscape. *Nature* 413, 723–725.

Kleijn, D., and W. Sutherland. 2003. How effective are European agri-environment schemes on conserving and promoting biodiversity? *Journal of Applied Ecology* 40: 947–969.

Kleijn, D., et al. 2006. Mixed biodiversity benefits of agri-environment schemes in five European countries. *Ecology Letters* 9: 243–254.

Lankoski, J., and M. Ollikainen. 2003. Agri-environmental externalities: A framework for designing targeted policies. *European Review of Agricultural Economics* 30(1): 51–75.

Latacz-Lohmann, U., and C. Van der Hamsvoort. 1998. Auctions as a means of creating a market for public goods from agriculture. *Journal of Agricultural Economics* 49(3): 334–345.

Latacz-Lohmann, U., and S. Schillizzi. 2007. Quantifying the benefits of conservation auctions. *EuroChoices* 6(3): 32–39.

Lowe, P., G. Cox, M. MacEwen, T. O'Riordan, and M. Winter. 1986. *Countryside conflicts: The politics of farming, forestry and conservation*. Aldershot, UK: Gower.

Madureira, L., T., Rambonilaza, and I. Karpinski. 2007. Review of methods and evidence for economic valuation of non-commodity outputs and suggestions to facilitate its application to broader decisional contexts. *Agriculture, Ecosystems and Environment* 120: 5–20.

McCann, L., B. Colby, K. Easter, A. Kasterine, and K. Kuperan. 2005. Transaction cost measurement for evaluation environmental policies. *Ecological Economics* 52: 527–542.

MAFF. 1989. *Environmentally sensitive areas*. London: HMSO.

Matzdorf, B., and J. Lorenz. 2010. How cost-effective are results-oriented agri-environment measures? An empirical analysis in Germany. *Land Use Policy* 27: 535–544.

Mettepenningen, E., V. Beckmann, and J. Eggers. 2011. Public transaction costs of agri-environmental schemes and their determinants—Analysing stakeholders' involvement and perceptions. *Ecological Economics* 70: 641–650.

Miettinen, A., and A. Huhtala. 2004. On joint production of cereals and grey partridges in Finland. Paper presented at 90th European Association of Agricultural Economists Seminar, Rennes.

Morris, J., J. Mills, and I. Crawford. 2000. Promoting farmer uptake of agri-environment schemes: The Countryside Stewardship arable options scheme. *Land Use Policy* 17: 241–254.

Moxey, A., B. White, and A. Ozanne. 1999. Efficient contract design for agri-environmental policy. *Journal of Agricultural Economics* 50(2), 187–202.

Netzwerk Land. 2011. What farmers are doing for the environment: The Austrian Agri-environmental Programme ÖPUL. Vienna: Netzwerk Land.

OECD. 1999. *Cultivating rural amenities: An economic development perspective.* Paris: Organisation for Economic Co-operation and Development.

OECD. 2001*a*. *Multifunctionality: Towards an analytical framework.* Paris: Organisation for Economic Co-operation and Development.

OECD. 2001*b*. *Improving the environmental performance of agriculture: Policy options and market approaches.* Paris: Organisation for Economic Co-operation and Development.

Ozanne, A., T. Hogan, and D. Colman. 2001. Moral hazard, risk aversion and compliance monitoring in agri-environmental policy. *European Review of Agricultural Economics* 28(3): 329–347.

Ozanne, A., and B. White. 2007. Equivalence of input quotas and input charges under asymmetric information in agri-environment schemes. *Journal of Agricultural Economics* 58(2): 260–268.

Peach, W., L. Lovett, S. Wotton, and C. Jeffs. 2001. Countryside Stewardship delivers cirl buntings (*Emberiza circlus*) in Devon, UK. *Biological Conservation* 101: 361–374.

Peerlings, J., and N. Polman. 2004. Wildlife and landscape services production in Dutch dairy farming: Jointness and transaction costs. *European Review of Agricultural Economics* 31(4): 427–449.

Perkins, A., H. Maggs, A. Watson, and J. Wilson. 2011. Adaptive management and targeting of agri-environment schemes does benefit biodiversity: A case study of the corn bunting *Emberiza calandra*. *Journal of Applied Ecology* 48: 514–522.

Polman, N., and L. Slangen. 2008. Institutional design of agri-environmental contracts in the European Union: the role of trust and social capital. *NJAS: Wageningen Journal of Life Sciences* 55(4): 413–420.

Primdahl, J. et al. 2010. Current use of impact models for agri-environment schemes and potential for improvements of policy design and assessment. *Journal of Environmental Management* 91: 1245–1254.

Puchta, A. 2011. The evaluation of the Austrian Agri-environmental programme. Paper presented at OECD Workshop on the Evaluation of Agri-environmental Policies, Braunschweig, June 20–22.

Pufahl, A., and C. Weiss. 2009. Evaluating the effects of farm programmes: Results from propensity score matching. *European Review of Agricultural Economics* 36(1): 79–101.

Purvis, G., G. Louwagie, G. Northey, S. Mortimer, J. Park, A. Mauchline, J. Finn, J. Primdahl, H. Vejre, J. P. Vesterager, K. Knickel, N. Kasperczyk, K. Balazs, G. Vlahos, S. Christopoulos, and J. Peltola. 2009. Conceptual development of a harmonised method for tracking change and evaluating policy in the agri-environment: The agri-environmental footprint index. *Environmental Science and Policy* 12: 321–337.

Quillérou, E., and R. Fraser. 2010. Adverse selection in the Environmental Stewardship Scheme: Does the Higher Level Stewardship Scheme design reduce adverse selection? *Journal of Agricultural Economics* 61(2): 369–380.

Renwick, A., T. Jansson, P. Verburg, C. Revoredo-Giha, W. Britz, A. Gocht, and D. McCracken. 2013. Policy reform and agricultural land abandonment. *Land Use Policy* 30: 446–457.

Rørstad, P. K., A. Vatn, and V. Kvakkestad. 2007. Why do transactions costs of agricultural policy vary? *Agricultural Economics* 36: 1–11.

Ruto, E., and G. Garrod. 2009. Investigating farmers' preferences for the design of agri-environment schemes: A choice experiment approach. *Journal of Environmental Planning and Management* 52: 631–647.

Schouten, M., P. Opdam, N. Polman, and E. Westerhof. 2013. Resilience-based governance in rural landscapes: Experiments with agri-environment schemes using a spatially explicit agent-based model. *Land Use Policy* 30: 934–943.

Schwarz, G., A. Moxey, D. McCracken, S. Huband, and R. Cummins. 2008. *An analysis of the potential effectiveness of a Payment-by-Results approach to the delivery of environmental public goods and services supplied by Agri-Environment Schemes.* Report to the Land Use Policy Group, UK. Macaulay Institute, Pareto Consulting and Scottish Agricultural College.

Shoard, M. 1980. *The theft of the countryside.* London: Maurice Temple Smith.

Stoate, C., and D. Parish. 2001. Monitoring is underway and results so far are promising. *Nature* 414: 687.

Stobbelaar, D. J., J. C. J. Groot, C. Bishop, J. Hall, and J. Pretty. 2009. Internalization of agri-environmental policies and the role of institutions. *Journal of Environmental Management* 90: S175–S184.

Taylor, M., and M. Morecroft. 2009. Effects of agri-environment schemes in a long-term ecological time series. *Agriculture, Ecosystems and Environment* 130: 9–15.

Vanslembrouck, I., G. van Huylenbroech, and W. Verbeke. 2002. Determinants of the willingness of Belgian farmers to participate in agri-environment measures. *Journal of Agricultural Economics* 53: 489–511.

Vatn, A. 2002. Multifunctional agriculture: Some consequences for international trade regimes. *European Review of Agricultural Economics* 29(3): 309–327.

Wätzold, F., N. Lienhoop, M. Dreschler, and J. Settele. 2008. Estimating optimal conservation in the context of agri-environmental schemes. *Ecological Economics* 68: 295–305.

Westbury, D., J. Park, A. Mauchline, R. Crane, and S. Mortimer. 2011. Assessing the environmental performance of English arable and livestock holdings using data from the Farm Accountancy Data Network (FADN). *Journal of Environmental Management* 92: 902–909.

Whitby, M. 1996 The prospect for agri-environmental policies within a reformed CAP. In *The European Environment and CAP Reform*, ed. M. Whitby, 227–240. Wallingford, UK: CAB International.

Whitby, M. 2000. Challenges and options for the UK agri-environment. *Journal of Agricultural Economics* 51(3): 317–332.

White, B. 2002. Designing voluntary agri-environmental policy with hidden information and hidden action: A note. *Journal of Agricultural Economics* 53(2): 353–360.

Whittingham, M. 2011. The future of agri-environment schemes: Biodiversity gains and ecosystem delivery? *Journal of Applied Ecology* 48: 509–513.

Williamson, O. 1996. *The mechanisms of governance.* Oxford: Oxford University Press.

Willis, K., J. Benson, and C. Saunders. 1988. The impact of agricultural policy on the costs of nature conservation. *Land Economics* 64(2): 147–157.

Wilson, G. 1997. Factors influencing farmer participation in the Environmentally Sensitive Areas scheme. *Journal of Environmental Management* 50: 67–93.

Wilson, G., and K. Hart. 2001. Farmer participation in agri-environment schemes: Towards conservation-oriented thinking? *Sociologia Ruralis* 41: 254–274.

Wossink, G., and H. van Wenum. 2003. Biodiversity conservation by farmers: Analysis of actual and contingent participation. *European Review of Agricultural Economics* 30: 461–485.

Wynn, G., B. Crabtree, and J. Potts. 2001. Modelling farmer entry into the environmentally sensitive areas in Scotland. *Journal of Agricultural Economics* 52: 65–82.

CHAPTER 23

AGRI-ENVIRONMENTAL POLICIES

A Comparison of US and EU Experiences

ROGER CLAASSEN, JOSEPH COOPER, CRISTINA SALVIONI, AND MARCELLA VERONESI

AGRICULTURE is more than just the production and sale of commodities; it also produces many intended and unintended positive and negative byproducts. Negative byproducts, or disamenities, include nutrient and pesticide runoff, soil erosion, air pollution, and the loss of biodiversity (ERS 2006). The positive byproducts, or amenities, provided by agriculture can be relatively tangible goods such as open space and scenic vistas, whereas others, such as the spiritual or symbolic value of preserving our farming heritage, are more abstract and nonpecuniary (Cooper et al. 2005). Many environmental amenities or disamenities of agricultural production affect society as a whole and have a social benefit or cost much greater than the private benefit or cost affecting those involved in agriculture. In such cases, there is an economic rationale for society to subsidize the environmental amenity (or tax an environmental disamenity) to produce the desired level of environmental protection.

The United States and the European Union have a long history of agri-environmental programs. In the 1980s, agri-environmental programs began to play a larger role in federal farm policies, in part due to greater concern about environmental damage from agricultural production. Agri-environmental programs are likely to play a vital role in future EU and US farm policy debates. In this chapter, we outline and compare EU and US agri-environmental programs. We then overview what is known about the environmental and land use impacts of these programs. We follow with a discussion of and EU data sources that are key to the analysis of agri-environmental programs and their land use impacts.

1. Different Instruments of Environmental Protection

Both the United States and the European Union rely primarily on a mixture of three types of programs to address agri-environmental issues: voluntary incentive-based programs, regulatory programs, and cross-compliance programs.[1] Other policy instruments in use include in-kind technical assistance and facilitative measures such as organic certification and labeling standards.

Agri-environmental incentives are payments to the farmer to adopt environmentally sound practices or to retire environmentally sensitive land from production. The advantage of incentives is that they lower resistance from farmers to adopting the desired practices or retiring land. Incentive payments can also facilitate targeting of conservation program effort to farms where relatively large benefits—relative to costs—can be achieved. The disadvantage of incentives is the cost to taxpayers. Incentives can also have the effect of expanding production, so that even if the disamenities produced by each farm (or on each field) decrease, more farms (or fields) may now produce disamenities.[2]

Regulatory requirements, or standards, represent an involuntary (or mandatory) approach to improving agri-environmental performance. Unlike policy choices in which farmer participation is uncertain, regulations simply require that all farmers participate. This feature can be particularly important if the consequences of not changing practices are drastic or irreversible. The ban on the production and application of the chemical DDT is one such example. However, regulatory requirements are a blunt tool and can be the least flexible of all policy instruments, requiring that producers reach a specific environmental goal or adopt specific practices without regard for cost or environmental effectiveness, which may vary significantly across farms but are seldom known by regulators. Consequently, regulation can be less flexible and less efficient than economic incentives. Regulatory requirements are used sparingly in both the European Union and the United States.

Cross-compliance requires that farmers use practices that meet a basic environmental standard as a condition of eligibility for other government programs that farmers may find economically desirable, such as those that provide income support payments. Technically, cross-compliance is a voluntary, indirect, incentive-based instrument, but because it represents a standard for receiving a subsidy, in practice, it may not strictly be

[1] Only a brief overview is provided here; for a more detailed overview of the economic instruments pertaining to US agri-environmental policy, see Claassen et al. (2001) and other papers at http://www.ers.usda.gov/Briefing/ConservationAndEnvironment/.

[2] A firm that would be unprofitable under a tax may be made profitable by an incentive or subsidy (Baumol and Oates, 1988). Although a tax may drive a firm out of a competitive industry, an incentive may increase entry and induce expansion in competitive outputs.

perceived as voluntary, particularly when the existing subsidy represents an important share of total farm income. It may be difficult for a farmer to forego cross-compliance when the value of the existing subsidies exceeds the farmer's costs of adopting the mandated practices.[3] An advantage of cross-compliance programs is that less government outlay is required than with subsidies to address environmental problems. A key disadvantage is that not all farmers receive program payments that are subject to cross-compliance. In the United States, for example, federally subsidized crop insurance, which is an increasingly important component of US government support for agriculture, is not currently subject to cross-compliance. Moreover, high market prices for commodity crops have reduced some US commodity program payments. If payments become low enough, farmers might forgo participation in these programs rather than use the practices entailed by cross-compliance (ERS 2012). Moreover, compliance requirements, if expensive to apply, may also undercut other program objectives, such as income support.

Other measures facilitate conservation without providing financial assistance directly to producers. For example, the United States provides in-kind conservation assistance to farmers through planning and technical assistance in the development and implementation of conservation practices to address specific agri-environmental problems (known as conservation technical assistance or CTA). Another example is eco-labeling (e.g., organic certification) that allows producers to differentiate their products in the marketplace and, possibly, command a higher price. The key advantage of these approaches is low cost (at least in relation to payment programs); the key disadvantage is that off-site environmental damages are not explicitly addressed, although producer benefits (e.g., from reduced soil erosion) may also lead to off-site benefits.

2. US Agri-Environmental Policy

Regulation is used sparingly in US federal agri-environmental policy. The Federal Insecticide, Fungicide, and Rodenticide Act (FIFRA) regulates the availability and use of agricultural pesticides. Regulatory authority under the Clean Water Act (CWA) has also been used in some instances to regulate loss of sediment, and influx of nutrients, pathogens, and pesticides into water. For example, CWA authority has been used to regulate

[3] Government payments can account for a large share of net farm income but vary widely across regions; for example, in 2010, in the United States, they account for less than 20% of net farm income in the Pacific region and 40% or more in the Southern Plains (Figure 1.11, ERS 2011). Farm payments have been in place long enough in both the European Union and the United States that they are largely capitalized into the value of land (Duffy et al. 1994; Barnard et al. 1997; Roberts 2004; Kirwan 2009). In the United States, crop insurance premium subsidies are probably also capitalized into land values to some extent. For many producers, the ability to purchase land, pay cash rent, or receive favorable interest rates on loans can depend significantly on receiving farm commodity program payments and purchasing (subsidized) crop insurance.

wetland drainage, occasionally preventing farmers from draining wetlands or requiring their mitigation. In 2008, the US Environmental Protection Agency (EPA) regulated effluent discharge from Confined Animal Feeding Operations (CAFOs), although only those CAFOs that discharge or plan to discharge must seek a permit—other CAFOs can self-certify that they do not and will not discharge (US EPA, undated). At the state level, a patchwork of regulation applies mostly to large CAFOs. For example, a number of states in the Chesapeake Bay watershed (Delaware, Maryland, Virginia, Pennsylvania, and New York) require livestock farms to devise and apply nutrient management plans.

Arguably, regulatory policies affecting agricultural land use in the United States are more significant at the state and local levels. In particular, zoning regulations are largely set by local jurisdictions, such as counties. These may place restrictions on nonagricultural uses in certain areas. Many states have right-to-farm rules that can protect the right of farmers to use standard farm management practices, some of which nonagricultural neighbors on the rural-urban fringe could otherwise seek to restrict (Hellerstein et al. 2002). For the sake of brevity, however, this chapter focuses on US federal policies affecting agricultural land use.

Economic incentive programs are the backbone of US federal agri-environmental policy, accounting for more than $5.5 billion in federal spending during fiscal year 2010 (OMB, 2012). We place these programs in one of three broad categories: land retirement (LR), working land (WL) conservation, and agricultural land preservation.

2.1 Land Retirement

The Conservation Reserve Program (CRP) offers annual payments and cost sharing to establish long-term, resource-conserving cover on environmentally sensitive land. Contracts are for 10–15 years. Economic use of the land is limited during the contract period, but landowners retain the right to return land to crop production at the end of the contract.

The CRP includes several components. Through the *general signup*, producers can enroll whole fields or whole farms but must compete for enrollment because acreage offered often exceeds the number of acres that can be added to CRP. *Continuous signup* offers enrollment without competition for certain high-priority practices (e.g., field-edge filter strips or wetland restoration). Through the Conservation Reserve Enhancement Program (CREP; a part of continuous signup), the US Department of Agriculture (USDA) can enter into partnership with states to support practices designed to address a specific environmental problem, such as water quality in a specific river or lake.

The Wetlands Reserve Program (WRP) provides cost sharing and long-term or permanent easements for restoration of wetlands on agricultural land. Through WRP, the USDA can offer a wide range of easement and contract options, ranging from permanent easements to relatively short-term contracts (e.g., 10-year agreements). Through the Wetlands Reserve Enhancement Program (WREP), the USDA can partner with states and nongovernmental organizations (NGOs) to carry out high-priority wetland protection, restoration, and enhancement activities. During the easement period, landowners retain land ownership and rights to recreational uses, such as hunting and fishing.

LR dominated federal agricultural conservation spending between 1985 and 2002. At the end of 2011, roughly 10% of US cropland—32.2 million acres—was enrolled in CRP (29.7 million acres) and WRP (2.6 million acres). Total CRP acreage has declined from a peak of 36.4 million acres and is currently limited to a maximum of 32 million acres. Program acreage and expenditures have also been shifted gradually from retirement of whole fields or whole farms to partial field practices through continuous signup. At the end of 2011, continuous signup (including CREP) accounted for 56% of CRP contracts, 32% of annual payments, and 18% of CRP acreage.

WRP enrollment is currently capped at 3.041 million acres. Unlike CRP, the WRP acreage cap was increased in the 2008 Farm Act from 2.275 million acres. Program enrollment is dominated by permanent easements, which account for roughly 80% of WRP acreage.

2.2 Working Land Conservation

The Environmental Quality Incentives Program (EQIP) provides technical assistance, cost sharing, and incentive payments to assist livestock and crop producers with adoption of a wide range of more environmentally friendly production practices or best management practices (BMPs). The Wildlife Habitat Incentives Program (WHIP) provides cost sharing to landowners and producers to develop and improve wildlife habitat. The Conservation Stewardship Program (CSP) provides payments to producers for maintaining or adopting a wide range of structural and land management practices that address a variety of local and/or national resource concerns. Unlike other USDA conservation programs, CSP payments are based on environmental benefits, as estimated using a series of indices to measure the potential value of installing or adopting a specific practice in a specific location. Producers can also receive payments based on the ongoing application of previously adopted practices. These payments are also based on an estimate of environmental benefits but are lower than payments for newly adopted practices. Also, unlike other programs, payments can be based on going beyond basic treatment of environmental problems to a higher or "enhanced" level of environmental performance.

Before 2002, funding for WL conservation was modest compared to LR. For EQIP, the largest US WL program, the 2002 Farm Act authorized a five-fold increase in funding over previous levels, funding levels that have been maintained in the 2008 Farm Act at least through fiscal year 2011, when it was $1.238 billion. The 2008 Farm Act directed the USDA to enroll 12.77 million acres per year in the CSP at an average annual cost (to the government) of $18 per acre. Program spending increased from $9 million in fiscal year (FY) FY2009 to $390 million in FY2010 and $601 million in FY2011. This program replaces the Conservation Security Program (authorized in the 2002 Farm Act), which will end when existing contracts have expired.

2.3 Agricultural Land Preservation

The Farm and Ranch Land Protection Program (FRPP) funds the purchase of development rights (i.e., purchases of easements) on agricultural land in urban fringe areas, thus preserving it for agricultural production. Under the 2008 Farm Act, FRPP has been funded at $121 million in FY2009, $150 million in FY2010, and $175 million in FY2011. The 2002 Farm Act extended FRPP eligibility to land with "historically important land areas and structures," providing one instance where US policy clearly attempts to preserve "positive" environmental amenities (e.g., open space, scenic vistas, or small-scale farms). In general, these types of "environmental" goals are left to other US federal or state programs.[4] The European Union, conversely, supports such amenities of agriculture as part of EU-wide agri-environmental policy, although the European Commission has limited control in the design and operation of specific programs.

The Grassland Reserve Program (GRP) assists owners, through long-term rental agreements or easements (i.e., voluntary sale or donation of specific use rights to land), in restoring grassland and conserving virgin grassland while maintaining areas for livestock grazing and hay production. GRP supports enhancement of plant and animal biodiversity and protection of grasslands under threat of conversion to cropping, urban development, and other activities. Funding has been $48 million, $100 million, and $79 million for fiscal years 2009, 2010, and 2011, respectively.

2.4 Compliance Mechanisms

Compliance mechanisms require farmers to conserve soil on highly erodible land and conserve wetlands to be eligible for federal agricultural payments, including commodity support payments (see, e.g., Cooper 2010, for an overview of commodity support payments; see Claassen et al. 2004, for an overview of programs potentially subject to compliance sanctions). Producers can become ineligible for commodity payments if they:

- convert wetlands to make agricultural production possible (a provision widely known as "swampbuster"); or
- produce crops on highly erodible land (HEL) without applying an approved conservation system.

[4] See American Farmland Trust http://www.farmland.org/programs/protection/farmland-information-center.asp for more information on US state farmland protection programs.

The conservation measures required under this program come closest in the United States to representing a basic level of "good farming practice" or environmental compliance such as exists in the European Union.

Since producers must pay the costs of compliance, it is difficult to quantify expenditures in comparison with direct incentive programs such as EQIP. Costs include applying an approved conservation system or the opportunity cost of not using HEL or wetlands for crop production. Some practices, such as conservation tillage, have probably lowered production costs for some (but not all) producers who have adopted them as part of a conservation system. The ERS (2006, Section 5.3) presents more detail about the benefits and costs of conservation compliance.

3. EU Agri-Environmental Policy

EU agri-environmental policy uses a combination of voluntary, regulatory, and cross-compliance programs to achieve environmental goals, similar in general principles to US agri-environmental policy. These programs can be summarized into two main categories: basic legal standards and the Common Agricultural Policy (CAP).

"Basic legal standards" are regulatory rules that apply to all EU Member States and their farmers. Farmers must comply with these environmental regulations without receiving any compensation for doing so. The EU Nitrate Directive[5] is an example of a basic legal standard that applies specifically to agriculture. Farmers have to meet the requirements of the Framework Directive on the Sustainable Use of Pesticides and of the Water Framework Directive,[6] as well as of those to ensure food traceability (General Food Law, EC/178/2002) and a whole range of far-reaching animal welfare rules.

The CAP consists into two pillars: Pillar I encourages farmers and other land managers to protect the environment and fight climate change through direct payments that are decoupled from production but linked to environmental requirements via cross-compliance; Pillar II deals with Rural Development Programs, which explicitly include agri-environmental measures, such as payments to farmers in return for adoption of desired farm management practices. One of the objectives of the ongoing CAP revision is to offer the opportunity to reinforce measures for "green growth" and to make the CAP more effective in providing existing environmental benefits. The EU Commission is now proposing a further layer of green measures to add to existing measures, as we will discuss in Section 3.6 ("Support for Nonproductive Investments"). later.

Cross-compliance is a mechanism that links direct payments to compliance by farmers with basic standards concerning the environment, food safety, animal and plant

[5] Legal basis: Directive 1991/676/EEC.

[6] Legal basis: Directive 2000/60/EC.

health, and animal welfare, as well as with the requirement of maintaining land in good agricultural and environmental condition. Cross-compliance includes:

1. Five sets of environmental concerns—for a total of 18 legislative standards—in the field of the environment, food safety, animal and plant health, and animal welfare, which are covered by Statutory Management Requirements (SMR). These requirements have a long history and apply to all farmers (even those not receiving the Pillar I support subject to cross-compliance).
2. Good Agricultural and Environmental Conditions (GAEC) are the obligations for farmers receiving CAP payments to keeping land in good agricultural and environmental condition, as defined by EU legislation. GAECs are compulsory for Member States—in many cases, they are simply the translation of EU environmental legislation or other EU requirements into specific national obligations.[7] GAEC standards are designed to prevent soil erosion, maintain soil organic matter and soil structure, ensure a minimum level of maintenance, avoid the deterioration of habitats, protect and manage water, and require that the ratio of permanent pastures at a national level is maintained within certain limits.

All farmers receiving direct payments, agri-environmental payments forming part of the Rural Development Policy (RDP), and certain wine payments are subject to compulsory cross-compliance.[8] Cross-compliance represents the "baseline" or "reference level" for agri-environment measures.

Farmers are expected to observe GAEC without receiving direct compensation for doing so. However, unlike basic legal standards, the European Commission does not mandate good farming practices but allows each Member State to decide what a good farming practice is. Member States can make good farming practices mandatory or cross-compliant by tying the adoption of such practices to CAP payments in a process known as "modulation." "Modulation" refers to the process whereby a proportion of CAP direct aids is rechanneled into agri-environmental programs.

3.1 Agri-Environmental Measures

In 2005, the RDP, the so-called Pillar II of the CAP, was restructured into three thematic "axes" for the period 2007–2013.[9] Axis 1 aims to improve the competitiveness of the

[7] As a matter of fact, many GAECs are already contemplated in the directives mentioned. Directives lay down certain end results, but Member States are free to decide how to meet these goals. The inclusion of GAEC in a regulation, that is, in a binding legislative act that must be applied in its entirety across the EU, requires all farmers to meet the same obligations.

[8] Legal basis: Council Regulation 73/2009 and Commission Regulation 1122/2009.

[9] Council Regulation (EC) No. 1698/2005 of September 20, 2005, on support for rural development by the European Agricultural Fund for Rural Development (EAFRD) lays down the general rules

agricultural and forestry sector; Axis 2, the environment and the countryside; and Axis 3, the quality of life in rural areas and diversification of the rural economy. Given the topic of this chapter, we focus our discussion on Axis 2. The three priority areas of intervention in Axis 2 of the RDP are "biodiversity and the preservation and development of high nature value farming and forestry systems and traditional agricultural landscapes; water; and climate change" (European Commission 2006).

Axis 2 includes measures aimed at contributing to the implementation of Natura 2000's "Network[10]" of protected areas (definitions of EU-specific terms such as "Natura 2000" follow); the commitment made during a European Council meeting in Gothenburg in June 2001 to reverse the decline of the EU's biodiversity by the year 2010; the objectives laid down in the Water Framework Directive; the Kyoto Protocol targets for climate change mitigation; and measures targeting the sustainable use of forestry land.

In contrast to the United States, where agri-environmental policy mainly targets the reduction of negative externalities produced by agriculture, from its origins, EU agri-environmental policy has rewarded farmers both for reducing negative externalities and for using farming practices that can help provide public goods (Baylis et al. 2008). The rationale for supporting land management practices that provide public goods is that intensification and concentration of land used in the most competitive areas and the marginalization or abandonment of land use in less competitive areas result in continued declines in many species and habitats, increased water scarcity, and significant problems with soil erosion and loss of soil organic matter. The RDP also supports social public goods, such as food security, farm animal welfare and health, and, especially, rural vitality (Cooper et al. 2009).

Central to this discussion of EU rural development is the assumption that economically and socially vibrant rural areas can help to promote the continuation of agriculture and forestry which, in turn, are important in providing the environmental public goods on which many sectors—such as rural tourism and recreation—depend (Cooper et al. 2009; ENRD 2010; Hart et al. 2011). The concept of "high nature value farming" has recently come to play a central role in the discourse of researchers and policy makers regarding EU rural development. This concept was introduced in the early 1990s and stems from a growing recognition that the conservation of biodiversity and of heritage landscapes in the EU depends on the continuation of low-intensity farming systems (Baldock et al. 1993). However, these

governing RDP for the period 2007–2013, as well as the policy measures available to Member States and regions. The RDPs that the Member States and regions prepared for the period 2007–2013 are currently under implementation.

[10] The Natura 2000's EU-wide network of nature protection areas was established under the 1992 Habitats Directive. The aim of the network is to assure the long-term survival of Europe's most valuable and threatened species and habitats. It is comprised of Special Areas of Conservation (SAC) designated by Member States under the Habitats Directive and also incorporates Special Protection Areas (SPAs), which they designated under the 1979 Birds Directive.

traditional management systems are disappearing due to agricultural intensification and rural abandonment. Therefore, the strategic approach to maintaining biodiversity across the EU includes both the protection of particular habitats or species and the maintenance of low-intensity land uses that are more favorable to wildlife and to maintaining biological and landscape diversity.

Axis 2 measures are largely voluntary, contractual, and co-financed, and are delivered within a strategic framework that links policy action to European, national, regional, and local needs. Agri-environment measures are, at present, the only compulsory measure under Pillar II. Member States have a wide degree of discretion in implementing these measures, permitting them to be tailored to different agronomic and environmental circumstances. Payments per hectare or farmer can vary substantially from one Member State to another. In the Annex to the Rural Development Regulation, maximum ceilings are set for each measure. In some cases, these ceilings can result in payments below actual costs.

The incentive payment levels are based on cost incurred and income foregone by the farmer for participating in the agri-environmental measure. Their calculation normally takes into account only variable costs or income forgone resulting from the participation in agri-environmental programs. A general condition for payments under Axis 2 is that farmers respect the relevant EU and national mandatory requirements (i.e., cross-compliance).

The Axis 2 measures targeting the sustainable use of agricultural land include Agri-Environmental Payments (AEPs), Natural Handicap Payments (NHPs) to farmers in mountainous areas or with other natural impediments to adoption of modern agricultural practices (less favored areas [LFAs]), Natura 2000 payments, payments linked to the Water Framework Directive, and other new measures related to animal welfare. We now outline the EU agri-environmental policy measures in more detail.

3.2 Agri-Environmental Payments

AEP schemes are designed to encourage farmers to protect and enhance the environmental attributes of their land. These provide payments to farmers in return for services such as carrying out agri-environmental commitments that go beyond the application of standard good farming practices. Each scheme has at least one of two broad objectives: reducing environmental risks associated with modern farming and preserving natural and cultivated landscapes. Specifically, these schemes include one category of measures related to productive land management and one related to nonproductive land management. The first category includes measures aimed at (1) input reduction; (2) organic farming; (3) extensification of livestock; (4) conversion of arable land to grassland and rotation measures; (5) undersowing and cover crops, strips, and preventing erosion and fire; (6) actions in areas of special biodiversity/nature interest; (7) rearing of rare local breeds and the preservation of plant genetic resources; (8) maintenance of existing sustainable and extensive systems; (9) farmed landscape; and (10) water use reduction. The group of measures related to nonproductive land management includes land set-aside managed for environmental purposes, upkeep of abandoned farmland and woodland, maintenance of countryside and landscape features, and public access.

3.3 Natural Handicap Measures

Natural Handicap Measures aim to provide an aid to farmers operating in LFAs, that is, in mountainous areas and in other areas with specific natural handicaps. LFA is a longstanding measure of CAP. The logic of intervention in the LFA scheme has undergone a significant evolution since its inception in 1975. Originally, the scheme explicitly addressed rural depopulation as a socioeconomic objective. In 2003, the implementation of the LFA scheme was subject to criticisms in a report of the European Court of Auditors (Court of Auditors 2003), particularly in regard to the designation of intermediate LFAs and the lack of aid targeting. Starting in 2005, within the new strategic approach adopted for the RDP for 2007–2013, LFA payments, renamed Natural Handicap Payments, became part of Axis 2 of RDP. The NHP scheme has a strong focus on land management and aims to maintain the countryside and promote sustainable agriculture, which delivers public goods such as valuable landscapes, biodiversity, soil conservation, and fire prevention in areas where farming is difficult.

3.4 Natura 2000 Payments

Natura 2000 payments aim to compensate farmers for the loss of income or the cost of extra management obligations necessary to deliver the objectives of the Natura 2000 Network. Similar considerations apply for the payments linked to Directive 2000/60/EC.

3.5 Animal Welfare Payments

Animal welfare payments are granted to farmers who commit to applying animal welfare standards that go beyond basic legal requirements. These commitments are described in Article 27 (7) of Commission Regulation (EC) No. 1974/2006. Any animal welfare commitment must provide upgraded standards in at least one of the following areas: water and feed closer to the animals' natural needs; housing conditions, such as space allowances, bedding, natural light; outdoor access; absence of systematic mutilations, isolation, or permanent tethering; and prevention of pathologies mainly determined by farming practices or/and keeping conditions.

3.6 Support for Nonproductive Investments

Support for nonproductive investments provides financial aid to farmers and other land managers who make on-farm agri-environmental, nonproductive investments; that is, investments that enhance the public amenity value of high nature value areas (e.g., NATURA 2000 areas). Examples of nonproductive investments include planting hedgerows; planting trees for wind-breaks/shelters; establishing grass margins; establishing grasslands for land use changes and nature conservation; and establishing green cover.

Regarding the rural development budget, 44% of the European Agricultural Fund for Rural Development (EAFRD) funding for the 2007–2013 period (about €43 billion) has been allocated by Member States to Axis 2 measures ("improving the environment and the countryside") (EC 2011). The CAP Health Check in 2008 assigned additional funding to five new "challenges," including biodiversity. The planned spending for the agri-environment payments over the 2007–2013 programming period amounts to €22.5 billion, representing half of the budget devoted to the environmental axis of rural development policy. LFA payments—in and outside mountainous areas—total €13.4 billion. These three measures account for 84% of all funds under Axis 2, and it is estimated that they will result in nearly 7 million agri-environment agreements over the 2007–2013 period, bringing approximately 42 million hectares (24% of total utilized agricultural area) under some form of environmental management. In addition, €472 million will be spent on Natura 2000 measures on farmland and €111 million on Natura 2000 measures on forestry land.

Regarding Axis 2 measures, AEPs represent the EAFRD policy instruments with the highest financial allocation in most Member States. At the EU-27 level, these represent 52.5% of the EAFRD contribution allocated to this axis, and its share is higher than 70% in Belgium (at 82.6%), the United Kingdom (at 74.4%), and the Netherlands (at 72.1%). In the recently added Member States, the share within Axis 2 is higher than 55% in Bulgaria (56%), Estonia (63.1%), and Hungary (67%).

In addition to cross-compliance and the agri-environmental measures under the RDP, Article 68 of Regulation 73/2009 allows Member States to retain up to 10% of their previously coupled payment ceilings under Pillar I for specific supports to farming and quality production. These retained payments can be used to:

- protect the environment, improve the quality and marketing of products, or for animal welfare support;
- help farmers producing milk, beef, sheep, goats, and rice in economically vulnerable or environmentally sensitive areas, as well as for economically vulnerable types of farming;
- top-up existing entitlements in areas where land abandonment is a threat;
- support risk assurance in the form of contributions to crop insurance premiums; and
- contribute to mutual funds to combat animal and plant diseases.

The CAP is due to be reformed by 2013. After a public debate on October 12, 2011, the Commission presented a set of legal proposals in the *CAP Towards 2020*. Following a debate in the European Parliament and the Council, approval of the different regulations and implementing acts is expected by the end of 2013, with the goal of having the CAP reform in place by January 2014.

One of the objectives of the new CAP is to improve efficiencies of support granted to farmers for practices aimed at environmental and climate change considerations. As for Pillar I, 30% of direct support is proposed to be made conditional on "greening" (i.e., environmentally supportive practices). According to the proposal, 30% of the total amount of resources devoted to direct payments in each Member State is constrained by the fulfilment of three mandatory measures: to maintain on-farm permanent grassland, to diversify crops in order to improve biodiversity, and to devote 7% of the Utilized Agricultural Area (UAA) to "Ecological Focus Areas" (EFA) (including terraces, buffer strips, hedges, and set-aside areas). The only actors who would not be submitted to these constraints are organic producers and farmers who accept the simplified scheme ("small farmers" scheme).[11]

The impact of greening measures on the income of European farms is estimated to be, on average, a €43 increase per hectare of potentially eligible area, although it may vary widely according to region and farming systems (European Commission 2011). Concerns about the negative impacts of greening on the competitiveness of the EU agricultural sector have been expressed by the major farmer associations (Copa-Cogeca 2012), as well as by the majority of the national ministries of agriculture of the Member States. In contrast, environmental NGOs such as BirdLife and the World Wildlife Fund (WWF) believe that the greening measures do not go far enough, and they propose replacing the crop diversification measure with a real crop rotation requirement, increasing the EFA to 10% of the agricultural area at farm level, and including a more stringent definition of permanent grassland (BirdLife International 2012). Academics and researchers have also contributed to this debate, and there is wide agreement that the strategy of green payments proposed by the European Commission could be improved (Groupe de Bruges 2012; Mahé 2012; Westhoek et al. 2012).

RDPs remain the key element of the new CAP for delivering public goods. In line with Europe 2020 and the overall CAP objectives, the sustainable management of natural resources and climate action have been restated as one of the three long-term strategic objectives of RDP, along with improved competitiveness of agriculture and balanced territorial development (Loriz-Hoffmann 2012) of rural areas.

Instead of three axes linked to economic, environmental, and social issues with minimum spending requirements for each axis, the new programming period will have six priorities: fostering knowledge transfer and innovation; enhancing competitiveness; promoting food chain organization and risk management; restoring, preserving, and enhancing ecosystems; promoting resource efficiency and a transition to a low-carbon

[11] http://ec.europa.eu/agriculture/analysis/perspec/cap-2020/impact-assessment/annex2en.pdf

economy; and promoting social inclusion, poverty reduction, and economic development in rural areas.

Under the proposals, Member States are still required to devote at least 25% of their rural development budget to land management and climate change mitigation.[12] However, the proposed rural development budget will suffer a decline in real terms for the period 2014–2020. This could be countered in those countries that take advantage of the option to move 10% of Pillar I funds to Pillar II. Conversely, some Member States will be allowed to transfer funding from Pillar II to Pillar I. Agri-environmental and climate payment schemes will have greater flexibility in contract design and will be linked to adequate training/information. In addition, new measures have been proposed to promote organic farming.

4. Impacts of US Agri-Environmental Programs on Land Use: A Review of the Empirical Literature

The focus of this review is on an empirical analysis of actual agri-environmental policies—and in particular, US federal policies—rather than on generic or stylized policies. However, some exceptions are made in cases in which the results may be particularly illuminating for US federal policy. Much more work has been done on CRP than on the federal WL conservation programs that we addressed earlier in this chapter. In this review, we do not attempt to include every academic paper ever written on US federal agri-environmental programs but focus rather on including examples covering the various general themes that turned up during our literature review.

Ideally, the government would target land for enrollment into agri-environmental programs in a manner that maximizes the social benefits of multiple environmental outcomes, subject to budget constraint. However, as noted by Babcock et al. (1996), the solution to this complex problem requires quantification of the physical tradeoffs between the various environmental benefits and a social value function that can capture the marginal rate of substitution of the various benefits, something that is generally not feasible in practice. Reichelderfer and Boggess (1988), Babcock et al. (1996), Wu and Boggess (1999), Feather, Hellerstein, and Hansen (1999), Wu, Zilberman, and Babcock (2001), and Feng et al. (2006) all provide examples of approaches to targeting, and although these cannot fully quantify the benefits, they at least permit a capturing of some of the physical and economic tradeoffs.

[12] http://europa.eu/rapid/pressReleasesAction.do?reference=MEMO/11/685&format=HTML&aged=0&language=EN&guiLanguage=en

Benefit-cost targeting has been a key component of US agri-environmental incentive programs since 1991, when the Environmental Benefits Index (EBI) was added to the CRP program. The index focuses mostly on maintaining soil productivity, water quality, and wildlife habitat. Feather, Hellerstein, and Hansen (1999) estimated that use of the EBI increased CRP benefits by 80% over a nontargeted CRP enrollment. The research also indicated that benefits could be increased by emphasizing water quality and wildlife habitat over the preservation of soil productivity. Similar indices are included in the EQIP, CSP, and other programs.

Competitive bidding has also been a part of CRP since the early 1990s. Producers who offer to take less than the (field-specific) bid limit or who waive cost-sharing of cover establishment can improve their EBI score (which includes a cost factor) and their chances of being selected for enrollment. Kirwan et al. (2005) argue that as farmers and landowners have become increasingly familiar with the EBI—which is largely unchanged since 1997—they have also been less likely to offer bids below their bid limit. Applicants offering land with high environmental benefits (EBI environmental scores are known before bids are finalized) and those offering low-value land have been particularly reluctant to offer bid discounts.

In the context of LR programs, *slippage* is the extent to which enrollment of land induces production change on land not enrolled. For example, LR may reduce crop production, thus increasing crop prices and encouraging farmers to convert other land (say pasture or range) to crop production. To the extent that this slippage occurs, the total environmental benefits associated with LR decline. Wu (2000), Roberts and Bucholtz (2005), and Wu (2005) econometrically examine CRP using National Resources Inventories (NRI) and Census of Agriculture data to test for the presence of slippage. Although there is some disagreement among the results of these studies, they appear to generally support the notion that the CRP does cause some slippage to occur.

WL conservation programs can also cause a slippage effect. Lichtenberg and Smith-Ramírez (2011) econometrically model the effect of a state-level BMP cost-sharing program that Maryland designed to address water quality problems in the Chesapeake Bay region. The allocation of land between pasture/wildlife habitat, contour farming/strip cropping, and cover crops was examined using farm-level data for both recipients and nonrecipients and found that farmers who received cost sharing allocated larger shares of their cropland to contour farming/strip cropping and to cover crops and less to the more environmentally benign pasture/wildlife habitat. Hence, the environmental quality improvements from this WL conservation program are likely offset to some degree. In another study of slippage potentially being associated with WL programs, Wallander and Hand (2011) examine how participation in EQIP by irrigators affects water application rates and decisions to expand or reduce a farm's irrigated acreage. Using farm-level panel data from a national survey of irrigators taken in 1998, 2003, and 2008, they estimate changes in water application rates and irrigated acreage that result when a farm receives EQIP payments. Their results suggest that, for the average farm participating in EQIP between 2004 and 2008, EQIP payments may have induced reduced water application rates but also may have increased total water use and led to an expansion in irrigated acreage. Khanna, Isik, and Zilberman (2002) and Lichtenberg (2004) also found that conservation subsidies can, in some instances, worsen environmental quality by giving farmers an incentive to expand production onto more erodible or otherwise environmentally fragile or more highly polluting land.

A political economy concern with LR is that it could have a negative impact on rural economies due to lowering local expenditures on farming-related businesses. Sullivan et al. (2004) estimated the impact that high levels of enrollment in the CRP have had on economic trends in rural counties since the program's inception in 1985 and through 2004. The results of the report's growth model and quasi-experimental control group analysis indicated no discernible impact by the CRP on aggregate county population trends. The report found that aggregate employment growth may have slowed in some high-CRP counties, but only temporarily. High levels of CRP enrollment appear to have affected farm-related businesses over the long run, but growth in the number of other nonfarm businesses moderated CRP's impact on total employment. If CRP contracts had ended in 2001, their simulation models suggest that roughly 51% of CRP land would have returned to crop production and that spending on outdoor recreation would decrease by as much as $300 million per year in rural areas. However, the resulting impacts on employment and income varied widely among regions having similar CRP enrollments, depending on local economic conditions. Bangsund et al. (2004) found that for CRP land in North Dakota, increased hunting revenues partially offset agricultural revenue, but the study did not estimate the regional economic impacts of either.

Some analysis has addressed the relationship between WL and LR programs. LR and WL programs can potentially compete with each other, given that they are mutually exclusive in the use of land, thus suggesting that these programs should be operated in a coordinated fashion. Feng et al. (2005) find that interactions between CRP and WL programs may be significant. For instance, based on results of an econometric analysis of 1997 NRI data, their simulation analysis finds that acres enrolled in CRP at a given rental rate would be about half in the presence of subsidies for conservation tillage. Using the Environmental Policy Integrated Climate (EPIC) simulation model in conjunction with their econometric model, they find that the presence of both large WL and LR programs can result in more environmental benefits (and income transfers) than an LR-only program can achieve.

Furthermore, WL and LR programs can target the same environmental benefits—a concept known as "stacking."[13] An interesting question, albeit hard to analyze, is to determine the cost differences of each—using either one exclusively or in combination—in achieving a given target. Feng et al. (2006) develop a formal theoretical framework combining an economic model and the EPIC model to simulate the marginal costs

[13] See Gillenwater (2012) and Cooley and Olander (2012) for a detailed discussion of "stacking" in the context of ecosystem services. Stacking occurs when multiple programs provide payments for the same ecosystem. Stacking can provide multiple revenue streams for landowners and encourage them to manage their lands for multiple ecosystem services (Cooley and Olander 2012). However, if the programs are not well coordinated, it may also lead to a net loss of services (ibid.) or cost inefficiencies.

of targeting an environmental objective (carbon sequestration) by LR alone, LR and WL in combination, and WL alone. Using this model with NRI data for Iowa, they find that, for achieving small carbon sequestration benefits, WL alone and an optimal budget split between WL and LR have the lowest marginal costs, but LR alone has the lowest marginal costs for achieving higher levels of sequestration. The results were similar when they modeled multiple environmental targets.

One might expect that the environmental benefits of LR increase the longer the land stays in retirement, assuming the alternative is likely to be the land returning back to crop production if the CRP contract expires and is not renewed. Roberts and Lubowski (2007) use parcel-level data from the USDA's NRI to examine actual land use choices following expiration of CRP contracts between 1995 and 1997 in the contiguous 48 states. These data reflect choices made by landowners who opted out of the CRP early, chose not to extend or renew their contracts, or submitted new contract bids that scored too low to be re-enrolled in the program. Based on the econometric analysis of actual land use decisions, they predicted that about 58% of all CRP acres would have converted to crop production in 1997 had they all, in fact, exited. Given that alternatives to crop production for lands with expiring contracts (e.g., pasture, range, or forest) are likely less environmentally damaging than crop production, CRP exits would likely increase environmental damages. Their results also suggested that the opportunity cost of enrolling land in CRP is higher for newly enrolling land as compared to re-enrolling land. If so, this result suggests that targeted signing bonuses for first-time enrollees would increase the longer term impacts of CRP and perhaps other incentive-based land use programs.

Agricultural commodity support and agri-environmental programs can be expected to have interaction effects, with the former potentially having negative environmental impacts that may offset the environmental benefits associated with the agri-environmental programs. Alternatively, agri-environmental programs can be used to offset the potentially negative environmental impacts of commodity support programs. Using NRI data and crop production patterns and crop yields taken from unpublished USDA/National Agricultural Statistics Service (NASS) files, as well as other data gathered from 1982 to 1992, Goodwin and Smith (2003) conduct an econometric analysis of the relative impacts of CRP and agricultural commodity support on erosion level. They find that CRP enrollment decreases erosion (as one would expect), Federal Crop Insurance causes a relatively small increase in erosion, but other government commodity support programs cause a relatively large increase in soil erosion. Conceivably, some of the negative impacts of government commodity support could be offset with increased support to WL conservation programs but, of course, at additional cost.

In considering potential interaction effects between agri-environmental programs and commodity support, these may be strongest between LR and commodity support given, in that they are mutually exclusive uses of land. Lubowski et al. (2008) use NRI data in an econometric analysis of land use and land characteristics on nonfederal lands conducted at 5-year intervals from 1982 to 1997 over the entire United States, excluding Alaska. In assessing the factors that affect land use decisions, they found strong evidence that cropland declines over that period were due to falling crop net returns and the existence of CRP. However, they also document the opposing influences of federal agricultural commodity payments (see, e.g., Cooper 2010 and ERS 2009*b* for a discussion of commodity payments). In particular, by raising farm income and/or lowering revenue risk through commodity support payments, the government increased acreage in crops and directly competed with itself in providing incentives for landowners to retire environmentally sensitive cropland under the CRP.

Not only may federal commodity support and CRP compete for land, CRP may compete with—or "crowd-out"—nonfederal conservation programs for crop land, such as land trusts. For example, Parker and Thurman (2011) examine the effects of US federal land programs (CRP and WRP) on private conservation using county-level panel regressions between 1990 and 2000. They use econometric analysis based on a Bayesian approach modeling private conservation acres held from several conservation NGOs as a function of CRP and WRP enrollment, acres in federal lands, demographic data, and other variables. They find some evidence of a small but measurable crowding-out effect from CRP land holding on the land trusts examined.

Of course, no discussion of agriculture is complete without a mention of biofuels. In particular, growing demand for biofuels production—mostly ethanol from corn in the United States—raises crop prices by increasing the demand for corn. Given the highly inelastic supply of land for crops, increasing corn acreage will increase the prices of other crops that are displaced by the increase in corn acreage. Increasing crop prices due to biofuels demand likely increases the total amount of land in crop production, potentially increasing negative environmental impacts as land is taken out of pasture and range and put into crops (e.g., Searchinger et al. 2008)—a change that has implications for WL conservation programs. The increasing crop prices have the potential for lowering re-enrollment rates in the CRP as farmers seek to expand planted acres, with consequent negative environmental impacts. For example, for central US grassland enrolled in the CRP for 15 years, Fargione et al. (2008) found that converting it to corn ethanol production creates a biofuels carbon debt that would take approximately 50 years to repay if subsequently replanted to perennial systems. Secchi et al. (2009) construct CRP land supply curves for various corn prices and then, using the EPIC model, estimate the environmental impacts of cropping land exiting CRP land. EPIC provides edge-of-field estimates of soil erosion, nutrient loss, and carbon sequestration. They find that incremental environmental impacts increase dramatically as higher corn prices bring into production more and more environmentally fragile land. Hence, maintaining current levels of environmental quality (as defined by EPIC) will require substantially higher spending levels on LR and WL programs.

Conversely, CRP land could, in principle, be a supplier of feedstocks for cellulosic-based production of biofuels, at least providing that harvesting of these feedstocks is consistent with conservation efforts. The renewable fuels standard (RFS) in the Energy Independence and Security Act of 2007 mandates an increasing amount of cellulosic biofuels production yearly through 2022, even though, to date, the EPA has granted waivers to this mandate. Additionally, cellulosic biofuels can be used to substitute for corn-based ethanol under the RFS, although it is not currently economically feasible to do so. If cellulosic-based production were to become feasible to the extent that it could be used to actually meet the cellulosic biofuels mandate and even substitute for corn ethanol, and assuming that much of the feedstock harvesting could be done on CRP land, then the pressure on landowners to not re-enroll CRP land could decrease. Mapemba et al. (2007) use a multiregion, multiperiod, mixed integer mathematical programming model to determine cost to deliver a flow of feedstock to a biorefinery. They found that restrictions on harvest days based on environmental impact concerns—for example, impacts on bird habitat—can significantly increase feedstock delivery costs. Careful management of the harvesting season will be necessary to balance environmental costs versus feedstock production costs.

The papers discussed here tend to be based on analysis of actual (revealed preference) data. Federal WL programs tend to offer incentive payments that do not vary intertemporally or cross-sectionally for the adoption of BMPs. As such, revealed preference data provide little guidance on how enrollment rates would change with different payment rates. Such knowledge would help in adjusting payment rates to achieve desired adoption levels for BMPs. Even if payments have variation, as in the case of the CRP, the stated preference approach using hypothetical incentive offers could be useful if there is concern that the actual offers are systematically higher than farmers' minimum willingness to accept (WTA).

One approach to assessing how farmers would respond to higher or lower payments than actually offered is to use a stated preference approach based on survey questionnaires. Examples of such approaches as applied to US federal WL programs include Cooper (2003) and Cooper and Keim (1996), although they have been applied to CRP as well (e.g., Cooper and Osborn 1998). As expected, the farmer's WTA to enroll in the WL programs, and to enroll more acres, increases with increasing incentive payments. Cooper (1997) provides an example of how to add revealed preference data—from those who have adopted the practices without program enrollment—in conjunction with the stated preference data.[14]

There is relatively little empirical research on transaction costs associated with agri-environmental programs. The research that does exist, however, indicates that transaction costs may by quite large. Because US programs require producers to propose the application of specific practices in specific fields to address specific resource concerns, a great deal of conservation planning must be done to complete an agri-environmental program application. McCann and Easter (2000) used data from the mid-1990s to estimate that NRCS transaction costs (for conservation planning,

[14] Although, in general, survey questions eliciting WTA may not be as incentive compatible as willingness to pay (WTP) questions, the latter are generally not an appropriate format for eliciting enrollment behavior from farmers because the expectation is that agri-environmental programs will pay them for conservation activities and that farmer will not have to pays fines for not adopting conservation practices. However, in the stated preference work cited here, the survey instruments made clear that the analysis was being conducted on behalf of the government. Strategic response bias in the upward direction—i.e., saying "no" to enrollment rates that exceed true minimum WTA—could be a welfare-lowering strategy because biasing WTA estimates in the upward direction could lower the government's interest in providing the program.

construction oversight, related overhead) were, on average, 38% of total conservation costs (including transaction costs, financial assistance, and private costs for practice installation or adoption). The estimate excludes producer costs related to developing the conservation program application and a broader set of costs (e.g., research, policy development) that could be considered a part of overall transaction costs (McCann et al. 2005). Farmer transaction costs associated with US agri-environmental program application have not been estimated (but see McCann 2009).

Finally, a recent study addresses the issue of *additionality* in US conservation payment incentive programs (Mezzatesta et al. 2011). Additionality is the degree to which conservation payments leverage the adoption of practices that would not have been adopted in the absence of these payments. Using propensity score matching with data from a survey of Ohio farmers, they estimate that additionality is high for structural and vegetative practices (e.g., filter strips and cover crops) but not for conservation tillage. Roughly 92% of filter strips, 87% of cover crop acres, but only 18% of conservation tillage acreage were found to be additional.

5. Impact of EU Agri-Environmental Programs: A Review of the Empirical Literature

There is an increasing debate on whether EU agri-environmental programs actually deliver the expected outcomes (e.g., Kleijn and Sutherland 2003; EC-DGAGRI 2005; Kleijn 2006; Boatman et al. 2008; Hodge and Reader 2010; ECA 2011). However, the impact assessment of EU agri-environmental programs is mainly based on "administrative" evaluations produced by public officials rather than on scientific research (Burrel 2011). The increasing budget stringency and the growing competition in the use of diminishing public funds have led the European Commission to adopt the Common Monitoring and Evaluation Framework (CMEF) (EC 2006). CMEF is a guide for the administrative evaluation of rural development policies in the current programming period 2007–2013. The "administrative" evaluation proposed by the CMEF relies on indicator-based evidence and analyses three types of outcomes: (1) "outputs" of program activities, such as number of participants in a scheme or hectares of land converted; (2) "results," that is, direct consequences for program participants, such as changes in management practices resulting from scheme participation (e.g., change to organic farming, training participation); and (3) "impacts," that is, longer lasting effects of the intervention with direct or indirect relevance to the program's overall objectives and their attainment (e.g., improved water quality). This framework has gained importance over time, and it is now an integral part of the policy process. The empirical evidence produced by the application of the CMEF is used for the administrative evaluation of RDPs to feed the policy monitoring cycle and to correct possible inefficiencies.

The scarce scientific evidence in the impact assessment of EU agri-environmental programs is supported by Primdahl et al. (2010), who examine a sample of 60 agri-environmental schemes implemented in EU Member States (Denmark, Finland, Germany, Greece, Hungary, Ireland, and the United Kingdom) within the 2000–2006 RDP period. These schemes mainly deal with natural resources (primarily water resources, 31%), whereas only a limited proportion of schemes deals with biodiversity (7%) and landscape (8%). This study shows that only a minority of schemes (15%) are based on scientific research that uses quantitative causal models of relationship between agricultural practices and environmental outcomes. In the majority of cases, impacts had been assessed on the basis of so-called commonsense impact models, reflecting policy design that was based more on general beliefs about causal relationships than on scientific evidence. Boatman et al. (2008) present a meta-analysis of the environmental benefits provided by UK agri-environmental schemes and find that, in general, they were successful in attaining the desired environmental benefits. In particular, additionality is shown to be present for landscape, biodiversity (particularly for plants and birds, less for mammals and invertebrates), and habitat objectives. However, they identify some cases in which progressive deterioration was evident, as in the cases of grassland and heather moorland.

The lack of scientific studies on the impact assessment of EU agri-environmental programs is partly explained by the fact that the objectives of EU agri-environment schemes are often unclear, imprecise, or too many and thus difficult to identify (Hodge 2001; Primdahl et al. 2003; Bartolini et al. 2005; Finn et al. 2007; ECA 2011). Even when the quantification of the outcomes is possible, baseline environmental data for before agri-environment payments were implemented are often missing. Primdahl et al. (2010) find that, in absence of any comprehensive environmental baseline study prior to the implementation of the scheme, participation has been used as an indicator of the environmental effectiveness of agri-environmental schemes. In addition, in most cases, the time frame for the achievement of the policy objectives is missing or is too short to evaluate effects within time horizons of 5–10 years on issues such as biodiversity and groundwater (Boatman et al. 2008; Primdahl et al. 2010).

Several academic studies analyze the drivers of agri-environmental measures' adoption (Crabtree et al. 1998; Delvaux et al. 1999; Wynn et al. 2001; Dupraz et al. 2002; Vanslembrouck et al. 2002; Wossink and van Wenum 2003; Defrancesco et al. 2008; Bertoni et al. 2008; Borsotto et al. 2008; Defrancesco et al. 2008; Barreiro-Hurlé et al. 2010; Giovanopoulou et al. 2011). The level of farmer participation is usually interpreted as a measure of the success of agri-environmental measures. Among the factors that negatively affect measure uptake, private transaction costs that reduce the net payment received by farmers have been identified as one of the most important (Falconer 2000). Empirical research has shown significant variations in private transaction costs (Hackl et al. 2007; Ducos et al. 2009), both across different agri-environmental schemes (Rørstad et al. 2007) and within single schemes (Falconer and Saunders 2002; Rørstad et al. 2007; Mettepenningen et al. 2009). In addition, a meta-analysis of environmental impacts of EU agri-environmental schemes finds a positive effect on the participants' behavior with respect to three indicators: nitrogen (N) fertilizer, livestock density, and area of grassland (Oltmer et al. 2000).

Although the academic literature dealing with impact assessment of actual policies is still scarce, many optimization and simulation economic models have been proposed to show, for example, how crop farms may respond to changes in incentives for the agri-environmental measure (Hansen and de Frahan 2011) or changes in other aspects of the designs of agri-environmental contracts (Bamière et al. 2011). Hynes et al. (2008) use simulated farm population microdata merged with habitat land cover data within a geographic information system (GIS) framework to examine what type of habitats are actually being protected under the Irish Rural Environmental Protection Scheme in 2005. They find that habitats such as forests or shallow waters are more likely to be protected than, for example, dry grassland or cut fen, although dry grassland is a dominant land cover type in Ireland. They also show that such a program could lead to poor targeting of benefits; that is, the program may be targeting farmers with marginal quality land for which there is no need of environmental improvement.

Only recently has the scientific community started to investigate, using quantitative methods such as quasi-experimental approaches (Pufahl and Weiss 2009; Chabé-Ferret and Subervie 2011), the additionality of program impacts relative to the counterfactual on what would have happened in the absence of the policy. Pufahl and Weiss (2009) assess the impact of agri-environment programs on input use and farm output in Germany, and they find a significant positive effect on the area farmed or grazed, particularly with respect to the latter. The need to reduce the density of cattle livestock to become eligible for agri-environmental payments and the fact that program payments are given on a per-area base can explain the increase in farm size.

Compared with the reference group, participants show a reduction in expenditures for farm chemicals (fertilizers, pesticides) per hectare. They do not find any significant effects on farm productivity (sales per hectare), capital endowment, off-farm labor, or cattle livestock units per farm. The insignificant effect on productivity might be explained by the extensification process undertaken. Chabé-Ferret and Subervie (2011) provide a disaggregated estimation of the effects of five agri-environmental programs on environmentally relevant practices for a nationally representative sample of French farmers. They find that the impact of payment schemes for organic farming is significantly large, whereas the impact of payment schemes for crop diversity is mixed. These results can be explained by the fact that schemes for crop diversification enable the entry of farmers who, in the absence of the agri-environmental scheme, would have highly diverse rotations. Future studies should include a cost-benefit analysis of agri-environmental programs by translating the causal effects of the agri-environmental programs in monetary terms.

Table 23.1 provides a summary comparison of US and EU agricultural policy, focusing on the US federal level and EU level, respectively. The first column lists the policy categories, as defined broadly, and the adjacent columns categorize the regulations, cross-compliance, and agri-environmental payment approaches for the European Union and the United States that are associated with each policy objective. The table

Table 23.1 Comparison of EU and US federal agri-environmental policies and programs[a]

	EU policies and programs			US policies and programs		
Policy objective	Regulation (basic legal standards)	Cross-compliance	Agri-environmental payments	Regulation	Cross-compliance	Agri-environmental payments
Preserve and restore natural areas including wildlife habitat	Natura 2000	Statutory Management Requirements; Good Agricultural and Environmental Conditions; Members set precise requirements which serve as a "reference" level or minimum standard for receipt of direct payments under Pillar I of the CAP.	Payments linked to Directive 2000/60/EC Natura 2000 Payments Support for Nonproductive Investments; AEP supporting biodiversity/nature	Clean Water Act (Wetland drainage)	Swampbuster	Conservation Reserve Program Conservation Reserve Enhancement Program (CREP) Wetland Reserve Program Wildlife Habitat Incentives Program
			AEP supporting biodiversity/nature and the conversion of arable land to grassland			Grassland Reserve Program

Reduce environmental risk/damage from agricultural production	EU Nitrate Directive Framework Directive on the Sustainable Use of Pesticides	AEP linked to Directive 2000/60/EC Support for Nonproductive Investments	Federal Inceticide, Fungicide, and Rodenticide Act (pesticide regulation)	Sodbuster	Conservation Reserve Program Environmental Quality Incentives Program
	Water Framework Directive	Natura 2000 Payments; AEP supporting extensification of livestock	Confined Animal Feeding Operations (CAFOs) regulations		Conservation Stewardship Program
Promote animal welfare	Animal Welfare Basic Legal requirements	Animal Welfare Payments	**[b]	**	**
Preserve agricultural landscape and prevent land abandonment	**	Natural Handicap Payments; AEP supporting farmed landscapes and the maintenance of the countryside and landscape features	**	**	Farm and Ranchland Protection Program
Food traceability	General Food Law	**	**	**	**

** =No policy or program

Note: AEP is Agri-environmental Payments

[a] This table does not address local policies that may exist outside the rubric of EU-level and U.S. Federal policy.

[b] The U.S. does have Federal Law protecting animal welfare (e.g., Animal Welfare Act, Horse Protection Act, Twenty-Eight Hour Law, and Humane Methods of Slaughter), but there have few explicit links land use and agri-environmental issues.

shows that the European Union and the United States both have policies in each of the three policy categories to achieve the same general objective. The two policy objectives for which the United States potentially does not have land use polices at the federal level are related to animal welfare and protection of farming in mountainous areas. Although there is US federal law protecting animal welfare (e.g., Animal Welfare Act, Horse Protection Act, Twenty-Eight Hour Law, and Humane Methods of Slaughter), these have few explicit links to land use and agri-environmental issues. In another difference, the US FRPP funds the purchase of development rights on agricultural land in urban fringe areas, thus preserving it for agricultural production, whereas the European Union does not have EU-level mechanisms for explicitly protecting agricultural land in urban fringe areas. However, this difference may be semantic and depends on the definition of "urban fringe"; certainly, the EU's NHPs have addressed agricultural landscape preservation on lands relatively close to urban areas. In addition, land use regulations operating outside the rubric of US federal level and EU-level agricultural policy can preserve agricultural landscapes. With regards to specific policy tools, the European Union does not appear to make use of easements as a mechanism, unlike in the United States (e.g., via the WRP).

6. Data Availability in the United States and European Union

Major USDA datasets that are often used to assess land use and other implications of federal agri-environmental programs include the NASS Agricultural Census and a variety of NASS surveys (e.g., agricultural chemical use, agricultural prices, crop yield, crop acreage) whose data are disseminated through the Quick Stats data tool, the Agricultural Resource Management Survey (ARMS), and the Conservation Effects Assessment Project (NRI-CEAP) Cropland Survey. Agricultural Census and Quick Stats provide aggregate data (county and above) on farm activities such as acreage and production, with the former being more detailed but updated at longer intervals than the latter. ARMS is the USDA's primary source of information on the financial condition, production practices, and resource use of America's farm businesses and the economic well-being of America's farm households. CEAP is a multiagency effort to quantify the environmental effects of conservation practices and programs and develop the science base for managing the agricultural landscape for environmental quality.

Increasingly, administrative and geospatial data also play a role in assessing the land use impacts of policy changes. Contract data for individual programs (e.g., CRP) may offer information on variations in the opportunity cost of practice adoption or insight on bidding behavior (Kirwan, Lubowski, and Roberts, 2005). Geospatial data on land use and soil properties have been critical in studies of land use change and the effect of LR programs (Lubowski, Plantinga, and Stavins 2008). The NRI includes information on land use and land quality for more than 800,000 points of nonfederal, rural land in the contiguous US. The USDA Cropland Data Layer provides land use interpretation of satellite imagery at 30-meter resolution.

One emerging issue is data integration—the process of combining data from different sources to increase opportunities for policy research. Combining farm survey and conservation program contact data, for example, could provide insight into the role of agri-environmental program incentives in land use and conservation practice adoption decisions. Although the promise of data integration is substantial, there are a number of barriers to its realization. Bohman and Claassen (2011) identify four potential barriers: (1) a lack of identifiers suitable for linking, particularly the lack of accurate geo-referencing on field-level data; (2) concerns about increasing the risk of disclosure for confidential survey data; (3) "informed consent" requirements that could mean agencies would need to revise notices about uses of collected data so program applicants and survey respondents are informed about possible plans to link administrative and survey data; and (4) the fact that survey and administrative data are often collected at different spatial scales.

Major EU datasets often used to assess land use and other implications of their agri-environmental programs include the European Network for Rural Development (ENRD), the Coordination of Information on the Environment (CORINE), the Farm Structure Survey (FSS), the Survey on Agricultural Production Methods (SAPM), and the Farm Accountancy Data Network (FADN).

The ENRD, set up by the European Commission in 2008 to help Member States implement their RDPs in an efficient manner, produces annual information on the RDPs' progress at the EU scale based on RDP monitoring data made available by the Commission. The snapshots show the current state of play of the EU rural development policies, highlight connections between resources and outcomes, and provide users with informed insights. Information is provided for all EU-27 Member States, covering 88 national and regional programs.

The CORINE is a European program initiated in 1985 by the European Commission. It is aimed at gathering information relating to the environment on certain priority topics—air, water, soil, land cover, coastal erosion, biotopes, and more—for the European Union. The Corine Land Cover (CLC) is a map of the European environmental landscape based on interpretation of satellite images. It provides comparable digital maps of land cover for each country for much of Europe. The CLC is useful for environmental analysis and for policy makers.

The FSS helps assess the agricultural situation across the EU by monitoring trends and transitions in the structure of agricultural holdings, while also modeling the impact of external developments or policy proposals. Two kinds of FSS are carried out by Member States: a basic survey (full-scope Agricultural Census) every 10 years and several sample-based intermediate surveys carried out every 2 or 3 years between the censuses to provide harmonized information about land use on all holdings of 1 ha or more. Topics covered include area farmed, area under various types of crops, numbers of livestock, the farm workforce, rural development, and the extent of involvement in nonagricultural activities (such as tourism, forestry, etc.).

EC Regulation No. 1166/2008 also outlined a one-off satellite Survey on Agricultural Production Methods (SAPM). The SAPM complements the FSS and collects information on soil tillage methods, landscape features, animal grazing, animal housing, manure application, manure storage and treatment, and irrigation. Both FSS and SAPM are statistically representative at the level of NUTS 2 ("Nomenclature for Units of Territorial Statistics").

The FADN is the primary source of economic data at the farm level in the EU. It is a European system of sample surveys that takes place each year and collects structural and accountancy data relating to farms. FADN includes only commercial farms, that is, farms which are large enough to provide the major income-generating activity for the farmer and a level of income sufficient to support his or her family. In practical terms, to be classified as commercial, a farm must exceed a minimum economic size, the threshold depending on the country and the year. Commercial farms cover the most relevant part of agricultural activity in each EU Member State, accounting for approximately 40–50% of FSS farms. FADN is the only source of microeconomic data that is harmonized, meaning that accounting principles are the same in all EU Member States; thus, FADN can be used to make comparison between Member States. It also provides information about payments received by the farmers participating in agri-environmental schemes (LFA and AEMs) (EC 2009). However, the FADN does not provide data on quantities of inputs used. Instead, only expenditures on nutrients and other chemicals are collected.

The data collected by FSS, SAPM, and FADN provide much useful information for the evaluation of agri-environmental schemes. Together, FSS and SAPM cover a large fraction of the data required for the AEIs and is fully representative of the farming community. However, they do not cover information on nutrients and other external farm inputs (apart from irrigation water) flows. The FADN gathers information about nutrients and other chemicals use, but only in monetary terms and for commercial farms. Linking satellite, survey, and administrative data at the individual level is receiving increasing attention (Selenius et al. 2011). Although the promise of data integration is substantial, the four potential barriers to this integration identified by Bohman and Claassen (2011) apply.

7. Conclusion

The United States and the European Union have many similar types of agri-environmental programs and goals, especially when it comes to preventing negative environmental byproducts such as soil erosion, overuse of chemical pesticides and fertilizers, and abuse of environmentally sensitive areas such as wetlands and wildlife habitats. Moreover, both the European Union and the United States offer flexibility in meeting the specific environmental needs of individual communities. In the United States, flexibility is given to the producer, whereas, in the EU, it is more likely given to the Member State. Either way, economically optimal management of these programs is based on notions of economic efficiency, in which program parameters are chosen with the aim of equating marginal benefits and their marginal costs. In practice, however, program designs may also be motivated by various political economy goals (e.g., income transfer).

However, there are also important differences between EU and US programs. The emphasis of EU agri-environmental programs on maintaining landscape features and the explicit focus on preventing land abandonment have little counterpart in US federal agri-environmental policy. US policy is largely focused on reducing the negative externalities of agriculture, rather than on maintaining or enhancing the positive externalities. However, it would be misleading to provide a takeaway message that Europeans have a higher preference for focusing on the amenities of agriculture relative to its disamenities than do Americans. To make such an assessment be informative would require considering agri-environmental program choices within the context of all the available substitutes and complements for agricultural and other activities.

In the past decade, both the European Union and the United States have moved forward with plans to expand their agri-environmental programs. Before 2002, funding for WL conservation was modest compared to LR. For the EQIP, the largest WL program, the 2002 Farm Act authorized a five-fold increase in funding over previous levels, funding levels that have been maintained in the 2008 Farm Act, at least through fiscal year 2011. Under the 2008 Farm Act, spending on the new CSP (which replaced the Conservation Security Program that authorized in the 2002 Farm Act) increased from FY2009 to FY2011. The funding situation for many US agri-environmental programs for 2013 and on is unknown at this writing. In the European Union, the 2003 CAP reform increased the CAP's focus on the interactions between agriculture and the environment by shifting some funds from support regimes to environmental programs through making "modulation" compulsory (EC 2003). The new reform of the CAP due by 2013 is expected to improve the environmental and climate change performance of the CAP (i.e., to further green the CAP payments).

Although our literature review demonstrates that a substantial body of work exists on the impacts of agri-environmental programs, a number of important issues have not been addressed or addressed in only a handful of studies. To date, we have identified only three papers that have addressed the issue of additionality in a US context and only one (Mezzatesta, Newburn, and Woodward, 2011) that addresses these issues in major USDA conservation programs. Liu and Lynch (2011) and Lynch, Gray, and Geoghegan (2007) address additionality in the context of federal-state farmland preservation programs. The literature review for the European Union also shows that research on additionality is in its early stages there (Pufahl and Weiss 2009; Chabé-Ferret and Subervie 2011).

As already noted, transaction cost analysis in conservation programs has also received very little attention in the literature (McCann and Easter 2000). To date, there are no studies of producer transaction costs for the United States, although existing work does show that agency transaction costs are large. Given that program application can be a lengthy process, producer transaction costs may also be large and could be a barrier to conservation program participation. The issue of transaction costs has been more deeply explored in the European Union, and the findings there show that significant variations in private transaction costs (Hackl et al. 2007; Ducos et al. 2009) exist both across different agri-environmental schemes (Falconer and Saunders 2002; Rørstad et al. 2007) and within single schemes (Rørstad et al. 2007; Mettepenningen et al. 2009).

Finally, there is a large literature on conservation practice adoption but very few articles actually address the role of federal cost-sharing and incentive payments. Cooper and Keim (1996) and Lohr and Park (1995), for example, base their studies on stated responses to hypothetical payments for conservation practices. The empirical analysis in Lichtenberg (2004) is based on cost sharing for structural soil conservation practices provided by the state of Maryland. Many other studies (e.g., Wu et al. 2004) use simulation models to estimate the effect of payments that lower the costs for production systems, which include conservation practices.

These studies consider the role of hypothetical payments in leveraging practice adoption rather than payments actually offered by the US government. Although these studies are valuable, they do not necessarily yield information on the role of existing programs in the adoption of conservation practices. In the European Union, optimization and simulation economic models have been proposed to explain, for example, how farmers respond to changes in incentives for adopting agri-environmental measure (e.g., Hansen and de Frahan 2011) to changes in other aspects of the designs of agri-environmental contracts (e.g., Bamière et al. 2011).

Acknowledgments

The views expressed herein are those of the authors and do not necessarily represent those of the Economic Research Service or the US Department of Agriculture.

References

American Farmland Trust. 1998. The farmland protection toolbox: Fact sheet. http://www.farmlandinfo.org/fic/tas/tafs-fptool.html

Babcock, B., P. Lakshminarayan, J. Wu, and D. Zilberman. 1996. The economics of a public fund for environmental amenities: A study of CRP contracts. *American Journal of Agricultural Economics* 78(November 1996): 961–971.

Baldock, D., G. Beaufoy, G. Bennett, and J. Clark. 1993. *Nature conservation and new directions in the EC common agricultural policy: The potential role of EC policies in maintaining farming and management systems of high nature value in the community*. London: Institute for European Environmental Policy.

Baumol, W. and W. Oates. 1988. *The theory of environmental policy*, 2nd ed. Cambridge University Press, Cambridge.

Bamière, L., P. Havlik, F. Jacquet, M. Lherm, G. Millet, and V. Bretagnolle. 2011. Farming system modeling for agri-environmental policy design: The case of a spatially non-aggregated allocation of conservation measures. *Ecological Economics* 70: 891–899.

Bangsund, D. A., N. M. Hodur, and L. Leistritz. 2004. Agricultural and recreational impacts of the conservation reserve program in rural North Dakota, USA. *Journal of Environmental Management* 71(4): 293–303.

Barnard, C. H., G. Whittaker, D. Westenbarger, and M. Ahearn. 1997. Evidence of capitalization of direct government payments into US cropland values. *American Journal of Agricultural Economics* 79(5): 1642–1650.

Barreiro-Hurle, J., M. Espinosa-Goded, and P. Dupraz. 2010. Does intensity of change matter? Factors affecting adoption of agri-environmental schemes in Spain. *Journal of Environmental Planning and Management* 53(7): 891–905.

Bartolini, F., V. Gallerani, M. Raggi, and D. Viaggi. 2005. Contact design and targeting for the production of public goods in agriculture: The impact of the 2003 CAP reform. Proceeding of 11th EAAE congress: The future of rural Europe in the global agri-food system, Copenhagen. August 24–27, 2005.

Baumol, W., and W. Oates. 1988. *The theory of environmental policy*, 2nd ed. Cambridge UK: Cambridge University Press.

Baylis, K., S. Peplow, G. Rausser, and L. Simon. 2008. Agri-environmental policies in the EU and United States: A comparison. *Ecological Economics* 65 :753-764.

Bertoni, D., D. Cavicchioli, R., Pretolani, and A. Olper. 2008. Agri-environmental measures adoption: new evidence from Lombardy Region. Paper prepared for the 109th EAAE Seminar "The CAP after the Fischler reform: National implementations, impact assessment and the agenda for future reforms," Viterbo, Italy, November 20–21st, 2008.

Birdlife International. 2012. Reform proposals for the common agricultural policy. *Birdlife Europe Briefing.*

Boatman, N., C. Ramwell, H. Parry, N. Jones, J. Bishop, P. Gaskell, C. Short, J. Mills, and J. Dwyer. 2008. A review of environmental benefits supplied by agri-environment schemes. FST20/79/041. Report to the Land Use Policy Group, UK.

Bohman, M., and R. Claassen. 2011. Drowning in data, coming up dry: Making connections for meaningful water policy analysis. Presented at the World Statistics Congress, August 21–26.

Burrel, A. 2012. Evaluating policies for delivering agri-environmental public goods. Paper presented at the OECD workshop on the Evaluation of Agri-environmental Policies, Paris, June 20–22, 2011. http://www.oecd.org/dataoecd/2/25/48185525.pdf

Borsotto P., R. Henke M. C. Macrì, and C. Salvioni. 2008. Participation in rural landscape conservation schemes in Italy. *Landscape Research* 33(3): 347–363.

Chabé-Ferret, S., and J. Subervie. 2011. Estimating the causal effects of the French agro-environmental schemes on farmers practices by difference in difference matching. Paper presented at the OECD workshop Evaluation of Agro-Environmental Policies, Paris, June 20, 2011.

Claassen, R. 2012. *The Future of Environmental Compliance Incentives in U.S. Agriculture*, EIB-94. Washington DC: Economic Research Service, United States Department of Agriculture.

Claassen, R., L. Hansen, M. Peters, V. Breneman, M. Weinberg, A. Cattaneo, P. Feather, D. Gadsby, D. Hellerstein, J. Hopkins, P. Johnston, M. Morehart, and M. Smith. 2001.

Agri-environmental policy at the crossroads: Guideposts on a changing landscape. AER-794. Washington, DC: Economic Research Service.

Claassen R., V. Breneman, S. Bucholtz, A. Cattaneo, R. Johansson, M. Morehart. 2004. Environmental compliance in agricultural policy: Past performance and future potential, agricultural economic report, AER-832. Washington, DC: Economic Research Service, US Department of Agriculture.

Cooley, D., and L. Olander. 2012. Stacking ecosystem services payments: Risks and solutions. *Environmental Law Reporter*, 42 ELR 10150.

Cooper, J., and R. Keim. 1996. Incentive payments to encourage farmer adoption of water quality protection practices. *American Journal of Agricultural Economics* 78(February): 54–64.

Cooper, J. 1997. Combining actual and contingent behavior data to model farmer adoption of water quality protection practices. *Journal of Agricultural and Resource Economics* 22(July): 30–43.

Cooper, J., and T. Osborn. 1998. The effect of rental rates on the extension of conservation reserve program contracts. *American Journal of Agricultural Economics* 80(February): 184–194.

Cooper, J. 2003. A joint framework for analysis of agri-environmental payment programs. *American Journal of Agricultural Economics* 85(November, 2003): 976–987.

Cooper, J., J. Berstein, V. Vasavada, and J. C. Bureau. 2005. The environmental by-products of agriculture: International policy responses. In *Global agricultural policy reform and trade—Environmental gains and losses*, ed. Joseph Cooper, 11–38. Cheltenham, UK: Edward Elgar.

Cooper, T., K. Hart, and D. Baldock. 2009. The provision of public goods through agriculture in the European Union. Report prepared for DG Agriculture and Rural Development, Contract No 30-CE-1233091/00-28. London: Institute for European Environmental Policy.

Cooper, J. 2010. Average crop revenue election: A revenue-based alternative to price-based commodity payment programs. *American Journal of Agricultural Economics* 92(4): 1214–1228.

Copa-Cogeca. 2012. The common agricultural policy after 2013; The reaction of EU farmers and agri-cooperatives to the commission's legislative proposals. Report prepared by Copa and Cogeca (European Farmers and European Agri-cooperatives), Brussels.

Court of Auditors, European Union. 2003. Special report No. 4/2003 concerning rural development: Support for less-favoured areas, together with the Commission's replies. *EUR-Lex Official Journal of the European Union C 151* Vol. 46. http://eurlex.europa.eu/JOHtml.do?uri=OJ:C:2003:151:SOM:EN:HTML

Crabtree, B., N. Chalmers, and N.-J. Barron. 1998. Information for policy design: Modelling participation in a farm woodland incentive scheme. *Journal of Agricultural Economics* 49(3): 306–320.

Defrancesco, E., P. Gatto, S. Trestini, and F. Runge. 2008. Factors affecting farmers' participation in agri-environmental measures: Evidence from a case study. *Journal of Agricultural Economics* 59(1): 114–131.

Delvaux, L., B. Henry de Frahan, P. Dupraz, and D. Vermersch. 1999. Adoption d´une MAE et consentement á recevoir des agriculteurs en région wallone. *Economie Rurale* 249: 71–81.

Ducos, G., P. Dupraz, and F. Bonnieux. 2009. Agri-environment contract adoption under fixed and variable compliance costs. *Journal of Environmental Planning and Management* 52(5): 669–687.

Duffy, P. A., C. R. Taylor, D. Cain, and G. J. Young. 1994. The economic value of farm program base. *Land Economics* 70: 318–29.

Dupraz P., I. Vanslembrouck, F. Bonnieux, and G. Van Huylenbroeck. 2002. Farmers' participation in European agri-environmental policies. Paper prepared for presentation at the Xth

EAAE Congress Exploring Diversity in the European Agri -Food System, Zaragoza, Spain, August 28–31, 2002.
EC-DGAGRI. 2005. Agri-environment measures overview on general principles, types of measures, and application. Unit G-4—Evaluation of Measures applied to Agriculture, Studies, Directorate General for Agriculture and Rural Development, European Commission.
ERS. 2002. Farm policy: Title II—Conservation. Washington, DC: Economic Research Service, United States Department of Agriculture. http://www.ers.usda.gov/Features/FarmBill/Titles/TitleIIConservation.htm
ERS. 2006. Agricultural resources and environmental indicators. Washington, DC: Economic Research Service, United States Department of Agriculture. http://www.ers.usda.gov/Publications/AREI/EIB16/
ERS. 2009*a*. WTO domestic support notifications. Washington, DC: Economic Research Service, United States Department of Agriculture. http://www.ers.usda.gov/db/Wto/AMS_database/
ERS. 2009*b*. Briefing room farm and commodity policy: Program provisions. Washington, DC: Economic Research Service, United States Department of Agriculture. http://www.ers.usda.gov/Briefing/FarmPolicy/ProgramProvisions.htm
ERS. 2011. Agricultural income and finance outlook, AIS-91. Washington, DC: Economic Research Service, United States Department of Agriculture.
European Commission. "Modulation and other financial transfers from EAGF to EAFRD", Directorate-General for Agriculture and Rural Development, European Commission, 2003.
European Commission. 2006. Rural development 2007–2013. Guidance document Handbook on Common Monitoring and Evaluation Framework. Brussels: DG for Agriculture and Rural Development, European Commission. http://ec.europa.eu/agriculture/rurdev/eval/guidance/document_en.pdf
European Commission. 2009. Rural development (2000–2006) in EU farms. Unit L3 D agri.l.3(2009)212727. Brussels: DG for Agriculture and Rural Development, European Commission.
European Commission. 2011. Common agricultural policy towards 2020—Impact assessment. SEC(2011) 1153 final. Brussels: Author.
European Court of Auditors. Is agri-environment support well designed and managed? Special Report No. 7/2011. http://eca.europa.eu/portal/pls/portal/docs/1/8760788.PDF
European Network for Rural Development (ENRD). 2010. Public goods and public intervention. Final report of Thematic Working Group 3. Brussels: Author.
Falconer, K. 2000. Farm-level constraints on agri-environmental scheme participation: A transactional perspective. *Journal of Rural Studies* 16(3): 379–394.
Falconer, K., and C. Saunders. 2002. Transaction costs for SSSIs and policy design. *Land Use Policy* 19(2): 157–166.
Fargione, J., J. Hill, D. Tilman, S. Polasky, and P. Hawthorne. 2008. Land clearing and the biofuel carbon debt. *Science* 319(5867): 1235–1238.
Feather, P., D. Hellerstein, and L. Hansen. 1999. *Economic valuation of environmental benefits and the targeting of conservation programs: The case of the CRP*. Agricultural Economics Report No. 778. Washington, DC: USDA, ERS.
Feng, H., C. L. Kling, K. Lyubov, A. Kurkalova, S. Secchi, and P. W. Gassman. 2005. The conservation reserve program in the presence of a working land alternative: Implications for environmental quality, program participation, and income transfer. *American Journal of Agricultural Economics* 87(5): 1231–1238.

Feng, H., L. A. Kurkalova, C. Kling, and P. Gassman. 2006. Environmental conservation in agriculture: Land retirement vs. changing practices on working land. *Journal of Environmental Economics and Management* 52(2): 600–614.

Finn, J. A., D. Bourke, I. Kurz, and L. Dunne. 2007. Estimating the environmental performance of agri-environmental schemes via use of expert consultations. Final report of the ITAES project, Institute National de le Recherche Agronomique, Rennes, France. http://merlin.lusignan.inra.fr/ITAES/website/Publicdeliverables

Gillenwater, M. 2012. What is additionality? Part 3: Implications for stacking and unbundling. Discussion Paper No. 003. Silver Spring, MD: Greenhouse Gas Management Institute.

Giovanopoulou, E., S. A. Nastis, and E. Papanagiotou. 2011. Modeling farmer participation in agri-environmental nitrate pollution reducing schemes. *Ecological Economics, Elsevier* 70(11): 2175–2180.

Goodwin, B. K., and V. H. Smith. 2003. An ex post evaluation of the conservation reserve, federal crop insurance, and other government programs: Program participation and soil erosion. *Journal of Agricultural and Resource Economics* 28(2003): 201–216.

Groupe de Bruges. 2012. A cap for the future!? Why we need a better CAP that can face the challenges of today and tomorrow. http://www.groupedebruges.eu/html/publicationscap-ref.html

Hackl, F., M. Halla, and G. J. Pruckner. 2007. Local compensation payments for agri-environmental externalities: A panel data analysis of bargaining outcomes. *European Review of Agricultural Economics* 34(4): 295–320.

Hansen, K., and B. Henry de Frahan. Evaluation of agro-environmental policy through a calibrated simulation farm model. Paper presented at the EAAE 2011, August 30 to September 2, 2011, Zurich, Switzerland.

Hart, K., D. Baldock, P. Weingarten, B. Osterburg, A. Povellato, F. Vanni, C. Pirzio-Biroli, and A. Boyes. 2011. What tools for the European agricultural policy to encourage the provision of public goods. Study prepared for the European Parliament, IP/B/AGRI/IC/2010_094, Brussels.

Hellerstein, Daniel, Cynthia Nickerson, Joseph Cooper, Peter Feather, Dwight Gadsby, Daniel Mullarkey, Abebayu Tegene, and Charles Barnard. 2002. *Farmland protection: The role of public preferences for rural amenities*. Agricultural Economic Report No. 815. Washington, DC: Economic Research Service, US Department of Agriculture.

Hodge, I. 2001. Beyond agri-environmental policy: Towards an alternative model of rural environmental governance. *Land Use Policy* 18: 99–111.

Hodge, Ian, and Mark Reader. 2010. The introduction of Entry Level Stewardship in England: Extension or dilution in agri-environment policy? *Land Use Policy* 27 (2): 270–282.

Hynes, S., N. Farrelly, E. Murphy, and C. O'Donoghue. 2008. Modelling habitat conservation and participation in agri-environmental schemes: A spatial microsimulation approach. *Ecological Economics* 66(2–3): 258–269.

Khanna, M., M. Isik, and D. Zilberman. 2002. Cost-effectiveness of alternative green payment policies for conservation technology adoption with heterogeneous land quality. *Agricultural Economics* 27(2): 157–174.

Kirwin, B., R. Lubowski, and M. Roberts. 2005. How cost-effective are land retirement auctions? Estimating the difference between payments and willingness to accept in the conservation reserve program. *American Journal of Agricultural Economics* 87: 1239–1247.

Kirwan. B. 2009. The incidence of US agricultural subsidies on farmland rental rates. *Journal of Political Economy* 117(1), 2009: 138–164.

Kleijn, D., and W. J. Sutherland. 2003. How effective are European agri-environment schemes in conserving and promoting biodiversity? *Journal of Applied Ecology* 40: 947–969.

Kleijn, D. 2006. Guidelines for the evaluation of agri-environment schemes. Manuscript, Wageningen University. http://www.ncp.wur.nl/NR/rdonlyres/EA88E46A-1B26-4A04-AF51-4FBB5AC50619/52783/Guidelines_evaluation_ae_schemes2.pdf

Lichtenberg, E. 2004. Cost-responsiveness of conservation practice adoption: A revealed preference approach. *Journal of Agricultural and Resource Economics* 29(3): 420–435.

Lichtenberg, E., and R. Smith-Ramírez. 2011. Slippage in conservation cost sharing. *American Journal of Agricultural Economics* 93(1): 113–129.

Liu, X., and L. Lynch. 2011. Do agricultural land preservation programs reduce farmland loss? Evidence from a propensity score matching estimator. *Land Economics* 87(2): 183–201.

Lohr, L., and T. Park. 1995. Utility-consistent discrete-continuous choices in soil conservation. *Land Economics* 71(4):474–490.

Loriz-Hoffmann, J. 2012. The CAP and balanced territorial development. DG AGRI unit G1: Consistency of rural development policy. The CAP towards 2020—taking stock with civil society. European Commission, Brussels.

Lynch, L., W. Gray, and J. Geoghegan. 2007. Are farmland preservation program easement restrictions capitalized into farmland prices? What can a propensity score matching analysis tell us? *Applied Economic Perspectives and Policy* 29(3): 502–509.

Lubowski, R. N., A. J. Plantinga, and R. Stavins. 2008. What drives land-use change in the United States? A national analysis of landowner decisions. *Land Economics* 84(4): 529–550.

Mahé, L. P. 2012. Do the proposals for the CAP after 2013 herald a 'major' reform? Policy paper No. 53. Paris: Notre Europe.

Mapemba, L. D., F. M. Epplin, C. M. Taliaferro, and R. L. Huhnke. 2007. Biorefinery feedstock production on conservation reserve program land. *Applied Economic Perspectives and Policy* 29(2): 227.

McCann, L., and K. W. Easter. 2000. Estimates of public sector transaction costs in NRCS programs. *Journal of Agricultural and Applied Economics* 32(3): 55–563

McCann, L. 2009. Transaction costs of environmental policies and returns to scale: The case of comprehensive nutrient management plans. *Review of Agricultural Economics* 31(3): 561–573.

Mettepenningen, E., A. Verspecht, and G. Van Huylenbroeck. 2009. Measuring private transaction costs of European agri-environmental schemes. *Journal of Environmental Planning and Management* 52(5): 649–667.

Mettepenningen, E., V. Beckmann, and J. Eggers. 2011. Public transaction costs of agri-environmental schemes and their determinants—Analysing stakeholders' involvement and perceptions. *Ecological Economics* 70(4): 641–650.

Mezzatesta, M., D. Newburn, and R. Woodward. 2011. Additionality and the adoption of farm conservation practices. Selected paper prepared for presentation at the Agricultural & Applied Economics Association's 2011 AAEA and NAREA joint annual meeting, Pittsburgh, PA, July 24–26, 2011.

Oltmer K., P. Nijkamp, R. Florax, and F. Brouwer. 2000. A meta analysis of environmental impacts of agri-environmental policies in the European Union. Discussion paper TI 2000-083/3, Tinbergen Institute.

OMB. 2012. The appendix, budget of the United States government, fiscal year 2013. Washington, DC: Department of Agriculture, Office of Management and Budget, Executive Office of the President. http://www.whitehouse.gov/omb/budget/Appendix

Parker, D. P., and W. N. Thurman. 2011. Crowding out open space: The effects of federal land programs on private land trust conservation. *Land Economics* 87: 202–22.

Primdahl, J., B. Peco, J. Schramek, E. Andersen, and J. J. Onate. 2003. Environmental effects of agri-environmental schemes in Western Europe. *Journal of Environmental Management* 67: 129–138.

Primdahl, J., J. P. Vesterager, J. A. Finn, G. Vlahos, L. Kristensen, and H. Vejre. 2010. Current use of impact models for agri-environment schemes and potential for improvements of policy design and assessment. *Journal of Environmental Management* 91: 1245–1254.

Pufahl, A., and C. R. Weiss. 2009. Evaluating the effects of farm programs: Results from propensity score matching. *European Review of Agricultural Economics* 36(1): 79–101.

Reichelderfer, K., and W. G. Boggess. 1988. Government decision making and program performance: The case of the conservation reserve program. *American Journal of Agricultural Economics* 70(1):1–11.

Roberts, M. 2004. Effects of government payments on land rents, distribution of payment. In *Decoupled payments in a changing policy setting*, eds. Mary E. Burfisher and Jeffrey Hopkins. Agricultural economic report No. (AER838). Washington, DC: USDA. http://www.ers.usda.gov/publications/aer838/

Roberts, M. J., and S. Bucholtz. 2005. Slippage in the Conservation Reserve Program or spurious correlation? A comment. *American Journal of Agricultural Economics* 87(1): 244–250.

Roberts, M. J., and R. N. Lubowski. 2007. Enduring impacts of land retirement policies: Evidence from the Conservation Reserve Program. *Land Economics* 83(4): 516.

Rørstad, P. K., A. Vatn, and V. Kvakkestad. 2007. Why do transaction costs of agricultural policies vary? *Agricultural Economics* 36(1): 1–11.

Searchinger, T., R. Heimlich, R. Houghton, F. Dong, A. Elobeid, J. Fabiosa, S. Tokgoz, D. Hayes, and T. Yu. 2008. Use of US croplands for biofuels increases greenhouse gases through emissions from land-use change. *Science* 319(5867):1238.

Secchi, S., P. Gassman, J. Williams, and B. Babcock. 2009. Corn-based ethanol production and environmental quality: A case of Iowa and the Conservation Reserve Program. *Environmental Management* 44(4): 732–744.

Selenius J., L. Baudouin, and A. Kremer (Eds.). 2011. Farm data needed for agri-environmental reporting. Methodologies and working papers. Luxembourg: EUROSTAT.

Sullivan, P., D. Hellerstein, L. Hansen, R. Johansson, S. Koenig, R. Lubowski, W. McBride, D. McGranahan, M. Roberts, S. Vogel, and S. Bucholtz. 2004. The conservation reserve program: Economic implications for rural America. Agricultural economic report No. AER-834. Washington, DC: USDA.

US EPA. Undated. "Concentrated Animal Feeding Operations (CAFO) - Final Rule", US Environmental Protection Agency. http://cfpub.epa.gov/npdes/afo/cafofinalrule.cfm

Vanslembrouck, I., G. Van Huylenbroeck, and W. Verbeke. 2002. Determinants of the willingness to participate in agri-environmental measures. *Journal of Agricultural Economics* 50(3): 489–511.

Vasavada, U., S. Warmerdam, and W. Nimon. 2001. Green box policies and the environment. Briefing paper, URAA Issues Series. Washington, DC: ERS, US Department of Agriculture, WTO Briefing Room. http://webarchives.cdlib.org/sw1wp9v27r/http://ers.usda.gov/Briefing/wto/environm.htm

Wallander, S., and M. S. Hand. 2011. Measuring the Impact of the Environmental Quality Incentives Program (EQIP) on irrigation efficiency and water conservation. Conference paper, 2011 meetings of the Agricultural and Applied Economics Association, Pittsburgh, Pennsylvania.

Westhoek H., H. van Zeijts, M. Witmer, M. van den Berg, K. Overmars, S. van der Esch, W. van der Bilt. 2012. Greening the CAP: An analysis of the effects of the European Commission's proposal for the Common Agricultural Policy. PBL note. The Hague: Netherlands Environmental Assessment Agency.

Wossink, G. A., and J. H. Van Wenum. 2003. European biodiversity conservation by farmers: Analysis of actual and contingent participation. *Review of Agriculture Economics* 30(4): 461–485.

Wu, J. J., and W. G. Boggess. 1999. The optimal allocation of conservation funds. *Journal of Environmental Economics and Management* 38(3): 302–321.

Wu, J. 2000. Slippage effects of the conservation reserve program. *American Journal of Agricultural Economics* 82(4):979–992.

Wu, J. J., D. Zilberman, and B. Babcock. 2001. Environmental and distributional impacts of conservation targeting strategies. *Journal of Environmental Economics and Management* 41(3): 333–350.

Wu, J., R. Adams, C. Kling, and K. Tanaka. 2004. From micro-level decisions to landscape changes: An assessment of agricultural conservation policies. *American Journal of Agricultural Economics* 86(February):26–41.

Wu, J. J. 2005. Slippage effects of the Conservation Reserve Program: Reply. *American Journal of Agricultural Economics* 87(1): 251–254.

Wynn, G., B. Crabtree, and J. Potts. 2001. Modeling farmer entry into the environmentally sensitive area schemes in Scotland. *Journal of Agricultural Economics* 52(1): 65–82.

CHAPTER 24

STIGMATIZED SITES AND URBAN BROWNFIELD REDEVELOPMENT

JOEL B. EISEN

THIS chapter addresses the "stigmatized sites" located in urban areas in the United States and Europe and the "brownfields" redevelopment programs aimed at removing the stigma and promoting remediation and reuse of these sites. Although the European Union has put regulatory frameworks in place (Pahlen 2004), the United States has led the global effort to address brownfields redevelopment (Eisen 1996; Sarni 2009; Davis 2011), and the discussion in this chapter will focus on American models for brownfields remediation and reuse.

Typically, the term "brownfields" has come to refer primarily to abandoned or underused urban sites (Eisen 1996; Paull 2008; Wernstedt et al. 2010; US Environmental Protection Agency 2011*b*), often located in declining cities with industries that have ceased operations (for example, the "Rust Belt" cities in the Northeast and Midwest of the United States) (Robertson 1999; US Environmental Protection Agency 2011*c*). Brownfields can be found throughout the nation, in rural and suburban areas, as well as in cities, but urban sites have attracted the most attention. These sites have often had a number of owners and a long history of industrial or commercial uses (Eisen 2007). Frequently, the former owners are not in possession of the sites (and, often, no longer in existence), and the sites are owned by cities or other public entities (Eisen 1996; Hollander 2009).

A brownfield site may be a small parcel, but many brownfield sites are the larger properties that once were the former "crown jewels" of the cities in which they are located (US Environmental Protection Agency 2005). In many cities in the United States, Europe, and elsewhere, brownfields are among the most visible urban properties, such as rotting hulks of abandoned steel mills or other manufacturing facilities, formerly grand railroad stations no longer carrying passengers and sitting idle, and other neglected properties (Wernstedt et al. 2004). These can be large, prominent sites located in the urban core near railroads, highways, other forms of transportation, and the bulk of the city's population (Eisen 1996). They frequently attract attention and interest in redevelopment from a wide range of public and private sector entities that may play roles in their redevelopment, including real estate developers, investors, business enterprises, nonprofit organizations, government representatives, and elected officials (Wernstedt et al. 2004).

What are the optimal use and societal benefits of redevelopment at a brownfield site? Brownfields redevelopment has many potential benefits. Reinvesting in an urban core can be the linchpin of a strategy to thwart sprawl (unchecked growth in suburban and exurban areas) and preserve open space (Paull 2008). In recent years, the idea of sustainability has gained traction as a means for pursuing a more holistic approach to urban redevelopment that may include brownfields remediation and reuse, among other strategies (Eisen 1999). Another challenge that brownfields redevelopment strategies may help address is the urgent need to reduce greenhouse gas (GHG) emissions to address climate change. In the United States, the second largest share of GHG emissions comes from transportation, and a large part of that comes from urban commuters. Redevelopment of brownfield sites, if done properly, could spur a decrease in emissions by reducing the amount of vehicle miles traveled (Wernstedt et al. 2004).

The challenges to redeveloping brownfield sites are as numerous as those present at any urban site. However, brownfield sites are not properly priced for current development, in large part because they carry a stigma reflecting the possible presence of environmental contamination (Davis 2011). The primary attribute and added challenge to development of a brownfield site, as compared to other urban sites, is that it is commonly believed that one or more entities contaminated brownfield sites in the past, making decisions that did not require them to reflect the full social costs of pollution, but that the extent of the contamination and added costs are unknown.

In the mid- to late-1980s, the idea began to take shape that the stigma associated with brownfield sites was not a result of larger societal forces, such as changes in consumer preferences or residential patterns, but was instead a byproduct of governmental laws and programs designed to force the remediation of contaminated sites (such as CERCLA, the "Superfund law," in the United States) (Eisen 1996). There are few reliable estimates of the number of brownfield sites, due to many factors, including the imprecision of data collection and the uncertainty whether any specific site carries the stigma of potential environmental contamination. Unofficial estimates of total brownfield sites in the United States are based on incomplete lists dating to the 1980s, including state inventories and the EPA's CERCLIS database that identified potentially contaminated sites. Based on these figures, it is often stated that there may be from 400,000 to more than a million in the United States alone (National Association of Local Government Professionals and Northeast-Midwest Institute 2004; Wernstedt et al. 2010; Davis 2011). Recent figures are more precise. For example, a 2010 report from the US Conference of Mayors, based on a survey of 150 major cities in 41 American states, identified a total of more than 22,000 sites in these cities alone (US Conference of Mayors 2010).

At brownfield sites, there is a daunting information asymmetry for would-be developers. Many brownfields sites sit abandoned for a decade or more without any environmental investigation, so it is often difficult to discern the extent of contamination or whether they would be subject to the requirements prevailing under environmental cleanup laws (Eisen 1996). Once the potential and uncertain costs of environmental monitoring and other policy costs (e.g., dealing with local land use authorities in the redevelopment process) are factored in, developers' reluctance to become involved with these sites is understandable.

1. Brownfields and the Broader Context of Urban Redevelopment

Redevelopment of brownfield sites cannot be considered in a vacuum, but must instead be examined against the broader context of urban redevelopment activities (Robertson 1999). The idea that a city that has fallen into decline and decay can stop or reverse that slide through revitalization efforts is not new to the twenty-first century (Kunstler 1993). Nor is it a new idea that some cities that face deplorable conditions eventually regain their prominence or that others fail to do so and are consigned to the dustbin of history.

The causes of urban decay in the modern era are well chronicled (Bradbury et al. 1982; Duany et al. 2001; Hollander 2009). A city may experience deindustrialization when its dominant manufacturing industry declines due to adverse business conditions, leading to vacancies in commercial and industrial areas, a declining tax base, high unemployment, and other indicia of decline (Hollander 2009). A city's geographic advantage may fade if the advantage conferred no longer works in the city's favor due to technological obsolescence or other factors (as in the case of Buffalo when the railroads carried freight traffic more expeditiously than the Erie Canal) or by construction of a transportation artery that bypasses it. After World War II, public policy at all levels of government encouraged building of housing in the suburbs, and urban residents migrated out as a result, further contributing to declines in economic activity in central core cities (Bradbury et al. 1982; Duany et al. 2001; Hollander 2009).

Continuation of a city's decay may appear inevitable. A center city area may decline as the outer areas grow, no matter what redevelopment activities are undertaken. This, of course, would suggest that it is futile to engage in redevelopment activities. However, the arc of a city's slide is often debatable. There have been substantial efforts made to revitalize inner cities in the United States, and demographic trends suggest that, in some cities, these efforts have had some success because some Americans have moved back into the cities and made them desirable again (Kromer 2010). Although some speak of decline and rebirth as evidence that a city "lifecycle" exists, this theory is neither universally accepted nor reliable as a marker for brownfields redevelopment (Hollander 2009).

When policy makers contemplate potential policies for addressing urban decline, two intriguing questions present themselves. The first is "what are the measures of decline?" Is decline measured in statistics about growth rates, population, employment, and so forth? Is it visual, or is it measured in more comprehensive ways (such as a perception among residents that standards of living have declined)? The answers to this are myriad but can help define the goals of redevelopment activities. The metrics a city chooses to measure success of redevelopment are presumably those it should pursue in its focus at individual brownfield sites. A second question is more properly oriented to the urban institutional architecture: "from whose perspective is decline measured?" Who is entitled to control the destiny of urban redevelopment activities? The city's government? The entity that proposes to undertake redevelopment activities? The community in and surrounding the area(s) planned for redevelopment? All of the above, in partnership? The answer to this question is important because different actors may have diverging ideas about the ideal plan for transforming an urban brownfield site (Eisen 1999).

There are no easy answers to these questions. Indeed, it may be the case that a particular site has been the locus of attention on more than one occasion and has been a component of more than one type of development strategy. It may even be the case that previous redevelopment strategies have been responsible for hastening the decline of a site (Kunstler 1993). Over time, American and European cities have engaged in experimentation, embracing numerous ideas about how to redevelop their cities. Not all of these programs were successful. The urban renewal programs of the 1950s in the United States rehabilitated some neighborhoods but exacerbated problems in others by targeting "slums," displacing residents, and creating public housing projects that became symbols of urban failure (Kunstler 1993; Kromer 2010). Rather than improve residents' standards of living, urban renewal and other policies (notably federal highway assistance and mortgage insurance programs) often contributed to out-migration from cities and further decay (Bradbury et al. 1982; Duany et al. 2001). The construction of highways through urban neighborhoods often split them, hastening their decline. Rust Belt cities in the United States declined, with migration taking place to the suburbs and new Sun Belt cities (Kunstler 1993).

Starting in the 1980s and continuing since then, cities have often pursued redevelopment through mega-projects: stadiums, convention centers, shopping districts and cultural hubs, and other attractions they view as essential to attract other activities for redevelopment (Duany et al. 2001; Kromer 2010). The evidence on these projects is mixed, with some being successes in attracting development to co-locate with them and others being expensive failures (Kromer 2010). Gentrification of urban neighborhoods with upscale housing projects, parks, and other amenities is controversial and often results in the same types of urban displacement as urban renewal strategies, shifting the locus of economic decline to suburbs (some of which now have the same types of urban concerns as the core cities) or more depressed areas of cities (Kunstler 1993; Duany et al. 2001). One important question then becomes whether governments at all levels should continue to subsidize these transformative activities. This continuing debate has the effect of making policy support inconsistent. To take just one of many examples, rehabilitation tax credits helped promote redevelopment activities between the mid-1970s and 1980s, but when they were rolled back in the 1986 tax code revision, they lost their effectiveness (Davis 2011).

This historical approach suggests that a city should be careful to take a long-term approach and view its abandoned or vacant brownfield sites as community and economic opportunities, connecting redevelopment initiatives to broader community visions and revitalization priorities (Eisen 1999; US Conference of Mayors 2010). When a city focuses on a specific urban site and considers whether to pursue a new land use at that site, the optimal strategy would recognize the role of that site in an overall plan for urban redevelopment. As noted earlier, a wide variety of socioeconomic forces may be responsible for the decay of a city and of specific sites in that city. It may be difficult or impossible to separate the problems that led to decline at individual sites from citywide or economy-wide trends, and therefore these broader trends should be addressed rather than pursuing parcel-by-parcel redevelopment (Eisen 1999). A city should also ideally recognize that it would need to revisit its plans and strategies even after they have been implemented because, as already noted, even well intentioned urban redevelopment strategies sometimes come to be viewed in hindsight as mistakes.

2. Brownfields and Their Developers

There may be important reasons to consider development at specific abandoned and underused brownfield sites. These sites may have advantages over other locations. For example, some existing geographic advantages that led predecessor businesses to locate there may be helpful to new enterprises, such as proximity to transportation links (Bartsch 1996; Eisen 1996; Robertson 1999). Yet, in many American and European cities, those who would become involved with transforming these sites to new, productive purposes (who will be termed "developers" for the remainder of this chapter, although they are not always real estate developers) have the choice of foregoing redevelopment altogether and selecting sites at suburban and exurban locations, which can be more attractive options than urban redevelopment for a variety of reasons (Eisen 1996; Davis 2011). So-called "greenfield" locations can often be developed without the need to deal with whatever infrastructure may exist at the urban site.

For many developers, the cost of redeveloping a brownfield site can be higher than that of a greenfield site. They must incur upfront investigation costs that can cause delays they do not encounter with undeveloped greenfields. Much of the infrastructure at a brownfield site is not likely to be suitable for the developer's intended purpose, which will be different from the preceding use, so new infrastructure must be built at a higher cost. However, it is not always the case that a greenfield is optimally priced for development in comparison to a brownfield site. The greenfield conversion itself can create negative externalities that may not be reflected in the site's purchase price. Moreover, if the greenfield site in question has been the site of prior development activities, the costs of environmental remediation and monitoring might even negate the apparent cost advantage of developing there (Boyd et al. 1996). And, as is often the case in transformative activities such as residential remodeling, it is also possible that some existing infrastructure can be preserved at a brownfield site, thus lessening the cost of redevelopment (Paull 2008).

From the outset of the development of brownfields law and policy, much was therefore made of the need to provide incentives to attract developers to pursue redevelopment efforts at urban sites. In this perspective, the developers' interests are elevated over those of other actors, including, for example, the residents of the surrounding community (Eisen 1996). Developers often find it necessary to invest their own capital, but they also typically can obtain resources for a site's evaluation, remediation, and reuse from a wide variety of federal and state agencies in the form of site assessment grants, loans, training and education programs, and tax and other financing incentives. As discussed later, the lesser cleanup standards at brownfield sites also operate as a sort of financial incentive to developers, cutting the costs of remediation. For their part, cities have been willing to provide prospective developers with tax breaks, create special districts, and establish other incentives for them to take on the task of transforming sites (Rosenberg 2000).

Studies have consistently found that one of the major drivers of success in brownfields redevelopment is the extent to which these sources of public funds are available to leverage the developer's investment (US Environmental Protection Agency 2005; US Conference of Mayors 2010). This can be especially important when the developer's investment is front-loaded, as, for example, when site assessment and remediation costs threaten to exceed the current values of the brownfield sites in question (National Association of Local Government Professionals and Northeast-Midwest Institute 2004). Conversely, some have argued that developers should not be extended financial incentives for actions they would take without the incentives, especially if a brownfields program makes less than full remediation of environmental contamination a possibility (Eisen 1996). The frequent response to this argument is that, at many sites, any remediation and reuse activities are preferable to allowing the sites to remain abandoned or underused (Davis 2011).

The prevailing justification for providing incentives to developers and tailoring the brownfields remediation system to their needs has been that developers savvy enough to understand the risks they might be taking on might balk at contacting state and federal environmental authorities, fearing the worst-case scenario of encountering toxic substances at the sites and being required to undertake multimillion dollar cleanups (Boyd et al. 1996). This argument is relatively straightforward. One cannot know in advance what might be present at a site that has a history of industrial or commercial uses and is therefore contaminated to some extent (Davis 2011). If investigating the conditions at a brownfield site, let alone making decisions about how to remediate them, might expose a developer to liability, then the environmental costs associated with a particular site cannot be quantified ahead of time (Davis 2011). Contemplating a worst-case scenario can lead to project cost estimates that threaten to jeopardize project profitability, if spiraling remediation costs are factored in.

The prevailing brownfields narrative focuses on assumptions about the present condition of the site and the idea that environmental laws are the problem, not the solution (Eisen 1996). It does not usually take into account whether there might be any connection between the conditions at a brownfield site and urban redevelopment activities of the near past. Nor does it account for any risk minimization tools that might be available to developers, such as environmental insurance. Finally, it does not account for an interesting paradox with respect to any specific site. Although the condition of the site is assumed to be an unquantifiable unknown, this is often not the case. At the very least, it is typically known that a brownfield site is not one that has been targeted for enforcement action. In the United States, the sites on the National Priorities List (NPL) are those eligible for funding from the government's Superfund and are the highest priorities for cleanup. Most brownfields programs targeted sites that were not on the NPL (Bartsch 1996; Eisen 1996; Geltman 2000; Davis 2011).

In this evolving policy framework, the need to attract developers takes precedence over other means for steering redevelopment of the site. Legal and policy evolution could well have addressed developers' cost concerns directly by simply providing significant funding for site investigations that would delineate the extent of the risk. The federal and state governments did make funds available for this purpose, but brownfields advocates sought more than that. One outgrowth of the focus on developers was that if the chief concern was the overreach of the environmental laws governing cleanup of hazardous waste sites, the natural tendency was to go beyond providing funds to evaluate sites and instead to suggest that these laws be relaxed to permit more streamlined redevelopment activities (Eisen 1996).

3. The Relationship Between Brownfields and State and Federal Environmental Laws

There is nothing new about attributing urban decline to governmental actions that were intended to revitalize cities. Today, as noted earlier, the urban renewal of the 1950s in the United States is widely regarded as a series of projects that, although well intentioned, led to failure that exacerbated the decline of many cities. With brownfields, the prevailing narrative that drove the creation of laws and policies for remediation and reuse was altogether different: that the stigma originated indirectly, from supposedly unintended consequences of actions that governments have taken for a beneficial purpose under the environmental laws (Eisen 1996; Robertson 1999; Davis 2011). The problem was not only that the extent of contamination at a brownfield site was unquantifiable (which could have been addressed with widespread use of site assessment grants), but also that attempting to evaluate brownfield sites might subject developers to strict liability for full cleanups at the sites regardless of their lack of prior involvement with the sites (Geltman 2000; Hollander et al. 2010; Davis 2011).

Laws such as the US Comprehensive Environmental Response, Compensation, and Liability Act (CERCLA, more popularly known as the "Superfund law" for the fund created under it to remediate hazardous waste sites) require full remediation of dangerous conditions at hazardous waste sites (Robertson 1999; Rosenberg 2000; Davis 2011). The CERCLA cleanup process can take years and millions of dollars to complete (Eisen 1996; Davis 2011). Because CERCLA has been interpreted to fasten joint and several liability on those responsible for the toxic conditions at the sites, including owners and "operators" of the sites, an entity that becomes involved with a brownfield site might face the full price tag of remediation even if it did nothing to cause the contamination there (Eisen 1996; Davis 2011). Knowing that price tag ahead of time is next to impossible because the CERCLA cleanup standard is determined through a lengthy process (which includes a number of requirements that apply under other federal environmental laws) that cannot be completed before site investigation and assessment activities are completed (Eisen 1996; Robertson 1999; Davis 2011).

Throughout the 1980s, courts in the United States had strengthened CERCLA, consistently interpreting it to give the Environmental Protection Agency (EPA) more power and more authority to investigate and remediate sites and confer on the EPA and private parties more tools to fasten liability on those responsible for the sites (known in Superfund parlance as "potentially responsible parties," or PRPs). By the end of the decade, the regulated community viewed CERCLA as a regulatory scheme with unprecedented and unfortunate power and breadth (Davis 2011). In addition to joint and several liability (which, as noted earlier, can fasten the entire price tag of a cleanup on a single PRP), CERCLA features strict liability without regard to fault, so the EPA need not prove that a PRP intended to dump waste at a site or was reckless about doing so (Eisen 1996; Rosenberg 2000). It is only necessary to connect the PRP with the site, for example, by showing that a company made wastes of the sort that were dumped at the site (Davis 2011).

The EPA has sweeping powers to ensure that a site is remediated. For example, it can use "notice letters" to force PRPs to discover and identify other PRPs, and it can issue unilateral administrative orders with onerous penalties for their violation (Davis 2011). The liability provisions were so broad that their net captured a wide group of entities, whether or not they had any involvement in the actual dumping of waste at the sites, and thousands of companies became PRPs (Davis 2011). Current property owners, for example, make up one category of PRPs, whether or not they owned the sites at the time of disposal, which potentially subjected brownfields developers to liability (Eisen 1996; Rosenberg 2000). In the 1980s and 1990s, CERCLA had extremely limited defenses, although a brownfields defense was finally added in 2002 (Small Business Liability Relief and Brownfields Revitalization Act [SBLRBRA] 2002; Eisen 2007). That defense protects otherwise innocent prospective purchasers who did not know and had no reason to know that hazardous substances were disposed of at the site and who take due care to protect against foreseeable contamination. This requires the purchaser to have made "all appropriate inquiry" to discern the extent of contamination. This term is defined in the EPA's regulations and typically requires some form of investigation at the site (US Environmental Protection Agency 2011*b*).

By the end of the 1980s, it was apparent that the Superfund law had spurred identification of many contaminated sites around the country, and some were in the process of being remediated. However, this was not an efficient process because it took years to move a site through the labyrinthine CERCLA cleanup framework. For this reason and others, CERCLA had created more litigation and work for lawyers than any other state or federal environmental statute.

In the 1980s, CERCLA successes were still largely to take place in the future, and the voices of backlash decried the slow progress of cleanups at hazardous waste sites and criticized the statute itself as harsh and even arbitrary at times (Eisen 1996). This was different from the public clamor a decade earlier, spurred by high-profile incidents such as the discovery of toxic contamination at Love Canal in western New York, which had led to the creation of the CERCLA regime. At the inception of the CERCLA program, the overriding purpose of the law was ensuring that sites such as Love Canal were remediated (Davis 2011). Throughout the 1980s and 1990s, proponents of the law successfully argued that any systematic exception to the joint and several liability framework would weaken it and frustrate the Congressional intent to ensure that dangerous sites be remediated (Eisen 1996).

Although amendments to CERCLA and EPA policies and interpretations of the statute attempted to alleviate some of the burden faced by PRPs, they were limited in scope (Davis 2011). The 1986 amendments added an "innocent landowner" defense to CERCLA that might have protected those, like brownfields developers, who purchased sites after waste dumping took place and were therefore not responsible for contaminating them. However, this defense was not widely used because meeting its requirements was difficult (Rosenberg 2000). Among other requirements, it called for those seeking to prove their innocence to demonstrate that they had engaged in "all appropriate inquiry" before purchasing the site. Most courts interpreted this to mean that if prospective purchasers had not discovered the contamination before purchasing the sites, they probably had not conducted sufficient inquiries (Schnapf 2007). This was exactly the type of activity that brownfields developers were loath to undertake before purchasing sites. Thus, rather than protect brownfields developers, the shortcomings of the innocent landowner defense appeared to be a primary reason why more reforms to the CERCLA structure were needed (Eisen 1996).

As a result, it is important to note that the advocacy for brownfields remediation and reuse became more intense at the same time that a backlash was taking place against CERCLA and burgeoning hazardous waste cleanup schemes in Europe. In general, it is difficult to separate the growing clamor at the time for relief for brownfields developers from the general calls for softening the tough liability-based approach of the Superfund law. Brownfields advocates sought partnerships with environmental agencies rather than adversarial enforcement-based relationships, shorter cleanup processes with more finality (including releases or other forms indicating that the brownfields purchaser would not face liability), and lesser cleanup standards that, in some cases, would allow less costly means of addressing contamination at the site (e.g., so-called institutional controls, such as fences and warning signs). That these were the same sorts of changes sought generally for the harsh and unyielding Superfund scheme did not go unnoticed (Eisen 1996).

Economic conditions in the broader US economy added fuel to the reform fire. The stock market crash of 1987, savings and loan collapse, and ensuing recession that lasted through the early 1990s prompted calls for development activities to spur job creation, and policy makers in the United States and Europe increasingly turned their attention to revitalizing urban cores (Bartsch 1996). In this struggling macroeconomic environment, the emerging cracks in the societal consensus that remediation of hazardous waste sites was always an unalloyed good grew even wider. In the United States, brownfield sites tended to be concentrated in states that were hit hardest by the recession of the 1990s, and, for many policy makers, it was important to put these sites to productive use (Bartsch and Collaton 1997). A frequently voiced concern at the time was that CERCLA and its state analogues required a level of cleanup that went too far at sites such as these (Eisen 1996).

The term "brownfield" itself was an invention of these times, being first coined at a 1992 Congressional field hearing in Ohio (Bartsch 1996). Although "brownfield" was meant as a counterpoint to "greenfield," a term then in vogue to describe untouched sites in the suburbs and exurbs, it had an unmistakably pejorative cast to it. It suggested that these sites did, in fact, have a stigma associated with them—no one eagerly associates with "brown" sites—and advocates for change maintained that this stigma could only be removed with reforms to environmental laws, although other legal reforms would be necessary as well (Bartsch 1996). One natural response to the clamor for brownfields reforms might have been that the calls for less regulation, and that it be more transparent and easier to comply with, were the typical unjustified response of a regulated community to environmental regulation. In this respect, developers and their advocates often did themselves no favors by calling for "streamlined" regulations to empower redevelopment (Eisen 1996). Therefore, at least some who were involved in the brownfields law and policy development process recognized that any relief would have to be carefully moderated and tailored rather precisely to the brownfields situation.

An ironic twist on the situation was that while brownfields developers were said to fear the federal Superfund scheme, far more brownfields sites were subject to the reach of state environmental laws (Bartsch and Collaton 1997). There was widespread recognition from the early days of the development of the regulatory frameworks for brownfields remediation and reuse that most sites would be addressed by the states (Bartsch and Collaton 1997). In the United States, virtually every state had created a state law analogue to the Superfund law, with comparable features (Wernstedt et al. 2010; Davis 2011). Some states, particularly in the Northeast, had property transfer laws as well, requiring evaluation (and remediation if necessary) of potentially contaminated sites prior to their transfer (Eisen 1996; Bartsch and Collaton 1997; Davis 2011). Therefore, brownfields policy reform began in the states, where individual states could tailor their programs to their own specific needs (Bartsch 1996).

4. The Rise of "Voluntary Cleanup Programs"

These conditions all made for an environment ripe for change, and it is not surprising that, between the late 1980s and mid-1990s, many states overhauled their environmental cleanup and property transfer laws (Eisen 1996; Eisen 2007), and the European Union later developed standards for brownfields remediation (Pahlen 2004).

Because the states were the drivers of brownfields legal changes, most activity in state brownfields programs before 2002 took place without significant reforms to the federal Superfund law, although some federal programs, such as the EPA's use of "prospective purchaser agreements," did make some progress toward protecting brownfields developers (Eisen 1996; Rosenberg 2000; Davis 2011). Thus, prospective brownfields developers during this time were in an interesting situation, to say the least. They could obtain comfort from state environmental agencies that no enforcement actions would be taken against them if they proceeded to investigate conditions at sites and remediate them if necessary, but there was always the potential that they might face federal liability (particularly if the cleanup in a state brownfields program was to a level less complete than required under the federal standard) (Eisen 1996). Eventually, however, many thousands of sites were processed successfully through state brownfields programs despite what some saw as the specter of federal liability. States negotiated with the EPA to create memoranda of understanding that secured a level of comfort for sites addressed in their programs (Eisen 1996; Davis 2011). It was also evident that changes enhancing the performance of state programs were almost guaranteed to eventually lead to changes to the Superfund law itself because the state laws being changed were analogous to the federal law.

The state brownfields programs are generally known as "voluntary cleanup programs" (VCPs) because their central feature is that developers voluntarily come to the states and initiate dialogues intended to lead to productive remediation and reuse of brownfields sites (Eisen 1996; Davis 2011). This differentiates the operational paradigm of these programs sharply from normal enforcement-driven CERCLA models, in which a PRP's first contact with the government is typically an adversarial notice that it faces liability (Eisen 1996). The intent of this model was to make the entire remediation and reuse process more flexible and less confrontational from the developer's perspective and to create a working relationship between state regulators and developers (Dana 2005).

The features of VCPs differ widely, but most include three central attributes (Eisen 1996; Gerrard 1998 and Supp. 2006; Robertson 1999; Rosenberg 2000; Wernstedt et al. 2010; Davis 2011).

4.1 Streamlined Administrative Processes

In VCPs, the steps between identification of a site as one to which the program will apply and final remediation and reuse are far less in number and shorter in duration than in enforcement-driven models. Often, developers were put in control of many steps of the process (in some states, by hiring a licensed environmental professional to administer the entire cleanup) (Eisen 1996). One major distinction of the process from the normal CERCLA model deserves special mention: the role of the community surrounding a brownfield site. In CERCLA cleanups, public participation in cleanup activities is mandatory and proceeds on a legally defined parallel track to the remediation itself; it can be an involved, complex process, depending on the nature of the sites. In VCPs, by contrast, many states empowered the developers themselves to determine on their own whether and how to involve the public in decision making at the sites (Eisen 1996).

4.2 Risk-Based Cleanup Standards

In VCPs, the end use to which sites will be put (such as commercial, industrial, or residential) is factored into the risk assessment of the sites, leading to standards that typically require less than complete remediation. Often, developers could cut costs by adopting remedies that were less comprehensive, such as entombing soils at brownfield sites rather than removing and treating them. In the states that empowered developers to employ licensed environmental professionals, these professionals were authorized to decide the level of cleanup standards within defined parameters, which took these critical decisions out of the hands of state environmental authorities (Eisen 1996; New Jersey Institute of Technology 2011).

4.3 Liability Protection

States offered a number of means for developers to secure protection against future enforcement actions by their environmental agencies, ranging from "no further action" letters (statements of intent that developers would not face liability in the future) to full releases from liability. These forms of protection do not offer any shield against federal liability but were typically viewed as sufficient for developers to continue with redevelopment activities (Eisen 1996).

The federal government has stepped in to assist brownfield developers as well. The 2002 amendments to CERCLA provided liability protection from CERCLA for developers of brownfields sites through a prospective purchaser exemption (SBLRBRA 2002). The EPA subsequently issued regulations to clarify how the protection would be obtained; for example, by requiring the prospective purchaser to allow access to and cooperate with regulators and to exercise care in dealing with the prior releases of contaminants at the site so as not to exacerbate the problem (US Environmental Protection Agency 2005; Eisen 2007; Schnapf 2007). The new law also supported the continued use of VCPs by restricting federal actions under CERCLA against developers who remediate sites under VCPs (SBLRBRA 2002).

The EPA implemented the 2002 law by providing additional federal grants and other tools to address the contamination of brownfields sites (US Environmental Protection Agency 2011*a*). These resources include grant programs for characterization of brownfields sites and site analytical tools that can help make the process of environmental investigation and remediation less onerous and costly (Hollander et al. 2010; US Environmental Protection Agency 2011*a*). Beyond the EPA's activities, federal governmental agencies at all levels have adapted existing programs in such areas as infrastructure, housing, and community development to promote site redevelopment and reuse (Robertson 1999; Sarni 2009; Hollander et al. 2010). Interagency partnerships have also become productive means of addressing important issues (US Environmental Protection Agency 2011*a*).

5. Public Input in the Brownfields Remediation and Reuse Process

The use to which a brownfields site would be put after its remediation has not been central to the decision-making architecture of most VCPs, except insofar as it has factored into the choice of the cleanup standard (Eisen 1996). It has been assumed that the developer controlled the choice of land use, in that it would not have approached the state in the first instance without a plan for site redevelopment. A VCP could, and in many cases, did, therefore sanction site plans that related only to the individual brownfields sites and bore little relationship (if any at all) to any comprehensive plan for urban redevelopment (Eisen 1999). There were exceptions to this, as some American cities eschewed parcel-by-parcel redevelopment in favor of more comprehensive approaches (US Conference of Mayors 2010). Also, some states created area-wide brownfields initiatives, in which environmental regulators and state development agencies worked together to address multiple brownfields in the same community (van Hook et al. 2003), but these states were in the minority. There is nothing about most VCPs that requires consistency with a holistic vision for the future of the particular city (Eisen 1999).

From the start, VCPs focused on user friendliness: alleviating the regulatory burden for developers, not creating relationships with communities (Davis 2011). As a result, public input in deciding the future of brownfields sites has often been limited (Eisen 1996). If residents in the community surrounding a brownfield site wanted a park instead of a mega-project, they had little power to influence the decision, and it was, in fact, rare for a prospective developer to change the plans for the site. In many cities, there were no obvious stakeholders to voice the concerns of the residents near brownfields sites, let alone engage in discussions with developers that had already prepared plans for the sites and approached state environmental authorities (Davis 2011). It is rare for residents living near brownfields sites to demonstrate the level of political mobilization that can derail projects, and the surrounding communities much more often consist of those who have historically been marginalized in urban planning efforts (Speiss 2008). Moreover, financial concerns are usually more important to a brownfields developer than satisfying the needs of the community (Wernstedt et al. 2010).

As VCPs have matured, savvy developers have turned to citizen "steering committees" or other community-based groups, particularly relying on existing groups that have knowledge and expertise of the affected communities (National Center For Neighborhood and Brownfields Redevelopment 2008; Speiss 2008). Studying the experiences over the years with VCPs, the EPA and others have come to view this identification and engagement with community groups, and the resulting degree of trust and consensus, as important to the success of brownfields reuse projects (National Association of Local Government Professionals and Northeast-Midwest Institute 2004; Speiss 2008; US Conference of Mayors 2010; US Environmental Protection Agency 2011*b*).

For this reason, and because the remediation and reuse of brownfields sites often has dramatic social and economic impacts on the surrounding area, community planners have viewed public outreach as an increasingly important feature of the process (Speiss 2008). A community group can bring a wider focus on community redevelopment than is possible at a site where remediation and reuse is governed solely by the developer (Sarni 2009). However, it should be emphasized that VCPs do not typically require this sort of public participation in the brownfields remediation and reuse process (Eisen 1996). Thus, the danger when public meetings or other means of involvement are conducted is that the level of participation can fall far short of meaningful input (Speiss 2008; Sarni 2009) or that the participation process can fail to identify a group that speaks meaningfully for the affected community (Davis 2011).

6. The Link Between Brownfields Redevelopment and Climate Change, "Smart Growth," and Sustainability

Brownfields redevelopment activities have gone beyond mere remediation to pursue a broader agenda much more closely related to urban sustainability (De Sousa 2008; Lewis 2008; Sarni 2009; Hollander et al. 2010). Given the link between brownfields redevelopment and reuse to preservation of greenfields spaces, there have been active links and synergies between the "smart growth" movement and brownfields redevelopment, particularly in addressing urban sprawl (Hollander et al. 2010; US Environmental Protection Agency 2011*b*). "Smart growth" is an umbrella-like term referring to strategies to pursue development that address negative externalities of unchecked suburban and exurban sprawl by preserving unspoiled land and protecting natural resources (Pollard 2000; Salkin 2002). It is one thing to articulate that brownfields redevelopment is consistent with smart growth principles, but quite another to achieve it in practice. The fact that brownfields projects use existing urban land and, at times, some of the existing infrastructure, does not necessarily make that growth "smart" (Eisen 2007; Paull 2008).

An evolving long-term trend in brownfields redevelopment is connecting brownfields with actions to address climate change (Paull 2008). There are many opportunities for reuse of brownfield sites that would not only conserve greenfields acreage but also deploy green technologies to reduce carbon emissions and produce other benefits (Lewis 2008; Sarni 2009). Employing green design and construction techniques in conjunction with overhauling existing buildings may conserve energy and feature sustainable building materials and creative waste reduction strategies. Some brownfields sites have been transformed into urban greenways or "brightfields" (sites for solar arrays to produce electricity) (Lewis 2008; Sarni 2009). To move forward on climate change action, cities and localities are increasingly forming sustainability or environmental quality departments that integrate energy reduction, deployment of clean energy, and other steps to reduce carbon footprints with existing land use planning. These departments, and their climate action plans and initiatives, have become important to integrating brownfields redevelopment planning into community-wide development agendas (Portland Bureau of Planning and Sustainability 2009).

Of course, there may be political, legal, or other obstacles to pursuing this broader approach to urban redevelopment. In some cases, the balkanization of urban policy making is a large part of what led to the city's decline in the first place, and simply forming a sustainability department may not be enough to override institutional inertia (Sarni 2009). Often, multiple institutions in a city have effective responsibility for urban planning, so it should be no surprise when these institutions cannot act nimbly to decide what to do with the brownfield sites they might choose to redevelop or when a developer cannot ascertain which entity it must deal with (Davis 2011).

7. Conclusion: Successes and Challenges of Brownfields Redevelopment Programs

Decades after their inception, brownfields redevelopment programs are mature environmental programs with many successes (US Environmental Protection Agency 2011*b*). In numerous American cities, sites that were abandoned for many years have been reclaimed for productive reuses. From their inception, VCPs grew quickly, and a number of success stories have been touted throughout the nation (Davis 2011). One well-known positive impact on the environment of brownfields remediation and reuse is the conservation of land at greenfield locations saved from development. Building on urban sites, with their existing footprints and infrastructure, can alleviate the damaging impacts of sprawl by conserving acres of greenfields (Deason et al. 2001; Paull 2008). Other benefits of brownfields redevelopment include reductions in vehicle miles traveled, storm water runoff, and air pollution (National Association of Local Government Professionals and Northeast-Midwest Institute 2004; Wernstedt et al. 2004; Paull 2008). Studies have also found that brownfields redevelopment can have a positive impact on property values in the areas surrounding brownfields sites at sites where the change in land use has yielded increased values (Paull 2008). Researchers using hedonic analysis have found that the stigma of a contaminated site depresses nearby property values and that removal of the stigma through expedited remediation would increase sites' present values (Kaufman and Cloutier 2006; Messer et al. 2006).

An ongoing concern is that, although VCPs have been successful, there are still numerous cities where brownfields continue to remain abandoned or underused. Many claim that far more brownfield sites remain to be addressed than have proceeded through the state VCP processes to completion (Paull 2008; Davis 2011). In many communities, the incentives for brownfields remediation and reuse have not succeeded in attracting investments because fear of environmental liability is not the only barrier to successful redevelopment (Robertson 1999; Auld et al. 2011). Some cities have brownfields that are too small to be suitable for the sort of projects that interest many developers (Wernstedt et al. 2010). These cities often also lack institutional capabilities for redevelopment activities (Auld et al. 2011). For example, they have less experience in matching prospective developers with opportunities to remediate and reuse brownfields sites because they have less skill at marketing their communities and identifying local officials who are sufficiently skilled to navigate VCP processes. Some prospective brownfields developers (such as nonprofit groups) lack experience in dealing with environmental agencies and can be overwhelmed by the VCP process. Making assistance available to these developers by, for example, assisting them with site evaluation methods, can be important to the success of their redevelopment activities (US Environmental Protection Agency 2005; New Jersey Institute of Technology 2011).

Another issue that has arisen at times, and is likely to recur, is whether remediation and reuse activities at individual brownfields sites have achieved final control of environmental contamination. The efficacy of some cleanups has come under fire years afterward as contamination has been discovered (Eisen 2007). Without aggressive provisions for revisiting sites that prove to be problematic in the future, there is no guarantee that the finality craved by brownfields developers will not come at a high societal cost. Cleanups in VCPs, with their risk-driven calculation of environmental harms, do not achieve complete eradication of all risks at the site. The typical means for these state programs to protect against backsliding is inclusion of reopeners in the laws creating them. These provisions allow state environmental departments to require developers or their successors to pursue additional cleanup activities at a later date if changed conditions warrant it (Eisen 2007).

Reopeners in VCPs have several drawbacks as protection against future discoveries of environmental contamination. First, and perhaps most obvious, the changed conditions, that is, the release of contaminants posing a threat to human health and the environment, would already have taken place by the time a state's environmental agency became involved in attempting to prevent them. Second, the reopeners are typically limited in scope because VCPs are designed to alleviate the regulatory burden faced by developers, not to ensure full and complete remediation of brownfields sites. A broad reopener provision allowing a state environmental agency to intervene at a brownfields site without a demonstration of imminent harm is typically perceived as a deterrent to initial finality of processing sites through a VCP.

Perhaps most importantly, any reopener provision depends both on resources available in the future to state environmental agencies and on the willingness of those agencies to tackle problems at sites they believed were successfully addressed in the past. The problem of resources to devote to enforcement is especially problematic in tight budgetary climates because cutbacks in state budgets can lead to a slower pace of cleanups and less vigilant oversight of brownfields sites (National Association of Local Government Professionals and Northeast-Midwest Institute 2004; Eisen 2007; US Environmental Protection Agency 2011*b*). Few state environmental agencies put oversight and monitoring of completed brownfields sites ahead of normal enforcement actions in their priorities. However, they would do well to devote more resources to oversight because some sites have been processed through state VCPs without any systematic examination of long-term impacts (Eisen 2007).

This highlights another shortcoming of VCPs: they generally lack structures for evaluation of sites over time to assess lifecycle impacts of brownfields remediation and reuse (Wernstedt et al. 2004; Auld et al. 2011). The VCP process focuses on the present-day problem of transforming an abandoned or underused site into a locus for commerce, and, as a result, methodologies to evaluate long-term impacts are only beginning to be developed, years after VCPs have been operating (Wernstedt et al. 2004; Auld et al. 2011). Deciding on modalities for assessing whether redevelopment activities at brownfields sites are beneficial can take the form of determining consistency with third-party verification systems such as the LEED system, the popular green building certification system that promotes sustainable building and development practices (Paull 2008). LEED's methodology takes positive note of buildings that are constructed on brownfields sites and also values features that are often positive advantages of existing brownfields sites, such as proximity to existing transportation systems (Paull 2008; Sarni 2009). However, a different approach will be necessary to determine whether brownfields policies meet the criteria outlined in climate action plans or, indeed, have been beneficial as a whole as a strategy for urban redevelopment (Auld et al. 2011).

Therefore, although VCPs have undeniably been responsible for successes and benefits, the final verdict on brownfields programs has yet to be rendered and will only be made in hindsight, years after the initial development decisions have been made. This is consistent with the societal perspective on other urban redevelopment programs, which can change as programs have impacts not foreseen by their initial drafters. Given the relative lack of in-depth research from economists on the impacts of brownfields programs, there is considerable room for targeted work that evaluates the value that these programs add at individual sites and the merits of specific redevelopment strategies.

References

Auld, Ronell, et al. 2011. Assessing brownfield sustainability: Life cycle analysis and carbon footprinting. http://www.cmu.edu/steinbrenner/brownfields/Current%20Projects/sustainability.html

Bartsch, C. 1996. Coming clean for economic development: A resource book on environmental cleanup and economic development opportunities. http://www.nemw.org/cmclean.htm

Bartsch, C., and E. Collaton. 1997. *Brownfields: Cleaning and reusing contaminated properties.* Santa Barbara, CA: Praeger.

Boyd, J., W. Harrington, and M. K. Macauley. 1996. The effects of environmental liability on industrial real estate development. *Journal of Real Estate Finance and Economics* 12(1): 37–58.

Bradbury, K. L., A. Downs, and K. A. Small. 1982. *Urban decline and the future of American cities*. Washington, DC: Brookings Institution Press.

Dana, D. A. 2005. State brownfields programs as laboratories of democracy? *New York University Environmental Law Journal* 14: 86–107.

Davis, T. S. (ed.). 2011. *Brownfields: A comprehensive guide to redeveloping contaminated property*, 3rd ed. Chicago: American Bar Association.

Deason, J. P., G. W. Sherk, and G. A. Carroll. 2001. Public policies and private decisions affecting the redevelopment of brownfields: An analysis of critical factors, relative weights and areal differentials. http://www.gwu.edu/~eem/Brownfields/

De Sousa, C. 2008. *Brownfields redevelopment and the quest for sustainability.* Bingley, UK: Emerald Group Publishing.

Duany, A., E. Plater-Zyberk, and J. Speck. 2001. *Suburban nation: The rise of sprawl and the decline of the American dream.* New York: North Point Press (Macmillan).

Eisen, J. B. 1996. "Brownfields of dreams?" Challenges and limits of voluntary cleanup programs and incentives. *University of Illinois Law Review* 1996: 883–1032.

Eisen, J. B. 1999. Brownfields policies for sustainable cities. *Duke Environmental Law & Policy Forum* 9: 187–229.

Eisen, J. B. 2007. Brownfields at 20: A critical reevaluation. *Fordham Urban Law Journal* 34: 721–756.

Geltman, E. Glass. 2000. *Recycling land: Understanding the legal landscape of brownfield development.* Ann Arbor: University of Michigan Press.

Gerrard, M. B. (ed.). 1998 & Suppl. 2006. *Brownfields law & practice: The cleanup & redevelopment of contaminated land.* New York: Matthew Bender.

Hollander, J. B. 2009. *Polluted & dangerous: America's worst abandoned properties and what can be done about them.* Burlington: University of Vermont Press.

Hollander, J., N. Kirkwood, and J. Gold. 2010. *Principles of brownfield regeneration: Cleanup, design, and reuse of derelict land.* Washington, DC: Island Press.

Kaufman, D. A., and N. Cloutier. 2006. The impact of small brownfields and greenspaces on residential property values. *Journal of Real Estate Finance and Economics* 33(1): 19–30.

Kromer, J. 2010. *Fixing broken cities: The implementation of urban development strategies.* New York: Routledge Press.

Kunstler, J. H. 1993. *The geography of nowhere: The rise and decline of America's man-made landscape.* New York: Touchstone Press.

Lewis, G. 2008. Brown to green: Sustainable redevelopment of America's brownfield sites. http://www.nemw.org/index.php/policy-areas/brownfields/brownfields-sustainable-urban-redevelopment-and-energyreports-papers

Messer, K. D., W. D. Schulze, K. F. Hackett, T. A. Cameron, and G. H. McClelland. 2006. Can stigma explain large property value losses? The psychology and economics of Superfund. *Environmental and Resource Economics* 33(3): 299–324.

National Association of Local Government Professionals & Northeast-Midwest Institute. 2004. Unlocking brownfields: Keys to community revitalization. http://www.nalgep.org/publications/

National Center For Neighborhood & Brownfields Redevelopment. 2008. Building capacity: Brownfields redevelopment for community-based organizations. http://policy.rutgers.edu/brownfields/projects/Manual_Building_Capacity.pdf

New Jersey Institute of Technology. 2011. Brownfield site contamination investigation. http://www.njit.edu/tab/managing/pre-development/contamination-investigation.php

Pahlen, G. 2004. RESCUE: Regeneration of European sites in cities and urban environments. http://www.grc.engineering.cf.ac.uk/events/rescue2/pdfs/R2-MS2-GP.pdf

Paull, E. 2008. The environmental and economic impacts of brownfields redevelopment. http://www.nemw.org/images/stories/documents/EnvironEconImpactsBFRedev.pdf

Pollard, O. A., III. 2000. Smart growth: The promise, politics, and potential pitfalls of emerging growth management strategies. *Virginia Environmental Law Journal* 19: 247–285.

Portland Bureau of Planning and Sustainability. 2009. Climate action plan 2009. http://www.portlandonline.com/bps/index.cfm?c=49989

Robertson, H. G. 1999. One piece of the puzzle: Why state brownfields programs can't lure businesses to the urban cores without finding the missing pieces. *Rutgers Law Review* 51(5): 1075–1132.

Rosenberg, R. 2000. *Community resource guide for brownfields redevelopment.* Williamsburg, VA: Center for Public Policy Research, College of William and Mary.

Salkin, P. E. 2002. Smart growth and sustainable development: Threads of a national land use policy. *Valparaiso University Law Review* 36: 381–412.

Sarni, W. 2009. *Greening brownfields: Remediation through sustainable development.* New York: McGraw-Hill Professional.

Schnapf, L. 2007. The new "all appropriate inquiries" rule. *The Practical Real Estate Lawyer* January: 7–24.

Small Business Liability Relief and Brownfields Revitalization Act of 2002 SBLRBRA, 42 USC. §§ 9604-05, 9607, 9622, 9628.

Speiss, D. M. 2008. Public participation in brownfields cleanup and redevelopment: The role of community organizations. http://deepblue.lib.umich.edu/handle/2027.42/60850

US Conference of Mayors. 2010. Recycling America's land: A national report on brownfields redevelopment (1993–2010). http://www.usmayors.org/pressreleases/uploads/November2010BFreport.pdf

U.S. Environmental Protection Agency. 2005. Investing in partnership, possibility, and people: A report to stakeholders (Moving Forward). www.epa.gov/brownfields/overview/05Stakeholder/StakeholderReport_MovingForward.pdf

U.S. Environmental Protection Agency. 2005. Standards and practices for all appropriate inquiries, 40 C.F.R. § 312. http://www.epa.gov/brownfields/aai/index.htm

U.S. Environmental Protection Agency. 2011a. A guide to federal tax incentives for brownfields redevelopment. www.epa.gov/brownfields/tax/tax_guide.pdf

U.S. Environmental Protection Agency. 2011b. Brownfields and land revitalization. http://epa.gov/brownfields/about.htm

U.S. Environmental Protection Agency. 2011c. State brownfields and voluntary response programs: An update from the states. http://www.epa.gov/brownfields/state_tribal/update2011/bf_states_report_2011.pdf

van Hook, D. E., J. A. Shaw, and K. J. Kloo. 2003. The challenge of brownfield clusters: Implementing a multi-site approach for brownfield remediation and reuse. *New York University Environmental Law Journal* 12: 111–152.

Wernstedt, K., L. Heberle, A. Alberini, and P. Meyer. 2004. The brownfields phenomenon: Much ado about something or the timing of the shrewd? Resources for the Future, Discussion Paper 04-46. http://www.rff.org/Documents/RFF-DP-04-46.pdf

Wernstedt, K., A. Blackman, T. P. Lyon, and K. Novak. 2010. Voluntary environmental programs at contaminated properties. Resources for the Future, Discussion Paper 10-18. http://www.rff.org/RFF/Documents/RFF-DP-10-18.pdf

CHAPTER 25

REGULATORY TAKINGS

THOMAS J. MICELI AND KATHLEEN SEGERSON

THE regulatory takings issue potentially arises whenever a government regulation restricts the use of private property without actually seizing title to it. Examples include zoning, environmental and safety regulations, historic landmark designation, rules requiring equal accommodation for the disabled, and so on.[1] From an economic perspective, regulations that reduce the value of private property are not fundamentally different from outright takings (i.e., seizures of property); the difference is one of degree rather than of kind. Thus, any deprivation or restriction of a particular right reduces the value of the property proportionately. A physical taking, which deprives the owner of all rights, is simply one end of a continuum.

Given this analytical equivalence between seizures and regulations, a separate treatment of the two types of actions does not appear to be warranted by economic theory. Yet the fact remains that courts have treated them quite differently: whereas compensation is virtually always required for seizures, it is rarely awarded for regulations. Indeed, courts have historically granted the government broad police powers to enact regulations in the public interest without the need to compensate property owners for lost value. Still, in some cases, courts have ruled that if a regulation goes "too far" in restricting private property, it will be ruled a "regulatory taking" and compensation will be due. The question, therefore, is where the dividing line is (or should be) between compensable and noncompensable regulations.

There exists a considerable body of case law and legal scholarship aimed at answering this "compensation question." A review of the various tests that have emerged from this investigation illustrates the range of perspectives that have been brought to bear on this debate and also reflects the apparent lack of consensus on an adequate answer. The goal of this chapter is to survey the contribution economic theory has made to this debate, highlighting

[1] See Miceli and Segerson (1996), Meltz et al. (1999), and Miceli (2011, Chapter 5) for detailed examinations of several of these regulations within the context of takings law. Note that, although the existing case law describes the range of government actions that have so far been challenged under takings law, it does not limit those things that can be challenged in the future. In principle, landowners can challenge any action that reduces the value of their land as constituting a taking.

the most significant insights and results. We do this using a simple model of takings or land use regulation that provides a unifying framework for discussing the economics of regulatory takings. We use the model to illustrate both basic economic principles related to compensation and a number of extensions that have been considered in the literature.

Much of this literature is normative in the sense that it proposes compensation rules aimed at achieving efficient regulatory and land use decisions and hence does not purport to provide a positive theory of the case law (which is viewed by many as incoherent) or to account for competing values like distributive justice. We will discuss one rule, however, that we believe goes a long way toward unifying the various tests that courts and legal scholars have proposed.

As a prelude to the economic analysis, we provide brief reviews of the case law and legal literature in this area.

1. Overview of the Case Law

1.1 The Physical Invasion Test

Nearly all courts have agreed that any government action that involves some sort of physical invasion of a landowner's property, even when it does not literally seize title, constitutes a compensable taking. For example, in *Loretto v. Teleprompter*,[2] the Court held that a state law allowing cable television providers to install wires and other equipment on a private building was a taking. Although the *physical invasion test* is well-established in takings law, it is of limited usefulness because it offers no guidance for the vast majority of government actions, like zoning and environmental regulations, that involve no invasion. The remaining legal tests concern these sorts of cases.

1.2 The Noxious Use Doctrine

An important early test was established in the case of *Mugler v. Kansas*,[3] which concerned a law passed by the state of Kansas, pursuant to a prohibition amendment to the Kansas constitution, forbidding the operation of breweries. The owner of a brewery sued for compensation on the grounds that the law constituted a taking of his property, but the US Supreme Court denied the claim based on the state's right to regulate, without compensation, those activities that are deemed "to be injurious to the health, morals, or safety of the community,"[4] so-called "noxious uses." This ruling, referred to as the

[2] 458 U.S. 419 (1982).
[3] 123 U.S. 623 (1887).
[4] Ibid., 668.

noxious use doctrine, recognized that the government has broad regulatory powers to prevent land uses seen as potentially harmful to the public.

Zoning ordinances provide the most common illustration of this principle, and courts have routinely upheld them as valid exercises of the government's right to regulate land use in the public interest. The first case to reach such a conclusion was *Village of Euclid v. Ambler Realty*,[5] which upheld a town ordinance zoning a portion of the plaintiff's land for residential use. The Court maintained that the ordinance fell within the municipality's inherent right, under the police power, to protect public health, safety, morals, and general welfare (Meltz et al. 1999, 214).

1.3 The Diminution of Value Test

Under the noxious use doctrine, the impact of a regulation on the landowner's value apparently had no bearing on the compensation question. As long as the landowner retained title, the government had broad regulatory authority to restrict his or her land. That view changed, however, when, in 1922, the Supreme Court decided the famous case of *Pennsylvania Coal v. Mahon*.[6] The case concerned a law passed by the State of Pennsylvania aimed at protecting the safety of surface owners against the risk of cave-ins (or subsidence) by requiring that coal companies leave enough coal in the ground to support the surface. The Pennsylvania Coal Company brought suit seeking compensation on the grounds that the regulation was a taking of its legal right to mine all of the coal under the surface. (Under a common legal arrangement, the mining company had sold the surface rights but had retained the mineral rights to the subsurface coal.) Although the case seemed to be an easy one under the noxious use doctrine, given that the law clearly met the standard of protecting the safety of the surface owners, the Court ruled that compensation was due.

Writing for the majority, Justice Oliver Wendell Holmes argued that, apart from the noxious use doctrine, there must be a limit to the government's power to regulate private property. That limit, he said, is embodied in the impact of the regulation on the landowner:

> One fact for consideration in determining such limits is the extent of the diminution [in the landowner's value]. When it reaches a certain magnitude, in most if not all cases there must be an exercise of eminent domain and compensation to sustain the act.[7]

This argument forms the basis for the *diminution of value test* for compensation, which says that compensation is due if the loss to the landowner as a result of a regulation

[5] 272 U.S. 365 (1926)

[6] 260 U.S. 393 (1922). Also see Friedman (1986), who characterized the *Penn Coal* decision as a "watershed" in takings law.

[7] Id., 413.

is sufficiently large. Of course, this raises the question of what amount of loss is large enough to meet the compensation threshold; Holmes only said that "if regulation goes too far it will be recognized as a taking."[8] He therefore left it to future courts to decide on a case-by-case basis what constitutes "too far."

More than six decades later, the Supreme Court confronted a case with an almost identical factual scenario as in *Pennsylvania Coal*. The issue again was whether an antisubsidence statute passed by the state legislature was a taking of the coal company's rights, but, in apparent contradiction of its earlier ruling, the Court in *Keystone Bituminous Coal Assn. v. DeBenedictus* (1987) ruled that it was not. In endeavoring to distinguish the two cases, the Court argued that the statute at issue in *Keystone* protected a broader public interest, whereas the earlier statute had been aimed at protecting only a few private parties. Although the distinction between public and private in this context is not strictly valid from an economic perspective, we will argue in Section 4.2.2 (see footnote 30) that changing values of both the surface and mining rights over the intervening time period can provide a legitimate basis for distinguishing the two cases.

1.4 The Penn Central Balancing Test

The need to balance the factors raised in these earlier cases—namely, the intent of the regulation and its impact on the landowner's property value—was made explicit in the case of *Penn Central Transportation Co. v. City of New York*.[9] This case arose out of the city's decision to designate Grand Central Terminal as a historic landmark, thereby limiting the sort of alterations that the owners could make.[10] Thus, when the Landmark Preservation Commission turned down a proposal by Penn Central to build a multistory office building above the terminal, the owners sued, claiming a taking of their right to develop. In deciding against compensation, the Supreme Court advanced a three-part test for determining whether a compensable taking has occurred. The relevant factors were (1) the character of the government action, (2) whether or not the regulation interfered with "investment-backed expectations," and (3) the extent of the diminution of value. The first and third of these factors clearly identified the importance of both the noxious use doctrine and the diminution of value test, although, once again, without offering explicit guidance on how to balance one against the other.

The second factor, emphasizing the importance of investment-backed expectations, captures the idea that any loss suffered by the landowner must have been based on reasonable expectations, backed up by actual investments (Mandelker 1987; Fischel 1995, 50). In other words, an owner could not claim to have been denied uses that he never would have contemplated or that would not have been allowed by law in the absence of

8 Id., 415.

9 438 U.S. 104 (1978).

10 On landmark designation and takings law, see Gold (1976).

the regulation. Thus, as a necessary condition for compensation, a claimant would have to show evidence that he had in fact planned to undertake the prohibited development.

In his dissenting opinion to the *Penn Central* ruling, Justice William Rehnquist added a further consideration when he stated that "a taking does not take place if the prohibition applies across a broad cross section of land and thereby 'secure[s] an average reciprocity of advantage.'"[11] The phrase "average reciprocity of advantage," first used by Holmes in his *Pennsylvania Coal* opinion, suggests that monetary compensation need not be paid if a regulation restricts all landowners equally, thereby spreading both the benefits and the costs of the regulation. The Supreme Court employed similar logic in the case of *Agins v. Tiburon* when it held that a landowner subject to a zoning restriction "will share with other owners the benefits and burdens of the city's exercise of its police power. In assessing the fairness of zoning ordinances, these benefits must be considered along with any diminution in market value that the appellants might suffer."[12] We will return to this logic in Section 5.

1.5 The Nuisance Exception

An important extension of takings law emerged from the case of *Lucas v. South Carolina Coastal Council* (1992).[13] The case involved a land developer who had purchased two beachfront lots in South Carolina with the intention of developing them for residential use. Such a use seemed reasonable at the time of purchase since several similarly situated neighboring lots had already been developed. However, after the developer's purchase but before he began development, the South Carolina legislature passed a law prohibiting further beachfront development in the area in an effort to control coastal erosion. The developer sued, claiming a taking because the lots were rendered valueless by the regulation. A trial court found in his favor and awarded full compensation. However, the South Carolina Supreme Court reversed the ruling, despite the trial court's finding of a nearly complete diminution of value, relying instead on the regulation's stated purpose of preventing harm to the public—the old noxious use doctrine.

The U.S. Supreme Court, in turn, reversed the South Carolina Supreme Court and said that compensation was due based on the fact that the regulation denied "all beneficial or productive use of land."[14] Still, the Court left open the possibility that the state could avoid paying compensation, despite the total loss, if it could show that the land use prevented by the regulation constituted a nuisance under the state's common law. This standard, known as the *nuisance exception*, provides an objective basis, founded in the common law, for determining what constitutes a noxious use.

One question not clarified by the *Lucas* decision, however, was the extent of diminution necessary to trigger automatic compensation. The regulation at issue in *Lucas*

[11] Id., 147.

[12] 157 Cal.Rptr. 373, 1979; affirmed 447 U.S. 255, 262 (1980).

[13] 505 U.S. 1003 (1992).

[14] Id., 1015.

clearly met any standard the Court could have applied because it caused a virtual total loss (the nuisance exception aside). The question therefore remained whether something short of full diminution would also qualify. The Supreme Court revisited this issue in *Palazzolo v. Rhode Island*,[15] which concerned a landowner who sought compensation when he was denied permission to develop waterfront property under a wetlands preservation law passed by the state of Rhode Island. The landowner claimed that the regulation met the requirement for compensation under *Lucas* because it denied him "all economically beneficial use" of the land, but the Court found that the regulation, in fact, left the owner with developable land worth $200,000, compared to his claimed loss of $3.15 million (a 94% diminution). Apparently, therefore, a diminution of at least 95% is required to constitute a "total" deprivation under *Lucas*.

The extent of the diminution arose in a different way in the case of *Tahoe-Sierra Preservation Council v. Tahoe Regional Planning Agency*,[16] which concerned a temporary moratorium on development that deprived a group of developers of the entire value of their holdings for a 32-month period. The plaintiffs claimed that this action constituted a taking under the *Lucas* rule, requiring compensation for regulations that deprive owners of all productive uses of their land, albeit for a limited period of time. The Supreme Court disagreed, however, arguing that the diminution was only partial in relation to the "parcel as a whole," accounting not only for its spatial dimension but for its temporal dimension as well. Recognizing that the value of the parcel would be restored once the moratorium was lifted, the Court argued that the *Lucas* rule did not apply, and that, under the *Penn Central* balancing test, no compensation was due.

1.6 Wetlands and Endangered Species Protection

Much recent litigation in the area of regulatory takings law has arisen in the context of regulations aimed at protecting wetlands and endangered species. Wetlands represent a natural resource that has only recently been recognized as providing important social benefits, including providing a habitat for wildlife, flood control, water quality maintenance, and both recreational and commercial use (Hartmann and Goldstein 1994). The recent recognition of these values has led to the enactment of government regulations at both the state and federal level aimed at preserving wetlands. However, since wetlands predominantly exist on privately owned land, and because their primary value to the owner is usually for future development, these regulations have naturally generated a large volume of takings claims.[17]

Efficiency dictates that conversion of wetlands to development should occur to the point at which the marginal social value of land in development equals its marginal

15 533 U.S. 606 (2001).

16 535 U.S. 302 (2002).

17 According to Meltz et al. (1999, 366, note 5), there were about 400 cases involving wetlands regulations between 1960 and 1990, of which about half raised the takings issue.

social value if left in an undeveloped state. Thus, although it is probably efficient to convert some wetlands to alternative uses, especially in early stages of economic development, private landowners almost certainly would go beyond that efficient point if unrestrained because they would not internalize the full social value of the resource. Regulation is therefore necessary to achieve the efficient balance. Still, the question remains whether landowners are entitled to compensation for their resulting loss.

Generally, courts have held that the denial of a permit to develop a wetland does not constitute a compensable taking of the owner's property. One argument in support of this position has been to claim that the proposed use of the land would represent a nuisance. However, in *Florida Rock Industries v. United States*, the U.S. Claims Court held that "the assertion that a proposed activity would be a nuisance merely because Congress chose to restrict, regulate, or prohibit it for the public benefit indicates circular reasoning that would yield the destruction of the fifth amendment."[18] As a result, the Court found that a taking had occurred. Although this argument is consistent with the *Lucas* nuisance exception in its reliance on the common law for defining a nuisance, it fails to recognize the possible efficiency benefits that a departure from nuisance law might allow. Although nuisance law will often provide a useful approximation for efficient regulation, this will not always be the case. Indeed, the fact that wetlands were once themselves thought to be nuisances worthy of removal, but are now highly valued as an important natural resource by many, illustrates the point (Meltz et al. 1999, 365).

Nuisance law is not the only applicable legal doctrine in wetlands cases; the "public trust doctrine" is also relevant. The public trust is an ancient doctrine that grants ownership of navigable waterways, shorelines, and the open sea to the public. According to this doctrine, landowners do not have a right to impair these resources (Lueck and Miceli 2007, 237). In *Just v. Marinette County*, for example, the court held that "[a]n owner of land has no absolute and unlimited right to change the essential character of his land so as to use it for a purpose for which it was unsuited in its natural state and which injures the rights of others."[19] Based on this logic, the court found that a regulation preventing the landowner from filling a wetland was not a taking, even though the proposed use would not have constituted a nuisance.

Like resource preservation, the protection of endangered species, especially those endangered by human activity, has become an important objective of government policy (Boyle and Bishop 1987). The most important legislative action in this regard was the passage of the Endangered Species Act (ESA) in 1973.[20] Under this Act, the Fish and Wildlife Service (FWS) was authorized to "list" a species as endangered or threatened and to designate the "critical habitat" of that species for special protection or management. The Act further stipulated that the criterion for listing a species is to be based on "the best scientific and commercial data, without reference to economic costs or private

18 21 Cl.Ct. 161, 168 (1990).

19 201 N.W.2d 761, 768 (Wisc. 1972).

20 16 U.S.C. §§ 1531–1544.

property impacts." In contrast, habitat designation is to be based on both scientific data and "economic impact and any other relevant impact," thus theoretically allowing consideration of landowners' interests (Meltz et al. 1999, 392).

As with wetlands, the preservation of endangered species warrants government intervention because of the externalities involved (Harrington 1981). However, the takings issue also arises because of the loss suffered by landowners as a result of the various restrictions on their allowed activities. For example, owners are prohibited from "taking" members of a listed species unless it is done in a good faith attempt to protect a person, where a "take" is defined to include, among other things, harassing, harming, pursuing, or hunting a listed animal. More ominously for landowners, the FWS has defined "harm" to include significant habitat modification or degradation (Meltz et al. 1999, 393), and, in 1995, the Supreme Court upheld that interpretation as reasonable.[21]

Conversely, land use restrictions under the ESA have generally produced relatively modest impacts on landowners' value, which, based on the prevailing legal standard requiring a landowner to show a virtual total loss in value, does not bode well for the success of taking claims.[22] Of course there are exceptions to this, such as when the owner of a stand of timber is prevented from harvesting it. The risk here, as will be discussed later, is that the threat of an uncompensated regulation can result in perverse (and costly) landowner incentives, such as a decision to clear cut the stand early to avoid its being declared a habitat or to conceal the fact that an endangered species might reside in a certain locale.

2. Other Proposed Tests for Compensation

This section describes several tests for compensation that have been proposed in the scholarly literature on takings. As will be seen, these tests vary in their economic content and logical consistency. A test first proposed by Sax (1964) asserts that the government owes compensation when it acquires property rights for use in its enterprise capacity, as when it provides a public good, but it does not owe compensation when it acts as a disinterested arbitrator in a private dispute, as when it prevents one private party from imposing external costs on other private parties.[23] Rubenfeld (1993) elaborates on this test by arguing that a taking occurs when the government takes property for some

[21] *Sweet Home Chapter of Communities for a Great Oregon v. Babbitt*, 515 U.S. 687 (1995).

[22] Meltz et al. (1999, 396) note that, as of 1999, not a single court decision finding a taking under the ESA had been reported.

[23] Rose (1983) makes a similar argument.

productive use—a so-called "using"—as opposed to merely depriving the owner of its use. Rose-Ackerman and Rossi (2000) propose a similar standard.

In a second article, Sax (1971) argues that the government does not owe compensation for any actions that it undertakes to regulate external costs. Daniel Bromley adopts a similar perspective in arguing that paying compensation for such regulations would represent "indemnification for an inability to continue to impose unwanted costs on others" (Bromley 1993, 677). According to this view, which echoes the noxious use doctrine, the law does not (and should not) protect the right of landowners to engage in activities that impose harm on others. However, the difficulty with this test, as noted by Fischel (1985, 153), is that it offers "no workable distinction... between land uses that create spillovers and those that do not. *Every* economic activity can be argued to affect someone else" [emphasis in original].

A similar delineation of property rights underlies the *harm-benefit rule*, which says that no compensation is due for regulations that prevent a landowner from imposing a harm on others (e.g., a regulation against pollution), but compensation is due for regulations that compel the landowner to confer a benefit on the public (e.g., a ban on development to preserve open space). Although this rule has some intuitive appeal, it, too, is unsupported by economic theory in the sense that a prevented harm can always be defined as a benefit, and a forgone benefit can be defined as a harm (Fischel 1985, 158). Based on this logic, Justice Scalia, in his *Lucas* opinion, dismissed the harm-benefit rule as lacking a coherent legal basis for deciding the compensability of regulations.[24]

What underlies the failure of the harm-benefit rule, or any nuisance-based approach to the compensation question, is Coase's insight that all harms are reciprocal in nature, meaning that both an injurer and victim must be present for an accident to occur (Coase 1960). Thus, regulations that prevent harms or confer benefits are indistinguishable in terms of the cost to the injurer and the gain to the victim. What is lacking in tests is a benchmark reflecting neutral conduct, which would serve as the basis for deciding when compensation should and should not be paid. Fischel (1985, 158–160) offers such a benchmark in the form of his *normal behavior standard*, which is based on arguments first made by Ellickson (1973, 1977). According to this standard, no compensation is due for regulations that prevent landowners from engaging in "subnormal" behavior, but compensation is due for regulations that compel them to undertake "above-normal" behavior, where "normal" behavior is defined by community standards based on what landowners can reasonably expect to be able to do with their land. This "reasonableness standard" therefore replaces the arbitrary distinction between harms and benefits in the

[24] "When it is understood that 'prevention of harmful use' was merely our early formulation of the police power justification necessary to sustain (without compensation) *any* regulatory diminution of value; and that the distinction between regulation that 'prevents harmful use' and that which 'confers benefit' is difficult, if not impossible, to discern an objective, value free basis; it becomes self evident that noxious use language cannot serve as a touchstone to distinguish regulatory takings—which require compensation—from regulatory deprivations that do not require compensation" (*Lucas v. South Carolina Coastal Council*, 505 U.S. 1003, 1026, 1992).

harm-benefit rule. What makes this an economic standard (rather than being another arbitrary distinction) is that it economizes on the transaction costs of achieving an efficient land use pattern. Specifically, by setting the "zero compensation point" at normal behavior, the costs of compliance will be minimized because most landowners will engage in normal behavior automatically (i.e., without the need for government action).

Wittman (1984) proposes a similar compensation rule that is based on the behavior of the government rather than of landowners. Specifically, he argues that the transaction costs of paying compensation will be minimized if compensation is limited to cases in which the government acts inefficiently, based on the presumption that "we would expect the government to act efficiently more often than not" (Wittman 1984, 74). An important drawback of both the Fischel and Wittman standards, however, is that they fail to account for the role of the compensation rule in *creating* the proper incentives for landowners and/or the government to act efficiently. The next section deals with this issue.

In a very influential article, Michelman (1967) proposed a standard that is based on a comparison of the settlement (or transaction) costs associated with paying compensation and the demoralization costs of not paying compensation, where the latter are defined to be those costs incurred by landowners and their sympathizers once they realize that they will not be compensated for their losses. According to Michelman's standard, if the settlement costs are lower, compensation should be paid, whereas if demoralization costs are lower, compensation should not be paid.[25]

Finally, Richard Epstein's view on the compensation question is based on the Lockean notion that the government should not stand in a preferred position compared to private citizens (Epstein 1985, Chapter 2). In this perspective, the government has no more rights in its interactions with private citizens than does any other private citizen, inasmuch as the government is merely an agent of those citizens when they act collectively. Thus, when a government action wrongfully deprives a private citizen of valuable property, it should have to pay compensation, just as a private citizen would have to pay for imposing similar harm under nuisance (tort) law. In contrast, when a government action prevents a private citizen from imposing harm on other citizens—as when it prevents that citizen from creating a nuisance (or noxious use)—it should not have to pay, based on the right that private citizens have to be free from nuisances caused by fellow citizens.[26] Epstein's view thus closely corresponds to the nuisance exception established in the *Lucas* case.

3. Role of Economics in the Takings Debate

Before turning to the economic models, we provide some comments on the role that economics can, and more importantly cannot, play in resolving issues related to the

[25] See Fischel and Shapiro (1988), who discuss Michelman's test in light of more recent theories.

[26] See Epstein (1985, 36) and Epstein (1995, 133).

takings debate. Fundamentally, debates about the scope of the government's power of eminent domain concern the relationship between the state and its citizens. In particular, "What can the state demand of the individual citizens whom it represents and governs?" (Epstein 1985, 3). As noted, under the Lockean conception of property, the government derives its power from the consent of the governed and therefore cannot infringe on individual property rights except insofar as that is necessary to prevent property owners from interfering with one another's rights. In contrast, a Benthamite view of property sees the government's role as defining property rights in such a way as to achieve the greatest good for the greatest number. It follows that infringement on the rights of some citizens is acceptable if it is part of an overall policy that results in an increase in social welfare (however that is measured).

An economic approach to the takings issue is potentially compatible with both views, depending on the concept of efficiency one employs. The conclusions one would reach regarding the compensation question, however, would likely be quite different. Under traditional Pareto optimality, government actions are only judged to be efficient if no one is made worse off by the action and some are made strictly better off. This criterion, which reflects the Lockean view regarding the protection of property rights, would clearly require full compensation to be paid for all government actions, regardless of any realized benefits. It would therefore be satisfied whenever the government regulation yields aggregate gains that exceed the losses, and compensation is paid. In contrast, the criterion of potential Pareto optimality (or Kaldor-Hicks efficiency) would not necessarily require actual compensation of losers but only that compensation be "possible." This approach is clearly more congenial to the Benthamite view of property. It would be satisfied whenever the government regulation yields aggregate gains that exceed the losses, *regardless* of whether compensation is paid. Thus, either notion of efficiency is consistent with an economic perspective. As a result, an economic approach does not offer a clear resolution of the fundamental question about property rights that is a critical dimension of the takings issue. It does, however, allow a consideration of how compensation decisions affect resource allocation and incentives for various parties, and thus, ultimately, the magnitude of aggregate welfare. This perspective and its implications constitute the primary contribution of economic models of regulatory takings.

4. Economic Models of Land Use and Regulation

Probably the most important contribution economists have made to the regulatory takings debate has been the examination of the impact of compensation on the investment incentives of landowners whose property is at risk of being taken or regulated. This line of research began with the seminal paper by Blume, Rubinfeld, and Shapiro (1984) (hereafter, BRS), which showed that paying full compensation for takings creates a moral hazard problem that causes landowners to overinvest in land that is targeted for regulation. An implication of the BRS analysis is the so-called no-compensation result, which demonstrated that zero compensation is efficient. The BRS model is actually more subtle than this conclusion suggests, but the no-compensation result has naturally received the most attention and has provided a stimulus for subsequent research, much of it aimed at providing countervailing arguments.

The no-compensation result was controversial principally because of its perceived unfairness and apparent inconsistency with the constitutional requirement of just compensation (at least for physical takings). From an economic perspective, however, the result is a simple consequence of the well-known moral hazard problem associated with full insurance. This section presents a simple version of the BRS model in which the government's decision to take or regulate the owner's property is treated as exogenous. The model provides a unifying framework for discussing the large literature on the economics of takings that has arisen since BRS. Consistent with this literature, the basic principles derived from it are equally valid in the contexts of outright takings and regulation of property. Subsequent sections then examine various extensions to the basic model.

4.1 Exogenous Probability of a Taking

The BRS model uses the following notation:

$V(x)$ = market value of a piece of land after x dollars of improvements have been made, where $V'>0$, and $V''<0$;
p = probability that the land will be taken for public use;
B = fixed value of the land in public use if taken;
$C(x)$ = compensation paid to the owner in the event of a taking.

The timing of events is as follows: first the landowner decides how much to invest in improving his land and then the taking/regulation decision occurs. The owner's initial investment is irreversible, so if the land is taken, its value in private use, $V(x)$, as well as the cost of the investment, x, are lost. Since the original BRS paper considered physical takings, the interpretations of the variables above reflect this. However, as just noted, the model and the results derived from it are equally valid in the context of regulatory takings using the following interpretations of the variables. Under a regulatory taking, $V(x)$ represents the *additional* market value that the landowner would realize in the absence of a regulation, or, equivalently, the loss in market value that would result from the regulation; B represents the benefit of the regulation or, equivalently, the external harm avoided by it; and p is the probability that the regulation is imposed.

Since the taking occurs randomly in this model, the only economic decision is the owner's choice of x. The socially optimal investment maximizes the expected social value of the land:

$$pB + (1-p)V(x) - x. \tag{1}$$

The resulting first-order condition is

$$(1-p)V'(x) = 1, \tag{2}$$

which defines the optimal investment, x^*. Note that the amount of investment is decreasing in p. Thus, as the probability of a taking increases, the landowner should invest less, so as to reduce the loss in the event of a taking.

Now consider the actual choice of x by the landowner. His goal is to maximize his expected private return from the land, which is given by

$$pC(x) + (1-p)V(x) - x. \tag{3}$$

Note that this expression differs from (1) by the first term. The first-order condition defining the owner's optimal investment is

$$pC'(x) + (1-p)V'(x) = 1. \tag{4}$$

Comparing (4) and (2) immediately shows that $C' = 0$ is a sufficient condition for efficiency; that is, lump sum compensation induces efficient investment. A special case of lump sum compensation is $C \equiv 0$, or zero compensation. Intuitively, zero compensation prevents the owner from overinvesting in his land because he internalizes the loss that would result if the land is taken. This is the "no-compensation result" of BRS.

4.2 Endogenous Probability of a Taking

Several counterarguments have been advanced in favor of compensation, the most common being that compensation is needed to prevent the government from overregulating (Johnson 1977). These models can be categorized based on the assumption that is made about the government's behavior.

4.2.1 Benevolent (Pigovian) Government

A benevolent government is defined as one that makes the taking decision to maximize social welfare. Fischel and Shapiro (1989) refer to such a government as "Pigovian" because it considers the social costs and benefits of its actions. To capture this formally, let the value of the land in public use, B, now be a random variable whose value is only learned after the landowner invests x. A benevolent government will only take the land if it turns out to be worth more in public than in private use, given x. Thus, once B is realized, a taking will occur if and only if $B \geq V(x)$. Let $F(B)$ be the distribution function of

B, where $F'(B) \equiv f(B)$ is the density. The landowner is assumed to know $F(B)$, so that, at the time he makes his investment decision, he knows that the probability of a taking is equal to $1 - F(V(x))$ for any x.

The socially optimal choice of x now maximizes

$$F(V(x))V(x) + [1 - F(V(x))]E[B \mid B \geq V(x)] - x$$
$$= F(V(x))V(x) + \int_{V(x)}^{\infty} B dF(B) - x. \quad (5)$$

The resulting first-order condition is

$$F(V(x))V'(x) = 1, \quad (6)$$

which has the same interpretation as (2), with $F(V(x))$ replacing $1 - p$ as the probability that the land will not be taken. The expected private value of the land in this case is given by

$$F(V(x))V(x) + [1 - F(V(x))]C(x) - x, \quad (7)$$

and the resulting first-order condition for x is

$$F(V(x))V'(x) + [1 - F(V(x))]C'(x) + F'(V(x))V'(x)[V(x) - C(x)] = 1. \quad (8)$$

Comparison of (8) and (6) shows that lump sum compensation ($C' = 0$) is no longer sufficient for efficiency. Instead, compensation must be equal to the full value of the land at its efficient level of investment, or $C = V(x^*)$. Intuitively, full compensation is necessary to prevent the landowner from either overinvesting or underinvesting to alter the probability of a taking (Miceli 1991). Specifically, if $C(x) < V(x)$ the final term on the left-hand side of (8) is positive. Thus, the landowner will have an incentive to overinvest in order to reduce the probability of a taking since he expects to be undercompensated. Conversely, if $C(x) > V(x)$, he will have an incentive to underinvest to increase the probability of a taking since he expects to be overcompensated. Only a rule of full compensation, or $C(x) = V(x)$, will eliminate this incentive. Combining this result with the lump sum requirement yields the efficient rule, $C = V(x^*)$.[27]

[27] This result was anticipated by Cooter's (1985) option approach, under which the government acquires an option from the landowner that allows it to take the land at any point for a prespecified price. If this approach were used, P would replace $C(x)$ in (7), and the first-order condition in (8) would become $F(V(x))V'(x) + F'(V(x))V'(x)[V(x) - P] = 1$. (Note that the C' term drops out here because the price is viewed as fixed with respect to the investment choice, x.) It follows that $P = C(x^*)$ for efficiency.

The preceding compensation rule is not the only one that induces efficient investment in this case. Hermalin (1995) showed that two other rules are also efficient. Under the first, $C = B$; that is, the government must pay the landowner the full value of the public project in the event of a taking (the gain-based compensation rule). In this case, the landowner internalizes the social value of the land given in (5) and therefore makes the efficient investment choice. Alternatively, suppose that compensation is zero in the event of a taking, but the owner has the option to keep the land by paying the government its social value, B. A rational owner will exercise this "buy-back" option if and only if $B < V(x)$. Thus, only efficient takings will go forward. (Note, therefore, that the government's decision about when to initiate a taking is immaterial, as long as it truthfully reveals B to the landowner.) Under this rule, the landowner's expected return is equal to

$$F(V(x))E[V(x)-B \mid V(x)>B]+[1-F(V(x))]\cdot 0-x$$
$$=\int_{0}^{V(x)}[V(x)-B]dF(B)-x. \qquad (9)$$

Maximizing (9) with respect to x yields the first-order condition in (6). Thus, the landowner makes the efficient investment choice.

In this analysis, the landowner is able to affect the probability of a taking through investments that increase the private value of the land, $V(x)$. However, Innes (2000) notes that a landowner might also be able to affect the probability of a taking through investments that change the public value of the land. For example, he might be able to affect the desirability of his property as habitat for an endangered species that the government might seek to protect. This implies that the investment x shifts the distribution function of B; that is, the distribution becomes $F(B,x)$. However, this does not change the fundamental result that, when the landowner can affect the probability of a taking, zero compensation does not lead to efficient landowner investment. In this context, Innes shows that efficiency can be restored by compensating the landowner for the public value of the land if it is taken or by employing a "negligence compensation" rule under which landowners receive compensation only if they have acted efficiently when investing in the public value of their land.

4.2.2 Nonbenevolent (Majoritarian) Government

More realistic models of government behavior suppose that it acts in the interests of the majority of landowners, subject to budgetary restrictions (Giammarino and Nosal 2005). Thus, suppose that the government makes its taking decision by comparing the value of the public project to the amount of compensation that it must pay in the event of a taking, rather than to the opportunity cost of the land. Such a government is said to have "fiscal illusion," in that it only considers the budgetary impacts of its actions (BRS 1984). In this case, the government will initiate a taking if and only if $B \geq C(x)$, which implies that the probability of a taking is $1 - F(C(x))$, given x.

An obvious way to induce the government to make the correct taking decision is to set $C = V(x)$ (full compensation), but this rule will revive the moral hazard problem. One solution is to set $C = V(x^*)$, which solves both the fiscal illusion problem (because compensation is full) and the moral hazard problem (because compensation is lump sum). As an alternative, consider the gain-based rule that sets $C = B$. As one saw earlier, this rule solves the moral hazard problem, but a nonbenevolent government will be indifferent between taking the land and not taking it. The landowner, however, will only want the taking to occur if $B \geq V(x)$, which is the efficient condition (given x). Thus, if the government follows the wishes of the landowner, the rule will be (weakly) efficient regarding the taking decision.

Consider next Hermalin's buy-back rule. Again, the landowner will control the taking decision in this case and will do so efficiently since he will buy back the land if and only if $B < V(x)$. Because we showed that this rule also solves the moral hazard problem, it will achieve efficiency of both the land use and takings decisions.

The final rule we consider involves a "threshold test" for compensation as first proposed by Miceli and Segerson (1994, 1996). The rule works as follows: if the government acts inefficiently to take or regulate land, it will be required to pay full compensation, but if it acts efficiently, it will not have to pay.[28] Formally, the rule can be written as

$$C = \begin{cases} V(x), & \text{if } B < V(x^*) \\ 0, & \text{if } B > V(x^*). \end{cases} \tag{10}$$

The efficiency of this rule can be established as follows.[29] First, assuming that the landowner invested efficiently, the government will take or regulate the land if and only if it is efficient to do so because it wishes to avoid paying compensation, which would result in a loss of $B - V(x^*)$ when the taking is inefficient (i.e., when $B < V(x^*)$). As a result, landowners will anticipate that only efficient takings (or regulations) will occur and that compensation for these actions will be zero. Thus, they will choose x^*. This logic establishes that the Nash equilibrium under rule (10) will be efficient regarding both the land use and taking decisions.

As a positive matter, the rule in (10) has considerable appeal because it goes a long way toward explaining actual legal doctrine in the area of regulatory takings. Most obviously, the rule resembles the diminution of value test from *Pennsylvania Coal* because it establishes a threshold for when a regulation "goes too far." Specifically, compensation will be due when the regulation is inefficiently imposed. The threshold rule also provides a standard for applying the noxious use doctrine. Specifically, a noxious use can be defined as an activity that is efficiently regulated by the government and for which compensation is therefore not required. Note that, according to this interpretation, the noxious use doctrine and the diminution of value test are two ways of saying the same

28 Miceli and Segerson (1994) also propose a threshold rule under which compensation hinges on whether the landowner acted efficiently in investing in the property. This rule is similar to the "negligence compensation" rule subsequently proposed by Innes (2000) in the context where the landowner's investment affects the public use value of the land.

29 For a more detailed proof, see Miceli and Segerson (1994).

thing: the noxious use doctrine emphasizes cases in which the government has acted efficiently in imposing a regulation, and so compensation is not due (corresponding to the second line of (10)), whereas the diminution of value test emphasizes cases in which the government has not acted efficiently, and so compensation is due (corresponding to the first line of (10)).[30]

Similar reasoning shows that the *Lucas* nuisance exception fits easily into this framework. Recall that the nuisance exception allows the government to avoid paying compensation when it regulates activities that would be judged a nuisance under the state's common law. But how is a nuisance defined by the common law? The usual standard is reasonableness, which is defined by asking whether a reasonable person would conclude that the amount of harm caused by the activity in question outweighs the benefit.[31] In other words, it is based on a cost-benefit calculation. Thus, the threshold for compensation implied by the nuisance exception is identical to that under the proposed threshold rule.

Extending this logic shows that the threshold rule provides an alternative "neutral conduct" point for applying the harm-benefit rule. Specifically, by setting *neutral conduct* equal to *efficient conduct*, a regulation can be said to "confer a benefit" (and hence require compensation) when it imposes inefficient restrictions on landowners, whereas it can be said to "prevent a harm" (and hence not require compensation) when it imposes an efficient restriction. The threshold rule is also consistent with Fischel's normal behavior standard, which, recall, set normal behavior based on a landowner's reasonable expectations (i.e., based on community norms) about permissible land uses.

4.3 Constitutional Choice Models

A different class of land use models is based on the notion that the government is not a distinct entity with motives of its own but is merely the vehicle by which the citizens in a given jurisdiction act collectively to govern themselves, including deciding on land use policies and how to finance the cost of any required compensation. These "constitutional choice models" envision a process in which citizens initially hold a hypothetical constitutional convention to choose the compensation rule from behind a veil of ignorance about which particular parcels will be taken or regulated (Rawls 1971). Then, these same citizens choose the amount (but not the specific parcels) of land to be regulated or taken. Given this, individual landowners then make their investment decisions without knowing if their land will be subject to the taking. Finally, the actual takings decisions are made. In this setting, landowners know that they are both potential targets

[30] Based on this interpretation, the rule in (10) provides a means of reconciling the apparently conflicting decisions in *Mugler, Pennsylvania Coal, and Keystone Bituminous Coal Assn.* See Miceli (2011, chapter 5) for a detailed discussion of this aspect of the threshold rule.

[31] See Landes and Posner (1987, Chapter 2) for an economic theory of nuisance law.

of regulation but also beneficiaries of that regulation, and any compensation awarded to victims of regulation must be financed out of taxes levied on all citizens. In designing the compensation rule at stage one, citizens will therefore presumably take account of both sides of the public ledger and thus will not be overly generous or stingy with regard to compensation (Fischel 1995, 211).

The formal model of this process, first developed by Fischel and Shapiro (1989),[32] uses the following notation:

n = total number of identical parcels subject to a taking risk;
s = number of parcels to be taken for public use, $s \leq n$;
$B(s)$ = social value of the taken land, $B' > 0$, $B'' < 0$.
T = per-person tax liability to finance compensation.

All other variables are defined as above. The public good, B, is assumed to be pure in the sense that it is enjoyed by all landowners, including those whose land is taken. The tax is also assessed on all landowners.

In this model, citizen landowners, acting from behind a veil of ignorance, choose the number of parcels to take. However, since the specific parcels that will be taken are only revealed after landowners have made their investment decisions, in the initial state, each landowner assesses an equal probability, p, that his or her parcel will be taken, where $p = s/n$. The probability that a parcel will not be taken is therefore $1-p = (n-s)/n$. The wealth of landowners in the "no-taking" and "taking" states, respectively, are given by

$$w_N = V(x) - T + B(s) - x \tag{11}$$

$$w_T = C(x) - T + B(s) - x. \tag{12}$$

The expected wealth of each landowner is therefore

$$E(w) = (1-p)V(x) + pC(x) - T + B(s) - x. \tag{13}$$

The public budget must be balanced, so $nT = sC$, or, using the definition of p,

$$T = pC. \tag{14}$$

(This assumes that the tax is assessed solely to finance compensation for takings.)

[32] Also see Nosal (2001).

As in the BRS model, landowners choose x to maximize their expected wealth, taking the compensation rule as given. In the current model, they also take as given the amount of land to be taken, s (or, equivalently, the probability of a taking). The new element here is the tax payment, T. If landowners also treat T as fixed (i.e., a lump sum tax), then the first-order condition emerging from (13) would be identical to that in (4), and the BRS result would be obtained. (That is, $C' = 0$ would be a sufficient condition for efficient investment.) However, suppose, more realistically, that taxes are assessed proportionately on property values. That is, let $T = tV(x)$, where t is the property tax rate. Also, suppose that compensation is defined as a proportion of land value, or $C(x) = \alpha V(x)$ for some parameter α. Substituting these expressions for T and $C(x)$ into (13) and taking the derivative with respect to x yields the first-order condition

$$(1-p)V'(x)+p\alpha V'(x)-tV'(x)=1,$$

or

$$(1-p)V'(x)+(p\alpha-t)V'(x)=1. \tag{15}$$

Now observe that, according to the balanced budget condition in (14), $tV(x)=p\alpha V(x)$, or $t = \alpha p$. Thus, the second term on the left-hand side of (15) vanishes, yielding (2). The landowner therefore makes the efficient investment choice for any value of α; that is, any compensation amount. In other words, the compensation rule is irrelevant with respect to the land use decision. The reason for this result is that the compensation and tax distortions exactly offset each other through the balanced budget condition (Miceli 2008).

Finally, consider the choice of s, or how much land to take. Landowners also make this choice from behind a veil of ignorance to maximize (13), subject to the balanced budget condition in (14). Note that, in making this choice, they recognize the fact that $p(s) = s/n$. The resulting first-order condition for s, after canceling terms, is

$$nB'(s)=V(x), \tag{16}$$

which is the Samuelson condition for a pure public good. That is, land should be devoted to public use until the marginal benefit of the last unit taken equals its opportunity cost in private use. Thus, landowners authorize the efficient amount of takings for any given x. As was true of the land use decision, this result is independent of the form of the compensation rule and for the same reason. Thus, any compensation rule, including zero and full compensation, would yield efficient decisions under this model.

4.4 Dynamic Models of Development

The discussion of land use incentives to this point has been based on a static model of land use in the sense that the timing of the landowner's development decision was not an issue. This section extends the model to address two dynamic land use issues. The first concerns the timing of development, and the second concerns the impact of the landowner's expectation regarding the threat of regulation on the purchase price of the land.

4.4.1 The Timing of Development

The timing of development is an important issue because landowners faced with the threat of a regulation may be impelled to develop prematurely in order to reduce or eliminate that threat. For example, a developer may fill a wetland in order to preempt an impending ban on development. Similarly, a landowner may harvest the timber on his land prematurely to reduce the likelihood that it would provide habitat for a protected species (see, for example, Innes et al. 1998). In fact, Lueck and Michael (2003) find statistical evidence that timber plots with greater proximity to colonies of the endangered red-cockaded woodpeckers are more likely to be harvested early. Preemptive habitat destruction of this type could actually lead to an overall reduction in the population of a species that the land use restrictions are intended to protect.

A number of authors have presented theoretical models that investigate the impact of compensation on the timing decision (e.g., Miceli and Segerson 1996; Innes 1997; Riddiough 1997; Turnbull 2002; Lueck and Michael 2003). The basic insight regarding premature or preemptive development can be illustrated using the following two-period model of the land use decision, based on Miceli and Segerson (1996, Chapter 8). Let

V_N = present value of the land if developed now;
V_L = present value of the land if developed later;
p = probability that there will be a social benefit from preventing development in the future, given no development now;
B = the resulting social benefit from prohibiting development in the future (either in the form of an explicit benefit or a foregone harm);
V_0 = residual value of the land to the landowner if development is prohibited, where $0 \leq V_0 < V_L$;
C = compensation paid to landowners who are prohibited from developing in the future.

Assume that development in the present period cannot be prevented and that, once it goes forward, the social benefit from prohibiting development can never be realized. Also assume that if the land is not developed in period one and B is not realized in period two, then the optimal course of action is to develop the land (i.e., there is no chance that B will be realized in some future period).

The key question in this setting is whether it is optimal for the landowner to develop the land now or to wait. If he develops now, the social (= private) value of the land is fixed at V_N, whereas if he waits, the expected social value is $p(B + V_0) + (1 - p)V_L$. Thus, waiting preserves the option to use the land for the public project. It is therefore socially optimal to wait if and only if

$$p(B+V_0)+(1-p)V_L > V_N. \tag{17}$$

From the landowner's perspective, if he develops now, his return is V_N, whereas if he waits, it is $p(C + V_0) + (1 - p)V_L$, which differs from the social value by the inclusion of C rather than B in the first term. He will therefore choose to wait if and only if

$$p(C+V_0)+(1-p)V_L > V_N. \tag{18}$$

Comparing (17) and (18) reveals that the only compensation rule that guarantees that the landowner will make the correct decision is $C = B$. Any lesser amount of compensation, including zero compensation, runs the risk of causing premature development.

In addition to affecting the timing of development, the compensation rule can also affect landowners' incentives to reveal information about the public (e.g., conservation) value of their land. For example, in the absence of compensation, landowners do not have an incentive to cooperate with regulators seeking to collect information about public values prior to regulation. Providing some form of compensation (perhaps conditional on landowner behavior or coupled with other conditions) can encourage landowners to cooperate with the collection of information or to reveal private information (Polasky et al. 1997; Polasky and Doremus 1998; Innes et al. 1998).

4.4.2 Capitalization and Compensation

In his highly influential article, Michelman (1967) argued that a landowner who bought a piece of property under the threat of an impending regulation would have no claim for compensation if the regulation is later enacted because the purchase price would have appropriately discounted the cost of the regulation. In other words, the price would have "capitalized" the taking risk. This is a persuasive argument that has found its way into the case law. For example, in *H.F.H. Ltd. v. Superior Court*,[33] the Court denied relief to a landowner whose commercial property was rezoned as residential based on the argument that "the long settled state of zoning law renders the possibility of change in zoning

33 542 P.2d 237, 246 (1975).

clearly foreseeable to land speculators and other purchasers of property, who discount their estimate of its value by the probability of such a change" (246).

To demonstrate the capitalization argument formally (Miceli and Segerson 1996, chapter 6), let

V = market value of a piece of property if unregulated;
V_R = market value of the property if regulated, where $0 \leq V_R < V$;[34]
p = probability that a regulation will be imposed.

Suppose that the current owner wishes to sell the property after the regulatory threat has become public knowledge. Assuming that both buyers and sellers are risk neutral, the maximum amount a rational buyer would be willing to pay for the property would be

$$(1-p)V + p(V_R + C), \tag{19}$$

which reflects both the risk of the regulation and the expected compensation. In the case of zero compensation, the buyer would only pay $(1-p)V + pV_R < V$. Thus, if the regulation were subsequently imposed, he would not have a good argument for compensation since the sale price was appropriately discounted.

Epstein (1985, 151–158) and Fischel and Shapiro (1988) both point out, however, that the seller *would* have a good argument for compensation since, at the time the possibility of the regulation was first announced, he suffered a capital loss equal to the difference between the discounted sale price and V, the value of the land in the absence of a regulatory threat. In particular, his loss would be $V - [(1-p)V + pV_R] = p(V - V_R)$. The compensation question thus reverts to the original owner.

One way to eliminate the original owner's loss would be to pay full compensation, or $C = V - V_R$, to the buyer at the time the regulation is actually enacted. Note that substituting this amount into (19) yields V, which means that the seller suffers no loss at the time of sale. Alternatively, suppose the original owner is given the right to assert a takings claim at the time of sale based on the probability that the regulation will be enacted later. Stein (2000) refers to this as a "sale ripened" claim. In that case, the buyer would pay a price equal to $(1-p)V + pV_R$ since he would have no takings claim later (i.e., $C = 0$), but the seller would receive compensation equal to $p(V - V_R)$ at the time of sale, yielding him an overall return of $(1-p)V + pV_R + p(V - V_R) = V$. Again, his loss is eliminated. In theory, therefore, both approaches to the problem of a sale in the face of a regulatory threat are equivalent in the sense that the original owner is fully compensated. In practice, however, the sale-ripened approach is probably inferior both because it would entail more frequent litigation and because it involves the difficult informational burden of calculating the risk of a future regulation.

[34] It is also possible that a regulation could enhance the value of other properties, a point we return to in Section 4. (See, especially, note 37 and the associated text; also see Fischel [1995, 81].)

4.5 Balancing Risk and Incentives

A final reason for paying compensation is to provide risk-averse landowners with insurance against a taking or regulatory risk. In advancing this argument, Blume and Rubinfeld (1984) contend that the government needs to provide this protection because private insurance for takings risk is generally not available. (Also see Rose-Ackerman [1992] and Kaplow [1986, [1992].) Further, compensation must be mandatory, as by constitutional dictate, because a nonbenevolent government might otherwise refuse to insure those parcels that it plans to take or regulate. As we have already seen, however, full compensation for takings creates the risk of landowner moral hazard, so the optimal compensation rule must balance risk-sharing and incentives.[35]

4.6 The Social Cost of Funds

Aside from landowner moral hazard, the preceding discussion focuses primarily on alternative economic arguments for paying compensation. However, requiring compensation for land use restrictions would impose substantial resource requirements on regulatory bodies. For example, an early estimate by Goldstein and Watson (1997) suggested that requiring compensation for restrictions on wetlands development could cost regulatory agencies $350–400 billion in 1994 dollars, or roughly $500–560 billion in today's (2013) dollars. The revenue to pay compensation for regulatory takings would generally have to be raised through distortionary taxation, implying a potentially significant deadweight loss. This loss constitutes a cost of paying compensation that would have to be weighed against any benefits. For this reason, Innes (2000) argues for use of a compensation rule that provides efficient incentives with the lowest possible cost to the government. Note, for example, that the threshold rule in (10) would not entail any deadweight loss because, under this rule, no compensation is paid in equilibrium.[36]

5. In-Kind Compensation

Government regulations are pervasive and in many cases impose substantial burdens on property owners in terms of lost value. It does not follow, however, that property owners as a whole are necessarily made worse off by the imposition of such

[35] For a formal analysis of this tradeoff in a takings context, see Miceli and Segerson (2007, 49–50). For more general discussions of the tradeoff, see Stiglitz (1974), Holmstrom (1979), and Shavell (1979).

[36] See Innes et al. (1998) and Innes (2000) for a more detailed discussion of the implications of the deadweight cost of government taxation for the design of compensation rules.

regulations[37] or even that landowners directly subject to the regulatory restrictions are necessarily uncompensated. The reason for this paradoxical assertion is that the constitutional requirement of just compensation does not specify that compensation must always be *monetary*; it can also be *in-kind* (Epstein 1985, Chapter 14).

To see what this means, note that in settings where regulations are widely imposed, as in the case of zoning restrictions, all property owners are equally burdened by the regulations, but they are also equally benefited by them. These benefits provide a form of implicit or in-kind compensation to all affected landowners. This argument implies that a compensable taking has not occurred when a regulation secures an "average reciprocity of advantage" across all property owners.[38] It also reflects Michelman's (1967, 1223) assertion that "[a] decision not to compensate is not unfair as long as the disappointed claimant ought to be able to appreciate how such decisions might fit into a consistent practice which holds forth a lesser long run risk to people like him than would any consistent practice which is naturally suggested by the opposite decision."

5.1 Neighborhood Externalities and Compensation

The economics of this perspective is based on the problem of "neighborhood externalities," which represent the spillover effects (costs or benefits) that neighboring property owners impose on one another as a result of their land use decisions (Miceli 2011, 136–139). For example, the manner in which owners use or maintain their property obviously affects their own values but also the values of neighboring owners. Because owners generally ignore these spillover effects, they may engage in socially inefficient practices. For example, they may skimp on maintenance or paint their houses unusual colors (Davis and Whinston 1961).

Often, the problem of neighborhood externalities is solved privately by means of agreements, explicit or implicit, among residents (e.g., Cannaday 1994; Hughes and Turnbull 1996). In some cases, however, transaction costs limit the ability of these sorts of private responses to the problem of neighborhood externalities. This is especially true for large-scale externalities, such as those created by business operations or in very dense neighborhoods where residents are strangers. In these settings, it is in the interests of property owners to allow the government, acting in their collective behalf, to impose regulations that allow (or rather, "force") them to achieve an efficient land use pattern.

Based on this logic, regulations aimed at achieving this outcome would not be compensable takings because landowners as a group actually benefit from them. Thus, for example, a zoning regulation that prevents a landowner from opening a gas station in a residential neighborhood would *not* give rise to a taking claim because, although the claimant might

[37] See, for example, Truesdell et al. (2006) for evidence that wetlands regulations resulted in both "takings" and "givings"; i.e., reductions in property values for some landowners but increases in values for others.

[38] *Pennsylvania Coal v. Mahon*, 260 U.S. 393, 415 (1922).

be able to demonstrate a loss in value due to the restriction, this loss would only exist relative to a background in which all other landowners are prevented from engaging in such use. In other words, the claimant's "loss" is calculated based on his unilateral departure from the efficient land use pattern. Thus, he would have no claim for compensation. Indeed, if the regulation is efficiently structured, it would actually *raise* the claimant's property value relative to the situation in which no regulation is in place and all landowners are free to pursue their private interests unimpeded (Schall 1976). It is in this sense that all landowners are said to receive in-kind compensation for the restrictions imposed by broad (and efficient) government actions.

At the start of this chapter we asserted that, from an economic perspective, regulatory takings lie on a continuum with physical takings and therefore should, in principle, be treated the same. The preceding argument, however, provides a possible economic basis for the dissimilar treatment of the two types of cases. Specifically, the nearly universal payment of compensation for physical takings, which typically involves the acquisition of only a few parcels, reflects the concentration of costs on those owners whose land is taken and for which they receive little or no in-kind compensation. Thus, monetary compensation is necessary to satisfy the just compensation requirement. In contrast, the denial of compensation for most regulations reflects their broad impact across property owners, with its promise of in-kind compensation through increased property value, as measured relative to a world in which no regulations are imposed on individual land use decisions.

5.2 The Essential Nexus and Proportionality Requirements

A different sort of argument for in-kind compensation was evaluated by the Supreme Court in the case of *Nollan v. California Coastal Commission*.[39] The case concerned the buyer of a beachfront cottage who wanted to build a larger house on the lot. The California Coastal Commission granted permission for the expansion, but only on the condition that Nollan would agree to allow public access to the adjoining beach. Although beach access would clearly represent a physical invasion of the owner's property, and hence would constitute a taking under ordinary circumstances, the Commission's logic was that the requisite compensation was implicit in the Commission's granting of the development right. Thus, it maintained, no further compensation was due. The Supreme Court disagreed based on the argument that there had to be an "essential nexus" between any conditions attached by the government to the development permit and the impact of the proposed development. Since in the *Nollan* case it found that no such nexus existed, the implicit transaction was not legally acceptable.

It is important to note that the Court's ruling did not invalidate the logic of the government's argument; rather, it suggested that the proposed transaction was not acceptable

[39] 483 U.S. 825 (1987).

based on the *facts* of the case. The Supreme Court further refined its position on this issue seven years later in the case of *Dolan v. Tigard*,[40] which involved a requirement by the City of Tigard that the owner of a hardware store had to deed a portion of her property to the City for use as a bike path and open space as a condition for its allowing her to expand the store. The City's argument in making this request was that the open space and bike path would mitigate the costs to the community arising from the expanded business operation. The Court in this case found, in contrast to *Nollan*, that there did exist a nexus between the city's demand and the proposed expansion since the bike path and open space would in fact mitigate the resulting damage. However, it also suggested that the costs imposed on the landowner by the demand were disproportionate in comparison to the social benefits. In order to avoid the need for explicit compensation, the government had to demonstrate a "rough proportionality" between the social harm from the proposed development and the value of the property that was being taken in exchange. In other words, the in-kind benefit received by the landowner had to provide sufficient compensation for her losses in order to meet the requirement of just compensation.

Note that the difference between the rulings in *Nollan* and *Dolan* is merely one of degree. Whereas *Nollan* found *no* relation between the government's demand and the landowner's proposed development, *Dolan* found an *inadequate* relation (Fischel 1995, 349). Been (1991) nevertheless criticized the Court's awarding of compensation in *Nollan* (and presumably would have likewise criticized the reasoning in *Dolan*) based on the argument that the claimant was protected against what he deemed to be an unreasonable government demand by his option to exit the jurisdiction (Ghosh 1997). However, Fischel (1995, 345) notes that, in *Nollan*, the regulation in question was tied to the particular location—namely, the beachfront—rather than to an activity that the claimant could easily have resumed in a different location. Thus, exit did not provide an adequate escape for Nollan. The exit argument applies better to the facts of *Dolan*, which involved a business that the claimant presumably could have relocated without substantially diminishing its value.[41]

6. Summary of Economic Research on Takings Law and Future Directions

Among legal scholars, the prevailing view is that the case law on regulatory takings is muddled at best and chaotic at worst. This has been true ever since the Supreme Court's decision in *Pennsylvania Coal*, which erased the apparently bright line separating compensable

[40] 512 U.S. 374 (1994).

[41] Of course, businesses often have location-specific goodwill that would be lost in the event of exit.

takings from mere regulations that had been established in *Mugler*. The current state of the law, which epitomizes this confusion, is the multipronged balancing test from *Penn Central*. In our view, the contribution of the economics literature on takings, especially since the BRS article, has been to bring some order to the debate, first, by formalizing the fundamental tradeoff between the land use decisions of owners whose land is at risk of a regulation and the regulatory decisions of the government; and second, by showing how compensation rules can provide incentives for both decisions to be made efficiently. Although, as we have noted, much of the literature has been normative in the sense of prescribing optimal rules along these lines, we also emphasize that some rules can be interpreted in a positive light as rationalizing the balancing approach that has emerged from the case law.

Aside from incentives, economic theory has also pointed out the risk sharing features of compensation. When landowners are risk averse, optimal risk sharing is an important aspect of efficiency, especially because land represents the largest component of most people's wealth. The absence of private insurance for takings risk provides an important efficiency rationale for compensation, although as we noted, this factor may conflict with incentives for efficient land use in the face of that risk.

Although we believe that the economic approach to takings law has been exceedingly fruitful, there are several issues that warrant further work. One concerns the information requirements of the proposed rules, many of which depend on the efficiency of either the landowner's or the regulator's decision. The question of how the court would acquire such information needs to be answered before these rules can be used in practice. Related to this is the increasing need for courts, in assessing the efficiency of various policies, to value noneconomic goods like the environment or endangered species, and, on the other side of the ledger, to account for the nonmarket (but legitimately economic) value that owners attach to their land.[42] Another issue concerns the motivation of judges who play a big role in the evolution of the common law (no matter what the area) but whose objectives are not well understood.[43]

Finally, it is important to recognize the limitations of economic theory in evaluating takings law. After all, the Fifth Amendment may never have been intended to advance an economic theory of takings. A broader perspective therefore requires the allowance for other values besides efficiency, like fairness or justice.[44] The challenge for future research on the takings issue is therefore to incorporate these competing values to develop a more complete understanding of the case law in this area.

[42] On this last point, see Plassmann and Tidemann (2008) and Shapiro and Pincus (2007).

[43] As a result, most models of legal change ignore the role of judges or treat them in an ad hoc way.

[44] See, for example, Tideman and Plassmann (2005) and Niemann and Shapiro (2008).

ACKNOWLEDGMENTS

We acknowledge the helpful comments of Josh Duke on an earlier draft of this chapter.

REFERENCES

Been, V. 1991. 'Exit' as a constraint on land use exactions: Rethinking the unconstitutional conditions doctrine. *Columbia Law Review* 91: 473–545.

Blume, L. and D. Rubinfeld. 1984. Compensation for takings: An economic analysis. *California Law Review* 72: 569–628.

Blume, L., D. Rubinfeld, and P. Shapiro. 1984. The taking of land: When should compensation be paid? *Quarterly Journal of Economics* 99: 71–92.

Boyle, K., and R. Bishop. 1987. Valuing wildlife in benefit-cost analysis: A case study involving endangered species. *Water Resources Research* 23: 943–950.

Bromley, D. 1993. Regulatory takings: Coherent concept or logical contradiction? *Vermont Law Review* 17: 647–682.

Cannaday, R. 1994. Condominium covenants: Cats, yes; dogs, no. *Journal of Urban Economics* 35: 71–82.

Coase, R. 1960. The problem of social cost. *Journal of Law and Economics* 3: 1–44.

Cooter, R. 1985. Unity in tort, contract, and property: The model of precaution. *California Law Review* 73: 1–51.

Davis, O., and A. Whinston. 1961. The economics of urban renewal. *Journal of Contemporary Problems* 26: 105–117.

Ellickson, R. 1973. Alternatives to zoning: Covenants, nuisance rules, and fines as land use controls. *University of Chicago Law Review* 40: 681–782.

Ellickson, R. 1977. Suburban growth controls: An economic and legal analysis. *Yale Law Journal* 86: 385–511.

Epstein, R. 1985. *Takings: Private property and the power of eminent domain.* Cambridge, MA: Harvard University Press.

Epstein, R. 1995. *Simple rules for a complex world.* Cambridge, MA: Harvard University Press.

Fischel, W. 1985. *The economics of zoning laws: A property rights approach to American land use controls.* Baltimore: Johns Hopkins University. Press.

Fischel, W. 1995. *Regulatory takings: Law, economics, and politics* . Cambridge, MA: Harvard University Press.

Fischel, W., and P. Shapiro. 1988. Takings, insurance, and Michelman: Comments on economic interpretations of 'just compensation' law. *Journal of Legal Studies* 17: 269–293.

Fischel, W., and P. Shapiro. 1989. A constitutional choice model of compensation for takings. *International Review of Law and Economics* 9: 115–128.

Friedman, L. 1986. A search for seizure: Pennsylvania Coal v. Mahon in context. *Law and History Review* 4: 1–22.

Ghosh, S. 1997. Takings, the exit option and just compensation. *International Review of Law and Economics* 17: 157–176.

Giammarino, R., and E. Nosal. 2005. Loggers versus campers: Compensation for the taking of property rights. *Journal of Law, Economics, and Organization* 21: 136–152.

Gold, A. 1976. The welfare economics of historic preservation. *Connecticut Law Review* 8: 348–369.

Goldstein, J. H., and W. D. Watson. 1997. Property rights, regulatory taking, and compensation: Implications for environmental protection. *Contemporary Economic Policy* 15: 32–42.

Harrington, W. 1981. The Endangered Species Act and the search for balance. *Natural Resources Journal* 21: 71–92.

Hartmann, J., and J. Goldstein. 1994. The impact of federal programs on wetlands, Vol. II. A report to congress by the Secretary of the Interior, Washington, D.C.

Hermalin, B. 1995. An economic analysis of takings. *Journal of Law, Economics, and Organization* 11: 64–86.

Holmstrom, B. 1979. Moral hazard and observability. *Bell Journal of Economics* 10: 74–91.

Hughes, W., and G. Turnbull. 1996. Restrictive land covenant. *Journal of Real Estate Finance and Economics* 12: 9–21.

Innes, R. 1997. Takings, compensation and equal treatment for owners of developed and undeveloped property. *Journal of Law and Economics* 40: 403–432.

Innes, R. 2000. The economics of takings and compensation when land and its public use value are in private hands. *Land Economics* 76: 195–212.

Innes, R., S. Polasky, and J. Tschirhart. 1998. Takings, compensation and endangered species protection on private lands. *Journal of Economic Perspectives* 12: 35–52.

Johnson, M. 1977. Planning without prices: A discussion of land use regulation without compensation. In *Planning without prices*, ed. B. Siegan, 63–111 Lexington, MA: Lexington Books.

Kaplow, L. 1986. An economic analysis of legal transitions. *Harvard Law Review* 99: 509–617.

Kaplow, L. 1992. Government relief for risk associated with government action. *Scandinavian Journal of Economics* 94: 525–541.

Landes, W., and R. Posner. 1987. *The economic structure of tort law*. Cambridge, MA: Harvard Univ. Press.

Lueck, D., and T. Miceli. 2007. Property law. In *Handbook of law and economics*, eds. A. M. Polinsky and S. Shavell, 183–257 Amsterdam: Elsevier.

Lueck, D., and J. Michael. 2003. Preemptive habitat destruction under the Endangered Species Act. *Journal of Law and Economics* 46: 27–61.

Mandelker, D. 1987. Investment-backed expectations: Is there a taking? *Journal of Urban and Contemporary Problems* 31: 3–43.

Meltz, R., D. Merriam, and R. Frank. 1999. *The takings issue: Constitutional limits on land use control and environmental regulation*. Washington, DC: Island Press.

Miceli, T. 1991. Compensation for the taking of land under eminent domain. *Journal of Institutional and Theoretical Economics* 147: 354–363.

Miceli, T. 2008. Public goods, taxes, and takings. *International Review of Law and Economics* 28: 287–293.

Miceli, T. 2011. *The economic theory of eminent domain: Private property, public use*. Cambridge, MA: Cambridge University Press.

Miceli, T., and K. Segerson. 1994. Regulatory takings: When should compensation be paid? *Journal of Legal Studies* 23: 749–776.

Miceli, T., and K. Segerson. 1996. *Regulatory takings: An economic analysis with applications*. Greenwich, CT: JAI Press.

Miceli, T., and K. Segerson. 2007. The economics of eminent domain: Private property, public use, and just compensation. In *Foundations and trends in microeconomics*, Vol. 3. ed. W. Kip Viscusi. Boston: Now Publishers.

Michelman, F. 1967. Property, utility, and fairness: Comments on the ethical foundations of 'just compensation' law. *Harvard Law Review* 80: 1165–1258.

Niemann, P., and P. Shapiro. 2008. Efficiency and fairness: Compensation for takings. *International Review of Law and Economics* 28: 157–165.

Nosal, E. 2001. The taking of land: Market value compensation should be paid. *Journal of Public Economics* 82: 431–443.

Plassmann, F., and T. N. Tideman. 2008. Accurate valuation in the absence of markets. *Public Finance Review* 36: 334–358.

Polasky, S., and H. Doremus. 1998. When the truth hurts: Endangered species policy on private land with imperfect information. *Journal of Environmental Economics and Management* 35: 22–47.

Polasky, S., H. Doremus, and B. Rettig. 1997. Endangered species conservation on private land. *Contemporary Economic Policy* 15: 66–76.

Rawls, J. 1971. *A theory of justice*. Cambridge, MA: Belknap Press.

Riddiough, T. 1997. The economic consequences of regulatory taking risk on land value and development. *Journal of Urban Economics* 41: 56–77.

Rose, C. 1983. Planning and dealing: Piecemeal land controls as a problem of local legitimacy. *California Law Review* 71: 837–912.

Rose-Ackerman, S. 1992. Regulatory takings: Policy analysis and democratic principles. In *Taking property and just compensation: Law and economic perspectives of the takings issue*, ed. N. Mercuro, 25–44 Boston: Kluwer Academic.

Rose-Ackerman, S., and J. Rossi. 2000. Disentangling deregulatory takings. *Virginia Law Review* 86: 1435–1495.

Rubenfeld, J. 1993. Usings. *Yale Law Journal* 102: 1077–1163.

Sax, J. 1964. Takings and the police power. *Yale Law Journal* 74: 36–76.

Sax, J. 1971. Takings, private property, and public rights. *Yale Law Journal* 81: 149–186.

Schall, L. 1976. Urban renewal policy and economic efficiency. *American Economic Review* 66: 612–628.

Shapiro, P., and J. Pincus. 2007. Efficiency and equity in the assemblage of land: The L2H2 auction. Working paper, Department of Economics, University of California, Santa Barbara.

Shavell, S. 1979. On moral hazard and insurance. *Quarterly Journal of Economics* 93: 541–562.

Stein, G. 2000. Who gets the taking claim? Changes in law use law, pre-enactment owners, and post-enactment buyers. *Ohio State Law Journal* 61: 89–165.

Stiglitz, J. 1974. Incentives and risk sharing in sharecropping. *Review of Economic Studies* 79: 578–595.

Tideman, T., and F. Plassmann. 2005. Fair and efficient compensation for taking property under uncertainty. *Journal of Public Economic Theory* 7: 471–495.

Truesdell, M. K., J. C. Bergstrom, and J. H. Dorfman. 2006. Regulatory takings and the diminution of value: An empirical analysis of takings and givings. *Journal of Agricultural and Applied Economics* 38: 585–595.

Turnbull, G. 2002. Land development under the threat of taking. *Southern Economic Journal* 69: 468–501.

Wittman, D. 1984. Liability for harm or restitution for benefit? *Journal of Legal Studies* 13: 57–80.

CHAPTER 26

EMINENT DOMAIN AND THE LAND ASSEMBLY PROBLEM

JOSHUA M. DUKE

In *Kelo v. New London*, 545 US 469 (2005), the US Supreme Court spurred a renewed political, legal, and economic focus on eminent domain. The case concerned confiscations for urban redevelopment and the interpretation of "public use" from the Fifth Amendment of the US Constitution. The decision precipitated widespread outrage, and some states fashioned legislation to tie the hands of local governments in using eminent domain. *Kelo* therefore simultaneously expanded eminent domain and created a backlash. Most outrage focused on the perceived unfairness of eminent domain, and the facts of *Kelo* do indeed suggest significant burdens borne by those whose property was confiscated. Economic research is especially well positioned to inform the contentious discourse that underlies the efficiency-derived normative arguments used to support the legal precedent on eminent domain. An economic assessment of land market failures from eminent domain helps to distill institutional meaning for a post-*Kelo* world and to predict the impact of the decision on land markets.

The Fifth Amendment reads, in part, "nor shall private property be taken for public use without just compensation." This is the "eminent domain" clause. Legal scholarship and case law focus on two aspects of the clause. The first concerns "just compensation" questions, such as when is compensation due, and what is "just"? The second analyzes what constitutes "public use." Since the 1980s, two principal approaches emerged to analyze the economics of land market problems related to eminent domain, and these mirror the two legal aspects.

Economic research investigates when the payment of just compensation is efficient, and Blume, Rubinfeld, and Shapiro (1984) present the seminal model. Their article and ones that extend it offer many results, but the main finding is that full compensation may introduce a moral hazard incentive problem. In Chapter 25 of this handbook, Miceli and Segerson thoroughly review their own and other extensions of the Blume, Rubinfeld, and Shapiro (1984) model. These models largely focus on compensation, especially in the context of the efficiency of regulatory takings law. Although regulatory takings indisputably emerged from eminent domain law, regulatory takings law has since evolved into a complex set of bright-line and ad hoc tests, and these tests do not generally apply to cases of physical appropriation. Thus, regulatory takings and eminent domain are largely distinct in current law. In law, regulatory takings scholarship tends to focus on whether compensation should be paid for a governmental action, whereas eminent domain scholarship assesses on the constitutionality (or permissibility) of the action. Because just compensation is not the central focus of eminent domain law, economic modeling must also examine questions about the performance of the underlying land market.

This chapter focuses on the second area of law—what is "public use"—and a second economic problem associated with land market performance—land assembly. Economic land assembly models can help inform questions about the permissibility of eminent domain actions. The underlying efficiency problem is the inability of markets to deliver optimally sized redevelopment, which warrants some exercises of eminent domain. In land assembly problems, a developer attempts to buy and combine a set of contiguous urban parcels, which time has seen partitioned to an extent that private redevelopment faces difficulties in capturing economies of scale. Why can a developer and sellers not write socially optimal assembly contracts? The conventional economic story involves the holdout problem; sellers act as local monopolists, holding their perfectly heterogeneous product out of the market to gain market power and thereby capture a share of the redevelopment rents (Posner 1992, 56). Despite the plausibility of the story, surprisingly few economists have replicated this simple intuition with formal models.

This chapter begins with a brief summary of the eminent domain jurisprudence. Next, the main economic approaches to analyzing eminent domain are reviewed (readers are directed to Miceli and Segerson's chapter in this handbook for an in-depth assessment of the just compensation models). Eminent domain potentially corrects two inefficiencies in land markets: (1) inefficiency from holdouts and (2) the undersupply of public goods from urban redevelopment. Yet, eminent domain will not be efficient in all settings.

This chapter then develops an original model of land assembly that is able to explain inefficiencies in land assembly that derive from informational asymmetry. The model identifies conditions under which eminent domain is likely to be more efficient than private assembly and vice versa. One key finding is that eminent domain affects the performance of the land assembly market, and thus market failure must be assessed in light of holdout, public good, *and* the option for eminent domain. Beyond efficiency, the results suggest that information asymmetry is the predominant reason for failure in the land assembly market—it is here that the warrant for eminent domain resides. This model helps assess recent controversies arising from eminent domain jurisprudence, and it offers a new opportunity for further economic investigation of urban land market failures. The model shows that the untoward intentions associated with the popular debate about *Kelo* have been given too much credit for market assembly and eminent domain problems. Instead, it is information asymmetry that drives much of these conflicts. Simply, private information prevents socially optimal contracts. A better understanding of the conditions under which land markets fail to deliver assembly will then lead to a better understanding of how new legislation and judicial rules will deliver improved outcomes. A final section concludes.

1. The Law of Eminent Domain

Although the eminent domain clause of the Fifth Amendment is simple and brief, the past century saw protracted academic disputes and legal cases that shaped the permissible scope of eminent domain. Controversy was particularly acute with respect to the definition of "public use." In what has become known as the "narrow" view of public use, the public must actually use the confiscated property. For instance, under the narrow view, the public must actually use land confiscated from a farmer, say, as a public road. The "narrow" view likely frames most examples in newspapers, public discourse, and classrooms, so it likely captures the public perception of eminent domain.

However, case law tends to favor the "broad" view of public use, which allows for private use of confiscated property so long as the use is to public advantage. The broad view of public use evolved from a series of early cases (see *Strickley v. Highland Boy Gold Mining Company*, 200 US 527, 1906) and, most recently, in *Kelo*. *Berman v. Parker*, 348 US 26 (1954) involved large-scale, urban redevelopment in Washington, DC, which sought to confiscate some non-"blighted" properties along with blighted ones. The US Supreme Court found the confiscation to be permissible, even though private parties would end up with the redeveloped property because, for public advantage, the "area must be planned as a whole," and large-scale redevelopment cannot be accomplished on a piecemeal basis. The Court in *Berman* explicitly recognized the land assembly problem and seemed to define the public interest as preventing local monopolies: "If owner after owner were permitted to resist these redevelopment programs on the ground that his particular property was not being used against the public interest, integrated plans for redevelopment would suffer greatly" (348 US 26, at 35). Subsequent cases reinforced this broad view. This includes validating as public use eminent domain actions that prevent a land oligopoly (*Hawaii Housing Authority v. Midkiff* 467 US 229, 1984) and enhance market competition (*Ruckelshaus v. Monsanto Co.*, 467 US 986, 1984).

In the *Kelo* case, a five-justice majority validated the New London Development Commission's (NLDC) use of delegated eminent domain power to condemn 15 non-blighted houses for a loosely conceptualized, large redevelopment project. A rule emerged that "public use" will be even more broadly interpreted. Specifically, blight was no longer necessary for using eminent domain in redevelopment, and a new sufficient condition became the prospect of increasing a jurisdiction's tax base. Specific examples of synergies were described, including jobs, tax revenue, and "build(ing) momentum for the revitalization of downtown New London" (*Kelo* 545 US 469, 2005). Following the case, many legislatures drafted statutes to restrain public agencies from using eminent domain except under a narrow set of circumstances.

Several features of the *Kelo* case drive the renewed focus on the use of eminent domain. The lower court opinions and other source material suggest that this redevelopment project was not profitable for a private developer (i.e., the project had net private costs without subsidies), nor was it thought providential for the city of New London (i.e., net social costs). The houses were in a well-maintained neighborhood, suggesting the absence of that standard justification—removing blight. Moreover, the proposed redevelopment plan was generally vague about what would be created—a parking lot, retail opportunities, "support the existing park." In short, the costs of eminent domain on existing owners seem large, whereas the benefits of an assembled (large) parcel seem ambiguous at best. Adding to the tenuous nature of the project, it turns out that the NLDC was prepared to bear a range of costs of redevelopment—relying on its ability to mobilize public resources for the task. The web-based accounts of the conflict suggested that the developers hired by the NLDC might be handed assembled parcels at an agreeable discount over what would have been required had eminent domain not been available.

A flawed legal context was not aided by the inflammatory language deployed by several justices in their struggle with the facts at hand. Justice O'Connor complained that such practices, if allowed to persist unchecked, would find cities condemning cheap hotels to allow for the appearance of elegant and expensive ones. The heated dissents then contributed to the public outrage mentioned earlier.

The *Kelo* decision not only focused public attention on eminent domain law and practice, it also suggested an expanded "public use" doctrine. A host of economic implications are associated with this new legal dispensation. Holdouts may hinder socially beneficial land assemblies (i.e., positive externalities of redevelopment), whereas the deployment of eminent domain will solve the problem of holdouts but captures some subjective values from those in a position of being a monopoly supplier of needed parcels (the holdout). Existing economic models—particularly, Miceli and Segerson (2007)—offer insights into the gains and losses associated with both approaches to the development challenge. But some issues have remained unexamined. Unlike previous models predicated on certainty, there is abiding uncertainty on the part of developers and landowners about whether eminent domain can and will be used to the developer's advantage.

2. Recent Economic Models of Land Assembly

Existing models explore the holdout problem in at least four ways. One approach focuses on delay, whereby sellers threaten to hold up a socially valuable project (Menezes and Pitchford 2003); then, Nash bargaining occurs to divide the rents (Miceli and Segerson 2007). A second approach is to conceptualize redevelopment as delivering positive pecuniary externalities to adjacent owners. Then, a developer cannot fully internalize pecuniary benefits through markets (O'Flaherty 1994). The problem also may be viewed as one of anticommons, in which any seller can veto a socially optimal transaction and thereby prevent efficient projects from occurring unless they are sufficiently valuable (Heller 1998; Buchanan and Yoon 2000). A fourth approach shows that asymmetric information may prevent optimal contracting (Eckart 1985; Strange 1995). Unfortunately, little synthesis exists to reconcile these four approaches.

This chapter contends that there are really two distinct underlying efficiency problems: When should eminent domain be used, and when does the private market for land assembly fail? The first problem may be termed the "eminent domain problem," whereas the second is the "land assembly problem." These problems are related because eminent domain is rationalized to overcome land assembly market failures, including monopoly, externalities, and information asymmetry. However, strictly interpreted, the problems are separate, and land assembly inefficiencies with and without eminent domain ought to be assessed. In the next section, I offer a model that does this with a focus on land assembly problems arising from information asymmetry.

One paper was identified that addresses both the land assembly problem (arising from monopoly) and eminent domain as a solution to problem (Miceli and Segerson 2007). The justification for the existence of eminent domain is to overcome monopoly by preventing delay—forcing the timing of the transaction—or by preventing sellers from securing such high prices that redevelopments are inefficiently small, thereby forcing sellers to accept the land-market price as just compensation. Miceli and Segerson (2007) model the assembly market as a two-period game in which sellers engage in cooperative Nash bargaining with the developer. Their model is particularly effective in explicitly demonstrating the holdout phenomenon, and it also demonstrates how eminent domain mitigates the incentive problem, although at a possible cost to sellers. Miceli and Segerson (2007) conclude that eminent domain may lead to inefficiently large redevelopments.

Eminent domain may also internalize the positive redevelopment externality by forcing projects to be the optimal size. O'Flaherty (1994) discusses this possibility, but not explicitly, in the context of his land assembly model. Overall, O'Flaherty seems pessimistic about the corrective capacity of eminent domain because he believes local governments face political constraints that result in inefficiently small redevelopments.

The role of information in assessing eminent domain has received scant attention. Munch (1976) offered the closest approximation, considering the performance of eminent domain relative to land assembly in light of transaction costs. Although not modeled as an information asymmetry, the analysis of transaction costs may hold implications about the role of information in comparing the performance of market assembly compared to public assembly. Munch (1976) concludes that eminent domain is less efficient than decentralized market-driven land assembly. A major shortcoming in this analysis is that Munch (1976) ignores externalities, endogenous behavior, and does not first demonstrate the land assembly problem with the model.

This review of existing economic models suggests a gap in explaining the conditions under which eminent domain outperforms market assembly in allocating scarce resources. Eminent domain performance must be assessed relative to market assembly under the same conditions and with explicit consideration of the market failures of monopoly (i.e., holdouts), externalities, and information asymmetries. As will be shown, information asymmetry offers a great deal of explanatory power for land assembly market failure.

3. Application: A Land Assembly Model of Eminent Domain

As the preceding section clarifies, only a small set of existing models explains the land market inefficiency warranting eminent domain. In contrast, well-developed legal scholarship exists on eminent domain. The model presented here combines key facets of existing models (such as delay, positive redevelopment externalities, and compensation) with information asymmetry. The application seeks to offer a more complete explanation of market failure in settings where eminent domain may or may not offer efficiency-enhancing institutional change. The original model is also designed to capture the key features of modern eminent domain law, such as those found in the *Kelo* case. The features of case law include the private and social efficiency of assembly, the role of delay costs for the developer introduced by uncertainty, and a new concept of delay benefits to sellers.

The model reveals that the option of eminent domain in the future helps explain the failure of market-based land assembly in the present. In addition, the model illustrates the effects of the imposition of different decision rules on the public body exercising eminent domain. Eminent domain proceedings can be used to force a transaction with the developer, but, as one sees in *Kelo,* eminent domain can also be used to force *and* subsidize land-assembly transaction. Recent legislative limits on eminent domain in response to *Kelo* alter the behavior in private assembly markets, but they will not prevent all opportunities for redevelopment. This section develops the general model structure and identifies key assumptions. Then, in turn, the model is evaluated under two possible information conditions: complete and incomplete information. The model is evaluated and questions are posed about possible policy impacts.

3.1 Model Structure

Developer, D, seeks to assemble parcels owned by A and B into a redevelopment project. These three parties constitute society, initially, although subsequent assumptions allow possible positive redevelopment externalities (following O'Flaherty 1994). The model (Figure 26.1) shows a two-period market assembly interaction and, later, an eminent

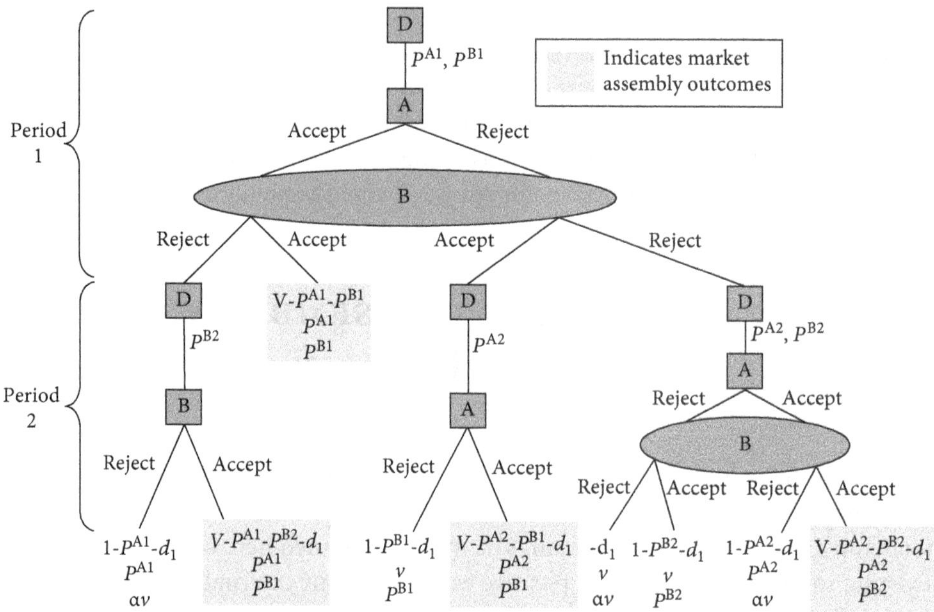

FIGURE 26.1 Market assembly subgame.

domain subgame (Figure 26.2) that will be imposed on the outcomes if market assembly fails. The initial period when nature selects the player type variables is omitted from the game in Figures 26.1 and 26.2:

- V is the value to D of the assembly measured in units of m, where m is the market value of one unassembled parcel;
- d_1, d_2 are the costs of project delay incurred by D (delay cost is explained below);
- v is the subjective value of A's parcel to A; and
- α is the subjective value parameter s.t. αv is the subjective value of B's parcel to B.

Nature also selects the high-type and low-type party. In period 1, D makes take-it-or-leave-it offers P^{A1} and P^{B1} to sellers, A and B, who then accept or decline. If one or both sellers decline, the developer bears delay cost, d_1, and makes new take-it-or-leave-it offers P^{A2} and P^{B2} to the remaining seller or sellers. This section develops a series of assumptions about parcel values and states of the world, which will guide the modeling sections.

3.2 Parcel Values

Let both parcels be homogeneous in market value, but let owners hold heterogeneous "subjective" values (following the term from Posner 1992, 57). Owners have

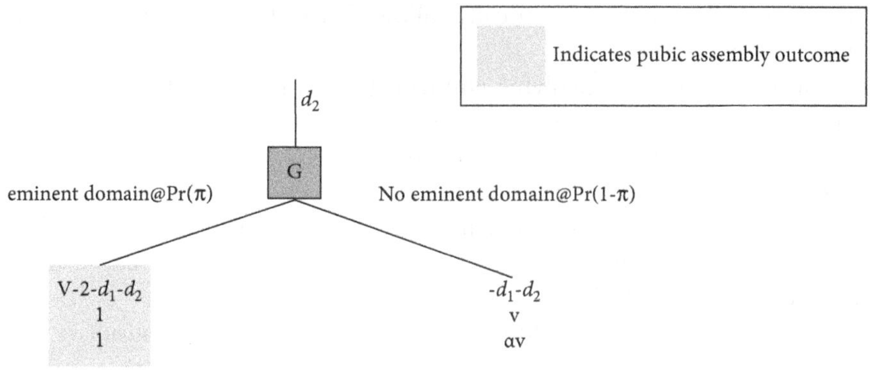

FIGURE 26.2 Eminent domain subgame.

heterogeneous values for many goods, such as housing, because individual preferences vary over the many amenities and disamenities that constitute the housing good. Heterogeneity for a given type of house manifests as owners' minima in their willingness to accept (WTA) compensation. Owners with WTA at or below current market prices (adjusted for transactions costs) are actively marketing their houses. Owners who are not in the market, therefore, reveal that they hold a subjective value in excess of the market value. As Miceli (2011, 57–58) explains, many scholars anticipate that the difference between subjective value and market value increases over time for homeowners as they gain idiosyncratic ties to their houses. For this model, simplifying assumptions are made to study owners with subjective values that would be most likely to lead to holdouts.

Assumption 1. *Sellers own homogeneous parcels with market value*, $m = 1$.

Assumption 2. *Sellers hold heterogeneous subjective values*: v for A, αv for B, where $\alpha \in (0,1)$.

The actual price level is immaterial, so a numéraire scaling is imposed such that all other values modeled are interpreted as relative to a single-parcel market value. The homogeneity assumption simplifies the model by controlling for a parcel characteristic that does not contribute to explaining the occurrence of the assembly problem. Subjective-value heterogeneity, however, does help explain why one seller might require a higher payment than another and, equally, captures seller willingness to hold out for a certain offer and to bear risk. In addition, heterogeneity allows for imperfect information on the part of *D* to have a more realistic complicating effect on assembly. A standard assumption in assembly models is that owners are not willing to sell at current market prices.

Assumption 3. *Sellers are not currently marginal sellers in the market*: $v > \alpha v > 1$.

This is consistent with the economic concept of upward sloping supply. The intuition that subjective value exceeds market value is well recognized in economics and law,[1] although it does not automatically follow that just compensation for eminent domain should exceed $m = 1$.[2]

Much of the controversy involving eminent domain in law and economics centers on the payment of $m = 1$, as "just compensation," to owners with higher, but unobservable, values. Posner (1992, 57) describes the quantity $v - 1$ as a tax on subjective value. This is also the distinction in institutional economics between value in use and value in exchange. From the perspective of a planner, representing the rest of society, this same quantity can be seen as a fiscal savings. However, this fiscal savings may lead to some projects that are inefficiently large.

What does it mean to be a "holdout"? This model will operationalize two forms of holdout behavior.

> **Definition 4.** *A seller is a* ***weak holdout*** *when the seller demands or is paid more than the market value, but less than the seller's reservation value:* $v > P^A > m$; $\alpha v > P^B > m$.
>
> **Definition 5.** *A seller is a* ***strong holdout*** *when the seller demands or is paid more than the seller's reservation value:* $P^A > v$; $P^B > \alpha v$.

This chapter introduces the strong versus weak holdout distinction to capture different distributional outcomes and potential unobservable resource allocation inefficiencies affected by eminent domain. A strong holdout seeks to extract rents from the redevelopment project, whereas a weak holdout is taxed by eminent domain. Because of the unobservability of subjective values, planners and other observers may perceive holdouts to be any seller demanding or getting paid more than the market value. The model focuses on the strong holdout phenomenon because it is most likely to trigger inefficiently small redevelopments, and it captures the monopoly-type rent extraction best.

3.3 Social Value of Assembly

Two sets of assumptions describe possible states of the world regarding the social value of redevelopment relative to that of the unassembled parcels and include possible positive redevelopment externalities. The following assumptions measure the relative value of V.

[1] Posner (1992, 56) captures this perspective well: "The familiar argument that the eminent domain power is necessary to overcome the stubbornness of people who refuse to sell at a 'reasonable' (that is, the market) price is bad economics. If I refuse to sell for less than \$250,000 a house that no one else would pay more than \$100,000 for, it does not follow that I am irrational, even if no 'objective' factors such as moving expenses justify my insisting on such a premium. It follows only that I value the house more than other people. This extra value has the same status in economic analysis as any other value."

[2] Some do not view the subjective value as a legitimate measure of value for conducting efficiency analyses.

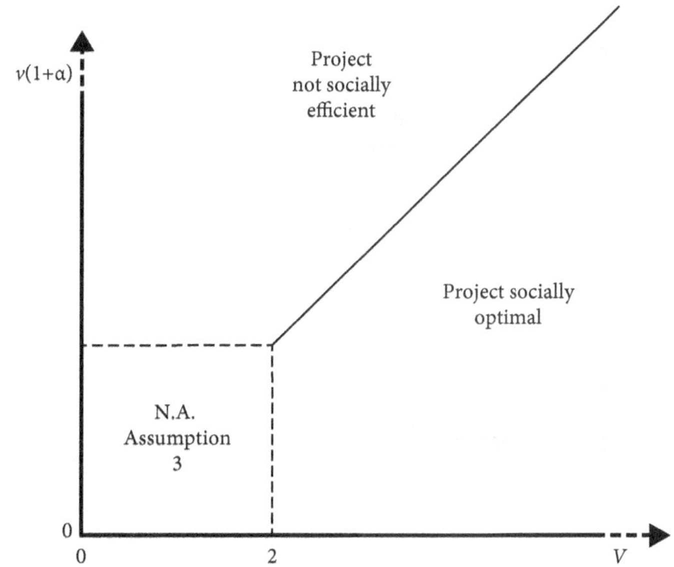

FIGURE **26.3** Social optimality of redevelopment.

Assumption 6. *Assembly is a potential Pareto improvement (PPI):* $V \geq v(1+\alpha)$.
Assumption 7. *Assembly is not a PPI, but is privately efficient for D:* $v(1+\alpha) > V \geq 2$.

A Pareto improvement (assumption 6) occurs if gains from the project are distributed to all three parties so that no one is made worse off. If the social value of the project is less than the subjective values but more than the market values, then assumption 7 holds. In other words, assembly appears financially efficient but is not economically efficient because it consumes more resources than it creates. Under eminent domain, developers and planners may perceive such projects to be "efficient" because the benefits of development exceed just compensation, which are v and αv when awarded at market values. These values are compared in Figure 26.3.

Redevelopment projects are often rationalized with positive externalities. For example, the redevelopment in *Kelo* was rationalized as a way to capture "synergies" with a recently sited, neighboring large firm. Following O'Flaherty (1994), let the value of the positive externality be Y measured in units of m.

Assumption 8. $Y \geq 0$, *where the addition of Y is large enough to make Assumption 7 into Assumption 6.*

If assumption 6 and 8 hold, then the PPI is enhanced by the externality but social efficiency is not affected: $V + Y \geq v(1+\alpha) > 2$. If assumptions 7 and 8 hold, then the PPI is directly affected by the externality: $V + Y \geq v(1+\alpha) > 2$. Although many possible impacts of externalities on the social value assumptions are possible, the model focuses only on these two. Figure 26.4 displays these relationships.

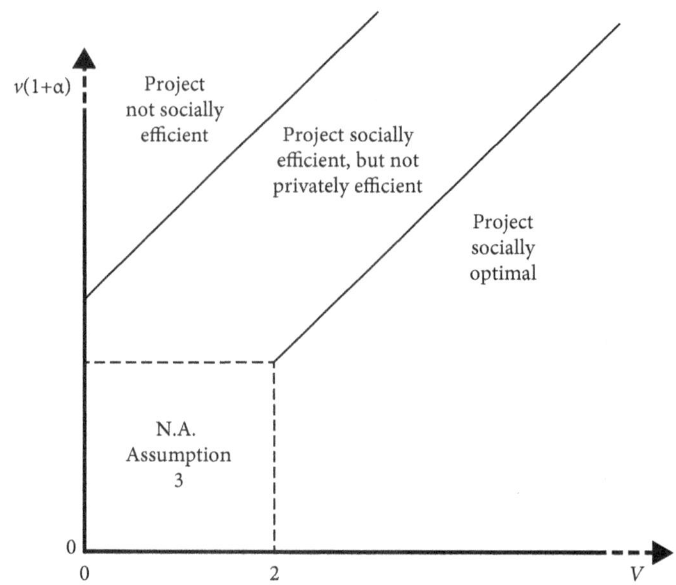

FIGURE 26.4 Social optimality of redevelopment with externalities.

3.4 Time and the Costs of Delay

The game consists of two periods of market assembly interactions and a third period of public assembly (eminent domain). Note that the game can run for 1, 2, or 3 periods. Delay costs, d_1, are imposed on developers unable to secure assembly during negotiation period 1. If period 2 negotiations also fail, then the wait for possible eminent domain imposes a second delay cost, d_2.

Delay does not affect sellers' decision making in market assembly. Specifically, any given price in period 1 is valued equivalently to that same price in the future because the discounting cost perfectly offsets the benefit of owning the parcel during the delay. This assumption is likely reasonable for most cases; otherwise, disequilibrium prevails and owners would have some incentive to enter the market in the present.

Consider the five instances of failed market assembly in the subgame in Figure 26.1 (occurring when one or both sellers reject the offer in period 2). Then, a legislative or quasi-judicial body (the "public authority") may use eminent domain. As in *Kelo*, the use of eminent domain for redevelopment may involve the public authority pursuing eminent domain and then turning over parcels to developers in exchange for market value, $m = 1$, or even less when the parcels are reallocated as a discount. The period of time waiting for public action at future time, T, imposes yearly eminent domain delay costs, ρ,[3] on

[3] In developing a land redevelopment plan involving assembly, D bears a host of project planning costs. Some of these costs are sunk, but others incur as yearly costs, ρ. The yearly costs, ρ, might include

the developer such that $d_2 = \rho(1 - \delta^T)/r$, where $r < 1$ is the discount rate and $\delta^t = 1/(1 - r)^t$ is the discount factor that raises nominal eminent domain subgame payoffs to those at the market assembly time.

Sellers view the delay of eminent domain differently than does the developer. At time T, eminent domain occurs and, in expectation, sellers will anticipate nominal gains that are less than their nominal subjective value (this is shown below). However, at all periods leading up to T, sellers enjoy their full subjective values (in annualized, nominal terms). In effect, the longer eminent domain is put off (i.e., as $T \to \infty$), the more subjective value under eminent domain approaches that of subjective value with no eminent domain. Consider an example. A seller facing eminent domain at time 10 derives greater utility from his or her parcel than if he or she faced eminent domain at time 3 because that seller will be able to enjoy full subjective value during time 3 to 10. This becomes a delay *benefit* for the seller. However, it is not valued at an annualized v; rather, the benefit becomes an avoided opportunity cost of the difference between residing in the parcel and moving. The next best option is best measured by the market value, $m = 1$, and thus the delay benefit is: $d_3 = (v - 1)(1 - \delta^T)/r$ and $d_4 = (\alpha v - 1)(1 - \delta^T)/r$. The author was unable to find the delay-benefit concept in the existing literature.

After T years, the public authority renders a decision—one unknown prior to T. The unknowable aspect of this decision pertains to (1) whether or not the project will proceed, (2) the scope of the project, or (3) whether a developer's desired parcels will be included in a broader project. Redevelopment occurs when assembly is mandated via eminent domain. The outcome is treated as an exogenous, common-knowledge parameter where the probability of redevelopment is distributed uniformly $\pi \epsilon (0,1)$.[4]

Let impacts on the developer and sellers incurred in market assembly increase with the discount rate, such that V, d_1, m, v, and α, are equivalent at any time. Then, the developer payoff in the public assembly subgame is $V - 2 - d_1 - d_2$ if urban redevelopment occurs, and $- d_1 - d_2$ otherwise—assuming the participation constraint is satisfied. Just compensation is a market-value measure, $m = 1$. The public assembly payoff assumes that the developer must pay for the parcels instead of a public body confiscating, paying $m = 1$, and then turning the parcels over to the developer at zero cost. The payoff to each seller is $m = 1$ if urban redevelopment occurs and is the subjective value otherwise. The expected payoff for all parties, with risk neutrality assumed, will simply weight the payoffs by the probabilities of their occurrence.

the costs of sustaining the development plan if delayed. For instance, the development requires access to capital and hedging against future increases in capital costs requires "lock-in" fees. A planning staff may need to be maintained during the delay period. Also, delay involves the recurrent costs of negotiation and gathering new information on an evolving local economy and land market.

[4] The options of no eminent domain ($\pi = 0$) and certain eminent domain ($\pi = 1$) are not allowed. The former is equivalent to the market assembly game. Both can potentially complicate the algebra.

3.5 Information

Asymmetric information exacerbates assembly conflicts, and much of the acrimony over eminent domain arises from fairness concerns: the presumption that subjective values exceed just compensation and the loss of autonomy in participating in a market. D has private information about V, d_1, and d_2, whereas m is common knowledge, as is the game structure. One limitation of the model (and an opportunity for future research) is that D cannot invest in gaining information and cannot alter the structure of the game to sort sellers. Furthermore, the model does not include a bargaining interaction, which, when coupled with the sequential structure of the game, implies that seller choice is not affected by knowledge of V. This contrasts with Eckart (1985) and Strange (1995) who produced land assembly problems from sellers' lack of knowledge about V, although these articles proposed different game structures.

For A and B, information is imperfect because they move simultaneously, and it is incomplete because they do not know the other's subjective value. The game structure and information availability thereby appear advantageous to D, who can make take-it-or-leave-it offers to sellers. This advantage probably captures reality better than that of market-savvy sellers, and the apparent structural advantage to D will be shown to balance with sellers' monopolist power.

This chapter conceptualizes the complications of information on assembly in two ways. First, governments do not exercise eminent domain with certainty. The process of eminent domain involves competing claims in the political process, where a developer may lobby for a project and sellers lobby against. Exogenous factors, such as the goals of political leaders and financial pressures within the community, also affect the decision to use eminent domain. In the model, eminent domain occurs with the common-knowledge probability of π. From D's perspective, the risk that eminent domain will not be used, $1 - \pi$, becomes a cost. This parameterization extends the Miceli and Segerson (2007) model, where eminent domain occurs with certainty and immediately at the developer's behest.

The second complication is an information asymmetry, which is modeled only as it affects D. The information in the game is complete when D knows v and α and is otherwise incomplete.

Assumption 9. *Complete information: D knows* v and α.

Assumption 10. *Incomplete information: D does not know* v and α, but knows assumption 3 (i.e., that A and B are not marginal sellers).

Incomplete information also implies D cannot identify the low type. In reality, a developer would likely have some information about sellers' subjective values. Future empirical and theoretical efforts may choose to explore these information assumptions and their impact on behavior and the efficiency of eminent domain.

4. Application: Land Assembly with Complete Information

Although complete information (D knows v, α) may not completely characterize reality, such an assumption is useful for establishing a baseline for market assembly performance. Proponents of market assembly (and opponents of public assembly) argue that markets produce superior results to those of eminent domain. However, perceptions of market superiority in assembly are likely driven by subtle assumptions about the insignificance of prevailing market imperfections, such as relatively low market power, no positive externalities, and low transaction costs. This is not surprising. Standard economic models show that perfect markets will automatically align private decisions with socially optimal allocations of resources. In part, market assembly advocates also may be driven by the Pareto improvement fairness characteristic of voluntary market transactions. In contrast, public assembly advocates might be driven by the same criteria of fairness and efficiency, seeing instead massive imperfections in market assemblies and monopolists holding up socially beneficial projects to extract undeserved holdout rents.

Assumptions about information lie at the heart of disputes about eminent domain. These assumptions are largely driven by one's worldview, and reconciling evidence is difficult to come by. However, theory can offer insight. The ability of markets to deliver optimal results without information problems must be assessed—and this assessment must be made *relative* to eminent domain under similar conditions. This section evaluates relative performance under assumptions of complete information. Then, in the next section, the relative ability of market and public assembly under a limited information condition is assessed.

4.1 Behavior in Market Assembly Without Eminent Domain Under Complete Information

For now, let eminent domain be unavailable if D fails to purchase both parcels during the market assembly period (only the Figure 26. 1 subgame). Seller payoffs are straightforward because, as argued earlier, delay does not affect seller decision making. If a seller accepts an offer, then the seller receives P^{It} for $I = A,B$, $t = 1,2$. If a seller rejects the offer, A receives v, and B receives αv. For D, market assembly payoffs are $V - P^{A1} - P^{B1}$ if in period 1 and $V - P^{A2} - P^{B2} - d_I$ if in period 2. If no seller accepts an offer, then D incurs delay cost, $-d_I$. If one seller accepts and the other rejects, then D may resell the purchased parcel for $m = 1$, but bears the costs of one purchase P^{It} for $I = A,B$, $t = 1,2$, and the delay, $-d_I$.

Will D participate in market assembly? Although Figure 26.1 does not allow explicitly for D to opt out of the interactions in periods 1 and 2, D would never participate in any market assembly game when it would be privately inefficient.

Participation Constraint D. *D participates in period 1 if $V - P^{A1} - P^{B1} \geq 0$, and in period 2 if $V - P^{A2} - P^{B2} - d_1 \geq 0$, where P^{It} for $I = A,B$, $t = 1,2$, are optimal offers.*

Characterizing equilibrium is straightforward, with backward induction identifying optimal strategies. Consider the three second-period subgames. Optimal seller choice is independent of the other seller's choice, and sellers cannot credibly reject any take-it-or-leave-it offer that makes them better off or (for simplicity) leaves them indifferent. A will accept only if $P^{At} \geq v$, and B will accept only if $P^{Bt} \geq \alpha v$, for $t = 1, 2$. Otherwise, each rejects. D deduces sellers' simple acceptance rule and will drive A and B to indifference in period 2: $P^{A2} = v$ and $P^{B2} = \alpha v$. D prefers to avoid d_1 and would thus also drive sellers to indifference in period 1. If the participation constraint holds, in equilibrium, sellers accept the subjective value offer in both periods.

One envisions three possible stories to support seller behavior. Sellers do not act strategically beyond the structure of this game. These sellers accept a price that drives them to indifference. In order to focus on other model aspects of interest, this story is maintained. However, two competing perspectives exist. Sellers might require an epsilon bonus in the period 1 to break the indifference within period 1 and between periods 1 and 2. This epsilon could be modeled, but it would needlessly complicate the presentation. A third possibility is that sellers would strategically seek to bargain over the delay costs, which they can impose unilaterally by rejecting the period 1 offer. Such bargaining has been thoroughly modeled by Miceli and Segerson (2007). If the epsilon bonus and strategic delay cost comprise part of the sellers' reservation prices, the two competing perspectives become analytically identical to the maintained assumption that sellers accept the indifference price.

Table 26.1 compares equilibria of this complete information game under the states-of-the-world assumptions about externalities and social value. Without externalities (assumption 8 does not hold), equilibria depend only on the assumption about the social value of the project, V, but, in both cases, market assembly is socially optimal. If the project is a PPI (assumption 6), then market assembly occurs and, if otherwise (assumption 7), D does not participate. Also, if the PPI assumption holds, then market assembly produces a Pareto improvement because sellers receive payments equivalent to their subjective values and D keeps all gains from pursuing the project. This analysis is not surprising; when no market imperfections exist, markets yield socially optimal outcomes.

If externalities exist, then social optimality depends on the social value assumption. If the project is already privately efficient (assumption 6), then the addition of externalities (assumption 8) does not alter market performance. However, if the project is not a PPI (assumption 7, 8), then the project does not occur despite its social optimality. The beneficiaries of the externality do not gain. This represents the prototypical public-goods type market failure and captures the argument made by planners and politicians in favor of using eminent domain for redevelopment.

Table 26.1 Equilibria in market assembly games of complete information

		Value of project			
		PPI		Not PPI, privately efficient	Privately inefficient
Equilibrium conditions		Complete info No externality	Externality	Complete Info No externality	Externality
D participates	Yes or no?	Yes	Yes	No	No
D offers					
	p^{A1}	v	v		
	p^{B1}	αv	αv		
	p^{A2}	v	v		
	p^{B2}	αv	αv		
A plays					
	Period 1	Accept	Accept		
	Period 2	Accept	Accept		
B plays					
	Period 1	Accept	Accept		
	Period 2	Accept	Accept		
Payoffs					
	D	$V-v-\alpha v$	$V-v-\alpha v$		
	A	v	v		
	B	αv	αv		
	3rd parties	N.A.	Y	N.A.	0
Analysis					
Assembly	Occurs?	Market	Market	No	No
	Is assembly optimal?	Yes	Yes	No	Yes
Social Welfare	Δ	$V-v(1+\alpha)$	$V-v(1+\alpha)+Y$	0	0
	Maximizes?	Yes	Yes	Yes	No*
	PI?	Yes	Yes	N.A.	No

* Fails to gain *Y*. PI, Pareto improvement; PPI, potential PI.

Overall, market assembly under complete information produces results that are intuitive and straightforward. Market assembly can achieve social optimality when markets lack imperfections and when redevelopment is privately efficient. However, market assembly does not always produce socially optimal results, even under complete information. Public goods associated with redevelopment may lead to an undersupply of assembly (in previous literature, inefficiently small redevelopments). In addition, there exists no holdout problem in this game because sellers always receive their subjective values, at minimum.

Two competing, but difficult to reconcile, visions of redevelopment likely dictate how severely one evaluates the ability of market assembly to generate social optimality. One vision views redevelopment externalities as substantive and pervasive. It is for exactly these reasons—revitalization of moribund urban economies—that redevelopment is proposed. This camp worries about the ability of market assembly alone to deliver optimal redevelopments even under the ideal conditions of perfect assembly. A second vision would likely argue that these externalities themselves produce the appropriate market incentives for developers to internalize them by expanding the scale of their redevelopments. If one truly believes that information is complete, then no obstacles in this model (except the two-seller structure) would stop developers from achieving a socially optimal scale of redevelopment.[5]

Collectively, this assessment warrants questions of how market assembly will perform under conditions of incomplete information. Yet, this model does not fully characterize the performance of assembly markets because eminent domain is not modeled. In Section 4.2, the assumption of complete information is maintained so the model can inform the performance of assembly markets when eminent domain becomes available. As one may suspect, under complete information, eminent domain will benefit D and harm A and B relative to the land assembly market alone.

4.2 Behavior in Market Assembly with Eminent Domain Under Complete Information

Eminent domain is rationalized as a way to achieve socially valuable land assembly when market assembly fails. Following the preceding subsection, the assembly market's failure under complete information refers to a public-goods market failure rather than holdouts from monopoly or delay. This subsection will show that, although eminent domain can overcome this market failure, the option of public assembly distorts the incentive for a developer to negotiate in the market. This option means that sellers can never do as well as they might in market assembly without eminent domain. The equilibrium described here shows that sellers accept offers below their subjective values, and this might lead to inefficiently large redevelopments (under assumption 7). The developer will do better with eminent domain. These results correspond to the public concerns in *Kelo* and other cases about the "unfairness" of eminent domain. Indeed, eminent domain does have unfavorable distributional impacts on sellers (under this model structure and assumptions). However, the model results will also show that greater uncertainty about eminent domain and longer delays attenuate the developer's advantage in eminent domain.

Eminent domain changes the strategies of D, A, and B. Sellers now trade off offers with expected payoffs under the risk of confiscation rather than subjective values. For now, assume there is no delay benefit to sellers. Sellers' expected eminent domain payoff is $\pi + (1 - \pi)v$ for A and $\pi + (1 - \pi)\alpha v$ for B. So, in period 2, sellers will accept if D's offer exceeds expected eminent domain payoff: A accepts if $P^{A2} \geq \pi + (1 - \pi)v$, and B accepts

[5] Obstacles outside the model might include capital and bargaining issues with holdouts (see Miceli and Segerson 2007).

if $P^{Bt} \geq \pi + (1 - \pi)\alpha v$. Otherwise, they each reject. Knowing this, D lowers the period 2 offers to force indifference. A similar assessment can be made in period 1; sellers must accept the expected indifference payoff from eminent domain.

Equilibria can now be described. D's participation constraint remains the same as in market assembly alone, except now the optimal offers are less (see proposition 1 below). This expands the set of interactions in which D will participate (see proposition 2), creating a difference between social optimality and private efficiency in the absence of externalities. D offers $P^{A1} = P^{A2} = \pi + (1 - \pi)v$, $P^{B1} = P^{B2} = \pi + (1 - \pi)\alpha v$. A and B "accept" in both periods. There are several implications.

Proposition 1. Under complete information, sellers receive and accept lower market assembly offers when eminent domain is available than when it was not. The developer does better.

Proof. It is sufficient to show for A that the acceptable offer under eminent domain is less than the acceptable offer without eminent domain: $\pi + (1 - \pi)v < v$. This implies $\pi(1 - v) + v < v \implies \pi(1 - v) < 0$. The LHS is negative because of assumptions: $\pi \epsilon (0,1)$ and $v > 1$. Also, because D pays less to A and B, D is better off.

Proposition 2. *With the eminent domain option, D will participate under more conditions than under market assembly alone. Let this set of land market conditions belong to set Z.*

Proof. Let points in set Z be project-seller value pairs: $\{v(1 + \alpha), V\}$. Consider only period 1, because assembly occurs in equilibrium in period 1. Under market assembly, the participation constraint showed that D participated in all market conditions when $V \geq v(1 + \alpha)$. Let these conditions be set, X. Proposition 2 is proved if X is a perfect subset of Z and $X \neq Z$. This holds if the market assembly participation constraint without eminent domain, $V \geq v(1 + \alpha)$, differs (and produces more possible pairs) from the one with eminent domain, $V \geq \pi + (1 - \pi)v + \pi + (1 - \pi)\alpha v$, or if $v(1 + \alpha) > \pi + (1 - \pi)v + \pi + (1 - \pi)\alpha v$. Simplifying, $v + v\alpha > \pi + v - v\pi + \pi + \alpha v - \alpha v\pi \implies 0 > 1 - v + 1 - \alpha v \implies v + \alpha v > 2$, which is true by assumption 3.

Proposition 3. When no externalities exist, eminent domain expands the set of market assemblies, and each of these new assemblies is socially inefficient.

Proof. From proposition 2, conflicts in Z but not in X satisfy: $V \geq \pi + (1 - \pi)v + \pi + (1 - \pi)\alpha v$, but not $V \geq v(1 + \alpha)$. Thus, the additional market assemblies conflicts created by eminent domain are those where $v(1 + \alpha) > V \geq \pi + (1 - \pi)v + \pi + (1 - \pi)\alpha v$. This condition matches the definition of social inefficiency. These conflicts are displayed in Figure 26.5.

These conditions show that merely having the possibility of eminent domain changes many aspects of market assembly. This is because complete information allows D to settle each privately efficient conflict in market assembly and at a lower cost to D because

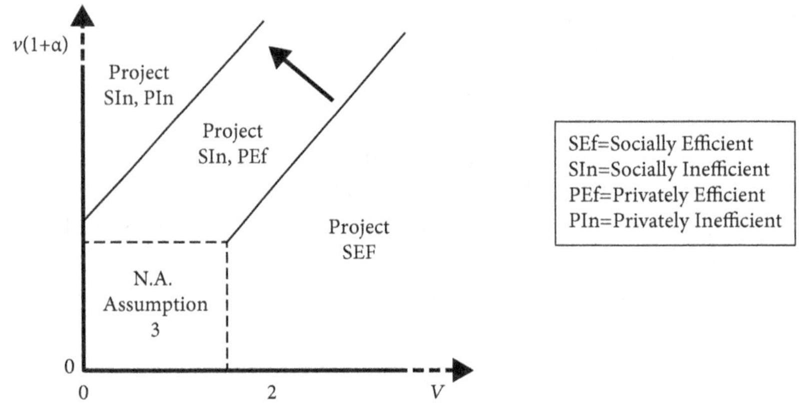

FIGURE 26.5 Social optimality of redevelopment with eminent domain (with and without externalities).

of the threat of eminent domain. Without externalities, eminent domain produces socially suboptimal outcomes. Market assembly had been optimal—because of the lack of imperfections—and now eminent domain leads to lower payments to sellers, which represents an apparent unfairness because wealth is transferred directly from sellers to a developer. In addition, eminent domain has allowed some socially inefficient market assemblies to proceed. Graphically, one sees the inefficiency by a parallel shifting up and to the left in the participation constraint line guiding D.

However, if redevelopment externalities exist, the results are not as clear about the shortcomings of eminent domain. Here the "distortionary" line in Figure 26.5 actually moves in the same direction as the externality line, in effect potentially improving the alignment of social optimality and private efficiency. In other words, the distortion created by eminent domain may attenuate the distortion created by the market failure. This is not to say that internalization occurs because of eminent domain. On the contrary, the two distortions would only align by chance. Nevertheless, the implication is clear. Eminent domain can improve efficiency when externalities exist. The following proposition formalizes these results.

Proposition 4. Given externalities, eminent domain improves the efficiency of market assembly if $\pi(v + \alpha v - 2) \leq Y$.

Proof. From proposition 3, eminent domain distorts efficiency with all conflicts where $v(1 + \alpha) > V \geq \pi + (1 - \pi)v + \pi + (1 - \pi)\alpha v$. Redevelopment externalities, Y, are added to V, which shrinks the number of conflicts satisfying the left inequality. The potential eminent domain distortion to efficiency corresponds to the possible values of V in the preceding inequality, which has magnitude: $v(1 + \alpha) - [\pi + (1 - \pi)v + \pi + (1 - \pi)\alpha v]$. This magnitude can be simplified to $\pi(v + \alpha v - 2)$. This quantity can be compared to Y, the efficiency loss from not using eminent domain for these conflicts. For $\pi(v + \alpha v - 2) < Y$, eminent domain in effect internalizes some of the externality, and at equality perfect internalization occurs. Thus, for $\pi(v + \alpha v - 2) \leq Y$, eminent domain improves efficiency. For $\pi(v + \alpha v - 2) > Y$, the internalization has occurred and an efficiency loss begins to mount for the eminent domain distortion alone: $Y - \pi(v + \alpha v - 2)$. Thus, optimally, society should balance the benefits of eminent domain Y with the costs $Y - \pi(v + \alpha v - 2)$.

Proposition 4 is the principal efficiency result of this analysis. It also implies that when externalities are small, eminent domain is less likely to provide an efficiency gain, all else equal. If externalities are sufficiently small, there may not be any land market assembly characteristics such that eminent domain will enhance social efficiency. Another implication is that eminent domain is more likely to enhance social efficiency when the externality is large relative to the eminent domain distortion.

5. Application: Land Assembly with Incomplete Information

Incomplete information is a severe case, contrasting starkly with the state of the world developed earlier because, strictly, an incomplete information world means that D knows absolutely nothing about v and α. Mathematically, D would not know if the maximum of v is infinite. Then, all attempts at achieving market assembly fail. In general, market assembly fails in many cases when information is incomplete—this is as to be expected because the information asymmetry manifests itself as potentially infinite transaction costs. Eminent domain corrects this failure in many cases, although it can potentially overcorrect, as seen earlier.

5.1 Behavior in Market Assembly Without Eminent Domain Under Incomplete Information

D does not know sellers' valuations other than that they exceed $m = 1$. Sellers' participation constraints (above) still guide their behavior. However, D's behavior is complicated by the information asymmetry. D no longer knows whether sellers will accept any offer and thus faces two risks: (1) bearing the delay cost, d_1, and (2) buying only from one seller and having to scrap the project for salvage value, $m = 1$. The first risk is known to D and could be optimally balanced with the expected benefit, $V - P^{A1} - P^{B1}$, to form a participation constraint. However, the second risk of salvaging $P^{It} - 1$, $I = A,B$, $t = 1,2$, is pure uncertainty and explodes with the infinite possible maximum of v. One must then posits a possible story about D's strategic thinking.

Assume that D believes that the v maximum might approach infinity, as the pure uncertainty condition suggests. Here, D will not participate in the assembly market at all because the expected benefit cannot mathematically outweigh the salvaging risk. (The salvaging risk is that D loses the difference between potentially infinite v and known market value $m = 1$, which means the potential loss also is potentially infinite.) Thus, D's participation constraint cannot be satisfied, and land assembly never occurs.

If the project would otherwise satisfy the social efficiency condition, then market assembly can be seen as inefficient. Redevelopment externalities exacerbate this inefficiency. If the project was not socially efficient, then market assembly is socially optimal. However, externalities might expand the set of socially efficient projects, pushing some from the socially inefficient to socially efficient category. The inefficiency result leads logically to calls for eminent domain.

5.2 Behavior in Market Assembly with Eminent Domain Under Incomplete Information

Under incomplete information, eminent domain would tend to generate more socially optimal outcomes than would market assembly. However, this improvement in social efficiency will sometimes require a transfer from sellers to D. Eminent domain would occur if D offered prices of 0 or 1 in the market and then simply waited for public assembly. Of course, D's participation constraint would need to be satisfied. Figure 26.6 shows that, with eminent domain, many socially optimal conflicts will now generate public assembly. Eminent domain improves social efficiency for all conflicts in the lower right area (i.e., all socially efficient conflicts)—subject to the preceding result that no assembly occurs without eminent domain when information is incomplete. However, eminent domain will lead to some socially inefficient assemblies. This region varies with π, as explained in Section 4 on complete information. Furthermore, as with complete information, externalities would exacerbate the

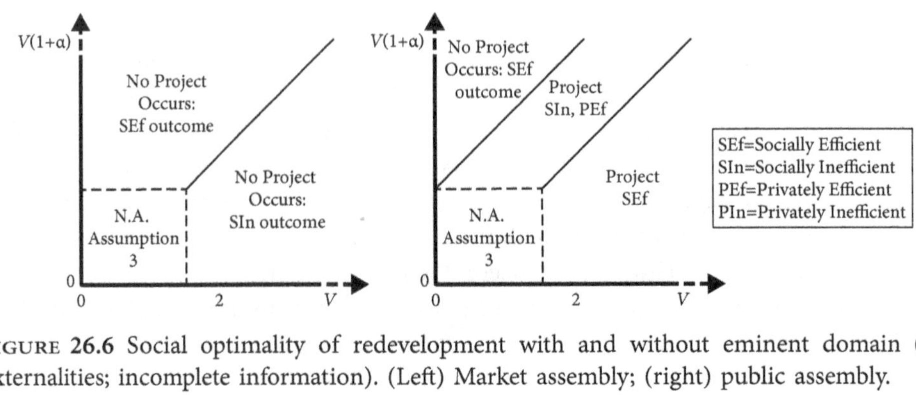

FIGURE 26.6 Social optimality of redevelopment with and without eminent domain (no externalities; incomplete information). (Left) Market assembly; (right) public assembly.

shortcomings of market assembly and would be attenuated for many conflicts under eminent domain.

6. Application Assessment

The analysis demonstrates that market assembly is relatively superior to public assembly, but only if one believes in a state of the world in which information is complete and if redevelopment externalities are small or can be internalized by larger private developments.[6] In other words, the complete-information state of the world suggests social optimality is more likely to occur when eminent domain (1) is not available, (2) has severe restrictions on its use, or (3) is used infrequently. If, however, one views the world as one in which information is incomplete, and if redevelopment externalities are substantive and cannot be internalized in private developments, then the analysis suggests that market assembly will be relatively worse than public assembly.

Although these two pure states of the world are somewhat unrealistic, it is exactly these sorts of assumptions that would be required to sustain absolute positions such as that *the market (or eminent domain) is always superior*. In contrast, much political discourse seems to claim knowledge that eminent domain either is or is not socially advantageous. The economist wonders if such claims have any relevance for social efficiency, and the model presented here suggests that it is information in the land use conflict setting that may determine efficiency.

Future research may find analytical traction in the case of partially incomplete information. The results of the model under partially incomplete information can then be compared to the two extreme benchmarks—thereby establishing the relative performance of market and public assembly. Unfortunately, current evidence does not suggest what type of information may be available to developers. The model allows several familiar issues to be examined, each of which will have different impacts on developers and sellers and that therefore may exacerbate or ameliorate conflict. Several possible approaches to analyzing land use policy are suggested in Section 6.1.

[6] This result comes from the model, but, intuitively, other conditions outside the model might lead to the same claim. For instance, if bargaining or negotiation leads to a sufficient attenuation of the information asymmetry, then market assembly is relatively superior.

6.1 Research Possibilities: Evaluating Eminent Domain and Institutional Change

The precedent set by *Kelo* seems to increase the likelihood of eminent domain because the set of assemblies qualifying for "public use" seems to expand. In the model, this means that π increases. The model suggests this increases assembly, which may be efficient if there are externalities and is inefficient otherwise. It is not clear how this will affect the behavior of developers if information is "partially" incomplete. One hypothesizes that it will increase D's use of low-ball offers because public assembly is more likely. This, in turn, would lower the likelihood of market assemblies.

Following *Kelo*, some states enacted legislation to curb the use of eminent domain. For some types of conflicts, such as redevelopment without blight, eminent domain would be prohibited. This would reduce the π for urban dwellers and would likely provide an incentive to D to make fewer low-ball offers and thus increase the use of market assembly.

Moratoria are a land use policy option used when land market behavior outstrips the planning process's ability to adapt. This strategy is one plausible response to the change emanating from courts and legislatures. Local governments might suspend the use of eminent domain for a period of time, thus increasing T. If T is large, then the payoffs D anticipates from eminent domain become small. This will result in a tendency for developers to abandon hopes for eminent domain and compel them to seek market assembly. This is not necessarily efficient because the land assembly market fails under many conditions.

Some authors (as described in Epstein 1985, 184) suggest that just compensation for eminent domain should be set at market value plus a bonus for reservation value, say 10%—an approach traditionally followed in England. This would render the new public assembly payment to be $m' = 1.1m$. Future work might explore how this institution might affect efficiency, and one anticipates that it may increase the likelihood of market assembly because eminent domain would become more costly to D—it is more costly because D must now pay $1.1m$ for each confiscated parcel, rather than m.

Free development represents an odd case, but one which may be common in redevelopment conflicts. One of the controversies in *Kelo* concerned the perception that the developers exaggerated the benefits of redevelopment because of the prospect of gaining "free" land through the eminent domain process. Indeed, the promise of redevelopment may lead public agencies to transfer the condemned land to developers at a very low (perhaps zero) cost. In such cases, assembly need not be privately efficient, yet D may still pursue a project of this type if D does not fully bear the costs of eminent domain. Ultimately, this is not necessarily inefficient. Local governments may subsidize developers because they perceive very large positive redevelopment externalities. But such a strategy would affect the performance of the land assembly market.

7. Conclusion

Eminent domain provides a mechanism to correct two substantive inefficiencies in urban land markets. One form of inefficiency arises from the holdout problem, or local monopolies associated with a heterogeneous land market. A second problem is that assembly is a part of efforts to revitalize areas through urban redevelopment, which in turn supplies public good benefits. A private assembly market fails to overcome these two failures. Eminent domain law can be supported by these economic rationales.

Yet eminent domain will not be efficient in all settings. The application presented in this chapter shows that there are conditions under which eminent domain is likely to be more efficient than private assembly and vice versa. One key finding is that eminent domain affects the performance of the land assembly market, and thus market failure must be assessed in light of holdout, public good, *and* the option for eminent domain. Other economic models have investigated efficiency implications of eminent domain, including delay and just compensation.

Beyond efficiency, this chapter offers results suggesting that information asymmetry is the predominant reason for failure in the land assembly market—it is here that the warrant for eminent domain resides. Economists should devote increasing attention to information and move the debate beyond issues of holdouts as monopoly, where pernicious sellers extract rents in markets and pernicious developers then capture rents by aligning with power-hungry planners and incompetent local governments. Such intentions have been ascribed particularly to developers, planners, and governments in the wake of *Kelo*. The model shows that the ascribed intentions, whether true or untrue, have been given too much credit for market—and public—assembly problems. Rather, it is a cognitive failing that drives these conflicts—private information prevents socially optimal contracts. A better understanding of the conditions under which land markets fail to deliver assembly will then lead to a better understanding of how new legislation and judicial rules will deliver improved outcomes.

Surprisingly, the land economic literature offers few economic studies of assembly and eminent domain. There are several potential reasons for this lack of literature. First, it is difficult to identify a behavioral reason why inefficiency exists—even though the assembly market failures of monopoly and public goods are readily understood. When one seeks to model behavior systematically, it becomes challenging to locate the precise failure leading to the inefficient outcome. As this chapter clarifies, several successful models have focused on delay and externalities. The application in this chapter focuses on information.

A second aspect of the literature has likely had a calming effect—specifically, the Blume, Rubinfeld, and Shapiro (1984) result of efficient zero compensation. Blume, Rubinfeld, and Shapiro (1984) offered an early and, some might say, definitive result on eminent domain. By finding that zero compensation is efficient because of the moral hazard problem, some economists may have been dissuaded from further study of eminent domain by the profundity and persuasiveness of the result. Yet, policy makers and the general public may have made little use of this result because it runs so counter to notions of fairness—notions that moreover are ingrained in the US Constitution.

As the literature review and the application show, there are other ways than just compensation to examine eminent domain. The "public use" part of the Fifth Amendment is also important to politicians and judges, but it has received little attention from economists. Economic research on eminent domain is not settled. Collectively, this lack of economic attention limited economists' impact on the public debate following *Kelo*. Ideally, future research will continue to investigate land assembly market failures.

Acknowledgments

Any errors are attributable to the author. Challenging discussions and feedback from Dan Bromley helped shape and improve this work. The author is also grateful for insightful feedback from Peter Schwarz and JunJie Wu, seminar participants at the University of Delaware Legal Studies Program, and workshop participants at the Society for Environmental Law and Economics.

References

Blume, L., D. Rubinfeld, and P. Shapiro. 1984. The taking of land: When should compensation be paid? *Quarterly Journal of Economics* 99: 71–92.

Buchanan, J. M., and Y. J. Yoon. 2000. Symmetric tragedies: Commons and anticommons. *Journal of Law and Economics* 43(1): 1–13.

Eckart, W. 1985. On the land assembly problem. *Journal of Urban Economics* 18: 364–378.

Epstein, R. A. 1985. *Takings: Private property and the power of eminent domain*. Cambridge, MA: Harvard University Press.

Heller, M. A. 1998. The tragedy of the anticommons: Property in the transition from Marx to markets. *Harvard Law Review* 111: 621–688.

Menezes, F., and R. Pitchford. 2003. The land assembly problem revisited. *Regional Science and Urban Economics* 34(2): 155–162.

Miceli, T. J. 2011. *The economic theory of eminent domain*. New York: Cambridge University Press.

Miceli, T. J., and K. Segerson. 2007. A bargaining model of holdouts and takings. *American Law and Economics Review* 9(1): 160–174.

Miceli, T.J. and K. Segerson. 2014. Regulatory takings. In *The Oxford handbook of land economics*, ed. J.M. Duke and J Wu. New York: Oxford University Press.

Munch, P. 1976. An economic analysis of eminent domain. *The Journal of Political Economy* 84(3): 473–497.

O'Flaherty, B. 1994. Land assembly and urban renewal. *Regional Science and Urban Economics* 24: 287–300.

Posner, R. A. 1992. *Economic analysis of law*, 4th ed. Boston: Little, Brown and Company.

Strange, W. C. 1995. Information, holdouts, and land assembly. *Journal of Urban Economics* 38: 317–332.

CHAPTER 27

FUTURE RESEARCH DIRECTIONS IN LAND ECONOMICS

JOSHUA M. DUKE AND JUNJIE WU

LAND is special in many ways. In the foreword, Bromley argues that our idea of "place" conflates with land, giving land primacy. Wars are fought over it. To the research economist, the commodity "land" poses special modeling challenges, not the least of which is that many do not see land as a commodity at all. As Bromley notes, land is different from other commodities that economists might model, like toothpaste. This special difference is not about market value. Land economists have long recognized the challenge of putting land on the quantity axis of a market model. Land has describable but also ineffable qualities (Bromley, foreword); or, as some see it, land is "extremely heterogeneous" (Irwin and Wrenn, Chapter 13). Irwin and Wrenn also argue that land modeling creates special challenges in that decisions about its uses are affected by market and nonmarket feedbacks, and it has important dynamic characteristics because past choices may accumulate.

Put differently, the special nature of land makes all owners interdependent monopolists foisting and bearing innumerable external costs and benefits, both spatial and temporal. Massive and complex challenges stand in the way of markets effectively allocating land among competing uses. And yet land markets function and not always poorly. Why? How well do they function? Can policy improve outcomes? Land economics has a long history of providing insights. As this handbook shows, land economists are poised to offer innovative, powerful answers in the near future.

Future research directions in land economics will expand the study of optimal land allocation, market failures preventing optimality, and policy impacts. The chapters in this handbook make clear that new data exist to better describe the spatial aspects of land, and new techniques allow economists to ask new questions or approach older questions looking for new insights. Together, these forces offer rich opportunities for economists to explain land use behavior and improve land market outcomes.

Although the handbook describes many advances, this chapter presents five prominent trends that will occupy a large share of future research. The ability to develop more sophisticated models that describe land outcomes is one of the most promising recent developments. These counterfactual analyses exemplify a key advantage of rigorous economic analysis. Another trend is toward more sophisticated models that explain how people and firms sort on the landscape. Integrated feedback modeling of human and ecological processes offers another rich field of study. Path-breaking articles from past decade have laid out these methods, and land economists are poised to extend and apply these techniques to a host of new problems.

These trends will help provide the answers to questions that society asks of economists. What changes would have happened to land uses in region R if clean water policy U had not been implemented? How will land use change in the future if location V has carbon policy W? How will incentive-based conservation policy X interact with zoning Y and, in turn, affect the supply of ecosystem services Z? How will provision Z affect the land choices made under X and Y? Land economists are better than ever poised to answer these questions.

The purpose of this chapter is to identify broad research priorities and directions for land economists, distilling lessons from recommendations in the preceding 26 chapters. Each chapter comprehensively covers one area of land economics, and this final chapter synthesizes five key directions for the field. The first two directions involve improved modeling capacity: spatially explicit structural modeling and integrated economic and ecological modeling. The third direction focuses on advancing methods to understand and uncover agents' behavior in settings involving land decisions. The fourth direction explores how to use abundant yet incomplete or inconsistent data. The fifth direction involves overcoming information challenges in policy design.

The focus on five directions is necessarily selective. For instance, most chapters discuss specific applications and topic-based directions and policy needs. These are difficult to synthesize, so we focus on broader trends. Another decision involved determining what exactly constitutes a "future research direction." Some chapters identify where the authors anticipate the literature to be moving, either in the short- or long-term. This positive approach differs from a normative one (i.e., where the authors think the literature should be going). We try to include both perspectives in this review.

1. Future Research Directions

An overarching trend that drives future research directions in land economics is the integrated approach that involves both integrated economic and ecological modeling and cross-fertilization among land-related economics fields. Several recent advancements in economics, including the emergence of the new economic geography and ecological economics, drive the integration among land-related economics fields. These advancements have led to the increasing recognition that land use patterns, economic growth, and the spatial distribution of economic activities and environmental impacts are highly interdependent. Recent advancements in information technology has also propelled integrated research and made it possible. Further development of integrated research will require additional theoretic, empirical, and methodological advances. Five future research directions are discussed here.

1.1 Spatially Explicit Structural Modeling

The increasing recognition of interdependency between land use patterns and economic growth highlights the need for spatially explicit structural modeling. Partridge and Rickman (Chapter 1) argue that land use and economic development research should be modeled, jointly, as complex systems; otherwise, "piecemeal" analyses lead to inconsistent lessons about development. In particular, Partridge and Rickman suggest that land economists should explain the location behavior of households and firms, whereas development economists should model the role of land in determining where economic activity occurs. Parker (Chapter 16) sees opportunities for agent-based models to explore the relationship between employment centers and residential locations. These studies suggest that a spatially explicit structural modeling approach would better explain economic performance, the distribution of economic activity in a region, impact of shocks (such as energy shocks and housing market bubbles), and poverty (Partridge and Rickman, Chapter 1). Although economists are accustomed to structural models, a great deal of the current empirical work relies on reduced-form models. Irwin et al. (2009) call for structural modeling to better identify the potential causal linkages among the many interdependent processes that affect urban-rural growth.

Economic models simplify reality, and economists keenly understand that their models are built on assumptions. Some noneconomists reject economic results, pointing to assumptions that they perceive as invalid. Objections are frequently framed as criticisms that economic models have oversimplified real-world complexities (Parker, Chapter 16). Many economists would contest the validity and applicability of such charges. They might argue that structural modeling is not an effort to address the longstanding "oversimplification" objection but to gain additional insights by capturing the essential linkages of the processes that shape economic and environmental outcomes.

Integrated research offers ways for economists to increase complexity, including linking quantitative modeling efforts in different economic fields and in noneconomic disciplines. Integration can take many forms, as explained in Khanna, Zilberman, and Crago (Chapter 4). They view the challenge of integration from the perspective of multiple models that all examine similar phenomena. How can these models be linked? Khanna, Zilberman, and Crago (Chapter 4) argue that a simple form of integration is triangulation, or examining a distribution of estimates provided by different models. A nesting or "off-line" linking of models provides a higher level of integration. Modularity offers even higher levels of integration in which the "subroutines" of one model become incorporated in another.

Irwin and Wrenn (Chapter 13) identify three general opportunities for integrating economic models. First, they see possibilities for simplifying difficult structural econometric modeling problems by selectively combining these models with reduced-form parameters estimates. A second opportunity identified by Irwin and Wrenn is to explore complementarities between structural spatial equilibrium models and agent-based models. Third, they believe spatial land use models can be linked to equilibrium models from other sectors.

1.2 Integrated Economic and Ecological Modeling

A great need also exists for integrated economic and ecological modeling. Economic activities affect ecosystems, and changes in ecosystems in turn affect economic performance. Thus, there is a need for integrated economic and ecological modeling, regardless of whether the focus of the study is on a natural resource-based economic system or a human-affected ecological system. Several chapters promote integrating economic models of land use and ecosystem services models, especially using ecological models from outside economics (Lewis and Nelson, Chapter 7; Johnston et al., Chapter 8; Attavanich et al. Chapter 10).

The chapters that use integrated models make clear that creating ecosystem service linkages is challenging. Even descriptions on a single dimension of ecological processes (such as habitat in one location for one species) require relatively large teams with significant time investments. Beyond time and effort, insufficient model integration was cited as a shortcoming (Attavanich et al., Chapter 10). Furthermore, integrated research should be careful not to proceed where the science cannot support its conclusions. Johnston, Swallow, Bauer, Uchida, and Anderson (Chapter 8) explain and offer examples about how truly integrated models of ecosystem services and land use can be constructed. But they also emphasize that our current ability to model these interactions accurately is limited. If "methodological sacrifices" are made to provide an integrated model, then the validity of the measures and, more broadly, the approach will be jeopardized.

Several chapters describe topical opportunities for integrated research. For example, McCarl et al. (Chapter 9) argue that land use research on climate has insufficiently modeled the interactions between adaptation and mitigation. They argue that this can be conceptualized as an optimal portfolio problem. Montgomery (Chapter 11) calls for feedback modeling between decisions to address fire fuel accumulation and fire suppression decisions. Barbier (Chapter 6) finds too few studies offer detailed, integrated modeling of land use change and economic development. Zilberman et al. (Chapter 2) argue that the role of technology adoption in vertical integration requires additional research and that this relationship should also model agricultural land use behavior.

This host of new methods offers better opportunities to examine complex linkages between policy choice and land use behavior. Gnedenko and Heffley (Chapter 20) advocate this form of integration, arguing for enhanced modeling of community-level decisions and of the decisions of nearby communities or higher level governments. They focus on decisions about fiscal policies for open space, but their point applies to other public goods. Traditionally, the link is established through an open-city condition, but Gnedenko and Heffley (Chapter 20) see opportunities for models that better capture linkages and potential spillovers arising from fiscal policies.

1.3 Methods to Uncover Agents' Behavior

The methods chapters cover spatial, econometric, simulation, and experimental approaches. Most of these methods have been developed to better understand selection issues. In other words, the methods allow economists to understand agents' interactions and decisions without necessarily observing in a given location a real-world policy or a real-world market. Inferences can be made without bias. Collectively, economists are better able to understand land behavior and phenomena, but the opportunities for applying these techniques have only just begun to be realized.

Irwin and Wrenn (Chapter 13) offer a comprehensive and synthetic review of land modeling, so this summary section on future directions will necessarily be brief. The modeling chapters also offer details about the future directions of various empirical, simulation, and experimental methods. Klaiber and Kuminoff (Chapter 14) explain equilibrium sorting models. The latest simulation methods are described in econometric-based settings (Plantinga and Lewis, Chapter 15) and agent-based settings (Parker, Chapter 16). Cho, Kim, and Roberts (Chapter 17) explain recent developments in spatial econometric modeling (see also Plantinga and Lewis, Chapter 15; Brady and Irwin 2011). Experimental methods, both quasi-experimental (Towe, Lewis, and Lynch, Chapter 18) and lab/field experiments (Messer, Duke, and Lynch, Chapter 19), are detailed. Many, but not all, of these methods involve some form of hedonic modeling.

The unifying message is that new spatial, econometric, simulation, and experimental methods exist so that economists no longer need to wait for actual institutional change to discern its likely impact on a landscape. The results of even untested land policies can be informed by sophisticated methods. The chapters do an excellent job of explaining how empirical evidence can be used to draw inference directly, to apply inferential results from one location to another, to motivate behavior rules in simulation, or to guide experimental design. Even when no empirical insight can be found, the chapters on lab/field experiments (Messer et al., Chapter 19) and agent-based modeling (Parker, Chapter 16) explain how economists can still analyze land policy.

The topical and applied chapters also highlight exactly how these methods will improve economic research. Nickerson and Zhang (Chapter 5), Barbier (Chapter 6), and Cho et al. (Chapter 17) all call for expanded temporal studies of spatially explicit land phenomena. However, Irwin and Wrenn (Chapter 13) note that these efforts require further work on overcoming the curse of dimensionality introduced by dynamics in empirical land use models.

Nickerson and Zhang (Chapter 5) offer recommendations for using new spatial techniques, regression discontinuity design, and matching methods to improve farmland value research. Ferris and Lynch (Chapter 21) argue that these new techniques are poised to make breakthroughs on our understanding of endogeneity of land policy and outcomes. Methods to addresses observed endogeneity and other inferential challenges are common themes in the handbook. In particular, authors recognize a need for better modeling of empirical outcomes from regulations (Lewis and Nelson, Chapter 7; Stone and Wu, Chapter 12). This relates to another important direction: research that uncovers structural parameters. Readers will find Irwin and Wrenn (chapter 13) and Klaiber and Kuminoff (Chapter 14) directly address these approaches. But Irwin and Wrenn also caution that the literature requires further empirical tests of the assumptions maintained to drive these models.

Some chapters highlighted methodological challenges that current theoretical and empirical models cannot address. In the case of estimating the sources and changes in farmland values, Nickerson and Zhang (Chapter 5) argue for a better merging of two largely distinct approaches—behavioral versus data-driven. They recommend building dynamic structural models of behavior that explain how landowner expectations are formed and that employ recent time series techniques to extend foundational models of value, such as Just and Miranowski (1993). Such models, Nickerson and Zhang suggest, would offer evidence on the speed with which farmland values change in response to changes in drivers.

Another example concerns the manner in which objective functions are specified. The land policies of governments include many articulated goals, but these goals are not always measured commensurately and benefit-cost data are often unavailable. A specific example might be farmland preservation policy, which seeks to achieve acreage goals while also delivering a series of amenities and other services such as food security, environmental services, and wildlife habitat (Nickerson and Hellerstein 2003).

Can economists contribute insight to these situations without a wholesale repudiation of the manner in which the objective is framed? Ferris and Lynch (Chapter 21) argue that, in these cases, programs will require multiple techniques to satisfy multiple goals. But current economic theory offers a poor understanding of the interactions among these techniques, and economists need theoretical advances and empirical insights. Fire hazard reduction and fire suppression response provides another example of a policy setting with complex goals. Although existing analytical approaches in dynamic programming do not readily address such problems, Montgomery (Chapter 11) sees potential for recent advances in approximate dynamic programming to be adapted to solve spatial and dynamic optimization problems. Other chapters in this handbook suggest similar ways that new methods can contribute insight to nagging challenges, even when the problem is specified in a complex manner.

1.4 How to Use Abundant Yet Incomplete or Inconsistent Data

Many causal mechanisms that influence land use and location patterns differ depending on the spatial scale of analysis (Irwin et al. 2009). Consequently, data are often collected at different spatial scales, depending on the issue of interest. What are the implications of scale-dependent processes for modeling and policy analysis? How should abundant, yet scale-incompatible data be used? These are important issues for future research. As Irwin et al. (2009) point out, we know relatively little about how microlevel processes and heterogeneity affect the current aggregate outcomes. Therefore, efforts are needed to develop models that capture decisions at the microlevel, that allow interactions at multiple scales, and that are able to predict aggregate outcomes.

Spatially explicit data on land prices, uses, and services are rich and increasingly available. Several chapters detail the datasets available for researchers to study specific areas of land economics (see, for instance, Klaiber and Kuminoff, Chapter 14, and Claassen et al., Chapter 23). Many chapters suggest that newly abundant data, especially spatially explicit data, offer tremendous opportunities for economists to create new insights on markets and policy performance. Some chapters also identify data needs for currently unanswerable questions.

Among the many chapters highlighting the need for better data, the unifying theme is space. The future importance of spatial data surprises no land economist. Economists eagerly anticipate new and better spatially explicit data, but they also identify specific data needs. For example, Nickerson and Zhang (Chapter 5) call for more spatially disaggregated data and spatially ordered transaction data in the study of farmland markets. Claassen et al. (Chapter 23) advocate for measures of transaction costs in landowners' supply of agri-environmental services. Barbier (Chapter 6) identifies the need for temporally explicit data on the geographical location of rural poor in the developing world, especially with reference to vulnerable ecological sites.

Several other chapters anticipate the need for better measures of land use with specific applications in mind. For instance, Stone and Wu (Chapter 12) call for improved measures of endogenous social amenities, or the intangible desirability of neighborhoods. Lewis and Nelson (Chapter 7) seek better measures on the benefits of conservation. Many application areas would benefit from better measures for dealing with counterfactuals (see, e.g., the discussion of conservation policy intervention from Lewis and Nelson, Chapter 7). More and better data from land markets can lead to resolution of persistent econometric issues, such as omitted variable bias, which is a nagging econometric challenge in many settings. Nickerson and Zhang (Chapter 5) explicitly cite this issue with respect to farmland value studies, but it applies broadly to most empirical land use models—especially the workhorse revealed preference models.

Other authors suggest that some spatial data exist but that economists have only just begun to take advantage of the opportunities for analysis. Partridge and Rickman (Chapter 1) recommend an expansion in the use of geo-coded firm-level data, especially when used in an integrated model with micro geo-coded housing data. Gnedenko and Heffley (Chapter 20) argue for further and better matching of land cover data and parcel-specific data on zoning and other land use controls. Yet existing data are not always readily useable in spatial formats. Ferris and Lynch (Chapter 21) suggest that farmland owners and other households' opinion, income, and preference survey data exist but that confidentiality rules prohibit most researchers from connecting these analytical units of observation with spatial data sources.

Several authors focused on making better efforts to measure unobserved costs (in supplying ecosystem services and other settings) at the farm or parcel level. Hodge (Chapter 22) identifies opportunities to use these cost data to better target agri-environmental policy at the farm level. Several other chapters (chapters 21 and 23) cite the importance of conservation targeting, but also the need to develop better targeting techniques; these techniques will require better measures of space, benefits, costs, and the like.

1.5 Overcoming Information Challenges in Policy Design

Economists have a long history of examining the burdens of information costs on resource allocation efficiency. Economists design contracts and institutions to improve allocation in light of information asymmetry and use terms such as "second best" to describe a situation in which one does as well as one can, given the information challenges (e.g., see Smith 1995; Wu and Babcock 1996). Many chapters in the handbook identify areas where future work can continue to create cost-effective solutions despite information asymmetry. For instance, these problems were mentioned in settings such as habitat conservation (Chapter 7), empirical modeling of landowner returns (Chapter 15), conservation auctions (Chapter 19), and urban landowner information on reservation value (Chapter 26).

Solutions to information problems can be derived from within existing markets, which means property rights are assigned and buyers/sellers are defined (Schmid 1999). This also means that the market provides some structure to the information problems facing participants and policy makers who seek to adjust market outcomes. Yet the chapters also make clear that land economists envision a future in which economists increasingly contribute to the design of policies, prior to the assignment of rights. Recent interest by policy makers in incentive problems such as additionality, baselines, leakage/slippage, and stacking seems to have energized land economists. Although economists have recognized these incentive problems for years, the needs and funding of policy is redirecting economic efforts (see, e.g., Claassen et al. Chapter 23).

Policy makers seek innovative solutions out of a desire for fiscal efficiency (i.e., obtaining a given level of agri-environmental services for the least cost) or fiscal illusion (i.e., creating demand for services by capping sources of emissions or development). But land economists recognize that the underlying problem arises from information asymmetry in the censoring of landowners' opportunity costs, which complicates optimal solutions (Lewis, Plantinga, and Wu 2009). Several chapters point out emerging trends where land economists can assess the performance of competing institutions and thus affect policy before the assignment of rights. For instance, recent literature examines market instrument comparisons in land conservation (consider Arnold et al.'s 2013 comparison of auctions, contracts, and taxes in government procurement of ecosystem services) and in work covering activities related to land (consider alternate baselines for incentivizing best management practices in water quality trading in Ghosh et al. 2011).

The handbook chapters offer many specific directions in the study of information and land economics. Fundamentally, the increasingly availability of information and interconnectedness of people affects and is affected by the way land is used. Mills (Chapter 3) examines the economic performance of differently sized metropolitan areas and, in the process, sketches a research agenda for anticipating future growth patterns. Mills predicts that suburban land use will continue to rapidly expand and thus poses a hypothesis for future research.

Many chapters consider future research directions arising from information asymmetry with respect to supply curve of land use. The chapters highlight the challenges of uncovering these opportunity costs in a number of settings, including the nonpecuniary benefits of agricultural land use and the role in technology adoption (Zilberman et al., Chapter 2). Several chapters call for studies of the unobservable costs of delivering conservation and other agri-environmental services (Lewis and Nelson, Chapter 7; Hodge, Chapter 22). Plantinga and Lewis (Chapter 15) discuss how to model landowners' private information.

In Chapter 22, Hodge offers some sobering thoughts about a desire to create even second-best contracts—issues that future research must come to terms with lest this work be unproductive. Hodge starts with a relatively uncontroversial position (that some asymmetric information is unavoidable), but notes that all agri-environmental efforts rely to some extent on an ability to write enforceable contracts. Hodge wonders if one also can define those agricultural practices that optimally deliver a given environmental benefit, for a given farm, and with cognizance of permanence. In other words, what happens when the contract ends? Eisen (Chapter 24) considers the effect of voluntary cleanup programs that lead to brownfield sites that are not contaminant free many years following a cleanup. In this situation, what is the implication for efficient "reopener" policy and land markets (i.e., policies that allow governments to require additional clean up in the future)?

What about additionality? Will increased contracting for agri-environmental services "crowd out" the norm among some land managers of delivering environmental services for free (Hodge Chapter 22)? In the case of unreclaimed brownfields, residual contamination identified at a later date would have occurred anyway. How should voluntary cleanup programs be evaluated in light of this contamination (Eisen, Chapter 24)?

These are two examples of land economics studies in very different settings, although the concerns are remarkably similar. Despite economists' often very clever work in market design, perhaps the remaining information problems of market failures are too severe. Even if one begins to understand fully how landowners respond to incentives—say, contracts for agri-environmental services under information asymmetry—Claassen et al. (Chapter 23) cite a need to understand the effect of different funding mechanisms, such as federal cost-share. Certainly, one future direction will be to seek better rights-based solutions. But another direction will likely be to devote greater attention to comparing the relative performance of rights-based solutions under alternate institutions.

Another quite different type of information problem that complicates land decisions and policy involves uncertainty. For instance, eminent domain (Duke, Chapter 26), regulatory diminutions (Miceli and Segerson, Chapter 25), and brownfield policy (Eisen, Chapter 24) are made under uncertain conditions about the future. How do future local economic conditions and uncertain future contamination affect optimal urban redevelopment policy in the present? Perhaps the regulatory takings literature has advanced the furthest in dealing with these issues because of robust work on efficient compensation for eminent domain following Blume, Rubinfeld, and Shapiro (1984).

Miceli and Segerson (Chapter 25) point out that the regulatory takings results depend on information about the impacts of a landowner's or regulator's decision, but it is unclear to what extent courts could have access to this information. One anticipates, nevertheless, that nonmarket valuation research, especially on ecosystem services (see Johnston et al., Chapter 8), would have a great deal of impact in providing this information in the future. In the eminent domain case, Duke (Chapter 26) argues that economists need more evidence on alternate rules about when confiscations are authorized because these not only impact efficiency (after the fact through compensation), but the expectations of outcomes in eminent domain also affect land assembly market performance. Some future work should explore broadly applicable rules for efficient urban redevelopment and efficient compensation for regulatory diminutions.

Nevertheless, one challenge is that the two key literatures mentioned in this section seem increasingly to have grown apart. Incentive-based agri-environmental policy now seems quite distant from the economics of land use law (often regulatory standards). The former focuses on incentivizing behavior, whereas the latter focuses on the implications of involuntary land use standards. In general, the regulatory law and economics research establishes a set of baseline market conditions from which marginal changes in the status quo occur through incentive-based policies. Towe et al. (Chapter 18) term this a "shift" from regulatory to incentive-based regulation. Future work may want to reexamine these approaches for opportunities to enhance efficiency through linked models.

One opportunity might be to recognize that the constitutionality of regulatory policies determines the price of incentive policies. For example, if regulatory takings law affords little protection to landowners in the form of no compensation for small to moderate diminutions in value, then a conservation easement should be less (fiscally) expensive. Future work may therefore seek to better understand the effectiveness of regulatory policies in terms of the direct benefits and costs of control and in terms of the impacts on future incentive-based efforts.

2. Reflections on Future Directions in Integrated Research and Policy

This handbook has been framed with the claim that land economics requires an integrated approach. The preceding sections suggest directions for integration, and this section provides some concluding thoughts about why this approach is needed. First, partial equilibrium analysis is not always adequate to examine the questions society needs answered. In these settings, all else is not equal. Land use decisions impact ecosystem services, economic development, and outcomes in other markets. There are feedback effects. As Klaiber and Kuminoff (Chapter 14) explain, institutions cause nonmarginal changes in public good provision, and partial equilibrium results will not apply. People will resort themselves on the landscape.

Second, land economic problem settings are often too fluid to warrant the simplification economists seek to derive tight and tractable results, ready lab experiments, and empirically testable theoretic results. For instance, the urban-rural land use interface is remarkably mutable. Although it is easier to model an urban market and a distinct agricultural land market, actual market behaviors stretch such economic simplifications. Why do some parcels at the fringe remain in farming despite higher apparent returns to conversion? Why are there farm parcels inside the fringe, exhibiting the hallmark of sustainable agriculture? What drives exurban residential development? Why do some farmers make preservation decisions that seem to make themselves worse off? Many economists have begun to explain these phenomena, and future work will likely need integrated models to develop higher level explanations. Similar needs with respect to these urban-rural modeling challenges could be claimed for explaining human-nature interactions.

Third, integrated work may help prevent unexpected suboptimal recommendations. Economic studies often focus on narrow policy applications for technical reasons. Social phenomena are largely uncontrollable, at least by researchers. Narrow foci allow for thoroughness of coverage. But we also live in a vast, complex, and integrated world. If we fix one failure, we may trigger others, and there may be perverse incentives.

Beyond our application areas, policy requires that we do not look at land use in isolation. We need to understand how agricultural land use affects ecosystems and urban uses. If economists explain these many linkages, policy is apt to follow. However, current land policy, especially in the United States, is notoriously divided. Local governments have direct control over most land decisions, but state and federal governments indirectly influence many land outcomes via major legislation and judicial review. Historical legacies led to our current incoherent land use control organization. That said, there is no clear answer on the best way to reorganize land policy.

The "extreme heterogeneity" of land seems to suggest that policy should be made locally, where information is best. Local communities also have the greatest incentives to solve local problems. But land also delivers positive and negative externalities beyond localities, suggesting that higher level policy is warranted. Are the costs of voting with one's feet less expensive than policy coordination or reinvention? What about the voiceless future? Many economists model only cross-sections or dynamics. Integrated models of space and time are difficult, but there is a cost to holding one dimension constant. If economists expand the size and scope of their questions, fewer questions will be answered.

Irwin and Wrenn (Chapter 13) call policy usefulness "one of the ultimate tests of any modeling approach." There is limited, unambiguous evidence that some work by land economists has had direct impacts on policy (Irwin and Wrenn, Chapter 13; Banzhaf 2010). But the pace of economic research diverges from policy needs. Irwin and Wrenn also argue that policy makers demand "real-time policy" and "quick approximate answers." Economic research largely does not match these requirements, and the integrated modeling called for in this handbook would slow economics down further.

Although these challenges are well-known to economists, they miss the role of agenda-setting research. Land economics has a strong record here. Consider agri-environmental policy. The shift from regulatory land use to incentive-based policies was most likely due to pioneering work by economists. As early incentive-based programs experimented with fixed-price and reverse auctions, economists weighed in with results. Today's economic research results will shape land policy in the coming decade. In this framing, integrated research can play a significant role.

The research agenda for the future has not been finalized, and this handbook offers many avenues for future work. Economists better understand how to compare institutional outcomes, but many applications are needed, and economists do not conduct enough replications (Irwin and Wrenn, Chapter 13; Messer et al., Chapter 19). Given the multiple sources of market failure in land, economists do not pay enough continuing attention to the normative content of the efficiency concept employed (Bromley 1990) or to problems with the general theory of second best (Lipsey and Lancaster 1956). Given that land policy delivers multiple outcomes, what is the marginal rate of substitution among the benefits (Claassen et al. Chapter 23)? Can society do better by turning agri-environmental payments around and focusing on the environmental results delivered rather than the costs of delivering them (Hodge, Chapter 22)? Given that land and land uses are highly inelastic in supply, economists should continue to explore the policy implications of capitalization—that is, to what extent do improvements flow as rents to landowners?

The integrated approach involves both a cross-fertilization across land-related economics fields and also an integration with models outside economics. The increasing recognition that land use patterns, economic growth, and the spatial distribution of economic activities and environmental impacts are highly interdependent has led to a convergence of interest among "land economists" working in several fields of economics, including agricultural economics, natural resource economics, environmental economics, regional science, and urban economics. This has made the potential gains from collaboration much greater. The purpose of this handbook has been to stimulate further integration and collaboration in land economics research.

References

Arnold, M., J. M. Duke, and K. Messer. 2013. Adverse selection in reverse auctions for ecosystem services. *Land Economics* 89(3):387–412

Attavanich, W., B. S. Rashford, R. M. Adams, and B. A. McCarl. 2014. Land use, climate change, and ecosystem services. In *The Oxford handbook of land economics*, eds. J. M. Duke and J. Wu, 255–280. New York: Oxford University Press.

Banzhaf, H. S. 2010. Economics at the fringe: Non-market valuation studies and their role in land use plans in the United States. *Journal of Environmental Management* 91: 592–602.

Barbier, E. B. 2014. Land use and sustainable economic development: developing world. In *The Oxford handbook of land economics*, eds. J. M. Duke and J. Wu, 139–159. New York: Oxford University Press.

Blume, L., D. Rubinfeld, and P. Shapiro. 1984. The taking of land: When should compensation be paid? *Quarterly Journal of Economics* 99: 71–92.

Brady, M., and E. Irwin. 2011. Accounting for spatial effects in economic models of land use: Recent developments and challenges ahead. *Environmental and Resource Economics* 48(3): 487–509.

Bromley, D. W. 1990. The ideology of efficiency: Searching for a theory of policy analysis. *Journal of Environmental Economics and Management* 19(1): 86–107.

Cho, S-H., S. G. Kim, and R. K. Roberts. 2014. Spatial econometric modeling of land use change. In *The Oxford handbook of land economics*, eds. J. M. Duke and J. Wu, 430–451. New York: Oxford University Press.

Claassen, R., J. Cooper, C. Salvioni, and M. Veronesi. 2014. Agri-environmental policies: A comparison of US and EU experiences. In *The Oxford handbook of land economics*, eds. J. M. Duke and J. Wu, 648–667. New York: Oxford University Press.

Duke, J. M. 2014. Eminent domain and the land assembly problem. In *The Oxford handbook of land economics*, eds. J. M. Duke and J. Wu, 723–735. New York: Oxford University Press.

Duke, J. M., and J. Wu. 2014. Future research directions in land economics. In *The Oxford handbook of land economics*, eds. J. M. Duke and J. Wu. New York: Oxford University Press.

Eisen, J. B. 2014. Stigmatized sites and urban brownfield redevelopment. In *The Oxford handbook of land economics*, eds. J. M. Duke and J. Wu, 668–697. New York: Oxford University Press.

Ferris, J., and L. Lynch. 2014. Land conservation in the United States. In *The Oxford handbook of land economics*, eds. J. M. Duke and J. Wu, 583–611. New York: Oxford University Press.

Ghosh, G., M. Ribaudo, and J. Shortle. 2011. Baseline requirements can hinder trades in water quality trading programs: Evidence from the Conestoga watershed. *Journal of Environmental Management* 92: 2076–2084.

Gnedenko, E., and D. Heffley. 2014. Open space preservation: Direct controls and fiscal incentives. In *The Oxford handbook of land economics*, eds. J. M. Duke and J. Wu, 547–582. New York: Oxford University Press.

Hodge, I. 2014. European agri-environmental policy: The conservation and re-creation of cultural landscapes. In *The Oxford handbook of land economics*, eds. J. M. Duke and J. Wu, 612–647. New York: Oxford University Press.

Irwin, E., K. P. Bell, N. E. Bockstael, D. Newburn, M. D. Partridge, and J. Wu. 2009. The economics of urban-rural space. *Annual Review of Resource Economics* 1(October): 1–26.

Irwin, E. G., and D. Wrenn. 2014. An assessment of empirical methods for modeling land use. In *The Oxford handbook of land economics*, eds. J. M. Duke and J. Wu, 327–351. New York: Oxford University Press.

Johnston, R. J., S. K. Swallow, D. M. Bauer, E. Uchida, and C. M. Anderson. 2014. Connecting ecosystem services to land use: Implications for valuation and policy. In *The Oxford handbook of land economics*, eds. J. M. Duke and J. Wu, 196–225. New York: Oxford University Press.

Just, R. E., and J. A. Miranowski. 1993. Understanding farmland price changes. *American Journal of Agricultural Economics* 75(1): 156–168.

Lewis, D. J., A. J. Plantinga, and J. Wu. 2009. Targeting incentives to reduce habitat fragmentation. *American Journal of Agricultural Economics* 91:1080–1096.

Lipsey, R. G., and K. Lancaster. 1956. The general theory of second best. *The Review of Economic Studies* 24(1): 11–32.

McCarl, B. A., W. Attavanich, M. Musumba, J. E. Mu, and R. Aisabokhae. 2014. Land use and climate change. In *The Oxford handbook of land economics*, eds. J. M. Duke and J. Wu, 226–254. New York: Oxford University Press.

Messer, K. D., J. M. Duke, and L. Lynch. 2014. Applying experiments to land economics: Public information and auction efficiency in ecosystem service markets. In *The Oxford handbook of land economics*, eds. J. M. Duke and J. Wu, 481–546. New York: Oxford University Press.

Miceli, T. J., and K. Segerson. 2014. Regulatory takings. In *The Oxford handbook of land economics*, eds. J. M. Duke and J. Wu, 698–722. New York: Oxford University Press.

Mills, E. S. Are large metropolitan areas still viable? 2014. In *The Oxford handbook of land economics*, eds. J. M. Duke and J. Wu, 74–84. New York: Oxford University Press.

Montgomery, C. A. 2014. Fire: An agent and a consequence of land use change. In *The Oxford handbook of land economics*, eds. J. M. Duke and J. Wu, 281–301. New York: Oxford University Press.

Nickerson, C. J., and D. Hellerstein. 2003. Protecting rural amenities through farmland preservation programs. *Agricultural and Resource Economics Review* 32(1): 129–144.

Nickerson, C. J., and W. Zhang. 2014. Modeling the determinants of farmland values in the United States. In *The Oxford handbook of land economics*, eds. J. M. Duke and J. Wu, 111–138. New York: Oxford University Press.

Parker, D. C. 2014. An economic perspective on agent-based models of land use and land cover change. In *The Oxford handbook of land economics*, eds. J. M. Duke and J. Wu, 402–429. New York: Oxford University Press.

Partridge, M. D., and D. S. Rickman. 2014. Integrating economic development analysis and land use economics. In *The Oxford handbook of land economics*, eds. J. M. Duke and J. Wu, 23–51. New York: Oxford University Press.

Plantinga, A. J., and D. J. Lewis. 2014. Landscape simulations with econometric-based land use models. In *The Oxford handbook of land economics*, eds. J. M. Duke and J. Wu, 380–401. New York: Oxford University Press.

Schmid, A. A. 1999. Government, property, markets... In that order... Not government versus markets. In *The fundamental interrelationships between government and property*, eds. N. Mercuro and W. J. Samuels, 237–242. Greenwich, CT: JAI Press.

Smith, R. B. W. 1995. The conservation reserve program as a least-cost land retirement mechanism. *American Journal of Agricultural Economics* 77(1995): 93–105.

Stone, E., and J. Wu. 2014. Land use and municipal profiles. In *The Oxford handbook of land economics*, eds. J. M. Duke and J. Wu, 302–324. New York: Oxford University Press.

Towe, C., R. Lewis, and L. Lynch. 2014. Using quasi-experimental methods to evaluate land policies: Application to Maryland's priority funding legislation. In *The Oxford handbook of land economics*, eds. J. M. Duke and J. Wu, 452–480. New York: Oxford University Press.

Zilberman, D., M. Khanna, S. Kaplan, and E. Kim. 2014. Technology adoption and land use. In *The Oxford handbook of land economics*, eds. J. M. Duke and J. Wu, 52–73. New York: Oxford University Press.

Wu, JunJie, and B. Babcock. 1996. Contract design for the purchase of environmental goods from agriculture. *American Journal of Agricultural Economics* 78(1996): 935–945.

Subject Index